"Things worthwhile generally don't just happen. Luck is a fact, but should not be a factor. Good luck is what is left over after intelligence and effort have combined at their best. Negligence or indifference are usually reviewed from an unlucky seat. The law of cause and effect and causality both work the same with inexorable exactitudes. Luck is the residue of design."

--- Branch Rickey

"I don't care if I was a ditch-digger at a dollar a day, I'd want to do my job better than the fellow next to me. I'd want to be the best at whatever I do."

-- Branch Rickey

To Avery & Shay,

My daughters, I love you – from the depths of my soul. I cannot figure out what I could have possibly done to have been blessed as much as I have. But for that, though, I am eternally grateful. Watching the both of you interact – the smiles, the laughing, the hugs, those tender moments – have been the highlights of my life. My hope for you two is that you'll always be inseparable – the best of friends, the closest of confidants, forever together.

Avery, with all your spunk, sass, and iron will, look after Shay. It's already apparent how much she adores you. Be the person she sees in you – always. Protect her.

Shay, with your curiosity and gentleness, follow your sister's example. She has a heart of gold, a sincerity that's rarely seen. Protect her.

It's amazing how goals in life evolve. But I can tell you both one thing that will never change: I promise to try and never disappointment either of you, to always guide and protect you both the best I can. And, most importantly, I promise that I will never stop trying to live up to the way each of you look at me.

Be good people. The world always needs good people. Be kind. Be generous. Volunteer. Make a positive impact. Be loving. Be curious. Be diligent in your beliefs and don't allow your faith to waiver. Be strong. Be tender. Trust your gut and instincts. Believe in yourselves.

I'm proud of you both – now, always, and forever.

Love,

Daddy

Julianne,

Our girls are lucky to have you as their mother. I see so much of you in both of them – and that's the best parts of them. Thank you for everything you do for us.

Cal,

My best friend, my late-night writing partner, my companion. I don't know what I'd do without you.

Author Bio: Joseph Werner provides further evidence that Jim Bouton was right when he wrote, "You spend your life gripping a baseball, and in the end it turns out that it was the other way around all the time."

As a lifelong Indians fan, Werner's lived and died multiple times over. First with the original revival of Cleveland baseball in the mid-1990s, then languishing through the lean years before having his life reinvigorated by their fantastically wonderful 2016 post-season run and continued success.

All along the way, though, he's heard two of the greatest radio voices in the game: Herb Score and Tom Hamilton. Despite his youth at the time, he proudly — and somewhat embarrassingly — remembers falling asleep with his arms clutched around a portable radio as Score made his last radio call during Game 7 of 1997 World Series.

Werner has been fortunate — and incredibly blessed — to have some of his work published and mentioned on several major media outlets, including: ESPN, Yahoo! Sports, Cleveland.com, The Baseball Research Journal, and Beyond the Box Score.

A Note from the Author: As I mentioned in every book, my continued goal is to provide the reader with the best product that I can. I want it to be something that not only is informative but also enjoyable to read. My hope is that I've achieved that goal with this year's Prospect Digest Handbook. Thank you for reading – as always.

I apologize about the delay in this year's edition. Life happily, wonderfully gets in the way.

I would just like to tip my hat to the following websites because without their invaluable data, none of this would have been possible:

- fangraphs.com
- baseballreference.com
- statcorner.com
- thebaseballcube.com
- claydavenport.com
- baseballprospectus.com

Another special thank you goes out to Josh Stollings for his his help on this year's cover.

I would like to thank you, the reader, once again. I enjoy hearing from you guys – be it before or after the book comes out. Please feel free to reach me at the following email address: JosephMWerner@yahoo.com. I absolutely love hearing everyone's thoughts/comments/concerns/feedback.

I'd also like to thank Michael Salfino. I appreciate you always championing my book. I'm forever indebted.

One final note: Because the book is self-published, I do not control the price of the Handbook; I wish I did, though. The price is based on the total amount of pages.

All the best,

JOE

Table of Contents

The Top 300 Prospects   13
The Top 10 Prospects by Position   19

Ranking the Farm Systems   23
The Top 25 Breakout Prospects for 2019   27

Organizational Analysis   31

Arizona Diamondbacks   33
Atlanta Braves   47
Baltimore Orioles   61
Boston Red Sox   75
Chicago Cubs   89
Chicago White Sox   101
Cincinnati Reds   115
Cleveland Indians   129
Colorado Rockies   143
Detroit Tigers   155
Houston Astros   167
Kansas City Royals   179
Los Angeles Angels   191
Los Angeles Dodgers   203
Miami Marlins   217
Milwaukee Brewers   231
Minnesota Twins   245
New York Mets   259
New York Yankees   271
Oakland Athletics   285
Philadelphia Phillies   299
Pittsburgh Pirates   313
San Diego Padres   327
San Francisco Giants   341
Seattle Mariners   355
St. Louis Cardinals   369
Tampa Bay Rays   383
Texas Rangers   397
Toronto Blue Jays   411
Washington Nationals   425

The Top 300 Prospects

Ranking the Top 300 Prospects (1-100)

Rank	Name	Team	Age	Pos	Rank	Name	Team	Age	Pos
1	Wander Franco	Tampa Bay Rays	19	SS	51	Deivi Garcia	New York Yankees	21	RHP
2	Gavin Lux	Los Angeles Dodgers	22	2B/SS	52	Jackson Kowar	Kansas City Royals	23	RHP
3	Jo Adell	Los Angeles Angels	21	OF	53	Nick Lodolo	Cincinnati Reds	22	LHP
4	Jarred Kelenic	Seattle Mariners	20	CF	54	Andres Gimenez	New York Mets	21	SS
5	MacKenzie Gore	San Diego Padres	21	LHP	55	Ronny Mauricio	New York Mets	19	SS
6	Adley Rutschman	Baltimore Orioles	22	C	56	Yusniel Diaz	Baltimore Orioles	23	CF/RF
7	Luis Robert	Chicago White Sox	22	CF	57	Gilberto Jimenez	Boston Red Sox	19	CF
8	Cristian Pache	Atlanta Braves	21	CF	58	Royce Lewis	Minnesota Twins	21	SS
9	Jesus Luzardo	Oakland Athletics	22	LHP	59	Nick Madrigal	Chicago White Sox	23	2B
10	Julio Rodriguez	Seattle Mariners	19	RF	60	Ke'Bryan Hayes	Pittsburgh Pirates	23	3B
11	Marco Luciano	San Francisco Giants	18	SS	61	Taylor Trammell	San Diego Padres	22	OF
12	Carter Kieboom	Washington Nationals	22	IF	62	Nolan Gorman	St. Louis Cardinals	20	3B
13	Dustin May	Los Angeles Dodgers	22	RHP	63	DL Hall	Baltimore Orioles	21	LHP
14	Nate Pearson	Toronto Blue Jays	23	RHP	64	Jasson Dominguez	New York Yankees	22	OF
15	Mitch Keller	Pittsburgh Pirates	24	RHP	65	Brent Honeywell	Tampa Bay Rays	23	RHP
16	Joey Bart	San Francisco Giants	23	C	66	Alek Thomas	Arizona Diamondbacks	20	CF
17	Alex Kirilloff	Minnesota Twins	22	1B/RF	67	Riley Greene	Detroit Tigers	19	CF
18	Dylan Carlson	St. Louis Cardinals	21	OF	68	Trevor Larnach	Minnesota Twins	23	RF
19	A.J. Puk	Oakland Athletics	25	LHP	69	Luis Garcia	Washington Nationals	20	2B/SS
20	Kristian Robinson	Arizona Diamondbacks	19	CF	70	Evan White	Seattle Mariners	24	1B
21	Matt Manning	Detroit Tigers	22	RHP	71	Tyler Freeman	Cleveland Indians	21	SS
22	Luis Patino	San Diego Padres	20	RHP	72	Logan Gilbert	Seattle Mariners	23	RHP
23	Grayson Rodriguez	Baltimore Orioles	20	RHP	73	Jazz Chisholm	Miami Marlins	22	SS
24	Sixto Sanchez	Miami Marlins	21	RHP	74	Jeter Downs	Boston Red Sox	21	SS
25	Oneil Cruz	Pittsburgh Pirates	21	SS	75	Jordan Groshans	Toronto Blue Jays	20	SS
26	Brendan McKay	Tampa Bay Rays	26	1B/LHP	76	Bryse Wilson	Atlanta Braves	22	RHP
27	Brandon Marsh	Los Angeles Angels	22	OF	77	Ian Anderson	Atlanta Braves	22	RHP
28	Spencer Howard	Philadelphia Phillies	23	RHP	78	Corbin Martin	Arizona Diamondbacks	22	RHP
29	Andrew Vaughn	Chicago White Sox	22	1B	79	Shane Baz	Tampa Bay Rays	21	RHP
30	CJ Abrams	San Diego Padres	19	SS	80	Tarik Skubal	Detroit Tigers	23	LHP
31	Bobby Witt Jr.	Kansas City Royals	20	SS	81	Diego Cartaya	Los Angeles Dodgers	18	C
32	Michael Kopech	Chicago White Sox	24	RHP	82	S. Woods Richardson	Toronto Blue Jays	19	RHP
33	Hunter Greene	Cincinnati Reds	21	RHP	83	Jose Urquidy	Houston Astros	25	RHP
34	Forrest Whitley	Houston Astros	22	RHP	84	Jose Garcia	Cincinnati Reds	22	SS
35	Brendan Rodgers	Colorado Rockies	23	IF	85	Brennen Davis	Chicago Cubs	20	OF
36	Edward Cabrera	Miami Marlins	22	RHP	86	Isaac Paredes	Detroit Tigers	21	IF
37	Casey Mize	Detroit Tigers	23	RHP	87	Josh Jung	Texas Rangers	22	3B
38	Drew Waters	Atlanta Braves	21	OF	88	Brett Baty	New York Mets	20	3B
39	Daulton Varsho	Arizona Diamondbacks	23	C	89	Brailyn Marquez	Chicago Cubs	21	LHP
40	Alec Bohm	Philadelphia Phillies	23	1B/3B	90	Daniel Espino	Cleveland Indians	19	RHP
41	JJ Bleday	Miami Marlins	22	RF	91	Nick Solak	Texas Rangers	25	2B/3B
42	Corbin Carroll	Arizona Diamondbacks	19	CF	92	Jonathan India	Cincinnati Reds	23	3B
43	Jhoan Duran	Minnesota Twins	22	RHP	93	Nick Allen	Oakland Athletics	21	SS
44	Nolan Jones	Cleveland Indians	22	3B	94	Ryan Mountcastle	Baltimore Orioles	23	1B/LF
45	Heliot Ramos	San Francisco Giants	20	CF	95	Sean Murphy	Oakland Athletics	25	C
46	Keibert Ruiz	Los Angeles Dodgers	21	C	96	Triston McKenzie	Cleveland Indians	26	RHP
47	Shane McClanahan	Tampa Bay Rays	23	LHP	97	Triston Casas	Boston Red Sox	20	1B
48	Brady Singer	Kansas City Royals	23	RHP	98	Daniel Lynch	Kansas City Royals	23	LHP
49	Josh Lowe	Tampa Bay Rays	22	OF	99	Tony Gonsolin	Los Angeles Dodgers	26	RHP
50	Luis Campusano	San Diego Padres	21	C	100	Vidal Brujan	Tampa Bay Rays	22	2B/SS

Ranking the Top 300 Prospects (101-200)

Rank	Name	Team	Age	Pos	Rank	Name	Team	Age	Pos
101	Jordan Balazovic	Minnesota Twins	21	RHP	151	Anthony Banda	Tampa Bay Rays	26	LHP
102	Ivan Herrera	St. Louis Cardinals	20	C	152	Clarke Schmidt	New York Yankees	24	RHP
103	Michael Siani	Cincinnati Reds	20	CF	153	Daulton Jefferies	Oakland Athletics	24	RHP
104	Liover Peguero	Pittsburgh Pirates	19	SS	154	Khalil Lee	Kansas City Royals	22	CF
105	Tahnaj Thomas	Pittsburgh Pirates	21	RHP	155	Genesis Cabrera	St. Louis Cardinals	23	LHP
106	Brusdar Graterol	Los Angeles Dodgers	22	RHP	156	Justus Sheffield	Seattle Mariners	24	LHP
107	Patrick Sandoval	Los Angeles Angels	23	LHP	157	Chris Vallimont	Minnesota Twins	23	RHP
108	Kyle Wright	Atlanta Braves	24	RHP	158	Cristian Javier	Houston Astros	23	RHP
109	Xavier Edwards	Tampa Bay Rays	20	2B/SS	159	Hunter Bishop	San Francisco Giants	22	CF
110	George Valera	Cleveland Indians	19	CF	160	Alexander Vizcaino	New York Yankees	23	RHP
111	Jay Groome	Boston Red Sox	22	LHP	161	Alek Manoah	Toronto Blue Jays	22	RHP
112	Geraldo Perdomo	Arizona Diamondbacks	20	SS	162	Zack Thompson	St. Louis Cardinals	22	LHP
113	Francisco Alvarez	New York Mets	18	C	163	Brennan Malone	Pittsburgh Pirates	23	RHP
114	Abraham Toro	Houston Astros	23	IF	164	Brayan Rocchio	Cleveland Indians	19	2B/SS
115	William Contreras	Atlanta Braves	22	C	165	Daz Cameron	Detroit Tigers	23	CF
116	Jesus Sanchez	Miami Marlins	22	RF	166	Jordyn Adams	Los Angeles Angels	20	CF
117	Lewin Diaz	Miami Marlins	23	1B	167	Josh Stephen	Philadelphia Phillies	22	LF
118	Matthew Liberatore	St. Louis Cardinals	21	LHP	168	Francisco Morales	Philadelphia Phillies	20	RHP
119	Adrian Morejon	San Diego Padres	21	LHP	169	Ronny Henriquez	Texas Rangers	20	RHP
120	Ryan Weathers	San Diego Padres	20	LHP	170	J.B. Bukauskas	Arizona Diamondbacks	24	RHP
121	Josiah Gray	Los Angeles Dodgers	22	RHP	171	Bryan Abreu	Houston Astros	23	RHP
122	Travis Swaggerty	Pittsburgh Pirates	22	CF	172	Drew Rasmussen	Milwaukee Brewers	24	RHP
123	Randy Arozarena	Tampa Bay Rays	25	OF	173	Thomas Szapucki	New York Mets	24	LHP
124	Braden Shewmake	Atlanta Braves	22	SS	174	Estevan Florial	New York Yankees	22	CF
125	Seth Corry	San Francisco Giants	21	LHP	175	Robert Puason	Oakland Athletics	17	SS
126	Logan Webb	San Francisco Giants	23	RHP	176	Jon Duplantier	Arizona Diamondbacks	25	RHP
127	Miguel Vargas	Los Angeles Dodgers	20	3B	177	Justin Dunn	Seattle Mariners	24	RHP
128	Bryan Mata	Boston Red Sox	21	RHP	178	Zac Lowther	Baltimore Orioles	24	LHP
129	Cody Bolton	Pittsburgh Pirates	22	RHP	179	Bowden Francis	Milwaukee Brewers	24	RHP
130	Ryan Rolison	Colorado Rockies	22	LHP	180	Bo Naylor	Cleveland Indians	20	C
131	Ethan Hankins	Cleveland Indians	20	RHP	181	Ryan Vilade	Colorado Rockies	21	3B/SS
132	Jackson Rutledge	Washington Nationals	21	RHP	182	Cody Morris	Cleveland Indians	23	RHP
133	Matthew Allan	New York Mets	23	RHP	183	Jarren Duran	Boston Red Sox	23	CF
134	Tyler Stephenson	Cincinnati Reds	23	C	184	Kyle Muller	Atlanta Braves	22	LHP
135	Noah Song	Boston Red Sox	23	RHP	185	Braxton Garrett	Miami Marlins	22	LHP
136	Kody Hoese	Los Angeles Dodgers	22	3B	186	David Peterson	New York Mets	24	LHP
137	Orelvis Martinez	Toronto Blue Jays	18	3B/SS	187	Quinn Priester	Pittsburgh Pirates	19	RHP
138	Brice Turang	Milwaukee Brewers	20	2B/SS	188	Trevor Rogers	Miami Marlins	22	LHP
139	Gabriel Moreno	Toronto Blue Jays	20	C	189	Tony Santillan	Cincinnati Reds	23	RHP
140	Wilderd Patino	Arizona Diamondbacks	18	CF	190	Luis Matos	San Francisco Giants	18	CF
141	Alejandro Kirk	Toronto Blue Jays	21	C	191	Greg Jones	Tampa Bay Rays	22	SS
142	Blake Walston	Arizona Diamondbacks	20	LHP	192	Gilberto Celestino	Minnesota Twins	21	CF
143	Hans Crouse	Texas Rangers	21	RHP	193	Michael Busch	Los Angeles Dodgers	22	1B/2B
144	Eric Pardinho	Toronto Blue Jays	19	RHP	194	Bobby Dalbec	Boston Red Sox	25	1B/3B
145	Seth Beer	Arizona Diamondbacks	23	1B/LF	195	Antonio Santos	Colorado Rockies	23	RHP
146	Andrew Knizner	St. Louis Cardinals	25	C	196	Ethan Small	Milwaukee Brewers	23	LHP
147	Nico Hoerner	Chicago Cubs	23	SS	197	Aaron Ashby	Milwaukee Brewers	22	LHP
148	Anthony Kay	Toronto Blue Jays	25	LHP	198	Ji-Hwan Bae	Pittsburgh Pirates	20	2B/SS
149	Pavin Smith	Arizona Diamondbacks	24	1B/LF	199	Cole Winn	Texas Rangers	20	RHP
150	George Kirby	Seattle Mariners	22	RHP	200	Kameron Misner	Miami Marlins	22	CF

Ranking the Top 300 Prospects (201-300)

Rank	Name	Team	Age	Pos
201	Kyle Isbel	Kansas City Royals	23	CF
202	Jack Herman	Pittsburgh Pirates	20	OF
203	Bryson Stott	Philadelphia Phillies	22	SS
204	Brenton Doyle	Colorado Rockies	22	CF
205	Drew Rom	Baltimore Orioles	20	LHP
206	Keoni Cavaco	Minnesota Twins	26	SS
207	Arol Vera	Los Angeles Angels	17	SS
208	Miguel Amaya	Chicago Cubs	21	C
209	Elehuris Montero	St. Louis Cardinals	21	3B
210	Yohanse Morel	Kansas City Royals	19	RHP
211	Helcris Olivarez	Colorado Rockies	19	LHP
212	Kevin Alcantara	New York Yankees	17	CF
213	Alexander Canario	San Francisco Giants	20	OF
214	Malcom Nunez	St. Louis Cardinals	19	3B
215	Erick Pena	Kansas City Royals	23	CF
216	Seth Romero	Washington Nationals	23	LHP
217	James Karinchak	Cleveland Indians	24	RHP
218	Emmanuel Clase	Cleveland Indians	22	RHP
219	Joe Ryan	Tampa Bay Rays	24	RHP
220	Kris Bubic	Kansas City Royals	22	LHP
221	Austin Allen	Oakland Athletics	26	C
222	Ryan Jeffers	Minnesota Twins	23	C
223	Brent Rooker	Minnesota Twins	25	1B/LF
224	Jared Oliva	Pittsburgh Pirates	24	CF
225	Owen Miller	San Diego Padres	23	IF
226	Michel Baez	San Diego Padres	24	RHP
227	Luis Toribio	San Francisco Giants	19	3B
228	Jairo Pomares	San Francisco Giants	19	RF
229	Adam Kloffenstein	Toronto Blue Jays	19	RHP
230	Luis Medina	New York Yankees	21	RHP
231	Michael Baumann	Baltimore Orioles	24	RHP
232	Lyon Richardson	Cincinnati Reds	20	RHP
233	Mauricio Dubon	San Francisco Giants	25	2B/SS
234	Chase Strumpf	Chicago Cubs	22	2B
235	Luis Garcia	Philadelphia Phillies	19	2B/SS
236	Michael Toglia	Colorado Rockies	21	1B/LF/RF
237	Ronaldo Hernandez	Tampa Bay Rays	22	C
238	Jorge Guzman	Miami Marlins	24	RHP
239	Tucker Davidson	Atlanta Braves	24	LHP
240	Huascar Ynoa	Atlanta Braves	22	RHP
241	Jake Fraley	Seattle Mariners	25	OF
242	Joey Cantillo	San Diego Padres	20	LHP
243	Joey Wentz	Detroit Tigers	22	LHP
244	Alex Faedo	Detroit Tigers	24	RHP
245	Colton Welker	Colorado Rockies	22	1B/3B
246	Peyton Burdick	Miami Marlins	23	LF
247	Darryl Collins	Kansas City Royals	18	LF
248	Kendall Williams	Toronto Blue Jays	25	RHP
249	Josh Smith	New York Yankees	22	SS
250	Miguel Hiraldo	Toronto Blue Jays	19	2B/SS
251	Lolo Sanchez	Pittsburgh Pirates	21	CF
252	Drey Jameson	Arizona Diamondbacks	22	RHP
253	Carlos Rodriguez	Milwaukee Brewers	19	OF
254	Anthony Volpe	New York Yankees	19	SS
255	Matt Tabor	Arizona Diamondbacks	21	RHP
256	Adbert Alzolay	Chicago Cubs	25	RHP
257	Brayan Bello	Boston Red Sox	21	RHP
258	Cal Mitchell	Pittsburgh Pirates	21	RF
259	Josh Wolf	New York Mets	23	RHP
260	Austin Hays	Baltimore Orioles	24	OF
261	Terrin Vavra	Colorado Rockies	23	2B/SS
262	Gabriel Arias	San Diego Padres	20	SS
263	Cadyn Grenier	Baltimore Orioles	23	SS
264	Thad Ward	Boston Red Sox	23	RHP
265	Logan Davidson	Oakland Athletics	22	SS
266	Will Wilson	San Francisco Giants	21	SS
267	Kevin Smith	New York Mets	23	LHP
268	Rece Hinds	Cincinnati Reds	21	3B
269	Tristen Lutz	Milwaukee Brewers	21	OF
270	Logan Wyatt	San Francisco Giants	22	1B
271	Andry Lara	Washington Nationals	17	RHP
272	Lane Thomas	St. Louis Cardinals	24	OF
273	Ben Rortvedt	Minnesota Twins	22	C
274	Logan Allen	Cleveland Indians	23	LHP
275	Brandon Bailey	Baltimore Orioles	25	RHP
276	Gunnar Henderson	Baltimore Orioles	19	SS
277	Shea Langeliers	Atlanta Braves	22	C
278	Tyler Ivey	Houston Astros	24	RHP
279	Luis Torrens	San Diego Padres	24	C
280	Jose Alberto Rivera	Houston Astros	23	RHP
281	Tanner Houck	Boston Red Sox	24	RHP
282	Mateo Gil	St. Louis Cardinals	19	SS
283	Ezequiel Tovar	Colorado Rockies	18	SS
284	Everson Pereira	New York Yankees	19	CF
285	Ronnie Quintero	Chicago Cubs	23	C
286	Lewis Thorpe	Minnesota Twins	24	LHP
287	Franklin Perez	Detroit Tigers	24	RHP
288	Brock Burke	Texas Rangers	23	LHP
289	Justin Williams	St. Louis Cardinals	24	LF/RF
290	Grant Holmes	Oakland Athletics	24	RHP
291	Mark Vientos	New York Mets	20	3B
292	Aaron Bracho	Cleveland Indians	19	2B
293	Daniel Johnson	Cleveland Indians	24	OF
294	Hunter Harvey	Baltimore Orioles	25	RHP
295	Mario Feliciano	Milwaukee Brewers	21	C
296	Michael Harris	Atlanta Braves	19	CF
297	Matt Wallner	Minnesota Twins	22	RF
298	Blayne Enlow	Minnesota Twins	21	RHP
299	Canaan Smith	New York Yankees	21	LF
300	Mickey Moniak	Philadelphia Phillies	22	CF

The Top 10 Prospects by Position

The Top 10 Prospects By Position

Catchers		
1.	Adley Rutschman	Baltimore Orioles
2.	Joey Bart	San Francisco Giants
3.	Daulton Varsho	Arizona Diamondbacks
4.	Keibert Ruiz	Los Angeles Dodgers
5.	Luis Campusano	San Diego Padres
6.	Diego Cartaya	Los Angeles Dodgers
7.	Sean Murphy	Oakland Athletics
8.	Ivan Herrera	St. Louis Cardinals
9.	Francisco Alvarez	New York Mets
10.	William Contreras	Atlanta Braves

Shortstop		
1.	Wander Franco	Tampa Bay Rays
2.	Gavin Lux	Los Angeles Dodgers
3.	Marco Luciano	San Francisco Giants
4.	Carter Kieboom	Washington Nationals
5.	Oneil Cruz	Pittsburgh Pirates
6.	CJ Abrams	San Diego Padres
7.	Bobby Witt Jr.	Kansas City Royals
8.	Brendan Rodgers	Colorado Rockies
9.	Andres Gimenez	New York Mets
10.	Ronny Mauricio	New York Mets

First Base		
1.	Alex Kirilloff	Minnesota Twins
2.	Andrew Vaughn	Chicago White Sox
3.	Alec Bohm	Philadelphia Phillies
4.	Evan White	Seattle Mariners
5.	Ryan Mountcastle	Baltimore Orioles
6.	Triston Casas	Boston Red Sox
7.	Lewin Diaz	Miami Marlins
8.	Seth Beer	Arizona Diamondbacks
9.	Pavin Smith	Arizona Diamondbacks
10.	Michael Busch	Los Angeles Dodgers

Outfield		
1.	Jo Adell	Los Angeles Angels
2.	Jarred Kelenic	Seattle Mariners
3.	Luis Robert	Chicago White Sox
4.	Cristian Pache	Atlanta Braves
5.	Julio Rodriguez	Seattle Mariners
6.	Alex Kirilloff	Minnesota Twins
7.	Dylan Carlson	St. Louis Cardinals
8.	Kristian Robinson	Arizona Diamondbacks
9.	Brandon Marsh	Los Angeles Angels
10.	Drew Waters	Atlanta Braves

Second Base		
1.	Gavin Lux	Los Angeles Dodgers
2.	Carter Kieboom	Washington Nationals
3.	Brendan Rodgers	Colorado Rockies
4.	Nick Madrigal	Chicago White Sox
5.	Luis Garcia	Washington Nationals
6.	Isaac Paredes	Detroit Tigers
7.	Nick Solak	Texas Rangers
8.	Vidal Brujan	Tampa Bay Rays
9.	Xavier Edwards	Tampa Bay Rays
10.	Abraham Toro	Houston Astros

Left-Handed Pitchers		
1.	MacKenzie Gore	San Diego Padres
2.	Jesus Luzardo	Oakland Athletics
3.	A.J. Puk	Oakland Athletics
4.	Brendan McKay	Tampa Bay Rays
5.	Shane McClanahan	Tampa Bay Rays
6.	Nick Lodolo	Cincinnati Reds
7.	DL Hall	Baltimore Orioles
8.	Tarik Skubal	Detroit Tigers
9.	Brailyn Marquez	Chicago Cubs
10.	Daniel Lynch	Kansas City Royals

Third Base		
1.	Alec Bohm	Philadelphia Phillies
2.	Nolan Jones	Cleveland Indians
3.	Ke'Bryan Hayes	Pittsburgh Pirates
4.	Nolan Gorman	St. Louis Cardinals
5.	Isaac Paredes	Detroit Tigers
6.	Josh Jung	Texas Rangers
7.	Brett Baty	New York Mets
8.	Jonathan India	Cincinnati Reds
9.	Abraham Toro	Houston Astros
10.	Miguel Vargas	Los Angeles Dodgers

Right-Handed Pitchers		
1.	Dustin May	Los Angeles Dodgers
2.	Nate Pearson	Toronto Blue Jays
3.	Mitch Keller	Pittsburgh Pirates
4.	Matt Manning	Detroit Tigers
5.	Luis Patino	San Diego Padres
6.	Grayson Rodriguez	Baltimore Orioles
7.	Sixto Sanchez	Miami Marlins
8.	Spencer Howard	Philadelphia Phillies
9.	Michael Kopech	Chicago White Sox
10.	Hunter Greene	Cincinnati Reds

Ranking the 2020 Farm Systems

Ranking the 2020 Farm Systems

Rank	Team
#1	Tampa Bay Rays
#2	Los Angeles Dodgers
#3	Arizona Diamondbacks
#4	San Diego Padres
#5	Pittsburgh Pirates
#6	San Francisco Giants
#7	Atlanta Braves
#8	Toronto Blue Jays
#9	Minnesota Twins
#10	Miami Marlins
#11	Cleveland Indians
#12	Boston Red Sox
#13	Detroit Tigers
#14	St. Louis Cardinals
#15	Oakland Athletics
#16	Baltimore Orioles
#17	New York Mets
#18	Cincinnati Reds
#19	Chicago White Sox
#20	New York Yankees
#21	Los Angeles Angels
#22	Houston Astros
#23	Kansas City Royals
#24	Colorado Rockies
#25	Seattle Mariners
#26	Philadelphia Phillies
#27	Washington Nationals
#28	Chicago Cubs
#29	Milwaukee Brewers
#30	Texas Rangers

The Top 25 Breakout Prospects for 2020

The Top 25 Breakout Prospects for 2020

1. **George Valera, CF, Cleveland Indians**
   Big time exit velocities – despite (A) being limited to handful of games during his 2019 debut and (B) squaring off against significantly older seasons. Valera's likely to be a Top 100 Prospect by year's end.

2. **Chris Vallimont, RHP, Minnesota Twins**
   Incredibly underrated right-hander acquired as the "second piece" from the Marlins last season. Lethal fastball/curveball combination.

3. **Drew Rasmussen, RHP, Milwaukee Brewers**
   Former collegiate ace that's undergone not one, but two Tommy John surgeries. Fastball was back up to the mid-90s in 2019. Look for the development of a third offspeed pitch. There's some Brandon Workman-type qualities here.

4. **Ivan Herrera, C, St. Louis Cardinals**
   One of the more underrated catching prospects in baseball. The then-19-year-old backstop slugged .284/.374/.405 between the Midwest and Florida State Leagues.

5. **Victor Vodnik, RHP, Atlanta Braves**
   Former late round pick that worked primarily in a multi-inning relief role in the South Atlantic League last season.

6. **Bryan Ramos, 3B, Chicago White**
   Love the swing. The teenage Cuban import batted .277/.353/.415 in the Arizona Summer League. Big time power potential. Elite bat speed.

7. **Lyon Richardson, RHP, Cincinnati Reds**
   A second round pick two years ago. A lot of potential due to his lack of pitching experience. Watch out for the Driveline Baseball boost, too.

8. **Cody Morris, RHP, Cleveland Indians**
   Plus- to plus-plus fastball and solid secondary offerings. Morris is exactly the type of pitcher the Indians have thrived at developing. Quietly dominant last season. And it wouldn't be out of the realm of possibility to see him called up down the stretch in 2020.

9. **Antonio Santos, RHP, Colorado Rockies**
   Nitrous-infused fastball. Throws strikes. Dark horse candidate for N.L. Rookie of the Year.

10. **Brenton Doyle, CF, Colorado Rockies**
    Former Shepherd University star slugged .383/.477/.611 during his debut in the Pioneer League. Power, speed, patience.

11. **Helcris Olivarez, LHP, Colorado Rockies**
    Teenage left-hander owns a plus fastball with a curveball that peak as an above-average offering. Big time potential, but there's risk.

12. **Terrin Vavra, 2B, SS, Colardo Rockies**
    Chris Coghlan clone that shows some defensive versatility, speed, solid glove, and a little bit of pop. Colorado's handled him conservatively at this point. But he's ticketed for High Class A to open 2020 with the likelihood of spending a good portion in Class AA.

13. **Ezequiel Tovar, SS, Colorado Rockies**
    Elite defensive shortstop that (A) may never hit but (B) likely ascends to the big leagues based on his glove.

14. **Kyle Isbel, CF, Kansas City Royals**
    Former University of Nevada-Las Vegas star was banged up during the regular season but dominated the Arizona Fall League by hitting .315/.429/.438. Underrated tools.

15. **Kevin Alcantara, CF, New York Yankees**
    Very impressive batted ball data as a 16-year-old in the Arizona Summer League last season: 88 mph average exit velocity and a peak exit velocity of 106 mph. He's going to *explode*.

16. **Josh Stephen, LF, Philadelphia Phillies**
    One of my favorite prospects in the minor leagues. There are some red flags – like his defensive shortcomings and lack of production against lefties – but he skipped all of High Class A and put together his finest season to date.

17. **Kendall Simmons, IF**

Loud tools. Slugged .280/.387/.660 over his final 30 games in short season action.

18. **Seth Johnson, RHP, Tampa Bay Rays**

Became a full-time pitcher in 2019 and shot up draft charts. A ton of projection remains.

19. **Adam Kloffenstein, RHP, Toronto Blue Jays**

Handled conservatively by the front office. Kloffenstein owns four above-average pitches with an idea on how to use them.

20. **Jordan Groshans, SS, Toronto Blue Jays**

Dominant production when he's on the field. He could jump into the Top 10 prospects in all of baseball with a healthy showing in 2020.

21. **Diego Cartaya, C, Los Angeles Dodgers**

The surging backstop could overtake Keibert Ruiz as the club's top catching prospect within a year. Big time power potential.

22. **Cody Bolton, RHP, Pittsburgh Pirates**

85% of Mitch Keller. He's poised to claim a spot in the Pirates' rotation by midseason.

23. **Blake Walston, LHP, Arizona Diamondbacks**

Raw lefty was taken early by the club. Tons of projection as his frame fills out.

24. **Tahnaj Thomas, RHP, Pittsburgh Pirates**

Former infielder with a big time fastball, an impressive curveball, and a strong feel for the strike zone.

25. **Yohanse Morel, RHP, Kansas City Royals**

If Morel navigates his way through the injury nexus, he has as high of a ceiling as any arm in the Royals' farm system.

Organizational Analysis

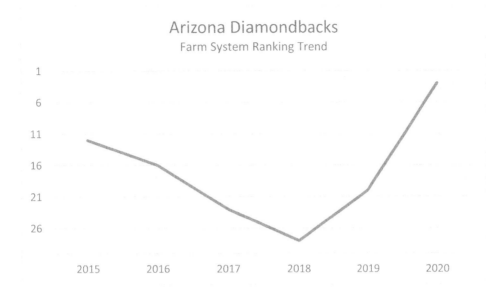

Arizona Diamondbacks
Farm System Ranking Trend

Rank	Name	Age	Pos
1	Kristian Robinson	19	CF
2	Daulton Varsho	23	C
3	Corbin Carroll	19	CF
4	Alek Thomas	20	CF
5	Corbin Martin	22	RHP
6	Geraldo Perdomo	20	SS
7	Wilderd Patino	18	CF
8	Seth Beer	23	1B/LF
9	Pavin Smith	24	1B/LF
10	Blake Walston	20	LHP
11	J.B. Bukauskas	24	RHP
12	Jon Duplantier	25	RHP
13	Drey Jameson	20	RHP
14	Matt Tabor	21	RHP
15	Jake McCarthy	22	CF
16	Levi Kelly	21	RHP
17	Dominic Fletcher	22	OF
18	Bo Takahashi	23	RHP
19	Ryne Nelson	22	RHP
20	Tommy Henry	22	LHP

1. Kristian Robinson, CF

Hit	Power	SB	Patience	Glove	Overall
45/55	55/60	50	55	50	60

Born: 12/11/00	Age: 19	Bats: R
Height: 6-3	Weight: 190	Throws: R

YEAR	LVL	PA	1B	2B	3B	HR	SB	CS	AVG	OBP	SLG	BB%	K%	GB%	LD%	FB%
2018	RK	182	29	11	0	4	7	5	0.272	0.341	0.414	8.79%	25.27%	43.2	21.2	28
2018	RK	74	14	1	0	3	5	3	0.300	0.419	0.467	14.86%	28.38%	50	17.5	25
2019	A-	189	32	10	1	9	14	3	0.319	0.407	0.558	12.17%	24.87%	44.8	19.8	31.9
2019	A	102	11	3	1	5	3	2	0.217	0.294	0.435	7.84%	29.41%	54.8	9.7	21

Background: After striking gold by signing Jazz Chisholm, who was dealt to the Marlins last season, from the Bahamas in 2015, Arizona handed fellow countryman Kristian Robinson a hefty $2.5 million bonus two seasons later. Standing a wiry 6-foot-3 and 190-pounds, the supremely gifted outfielder bypassed the foreign rookie leagues and split time between the Arizona Summer and Pioneer Leagues during his debut; he batted an aggregate .279/.363/.428 with 12 doubles and seven homeruns with 12 stolen bases. Last season, Robinson opened the year up by slugging .319/.407/.558 with 10 doubles, one triple, and nine homeruns in only 44 games before he was promoted up to the Midwest League. Robinson capped off second professional season with a .282/.368/.514 triple-slash line, belting out 13 doubles, two triples, and 14 homeruns to go along with 17 stolen bases in 22 total attempts.

Snippet from The 2018 Prospect Digest Handbook: There's a lot to like about the teenage center fielder: solid patience at the plate, OK hit tool and contact rates, above-average speed, and promising power potential. Robinson is still quite raw. And he's going to have to cut down his strikeouts. But it's incredibly promising that he handled jumping straight into the stateside rookie league and then a brief tour through the Pioneer League.

Scouting Report: With respect to his work in short-season ball, consider the following:

- Since 2006, here are the top two offensive seasons in the Northwest League by an 18-year-old with a minimum of 175 PA: Kristian Robinson and Kevin Padlo. But here's the impressive part: Robinson's production was an eye-catching 44-percentage points better than the runner-up.

As I indicated in last year's Handbook, there's a lot to like about Robinson: burgeoning plus power, plus speed, strong glove in center field, and top notch production against older competition. However – and there's *always* a "however" – the strikeout rates continues to be an issue. He whiffed in a quarter of his plate appearances with Hillsboro and slightly less than 30% of his plate appearances with Kane County. He has superstar potential and I think he eventually works past the strikeout issues. One more final note: per FanGraphs, Robinson's average exit velocity was a whopping 92 mph with a peak of 109 mph last season.

Ceiling: 5.0-win player
Risk: Moderate
MLB ETA: 2022

2. Daulton Varsho, C

Hit	Power	SB	Patience	Glove	Overall
55	55	50	50	50	60

Born: 07/02/96	Age: 23	Bats: L
Height: 5-10	Weight: 190	Throws: R

YEAR	LVL	PA	1B	2B	3B	HR	SB	CS	AVG	OBP	SLG	BB%	K%	GB%	LD%	FB%
2017	A-	212	34	16	3	7	7	2	0.311	0.368	0.534	8.02%	14.15%	47.6	17.1	25
2018	RK	12	2	2	1	1	0	0	0.500	0.500	1.083	0.00%	8.33%	36.4	18.2	36.4
2018	A+	342	62	11	3	11	19	3	0.286	0.363	0.451	8.77%	20.76%	39.3	21.4	26.9
2019	AA	452	72	25	4	18	21	5	0.301	0.378	0.520	9.29%	13.94%	39.2	13.8	32.9

Background: The son of ex-big leaguer Gary Varsho, who batted .244/.294/.355 across parts of eight seasons with the Cubs, Pirates, Reds, and Phillies, The younger Varsho was one of the more intriguing names in the 2017 draft class. A product of the University of Wisconsin at Milwaukee, the lefty-swinging backstop put up some eye-popping numbers beginning with his first stint in the Northwoods Summer League and continued all the way through the his final two years in college. Arizona drafted the Wisconsin native in the second round, 68th overall, and he's continued to produce as he made his way up the minor league ladder. Varsho batted .311/.368/.534 in short-season ball. And he followed that up with a .294/.367/.475 slash line as he was aggressively pushed up to the California League. Last season, Varsho appeared in a career best 108 games for the Jackson Generals in the Southern League, slugging .301/.378/.520 with career highs in doubles (25) and homeruns (18) to go along with a quartet of triples. The speedy backstop also swiped an impressive 21 bags in only 26 attempts. His overall production, as measured by Baseball Prospectus' *Deserved Runs Created Plus*, topped the league average threshold by a whopping 56%.

Snippet from The 2018 Prospect Digest Handbook: As I remarked heading into the 2017 draft, Varsho has "double-digit power, an average eye at the plate, and strong contact skills – all wrapped up at a premium position." And that analysis/scouting report still holds true a year later – despite an aggressive promotion up to High Class A. The lefty-swinging Varsho shows no semblance of platoon splits and has looked like a brick wall behind the dish, posting a +16 in the runs saved department since entering the professional ranks. Varsho remains one of the more underrated backstops in the minor leagues. Plus, he's only entering his age-22 season.

Scouting Report: Consider the following:

- Since 2006, here's the list of 22-year-old hitters to post a 150 to 160 DRC+ in the Southern League (min. 350 PA): Desmond Jennings, Angel Salome, and Daulton Varsho. Jennings was a prolific athlete that was a better than league average bat during his peak. Salome was once considered a top prospect with a dynamic bat, but battled his own demons and only briefly got called up to the big leagues.

As for Varsho, well, what can't he do? Nothing, really. He hits for average and power. He runs well for an outfielder, let alone a full time catcher. He's willing to walk and owns fantastic contact rates. And the lefty-swinging prospect doesn't own any serious platoon splits. Arizona now controls one of the better young catchers in the big leagues – Carson Kelly – as well as one of the best prospects at the same position. One more thought: Varsho does have the athleticism, a la Craig Biggio, to move to another position and succeed.

Ceiling: 4.0-win player
Risk: Moderate
MLB ETA: 2020

3. Corbin Carroll, CF

	Hit	Power	SB	Patience	Glove	Overall
	50/60	45/50	55	55	55	60

Born: 08/21/00	Age: 19	Bats: L
Height: 5-10	Weight: 165	Throws: L

YEAR	LVL	PA	1B	2B	3B	HR	SB	CS	AVG	OBP	SLG	BB%	K%	GB%	LD%	FB%
2019	Rk	137	21	6	3	2	16	1	0.288	0.409	0.450	17.52%	21.17%	60.7	16.7	17.9
2019	A-	49	7	3	4	0	2	0	0.326	0.408	0.581	10.20%	24.49%	38.7	32.3	22.6

Background: Typically, top prep prospects have the hulking frames or wiry, quick-twitchy builds that ooze potential. For example, there were seven high school players chosen in the Top 10 selections between 2017 and 2018. The smallest player, Jarred Kelenic, measured in at 6-foot-1 and 196 pounds. Enter: Corbin Carroll. A UCLA commit since his sophomore season at Lakeside High School, Carroll stands a diminutive – though rock solid – 5-foot-10 and 165 pounds. Carroll's smaller frame size, however, didn't limit or hinder his skyrocketing draft status, nor has it negatively impacted his on-field performance. Winner of Washington's Gatorade Baseball Player of the Year, the Seattle native also starred for the 18U Team USA National Squad in 2018 as well. Playing alongside likes of other elite prospects, he batted .500/.615/1.000 with four doubles and one triple while tying for the team best in homeruns (3). He also swiped a team-leading nine bags and sported a solid 2-to-3 strikeout-to-walk ratio. Arizona drafted him in the opening round, 16th overall, and signed him to a deal worth $3,745,500 – the recommended slot bonus. The toolsy outfielder split time between the stateside rookie league and Hillsboro, hitting a combined .299/.409/.487 with nine doubles, seven triples, and a pair of homeruns with 18 stolen bases in 19 total attempts.

Scouting Report: One of my favorite, if not my absolute favorite, player in the entire 2019 draft class. Here's what I wrote about the Lakeside School product prior to the draft:

"Surprising power thank to his elite bat speed and natural loft in a silky smooth left-handed swing. Carroll's a legitimate five-tool prospect, showcasing above-average tools across the board. He has a tendency to expand the strike zone at times, especially against fastballs up. Carroll's very reminiscent of an early career Adam Eaton. Between 2015 and 2016, the above-average center fielder slugged .286/.362/.430 while averaging 30 doubles, nine triples, 15 homeruns, and 17 stolen bases every 162 games."

The club top pick from last June showed no massive red flags. He's an absolute gamer. Love him. One more thought: per FanGraphs, his average exit velocity was an impressive 91 mph with a peak of 108 mph.

Ceiling: 4.0-win player
Risk: Moderate
MLB ETA: 2022

4. Alek Thomas, CF

Hit	Power	SB	Patience	Glove	Overall
55	55	50	50	50	55

Born: 04/28/00	Age: 20	Bats: L
Height: 5-11	Weight: 175	Throws: L

YEAR	LVL	PA	1B	2B	3B	HR	SB	CS	AVG	OBP	SLG	BB%	K%	GB%	LD%	FB%
2018	RK	138	32	3	5	0	8	2	0.325	0.394	0.431	9.42%	13.04%	57.1	17.1	21
2018	RK	134	28	11	1	2	4	3	0.341	0.396	0.496	8.21%	14.18%	51.9	23.1	22.1
2019	A	402	74	21	7	8	11	6	0.312	0.393	0.479	10.70%	17.91%	56.3	17	23.1
2019	A+	104	20	2	0	2	4	5	0.255	0.327	0.340	8.65%	31.73%	47.5	34.4	14.8

Background: Sharing a couple similarities with Daulton Varsho: #1 Thomas was also taken in the second round of the draft (2018) and #2 the young center fielder also has some interesting, baseball-related bloodlines; his father, Allen, is the Director of Conditioning for the Chicago White Sox. The 63rd overall selection out of Mount Carmel High School two years ago, Thomas, a 5-foot-11, 175-pound toolsy center fielder, turned in a dynamic debut as he split time between the Arizona Summer and Pioneer Leagues. In a combined 56 games, he slugged .333/.395/.463 with 14 doubles, six triples, and a pair of homeruns. He also swiped 12 bags in 17 attempts. Last season, Thomas, once again, split time at two separate levels: he appeared in 91 games in the Midwest League and another 23 contests in the California League. He batted a combined .300/.379/.450 with 23 doubles, seven triples, 10 homeruns, and 15 stolen bases.

Snippet from The 2018 Prospect Digest Handbook: Thomas showed a promising, well-rounded game on both sides of the ball. He has the potential to develop an above-average hit tool to go along with plenty of speed and solid defense. If he develops power – which may or may not happen because he put more than 50% of his balls in play on the ground – Thomas looks like a five-tool threat.

Scouting Report: With respect to his work in Low Class A last season, consider the following:

- Since 2006, here's the list of 19-year-old hitters to post a 150 to 160 DRC+ in the Midwest League with a sub-20% strikeout rate (min. 350 PA): Luis Arraez and – of course – Alek Thomas. Arraez, by the way, finished sixth in the A.L. Rookie of the Year voting after hitting .334/.399/.439 for the Twins last season.

Like Varsho, Thomas offers up an incredibly well-rounded approach at the plate, showing an above-average hit tool, power that should grow into a perennial 20-homer threat, and above-average speed. Thomas does show a slight platoon split, but it barely registers a blip on his future ceiling. Defensively, he's average.

Ceiling: 3.5- to 4.0-win player
Risk: Moderate
MLB ETA: 2020

5. Corbin Martin, RHP

FB	CB	SL	CH	Command	Overall
65	55	60	55/60	45/50	60

Born: 12/28/95	Age: 24	Bats: R
Height: 6-2	Weight: 200	Throws: R

YEAR	LVL	IP	W	L	SV	ERA	FIP	WHIP	K/9	K%	BB/9	BB%	K/BB	HR/9	BABIP
2017	Rk	5.0	0	0	0	0.00	2.02	0.20	9.0	29.41%	1.8	5.88%	5.00	0.00	0.000
2017	A-	27.7	0	1	0	2.60	2.02	1.01	12.4	34.23%	2.6	7.21%	4.75	0.33	0.297
2018	A+	19.0	2	0	1	0.00	1.88	0.58	12.3	37.14%	3.3	10.00%	3.71	0.00	0.111
2018	AA	103.0	7	2	0	2.97	3.28	1.09	8.4	23.47%	2.4	6.85%	3.43	0.61	0.277
2019	AAA	37.3	2	1	0	3.13	3.69	1.37	10.8	28.48%	4.3	11.39%	2.50	0.48	0.341

Background: Arizona pulled the trigger on a massive deal at the trade deadline last season, agreeing to send future Hall of Famer Zack Greinke and cash to the eventual American League Champion Houston Astros for a four-player package of prospects: Corbin Martin, J.B. Bukauskas, Seth Beer, and Josh Rojas. According to reports, Martin was viewed as the centerpiece of the deal by the Diamondbacks' front office – despite undergoing Tommy John surgery weeks before. Prior to the injury the 6-foot-2, 200-pound right-hander tossed 37.1 innings with Round Rock in the Pacific Coast League, averaging 10.8 strikeouts and 4.3 walks per nine innings. He also made five starts with the Astros as well, fanning 19 and walking 12 in 19.1 innings of work.

Snippet from The 2018 Prospect Digest Handbook: Martin hardly looks the same pitcher he was coming out of college. He's not only a consistent strike-thrower, but he's consistently making pitcher's pitches – with his entire arsenal. Martin very well could ascend upwards of a #2/#3-type starting pitcher at full maturity – especially if he was locating as well as he was in 2018.

Scouting Report: I aggressively listed Martin as the third best prospect in a *loaded* Houston Astros farm system. And his repertoire – before succumbing to the elbow woes – looked as explosive as ever. His riding four-seamer was sitting comfortably in the mid-90s, touching a tick or two higher on occasion. His curveball is straight filth; the slider is an above-average weapon. And his changeup flashed plus on a couple occasions. All of this could be moot is the surgical procedure and / or rehab doesn't go as expected. But, personally, I would have absolutely made the deal the Diamondbacks did.

Ceiling: 4.0-win player
Risk: Moderate to High
MLB ETA: Debuted in 2019

6. Geraldo Perdomo, SS

Hit	Power	SB	Patience	Glove	Overall
45/55	35/45	50	60	55	55

Born: 10/22/99	Age: 20	Bats: B
Height: 6-3	Weight: 184	Throws: R

YEAR	LVL	PA	1B	2B	3B	HR	SB	CS	AVG	OBP	SLG	BB%	K%	GB%	LD%	FB%
2017	RK	278	45	3	2	1	16	8	0.238	0.410	0.285	21.58%	13.31%	58.4	12.4	21.9
2018	RK	101	20	4	2	1	14	1	0.314	0.416	0.442	13.86%	16.83%	36.2	23.2	30.4
2018	A-	127	23	3	2	3	9	4	0.301	0.421	0.456	14.17%	18.11%	43.9	19.5	29.3
2019	A	385	63	16	3	2	20	8	0.268	0.394	0.357	14.55%	14.55%	49.6	16	23.3
2019	A+	114	22	5	0	1	6	5	0.301	0.407	0.387	12.28%	9.65%	50.6	19.8	22.2

Background: Handed a scant five-figure bonus on the international scene four years ago, Perdomo, a 6-foot-3, 184-pound shortstop, is proving to be quite the bargain. After struggling during his debut in the foreign rookie the league, the young switch-hitter had a coming out party as he made three stops in 2018: he batted an aggregate .322/.438/.460 with seven doubles, five triples, four homeruns, and 24 stolen bases in 30 attempts between his time in the Arizona Summer, Pioneer, and Northwest Leagues. Last season – once again – Perdomo was aggressively pushed through two levels. And he handled the challenge with aplomb. In 116 games with Kane County and Visalia, the Santo Domingo, Dominican Republic, native hit .275/.397/.364 with 21 doubles, three triples, and three homeruns. He also swiped 26 bags in 39 attempts. Perdomo spent the fall playing for the Salt River Rafters, batting .316/.417/.418 with five extra-base hits and a pair of stolen bases.

Scouting Report: Remarkably consistent during his stops in the Midwest and California Leagues last season; his overall production topped the league average threshold by 27% and 28%, respectively. Tremendously talented as a defender, Perdomo, according to Clay Davenport's defensive metrics, saved a total of 14 runs between both stops. The bat is looks like an above-average weapon; the speed is a game changer; and he's surprisingly patient for a teenage player squaring off against significantly older competition. The power's below-average, but he did show strong batted ball data two years ago to suggest double-digit dingers are in the near future. One more final thought: the defense, alone, could be enough to carry him to the big leagues.

Ceiling: 3.5-win player
Risk: Moderate to High
MLB ETA: 2022

7. Wilderd Patino, CF

Hit	Power	SB	Patience	Glove	Overall
45/55	35/50	55	50	55	50

Born: 07/18/01	Age: 18	Bats: R
Height: 6-1	Weight: 175	Throws: R

YEAR	LVL	PA	1B	2B	3B	HR	SB	CS	AVG	OBP	SLG	BB%	K%	GB%	LD%	FB%
2018	RK	111	15	5	0	0	2	3	0.225	0.360	0.281	12.61%	17.12%	50	16.7	16.7
2018	RK	27	8	1	0	0	4	2	0.409	0.519	0.455	7.41%	18.52%	64.7	17.6	11.8
2019	Rk	125	29	4	3	1	13	3	0.349	0.403	0.472	8.80%	25.60%	61.3	15	20
2019	Rk+	40	5	1	2	0	1	1	0.229	0.300	0.371	5.00%	35.00%	68.2	18.2	9.1

Background: What was the Texas Rangers' loss turned out to be a windfall for the Arizona Diamondbacks. Patino, a toolsy center fielder out of Puerto Ordaz, Venezuela, originally signed a hefty $1.3 million deal with Texas, but it was eventually voided due to an arm injury. Arizona swooped in and signed him to a deal in early October 2017. Lanky, twitchy, and oozing tools, the 6-foot-1, 175-pound outfielder struggled a bit during his debut in the foreign rookie league, hitting a paltry .261/.391/.315 with just six doubles in 34 games as a 16-year-old. The front office brass pushed Patino to the Arizona Summer League to begin last season and the results were significantly improved: in 30 games he slugged .349/.403/.472 with four doubles, three triples, one homerun, and 13 stolen bases. The then-17-year-old capped off his showing with a 10-game cameo in the Pioneer League, batting .229/.300/.371.

Scouting Report: With respect to his work in the rookie league last season, consider the following:

- Since 2006, only eight 17-year-old hitters posted a DRC+ between 142 and 152 in the Arizona Summer League (min. 125 PA): Gleyber Torres, Jeisson Rosario, Isaac Paredes, Tirso Ornelas, Darryl Collins, Nino Leyja, Jordan Diaz, and Wilderd Patino.

For those counting at home that's: one two-time All-Star and one of the best young stars in baseball (Torres), one prospect (Paredes), four additional intriguing prospects (Rosario, Ornelas, Collins, and Diaz), one failed prospect (Leyja), and – of course – Patino. Average power that may develop into a 50-grade. The hit tool looks incredibly promising, offering glimpses of quickly becoming an above-average weapon. Plus speed. Solid eye at the plate. Above-average defense. The lone red flag: his borderline strikeout rate; he fanned in more than a quarter of his plate appearances.

Ceiling: 3.0-win player
Risk: Moderate
MLB ETA: 2022/2023

8. Seth Beer, 1B/LF

Hit	Power	SB	Patience	Glove	Overall
50	60	30	50	50	50

Born: 09/18/96	Age: 23	Bats: L
Height: 6-3	Weight: 195	Throws: R

YEAR	LVL	PA	1B	2B	3B	HR	SB	CS	AVG	OBP	SLG	BB%	K%	GB%	LD%	FB%
2018	A-	51	5	3	0	4	0	0	0.293	0.431	0.659	11.76%	19.61%	45.2	16.1	35.5
2018	A	132	29	7	0	3	1	0	0.348	0.443	0.491	11.36%	12.88%	34.7	27.4	31.6
2018	A+	114	19	4	0	5	0	1	0.262	0.307	0.439	3.51%	19.30%	36.5	20	36.5
2019	A+	152	25	8	0	9	0	3	0.328	0.414	0.602	9.21%	19.74%	36.6	19.8	36.6
2019	AA	280	45	9	0	16	0	0	0.299	0.407	0.543	8.57%	20.71%	42.1	21.9	30.3
2019	AA	101	10	7	0	1	0	1	0.205	0.297	0.318	7.92%	24.75%	39.3	11.5	42.6

Background: The hulking first baseman / left fielder put together one of the most dynamic offensive campaigns by a true freshman in recent memory when he bashed and battered the competition to the tune of .369/.535/.700 with 31 extra-base hits as a Clemson Tiger. His numbers production regressed a bit the following two seasons, going from otherworldly to just first round status. Arizona received Beer as part of the Zack Greinke extravaganza last July. The 28th overall player chosen in 2018 is now coming off of two rock solid seasons in the minor leagues. He batted .304/.389/.496 with 14 doubles and 12 homeruns between three levels during his debut. Beer, 6-foot-3 and 195 pounds, hit an aggregate .289/.388/.516 with 24 doubles and 26 homers between High Class A and Class AA.

Snippet from The 2018 Prospect Digest Handbook: In terms of big league comps, Beer looks like a poor man's Kris Bryant or Paul Goldschmidt. Or better yet: an improved version of Eric Thames, the 2017 version. In terms of big league ceiling, I'd think .260/.370/.530.

Scouting Report: One of the most saber-friendly hitters in the entire minor leagues. Beer does everything you'd want a middle-of-the-lineup thumper to do: make consistent contact, hit for plus-power, walk a bit, and do so without concerning platoon splits. The former Clemson Tiger faltered a bit after the trade to Arizona – which doesn't even move the needle on the "Concern-o-Meter" – but his production in the Texas League was prolific. Consider the following:

- Since 2006, here's the list of 22-year-old hitters to post at least a 150 DRC+ in the Texas League (min. 250 PA): Alex Bregman, Alex Gordon, Dexter Fowler, Chris Carter, Abraham Toro, and – of course – Seth Beer.

For those counting at home: Bregman owns a 138 DRC+; Gordon has a career 104 DRC+ including four-year stretch where he was far above the league average; Fowler sports a 101 DRC+ in his career; Carter, surprising, owns a 112 DRC+ in his career; and Toro is a easy top prospect in Houston's system. And, just for the record, only two of the aforementioned players topped the 170 DRC+ mark: Bregman and Beer. And the Diamondbacks' budding slugger bested the Astros' superstar by five percentage points.

Ceiling: 2.5-win player
Risk: Low to Moderate
MLB ETA: 2020

9. Pavin Smith, 1B/RF

Hit	Power	SB	Patience	Glove	Overall
60	45	30	55	55	50

Born: 02/06/96	Age: 24	Bats: L	Top CALs:
Height: 6-2	Weight: 210	Throws: L	

YEAR	LVL	PA	1B	2B	3B	HR	SB	CS	AVG	OBP	SLG	BB%	K%	GB%	LD%	FB%
2017	A-	223	45	15	2	0	2	1	0.318	0.401	0.415	12.11%	10.76%	49.7	19.3	24
2018	A+	504	75	25	1	11	3	2	0.255	0.343	0.392	11.31%	12.90%	49.2	17.5	23.5
2019	AA	507	81	29	6	12	2	1	0.291	0.370	0.466	11.64%	12.03%	44.6	18.8	27.2

Background: Four of the first nine players taken in the 2017 draft have already made their respective big league debuts (Brendan McKay, Kyle Wright, Adam Haseley, and Kesto Hiura). And Smith, the seventh overall player selected that June, is poised to become the fifth. A product of the University of Virginia, a collegiate superpower, Smith left the school with a career .326/.403/.515 triple-slash line. And he's been remarkably consistent in his three-year professional career; he owns a professional slash line of .281/.364/.426. Last season the 6-foot-2, 210-pound first baseman / corner outfielder hit a rock solid .291/.370/.466 with career bests in doubles (29), triples (6), and homeruns (12). His production, according to *Deserved Runs Created Plus*, topped the league average mark by 42%.

Snippet from The 2018 Prospect Digest Handbook: Nearly 50% of the balls he's put into play in his career have been on the ground. If he were a shortstop, he'd be a Top 50 prospect. But he's mired at a power-oriented position. I still think he'll be an above-average big leaguer on the patience/defense combination, but he needs to prove he walk more than 10% of his plate appearances if pitchers aren't afraid of him.

Scouting Report: As indicated above; I've been fairly bearish on Smith's big league prospects. He's at the preeminent power position in baseball and...well...doesn't hit for much power. *BUT*...he does a lot of other things well. Namely, he owns one of the best hit tools in the minor leagues; he walks a ton; he makes a *ton* of contact; he fields his position well; and his power is creeping towards respectability. Mark Grace seems like the ideal comparison, but that's a best case scenario. One more final note: he did trim his groundball rate from nearly 49% to just under 44% last season. But former big leaguer John Jaso seems more likely. Consider the following:

- Since 2006, here's the list of 23-year-old hitter to post a DRC+ between 137 and 147 with a double-digit walk rate and a sub-15% strikeout rate in the Southern League (min. 350 PA): LaMonte Wade, John Jaso, and Pavin Smith.

Jaso, by the way, owns a career 105 DRC+ mark in nine big league seasons. He was a well above-average hitter in 2012, 2014, and 2015. If Smith's power bumps up to a 50-grade, his ceiling moves significantly higher.

Ceiling: 2.5-win player
Risk: Low to Moderate
MLB ETA: 2020

10. Blake Walston, LHP

FB	CB	SL	CH	Command	Overall
55/60	60	N/A	50	50	50

Born: 06/28/01	Age: 19	Bats: L	
Height: 6-5	Weight: 175	Throws: L	

YEAR	LVL	IP	W	L	SV	ERA	FIP	WHIP	K/9	K%	BB/9	BB%	K/BB	HR/9	BABIP
2019	Rk	5.0	0	0	0	1.80	0.15	0.40	19.8	68.75%	0.0	0.00%	#DIV/0!	0.00	0.333
2019	A-	6.0	0	0	0	3.00	2.62	1.33	9.0	24.00%	3.0	8.00%	3.00	0.00	0.353

Background: Armed with four picks among the top 34 selections, the Diamondbacks dipped into the prep ranks early and often, grabbing high schoolers Corbin Carroll, Blake Walston, and Brennan Malone. Walston, the 26th overall pick, signed for a slightly below-slot deal worth $2.45 million, roughly saving the club $200,000 to spend elsewhere in the draft. A tall, lanky left-hander, Walston was previously committed to play ball at N.C. State after posting absurd numbers during his three seasons at New Hanover High School: he fanned 355 hitters in just 227 innings to go along with 0.89 ERA. And that includes a monster senior season when he fanned 137 in only 75.1 innings with a perfect 13-0 record. For those counting at home that's averaging a little more than 14 punch outs per nine innings. Walston made six brief appearances in the Arizona Summer and Northwest Leagues, throwing 11.0 innings with 17 punch outs and a pair of walks.

Scouting Report: A dynamic two-sport star at New Hanover; Walston, who quarterbacked the school to a 3AA state championship, oozes potential and projectability. Long limbs and a loose, easy arm, Walston's fastball was sitting 91 mph to 94 mph and should – easily – bump up two ticks as he begins to fill out. His curveball is the stuff of dreams, a true plus offering with late, sharp, hard bite. And his changeup, an easy 50-grade, was better than advertised. Reports had him throwing a slider, though I didn't see one. Strike thrower with the ability to make pitcher's pitches consistently. Walston's one of my favorite prep arms in the entire class. If the control / command remains strong he could move quickly.

Ceiling: 3.0-win player
Risk: Moderate
MLB ETA: 2022

11. J.B. Bukauskas, RHP

FB	SL	CH	Command	Overall
65	70	55	50	60

Born: 10/11/96	Age: 23	Bats: R
Height: 6-0	Weight: 196	Throws: R

YEAR	LVL	IP	W	L	SV	ERA	FIP	WHIP	K/9	K%	BB/9	BB%	K/BB	HR/9	BABIP
2018	A-	8.3	0	0	0	0.00	2.04	1.20	9.7	27.27%	2.2	6.06%	4.50	0.00	0.364
2018	A	15.0	1	2	0	4.20	2.28	1.47	12.6	31.34%	4.2	10.45%	3.00	0.00	0.395
2018	A+	28.0	3	0	0	1.61	3.00	0.93	10.0	28.97%	4.2	12.15%	2.38	0.32	0.194
2018	AA	6.0	0	0	0	0.00	1.78	0.50	12.0	40.00%	3.0	10.00%	4.00	0.00	0.100
2019	AA	85.7	2	4	1	5.25	4.30	1.58	10.3	25.72%	5.7	14.17%	1.81	0.84	0.332
2019	AA	7.0	0	1	0	7.71	2.72	2.14	14.1	31.43%	6.4	14.29%	2.20	0.00	0.556

Background: Viewed as the second – or third – best prospect in the Zack Greinke return last July. Bukauskas is hardly a complementary addition to the Diamondbacks' blossoming farm system. The 15th overall pick out of the University of North Carolina three years ago, the 6-foot, 196-pound right-hander spent the entirety of last season working between both organizations' Class AA affiliates. In 92.2 combined innings Bukauskas fanned 109 and walked a whopping 59 en route to tallying an unsightly 5.44 ERA. His season prematurely ended in early August thanks to a wonky elbow.

Snippet from The 2018 Prospect Digest Handbook: Beyond Bukauskas' small stature, at least in terms of big league starting pitchers, is whether his control takes another leap forward. His walk rates have been just north of the league average since his days as an amateur, but I ultimately think he winds up with above-average control/command. His mechanics are clean and repeatable. As it stands today, even without a tick up in control, I think he's quite capable of putting together a Mike Foltynewicz-type performance (circa 2019) where he average 9.9 K/9 and 3.3 BB/9 with a sub-3.00 ERA.

Scouting Report: So...the control / command not only didn't improve but it regressed – tremendously. He walked 14.2% of the total batters he faced last season. Across the handful of games I scouted, Bukauskas wouldn't just barely miss his spots; he was missing by margins I haven't previously seen by him. The repertoire – injury notwithstanding – is still electric: mid-90s fastball with exceptional late-life, his slider is practically gifted from Steve Carlton – a genuine thing of beauty; and his change is a nice third weapon. With respect to his work in the Texas League (where he made all but two appearances), consider the following:

- Since 2006, here's the list of 22-year-old pitchers to post a strikeout percentage between 24.5% and 26.5% in the Texas League (min. 75 IP): Mitch Talbot, Luke Jackson, Tim Cooney, Carlos Pimental, and J.B. Bukauskas. And it should be noted that the latter were only arms to walk at least 10%. In fact, they both walked 14.1% of the hitters they faced.

The repertoire – and pedigree – all suggest #2/#3-type potential. But if he doesn't start throwing consistent strikes he's going to be staring at a high-leverage relief role soon.

Ceiling: 3.0-win player
Risk: Moderate to High
MLB ETA: Debuted in 2019

12. Jon Duplantier, RHP

FB	CB	CU	CH	Command	Overall
55	55	55	50	45	50

Born: 07/11/94	Age: 25	Bats: L
Height: 6-4	Weight: 225	Throws: R

YEAR	LVL	IP	W	L	SV	ERA	FIP	WHIP	K/9	K%	BB/9	BB%	K/BB	HR/9	BABIP
2017	A	72.7	6	1	0	1.24	2.85	0.83	9.7	28.68%	1.9	5.51%	5.20	0.50	0.240
2017	A+	63.3	6	2	0	1.56	2.96	1.15	12.4	34.12%	3.8	10.59%	3.22	0.28	0.324
2018	AA	67.0	5	1	0	2.69	3.50	1.19	9.1	24.91%	3.8	10.26%	2.43	0.54	0.282
2019	A+	3.0	0	0	0	0.00	1.66	0.67	9.0	33.33%	0.0	0.00%	#DIV/0!	0.00	0.333
2019	AAA	38.0	1	2	0	5.21	4.19	1.55	10.4	26.19%	6.6	16.67%	1.57	0.24	0.323

Background: Riding a wave of hype and recognition following a dominant 2018 season, Duplantier, who finished that year with a 77-to-30 strikeout-to-walk ratio in 74.0 innings of work, battled control / command issues as he was once again held to fewer than 100.0 innings. A third round pick out of Rice University – home to two many failed pitching prospects – Duplantier has a chance to move beyond the school's reputation and establish himself as a useful big league arm. The good news: the lanky right-hander made his highly anticipated big league debut. The bad news: arm woes, once again, forced him onto the shelf last season. In 13 appearances with the Reno Aces of the Pacific Coast League, the 6-foot-4, 225-pound righty posted a 44-to-28 strikeout-to-walk ratio in 38.0 innings of work. He was called up to The Show on six separate occasions throughout the season, throwing another 36.2 innings with 34 punch outs and 18 walks.

Snippet from The 2018 Prospect Digest Handbook: Duplantier's ceiling is limited by two factors: his below-average control/command and he's going to have to prove that he can continually stay healthy from year-to-year. I think he's a bit overrated.

Scouting Report: Same story, different year. Duplantier has the requisite size, build, and repertoire to succeed as a mid-rotation caliber starting pitcher at the big league level. But, again, it's going to come down to his ability to throw quality strikes and – perhaps, more importantly – stay on the mound. Duplantier's fastball downgraded for me in 2019. A strong 60 heading into the year, Duplantier's velocity was hovering in the 92 mph during a couple MiLB stints and, according to BaseballSavant data, it averaged the same during his big leagues stints. Both of his breaking balls grade out as above-average. And his changeup, previously a 45, bumped up to average. The cold hard fact remains: he's entering his age-25 season, has been banged up throughout his career at various points, and he hasn't thrown more than 79.2 innings in each of the past two years. Ceiling of a #4 with the likelihood of a long reliever.

Ceiling: 2.5-win player
Risk: Moderate
MLB ETA: Debuted in 2019

13. Drey Jameson, RHP

	FB	CB	SL	CH	Command	Overall
	65	55/60	55	45	45/50	50

Born: 08/17/97	Age: 22	Bats: R	Top CALs:
Height: 6-0	Weight: 165	Throws: R	

YEAR	LVL	IP	W	L	SV	ERA	FIP	WHIP	K/9	K%	BB/9	BB%	K/BB	HR/9	BABIP
2019	A-	11.7	0	0	0	6.17	5.25	1.97	9.3	20.69%	6.9	15.52%	1.33	0.77	0.371

Background: The final of the club's four first round picks last June, Jameson was also the lone collegiate selection by the Diamondbacks in the opening round as well. A draft eligible sophomore, Jameson burst onto the scene for Ball State two years ago when he fanned 97 hitters in only 72.0 innings of work. Of course, he handed out free passes like they were going out of style; he averaged 5.5 walks per nine innings. Last season the 6-foot, 165-pound hurler honed in on the strike zone with a greater regularity as he became one of college baseball's most dominant arms. In a career high 16 starts, Jameson averaged a whopping 14.3 strikeouts and just 3.1 walks per nine innings to go along with a 3.24 ERA and a 6-3 win-loss record. After signing with the club for $1.4 million, which was well below the recommended slot, the diminutive righty made eight brief appearances in the Northwest League, posting a 12-to-9 strikeout-to-walk ratio in 11.2 innings of work.

Scouting Report: There's a little of The Freak (Tim Lincecum) in him. Jameson generate a borderline plus-plus fastball with relative ease, despite his slight stature; he generously listed a 6-feet and 165 pounds. He'll mix in a couple of breaking balls, both average, though the curveball flashed plus during his debut with Hillsboro. The changeup's a bit too firm, though it'll likely grade out as average at full maturity. It's easy to ticket the Ball State product for an eventual role in the bullpen, but if the command bumps up to slightly below-average he has the chops to make it as a solid #3/#4-type starting pitcher. If the club does push him into a relief role, he could be throwing some big league innings within 18 months.

Ceiling: 2.0-win player
Risk: Moderate
MLB ETA: 2022

14. Matt Tabor, RHP

	FB	SL	CH	Command	Overall
	60	50	55/60	55	50

Born: 07/14/98	Age: 21	Bats: R
Height: 6-2	Weight: 180	Throws: R

YEAR	LVL	IP	W	L	SV	ERA	FIP	WHIP	K/9	K%	BB/9	BB%	K/BB	HR/9	BABIP
2017	Rk	4.7	0	1	0	1.93	0.36	1.71	17.4	39.13%	0.0	0.00%	#DIV/0!	0.00	0.571
2018	A-	60.7	2	1	0	3.26	3.73	1.19	6.8	18.18%	1.9	5.14%	3.54	0.59	0.296
2019	A	95.3	5	4	0	2.93	2.70	1.00	9.5	26.79%	1.5	4.24%	6.31	0.57	0.290

Background: Simply put: the Arizona Diamondbacks had one helluva strong draft class in 2017, adding the likes of Pavin Smith, Drew Ellis, Daulton Varsho, Matt Tabor, Jeff Bain, and Brian Shaffer into the fold. Tabor, who was handed a nice seven-figure bonus as a third round selection, showed some promise as a 19-year-old in the Northwest League; he posted a 46-to-13 strikeout-to-walk ratio in 60.2 innings. Last season, though, the 6-foot-2, 180-pound right-hander had a breakout campaign in the Midwest League. Making 21 starts with the Kane County Cougars, the Milton

Academy product averaged 9.5 strikeouts and just 1.5 walks per nine innings to go along with a 2.93 ERA and a 3.30 DRA (Deserved Runs Average).

Snippet from The 2018 Prospect Digest Handbook: Tabor's strikeout rate, 6.8 K/9, is a bit concerning. But there's plenty of room for hope: along with three above-average or better pitches, Tabor's swinging strike percentage last season, 13.2%, was the fourth best in the Northwest League (min. 40 IP). He has the potential to be a league-average starter, though he's several years away.

Scouting Report: Tabor's fastball grew some legs last season, sitting in the 93-94 mph range and touching as high as 97 mph on occasion. And his changeup continues to be an impressive, swing-and-miss type offering. His slider, on the other hand, looked like it backed up a touch when I saw him – though it didn't impact the results thanks to his ability to control the strike zone. 60-grade control with 55-grade command. Tabor's wildly successful 2019 season has only solidified his odds of becoming a viable big league starting option in the coming years. With respect to his work last season, consider the following:

- Since 2006, here's the list of 20-year-old pitchers to post a strikeout percentage between 26% and 28% with a sub-6.0% walk percentage in the Midwest League (min. 75 IP): Jordan Yamamoto, A.J. Cole, Daniel Corcino, and Matt Tabor. Yamamoto, for the record, is coming off of a debut season in which he posted an 82-to-36 strikeout-to-walk ratio while tallying one win above replacement in 15 starts.

Ceiling: 2.0-win player
Risk: Moderate
MLB ETA: 2021/2022

15. Jake McCarthy, CF

	Hit	Power	SB	Patience	Glove	Overall
	55/60	40/45	50	50	50	50

Born: 07/30/97	Age: 22	Bats: L	Top CALs:
Height: 6-2	Weight: 195	Throws: L	

YEAR	LVL	PA	1B	2B	3B	HR	SB	CS	AVG	OBP	SLG	BB%	K%	GB%	LD%	FB%
2018	RK	12	2	0	1	0	1	0	0.273	0.333	0.455	8.33%	8.33%	70	10	20
2018	A-	241	37	17	3	3	20	8	0.288	0.378	0.442	9.13%	16.60%	54.1	18.8	21.2
2019	A+	214	36	13	3	2	18	2	0.277	0.341	0.405	7.94%	24.30%	48.3	20.3	25.2

Background: A dynamic, sweet swinging outfielder from the Virginia Cavaliers, McCarthy was an impact bat – when he appeared in the school's lineup. He played in just six games as a true freshman, remained healthy the following season, and made it to the park for just 20 contests in 2018. Despite the lack of a lengthy track record, the organization gambled on the saber-friendly outfielder in the opening round, 39th overall, two years ago. McCarthy responded by hitting .288/.378/.442 with 17 doubles, three triples, and three homeruns with Hillsboro during his debut. Last season the front office aggressively pushed the Pennsylvania native up to High Class A. And – once again – he performed well...when he was in the lineup. A vague injury described as a leg issue limited him to just 53 games with Visalia. He batted .277/.341/.405 with 13 doubles, three triples, two homeruns, and 18 stolen bases. His overall production, according to Baseball Prospectus' *Deserved Runs Created Plus*, topped the league average mark by 4%. McCarthy also spent the fall playing for the Salt River Rafters, batting .265/.324/.397.

Scouting Report: McCarthy got off to a bit of a slow start as he bypassed Low Class A; he hit a lowly .231/.300/.341 over his first 24 games. But after returning from the his first disabled list stint, he rebounded to slug .317/.377/.462 with seven doubles, one triple, and two homeruns over his final 29 games – numbers more indicative of his true talent level. McCarthy is a surprisingly good athlete, possessing above-average or better speed, as well as tremendous instincts on the base paths; gap-to-gap power that could grow into 12 or so homeruns down the line; and a hit tool that looks like it could be plus at full maturity. The question, though, is can he stay healthy? For now the answer's been a resounding no in three of his last four seasons.

Ceiling: 2.0-win player
Risk: Moderate
MLB ETA: 2021/2022

16. Levi Kelly, RHP

FB	SL	SF	Command	Overall
55/60	70	N/A	45	45

Born: 05/14/99	Age: 21	Bats: R
Height: 6-4	Weight: 205	Throws: R

YEAR	LVL	IP	W	L	SV	ERA	FIP	WHIP	K/9	K%	BB/9	BB%	K/BB	HR/9	BABIP
2018	Rk	6.0	0	0	0	0.00	3.07	0.83	9.0	26.09%	3.0	8.70%	3.00	0.00	0.200
2019	A	100.3	5	1	0	2.15	2.78	1.11	11.3	30.88%	3.5	9.56%	3.23	0.36	0.292

Background: Handed the largest bonus among all eighth round picks two years ago, Kelly, a product of the ultra-competitive IMG Academy, turned in a dynamic showing as he made the leap straight into the Midwest League last season. Kelly, a 6-foot-4, 205-pound right-hander, made 22 starts for the Kane County Cougars, throwing 100.1 innings while racking up plenty of strikeouts (126) with solid control (39 free passes). He finished his first full season in pro ball with a sparkling 2.15 ERA and a 3.17 DRA.

Scouting Report: A tremendous find in the mid-rounds of the 2018 draft; Kelly, who was the 249th overall player chosen, mainly attacks hitters with an above-average fastball and a lethal, wipeout slider. The young righty's heater was sitting in the 92- to 94-mph range across a couple games I scouted and it touched as high as 97 mph in a mid-July start. His slider is wicked, leaving hitters with the pain of a decade long relationship gone in an instant. Numerous reports indicated Kelly mixed in a split-finger, but I didn't see in at any time. The control's not horrible, but I'm not sure it ever bumps up to a 50. Kelly needs to develop a workable third offering to reach his ceiling as a #4-type arm. Otherwise, he could be a lethal late-inning option. With respect to his work in Low Class A last season, consider the following:

- Since 2006, just three 20-year-old hurlers posted a strikeout percentage between 29% and 32% with a walk rate between 9.5% and 11.5% in the Midwest League (min. 75 IP): Sandy Alcantara, the Marlins' All-Star representative last season, Keyvius Sampson, and – of course – Levi Kelly.

Ceiling: 1.5- to 2.0-win player
Risk: Moderate
MLB ETA: 2022

17. Dominic Fletcher, OF

Hit	Power	SB	Patience	Glove	Overall
45	50	30	50	50	45

Born: 09/02/97	Age: 22	Bats: L
Height: 5-9	Weight: 185	Throws: L

YEAR	LVL	PA	1B	2B	3B	HR	SB	CS	AVG	OBP	SLG	BB%	K%	GB%	LD%	FB%
2019	A	239	48	14	1	5	1	1	0.318	0.389	0.463	9.21%	20.92%	43.3	15.2	34.1

Background: Studying sports management at the University of Arkansas, Fletcher, a stocky outfielder hailing from Cypress, California, was a three-year starter in the middle of the Razorbacks' lineup. Measuring 5-feet-9 and 185 pounds, Fletcher hit an impressive .291/.356/.495 with seven doubles, one triple, and 12 homeruns as a true freshman. That production earned him the NCBWA Freshman and Baseball America All-American status, as well as being named on the SEC All-Freshman Team. The squat outfielder followed that up with a nearly identical slash line during his sophomore campaign; he slugged .288/.338/.468 with 16 doubles, one triple, and 10 homeruns. Last season Fletcher raised the offensive ante by setting career highs in batting average (.318), on-base percentage (.389), slugging percentage (.537), doubles (24), and stolen bases (two). Arizona drafted the Razorback in the second round, 75th overall. He spent the entirety of his debut in the Midwest League where he – unsurprisingly – maintained status quo; he hit .318/.389/.463 with 14 doubles, one triple, and five homers.

Scouting Report: With respect to his work in school last season, consider the following:

- Between 2011 and 2018, only six SEC hitters met the following criteria in a season (min. 275 PA): hit .300/.375/.500 with a sub-20% strikeout rate and walk rate between 8% and 10%. Those six hitters: Michael Helman, Austin Cousino, J.J. Schwarz, Preston Tucker, Will Holland, and Heston Kjerstad.

Now let's take a look at his work during his debut:

- Since 2006, only three 21-year-old hitters posted a 140 to 150 DRC+ with a strikeout rate between 17% and 22% with a sub-10% walk rate in the Midwest League (min. 200 PA): Eduardo Diaz, Vinnie Catricala, and – of course – Dominic Fletcher.

A potential solid, above-average fourth outfielder / low-end starting caliber outfielder. Fletcher offers up surprising power with solid contact rates.

Ceiling: 1.5-win player
Risk: Moderate
MLB ETA: 2022

18. Bo Takahashi, RHP

	FB	SL	CH	Command	Overall
	50	50	55	55	40

Born: 01/23/97	**Age:** 23	**Bats:** R
Height: 6-0	**Weight:** 197	**Throws:** R

YEAR	LVL	IP	W	L	SV	ERA	FIP	WHIP	K/9	K%	BB/9	BB%	K/BB	HR/9	BABIP
2017	A	16.3	0	2	0	3.86	5.46	1.29	7.7	18.92%	2.8	6.76%	2.80	1.65	0.260
2017	A+	109.7	7	10	0	5.33	5.05	1.31	7.6	19.66%	3.0	7.82%	2.51	1.07	0.294
2018	A+	47.7	3	3	0	3.02	3.37	1.15	10.0	27.46%	1.9	5.18%	5.30	0.76	0.331
2018	AA	73.0	3	3	0	4.68	4.46	1.16	9.5	25.67%	2.5	6.67%	3.85	1.48	0.286
2019	AA	118.7	9	7	0	3.72	3.97	1.23	7.9	21.36%	2.9	7.80%	2.74	0.91	0.294

Background: Different year, same Takahashi. One of the more consistently underrated arms in the minor leagues, Takahashi, a 6-foot, 197-pound right-hander from Presidente Prudente, Brazil, first turned some heads – and caught my attention – as a 19-year-old rocketing through the Northwest, Midwest, and California Leagues when he averaged 7.2 strikeouts and 3.1 walks per nine innings. The savvy righty spent the majority of the following season, 2017, in High Class A, averaging 7.6 strikeouts and just 3.0 walks per nine innings. Takahashi returned back to Visalia for a third tour in 2018, though after nine starts he was promoted up to the Southern League for 14 appearances. Last season the slight-framed hurler made 23 starts with the Class AA Jackson Generals, posting a 104-to-38 strikeout-to-walk ratio in 118.2 innings of work. He compiled a 3.72 ERA and a 5.07 DRA (*Deserved Run Average*).

Snippet from The 2018 Prospect Digest Handbook: Arms like Takahashi tend to get overlooked in today's game. He's approaching big league readiness and could help round out the Diamondbacks' rotation without any issue.

Scouting Report: Consider the following:

- Since 2006, here's the list of 22-year-old pitchers to post a 20.5% to 22.5% strikeout percentage with a walk percentage between 7% and 9% in the Southern League (min. 100 IP): Fernando Romero, Travis Wood, Rob Whalen, Sam McWilliams, James Houser, Paul Mildren, and Bo Takahashi.

Still ready to step in the Diamondbacks' rotation at `the drop of a hat. His ceiling is certainly low, but the floor is incredibly high. The arsenal lacks a true standout pitch – just his changeup grades out above average – but he knows how to use what he has. He's an easy guy to root for.

Ceiling: 1.0- to 1.5-win player
Risk: Moderate
MLB ETA: 2021/2022

19. Ryne Nelson, RHP

	FB	CB	SL	CH	Command	Overall
	70	60	50	45	40	40

Born: 02/01/98	**Age:** 22	**Bats:** R	**Top CALs:**
Height: 6-3	**Weight:** 184	**Throws:** R	

YEAR	LVL	IP	W	L	SV	ERA	FIP	WHIP	K/9	K%	BB/9	BB%	K/BB	HR/9	BABIP
2019	A-	18.7	0	1	0	2.89	3.30	1.34	12.5	38.24%	4.8	14.71%	2.60	0.48	0.382

Background: A star two-way player for Basic High School a handful of years back. Nelson, a wiry 6-foot-3, 184-pound prospect, dominated the Nevada high school scene during his four-year prep career, earning four varsity letters and was named as a First-Team All-State as a utility player after slugging .415 with 12 doubles and 20 RBIs. He also recorded a 7-2 win-loss record on the Nevada Division I State Championship squad as well, finishing with a 1.91 ERA and 57 strikeouts. Nelson spent his first two seasons with Oregon as a light-hitting shortstop and a dominant relief arm: between his freshman and sophomore seasons for Head Coach George Horton, Nelson batted a paltry .170/.300/.204 with just six doubles and he tallied an impressive 54-to-19 strikeout-to-walk ratio in just 36.0 innings of work on the mound. The hard-throwing right-hander spent the 2018 summer dominating as a late-inning relief specialist for the Yarmouth-Dennis Red Sox, fanning 26 against just nine walks in 17.0 innings while earning a trip to the premier league's All-Star contest. Last season Nelson transitioned into a full time pitching gig, making 23 appearances – four of which are starts – while recording a mindboggling 104 strikeouts and 41 walks in only 65.0 innings of work. Arizona drafted Nelson in the second round, 56th overall, and sent him to the Northwest League for an additional 18.2 innings; he fanned 26 and walked 10 to go along with a 2.89 ERA.

Scouting Report: Here's what I wrote about the Oregon relief ace heading into the draft last season:

"Owner of one of the best fastballs in the entire 2019 draft class. Nelson uncorks a 70-grade heater that can reach the upper 90s with relative ease. He combines the plus offering with a wipeout 60-grade curveball that flashes incredible late movement. His changeup, a hard-diving offspeed pitch, needs further refinement – as does his ability to control the strike zone. Nelson's wicked two-pitch combo screams potential late-inning, high leverage relief option. But his lack of experience on the mound should grant him a few years to develop into a starting pitcher. With respect to his work in 2019, consider the following:

- *Between 2011 and 2018, here's the list of PAC12 pitchers to average at least 12 strikeouts every nine innings (min. 50 IP): former Oregon ace David Peterson, who was taken by the New York Mets with the 20th overall pick in 2017; right-hander Jimmie Sherfy, another Oregon alum, who owns a 1.06 ERA through his first 35.1 big league innings; and Kevin Abel, a Freshman All-American in 2018 before succumbing to Tommy John surgery this season.*

Nelson's strikeout rate, by the way, is the only one to eclipse the 14.0 threshold. Intriguing high ceiling with a high relief floor."

One final additional observation: Nelson started throwing a 50-grade slider more frequently in the pros. I did not see it during several games I scouted in college.

Ceiling: 1.0- to 1.5-win player
Risk: Moderate
MLB ETA: 2022

20. Tommy Henry, LHP

FB	SL	CH	Command	Overall
50	50	55	50/55	40

Born: 07/29/97	Age: 22	Bats: L
Height: 6-3	Weight: 205	Throws: L

YEAR	LVL	IP	W	L	SV	ERA	FIP	WHIP	K/9	K%	BB/9	BB%	K/BB	HR/9	BABIP
2019	A-	3.0	0	0	0	6.00	0.95	1.33	12.0	36.36%	0.0	0.00%	#DIV/0!	0.00	0.429

Background: It was a fantastic year for the University of Michigan's baseball squad: the club squared off against Vanderbilt University in the College World Series Finals, coming up short; and three players – Tommy Henry, Karl Kauffmann, and Jordan Brewer – were all selected within the opening three rounds of the June draft. But, perhaps the most fascinating tidbit: Henry and Kauffmann, the 74th and 77th overall selections, became the highest drafted Wolverine pitchers since the Athletics selected right-hander with the 70th overall pick all the way back in 1990. Henry, a 6-foot-3, 205-pound left-hander, was particularly dominant during the school's epic season: making a career high 19 starts, along with one relief appearance, he tossed 124.0 innings, recording 135 strikeouts to just 26 walks en route to tallying a 3.27 ERA. The savvy lefty made three abbreviated appearances with the Hillsboro Hops in the Northwest League, posting a 4-to-2 strikeout-to-walk ratio in three innings of work.

Scouting Report: Far from overpowering, Henry's fastball sits in the 91- to 92-mph neighborhood (with a peak of 93), though some deception in his herky-jerky mechanics helps. The lanky lefty also mixes in an average, mid-80s slider, and an above-average 83- to 84-mph fading changeup. Henry's arsenal isn't particularly dominant. And Big10 arms have typically struggled in the professional ranks, so this pick looks like a bit of a stretch. Strictly a backend option, and just as likely to slide into a multi-inning reliever.

Ceiling: 1.0- to 1.5-win player
Risk: Moderate
MLB ETA: 2021/2022

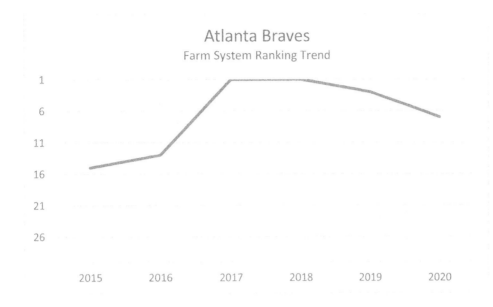

Atlanta Braves
Farm System Ranking Trend

Rank	Name	Age	Pos
1	Cristian Pache	21	CF
2	Drew Waters	21	OF
3	Bryse Wilson	22	RHP
4	Ian Anderson	22	RHP
5	Kyle Wright	24	RHP
6	William Contreras	22	C
7	Braden Shewmake	22	SS
8	Kyle Muller	22	LHP
9	Tucker Davidson	24	LHP
10	Huascar Ynoa	22	RHP
11	Shea Langeliers	22	C
12	Michael Harris	19	CF
13	Victor Vodnik	20	RHP
14	Jasseel De La Cruz	23	RHP
15	Alex Jackson	24	C
16	Kasey Kalich	22	RHP
17	Freddy Tarnok	21	RHP
18	Bryce Ball	21	1B
19	Greyson Jenista	23	1B/OF
20	Beau Philip	21	SS

1. Cristian Pache, CF

Hit	Power	SB	Patience	Glove	Overall
50/55	45/55	50	45+	60	70

Born: 11/19/98	Age: 21	Bats: R
Height: 6-2	Weight: 185	Throws: R

YEAR	LVL	PA	1B	2B	3B	HR	SB	CS	AVG	OBP	SLG	BB%	K%	GB%	LD%	FB%
2017	A	514	111	13	8	0	32	14	0.281	0.335	0.343	7.59%	20.23%	53.4	19.4	18.6
2018	A+	387	72	20	5	8	7	6	0.285	0.311	0.431	3.88%	17.83%	49	21.5	19.2
2018	AA	109	22	3	1	1	0	2	0.260	0.294	0.337	4.59%	25.69%	51.3	23.7	19.7
2019	AA	433	62	28	8	11	8	11	0.278	0.340	0.474	7.85%	24.02%	40.8	22	28.9
2019	AAA	105	16	8	1	1	0	0	0.274	0.337	0.411	8.57%	17.14%	51.3	25.6	15.4

Background: Slowly reaching a boiling point. The Dominican-born outfielder's production – and underlying skill set – has continued to improve in each of his four professional seasons. A highly touted amateur free agent on the international scene, Pache, who was signed by the club in 2015 for $1.4 million, was pushed straight into the stateside rookie leagues the following season for his debut. Splitting time between the Gulf Coast and Appalachian Leagues, the wiry center fielder slashed .309/.349/.391 with four doubles and seven triples in 57 total games. The front office brass pushed the Santo Domingo Centro native up to the Sally at the beginning of 2017. And – at the ripe ol' age of 18 – Pache posted a .281/.335/.343 line with 13 doubles, eight triples, and 32 stolen bases. He split the next season between the Florida State and Southern Leagues, batting an aggregate .279/.307/.410 with 23 doubles, six triples, and a then-career best nine homeruns. He spent the ensuing fall with the Peoria Javelinas in the Arizona Fall League, hitting .279/.323/.360 in 20 games. Atlanta sent the young outfielder, who's put on considerable bulk over the past couple of seasons, back to Class AA for additional seasoning. And he passed the minors' toughest challenge with aplomb. In 104 games with the Mississippi Braves, Pache slugged .278/.340/.474 with 28 doubles, eight triples, 11 homeruns, and eight stolen bases. He spent an additional 26 games with Gwinnett in the International League, slashing .274/.337/.411.

Snippet from The 2018 Prospect Digest Handbook: The power's likely to continue to blossom as his lean frame approaches maturity as well. The Dominican native, despite reaching Class AA before his age-20 season, hasn't quite put everything together successfully – yet. Instead, there are glimpses of the full package sprinkled throughout his career. At various points his eye at the plate is solid, the speed on the base paths exceptional, and – of course – the power too. But once he does put it all together – watch out.

Scouting Report: Let's take a look at his numbers and production in Class AA, the make-it-or-break-it level for a prospect, last season. Consider the following:

- Since 2006, here's the list of 20-year-old hitters to post a DRC+ between 135 and 145 in the Southern League (min. 300 PA): Jake Bauers, the young outfielder who struggled a bit for the Indians in 2019, Drew Waters, and – of course – Cristian Pache.

A plus glove with the offensive tools to settle in atop – or in the middle – of championship big league team. But the most exciting aspect for Pache's development: his blossoming power. A speed-based, slashing hitter for the majority of his career, Pache underwent an interesting transformation in 2019 – he stopped putting the ball on the ground. After posting a groundball rate of at least 48% and as high as 64.5 in his previous seasons, Pache posted a 39.4% groundball rate last year. So it's not surprising that he posted a career best .462 slugging percentage and 12 homeruns. There's 20- to 25-homer potential thanks his lightning bat and new approach. In terms of ceiling, think Yoan Moncada's numbers from 2019: he slugged .315/.367/.548 with 25 homeruns and 10 stolen bases.

Ceiling: 6.0-win player
Risk: Low to Moderate
MLB ETA: 2020

2. Drew Waters, OF

Hit	Power	SB	Patience	Glove	Overall
50/55	45/50	60	60	50	60

Born: 12/30/98	Age: 21	Bats: B
Height: 6-2	Weight: 183	Throws: R

YEAR	LVL	PA	1B	2B	3B	HR	SB	CS	AVG	OBP	SLG	BB%	K%	GB%	LD%	FB%
2017	RK	58	11	3	1	2	2	1	0.347	0.448	0.571	12.07%	18.97%	55.3	26.3	18.4
2017	RK	166	24	11	1	2	4	2	0.255	0.331	0.383	9.64%	35.54%	43.3	24.4	31.1
2018	A	365	55	32	6	9	20	5	0.303	0.353	0.513	5.75%	19.73%	51.9	21.1	23.7
2018	A+	133	23	7	3	0	3	0	0.268	0.316	0.374	6.02%	24.81%	48.4	22	25.3
2019	AA	454	85	35	9	5	13	6	0.319	0.366	0.481	6.17%	26.65%	47	24.7	25
2019	AAA	119	22	5	0	2	3	0	0.271	0.336	0.374	9.24%	36.13%	44.6	33.8	20

Background: After selecting Vanderbilt University ace Kyle Wright – and handing over a massive bonus – with the fifth overall pick in the 2017 draft, the front office dipped into the prep ranks and drafted toolsy outfielder Drew Waters 36 selections later. A product of Etowah High School, which has produce three other minor leaguers, Waters put together one of the better debut showings for a teenage hitter that summer: he slugged .278/.362/.429 between both stateside rookie leagues. He split time between Rome and Florida the following season and his production showed no signs of slowing as he slugged a hearty .293/.343/.476 with

39 doubles, nine triples, and nine homeruns. Despite only appearing in 30 games in High Class A, the front office aggressively pushed the 20-year-old outfielder up to Class AA, the most important development step for a prospect, at the start of 2019. And he didn't blink. In 108 games with Mississippi, the 6-foot-2, 183-pound switch-hitter bashed .319/.366/.481 with 35 doubles, nine triples, and five homeruns. He spent the remaining 26 games with Gwinnett in the International League.

Snippet from The 2018 Prospect Digest Handbook: A toolsy switch-hitter that's flirted with some concerning strikeout rates at various points in his young career. Waters is likely to grow into above-average power to go along with his plus speed. Even if the hit tool remains average – which it likely will – Waters has a shot to be a nice little league average center fielder in the coming years.

Scouting Report: Eerily similar production and peripherals to his teammate, Cristian Pache, consider the following:

NAME	YEAR	LVL	AGE	PA	AVG	OBP	SLG	BB%	K%	DRC+
Cristian Pache	2019	AA	20	433	0.278	0.340	0.474	7.85%	24.02%	139
Drew Waters	2019	AA	20	454	0.319	0.366	0.481	6.17%	26.65%	143

Waters doesn't possess his counterpart's defensive prowess, though he's far from a slouch either. Offensively speaking, Waters is still showing some borderline concerning swing-and-miss numbers; he whiffed in nearly 27% of his Class AA plate appearances and that number ballooned by nearly 10-percentage points during his 26-game cameo in the International League. Below-average patience. Plus-speed. And there's some solid raw power, though he's still putting the ball on the ground too frequently. He looks like .280/.320/.420 -type hitter. One more final thought: per FanGraphs, Waters average exit velocity was 89 mph with a peak of 109 mph last season.

Ceiling: 4.0-win player
Risk: Moderate
MLB ETA: 2020

3. Bryse Wilson, RHP

	FB	CB	SL	CH	Command	Overall
	60	50	60	55	55	55

Born: 12/20/97	Age: 22	Bats: R
Height: 6-1	Weight: 225	Throws: R

YEAR	LVL	IP	W	L	SV	ERA	FIP	WHIP	K/9	K%	BB/9	BB%	K/BB	HR9	BABIP
2017	A	137.0	10	7	0	2.50	3.20	1.04	9.1	25.46%	2.4	6.78%	3.76	0.53	0.272
2018	A+	26.7	2	0	0	0.34	2.42	0.86	8.8	25.00%	2.4	6.73%	3.71	0.00	0.229
2018	AA	77.0	3	5	0	3.97	2.73	1.34	10.4	26.57%	3.0	7.76%	3.42	0.35	0.347
2018	AAA	22.0	3	0	0	5.32	4.74	1.05	11.5	32.18%	1.2	3.45%	9.33	2.45	0.280
2019	AAA	121.0	10	7	0	3.42	3.68	1.21	8.8	24.63%	1.9	5.43%	4.54	0.89	0.316

Background: It's easy to stock a farm system with a bevy of early first round picks. But the Braves also haven't had an issue unearthing plenty of intriguing talent beyond the opening round. Enter: Bryse Wilson, the 109th player chosen in the 2016 draft. A product of Orange High School in Hillsborough, North Carolina, the burly, powerfully built right-hander has moved through the minor leagues with the efficiency of a shark's fin through water. The 6-foot-1, 225-pound hurler was nearly unhittable during his debut in the Gulf Coast League; he followed that up with a dominating showing in the South Atlantic League. And then, once the front office took the training wheels off, Wilson shot through four separate levels in 2018, going from Low Class A all the way to a three-game cameo with the Braves. Last season the North Carolinian spent the majority of the time yo-yoing between Gwinnett and Atlanta. He made 21 starts with the club's International League affiliate, throwing 121.0 innings with 118 strikeouts and just 26 walks. He tossed another 20.0 innings, fanning 16 and walking just 10.

Snippet from The 2018 Prospect Digest Handbook: Wilson's fastball is a like a punch to the jaw from a heavyweight champion boxer.

Scouting Report: Consider the following:

- Since 2006, here's the list of 21-year-old pitchers to post a sub-6.0% walk percentage in the either Class AAA league (min. 100 IP): Bryse Wilson.

Wilson commands the strike zone – with all four pitches – like a savvy, soft-tossing veteran; not a haymaker-throwing, power-based right-hander. With the physical build of Roger Clemens, Wilson has makings of an underrated #2-type arm. And the former fourth rounder has – quietly – become the best pitching prospect in a system rich on pitching prospects. There's some Jose Berrios-type level of potential here. Plus fastball, plus-slider, above-average changeup, and a decent get-me-over curveball.

Ceiling: 3.5-win player
Risk: Moderate
MLB ETA: Debuted in 2018

4. Ian Anderson, RHP

	FB	CB	SL	CH	Command	Overall
	55+	60	50/55	55	45+	55

Born: 05/02/98	Age: 22	Bats: R
Height: 6-3	Weight: 170	Throws: R

YEAR	LVL	IP	W	L	SV	ERA	FIP	WHIP	K/9	K%	BB/9	BB%	K/BB	HR9	BABIP
2017	A	83.0	4	5	0	3.14	3.05	1.35	11.0	28.45%	4.7	12.11%	2.35	0.00	0.345
2018	A+	100.0	2	6	0	2.52	2.63	1.13	10.6	28.50%	3.6	9.66%	2.95	0.18	0.282
2018	AA	19.3	2	1	0	2.33	2.43	1.19	11.2	30.00%	4.2	11.25%	2.67	0.00	0.304
2019	AA	111.0	7	5	0	2.68	2.91	1.16	11.9	31.82%	3.8	10.17%	3.13	0.65	0.287
2019	AAA	24.7	1	2	0	6.57	6.42	1.66	9.1	22.12%	6.6	15.93%	1.39	1.82	0.277

Background: When the Braves made Anderson the third overall pick in 2016 it was earliest selection for the storied franchise since 1991 when they chose Arizona State University outfielder second overall. And Anderson tied former All-Star left-hander Steve Avery for the highest drafted pitcher in franchise history. A 6-foot-3, 170-pound right-hander out of Shenendehowa High School, Anderson immediately started making waves in the Braves' farm system: he posted a dominating 36-to-12 strikeout-to-walk ratio in 39.2 innings of work. He spent the following season, 2017, dominating the challenging South Atlantic League and split the 2018 campaign between High Class A and Class AA. The then-22-year-old righty opened up last year back in Mississippi, making 21 starts with the club's Southern League affiliate, throwing 111.0 innings with 147 strikeouts and 47 walks to go along with a 2.68 ERA. He made five additional starts with Gwinnett in Class AAA, though they were mostly disastrous. Overall, he averaged 11.4 strikeouts and 4.3 walks per nine innings.

Snippet from The 2018 Prospect Digest Handbook: Anderson has clean, repeatable mechanics so his control/command should continue its upward trend. At his peak he looks like another #2/#3-type arm.

Scouting Report: The numbers remain impressive, certainly, but his velocity – particularly down the stretch – is a bit troubling. Two years ago Anderson's heater was kissing the mid-90s with some regularity. Across several starts that I saw last season, though, Anderson's fastball was sitting 91- to 92-mph and touching 93. His curveball still looks like a hammer and his changeup adds another 55-grade weapon to his arsenal. And it looks like he added a slider to his repertoire late in the season. With respect to his work in Class AA, consider the following:

- Since 2006, only three 21-year-old hurlers have fanned at least 30% of the hitters they faced in the Southern League (min. 100 IP): Michael Kopech, Gio Gonzalez, and Ian Anderson.

Gonzalez, who was a 3.5-win player for the majority of his career, seems like a reasonable comparison.

Ceiling: 3.5-win player
Risk: Moderate
MLB ETA: 2020

5. Kyle Wright, RHP

	FB	CB	SL	CH	Command	Overall
	65	65	60	55	55	55

Born: 10/02/95	Age: 24	Bats: R
Height: 6-4	Weight: 200	Throws: R

YEAR	LVL	IP	W	L	SV	ERA	FIP	WHIP	K/9	K%	BB/9	BB%	K/BB	HR9	BABIP
2017	Rk	5.7	0	0	0	1.59	1.65	0.88	12.7	36.36%	3.2	9.09%	4.00	0.00	0.250
2017	A+	11.3	0	1	0	3.18	2.87	1.06	7.9	21.74%	3.2	8.70%	2.50	0.00	0.258
2018	AA	109.3	6	8	0	3.70	3.34	1.34	8.6	22.53%	3.5	9.23%	2.44	0.49	0.311
2018	AAA	28.7	2	1	0	2.51	3.22	0.80	8.8	25.45%	2.5	7.27%	3.50	0.63	0.183
2019	AAA	112.3	11	4	0	4.17	4.32	1.26	9.3	24.42%	2.8	7.37%	3.31	1.04	0.313

Background: One of the more highly touted collegiate arms in recent memory. Wright, a well-built 6-foot-4, 200-pound right-hander, was consistently dominant during his three-year tenure at Vanderbilt University – a.k.a. Pitcher U. After making him the fifth overall pick in 2017 draft, Atlanta signed the hard-throwing righty for a hefty $7 million bonus. And as expected, Wright moved quickly through the minor leagues – perhaps even faster than many people were prognosticating. He rocketed through Class AA and Class AAA during his first full season in the minor leagues and he even capped it off with a four-game cameo with Atlanta at the end of the year. The former Commodore opened up last season in The Show, but after a trio of starts – two of which were disastrous – he was demoted back down to the International League. In total, Wright tossed 112.1 innings with Gwinnett, posting a 116-to-35 strikeout-to-walk ratio. And he tossed another 19.2 innings with the Braves, fanning 18 and walking 13.

Snippet from The 2018 Prospect Digest Handbook: A little more than a year after being drafted Wright was toeing a rubber for the Braves and looks to be a big part of the club's plans in 2019. Wright shows a standard four-pitch mix: fastball, curveball, slider, and a changeup. Wright's heater, a plus-offering, sits in the 93- to 95-mph range with the ability to reach back for a little more when needed. His curveball trails only teammate Touki Toussaint's as tops in the organization and he's not afraid to bounce it to get hitters to chase. His slider, a mid-80s weapon, adds a third above-average pitch. The changeup settles in comfortably as the fourth option.

Scouting Report: Wright's added a couple ticks of consistent velocity onto his fastball. As I remarked in last year's Handbook, his fastball was sitting in the 93- to 95-mph range. Across a couple minor league starts last season Wright's heater was sitting a blistering 97-mph and touching 98-mph on occasion. He featured his changeup more frequently too, which also showed some developmental growth as well. The former collegiate ace's breaking balls are nasty, plus offerings. The break on his slider will vary from a hard cutter to a more traditional slider. With respect to his work in Class AAA, consider the following:

- Since 2006, here's the list of 23-year-old arms to post a strikeout percentage between 23.5% and 25.5% with a walk percentage between 6.5% and 8.5% in the International League (min. 100 IP): Jake Odorizzi, Mike Minor, Garrett Olson, and – of course – Kyle Wright.

Wright's repertoire and pedigree all suggest #1/#2-type status. But I don't think he ascends to that level. I think a Jake Odorizzi ceiling is more than reasonable. The cause: the fastball looks more hittable than the velocity would suggest. For example: during his May 3rd start against the Durham Bulls, hitters – without much hope for establishing themselves as big leaguers – looked awfully comfortable against what should be a plus to plus-plus fastball.

Ceiling: 3.5-win player
Risk: Moderate
MLB ETA: Debuted in 2018

6. William Contreras, C

Hit	Power	SB	Patience	Glove	Overall
50	45/50	30	45+	50	50

Born: 12/24/97	Age: 22	Bats: R
Height: 6-0	Weight: 180	Throws: R

YEAR	LVL	PA	1B	2B	3B	HR	SB	CS	AVG	OBP	SLG	BB%	K%	GB%	LD%	FB%
2017	RK	198	34	10	1	4	1	0	0.290	0.379	0.432	12.12%	15.15%	47.9	21.1	29.6
2018	A	342	61	17	1	11	1	1	0.293	0.360	0.463	8.48%	21.35%	46.6	20.8	27.1
2018	A+	90	14	7	0	0	0	0	0.253	0.300	0.337	6.67%	17.78%	38.2	26.5	30.9
2019	A+	207	36	11	0	3	0	0	0.263	0.324	0.368	6.76%	21.26%	50.7	22.6	21.9
2019	AA	209	35	9	0	3	0	0	0.246	0.306	0.340	7.18%	19.14%	47	14.6	30.5

Background: After a bit of a slow-and-steady approach in the early years of Contreras' career, the front office began easing the reins two years ago as the Venezuelan-born backstop split time between the South Atlantic and Florida State Leagues. And last season Contreras – once again – spent time between two separate levels. The 6-foot, 180-pound catcher opened the year back up with the Florida Fire Frogs, hitting a solid .263/.324/.368 with 11 doubles and three homeruns in 50 games. Contreras was promoted up to the Southern League in early June; he hit .246/.306/.340 with nine doubles and three homers in 60 games with the club's Class AA affiliate.

Snippet from The 2018 Prospect Digest Handbook: The biggest develop for the lean catcher was the surge in pop last season and that's only the beginning. At full maturity Contreras' power has the potential to blossom into a perennial 20-homer threat at the big league level. Throw in an above-average hit tool, a good glove behind the dish, and his willingness to take balls the other way; and there's *a lot* to like about the young Venezuelan.

Scouting Report: A few things to note:

- Contreras sandwiched three miserable offensive months with two scorching ones; he hit .329/.394/.447 in April and .290/.329/.420 in August, but managed to cobble together a putrid .212/.279/.297 triple-slash line in May, June, and July.
- The uptick in power Contreras showed in 2018 regressed to his previous subpar showing.

- Even though the numbers weren't all that impressive during his Class AA debut, Contreras, the younger brother of Cubs catcher Willson, was (A) a league average bat, (B) in the most important level, (C) at a premium position, and (D) at just 21-years-old.

Strong bat-to-ball skills with a decent eye at the plate and a solid glove behind the dish. Contreras is a league average – or better – starting catcher in the making.

Ceiling: 3.0-win player
Risk: Moderate
MLB ETA: 2020/2021

7. Braden Shewmake, SS	Hit	Power	SB	Patience	Glove	Overall
	50	45/50	50	50	50	50

Born: 11/19/97	Age: 22	Bats: L	Top CALs:
Height: 6-4	Weight: 190	Throws: R	

YEAR	LVL	PA	1B	2B	3B	HR	SB	CS	AVG	OBP	SLG	BB%	K%	GB%	LD%	FB%
2019	A	226	41	18	2	3	11	3	0.318	0.389	0.473	9.29%	12.83%	46.5	18	32
2019	AA	52	10	0	0	0	2	0	0.217	0.288	0.217	7.69%	21.15%	61.1	13.9	22.2

Background: Starred on the diamond and the gridiron during his four-year career at Wylie East High School; Shewmake quarterbacked his way into earning All-District 10-5A First Team honors as well as hitting .495 for the baseball team during his senior season. The 6-foot-4, 190-pound infielder turned quite a few heads after his dominant freshman season at Texas A&M in 2017. In 64 games for the SEC powerhouse, Shewmake slugged .328/.374/.529 with 18 doubles, two triples, and 11 homeruns to go along with 11 stolen bases. Baseball America, Collegiate Baseball, and NCBWA tabbed him as a First Team All-American. And he earned second team honors from ACBA and D1Baseball. The Texas native was also named as an ALL-SEC First Team and Freshman All-SEC. He spent the ensuing summer playing the USA National Collegiate Team, hitting a lowly .209/.327/.308 in 15 games. Shewmake's numbers – particularly in the power department – took a little bit of step backward during his follow up campaign two years ago: in 60 games for Head Coach Rob Childress, the lefty-swinging middle infield batted .325/.395/.450 with just 16 extra-base hits (seven doubles, four triples, and five homeruns). He also – briefly – popped up on Team USA's roster for the second time as well. Last season Shewmake's numbers maintained status quo: .313/.374/.474 with 24 extra-base hits (14 doubles, four triples, and six homeruns) to go along with 13 stolen bases in 16 attempts. Atlanta used their second first round pick on the Aggies shortstop, 21st overall, last June. Shewmake acquitted himself nicely in the South Atlantic League, slugging .318/.389/.473 with 18 doubles, two triples, and three homeruns. He also spent a couple weeks in the Southern League too.

Scouting Report: Per the usual, here's what I wrote about the lefty-swinging shortstop heading into last June's draft:

"Three years ago Shewmake looked like a burgeoning star, offering up above-average in-game power, speed, a strong hit tool, and incredible bat-to-ball skills. In fact, consider the following:

- *Between 2011 and 2018 there were only four instances in which a SEC hitter batted at least .320/.360/.500 with a sub-12% walk rate and a single digit strikeout rate (min. 275 PA): Alex Bregman, Alex Yarbrough, Michael Helman, and Braden Shewmake. Bregman, of course, is a bonafide star for the Astros. Alex Yarbrough, who accomplished the feat as a junior, was a fourth round pick by the Angels in 2012. And Helman, also a junior, was taken in the 11th round.*

Again, the only two players to meet the criteria during their respective freshman seasons were Bregman and Shewmake. The Texas A&M star's production, though, has stagnated the past two years, going from dominant to merely solid. His power has dried up. And while the incredible bat-to-ball skills remain intact, his lack of patience at the plate significantly cuts into his overall offensive value. Consider the following:

- *Between 2011 and 2018, only five SEC hitters have met the following criteria (min. 200 PA): hit at least .300/.350/.450 with a walk rate between 8% and 11% and a strikeout rate between 6% and 8%. Those five hitters: Alex Yarbrough, Kade Scivicque, Jake Magnum, Auston Bousfield, and Daniel Pigott.*
- *Again, Yarnrough was a fourth round pick. Scivicque, too, was taken in the fourth round. Mangum was drafted in the 32nd round by the Twins last season. And Pigott was selected in the ninth round by the Reds in 2012.*

Obviously, that's a less-than-stellar group of comparisons. There was a time in the not-so-distant past that Shewmake looked like a lock as a first rounder. But now, he's likely going to hear his name between the late second or early third rounds. Teams may be hoping to unlock his previous thump."

Shewmake's stellar debut – particularly in the Sally – like suggests that I may have shot a little too low on the young shortstop. I'd bump his ceiling up for a low-end starting caliber shortstop to a potentially league average one. Solid hit tool and power with a smattering of speed.

Ceiling: 2.5- to 3.0-win player
Risk: Low to Moderate
MLB ETA: 2021

8. Kyle Muller, LHP

	FB	CB	CH	Command	Overall
	70	60	45/55	40/45	50

Born: 10/07/97	Age: 22	Bats: R
Height: 6-6	Weight: 225	Throws: L

YEAR	LVL	IP	W	L	SV	ERA	FIP	WHIP	K/9	K%	BB/9	BB%	K/BB	HR9	BABIP
2017	Rk	47.7	1	1	0	4.15	4.40	1.28	9.3	23.67%	3.4	8.70%	2.72	0.94	0.284
2018	A	30.0	3	0	0	2.40	4.23	1.07	6.9	19.33%	2.4	6.72%	2.88	0.90	0.253
2018	A+	80.7	4	2	0	3.24	3.06	1.39	8.8	23.44%	3.6	9.50%	2.47	0.22	0.350
2018	AA	29.0	4	1	0	3.10	3.68	0.97	8.4	23.28%	1.9	5.17%	4.50	0.93	0.244
2019	AA	111.7	7	6	0	3.14	3.74	1.33	9.7	25.64%	5.5	14.53%	1.76	0.40	0.284

Background: Atlanta opened up the 2016 draft by taking three consecutive prep arms: Ian Anderson with the 3rd overall pick; Joey Wentz, who was selected 37 picks later; and – of course – Kyle Muller, a behemoth southpaw out of Dallas Jesuit College Prep. Muller squared off against the Southern League competition in 2019, showing an impressive ability to miss bats and the strike zone. The large left-hander struck out 120 and walked 68 in only 111.2 innings of work. That's an average of 9.7 strikeouts and a whopping 5.5 walks per nine innings. He finished the year with a 3.14 ERA and a 4.85 DRA (*Deserved Run Average*).

Snippet from The 2018 Prospect Digest Handbook: Muller looks like a backend starter, though if the curveball doesn't lurch forward he could be a fastball/changeup guy out of the pen.

Scouting Report: One of my favorite accounts to follow on Twitter because, well, I follow anyone associated with Driveline Baseball. Muller famously touched 107.3 mph on a pull down, a max effort throw with a running start, last offseason. The reason why I bring up Muller's Twitter account: he's been working diligently on an improved changeup. Ignoring his inability to consistently find the strike zone last season, Muller's below-average changeup was a massive issue. It was too firm, too...terrible. But he's been tweeting out videos of a vastly improved one, showing significant fade and dive. I think there's an outside chance for three plus-pitches. Now the control issues: there was a dramatic step back up from his control/command – particularly involving his fastball. He never showed a solid feel for zone, but there's no reason to think the control/command won't bounce back up to a 45-grade. There's some league average starting caliber potential, especially if the changeup is as good as it's looked in practice (assuming the control/command comes back).

Ceiling: 2.5-win player
Risk: Moderate
MLB ETA: 2020

9. Tucker Davidson, LHP

	FB	CB	CH	Command	Overall
	60	50	50	45	50

Born: 03/25/96	Age: 24	Bats: L
Height: 6-2	Weight: 215	Throws: L

YEAR	LVL	IP	W	L	SV	ERA	FIP	WHIP	K/9	K%	BB/9	BB%	K/BB	HR9	BABIP
2017	A	103.7	5	4	2	2.60	2.98	1.22	8.8	23.93%	2.6	7.11%	3.37	0.35	0.322
2018	A+	118.3	7	10	0	4.18	3.97	1.50	7.5	19.26%	4.4	11.28%	1.71	0.38	0.332
2019	AA	110.7	7	6	0	2.03	3.00	1.20	9.9	27.17%	3.7	10.02%	2.71	0.41	0.304
2019	AAA	19.0	1	1	0	2.84	4.10	1.53	5.7	14.63%	4.3	10.98%	1.33	0.00	0.339

Background: Surprisingly, the hefty lefty out of Midland College isn't the only success story to happen in the 19th round of the 2016 draft. Harvard right-hander Scott Pippen, who was taken drafted by the Minnesota Twins, earned a four-game cup of coffee with the big league club in 2019. Davidson, however, is clearly on his heels. The 559th overall pick that year, the 6-foot-2, 215-pound thick-bodied left-hander spent the majority of his fourth professional season squaring off – and often dominating – the minors' most important challenge, Class AA. In 21 starts with the Mississippi Braves, Davidson fanned 122 and walked 45 in 110.2 innings of work. He tallied a barely-there 2.03 ERA and a 4.43 DRA (*Deserved Run Average*). The Texas-born southpaw made four final starts with Gwinnett in Class AAA as well, tossing 19.0 innings with 12 punch outs and nine free passes.

Scouting Report: So I have to admit something that I wasn't aware of: as I was doing my background research on Davidson, a Reddit thread popped up that (A) showed he was a Driveline guy (which I love) and (B) he was posting some absurd metrics like: he set the MoCap (Motion Capture) record of 100.2 mph and bested Rays ace – and famed flame-thrower Tyler Glasnow – in several plyoball records. This is fascinating because in a late-season start against the Durham Bulls, his fastball was sitting firmly in average territory (91- to 92-mph). His curveball is slow and loopy, a 50-grade. And he'll mix in a decent changeup. However, a month earlier, on July 24th, Davidson's fastball was touching 96 mph and his curveball was flashing plus. Assuming the fastball isn't the one I saw at the end of the year, Davidson has the ceiling as a #4-type arm with the floor of a as a hard-throwing lefty reliever. The command still needs some work.

Ceiling: 2.0-win player
Risk: Moderate
MLB ETA: 2020

10. Huascar Ynoa, RHP

FB	SL	CH	Command	Overall
80	55	60	45	50

Born: 05/28/98	Age: 22	Bats: R
Height: 6-3	Weight: 175	Throws: R

YEAR	LVL	IP	W	L	SV	ERA	FIP	WHIP	K/9	K%	BB/9	BB%	K/BB	HR9	BABIP
2017	Rk	25.7	0	1	0	5.26	4.37	1.64	8.1	19.66%	4.9	11.97%	1.64	0.35	0.346
2017	Rk	25.7	0	3	0	5.26	4.41	1.52	9.5	22.69%	5.3	12.61%	1.80	0.35	0.315
2018	A	91.7	7	8	0	3.63	3.87	1.21	9.8	25.58%	4.1	10.74%	2.38	0.69	0.264
2018	A+	24.7	1	4	0	8.03	2.94	1.82	11.3	26.50%	4.4	10.26%	2.58	0.36	0.438
2019	A+	11.0	0	1	0	3.27	2.58	1.45	13.1	31.37%	4.9	11.76%	2.67	0.00	0.370
2019	AA	13.7	1	2	1	5.27	4.10	1.61	9.9	23.81%	3.3	7.94%	3.00	1.32	0.366
2019	AAA	72.7	3	5	0	5.33	5.52	1.57	9.8	23.94%	4.2	10.30%	2.32	1.73	0.332

Background: Signed by the Twins off the international market during the summer of 2014. Minnesota shipped the hard-throwing right-hander down south for veteran southpaw Jaime Garcia, Anthony Recker, and cash near the trade deadline three years ago. (On a side note: three days after acquiring Garcia, the Twinkies dealt him to the Yankees for Dietrich Enns and Zack Littell.) Ynoa rocketed through four separate levels last season, going from Low Class A all the way up to the big leagues, where he earned a brief two-game cameo. In total, Ynoa tossed 97.1 minor leagues innings, fanning 110 and walking 45 to go along with an aggregate 5.09 ERA. He tossed another three innings with the Braves, coughing up six earned runs while fanning three and walking one.

Snippet from The 2018 Prospect Digest Handbook: I'm a big, *big* believer of Ynoa's potential as a starting pitcher. The two knocks on the Dominican-born hurler are: #1 he's a max effort guy, which may persuade the Braves to push him into a bullpen role and #2 his control. Ynoa's ability to throw strikes took some baby steps forward last season, so the trend needs to continue. But he's going to be a light's out arm at the big league level – regardless of whether he's in the rotation or bullpen.

Scouting Report: The front office seemed like it had no idea on how to handle the hard-throwing hurler last season. He began the year in the rotation, was promptly pushed into a multi-inning reliever upon his promotion up to Class AA, and then made starts in Class AAA. He was then bounced back to the bullpen, then back to the rotation. Ynoa's fastball was sitting 94- to 95-mph during stint as a starter and sitting 97- to 98-mph as a reliever. Above-average slider. One of the more underrated changeups in the minor leagues. The Braves have a bevy of starting pitching options so it wouldn't be surprising to see him wind up as a full-time reliever. There's some league average starting caliber potential, though.

Ceiling: 2.0-win player
Risk: Moderate
MLB ETA: Debuted in 2019

11. Shea Langeliers, C

Hit	Power	SB	Patience	Glove	Overall
50	50	30	50	50	45

Born: 11/18/97	Age: 22	Bats: R
Height: 6-0	Weight: 190	Throws: R

YEAR	LVL	PA	1B	2B	3B	HR	SB	CS	AVG	OBP	SLG	BB%	K%	GB%	LD%	FB%
2019	A	239	40	13	0	2	0	0	0.255	0.310	0.343	7.11%	23.01%	42	19.1	28.4

Background: Not to be confused with Stephen King's novella, which was later turned into a miniseries on TV, *The Langoliers*; Langeliers, a six-foot, 190-pound backstop from Keller, Texas, put a disappointing sophomore campaign firmly in the rearview mirror. A three-year letter winner at Keller High School, Langeliers turned in a dynamic, power-packed freshman campaign at Baylor three years ago: in 55 games, the then-19-year-old slugged .313/.388/.540 with 14 doubles, a pair of triples, and 10 homeruns for Head Coach Steve Rodriguez. The promising backstop spent the ensuing summer playing for the Chatham Anglers in the premier Cape Cod League, hitting a respectable .234/.324/.469 with 16 extra-base hits (eight doubles, two triples, and six homeruns) in 34 contests. Langeliers' numbers dipped a bit during his sophomore season in 2018: he batted .252/.351/.496 with a career high 18 doubles, two triples, and 11 homeruns in 58 games the Bears, who reached the College World Series Regionals. An early season wrist injury, which forced him to miss some time, may have contributed to the decline. Langeliers spent that summer as the second best hitter on the Team USA National squad, slugging a scorching

.346/.393/.500 with four doubles and a 5-to-5 strikeout-to-walk ratio in eight games. Last season Langeliers has maintained status quo: he hit .308/.374/.530 with nine doubles, one triple, and 10 homeruns. Atlanta snagged him with the ninth overall selection last June. Langeliers batted a respectable .255/.310/.343 with 13 doubles and a pair of homeruns during his 55-game debut with Rome. Per *Deserved Runs Created Plus*, Langeliers was exactly a league bat.

Scouting Report: Per the usual, here's what I wrote prior to last June's draft:

> *"Playing in the shadow for fellow backstop – and likely #1 overall pick – Adley Rutschman; Langoliers, nonetheless, is poised to hear his name in the second round. Baylor's backstop shows above-average power with the potential to belt out 18- to 20-homeruns in a full professional season. He combines that with strong contact skills and a decent eye at the plate. Consider the following:*
>
> * *Between 2011 and 2018, there were six Big12 hitters that met the following criteria in a season (min. 200 PA): Tyler Naquin, Matt Juengel, Austin Fisher, Ryan McBroom, Kolbey Carpenter, and Devin Foyle. Only Naquin, a former first round pick, developed into a notable prospect. "*

I still believe that the former Baylor slugger went about a round too early. But he profiles as a low end, capable starter at the MLB level.

Ceiling: 1.5- to 2.0-win player
Risk: Moderate
MLB ETA: 2022

12. Michael Harris, OF

Hit	Power	SB	Patience	Glove	Overall
45/50	45/50	50	50	55	45

Born: 03/07/01	Age: 19	Bats: B
Height: 6-0	Weight: 195	Throws: L

YEAR	LVL	PA	1B	2B	3B	HR	SB	CS	AVG	OBP	SLG	BB%	K%	GB%	LD%	FB%
2019	Rk	119	27	6	3	2	5	2	0.349	0.403	0.514	7.56%	16.81%	46.1	25.8	25.8
2019	A	93	12	2	1	0	3	0	0.183	0.269	0.232	9.68%	23.66%	55.7	14.8	27.9

Background: Back in 2001 the Braves selected once-promising right-hander Kyle Davies in fourth round out of Stockbridge High School. Fast forward nearly two decades later and the front office – once again – found themselves calling one of the school's alums early in the draft when they selected switch-hitting outfielder Michael Harris. The 98th overall player chosen last summer, Harris batted a scorching .432 with seven doubles, four triples, and four homeruns during his senior season. And he starred on the mound for the Georgia high school as well, fanning 75 with a 1.87 ERA in 45.0 innings. He signed with the ballclub for $550,000, adding roughly $43,000 back into their draft pool. The 6-foot, 195-pound outfielder turned in one of the more dynamic showings in the Gulf Coast League as he slugged a sweltering .349/.403/.514 with six doubles, three triples, and a pair of homeruns to go along with five stolen bases. His bat, however, cooled considerably upon his promotion up to the South Atlantic League as he hit a lowly .183/.269/.232 in 22 games with Rome.

Scouting Report: Plus speed with the arm strength to match, Harris' defensive metrics were above-average in his limited debut – though he should be able to maintain a floor of a 55-grade defender given his sheer athleticism. The Georgia prep star' swing looks considerably smoother from the left side, offering up more natural loft, bat speed, and power potential. Harris takes more of a slashing approach from the right-side. The front office seemed to experiment with him primarily as a lefty-swinging during his debut, so that will need to be monitored going forward, but he could move quickly is he sticks to the left side. The raw athleticism is off the charts. He could prove to be one of the better value picks.

Ceiling: 1.5- to 2.0-win player
Risk: Moderate
MLB ETA: 2022

13. Victor Vodnik, RHP

FB	SL	CH	Command	Overall
60	55	50/55	50	45

Born: 10/09/99	Age: 20	Bats: R
Height: 6-0	Weight: 200	Throws: R

YEAR	LVL	IP	W	L	SV	ERA	FIP	WHIP	K/9	K%	BB/9	BB%	K/BB	HR9	BABIP
2018	Rk	4.7	1	1	0	9.64	3.21	1.93	17.4	39.13%	1.9	4.35%	9.00	1.93	0.583
2019	A	67.3	1	3	3	2.94	2.77	1.17	9.2	25.18%	3.2	8.76%	2.88	0.13	0.303

Background: Just another example of Atlanta's astute ability to find premium talent beyond the first round. The Braves scooped up – and somehow convinced – the hard-throwing right-hander to sign with the organization as a 14th round selection two years ago. A product of Rialto High School, which has produced long time veteran Ricky Nolasco, Vodnik was limited to just four brief relief appearances during his professional debut in the Gulf Coast League, posting a ridiculous 9-to-1 strikeout-to-walk ratio in only 4.2 innings of work. Last season, despite the low draft slot and limited action in the rookie league, the Braves pushed the 6-foot, 200-pound right-hander to South Atlantic League. And Vodnik didn't miss a beat. Making 23 appearances, most of which were multi-inning relief outings, the California native struck out 69 and walked 24 in 67.2 innings of work. He compiled a 2.94 ERA and a 4.44 DRA (*Deserved Run Average*).

Scouting Report: A few thoughts on Vodnik:

- The organization is clearly grooming him as a starting pitcher. Each of his outings last season extended beyond one inning of work.
- There's a possibility that Vodnik develops three above-average or better offerings. His fastball showed exceptional late life, touching the mid-90s. His slider is inconsistent, but flashed a few plus grades with two plane break. And his changeup, while firm, shows some arm side run and fade with a little bit of deception.
- He's poised to be one of the bigger breakout prospects in 2020.
- He's one of my favorite arms in the minor leagues.

Physically, Vodnik is maxed out so he's not likely to add much velocity moving forward (unless he gets together with Kyle Muller, Tucker Davidson and the rest of the Driveline guys). There's the ceiling as a backend arm with the floor of as a seventh/eighth inning arm.

Ceiling: 1.5- to 2.0-win player
Risk: Moderate
MLB ETA: 2022

14. Jasseel De La Cruz, RHP

FB	SL	CH	Command	Overall
65	55	50	45+	45

Born: 06/26/97	Age: 23	Bats: R
Height: 6-1	Weight: 215	Throws: R

YEAR	LVL	IP	W	L	SV	ERA	FIP	WHIP	K/9	K%	BB/9	BB%	K/BB	HR9	BABIP
2017	Rk	23.7	0	2	0	5.32	4.49	1.52	7.2	17.43%	4.2	10.09%	1.73	0.38	0.316
2017	Rk	19.0	2	1	0	1.89	3.58	1.05	8.1	21.79%	3.3	8.97%	2.43	0.47	0.231
2018	A	69.0	3	4	0	4.83	4.40	1.43	8.5	21.59%	4.4	11.30%	1.91	0.78	0.309
2019	A	18.0	0	1	0	2.50	2.75	1.33	11.0	29.33%	2.5	6.67%	4.40	0.50	0.391
2019	A+	28.0	3	1	0	1.93	2.31	0.68	8.4	25.24%	2.3	6.80%	3.71	0.00	0.174
2019	AA	87.0	4	7	0	3.83	4.11	1.24	7.6	19.89%	3.8	10.08%	1.97	0.72	0.262

Background: After spending parts of three seasons in the rookie leagues – both the foreign and stateside levels – De La Cruz cracked a full-season roster for the first time at the start of 2018. And he more than held his own in the tough South Atlantic League. In 15 appearances, 13 of which were starts, the 6-foot-1, 215-pound right-hander posted a solid 65-to-37 strikeout-to-walk ratio in 69.0 innings of work. He finished the season with a 4.83 ERA and an unsightly 5.81 DRA (*Deserved Run Average*). Last season the Dominican-born hurler made four starts back with Rome before moving up to High Class A for another four games. He eventually settled in at Class AA in late May for the remainder of the year. In total, the hard-throwing youngster fanned 121 and walked 49 in 133.0 innings. He compiled an aggregate 3.25 ERA.

Snippet from The 2018 Prospect Digest Handbook: De La Cruz's age is a bit of an inhibiting factor because there's little projection left. The Dominican-born hurler is very likely to wind up as a potential late-inning two-pitch pitcher.

Scouting Report: In a farm system chock full of high octane, nitrous infused fastballs, De La Cruz's heater deserved to be in the conversation. Late in the season his fastball was up to 98 mph. With that being said, (A) he's closing in on his age-23 season in a system full of high upside arms, (B) is more of a strike-thrower rather than a command guy, and (C) owns two above-average of better pitches that just screams late-inning, high leverage relief arm.

Ceiling: 1.5-win player
Risk: Moderate
MLB ETA: 2020

15. Alex Jackson, C

	Hit	Power	SB	Patience	Glove	Overall
	40	65	30	45	50+	40

Born: 12/25/95	Age: 24	Bats: R
Height: 6-2	Weight: 215	Throws: R

YEAR	LVL	PA	1B	2B	3B	HR	SB	CS	AVG	OBP	SLG	BB%	K%	GB%	LD%	FB%
2017	A+	282	39	17	0	14	0	1	0.272	0.333	0.502	4.61%	26.24%	39.1	20.1	31
2017	AA	120	19	4	0	5	0	0	0.255	0.317	0.427	8.33%	26.67%	39.7	16.7	34.6
2018	AA	252	27	12	1	5	0	0	0.200	0.282	0.329	7.94%	30.95%	40.5	20.3	31.1
2018	AAA	125	6	11	2	3	0	0	0.204	0.296	0.426	9.60%	33.60%	25	14.7	45.6
2019	AAA	345	33	9	0	28	1	0	0.229	0.313	0.533	5.80%	34.20%	28.1	22.7	36.2

Background: It seems like a lifetime ago, but Jackson was one of the most heralded bats in the 2014 draft, which is why the Mariners selected the power-hitting backstop with the sixth overall pick – immediately ahead of, by the way, guys like Aaron Nola, Kyle Freeland, and Michael Conforto. Seattle dealt the young catcher to the Braves a couple years later. Last season Jackson turned in a rather Jackson-like showing in the bandbox known as Class AAA. In 85 games with the Gwinnett Stripers, the 6-foot-2, 215-pound slugger bashed out nine doubles and a whopping 28 homeruns en route to batting .229/.313/.533. Per *Deserved Runs Created Plus*, his overall production was 6% better than league average.

Scouting Report: I went back and forth multiple times as to whether I should include Jackson on the Braves' Top 20 list because…well…he's a career .233/.317/.433 hitter in parts of six minor league seasons. He's flawed. Everyone knows this. He whiffs entirely too often. He doesn't walk nearly enough to help compensate. But he has some of the best raw and in-game power around. He was, by the way, on pace for 53 homeruns in a 162-game season last year. Catching at the big league level is just so desperate for any type of punch that I ultimately decided his inclusion. Per FanGraphs, Jackson's average exit velocity was a phenomenal 91 mph last season.

Ceiling: 1.0- to 1.5-win player
Risk: Low to Moderate
MLB ETA: Debuted in 2019

16. Kasey Kalich, RHP

	FB	SL	Command	Overall
	70	60	45+	40

Born: 04/25/98	Age: 22	Bats: R
Height: 6-3	Weight: 220	Throws: R

YEAR	LVL	IP	W	L	SV	ERA	FIP	WHIP	K/9	K%	BB/9	BB%	K/BB	HR9	BABIP
2019	Rk	1.0	0	0	0	0.00	2.50	2.00	18.0	40.00%	9.0	20.00%	2.00	0.00	0.500
2019	A	20.7	1	1	1	1.31	2.79	0.92	9.6	27.50%	4.4	12.50%	2.20	0.00	0.188

Background: If there was a theme to the club's draft class last season it has to center around how the front office keyed in on former JuCo stars that (A) were draft eligible after a year of Division I action and (B were below-slot signings. A product of Victoria West High School, where he was a unanimous choice for All=District 27-5A First Team following his senior season, the 6-foot-3, 220-pound flame-throwing right-hander spent a year at Blinn College. Following a year in which he fanned 48 in 46.1 innings for the JuCo squad, Kalich transferred to Texas A&M and – almost immediately –stepped into the closer's gig. He made 28 appearances for the SEC powerhouse, throwing 34.0 innings with 51 strikeouts, 13 walks, and 12 saves to go along with a 3.18 ERA. Atlanta drafted him in the fourth round and – of course – signed him to a below-slot deal. After a one-inning stint in the Gulf Coast League, the Texas-born righty made 13 appearances in the Sally, posting a 22-to-10 strikeout-to-walk ratio with a 1.31 ERA.

Scouting Report: Two plus pitches with the mentality to close out games at the big league level. Kalich sports a hard, late-lifed fastball in the mid- to upper-90s – which is thrown with exceptional ease. And he complements the 65-grade offering with late, downward-biting slider with two-plane break. Kalich has never been an extreme strike thrower, so that may slow his ascension towards the big leagues a little. He has the floor of a seventh inning arm and the ceiling as a bonafide closer.

Ceiling: 1.0- to 1.5-win player
Risk: Moderate
MLB ETA: 2021

17. Freddy Tarnok, RHP

FB	CB	CH	Command	Overall
55	50/55	45/50	45+	40

Born: 11/24/98	Age: 21	Bats: R
Height: 6-3	Weight: 185	Throws: R

YEAR	LVL	IP	W	L	SV	ERA	FIP	WHIP	K/9	K%	BB/9	BB%	K/BB	HR9	BABIP
2017	Rk	14.0	0	3	0	2.57	2.85	1.00	6.4	17.24%	1.9	5.17%	3.33	0.00	0.250
2018	A	77.3	5	5	0	3.96	4.02	1.44	9.7	23.31%	4.8	11.52%	2.02	0.58	0.297
2019	Rk	8.0	0	1	0	3.38	4.00	0.50	10.1	30.00%	1.1	3.33%	9.00	1.13	0.118
2019	A+	98.0	3	7	0	4.87	3.71	1.44	7.5	19.03%	3.3	8.35%	2.28	0.55	0.329

Background: A third round pick out of Riverview High School three years ago. Tarnok's another one of the lower level wild card arms currently making their way through the system. The wiry 6-foot-3, 185-pound right-hander turned some heads after a solid showing in the Sally when he averaged 9.7 strikeouts and 4.8 walks in a similar multi-inning reliever/spot-starter role that Victor Vodnik occupied last season. Tarnok, in an injury-shortened campaign in 2019, made 19 starts with the Florida Fire Frogs in High Class A, posting a solid 82-to-36 strikeout-to-walk ratio. He compiled a 4.87 ERA and an unsightly 6.06 DRA (*Deserved Run Average*).

Snippet from The 2018 Prospect Digest Handbook: An above-average fastball leads Tarnok's promising, albeit quite raw, arsenal. He'll also throw an overhand curveball which grades out as a future 55. The breaking pitch is inconsistent; at times it looks like a more slider and other times it resembles a more traditional curveball. His changeup will flash average at times. Tarnok works exclusively from the stretch. A recent convert to the mound in the latter years of his high school career, there's still quite a bit of projection left. At his peak, the Florida native looks like a backend starter/multiple inning reliever.

Scouting Report: (Author's Note: Tarnok is one of the only arms I did not personally scout last season. The above grades are from held over from the previous year's scouting notes.) Consider the following:

- Since 2006, here's the list of 20-year-old arms that posted a strikeout percentage between 18% and 20% with a walk percentage between 7.5% and 9.5% in the Florida State League (min. 75 IP): Nicholas Bucci, Chad James, and Freddy Tarnok.

Not exactly an inspiring collection of arms, is it? The control/command ticked up a little bit but his strikeout numbers drooped a touch. Tarnok was far better upon his month long stint on the disabled list as he struck out 41 and walked just 10 in 45.1 innings of work. I'm not certain the wiry right-hander is ready for the minors' toughest challenge, Class AA, so a return to the Florida State League is a possibility. If the second half production is indicative of his future performance, there's a chance he develops into a #5/#6-type arm.

Ceiling: 1.0- to 1.5-win player
Risk: Moderate
MLB ETA: 2021

18. Bryce Ball, 1B

Hit	Power	SB	Patience	Glove	Overall
45	60	30	55	50	40

Born: 07/08/98	Age: 21	Bats: L
Height: 6-6	Weight: 235	Throws: R

YEAR	LVL	PA	1B	2B	3B	HR	SB	CS	AVG	OBP	SLG	BB%	K%	GB%	LD%	FB%
2019	Rk+	173	22	12	0	13	0	0	0.324	0.410	0.676	12.72%	17.34%	37.8	25.2	31.1
2019	A	90	19	6	0	4	0	0	0.337	0.367	0.547	4.44%	22.22%	42.4	21.2	33.3

Background: There were a few parallels between Bryce Ball and Beau Philip, the club's second round selection last June. Both attended junior colleges – Philip went to San Joaquin Jacinto and Ball attended North Iowa Area Community College. Both put up tremendous numbers during their lone Division I seasons: Philip hit .311/.369/.486 with Oregon State and Ball mashed .325/.443/.614 at Dallas Baptist. Both were drafted following their age-20 season, which makes them young for their class. And, of course, both were drafted by the Braves last season. But that's where the parallels die. Philip was an under-slot signing as a second round pick and Ball lasted all the way to the 24th round. Philip looked completely hapless during his debut in the Appalachian League, hitting just .193/.297/.280; and Ball ripped through the Appalachian League to the tune of .324/.410/.676 and didn't stop hitting in a 21-game cameo with Rome. The massive 6-foot-6, 235-pound first baseman slugged an aggregate .329/.395/.628 with 18 doubles and 17 homeruns in 62 games.

Scouting Report: With respect to his work with Dallas Baptist last season, consider the following:

- Between 2011 and 2018, only three Missouri Valley Conference hitters met the following criteria in a season (min. 250 PA): hit at least .300/.425/.600 and post a walk rate north of 15%. Those three hitters: Casey Gillaspie, a first round pick in 2014, Austin Listi, who is coming off of a solid showing between Class AA and Class AAA in 2019, and Devlin Granberg, a sixth round by the Red Sox in 2018.

Not a bad find in the 24th round last season, huh? Plus in-game raw power, a history of strong walk rates and decent contact levels, and the left-swinging first baseman didn't show any concerning platoon splits during his debut. He's locked in at first base, so he's going to have to continue to mash as he moves up the ladder – and he clearly won't do so at last season's benchmark. Impressive opposite field power too. He stays inside the ball well. There might be some low end starting material here. Oh, yeah, his average exit velocity was a whopping 92 mph during his impressive debut.

Ceiling: 1.0- to 1.5-win player
Risk: Moderate
MLB ETA: 2022

19. Greyson Jenista, 1B/OF

Hit	Power	SB	Patience	Glove	Overall
40/45	45	35	55	50	40

Born: 12/07/96	Age: 23	Bats: L	Top CALs:
Height: 6-3	Weight: 210	Throws: R	

YEAR	LVL	PA	1B	2B	3B	HR	SB	CS	AVG	OBP	SLG	BB%	K%	GB%	LD%	FB%
2018	RK	47	6	1	0	3	0	1	0.250	0.348	0.500	12.77%	19.15%	50	25	21.9
2018	A	130	30	5	3	1	4	1	0.333	0.377	0.453	7.69%	13.08%	51.5	23.3	23.3
2018	A+	74	6	3	1	0	0	0	0.152	0.230	0.227	9.46%	20.27%	57.7	13.5	25
2019	A+	231	26	14	1	4	1	4	0.223	0.312	0.361	11.69%	30.30%	44	21.6	30.6
2019	AA	256	44	4	1	5	2	4	0.243	0.324	0.338	10.55%	29.30%	42.7	16	36.7

Background: A stout – albeit – incredibly consistent bat in the middle of Wichita State's lineup for his three-year collegiate career. Jenista, who left the school as a .318/.430/.487 hitter, was drafted by the Braves in the second round, 49th overall, two years ago. The 6-foot-3, 210-pound first baseman / outfielder ripped through the Appalachian League for 10 games (.250/.348/.500), scorched the South Atlantic League pitching in 32 contests (.333/.377/.453), and finally cooled in a late-season promotion up to High Class A. The former Wichita State slugged opened the 2019 season back up in High Class A. And, unfortunately, his numbers barely improved. In 56 games with the Fire Frogs Jenista hit a lowly .223/.312/.361 with 14 doubles, one triple, and four homeruns. Atlanta bounced the disappointing hitter – for some reason – up to Class AA in early June and he continued to struggle (.243/.324/.338).

Snippet from The 2018 Prospect Digest Handbook: Jenista looks like a tweener in terms of big league ceiling – though he's very likely going to slide into a fourth outfielder role.

Scouting Report: Well, it's not great. Even by basic metrics, Jenista's 2019 season was craptacular: his monthly OPS totals eclipsed .700 just one time (July). He still hasn't tapped into his average in-game power, despite putting the ball on the ground in roughly 40% of his plate appearances in 2019. Above-average patience that's undone by his swing-and-miss issues – which he hasn't shown at any point in his previous four seasons. Oh, and then there's this: two seasons into his professional career and the lefty-swinging first baseman/outfielder is showing some concerning platoon splits. Fourth outfielder ceiling seems a bit optimistic at this point.

Ceiling: 1.0- to 1.5-win player
Risk: Moderate
MLB ETA: 2020/2021

20. Beau Philip, SS

Hit	Power	SB	Patience	Glove	Overall
35/45	40/45	40	50	50	40

Born: 10/23/98	Age: 21	Bats: R	
Height: 6-0	Weight: 190	Throws: R	

YEAR	LVL	PA	1B	2B	3B	HR	SB	CS	AVG	OBP	SLG	BB%	K%	GB%	LD%	FB%
2019	Rk+	239	30	6	0	4	5	5	0.193	0.297	0.280	10.88%	21.34%	56.1	15.9	22.9

Background: A product of Oak Ridge High School, Philip, who left the California prep school as a career .324 hitter and a Division I section champion runner-up, spent his freshman and sophomore collegiate seasons at San Joaquin Jacinto College where he earned a bevy of awards and recognitions including: First-Team All-League, All-Nor Cal, Rawlings Pacific Division All-American First Team, All Big 8, and a Gold Glove. The 6-foot, 190-pound middle infielder transferred to Pac12 powerhouse Oregon State for the 2019 season. In an injury-abbreviated campaign with the Beavers, Philip slugged a healthy .311/.369/.486 with 14 doubles, one triple, and five homeruns. He also swiped six bags in nine total attempts. Atlanta drafted him in the second round, 60th overall, and signed him to a below slot deal for $700,000 – more than half of the recommended bonus. Philip looked helpless against the Appalachian League pitching during his debut as he batted a lowly .193/.297/.280 with six doubles and four homeruns.

Scouting Report: A good, sometimes great hitter during his injury-interrupted campaign with Oregon State. Philip shows average tools across the board: hit tool, power (though it's mainly gap to gap), patience, and glove. His showing in the Advanced Rookie League was – simply – downright scary, particularly for a hitter coming from a top notch collegiate program. Philip was young for the class and only entering his age-21 season, but it's not looking good for the second rounder. Utility ceiling.

Ceiling: 1.0- to 1.5-win player
Risk: Moderate
MLB ETA: 2022

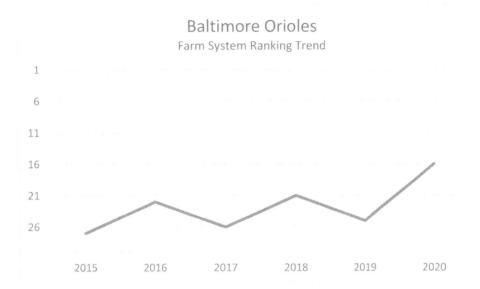

Baltimore Orioles
Farm System Ranking Trend

Rank	Name	Age	Pos
1	Adley Rutschman	22	C
2	Grayson Rodriguez	20	RHP
3	Yusniel Diaz	23	CF/RF
4	DL Hall	21	LHP
5	Ryan Mountcastle	23	1B/LF
6	Zac Lowther	24	LHP
7	Drew Rom	20	LHP
8	Michael Baumann	24	RHP
9	Austin Hays	24	OF
10	Cadyn Grenier	23	SS
11	Gunnar Henderson	19	SS
12	Hunter Harvey	25	RHP
13	Adam Hall	21	2B/SS
14	Kyle Stowers	22	LF/RF
15	Dean Kremer	24	RHP
16	Keegan Akin	25	LHP
17	Ryan McKenna	23	CF
18	Rylan Bannon	24	3B
19	Brett Cumberland	25	C
20	Bruce Zimmermann	25	LHP

1. Adley Rutschman, C

Hit	Power	SB	Patience	Glove	Overall
55	60	30	60	55	70

Born: 02/06/98	Age: 22	Bats: B
Height: 6-2	Weight: 216	Throws: R

YEAR	LVL	PA	1B	2B	3B	HR	SB	CS	AVG	OBP	SLG	BB%	K%	GB%	LD%	FB%
2019	Rk	16	1	0	0	1	1	0	0.143	0.250	0.357	12.50%	12.50%	50	8.3	41.7
2019	A-	92	16	7	1	1	0	0	0.325	0.413	0.481	13.04%	17.39%	28.6	34.9	30.2
2019	A	47	3	1	0	2	0	0	0.154	0.261	0.333	12.77%	19.15%	51.6	6.5	35.5

Background: A do-everything-type of athlete cut from the same cloth as former big league All-Star – and stout University of Nebraska punter – Darin Erstad. Rutschman, like Erstad, spent some time on the gridiron for Oregon State; he was a placekicker – and actually recorded a couple tackles – during his freshman season in 2016. A native of Portland, Oregon, the Seattle Mariners snagged the switch-hitting catcher in the late, late rounds in the June draft following a superb career at Sherwood High School; Rutschman was rated the second best prep prospect in the state by *Baseball Northwest*. Following the conclusion of his lone collegiate football campaign, the 6-foot-2, 216-pound backstop earned the starting gig behind the dish for long-time Manager Pat Casey, hitting .234/.322/.306 with 10 extra-base hits (seven doubles, one triple, and a pair of long balls) in 61 games of work. Rutschman spent the ensuing summer playing for the Corvallis Knights in the West Coast League, batting .256/.256/.308 with a pair of doubles in 39 plate appearances. The switch bopper turned in – arguably – the biggest breakout campaign of the year as he led Oregon State to a National Championship in 2018: in 67 games for the Pac-12 powerhouse, Rutschman slugged a robust .408/.505/.628 with 22 doubles, three triples, and nine homeruns; he finished his sophomore campaign with a stout 40-to-53 strikeout-to-walk ratio as well. And, of course, the Portland-native earned a bevy of awards and recognitions, including:

- College World Series Most Outstanding Player
- First-Team All-America by D1Baseball and ABCA
- Second-Team All-America by Baseball America and Perfect Game
- Third-Team All-America by NCBWA and Collegiate Baseball
- All-Pac-12 First Team, Pac-12 All-Defensive Team, Pac-12 All-Academic Honorable Mention
- Semifinalist for the Dick Howser Trophy and Johnny Bench Award

Rutschman continued to swing a scorching bat for Team USA that summer as well, putting together a team-leading .355/.432/.516 triple-slash line to go along with five doubles and a 5-to-5 strikeout-to-walk ratio in 31 at bats. Last season Rutschman raised the bar even further, putting up videogame-esque numbers: in 57 games, he slugged .411/.575/.751 with 10 doubles, one triple, and 7 homeruns. Baltimore made the easy decision and selected the uber-prospect with the #1 overall pick in June. Rutschman split his debut between three levels, hitting a respectable .254/.351/.423 with eight doubles, one triple, and four homeruns.

Scouting Report: My pre-draft analysis for Rutschman:

"The obvious front runner for the top pick in the June draft. Between 2000 and 2010 nearly 10% of all Team USA hitters had at least one season in which they topped five wins above replacement (FanGraphs version). And Rutschman ticks off a lot of important checkboxes: elite plate discipline, above-average power potential, above-average hit tool, and some strong defensive chops – which includes smooth footwork and a strong arm behind the plate With respect to his offensive work thus far in 2019, consider the following:

- *Between 2011 and 2018, only two Division I hitters have posted a walk rate north of 25% in a season (min. 200 PA): Anthony Rendon, the sixth overall pick in the 2011 draft, and Zack Collins, the tenth pick in 2016.*
- *Rendon, though, finished the year with a strikeout rate below 15%.*

Let's continue:

Player	Age	Year	PA	AVG	OBP	SLG	K%	BB%
Adley Rutschman	21	2019	198	0.429	0.576	0.800	27.27%	14.14%
Anthony Rendon	21	2011	302	0.327	0.520	0.523	26.49%	10.93%

Obviously, Rutschman's production dwarf's his counterpart's numbers, though in a smaller sample size. Rutschman shows a smooth, easy swing without much effort that generates above-average bat speed. There's no such thing as a lock for superstardom when it comes to prospects, but Rutschman looks like a strong possibility to get there."

Ceiling: 6.0-win player
Risk: Low to Moderate
MLB ETA: 2021/2022

2. Grayson Rodriguez, RHP

FB	CB	SL	CH	Command	Overall
70	55	65	55	50/55	60

Born: 11/16/99	Age: 20	Bats: R
Height: 6-5	Weight: 220	Throws: R

YEAR	LVL	IP	W	L	SV	ERA	FIP	WHIP	K/9	K%	BB/9	BB%	K/BB	HR9	BABIP
2018	Rk	19.3	0	2	0	1.40	2.66	1.24	9.3	25.00%	3.3	8.75%	2.86	0.00	0.321
2019	A	94.0	10	4	0	2.68	2.62	0.99	12.4	34.22%	3.4	9.55%	3.58	0.38	0.262

Background: A product of Central Heights High School, home to former Indians second round pick Trey Haley, Rodriguez was nearly unhittable during his junior campaign; he went a whopping 14-1 during the 2017 season, posting a barely-there 0.38 ERA, and was named Texas Sports Writers Association Player of the Year. His draft stock rocketed up during his final prep season as his fastball climbed – comfortably – into the mid- to upper-90s. Baltimore snagged the broad-shouldered right-hander in the opening round, 11th overall, in 2018. After dominating the Gulf Coast League in a couple of brief outings during his debut, Rodriguez continued wreak havoc on the opposition as he moved up to full-season action in 2019. In 20 starts with the Delmarva Shorebirds, the 6-foot-5, 220-pound right-hander fanned an incredible 129 – against just 36 free passes – in only 94.0 innings of work. He finished the year with a 2.68 ERA and a nearly identical 2.69 DRA (Deserved Runs Average).

Snippet from The 2018 Prospect Digest Handbook: The well-built righty showcases a standard four-pitch mix: an electric, plus-fastball with some arm side movement; a 12-6 curveball, a slider, and a changeup. Both of Rodriguez's breaking pitches flash above-average but need further refinement as they tend to float on occasion and remain quite raw. His fastball reportedly touched 98 heading into the spring. And his changeup is thrown with a split-finger grip. His breaking pitches seem a bit rawer than I would have expected for an early first round pick.

Scouting Report: First off: Ranked as the club's seventh best prospect heading into the year, I *clearly* underrated Rodriguez's potential. Consider the following:

- Since 2006, Rodriguez's 2.69 DRA is seventh best mark among all 19-year-old pitchers in either Low Class A league (min. 75 IP), trailing only Joey Cantillo, Will Inman, Jose Fernandez, Lucas Giolito, Tyler Glasnow, and Jen-Ho Tseng.

There are more than a few impressive names sprinkled among the group. Three would go on to become viable stars (Fernandez, Giolito, and Glasnow), another is a former top prospect (Inman), and a fifth, Cantillo, is currently rocketing up prospect charts. So let's look at Rodriguez's dominance another way:

- Since 2006, here's the list of 19-year-old pitchers to fan at least a third of the hitters they faced in Low Class A (min. 75 IP): Jose Fernandez, Tyler Glasnow, Joey Cantillo, and – of course – Grayson Rodriguez. The Orioles budding ace, by the way, owns the second best strikeout percentage for 19-year-olds in the South Atlantic League since 2006.

Rodriguez is physically reminiscent of former MLB All-Star – forever enigma – right-hander Ubaldo Jimenez: long arms, shoulders that look like that could bear the load of a highway overpass, and tree-trunk legs. The former 11th overall pick owns a wipeout arsenal as his secondary weapons improved: his fastball was sitting in upper-90s late year; his slider was so overpowering at times it was comically unfair, the changeup shows impressive deception, and the curveball is quietly an above-average offering. There's no question about it: he's an ace-in-the-making and there are few – if any – minor league pitchers I would take over Rodriguez.

Ceiling: 5.0-win player
Risk: Moderate
MLB ETA: 2022

3. Yusniel Diaz, RF

Hit	Power	SB	Patience	Glove	Overall
60	55	30	50	50	60

Born: 10/07/96	Age: 23	Bats: R
Height: 6-1	Weight: 195	Throws: R

YEAR	LVL	PA	1B	2B	3B	HR	SB	CS	AVG	OBP	SLG	BB%	K%	GB%	LD%	FB%
2017	AA	118	25	8	0	3	2	5	0.333	0.390	0.491	8.47%	24.58%	39.2	31.6	22.8
2018	AA	264	49	10	4	6	8	8	0.314	0.428	0.477	15.53%	14.77%	40.3	23.2	26
2018	AA	152	21	5	1	5	4	5	0.239	0.329	0.403	11.84%	18.42%	43.4	20.8	28.3
2019	AA	322	41	19	4	11	0	3	0.262	0.335	0.472	9.94%	20.81%	43.2	16.7	32.4

Background: In one the final acts as General Manager of the Orioles, Dan Duquette was tasked with dealing superstar – and hometown icon – Manny Machado as the trade deadline approached. Duquette did as well as anyone could have in the same situation, acquiring a bevy of prospects – Yusniel Diaz, Dean Kremer, Zach Pop, Rylan Bannon, and Breyvic Valera – for a couple months of Machado. Diaz, obviously, was the major "get" in the deal for Baltimore. A sweet-swinging corner outfielder with gobs of potential that could become the next face of the franchise; he clearly felt the pressure of the deal and looked overwhelmed in 38 Class AA games in the Orioles' system. Last season Diaz, an athletic 6-foot-2, 195-pound import from La Habana, Cuba, battled a couple lower body injuries – a strained hamstring and a quadriceps issues – that limited him to just 76 Eastern League games (as well as a handful of rehab appearances). He batted a respectable .262/.335/.472 with 19 doubles, four triples, and 11 homeruns with Bowie.

Snippet from The 2018 Prospect Digest Handbook: Plus hit tool, above-average power and speed (though he's an atrocious base runner), incredible eye at the plate with strong bat-to-ball skills, and he plays a competent center and right fields. If the power takes another step forward Diaz could be a perennial MVP candidate.

Scouting Report: It wasn't necessarily a lost year for Diaz in 2019, but it's tough to remain productive with a pair of lengthy disabled stints on the docket. But, surprisingly, Diaz remained one of the most potent bats in Class AA in 2019, topping the league average a mark by 50%.

- Since 2006, there have been three 22-year-old hitters to post a 145- to 150-DRC+ with an average walk rate (7% to 10%) to go along with a 17% to 22% strikeout rate in the Eastern League (min. 300 PA): Travis d'Arnaud, Brandon Laird, and Yusniel Diaz. d'Arnaud has been exactly a league average hitter through his 500-big league games. And Laird received a couple cups of big league coffee with the Yankees and Astros.

Above-average or better tools across the board: plus bat, above-average pop, solid eye and contact skills at the plate, and he can play a solid center and right fields. Diaz is at an interesting precipice in his career as he enters his age-23 season. He's either going to take that next step forward into stardom, which could very well happen under the new guidance of the player development engine, or he simply stays very good.

Ceiling: 4.0-win player
Risk: Moderate
MLB ETA: 2020

4. DL Hall, LHP

	FB	CB	CH	Command	Overall
	65	60	60	40/45	60

Born: 09/19/98	Age: 21	Bats: L
Height: 6-2	Weight: 195	Throws: L

YEAR	LVL	IP	W	L	SV	ERA	FIP	WHIP	K/9	K%	BB/9	BB%	K/BB	HR9	BABIP
2017	Rk	10.3	0	0	0	6.97	5.55	1.94	10.5	24.49%	8.7	20.41%	1.20	0.87	0.360
2018	A	94.3	2	7	0	2.10	3.66	1.17	9.5	25.58%	4.0	10.74%	2.38	0.57	0.262
2019	A+	80.7	4	5	1	3.46	3.21	1.33	12.9	33.53%	6.0	15.61%	2.15	0.33	0.299

Background: His wavering command / control in 2018 developed into a full meltdown last season. Hall, the 21st overall pick out of Valdosta High School three years ago, established himself as one of the more dynamic young arms in the minor leagues after his first full season in professional ball: making 22 appearances for the Delmarva Shorebirds in 2018, the 6-foot-2, 195-pound southpaw fanned 100 – against 42 free passes – across 94.1 innings of work. Last season, though, Hall's walk rate ballooned from 4.0 BB/9 all the way to Steve Blass territory: the former first rounder handed out 54 walks in just 80.2 innings of work. Amazingly enough, though, Hall finished the year with a 3.46 ERA on the back of his incredible ability to miss bats (12.9 K/9). He was knocked out of action in mid-August because of a mild left lat muscle strain.

Snippet from The 2018 Prospect Digest Handbook: With respect to his production, consider the following:

- Between 2006 and 2017, here's the list of 19-year-old pitchers to post a strikeout percentage between 24.5% and 26.5% in the South Atlantic League (min. 75 IP): Carlos Carrasco, Jeremy Jeffress, Kelvin De La Cruz, Randall Delgado, Jameson Taillon, Robbie Ray, and Bryse Wilson.

Scouting Report: Let's update that a bit, shall we? Consider the following:

- Since 2006, there have been just five 20-year-pitchers to post a 30% strikeout percentage in any High Class A league (min. 75 IP): Tyler Glasnow, Yovani Gallardo, MacKenzie Gore, Will Inman, and DL Hall.

Equipped with three-plus pitches – a mid- to upper-90s fastball with explosive, late life; a hard, *hard* biting curveball, and an incredibly underrated changeup – but can't take full advantage of them (scary thought, right?) because of his control / command woes. Prior to hitting the DL in mid-August, Hall made a total of 19 appearances. Of those 19, he walked at least four hitters in six of them. He has the potential to develop into a Blake Snell-type lefty; he just has to throw more strikes. Snell, by the way, battled severe control issues early in his career too.

Ceiling: 4.5-win player
Risk: Moderate to High
MLB ETA: 2022

5. Ryan Mountcastle, 1B/LF

Hit	Power	SB	Patience	Glove	Overall
55	55	30	40	45	50

Born: 02/18/97	Age: 23	Bats: R
Height: 6-3	Weight: 195	Throws: R

YEAR	LVL	PA	1B	2B	3B	HR	SB	CS	AVG	OBP	SLG	BB%	K%	GB%	LD%	FB%
2017	A+	379	62	35	1	15	8	2	0.314	0.343	0.542	3.69%	16.09%	36.5	25.2	29.9
2017	AA	159	18	13	0	3	0	0	0.222	0.239	0.366	1.89%	22.01%	37.5	13.3	34.2
2018	AA	428	81	19	4	13	2	0	0.297	0.341	0.464	6.07%	18.46%	40.6	20	30.3
2019	AAA	553	101	35	1	25	2	1	0.312	0.344	0.527	4.34%	23.51%	37.2	28.2	25.2

Background: An incredibly underrated prospect during the early years of his pro career, Mountcastle, who was taken by the Orioles with the 36th overall pick in 2015, has quietly established himself among the game's best prospects over the past few seasons. Originally drafted a shortstop and converted to a full-time third baseman, the Orioles continued to move Mountcastle around the diamond last season, settling on a pair of un-athletic corner positions: first base and left field. Wherever he stands on defense, though, the bat won't have a problem contributing. After passing the Class AA exam with convincing production – he batted .297/.341/.464 with Bowie as a 21-year-old – Mountcastle plowed through the minors' last stop, Class AAA, while feasting on the notorious hitter-friendly environments: in a career-best tying 127 games, the 6-foot-3, 195-pound slugger hit .312/.344/.527 with 35 doubles, one triple, and a career-best 25 dingers. His overall production, according to *Baseball Prospectus'* Deserved Runs Created Plus (DRC+), topped the league average threshold by 15%.

Snippet from The 2018 Prospect Digest Handbook: A long-time perennial favorite of mine. He hits for average and has underrated power. The lone knock is his defense at third base, where he'll never be confused with Matt Chapman or Brooks Robinson. He may never develop into a full-fledged star, but there are a lot of similar qualities with Seattle Mariners third baseman Kyle Seager.

Scouting Report: Consider the following:

- Since 2006, only two 22-year-old hitters posted a 110 to 120 DRC+ total with a sub-7.0% walk rate in the International League (min. 300 PA): new Yankees' cult star Gio Urshela and Ryan Mountcastle. Urshela, of course, is fresh off a massive breakout campaign for New York, slugging .314/.355/.534 during his age-27 season.

There are still two pockmarks that are plaguing Mountcastle's eventually big league value: (A) his inability to play even passable defense (he was atrocious at first and below-average in a short sample size in left field) and (B) his unwillingness to walk. Everything else about Mountcastle screams potential All-Star during his peak: above-average hit tool, above-average in-game power, and strong contact rates. He's going to be a cornerstone in the Orioles resurgence for a long time.

Ceiling: 3.0-win player
Risk: Low to Moderate
MLB ETA: 2020

6. Zac Lowther, LHP

FB	CB	CH	Command	Overall
50	60	50	50	50

Born: 04/30/96	Age: 24	Bats: L
Height: 6-2	Weight: 235	Throws: L

YEAR	LVL	IP	W	L	SV	ERA	FIP	WHIP	K/9	K%	BB/9	BB%	K/BB	HR9	BABIP
2017	A-	54.3	2	2	0	1.66	1.62	0.85	12.4	35.89%	1.8	5.26%	6.82	0.17	0.283
2018	A	31.0	3	1	0	1.16	1.98	0.68	14.8	44.35%	2.6	7.83%	5.67	0.58	0.192
2018	A+	92.7	5	3	0	2.53	3.01	1.08	9.7	26.88%	2.5	6.99%	3.85	0.58	0.288
2019	AA	148.0	13	7	0	2.55	3.16	1.11	9.4	25.97%	3.8	10.62%	2.44	0.49	0.259

Background: The highest drafted player out of Xavier University in Cincinnati, Ohio, Lowther, the 74th overall pick in the 2017 draft, is already knocking on the big league club's door. The former Big East Conference ace split the 2018 season between the South Atlantic and Carolina Leagues, throwing a combined 123.2 innings with a whopping 151 strikeouts and just 35 walks. Lowther spent the entirety of last season squaring off against the minors' toughest challenge, Class AA. In 26 starts, the big bodied left-hander fanned 154, walked 63, and compiled a 4.16 DRA (Deserved Run Average) in 148.0 innings of work.

Snippet from The 2018 Prospect Digest Handbook: The numbers – especially the strikeout percentages – are a bit misleading because the big lefty is far from a traditional power pitcher. Instead, Lowther commands three average or better offerings reasonably well. And he's willing to vary the arm angle/release point on his fastball as well.

Scouting Report: Despite moving up to Class AA, the make-it-or-break-it level, last season, Lowther's arsenal and pitchability still racked up plenty of swings-and-misses. His fastball was sitting 87-90 mph in a late season start against Reading, kissing 92 mph on occasion. His straight changeup is workable. And his curveball, a mid-70s offering, is a swing-and-miss type breaking ball and something he should throw more frequently. With respect to his production last season, consider the following:

- .0-Since 2006, only four 23-year-old pitchers – three of which were southpaws, by the way – posted a strikeout percentage between 25% and 27% in the Eastern League (min. 100 IP): Glen Perkins, Taylor Hearns, Dellin Betances, and Zac Lowther.

Lowther is what Lowther's always been: a safe, low ceiling, fast moving pitching prospect. He's going to be a backend starting pitcher for a long time, hovering near league average status. The command, by the way, wavered at points with Bowie last season. And he's the type of pitcher where that can't happen too often.

Ceiling: 2.5-win player
Risk: Moderate
MLB ETA: 2020

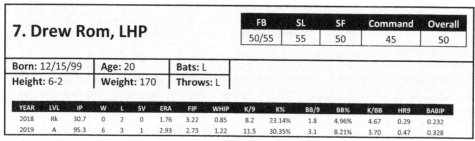

7. Drew Rom, LHP

	FB	SL	SF	Command	Overall
	50/55	55	50	45	50

Born: 12/15/99	Age: 20	Bats: L
Height: 6-2	Weight: 170	Throws: L

YEAR	LVL	IP	W	L	SV	ERA	FIP	WHIP	K/9	K%	BB/9	BB%	K/BB	HR9	BABIP
2018	Rk	30.7	0	2	0	1.76	3.22	0.85	8.2	23.14%	1.8	4.96%	4.67	0.29	0.232
2019	A	95.3	6	3	1	2.93	2.73	1.22	11.5	30.35%	3.1	8.21%	3.70	0.47	0.328

Background: Handed an above-slot bonus worth about $170,000 to persuade him from heading to the University of Michigan. Rom, the 115th overall player taken in the June draft two years ago, has been nearly unhittable during his two seasons in the minors. The 6-foot-2, 170-pound left-hander posted a 28-to-6 strikeout-to-walk ratio across 30.2 innings in the Gulf Coast League. The front office brass pushed the teenager up to the South Atlantic League and he chewed through hitters like an angry pit bull. In 21 appearances, 15 of them coming via the start, the Highlands High School product fanned an incredible 122 and handed out just 33 walks while coming a 2.93 ERA – as well as a 4.17 DRA – in 95.1 innings of work.

Scouting Report: Consider the following:

- Since 2006, here's the list of 19-year-old pitchers to post at least a 30% strikeout percentage with a walk percentage between 7% and 10% in the South Atlantic League (min. 75 IP): Grayson Rodriguez and Drew Rom.

Notice a reoccurring them among the club's top low level pitching prospects: massive strikeout percentages. Rom doesn't have the repertoire of Grayson Rodriguez or DL Hall, but he knows how to maximize his talents. His fastball sits in the 90 mph range. He'll mix in an above-average slider and a decent split finger that he uses as a changeup. His pitching style is reminiscent of Andy Pettitte. Rom looks like a #3/#4-type arm if the fastball can bump a couple ticks, something in the 92- to 93-mph range. Nonetheless he's a very interesting prospect.

Ceiling: 2.5-win player
Risk: Moderate
MLB ETA: 2020

8. Michael Baumann, RHP

	FB	CB	SL	CH	Command	Overall
	60	50/55	55	50	50	50

Born: 09/10/95	Age: 24	Bats: R
Height: 6-4	Weight: 225	Throws: R

YEAR	LVL	IP	W	L	SV	ERA	FIP	WHIP	K/9	K%	BB/9	BB%	K/BB	HR9	BABIP
2017	Rk	1.0	0	0	0	0.00	0.58	2.00	18.0	40.00%	0.0	0.00%	#DIV/0!	0.00	0.667
2017	A-	41.3	4	2	0	1.31	3.45	1.06	8.9	24.40%	4.1	11.31%	2.16	0.44	0.217
2018	A	38.0	5	0	0	1.42	2.09	0.95	11.1	32.64%	3.1	9.03%	3.62	0.00	0.277
2018	A+	92.7	8	5	0	3.88	4.71	1.32	5.7	15.13%	3.9	10.26%	1.48	0.87	0.261
2019	A+	54.0	1	4	0	3.83	2.34	1.19	12.8	34.38%	4.0	10.71%	3.21	0.33	0.314
2019	AA	70.0	6	2	1	2.31	2.62	0.94	8.4	25.00%	2.7	8.08%	3.10	0.26	0.229

Background: A tremendous find in the third round of the 2017 draft. Baumann, a product of Jacksonville University, began to put things together during his junior campaign for the Atlantic Sun Conference school; he posted a 97-to-35 strikeout-to-walk ratio in 87.1 innings of work. The broad-shouldered right-hander continued to impress during his debut in the minor leagues as well, fanning 43 and walking just 19 in 42.1 innings of work – most of which came in the New York-Penn League. Baumann split the following year between Delmarva and Frederick, posting a 106-to-53 strikeout-to-walk ratio in 130.2 innings of work. Last season, easily his best as a professional, Baumann established himself as a legitimate big league option: in 24 appearances between Frederick and Bowie, the 6-foot-4, 225-pound righty fanned 142 and walked 45 to go along with a 2.98 ERA.

Scouting Report: Very impressive repertoire: Baumann's fastball sits in the 92- to 94-mph range and touched as high as 97 mph late in the year with Bowie; his slider shows some impressive two-plane depth and sits in the 86- to 88-mph range; his curveball flashes above-average when he's not overthrowing it; and his changeup has some strong arm-side run. Consider the following:

- Since 2006, here's the list of 23-year-old pitchers to fan between 23% and 25% and walk between 7% and 9% of the hitters they faced in the Eastern League (min. 50 IP): Dean Kremer, Patrick McCoy, Tristan Crawford, Travis Foley, David Parkinson, Adrian Salcedo, Nabil Crismatt, Eli Morgan, David Peterson, George Kontos, and – of course – Michael Baumann.

It's obviously a less-than-stellar collection of arms. But Baumann has a bright future as a #4-type starting pitcher.

Ceiling: 2.0 to 2.5--win player
Risk: Moderate
MLB ETA: 2020

9. Austin Hays, OF

Hit	Power	SB	Patience	Glove	Overall
50	55	30	45	50	50

Born: 07/05/95	Age: 24	Bats: R
Height: 6-1	Weight: 195	Throws: R

YEAR	LVL	PA	1B	2B	3B	HR	SB	CS	AVG	OBP	SLG	BB%	K%	GB%	LD%	FB%
2017	A+	280	52	15	3	16	4	6	0.328	0.364	0.592	4.29%	14.29%	39.7	22.3	32.6
2017	AA	283	51	17	2	16	1	1	0.330	0.367	0.594	4.59%	15.90%	41.2	23.1	25.8
2018	AA	288	40	12	2	12	6	3	0.242	0.271	0.432	4.17%	20.49%	42.9	17.5	32.3
2019	AAA	257	34	16	1	10	6	4	0.254	0.304	0.454	4.28%	23.74%	43.8	20.5	27.3

Background: There's very few – if any – bats in the minor leagues that have endured the roller coaster that Hays has over the past few seasons. A 20-year-old third round pick out of Jacksonville University in 2016, Hays, who batted .350/.406/.655 during his final collegiate season, skyrocketed through the Orioles' farm system – as well as launching himself up every prospect list – through his first two professional seasons. But something happened to the 6-foot-1, 195-pound outfielder in 2018: he stopped producing. He hit a paltry .224/.259/.374 through his first 43 games before hitting the DL and, well, never quite recovered. Last season, once again, Hays spent considerable time on the disabled list. He finished the year with an aggregate .248/.299/.464 across four minor league levels and slugged .309/.373/.574 in 21 games in Baltimore.

Snippet from The 2018 Prospect Digest Handbook: There are essentially two schools of thought surrounding Hays meteoric crash: (#1) The league adjusted to Hays or (#2) a Spring Training shoulder strain and a midseason ankle issue, which resulted in the lengthy DL stint, were to blame. I'm willing to bet on the latter. Even in a lost season, Hays' offensive toolkit remained largely intact: below-average walk rates, solid bat-to-ball skills, and average-ish power.

Scouting Report: Honestly, at this point, I'm not certain the Orioles even know what to expect from Hays. Injuries notwithstanding, Hays looks like a legitimate starting caliber outfielder: he slugged .247/.300/.452 in 24 games in Class AA, but promptly hit the disabled list. He followed that up with a .261/.312/.473 mark in 49 games in Class AAA following a rehab stint. But the truth is simple: the nagging injuries have severely limited his development time. At one point the bat looked like a plus tool, but now it's more average. The power is above-average. But the lack of patience chews into a lot of his offensive value. One more thought: across 138 total MLB plate appearances his batted ball data is mediocre.

Ceiling: 2.0-win player
Risk: Moderate
MLB ETA: Debuted in 2017

10. Cadyn Grenier, SS

Hit	Power	SB	Patience	Glove	Overall
40/45	45/50	35	50	70	50

Born: 10/31/96	Age: 23	Bats: R
Height: 5-11	Weight: 188	Throws: R

YEAR	LVL	PA	1B	2B	3B	HR	SB	CS	AVG	OBP	SLG	BB%	K%	GB%	LD%	FB%
2018	A	183	20	12	2	1	3	2	0.216	0.297	0.333	9.29%	28.96%	32.4	18.9	37.8
2019	A	364	50	18	3	7	5	1	0.253	0.360	0.399	13.19%	29.40%	35.3	19.6	34.8
2019	A+	92	10	4	1	1	2	1	0.208	0.337	0.325	11.96%	33.70%	41.3	21.7	26.1

Background: A smooth, slick fielding middle infielder from Oregon State University; Baltimore took a flier on Grenier's defensive upside – as opposed to some questions about his bat – at the end of the first round two years. The 37th overall player drafted, Grenier's debut went as expected: he was an absolute wizard at shortstop and struggled a bit with the bat, hitting a lowly .216/.297/.333 with 15 extra-base hits. Unsurprisingly, Grenier found himself back in the South Atlantic League for a do over in 2019. This time, though, the results were improved: in 82 games with the Delmarva Shorebirds, the 5-foot-11, 188-pound shortstop batted .253/.360/.399 with 18 doubles, three triples, and seven homeruns. He also swiped five bags in six attempts. Baltimore bounced the former Beaver up to the Carolina League in mid-July. He would struggle after the promotion, cobbling together a puny .208/.337/.325 triple-slash line.

Snippet from The 2018 Prospect Digest Handbook: A questionable first round pick for a couple reasons: (#1) Grenier has a limited offensive track record; (#2) He's approach at the plate remained stagnant during his three-year career; (#3) He doesn't own a true standout tool.

Scouting Report: On the short, short list for top defender – at any position – in the minor leagues. Grenier put up some eye-popping defensive value in 2019. According to Clay Davenport's metrics, Grenier was a plus-10 shortstop. *Baseball Prospectus* had the former Oregon State star as saving 7.7 Defensive Runs Above Average. He was nothing short of spectacular. Offensive speaking, he showed some progress at the plate: he walked more frequently (though his swing-and-miss numbers spiked to red flag territory) and the power looks like it could develop into a 15 or so homeruns. It looked like Grenier would eventually slide into a utility role, but there's now enough offensive hope to suggest a strong starting option in a few year. The defensive cannot afford to degrade though.

Ceiling: 2.0-win player
Risk: Moderate
MLB ETA: 2022

11. Gunnar Henderson, SS

	Hit	Power	SB	Patience	Glove	Overall
	40/55	40/50	35	50	50	50

Born: 06/29/01	Age: 19	Bats: L
Height: 6-3	Weight: 195	Throws: R

YEAR	LVL	PA	1B	2B	3B	HR	SB	CS	AVG	OBP	SLG	BB%	K%	GB%	LD%	FB%
2019	Rk	121	20	5	2	1	2	2	0.259	0.331	0.370	9.09%	23.14%	44.4	17.3	33.3

Background: The first and only player taken out of John T. Morgan Academy in Selma, Alabama, Baltimore signed the lefty-swinging shortstop to a deal worth roughly $500,000 above the slotted value as the top pick in the second round. The deal, as reported, totaled $2.3 million, a large enough sum to persuade the prep player from his commitment to Auburn. Henderson, who measured in at 6-foot-3 and 195-pounds, appeared in 29 games in the Gulf Coast League during his debut, batting .259/.331/.370 with five doubles, a pair of triples, and one homerun. He also swiped two bags in four attempts. His overall production, as measured by *Baseball Prospects'* Deserved Runs Created Plus, was a whopping 35% *below* the league average threshold.

Scouting Report: Ignoring Henderson's first handful of games: over his final 104 plate appearances he hit .286/.365/.418. The toolsy shortstop didn't show any meaningful red flags during his debut: he handled left- and right-handers equally well; showed a solid approach at the plate; flashed some average-ish power; and played a competent shortstop. He's likely ticketed for a spot on the Top 100 list in 2021. One more thought: very short, quick, compact swing.

Ceiling: 2.0-win player
Risk: Moderate
MLB ETA: 2023

12. Hunter Harvey, RHP

	FB	CB	CH	Command	Overall
	65	70	45	55	45

Born: 12/09/94	Age: 25	Bats: R
Height: 6-3	Weight: 175	Throws: R

YEAR	LVL	IP	W	L	SV	ERA	FIP	WHIP	K/9	K%	BB/9	BB%	K/BB	HR9	BABIP
2017	Rk	5.0	0	0	0	0.00	1.02	1.20	10.8	30.00%	0.0	0.00%	#DIV/0!	0.00	0.429
2017	A-	5.0	0	0	0	0.00	1.23	0.80	18.0	52.63%	5.4	15.79%	3.33	0.00	0.167
2017	A	8.7	0	1	0	2.08	1.68	0.81	14.5	41.18%	3.1	8.82%	4.67	0.00	0.250
2018	AA	32.3	1	2	0	5.57	3.68	1.39	8.4	21.74%	2.5	6.52%	3.33	0.84	0.351
2019	AA	59.0	2	5	1	5.19	5.55	1.42	9.3	23.74%	3.2	8.17%	2.90	2.14	0.316
2019	AAA	16.7	1	1	0	4.32	3.62	1.08	11.9	31.43%	2.7	7.14%	4.40	1.08	0.275

Background: At one point it seemed like it was indisputable. A short while later it looked like it was impossible. And last season, after a career worth of injuries and question marks, Hunter Harvey, the once much ballyhooed prospect, made his highly anticipated debut. A multitude of injuries limited the former 22nd overall pick to just over 30 innings of work between 2015 and the end of 2017. Finally healthy, Harvey tossed a career best 75.2 innings between Class AA and Class AAA last season, fanning 83 and walking just 26. He tossed an additional 6.1 innings with Baltimore, posting a ridiculous 11-to-4 strikeout-to-walk ratio.

Snippet from The 2018 Prospect Digest Handbook: The only question that remains is whether Harvey's body will cooperate.

Scouting Report: His numbers to start the year are mediocre, at best. Through his first 11 appearances, which were all starts, the firebolt-slinging right-hander compiled a 6.12 ERA in 50.0 innings with Bowie. Baltimore – perhaps correctly – decided to convert the once-budding-ace into a full-time reliever. And Harvey – promptly – became unhittable. Over his final 25.2 innings in the minor leagues, the 6-foot-3, 175-pound hurler fanned 33, walked just seven, and allowed only eight runs – five of which came in one single appearance. The opposition, by the way, batted just .157/.227/.281 against him during that stretch. Harvey's plus fastball was sitting in the upper-90s with ease. His curveball is like a gift from Sandy Koufax. The changeup, well, should be scrapped all together. Combine that repertoire with his pinpoint command and Harvey could – very well – be a 2.0-win reliever in 2020.

Ceiling: 1.5- to 2.0-win player
Risk: Moderate
MLB ETA: 2020

13. Adam Hall, 2B/SS

Hit	Power	SB	Patience	Glove	Overall
55	40/45	60	50	50	45

Born: 05/22/99	Age: 21	Bats: R
Height: 6-0	Weight: 170	Throws: R

YEAR	LVL	PA	1B	2B	3B	HR	SB	CS	AVG	OBP	SLG	BB%	K%	GB%	LD%	FB%
2017	RK	9	4	1	1	0	1	0	0.667	0.667	1.000	0.00%	22.22%	71.4	0	28.6
2018	A-	256	52	9	3	1	22	5	0.293	0.368	0.374	6.64%	22.66%	62.9	14.1	18.8
2019	A	534	107	22	4	5	33	9	0.298	0.385	0.395	8.43%	21.91%	52.9	19.1	24.9

Background: A product of A B Lucas Secondary School, home to former big leaguer – and 2003 fourth round pick Jamie Romak – Hall was snagged by the Orioles in the second round of the June draft three years ago. The wiry middle infielder showed some offensive promise during his stint in the New York-Penn League in 2018, batting .293/.368/.374 with 13 extra-base hits in 62 games of action. And he was able to nearly replicate that triple-slash line as he moved up to the South Atlantic League last year. In 122 games with the Delmarva Shorebirds, the 6-foot, 170-pound middle-infielder hit .298/.385/.395 with 22 doubles, four triples, and five homeruns. Hall also swiped 33 bags in 42 total attempts. His overall production, as measured by *Deserved Runs Created Plus*, topped the league average threshold by a surprising 40%.

Snippet from The 2018 Prospect Digest Handbook: An exceptionally similar skill set as fellow Orioles up-the-middle prospect Ryan McKenna. Hall, who isn't overly big and is likely maxed out physically, has a slightly below-average eye at the plate, below-average power, a decent glove at shortstop, and a potentially above-average hit tool.

Scouting Report: Consider the following:

- Since 2006, there have been three 20-year-old hitters that met the following criteria in the South Atlantic League (min. 300 PA): 135- to 145-DRC+, a walk percentage between 7% and 9%; and a strikeout percentage between 20% and 22%. Those three hitters are William Contreras, a top catching prospect, Aderlin Rodriguez, and Adam Hall.

The power is still below-average, but it's trending in the right direction. The hit tool has a chance – albeit a bit of a long shot – to become a plus weapon. The speed is already there. Defensively, he grades out between average and slightly better than average at either up the middle position. Hall is very reminiscent of Tampa Bay Rays infielder – and former top prospect – Daniel Robertson with a little less pop.

Ceiling: 1.5- to 2.0-win player
Risk: Moderate
MLB ETA: 2022

14. Kyle Stowers, LF/RF

Hit	Power	SB	Patience	Glove	Overall
40/45	55	35/30	50	50	45

Born: 01/02/98	Age: 22	Bats: L
Height: 6-3	Weight: 200	Throws: L

YEAR	LVL	PA	1B	2B	3B	HR	SB	CS	AVG	OBP	SLG	BB%	K%	GB%	LD%	FB%
2019	A-	228	24	13	1	6	5	1	0.216	0.289	0.377	8.77%	23.25%	51.7	21.2	23.2

Background: A pedigreed, polished collegiate bat out of a top program – albeit one that's struggled to churn out a lot of meaningful hitters. Stowers, who saw limited time as a true freshman, stepped into Stanford's lineup as a sophomore and never looked back. The 6-foot-3, 200-pound corner outfielder hit .286/.383/.510 with 10 doubles, three triples, and 10 homeruns in 58 games. Stowers spent the ensuing summer playing – and starring – for the Falmouth Commodores, slugging .326/.361/.565 with 13 doubles, one triple, and six homeruns in 34 games in the Cape Cod League. Last season Stowers maintained status quo for the PAC-12 school: in 55 games, the California native batted .303/.369/.523 with 19 doubles, one triple, and nine homeruns. He also swiped 13 bags in 17 attempts. Baltimore drafted 2019 PAC-12 Honorable Mention in the second round, 71st overall, and signed him to a deal worth $884K. Stowers spent the entirety of his debut in the New York-Penn League, hitting a lowly .216/.289/.377 with 13 doubles, one triple, and six homeruns.

Scouting Report: Stowers showed some concerning swing-and-miss tendencies as a sophomore, fanning in over 20% of his plate appearances – a number that's borderline concerning for a player that's considered a top prospect. He trimmed that number considerably during his junior season (12.4%) and maintained solid contact rates as a pro. With respect to his work in college last season, consider the following:

- Since 2011, there have been 12 PAC-12 hitters to meet the following criteria (min. 200 PA): hit at least .300/.350/.500 with a walk rate between 8% and 11%, and a sub-15% strikeout rate. Of those 12, six of them have gone on to play – some rather successfully – in the big leagues (Michael Conforto, Rob Refsnyder, Ryon Healy, Brandon Dixon, Alex Blandino, and Johnny Field). One more, Nick Madrigal, will likely spend more than a decade in the bigs. And three more are still working their way through the minors (J.J. Matijevic, Quinn Brodey, and Alfonso Rivas).

The initial results for Stowers are pretty poor: he looked completely helpless against fellow left-handers (.143/.231/.200) and looked overwhelmed at times. Solid peripherals with above-average power. He could be a low end starting outfielder.

Ceiling: 1.5- to 2.0-win player
Risk: Moderate to High
MLB ETA: 2022/2023

15. Dean Kremer, RHP

	FB	CB	SL	CH	Command	Overall
	50	60	45	45	45	45

Born: 01/07/96	Age: 24	Bats: R
Height: 6-3	Weight: 180	Throws: R

YEAR	LVL	IP	W	L	SV	ERA	FIP	WHIP	K/9	K%	BB/9	BB%	K/BB	HR9	BABIP
2017	A+	80.0	1	4	3	5.18	3.88	1.50	10.8	26.97%	3.8	9.55%	2.82	0.68	0.369
2018	A+	79.0	5	3	0	3.30	3.08	1.18	13.0	35.51%	3.0	8.10%	4.38	0.80	0.351
2018	AA	45.3	4	2	0	2.58	3.03	1.21	10.5	28.34%	3.4	9.09%	3.12	0.60	0.310
2018	AA	7.0	1	0	0	0.00	1.59	0.86	14.1	42.31%	3.9	11.54%	3.67	0.00	0.250
2019	A+	9.7	0	0	0	0.00	2.03	1.03	13.0	35.90%	3.7	10.26%	3.50	0.00	0.300
2019	AA	84.7	9	4	0	2.98	3.55	1.23	9.2	25.00%	3.1	8.33%	3.00	0.96	0.297
2019	AAA	19.3	0	2	0	8.84	3.42	1.76	9.8	23.86%	1.9	4.55%	5.25	0.93	0.459

Background: The second best prospect acquired from the Dodgers in the Manny Machado saga two years ago. Kremer quietly put together one of the more dominant showings in 2018: splitting time between two levels – as well as two different organizations – the thin, long-limbed right-hander posted an incredible 178-to-46 strikeout-to-walk ratio in only 131.1 innings of work. A mid-February oblique injury lingered for several months last season, forcing him out of action until early May. Kremer would eventually make 21 starts across three different levels (High Class A, Class AA, and Class AAA), throwing 113.2 innings with 122 strikeouts and just 37 walks. He finished his fourth professional season with a 3.72 ERA. Kremer also tossed an additional 19.0 innings in the Arizona Fall League, posting a dominating 23-to-4 strikeout-to-walk ratio while surrendering five earned runs.

Snippet from The 2018 Prospect Digest Handbook: It's all going to come down to Kremer's further development of his changeup or slider. If one of those ticks up a notch, he becomes a legitimate #3-type arm.

Scouting Report: Bad news: the changeup, nor the slider ticked up during the 2019 season. Both secondary offerings are in the average-ish to slightly below-average territory. Thanks to his long limbs, Kremer's fastball is sneaky quick – despite sitting in the 91-mph range last season. And his curveball, a 12-to-6 hammer-of-an-offering, is easily a plus pitch. Kremer is going to be a solid test for the new Orioles regime: can Mike Elias & Co. squeak out some additional value through pitch design/develop a la the GM's former organization (Houston Astros)? Or will Kremer languish in 45-grade territory moving forward?

Ceiling: 1.5-win player
Risk: Moderate
MLB ETA: 2020

16. Keegan Akin, LHP

FB	SL	CH	Command	Overall
55	55	55	45	45

Born: 04/01/95	Age: 25	Bats: R
Height: 6-0	Weight: 225	Throws: R

YEAR	LVL	IP	W	L	SV	ERA	FIP	WHIP	K/9	K%	BB/9	BB%	K/BB	HR9	BABIP
2017	A+	100.0	7	8	0	4.14	4.20	1.35	10.0	26.24%	4.1	10.87%	2.41	1.08	0.307
2018	AA	137.7	14	7	0	3.27	4.11	1.25	9.3	24.78%	3.8	10.12%	2.45	1.05	0.278
2019	AAA	112.3	6	7	0	4.73	4.13	1.51	10.5	26.04%	4.9	12.13%	2.15	0.80	0.331

Background: A rotund lefty with tree trunks for legs out of Western Michigan University. Akin, who stands just 6 feet but tips the scales at a generous 225 pounds, has spent a year at each level since popping up in High Class A three seasons ago. Taken in the second round, 54th overall, four years ago, Akin made 25 appearances with the Norfolk Ties in the International League last season, throwing 112.1 innings with a solid 131-to-61 strikeout-to-walk ratio. He finished his fourth minor league season with a mediocre 4.73 ERA and a 4.36 DRA (Deserved Runs Average).

Snippet from The 2018 Prospect Digest Handbook: The interesting trend among [similarly performing players]: Perkins, Betances, and May have had a lot of success at the big league level as relievers. Baltimore won't be contending for the next four or five years, so Akin should be given every opportunity in the rotation.

Scouting Report: As I suggested / implied last year, Akin's likely going to wind up in Baltimore's bullpen where he could become one of the better – and cheaper – left-handed relievers in the game. He's now entering his age-25 season, owns three above-average offerings, but complements it with spotty command. Bold Prediction: Akin unseats Mychal Givens as the club's closer by the All-Star game.

Ceiling: 1.5-win player
Risk: Moderate
MLB ETA: 2020

17. Ryan McKenna, CF

Hit	Power	SB	Patience	Glove	Overall
45	45	50	50	55	45

Born: 02/14/97	Age: 23	Bats: R
Height: 5-11	Weight: 185	Throws: R

YEAR	LVL	PA	1B	2B	3B	HR	SB	CS	AVG	OBP	SLG	BB%	K%	GB%	LD%	FB%
2017	A	530	78	33	2	7	20	2	0.256	0.331	0.380	8.11%	24.15%	48	15.8	30.2
2018	A+	301	69	18	2	8	5	6	0.377	0.467	0.556	12.29%	14.95%	47.2	26.4	24.1
2018	AA	250	38	8	2	3	4	1	0.239	0.341	0.338	11.60%	22.40%	51.6	19.3	24.8
2019	AA	567	72	26	6	9	25	11	0.232	0.321	0.365	10.41%	21.34%	44	17.2	32.1

Background: From Babe Ruth to Mario Mendoza. It's the perfect description of how McKenna's last two seasons have gone. A fourth round pick out of St. Thomas Aquinas High School in 2015, McKenna showed a little bit of offensive production throughout his first three minor league seasons but something clicked – in a massive way – during his stint in the Carolina League two years ago. In 60 games with the Frederick Keys, the 5-foot-11, 185-pound center fielder slugged a scorching .377/.467/.556 while tapping into an unknown power reserve as he belted out 18 doubles, two triples, and eight homeruns. The front office bounced him up to the minors' toughest challenge, Class AA, in early July and his production – unsurprisingly – cratered. Still, though, it's difficult to image a player whose production was a staggering 118% better than the league average not being able to recapture some of that magic in a do over in the Eastern League. He didn't. In a career best 135 games, McKenna cobbled together a disappointing .232/.321/.365 triple-slash line with just 26 doubles, six triple, and nine homeruns. He swiped a career best 25 bags (in 35 attempts). His overall production, as measured by *Deserved Runs Created Plus*, still bested the league average by 12%.

Snippet from The 2018 Prospect Digest Handbook: McKenna looks like a tweener right now: if the power takes another small step forward he could be a solid everyday center fielder; if not, he should get more than enough opportunities to prove himself as a capable fourth outfielder.

Scouting Report: Consider the following:

- Since 2006, six 22-year-old hitters to post a DRC+ between 107 and 117 with a double-digit strikeout rate in the Eastern League (min. 300 PA): Bobby Bradley, Luis Guillorme, Brian Goodwin, Corban Joseph, Yamaico Navarro, and Ryan McKenna.

Brian Goodwin seems like a best case scenario for McKenna. The Orioles prospect can run it down in center field, handles left-handed pitching impressively well, and is willing to take a walk. A year later, McKenna is starring down the potential as a decent little fourth outfield option.

Ceiling: 1.5-win player
Risk: Moderate
MLB ETA: 2020

Baltimore Orioles

18. Rylan Bannon, 3B

	Hit	Power	SB	Patience	Glove	Overall
	45+	45+	40	55	50	45

Born: 04/22/96	**Age:** 24	**Bats:** R
Height: 5-7	**Weight:** 180	**Throws:** R

YEAR	LVL	PA	1B	2B	3B	HR	SB	CS	AVG	OBP	SLG	BB%	K%	GB%	LD%	FB%
2018	A+	403	57	17	6	20	4	4	0.296	0.402	0.559	14.64%	25.56%	37	18.1	34.9
2018	AA	122	12	6	0	2	0	0	0.204	0.344	0.327	18.03%	19.67%	44.7	18.4	27.6
2019	AA	444	65	22	4	8	8	4	0.255	0.345	0.394	10.59%	16.22%	46.2	18.4	25.9
2019	AAA	90	13	10	0	3	0	1	0.317	0.344	0.549	3.33%	15.56%	42.3	23.9	28.2

Background: Unequivocally, without a smidgeon of doubt, Bannon is *exactly* the type of prospect a rebuilding team should gamble on. The production has been well above-average throughout the majority of his career. He's flawed, though. At least in a traditional sense. Bannon, who was acquired as a secondary or tertiary prospect in the Manny Machado deal from the Dodgers, owns a career .280/.375/.481 triple-slash line in the minor leagues, but he stands a less-than-ideal 5-foot-7 and 180 pounds. Last season, his first full year in the Orioles' farm system, Bannon appeared in 110 games with Bowie, batting .255/.345/.394 with 22 doubles, four triples, and eight homeruns. He also earned a 20-game cameo in the International League at the end of the year, hitting .317/.344/.549.

Snippet from The 2018 Prospect Digest Handbook: Between 2006 and 2016, only two 22-year-old hitters met the following criteria in the California League (min. 350 PA): a wRC+ between 150 and 165 and double-digit walk rate. Those two aforementioned hitters are All-Star Carlos Santana and Kyle Parker.

Scouting Report: Let's update that, shall we? Consider the following:

- Since 2006, there have been five 23-year-old hitters that met the following criteria in the Eastern League (min. 350 PA): 120- to 130-DRC+, a walk rate between 9.5% and 11.5%; and a sub-20% strikeout rate. Those five hitters are: Jesus Aguilar, Jose Pirela, Chris Parmelee, Brock Peterson, and Rylan Bannon.

Here's the intriguing part among the aforementioned group (sans Bannon): three of the four have spent time in the big leagues (Aguilar, Pirela, and Parmelee). Aguilar owns a 113 DRC+ in his career; Parmelee was essentially a league average bat in 311 career games; and Pirela owns a 82 DRC+ in his career. Bannon owns a decent hit tool; the power has a chance to be 15-homer territory; the patience is above-average; and his defense remains solid. That's a recipe for a strong role player / low-end starter.

Ceiling: 1.5-win player
Risk: Moderate
MLB ETA: 2020

19. Brett Cumberland, C

	Hit	Power	SB	Patience	Glove	Overall
	45	50	30	70	45	45

Born: 06/25/95	**Age:** 25	**Bats:** B
Height: 5-11	**Weight:** 205	**Throws:** R

YEAR	LVL	PA	1B	2B	3B	HR	SB	CS	AVG	OBP	SLG	BB%	K%	GB%	LD%	FB%
2018	A+	341	40	15	0	11	0	1	0.236	0.367	0.407	15.25%	24.93%	36	19.3	36.5
2018	AA	49	5	0	0	3	0	0	0.190	0.292	0.405	8.16%	24.49%	45.2	9.7	32.3
2018	AA	20	2	0	0	0	0	0	0.111	0.200	0.111	5.00%	25.00%	46.2	15.4	30.8
2019	AA	157	19	8	0	4	0	0	0.248	0.395	0.408	14.65%	21.66%	35.9	19.6	31.5

Background: When Dan Duquette traded enigmatic right-hander – and former top prospect – Kevin Gausman to the Braves I voiced some concern that Baltimore traded for quantity, rather than quality. A year later the Braves placed the former #4 overall pick on unconditional waivers and he was claimed by Cincinnati and immediately converted into a reliever. Anyway, the return for Gausman (and Darren O'Day) seems reasonably fair at this point: Brett Cumberland, Bruce Zimmerman, JC Encarnacion, Evan Phillips, and international bonus slot money. Cumberland, a switch-hitting backstop out of UC Berkley in 2016, continues to produce through his saber-slanted approach at the plate – despite failing to eclipse more than 111 games in any of his three full professional seasons. Last season the former second round pick was limited to just 60 games, 41 of which came in the Eastern League, hitting a combined .257/.404/.415 with 14 doubles and five homeruns.

Snippet from The 2018 Prospect Digest Handbook: Cumberland does two things really well: he walks at an elite level, including 13.9% of the time last season, and hits for above-average power. Other than that the rest of the skill set is average or worse. He's essentially the poor's man version of White Sox prospect Zack Collins.

Scouting Report: Cumberland was one of the most productive bats during his 41-game stint in the Eastern League last season; topping the average line by a whopping 45%. It's a similar level of production that he showed in the Florida State League two years ago (138 DRC+) as well as the South Atlantic League in 2017 (172 DRC+). There's a market inefficiency that no one seems to be talking about: older, productive prospects – which were typically written off in the past – have stepped in and done wonders when given the chance. Justin Turner, T.J. Rivera, Mitch Garver, and Mike Tauchman all immediately come to mind. And Cumberland could very well be the next one in line. The switch-hitting backstop is still walking a ridiculous amount of the time (14.6% in Class AA in 2019) and he's still showing 20-homerun potential. The hit tool is nothing to get excited about, but in world so bereft of catching talent he should become a lower tier starting option.

Ceiling: 1.5-win player
Risk: Moderate
MLB ETA: 2020

20. Bruce Zimmermann, LHP	FB	CB	SL	CH	Command	Overall
	50	55	45	50	50	40+

Born: 02/09/95	Age: 25	Bats: L
Height: 6-2	Weight: 215	Throws: L

Background: Another one of the many pieces acquired from the Braves for Kevin Gausman at the trade deadline two years ago. Zimmermann, who was acquired with Brett Cumberland, JC Encarnacion, and Evan Phillips, was taken by Atlanta in the fifth round in 2017. A product of Mount Oliver College, home to Carter Capps, Zimmermann split his third minor league season with the Bowie Baysox and Norfolk Tides. In 24 starts and one relief appearance, the 6-foot-2, 215-pound southpaw tossed a career best 140 innings, recording 134 strikeouts against 54 walks to go along with an aggregate 3.21 ERA. For his career, Zimmermann's averaging 9.2 strikeouts and just 3.2 walks per nine innings with a 3.20 ERA.

Scouting Report: Zimmermann offers up an average-ish four-pitch mix: a 90- to 92-mph fastball that shows a bit of life at times; an above-average curveball that should be thrown more frequently; a decent little changeup that doesn't generate a lot of swings-and-misses but draws a surprising amount of weak contact; and a poor slider that lacks depth. The Orioles are in full-blown rebuild mode, so Zimmermann should be given every single opportunity to prove his worth as a #5-type starting pitcher. At worst, he's been death to left-handed hitters so he should be able to carve out a role as a solid relief option.

Ceiling: 1.0- to 1.5-win player
Risk: Low to Moderate
MLB ETA: 2020

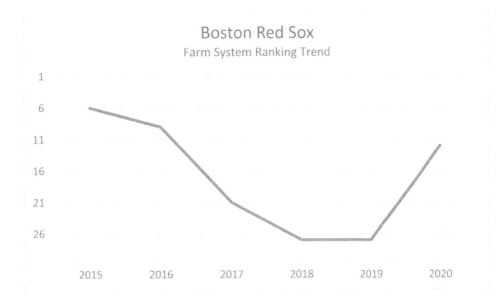

Boston Red Sox
Farm System Ranking Trend

Rank	Name	Age	Pos
1	Gilberto Jimenez	19	CF
2	Jeter Downs	21	SS
3	Triston Casas	20	1B
4	Jay Groome	22	LHP
5	Bryan Mata	21	RHP
6	Noah Song	23	RHP
7	Jarren Duran	23	CF
8	Bobby Dalbec	25	1B/3B
9	Brayan Bello	21	RHP
10	Thad Ward	23	RHP
11	Tanner Houck	24	RHP
12	Alex Scherff	22	RHP
13	Matthew Lugo	19	SS
14	Aldo Ramirez	19	RHP
15	Connor Wong	24	C
16	Nick Decker	20	RF
17	Kole Cottam	23	C
18	Jhonathan Diaz	23	LHP
19	Cameron Cannon	25	2B/SS
20	Mike Shawaryn	25	RHP

1. Gilberto Jimenez, CF

	Hit	Power	SB	Patience	Glove	Overall
	60/70	45/55	55	40/50	40/50	60

Born: 07/08/00	Age: 19	Bats: B
Height: 5-11	Weight: 160	Throws: R

YEAR	LVL	PA	1B	2B	3B	HR	SB	CS	AVG	OBP	SLG	BB%	K%	GB%	LD%	FB%
2018	RK	284	64	10	8	0	16	14	0.319	0.384	0.420	6.69%	14.08%	61.8	22.6	12.9
2019	A-	254	67	11	3	3	14	6	0.359	0.393	0.470	5.12%	14.96%	64.5	16.0	17.0

Background: Despite a downward trending farm system, the Red Sox player development has churned out a pair of superstar caliber homegrown players over the past few seasons in Rafael Devers and Andrew Benintendi. And Jimenez, a native of San Cristobal, Dominican Republic, is poised to be the next great Red Sox product. Handed a paltry, paltry sum of just $10,000 on August 2, 2017, Gimenez ripped through the Dominican Summer League a season later, slugging .319/.384/.420 with 10 doubles and eight triples in 67 games. Last season the club aggressively pushed the then-18-year-old up to Lowell and the 5-foot-11, 160-pound wiry outfielder barely broke a sweat. In 59 games with the Spinners, Jimenez hit a scorching .359/.393/.470 with 11 doubles, three triples, and three homeruns. He also swiped 14 bags in 20 total attempts. His overall production, as measured by Baseball Prospectus' *Deserved Runs Created Plus*, was a whopping 91% better than the league average, the third best mark among all hitters in the New York-Penn League with at least 150 plate appearances.

Scouting Report: Consider the following:

- Since 2006, the two best performing 18-year-old hitters in the New York-Penn League (min. 150 PA) were Victor Robles in 2015 and Gilberto Jimenez last season.

Just how good was Jimenez? His overall production was 26-percentage points better than his teenage counterpart. To put that in perspective: Pete Alonso captured the N.L. Rookie of the Year on the back of a 141 DRC+ last season. The difference between Jimenez and Robles is the same as Alonso and Kurt Suzuki. Jimenez is a rare five-tool athlete with the potential for above-average to plus tools across the board. As a young switch-hitter, he handles lefties and righties well, plays an up-the-middle position (albeit incredibly raw), and shows a knack for consistently barreling up the baseball. The lone knock on Jimenez: he's not overly patient, but it should improve with time. Within a year he could be a challenger for top prospect in baseball.

Ceiling: 4-0-win player
Risk: Moderate
MLB ETA: 2022/2023

2. Jeter Downs, SS

	Hit	Power	SB	Patience	Glove	Overall
	50	50	60	55	45/50	55

Born: 07/27/98	Age: 21	Bats: R
Height: 5-11	Weight: 180	Throws: R

YEAR	LVL	PA	1B	2B	3B	HR	SB	CS	AVG	OBP	SLG	BB%	K%	GB%	LD%	FB%
2017	RK	209	34	3	3	6	8	5	0.267	0.370	0.424	12.92%	15.31%	34.9	11.6	39.0
2018	A	524	79	23	2	13	37	10	0.257	0.351	0.402	9.92%	19.66%	32.7	17.5	33.2
2019	A+	479	55	33	4	19	23	8	0.269	0.354	0.507	11.27%	20.25%	26.5	21.5	41.4
2019	AA	56	9	2	0	5	1	0	0.333	0.429	0.688	10.71%	17.86%	18.4	26.3	39.5

Background: I wish I could claim it, but I'm clearly not that witty. Or at least lack that type of quick wit. But someone on Reddit or Twitter summed it up succinctly: The Red Sox now have a Jeter they can root for. Of course it took dealing away the face of the franchise – and one of the best players in baseball – as well as a still dominant, albeit aging, top pitcher to get him. The Sox and Dodgers got together in one of the bigger trades in recent memory when the two historical franchises agreed to a deal that sent Mookie Betts, David Price, and boatload of cash to the Dodgers in exchange for outfielder Alex Verdugo, backstop Connor Wong, and – of course – shortstop Jeter Downs. Taken at the back end of the opening round three years ago, Downs, who was originally drafted by the Reds, is now onto his third organization; he was originally traded by Cincinnati as part of the Yasiel Puig mega-swap last offseason. Downs spent the majority of his 2019 campaign with the Dodgers' High Class A affiliate, Rancho Cucamonga, hitting a solid .269/.354/.507 with career highs in doubles, (33), triples (four), and homeruns (19) while swiping 23 bags. Per *Deserved Runs Created Plus*, his overall production topped the league average mark by 27%. Downs also appeared in a dozen Class AA contests at the end of the year as well.

Snippet from The 2018 Prospect Digest Handbook: Cut from a similar cloth as Reds center fielder of the future Taylor Trammell. Downs acquitted himself nicely against the older competition that the Midwest League has to offer. He shows a solid approach at the plate, making consistent contact with an average eye. The overwhelming majority of his power is of the pull-variety, so teams will likely start employing a shift to the left-side of the infield. Defensively speaking, he's a liability – and that's putting it nicely – so a shift to center field, forsaking his namesake, is a very distinct possibility in the coming years.

Scouting Report: Consider the following:

- Since 2006, only three 20-year-old hitters met the following criteria in the California League (min. 300 PA): 122 to 132 DRC+ and a double digit walk rate. Those three hitters: Rio Ruiz, Delino DeShields Jr., and Jeter Downs.

Solid batted ball data for a 20-year-old in High Class A, Downs, according to *FanGraphs*, posted an average exit velocity of 88 mph with a peak exit velocity of 106 mph. Strong, above-average eye at the plate backed up by solid bat-to-ball skills and plus speed. Downs' power – and his glove work – took a development leap. He's not going to be a star, but he could anchor Boston's infield for the better part of a decade or so.

Ceiling: 3.5-win player
Risk: Moderate
MLB ETA: 2021

3. Triston Casas, 1B/3B

Hit	Power	SB	Patience	Glove	Overall
45/50	60/70	30	55	50	55

Born: 01/15/00	Age: 20	Bats: L
Height: 6-4	Weight: 238	Throws: R

YEAR	LVL	PA	1B	2B	3B	HR	SB	CS	AVG	OBP	SLG	BB%	K%	GB%	LD%	FB%
2018	RK	5	0	0	0	0	0	0	0.000	0.200	0.000	20.00%	40.00%	50.0	0.0	50.0
2019	A	493	58	25	5	19	3	2	0.254	0.349	0.472	11.76%	23.53%	43.3	19.6	27.6
2019	A+	7	1	1	0	1	0	0	0.429	0.429	1.000	0.00%	28.57%	40.0	20.0	40.0

Background: A product of American Heritage High School, home to several notable players including Eric Hosmer, Zack Collins, Shaun Anderson, Darnell Sweeney, and former Boston farmhand Deven Marrero, Casas had the pedigree – and the production – that suggested first round pick. The slugging corner infielder was a two-time Under Armour All-America All-Star and captured the Most Valuable Player Award for the 2017 U-18 Baseball World Cup. The Red Sox snagged the 6-foot-4, 238-pound Floridian in the opening round, 26th overall, and signed him to a deal worth $2.55 million. Casas appeared in just a pair of Gulf Coast League games during his debut courtesy of a UCL injury in his right thumb. Despite the lack of professional experience, the front office aggressively pushed the promising youngster up to the South Atlantic League last season. And Casas made the transition with aplomb. In 118 games with Greenville, he slugged .254/.349/.472 with 25 doubles, five triples, and 19 homeruns to go along with a trio of stolen bases. His overall production, according to Baseball Prospectus's *Deserved Runs Created Plus*, topped the league average mark by 45%. He also appeared in a pair of games in High Class A at the end of the year as well, going 3-for-7 with a double and a homerun.

Snippet from The 2018 Prospect Digest Handbook: While the Red Sox seem content on having the sweet-swinging lefty play third base, he's likely to eventually slide across the diamond to first base as he reaches full maturity. Casas shows impressive bat speed with above-average or better power to all fields. I do wonder if contact issues in his all-or-nothing approach won't be an issue. But make no mistake, there's serious light tower power here.

Scouting Report: A few things to note:

- The defensive shift has already occurred as he made 94 appearances at first base and just a pair of games at the hot corner.
- I was wrong about his approach at the plate. Casas's approach resulted in a modest 23.5% strikeout rate to go along with an above-average walk rate (11.8%) last season.

Now let's compare his production against his peers over the past two decades. Consider the following:

- Since 2000, there have been four 19-year-old hitters to post a *Deserved Runs Created Plus* between 140 and 150 with a double-digit walk rate in the South Atlantic League (min. 250 PA): Luis Alejandro Basabe, J.P. Crawford, Travis Denker, and – of course – Triston Casas.

It's obviously a less-than-stellar collection of comparables. Basabe's a middle-tier prospect the Diamondbacks' organization; Crawford, the Mariner's starting shortstop, owns a career .222/.320/.367 triple-slash line; and Denker made it to the big leagues for 24 games in 2008. With respect to Casas's peripherals: they're all quite promising – a strong eye, plus in-game power, and a solid enough hit tool. He did struggle against fellow southpaws, so that needs to be monitored closely (he batted .213/.317/.416 vs. LHP). And now that he's a full-time first baseman the bat needs to carry him the rest of the way. Per FanGraphs, his average exit velocity was 87 mph with a peak of 107 mph.

Ceiling: 3.0- to 3.5-win player
Risk: Moderate
MLB ETA: 2022/2023

4. Jay Groome, LHP

FB	CB	CH	Command	Overall
60	70	50	45/50	55

Born: 08/23/98	Age: 21	Bats: L
Height: 6-6	Weight: 220	Throws: L

YEAR	LVL	IP	W	L	SV	ERA	FIP	WHIP	K/9	K%	BB/9	BB%	K/BB	HR9	BABIP
2017	A-	11.0	0	2	0	1.64	2.52	0.91	11.5	31.82%	4.1	11.36%	2.80	0.00	0.208
2017	A	44.3	3	7	0	6.70	4.56	1.56	11.8	29.15%	5.1	12.56%	2.32	1.22	0.355
2019	Rk	2.0	0	0	0	0.00	0.50	1.00	13.5	37.50%	0.0	0.00%	N/A	0.00	0.400
2019	A-	2.0	0	0	0	4.50	1.90	2.00	13.5	27.27%	4.5	9.09%	3.00	0.00	0.429

Background: It's been a rough couple of seasons for the promising, oft-times dominant southpaw. The front office pumped the brakes on his 2017 season in August after the former first round pick succumbed to some arm issues, which were initially diagnosed as a forearm stain. Fast forward roughly nine months and Groome's woes eventually pushed him under the knife for Tommy John surgery, forcing him to miss the entire 2018 season and most of 2019. Finally healthy, the Barnegat High School product made his way back to the Gulf Coast League in last August for a couple of one-inning appearances before a final two-inning start with the Lowell Spinners in the New York-Penn League. He tossed four innings, recording six strikeouts against just one free pass.

Scouting Report: Prior to the injury; he attacked hitters with two plus-offerings – a heavy, mid-90s fastball and an elite curveball – to go along with a decent changeup. During his return to action at the end of the year Groome's fastball was back up to the mid-90s, peaking at 95 mph. Injury issues notwithstanding, the lone knock on the 12th overall pick in the 2016 draft was his sometimes problematic control. He's now lost the better part of two years of development and pitchers tend to struggle commanding the zone after Tommy John surgery – so it's not a promising recipe. His curveball is very reminiscent of fellow southpaw Rich Hill's.

Ceiling: 3.5-win player
Risk: Moderate to High
MLB ETA: 2022/2023

5. Bryan Mata, RHP

FB	CB	SL	CH	Command	Overall
70	60	55	55	45/50	50

Born: 05/03/99	Age: 21	Bats: R
Height: 6-3	Weight: 160	Throws: R

YEAR	LVL	IP	W	L	SV	ERA	FIP	WHIP	K/9	K%	BB/9	BB%	K/BB	HR9	BABIP
2017	A	77.0	5	6	0	3.74	3.40	1.31	8.6	22.70%	3.0	7.98%	2.85	0.35	0.333
2018	A+	72.0	6	3	0	3.50	4.76	1.61	7.6	18.65%	7.3	17.74%	1.05	0.13	0.292
2019	A+	51.3	3	1	0	1.75	3.06	1.09	9.1	24.19%	3.2	8.37%	2.89	0.18	0.268
2019	AA	53.7	4	6	0	5.03	3.98	1.45	9.9	25.21%	4.0	10.26%	2.46	1.01	0.340

Background: Signed out of Maracay, Venezuela, in late January, 2016. The lightning quick arm of Mata's has propelled the promising youngster to the upper levels of the minor leagues just a few scant seasons later. Mata, a wiry, baby-faced right-hander, spent his professional debut in the club's foreign rookie league before moving stateside in 2017. As an 18-year-old, Mata ripped through the South Atlantic League with a surprising amount of ease – especially considering his aggression promotion schedule. In 17 starts with Greenville, the 6-foot-3, 160-pound hurler posted a 74-to-26 strikeout-to-walk ratio in 77.0 innings of work. Mata spent the following season, 2018, battling control demons in the Carolina League; he would walk nearly as many hitters as he fanned (61-to-58) through 17 starts – though he somehow managed to cobble together a superficially nice 3.5 0ERA. Last season the young fireballer regained command of the strike zone and torched the High Class A competition for 10 starts before settling in – and often dominating – the minors' most difficult test, Class AA. In a career best 21 starts, Mata averaged 9.5 strikeouts and 3.6 walks per nine innings to go along with a 3.43 ERA.

Snippet from The 2018 Prospect Digest Handbook: Watching Mata pitch, even as painful as it was at times, it's clear to see how he passed through the Sally with barely a scratch as an 18-year-old two years ago. His fastball, an above-average pitch, shows a bit of life, though there isn't any projection left because he's physically maxed out. His curveball, a sharp 12-6 break, flashes plus at times.

Scouting Report: From painful to watch to a pure joy. Mata's on the cusp on putting everything together. The young right-hander's fastball was up to 97 mph during his final start of the year, a seven-inning, nine-strikeout performance against the New Hampshire Fisher Cats. His curveball, which previously flashed plus, has become a consistent swing-and-miss weapon. His changeup is a fine above-average offering. And he's added a hard slider/cutter that shows late, hard bite. The command can waver a bit at times, but he continues to show the mental fortitude to move beyond the brief hiccups. With respect to his work in the Eastern League last season, consider the following:

- Since 2000, only three 20-year-old pitchers have posted a strikeout percentage between 24% and 27% with a walk percentage between 10% and 12% in the Eastern League (min. 50 IP): Chris Tillman, Gio Gonzalez, and Bryan Mata.

Tillman, a former top prospect in the Mariners' and Orioles' farm system, was a consistent mid-rotation arm from 2013 through 2016. And Gonzalez, another former top prospect, has been an above-average, often dominating hurler across 12 big league seasons. Mata has the build and repertoire to develop into a strong #3-type arm that could peak as a #2 if the command continues to improve.

Ceiling: 3.0-win player
Risk: Moderate
MLB ETA: 2020

6. Noah Song, RHP

	FB	CB	SL	CH	Command	Overall
	70	65	60	50	55	60

Born: 05/28/97	**Age:** 23	**Bats:** R	
Height: 6-4	**Weight:** 200	**Throws:** R	

Background: Arguably the most talented pitcher in the entire draft class last season; Song, a firebolt-slinging right-hander, slipped all the way to the last pick in the fourth round, 137th overall, due to the two-year active-duty service requirement as a member of the United States Naval Academy. Song simply posted the sixth best strikeout rate in Division I history last season, whiffing an astonishing 15.4 hitters every nine innings. In total, the 6-foot-4, 200-pound right-hander struck out a whopping 161, against just 31 free passes, in 94.0 innings of work. He tallied a barely-there 1.44 ERA to go along with an 11-1 win-loss record for the Naval Academy. He made seven starts for Lowell in the New York-Penn League during his pro debut, posting a 19-to-5 strikeout-to-walk ratio in 17.0 innings.

Scouting Report: Straight filth. His fastball was kissing 98 or 99 mph during his recent appearance for Team USA in the WBSC Premier 12. He'll also mix in a hard, oft-times absurdly good slider, a mid-70s curveball that might just be better than the slider with hard downward tilt, and an average changeup. To go along with the plus- to plus-plus velocity; his fastball shows impressive arm side run at times. He also commands the zone surprising well. He has the potential to be an upper-rotation-caliber arm.

Ceiling: 4.0-win player
Risk: Moderate
MLB ETA: 2023 (depending upon service duty)

7. Jarren Duran, CF

	Hit	Power	SB	Patience	Glove	Overall
	60	35/40	60	45	45/55	50

Born: 09/05/96	**Age:** 23	**Bats:** L	
Height: 6-2	**Weight:** 200	**Throws:** R	

YEAR	LVL	PA	1B	2B	3B	HR	SB	CS	AVG	OBP	SLG	BB%	K%	GB%	LD%	FB%
2018	A-	168	37	5	10	2	12	4	0.348	0.393	0.548	6.55%	15.48%	52.3	19.2	26.2
2018	A	134	36	9	1	1	12	6	0.367	0.396	0.477	3.73%	16.42%	51.9	21.7	23.6
2019	A+	226	57	13	3	4	18	5	0.387	0.456	0.543	10.18%	19.47%	48.7	29.5	18.6
2019	AA	352	63	11	5	1	28	8	0.250	0.309	0.325	6.53%	23.86%	51.3	22.5	21.2

Background: One of the more fascinating prospects in the entire minor leagues because, well, Duran's professional success wasn't foreseen by *anyone*. A three-year starter for Long Beach State, Duran left the school as a solid, though remarkably mediocre .294/.376/.377 hitter when the Sox called his name in the seventh round of the 2018 draft. The 220th overall player chosen that year, Duran looked like the second coming of Cobb during his professional debut, slugging a scorching .357/.394/.516 triple-slash line in 67 games between Lowell and Greenville. And truth be told, it smacked of beginner's luck, something he wouldn't – and couldn't – come close to replicating in another extend stint. Until he did. Opening last season up with Salem in the Carolina League, Duran slugged a whopping .387/.456/.543 in 50 games while topping the league average production by a staggering 101%. Boston bounced the former second-baseman-turned-center-fielder up to the minors' toughest challenge and, finally, the former Dirt Bag's bat began cool. In 82 games with Portland, the 6-foot-2, 200-pound outfielder hit a disappointing .250/.309/.325. Duran finished the year with an aggregate .303.367/.408 mark, belting out 24 doubles, eight triples, and five homerun while swiping 46 bags in 59 attempts. The organization sent him to the Arizona Fall League after the year; he hit .267/.337/.400 in 24 games with Peoria.

Scouting Report: Wildly fascinating. Consider the following:

- Since 2007 only two other hitters, Joey Gallo and Ryan McKenna, has posted a higher *Deserved Runs Created Plus* in the Carolina League (min. 200 PA).

For those counting at home: there have been a total of 1,295 instances in which a hitter received at least 200 plate appearances in a season in the Carolina League. Now let's take a look at his work in the Class AA:

- Since 2007 only three 22-year-old hitters have met the following criteria in the Eastern League (min. 300 PA): a DRC+ total between 70- and 80; a walk rate between 5% and 8%; and a strikeout rate between 21% and 25%. Those three hitters are: Darick Hall, Destin Hood, and Jarren Duran.

So which is the real Duran: the guy that torched three levels or the one that barely scraped by with enough production in Class AA? The answer's probably somewhere firmly in the middle. Duran's stint in Class AA was sandwiched by several poor weeks: he batted just .186/.294/.271 during his first 15 games and finished the year by hitting .218/.295/.347 over his final 27 contest. In between that, though, he hit .294/.325/.331 in 40 contests. The hit tool looks like it has a chance to be a plus skill and speed is already bordering on plus-plus. But the power has ways to go still, though it's flashed double-digit homer potential. The defense is still raw, but the combination of elite speed and lack of center field experience bodes well for the future. He could be a dynamic table setter if everything breaks the right way.

Ceiling: 2.5-win player
Risk: Moderate
MLB ETA: 2020

8. Bobby Dalbec, 1B/3B

Hit	Power	SB	Patience	Glove	Overall
40	70	30	70	50	50

Born: 06/29/95	Age: 25	Bats: R	Top CALs:
Height: 6-4	Weight: 225	Throws: R	

YEAR	LVL	PA	1B	2B	3B	HR	SB	CS	AVG	OBP	SLG	BB%	K%	GB%	LD%	FB%
2018	A+	419	33	27	2	26	3	1	0.256	0.372	0.573	14.32%	31.03%	29.0	28.1	37.6
2018	AA	124	14	8	1	6	0	0	0.261	0.323	0.514	4.84%	37.10%	34.3	16.4	41.8
2019	AA	439	47	15	2	20	6	4	0.234	0.371	0.454	15.49%	25.06%	39.9	12.9	35.5
2019	AAA	123	18	4	0	7	0	2	0.257	0.301	0.478	4.07%	23.58%	39.5	22.1	26.7

Background: The former University of Arizona two-way star earned some nice hardware two years ago: The hulking corner infielder was named the Carolina League MVP and Boston recognized him as the franchise's Top Minor League Offensive *and* Defensive Player of the Year. Not a bad showing for a fourth round pick. After spending just over two dozen games in the Eastern League to cap of his successful 2018 season, Dalbec was sent back to Portland for some more seasoning. He obliged by slugging .234/.371/.454 with 15 doubles, a pair of triples, and 20 homeruns in 105 games. His overall production in the most challenging minor league test, according to *Deserved Runs Created Plus*, was a whopping 51% better than the average. Boston bumped him up to Pawtucket in early August for his final 30 contests. He finished the year with a .239/.356/.460 triple-slash line with 19 doubles, two triples, and 27 homers.

Snippet from The 2018 Prospect Digest Handbook: Dalbec's calling card – as always – has been his light-tower power. And he complements the plus skill with tremendous patience at the dish as well. The problem for Dalbec, however, is his inability to make consistent enough contact.

Scouting Report: Light tower power still intact? Check. Elite patience at the dish? Double check. Problematic strikeout rates? Far from it. It's wildly uncommon and, frankly, nearly unheard of, but during his fourth professional season and at the age of 24, Dalbec took *tremendous* strides in trimming his ceiling-limiting strikeout rates down to...well...average-ish territory. Against the Eastern League pitching he whiffed in slightly more than 25% of his plate appearances, roughly eight-percentage points better than his career numbers. With respect to his work in Class AA, consider the following:

- Since 2000 only four 24-year-old hitters have posted a DRC+ between 145 and 155 in the Eastern League (min. 300 PA): Josmil Pinto, Zach Green, Thomas Neal, and Bobby Dalbec.

The good news: Pinto, Green, and Neal all reached the major leagues. The bad news: they played a collective 107 games there. Despite trimming his red flag-waving punch out rate, Dalbec's below-average hit tool – regardless of the power and patience combo – make him a tough bet to carve out a lengthy big league career.

Ceiling: 2.5-win player
Risk: Moderate
MLB ETA: 2020

9. Brayan Bello, RHP

FB	SL	CH	Command	Overall
60/65	55/60	50	50	50

Born: 05/17/99	Age: 21	Bats: R
Height: 6-1	Weight: 170	Throws: R

YEAR	LVL	IP	W	L	SV	ERA	FIP	WHIP	K/9	K%	BB/9	BB%	K/BB	HR9	BABIP
2018	Rk	64.3	6	2	0	1.68	1.93	0.73	9.5	28.10%	1.4	4.13%	6.80	0.00	0.228
2018	Rk	3.0	1	0	0	0.00	0.36	0.67	18.0	54.55%	0.0	0.00%	N/A	0.00	0.400
2019	A	117.7	5	10	0	5.43	3.64	1.47	9.1	22.62%	2.9	7.22%	3.13	0.69	0.359

Background: One of the more promising, albeit raw, arms Boston's system is boasting. The organization signed the wiry, projectable right-hander three years ago out of Samana, Dominican Republic. The 6-foot-1, 170-pound hurler made his professional debut two years ago, making 13 starts in the Dominican Summer League and one final relief appearance in the Gulf Coast League; he would finish the year with a 1.60 ERA, averaging 9.9 strikeouts and just 1.3 walks per nine innings. Last season the front office turned the kid gloves into a lead foot and pushed him straight into the South Atlantic League. And Bello continued to post impressive peripherals – especially considering his lack of professional experience. In a career-high 117.2 innings, he fanned 119 and walked just 38.

Scouting Report: Consider the following:

- Since 2000, there have been nine 20-year-old pitchers to post a strikeout percentage between 21% and 23% with a walk percentage between 6% and 8% in the South Atlantic League (min. 100 IP): Jhoulys Chacin, Nick Kingham, Domingo Tapia, Zachary Fuesser, Jorge Bucardo, Nick Pesco, Anthony Lerew, Mike Hinckley, and Brayan Bello.

Bello, showing a lightning-quick arm, has an explosive, above-average fastball that has a solid chance of bumping up to plus—territory as he fills out. It was hovering in the 93- to 94-mph range with relative ease. Bello's slider, an above-average offering, shows some solid depth and looks more like a traditional curveball. Like the fastball, there's a chance it gets better as he further refines it. And his changeup, a 50-grade weapon, is raw with some fade and sink. He's more of a strike-thrower as opposed to someone that commands the strike zone. Bello has the makings of a #4-type arm, maybe more. There's a lot to like.

Ceiling: 2.0-win player
Risk: Moderate
MLB ETA: 2022/2023

10. Thad Ward, RHP

FB	SL	CH	Command	Overall
55	60	50	45	50

Born: 01/16/97	Age: 23	Bats: R
Height: 6-3	Weight: 182	Throws: R

YEAR	LVL	IP	W	L	SV	ERA	FIP	WHIP	K/9	K%	BB/9	BB%	K/BB	HR9	BABIP
2018	A-	31.0	0	3	0	3.77	3.83	1.45	7.8	20.15%	3.5	8.96%	2.25	0.58	0.337
2019	A	72.3	5	2	0	1.99	2.84	1.05	10.8	29.19%	3.1	8.39%	3.48	0.25	0.280
2019	A+	54.0	3	3	0	2.33	3.86	1.30	11.7	30.84%	5.3	14.10%	2.19	0.67	0.296

Background: A solid find in the fifth round out of the University of Central Florida two years ago, Ward spent the overwhelming majority of collegiate career pitching in short stints; he made just seven career starts and 54 relief appearances. He finished his collegiate career with a 127-to-52 strikeout-to-walk ratio in 118.2 innings of work. Boston immediately converted Ward – and his four-pitch repertoire – into a fulltime starting pitcher. And the 6-foot-3, 182-pound right-hander shot through two low levels en route to a statistically dominant sophomore professional season. Making a combined 25 starts between Greenville and Salem, Ward fanned a remarkable 157 against 57 walks to go along with a 2.14 ERA.

Scouting Report: One of the fastest working arms in the minor leagues; Ward quickly gets into a rhythm early in the game by attacking hitters with his above-average low-90s fastball, which will top 96 at times, and a slider that pushes the boundaries between a traditional cutter and a harder curveball at times. . Ward commands his heater well, particularly low-and-away to hitters, which helps the effectiveness of his slider against right-handers. He'll mix in a changeup, which is a solid average. Ward looks like a solid #4/#5-type arm in the coming years.

Ceiling: 2.0-win player
Risk: Moderate
MLB ETA: 2021

11. Tanner Houck, RHP

	FB	CB	SL	CH	Command	Overall
	60	50	55	50	50	45

Born: 06/29/96	Age: 24	Bats: R
Height: 6-4	Weight: 210	Throws: R

YEAR	LVL	IP	W	L	SV	ERA	FIP	WHIP	K/9	K%	BB/9	BB%	K/BB	HR9	BABIP
2017	A-	22.3	0	3	0	3.63	2.53	1.30	10.1	25.51%	3.2	8.16%	3.13	0.00	0.333
2018	A+	119.0	7	11	0	4.24	4.31	1.43	8.4	21.39%	4.5	11.56%	1.85	0.83	0.298
2019	AA	82.7	8	6	0	4.25	3.35	1.43	8.7	22.10%	3.5	8.84%	2.50	0.44	0.346
2019	AAA	25.0	0	0	1	3.24	5.30	1.32	9.7	23.89%	5.0	12.39%	1.93	1.08	0.250

Background: A stalwart atop Missouri's rotation in each of his three years at the school, Houck, a 6-foot-4, 210-pound right-hander, made 44 starts in his collegiate career, averaging 8.7 strikeouts and just 1.9 walks per nine innings to go along with a 3.26 ERA. Boston snagged the savvy hurler in the opening round, 24th overall, three years ago. After making 10 brief starts in the New York-Penn League during his debut, Houck spent the entirety of 2018 working out of Salem's rotation. In 23 High Class A starts, he posted a solid 111-to-60 strikeout-to-walk ratio in 119 innings of work. Last season Houck split time between Portland and Pawtucket, making 33 appearances – 17 of which were starts – while fanning 107 and walking 46 with an aggregate 4.01 ERA.

Snippet from The 2018 Prospect Digest Handbook: Heading into the [2017] draft I opined that Houck looked like a mid-rotation caliber arm, perhaps peaking as a #2/#3-type hurler. A year later and the former Mizzou ace looks more like a capable backend arm.

Scouting Report: The former Mizzou Tiger maintained status quo during his stint as a starting pitcher in Class AA last season, posting a respectable 78-to-30 strikeout-to-walk ratio through 81.0 innings. But the with the big league club's bullpen potentially looking for help down the stretch Houck was pushed into a bullpen in July for the remainder of the season. Houck still looks like a capable backend starting pitcher. His fastball peaked at 95 mph as a starting pitcher, showing plus to plus-plus movement at times. His slider was notably different this season, no longer resembling a cutter. According to reports, Brian Bannister, Boston's Vice President of Pitching Development, said Houck tweaked the pitch in Spring Training. For what it's worth I think the slider was a more viable weapon two years ago as it was more difficult to differentiate from his fastball. His other two offspeed pitches, a curveball and changeup, are average. With respect to his work as a starting pitcher in Class AA last season, consider the following:

- Since 2000, only six 23-year-old pitchers have posted a strikeout rate between 8.5 and 9.0 K/9 and a walk rate between 3.35 and 3.6 BB/9 in the Eastern League (min. 75 IP): Yefrey Ramirez, Parker Bridwell, Hansel Robles, George Kontos, Billy Sadler, and – of course – Tanner Houck.

Ceiling: 1.5 to 2.0-win player
Risk: Low to Moderate
MLB ETA: 2020

12. Alex Scherff, RHP

	FB	CB	SL	CH	Command	Overall
	60	55/60	50	55/60	45/50	45

Born: 02/05/98	Age: 22	Bats: B
Height: 6-3	Weight: 205	Throws: R

YEAR	LVL	IP	W	L	SV	ERA	FIP	WHIP	K/9	K%	BB/9	BB%	K/BB	HR9	BABIP
2018	Rk	5.0	0	0	0	1.80	3.04	1.20	5.4	16.67%	1.8	5.56%	3.00	0.00	0.357
2018	A	65.0	1	5	0	4.98	4.44	1.40	7.1	18.82%	3.2	8.49%	2.22	0.97	0.324
2019	A	123.0	5	12	0	4.83	4.69	1.60	8.0	19.50%	3.9	9.48%	2.06	1.02	0.348
2019	A+	6.3	1	0	0	1.42	3.37	1.11	4.3	12.50%	2.8	8.33%	1.50	0.00	0.263

Background: Handed a six-figure over-slot bonus as a fifth round pick three years ago. Scherff, a product of Colleyville Heritage High School, wouldn't make his debut until the following year. He would make two rehab appearances in the Gulf Coast League sandwiched around 15 starts in the Sally. He finished the 2018 season with a 54-to-24 strikeout-to-walk ratio in 70.0 innings of work. Last year the front office sent the hard-throwing right-hander back down to Low Class A for 26 of his 27 starts. He finished the year with 112 punch outs against 55 walks to go along with a 4.66 ERA in a career-best 129.1 innings.

Snippet from The 2018 Prospect Digest Handbook: Scherff attacks hitters with an easy plus fastball, showing quick arm action. His curveball, which was reported to be an underwhelming offering heading into the year, was surprising – in a good way. It's a hard, 12-6 overhand offering with bite – easily an above-average breaking ball that – on occasion – flashes plus.

Scouting Report: The fastball is still a plus-offering - it sits easily in the mid-90s – but it's straight and doesn't miss many bats. The curveball is still one helluva a breaking ball when it's on. And his changeup has quietly become one of my favorites in the minor leagues. It's hard with tremendous dive when he's locating it low in the zone. Scherff's also added a hard, tightly spun slider as well – another solid weapon in his arsenal. He looks like a solid #4-type arm in the coming years, maybe a bit more if he can improve his fastball command. With respect to his work in the Sally last season, consider the following:

- Since 2000, there have been five 21-year-old pitchers to post a strikeout percentage between 18.5% and 20.5% with a walk percentage between 8.5% and 10.5% in the South Atlantic League (min. 100 IP): Navery Moore, Zachary Fuesser, Ryan Pressly, John Lannan, and Alex Scherff. Pressly and Lannan both accrued significant MLB time.

Ceiling: 1.5 to 2.0-win player
Risk: Moderate
MLB ETA: 2022

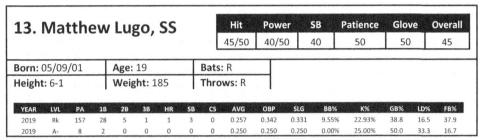

13. Matthew Lugo, SS

Hit	Power	SB	Patience	Glove	Overall
45/50	40/50	40	50	50	45

Born: 05/09/01	Age: 19	Bats: R
Height: 6-1	Weight: 185	Throws: R

YEAR	LVL	PA	1B	2B	3B	HR	SB	CS	AVG	OBP	SLG	BB%	K%	GB%	LD%	FB%
2019	Rk	157	28	5	1	1	3	0	0.257	0.342	0.331	9.55%	22.93%	38.8	16.5	37.9
2019	A-	8	2	0	0	0	0	0	0.250	0.250	0.250	0.00%	25.00%	50.0	33.3	16.7

Background: Taken by Boston in the second round last June, Lugo already has strong ties to big league greatness – potentially even Hall of Fame bloodlines: the talented middle-infielder's uncle is Carlos Beltran, the 1999 American League Rookie of the Year, eight-time All-Star, and owner of a career .279/.350/.486 triple-slash line. Lugo, who was drafted out of the Carlos Beltran Baseball Academy, signed for a slightly above-slot bonus worth $1.1 million. The wiry 6-foot-1, 185-pound shortstop batted .257/.342/.331 in 39 games in the Gulf Coast League and popped up for a two-game cameo in the New York-Penn League.

Scouting Report: Consider the following:

- Since 2000 there have been six 18-year-old hitters to post a DRC+ between 120 and 130 with a walk rate between 8.5% and 10.5% in the Gulf Coast League (min. 150 PA): Lolo Sanchez, Michael De La Cruz, Kenny Wilson, Bo Greenwell, Mitch Dening, and Matthew Lugo.

Impressive bat speed that suggests he'll develop at least 50-grade power. Lugo, with no surprise given his bloodlines, owns a short, compact swing and a solid approach at the plate. Defensively, he was better than average. If he's able to tap into the power, he could be a solid starting shortstop. If not, his gap-to-gap approach could make him a lower-end starter on a non-championship caliber quad.

Ceiling: 1.5- to 2.0-win player
Risk: Moderate
MLB ETA: 2023

14. Aldo Ramirez, RHP

FB	CB	CH	Command	Overall
55/60	50/55	50/55	50/55	45

Born: 05/06/01	Age: 19	Bats: R
Height: 6-0	Weight: 180	Throws: R

YEAR	LVL	IP	W	L	SV	ERA	FIP	WHIP	K/9	K%	BB/9	BB%	K/BB	HR9	BABIP
2018	Rk	23.0	1	2	0	0.39	2.66	0.57	6.7	20.00%	1.2	3.53%	5.67	0.00	0.159
2019	A-	61.7	2	3	0	3.94	3.33	1.22	9.2	24.05%	2.3	6.11%	3.94	0.73	0.309

Background: A native of Aguascalientes, Mexico, the Sox signed the promising right-hander in the early part of the season two years ago. A member of Rieleros de Aguascalientes prior to joining the Red Sox organization, Ramirez spent the remainder of the year in the Dominican Summer League: in five starts, the 6-foot, 180-pound teenager tossed 23.0 innings, recording 17 strikeouts against just three free passes. Boston aggressively pushed the then-18-year-old up to the New York-Penn League last season and the results were impressive: in 14 appearances, 13 of which were starts, the righty posted a 63-to-16 strikeout-to-walk ratio in 61.2 innings of work. He finished the year with a 4.76 *Deserved Runs Allowed*, or DRA.

Scouting Report: There is a reasonable chance that Ramirez develops three above-average or better offerings in the coming years. In an early July start against the Staten Island Yankees, his fastball was sitting 92 with arm-side action and a bit of late life; his upper-70s curveball showed some bite with 1-to-7 break; and his mid-80s changeup – although he struggles locating it – blends well with the action on his two-seam fastball. With respect to his work last season, consider the following:

- Since 2006, Ramirez's strikeout percentage, 24.1%, is the second highest percentage among all 18-year-old pitchers with at least 50 innings pitched in the New York-Penn League.

Ceiling: 1.5- to 2.0-win player
Risk: Moderate
MLB ETA: 2022/2023

15. Connor Wong, C/IF

	Hit	Power	SB	Patience	Glove	Overall
	45	50	30	45+	50	45

Born: 05/19/96	**Age:** 24	**Bats:** R
Height: 6-1	**Weight:** 181	**Throws:** R

YEAR	LVL	PA	1B	2B	3B	HR	SB	CS	AVG	OBP	SLG	BB%	K%	GB%	LD%	FB%
2017	A	107	16	6	0	5	1	1	0.278	0.336	0.495	6.54%	24.30%	52.8	12.5	33.3
2018	A+	431	62	20	2	19	6	2	0.269	0.350	0.480	8.82%	32.02%	35.9	28.6	29.0
2019	A+	302	31	15	6	15	9	2	0.245	0.306	0.507	6.95%	30.79%	31.5	27.2	32.1
2019	AA	163	33	9	1	9	2	1	0.349	0.393	0.604	6.75%	30.67%	40.0	29.0	26.0

Background: The third – and final – player the Sox acquired in the Mookie Betts/David Price sweepstakes. Wong, a third round pick out of the University of Houston three years ago, opened some eyes during a strong showing in High Class A in 2018 when he slugged .269/.350/.480 with 20 doubles, two triples, and 19 homeruns in 102 games. Despite topping the league average production by 13%, Wong found himself back in the California League for the start of 2019 – which was the result of Keibert Ruiz's presence more than anything else. And the numbers were…not as good. In 71 games with Rancho Cucamonga, he batted .245/.306/.507 with 15 doubles, six triples, and 15 homeruns. Los Angeles promoted him up to the minors' toughest challenge, Class AA, for his final 40 contests; Wong slugged a scorching .349/.393/.604 with 19 extra-base knocks with Tulsa.

Snippet from The 2018 Prospect Digest Handbook: And it's clear to see the Dodgers have tweaked Wong's approach at the plate into the organizational mantra of more fly balls = more homeruns = more production. Wong's groundball rate was just 34.7% last season. Average eye and hit tool with a tendency to swing-and-miss (hello, mantra). Wong looks like a lower-tier starting catcher if everything breaks the right way for him and the Dodgers.

Scouting Report: The change in his approach at the plate was able to carry over into the 2019 season as he continued to (A) put the ball in the air more frequently and (B) slugged a career best 24 homeruns. The problem, of course, is still quite evident: he's punching out in nearly 31% of his plate appearances. 45-grade hit tool, 50-power, solid glove. Wong's fortunate because his main position, catcher, is a black hole across baseball, so his big punch out rates may not inhibit big league playing time. Strictly a power-oriented backup.

Ceiling: 1.5-win player
Risk: Moderate
MLB ETA: 2020

16. Nick Decker, RF

	Hit	Power	SB	Patience	Glove	Overall
	45	40/50	30	55	45	45

Born: 10/02/99	**Age:** 20	**Bats:** L
Height: 6-0	**Weight:** 200	**Throws:** L

YEAR	LVL	PA	1B	2B	3B	HR	SB	CS	AVG	OBP	SLG	BB%	K%	GB%	LD%	FB%
2018	RK	5	0	1	0	0	0	0	0.250	0.400	0.500	20.00%	20.00%	66.7	33.3	0.0
2019	A-	197	21	10	5	6	4	5	0.247	0.328	0.471	10.66%	29.95%	31.6	21.1	39.5

Background: The club's second round pick two years ago out of Seneca High School, home to former Blue Jays first rounder Kevin Comer, Decker was limited to just a pair of Gulf Coast League games during his debut courtesy of a fractured wrist he suffered on a swing. Last season, though, Decker showed very little – if any – side effects as the club bounced him up to Lowell. In 53 games with the Spinners, the former 64th overall pick batted .247/.328/.471 with 10 doubles, five triples, and six homeruns to go along with a quartet of stolen bases. His overall production, per *Deserved Runs Created Plus,* was 21% better than the league average.

Snippet from The 2018 Prospect Digest Handbook: Decker shows a quick bat, though his swing can get a little long at times.

Scouting Report: Consider the following:

- Since 2000 there have been 18 different 19-year-old hitters to post a DRC+ between 115 and 125 in the New York-Penn League (min. 175).
- Of those 18 aforementioned hitters, only four of them fanned in at least 25% of their NYPL plate appearances: Josh Ockimey, Manuel Sanchez, Larry Greene, and – of course – Nick Decker.

Obviously it's a less-than-impressive collection of players: Ockimey, a fellow Sox farmhand has consistently struggled with contact issues; Sanchez washed out of pro ball after a brief – and incredibly unsuccessful – season in High Class A; and Greene failed to make it past Low Class A. There is a silver lining of sorts: Decker slugged .271/.358/.534 over his final 37 games, but, again, he whiffed in 30% of his plate appearances. And not to pile on, but he struggled against LHP too (.226/.226/.387). It's not looking overly optimistic at this point, but Decker flashes glimpses of 15- to 20-homerun potential.

Ceiling: 1.5-win player
Risk: Moderate
MLB ETA: 2023

17. Kole Cottam, C

Hit	Power	SB	Patience	Glove	Overall
45	45/50	30	55	40/45	45

Born: 05/30/97	**Age:** 23	**Bats:** R	
Height: 6-3	**Weight:** 220	**Throws:** R	

YEAR	LVL	PA	1B	2B	3B	HR	SB	CS	AVG	OBP	SLG	BB%	K%	GB%	LD%	FB%
2018	A-	129	17	8	1	3	2	1	0.242	0.279	0.400	3.88%	20.93%	46.3	16.8	33.7
2018	A	4	0	0	0	0	0	0	0.000	0.250	0.000	0.00%	25.00%	50.0	0.0	50.0
2019	A	316	39	21	1	6	0	0	0.255	0.377	0.411	13.92%	24.68%	34.9	21.5	37.1
2019	A+	42	4	4	0	2	0	1	0.256	0.262	0.513	2.38%	26.19%	30.0	36.7	30.0

Background: The University of Kentucky, Cottam's alma mater, has quietly become a hotbed for big league talent over the past three seasons: the school's had a pair of first round picks (Zack Thompson and Evan White), a second rounder (Sean Hjelle), two third round selections (Tristan Pompey and Riley Mahan), and a four rounder (Cottam). Taken as the 130th overall player in 2018, Cottam cemented himself as a reliable bat during his three-year tenure as the school's starting catcher. The 6-foot-3, 220-pound backstop left the school with an impressive .326/.399/.553 triple-slash line, belting out 30 doubles, one triple, and 27 homeruns in 151 games. The former Wildcat spent the majority of his pro debut with Lowell two years ago, hitting .242/.279/.400 in 40 games. Last season he appeared in 76 contests with Greenville and another 11 with Salem, hitting a combined .255/.363/.424 with 25 doubles, one triple, and eight homeruns.

Scouting Report: With respect to his work in the Sally last season, consider the following:

- Since 2000 there have been five 22-year-old hitters to meet the following criteria in the South Atlantic League (min. 300 PA): a DRC+ between 140 and 150; a walk rate greater than 12% and strikeout percentage of at least 24%. Those five hitters are: Josh Stowers, Brenden Webb, Chris Gittens, Kody Hinze, and – of course – Kole Cottam.

Cottam's bat was incredibly lethal during his stint in the Sally last season, ranking among the league's most productive hitters. He generates a lot of value from his patient approach and there's at least 45-grade power developing in the bat. Offense is going to have to carry him the rest of the way because he's going to cost a team some runs behind the dish. At worst, he's a solid backup.

Ceiling: 1.5-win player
Risk: Moderate
MLB ETA: 2022

18. Jhonathan Diaz, LHP

FB	CB	SL	CH	Command	Overall
50	55	55	55	45	45

Born: 09/13/96	**Age:** 23	**Bats:** L	
Height: 6-0	**Weight:** 170	**Throws:** L	

YEAR	LVL	IP	W	L	SV	ERA	FIP	WHIP	K/9	K%	BB/9	BB%	K/BB	HR9	BABIP
2017	A	88.7	6	6	0	4.57	3.53	1.45	8.1	20.57%	2.8	7.20%	2.86	0.41	0.361
2018	A	153.0	11	8	0	3.00	3.13	1.06	8.6	23.82%	2.3	6.32%	3.77	0.35	0.287
2018	A+	4.3	0	1	0	6.23	6.59	2.08	8.3	17.39%	4.2	8.70%	2.00	2.08	0.400
2019	A+	128.3	9	8	0	3.86	3.85	1.36	8.3	21.00%	3.8	9.61%	2.19	0.42	0.315

Background: Signed by the club all the way back on August 9, 2013. Diaz has taken the slow-and-steady approach through the low levels of the minor leagues with a detour through the surgeon's office for Tommy John woes. Diaz first popped up in the South Atlantic League in 2017. And despite some strong peripherals – he average 8.1 strikeouts and just 2.8 walks per nine innings – the club bounced him back down to Greenville the following season. His numbers, by the way, were only slightly improved during his second tour the Low Class A league (8.6 K/9 and 2.3 BB/9). Last season Diaz spent the entirety squaring off against the Carolina League hitters: in career-best-tying 27 starts, the 6-foot, 170-pound, southpaw posted a respectable 118-to-54 strikeout-to-walk ratio to go along with a 4.98 *Deserved Runs Average* (DRA). He appeared in eight games with Peoria in the Arizona Fall League, fanning 16 and walking six in 10.1 innings.

Snippet from The 2018 Prospect Digest Handbook: It would be easy to pigeonhole Diaz into the Dedgar Jimenez/Enmanuel De Jesus group, but Diaz's upside is a little higher thanks to a better arsenal. If everything breaks the right way – and he doesn't get pigeonholed into a relief role – Diaz looks like a nice little #5-type arm.

Scouting Report: The type of pitcher that gets buried in big market franchises like Boston. Diaz, like a lot of 50-grade fastball pitchers, is at his best when he's getting ahead earlier in the count with his fastball and then throwing a bevy of offspeed pitches. All three of his secondary weapons – curveball, changeup, and a newly developed slider – grade out as above-average. The command is still not overly sharp – at least not enough to earn a long look in Boston's rotation at some point in the future – but he could become an Oliver Perez-type reliever.

Ceiling: 1.5-win player
Risk: Low to Moderate
MLB ETA: Debuted in 2019

19. Cameron Cannon, 2B/SS

Hit	Power	SB	Patience	Glove	Overall
45/50	50	35	45	45/50	45

Born: 10/16/97	Age: 22	Bats: R
Height: 5-10	Weight: 196	Throws: R

YEAR	LVL	PA	1B	2B	3B	HR	SB	CS	AVG	OBP	SLG	BB%	K%	GB%	LD%	FB%
2019	Rk	10	1	0	0	0	0	0	0.111	0.200	0.111	0.00%	50.00%	50.0	0.0	25.0
2019	A-	180	18	12	0	3	1	0	0.205	0.289	0.335	6.67%	20.56%	32.8	23.0	32.8

Background: The Arizona native had a bit of a coming out party for the Wildcats during his sophomore season two years ago: after hitting a respectable .274/.384/.345 as a true-freshman, he slugged .321/.427/.549 with 21 doubles, two triples, and eight homeruns for Head Coach Jay Johnson. Cannon's production, though, faltered a bit during the following summer as he squared off against the elite Cape Cod League pitching. In 42 games with the Falmouth Commodores, the 5-foot-10, 196-pound middle infielder batted a mediocre .263/.298/.338 with just eight extra-base hits. Last season at the University of Arizona, Cannon helped alleviate a lot of concerns with a stellar junior campaign: he slugged a robust .397/.478/.651 with career-highs in doubles (29), triples (three), and tied a previous best in homeruns (eight). Boston snagged the versatile infielder in the second round, 43rd overall, and signed him to a deal worth $1.3 million – roughly a million less than the following picks received. Cannon spent the majority of his debut in the New York-Penn League, batting a lowly .205/.289/.335 with 12 doubles and three homeruns.

Scouting Report: Cannon got off to a strong start upon his promotion up to short-season ball last year, batting .265/.318/.422 through his first 25 games before fading into mediocrity. However, just as his patience eroded during his stint in the Cape Cod League, Cannon, who walked in nearly 13% of his plate appearances as junior, was too trigger happy as a pro; he walked in 6.7% of his plate appearances with Lowell. He has surprising power for an up-the-middle player. His glove is barely average as a shortstop and a tick better at the keystone. Low end starting infielder with the floor as a utility guy.

Ceiling: 1.5-win player
Risk: Moderate
MLB ETA: 2023

20. Mike Shawaryn, RHP

FB	SL	CH	Command	Overall
50	55	55	45+	40

Born: 09/17/94	Age: 25	Bats: B
Height: 6-2	Weight: 200	Throws: R

YEAR	LVL	IP	W	L	SV	ERA	FIP	WHIP	K/9	K%	BB/9	BB%	K/BB	HR9	BABIP
2017	A	53.3	3	2	0	3.88	2.78	1.07	13.2	35.78%	2.2	5.96%	6.00	0.84	0.331
2017	A+	81.3	5	5	0	3.76	4.23	1.30	10.1	25.85%	3.9	9.94%	2.60	1.11	0.289
2018	AA	112.7	6	8	0	3.28	3.21	1.13	7.9	21.43%	2.2	5.84%	3.67	0.56	0.287
2018	AAA	36.7	3	2	0	3.93	4.64	1.12	8.1	22.30%	2.7	7.43%	3.00	1.47	0.247
2019	AAA	89.7	1	2	0	4.52	5.65	1.39	7.6	19.84%	4.9	12.79%	1.55	1.30	0.264

Background: The bulky right-hander had a coming out party during his sophomore season for the Maryland Terrapins in 2015: in 17 starts he fanned a whopping 138 against just 29 free passes for the school. It looked like he was poised to become a mid-first round selection heading into his junior season, but his numbers backed up a bit – he finished with a 97-to-26 strikeout-to-walk ratio in 99.0 innings – and wouldn't hear his name called until the fifth round. The bulky right-hander vaulted through the Sox's system during his first full season in pro ball as he reach Class AAA for seven starts two years ago. Last season Shawaryn opened the year up in Pawtucket's rotation, making 10 starts before earning the first of two big league call-ups to work as a reliever. He would throw 89.2 minor league innings, averaging just 7.6 strikeouts and 4.9 walks per nine innings. Shawaryn would toss an additional 20.1 innings in Boston, posting a 29-to-13 strikeout-to-walk ratio.

Snippet from The 2018 Prospect Digest Handbook: Shawaryn shows a pair of above-average pitches: a heavy 93 mph fastball, which he spots well, and a solid changeup. But it's his ability to locate – with *high regularity* – his plus-slider that makes him attractive as a mid-rotation option.

Scouting Report: The stuff's backed up from the previous seasons, showing downgrades nearly across the board. His fastball was average during his second to last minor league start against the Buffalo Bisons, lacking the little bit of life it previously owned. His slider was still an above-average weapon, but it, too, lacked the added zip in past years. His changeup still fades fast and dives hard. Heading into the year Shawaryn looked like a viable mid-rotation arm but he now looks like a #5, at best. His command also degraded too.

Ceiling: 1.0 to 1.5-win player
Risk: Low to Moderate
MLB ETA: Debuted in 2019

Chicago Cubs
Farm System Ranking Trend

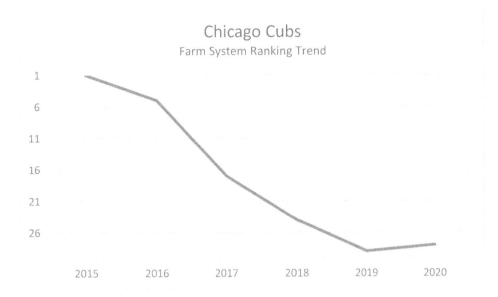

Rank	Name	Age	Pos
1	Brennen Davis	20	OF
2	Brailyn Marquez	21	LHP
3	Nico Hoerner	23	SS
4	Miguel Amaya	21	C
5	Chase Strumpf	22	2B
6	Adbert Alzolay	25	RHP
7	Ronnie Quintero	23	C
8	Ryan Jensen	22	RHP
9	Cory Abbott	24	RHP
10	Alfonso Rivas	23	1B
11	Pedro Martinez	19	2B/SS
12	Riley Thompson	23	RHP
13	Cole Roederer	20	CF
14	Justin Steele	24	LHP
15	Aramis Ademan	21	SS
16	Nelson Velazquez	21	OF
17	Kohl Franklin	20	RHP
18	Robel Garcia	27	2B/LF
19	Christopher Morel	21	3B/SS
20	Oscar De La Cruz	25	RHP

1. Brennen Davis, OF

Hit	Power	SB	Patience	Glove	Overall
50/55	50/55	45/40	50	50	55

Born: 11/02/99	Age: 20	Bats: R
Height: 6-4	Weight: 175	Throws: R

YEAR	LVL	PA	1B	2B	3B	HR	SB	CS	AVG	OBP	SLG	BB%	K%	GB%	LD%	FB%
2018	RK	72	15	2	0	0	6	1	0.298	0.431	0.333	13.89%	16.67%	54.3	19.6	21.7
2019	A	204	34	9	3	8	4	1	0.305	0.381	0.525	8.82%	18.63%	37.8	17.5	37.1

Background: A second round pick out of Basha High School two years ago, the Cubs signed the toolsy, projectable outfielder for a slightly above-slot bonus worth $1.1 million. Davis turned in a solid debut in the Arizona Summer League, hitting a respectable .298/.431/.333 with a pair of doubles and six stolen bases in 18 games. Last season the 6-foot-4, 175-pound outfielder turned in a breakout campaign for the South Bend Cubs in the Midwest League – despite succumbing to a litany of hand injuries. He was hit on the hand not once, but twice – *during the same homestand* in mid-July. And then a few weeks later his season ended prematurely *because he was hit on the hand by a pitch*. That's not counting his late start to the year too! In all, the Arizona native slugged an impressive .305/.381/.525 with nine doubles, three triples, and eight homeruns in 50 games. He also swiped four bags in five attempts. Per *Deserved Runs Created Plus*, his overall production topped the league average threshold by a whopping 55%.

Scouting Report: Consider the following:

- Since 2006, here's the list of 20-year-old hitters to post at least a 150 DRC+ with a sub-20% strikeout percentage and a single-digit walk percentage in the Midwest League (min. 200 PA): Royce Lewis, Bo Bichette, Luis Arraez, Oscar Taveras, Elehuris Montero, and – of course – Brennen Davis.

For those counting at home that's: three former widely regarded top prospects (Bichette, Taveras, who was taken tragically after briefly reaching the big leagues, and Lewis), a guy hit just slugged .334/.399/.439 during his rookie season (Arraez), and Montero, a personal favorite of mine that struggled through a lost, injury-plagued season in Class AA as a 20-year-old. As for Davis, he has the potential to be a special, special talent: blossoming power that should settle in as an above-average weapon, above-average hit tool, solid speed, a decent glove, phenomenal contact rates, and a willingness to walk a bit.

Ceiling: 3.5-win player
Risk: Moderate
MLB ETA: 2022

2. Brailyn Marquez, LHP

FB	CB	CH	Command	Overall
80	55	50	45/50	55

Born: 01/30/99	Age: 21	Bats: R
Height: 6-4	Weight: 185	Throws: R

YEAR	LVL	IP	W	L	SV	ERA	FIP	WHIP	K/9	K%	BB/9	BB%	K/BB	HR9	BABIP
2017	Rk	44.0	2	1	0	5.52	3.83	1.41	10.6	26.13%	2.5	6.03%	4.33	0.61	0.367
2018	A-	47.7	1	4	0	3.21	3.80	1.26	9.8	26.40%	2.6	7.11%	3.71	0.94	0.333
2018	A	7.0	0	0	0	2.57	2.76	1.29	9.0	22.58%	2.6	6.45%	3.50	0.00	0.333
2019	A	77.3	5	4	0	3.61	3.29	1.38	11.9	30.72%	5.0	12.95%	2.37	0.47	0.335
2019	A+	26.3	4	1	0	1.71	2.80	1.06	8.9	24.53%	2.4	6.60%	3.71	0.34	0.282

Background: The Cubs have had a lot of trouble developing young arms over the past several seasons. Oscar De La Cruz can't stay healthy; Duane Underwood Jr. couldn't hack it in the rotation; Bryan Hudson's development simply never happened; and Adbert Alzolay, with a tremendous amount of potential, just can't seem to put it all together. Enter: Brailyn Marquez, a big, projectable, flame-throwing, thunderbolt-slinging southpaw. Hailing from Santo Domingo, Dominican Republic, Marquez turned a lot of heads last summer as his heater touched a scorching 102 mph as a starting pitcher. The 6-foot-4,185-pound left-hander began showing serious potential during his stint in the Arizona Summer League three years ago when he posted a 52-to-12 strikeout-to-walk ratio in 44.0 innings as an 18-year-old. He followed that up with 12 strong starts between Eugene and South Bend the following season; he fanned 59 and walked 16 in 54.2 innings. Last season the then-20-year-old opened the year up with 17 starts back in the Midwest League before capping off his finest season to date with a five-game cameo in the Carolina League. In total, he tossed 103.2 innings with 128 strikeouts and 50 walks to go along with an aggregate 3.13 ERA.

Snippet from The 2018 Prospect Digest Handbook: Big time fastball that explodes through the zone thanks to his whip-like long arms. Marquez's heat sits comfortably in the 94- to 96-mph range and can reach upwards of triple-digits when needed. His secondary offerings, though, remain incredibly raw – like an open wound. Marquez's curveball is slow and lacks depth and looks slider-esque in movement at times.

Scouting Report: Consider the following:

- Since 2006, here's the list of 20-year-old pitchers to post at least a 29% strikeout percentage and a double-digit walk percentage in the Midwest League (min. 75 IP): Sandy Alcantara, Keyvius Sampson, Hector Yan, Fabio Martinez Mesa, Alexander Smit, Robinson Pina, and – of course – Brailyn Marquez.

Obviously, it's a less than stellar collection of arms, the best being Marlins All-Star fireballer Sandy Alcantara, who also owns a plus-plus-fastball and some decent, not great, offspeed options. The good news for Marquez: his curveball looked consistent last season and his changeup progressed as well. The potential is there to be one of the game's premier southpaws, but more work has to be done. As Major League Baseball and their organizations continue to buy into the pitch design / pitch development by Driveline Baseball and the like, the odds of Marquez taking that elite step forward increases dramatically.

Ceiling: 3.5-win player
Risk: Moderate
MLB ETA: 2021/2022

3. Nico Hoerner, 2B/SS

Hit	Power	SB	Patience	Glove	Overall
55	45	40	45/50	50	50

Born: 05/13/97	Age: 23	Bats: R
Height: 5-11	Weight: 200	Throws: R

YEAR	LVL	PA	1B	2B	3B	HR	SB	CS	AVG	OBP	SLG	BB%	K%	GB%	LD%	FB%
2018	RK	15	1	1	1	0	2	0	0.250	0.400	0.500	13.33%	0.00%	75.0	8.3	8.3
2018	A-	28	5	0	1	1	4	1	0.318	0.464	0.545	17.86%	10.71%	42.1	31.6	26.3
2018	A	17	4	1	0	1	0	0	0.400	0.471	0.667	11.76%	5.88%	57.1	28.6	14.3
2019	AA	294	54	16	3	3	8	4	0.284	0.344	0.399	7.14%	10.54%	41.9	22.6	27.8

Background: "Chicago has, in essence, stacked the odds of player development in their favor by going with the group of prospects that holds the least amount of risk: hitters." – *The Chicago Cubs: The Right Way to Rebuild*, The 2014 Prospect Digest Annual. In my very first prospect book I opined that the Cubs were going about their rebuilding process the way all teams should: corner the market on impact hitters early in the draft and then when those hitters begin to produce at the big league level the front office should use the free agent and trade market and to fill in the gaps with veteran pitchers. The Cubs were highly successful developing or trading for young offensive-minded prospects like Anthony Rizzo, Kris Bryant, Javier Baez, Willson Contreras, Kyle Schwarber, Albert Almora and, to a lesser extent, Addison Russell and Ian Happ. But here's the thing with that plan: it worked – astoundingly well. And then they deviated from it for a few seasons. The ballclub didn't own a first or second round pick in 2016, and then they snagged right-hander Tom Hatch in the third round. In 2017 they snagged southpaw Brendon Little with the 27th overall pick and Alex Lange three picks later. And then promptly doubled down on the arms and drafted Cory Abbott, Keegan Thompson, and Erich Uelmen over the next three rounds. Finally, in 2018 the Cubs got back to what they do best: drafting and developing hitters. They snagged Hoerner, Brennan Davis, and Cole Roederer. Hoerner, the 24th overall pick out of Stanford University, rocketed through the Cubs' minor league system, appearing at three different levels during his debut and then splitting time between Chicago and Class AA last season. The 5-foot-11, 200-pound shortstop batted .284/.344/.399 with 16 doubles, three triples, and three homeruns with Tennessee. His overall production according to Baseball Prospectus' *Deserved Runs Created Plus*, topped the league average mark by 4%.

Snippet from The 2018 Prospect Digest Handbook: If Hoerner's defense grades out as above-average – which it quite possibly will – he has a chance to develop into a fringy starting shortstop. He makes consistent contact and doesn't swing-and-miss often. The walk rate is average, at best. And his power likely falls into the below-average territory. In terms of big league ceiling, think Adeiny Hechavarria circa 2015 (.281/.315/.374).

Scouting Report: I've never been particularly high on the former Stanford Cardinal. In large part due to his alma mater and the dreaded Stanford Swing. But the Cubs are exactly the type of organization that can capitalize on a young hitter's offensive ceiling. Hoerner's far from a finished product. The bat has a chance to be an above-average tool, but it hasn't been nearly as productive as hoped. His overall production was roughly league average in Class AA. And the batted ball data was mediocre, at best, during his 20-game cameo in Chicago. And the power is still below-average as well; he's slugged just eight homeruns since the start of his junior season in college. Defensively, he's average. With respect to his work in Class AA last season, consider the following:

- Since 2006, here's the list of 22-year-old hitters to post a 100 to 110 DRC+ with a sub-8.5% walk rate and a punch out rate below 15% (min. 275 PA): Dawel Lugo, Mauricio Dubon, Willie Cabrera, Ozzie Martinez, and Nico Hoerner.

Ceiling: 2.5-win player
Risk: Low to Moderate
MLB ETA: Debuted in 2019

4. Miguel Amaya, C

	Hit	Power	SB	Patience	Glove	Overall
	40/45	55	30	60	45/50	50

Born: 03/09/99	Age: 21	Bats: R
Height: 6-1	Weight: 185	Throws: R

YEAR	LVL	PA	1B	2B	3B	HR	SB	CS	AVG	OBP	SLG	BB%	K%	GB%	LD%	FB%
2017	A-	244	34	14	1	3	1	0	0.228	0.266	0.338	4.51%	20.08%	41.8	19.2	29.7
2018	A	479	71	21	2	12	1	0	0.256	0.349	0.403	10.44%	19.00%	39.4	19.0	32.4
2019	A+	410	45	24	0	11	2	0	0.235	0.351	0.402	13.17%	16.83%	46.0	16.4	29.9

Background: A saber-slanted backstop performing well above the league average threshold over the past couple of seasons. Amaya, a 6-foot-1, 185-pound prospect out of Chitre, Panama, opened a lot of eyes after a strong showing in the Midwest League two years ago; he batted .256/.349/.403 with 21 doubles, a pair of triples, and 12 homeruns in 116 games as a 19-year-old. The front office bounced the promising catcher up to the Carolina League where he – once again – was one of the youngest everyday players. Amaya hit .235/.351/.402 with a career best 24 doubles and 11 homeruns. He also swiped a pair of bags. His overall production, per *Deserved Runs Created Plus*, topped the league average mark by a surprising 24%.

Snippet from The 2018 Prospect Digest Handbook: Amaya actually got off to a strong start to the year, slugging .284/.352/.484 over his first 78 games but cobbled together a pathetic .192/.342/.216 line over his final 38 contests – which isn't surprising given his (A) age, (B) level of competition, and (C) defensive position. Chicago also develops hitters better than many other organizations as well. Amaya's typically been an above-average defensive backstop. Throw in 20-homer potential, patience at the plate, strong contact skills, and age relative to level of competition and there's a lot to like. I'm betting on the first 78 games, rather the entire season.

Scouting Report: Consider the following:

- Since 2006, here's the list of 20-year-old hitters to post a DRC+ between 120 and 130 with a double-digit walk rate and a strikeout rate below 20% in any High Class A league (min. 300 PA): Jorge Polanco, Delino DeShields Jr., Lucius Fox, and Miguel Amaya.

The bat still has ways to go but the secondary skills remain incredibly promising: above-average power, elite walk rates, and – surprisingly – consistently well-above-average contact rates, all wrapped up at *the* premium position on the diamond. Defensively, he remains raw – and had a bit of down year behind the dish last season – but he should have no problem sticking behind the plate. He may not be a star, but he has the potential to be an above-average starter at the big league level.

Ceiling: 2.5- to 3.0-win player
Risk: Moderate to High
MLB ETA: 2022

5. Chase Strumpf, 2B

	Hit	Power	SB	Patience	Glove	Overall
	45/50	50/55	30	45	50	50

Born: 03/08/98	Age: 22	Bats: R
Height: 6-1	Weight: 191	Throws: R

YEAR	LVL	PA	1B	2B	3B	HR	SB	CS	AVG	OBP	SLG	BB%	K%	GB%	LD%	FB%
2019	Rk	32	1	3	0	0	0	0	0.182	0.406	0.318	21.88%	21.88%	31.3	0.0	68.8
2019	A-	111	16	8	0	2	2	0	0.292	0.405	0.449	13.51%	25.23%	28.1	28.1	35.9
2019	A	28	1	1	0	1	0	0	0.125	0.214	0.292	3.57%	25.00%	38.9	11.1	44.4

Background: Quite the notable player prior to his illustrious career at UCLA. Strumpf, a 6-foot-1, 191-pound middle infielder, helped the 15U Team USA win Gold. That in itself is impressive enough. But consider this: the eventual early round draft selection committed to the Bruins prior to playing a single game at San Juan Capistrano JSerra High School. The California native struggled a bit during his first season with the PAC12 school: he batted just .239/.315/.399 with nine doubles and seven homeruns. Strumpf had a massive breakout campaign the following year, slugging .363/.475/.633 with 23 doubles, one triple, and 12 homeruns with a pair of stolen bases. Last season Strumpf's numbers took a bit of downturn as he hit .279/.416/.472 with 14 doubles, a pair of triples, and nine homeruns. Chicago snagged him in the second round, 64th overall. Strumpf hit a combined .244/.374/.400 with 12 doubles and three homeruns between three low level leagues.

Scouting Report: A patient hitter, who left college with a career walk rate of nearly 14.5%, continued to work the count well as he transitioned into professional ball; he posted a 13.45% walk rate during his debut. Solid-average power that could develop into a perennial 20-homer threat down the road. Strumpf's college strikeout rate is a bit high for an early round pick (20.5%), and that number was close to red flag territory during his debut (24.6%). With respect to his production in college during his sophomore season, his best amateur showing, consider the following:

- Between 2011 and 2018, here's the list of PAC12 hitters to slug at least .350/.450/.600 in a season (min. 250 PA): Adley Rutschman, the top pick in the draft last season, Andrew Vaughn, who was taken two picks later last June, and – of course – Chase Strumpf, who the Cubs happily snagged him in the second round.

If the Cubs can unlock his production from two years ago, Strumpf could prove to be a tremendous value.

Ceiling: 2.0- to 2.5-win player
Risk: Moderate
MLB ETA: 2022

6. Adbert Alzolay, RHP

	FB	CB	CH	Command	Overall
	60	55	55	45	50

Born: 03/01/95	Age: 25	Bats: R
Height: 6-0	Weight: 179	Throws: R

YEAR	LVL	IP	W	L	SV	ERA	FIP	WHIP	K/9	K%	BB/9	BB%	K/BB	HR9	BABIP
2017	A+	81.7	7	1	0	2.98	3.67	1.07	8.6	23.78%	2.4	6.71%	3.55	0.88	0.263
2017	AA	32.7	0	3	0	3.03	2.56	1.19	8.3	22.22%	3.3	8.89%	2.50	0.00	0.297
2018	AAA	39.7	2	4	0	4.76	4.67	1.41	6.1	15.79%	2.9	7.60%	2.08	0.91	0.307
2019	A+	4.0	0	1	0	11.25	6.62	2.25	6.8	15.00%	4.5	10.00%	1.50	2.25	0.429
2019	AAA	65.3	2	4	0	4.41	4.60	1.29	12.5	32.27%	4.3	10.99%	2.94	1.38	0.295

Background: After a long eight years in the Cubs' organization Alzolay, a 6-foot, 179-pound right-hander, finally reached the pinnacle of professional baseball, ascending up to the big leagues for a brief four-game cameo last season. A native of Puerto Ordaz, Venezuela, Alzolay's 2019 season got off to a late start and he later dealt with what was described as "slight biceps soreness" according to reports. The hard-throwing righty would eventually make a total of 15 starts with Iowa in the hitter-friendly Pacific Coast League, throwing just 65.1 innings with a staggering 91 strikeouts and 31 walks. He compiled a 4.41 ERA and an impressive 2.70 Deserved Runs Average (DRA). During his two short stints with Chicago Alzolay fanned 13 and walked nine in 12.1 innings of work.

Snippet from The 2018 Prospect Digest Handbook: Watching the 6-foot, 179-pound right-hander pitch, one would guess he'd be in line for a punch out per inning based on pure stuff. His riding fastball sits 93 to 95 mph with ease. His snapdragon of a curveball has wicked 12-6 bite. And his changeup is at least an average offering. But Alzolay's never truly dominated at any level – even though most of the time he's been a touch old. His arrow's been trending upward for the past 18 or so months. Right now, he looks like a #4-type arm.

Scouting Report: For the first time since 2014 Alzolay's minor league strikeout rate surpassed a punch out per inning. And he was incredibly dominant as well. Unfortunately, though, Alzolay's control / command wavered after his first call up to Chicago; he walked just six hitters across his first six starts in Class AAA and then handed out a whopping 25 free passes in 33.1 innings. The repertoire still screams dominant big league starting pitcher: mid-90s fastball; an 80 mph, late breaking curveball that averaged more than 3,000 RPMs during his debut; and a mid-80s changeup. Consider the following:

- Since 2006, only five 24-year-old pitchers fanned at least 30% of the hitters they faced in the Pacific Coast League (min. 50 IP): Brian Moran, Conner Menez, Josh Staumont, Jose Urquidy, and Adbert Alzolay.

You don't have to squint too hard to see a solid #3 starting pitcher, but there's the risk if his control / command doesn't rebound.

Ceiling: 2.0-win player
Risk: Moderate
MLB ETA: Debuted in 2019

7. Ronnie Quintero, C

	Hit	Power	SB	Patience	Glove	Overall
	40/55	45/55	30	N/A	50	50

Born: 11/13/02	Age: 17	Bats: L
Height: 6-0	Weight: 175	Throws: R

Background: Widely regarded as the best catching prospect on the international scene last summer, the Cubs – who certainly agreed – broke the proverbial bank and signed the teenager to a hefty $2.9 million deal, surpassing the organization's previous high water mark given to former top prospect Eloy Jimenez ($2.8 million). Hailing from Venezuela, Quintero stands a wiry 6-foot and 175-pounds and offers up a smooth left-handed swing from a premium position. Chicago aggressively assigned Jimenez to the Arizona Summer League for his debut season in 2014. And it's likely that Quintero, another advanced stick, follows the same path.

Scouting Report: Strong, accurate arm behind the plate with solid footwork. Quintero shows a silky smooth left-handed swing with gobs of power. There's limited video of Quintero, but what I've seen has been quite promising. His swing is reminiscent of Robinson Cano, though with a larger, more emphasized leg kick. Above-average or better bat speed. Big time pull power to right field.

Ceiling: 2.0- to 2.5-win player
Risk: Moderate to High
MLB ETA: 2022/2023

8. Ryan Jensen, RHP

FB	SL	CH	Command	Overall
70	55/60	50	45	45

Born: 11/23/97	Age: 22	Bats: R
Height: 6-0	Weight: 180	Throws: R

YEAR	LVL	IP	W	L	SV	ERA	FIP	WHIP	K/9	K%	BB/9	BB%	K/BB	HR9	BABIP
2019	A-	12.0	0	0	0	2.25	4.45	1.75	14.3	33.33%	10.5	24.56%	1.36	0.00	0.318

Background: One of the bigger pop-up guys in the draft class last June. Jensen, a squat, strong right-hander out of Fresno State, was largely mediocre during his first two collegiate seasons. Making 29 appearances, only one of which was a start, as a true freshman, the California native tossed 43.2 innings with 35 strikeouts and a whopping 36 walks to go along with a horrific 6.60 ERA. The coaching staff transitioned the 6-foot, 180-pound righty into a bit of a swing-man during his sophomore season as he made seven relief appearances and 11 starts, averaging 8.8 strikeouts and nearly five walks per nine innings. Last season, though, Jensen seemingly put it all together for the Mountain West Conference school: making a career high 15 starts – as well as one lone relief appearance – he tossed an even 100 innings with a dominating 107-to-27 strikeout-to-walk ratio. Chicago drafted him in the opening round, 27th overall, and sent him to the Northwest League for six brief appearances (12.0 IP, 19 K, 14 BB).

Scouting Report: Wildly different from the arms the club has zeroed in on in the early parts of the draft over the last several years; Jensen's a let-'er-rip type of pitcher. Armed with a plus-plus-fastball and an above-average slider, he challenges hitters early and often in a "I dare you to hit it" mentality. The changeup is fringy average and needs some work. He has bouts of wildness and I'm far from convinced that he'll remain the type of strike thrower he showed during his junior campaign moving forward. And he may wind up as a fastball/slider type reliever. With respect to his work in college last season consider the following:

- Between 2011 and 2018, only seven Mountain West Conference pitchers averaged at least nine strikeouts and fewer than three walks per nine innings (min. 75 IP): Erick Fedde, Ben Bertelson, Bubba Derby, Edgar Gonzalez, Gera Sanchez, Tyler Stevens, and Kyle Winkler.

Ceiling: 1.5- to 2.0-win player
Risk: Moderate
MLB ETA: 2022

9. Cory Abbott, RHP

FB	CB	CU	CH	Command	Overall
50	55	55	50	50	45

Born: 09/20/95	Age: 24	Bats: R	Top CALs:
Height: 6-2	Weight: 220	Throws: R	

YEAR	LVL	IP	W	L	SV	ERA	FIP	WHIP	K/9	K%	BB/9	BB%	K/BB	HR9	BABIP
2017	A-	14.0	0	0	0	3.86	3.00	1.21	11.6	31.03%	1.9	5.17%	6.00	0.64	0.371
2018	A	47.3	4	1	0	2.47	3.33	1.01	10.8	30.81%	2.5	7.03%	4.38	0.95	0.275
2018	A+	67.7	4	5	0	2.53	2.99	1.26	9.8	26.24%	3.5	9.22%	2.85	0.40	0.316
2019	AA	146.7	8	8	0	3.01	3.51	1.12	10.2	28.92%	3.2	9.06%	3.19	0.92	0.274

Background: A second rounder in 2017 that was sandwiched in between more than a handful of players that would become legitimate big league prospects like Rangers right-hander Hans Crouse, Arizona's backstop-of-the-future Dalton Varsho, the Indians' heir apparent at shortstop Tyler Freeman, and Orioles southpaw Zac Lowther; Abbott – nonetheless – turned in his finest professional season to date. Making a career best 26 starts with the Tennessee Smokies in the Southern League, the stocky 6-foot-2, 220-pound right-hander tossed 146.2 with an impressive 166 punch outs and just 52 walks. He finished the year with a solid 3.01 FRA and a mediocre 4.19 DRA.

Snippet from The 2018 Prospect Digest Handbook: His strikeout percentages last season – 30.8% in the Midwest League and 26.2% in the Carolina League – are deceiving as he was feasting off of inferior hitters. It'll likely settle around the league average mark as he jumps into Class AA and above. He's a safe, fast moving backend option. Nothing more. Nothing less.

Scouting Report: Well, I was wrong. Not only was his strikeout percentage not deceiving but it actually ticked up a bit – 27.8% – as he jumped up to the minors' most challenging level. Consider the following:

- Since 2006, here's the list of 23-year-old pitchers to post a strikeout percentage of at least 27% in the Southern League (min. 100 IP): Tucker Davidson, Brandon Woodruff, and Cory Abbott.

That's a solid duo of arms to line up with – except, well, Abbott doesn't really belong in the group. Davidson and Woodruff both own plus- or better fastballs. Abbott, on the other hand, gets by using his solid four-pitch mix, changing speeds and eye levels. His fastball is average, nothing to write home about. His cutter is an equalizer for him and his go-to weapon; it's a 55-grade, maybe a touch better. His curveball adds a second above-average weapon. And the changeup is solid-average. The production is far better than the individual pieces. But it's still incredibly dominant numbers. Abbott looks like a backend arm, though he likely doesn't get to long of a leash in Chicago.

Ceiling: 1.5-win player
Risk: Low to Moderate
MLB ETA: 2020

10. Alfonso Rivas, 1B

	Hit	Power	SB	Patience	Glove	Overall
	55/60	35/50	30	60	55	45

Born: 09/13/96	Age: 23	Bats: L
Height: 6-0	Weight: 188	Throws: L

YEAR	LVL	PA	1B	2B	3B	HR	SB	CS	AVG	OBP	SLG	BB%	K%	GB%	LD%	FB%
2018	A-	257	43	16	1	1	7	4	0.285	0.397	0.383	14.01%	17.12%	34.9	31.4	30.2
2019	A+	509	87	24	3	8	2	2	0.283	0.383	0.408	12.97%	22.20%	46.3	16.3	35.6
2019	AAA	34	9	2	1	1	0	0	0.406	0.441	0.625	5.88%	20.59%	48.0	32.0	20.0

Background: A fourth round pick out of the University of Arizona two years ago by the Athletics, he left the Wildcats as a career .325/.418/.472 hitter, belting out 37 doubles, five triples, and 15 homeruns in 172 total games. Rivas, the 113th overall player chosen that year, continued to produce as he moved into the New York-Penn League during his debut, batting .285/.397/.383 with 16 doubles, one triple, and one homerun. Last season Oakland's front office bumped the 6-foot, 188-pound first baseman up to High Class A. And he handled the aggressive promotion with aplomb. In 114 games with the Stockton Ports, the California native slugged .283/.383/.408 with 24 doubles, three triples, and eight homeruns. As measured by *Deserved Runs Created Plus*, his overall production topped the league average threshold by 35%. Chicago acquired the young first baseman for utility man Tony Kemp this offseason.

Scouting Report: Not all that different from Pavin Smith, the player chosen directly after Austin Beck in the opening round of the 2017 draft. Rivas is an advanced, "professional hitter" with a solid pedigree, tremendous patience, and very little, though improving, power. Rivas puts the ball on the ground too frequently, like Sheldon Neuse's former approach, so I'd expect the Cubs to rework his swing to generate more loft. The overall power may never top 15- or 18-homeruns, but the hit tool, patience, and glove should be enough to push him toward league average starting caliber potential. Maybe.

Ceiling: 1.5- to 2.0-win player
Risk: Moderate
MLB ETA: 2021

11. Pedro Martinez, 2B/SS

	Hit	Power	SB	Patience	Glove	Overall
	45	45/50	35	45	45/50	45

Born: 01/28/01	Age: 19	Bats: B
Height: 5-11	Weight: 165	Throws: R

YEAR	LVL	PA	1B	2B	3B	HR	SB	CS	AVG	OBP	SLG	BB%	K%	GB%	LD%	FB%
2018	RK	228	51	3	5	2	31	9	0.310	0.398	0.406	11.40%	11.40%	59.5	20.2	16.8
2019	Rk	121	27	6	3	2	8	5	0.352	0.417	0.519	9.92%	22.31%	57.3	20.7	19.5
2019	A-	112	21	2	3	0	11	5	0.265	0.357	0.347	10.71%	32.14%	62.1	20.7	13.8

Background: Signed out of Porlamar, Venezuela, in the middle of May 2018, Martinez, a switch-hitting, wiry middle infielder, turned in an impressive debut with the Cubs' foreign rookie league affiliate: in 54 games, he slugged .310/.398/.406 with three doubles, five triples, and a pair of homeruns. He also swiped an impressive 31 bags in 40 tries. During his sophomore campaign last season, Martinez split time between the Arizona Summer and Northwest League, hitting an aggregate .311/.388/.437 triple-slash line with eight doubles, six triples, and two homeruns with 19 stolen bases in 29 total attempts.

Scouting Report: A really impressive breakout-type season for the teenager. Despite standing just 5-foot-11 and 165 pounds, Martinez shows some intriguing power potential – perhaps offering up 15-to 17-homerun type potential. Above-average speed, though he needs to improve his base running efficiency. Some of Martinez's flaws were exposed against the older Northwest League competition; he fanned in nearly a third of plate appearances – including punching out in 21 of his final 44 trips to the plate. Defensively, he's been roughly average. Martinez has the ceiling as a low end starting shortstop / solid utility bat, though he's very raw.

Ceiling: 1.5- to 2.0-win player
Risk: Moderate to High
MLB ETA: 2022/2023

12. Riley Thompson, RHP

FB	CB	CH	Command	Overall
65	60	55	50	45

Born: 07/09/96	Age: 23	Bats: R
Height: 6-3	Weight: 205	Throws: R

YEAR	LVL	IP	W	L	SV	ERA	FIP	WHIP	K/9	K%	BB/9	BB%	K/BB	HR9	BABIP
2018	A-	25.3	0	2	0	2.84	3.51	1.30	8.9	22.94%	3.2	8.26%	2.78	0.36	0.324
2019	A	94.0	8	6	0	3.06	3.88	1.23	8.3	22.25%	3.0	7.93%	2.81	0.86	0.290

Background: Snake-bitten like few others over the past couple of seasons. Thompson was a highly touted prep arm coming out of Christian Academy High School. Blessed with the prototypical power pitcher's build and a plus- to plus-plus fastball, Thompson's elbow flared up heading into the draft and eventually succumbed to Tommy John surgery which caused his stock to plummet. The Reds took a late round flier on him, though the two sides failed to come to an agreement. After missing the entirety of the following season, 2016, Thompson appeared In 14 games for the Louisville Cardinals, throwing 15.2 innings with 23 strikeouts and nine walks. The Yankees came calling in the 25th round. And, once again, Thompson declined. Shoulder woes limited him to just 11 appearances, seven of which were starts, in 2018; he tossed 33.0 innings with 35 punch outs and 25 walks. Chicago snagged him in the 11th round and sent him to Eugene for his debut. Last season the 6-foot-3, 205-pound righty tossed a career best 94.0 innings while recording 87 punch outs against just 31 walks.

Scouting Report: On a bit of side note: Thompson was busted with an illegal or foreign substance near the latter part of the season and missed a little more than a week-and-a-half due to suspension. In terms of potential, it's easy to see how an injured, hardly used pitcher can generate so much interest over multiple draft classes. Thompson's fastball was sitting 95 and touching a couple ticks higher once he returned from his aforementioned suspension. His curveball is an absolute hammer-of-a-pitch. And his changeup, the lone knock on his otherwise stellar repertoire heading into the year, was impressive – easily grading out as a 55 and flashing plus at times. The track record for oft-injured pitchers is spotty, at best, but Thompson has some #4-type potential if he can stay healthy.

Ceiling: 1.5 to 2.0-win player
Risk: Moderate to High
MLB ETA: 2021/2022

13. Cole Roederer, CF

Hit	Power	SB	Patience	Glove	Overall
40/45	50	50	55	50	45

Born: 09/24/99	Age: 20	Bats: L
Height: 6-0	Weight: 175	Throws: L

YEAR	LVL	PA	1B	2B	3B	HR	SB	CS	AVG	OBP	SLG	BB%	K%	GB%	LD%	FB%
2018	RK	161	26	4	4	5	13	4	0.275	0.354	0.465	11.18%	22.98%	36.8	22.6	36.8
2019	A	448	54	19	4	9	16	5	0.224	0.319	0.365	11.61%	25.00%	41.7	15.2	34.8

Background: Refocusing on the club's strength of developing hitters, Chicago took a calculated gamble on Roederer in the second round of the 2018 draft. Viewed as one of the best prep bats in the entire class, the organization handed the William S. Hart High School product a hefty $1.2 million signing bonus, nearly $500,000 above the recommended slot bonus. The 6-foot, 175-pound center fielder quickly went to work, slugging .275/.354/.465 with four doubles, four triples, and five homeruns to go along with 13 stolen bases during his 36-game debut in the Arizona Summer League. The front office brass bounced Roederer up to the Midwest League last season. And the wheels...promptly fell off. In 108 games with South Bend, the young outfielder hit a paltry .224/.319/.365 with 19 doubles, four triple, nine homeruns, and 16 stolen bases. His overall production, as measured by *Deserved Runs Created Plus*, was 9% below the league average.

Snippet from The 2018 Prospect Digest Handbook: Between 2006 and 2015, only five 18-year-old hitters met the following criteria in the Arizona Summer League (min. 150 PA): 125 to 135 wRC+ total, a walk rate between 10% and 14%, and a strikeout rate between 21% and 26%. Those five hitters: Robel Garcia, Daniel Carroll, B.J. Boyd, Jose Carlos Urena, and Monte Harrison.

Scouting Report: Consider the following:

- Since 2006, there were four 19-year-old hitters to meet the following criteria in the Midwest League (min. 300 PA): 85 to 95 DRC+, a strikeout rate between 24% and 26%, and a double-digit walk rate. Those four hitters are LeVon Washington, a toolsy prospect that could never shake a relentless string of injuries, Agustin Ruiz, Je'Von Ward, and Cole Roederer.

He can stuff a stat sheet with the best of them. Above-average speed, power, and patience that's currently hampered by a disappointing hit tool. Roederer did manage to have two incredibly productive months, batting .273/.314/.470 and .256/.349/.400 in June and August, but he looked completely helpless in April (.229/.296/.314), May (.203/.276/.362), and July (.176/.351/.306). He owns a similar skillset – though with more power potential – as former Cubs farmhand Matt Szczur. One other red flag: Roederer was practically useless against southpaws, hitting .149/.253/.179 in 79 plate appearances.

Ceiling: 1.5-win player
Risk: Moderate
MLB ETA: 2022/2023

14. Justin Steele, LHP

FB	CB	CH	Command	Overall
55	55	50	50	45

Born: 07/11/95	Age: 24	Bats: L
Height: 6-2	Weight: 205	Throws: L

YEAR	LVL	IP	W	L	SV	ERA	FIP	WHIP	K/9	K%	BB/9	BB%	K/BB	HR9	BABIP
2017	A+	98.7	6	7	0	2.92	3.92	1.38	7.5	18.98%	3.3	8.33%	2.28	0.55	0.315
2018	Rk	18.3	0	0	0	1.47	2.65	0.71	13.3	39.13%	2.0	5.80%	6.75	0.49	0.222
2018	A+	18.3	2	1	0	2.45	2.76	0.98	9.3	25.68%	2.9	8.11%	3.17	0.00	0.261
2018	AA	10.0	0	1	0	3.60	4.46	1.10	6.3	16.67%	2.7	7.14%	2.33	0.90	0.233
2019	AA	38.7	0	6	0	5.59	3.76	1.68	9.8	24.71%	4.7	11.76%	2.10	0.70	0.404

Background: The Man of Steele is anything but. The 6-foot-2, 205-pound southpaw missed the final handful of weeks of 2017 and the majority of the following year due to Tommy John surgery. And after struggling through the opening two months with the Smokies last season, Steele, a former fifth round pick all the way back in 2014, began to recapture some previous magic. He posted a 24-to-11 strikeout-to-walk ratio and only five earned runs over his final 20.1 innings of work. Then disaster struck: a severe oblique injury prematurely ended his sixth minor league season in late June. Steele finished the year with 42 strikeouts, 20 walks, and an unsightly 5.59 ERA in only 38.2 innings of work.

Snippet from The 2018 Prospect Digest Handbook: During his first Class AA start, it was apparent that Steele was (A) still trying to shake the rust off his left arm and (B) his secondary offerings were inconsistent. His fastball shot out of his hand with relative ease, though he had trouble locating (again, which is to be expected). His curveball showed sharp, late 11-to-5 break. He looked to be exclusively fastball/curveball. Steele's sort of a tweener: he's always had good stuff, but he doesn't profile as anything other than a spot-start/relief option.

Scouting Report: Steele was incredibly effective in his second-to-last start of the year against the Pensacola Blue Wahoos. Working primarily off of his fastball that day, the broad-shouldered southpaw fanned seven and looked nearly unhittable. His curveball has settled in as a strong above-average option. And the changeup is average. He's now entering his age-24 season and has thrown only 85.1 innings over the past two years. The 2020 season may be his final shot at a starting gig.

Ceiling: 1.5-win player
Risk: Moderate to High
MLB ETA: 2020

15. Aramis Ademan, SS

Hit	Power	SB	Patience	Glove	Overall
30/45	35/45	40	50	45/50	40

Born: 09/13/98	Age: 21	Bats: L
Height: 5-11	Weight: 160	Throws: R

YEAR	LVL	PA	1B	2B	3B	HR	SB	CS	AVG	OBP	SLG	BB%	K%	GB%	LD%	FB%
2017	A-	183	29	9	4	4	10	6	0.286	0.365	0.466	7.65%	16.39%	45.1	18.0	30.8
2017	A	134	21	6	1	3	4	2	0.244	0.269	0.378	2.99%	17.91%	44.8	14.3	34.3
2018	A+	452	65	11	3	3	9	5	0.207	0.291	0.273	8.41%	21.02%	51.9	15.5	25.8
2019	A+	422	57	10	8	5	16	9	0.221	0.318	0.334	11.37%	21.80%	42.0	16.7	29.3

Background: Signed out of Santiago, Dominican Republic, near the end of August five years ago, Ademan, a 5-foot-11, 160-pound lefty-swinging shortstop, opened up some eyes after an impressive jaunt through the Northwest League in 2017. The then-18-year-old batted .286/.365/.466 with nine doubles, four triples, and four homeruns to go along with 10 stolen bases. Since then, though, the youngster has struggled at the plate: he hit .244/.269/.378 in the second half of 2017; he looked completely overwhelmed in his aggressive promotion up to High Class A the following year (.207/.291/.273); and he only slightly improved during his do-over stint with Myrtle Beach last season, batting just .221/.318/.334.

Snippet from The 2018 Prospect Digest Handbook: Since 2006, here's a list of 19-year-old players to post a walk rate between 7% and 10% and a punch out rate between 17% and 23% in the Carolina League (min. 250 PA): Chris Marrero, Wendell Rijo, Rafael Devers, Xander Bogaerts, and Aramis Ademan. But here's the death blow: Ademan's Isolated Power was a lowly .066. The second worst among the group was Rijo's .121 mark. Right now, it doesn't look good for Ademan. He's clearly in over his head and he's – without a doubt – in need of a repeat in High Class A.

Scouting Report: A repeat of High Class A didn't lead to any developmental progress last season. And even more alarming: his overall production dropped precipitously as the season progressed. He posted monthly OPS totals of .926, .683, .638, .569, and .507. There's still a solid foundation in place for Ademan. He owns solid peripherals, above-average speed, and some developing power that might grade out as a 50 at maturity. The problem, of course, is the actual hit tool. It's terrible. He once looked like a potential Top 100 prospect. Now, though, he's firmly down the path of future utility-dom. And that's a best case scenario.

Ceiling: 1.0- to 1.5-win player
Risk: Moderate
MLB ETA: 2022/2023

16. Nelson Velazquez, OF

	Hit	Power	SB	Patience	Glove	Overall
	45	45/50	35	45	45/50	40

Born: 12/26/98	Age: 21	Bats: R
Height: 6-0	Weight: 190	Throws: R

YEAR	LVL	PA	1B	2B	3B	HR	SB	CS	AVG	OBP	SLG	BB%	K%	GB%	LD%	FB%
2017	RK	126	11	5	2	8	5	2	0.236	0.333	0.536	11.90%	30.95%	31.0	18.3	47.9
2018	A-	293	35	18	2	11	12	4	0.250	0.322	0.458	7.85%	27.65%	44.6	15.8	33.2
2018	A	120	20	1	0	0	3	0	0.188	0.242	0.196	5.83%	35.83%	53.6	17.4	26.1
2019	A	285	51	16	4	4	5	3	0.286	0.338	0.424	7.37%	27.02%	49.5	16.1	28.5

Background: Taken in the fifth round three years ago out of PJ Education School as a development project, Nelson, the 165th overall player drafted, was in the midst of a surprising breakout season with South Bend before an injury midseason forced him onto the Disabled List for several months. The 6-foot, 190-pound outfielder, who hit a paltry .188/.242/.196 with the club's Low Class A affiliate in 2018, fared significantly better in his do-over campaign. In 72 games, the native of Carolina, Puerto Rico, slugged .286/.338/.424 with 16 doubles, four triples, and four homeruns. He also swiped five bags in eight total attempts. His overall production, according to D*eserved Runs Created Plus*, topped the league average by 26%.

Scouting Report: The season-interrupting injury, which was described as a muscle issue according to reports, hardly slow the young developing outfielder: he hit .293/.333/.401 in 41 games prior to going on the DL and he managed to cobble together a .278/.344/.452 triple-slash line in his final 31 contests. Velazquez continues to have some issues making consistent contact, though the numbers are trending in the right direction; he whiffed in 31% of his plate appearances in 2017; lowered that to 27.6% after his demotion to short-season ball two years ago, and posted the lowest rate of his career in 2019 (27%). Glimpses of solid-average, maybe even a touch better, power are visible. Velazquez looks like a fourth outfielder, maybe squeaking out a 50-grade if everything breaks the right way. Consider the following:

- Since 2006, only three 20-year-old hitters met the following criteria in the Midwest League (min. 250 PA): DRC+ between 120 and 130, and a strikeout rate of at least 26%. Those three hitters: Alex Jackson, who continues to struggle with his contact rate in the upper levels of the minor leagues; Michael Crouse, who petered out in Class AA; and Nelson Velazquez.

Ceiling: 1.0- to 1.5-win player
Risk: Moderate
MLB ETA: 2022

17. Kohl Franklin, RHP

	FB	CB	CH	Command	Overall
	55/60	45/50	55/60	45/50	40

Born: 09/09/99	Age: 20	Bats: R
Height: 6-4	Weight: 190	Throws: R

YEAR	LVL	IP	W	L	SV	ERA	FIP	WHIP	K/9	K%	BB/9	BB%	K/BB	HR9	BABIP
2018	Rk	8.7	0	1	0	6.23	4.30	1.27	8.3	21.05%	6.2	15.79%	1.33	0.00	0.208
2019	A-	39.0	1	3	0	2.31	3.16	1.15	11.3	29.70%	3.2	8.48%	3.50	0.46	0.302
2019	A	3.0	0	0	0	3.00	6.43	1.67	9.0	20.00%	15.0	33.33%	0.60	0.00	0.000

Background: Strong bloodlines that run pretty deep: Franklin's father, Jay, spent a handful of seasons in the minor leagues as an eighth round pick and is currently an agent; and Kohl's uncle, Ryan, spent 12 years in the big leagues and earned a trip to the 2009 All-Star game. The youngest Franklin, a 6-

foot-4, 190-pound right-hander, received a hefty $500,000 bonus as a sixth round pick out of Broken Arrow High School two years ago. The projectable righty made 10 impressive starts with the Eugene Emeralds last season, throwing 39.0 innings with 49 strikeouts and just 14 free passes. Chicago bumped him up to the Midwest League for one brief three-inning appearance to cap off his first full season in professional baseball.

Scouting Report: Franklin's alma mater, Broken Arrow High School, has churned out a few impressive big league arms: Diamondbacks relief ace Archie Bradley, former two-time All-Star Brad Penny, and Jim Brewer, who spent parts of 17 seasons in the big leagues. As for Kohl, he's long-limbed, loose-armed, and quite projectable. The young right-hander's fastball, across a few starts I scouted last season, sat in the 90- to 92-mph range, kissing 94 mph on occasion. As his body continues to fill out it has the chance to be a plus offering. His changeup is his best secondary offering, showing a solid amount of velocity separation and plenty of fade. His curveball is a weakness, grading out – generously – as a 45. He remains very raw and this should be a solid litmus test for the club's player development engine. He looks like a solid backend arm if his curveball takes another step forward.

Ceiling: 1.0- to 1.5-win player
Risk: Moderate
MLB ETA: 2023

18. Robel Garcia, 2B/LF

Hit	Power	SB	Patience	Glove	Overall
40/45	50	50	55	50	40

Born: 03/28/93	Age: 27	Bats: B
Height: 6-0	Weight: 168	Throws: R

YEAR	LVL	PA	1B	2B	3B	HR	SB	CS	AVG	OBP	SLG	BB%	K%	GB%	LD%	FB%
2019	AA	92	12	5	0	6	1	1	0.295	0.391	0.590	13.04%	23.91%	29.8	10.5	42.1
2019	AAA	296	38	12	2	21	3	3	0.281	0.361	0.585	10.14%	33.11%	30.5	23.8	36.6

Background: One of the best stories of the 2019: Garcia epitomized the value of persistence as he cracked a big league lineup for 30 games. Hailing from Las Matas de Farfan, Dominican Republic, Garcia was a member of the Cleveland Indians organization from 2010 up to his release following the 2013 season. The 6-foot, 168-pound infielder / outfielder spent a couple years playing ball in Italy, including a stint for the National Team that played in the 2018 Super 6 Baseball Tournament. A little more than a month after the tournament concluded the Cubs tracked Garcia down and signed him to a minor league deal. In his stateside return he ripped through the Southern League with a .295/.391/.590 triple-slash line and spent the remainder of the year yo-yoing between Iowa and Chicago. The new cult, fan favorite hit an aggregate .284/.369/.586 with 17 doubles, two triples, and 27 homeruns in 98 minor league games and compiled a .208/.275/.500 triple-slash line with the Cubs.

Scouting Report: More than just a heartwarming, root-for-the-underdog story, Garcia put up some noteworthy batted ball data during his extended stay in Chicago: his Hard Hit %, 42.1%, was nearly eight percentage points better than the MLB average and his Barrel %, 15.8%, was well above the average too. Now the bad news: Garcia was – clearly – swinging out of his shoes the majority of the time as he whiffed in nearly 44% of his big league plate appearances and more than a third of his trips to the plate in Class AAA. He was particularly lethal against left-handers so he may very well carve out a couple years in the bigs as a platoon / role player.

Ceiling: 1.0- to 1.5-win player
Risk: Low to Moderate
MLB ETA: Debuted in 2019

19. Oscar De La Cruz, RHP

FB	CB	CH	Command	Overall
55	60	45	50	40

Born: 03/04/95	Age: 25	Bats: R
Height: 6-4	Weight: 200	Throws: R

YEAR	LVL	IP	W	L	SV	ERA	FIP	WHIP	K/9	K%	BB/9	BB%	K/BB	HR9	BABIP
2017	Rk	2.0	0	0	0	0.00	3.22	0.00	4.5	16.67%	0.0	0.00%	#DIV/0!	0.00	0.000
2017	A+	54.7	4	3	0	3.46	4.20	1.24	7.7	20.26%	2.1	5.60%	3.62	0.99	0.308
2018	AA	77.3	6	7	0	5.24	4.57	1.38	8.5	21.28%	3.6	9.04%	2.35	0.93	0.313
2019	A+	15.0	1	0	0	1.20	2.31	1.27	10.2	26.56%	3.0	7.81%	3.40	0.00	0.341
2019	AA	81.3	4	5	2	4.09	3.92	1.16	9.7	25.58%	3.2	8.43%	3.03	0.89	0.275

Background: The year began off on an impressive note for the enigmatic right-hander: he dominated the Carolina League for three starts before getting a promotion back up to Class AA. He continued to throw well for a few starts with the Smokies before all hell broke loose. Between May 22nd and June 12th De La Cruz allowed 18 earned runs in 26.2 innings of work. Finally, the front office relented and made the move that was, frankly, long overdue: the lanky, 6-foot-4, 200-pound righty was converted into a full time reliever. And he shined. In 23 games in Tennessee's pen, the Dominican Republic native posted an absurd 49-to-9 strikeout-to-walk ratio in 37.1 innings of work. He allowed 6 earned runs, though 10 of them came in three of his appearances.

Snippet from The 2018 Prospect Digest Handbook: He's another one of their former prominent pitching prospects headed toward the bullpen, though with his injury history it's far from a certainty that his body could withstand throwing two out of every three days.

Scouting Report: Primarily a two-pitch pitcher once he moved into a short relief role. De La Cruz's fastball was sitting 93 and kissing 95, maybe a tick better, at times. His curveball is late, hard, and sharp. It's a definite swing-and-miss option. De La Cruz has always shown a strong feel for the strike zone and that was only amplified as a reliever. He's ready to start working some high leverage innings at the big league level.

Ceiling: 1.0- to 1.5-win player
Risk: Moderate
MLB ETA: 2020

20. Christopher Morel, SS

	Hit	Power	SB	Patience	Glove	Overall
	45	50	35	40/45	50	40

Born: 06/24/99	Age: 21	Bats: R
Height: 6-0	Weight: 140	Throws: R

YEAR	LVL	PA	1B	2B	3B	HR	SB	CS	AVG	OBP	SLG	BB%	K%	GB%	LD%	FB%
2017	RK	268	34	6	2	7	23	10	0.220	0.332	0.359	13.06%	13.81%	43.5	18.3	20.9
2018	RK	128	21	6	0	2	1	4	0.257	0.331	0.363	8.59%	21.88%	48.3	20.7	24.1
2018	A-	93	12	2	0	1	0	1	0.165	0.172	0.220	0.00%	31.18%	41.3	17.5	23.8
2019	A	278	45	15	7	6	9	6	0.284	0.320	0.467	3.96%	21.58%	44.3	14.3	32.0

Background: A product of Santiago, Dominican Republic, Morel, an international free agent that signed with the organization all the way back in 2015, finally began to put the pieces together in the Midwest League last season. After struggling – massively – during his first two professional seasons when he batted a putrid .220/.332/.359 and .216/.264/.299, the 6-foot, 140-pound infielder slugged an impressive .284/.320/.467 with 15 doubles, seven triples, and six homeruns. He also swiped nine bags in 15 total attempts. His production, as measured by Baseball Prospectus' *Deserved Runs Created Plus*, topped the league average mark by 13%.

Scouting Report: Consider the following:

- Since 2006, there have been three hitters that posted a DRC+ between 108 and 118 with a sub-6.0% walk rate and an Isolated Power between .160 and .200 during their respective age-20 seasons in the Midwest League (min. 250 PA): Fernando Perez, Steven Moya, and – of course – Christopher Morel.

Still incredibly raw – despite the breakout showing – but the fact that he hit like he did is a minor testament to the club's development capabilities. Above-average power with the potential to slug 20 homeruns in a full year. There's some interesting bits-and-pieces to Morel's toolkit, but he looks like a solid Quad-A / utility guy.

Ceiling: 1.0- to 1.5-win player
Risk: Moderate
MLB ETA: 2022/2023

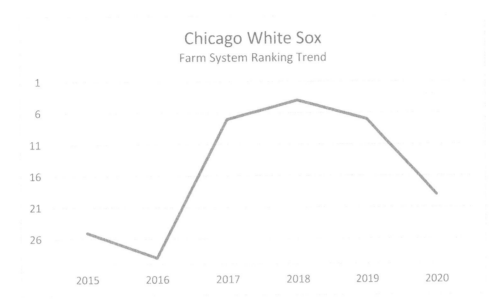

Chicago White Sox
Farm System Ranking Trend

Rank	Name	Age	Pos
1	Luis Robert	22	CF
2	Andrew Vaughn	22	1B
3	Michael Kopech	24	RHP
4	Nick Madrigal	23	2B
5	Blake Rutherford	23	CF
6	Jonathan Stiever	23	RHP
7	Matthew Thompson	19	RHP
8	Dane Dunning	23	RHP
9	Gavin Sheets	24	1B
10	Bryan Ramos	18	3B
11	Luis Alexander Basabe	23	OF
12	Andrew Dalquist	22	RHP
13	Yermin Mercedes	27	C
14	Zack Collins	25	CF
15	Luis Gonzalez	24	OF
16	Konnor Pilkington	22	LHP
17	Jose Rodriguez	19	2B/SS
18	Micker Adolfo	23	RF
19	Jake Burger	19	1B
20	Jimmy Lambert	25	RHP

1. Luis Robert, CF

Hit	Power	SB	Patience	Glove	Overall
55	60	60	45	55	70

Born: 08/03/97 | **Age:** 22 | **Bats:** R

Height: 6-3 | **Weight:** 185 | **Throws:** R

YEAR	LVL	PA	1B	2B	3B	HR	SB	CS	AVG	OBP	SLG	BB%	K%	GB%	LD%	FB%
2018	RK	18	4	2	1	0	3	0	0.389	0.389	0.611	0.00%	16.67%	53.3	33.3	13.3
2018	A	50	9	3	1	0	4	2	0.289	0.360	0.400	8.00%	24.00%	51.5	18.2	18.2
2018	A+	140	23	6	1	0	8	2	0.244	0.317	0.309	5.71%	26.43%	47.2	20.2	25.8
2019	A+	84	18	5	3	8	8	2	0.453	0.512	0.920	4.76%	23.81%	27.3	18.2	43.6
2019	AA	244	44	16	3	8	21	6	0.314	0.362	0.518	5.33%	22.13%	32.9	18.5	32.9
2019	AAA	223	29	10	5	16	7	3	0.297	0.341	0.634	4.93%	24.66%	28.9	24.8	38.9

Background: Committed to a full-blown rebuild – finally – the White Sox pulled the trigger and dealt away the best pitcher in franchise history when they agreed to send ace southpaw Chris Sale to the Red Sox for a package of four prospects (Michael Kopech, Yoan Moncada, Luis Alexander Basabe, and Victor Diaz). The date: December 6th, 2016. A little more than five months later the club made the second most important move towards their rebuild: they handed Cuban star, fresh off of a .401/.526/.687 showing – at the age of 18 – in the Cuban National Series, Luis Robert a $26 million. The toolsy, wide receiver-sized center fielder promptly dominated the Dominican Summer League the following year when he slugged .310/.491/.536 with eight doubles, one triple, and three homeruns. After that the front office took the training wheels off. And, well, Robert struggled. He quickly moved through the South Atlantic League, but struggled during his stint in High Class A – which was undoubtedly hindered by a month long stint on the disabled list. Regardless, though, nothing could have prepared anyone for the massive, wildly successful breakout last season. Robert ripped through the Carolina League, battered Class AA, the toughest challenge for a prospect, and continued to drop bombs in 47 games in the International League. He finished the year with an aggregate .328/.376/.624 with 31 doubles, 11 triples, 32 homers, and 36 stolen bases. The 30/30/30 club.

Snippet from The 2018 Prospect Digest Handbook: Basically a lost season for one of the minors' most talented outfielders. Robert got off to a late start and then just a month into his season he missed another significant stretch of the schedule. Under normal circumstances the lack of power wouldn't be too concerning given the hand/thumb injury, but Robert's groundball rate last season was up precipitously from the previous year. And it's also not surprising that he suffered some serious first. vs. second half production woes as well (because of the second layoff). Robert batted .308/.382/.385 in 22 High Class A games to start the year, but managed a meager .211/.280/.289 showing after missing the month of July. Expect significantly better production in 2018 as long as (A) he's healthy and (B) the groundball rate normalizes again. One final thought: Robert's bat speed looked impressive during his stint in the Arizona Fall League.

Scouting Report: With respect to his work in Class AA last season, consider the following:

- Since 2006, here's the list of 21-year-old hitters to post a DRC+ between 123 and 133 in the Southern League (min. 200 PA): Joc Pederson, Mat Davidson, Chris Young, Josh Lowe, Dustin Peterson, Jordan Schafer, and Luis Robert.
- And it should be noted that: only two players posted below 8% walk rates (Peterson and Robert).

Now let's look at his work in Class AAA:

- Since 2006, here's the list of 21-year-olds to post a DRC+ between 110 and 120 in the International League (min. 200 PA): Jose Ramirez, Melvin Upton, Jose Tabata, Ryan Sweeney, and Luis Robert.
- And, again, it should be noted that Robert owns the worst strikeout and walk rates.

Let's break Robert down: he's a five-tool player – above-average or better tools across the board. That's known. But his production, while good, was not great last season – let alone elite. There's a chance for a 55-hit tool, 60-power, 60-speed, 55-defense. The bat speed is incredible and the power/speed combination separates him from the rest of the group. Do I think he becomes a perennial All-Star? Yes. Do I think he becomes a transcendent superstar along the lines of a Mike Trout, which seems to be the comp being thrown around frequently? I think that's far less of a lock. It could happen, but I think the odds aren't quite what everyone makes them out to be. I would put his ceiling around the Rafael Devers / Ozzie Albies 2019 production with more stolen bases. Something along the lines of .310/.370/.550. Per FanGraphs data, Robert's average exit velocity, 90 mph, was tied for the 56th best mark and his peak exit velocity, 111 mph, tied for the ninth best.

Ceiling: 6.0-win player
Risk: Low to Moderate
MLB ETA: 2020

2. Andrew Vaughn, 1B

Hit	Power	SB	Patience	Glove	Overall
60	55	30	60	50	60

Born: 04/03/98	Age: 22	Bats: R
Height: 6-0	Weight: 214	Throws: R

YEAR	LVL	PA	1B	2B	3B	HR	SB	CS	AVG	OBP	SLG	BB%	K%	GB%	LD%	FB%
2019	Rk	16	6	2	0	1	0	0	0.600	0.625	0.933	0.00%	18.75%	33.3	33.3	25.0
2019	A	103	12	7	0	2	0	0	0.253	0.388	0.410	13.59%	17.48%	45.5	22.7	30.3
2019	A+	126	16	8	0	3	0	1	0.252	0.349	0.411	12.70%	13.49%	39.3	20.2	33.7

Background: The stocky, broad-shouldered slugger was already a star long before his days with the California Golden Bears. Vaughn, who measures in at six feet and 214 pounds, earned MVP honors by slugging a three-run homerun in the championship game for the 15-U Team USA National club in 2013. The Santa Rosa, California, native would continue to dominate during his time in high school as well, posting a career .380 batting average to go along with 29 doubles, three triples, and one homerun while whiffing only 15 times. He also showed some intriguing potential on the bump too: he finished his prep career with a 2.06 ERA to go along with 166 punch outs. Vaughn continued to swing an impressive stick during his freshman year with Cal, batting .349/.414/.555 with seven doubles, one triple, and 12 homeruns in 54 games for former Manager David Esquer. He also made 10 brief appearances on the mound, posting a 4-to-5 strikeout-to-walk ratio in eight innings of work. Vaughn earned Pac-12 Freshman of the Year and Freshman All-American (NCBWA, Baseball America, Perfect Game/Rawlings). He also appeared in 19 games for Team USA, batting .242/.320/.364 in 66 at bats. His production skyrocketed into another stratosphere during his sophomore campaign: in 54 contests he slugged a whopping .402/.531/.819 with 14 doubles and 23 homeruns to go along with a videogame-esque 18-to-44 strikeout-to-walk ratio. And he – once again – earned significant time for Team USA during the summer, though his production cratered. In 49 at bats he hit .224/.316/.367. Last season Vaughn's production declined ever-so-slightly: he batted .374/.539/.704 with 14 doubles and 15 homeruns to go along with a 33-to-60 strikeout-to-walk ratio in 52 games. Chicago made the slugging first baseman the third overall pick last June. After a three-game cameo in the Arizona Summer League, Vaughn split the remainder of his debut between Kannapolis and Winston-Salem. He hit an aggregate .278/.384/.449 with 17 doubles and six homeruns between all three stops.

Scouting Report: Here's what I wrote prior to the draft last June:

"Let's take a look back at his historic 2018 campaign. Consider the following:

- Between 2011 and 2018, only six Division I hitters have slugged at least .800 in a season (min. 200 PA): Kris Bryant, Brent Rooker, D.J. Peterson, C.J. Cron, Bren Spillane, and Andrew Vaughn.

Let's continue…

- Of those aforementioned six, three of them walked at least 16% of the time and recorded a strikeout percentage below 15%: Bryant, Peterson, and Vaughn. Bryant was the second overall pick in 2013. Seattle selected Peterson with the 12th overall pick. And it should be noted that both accomplished the feat during their junior seasons.

Now let's take a look at his work thus far in 2019:

- Between 2011 and 2018, only three Division I hitters met the following criteria in a season (min. 175 PA): 20% walk rate, sub-15% strikeout rate, a .350 batting average, and a .650 slugging percentage. Those three hitters: Seth Beer, James Ramsey, and Casey Gillaspise, all three getting drafted in the opening round.

Bat speed, bat speed, bat speed – that's the name of the game for Vaughn. It's not on the same level as Clint Frazier, who's long been lauded for his bat speed, but it is close. Vaughn shows above-average to plus raw power – though it may slide comfortably into the 15- to 20-homer territory in the professional ranks. But he has the potential to be a perennial .290- to .300-hitter with plus on-base skills and some defensive value. One more final note: Since 2010, only two first baseman who were 6-foot or less slugged at least 25 homeruns in a big league season: Prince Fielder, who accomplished it four times, and Eric Thames."

For the record, per FanGraphs, Vaughn's average exit velocity was 91 mph with a peak of 111 mph.

Ceiling: 4.0-win player
Risk: Low to Moderate
MLB ETA: 2021

3. Michael Kopech, RHP

	FB	CB	SL	CH	Command	Overall
	N/A	N/A	N/A	N/A	N/A	60

Born: 04/30/96	Age: 24	Bats: R
Height: 6-3	Weight: 205	Throws: R

YEAR	LVL	IP	W	L	SV	ERA	FIP	WHIP	K/9	K%	BB/9	BB%	K/BB	HR9	BABIP
2017	AA	119.3	8	7	0	2.87	2.83	1.15	11.7	31.76%	4.5	12.30%	2.58	0.45	0.272
2017	AAA	15.0	1	1	0	3.00	2.07	1.33	10.2	27.42%	3.0	8.06%	3.40	0.00	0.375
2018	AAA	126.3	7	7	0	3.70	3.29	1.27	12.1	31.31%	4.3	11.05%	2.83	0.64	0.316

Background: It was the deal that – officially – kicked off the club's rebuild after years, and years, of being mired in baseball purgatory. And the White Sox, as difficult as it was dealing off one of the greatest players in franchise history, knocked it out of the park when they received Yoan Moncada, Luis Alexander Basabe, Victor Diaz, and Michael Kopech for ace southpaw Chris Sale. Equipped with a limitless arsenal and 45-grade control/command, Kopech rocketed through the minor leagues beginning in 2016 when he spent the majority of a shortened season in High Class A as a 20-year-old. The 6-foot-3, 205-pound righty, now in Chicago's farm system, split time between the club's Class AA and Class AAA affiliates the following season, posting a dominating 172-to-65 strikeout-to-walk ratio in 134.1 innings of work. And just as he was dipping his toes in the waters of Chicago – he posted a 15-to-2 strikeout-to-walk ratio during a four-game start with the Sox – the former first rounder's season was prematurely cut short due to Tommy John surgery. The injury and subsequent rehab knocked him out for the entirety of 2019.

Snippet from The 2018 Prospect Digest Handbook: Possesses one of the best fastballs in organized baseball. Kopech's heater sits comfortably in the mid- to upper-90s with the ability to touch several ticks above 100 mph at times. But the Mount Pleasant High School product is more than just a one-trick pony. His slider is a hellacious, knee-buckling bender that hovers in the 81- to 85-mph range. And his changeup is a solid third offering. The lone knock on Kopech has been his ability – or inability – to command the strike zone, though he may be able to ascend up to true ace-dom without average control/command.

Scouting Report: According to FanGraphs' Eric Longenhagen, Kopech's fastball – post op – was still sitting in the upper 90s and touching triple digits during his return to action in the Instruction League following the regular. Essentially, at this point, there's nothing new to report on skill wise. It's an elite arsenal, assuming it all comes back, that should push him up to bonafide ace status depending upon his feel for the strike zone with the floor of a Yordano Ventura.

Ceiling: 5.0-win player
Risk: Moderate to High
MLB ETA: Debuted in 2018

4. Nick Madrigal, 2B

	Hit	Power	SB	Patience	Glove	Overall
	70	40	60	50	50+	55

Born: 03/05/97	Age: 23	Bats: R
Height: 5-7	Weight: 165	Throws: R

YEAR	LVL	PA	1B	2B	3B	HR	SB	CS	AVG	OBP	SLG	BB%	K%	GB%	LD%	FB%
2018	RK	17	2	0	0	0	0	1	0.154	0.353	0.154	5.88%	0.00%	76.9	7.7	15.4
2018	A	49	12	3	0	0	2	2	0.341	0.347	0.409	2.04%	0.00%	53.2	21.3	19.1
2018	A+	107	26	4	0	0	6	3	0.306	0.355	0.347	4.67%	4.67%	58.5	18.1	16.0
2019	A+	218	38	10	2	2	17	4	0.272	0.346	0.377	7.80%	2.75%	47.6	16.9	29.6
2019	AA	180	42	11	2	1	14	6	0.341	0.400	0.451	7.78%	2.78%	47.2	24.5	20.1
2019	AAA	134	31	6	1	1	4	3	0.331	0.398	0.424	9.70%	3.73%	62.2	13.5	16.2

Background: It's not often that a 5-foot-7, 165-pound collegiate player will hear his name in the opening picks of the June draft. But Madrigal isn't your typical player. A consistent – often times dominating – bat during his three-year career with the Oregon State Beavers, Madrigal left the collegiate powerhouse with a career .361/.422/.502 triple-slash line, belting out 40 doubles, 11 triples, eight homeruns, and 39 stolen bases. Chicago made the middle infielder the fourth overall pick two years ago, sandwiching him between another pair of dominating collegiate bats (Wichita State's Alec Bohm and Florida's Jonathan India). Madrigal continued to impress as he vaulted through three different levels during his professional debut, batting a collective .303/.353/.348 with seven doubles in 43 total games. And last season – once again – the 5-foot-7, 165-pound second baseman skipped his way through three levels, going from High Class A up to the Southern League before settling in nicely in Class AAA. In 120 total games, Madrigal hit .311/.377/.414 with 27 doubles, five triples, four homeruns, and 35 stolen bases (in 48 attempts).

Snippet from The 2018 Prospect Digest Handbook: To put it frankly: if Madrigal was two or three inches taller, he would have likely been a first or second round pick coming out of high school. But his offensive firepower continues to prove any – and all – doubters wrong. The kid's a stud. Beyond his diminutive stature, the lone knocks on him are an average-ish eye at the plate and the fact that he's likely relegated to the right side of the infield. But make no mistake about it: if I'm picking first, Madrigal would easily be my pick.

Scouting Report: An on-base machine who possesses the type of speed to wreak havoc on the base paths. Madrigal remains one of my favorite prospects in the game, a player easy to root for. The former Oregon State star is a throwback to yesteryear: he struck out just 16 times in 532 plate appearances last season – or exactly 3.0% of the time. Somewhere, I figure, Joe DiMaggio is smiling. Madrigal owns one of the best – if not *the best* – hit tool in the all the minor leagues. It's a genuine plus-plus tool with the likelihood of competing for several batting titles before the end of his career. He doesn't show a ton of over-the-fence pop, but uses the entire field effectively, shooting the ball from gap to gap. Above-average or better speed. Slightly better than average glove. He looks like a Whit Merrifield clone.

Ceiling: 3.5-win player
Risk: Low to Moderate
MLB ETA: 2020

5. Blake Rutherford, OF

Hit	Power	SB	Patience	Glove	Overall
45	40	40	50	50	45

Born: 05/02/97	Age: 23	Bats: L
Height: 6-2	Weight: 210	Throws: R

YEAR	LVL	PA	1B	2B	3B	HR	SB	CS	AVG	OBP	SLG	BB%	K%	GB%	LD%	FB%
2017	A	304	53	20	2	2	9	4	0.281	0.342	0.391	8.22%	18.09%	52.3	21.2	23.0
2017	A	136	21	5	0	0	1	0	0.213	0.289	0.254	9.56%	15.44%	52.9	15.7	22.5
2018	A+	487	90	25	9	7	15	8	0.293	0.345	0.436	6.98%	18.48%	55.0	19.7	21.9
2019	AA	480	89	17	3	7	9	2	0.265	0.319	0.365	7.71%	24.58%	49.8	19.6	27.1

Background: Taken between a couple of power arms in the opening round of the 2016 draft. Rutherford, who was sandwiched by Forrest Whitley and former Boston College star Justin Dunn, was the 18th overall pick. Out of Chaminade College Preparatory School in West Hills, California, the lefty-swinging outfielder was acquired from the Yankees near the trade deadline three years ago in the deal that sent Todd Frazier, David Robertson, and Tommy Kahnle to New York. Rutherford, who was coming off of a quietly solid performance in the Carolina League, spent the entirety of 2019 in the Southern League. In a career-best 118 games with the Barons, the 6-foot-2, 210-pound outfielder batted .265/.319/.365 with 17 doubles, three triples, and seven homeruns. He also swiped nine bags in 11 total attempts. Per Baseball Prospectus' *Deserved Runs Created Plus*, his overall production was 5% *below* the league average mark. Rutherford spent time with Glendale in the Arizona Fall League, hitting a lowly .179/.281/.385.

Snippet from The 2018 Prospect Digest Handbook: There's enough here to be a batting average-driven starter, though he could very easily settle in as a fourth outfielder.

Scouting Report: The overall numbers are pretty mediocre. But Rutherford's batting average-driven, slashing approach at the plate shined brightly after a terrible start to the year. After hitting a lowly.160/.212/.255 over his first 29 games, the former first rounder slugged a healthy .298/.351/.401 with 15 doubles, a pair of triples, and five homeruns over his final 89 games. And just prorating those numbers over a full 162-game schedule: 27 doubles, four triples, and nine homeruns. Rutherford remains a bit of an underrated prospect. There's a chance for a 55-hit tool, with 8 to 10 homeruns, and 15 stolen bases. In terms of ceiling, think Adam Eaton's stat line from 2019: .279/.365/.428.

Ceiling: 1.5- to 2.0-win player
Risk: Moderate
MLB ETA: 2020

6. Jonathan Stiever, RHP

FB	CB	SL	CH	Command	Overall
60	60	55	50	55+	45

Born: 05/12/97	Age: 23	Bats: R
Height: 6-2	Weight: 205	Throws: R

YEAR	LVL	IP	W	L	SV	ERA	FIP	WHIP	K/9	K%	BB/9	BB%	K/BB	HR9	BABIP
2018	Rk	28.0	0	1	0	4.18	4.21	1.14	12.5	33.62%	2.9	7.76%	4.33	0.96	0.323
2019	A	74.0	4	6	0	4.74	3.84	1.38	9.4	24.06%	1.7	4.38%	5.50	1.22	0.361
2019	A+	71.0	6	4	0	2.15	3.12	0.97	9.8	28.00%	1.6	4.73%	5.92	0.89	0.278

Background: Indiana University has churned out an impressive list of hitters throughout the years, like: Kyle Schwarber, Sam Travis, Micah Johnson, Alex Dickerson, Kevin Orie, and Mickey Morandini. But the Big10 school hasn't burped out a ton of interesting arms. Jonathan Stiever, however, could change that perception. A fifth round pick two years ago, Stiever, who was the 138th overall player, turned in one of the more pleasant surprises in the White Sox's system last season. Beginning with a 14-game stint with the Kannapolis Intimidators, Stiever's punched out 77 and walked just 14 in 74.0 innings of work. The front office bumped the hard-throwing right-hander up to the Carolina League in late June for another 12 starts; he posted a 77-to-13 strikeout-to-walk ratio in 71.0 innings of work.

Scouting Report: A far better arsenal than I would have guessed given (A) his lack of strikeouts in college, (B) his feel for the strike zone, and (C) his relatively modest draft status. Stiever features four quality pitches: a plus fastball that he commands well and prefers to keep low; a 60-grade curveball; an above-average slider, and a decent changeup. His curveball is particularly interesting because the ferocity of spin. Mix in some pinpoint accuracy, and Stiever – the former fifth rounder – has developed into a legitimate pitching prospect. With respect to his work in High Class A, consider the following:

- Since 2006, here's the list of 22-year-old pitchers to post a strikeout rate between 27% and 29% with a 4% to 6% walk percentage in any of the three High Class A leagues (min. 60 IP): Leo Crawford, Harold Arauz, Jarod Plummer, Matt Frisbee, Adam Morgan, Eric Surkamp, and – of course – Jonathan Stiever.

Stiever has the potential to develop into a nice, innings-eater type backend starting pitcher with the floor of a solid 8th inning arm.

Ceiling: 1.5- to 2.0-win player
Risk: Moderate
MLB ETA: 2021

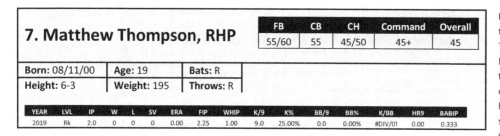

7. Matthew Thompson, RHP

FB	CB	CH	Command	Overall
55/60	55	45/50	45+	45

Born: 08/11/00	Age: 19	Bats: R
Height: 6-3	Weight: 195	Throws: R

YEAR	LVL	IP	W	L	SV	ERA	FIP	WHIP	K/9	K%	BB/9	BB%	K/BB	HR9	BABIP
2019	Rk	2.0	0	0	0	0.00	2.25	1.00	9.0	25.00%	0.0	0.00%	#DIV/0!	0.00	0.333

Background: Fun Fact: Prior to the Sox taking Matthew Thompson and Andrew Dalquist in the second and third rounds last June, the organization hadn't drafted a high school arm that early since 2014 when they selected Georgia prep right-hander Spencer Adams with the 44th overall pick. Thompson, a long-limbed, wiry right-hander, signed with the franchise for a hefty $2.1 million – roughly $500,000 above the recommended slot value. Thompson made two brief, single-inning appearances in the Arizona Summer League, fanning two without issuing a walk.

Scouting Report: Thompson's fastball sits in the low-90s; it's fairly straight, but it's likely to be a plus pitch as he fills out. His curveball is hard and tight, almost like a 12-to-6 breaking slider. And he'll mix in a below-average changeup that's a bit too raw, too firm. Thompson's raw, but has the potential to develop into a backend starting pitcher. He seems confident in his ability to spin the breaking ball.

Ceiling: 1.5- to 2.0-win player
Risk: Moderate
MLB ETA: 2023

8. Dane Dunning, RHP

FB	CB	SL	CH	Command	Overall
N/A	N/A	N/A	N/A	N/A	50

Born: 12/20/94	Age: 25	Bats: R
Height: 6-4	Weight: 200	Throws: R

YEAR	LVL	IP	W	L	SV	ERA	FIP	WHIP	K/9	K%	BB/9	BB%	K/BB	HR9	BABIP
2017	A	26.0	2	0	0	0.35	1.34	0.58	11.4	35.11%	0.7	2.13%	16.50	0.00	0.224
2017	A+	118.0	6	8	0	3.51	3.98	1.27	10.3	26.42%	2.7	7.05%	3.75	1.14	0.316
2018	A+	24.3	1	1	0	2.59	2.49	0.95	11.5	31.63%	1.1	3.06%	10.33	0.74	0.300
2018	AA	62.0	5	2	0	2.76	2.40	1.29	10.0	26.34%	3.3	8.78%	3.00	0.00	0.343

Background: Drafted with the 29th overall pick coming out of the University of Florida four years ago by the Nationals. Washington dealt the savvy right-hander to the Pale Hose as part of a four-player return for outfielder Adam Eaton in early December 2016. Dunning, who was acquired along with burgeoning ace Lucas Giolito and righty Reynaldo Lopez, was in the midst of playing himself into a September call-up two years ago. But a wonky elbow, which was originally diagnosed as a sprained ligament but eventually required Tommy John surgery, forced him to miss the second half of 2018 and all of 2019.

Snippet from The 2018 Prospect Digest Handbook: Dunning owns one of the more underrated fastballs in the minor leagues. Not because of sheer velocity – it sits in the low 90s and grades out as a 55 – but the late movement and action pushes it up into 60-grade territory. The University of Florida product complements the plus-pitch with two above-average secondary offerings – a high 70s slider (that looks more like a traditional curveball) and a fading, sinking changeup. Dunning is a strike thrower that has the makeup necessary to fill out a spot in the middle of the White Sox's rotation. Reports released in early October indicated Dunning resumed throwing – pain-free – so hopefully the elbow woes won't be an issue moving forward.

Scouting Report: The October 2018 reports indicating that Dunning was throwing pain-free proved to a be a false warning of sorts; the former Gator underwent Tommy John surgery, which was performed by Dr. James Andrews, near the end of Spring Training last season. The 6-foot-4, 200-pound right-hander is now entering his age-25 with just over 50 innings above High Class A. Assuming health isn't an issue moving forward, it wouldn't be surprising to see Dunning pop up in Chicago down the stretch for a couple short relief outings to get his feet wet in the big leagues.

Ceiling: 2.0-win player
Risk: Moderate to High
MLB ETA: 2020

9. Gavin Sheets, 1B

	Hit	Power	SB	Patience	Glove	Overall
	50	45	30	55	50	45

Born: 04/23/96	Age: 24	Bats: L	
Height: 6-4	Weight: 230	Throws: L	

YEAR	LVL	PA	1B	2B	3B	HR	SB	CS	AVG	OBP	SLG	BB%	K%	GB%	LD%	FB%
2017	RK	17	3	2	0	1	0	0	0.500	0.625	0.917	17.65%	0.00%	38.5	23.1	38.5
2017	A	218	38	10	0	3	0	0	0.266	0.346	0.365	9.17%	15.60%	41.9	17.5	33.1
2018	A+	497	92	28	2	6	1	0	0.293	0.368	0.407	10.46%	16.30%	45.4	20.8	30.5
2019	AA	527	89	18	1	16	3	1	0.267	0.345	0.414	10.25%	18.79%	42.7	19.8	28.3

Background: A consistent, smooth hitter in the middle of Wake Forest's lineup for the majority of his collegiate career, the Pale Hose selected the 6-foot-4, 230-pound first baseman in the second round, 49th overall, three years ago. The former Demon Deacon, who's father Larry slugged 31 homeruns for the Orioles in 1987, squared off against the most difficult minor league challenge last season, Class AA, and quietly succeeded. In 126 games with the Birmingham Barons, Sheets posted a solid .267/.345/.414 triple-slash line, belting out 18 doubles, one triple, and a career best 16 homeruns – an increase of 10 dingers from his previous season's output. Per *Deserved Runs Created Plus*, Sheets topped the league average threshold by 29%.

Snippet from The 2018 Prospect Digest Handbook: Sheets' ceiling as a solid, league average MLB bat is largely predicated upon his future power. And if he doesn't show some of that previous thump soon, he's likely going to head down the path as a Quad-A bat.

Scouting Report: Consider the following:

- Since 2006, only four 23-year-olds met the following criteria in the Southern League (min. 300 PA): 125 to 135 DRC+, double-digit walk rate, a sub-20% strikeout rate, and an ISO between .130 and .160. Those four players: Jonathan Lucroy, Chris Coghlan, Phil Ervin, and – of course – Phil Ervin.
- Sans Sheets, here are their respective career DRC+ totals at the big league level: 103 (Lucroy), 94 (Coghlan), and 95 (Ervin)

That level of production, while decent for up-the-middle and/or role players, hardly screams middle-of-the-lineup first baseman. Best case scenario: Mitch Moreland, who's been a league average-ish bat during his big league career.

Ceiling: 1.5-win player
Risk: Low to Moderate
MLB ETA: 2020

10. Bryan Ramos, 3B

	Hit	Power	SB	Patience	Glove	Overall
	45/50	45/55	30	50	50	50

Born: 03/12/02	Age: 18	Bats: R	Top CALs:
Height: 6-2	Weight: 190	Throws: R	

YEAR	LVL	PA	1B	2B	3B	HR	SB	CS	AVG	OBP	SLG	BB%	K%	GB%	LD%	FB%
2019	Rk	218	36	10	2	4	3	4	0.277	0.353	0.415	8.72%	20.18%	46.3	16.1	28.2

Background: The franchise has never been shy about signing Cuban players. Alexei Ramirez, a 2014 All-Star and two-time Silver Slugger Award winner; Dayan Viciedo, and – of course – the club's current top prospect, Luis Robert, immediately jump to mind. Enter: Bryan Ramos, a 6-foot-2, 190-pound teenager from La Habana. Signed for $300,000 on the international market in early July two years ago, the young third baseman made his debut in the Arizona Summer League last season, slugging a solid .277/.353/.415 with 10 doubles, a pair of triples, and four homeruns. He also swiped three bags in seven attempts. His overall production, according to *Deserved Runs Created Plus*, topped the league average mark by 19%.

Scouting Report: Consider the following:

- Since 2006, here's the list of 17-year-old hitters that owned a DRC+ between 115 to 125 in the Arizona Summer League (min. 175 PA): Fernando Tatis Jr., Martin Peguero, Gionti Turner, and Bryan Ramos.

Does. Not. Get. Cheated. The ideal goal for Ramos' swing would be controlled chaos, though there's still work to be done on the control side. But the bat speed; raw, muscular power, and natural loft all scream future above-average power. I really, really like the upside in Ramos. There's starting potential here, possibly more. He could be one of the bigger breakouts in the minor leagues in 2020.

Ceiling: 2.0-win player
Risk: High
MLB ETA: 2023

11. Luis Alexander Basabe, OF

Hit	Power	SB	Patience	Glove	Overall
45	50	55	55	50	45

Born: 08/26/96	Age: 23	Bats: B
Height: 6-0	Weight: 160	Throws: R

YEAR	LVL	PA	1B	2B	3B	HR	SB	CS	AVG	OBP	SLG	BB%	K%	GB%	LD%	FB%
2017	A+	435	61	12	5	5	17	6	0.221	0.320	0.320	11.26%	23.91%	43.8	21.4	29.0
2018	A+	245	29	12	5	9	7	8	0.266	0.370	0.502	13.88%	26.12%	42.5	17.8	37.0
2018	AA	270	40	9	3	6	9	4	0.251	0.340	0.394	11.11%	28.15%	36.4	25.9	30.2
2019	A	24	5	0	1	0	1	1	0.300	0.417	0.400	16.67%	29.17%	76.9	23.1	0.0
2019	AA	291	47	12	1	3	9	4	0.246	0.324	0.336	9.97%	29.21%	48.9	19.5	29.3

Background: The third of four notable prospects acquired in the Chris Sale mega-swap with the Red Sox a couple years ago. Basabe, a switch-hitting outfielder from El Vigia, Venezuela, flashed some five-tool potential during his breakout 2016 campaign in the South Atlantic League when he slugged .258/.325/.447 with 24 doubles, eight triples, 12 homeruns, and 25 stolen bases as a teenager. But Basabe's production cratered during his first stint in High Class A the following year as he batted a lowly .221/.320/.320 – taking with it some of the shine from his prospect status. Unsurprisingly, the 6-foot, 160-pound outfielder found in himself back in High Class A the following season, 2018, and this time he faired significantly better (.266/.370/.502). Basabe spent the second half of the year squaring off against the minors' toughest challenge, Class AA. The results were...OK. Last season, in an injury-shortened showing, Basabe appeared in 69 games with the Birmingham Barons, batting .246/.324/.336 with 12 doubles, one triple, three homeruns, and nine stolen bases. His overall production, per *Deserved Runs Created Plus*, was 8% *below* the league average threshold.

Snippet from The 2018 Prospect Digest Handbook: Basabe generates a ton of value through finding first base via the free pass and flashing decent pop. Basabe's swing-and-miss totals continued its troubling trend that first popped up in 2015. The Venezuela-born center fielder is a flawed prospect: he can run a bit, but doesn't do it efficiently in the outfield or on the base paths; he can knock a few out of the park, but whiffs too frequently. Basabe falls into the same category as Blake Rutherford – a tweener type outfielder who may carve out a career as a starter on a non-contending team.

Scouting Report: Consider the following:

- Since 2006, only a pair of 22-year-old hitters have posted a DRC+ between 87 and 92, with a 9% to 11% walk rate and a strikeout rate north of 28% in the Southern League (min. 250 PA): Trey Michaelczewski and Luis Alexander Basabe.

A few things: Basabe's a talented, albeit flawed, hitter with an impressive power/speed/patience combo. But (A) it's incredibly inconsistent and (B) and limited by his ability to make consistent contact. And last season's swing-and-miss rate, 29.2%, was the worst showing of his career. Simply put, he's a tantalizing enigma. Sometimes these guys put it all together, a lot of times they don't. I'm more inclined to go with the latter when it comes to Basabe. He profiles as a solid fourth outfielder.

Ceiling: 1.5-win player
Risk: Moderate
MLB ETA: 2020

12. Andrew Dalquist, RHP

	FB	CB	CH	Command	Overall
	55/60	55/60	55	45	45

Born: 11/13/00	Age: 19	Bats: R
Height: 6-1	Weight: 175	Throws: R

YEAR	LVL	IP	W	L	SV	ERA	FIP	WHIP	K/9	K%	BB/9	BB%	K/BB	HR9	BABIP
2019	Rk	3.0	0	0	0	0.00	4.92	1.33	6.0	15.38%	6.0	15.38%	1.00	0.00	0.222

Background: After taking right-hander Matthew Thompson in the second round last June, the front office doubled up on wiry prep arms when they picked Andrew Dalquist a round later. The organization went well above the recommended slot bonus of $750,000 and handed 6-foot-1, 175-pound hurler, who was taken with the 81st overall pick, a hefty $2 million signing bonus. The young hurler made just three brief appearances in the Arizona Summer League during his debut, throwing just a trio of innings with a pair of walks and strikeouts without surrendering a run.

Scouting Report: Watching Dalquist carve up his peers during his senior season at Union High School, it's easy to see why the front office went after the hard-throwing righty. Dalquist's fastball hovered in the 92- to 93-mph range with consistency, and it touched a high as 95-mph rather frequently. His curveball remains raw, flashing plus with hard tilt at times and then showing too much loop at other times. The changeup, which was thrown 81- to 83-mph, shows nice velocity separation and arm side fade. The control, like his curveball, is still raw. Dalquist has the makings of a #4/#5-type starting pitcher.

Ceiling: 1.5-win player
Risk: Moderate
MLB ETA: 2023

13. Yermin Mercedes, C

	Hit	Power	SB	Patience	Glove	Overall
	50	45+	30	50	50	40

Born: 02/14/93	Age: 27	Bats: R
Height: 5-11	Weight: 225	Throws: R

YEAR	LVL	PA	1B	2B	3B	HR	SB	CS	AVG	OBP	SLG	BB%	K%	GB%	LD%	FB%
2017	A+	378	60	17	0	15	4	3	0.274	0.341	0.458	8.73%	15.61%	29.8	21.6	36.9
2017	AA	46	9	3	0	1	1	0	0.295	0.326	0.432	4.35%	17.39%	38.9	16.7	30.6
2018	A+	410	65	24	1	14	4	0	0.289	0.362	0.478	9.76%	16.34%	38.6	19.8	31.2
2019	AA	167	35	7	0	6	2	0	0.327	0.389	0.497	10.18%	14.97%	34.4	23.2	32.0
2019	AAA	220	29	12	0	17	0	0	0.310	0.386	0.647	10.91%	19.09%	30.2	26.2	40.3

Background: At what point will Mercedes be considered a legitimate prospect? It wasn't after he topped the South Atlantic League's average production by a staggering 85% or when he bettered the High Class A league production line by 53% during his tremendous 2016 season. It wasn't when he was forced to repeat – for a second time – the High Class A level and posted a 151 DRC+ in 2018. His 42-game cameo in the Southern League didn't even register a blip on the radars when he slugged .327/.389/.497 at the start of 2019. And no one noticed his .310/.386/.647 triple-slash during in the second half of last season either. For his career, the 5-foot-11, 225-pound backstop owns a .302/.366/.491 slash line, belting out 130 doubles, 11 triples, and 83 homeruns in 617 games.

Scouting Report: Mercedes is now entering his age-27 season and, by default, very few would actually consider him a prospect at this point. So maybe the question isn't when will he be considered a legitimate prospect but, rather, when will he be given a shot at big league pitching? Solid eye, tremendous contact skills, a little bit of thump to his bat, and a solid glove behind the dish. Across the league MLB catchers batted a horrific .236/.308/.405 last season with an 8.4% walk rate and a 24.5% K-rate. Surely, without a doubt, Mercedes could easily match – and exceed – such low expectations.

Ceiling: 1.0- to 1.5-win player
Risk: Low to Moderate
MLB ETA: 2020

14. Zack Collins, C

	Hit	Power	SB	Patience	Glove	Overall
	40+	55	20	65	45	40+

Born: 02/06/95	Age: 25	Bats: L
Height: 6-3	Weight: 220	Throws: R

YEAR	LVL	PA	1B	2B	3B	HR	SB	CS	AVG	OBP	SLG	BB%	K%	GB%	LD%	FB%
2017	A+	426	38	18	3	17	0	2	0.223	0.365	0.443	17.84%	27.70%	38.3	17.4	40.0
2017	AA	45	4	2	0	2	0	0	0.235	0.422	0.471	24.44%	24.44%	30.4	13.0	43.5
2018	AA	531	58	24	1	15	5	0	0.234	0.382	0.404	19.02%	29.76%	33.5	24.5	35.7
2019	AAA	367	44	19	1	19	0	0	0.282	0.403	0.548	16.89%	26.70%	39.6	23.3	34.2

Background: Every so often the MLB draft drums up a generational type catcher. Last season it was Oregon State's Adley Rutschman. The year before that it was Georgia Tech's Joey Bart. Go back a few more seasons, to 2016, and Zack Collins was supposed to be that guy. A force to be reckoned with during his three-year tenure at Georgia Tech, the lefty-swinging backstop finished his collegiate career as a .320/.473/.604 hitter and was particularly dominant during his final two seasons. The White Sox selected him in the opening round, 10th overall, with visions of him quickly moving through the minor leagues – in convincing fashion. After a strong debut in the Carolina League, Collins' hit tool was exposed as he returned back to High Class A in 2017. And it stagnated the following year in Class AA. Last season, though, feasting off of the "juiced" balls of the International League, the Florida native slugged .282/.403/.548 with 19 doubles, one triple, and 19 homeruns in only 88 games with the Charlotte Knights. Per *Deserved Runs Created Plus*, his overall production topped the league average threshold by 34%. He also spent 27 games with the White Sox, hitting a lowly .186/.307/.349 with seven extra-base hits in 27 games.

Snippet from The 2018 Prospect Digest Handbook: A Three True Outcomes-type hitter who may end up moving away from behind the dish thanks to some questionable defense. The crux of Collins' production comes from his ability to work the count and take plenty of walks. His walk rate last season, 19.0%, was the third best mark among all minor league bats (min. 350 PA). Collins will likely face a bevy of infield shifts as well due to his inability to take the ball the other way. And not to pile on, but the lefty-swinging catcher looks hapless against fellow left-handers as well. Collins could find some work – and make plenty of dough – as a part-time catcher/first baseman against right-handed pitching.

Scouting Report: Consider the following:

- Since 2006, here's the list of 24-year-olds who posted a 130 to 140 DRC+ with a double-digit walk rate and a strikeout rate north of 25% in the International League (min. 300 PA): Travis Demeritte, who hit .225/.286/.343 during his respective last season, and Zack Collins.

So his strikeout rate improved a couple percentage points, but the fact remains that (A) the hit tool is, maybe, a 40+ and (B) he still can't hit southpaws (he batted .206/.310/.383 against them last season). Below average defense, a 45-grade arm. He's going to be a solid platoon bat behind the plate/designated hitter, perhaps even underrated at that point.

Ceiling: 1.0- to 1.5-win player
Risk: Low to Moderate
MLB ETA: Debuted in 2019

15. Luis Gonzalez, OF

	Hit	Power	SB	Patience	Glove	Overall
	45	45	50	50	50	40+

Born: 09/10/95	Age: 24	Bats: L
Height: 6-1	Weight: 195	Throws: L

YEAR	LVL	PA	1B	2B	3B	HR	SB	CS	AVG	OBP	SLG	BB%	K%	GB%	LD%	FB%
2017	A	277	38	13	4	2	2	3	0.245	0.356	0.361	13.72%	18.05%	40.9	19.4	33.3
2018	A	255	43	16	2	8	7	2	0.300	0.358	0.491	8.24%	22.35%	51.1	18.8	22.7
2018	A+	288	46	24	3	6	3	5	0.313	0.376	0.504	9.38%	15.97%	42.5	21.7	27.4
2019	AA	535	86	18	4	9	17	9	0.247	0.316	0.359	8.79%	16.64%	48.2	19.5	24.9

Background: Class AA has always been the "make it or break it" level for me. Pitchers arsenals are crispier and quality strikes, especially with secondary offerings, are bountiful. Hitters frequently punish "mistake" pitches and learn to layoff of breaking balls in the dirt. At least, the successful ones do. Enter: Luis Gonzalez, a third round pick out of the University of New Mexico three years ago. The 6-foot-1, 195-pound outfielder, who left college as a .356/.468/.564 career hitter, tore through the Low Class A and High Class A pitching in 2018 as he slugged a hearty .307/.368/.498 with a whopping 40 doubles, five triples, and 14 homeruns. He also swiped 14 bags as well. And then...Class AA came calling. The then-23-year-old spent the entirety of 2019 squaring off against the Southern League. And the results were...mediocre, at best. In a career best 126 games with the Barons, Gonzalez batted .247/.316/.359 with 18 doubles, four triples, nine homeruns, and 17 stolen bases. Per *Deserved Runs Created Plus*, his overall production bested the league average mark by 3%.

Snippet from The 2018 Prospect Digest Handbook: There may be some low-end starting caliber potential brewing here, though he needs to prove that he can handle the rigors of Class AA first.

Scouting Report: A brief summary of Gonzalez's showing in Class AA in 2019: the BABIP normalized and power evaporated. And now he enters his age-24 season with an average toolkit fresh off of a disappointing showing in the Southern League. Consider the following:

- Since 2006, only four 23-year-olds have met the following criteria in the Southern League (min. 300 PA): 98 to 108 DRC+, sub-20% strikeout rate, a walk rate between 8% and 10%, and an Isolated Power below .140. Those four hitters: Luke Maile, Cory Harrilchak, Tyler Kuhn, and Luis Gonzalez.

It's not a ringing endorsement, is it? There is a bit of a silver lining: Gonzalez batted a respectable .285/.369/.423 over his final 34 games. The former New Mexico slugger looks like the typical fourth/fifth outfielder.

Ceiling: 1.0- to 1.5-win player
Risk: Moderate
MLB ETA: 2020

16. Konnor Pilkington, LHP

FB	CB	CH	Command	Overall
50	50	55	45+	40

Born: 09/12/97	Age: 22	Bats: L
Height: 6-3	Weight: 225	Throws: L

YEAR	LVL	IP	W	L	SV	ERA	FIP	WHIP	K/9	K%	BB/9	BB%	K/BB	HR9	BABIP
2018	Rk	12.0	0	1	0	5.25	4.90	1.50	6.8	16.98%	3.0	7.55%	2.25	0.75	0.333
2018	Rk	2.0	0	0	0	18.00	5.07	4.00	9.0	13.33%	4.5	6.67%	2.00	0.00	0.636
2019	A	33.3	1	0	0	1.62	3.08	0.78	11.3	32.56%	3.0	8.53%	3.82	0.54	0.186
2019	A+	95.7	4	9	0	4.99	3.60	1.44	9.0	23.19%	3.7	9.42%	2.46	0.66	0.341

Background: A hefty, thick-bodied left-hander out of Mississippi State University, Pilkington's collegiate ERA got progressively worse as his peripherals improved in each of his seasons. Taken with the third pick in the third round two years ago, the 6-foot-3, 225-pound left-hander ripped through the Sally early in 2019 before settling in for 19 starts with the Winston-Salem Dash. In 19 starts with the club's Carolina League affiliate, Pilkington, a native of Mississippi, tossed 95.2 innings with 96 strikeouts and 39 walks. He finished his stint in High Class A with a 4.99 ERA and a 5.69 DRA (*Deserved Run Average*).

Snippet from The 2018 Prospect Digest Handbook: A sturdy, well-built left-hander who will need to watch a soft-midriff, Pilkington's been as consistent as they come throughout his tenure for Mississippi State. He looks like a competent backend starting pitcher.

Scouting Report: Sort of your run-of-the-mill left-hander at this point in his career. Pilkington's sporting two average offerings, a low 90s fastball and a 12-6 curveball, with a 55-grade changeup, easily his go-to pitch. The former Bulldog's control/command has backed up since entering the Sox's organization, pushing his ceiling from a backend starter down to an up-and-down arm.

Ceiling: 1.0- to 1.5-win player
Risk: Moderate
MLB ETA: 2021

17. Jose Rodriguez, 2B/SS

Hit	Power	SB	Patience	Glove	Overall
45	50/55	40	40	50/55	40

Born: 05/13/01	Age: 19	Bats: R
Height: 5-11	Weight: 175	Throws: R

YEAR	LVL	PA	1B	2B	3B	HR	SB	CS	AVG	OBP	SLG	BB%	K%	GB%	LD%	FB%
2018	RK	240	48	13	3	2	16	4	0.291	0.318	0.401	3.75%	12.08%	47.8	21.4	23.4
2019	Rk	200	36	7	3	9	7	1	0.293	0.328	0.505	4.50%	22.50%	37.9	17.2	33.1

Background: Signed in the middle of February two years ago out of Valverde, Dominican Republic, Rodriguez debuted in the foreign rookie league a few months later. The 5-foot-11, 175-pound middle infielder batted a respectable .291/.318/.401 with 13 doubles, three triples, and a pair of homeruns. The young Dominican moved stateside last season and the production largely remained unchanged – except for a massive surge in power. In 44 games with the club's Arizona Summer League affiliate, Rodriguez slugged .293/.328/.505 with seven doubles, three triples, and nine homeruns. He also swiped seven bags in eight attempts. According to Baseball Prospectus' *Deserved Runs Created Plus*, his overall production topped the league average threshold by 7%.

Scouting Report: Consider the following:

- Since 2006, only three 18-year-old hitters posted a DRC+ between 102 and 112 with an Isolated Power of at least .180 in the Arizona Summer League (min. 175 PA): Matt Olson, who owns a career 126 DRC+ at the big league level; Lazaro Armenteros, a huge international free agent signed by the A's a couple years ago; and – of course – Joe Rodriguez.
- And it should be noted that the former two walked nearly twice as often as Rodriguez.

Rodriguez's unwillingness to walk mitigates some of his overall production, despite flashing some impressive power potential at an up-the-middle position. His ability to make consistent contact may be an issue as he moves up the ladder, so that bears watching. A potential 55-grade glove at either position.

Ceiling: 1.0- to 1.5-win player
Risk: Moderate
MLB ETA: 2023

18. Micker Adolfo, RF

Hit	Power	SB	Patience	Glove	Overall
45	55	30	55	50	40

Born: 09/11/96	Age: 23	Bats: R
Height: 6-4	Weight: 255	Throws: R

YEAR	LVL	PA	1B	2B	3B	HR	SB	CS	AVG	OBP	SLG	BB%	K%	GB%	LD%	FB%
2017	A	473	66	28	2	16	2	0	0.264	0.331	0.453	6.55%	31.50%	41.1	18.6	32.5
2018	A+	336	52	18	1	11	2	1	0.282	0.369	0.464	10.12%	27.38%	46.5	22.8	25.7
2019	Rk	58	6	5	0	2	0	0	0.260	0.362	0.480	12.07%	36.21%	41.4	27.6	24.1
2019	AA	95	9	7	0	0	0	3	0.205	0.337	0.295	14.74%	37.89%	25.6	32.6	34.9

Background: At the time of his signing, July 2nd, 2013, the White Sox handed the then-16-year-old prospect a hefty $1.6 million, a franchise record for an international free agent at that time. So how has the investment paid off? Well, he bottomed out early, showed some positive signs of a solid future, and then promptly missed all but 36 games in 2019. The cause of injury: arthroscopic surgery on his throwing elbow, which was, according to reports, needed to clean up some potential scar tissue. Before hitting the disabled list, Adolfo batted a terribly disappointing – although, likely effected by injury – .227/.346/.367 between the Southern and Arizona Summer Leagues. The Dominican outfielder did appear in 15 games with the Glendale Desert Dogs in the Arizona Fall League, hitting a lowly .167/.262/.389 with four homeruns.

Snippet from The 2018 Prospect Digest Handbook: Just when things had moved from a slow simmer to a boiling point Adolfo hit the DL for a lengthy stay. There are still several areas that remain problematic for the upward trending prospect – like his contact rates – but he's come a *long* way since his horrific debut. Adolfo showed a new found patience at the plate as his walk rate morphed from below-average to above-average. He still hasn't fully tapped into his pure raw power, but it's a 55-grade tool now. A couple years ago Adolfo was – more or less – written off as a bust. Now, though, he has a shot to be a solid low end starting outfielder.

Scouting Report: After showing some progress in his problematic swing-and-miss rates in 2018, Adolfo fanned in nearly 38% of his Class AA plate appearances last season. Again, it could be injury related. Except when he popped back up in the rookie leagues on his rehab appearances he whiffed 36.2% of the time – which was promptly followed up by 27 strikeouts in 61 plate appearances during the fall. Ouch. Adolfo's entering his age-23 season, so a return to his 2018 form is pertinent.

Ceiling: 1.0- to 1.5-win player
Risk: Moderate to High
MLB ETA: 2021/2022

19. Jake Burger, 3B

Hit	Power	SB	Patience	Glove	Overall
N/A	N/A	N/A	N/A	N/A	40

Born: 04/10/96	Age: 24	Bats: R
Height: 6-2	Weight: 210	Throws: R

YEAR	LVL	PA	1B	2B	3B	HR	SB	CS	AVG	OBP	SLG	BB%	K%	GB%	LD%	FB%
2017	RK	17	0	1	0	1	0	0	0.154	0.353	0.462	5.88%	11.76%	45.5	9.1	36.4
2017	A	200	34	9	2	4	0	1	0.271	0.335	0.409	6.50%	14.00%	51.3	16.2	24.0

Background: After a dynamic career at Missouri State University, Burger positioned himself as one of the premier – if not *the* premier – collegiate power bat available in the 2017 draft. The 6-foot-2, 210-pound third baseman slugged a scorching .349/.420/.689 with 21 dingers as a sophomore and he remained impressively consistent during his junior campaign by batting .328/.443/.648 with 22 bombs. The prolific power convinced the Sox to use the 11th overall pick on Burger three years ago. And, well, things haven't gone as planned. After a sold initial showing in the South Atlantic League – he hit .271/.335/.409 in 47 games – Burger hasn't appeared in a meaningful game since. He missed the all of 2018 and 2019 with a combination of two left Achilles tears and a severely bruised left heel.

Scouting Report: There's really nothing new to report on. It's just an incredibly unlucky string of shit luck. Here's what I wrote about Burge heading into the 2017 draft:

"Again, the prolific collegiate power hitter in this year's draft class. Burger has not one, but two seasons in which he's reached the 20-homer mark – the only hitter to accomplish that feat since 2011. In fact, here's some more contextual evidence to support Burger's dominance throughout his amateur career:

- *Since 2011, there are only 61 instances in which a slugger – at any level – batted at least .340/.400/.675 in a season (minimum 240 plate appearances).*
- *Continuing with the aforementioned factoid, only four hitters have accomplished that twice in their respective careers: Adam Giacalone, Dylan Johnson, Kyle Lewis, D.J. Peterson.*
- *Of those aforementioned four, only Kyle Lewis and D.J. Peterson played at the Division I level. Burger, of course, would be the third. Keeping with the original production levels (.340/.400/.675), only six of those hitters have slugged 20 homeruns in their respective seasons: Casey Allison, Miguel Beltran, Jake Burger (twice, potentially), Nick Feight, Jake Lowery, Heath Quinn. Again, extending the constraints a little more, no player has accomplished that with a walk rate north of 15.0%. If the season ended at the time of this writing, Burger would eclipse that mark.*

There's really nothing to not like about Burger: above-average to plus power, a premium defensive position, and impressive plate discipline. Depending upon his defensive ratings, Burger has the potential to be an All-Star."

Ceiling: 1.0- to 1.5-win player
Risk: High
MLB ETA: 2022

20. Jimmy Lambert, RHP

	FB	CB	SL	CH	Command	Overall
	N/A	N/A	N/A	N/A	N/A	40

Born: 11/18/94	Age: 25	Bats: R
Height: 6-2	Weight: 190	Throws: R

YEAR	LVL	IP	W	L	SV	ERA	FIP	WHIP	K/9	K%	BB/9	BB%	K/BB	HR9	BABIP
2017	A	74.0	7	2	0	2.19	3.15	1.19	5.2	14.33%	1.3	3.67%	3.91	0.12	0.315
2017	A+	76.0	5	4	0	5.45	4.77	1.51	7.0	17.72%	3.4	8.71%	2.03	1.18	0.326
2018	A+	70.7	5	7	0	3.95	2.99	1.10	10.2	27.97%	2.7	7.34%	3.81	0.64	0.292
2018	AA	25.0	3	1	0	2.88	2.72	1.04	10.8	29.70%	2.2	5.94%	5.00	0.72	0.286
2019	AA	59.3	3	4	0	4.55	4.71	1.50	10.6	27.03%	4.1	10.42%	2.59	1.67	0.338

Background: The franchise has been struck by a string of Tommy John surgeries over the past couple of seasons: Carlos Rondon, Michael Kopech, Dane Dunning, Ryan Burr, Zack Burdi, and – unfortunately – Jimmy Lambert's name was added to the list during the middle of 2019. A fifth round pick of California State University four years ago, Lambert was in the midst of a solid showing in the Southern League before his elbow flared up. He posted a 70-to-27 strikeout-to-walk ratio in 59.1 innings of work with a 4.55 ERA and a 5.57 DRA (*Deserved Run Average*).

Snippet from The 2018 Prospect Digest Handbook: Lambert's no run-of-the-mill organizational arm. The slight-framed right-hander features a solid four-pitch arsenal fronted by three above-average or better offerings. The 6-foot-2, 170-pound hurler throws a heavy 94 mph four-seam fastball (he's ditched his two-seamer) to go along with a big 12-6 curveball and a promising slider. He'll also throw a decent little changeup. There's enough promise here to bloom into a nice little backend starting pitching prospect – one that could, potentially, peak as a #4-type arm in the next year or two (assuming health isn't an issue).

Scouting Report: The Sox's rotation – barring a continuation of elbow injuries – is deep and, potentially, as talented as any in baseball. Lucas Giolito, Dallas Keuchel, Dylan Cease, Gio Gonzalez, and Renaldo Lopez look to hold down the top five until Michael Kopech and Carlos Rodon work their way back. So what does that mean for Lambert, a minor league strikeout artist with some fringy control/command? He's likely going to be converted into a relief option after his return to action.

Ceiling: 1.0-win player
Risk: Moderate to High
MLB ETA: 2020

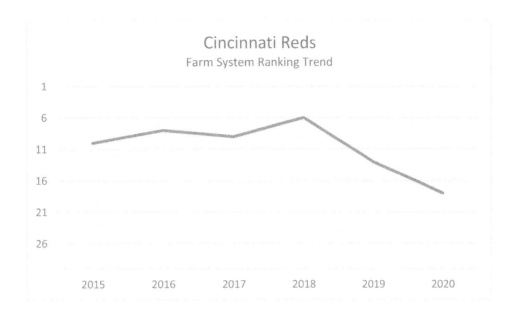

Rank	Name	Age	Pos
1	Hunter Greene	21	RHP
2	Nick Lodolo	22	LHP
3	Jose Garcia	22	SS
4	Jonathan India	23	3B
5	Michael Siani	20	CF
6	Tyler Stephenson	23	C
7	Tony Santillan	23	RHP
8	Lyon Richardson	20	RHP
9	Rece Hinds	21	3B
10	Vladimir Gutierrez	24	RHP
11	Tyler Callihan	20	2B/3B
12	Stuart Fairchild	24	OF
13	TJ Friedl	24	OF
14	Jameson Hannah	22	OF
15	Ivan Johnson	21	SS
16	Lorenzo Cedrola	22	CF
17	Hendrik Clementina	23	C
18	Reiver Sanmartin	24	LHP
19	Ibandel Isabel	25	1B/OF
20	Jacob Heatherly	21	LHP

1. Hunter Greene, RHP

	FB	CB	SL	CH	Command	Overall
	N/A	N/A	N/A	N/A	N/A	60

Born: 08/06/99	Age: 20	Bats: R	Top CALs:
Height: 6-4	Weight: 215	Throws: R	

YEAR	LVL	IP	W	L	SV	ERA	FIP	WHIP	K/9	K%	BB/9	BB%	K/BB	HR9	BABIP
2017	Rk	4.3	0	1	0	12.46	2.34	2.08	12.5	28.57%	2.1	4.76%	6.00	0.00	0.571
2018	A	68.3	3	7	0	4.48	3.29	1.30	11.7	30.27%	3.0	7.82%	3.87	0.79	0.353

Background: Arguably the most highly touted prep prospect since Bryce Harper. Greene, a 6-foot-4, 215-pound right-hander, donned the cover of *Sports Illustrated* in April 2017, becoming just the 13th prep athlete to do so and the first since Chicago hoops star Jabari Parker accomplished the feat in 2012. A product of Notre Dame High School, Greene, who flirted with a potential two-way gig during his professional debut in the Pioneer League, hit the disabled list with elbow woes prior to the kickoff of the 2019 season. And he eventually succumbed to Tommy John surgery in early April. According to reports, Greene is scheduled to begin a throwing program in the middle of January. And his return to full-season action won't – likely – happen until mid-year.

Snippet from The 2018 Prospect Digest Handbook: If there's such a thing as an "easy 100 mph" Greene's name certainly belongs on the short list. Blessed with a lightning-quick arm that allows his fastball to comfortably – and easily – sit in the 97- to 99-mph range with a peak at 102, Greene's polish differentiates himself from all other hard-throwers. He's only entering his age-19 season, but he has an idea on how to pitch, showing poise and guile already. His curveball, a sharp overhand offering, is above-average with flashes of more on occasion. His slider's usable and hovers around 89- to 90-mph. And his changeup has the makings of an above-average offering. Like Strasburg, Greene's one of the rare pitching prospects that has a chance to achieve true ace-dom, as long as he can work his way through the injury nexus.

Scouting Report: The Cincinnati Reds made one of the most important acquisitions on the offseason market – a move that, potentially, changes the entire culture and pitching fortunes of the franchise. In early October the club announced that they hired Driveline Baseball founder Kyle Boddy, who will work primarily with the club's minor league arms. I'm a *massive* believer in the Driveline's ability to (A) improve pitching performance through training, throwing regimens, and analytics; and (B) help pitcher's comeback from serious injuries. Royals long time top prospect, who was snake-bitten *for years*, returned to form with the help of Driveline. This is going to be a massive windfall for the organization. And will only improve the odds of all pitchers, not just Greene, to exceed expectations.

Ceiling: 5.0-win player
Risk: Moderate to High
MLB ETA: 2022

2. Nick Lodolo, LHP

	FB	SL	CH	Command	Overall
	60	55/60	55/60	55/60	60

Born: 02/05/98	Age: 22	Bats: L	Top CALs:
Height: 6-6	Weight: 202	Throws: L	

YEAR	LVL	IP	W	L	SV	ERA	FIP	WHIP	K/9	K%	BB/9	BB%	K/BB	HR9	BABIP
2019	Rk	11.3	0	1	0	2.38	1.46	1.06	16.7	45.65%	0.0	0.00%	N/A	0.79	0.458
2019	A	7.0	0	0	0	2.57	1.29	0.86	11.6	32.14%	0.0	0.00%	N/A	0.00	0.333

Background: A projectable, lanky left-hander coming out of Damien High School, the Pirates snagged the 6-foot-6, 202-pound hurler in the opening round of the 2016 draft. Sandwiched between top prospect Joey Wentz and snake-bitten Phillies right-hander Kevin Gowdy, Pittsburgh took a calculated gamble on the California native, knowing that he'd be a tough sign. He didn't. Three years later Lodolo positioned himself as one of the top arms amateur available in the 2019 draft class. The big lefty transitioned to the collegiate level with a surprising amount of ease: he made 17 appearances for the Horned Frogs, 15 of which were starts, as a true freshman, throwing 78.2 innings to go along with 72 strikeouts and just 28 free passes. Following his wildly successful campaign, Lodolo earned a bevy of awards including:

- Freshman All-American (Collegiate Baseball)
- Second-Team Freshman All-American (Baseball America)
- Second-Team All-Big 12 Conference
- Big 12 Academic All-Rookie Team
- Big 12 All-Freshman Team

Lodolo's production crept forward during his sophomore season for Head Coach Jim Schlossnagle: in 15 starts and one relief appearance, the big southpaw hurled 77.0 innings while fanning 93 and walking only 28. Last season Lodolo maintained his impressive ability to miss bats – he averaged 11.4 strikeouts per nine innings – while drastically improving his control; he walked a career best 2.2 per nine innings. Cincinnati snagged the young southpaw in the opening round, seventh overall, and set him loose on the low levels of the minor leagues. Lodolo made eight brief appearances between Billings and Dayton, throwing 18.1 innings with 30 strikeouts and he didn't hand out a single free pass.

Scouting Report: Here's what I wrote about the dominating lefty prior to the draft last June:

"Long, gangly limbs that allows his low 90s fastball to sneak up on hitters. Lodolo's bread-and-butter offering is his wipeout slider, which is particularly lethal down-and-in to right-handed hitters. He also features an above-average changeup that might grow into a consistent plus-pitch. With respect to his production thus far in 2019, consider the following:

- *Between 2011 and 2018, only three Big 12 pitchers met the following criteria: at least 10 strikeouts per nine innings and a sub-2.00 walk rate with at least 70 innings. Those three pitchers: Jon Gray, the third overall pick in 2016; Andrew Heaney, the ninth overall pick in 2012; and Chad Donato, a sleeper in the Houston Astros system that was taken in the 11th round in 2016.*

One more thought:

- *Gray has been an above-average, sometimes dominant, starter in each of his first five big league seasons. And Heaney tallied near three wins above replacement (FanGraphs) in 2018.*

Lodolo looks like a potential #2/#3-type arm at his peak."

A few things to note: During his debut last season, Lodolo's fastball ticked up a bit as it hit – consistently – 95 mph; his slider was 80- to 82 mph; and his changeup was filthy. There's a nonzero chance he develops three plus pitches.

Ceiling: 4.0-win player
Risk: Moderate
MLB ETA: 2021/2022

3. Jose Garcia, SS

	Hit	Power	SB	Patience	Glove	Overall
	50	45/50	45	40+	50	55

Born: 04/05/98	Age: 22	Bats: R	Top CALs:
Height: 6-2	Weight: 175	Throws: R	

YEAR	LVL	PA	1B	2B	3B	HR	SB	CS	AVG	OBP	SLG	BB%	K%	GB%	LD%	FB%
2018	A+	15	1	0	0	0	1	0	0.071	0.133	0.071	6.67%	46.67%	71.4	0.0	28.6
2019	A+	452	67	37	1	8	15	2	0.280	0.343	0.436	5.53%	18.36%	46.1	18.3	28.8

Background: Described by Cincinnati.com as "one of the Reds' prized international free agents" when the club inked the Cuban star to a hefty $5 million deal during the summer of 2017. Garcia, who popped up briefly with the Industriales of the Cuban National Series as an 18-year-old, made his stateside debut with the Dayton Dragons two season ago; he batted a disappointing .245/.290/.344 with 22 doubles, four triples, and six homeruns with 13 stolen bases in 125 games. And despite some lackluster production, the front office pushed the young infielder up to High Class A. And Garcia, who stands 6-foot-2 and 175 pounds, raised his offensive game to new heights. In 104 games with the Daytona Tortugas, the La Habana native slugged .280/.343/.436 with 37 doubles, one triple, and eight homeruns while swiping 15 bags. Per *Deserved Runs Created Plus*, his overall production topped the league average mark by 43%.

Scouting Report: Consider the following:

- Since 2006, only four 21-year-old hitters met the following criteria in the Florida State League (min. 350 PA): 140 to 150 DRC+, a sub-20% strikeout rate, and a single-digit walk rate. Those four hitters: Adam Lind, Josh Bell (the Pirates first baseman), Daryl Jones, and Jose Garcia. Sans Garcia, here are their respective big league career DRC+ totals: Lind: 110; Bell: 112; Jones: N/A

Last season Garcia looked like a completely different, and *vastly* improved, hitter. He was driving the ball more authoritatively, with far more consistency. His was more patient, though it's still below average. And he improved his contact rate as well. And here's the kicker: after a slow start to the year – he batted just .238/.307/.388 over his first 36 games – Garcia slugged an impressive .304/.363/.463 over his remaining 68 games. Throw in some solid defense, and he looks like a potential above-average MLB shortstop, perhaps even a burgeoning star.

Ceiling: 3.5-win player
Risk: Moderate
MLB ETA: 2020

4. Jonathan India, 3B

Hit	Power	SB	Patience	Glove	Overall
50	45/50	40	60	50	50

Born: 12/15/96	Age: 23	Bats: R	Top CALs:
Height: 6-0	Weight: 200	Throws: R	

YEAR	LVL	PA	1B	2B	3B	HR	SB	CS	AVG	OBP	SLG	BB%	K%	GB%	LD%	FB%
2018	RK	10	2	0	0	0	0	1	0.250	0.400	0.250	0.00%	40.00%	0.0	50.0	25.0
2018	RK	62	6	2	1	3	1	0	0.261	0.452	0.543	24.19%	19.35%	47.1	23.5	23.5
2018	A	112	12	7	0	3	5	0	0.229	0.339	0.396	11.61%	25.00%	33.8	20.6	39.7
2019	A+	367	53	15	5	8	7	5	0.256	0.346	0.410	10.08%	22.89%	36.7	19.4	33.8
2019	AA	145	24	3	0	3	4	0	0.270	0.414	0.378	15.17%	17.93%	42.9	22.6	26.2

Background: With a pitching staff sporting a couple of bonafide collegiate aces like Brady Singer and Jackson Kowar, it was the University of Florida's young third baseman that heard his name called first in the opening round of the 2018 draft. India, the fifth overall pick that year, was a solid, sometimes spectacular offensive performer across his freshman and sophomore seasons with the Gators: he batted a solid .303/.367/.440 with 22 extra-base knocks in 2016 and followed that up with a .274/.354/.429 showing a year later. But it was his work during his junior campaign that sent the young third baseman rocketing up everyone's draft list. In a career best 68 games, the 6-foot, 200-pound infielder slugged a whopping .350/.497/.771 with 12 doubles, four triples, and 21 homeruns – more than double his entire career total up to that point. India made three brief stops during his pro debut as he hit a mediocre .240/.380/.433 with nine doubles, one triple, and six homeruns in 44 games. And despite only spending 27 games in Low Class A, the front office aggressively challenged the top prospect by sending him up to High Class A to start the 2019 season. India responded by batting .256/.346/.410 with 15 doubles, five triples, and eight homeruns in 87 games. He spent his final 34 contests in the Southern League, where he batted .270/.414/.378.

Snippet from The 2018 Prospect Digest Handbook: He's – by far – the top collegiate prospect in this year's draft class, a potential All-Star especially if he slides back over to a middle infield position. I wouldn't rule out a switch to the keystone either.

Scouting Report: It was a roller coaster ride of a season for India. There were months were he looked every bit the top prospect – like in May when he hit .274/.391/.453 or in August as he slugged .289/.418/.434. There were other extended periods of mediocrity such as April (.247/.323/.416) or June (.247/.323/.412). And there were certainly low parts as well (he hit .228/.360/.266 in July). So here's what we know about the former Florida Gator: he plays with a definite saber-slant at the plate, walking in more than 12% of his career plate appearances; his power is fringy average at this point, despite very few groundballs; and he's an average-ish third baseman. While India's triple-slash lines in High Class A and Class AA don't exactly scream dominant hitter, his overall production – as measured by Baseball Prospectus' *Deserved Runs Created Plus* – topped the league average mark by 30% and 41%, respectively. And, of course, the overwhelming majority of his production is derived from his ability to sniff out first base. With respect to his work in High Class A last season, consider the following:

- Since 2006, here's the list of 22-year-old hitters to post a 125 to 135 DRC+ with a double-digit walk rate and a strikeout rate between 20% and 24% in the Florida State League (min. 300 PA): Jason Donald, Jhoan Urena, Stefan Welch and – of course – Jonathan India.

A year-plus into his professional career and it doesn't look like India's destined to be a star. Rather, he looks like a hitter with the offensive ceiling similar to Johan Camargo circa 2018 when he batted .272/.349/.457 with 19 homeruns.

Ceiling: 3.0-win player
Risk: Low to Moderate
MLB ETA: 2020

5. Michael Siani, CF

Hit	Power	SB	Patience	Glove	Overall
45/50	40/45	70	50	80	55

Born: 07/16/99	Age: 20	Bats: L	Top CALs:
Height: 6-1	Weight: 188	Throws: L	

YEAR	LVL	PA	1B	2B	3B	HR	SB	CS	AVG	OBP	SLG	BB%	K%	GB%	LD%	FB%
2019	A	531	96	10	6	6	45	15	0.253	0.333	0.339	8.66%	20.53%	52.9	12.9	25.8

Background: Cincinnati went well above the recommended slot bonus to sign the former Philadelphia prep star. To be exact: the front office nearly quadrupled the recommended slot bonus when they handed him $2 million when they selected him in the fourth round, 109th overall, two years ago. A product of William Penn Charter School, Siani turned in a solid debut showing in the Appalachian League when he batted .288/.351/.386 with six doubles, three triples, a pair of homeruns, and half-a-dozen stolen bases. The front office pushed the then-19-year-old outfielder up to Dayton. And the results were...mediocre. In 121 games with the Dayton Dragons, the 6-foot-1, 188-pound table setter batted .253/.333/.339 with 10 doubles, six triples, and six homeruns. His overall production, according to Baseball Prospectus' *Deserved Runs Created Plus*, was 4% *below* the league average threshold.

Snippet from The 2018 Prospect Digest Handbook: Siani acquitted himself nicely during his first taste of pro ball, showing a well-rounded offensive game with the potential to have an above-average hit tool and speed to go along with decent power. Yes, it was a short same size but Siani was out-of-the-universe good in center field, posting a +11 in runs saved. He's poised to be one of the bigger breakouts in 2019.

Scouting Report: So he wasn't one of the bigger breakouts in 2019. In fact, he quite the opposite. Consider the following:

- Since 2006, only five 19-year-old hitters met the following criteria in the Midwest League (min. 350 PA): a DRC+ total between 90 and 100; a strikeout rate between 18% and 22%; and a walk rate between 7% and 10%. Those five hitters: Josh Van Meter, Matt Tuiasosopo, Juniel Querecuto, Jack Suwinski, and – of course – Michael Siani.

So this is the basics of it: Michael Siani, who's younger brother Sami was taken in the opening round by the Pirates last June, is – arguably – the best defensive player not yet at the big league level. He's otherworldly, blessed with the talents of Willie Mays' famous "where triples go to die" adage. He's so damn good, in fact, that he could hit .220 and still carve out a starting gig in center field for a championship contending big league team. According to Baseball Prospectus' Fielding Runs Above Average, he was a +24. Clay Davenport's metrics show him even better, at +26. To put that into some contact: Harrison Bader, arguably the best defensive center fielder in MLB, posted a +14 FRAA and a +4 according to Davenport. Siani shows plus- to plus-plus speed, solid peripherals, and projects to be a 10/50 guy (homeruns/stolen bases).

Ceiling: 3.0- to 3.5-win player
Risk: Moderate
MLB ETA: 2022

6. Tyler Stephenson, C

	Hit	Power	SB	Patience	Glove	Overall
	50	50	20	55	40	50

Born: 08/16/96	Age: 23	Bats: R	Top CALs:
Height: 6-4	Weight: 225	Throws: R	

YEAR	LVL	PA	1B	2B	3B	HR	SB	CS	AVG	OBP	SLG	BB%	K%	GB%	LD%	FB%
2017	A	348	54	22	0	6	2	1	0.278	0.374	0.414	12.64%	16.67%	49.2	19.0	28.9
2018	A+	450	65	20	1	11	1	0	0.250	0.338	0.392	10.00%	21.78%	37.4	20.9	35.0
2019	AA	363	63	19	1	6	0	0	0.285	0.372	0.410	10.19%	16.53%	37.5	21.9	37.5

Background: The first backstop off the board in the 2015 draft, Stephenson, who was taken between Cornelius Randolph and Josh Naylor with the 11th overall pick, continues to be one of the most underrated catching prospects in the minor leagues. A product of Kennesaw Mountain High School in Kennesaw, Georgia, Stephenson continues to battle injuries over his young career – he's only topped the 100-game threshold once in five years – but has maintained an above-average production line at the dish nonetheless. After batting .250/.338/.392 as a 21-year-old in High Class A, the 6-foot-4, 225-pound brick wall turned in – arguably – his finest professional season to date, *at the minors' most challenging level*. In 89 games with the Chattanooga Lookouts, Stephenson slashed .285/.372/.410 with 19 doubles, one triple, and six homeruns. His overall production, according to Baseball Prospectus' *Deserved Runs Created Plus*, topped the league average threshold by 28%. Cincinnati sent him to the Arizona Fall League. And he further cemented his status as a top catching prospect by batting .347/.418/.490 in 13 games with Glendale.

Snippet from The 2018 Prospect Digest Handbook: The defense is still quite terrible – among the worst for backstops. Above-average patience, solid contact skills, and the potential to blossom into a 20-homer threat.

Scouting Report: First, the offense. Consider the following:

- Since 2006, here's the list of 22-year-old hitters to post a 123 to 133 DRC+ total with a double-digit walk rate and a sub-20.0% strikeout rate in the Southern League (min. 350 PA): Russell Martin, Steve Moss, Josh Bell (the former Orioles and Dodgers prospect, not the current Pirates first baseman), and Tyler Stephenson.

Using FanGraphs' version of Wins Above Replacement, there were just 11 catchers that eclipsed the 2.0-win threshold last season. Beyond the notable guys like Gary Sanchez, J.T. Realmuto, and Roberto Perez; such luminaries like James McCann, Tyler Flowers, and Robinson Chirinos accomplished the feat. So, the question is quite simple: Can Tyler Stephenson, who easily passed the Class AA test as a 22-year-old at the most challenging position, establish himself as a league average starting catcher? Injuries notwithstanding, it's a resounding yes. Average offensive tools across the boards with a chance to see a bump in future power. Now the defense: it's bad. Baseball Prospectus had him tallying -11.8 FRAA. And Clay Davenport was in the same neighborhood (-11). To put that into context, there were 36 catchers that received at least 250 PA last season. Only three approached Stephenson's level of ineptitude: Welington Castillo, Elias Diaz, and Omar Narvaez.

Ceiling: 3.0-win player
Risk: Moderate
MLB ETA: 2020

7. Tony Santillan, RHP

	FB	SL	CH	Command	Overall
	70	60	50	40+	50

Born: 04/15/97	Age: 23	Bats: R	Top CALs:
Height: 6-3	Weight: 240	Throws: R	

YEAR	LVL	IP	W	L	SV	ERA	FIP	WHIP	K/9	K%	BB/9	BB%	K/BB	HR9	BABIP
2017	A	128.0	9	8	0	3.38	3.77	1.25	9.0	24.02%	3.9	10.51%	2.29	0.63	0.281
2018	A+	86.7	6	4	0	2.70	3.50	1.19	7.6	20.22%	2.3	6.09%	3.32	0.52	0.298
2018	AA	62.3	4	3	0	3.61	3.94	1.30	8.8	22.76%	2.3	5.97%	3.81	1.16	0.315
2019	AA	102.3	2	8	0	4.84	4.24	1.60	8.1	19.78%	4.7	11.61%	1.70	0.70	0.333

Background: Built out of the typical Texas-born power-pitching mold. Santillan, a hulking 6-foot-3, 240-pound native of Fort Worth, was added to the organization via the second round of the 2015 draft. And after years of subpar control/command trending in the right direction, the young fireballer put it all together during a breakout 2018 campaign. Splitting time between Daytona and Pensacola, Santillan tossed a career best 149.0 innings while racking up 134 strikeouts and handing out just 38 free passes to go along with a 3.08 ERA. That surge in production, placed firmly on the back of his newfound ability to throw strikes, made him a prime candidate for a 2019 call up heading into last season. Unfortunately, for the hefty righty he lost sight of the strike zone and a triceps injury curtailed his season after just 21 starts in the Southern League. In total, Santillan tossed 102.1 innings, averaging 8.1 strikeouts and 4.7 walks per nine innings. He compiled a 4.84 ERA and a 5.75 DRA (*Deserved Run Average*).

Snippet from The 2018 Prospect Digest Handbook: His third offering, a straight changeup, needs further refinement/development. His control is also below-average as well. As it stands, Santillan looks like a good #3 type arm in the coming years, though that could move up a notch or two if he sees some improvement in the changeup and/or control/command.

Scouting Report: Along with his questionable – or, at least, wavering – feel for the strike zone, Santillan's changeup continues to be a bit of a rough subject. However, with the addition to Driveline's Kyle Boddy as well as the club's new emphasis on pitcher/pitch development, I truly believe Santillan's changeup bumps up half-of-a-grade in the next year or so. His fastball's one of the better heaters among minor league starting pitchers. And his wipeout slider is still intact. He has the potential to become an above-average big league starting pitcher. And his work last season compares favorably to All-Star right-hander Chris Archer's stint in the Southern League:

NAME	LGE	YEAR	AGE	IP	DRA	K%	BB%
Tony Santillan	Southern	2019	22	102.3	5.75	19.78%	11.61%
Chris Archer	Southern	2011	22	134.3	5.74	19.28%	13.07%

Ceiling: 2.5-win player
Risk: Moderate
MLB ETA: 2020

8. Lyon Richardson, RHP

	FB	CB	SL	CH	Command	Overall
	60	50/55	55	50/55	50/55	50

Born: 01/18/00	Age: 20	Bats: R	Top CALs:
Height: 6-2	Weight: 192	Throws: R	

YEAR	LVL	IP	W	L	SV	ERA	FIP	WHIP	K/9	K%	BB/9	BB%	K/BB	HR9	BABIP
2018	Rk	29.0	0	5	0	7.14	5.54	1.83	7.4	17.27%	5.0	11.51%	1.50	0.93	0.362
2019	A	112.7	3	9	0	4.15	3.74	1.41	8.5	21.33%	2.6	6.64%	3.21	0.80	0.340

Background: After grabbing Florida Gator Jonathan India with the fifth overall selection two years ago, Cincinnati selected University of Florida commit Lyon Richardson 42 picks last in the second round. A well-built 6-foot-2, 195-pound righty, Richardson made 11 brief starts in the Appalachian League during his debut two years, throwing 29.0 innings with 24 strikeouts and 16 free passes to go along with an unsightly 7.14 ERA. Last season, despite the mediocre debut showing, the front office pushed the young fireballer up to Low Class A. And, well, Richardson offered up more than a few glimpses of dominance. In 26 starts with the Dayton Dragons, Richardson posted a 106-to-33 strikeout-to-walk ratio in 112.2 innings. He finished the year with a 4.15 ERA and a 5.70 DRA.

Snippet from The 2018 Prospect Digest Handbook: Richardson's still has plenty of untapped potential brewing in his right arm thanks to his lack of pitching experience; he was used primarily as a closer prior to his senior year in high school. Because of his aforementioned lack of experience he's rawer than the typical prep arm taken in the second round. He looks like a nice backend starter or dominant relief arm if his control/command doesn't come around.

Scouting Report: Consider the following:

- Since 2006, here's the list of 19-year-old pitchers to post a 20% to 22% strikeout percentage with a walk percentage between 5.5% and 7.5% in the Midwest League (min. 100 IP): J.C. Ramirez, Garrett Gould, Maximo Castillo, Andrew Jordan, and Lyon Richardson.

Richardson owns an impressive four-pitch mix: a low- to mid-90s fastball that was touching 95 mph regularly late in the year; an improved curveball showing better bite that flashed above-average; a tightly spun slider, and a quietly solid changeup. The Jensen Beach High School product really seemed to be emphasizing his changeup develop in the latter part of the year, often going to it as an "out pitch". At times it showed some promising fade and run. Richardson's control/command was far better than advertised in 2019. In fact, he only walked more than two hitters just twice last season. And in both instances, he handed out just three free passes in six-inning starts. He's poised to become one of the bigger breakout prospects in 2020.

Ceiling: 2.0- to 2.5-win player
Risk: Moderate
MLB ETA: 2022

9. Rece Hinds, SS

Hit	Power	SB	Patience	Glove	Overall
50	60	30	55	45+	50

Born: 09/05/00	Age: 19	Bats: R	Top CALs:
Height: 6-4	Weight: 215	Throws: R	

YEAR	LVL	PA	1B	2B	3B	HR	SB	CS	AVG	OBP	SLG	BB%	K%	GB%	LD%	FB%
2019	Rk+	10	0	0	0	0	0	0	0.000	0.200	0.000	20.00%	30.00%	60.0	0.0	40.0

Background: The front office took the "Go Big or Go Home" approach in the early parts of the draft last June. The organization signed first rounder Nick Lodolo to a recommended slot bonus worth slightly more than $5 million. They inked Rece Hinds, their second round pick, to an above-slot deal worth $1.797 million. And then they more than doubled the recommended bonus for third rounder Tyler Callihan. A product of IMG Academy – which churned out fellow 2019 picks Brennan Malone, the Arizona's first round pick; and Kendall Williams, Toronto's second round selection – Hinds was committed to attend Louisiana State University prior to signing with the club. He appeared in just three Appalachian League games, going 0-for-8 with three strikeouts and two walks.

Scouting Report: Big time plus power potential that helped him capture the Under Armour All-America homerun derby two years ago. Hinds has terrific size and some of the draft class's best pure bat speed. There's a lot rumblings that scouts are worried about his hit tool and whether he's going to make enough consistent contact. Make no mistake about it: he's a dead red hitter. But he didn't (A) show a propensity to chase offspeed pitches out of the zone and (B) when he was fooled on offspeed stuff battled enough to foul off plenty of offerings. He looks solid enough to remain at third, though his athleticism would allow him to slide into a corner outfielder position.

Ceiling: 2.0-win player
Risk: Moderate
MLB ETA: 2023

10. Vladimir Gutierrez, RHP

FB	CB	CH	Command	Overall
60	60	55	45	45

Born: 09/18/95	Age: 24	Bats: R	Top CALs:
Height: 6-0	Weight: 190	Throws: R	

YEAR	LVL	IP	W	L	SV	ERA	FIP	WHIP	K/9	K%	BB/9	BB%	K/BB	HR9	BABIP
2017	A+	103.0	7	8	0	4.46	3.44	1.23	8.2	21.66%	1.7	4.38%	4.95	0.87	0.320
2018	AA	147.0	9	10	0	4.35	4.09	1.20	8.9	23.24%	2.3	6.09%	3.82	1.10	0.298
2019	AAA	137.0	6	11	0	6.04	5.72	1.40	7.7	19.18%	3.2	7.87%	2.44	1.71	0.291

Background: Signed on the international free agent market for $4.75 million near the end of August 2016. Gutierrez, the Serie Nacional Rookie of the Year for the 2013-14 season, has moved methodically through the Reds' farm system: he spent a year each in the Florida State, Southern, and International Leagues. Last season the Cuban import made a career high-tying 27 starts with the Louisville Bats, throwing 137.0 innings while racking up 117 punch outs and handing out 48 free passes. However, he compiled a 6.04 ERA and a slightly better 4.93 DRA (*Deserved Run Average*). For his stateside career, Gutierrez is averaging an impressive 8.3 strikeouts and just 2.4 walks per nine innings with a 4.98 ERA.

Snippet from The 2018 Prospect Digest Handbook: While possessing a plus-fastball, Gutierrez's lack of a dominant secondary offering pushes his ceiling towards back-of-the-rotation caliber arm or dominant late-inning reliever.

Cincinnati Reds

Scouting Report: Consider the following:

- Since 2006, only six 23-year-old pitchers met the following criteria in the International League (min. 100 IP): a strikeout percentage between 18% and 20% with a walk percentage between 7% and 9%. Those six pitchers: Michael Bowden, Jeanmar Gomez, Ivan Nova, Chris Mason, Kevin Mulvey, and Vladimir Gutierrez.

So...a couple things:

- The secondary stuff looked remarkably better, especially late in the season. The curveball was ridiculous and the changeup showed some better fade.
- He's an enigma of sorts. The repertoire, even in past years, has never played as well as expected. He's similar to Rockies right-hander Jeff Hoffman. They're both eerily too hittable.

Gutierrez is now entering his age-24 season. His control/command has declined in each of the last two seasons. And as basic and untrustworthy as it is, his ERA since 2019 is nearly 5.00 ERA. Again, I think he's a prime candidate to improve under the Kyle Boddy-led pitching clinics. If not, he's a multiple inning reliever at the big league level.

Ceiling: 1.5- to 2.0-win player
Risk: Moderate to High
MLB ETA: 2020

11. Tyler Callihan, 2B/3B

Hit	Power	SB	Patience	Glove	Overall
40/45	50/60	40	40/45	50	45

Born: 06/22/00   **Age:** 20   **Bats:** L   **Top CALs:**
Height: 6-1   **Weight:** 205   **Throws:** R

YEAR	LVL	PA	1B	2B	3B	HR	SB	CS	AVG	OBP	SLG	BB%	K%	GB%	LD%	FB%
2019	Rk+	21	6	0	1	1	2	0	0.400	0.429	0.650	4.76%	19.05%	43.8	12.5	37.5
2019	Rk+	217	31	10	5	5	9	3	0.250	0.286	0.422	4.15%	21.20%	46.9	19.4	27.5

Background: After eclipsing the recommended slot bonus – slightly – for second rounder Rece Hinds, the Reds went all in for Callihan. Taken in the third round, 85th overall, out of Providence High School, Callihan became a member of the organization after signing for a hefty $1.5 million – more than double the recommended slot bonus. A commit to the University of South Carolina, Calllihan batted .528 for the 2018 COPABE U-18 Pan-American tournament. The 6-foot-1, 205-pound lefty-swinging infielder appeared in 52 games in the Appalachian League, batting .250/.286/.422 with 10 doubles, five triples, five homeruns, and nine homeruns. His overall production in the rookie league was 14% *below* the league average mark. He also appeared in five games in the Pioneer League at the end of the year as well, going 8-for-20.

Scouting Report: Despite accruing fewer than 60 games in his professional career, here's what's already apparent: impressive power, perhaps even approaching plus power down the line; decent glove that likely handles the hot corner or the keystone; very little patience at the plate; and the hit tool is underdeveloped. In short, he immediately reminds me of Boston's Bobby Dalbec with worse patience and better contact skills.

Ceiling: 1.5-win player
Risk: Moderate
MLB ETA: 2023

12. Stuart Fairchild, OF

Hit	Power	SB	Patience	Glove	Overall
50	45	50	50	50	45

Born: 03/17/96   **Age:** 24   **Bats:** R   **Top CALs:**
Height: 6-0   **Weight:** 190   **Throws:** R

YEAR	LVL	PA	1B	2B	3B	HR	SB	CS	AVG	OBP	SLG	BB%	K%	GB%	LD%	FB%
2018	A	276	41	12	5	7	17	4	0.277	0.377	0.460	11.23%	23.55%	41.9	20.3	30.8
2018	A+	242	38	14	1	2	6	2	0.250	0.306	0.350	7.02%	26.03%	31.3	25.6	35.6
2019	A+	281	37	17	2	8	3	5	0.258	0.335	0.440	8.90%	21.35%	39.3	19.4	31.9
2019	AA	179	25	12	1	4	3	2	0.275	0.380	0.444	10.61%	12.85%	37.0	18.1	35.4

Background: A dynamic bat in his three-year career at Wake Forest. Fairchild left the Demon Deacons as a .334/.424/.541 hitter when the Reds selected him in the second round, 38th overall, in the 2017 draft. After tearing through the Pioneer League to the tune of .304/.393/.412 during his debut, the 6-foot, 190-pound outfielder split his follow-up campaign between Dayton and Daytona. In a combined 130 games, the former ACC standout batted .264/.344/.407 with 26 doubles, six triples, and nine homeruns with 23 stolen bases. The front office sent Fairchild back down to the Florida

State League for a recap to begin last season. And after hitting an improved .258/.335/.440 in 67 games, he was promoted up to the minors' toughest challenge, Class AA, at the end of June for the remainder for the year. He hit an impressive .275/.380/.444 with 12 doubles, one triple, and four homeruns.

Snippet from The 2018 Prospect Digest Handbook: Fairchild's hit tool wasn't as polished as it appeared; his swing-and-miss rate ballooned up to 26.0% during his stint in High Class A. And his defense was fringy – at best. Fairchild looks like another outfielder in the mold of Naquin or organization-mate T.J. Friedl.

Scouting Report: Cut from the quintessential fourth outfielder cloth; Fairchild does everything well without owning a true standout tool. He'll flash a decent hit tool with gap-to-gap pop that will turn into a handful of homeruns. He'll also swipe the occasional bag as well. Defensively, he's a bit stretched in center field, but won't kill a team in shorter looks.

Ceiling: 1.5-win player
Risk: Moderate
MLB ETA: 2020

13. T.J. Friedl, OF

Hit	Power	SB	Patience	Glove	Overall
50	40	50	55	50+	45

Born: 08/14/95	Age: 24	Bats: L	Top CALs:
Height: 5-10	Weight: 180	Throws: L	

YEAR	LVL	PA	1B	2B	3B	HR	SB	CS	AVG	OBP	SLG	BB%	K%	GB%	LD%	FB%
2017	A	292	40	20	6	5	14	8	0.284	0.378	0.472	9.93%	15.75%	48.8	12.1	28.0
2017	A+	199	36	6	2	2	2	1	0.257	0.313	0.346	5.03%	19.60%	51.0	17.2	25.5
2018	A+	274	50	10	4	3	11	4	0.294	0.405	0.412	13.87%	16.06%	43.5	17.7	30.6
2018	AA	296	57	10	3	2	19	5	0.276	0.359	0.360	9.46%	18.92%	42.2	20.9	27.7
2019	AA	269	33	11	4	5	13	4	0.235	0.347	0.385	10.78%	18.59%	41.3	17.9	30.7

Background: The story is well-known at this point: Friedl – and the rest of baseball – didn't know he was eligible for the 2016 draft because he exhausted his academic eligibility. And when word spread, a bevy of teams with left over money to burn came calling. The Reds won the bidding and signed him to a hefty six-figure bonus. And prior to last season, Friedl's production line screamed solid MLB bat / role player. But after a lost – and injury-interrupted 2019 – the former University of Nevada-Reno star's future is quite cloudy. Friedl, who stands 5-foot-10 and 180 pounds, maintained a decent triple-slash line (.276/.359/.360) in a second half promotion up to Class AA in 2018. But he managed to cobble together a lowly .235/.347/.385 mark with 11 doubles, four triples, five homeruns, and 13 stolen bases in 65 games. His overall production, according to *Deserved Runs Created Plus*, his production topped the league average mark by 13%. His season ended in early July courtesy of peroneal tendinitis.

Snippet from The 2018 Prospect Digest Handbook: Friedl could be a low end starter. But he's very likely going to settle in as a capable fourth outfielder. Long time big league vagabond Gerardo Parra seems like a reasonable comp at this point.

Scouting Report: So...question is: how much did the ankle injury impact his production? Or was an early season shoulder sprain that curtailed his normally average bat? Or...did Class AA just figure him out? Here's what we know:

- Friedl got off to a wickedly slow start to last year, hitting a pathetic .181/.302/.264 over his first month of action.
- But after returning to action in early May, he hit a Friedl-esque .260/.368/.442 over his remaining 44 games before his season ended.

So, I think it's easy to chalk up Friedl's poor showing to (A) a slow start and (B) an abbreviated season that didn't allow his numbers to fully normalize. At this point, the book's written on Friedl: saber-slanted hitter who can handle all three outfield positions with solid contact rates, swipes a couple dozen bags, and knock out a couple of dingers. He's very similar to fellow outfielder Stuart Fairchild.

Ceiling: 1.5-win player
Risk: Moderate
MLB ETA: 2020

14. Jameson Hannah, OF

Hit	Power	SB	Patience	Glove	Overall
45/50	40/45	40	50	50	45

Born: 08/10/97	Age: 22	Bats: L	Top CALs:
Height: 5-9	Weight: 185	Throws: L	

YEAR	LVL	PA	1B	2B	3B	HR	SB	CS	AVG	OBP	SLG	BB%	K%	GB%	LD%	FB%
2018	A-	95	18	4	1	1	6	0	0.279	0.347	0.384	9.47%	25.26%	51.6	25.8	17.7
2019	A+	78	11	3	1	0	2	1	0.224	0.325	0.299	11.54%	20.51%	64.0	14.0	18.0
2019	A+	414	76	25	3	2	6	7	0.283	0.341	0.381	7.00%	21.26%	54.8	13.8	25.5

Background: A product of Dallas Baptist University, home to veteran super-sub Ben Zobrist. Cincinnati acquired the pint-sized dynamo from the Athletics at the trade deadline last July for veteran right-hander Tanner Roark. Hannah, who was originally drafted by Oakland in the second round

two years ago, spent the entirety of 2019 in High Class A – splitting time between both organizations' affiliates. In a combined 110 games, the 5-foot-9, 185-pound outfielder batted a respectable, though far from impressive, .274/.339/.369 with 28 doubles, four triples, and a pair of homeruns. He also swiped eight bags in 16 attempts.

Snippet from The 2018 Prospect Digest Handbook: Hannah looks like a potential better-than-average big league regular – if his defense grades out as well as his peers/voters think and he continue to progress as a hitter. He seems like a player the Rays or Cardinals would hone in on in the second or third rounds.

Scouting Report: Hannah spent the majority of last season in the California League with Oakland's High Class A affiliate. So let's see how his production there stacked up to his peers through a historical lens. Consider the following:

- Since 2006, here's the list of 21-year-old hitters to post a 105 to 115 DRC+ with a 6% to 9% walk rate and an average strikeout rate in the California League (min. 350 PA): Victor Reyes, Socrates Brito, Orlando Martinez, Gianfranco Wawoe, and – of course – Jameson Hannah.

Hannah falls into the useful, sometimes valuable, fourth outfielder role, a la Reyes and Brito. He's toolsy in the same manner: he'll flash a 55-grade bat and plus speed, but he's never run all that frequently – even going back to his collegiate days. The power's – maybe – a 40. And there's not much hope of future development given (A) his frame size and (B) his track record. Solid defender, not elite like I would have suspected.

Ceiling: 1.5-win player
Risk: Moderate
MLB ETA: 2021

15. Ivan Johnson, SS

Hit	Power	SB	Patience	Glove	Overall
45/50	50	45	50	50	45

Born: 10/11/98	Age: 21	Bats: B	Top CALs:
Height: 6-0	Weight: 190	Throws: R	

YEAR	LVL	PA	1B	2B	3B	HR	SB	CS	AVG	OBP	SLG	BB%	K%	GB%	LD%	FB%
2019	Rk+	210	31	10	1	6	11	4	0.255	0.327	0.415	8.57%	21.90%	44.4	20.8	29.9

Background: After taking the premier arm in the opening round of the draft last June, the front office honed in on middle infield talent. They snagged IMG Academy shortstop Rece Hinds in the second round; drafted Tyler Callihan a round later; and

then chose Ivan Johnson out of JuCo powerhouse Chipola College with the 114th overall pick. Johnson, a 6-foot, 190-pound athlete, slugged a hefty .381/.491/.587 with 10 doubles, one triple, and nine homeruns to go along with 14 stolen bases for the Indians. After signing with the club, Johnson spent the entirety of his professional debut with the Greeneville Reds in the Appalachian League, batting a respectable .255/.327/.415 with 10 doubles, one triple, six homeruns, and 11 stolen bases. His overall production, according to *Deserved Runs Created Plus*, topped the league average mark by 6%.

Scouting Report: Chipola College has churned out some impressive talent throughout the years including: Russell Martin, who was taken in the 17th round by the Dodgers, Jose Bautista, Patrick Corbin, and Tyler Flowers. Johnson is built in a similar mold as his fellow 2019 draftmates: impressive pop for an up-the-middle-bat, a decent hit tool, a little bit of speed, and an average glove. Consider the following:

- Since 2006, only two 20-year-old hitters posted a 100 to 110 DRC+ with a 7.5% to 9.5% walk rate and a strikeout rate between 21% and 23% in the Appalachian League (min. 200 PA): D'Andre Toney and Ivan Johnson.

After a start to his debut – he hit a horrible .221/.302/.319 through his first 27 games – Johnson rebounded to slug .307/.366/.560 over his remaining 19 contests. Defensively, he's incredible fluid – though he may end up shifting over to second base. There's a little bit of Brandon Phillips here.

Ceiling: 1.5-win player
Risk: Moderate
MLB ETA: 2022

16. Lorenzo Cedrola, CF

	Hit	Power	SB	Patience	Glove	Overall
	50/55	35	50	40	50	40

Born: 01/12/98	Age: 22	Bats: R	Top CALs:
Height: 5-8	Weight: 152	Throws: R	

YEAR	LVL	PA	1B	2B	3B	HR	SB	CS	AVG	OBP	SLG	BB%	K%	GB%	LD%	FB%
2017	A	379	76	18	3	4	19	7	0.285	0.322	0.387	2.90%	12.66%	49.2	15.8	24.8
2018	A	188	37	4	2	1	13	7	0.260	0.310	0.325	4.79%	14.89%	44.9	14.3	29.3
2018	A	229	47	17	3	0	10	8	0.318	0.350	0.427	2.18%	12.66%	45.2	21.3	25.0
2019	A+	381	77	10	7	1	18	10	0.277	0.330	0.356	4.46%	11.29%	50.8	15.1	23.0

Background: Acquired from the Red Sox for an undisclosed amount of international bonus pool money in early July 2018. Cedrola, a native of Caracas, Venezuela, has been a consistent top-of-the-lineup minor league bat since making his debut in the foreign rookie league five years ago when he batted .321/.420/.415. Boston bounced him up to the Gulf Coast League the following year, 2016, and he maintained status quo as he hit .290/.350/.393 in 53 games. The 5-foot-8, 152-pound center field spent the next two seasons in Low Class A, slashing a combined .289/.327/.384 with 39 doubles, eight triples, five homeruns, and 42 stolen bases. Finally, with little left to prove, Cincinnati promoted – relented? – the wispy prospect up to High Class A. And he held his own. In a career best 102 games with the Daytona Tortugas, he batted .277/.330/.356 with 10 doubles, seven triples, one homer, and 18 stolen bases. Per Baseball Prospectus' *DRC+*, his overall production topped the league average mark by 12%.

Snippet from The 2018 Prospect Digest Handbook: The typical fourth/fifth outfielder type. Cedrola shows a little bit of offensive prowess – a solid-average hit tool and plus speed. But his power is well below-average. Defensively speaking, his speed plays well in center field, allowing him to be a strong glove. These types of prospects are typically a dime-a-dozen, but every organization needs them – especially if it only costs "future considerations."

Scouting Report: Consider the following:

- Since 2006, only four 21-year-old hitters met the following criteria in the Florida State League (min. 350 PA): 107 to 117 DRC+; a sub-6.0% walk rate; and a strikeout rate below 15.0%. Those four hitters: Danny Santana, Scooter Gennett, Tony Cruz, and – of course – Lorenzo Cedrola.
- So here's the impressive part: Santana, Gennett, and Cruz have all accrued at least six years at the big league level.

Well, you have to like those odds. Again, Cedrola does everything necessary for a fourth/fifth outfielder to survive at the big league level: batting average-driven production; can handle multiple positions well; doesn't show any meaningful platoon splits; and he can run. A decade ago Cedrola's the type of player that would be handed a starting gig for multiple seasons on a non-contending team. Now, though, that's not likely to happen. Offensive ceiling: think Leury Garcia's showing with the White Sox last season (.279/.310/.378).

Ceiling: 1.0- to 1.5-win player
Risk: Low to Moderate
MLB ETA: 2021

17. Hendrik Clementina, C

	Hit	Power	SB	Patience	Glove	Overall
	40	55	30	45	50	40

Born: 06/17/97	Age: 23	Bats: R	Top CALs:
Height: 6-0	Weight: 250	Throws: R	

YEAR	LVL	PA	1B	2B	3B	HR	SB	CS	AVG	OBP	SLG	BB%	K%	GB%	LD%	FB%
2017	RK	106	15	6	0	2	0	0	0.240	0.302	0.365	6.60%	23.58%	52.8	13.9	27.8
2017	RK	108	25	5	0	4	0	0	0.370	0.439	0.554	9.26%	14.81%	48.1	22.8	26.6
2018	A	376	50	22	1	18	1	0	0.268	0.327	0.497	7.98%	26.33%	39.6	15.5	35.9
2019	A+	365	57	13	0	14	1	0	0.249	0.296	0.411	5.21%	25.21%	37.8	20.9	34.5

Background: Molded like a wrecking ball, the Dodgers originally signed the 6-foot, 250-pound backstop out of Willemstad, Curacao, during the winter of 2013-14. Cincinnati acquired the stocky catcher – along with Scott Van Slyke – for veteran southpaw Tony Cingrani at the trade deadline three years ago. After showing some offensive promising in the foreign and stateside rookie leagues, Clementina began to flash some intriguing production lines at he moved into the Pioneer League in 2017, hitting a combined .303/.371/.457 with 11 doubles and six homeruns between both organizations' Rookie Advanced League affiliates. He followed that up with a stout showing in the Midwest League, slugging .268/.327/.497 with 22 doubles, one triple, and 18 homeruns in 96 games with the Dragons. And it was business as usual as he bumped up to the Florida State League in 2019: he batted .249/.296/.411 with 13 doubles and 14 homeruns in 91 contests. Per *Deserved Runs Created Plus*, his overall production topped the league average mark by 13%.

Scouting Report: Consider the following:

- Since 2006, only two 22-year-old hitters met the following criteria in the Florida State League (min. 350 PA): a DRC+ between 108 and 118; a sub-6.5% walk rate; and a strikeout rate north of 23%. Those two hitters: long time minor leaguer Zach Green, who cracked the Giants' lineup a handful of times in his eighth professional season in 2019, and – of course Hendrik Clementina.

A year later Clementina's skill set is becoming increasing clear: above-average power at a premium position, terrible patience at the plate, and some questionable strikeout rates. He's never been spectacular with the glove, which further pushes him into the realm up a future backup. In terms of offensive, think something along the lines up .245/.300/.430 – which, believe it or not, is still quite valuable for a big league backstop.

Ceiling: 1.0- to 1.5-win player
Risk: Moderate
MLB ETA: 2021

18. Reiver Sanmartin, LHP

FB	SL	CH	Command	Overall
50	50	50	55	40

Born: 04/15/96	Age: 24	Bats: L	Top CALs:
Height: 6-2	Weight: 160	Throws: L	

YEAR	LVL	IP	W	L	SV	ERA	FIP	WHIP	K/9	K%	BB/9	BB%	K/BB	HR9	BABIP
2018	A-	7.3	1	0	1	0.00	0.07	0.68	16.0	48.15%	0.0	0.00%	N/A	0.00	0.357
2018	A	43.0	2	6	0	4.19	3.53	1.21	6.5	16.76%	0.8	2.16%	7.75	0.42	0.331
2018	A+	12.0	2	0	0	0.00	1.80	0.67	7.5	23.81%	0.0	0.00%	N/A	0.00	0.250
2018	AA	5.0	0	1	0	1.80	1.71	0.80	7.2	22.22%	0.0	0.00%	N/A	0.00	0.286
2019	A+	64.3	2	5	0	3.78	3.20	1.27	8.4	21.82%	2.0	5.09%	4.29	0.70	0.325
2019	AA	58.0	2	7	0	4.34	3.76	1.34	8.4	21.09%	2.6	6.64%	3.18	0.93	0.311

Background: The low-slinging lefty has been passed around quite a bit over the past couple of seasons. The Rangers sent the 6-foot-2, 160-pound pinpoint control artist to the Yankees following the conclusion of the 2017 season for right-hander Ronald Herrera. New York turned around 14 months later and dealt Sanmartin, as well a resurgent Sonny Gray, for infielder Shed Long and a 2019 Competitive Balance Round A pick. Last season the wiry left-hander split time between Daytona and Chattanooga, making 25 starts with 114 strikeouts and 31 walks with a 4.05 ERA in 122.1 innings of work.

Snippet from The 2018 Prospect Digest Handbook: Richardson's still has plenty of untapped potential brewing in his right arm thanks to his lack of pitching experience; he was used primarily as a closer prior to his senior year in high school. Because of his aforementioned lack of experience he's rawer than the typical prep arm taken in the second round. He looks like a nice backend starter or dominant relief arm if his control/command doesn't come around.

Scouting Report: With respect to his work in Class AA last season, consider the following:

- Since 2006, only three 23-year-old pitchers posted a strikeout percentage between 20% and 22% with a walk percentage between 5.5% and 7.5% in the Southern League (min. 50 IP): Ivan Pineyro, Sean Thompson, and – of course - Reiver Sanmartin.

The lanky lefty is an intriguing, deceptive pitcher: he doesn't throw the ball; he slings it from a low three-quarter arm action that makes his susceptible to right-hander hitters (which is confirmed by his platoon splits over the past couple of years). Sanmartin shows an across-the-board average repertoire: a 90 mph fastball with some sink and cut; a solid little slider; and a workable changeup. His pinpoint control/command, particularly on his offspeed pitches, allows the arsenal to play up. He's strictly a future reliever, but could carve out a role as an Oliver Perez type arm – perhaps as early as 2020.

Ceiling: 1.0- to 1.5-win player
Risk: Moderate
MLB ETA: 2020

19. Ibandel Isabel, 1B/RF

Hit	Power	SB	Patience	Glove	Overall
40	70	30	50	50	40

Born: 06/20/95   **Age:** 25   **Bats:** R   **Top CALs:**

Height: 6-4   **Weight:** 225   **Throws:** R

YEAR	LVL	PA	1B	2B	3B	HR	SB	CS	AVG	OBP	SLG	BB%	K%	GB%	LD%	FB%
2017	A+	492	70	16	1	28	0	2	0.259	0.327	0.489	8.13%	34.96%	50.7	18.2	25.9
2018	A+	420	51	11	0	35	1	1	0.258	0.333	0.566	8.57%	36.19%	43.1	20.0	31.1
2018	A+	23	2	2	0	1	0	0	0.238	0.304	0.476	8.70%	39.13%	33.3	8.3	41.7
2019	AA	368	42	12	1	26	0	0	0.243	0.307	0.518	7.07%	41.58%	42.0	25.4	28.2

Background: Acquired along with right-hander Zach Neal from the Dodgers for Ariel Hernandez in mid-April 2018. Isabel's going to do what Isabel's going to do. Namely: hit the crap out of baseballs, or go down trying. The muscular first baseman / corner outfielder captured a lot of media attention as he assaulted High Class A pitching two years ago, slugging 36 homeruns in just 104 games en route to batting .257/.332/.562. Cincinnati bounced the all-or-nothing slugger up to Class AA, the level where flawed hitters go to die, and – surprisingly – Isabel held his own, despite a massive strikeout rate. In 91 games with the Chattanooga Lookouts, the 6-foot-4, 225-pound Dominican thumper smashed 12 doubles, one triple, and 26 homeruns as he batted .243/.307/.518. His production, according to *Deserved Runs Created Plus*, topped the league average mark by 5%.

Scouting Report: An absolute monster at the plate, almost to a cartoonish level, when he connects with the baseball. Prorating his production last season over a full 162-game season, his numbers are 21 doubles, two triples, and 46 homers. Of course, he punched out in nearly 42% of his plate appearances. It's actually remarkable if you think about: he's whiffing – on average – two times a game. And he still, somehow, managed to his .243. Maybe he's not quite cartoonish. But there's some Happy Gilmore to him. I'd pay to watch him blast some dingers in a homerun derby. No question about that.

Ceiling: 1.0-win player
Risk: Moderate
MLB ETA: 2020

20. Jacob Heatherly, LHP

FB	CB	SL	CH	Command	Overall
N/A	N/A	N/A	N/A	N/A	40

Born: 05/20/98   **Age:** 22   **Bats:** L   **Top CALs:**

Height: 6-1   **Weight:** 215   **Throws:** L

YEAR	LVL	IP	W	L	SV	ERA	FIP	WHIP	K/9	K%	BB/9	BB%	K/BB	HR9	BABIP
2017	Rk	30.7	2	1	0	2.93	5.46	1.37	7.6	19.40%	4.7	11.94%	1.63	0.88	0.261
2017	Rk	9.0	0	1	0	12.00	4.98	2.33	5.0	10.64%	4.0	8.51%	1.25	0.00	0.459
2018	Rk	38.7	1	5	0	5.82	5.80	1.91	11.4	26.63%	9.3	21.74%	1.23	0.70	0.348
2019	A	8.7	1	2	0	8.31	3.54	2.08	10.4	21.28%	6.2	12.77%	1.67	0.00	0.400

Background: A product of Cullman High School, which produced 2006 Red Sox first rounder Caleb Clay, Heatherly committed to in-state University of Alabama after flashing some promising production throughout his prep career. The Reds were able to persuade the 6-foot-1, 215-pound left-hander with a hefty $1.1 million bonus, roughly $300,000 above the recommended slot bonus for the 77th overall selection. Two years ago Heatherly looked lost on the bump as he walked 40 hitters in only 38.2 innings with the Greeneville Reds in the Appalachian League. And his 2019 season with the Dayton Dragons began in similar fashion: he walked six in 8.2 innings across four appearances with the Midwest League affiliate. A sore shoulder cut his season short in late April.

Scouting Report: I have to be completely honest now: Heatherly's inclusion on the Top 20 list is more about the Reds' new mindset when it comes to developing pitching, rather than his production line. I'm a massive, *massive* believer in Kyle Boddy and the rest of the Driveline Baseball crew. And Heatherly is exactly the type of pitcher that could succeed in their care. Heatherly showed a plus fastball and solid offspeed offerings coming out of high school, so let's see if he can hone in on the strike zone with higher regularity.

Ceiling: 1.0-win player
Risk: Moderate to High
MLB ETA: 2022

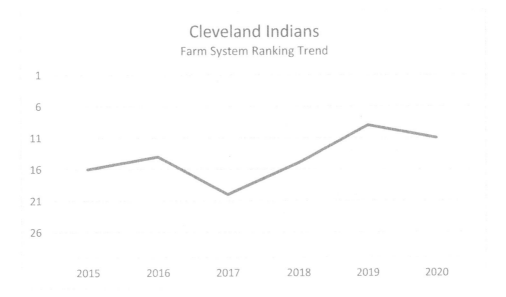

Cleveland Indians
Farm System Ranking Trend

Rank	Name	Age	Pos
1	Nolan Jones	22	3B
2	Tyler Freeman	21	SS
3	Daniel Espino	19	RHP
4	Triston McKenzie	22	RHP
5	George Valera	19	CF
6	Ethan Hankins	20	RHP
7	Brayan Rocchio	19	2B/SS
8	Bo Naylor	20	C
9	Cody Morris	23	RHP
10	James Karinchak	24	RHP
11	Emmanuel Clase	22	RHP
12	Logan Allen	23	LHP
13	Aaron Bracho	19	2B
14	Daniel Johnson	24	OF
15	Gabriel Rodriguez	18	3B/SS
16	Lenny Torres	23	RHP
17	Bobby Bradley	24	1B
18	Adam Scott	24	LHP
19	Sam Hentges	23	LHP
20	Luis Oviedo	21	RHP

1. Nolan Jones, 3B

Hit	Power	SB	Patience	Glove	Overall
50/60	50/60	35	70	50	60

Born: 05/07/98	Age: 22	Bats: L
Height: 6-2	Weight: 185	Throws: R

YEAR	LVL	PA	1B	2B	3B	HR	SB	CS	AVG	OBP	SLG	BB%	K%	GB%	LD%	FB%
2017	A-	265	44	18	3	4	1	0	0.317	0.430	0.482	16.23%	22.64%	54.4	21.3	24.4
2018	A	389	62	12	0	16	2	1	0.279	0.393	0.464	16.20%	24.94%	49.3	22.3	26.2
2018	A+	130	19	9	0	3	0	0	0.298	0.438	0.471	20.00%	26.15%	42.9	25.7	30.0
2019	A+	324	52	12	1	7	5	3	0.286	0.435	0.425	20.06%	26.23%	48.2	21.2	23.5
2019	AA	211	25	10	2	8	2	0	0.253	0.370	0.466	14.69%	29.86%	40.7	26.5	27.4

Background: The Indians have had several notable second round selections sprinkled throughout their storied history: Albert Belle, who looked like a surefire Hall of Famer before injuries derailed his career; Jason Kipnis, who just left the ballclub after nine years and a pair of All-Star appearances; sweet-swinging first baseman and three-time All-Star Sean Casey; southpaw Neil Heaton, who cracked the 1990 N.L. All-Star roster; World Series winning manager John Farrell; and former cult hero Herbert Perry. Most recently, the club added a couple of high profile second round draft picks in Nolan Jones and Tyler Freeman. Taken with the 55th overall selection four years ago and signed to an above-slot deal, Jones began to turn some heads after a solid showing in the New York-Penn League during his first full season in the organization as he slugged a hearty .317/.430/.482 as a 19-year-old. The silky smooth, lefty-swinging third baseman continued to impressive the following season, 2018, as he moved into Low Class A and eventually up to High Class A; he batted .283/.405/.466 with 21 doubles and 19 homeruns. Last year, the Holy Ghost Prep High School product opened the season up with dramatic flair as he returned to the Carolina League, going 3-for-6 with a double and pair of RBIs on Opening Day. He would spend slightly more than three months with the Lynchburg Hillcats, hitting an impressive .286/.435/.425 with 20 extra-base knocks. Jones was promoted up to the minors' toughest challenge, Class AA, in early July for the remainder of the year. And, of course, he didn't miss a beat as he slashed .253/.370/.466 in 49 contests. He spent the fall with the Mesa Solar Sox, going 12-for-60 with p air of doubles and four homeruns.

Snippet from The 2018 Prospect Digest Handbook: There's reason for concern with Jones moving forward, the same thing that plagued [Lonnie] Chisenhall as well: he's showing some massive platoon splits; Jones batted .341/.450/.506 vs. RHP and .214/.352/.381 vs. LHP. At first blush Jones looks like a safe, high-ceiling hitter, but he's more volatile than most realize. I ultimately think the smooth-swinging lefty figures out southpaws enough to ward off any platoon talk.

Scouting Report: Jones' lengthy, red flag raising history of platoon splits continued once again and, frankly, it showed zero signs of improvement in 2019. The former second round pick slashed a scorching .312/.439/.497 vs. right-handers, but cobbled together a paltry .151/.324/.274 against southpaws. And what's more concerning: he whiffed in 35.3% of his plate appearances against lefties. So now the good, well, great news: his batted ball data is *off the charts*. According to FanGraphs, Jones' average exit velocity was 92 mph last season, tied for the seventh highest mark among the 285 hitters where data is available. His peak exit velocity was 114 mph, tied for third best among the group. With an incredibly patient approach at the plate, Jones, who walked in nearly 18% of his plate appearances last season, is just beginning to tap into his plus in-game power potential. As I stated in last year's Prospect Digest Handbook, the platoon rates are quite concerning and he remains more volatile than most realize, I ultimately think Jones figures it out. All-Star potential with a ceiling of a Trevor Story-type player (.300/.370/.560).

Ceiling: 4.0-win player
Risk: Moderate
MLB ETA: 2020

2. Tyler Freeman, SS

Hit	Power	SB	Patience	Glove	Overall
55/70	40/45	40	40/45	50	55

Born: 05/21/99	Age: 21	Bats: R
Height: 6-0	Weight: 170	Throws: R

YEAR	LVL	PA	1B	2B	3B	HR	SB	CS	AVG	OBP	SLG	BB%	K%	GB%	LD%	FB%
2017	RK	144	27	9	0	2	5	1	0.297	0.364	0.414	4.86%	8.33%	46.6	21.2	22.0
2018	A-	301	60	29	4	2	14	3	0.352	0.405	0.511	2.66%	7.31%	43.7	24.2	27.4
2019	A	272	47	16	3	3	11	4	0.292	0.382	0.424	6.62%	10.29%	37.8	26.3	28.7
2019	A+	275	64	16	2	0	8	1	0.319	0.354	0.397	2.91%	9.09%	48.5	23.4	21.2

Background: At some point in the near future Indians fans are going to look back and realize the impact the second rounds of the 2016 and 2017 drafts had on the organization. The club, of course, drafted top prospect Nolan Jones four years ago in the middle of the second round. And they followed that up a season later by selecting prep shortstop Tyler Freeman with the 71st overall pick. A product of Etiwanda High School, the speedy, slashing 6-foot, 170-pound infielder immediate made an impact during his debut in the Arizona Summer League as he batted .297/.364/.414 with nine doubles, a pair of homeruns, and five stolen bases. But, perhaps most impressively, he fanned just 12 times. The following year Freeman raised expectations even higher as he slugged a scorching .352/.405/.511 with 29 doubles, four triples, two homeruns, and 14 stolen bases as a 19-year-old in the New

York-Penn League. His production that year, according to Baseball Prospectus' *Deserved Runs Created Plus*, topped the league average threshold by a whopping 89%. Freeman opened up last season with Lake County, but after batting .292/.382/.424 in 61 games with the club's Midwest League affiliate he moved up to High Class A in the second half. In total, the young shortstop hit an impressive .306/.368/.410 with 32 doubles, five triples, three homeruns, and 19 stolen bases.

Snippet from The 2018 Prospect Digest Handbook: Freeman's such an odd, fascinating prospect: he has a shot at developing a plus-hit tool to go along with matching speed and average power – all wrapped up at a premium position, whether he settles in at second base (likely) or stays at shortstop. It's a recipe for a long, successful big league career. But here's where it gets weird: he doesn't walk *and* he rarely, if ever, strikes outs. Expect his walk rate to climb into the 5.5% to 6.0% range as he squares off more advanced pitching in the Midwest League.

Scouting Report: First: his walk rate did climb a bit during his stint in the Midwest League, jumping all the way up to 6.6%. Second: let's take a look at Freeman's production in High Class A through a historical lens. Consider the following:

- Since 2006, here's the list of 20-year-old hitters to post a 125 to 135 DRC+ with a sub-15% strikeout rate in the Carolina League (min. 250 PA): Neil Walker, who owns a career 106 DRC+ at the big league level; Cheslor Cuthbert, a below average big league bat; and – of course – Tyler Freeman.

The batted ball data is about average, maybe a touch better given his age and level of competition: his average exit velocity was 86 mph last season. But, surprisingly, he doesn't put the ball on the ground nearly as much as you'd think; roughly just 43% of the time in 2019. The bat speeds average, but he excels at indiscriminately shooting the ball where it's pitched. The hit tool is going to determine whether he develops into an above-average starter or a super-sub type of player. There's a chance it develops into a 70-grade and he's currently profiling as a Kevin Newman-type bat: .310/.350/.430 with double-digit stolen bases.

Ceiling: 3.0- to 3.5-win player
Risk: Low to Moderate
MLB ETA: 2020

3. Daniel Espino, RHP

FB	CB	SL	CH	Command	Overall
70	60	60	45/50	45/50	55

Born: 09/03/95	Age: 24	Bats: L
Height: 6-6	Weight: 240	Throws: L

YEAR	LVL	IP	W	L	SV	ERA	FIP	WHIP	K/9	K%	BB/9	BB%	K/BB	HR9	BABIP
2019	Rk	13.7	0	1	0	1.98	4.18	0.88	10.5	30.77%	3.3	9.62%	3.20	0.66	0.207
2019	A-	10.0	0	2	0	6.30	2.60	1.40	16.2	40.00%	4.5	11.11%	3.60	0.90	0.381

Background: Near the late 1990s and early 2000s a 6-foot-3, 229-pound high school-aged hurler captured the sheer imagination of the baseball world every time he toed the rubber. Blessed with ability to unfurl lightning bolt after lightning bolt from his Zeus-ian right arm, Colt Griffin's fastball would sit – comfortably – in the upper 90s, often times touching triple digits – a rarity now a days, but practically unheard of then. The Kansas City Royals drafted the highly touted youngster with the ninth overall pick in 2001. Five seasons later he would retire from professional baseball after plateauing in Class AA. Roughly a decade-and-a-half later another massive Texas-born hurler shot up the draft charts as one of 2014's biggest helium guys on the back of his ability to touch triple-digits. But since the Marlins selected righty Tyler Kolek with the second overall pick that year, he's been limited to just 163.2 career innings. Enter: Fireballer Daniel Espino, who touched triple-digits with his heater as a junior for Georgia Premier Academy. Espino's earned a bevy of awards and recognitions, including:

- 2019 Perfect Game Preseason All-American
- 2019 Perfect Game High School Showdown All-Tournament Team
- 2018 Perfect Game High School Showdown Tournament Most Valuable Pitcher
- 2018 Perfect Game Preseason All-American
- 2018 Perfect Game High School Showdown All-Tournament Team
- 2018 Perfect Game National Showcase
- 2018 Perfect Game All-American Classic
- Perfect Game Top Right-Handed Pitcher

But despite notoriety, the 6-foot-2, 205-pound hurler's stock tumbled a bit in last June's draft, falling all the way down to the Indians at the 24th overall pick. The ballclub signed him to a deal worth $2.5 million. Espino, who was previously committed to play at Louisiana State University, made nine brief appearances between the Arizona Summer and New York-Penn Leagues during his debut, posting a 34-to-10 strikeout-to-walk ratio with a 3.80 ERA in 23.2 innings of work.

Scouting Report: Per the usual, here's what I wrote about Espino prior to the draft last season:

"Easy plus-plus velocity with a wipeout slider, and a knee-buckling curveball. Espino's fastball shows incredible late action and both breaking balls grade out as plus. He'll also mix in a rare below-average changeup, though I only witnessed the upper 80s offering once. He shows solid feel for pitching, especially considering his ability to overpower his peers with one pitch. The major knock on the wiry hurler – seemingly – is his long arm action. But his mechanical fluidity, athleticism, and flexibility alleviates a lot of my concerns, personally. Espino's the best pitching prospect in a weak class – by a wide margin. Of course, there's concern and risk associated with any hard-throwing youngster but Espino's ceiling is incredibly high."

Ceiling: 3.5-win player
Risk: Moderate
MLB ETA: 2022

4. Triston McKenzie, RHP

	FB	CB	CH	Command	Overall
	N/A	N/A	N/A	N/A	55

Born: 08/02/97	Age: 22	Bats: R
Height: 6-6	Weight: 165	Throws: R

YEAR	LVL	IP	W	L	SV	ERA	FIP	WHIP	K/9	K%	BB/9	BB%	K/BB	HR9	BABIP
2017	A+	143.0	12	6	0	3.46	3.03	1.05	11.7	32.75%	2.8	7.92%	4.13	0.88	0.283
2018	AA	90.7	7	4	0	2.68	3.60	1.00	8.6	24.03%	2.8	7.73%	3.11	0.79	0.234

Background: It's been a rough couple of years for the long time top prospect. McKenzie missed the opening couple months of the 2018 season due to a forearm strain. And another major injury – a severe upper back strain – forced the ballclub to shut him down in early March last year. Just as the snake-bitten hurler was on the mend and set to return to action, a strained pectoral shut him down for the remainder of the year. Injuries in back-to-back years not only cost the skinny right-hander precious development time, but it also likely kept him from making his highly anticipated debut. Prior to the 2018 season, the former first round selection was coming off of an incredibly dominant showing in the Carolina League as he averaged 11.7 strikeouts and just 2.8 walks per nine innings with a 3.46 ERA in 25 starts as a 19-year-old. According to reports at the start of Spring Training, McKenzie's fully healthy for the 2020 season.

Snippet from The 2018 Prospect Digest Handbook: McKenzie's fastball is a lot like *Miracle Whip* – it's got that tangy zip. It's a lively mid-90s offering thrown with a surprising amount of ease that plays up even more due to his long limbs. He complements the plus-pitch with a hellacious, knee-buckling curveball and a changeup that flashes above-average. McKenzie pitches off his fastball as well as any young arm in the minor leagues, throwing it to all four quadrants equally well. Barring any injury – or injuries – McKenzie has the chance to develop into a strong #2-type arm.

Scouting Report: The Indians rotation isn't quite what it at the start of the 2019 season. Corey Kluber and Trevor Bauer were traded. And Mike Clevenger will miss some significant time as he recovers from a surgical procedure to repair a torn meniscus in his left knee. Meaning: despite missing half of 2018 and all of 2019 due to injuries, there's a non-zero chance that McKenzie makes 10 or so appearances with the Tribe throughout the year. He's lost a little of the prospect luster he once owned, but at least last year's lengthy stay on the disabled list wasn't a result of a arm injury.

Ceiling: 3.5- to 4.0-win player
Risk: Moderate to High
MLB ETA: 2020/2021

5. George Valera, CF

	Hit	Power	SB	Patience	Glove	Overall
	45/55	50/60	40	60/55	50	55

Born: 11/13/00	Age: 19	Bats: L
Height: 5-10	Weight: 160	Throws: L

YEAR	LVL	PA	1B	2B	3B	HR	SB	CS	AVG	OBP	SLG	BB%	K%	GB%	LD%	FB%
2018	RK	22	4	1	0	1	1	1	0.333	0.409	0.556	13.64%	13.64%	50.0	18.8	12.5
2019	A-	188	21	7	1	8	6	2	0.236	0.356	0.446	15.43%	27.66%	46.2	21.7	27.4
2019	A	26	1	0	1	0	0	2	0.087	0.192	0.174	7.69%	34.62%	35.7	7.1	57.1

Background: One of the bigger names on the international market three years ago, the club signed the Queens, New York, native for a hefty $1.3 million after moving to the Dominican Republic. Valera, though, had his professional debut abruptly cut short courtesy of a broken hamate bone two years ago. But despite appearing in just six rookie league games – as well as suffering an injury that typically saps a hitter's power – the front office bumped the 5-foot-10, 160-pound outfielder up to the New York-Penn League to begin 2019. And, of course, he struggled a bit as he hit a power-driven .236/.356/.446 with seven doubles, one triple, eight homeruns, and six stolen bases (in eight attempts). Valera also appeared in half-of-a-dozen games in the Midwest League. His overall production in the New York-Penn League, according to *Deserved Runs Created Plus*, topped the league average mark by a surprising 32%.

Snippet from The 2018 Prospect Digest Handbook: When Valera connects it's a loud audible crack off the bat.

Scouting Report: That loud audible crack I mentioned in last year's Handbook turned out to be some *phenomenal* exit velocities in 2019: it averaged a whopping 91 mph with a peak of 107 mph. That's as an 18-year-old squaring off against competition that averaged three years his senior. There's some big time, plus power potential and well above-average patience mix in. And his strikeout rate last season in the NYPL, 27.7%, barely moves the needle in terms of concern. He was (A) 18-years-old, (B) coming off of a semi-serious injury, (C) which limited to six games in rookie ball, and (D) jumped an entire level. There's some massive, *massive* upside here. He's going to be one of the biggest breakout prospects in 2020. Remember the name.

Ceiling: 3.5-win player
Risk: Moderate to High
MLB ETA: 2020

6. Ethan Hankins, RHP

	FB	CB	SL	CH	Command	Overall
	70	50/55	55	45/50	45/50	50

Born: 05/23/00	Age: 20	Bats: R
Height: 6-6	Weight: 200	Throws: R

YEAR	LVL	IP	W	L	SV	ERA	FIP	WHIP	K/9	K%	BB/9	BB%	K/BB	HR9	BABIP
2018	Rk	3.0	0	0	0	6.00	1.07	1.33	18.0	42.86%	0.0	0.00%	N/A	0.00	0.571
2019	A-	38.7	0	0	0	1.40	3.21	1.06	10.0	30.94%	4.2	12.95%	2.39	0.23	0.232
2019	A	21.3	0	3	0	4.64	4.46	1.50	11.8	29.79%	5.1	12.77%	2.33	1.27	0.340

Background: There was a time when Hankins looked like a potential early first round pick. He owned the size – he stands an imposing 6-foot-6 and 200 pounds – with the requisite plus-plus fastball. But a stiff shoulder caused the Georgia-born hurler to tumble towards the back of the first round; the Tribe drafted him with the 35th overall pick two years ago and signed him to an above-slot deal worth $2,246,022. After an abbreviated debut in rookie ball, Hankins opened last season in the New York-Penn League. And he was...dominating. In eight starts and one relief appearance with the Mahoning Valley Scrappers, the burly righty fanned 43 and walked just 18 to go along with a 1.40 ERA in 38.2 innings of work. Hankins made five additional starts in the Midwest League at the end of the year, fanning 28 and walking 12 in 21.2 innings. For the year he averaged 10.7 strikeouts and 4.5 walks per nine innings with a 2.55 ERA.

Snippet from The 2018 Prospect Digest Handbook: Hankins has a little of swagger on the mound. And I like that. With clean, repeatable mechanics his control/command should be no worse than average. Hankins has the potential to ascend towards the top of a big league rotation with the floor as a #4 – barring any injury setbacks.

Scouting Report: A thick lower half that looks like he can squat a Buick without breaking a sweat, Hankins can run his plus-plus heater towards the upper-90s and maintain 95-mph heat late into games. At times it looks like Hankins is merely playing catch with his battery mate, and I'll look up and he's touching 96. His average curveball shows a nice shape and has the makings of an above-average pitch with a bit more refinement, something the Indians do exceptionally well (see: Shane Bieber). His 79- to 80-mph slider is tightly wound, an above-average offering. Hankins' 88- to 89-mph changeup doesn't show a lot of decpetion, though there's some arm-side run to it. The fastball and fastball command suggest a mid-rotation caliber ceiling, something along the lines of #3/#4. But his changeup needs to tick up for that to happen.

Ceiling: 3.0-win player
Risk: Moderate
MLB ETA: 2022

7. Brayan Rocchio, SS

	Hit	Power	SB	Patience	Glove	Overall
	50/60	35/40	45	45+	55/60	50

Born: 01/13/01	Age: 19	Bats: B
Height: 5-10	Weight: 150	Throws: R

YEAR	LVL	PA	1B	2B	3B	HR	SB	CS	AVG	OBP	SLG	BB%	K%	GB%	LD%	FB%
2018	RK	111	26	2	3	1	8	5	0.323	0.391	0.434	4.50%	12.61%	45.3	20.9	29.1
2018	RK	158	37	10	1	1	14	8	0.343	0.389	0.448	6.33%	10.76%	42.6	20.9	26.4
2019	A-	295	47	12	3	5	14	8	0.250	0.310	0.373	6.78%	13.56%	44.1	15.3	33.2

Background: The Indians front office hit a homerun on the international market three years ago as they added the likes of George Valera, Aaron Bracho, and – of course – Brayan Rocchio. A 5-foot-10, 150-pound switch-hitter from Caracas, Venezuela, Rocchio ripped through the foreign and stateside rookie leagues during his debut two years ago as he slugged a hearty .335/.390/.442 with 12 doubles, four triples, two homeruns, and 22 stolen bases (in 35 attempts). Rocchio spent his sophomore professional season as one of the younger players in the New York-Penn League. In 69 games with the Mahoning Valley Scrappers, the then-18-year-old middle infielder batted .250/.310/.373 with 12 doubles, three triples, five homeruns, and 14 stolen bases in 22 attempts. Per *Deserved Runs Created Plus*, his production topped the league average threshold by 7%.

Snippet from The 2018 Prospect Digest Handbook: Needless to say, but I really like Rocchio moving forward. His glove is a bit raw at shortstop, but should develop enough to keep him at the position. Rocchio has impressive bat speed, perhaps among the top five in the system. His line drive stroke should allow him to spray the ball all over the field with average-ish power. Rocchio's poised to be one of the bigger breakout prospects in 2019. He has the ceiling as a .290/.330/.440-type hitter. He's one of the names you haven't heard, but will.

Scouting Report: Consider the following:

- Since 2006, only two 18-year-old hitters posted a DRC+ between 102 and 112 with a sub-20% strikeout rate in the New York-Penn League (min. 200 PA): Cito Culver, a first round pick by the Yankees who flamed out, and Brayan Rocchio.

Solid, though far from elite batted ball data last season. Rocchio's average exit velocity was 85 mph and his peak exit velocity was 102 mph. A slow start to his year, which isn't surprising, put a damper on his overall numbers. But it's important to point out that he hit a respectable .271/.329/.403 with five doubles and four homeruns over his final 32 games. Short compact swing with the same lightning quickness he displayed the previous year. Very twitchy. A year later, though, I'm not certain on how the power will develop. He's more of a slasher. His potential plus-glove pushes him up to starter status.

Ceiling: 2.5- to 3.0-win player
Risk: Moderate
MLB ETA: 2022

8. Bo Naylor, C

	Hit	Power	SB	Patience	Glove	Overall
	45/50	50/55	40/35	50	50+	50

Born: 02/21/00	Age: 20	Bats: L
Height: 6-0	Weight: 195	Throws: R

YEAR	LVL	PA	1B	2B	3B	HR	SB	CS	AVG	OBP	SLG	BB%	K%	GB%	LD%	FB%
2018	RK	139	24	3	3	2	5	1	0.274	0.381	0.402	15.11%	20.14%	45.6	20.0	27.8
2019	A	453	58	18	10	11	7	5	0.243	0.313	0.421	9.49%	22.96%	40.7	20.2	36.8

Background: The younger brother of Padres first baseman/corner outfielder Josh Naylor, Bo joined his brother as a fellow first rounder when the Indians called his name at the 29th overall pick two years ago. The younger Naylor acquitted himself nicely during his debut in the Arizona Summer League as he batted a solid .274/.391/.402 with three doubles, three triples, and a pair of homeruns. The front office bumped the lefty-swinging backstop up to the Midwest League for the 2019 season. And unsurprisingly, his numbers took a bit of a hit. In 107 games with the Lake County Captain, Naylor batted .243/.313/.421 with 18 doubles, 10 triples, 11 homeruns, and seven stolen bases. Per *Deserved Runs Created Plus*, the young catcher's overall production was 2% below the league average mark.

Snippet from The 2018 Prospect Digest Handbook: Naylor's got a chance to not only outperform his older brother, but also develop into a better-than-average big league catcher.

Scouting Report: The foundation is in place to develop into a better-than-average backstop: above power with the potential to jump into 55-grade territory, a surprising amount of speed, solid hit tool, and a slightly better-than-average glove at a premium position. Not shockingly, Naylor got off to a bit of a slow start as he jumped up to Low Class A last season, batting a lowly .214/.313/.321 over his first 32 games. But once he got his feet underneath of him, he slugged a solid .254/.313/.460 over his final 75 games. Very good athlete. Naylor's offensive ceiling should settle in the neighborhood of Travis d'Arnaud's 2019 season in which he batted .251/.312/.433.

Ceiling: 2.5-win player
Risk: Moderate
MLB ETA: 2022

9. Cody Morris, RHP

FB	CB	SL	CH	Command	Overall
60	55	50	50	55	50

Born: 11/04/96	Age: 23	Bats: R
Height: 6-5	Weight: 222	Throws: R

YEAR	LVL	IP	W	L	SV	ERA	FIP	WHIP	K/9	K%	BB/9	BB%	K/BB	HR9	BABIP
2019	A	45.0	5	2	0	3.20	2.10	1.13	11.2	30.27%	2.0	5.41%	5.60	0.20	0.348
2019	A+	44.0	2	2	0	5.52	3.94	1.61	11.3	27.09%	3.5	8.37%	3.24	1.23	0.390

Background: Originally taken by the Baltimore Orioles in the 32nd round coming out of Reservoir High School in 2015. Morris, instead, headed to the University of South Carolina to square off against the stiff SEC competition. The real surprise: the Orioles drafted the promising right-hander despite the need for Tommy John surgery, which would eventually keep him out of commission until the 2017 season. After two years in the school's rotation, the Indians drafted the 6-foot-5, 222-pound right-hander in the seventh round of the 2018 draft. The Indians held the big righty out of action until last season. Morris made his professional debut in the Midwest League, posting an impressive 56-to-10 strikeout-to-walk ratio in 45.0 innings of work. The former Gamecock made another 11 starts in the Carolina League with the Lynchburg Hillcats, fanning 55 and walking 17 in 44.0 innings of work. Overall, Morris finished the year by averaging 11.2 strikeouts and just 2.7 strikeouts per nine innings with a 4.35 ERA.

Scouting Report: One of the more underrated arms in the entire minor leagues. And he's exactly the type of pitcher the Indians have excelled at developing. Morris shows an impressive four-pitch arsenal: his fastball sits in the 93- to 95-mph range and peaked as high as 97-mph during one of the games I saw. His upper-70s curveball buckled a few knees and his Bugs Bunny-esque changeup adds a pair of strong, above-average offerings. He'll also mix in a decent, average-ish slider as well. The Indians' brass monitored Morris' workload rather closely last season, limiting him to just 89.0 innings and allowing him to surpass just 90 pitches in an outing just once. Morris is likely ticketed for a brief return back to High Class A, but he should spend some significant time in the Eastern League as well. Sneaky, sneaky upside. #4-type ceiling.

Ceiling: 2.5-win player
Risk: Moderate
MLB ETA: 2021

10. James Karinchak, RHP

FB	CB	Command	Overall
70	80	40	50

Born: 09/22/95	Age: 24	Bats: R
Height: 6-3	Weight: 230	Throws: R

YEAR	LVL	IP	W	L	SV	ERA	FIP	WHIP	K/9	K%	BB/9	BB%	K/BB	HR9	BABIP
2017	A-	23.3	2	2	0	5.79	2.48	1.67	12.0	30.10%	3.5	8.74%	3.44	0.39	0.468
2018	A	11.3	3	0	1	0.79	1.80	1.32	15.9	42.55%	5.6	14.89%	2.86	0.00	0.400
2018	A+	27.0	1	1	13	1.00	2.39	1.15	15.0	42.06%	5.7	15.89%	2.65	0.33	0.295
2018	AA	10.3	0	1	0	2.61	4.96	1.84	13.9	32.00%	10.5	24.00%	1.33	0.87	0.300
2019	AA	10.0	0	0	6	0.00	1.04	0.40	21.6	66.67%	1.8	5.56%	12.00	0.00	0.222
2019	AAA	17.3	1	1	2	4.67	2.53	1.56	21.8	53.85%	6.8	16.67%	3.23	1.04	0.571

Background: Fun Fact Part I: Bryant College, which is located in Smithfield, Rhode Island, has produced just 23 draft picks since 1976. Fun Fact Part II: only two of the players – Keith MacWhorter, a 15th round pick by the Dodgers in 1976, and James Karinchak – have cracked a big league roster. A ninth round pick in 2017, Karinchak, the 282nd overall player chosen, began his rapid ascent to the big leagues two years ago as he sprinted through three separate levels in dominant fashion: he averaged a mindboggling 15.0 strikeouts and 6.7 walks per nine innings in 42 games between the Midwest, Carolina, and Eastern Leagues. Last season the hard-throwing reliever battled an early hamstring issue that put him on the DL for roughly two months. But when he was healthy, he was unbelievably dominant. In 30.1 innings between Akron and Columbus, the 6-foot-3, 230-pound hurler struck out an unbelievable 74 hitters – an average of 22.0 strikeouts every nine innings. Twenty-two. Strikeouts. Per. Nine. Innings. Karinchak also made a brief, five-game cameo with the Indians down the stretch as well, fanning eight and walking just one in 5.1 innings of work.

Scouting Report: The level of production far surpassed absurdity that it deserves a newly minted word in the English language. Karinchak struck out 59.2% of the minor league hitters he faced last year. In other words: 74 of the 125 batters he faced off against resulted in a punch out. Two plus-plus pitches: an explosive upper-90s that's practically unhittable at the top of the strike zone and the filthiest curveball I've ever seen in my entire life. The control/command, of course, is problematic , but his high strikeout frequency and lack of hits surrendered help negate it. He's going to be a 2.0-plus win reliever. If you've never seen Karinchak pitch, you're definitely missing something spectacular.

Ceiling: 2.0-win player
Risk: Low to Moderate
MLB ETA: Debuted in 2019

11. Emmanuel Clase, RHP

FB	SL	CU	Command	Overall
80	70	80	55	50

Born: 03/18/98	Age: 22	Bats: R
Height: 6-2	Weight: 206	Throws: R

YEAR	LVL	IP	W	L	SV	ERA	FIP	WHIP	K/9	K%	BB/9	BB%	K/BB	HR9	BABIP
2017	Rk	35.7	2	4	0	5.30	5.68	1.74	10.6	24.14%	5.6	12.64%	1.91	1.01	0.360
2017	A-	3.3	0	1	0	13.50	5.28	2.70	10.8	21.05%	0.0	0.00%	N/A	2.70	0.571
2018	A-	28.3	1	1	12	0.64	2.28	0.78	8.6	25.71%	1.9	5.71%	4.50	0.00	0.222
2019	A+	7.0	2	0	1	0.00	0.66	0.71	14.1	44.00%	1.3	4.00%	11.00	0.00	0.308
2019	AA	37.7	1	2	11	3.35	2.36	1.12	9.3	25.49%	1.9	5.23%	4.88	0.24	0.314

Background: It's been one helluva whirlwind couple of seasons for the absurdly talented right-hander. The Rangers acquired the dominant reliever in a May 7th, 2018 deal with the Padres in exchange for lefty-swinging catcher Brett Ncholas. Texas flipped the triple-digit reaching hurler, along with outfielder Delino DeShields Jr., to the Indians in exchange for...two-time Cy Young award winner Corey Kluber. Clase, a native of Rio San Juan, Dominican Republic, appeared in 39 games with the Rangers' High Class A and Class AA affiliates in 2019, posting a 50-to-9 strikeout-to-walk ratio to go along with a 2.82 ERA in 44.2 innings. Clase also appeared in 21 games in The Show as well, averaging 8.1 K/9 and just 2.3 BB/9 per nine innings with a 2.31 ERA and a 3.91 DRA (*Deserved Run Average*). Unfortunately for Clase, as well as the organization, he suffered a Spring Training back issue – which was diagnosed with a Teres Major Strain – that will knock him out of commission for up to three months.

Scouting Report: I've watched a bevy of Clase's games last season. And every single time I walked away thinking the same thing: how in the hell can anyone make contact, let alone square up one of his plus-plus offerings? Explosive, 80-grade fastball that sits in the 98- to 99-mph range and consistently touches triple-digits. His otherworldly 90 mph slider shows the type of late, hard downward bite that haunts a hitter's dreams. But it's all about his superhuman cutter: it sits in the upper 90s with late, bat-busting movement. And for all the talk about his power-based repertoire, Clase has had little trouble in throwing strikes. He's going to team with James Karinchak, at some point, to give the Tribe a pair of unhittable, late-inning, high leverage options.

Ceiling: 2.0-win player
Risk: Low to Moderate
MLB ETA: Debuted in 2019

12. Logan Allen, LHP

FB	CB	SL	CH	Command	Overall
55	50	50	55	45/50	45

Born: 05/25/97	Age: 23	Bats: L
Height: 6-3	Weight: 200	Throws: R

YEAR	LVL	IP	W	L	SV	ERA	FIP	WHIP	K/9	K%	BB/9	BB%	K/BB	HR9	BABIP
2017	A	68.3	5	4	0	2.11	2.60	1.10	11.2	30.14%	3.4	9.22%	3.27	0.13	0.294
2017	A+	56.7	2	5	0	3.97	3.32	1.38	9.1	23.55%	2.9	7.44%	3.17	0.32	0.352
2018	AA	121.0	10	6	0	2.75	3.20	1.05	9.3	26.04%	2.8	7.92%	3.29	0.52	0.269
2018	AAA	27.7	4	0	0	1.63	5.15	1.23	8.5	22.61%	4.2	11.30%	2.00	1.30	0.236
2019	AAA	57.7	4	3	0	5.15	4.87	1.44	9.8	24.51%	3.4	8.56%	2.86	1.25	0.338
2019	AAA	22.3	1	1	0	7.66	7.38	1.93	7.3	16.82%	4.8	11.21%	1.50	2.42	0.362

Background: The Indians' front office isn't shy about pulling the trigger on big time deals – even going back to the Mark Shapiro-led days. And, historically speaking, the Tribe has come out on top. Last summer's mega, three-team swap has the makings of a similar trade. Cleveland dealt away ace right-hander Trevor Bauer to the Reds. Cincinnati, in turn, sent top prospect Taylor Trammell to the Padres, and then shipped Yasiel Puig and Scott Moss to Indians. The Padres traded power-hitting corner outfielder Franmil Reyes, rookie ball infielder/outfielder Victor Nova, and southpaw Logan Allen to Cleveland. Allen was originally drafted by the Red Sox in the eighth round and shipped to the Padres as part of the package for ace reliever Craig Kimbrel. Last season the 6-foot-3, 200-pound lefty made 18 starts between both organizations' Class AAA affiliates, throwing 80.0 innings with 81 strikeouts and 34 walks to go along with a disappointing 5.85 ERA. Allen also made nine appearances with the Indians following the deal, throwing an additional 27.2 innings with 17 strikeouts and 13 walks with a 6.18 ERA.

Snippet from The 2018 Prospect Digest Handbook: Typical crafty left-hander than has an idea and executes it. Allen moves the ball around well, allowing his repertoire to play up even higher. He's a strike-thrower but the command is merely average now. Allen is a safe bet to develop into a #4-type arm.

Scouting Report: After three straight years of solid-average command, Allen's feel for the strike zone backed up a bit last season. But given the rather lengthy track record, there's no reason to suspect a bounce back isn't in the near future. He sports an above-average fastball that sits in the 91- to 93-mph range, an average pair of breaking balls and a strong 55-grade changeup. His slider is particularly useful against left-handed hitters due to the horizontal movement, especially when he's location it on the outer third of the plate and letting it sweep outside. Pitchable backend arm, something along the lines of a Jake Junis.

Ceiling: 1.5-win player
Risk: Low to Moderate
MLB ETA: Debuted in 2019

13. Aaron Bracho, 2B

Hit	Power	SB	Patience	Glove	Overall
50/55	45/50	40	55	50	45

Born: 04/24/01	Age: 19	Bats: B
Height: 5-11	Weight: 175	Throws: R

YEAR	LVL	PA	1B	2B	3B	HR	SB	CS	AVG	OBP	SLG	BB%	K%	GB%	LD%	FB%
2019	Rk	137	14	10	2	6	4	1	0.296	0.416	0.593	16.79%	15.33%	29.7	20.9	37.4
2019	A-	32	3	1	0	2	0	0	0.222	0.344	0.481	15.63%	25.00%	31.6	5.3	52.6

Background: Signed out of El Tigrito, Venezuela, for $1.5 million three years ago as part of the Indians' major haul on the international market. Bracho, who was added to the organization along with George Valera and Jose Tena, was set to make his professional debut in 2018. But a broken arm forced him to sit out the entire season. Finally healthy, the club sent the then-18-year-old middle infielder to the Arizona Summer League to make his highly anticipated debut. In 30 games with the club's rookie league affiliate, the 5-foot-11, 175-pound prospect batted an impressive .296/.416/.593 with 10 doubles, two triples, six homeruns, and four stolen bases. His overall production, according to *Deserved Runs Created Plus*, topped the league average mark by a staggering 86%. Bracho also spent a week-plus in the New York-Penn League at the end of the year as well.

Scouting Report: A short quick bat path with plus bat speed that looks remarkably effortless. The young switch-hitter offers up some surprising power potential for a sub-6-foot middle infielder. Bracho also looked adept at laying off breaking balls down in the zone last season, which is incredibly encouraging given his lack of professional experience. The offensive performance/track record remains quite limited, but there's some solid starter potential here. It wouldn't be surprising to see the Indians push the teenager up to the Midwest League at the start of 2020 in an effort to make up for lost time.

Ceiling: 1.5- to 2.0-win player
Risk: Moderate
MLB ETA: 2022

14. Daniel Johnson, OF

Hit	Power	SB	Patience	Glove	Overall
50	50	40	50	50	45

Born: 07/11/95	Age: 24	Bats: L
Height: 5-10	Weight: 200	Throws: L

YEAR	LVL	PA	1B	2B	3B	HR	SB	CS	AVG	OBP	SLG	BB%	K%	GB%	LD%	FB%
2017	A	364	61	16	4	17	12	9	0.300	0.361	0.529	6.04%	19.23%	39.5	20.3	29.5
2017	A+	185	32	13	0	5	10	2	0.294	0.346	0.459	7.03%	16.22%	42.6	20.6	26.2
2018	RK	24	5	0	0	1	1	0	0.300	0.417	0.450	8.33%	8.33%	38.9	22.2	33.3
2018	AA	391	63	19	7	6	21	4	0.267	0.321	0.410	5.88%	23.02%	44.6	18.8	28.0
2019	AA	167	18	7	2	10	6	3	0.253	0.337	0.534	9.58%	23.35%	31.2	21.1	38.5
2019	AAA	380	62	27	5	9	6	7	0.306	0.371	0.496	8.95%	20.79%	41.0	23.8	27.6

Background: It was a move that was *widely* panned from the moment it was announced – particularly amongst locals. But a little more than a year later it just reaffirmed one thing: the Indians' front office trades as well as any in baseball. Cleveland dealt away a resurgent, long time fan favorite in Yan Gomes for a trio of prospects: hard-throwing right-hander Jefry Rodriguez, outfielder Daniel Johnson, and a player to be named later – who would eventually become infielder Andruw Monasterio. Gomes, a 2018 A.L. All-Star, would eventually win a World Series ring with the Washington Nationals, managed to bat a paltry .223/.316/.389 while earning slightly more than $7 million. Johnson, on the other hand, put together his finest professional season to date as he split time between the minors' top two levels. In 123 games with the RubberDucks of Akron and the Clippers of Columbus, the 5-foot-10, 200-pound outfielder slugged .290/.361/.507 with 34 doubles, seven triples, 19 homeruns, and 12 stolen bases (in 22 total attempts).

Snippet from The 2018 Prospect Digest Handbook: The lone knock on Johnson – beyond a smaller frame – was his inability to handle southpaws in 2018; he batted a decrepit .161/.255/.237 against them. He's always shown a slight platoon split, but nothing to that degree, so there's hope it was just an outlier moving forward. Average bat and defense; below-average power; and 25- to 30-stolen base potential. Johnson becomes the latest intriguing outfielder lottery ticket the club seems to be holding along with Jordan Luplow.

Scouting Report: Consider the following:

- Since 2006, here's the list of 23-year-old hitters to post a 118 to 128 DRC+ with an 8% to 10% walk rate and a strikeout rate between 16% and 21% in the International League (min. 350 PA): Yonder Alonso, Rowdy Tellez, Cesar Hernandez, and – of course – Daniel Johnson.
- Sans Johnson, who's yet to make his big league debut, here are their respective DRC+ marks in the big leagues: 100 (Alonso), 93 (Tellez), and 94 (Hernandez).

Johnson falls into the same category as a fringy, league average bat – though his speed and defensive contributions push him towards starter status. The Indians currently have a glut of outfielder, with widely varying ceilings, so Johnson's likely going to find himself back in Class AAA awaiting a shot at The Show.

Ceiling: 1.5- to 2.0-win player
Risk: Moderate
MLB ETA: 2020

---

15. Gabriel Rodriguez, SS

Hit	Power	SB	Patience	Glove	Overall
30/50	45/55	40/35	45+	45/50	45

Born: 02/22/02	Age: 18	Bats: R
Height: 6-2	Weight: 174	Throws: R

YEAR	LVL	PA	1B	2B	3B	HR	SB	CS	AVG	OBP	SLG	BB%	K%	GB%	LD%	FB%
2019	Rk	73	11	3	0	0	1	1	0.215	0.288	0.262	5.48%	30.14%	59.1	20.5	18.2

Background: The Indians have aggressively attacked the international free agent market in recent years, adding the likes of George Valera, Brayan Rocchio, Aaron Bracho, Angel Martinez, and Jose Tena, to a quietly underrated farm system. But it was Gabriel Rodriguez that surpassed not only the group's individual bonuses, but he was handed the largest bonus given to a position player by the organization. A 6-foot-2, 174-pound shortstop/third baseman, Rodriguez looked overwhelmed during his professional debut last season. He batted a puny .238/.335/.406 with seven doubles, four triples, and three homeruns in 38 games in the offensive-friendly confines of the Dominican Summer League. And he cobbled together a lowly .215/.288/.262 triple-slash line in 18 Arizona Summer League games.

Scouting Report: Well, that didn't exactly go like the Indians' front office brass envisioned. But there's a lot to like about the Bonus Baby. Short, simple, compact swing with above-average bat speed. Rodriguez seems to be unsettled on his mechanical approach at the plate, some games he's using an awkward, ill-timed large leg kick and other times it's far more subtle. There's a tremendous amount of projection left. And he has the frame that should be able to add a significant amount of strength as he matures. One more thought: I find it curious that the Indians would bounce the then-17-year-old to the stateside league despite having terrible numbers. I suspect it's because the batted ball data, which I don't have access to, must be strong.

Ceiling: 1.5- to 2.0-win player
Risk: Moderate to High
MLB ETA: 2023

---

16. Lenny Torres, RHP

FB	SL	CH	Command	Overall
N/A	N/A	N/A	N/A	45

Born: 10/15/00	Age: 19	Bats: R
Height: 6-1	Weight: 190	Throws: R

YEAR	LVL	IP	W	L	SV	ERA	FIP	WHIP	K/9	K%	BB/9	BB%	K/BB	HR9	BABIP
2018	Rk	15.3	0	0	0	1.76	2.37	1.17	12.9	34.92%	2.3	6.35%	5.50	0.00	0.400

Background: Fun Fact: The Indians have drafted multiple high school arms in the opening round on three separate occasions – 2001 when they selected Dan Denham, Alan Horne, and J.D. Martin; 2015 when they tabbed Brady Aiken and Triston McKenzie; and 2018 when they chose Ethan Hankins and Lenny Torres. Standing a wiry 6-foot 1 and 190 pounds, Torres, the 41st overall pick, turned in a solid, albeit abbreviated debut in the Arizona Summer League two years ago as he posted a dominating 22-to-4 strikeout-to-walk ratio with a 1.76 ERA in just 15.1 innings of work. Unfortunately for the former St. John's University commit, Torres underwent Tommy John surgery and missed the entirety of the 2019 season.

Snippet from The 2018 Prospect Digest Handbook: Only entering his age-18 season thanks to a late birthday. Torres attacks hitters with a solid three-pitch mix: his fastball sits between 92- and 96-mph, an above-average 84-mph slider, and a solid, upper-80s changeup. Torres shows some promising control/command, especially for a prep arm, though his mechanics need a bit of fine-tuning. The Indians, in recent years, have shown a far better aptitude in developing young arms, which bodes well for Torres and fellow first round Ethan Hankins. Torres looks like a backend starting pitcher who could easily slide into a fastball/slider-type high-leverage relief role.

Scouting Report: There's nothing new to report. Here's hoping for a full return to health in 2020. He's likely ticketed for a spot on Mahoning Valley's squad in the New York-Penn League.

Ceiling: 1.5- to 2.0-win player
Risk: Moderate to High
MLB ETA: Debuted in 2019

17. Bobby Bradley, 1B

Hit	Power	SB	Patience	Glove	Overall
45	60	30	55	50	45

Born: 05/29/96	Age: 24	Bats: L
Height: 6-1	Weight: 225	Throws: R

YEAR	LVL	PA	1B	2B	3B	HR	SB	CS	AVG	OBP	SLG	BB%	K%	GB%	LD%	FB%
2017	AA	532	66	25	3	23	3	3	0.251	0.331	0.465	10.34%	22.93%	45.6	19.4	30.5
2018	AA	421	33	19	3	24	1	0	0.214	0.304	0.477	10.69%	24.94%	40.4	15.0	36.7
2018	AAA	128	17	7	2	3	0	0	0.254	0.323	0.430	8.59%	33.59%	31.5	30.1	30.1
2019	AAA	453	50	23	0	33	0	0	0.264	0.344	0.567	10.15%	33.77%	39.5	22.2	30.2

Background: One of the most physically imposing prospects in all of baseball – despite standing just 6-foot-1 – Bradley owns the best in-game and raw power in the entire Cleveland farm system. A third round pick out of Harrison Central High School in 2014, the hulking first baseman put on an offensive show in the offensive-friendly International League last season. Appearing in 107 games with the Columbus Clippers, Bradley belted out 23 doubles and a career best 33 dingers en route to batting .264/.344/.567. Per *Deserved Runs Created Plus*, his overall production topped the league average threshold by 24%. Cleveland called lefty-swinging Bradley up in late June for a couple – mostly miserable – weeks.

Snippet from The 2018 Prospect Digest Handbook: The lefty-swinging slugger generates easy homerun power which – at some point in his professional career – will crack 30- to 35-long balls. And while he's made strides in trimming down his problematic punch out rate, the hit tool itself is underwhelming. Throw in some ugly – albeit improving – platoon splits, and the future looks less and less bright for Bradley.

Scouting Report: Let's have a little (nerdy) fun. Consider the following:

- Since 2006, there were thirteen 23-year-old hitters to post a DRC+ total between 120 and 130 in the International League (min. 300 PA): Joey Votto, Jesse Winker, Gary Sanchez, Michael Brantley, Martin Prado, Yonder Alonso, Cesar Hernandez, Rowdy Tellez, Daniel Johnson, Cody Asche, Brent Morel, Lars Anderson, and – of course – Bobby Bradley.
- Of those 13 aforementioned hitters, here's the list of them that walked in at least 10% of their plate appearances: Votto, Winkler, Brantley, Anderson, and Bradley.
- Going back to the original 13 hitters, here's the list of them that fanned in at least 22% of their plate appearances: Bobby Bradley, who punched out nearly 34% of the time.

Light tower power – the kind that you're born with, not taught. The good news: Bradley handled left-handers exceptionally well last season, slugging .284/.327/.582 against them. The bad news: well, it's the punch out rate. When he's making contact, which isn't all that often, it's loud. He's the type of hitter that could anchor a rebuilding team's lineup until better talent arrives. Unfortunately, for him though, Cleveland's not at that point. Yet.

Ceiling: 1.5-win player
Risk: Moderate
MLB ETA: Debuted in 2019

18. Adam Scott, LHP

FB	SL	CH	Command	Overall
55	55	50	55	45

Born: 10/10/95	Age: 24	Bats: L
Height: 6-4	Weight: 220	Throws: L

YEAR	LVL	IP	W	L	SV	ERA	FIP	WHIP	K/9	K%	BB/9	BB%	K/BB	HR9	BABIP
2018	Rk	7.3	1	0	0	0.00	0.66	0.68	17.2	50.00%	1.2	3.57%	14.00	0.00	0.308
2018	A-	11.7	2	0	0	3.09	2.96	1.11	10.8	29.79%	1.5	4.26%	7.00	0.77	0.333
2018	A	11.0	0	1	0	2.45	2.20	1.00	12.3	34.09%	0.8	2.27%	15.00	0.82	0.333
2018	A+	4.0	0	0	0	0.00	5.11	1.75	9.0	21.05%	9.0	21.05%	1.00	0.00	0.300
2019	A+	57.3	3	7	0	3.45	3.01	1.36	11.6	29.48%	3.1	7.97%	3.70	0.63	0.365
2019	AA	75.3	4	6	0	3.94	3.83	1.21	8.8	23.64%	2.5	6.71%	3.52	1.08	0.300

Background: Fun Fact Part I: Wofford College has had just 14 players drafted in the school's history. Fun Fact Part II: The first player chosen was backstop Tim Wallace, a second round pick by the Cardinals in 1982. Fun Fact Part III: The school's most recent pick was big left-hander Adam Scott, a fourth round pick in 2018. Fun Fact Part IV: Scott was the second highest pick in Wofford's history. Chosen with the 133rd overall pick, Scott – quietly – turned in a breakout campaign last season. Splitting time between Lynchburg and Akron, the 6-foot-4, 220-pound southpaw struck out an impressive 148, walked 41, and tallied an aggregate 3.73 ERA.

Scouting Report: With respect to his work in Class AA last season, consider the following:

- Since 2006, here's the list of 23-year-old pitchers to post a 22.5% to 24.5% strikeout percentage with a walk percentage between 5.5% and 7.5% in the Eastern League (min. 75 IP): David Peterson, Austin Voth, Shaun Anderson, Thomas Pannone, David Phelps, and – of course – Adam Scott.

A very intriguing middle-tier type pitching prospect. Scott's primarily a two-pitch pitcher: his fastball sits in the 93- to 94-mph range with some mechanical deception and his slider adds a second above-average weapon, capable of missing a surprising amount of bats. He'll also mix in a 50-grade changeup. Throw in a strong feel for the strike zone and Scott has a chance to develop into a competent backend starting pitcher.

Ceiling: 1.5-win player
Risk: Moderate
MLB ETA: 2022

19. Sam Hentges, LHP

FB	CB	CU	CH	Command	Overall
55	55	50	50	45	40

Born: 07/18/96	Age: 23	Bats: L
Height: 6-8	Weight: 245	Throws: L

YEAR	LVL	IP	W	L	SV	ERA	FIP	WHIP	K/9	K%	BB/9	BB%	K/BB	HR9	BABIP
2017	Rk	13.0	0	3	0	4.85	4.14	1.46	12.5	31.03%	2.1	5.17%	6.00	1.38	0.400
2017	A-	17.7	0	1	0	2.04	3.60	0.96	11.7	33.33%	6.1	17.39%	1.92	0.51	0.121
2018	A+	118.3	6	6	0	3.27	3.21	1.41	9.3	24.16%	4.0	10.50%	2.30	0.30	0.343
2019	AA	128.7	2	13	0	5.11	3.83	1.65	8.8	21.43%	4.5	10.88%	1.97	0.77	0.358

Background: It took a while for the gargantuan lefty to gain some minor league traction – though, missing a year or so due to Tommy John surgery will do that to a young arm – but Hentges put it all together two years ago in the Carolina League as he averaged 9.3 strikeouts and 4.0 walks per nine innings. The front office deemed the then-22-year-old hurler ready for the minors' toughest challenge, Class AA, for the 2019 season. And the results were…mixed. Standing an imposing 6-foot-8 and 245-pounds, the former fourth round selection made a career best 26 starts with the Akron RubberDucks, posting a 126-to-64 strikeout-to-walk ratio in 128.1 innings of work. He finished the year with an unsightly 5.11 ERA and a laughably poor 7.13 DRA (*Deserved Run Average*).

Snippet from The 2018 Prospect Digest Handbook: The Mounds View High School product looks like a potential backend starting pitcher, perhaps peaking as a #4.

Scouting Report: Consider the following:

- Since 2006, here's the list of 22-year-old pitchers that posted a 20.5% to 22.5% strikeout percentage with a walk percentage between 10% and 12% in the Eastern League (min. 100 IP): Justin Wilson and Sam Hentges.

While the arsenal suggests a competent big league backend starting option, the command hasn't come around as hoped. And all of its ugliness was exposed in Class AA, which isn't surprising. Low-90s fastball that plays up given his massive wingspan/stride. Above-average slurvy-type curveball. Average cutter and changeup. He could be an interesting fastball/curveball arm out of the Indians pen in a year or two though.

Ceiling: 1.0- to 1.5-win player
Risk: Moderate
MLB ETA: 2022

20. Luis Oviedo, RHP

	FB	CB	SL	CH	Command	Overall
	50/55	50	55/60	50	45	40

Born: 05/15/99	Age: 21	Bats: R
Height: 6-4	Weight: 170	Throws: R

YEAR	LVL	IP	W	L	SV	ERA	FIP	WHIP	K/9	K%	BB/9	BB%	K/BB	HR9	BABIP
2017	Rk	51.7	4	2	0	7.14	3.75	1.63	12.2	28.11%	3.8	8.84%	3.18	0.35	0.411
2018	A-	48.0	4	2	0	1.88	2.43	0.92	11.4	32.45%	1.9	5.32%	6.10	0.56	0.274
2018	A	9.0	1	0	0	3.00	4.48	1.33	6.0	16.67%	7.0	19.44%	0.86	0.00	0.217
2019	A	87.0	6	6	0	5.38	4.40	1.38	7.4	18.95%	4.1	10.53%	1.80	0.62	0.294

Background: A quasi-trendy pick, especially by me, for a breakout in 2019. Instead, though, Oviedo disappointed as he moved into full season action for the first time in his four-year career. Oviedo, a native of Barquisimeto, Venezuela, seemed to put it all together as he spent time with Mahoning Valley and Lake County two years ago when he posted a 67-to-17 strikeouts with a sparkling 2.05 ERA in 57.0 innings of work. Last season Oviedo returned to the Midwest League, though the production left a lot to be desired. In a career best 19 starts with the Captains, the 6-foot-4, 170-pound right-hander averaged just 7.4 strikeouts and 4.1 walks per nine innings. He compiled a 5.38 ERA and a slightly better 4.98 DRA (*Deserved Run Average*).

Snippet from The 2018 Prospect Digest Handbook: The 6-foot-4, 170-pound right-hander has some potential to be a solid mid-rotation caliber arm, but he is years – and years – away from making an impact. He could be one of the bigger breakout prospects in 2019.

Scouting Report: While Oviedo's known to add and subtract from his fastball, it lacked the second gear that he showed in 2019. He labored to get it up to 92 mph in a couple starts I saw last season. He'll also cut it at times as well, which adds a nice dimension to his repertoire. He complements the heater with an above-average, swing-and-miss slider. He'll also feature a big bending 12-6 curveball can be picked up from his hand early, though he can consistently throw it for strikes, and an 80-mph changeup. Oviedo just doesn't look like the same hurler from two years ago. There's an added layer of rigidity in his mechanics that seems to replace the explosive fluidity.

Ceiling: 1.0- to 1.5-win player
Risk: Moderate
MLB ETA: 2022

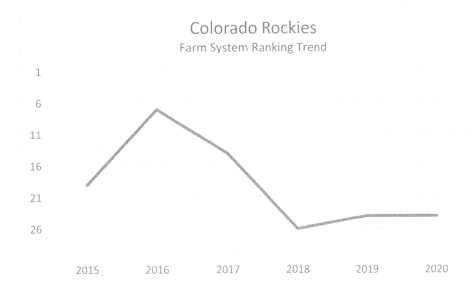

Colorado Rockies
Farm System Ranking Trend

Rank	Name	Age	Pos
1	Brendan Rodgers	23	IF
2	Ryan Rolison	22	LHP
3	Ryan Vilade	21	3B/SS
4	Antonio Santos	23	RHP
5	Brenton Doyle	22	CF
6	Helcris Olivarez	19	LHP
7	Michael Toglia	21	1B/LF/RF
8	Colton Welker	22	1B/3B
9	Terrin Vavra	23	2B/SS
10	Ezequiel Tovar	18	SS
11	Tyler Nevin	23	1B/3B/OF
12	Ryan Castellani	24	RHP
13	Grant Lavigne	20	1B
14	Riley Pint	22	RHP
15	Aaron Schunk	22	3B/SS
16	Ben Bowden	25	LHP
17	Tommy Doyle	24	RHP
18	Jacob Wallace	21	RHP
19	Eddy Diaz	20	2B/SS
20	Karl Kauffman	23	RHP

1. Brendan Rodgers, IF

Hit	Power	SB	Patience	Glove	Overall
55	55	40	45	50	55

Born: 08/09/96	Age: 23	Bats: R
Height: 6-0	Weight: 180	Throws: R

YEAR	LVL	PA	1B	2B	3B	HR	SB	CS	AVG	OBP	SLG	BB%	K%	GB%	LD%	FB%
2017	A+	236	50	21	3	12	2	1	0.387	0.407	0.671	2.54%	14.83%	42.9	19.4	31.9
2017	AA	164	28	5	0	6	0	2	0.260	0.323	0.413	4.88%	21.95%	37.7	20.2	27.2
2018	AA	402	56	23	2	17	12	3	0.275	0.342	0.493	7.46%	18.91%	43.9	18.8	32.1
2018	AAA	72	12	4	0	0	0	0	0.232	0.264	0.290	1.39%	22.22%	45.3	28.3	22.6
2019	AAA	160	30	10	1	9	0	0	0.350	0.413	0.622	8.75%	16.88%	46.2	24.8	23.1

Background: A member of every Top 100 list since hearing his name called as the third overall pick all the way back in 2015. It's hard to believe that the Lake Mary High School product is only entering his age-23 season. Now a defensive vagabond of sorts, Rodgers has been a consistent – sometimes potent – offensive weapon during his five-year professional career. Last season the 6-foot, 180-pound infielder opened the year up on one helluva offensive tear with the Albuquerque Isotopes in the Pacific Coast League: he slugged a Ruthian .356/.421/.644 with 10 doubles, one triple, and nine homeruns in only 35 games. Colorado called their long time top prospect up to The Show in mid-May, though the results we a bit underwhelming: he hit a lowly .246/.300/.277 with just a pair of doubles in 70 plate appearances. He was briefly demoted and then recalled before hitting the disabled list with a "shoulder impingement." He would eventually undergo a procedure to repair his right labrum.

Snippet from The 2018 Prospect Digest Handbook: Rodgers doesn't have any glaring red flags. But he could very well take the Addison Russell career trajectory from top prospect to qualified big league starter without actually reaching stardom.

Scouting Report: The ink has dried on Nolan Arenado's eight-year extension and Trevor Story is still under team control for three more seasons, and neither is going to be vacating their positions on the left-side of the infield. Daniel Murphy, fresh off of a season in which he slugged .279/.328/.452, is under contract for at least one more year, maybe two thanks to a contract option. And the team has other interesting options to fill the second base void in Garret Hampson and Ryan McMahon as well. But make no mistake about it: Rodgers will assume a starting gig as soon as the team's convinced he can handle it. Above-average offensive tools with a solid glove to handle any infield position.

Ceiling: 3.5- to 4.0-win player
Risk: Low to Moderate
MLB ETA: Debuted in 2019

2. Ryan Rolison, LHP

FB	CB	SL	CH	Command	Overall
55	60	50	50	55	50

Born: 07/11/97	Age: 22	Bats: R
Height: 6-2	Weight: 195	Throws: L

YEAR	LVL	IP	W	L	SV	ERA	FIP	WHIP	K/9	K%	BB/9	BB%	K/BB	HR9	BABIP
2018	Rk	29.0	0	1	0	1.86	3.70	0.79	10.6	31.19%	2.5	7.34%	4.25	0.62	0.200
2019	A	14.7	2	1	0	0.61	1.97	0.68	8.6	26.42%	1.2	3.77%	7.00	0.00	0.216
2019	A+	116.3	6	7	0	4.87	5.12	1.44	9.1	24.38%	2.9	7.85%	3.11	1.70	0.320

Background: There was a brief two-year stretch where the Rockies were simply picking the wrong arms in the opening round of the draft. The club selected Mike Nikorak with the 27th overall pick in 2015. And doubled down on a pair of high upside arms in Riley Pint and Robert Tyler with the 4th and 38th selections the following year. But they finally found a keeper in Rolison, a lanky left-hander out of Ole Miss. Taken with the 22nd pick two years ago, it took just three – absurdly good – starts in the Sally last season for Rolison to convince the powers that be that he was ready for High Class A. He would go on to make 22 starts with Lancaster, home to the infamous bandbox, posting a 118-to-38 strikeout-to-walk ratio. He finished the year with a total of 131.0 innings of work, averaging 9.1 strikeouts and just 2.7 walks per nine innings.

Snippet from The 2018 Prospect Digest Handbook: He has the look and production that screams #4-type pitcher, maybe a little more if his command improves.

Scouting Report: The command improved – significantly. Rolison battled some questionable control / command issues during his collegiate career, particularly in his final season at Ole Miss. But it's been impeccable since he's entered the Rockies' organization. The young lefty owns a standard four-pitch mix: a low-90s fastball, a plus curveball, an average slider (that he sometimes chokes), and a nice little deceptive changeup. If he continues the trend of throwing more quality strikes, which has been the case, Rolison is looking like a strong candidate to develop into a #3-type starting pitcher.

Ceiling: 3.0-win player
Risk: Moderate
MLB ETA: 2021

3. Ryan Vilade, SS

	Hit	Power	SB	Patience	Glove	Overall
	55/60	45/50	50	50	45	50

Born: 02/18/99	Age: 21	Bats: R
Height: 6-2	Weight: 194	Throws: R

YEAR	LVL	PA	1B	2B	3B	HR	SB	CS	AVG	OBP	SLG	BB%	K%	GB%	LD%	FB%
2017	RK	146	26	3	2	5	5	5	0.308	0.438	0.496	18.49%	21.23%	44.8	25.3	26.4
2018	A	533	96	20	4	5	17	13	0.274	0.353	0.368	9.19%	18.01%	55.3	16.4	24.1
2019	A+	587	105	27	10	12	24	7	0.303	0.367	0.466	9.54%	16.18%	44.4	16.6	32.7

Background: Penn State was famously regarded as Linebacker U. for decades. Perhaps the Colorado Rockies farm system should adopt their own moniker? Middle-infielder U.? Doesn't really have the same ring to it, but the premise certainly holds – at least for the last several seasons. Trevor Story, Brendan Rodgers, Ryan McMahon, Garrett Hampson, and – quietly – Ryan Vilade. Taken in the second round of the 2017 draft, the 48th overall pick, Vilade handled the Pioneer League with relative ease during his professional debut, hitting .308/.438/.496 with 10 extra-base hits in only 33 games. He followed that up with a solid .274/.353/.368 triple-slash line as he moved into the Sally the following year. Last season, as a 20-year-old, the Stillwater High School product turned in his finest season to date – though it comes with a large caveat – in High Class A. That aforementioned caveat: Lancaster is one of the most hitter-friendly, run-inducing environments in professional baseball. Vilade slugged .303/.367/.466 with career highs in doubles (27), triples (10), homeruns (12), and stolen bases (24). His overall production, per Baseball Prospectus' *Deserved Runs Created Plus*, topped the league average mark by 18%.

Snippet from The 2018 Prospect Digest Handbook: It took longer than expected for Vilade to find his true skill set with the Tourists, but he eventually developed into one of the better bats in the Sally in the second half of last season. After batting a disappointing .232/.342/.314 over his first 52 games, he slugged an impressive .304/361/.407 over his remaining 67 contests. There's more in the tank for Vilade, especially considering his steady improvement throughout the year. But his value will take a considerable hit if he moves away from shortstop.

Scouting Report: Consider the following:

- Since 2006, here's the list of 20-year-old hitters to meet the following criteria in the California League (min. 350 PA): 113 to 123 DRC+; a sub-20% strikeout rate; and a walk rate between 8% and 10%. Those three hitters are Franmil Reyes, Nolan Arenado, and – of course – Ryan Vilade. For the record: Reyes has been 11% better than the league average in his young big league career and Arenado has topped the league average by 25%.

Despite the strong comparisons, Vilade did show – unsurprisingly – some massive home/road splits: he hit .304/.358/.474 in Lancaster and only .250/.314/.371 on the road. Strong bat-to-ball skills with developing power to belt out 12- to 15-homeruns and a solid willingness to walk. The biggest improvement in Vilade's game last season was his work with the leather: he was abysmal at shortstop two years ago, but graded out as slightly below-average last season.

Ceiling: 3.0-win player
Risk: Moderate
MLB ETA: 2021/2022

4. Antonio Santos, RHP

	FB	CB	SL	CH	Command	Overall
	80	50	45	50+	55	50

Born: 10/06/96	Age: 23	Bats: R
Height: 6-3	Weight: 180	Throws: R

YEAR	LVL	IP	W	L	SV	ERA	FIP	WHIP	K/9	K%	BB/9	BB%	K/BB	HR9	BABIP
2017	A	147.0	9	10	0	5.39	4.32	1.54	6.5	16.31%	1.6	4.00%	4.08	1.04	0.373
2018	A	86.3	1	10	0	4.48	3.19	1.30	9.0	23.18%	1.3	3.23%	7.17	0.83	0.351
2018	A+	65.7	4	3	0	5.21	5.97	1.45	7.7	19.44%	2.9	7.29%	2.67	2.06	0.301
2019	A+	99.3	3	6	0	4.35	3.80	1.35	8.7	22.33%	1.6	4.19%	5.33	1.00	0.348
2019	AA	45.7	3	3	0	4.93	2.88	1.25	8.7	25.88%	2.0	5.88%	4.40	0.59	0.342

Background: Ignore the stigma that's plagued the organization since its inception. You know, the one about struggling to develop arms. Now let's take a look at the Rockies' homegrown arms that have popped up during the past couple seasons: German Marquez, who's tallied 9.9 wins above replacement since 2017; Jon Gray, who's totaled more than 12 WAR since 2016; Kyle Freeland, who earned more than four wins in 2018; Antonio Senzatela, a solid backend starting pitcher; and dominant backend reliever Carlos Estevez. Enter: Antonio Santos, a ridiculously hard-throwing right-hander who's already earned some significant time at Class AA. Last season, the hard-throwing Dominican right-hander spent time between Lancaster and Hartford, throwing 145.0 innings with an impressive 140-to-28 strikeout-to-walk ratio to go along with an aggregate 4.53 ERA.

Scouting Report: On the short, short list for most underrated prospect in the entire minor leagues; Santos owns a high octane, nitrous infused repertoire that's not dissimilar to Marlins All-Star Sandy Alcantara. The Rockies' prospect owns an 80-grade fastball that sits 95- to 97-mph and reached as high as 102 mph last season. He'll mix in a surprisingly solid mid- to upper-80s changeup that generates a decent amount of weak contact and swings-and-misses. He also throws two distinct breaking balls: a power curveball sitting in the low-80s with some solid action and a cutter-like slider that's easily his worst offering. The best part: he commands the strike zone really well. I like this kid. He's a name to remember and a dark horse candidate for N.L. Rookie of the Year.

Ceiling: 2.5-win player
Risk: Moderate
MLB ETA: 2020

5. Brenton Doyle, CF

Hit	Power	SB	Patience	Glove	Overall
50/55	50	50	55	50	50

Born: 05/14/98	Age: 22	Bats: R
Height: 6-3	Weight: 200	Throws: R

YEAR	LVL	PA	1B	2B	3B	HR	SB	CS	AVG	OBP	SLG	BB%	K%	GB%	LD%	FB%
2019	Rk+	215	47	11	3	8	17	3	0.383	0.477	0.611	14.42%	21.86%	52.6	24.4	21.5

Background: A dominant bat for Shepherd University during his three-year tenure at the Mountain East Conference school. Doyle, a native of Warrenton, Virginia, began his collegiate career with a stellar .327/.373/.480 with 13 doubles, one triple, and five homeruns with 11 stolen bases. Doyle did his best Babe Ruth impression the next year for the Rams: in 55 games, the 6 foot 3, 200 pound center fielder slugged .415/.434/.699 with 17 doubles, four triples, and 14 homeruns to go along with 22 stolen bases in 23 total attempts. He followed that up with another dynamic showing during his junior season: in 52 games he batted .392/.502/.758 with 17 doubles, six triples, and 13 homeruns with 19 stolen bases in 24 attempts. Colorado drafted the Division II star in the fourth round, 129th overall, and sent him to the Pioneer League. And Doyle did what Doyle's always done: smoke the ball. In 51 games with Grand Junction the toolsy center fielder slugged .383/.477/.611 with 11 doubles, three triples, and eight homeruns. He also swiped 17 bags in 20 tries. His production, as measured by Baseball Prospectus' *Deserved Runs Created Plus*, topped the league average mark by a whopping 98%.

Scouting Report: Consider the following:

- Since 2006, here's the list of 21-year-old hitters to post at least a 190 DRC+ with 15 or more stolen bases in Pioneer League (min. 200 PA): Adam Eaton and Brenton Doyle. Eaton, of course, has been a dynamic top-of-the-lineup table setter through his big league career.

As for Doyle, well, the former Shepherd University star looked incredibly comfortable as he transitioned into the professional ranks: there's the potential for above-average tools across the board. Tremendous plate discipline; he was on pace to swipe 50 bags in a full season; showed impressive power and played a passable center field as well. Doyle could prove to be one of the bigger value picks in the entire 2019 draft class.

Ceiling: 2.5-win player
Risk: Moderate
MLB ETA: 2021/2022

6. Helcris Olivarez, LHP

FB	CB	CH	Command	Overall
60/70	45/55	45/50	40/50	50

Born: 08/08/00	Age: 19	Bats: L
Height: 6-2	Weight: 192	Throws: L

YEAR	LVL	IP	W	L	SV	ERA	FIP	WHIP	K/9	K%	BB/9	BB%	K/BB	HR9	BABIP
2017	Rk	33.0	0	1	0	3.55	2.84	1.24	9.5	24.82%	4.6	12.06%	2.06	0.00	0.276
2018	Rk	19.0	2	0	0	1.42	1.75	0.79	11.4	32.88%	1.9	5.48%	6.00	0.00	0.250
2018	Rk	35.7	4	1	0	2.78	3.77	1.32	9.1	24.49%	5.6	14.97%	1.64	0.25	0.276
2019	Rk	46.7	3	4	0	4.82	5.78	1.52	11.8	28.77%	4.6	11.32%	2.54	1.74	0.336

Background: Signed out of San Francisco de Macoris, Dominican Republic, in the middle of August in 2016 for a rather paltry sum of $77,000. Olivarez, though, has big, *big* time potential thanks to his firebolt-slinging left arm. After spending the previous two summers and the first three games last season in the Dominican Summer League, the 6-foot-2, 192-pound southpaw finally made the leap stateside and opened a lot of eyes. In 11 starts with the Grand Junction Rockies, Olivarez posted a strong 61-to-24 strikeout-to-walk ratio in only 46.2 innings of work. He tallied an unsightly 4.82 ERA and a nearly identical 4.88 Deserved Runs Average.

Scouting Report: Big, big time fastball potential. Olivarez's heater would sit 92- to 94-mph and easily touch 97 mph at will. And it's not just the velocity that's impressive, it's the ease that he generates velocity. His curveball is loopy but shows the requisite shape. It grades out as a strong 45 now, but it could easily wind up as plus as he matures. The changeup, which was widely regarded a well below-average prior to the year, was far better than expected. It shows some arm-side run and fade with the potential to be average, maybe better if everything breaks the right way. Olivarez is raw, but there's sneaky potential brewing in his powerful arm. Had he lived stateside and eligible for the June draft, I would have put a second/third round grade on him. Consider the following:

- Since 2006, here's the list of 18-year-old pitchers to fan at least 26% of the hitters they faced in the Pioneer League (min. 40 IP): fellow left-hander John Lamb, who was widely regarded at one point as a Top 20 prospect in all of baseball, and – of course – the Rockies' burgeoning arm Helcris Olivarez.

Ceiling: 2.5- to 3.0--win player
Risk: Moderate to High
MLB ETA: 2023

7. Michael Toglia, 1B/LF

Hit	Power	SB	Patience	Glove	Overall
45	55/60	30	55	50	50

Born: 08/16/98	Age: 21	Bats: B
Height: 6-5	Weight: 226	Throws: L

YEAR	LVL	PA	1B	2B	3B	HR	SB	CS	AVG	OBP	SLG	BB%	K%	GB%	LD%	FB%
2019	A-	176	20	7	0	9	1	1	0.248	0.369	0.483	15.91%	25.57%	42.0	25.0	30.0

Background: If you don't succeed, try, try, try again. Well, the Colorado Rockies have taken that advice to heart. The organization originally took a late, late flier on Toglia as he was coming out of Gig Harbor High School in 2016; they used the 1,040[th]

pick on him. Toglia, of course, never signed and attended UCLA. Fast forward three years and Rockies once again called out Toglia's name in the draft. This time, though, it was in the first round when they used the 23rd overall pick on him. Toglia, a 6-foot-5, 226-pound switch-hitting first baseman / corner outfielder, turned in an impressive collegiate career for the Bruins. As a true freshman, the Gig Harbor, Washington, native batted .261/.382/.483 with 21 extra-base hits and spent the ensuing summer with the Cotuit Kettleers in the Cape Cod League. Toglia ratcheted up his performance during his sophomore season for the PAC12 school, slugging .336/.449/.588 with 24 doubles and 11 homeruns. And, once again, he spent the summer with the Kettleers, though he struggled to the tune of .209/.323/.388. Last season Toglia's number regressed a touch as he hit .314/.392/.624 with 16 doubles, four triple, and 17 homeruns. As far as his performance during his debut, Toglia batted .248/.369/.483 with seven doubles and nine homeruns in 41 games with Boise in the Northwest League.

Scouting Report: Built in the typical saber-slanted slugging mold, Toglia posses above-average to plus in-game power, a tremendously patient approach at the plate, and some red flag-territory strikeout numbers. It's the basic scouting report throughout his three seasons with the Bruins and he maintained status quo in the Northwest League as well. Looking back at his work as junior last season, consider the following:

- Between 2011 and 2018, here's the list of PAC12 hitters to hit at least .300/.380/.600 with a strikeout rate north of 20% in season in which they received at least 250 plate appearances: Bobby Dalbec, Trevor Larnach, and Gage Canning. Dalbec's an overhyped, flawed prospect in the Red Sox's system. Larnach decimated High Class A and Class AA (briefly) during his second professional season. And Canning has disappointed since becoming a fifth round pick.

His offensive struggles in the Cape Cod in back-to-back seasons is a major red flag for me.

Ceiling: 2.0-win player
Risk: Moderate
MLB ETA: 2022

8. Colton Welker, 1B/3B

Hit	Power	SB	Patience	Glove	Overall
55	50/55	30	50	50	50

Born: 10/09/97	Age: 22	Bats: R
Height: 6-1	Weight: 195	Throws: R

YEAR	LVL	PA	1B	2B	3B	HR	SB	CS	AVG	OBP	SLG	BB%	K%	GB%	LD%	FB%
2017	A	279	64	18	1	6	5	7	0.350	0.401	0.500	6.45%	15.05%	43.9	25.7	26.2
2018	A+	509	106	32	0	13	5	1	0.333	0.383	0.489	8.25%	20.24%	41.4	27.1	28.2
2019	AA	394	55	23	1	10	2	1	0.252	0.313	0.408	8.12%	17.26%	40.4	18.5	37.0

Background: A long time personal favorite of mine, as well as a bevy of the club's infield prospects, Welker has moved through the minor leagues with the quiet efficiency of a trained assassin. Hailing from Stoneman-Douglas High School, which includes such luminaries as

Anthony Rizzo, Jesus Luzardo, and former Rookie of the Year contender Mike Caruso, Welker has spent an entire season in each of following levels: Rookie Advanced, Low Class A, High Class A, and – of course – Class AA. In 98 games with the Hartford Yard Goats, the former fourth round pick hit a respectable .252/.313/.408 with 23 doubles, one triple, and 10 homeruns. His overall production, per *Deserved Runs Created Plus*, topped the league average mark by 13%.

Snippet from The 2018 Prospect Digest Handbook: Welker's undergoing an important transition at the plate as he's continually decreased his groundball rates in each of the last two seasons. He's eventually going to see a spike in the homerun department in the next year or two. The hit tool is above-average; the power has a shot at developing into 20-HR territory; and the eye at the plate is trending in the right direction. Plus, he plays a passable hot corner as well.

Scouting Report: Consider the following:

- Since 2006, here's the list of 21-year-old hitters to post a DRC+ between 108 and 118 with a walk rate between 7% and 9% in the Eastern League (min. 350 PA): Brendan Rodgers and Colton Welker.

Cut from the same mold, apparently. The problem, at least temporarily, is Rodgers is an up-the-middle player where as Welker's stuck in a more power-oriented corner infield spot (e.g. first base because of Nolan Arenado). Strong contact rates, average patience, average glove at third base. But there's a silver lining: Welker started out like a bat-of-a-hell last season, slugging .308/.358/.510 across his first 56 games. He would hit a lowly .151/.212/.204 over his next 26 contests before hitting the DL with "an undisclosed injury" for a month and never quite recovered. Given Welker's career trajectory, his first 56 games is more in line with expectations. The power is coming.

Ceiling: 2.0-win player
Risk: Moderate
MLB ETA: 2020

9. Terrin Vavra, 2B/SS

Hit	Power	SB	Patience	Glove	Overall
55/60	45	50	55	50	50

Born: 05/12/97	Age: 23	Bats: L
Height: 6-1	Weight: 185	Throws: R

YEAR	LVL	PA	1B	2B	3B	HR	SB	CS	AVG	OBP	SLG	BB%	K%	GB%	LD%	FB%
2018	A-	199	35	8	4	4	9	1	0.302	0.396	0.467	13.07%	20.10%	50.0	18.2	31.1
2019	A	453	76	32	1	10	18	9	0.318	0.409	0.489	13.69%	13.69%	42.0	18.2	35.5

Background: A standout offensive performer during his three-year tenure at the University of Minnesota, Vavra twice topped the .350 batting average threshold during his career. Colorado snagged the lefty-swinging middle infielder in the third round, 96th overall, in the 2018 draft. Vavra, of course, continued to swing an impressive stick as he entered the professional ranks. The 6-foot-1, 185-pound, lefty-swinging middle infielder hit .302/.396/.467 with eight doubles, four triples, and four homers in 44 games in the Northwest League. The front office bumped him up to the South Atlantic League last season and Vavra performed, well, like Terrin Vavra: in 102 games with the Asheville Tourists, the former Golden Gopher batted .318/.409/.489 with 32 doubles, one triple, and 10 homers. He also swiped 18 bags in 27 attempts. Per *Deserved Runs Created Plus*, his overall production topped the league average mark by 52%.

Snippet from The 2018 Prospect Digest Handbook: Vavra slides into the same prospect class as [Garrett] Hampson – a potential above-average middle infielder. The lefty-swinging Vavra showed no platoon spits as well. In terms of draft slot and bonus, he could be one of the biggest steals in the 2018d draft. Expect him to take a quick path to the big league a la Hampson.

Scouting Report: It's a surprising, at least a little bit, that the brass didn't bounce the sweet-swinging infielder up to High Class A at some point in the second half of the season. Vavra, though, still has the potential to move quickly. The stick is an above-average tool, maybe even peaking as a 60-grade; he's fleet-footed enough to swipe 25 bags in a season, though he needs to work on his jumps; above-average eye and surprising power. Throw in some solid defense and that's a recipe for big league value. Consider the following:

- Since 2006, here's the list of 22-year-olds to post at least a 145 DRC+ with at least a 12% walk rate and sub-16% strikeout rate in the South Atlantic League (min. 350 PA): Chris Coghlan, Shawn Payne, and Terrin Vavra.

Coghlan, a league average hitter in over 800 big league games, seems like a reasonable comp and best case scenario.

Ceiling: 2.0-win player
Risk: Moderate
MLB ETA: 2022

Colorado Rockies

10. Ezequiel Tovar, SS

Hit	Power	SB	Patience	Glove	Overall
30/50	30/40	50	50	70	50

Born: 08/01/01	Age: 18	Bats: B
Height: 6-0	Weight: 162	Throws: R

YEAR	LVL	PA	1B	2B	3B	HR	SB	CS	AVG	OBP	SLG	BB%	K%	GB%	LD%	FB%
2018	RK	158	26	4	4	0	16	9	0.262	0.369	0.354	13.92%	20.89%	38.6	26.7	29.7
2019	Rk+	86	15	2	2	0	4	1	0.264	0.357	0.347	11.63%	19.77%	46.6	15.5	34.5
2019	A-	243	46	4	2	2	13	0	0.249	0.304	0.313	6.58%	21.40%	45.3	21.8	25.3

Background: Just another member of the club's bevy of intriguing middle infield prospects. Tovar, who signed with the organization for $800,000 on August 1st, 2017, has quickly become of the best defensive players in the entire minor leagues – which is great news because he can't hit. The 6-foot, 162-pound switch-hitter opened up his professional career in the Dominican Summer League, one of the most hitter-friendly environments in the minor leagues, by hitting a lowly .262/.369/.354 two years ago. The front office bounced him stateside to the Northwest League last season, an uncharacteristic move for Colorado. And Tovar flailed away, batting a lowly .249/.304/.313 with just four doubles, two triples, and two homeruns in 55 games. He was demoted down to the Pioneer League for his final 18 games; he hit an improved .264/.357/.347.

Scouting Report: One of my favorite prospects in the entire minor leagues. Tovar's an absolute wizard at shortstop. So much so, in fact, if he could post production lines below 10% of the league average mark he'd be a 2.5- to 3.0-win player. Very young, very, very raw. But there's a lot to like here. Above-average to plus speed; the hit tool is below-average but should be a 50-grade at maturity. And despite the lagging slugging numbers there's so interesting pop brewing. Defensively, he was jaw-dropping good in 2019; according to Clay Davenport's metrics he saved 15 runs better than the average in only 73 games. Remember this kid.

Ceiling: 2.0- to 2.5-win player
Risk: Moderate to High
MLB ETA: 2022/2023

11. Tyler Nevin, 1B/3B

Hit	Power	SB	Patience	Glove	Overall
50	50	50	55	50	45

Born: 05/29/97	Age: 23	Bats: R
Height: 6-4	Weight: 200	Throws: R

YEAR	LVL	PA	1B	2B	3B	HR	SB	CS	AVG	OBP	SLG	BB%	K%	GB%	LD%	FB%
2017	A-	30	3	3	0	1	0	1	0.233	0.233	0.433	0.00%	30.00%	52.4	28.6	19.0
2017	A	335	63	18	3	7	10	5	0.305	0.364	0.456	8.06%	16.72%	46.0	21.4	27.4
2018	A+	417	85	25	1	13	4	3	0.328	0.386	0.503	8.15%	18.47%	48.2	20.1	27.4
2019	AA	540	76	26	2	13	6	2	0.251	0.345	0.399	12.04%	16.67%	43.7	16.8	34.5

Background: Practically going hand-in-hand with fellow middle-of-the-lineup thumper Colton Welker, Nevin has quickly moved through the low levels of the minor leagues after a small hiccup of injuries in 2016 and 2017. Taken in the first round of the 2015 draft, 38th overall and sandwiched between Daz Cameron and Jake Woodford, Nevin spent the entirety of last season in the minors' most challenging level: Class AA. In a career best 130 games, Phil's kid hit a saber-driven .251/.345/.399 with a career high in doubles (26) to go along with a pair of triples and 13 dingers. His overall production, as measured by *Deserved Runs Created Plus*, topped the league average mark by a surprising 20%. Not bad work for a 22-year-old prospect.

Snippet from The 2018 Prospect Digest Handbook: Nevin's overall offensive approach is similar to teammate Colton Welker: average-eye at the plate, budding 25 homerun potential, and – surprisingly – solid contact skills.

Scouting Report: Consider the following:

- Since 2006, there were four 22-year-old hitters to meet the following criteria in the Eastern League (min. 350 PA): 115 to 125 DRC+; double-digit walk rate; and a sub-20% strikeout rate. Those four hitters: Luis Guillorme, Robbie Grossman, Corban Joseph, and Tyler Nevin. The best of the bunch (sans Nevin): saber-friendly outfielder Robbie Grossman, who's been exactly a league average hitter in 675 big league games.

An abysmal month of May significantly deflated Nevin's overall production; he hit a depressingly low .185/.279/.261. And his overall power was rather pathetic before uncorking a huge month of August. He slugged 11 of his 26 doubles in eight of his 13 dingers in August. I've always favored Welker over Nevin and nothing's changed. A lot of the latter's future value will be tied up in his power.

Ceiling: 1.5- to 2.0-win player
Risk: Moderate
MLB ETA: 2020

12. Ryan Castellani, RHP

	FB	SL	CH	Command	Overall
	N/A	N/A	N/A	N/A	45

Born: 04/01/96	Age: 24	Bats: R
Height: 6-4	Weight: 223	Throws: R

YEAR	LVL	IP	W	L	SV	ERA	FIP	WHIP	K/9	K%	BB/9	BB%	K/BB	HR9	BABIP
2017	AA	157.3	9	12	0	4.81	4.00	1.33	7.6	19.35%	2.7	6.89%	2.81	0.92	0.309
2018	AA	134.3	7	9	0	5.49	5.20	1.53	6.1	15.17%	4.7	11.67%	1.30	1.00	0.291
2019	AAA	43.3	2	5	0	8.31	8.25	1.94	9.8	21.76%	6.2	13.89%	1.57	2.91	0.333

Background: Castellani has always been an interesting prospect. The production throughout the first five seasons of his career all suggested a finesse right-hander succeeding with guile, pitchability, and little oomph in his repertoire. Except it was the opposite: the former second round pick owns a plus fastball and a slider that would flash plus at times (to go along with an average changeup). Something finally changed in Castellani's development / production in the Arizona Fall League two years ago: he started missing sticks, a lot of them. And that continued through his first 10 starts of 2019 as well: in 43.1 innings with the Isotopes, the hard-throwing right-hander posted a 47-to-30 strikeout-to-walk ratio. Then he hit the DL with a problematic right elbow. He would eventually undergo surgery to remove particulates around the joint in late June.

Snippet from The 2018 Prospect Digest Handbook: Castellani's tough to get a read on. Earlier in the season his fastball was sitting 92- to 94-mph and bumping 95 at times. But his fastball was in the upper 80s touching 90 in his last start of the year against the New Hampshire Fisher Cats. When he's on his fastball can sneak up on hitters. And he'll complement it with a hard biting slider – easily an above-average to plus-offering.

Scouting Report: Hindsight being 20-20. Perhaps the elbow injury last season started rearing its ugly head in the second half of 2018. Castellani made it back to the Arizona Fall League where – of course – he continued his newfound ability to punch out hitters. In 16.2 innings with the Salt River Rafters, the former second rounder fanned 20 and walked only seven to go along with a 2.16 ERA. The stuff's been there for a long time. And the command's been above-average at times. If he puts it all together he's going to be something. But time is no longer on his side.

Ceiling: 1.5- to 2.0--win player
Risk: Moderate to High
MLB ETA: 2020

13. Grant Lavigne, 1B

	Hit	Power	SB	Patience	Glove	Overall
	40/50	45/55	35	55	50	45

Born: 08/27/99	Age: 20	Bats: L
Height: 6-4	Weight: 220	Throws: R

YEAR	LVL	PA	1B	2B	3B	HR	SB	CS	AVG	OBP	SLG	BB%	K%	GB%	LD%	FB%
2018	RK	258	51	13	2	6	12	7	0.350	0.477	0.519	17.44%	15.50%	55.1	18.0	23.4
2019	A	526	78	19	0	7	8	9	0.236	0.347	0.327	12.93%	24.52%	53.2	16.8	25.3

Background: Sandwiched between the Indians taking prep right-hander Lenny Torres and the Cardinals snagging Griffin Roberts, Colorado selected the top first baseman with the 42nd overall pick two years ago. And Lavigne, a hulking 6-foot-4, 220-pound basher out of Bedford High School, not only looked like a gamble but also a burgeoning star as he slugged a robust .350/.477/.519 with 13 doubles, a pair of triples, and half-a-dozen homeruns. He was promoted up to the South Atlantic league last season. And the league's arms clapped back. In 126 games with the Asheville Tourists, Lavigne cobbled together a hugely disappointing .236/.347/.327 triple-slash line, belting out just 19 doubles and seven homeruns. Making matters worse: he swiped eight bags in 17 total attempts. His overall production, as measured by *Deserved Runs Created Plus*, was 13% below the league average threshold.

Snippet from The 2018 Prospect Digest Handbook: Tremendous, tremendous eye at the plate with genuine middle-of-the-lineup power, Lavigne certainly looks like the complete package – or at least that's how he performed during his debut.

Scouting Report: He – clearly – looked like the opposite of a complete package, something like a flattened cardboard box. And here's a bit of a troubling trend in Lavigne's performance: after slugging Dan Vogelbach-esque .252/.382/.405 across his first 33 games last season, he managed to bat a putrid .231/.334/.301 over his remaining 93 contests – numbers more in line with teenage shortstops in Low Class A, not supposed middle-of-the-lineup bats. It's too early to discount his future, as well as the numbers he posted with Grand Junction, but one gets the feeling that Lavigne is quickly approaching a crossroads in his brief career.

Ceiling: 1.5- to 2.0-win player
Risk: Moderate to High
MLB ETA: 2022

14. Riley Pint, RHP

	FB	CB	SL	CH	Command	Overall
	N/A	N/A	N/A	N/A	N/A	50

Born: 11/06/97	Age: 22	Bats: R	
Height: 6-5	Weight: 225	Throws: R	

YEAR	LVL	IP	W	L	SV	ERA	FIP	WHIP	K/9	K%	BB/9	BB%	K/BB	HR9	BABIP
2017	A	93.0	2	11	0	5.42	4.41	1.67	7.6	18.16%	5.7	13.56%	1.34	0.29	0.325
2018	A-	8.0	0	2	0	1.13	4.92	1.63	9.0	23.53%	10.1	26.47%	0.89	0.00	0.235
2018	A	0.3	0	1	0	81.00	21.46	12.00	0.0	0.00%	54.0	33.33%	0.00	0.00	0.500
2019	A	17.7	0	1	0	8.66	7.15	2.43	11.7	23.47%	15.8	31.63%	0.74	0.00	0.316

Background: Different year, same story – unfortunately. Once viewed as the single most dynamic arm in the entire 2016 draft class, Pint was hampered by a combination of injuries and untamed wildness. The 6-foot-5, 225-pound right-hander was limited to just 8.1 innings in the Northwest League two years ago. And his 2019 season ended prematurely in the middle of June after 21 mostly disastrous relief outings. He finished his fourth professional season with 23 strikeouts and a whopping 31 walks in only 17.2 innings.

Snippet from The 2018 Prospect Digest Handbook: While not necessarily the outcome, forearm tightness – especially the kind that limits a pitcher to single-digit innings – will often lead to Tommy John surgery. That only further clouds the supremely talented, enigmatic right-hander's future.

Scouting Report: The repertoire's still intact, at least it was prior to his latest season-ending injury. And it still screams – loudly – elite pitcher. At. Any. Level. The question is – and will always be – can he throw enough strikes? Period.

Ceiling: 3.0-win player
Risk: Extremely High
MLB ETA: 2023

15. Aaron Schunk, 3B

	Hit	Power	SB	Patience	Glove	Overall
	50	45/50	35	50	55	45

Born: 07/24/97	Age: 22	Bats: R	
Height: 6-2	Weight: 205	Throws: R	

YEAR	LVL	PA	1B	2B	3B	HR	SB	CS	AVG	OBP	SLG	BB%	K%	GB%	LD%	FB%
2019	A-	192	33	12	2	6	4	1	0.306	0.370	0.503	7.29%	13.02%	39.6	26.2	28.2

Background: A solid offensive contributor in his first two seasons at the University of Georgia for Head Coach Scott Stricklin, Schunk earned a trip to the Cape Cod League after hitting .299/.340/.411 as a sophomore. And the third baseman / part-time reliever held his own against the elite summer league competition: in 29 games with the Harwich Mariners, the 6-foot-2, 205-pound Bulldog batted .287/.338/.336 with six doubles. Last season, though, Schunk elevated his game from a middle-tier draft pick to an eventual second round selection. In 57 games for the SEC club, Schunk slugged .339/.373/.600 with 11 doubles, a pair of triples, and a career best 15 dingers. Colorado grabbed him with the 62nd overall pick last June. Schunk spent the entirety of his debut in the Northwest League, slugging .306/.370/.503 with 12 doubles, two triples, and six homers. His production, according to *Deserved Runs Created Plus*, topped the league average mark by 38%.

Scouting Report: A surprisingly strong ability to put the bat on the ball; Schunk whiffed in just 12.5% of his career plate appearances with the Bulldogs. And that ability carried over into the Northwest League during his debut as well; he fanned just 13.0% of the time. Schunk is surprisingly spry at third base and – of course – he owns an above-average arm. He saved 12 games for Georgia last season. Consider the following:

- Since 2011, here's the list of SEC hitters to post a .325/.350/.575 triple-slash line with a single-digit walk rate and a strikeout rate below 14% (min. 200 PA): J.J. Schwarz, Zach Lavy, and Riley Mahan.

If the power ticks up to a strong 50-grade, Schunk has the league-average potential.

Ceiling: 1.5-win player
Risk: Moderate
MLB ETA: 2022

16. Ben Bowden, LHP

	FB	SL	CH	Command	Overall
	60	55	60	45	40

Born: 10/21/94	Age: 25	Bats: L
Height: 6-4	Weight: 235	Throws: L

YEAR	LVL	IP	W	L	SV	ERA	FIP	WHIP	K/9	K%	BB/9	BB%	K/BB	HR9	BABIP
2018	A	15.3	3	0	0	3.52	3.07	1.43	14.7	36.76%	2.9	7.35%	5.00	1.17	0.429
2018	A+	36.7	4	2	0	4.17	4.21	1.36	13.0	33.13%	3.7	9.38%	3.53	1.47	0.337
2019	AA	25.7	0	0	20	1.05	1.22	0.58	14.7	46.15%	2.5	7.69%	6.00	0.35	0.171
2019	AAA	26.0	1	3	1	5.88	4.91	1.77	12.8	29.84%	5.9	13.71%	2.18	1.38	0.379

Background: Taken near the backend of the second round in the 2016 draft, Bowden had the build, pedigree, and repertoire to shoot quickly through the minor leagues. He was coming off of a season at Vanderbilt – a.k.a. Pitcher U. – in which he posted an impressive 65-to-14 strikeout-to-walk ratio as the school's fireman. But an undisclosed injury forced him to miss the entire 2017 season. He opened the following year up with Asheville and finished in High Class A. Last season, the 6-foot-4, 235-pound southpaw split time between Hartford and Albuquerque, throwing 51.2 innings with a whopping 79 punch outs and 24 walks to go along with a combined 3.48 ERA.

Snippet from The 2018 Prospect Digest Handbook: Despite the missed time [in 2017] there's an outside shot he sniffs the big leagues as a September call-up in 2019. If he can maintain average control, Bowden figures to make a lot of money in the future as a left-handed setup arm.

Scouting Report: Bowden didn't make it up to Colorado late last season largely because his control / command regressed down the stretch. He walked 13 in 15.1 innings beginning on July 28th. Bowden has a starter's repertoire: a low- to mid-90s fastball that sneaks up on people; an underrated slider, which as I noted in last year's book, should be thrown more frequently; and one of the better changeups in the minor leagues. As long as his control / command remain average-ish, Bowden's going to pitch quite awhile in the big leagues.

Ceiling: 1.0- to 1.5--win player
Risk: Low to Moderate
MLB ETA: 2020

17. Tommy Doyle, RHP

	FB	SL	CH	Command	Overall
	60	55	50	50	40

Born: 05/01/96	Age: 24	Bats: R
Height: 6-6	Weight: 235	Throws: R

YEAR	LVL	IP	W	L	SV	ERA	FIP	WHIP	K/9	K%	BB/9	BB%	K/BB	HR9	BABIP
2017	Rk	21.0	3	3	3	5.14	5.52	1.86	7.7	17.14%	4.3	9.52%	1.80	0.86	0.365
2018	A	58.3	7	6	18	2.31	2.41	1.10	10.2	27.16%	1.9	4.94%	5.50	0.31	0.313
2019	A+	36.0	2	3	19	3.25	3.61	1.03	12.0	32.88%	3.3	8.90%	3.69	1.00	0.250

Background: A bit of a swing-man during his freshman and sophomore seasons at the University of Virginia, Doyle, a 6-foot-6, 235-pound right-hander, settled in nicely as the club's full-time fireman during his junior campaign as he posted a 38-to-10 strikeout-to-walk ratio in 33.2 innings while saving 14 games. Colorado snagged the former Cavalier in the second round, 70th overall, in 2017. Doyle spent his first full season in pro ball, 2018, dominating the South Atlantic League, averaging more than 10 strikeouts and fewer than 2.0 walks per nine innings. Last season the front office bounced him up to High Class A. And Doyle's numbers remained impressive: in 36.0 innings with Lancaster, the Virginia native fanned 48 and walked 13 to go along with a 3.25 ERA and a miniscule 1.83 DRA.

Snippet from The 2018 Prospect Digest Handbook: Doyle should settle in nicely as a lite version of Vinnie Pestano. Meaning: a good seventh or eighth inning arm.

Scouting Report: It's seems a bit odd – at least to me – that the Rockies continue to take the slow-and-steady approach with Doyle. He has the pedigree, arsenal, and solid command to be challenged more aggressively rather than just staying an entire season at a level. Doyle shows a starter's standard three-pitch mix: a mid-90s fastball, an above-average slider, and a decent changeup. He may end up scrapping the changeup altogether and focusing solely on his two strengths (fastball / slider). A year later he looks like a strong seventh / eighth inning option.

Ceiling: 1.0- to 1.5-win player
Risk: Moderate
MLB ETA: 2020/2021

Colorado Rockies

18. Jacob Wallace, RHP

FB	SL	Command	Overall
70	55	50	40

Born: 08/13/98	Age: 21	Bats: R
Height: 6-1	Weight: 190	Throws: R

YEAR	LVL	IP	W	L	SV	ERA	FIP	WHIP	K/9	K%	BB/9	BB%	K/BB	HR9	BABIP
2019	A-	21.0	0	0	12	1.29	2.90	0.86	12.4	36.25%	3.9	11.25%	3.22	0.43	0.200

Background: Over the past several seasons the Rockies' draft modus operandi has zeroed in on collegiate relievers in the early rounds. Ben Bowden, Vanderbilt's closer, was drafted in the second round in 2016. The front office snagged Virginia relief ace Tommy Doyle in the second round a year later. And last season the Rockies snagged Connecticut fireballer Jacob Wallace in the third round. The 100th overall player chosen, Wallace's draft stock rocketed skyward after an incredible run in the Cape Cod League two summers ago. Appearing in 12 games with the Bourne Braves, the 6-foot-1, 190-pound right-hander didn't allow a run – either earned or unearned – in 13.2 innings while saving six games and posting an absurd 25-to-5 strikeout-to-walk ratio against some of the elite collegiate hitters in the nation. Last season Wallace continued that torrid streak with the Huskies: in 42.0 innings for the AAC squad he posted an absurd 68-to-10 strikeout-to-walk ratio with 16 saves. After signing with the Rockies, Wallace appeared in another 22 games with Boise, averaging 12.4 strikeouts and 3.9 walks per nine innings with a 1.29 ERA.

Scouting Report: The quintessential two-pitch reliever. Wallace sports a plus-plus fastball with incredible late life and an above-average slider. The latter is a solid offering, but it's not a genuine swing-and-miss type pitch – which may limit his ceiling as a seventh or eighth inning arm, as opposed to a closer. There's some Matt Mantei here. Like Bowden and Doyle, Wallace could be pushed aggressively but the Rockies seem to prefer to bump these guys one level at a time.

Ceiling: 1.0- to 1.5--win player
Risk: Moderate
MLB ETA: 2021/2022

19. Eddy Diaz, 2B/SS

Hit	Power	SB	Patience	Glove	Overall
50/60	30/40	40	40	50/55	40

Born: 02/14/00	Age: 20	Bats: R
Height: 6-0	Weight: 175	Throws: R

YEAR	LVL	PA	1B	2B	3B	HR	SB	CS	AVG	OBP	SLG	BB%	K%	GB%	LD%	FB%
2017	RK	155	30	7	4	0	30	6	0.311	0.403	0.424	12.26%	13.55%	59.3	14.2	15.0
2018	RK	223	38	13	5	0	54	8	0.309	0.417	0.436	13.90%	7.62%	53.2	21.1	15.2
2019	Rk+	177	40	12	3	0	20	9	0.331	0.366	0.440	4.52%	18.64%	54.1	24.4	11.1

Background: Diaz earned the distinction of becoming the first Cuban to sign with the organization when he came to terms on a deal worth three-quarters of a million dollars in early July 2017. Diaz spent the rest of that summer and the following season in the Dominican Summer League, hitting .311/.403/.424 and .309/.417/.436, respectively. Colorado bounced the 6-foot, 175-pound middle infielder up to Grand Junction last season. And Diaz continued to hold his own with the bat. In 39 games with the organization's Pioneer League affiliate, he slugged .331/.366/.440 with 12 doubles and three triples. He also swiped nine bags in 17 attempts. His overall production, according to Baseball Prospectus' *Deserved Runs Created Plus*, topped the league average mark by 31%.

Scouting Report: A low level wild card of sorts that derives the majority – the *overwhelming* majority – of his offensive value with his line-drive approach at the plate (also known as his batting average) and plus- to plus-plus speed. Otherwise, he rarely walks and hasn't hit a homerun in 126 career minor league games. Defensively, he's solid. With respect to his production last season, consider the following:

- Since 2006, here's the list of 19-year-olds to post a DRC+ between 125 to 135 with a sub-8.0% walk rate in the Pioneer League (min. 150 PA): Chris McFarland, Sal Perez, and Eddy Diaz.

Ceiling: 1.0- to 1.5-win player
Risk: Moderate
MLB ETA: 2023

20. Karl Kauffman, RHP

FB	SL	CH	Command	Overall
50	50	50	50	40

Born: 08/15/97	Age: 22	Bats: R
Height: 6-2	Weight: 200	Throws: R

Background: An interesting prospect, though not for the right reasons. Kauffman, as it seems, has always been regarded with rather high promise. He cracked Yarmouth-Dennis' roster in the Cape Cod following his true freshman season at the University of Michigan – despite throwing only 13.1 innings in relief. He was moved into the Wolverines' rotation the following season, 2018, had he had a bit of a coming out party: in 15 appearances, 14 of which were starts, he posted a 78-to-32 strikeout-to-walk ratio in 79.0 innings of work. He spent the summer back with Yarmouth-Dennis where his numbers were – once again – mediocre or worse: 20 strikeouts, 18 walks, and a 5.40 ERA in 26.2 innings. His numbers backed up a bit during his junior campaign last season, averaging just 7.9 strikeouts and 2.4 walks per nine innings. Colorado snagged him near the end of the second round.

Scouting Report: Frankly, I don't get it. Maybe the club's privy to some Rapsodo data that suggests there's a lot of potential in Kauffman's repertoire because the naked eye says it's blasé. His fastball sits in the upper-80s to 92 mph with a rare peak of 94. His slider may tick up to above-average, though it needs to be tightened a bit. The changeup is pretty solid. Kauffman looks to be a reach as a second rounder. I would have likely thrown a fifth round grade on him prior to the draft.

Ceiling: 1.0- to 1.5--win player
Risk: Moderate
MLB ETA: 2023

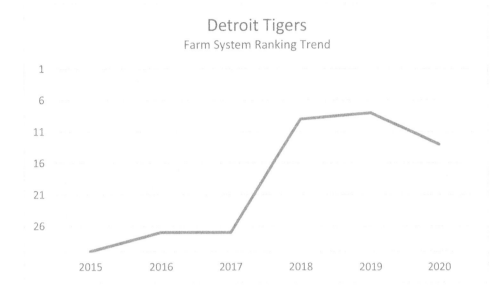

Detroit Tigers
Farm System Ranking Trend

Rank	Name	Age	Pos
1	Matt Manning	22	RHP
2	Casey Mize	23	RHP
3	Riley Greene	19	CF
4	Tarik Skubal	23	LHP
5	Isaac Paredes	21	IF
6	Daz Cameron	23	CF
7	Joey Wentz	22	LHP
8	Alex Faedo	24	RHP
9	Franklin Perez	24	RHP
10	Parker Meadows	20	CF
11	Alex Lange	24	RHP
12	Nick Quintana	20	3B
13	Beau Burrows	23	RHP
14	Jake Rogers	24	C
15	Willi Castro	23	SS
16	Rony Garcia	22	RHP
17	Bryant Packard	21	LF
18	Wenceel Perez	20	SS
19	Ulrich Bojarski	21	RF
20	Roberto Campos	22	RF

1. Matt Manning, RHP

	FB	CB	CH	Command	Overall
	65	65	50	55	60

Born: 01/28/98	Age: 22	Bats: R
Height: 6-6	Weight: 215	Throws: R

YEAR	LVL	IP	W	L	SV	ERA	FIP	WHIP	K/9	K%	BB/9	BB%	K/BB	HR9	BABIP
2017	A-	33.3	2	2	0	1.89	2.71	1.23	9.7	25.90%	3.8	10.07%	2.57	0.00	0.310
2017	A	17.7	2	0	0	5.60	2.59	1.42	13.2	32.91%	5.6	13.92%	2.36	0.00	0.341
2018	A	55.7	3	3	0	3.40	3.06	1.35	12.3	32.07%	4.5	11.81%	2.71	0.49	0.344
2018	A+	51.3	4	4	0	2.98	3.12	0.99	11.4	31.71%	3.3	9.27%	3.42	0.70	0.241
2018	AA	10.7	0	1	0	4.22	2.28	1.41	11.0	28.26%	3.4	8.70%	3.25	0.00	0.393
2019	AA	133.7	11	5	0	2.56	2.53	0.98	10.0	28.08%	2.6	7.21%	3.89	0.47	0.259

Background: Not quite as tall as his dad, Rich, the 6-foot-11 former power forward for the defunct Vancouver Grizzlies and Los Angeles Clippers, the younger Manning, however, remains an imposing figure atop the bump. Standing 6-foot-6 and 215 pounds, the Tigers selected the budding ace in the opening round, ninth overall, of the 2016 draft.

Manning has showed some encouraging progress in each of his professional seasons. The then-19-year-old right-hander averaged 10.9 strikeouts and 4.4 walks per nine innings as he split time between Connecticut and West Michigan in 2017. Manning raised his strikeout rate, 11.8 K/9, and lowered his walk rate, 3.9 BB/9, as he sprinted through Low Class A, High Class A, and Class AA the following season. And last year – the first time he's stayed at one level since his brief debut – Manning put together his finest showing to date, despite squaring off against the minors' most challenging level: Class AA. Making a career-best 24 starts with Erie, the hard-throwing hurler posted a dominating 148-to-38 strikeout-to-walk ratio in 133.2 innings. He compiled a 2.56 ERA and a 2.75 DRA (*Deserved Run Average*).

Snippet from The 2018 Prospect Digest Handbook: The big right-hander has the look, build, and repertoire of a future #2-type arm, though he'll need to further refine his changeup to ascend to that status.

Scouting Report: In a system chock full of premium, high octane arms; Manning has the potential to be the best of the bunch. The former first rounder owns one of the best fastball/curveball combos in the minor leagues. His heater sits in the 94- to 95-mph range and will touch as high as 97- or 98-mph on occasion. His long arms and massive stride allow the plus offering to play up more effectively too. His curveball, another 65-grade offering, is a genuine knee-buckling, put-your-head-down-on-the-way-back-to-the-dugout, swing-and-miss pitch. It's hard, biting downward break. And generally sits in the 79- to 80-mph neighborhood. He'll also mix in a firm, upper-80s changeup. Manning typically relies on his fastball/curveball combo, so he needs to show more trust in his changeup to allow for further development. His command jumped several grades last season for me as well. He was consistently throwing quality strikes, not just strikes. He has a chance to be a bonafide ace, a true #1.

Ceiling: 5.0-win player
Risk: Moderate
MLB ETA: 2020

2. Casey Mize, RHP

	FB	SL	SF	Command	Overall
	60	65	80	60	60

Born: 05/01/97	Age: 23	Bats: R
Height: 6-3	Weight: 220	Throws: R

YEAR	LVL	IP	W	L	SV	ERA	FIP	WHIP	K/9	K%	BB/9	BB%	K/BB	HR9	BABIP
2018	Rk	2.0	0	0	0	0.00	1.14	0.50	18.0	57.14%	4.5	14.29%	4.00	0.00	0.000
2018	A+	11.7	0	1	0	4.63	5.01	1.29	7.7	20.83%	1.5	4.17%	5.00	1.54	0.344
2019	A+	30.7	2	0	0	0.88	1.94	0.52	8.8	28.04%	1.5	4.67%	6.00	0.00	0.155
2019	AA	78.7	6	3	0	3.20	2.97	1.11	8.7	23.53%	2.1	5.57%	4.22	0.57	0.294

Background: Equipped with the #1 overall pick for just the second time in franchise history – the first was in 1997 when they selected fire-bolt slinging right-hander Matt Anderson out of Rice University – the Tigers once again went the collegiate route and selected Auburn University ace righty Casey Mize. Opting to go with the polish and upside of Mize – as opposed to some of the high profile bats of Joey Bart, Alec Bohm, Nick Madrigal, Jonathan India, and Jarred Kelenic – Detroit quickly placed him on the fast track to the big leagues. After a brief two-inning appearance in the Gulf Coast, Mize made four brief appearances in High Class A. Mize opened up last season back in High Class A. And was, simply, unhittable. In four starts the former SEC star posted a 25-to-1 K/BB ratio while surrendering just one earned run in 26.0 innings of work. Detroit bounced him up to the Eastern League in late April. But a wonky shoulder – which was tabbed as "soreness" and diagnosed by Dr. James Andrews as "minor inflammation at the back of the shoulder" – shelved him for roughly a month. He popped back up in the Florida State League for a pair of rehab starts before moving back up to Class AA. In total he made 21 starts, throwing 109.1 innings with 106 whiffs and 23 walks with a 2.55 ERA.

Snippet from The 2018 Prospect Digest Handbook: Stud. One of my favorite collegiate arms in this year's draft class. Mize ticks off all the important boxes: big and projectable, handled conservatively during his amateur career, pounds the strike zone, power pitcher's arsenal, and high levels of success [against] elite competition.

Scouting Report: Three plus or better pitches with the command to match. But Mize isn't without his red flags either. The shoulder issue may – or may not – be something. And that's not including his arm issues during his time in college and Team USA. That's a whole lot of arm woes for a top prospect in a rather short time frame. Then there's his production, which is good, even borderline great, but it's not what you would expect out of the #1 player chosen in the draft two years ago. For instance: his strikeout percentage in the Eastern League, 23.5%, ranked as the 19th best mark among all pitchers with at least 70 IP, placing him right in between Patrick Murphy and Wil Crowe. And his K% was actually less than Orioles soft-tossing lefty Bruce Zimmerman. Frankly, it doesn't make sense either. His fastball sits in the 93- to 95-mph range. His slider, which has improved significantly within the last season, is 87- 90-mph and varies from a traditional hard slider and late-tilting cutter. And then there's his trademark splitter, an easy 80-grade pitch. Everything other than the production suggests a bonafide ace, but I think he probably settles in as a good #2/#3 arm.

Ceiling: 4.0-win player
Risk: Moderate
MLB ETA: 2020

3. Riley Greene, CF

Hit	Power	SB	Patience	Glove	Overall
45/55	45/50	50	50/55	55	55

Born: 09/28/00	Age: 19	Bats: L
Height: 6-3	Weight: 200	Throws: L

YEAR	LVL	PA	1B	2B	3B	HR	SB	CS	AVG	OBP	SLG	BB%	K%	GB%	LD%	FB%
2019	Rk	43	8	3	0	2	0	0	0.351	0.442	0.595	11.63%	27.91%	56.0	20.0	20.0
2019	A-	100	21	3	1	1	1	0	0.295	0.380	0.386	11.00%	25.00%	46.0	30.2	17.5
2019	A	108	15	2	2	2	4	0	0.219	0.278	0.344	5.56%	24.07%	43.8	16.4	34.2

Background: Part of the dynamic 18U Team USA squad two summers ago. Greene, who teamed with the likes of fellow first rounders like Bobby Witt Jr., C.J. Abrams, and Brennan Malone (as well as Jack Leiter, who was a surefire top pick had he not informed clubs of his desire to play for Vanderbilt), put his offensive prowess on full display: in nine games the 6-foot-3, 200-pound outfielder slugged an impressive .424.548/.848 with five doubles and three homeruns while plating a whopping 28 RBIs. The Hagerty High School product also fanned just four times against nine walks. Greene was finalist for the Gatorade Baseball Player of the Year. Detroit drafted the toolsy outfielder in the opening round last June, 5th overall, to a hefty $6.1 million, the full slot value. Greene sprinted through three separate low levels during his professional debut last season, batting a solid .271/.347/.403 with eight doubles, three triples, five homeruns, and five stolen bases in as many attempts in 57 games.

Scouting Report: Here's what I wrote prior to the draft last June:

"Earned a nod from Baseball America as a Third-Team High School All-American two years ago, Greene has altered his stance at the plate this season, starting from a wider base than he showed during his time with Team USA. He shows above-average bat speed and keeps the barrel in the hitting zone as well as any high school hitter in this year's draft class. The toolsy outfielder also shows some remarkable patience, especially at secondary pitches off the plate or below the strike zone. Greene, according to a variety of reports, has touched the upper 80s as a hurler as well. It'll be interesting to see if a big league club will shorten his base, which allows for a smoother weight transfer. He has the potential to develop into an above-average big league starting outfielder.

Greene, by the way, walked in 8.8% of his plate appearances during his debut.

Ceiling: 3.5- to 4.0-win player
Risk: Moderate
MLB ETA: 2020

4. Tarik Skubal, LHP

FB	CB	SL	CH	Command	Overall
65	55	50/55	50	45	55

Born: 11/20/96	Age: 23	Bats: L	Top CALs:
Height: 6-3	Weight: 215	Throws: L	

YEAR	LVL	IP	W	L	SV	ERA	FIP	WHIP	K/9	K%	BB/9	BB%	K/BB	HR9	BABIP
2018	Rk	3.0	1	0	0	0.00	1.31	1.00	15.0	38.46%	3.0	7.69%	5.00	0.00	0.286
2018	A-	12.0	0	0	1	0.75	1.14	0.83	12.8	39.53%	1.5	4.65%	8.50	0.00	0.333
2018	A	7.3	2	0	1	0.00	0.89	0.82	13.5	42.31%	1.2	3.85%	11.00	0.00	0.357
2019	A+	80.3	4	5	0	2.58	2.56	1.01	10.9	30.31%	2.1	5.94%	5.11	0.56	0.292
2019	AA	42.3	2	3	0	2.13	1.25	1.02	17.4	48.24%	3.8	10.59%	4.56	0.43	0.343

Background: Easily the most exciting breakout player in the minor leagues last season. Detroit unearthed a potential gem, a unicorn of sorts thanks to his long, wiry frame and explosive, meteoric fastball. A late round pick out of Seattle University two years ago, Skubal, who was chosen as the 255th overall player, was sporting a couple of hefty red flags following his redshirt junior season: he missed all of 2017 as he was recovering/rehabbing from Tommy John surgery and his control/command, which wavered at points in 2016, imploded upon itself as he averaged more than six walks per nine innings. So...there he sat at the top of the ninth round. And the Tigers' brass decided he was worth the risk as they handed him an above-slot deal worth $350,000 – more than double the recommended slot bonus. The 6-foot-3, 215-pound southpaw made stops at three separate levels during his debut, posting an incredible 33-to-4 strikeout-to-walk ratio with a 0.40 ERA. And it was just a harbinger of things to come. The front office pushed the flame-throwing lefty straight into High Class A at the start of 2019 and after 15 absurdly dominating starts he earned a mid-season promotion up to the minors' toughest test, Class AA. In total, Skubal made 24 starts, throwing 122.2 innings while recording a whopping 179 punch outs and handing out just 37 walks. He compiled an aggregate 2.42 ERA.

Scouting Report: One of the more explosive fastballs for a left-handed prospect last season. Skubal takes a no nonsense approach to challenging hitters, particularly early in the count: here's a fastball, try to hit it. The borderline plus-plus offering sat in the late 90s – and touched as high as 98 mph – with some of the best late, riding life I saw all season long. The former Seattle University ace features two breaking balls: a sharp curveball with tremendous downward force and cutter-like slider. He uses his slider, which flashes above-average when he stays on top of it, almost primarily as an equalizer on left-handed hitters. He'll also mix in an average low- to mid-80s change with some sink. As good as Skubal is – and he was exceptionally dominating for most of the time – he's still quite raw. The control/command is fringy average, but he'll continue to succeed because of the quality of his arsenal. But the way to beat him is simple: make him throw his breaking balls for strikes. Skubal got ahead with his fastball last season, and got the hitters to chase outside the zone. While Skubal has the potential to be, say, 80% of Chris Sale, I think he's going to have a few rough patches ahead until he can throw this curveball/slider consistently for strikes. #3-type ceiling.

Ceiling: 3.5- to 4.0-win player
Risk: Moderate
MLB ETA: 2020

5. Isaac Paredes, IF

Hit	Power	SB	Patience	Glove	Overall
55	50	35	55	50	55

Born: 02/18/99	Age: 21	Bats: L
Height: 5-11	Weight: 225	Throws: R

YEAR	LVL	PA	1B	2B	3B	HR	SB	CS	AVG	OBP	SLG	BB%	K%	GB%	LD%	FB%
2017	A	384	57	25	0	7	2	1	0.264	0.343	0.401	7.55%	14.06%	34.0	19.8	29.5
2017	A	133	18	3	0	4	0	0	0.217	0.323	0.348	9.77%	9.77%	34.3	18.6	31.4
2018	A+	347	45	19	2	12	1	0	0.259	0.338	0.455	9.22%	15.56%	37.4	16.1	31.1
2018	AA	155	30	9	0	3	1	0	0.321	0.406	0.458	12.26%	14.19%	36.6	22.3	31.3
2019	AA	552	98	23	1	13	5	3	0.282	0.368	0.416	10.33%	11.05%	41.7	19.5	28.6

Background: It was a text book, sit-down-take-notes type of trade that was perfectly executed by the Al Avila-led front office. The Tigers dealt away Alex Avila, Al's kid, and talented, enigmatic left-handed reliever Justin Wilson to the Cubs for Isaac Paredes and Jeimer Candelario at the trade deadline three years ago. And while Candelario has looked beyond atrocious during his two-plus seasons in Detroit, Paredes – on the other hand – looks like a bonafide All-Star in the making. Standing a stocky 5-foot-11 and 225 pounds, the lefty-swinging infielder was promoted up to the minors' toughest challenge – Class AA – at the end of the 2018 season. And, frankly, he looked All-World as he slugged .321/.406/.458 in 39 games. The Hermosillo, Mexico, native spent all of last year back in the Eastern League and he continued to impress. In 127 games with the Erie SeaWolves, Paredes batted .282/.368/.416 with 23 doubles, one triple, 13 homeruns, and five stolen bases. Per Baseball Prospectus' *Deserved Runs Created Plus*, his production topped the league average threshold by 38%. He also popped up with the Mesa Solar Sox in the Arizona Fall League, batting .208/.377/.396 in 15 games.

Snippet from The 2018 Prospect Digest Handbook: There's some – growing – concern that Paredes, who's listed at just 5-foot-11 but tips the scales at a hefty 225 pounds, may never reach his potential as a table setter because of conditioning issues. Despite that, though, Paredes elevated his entire approach at the plate last season, showing more patience and significantly more pop than in past years. He's got a chance to be an above-average starter, but the weight is concerning

Scouting Report: Consider the following:

- Since 2006, here's the list of 20-year-old hitters that posted a 133 to 143 DRC+ total with a sub-20% strikeout rate in any Class AA league (min. 300 PA): Colby Rasmus, Billy Butler, Jake Bauers, and Issac Paredes.
- Sans Paredes, here's the group's career big league DRC+ total: 100 (Rasmus), 115 (Butler), and 86 (Bauers).

Side note: I still think Bauers becomes a valuable big league bat, by the way. But ignoring that for a moment, two of the three went on to become better than average big leaguers during their peak seasons. Paredes combines a strong feel for contact – he whiffed in few than 12% of his plate appearances in 2019 – with 20-homerun pop and a strong walk rate. Throw in some solid glove work. And all of sudden Paredes looks like a borderline All-Star at his peak. Corey Seager's showing last season with the Dodgers seems like a reasonable comp for the young infield vagabond: .272/.335/.483. I'm still worried about the weight, though.

Ceiling: 3.5-win player
Risk: Moderate
MLB ETA: 2020

6. Daz Cameron, CF

Hit	Power	SB	Patience	Glove	Overall
45	50	55	55	55	50

Born: 01/15/97	Age: 23	Bats: R
Height: 6-2	Weight: 195	Throws: R

YEAR	LVL	PA	1B	2B	3B	HR	SB	CS	AVG	OBP	SLG	BB%	K%	GB%	LD%	FB%
2018	A+	246	41	9	3	3	10	4	0.259	0.346	0.370	10.16%	28.05%	36.5	20.3	37.2
2018	AA	226	35	12	5	5	12	5	0.285	0.367	0.470	11.06%	23.45%	39.5	26.5	29.3
2018	AAA	62	7	4	1	0	2	2	0.211	0.246	0.316	3.23%	24.19%	38.6	9.1	43.2
2019	AAA	528	55	22	6	13	17	8	0.214	0.330	0.377	11.74%	28.79%	42.6	18.9	29.4

Background: Cut from a similar cloth as his father, Mike Cameron, who was a 2001 A.L. All-Star for the Seattle Mariners and three-time Gold Glove Winner – which is a *travesty* given his defensive aptitude; it should have been – at least by my count – nine Gold Gloves. The younger Cameron was originally selected by the Houston Astros in the opening round, 37th overall, in the 2015 draft. A little more than two seasons later Detroit acquired the toolsy center fielder – along with Franklin Perez and defensive wizard Jake Rogers – in the Justin Verlander swap. Two years ago the Tigers' brass held the accelerator down on his development as they pushed him through three different levels. And it looked – at that time – that the former first rounder was positioning himself as a potential mid-season call up in 2019. Then...he stopped hitting. Last season Cameron appeared in 120 games with the Toledo Mud Hens in the International League, batting a disappointing .214/.330/.377 with 22 doubles, six triples, 13 homeruns, and 17 stolen bases. Per *Deserved Runs Created Plus*, his overall production was 14% *below* the league average threshold.

Snippet from The 2018 Prospect Digest Handbook: Loud – and underrated – tools like his old man. Cameron – along with fellow top prospect Isaac Paredes – showed some serious developmental progress in terms of patience at the plate last season. The young outfielder walked in a career best 9.7% of his plate appearances in 2018. I very much think that Cameron winds up as a slightly lesser version of his old man.

Scouting Report: Well, not only didn't that go as planned, but it's concerning that Cameron didn't show any type of ability to make adjustments during his horrific 2019 season. For instance he batted below .200 in three of the five full months (April, July, and August) and hit just .226 in June. Only one month of the season, May, did he hit as one would expect; he batted .269/.333/.495 in May. He can still stuff a stat sheet with the best of them, especially with his 20/20 potential, but – man – was he bad last year. His strikeout rate exploded to a career worst 28.8% as well. His dad was a career .249/.338/.444 hitter in 17 big league seasons. That seems like a reasonable ceiling at this point, but he certainly needs to show something in 2020 to get his career on track.

Ceiling: 2.5- to 3.0-win player
Risk: Moderate
MLB ETA: 2020

7. Joey Wentz, LHP

FB	CB	CH	Command	Overall
55	50	65	50	50

Born: 10/06/97	Age: 22	Bats: L
Height: 6-5	Weight: 210	Throws: L

YEAR	LVL	IP	W	L	SV	ERA	FIP	WHIP	K/9	K%	BB/9	BB%	K/BB	HR9	BABIP
2017	A	131.7	8	3	0	2.60	2.68	1.10	10.4	28.84%	3.1	8.73%	3.30	0.27	0.293
2018	A+	67.0	3	4	0	2.28	3.63	1.09	7.1	19.92%	3.2	9.02%	2.21	0.40	0.250
2019	AA	103.0	5	8	0	4.72	4.39	1.31	8.7	22.94%	3.9	10.32%	2.22	1.14	0.280
2019	AA	25.7	2	0	0	2.10	2.27	0.94	13.0	37.76%	1.4	4.08%	9.25	1.05	0.315

Background: The second of three straight prep arms the Braves selected in the opening rounds of the 2016 draft. Wentz, the 40th overall pick, was sandwiched around Braves hurlers Ian Anderson and Kyle Muller. Detroit acquired the intriguing – albeit enigmatic – southpaw, along with Travis Demeritte at the trade deadline last June in exchange for veteran reliever Shane Greene. A product of Shawnee Mission East High School in Prairie Village, Kansas, Wentz made a total of 25 starts between both organizations' Class AA affiliates. He tossed 128.2 innings with a solid 137-to-49 K/BB ratio to go along with a 4.20 ERA. For his career, the former first round pick is averaging 9.6 strikeouts and 3.5 walks per nine innings with a 3.22 ERA.

Snippet from The 2018 Prospect Digest Handbook: Wentz's stock took quite a hit after his showing [in 2018]. And unless his swing-and-miss tendencies return in full force in 2019 he could very easily be dealt away. He's purely a backend starting pitcher at this point.

Scouting Report: Well, the strikeout rate did come storming back. But that didn't stop the Braves from dealing him away either. Wentz is an interesting pitcher. At times he looks like a solid #4-type arm. And at other times he's looks like an up-and-down arm. Above-average fastball, a strong 50-grade curveball that may peak as an above-average offering if everything develops well; and a changeup that was (A) way better than

I expected and (B) one of the better ones I saw all of last season. It's Cole Hamels-esque, which is the bar for plus, left-handed changeups. The command wavers at points, but should settle in as he continues to mature. With respect to his work in the Southern League last season, which he made 20 of his 25 starts, consider the following:

- Since 2006, only two 21-year-olds met the following criteria in the Southern League (min. 100 IP): a strikeout percentage between 21% and 23% with a walk percentage between 9% and 11%. Those two arms: Nathan Eovaldi and – of course – Joey Wentz.

Wentz clearly doesn't possess the 80-grade fastball of Eovaldi. But it's encouraging nonetheless. One more final thought: I'd really like to see Wentz throw his fantastic changeup more frequently.

Ceiling: 2.0-win player
Risk: Moderate
MLB ETA: 2020

8. Alex Faedo, RHP

FB	SL	CH	Command	Overall
55	55	55	55	50

Born: 11/12/95	Age: 24	Bats: R
Height: 6-5	Weight: 230	Throws: R

YEAR	LVL	IP	W	L	SV	ERA	FIP	WHIP	K/9	K%	BB/9	BB%	K/BB	HR9	BABIP
2018	A+	61.0	2	4	0	3.10	3.27	1.02	7.5	20.73%	1.9	5.28%	3.92	0.44	0.263
2018	AA	60.0	3	6	0	4.95	5.80	1.27	8.9	23.23%	3.3	8.66%	2.68	2.25	0.250
2019	AA	115.3	6	7	0	3.90	3.56	1.12	10.5	29.32%	2.0	5.47%	5.36	1.33	0.293

Background: I mention it every chance I can, so I'm certainly not going to pass up another chance. The 2016 Florida Gators team will go down as one of the single most talented collegiate squads in history. The pitching staff was loaded with the likes of Faedo, A.J. Puk, Brady Singer, Jackson Kowar, Logan Shore, Dane Dunning, Shaun Anderson, and Scott Moss. And the lineup featured power-hitting first baseman Peter Alonso, Jonathan India, Buddy Reed, J.J. Schwarz, and Mike Rivera, a defensive wizard behind the dish. As for Faedo, the Tigers originally drafted the crafty right-hander in the 40th round coming out of Braulio Alonso High School. They then circled back around three years later and made him the 18th overall pick. Last season Faedo teamed with Matt Manning, Tarik Skubal, Casey Mize, Joey Wentz, and Logan Shore to form one of the deepest, most talented staffs in the minor leagues. Faedo made 22 starts for the Erie SeaWolves, throwing 115.1 innings with an absurd 134-to-25 strikeout-to-walk ratio. He finished the year with a 3.90 ERA and a 3.75 DRA.

Snippet from The 2018 Prospect Digest Handbook: Faedo's production in Class AA was skewed a bit thanks to some wonky homerun numbers: he surrendered 15 dingers in just 60.0 innings in Class AA. He's always coughed up more homeruns than expected, even going back to his college days, but even that was way out of whack. He's positioned himself for a second-half call-up to Motown.

Scouting Report: So he never got that call up to Motown last season. But his production came roaring back. Faedo shows straight 55's across the board: fastball, slider, changeup, and command. He's the ideal, innings eater fourth starter type pitcher that may squeak out a few years of slightly better production. As I noted in last year's Handbook, as well as documenting it above, Faedo got dinged by the long ball yet again: he averaged 1.33 homeruns per nine innings, the worst mark among all qualified Class AA pitchers. He's ready to be handed a gig in the Tigers' rotation, though that likely won't happen until his Super2 status passes. I wouldn't be surprised to see him put up some Anthony DeSclafani-type production in the coming years – but watch the long ball.

Ceiling: 2.0-win player
Risk: Moderate
MLB ETA: 2020

9. Franklin Perez, RHP

FB	CB	SL	CH	Command	Overall
N/A	N/A	N/A	N/A	N/A	50

Born: 12/06/97	Age: 22	Bats: R
Height: 6-3	Weight: 197	Throws: R

YEAR	LVL	IP	W	L	SV	ERA	FIP	WHIP	K/9	K%	BB/9	BB%	K/BB	HR9	BABIP
2017	A+	54.3	4	2	2	2.98	3.34	0.99	8.8	24.31%	2.7	7.34%	3.31	0.66	0.236
2017	AA	32.0	2	1	1	3.09	3.69	1.38	7.0	18.25%	3.1	8.03%	2.27	0.56	0.316
2018	Rk	8.0	0	1	0	4.50	2.77	0.38	5.6	17.86%	0.0	0.00%	#DIV/0!	0.00	0.136
2018	A+	11.3	0	1	0	7.94	6.29	2.03	7.1	16.67%	6.4	14.81%	1.13	1.59	0.371
2019	A+	7.7	0	0	0	2.35	5.39	1.57	7.0	18.18%	5.9	15.15%	1.20	1.17	0.286

Background: When the Tigers acquired Perez he was (A) the centerpiece of the Justin Verlander swap with Houston, (B) failed to appear in a Tigers affiliate uniform due to a blister issue, and (C) has – somehow – only totaled just 27.0 innings over the past two seasons. The 6-foot-3, 197-pound right-hander, who whipped fire-bolts consistently for strikes, was limited to just seven brief appearances in 2018 courtesy of a severe lat strain. And last season – of course – something entirely new popped up that hampered Perez: a nagging right shoulder injury, which seemed curious because team doctors haven't found any structural issues. He made two brief appearances in the Florida State League last season, throwing 7.2 innings with six strikeouts and five walks with a 2.35 ERA.

Snippet from The 2018 Prospect Digest Handbook: I happened to catch one of the few starts Perez made in High Class A last season. And, simply put, the stuff never went away. Perez challenged hitters with an explosive plus fastball that sat anywhere from 92- to 95-mph. His curveball showed that trademark hellacious bend, making it the second of three plus-offerings wielded by Perez. His changeup, a mid-80s offering, showed impressive fade. And his slider flashed above-average at times.

Scouting Report: Suffering through a string of back luck that's basically been unparalleled among professional pitchers. Actually only other one arm comes to mind immediately: Royals right-hander Kyle Zimmer. Who knows what to expect at this point? Hopefully he can shake the physical bugs that seem to continually pop up, though it's incredibly reassuring that doctors don't see any issues.

Ceiling: 2.5-win player
Risk: High
MLB ETA: 2020/2021?

10. Parker Meadows, CF

Hit	Power	SB	Patience	Glove	Overall
35/45	45/50	50	50	50	45

Born: 11/02/99	Age: 20	Bats: L
Height: 6-5	Weight: 205	Throws: R

YEAR	LVL	PA	1B	2B	3B	HR	SB	CS	AVG	OBP	SLG	BB%	K%	GB%	LD%	FB%
2018	RK	85	14	2	1	4	3	1	0.284	0.376	0.500	9.41%	29.41%	36.7	20.4	36.7
2018	A-	21	5	1	0	0	0	0	0.316	0.381	0.368	9.52%	28.57%	38.5	38.5	23.1
2019	A	504	74	15	2	7	14	8	0.221	0.296	0.312	9.33%	22.42%	47.0	15.4	28.7

Background: The Meadows brothers went toe-to-toe when it comes to their respective performances during debuts. Austin, the ninth overall pick in 2013, slugged a robust .316/.424/.554 between his time in the Gulf Coast and New York-Penn Leagues. And Parker, the 44th overall choice two years ago, batted .290/.377/.473 as he spent time between the same two leagues. But there's where the parallels in their production end. While Austin went on to slash .322/.388/.486 in an injury-shortened campaign in the South Atlantic League. Parker, on the other hand, barely hit his weight in the Midwest League: in 126 games with the West Michigan Whitecaps, the 6-foot-5, 205-pound center fielder cobbled together a .221/.296/.312 slash-line with 15 doubles, two triples, and seven homers. He swiped 14 bags in 22 attempts. His overall production, according to *Deserved Runs Created Plus*, was 22% below the league mark.

Snippet from The 2018 Prospect Digest Handbook: Meadows struggled with some swing-and-miss issues during his debut, but his patient approach should push his K-rate down towards the league average mark. The initial results from his work in center field looks like he'll be a competent, perhaps even an above-average defender. Tremendous, tremendous grab early in the second round last June.

Scouting Report: On the positive side of things: Meadows' strikeout rate normalized down to an average-ish 22.4% last season; he also showed some stat-stuffing ability with above-average power potential and speed to burn. On the opposite end of the spectrum: well, he was pretty terrible. The "Baby Giraffe", as he's known, appears quite lean and will likely add strength as he begins to fill out. He's still quite raw.

Ceiling: 1.5- to 2.0-win player
Risk: Moderate
MLB ETA: 2022

11. Alex Lange, RHP

FB	CB	CH	Command	Overall
60	55	60	55	45

Born: 10/02/95	Age: 24	Bats: R
Height: 6-3	Weight: 197	Throws: R

YEAR	LVL	IP	W	L	SV	ERA	FIP	WHIP	K/9	K%	BB/9	BB%	K/BB	HR9	BABIP
2017	A-	9.3	0	1	0	4.82	2.28	1.29	12.5	31.71%	2.9	7.32%	4.33	0.00	0.375
2018	A+	120.3	6	8	0	3.74	3.47	1.18	7.6	20.40%	2.8	7.68%	2.66	0.45	0.287
2019	A+	47.7	1	9	0	7.36	4.09	1.76	9.6	22.37%	4.9	11.40%	1.96	0.76	0.372
2019	AA	39.0	2	3	0	3.92	4.96	1.41	6.5	16.67%	4.4	11.31%	1.47	0.92	0.283
2019	AA	15.7	2	1	0	3.45	2.78	1.34	8.6	24.59%	4.6	13.11%	1.88	0.00	0.342

Background: Detroit dealt away their largest trade chip last July, Nick Castellanos, as they acquired a pair of former high round collegiate arms from the Cubs: Alex Lange and Paul Richan. Originally taken as the 30th overall selection in the 2017 draft, the former LSU ace hasn't continued his development as expected thanks to some subpar command. And that trend continued last season for the former SEC star. Splitting time between High Class A and both organizations' Class AA affiliates, the 6-foot-3, 197-pound right-hander averaged 8.3 strikeouts and 4.7 walks per nine innings to go along with a 5.45 ERA. For his professional career he's averaging 8.1 strikeouts and 3.6 walks per nine innings. Lange also appeared in nine games in the Arizona Fall League, posting a 13-to-3 strikeout-to-walk ratio in 9.2 innings of work.

Snippet from The 2018 Prospect Digest Handbook: He's probably a year away from stepping into a #3/#4-type role, though a late season call-up isn't out of the question either.

Scouting Report: It was easier for his new team to make the tough call and move him into the bullpen full time. I have to be honest: I don't know if that was the right move. Lange has a solid #4/#5-type starting arsenal: a straight 94 mph fastball, a dynamite above-average curveball, and late fading, diving changeup. But the regression in his control/command is concerning to say the least, though it wasn't any better during his multiple-inning relief appearances. He could eventually work as a Joakim Soria-type closer thanks to his deep arsenal, though – again – I'd give him one final crack at a starting gig.

Ceiling: 1.5- to 2.0-win player
Risk: Moderate
MLB ETA: 2020

12. Nick Quintana, 3B

Hit	Power	SB	Patience	Glove	Overall
40/45	45	35	55	50	45+

Born: 10/3/97	Age: 22	Bats: R
Height: 5-10	Weight: 187	Throws: R

Background: A highly touted prep prospect coming out of Arbor View High School; the Red Sox snagged the stocky third baseman in the 11th round. Quintana spurned the club's interest, opting instead to attend the University of Arizona. Quintana immediately settled into the heart of the Wildcats' lineup as he slugged .293/.394/.471 with 17 doubles, one triple, and six homeruns as a true freshman. He spent the ensuing summer playing the Yarmouth-Dennis Red Sox, a little apropos, hitting .200/.267/.410 in 34 games. The 5-foot-10, 187-pound corner infielder raised the bar during his sophomore season with the Pac12 squad as he batted .313/.413/.592 with 17 doubles and 14 homeruns. And, once again, he spent the summer playing in the Cape Cod League with Yarmouth-Dennis, hitting .259/.351/.435 in 35 games. Quintana turned in an epic showing as a junior last season, belting out 18 doubles and 15 homeruns en route to posting a .342/.462/.626 triple-slash line in 56 games. Detroit drafted him in the second round, 47th overall, and then it went downhill – quickly. The front office pushed Quintana straight into the Midwest League for his debut. But after batting a puny .158/.228/.226 in 41 games, he was finally demoted down to the New-York-Penn League (where he hit .256/.347/.372).

Scouting Report: With respect to his work in college last season, consider the following:

- Between 2011 and 2018, here's the list of Pac12 hitters that posted at least a .325/.450/.600 triple-slash line in a season (min. 200 PA): Adley Rutschman, Andrew Vaughn, Trevor Larnach, Brett Cumberland, and Chase Strumpf. Three first rounders and a pair of second round picks.

Not bad company to keep. Always sort of a saber-slanted hitter during his collegiate days, Quintana, who walked in 14.1% and struck out in 19.8% of his career plate appearances, looked utterly lost at the plate during his debut. As evidenced by his massive 31.6% of his plate appearances. And despite some gaudy power numbers at a strong baseball school, Quintana's a sub-6-foot third baseman that...well...is going to have to continue to prove doubters wrong. Fans – and front office personnel – have to be wondering whether he'll be the next Ronnie Bourquin.

Ceiling: 1.5- to 2.0-win player
Risk: Moderate to High
MLB ETA: 2022

13. Beau Burrows, RHP

FB	CB	SL	CH	Command	Overall
55	55	N/A	50	45	45

Born: 09/18/96	Age: 23	Bats: R
Height: 6-2	Weight: 215	Throws: R

YEAR	LVL	IP	W	L	SV	ERA	FIP	WHIP	K/9	K%	BB/9	BB%	K/BB	HR9	BABIP
2017	A+	58.7	4	3	0	1.23	2.57	0.95	9.5	28.18%	1.7	5.00%	5.64	0.46	0.298
2017	AA	76.3	6	4	0	4.72	3.41	1.47	8.8	22.66%	3.9	9.97%	2.27	0.59	0.339
2018	AA	134.0	10	9	0	4.10	4.01	1.36	8.5	22.24%	3.8	9.81%	2.27	0.81	0.310
2019	A+	4.0	0	0	0	0.00	2.31	0.75	11.3	35.71%	4.5	14.29%	2.50	0.00	0.143
2019	AA	5.0	1	0	0	0.00	3.16	0.80	5.4	16.67%	3.6	11.11%	1.50	0.00	0.154
2019	AAA	65.3	2	6	0	5.51	5.84	1.53	8.4	20.68%	4.4	10.85%	1.91	1.65	0.303

Background: While the opening round of the 2015 draft is sprinkled with plenty of star caliber talent – like Alex Bregman, Brendan Rodgers, Andrew Benintendi, Kyle Tucker, Mike Soroka, Ke'Bryan Hayes, Walker Buehler, and Dansby Swanson – there's a tremendous amount of failed and/or disappointments, like: Dillon Tate, Tyler Jay, Carson Fulmer, Cornelius Randolph, Brady Aiken, Ashe Russell, Nick Plummer, and Nolan Watson, among others. It's becoming readily apparent five seasons into his professional career that Burrows is teetering towards the latter group. The 22nd overall pick that year, Burrows' control has slowly regressed in each of the past two seasons as he's jumped through the minor leagues. After averaging 1.9 BB/9 in High Class A in the opening half of 2017, he finished the season with a 3.9 BB/9 rate in Class AA in the second half. Burrows walked 56 in 134.0 innings in a return to the Eastern League the following season. Last year, in an injury-interrupted campaign (oblique), Burrows averaged 4.4 walks per nine innings in 15 starts in Class AAA.

Snippet from The 2018 Prospect Digest Handbook: Burrows lacks a strong secondary option that would allow him to ascend toward the middle of a big league rotation.

Scouting Report: Again, it all comes down to his inconsistent and/or run-of-the-mill secondary offerings. The former first rounder's fastball shows solid life, particularly up in the zone. His curveball oscillated between below-average to above-average last season, which could be a result of the mid-season oblique issue. I didn't see a slider, which he showcased the previous year. And his change has a little bit of sink. Detroit has a bevy of high upside minor league arms, so it isn't out of the question that Burrows slides into a relief role as a fastball/curveball combo arm. Ceiling as a #5-type arm on a non-contending team.

Ceiling: 1.5-win player
Risk: Moderate
MLB ETA: 2020

14. Jake Rogers, C

Hit	Power	SB	Patience	Glove	Overall
40	50	30	55	80	45

Born: 04/18/95	Age: 25	Bats: R
Height: 6-1	Weight: 205	Throws: R

YEAR	LVL	PA	1B	2B	3B	HR	SB	CS	AVG	OBP	SLG	BB%	K%	GB%	LD%	FB%
2017	A	116	12	7	1	6	1	0	0.255	0.336	0.520	7.76%	24.14%	34.7	17.3	40.0
2017	A+	367	50	18	3	12	13	8	0.265	0.357	0.457	11.99%	19.62%	39.3	20.6	32.4
2017	A+	8	1	0	0	0	0	0	0.143	0.250	0.143	12.50%	25.00%	0.0	0.0	60.0
2018	AA	408	44	15	1	17	7	1	0.219	0.305	0.412	10.05%	27.45%	33.3	18.1	41.8
2019	AA	112	17	3	1	5	0	0	0.302	0.429	0.535	16.96%	23.21%	32.8	15.6	39.1
2019	AAA	191	17	10	1	9	0	0	0.223	0.321	0.458	9.42%	27.75%	27.2	24.6	38.6

Background: Not only the top defensive catcher with rookie eligibility remaining, but Rogers is on the short list of top defenders in all of the minor leagues – regardless of position. The former Tulane backstop made stops at three separate levels during his sixth professional season, going from the Eastern League to the International League before settling in for an extended look at the big league level. Rogers, a third round pick in 2016, batted a solid .250/.361/.484 with 13 doubles, two triples, and 14 homeruns in 76 minor league games. He cobbled together a puny .125/.222/.259 slash line during his 35-game MLB cameo.

Snippet from The 2018 Prospect Digest Handbook: Regardless of how poor the hit tool is – and it most definitely is – Rogers will likely carve out a lengthy big league career as a starting caliber catcher thanks to his terrific defense.

Scouting Report: Defense, defense, defense. The book on Rogers is complete and thorough. A stout brick wall of a catcher with little offensive value. But the defensive showing will open plenty of starting options for him. Baseball Prospectus' FRAA (*Fielding Runs Above Average*) had him as a +11.8 defender in only 76 games. He also tossed out 53% of would-be base stealers during the same timeframe as well. Given enough time he'll run into enough fastballs to belt out 12 or so homeruns as well.

Ceiling: 1.5-win player
Risk: Low to Moderate
MLB ETA: Debuted in 2019

15. Willi Castro, SS

Hit	Power	SB	Patience	Glove	Overall
50+	45	50	45+	50	45

Born: 04/24/97 | **Age:** 23 | **Bats:** B
Height: 6-1 | **Weight:** 205 | **Throws:** R

YEAR	LVL	PA	1B	2B	3B	HR	SB	CS	AVG	OBP	SLG	BB%	K%	GB%	LD%	FB%
2018	AA	410	64	20	2	5	13	4	0.245	0.303	0.350	6.83%	20.49%	47.1	21.0	24.4
2018	AA	114	19	9	2	4	4	1	0.324	0.366	0.562	5.26%	21.93%	35.4	30.5	28.0
2018	AAA	21	6	0	0	0	1	0	0.286	0.286	0.286	0.00%	23.81%	31.3	25.0	43.8
2019	AAA	525	93	28	8	11	17	4	0.301	0.366	0.467	7.05%	20.95%	45.2	22.2	26.3

Background: Smooth-swinging shortstop brought over from the Cleveland farm system at the trade deadline two years ago. Detroit sent center field Leonys Martin and intriguing, hard-throwing right-hander Kyle Dowdy to the Indians to complete the inter-divisional deal. The 6-foot-1, 205-pounder captured the imagination of the Tigers faithful following the trade as he put together one the best hot streaks in in his career; he slugged .324/.344/.562 with 15 extra-base hits in only 26 games with Toledo (as opposed to the .245/.303/.350 triple-slash line he sports in 97 games with Akron). Detroit pushed Castro up to the International League for 2019. In 119 games with the Mud Hens, he slugged .301/.366/.467 with 28 doubles, eight triples, and 11 homeruns. He also swiped 17 bags in 21 attempts. According to *Deserved Runs Created Plus*, his overall production topped the league average mark by 11%. Castro spent the last several weeks in Detroit, batting a lowly .230/.284/.340.

Snippet from The 2018 Prospect Digest Handbook: Castro has always been an intriguing, projection-before-production prospect with impressive raw tools. And it looked like things were beginning to click for the Puerto Rican middle infielder two years ago. But he – simply – looked overwhelmed at times in the Eastern League, which is to be expected given his age. He lacks a whole lot of patience at the dish, but can certainly pick-it at shortstop. Right now Castro looks like he could go two ways – a solid league-average or better shortstop driven by his defense and hit tool or a strong backup. I'm more inclined to believe he falls into the latter category unless the power creeps.

Scouting Report: Consider the following:

- Since 2006, only three 22-year-old hitters met the following criteria in the International League (min. 300 PA): 105 to 115 DRC+, 19% to 23% strikeout rate, and a walk rate between 6% and 8%. Those three hitters: Arismendy Alcantara and Austin Jackson.
- Jackson owns a career 95DRC+ at the big league level. And Alcantara owns a 59 DRC+.

Low end starter with a decent all-around skill set without a true standout. Maybe, best case scenario, he peaks with a 55-grade bat. But he should claim the Tigers starting gig for a couple years until a long term replacement comes along.

Ceiling: 1.5-win player
Risk: Moderate
MLB ETA: Debuted in 2019

16. Rony Garcia, RHP

FB	SL/CU	CH	Command	Overall
65	60	N/A	50+	45

Born: 12/19/97 | **Age:** 22 | **Bats:** R
Height: 6-3 | **Weight:** 200 | **Throws:** R

YEAR	LVL	IP	W	L	SV	ERA	FIP	WHIP	K/9	K%	BB/9	BB%	K/BB	HR9	BABIP
2017	Rk	11.3	0	0	0	3.97	4.17	1.15	8.7	23.40%	1.6	4.26%	5.50	0.79	0.323
2017	A	64.3	2	3	0	2.24	3.67	1.04	6.3	17.24%	2.1	5.75%	3.00	0.42	0.254
2018	A	71.0	3	4	0	4.18	3.43	1.21	7.9	20.39%	1.6	4.28%	4.77	0.63	0.312
2018	A+	48.0	1	5	0	4.50	3.32	1.29	8.4	21.84%	2.8	7.28%	3.00	0.38	0.321
2019	A+	25.0	0	2	0	2.16	3.19	1.12	9.0	25.00%	2.5	7.00%	3.57	0.72	0.288
2019	AA	105.3	4	11	0	4.44	4.20	1.25	8.9	23.21%	3.2	8.48%	2.74	1.20	0.281

Background: Exactly the type of move – and player – a rebuilding club should hone in on at the top of the Rule 5 Draft. The Tigers selected the hard-throwing, 6-foot-3, 200-pound right-hander from the Yankees with the first overall selection in the Rule 5 Draft this offseason. A native of Mao, Dominican Republic, Garcia is coming off of his finest professional season date. After rattling off four strong appearances with New York's Florida State League affiliate, he was promoted up to Class AA for seven starts. He was then briefly demoted to High Class A for a start, and returned to the Eastern League two weeks later. In total, Garcia made a career-high 25 appearances, 24 of which were starts, throwing 130.1 innings with 129 strikeouts and 45 free passes. He compiled an aggregate 4.01 ERA.

Scouting Report: With respect to his work in Class AA last season, consider the following:

- Since 2006, here's the list of 21-year-old arms to post a strikeout percentage between 22$ and 24% with a walk percentage between 7.5% and 9.5% in the Eastern League (min. 100 IP): Carlos Carrasco, Jameson Taillon, JoJo Romero, and – of course – Rony Garcia.

Not bad company to keep. At. All. Garcia's repertoire is far better than reported. Following his selection by the Tigers, Vice President of Player Development David Littlefield was quoted by MLB.com as saying his fastball sits "91-95". It was better than that during the time I saw him – particularly an early August contest against the Hartford Yard Goats. Garcia's heater was sitting 94-95 and bumping 97 with regularity. Reports also indicate he throws two separate breaking balls: a slider and a cutter. I believe they're one in the same, albeit plus. The offering(s) sit in the 87- to 91-mph range with late, sharp lateral movement. He also shows a changeup, though I didn't see one. Garcia throws from a low three-quarter, slinging arm slot, which explains his platoon numbers against LHs (.2667/.334/.457). At best, he's a #5 arm because of the splits. But my money's on him sliding into a late-inning relief role. Great pick.

Ceiling: 1.5-win player
Risk: Moderate
MLB ETA: 2020

17. Bryant Packard, LF

Hit	Power	SB	Patience	Glove	Overall
50	50	35	50+	45	45

Born: 10/06/97	Age: 22	Bats: L
Height: 6-3	Weight: 200	Throws: R

YEAR	LVL	PA	1B	2B	3B	HR	SB	CS	AVG	OBP	SLG	BB%	K%	GB%	LD%	FB%
2019	A-	44	11	2	0	0	1	0	0.351	0.432	0.405	13.64%	20.45%	48.3	34.5	13.8
2019	A	94	16	6	0	3	1	0	0.309	0.404	0.494	13.83%	25.53%	47.4	28.1	17.5
2019	A+	20	2	0	0	0	0	0	0.118	0.250	0.118	10.00%	25.00%	58.3	8.3	33.3

Background: The ninth highest player chosen in East Carolina University's history. Detroit made Packard their fifth round choice, 142nd overall, last June. One of the most productive collegiate hitters over his final two seasons for the Pirates, which includes his stout showing in the Cape Cod League in which he slugged .305/.421/.576, Packard left the school as a career .359/.427/.566 hitter. And, of course, he continued to mash as a professional. Sprinting through three separate levels – New York-Penn, Midwest, and Florida State Leagues – the 6-foot-3, 200-pound corner outfielder batted .296/.392/.422 with eight doubles and three triples in 39 games of work.

Scouting Report: He could prove to be one of the better value selections in last year's draft class. There's the potential that (A) Packard flashes average or better tools with the bat and (B) spends some significant time in Class AA by the end of 2020. Packard's swing has a lot of natural loft that should allow him to hit 20 or so dingers in a season with a .260 or so batting average. There's some low-end starting caliber potential here.

Ceiling: 1.5-win player
Risk: Moderate
MLB ETA: 2021/2022

18. Wenceel Perez, SS

Hit	Power	SB	Patience	Glove	Overall
40/50	40/45	60	50	45/50	45

Born: 10/30/99	Age: 20	Bats: B
Height: 5-11	Weight: 195	Throws: R

YEAR	LVL	PA	1B	2B	3B	HR	SB	CS	AVG	OBP	SLG	BB%	K%	GB%	LD%	FB%
2017	RK	258	62	8	1	0	16	6	0.314	0.387	0.358	10.47%	8.14%	50.7	17.2	24.4
2018	RK	93	22	7	0	2	2	1	0.383	0.462	0.543	12.90%	15.05%	38.8	31.3	22.4
2018	A-	87	17	2	0	1	7	3	0.244	0.287	0.305	5.75%	13.79%	50.0	12.9	31.4
2018	A	71	15	3	3	0	4	1	0.309	0.324	0.441	2.82%	11.27%	52.5	19.7	23.0
2019	A	516	82	16	6	3	21	13	0.233	0.299	0.314	8.72%	16.86%	52.2	14.8	23.2

Background: Coming off of two impressive offensive campaigns against the lowest levels, the young switch-hitting middle infielder looked primed for shooting up a lot of prospect lists heading into the 2019 season. And then he promptly fell flat on his face. Perez, a 5-foot-11, 195-pound shortstop out of Azua, Dominican Republic, looked comfortable during his tour through the foreign rookie league two years ago as he batted .314/.387/.358 with nine extra-base hits. He followed that up with an even better showing as he spent time in the Gulf Coast, New York-Penn and Midwest Leagues, batting an aggregate .312/.363/.429 in 57 combined games in 2018. Perez spent all of last season back in Low Class A – where he managed to barely hit his weight: .233/.299/.314 with 16 doubles, six triples, three homers, and 21 stolen bases. Per *DRC+*, his production was 22% *below* the league mark.

Snippet from The 2018 Prospect Digest Handbook: The 5-foot-11, 170-pound switch-hitter showed some solid power potential last season – with the promise to be a double-digit homerun threat in the coming years if he can elevate the ball with a higher frequency. Perez's hit tool should grow into an above-average weapon, which teams well with his solid eye and plus-speed. And it looks like his glove is solid enough to keep him at shortstop as well. There's some starting caliber potential here, though it's raw and several years ago.

Scouting Report: When it comes to disappointing seasons – particularly those involving young players making the leap into more advanced levels – one of the key indicators I look for is progress throughout the year. And Perez, despite the poor showing, slowly-but-surely continued to improve. Here are his monthly OPS totals beginning with April: .481, .590, .634, .599, and .694. It's not great, but it's something nonetheless. Strong contact skills, plus speed, and a decent eye at the plate. Throw in his ability to switch-hit and Perez has the makings of a useful utility player for the Tigers in the coming years.

Ceiling: 1.5-win player
Risk: Moderate
MLB ETA: Debuted in 2019

19. Ulrich Bojarski, RF

Hit	Power	SB	Patience	Glove	Overall
45	50/55	35	40	50	45

Born: 09/15/98	Age: 21	Bats: R
Height: 6-3	Weight: 200	Throws: R

YEAR	LVL	PA	1B	2B	3B	HR	SB	CS	AVG	OBP	SLG	BB%	K%	GB%	LD%	FB%
2018	A-	83	8	3	0	1	3	0	0.162	0.241	0.243	6.02%	39.76%	0.0	0.0	0.0
2018	A	37	3	3	1	1	0	0	0.222	0.216	0.444	0.00%	40.54%	36.4	22.7	27.3
2019	A	420	74	17	3	10	6	3	0.271	0.304	0.409	3.81%	20.71%	0.0	0.0	0.0
2019	A+	80	9	4	1	0	1	0	0.182	0.200	0.260	1.25%	25.00%	37.9	27.6	29.3

Background: Of South African decent, Bojarski first popped up on MLB teams' radar after the then-17-year-old corner outfielder hit .243/.268/.360 in the Australian Baseball League. The next time Bojarski, a native of East London, popped up on a baseball field he was donning a Tigers' Gulf Coast League uniform. The numbers weren't great – he hit a lowly .225/.298/.333 – and he followed that up with an equally disappointing showing in 2018 as he spent time with three low level affiliates (.202/.281/.365). Last season, though, things seemed to click for Bojarski in the Midwest League. In 104 games, the 6-foot-3, 200-pound corner outfielder slugged .271/.304/.409 with 17 doubles, three triples, 10 homeruns, and six stolen bases. His production, per *Deserved Runs Created Plus*, topped the league average threshold by 1%. Bojarski also spent 22 games in High Class A, though they were mostly forgettable.

Scouting Report: Prior to the 2019 season, Bojarski never topped more than 60 games in a professional season – which may explain his late season collapse. The young corner outfielder slugged a healthy .311/.346/.498 with 27 extra-base hits through his first 73 contests. He followed that up with a lowly .180/.203/.227 over his remaining 53 contests (including the 22 in High Class A). I'm betting on the former numbers, not the latter. There's some intriguing potential as a low-end starting option with 20-homerun potential, low OBPs, and decent glove.

Ceiling: 1.5-win player
Risk: Moderate
MLB ETA: Debuted in 2019

20. Roberto Campos, RF

Hit	Power	SB	Patience	Glove	Overall
N/A	N/A	N/A	N/A	N/A	N/A

Born: XX/XX/XX	Age: 17	Bats: R
Height: 6-3	Weight: 200	Throws: R

Background: 52.8%. That's the percentage of the club's international bonus pool the front office handed the Cuban import. According to reports, Campos defected from Cuba as a 13-year-old following an amateur tournament.

Scouting Report: There's very little know about the teenage corner outfielder. And what is known is largely mixed. An article by Lynn Henning of *The Detroit News* quotes an anonymous scout, saying "the Tigers got a player for $2.8 million who probably was worth $750,000 to $1 million." I've scoured the internet and there are zero videos of Campos. I've decided to include him due to (A) his age and (B) there seems to be zero knowledge outside the Tigers' organization about him. So far he's the international man of mystery.

Ceiling: N/A
Risk: High
MLB ETA: Debuted in 2019

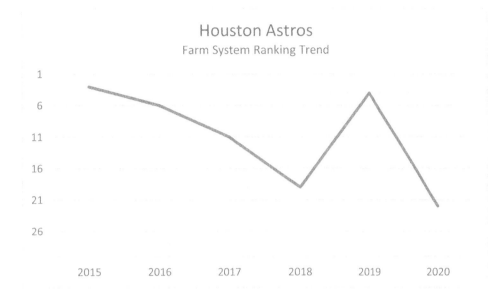

Houston Astros
Farm System Ranking Trend

Rank	Name	Age	Pos
1	Forrest Whitley	22	RHP
2	Jose Urquidy	25	RHP
3	Abraham Toro	23	IF
4	Cristian Javier	23	RHP
5	Bryan Abreu	23	RHP
6	Brandon Bailey	25	RHP
7	Tyler Ivey	24	RHP
8	Jose Alberto Rivera	23	RHP
9	Jairo Solis	20	RHP
10	Freudis Nova	20	IF
11	Korey Lee	21	C
12	Cionel Perez	24	LHP
13	Enoli Paredes	24	RHP
14	Jordan Brewer	21	CF
15	Luis Garcia	23	RHP
16	Brandon Bielak	24	RHP
17	Jeremy Pena	22	SS
18	Grae Kessinger	22	IF
19	J.J. Matijevic	24	1B/LF
20	Nathan Perry	20	C/1B

1. Forrest Whitley, RHP

	FB	CB	SL	CU	CH	Control	Overall
	70	70	60	60	60	50/60	60

Born: 09/15/97	Age: 22	Bats: R
Height: 6-7	Weight: 195	Throws: R

YEAR	LVL	IP	W	L	SV	ERA	FIP	WHIP	K/9	K%	BB/9	BB%	K/BB	HR9	BABIP
2017	A	46.3	2	3	0	2.91	2.66	1.36	13.0	34.36%	4.1	10.77%	3.19	0.39	0.388
2017	A+	31.3	3	1	0	3.16	2.08	1.18	14.4	38.76%	2.6	6.98%	5.56	0.57	0.394
2017	AA	14.7	0	0	0	1.84	1.68	0.82	16.0	46.43%	2.5	7.14%	6.50	0.61	0.292
2018	AA	26.3	0	2	0	3.76	3.33	0.99	11.6	31.48%	3.8	10.19%	3.09	0.68	0.220
2019	A+	8.3	1	0	0	2.16	1.45	0.60	11.9	35.48%	1.1	3.23%	11.00	0.00	0.222
2019	AA	22.7	2	2	0	5.56	4.33	1.63	14.3	34.95%	7.5	18.45%	1.89	0.79	0.372
2019	AAA	24.3	0	3	0	12.21	8.07	2.05	10.7	24.37%	5.5	12.61%	1.93	3.33	0.394

Background: The crown jewel of Houston's farm system has had a rough go of it the past couple of seasons. Whitley, who was committed to Florida State University prior to the club taking him with the 17th overall pick four years ago, was popped for a banned substance during Spring Training heading into 2018. He eventually made his way back to regular season action but an oblique issue knocked him out for a month in early July. And then last season the behemoth right-hander, who still looked poised to become a valuable contributor for the club, battled shoulder fatigue issues in late May – an injury that put him on the DL for nearly two full months. Negating his two-game rehab stint in the Gulf Coast League, Whitley was limited to just 16 appearances, throwing 55.1 innings with 76 strikeouts and 35 walks. The Alamo Heights High School product made six more appearances with the Peoria Javelinas in the Arizona Fall League, throwing 25.0 innings with 32 strikeouts and nine walks with a 2.88 ERA.

Snippet from The 2018 Prospect Digest Handbook: He's a legitimate top-of-the-line caliber arm.

Scouting Report: Not including his abbreviated debut following his selection in the middle of the first round, last season marked the third consecutive time that Whitley has failed to throw more than 92.2 innings of work. And thanks to his early season suspension in 2018 – and including both stints in the Arizona Fall League – Whitley's thrown just 137.0 innings over the past two years. That's problematic – especially considering that he's dealt with a couple arm / body issues (oblique and right shoulder) as well the avoidable suspension. With that being said, it's the single best arsenal in the minor leagues. Five plus pitches – which is almost unheard of. Whitley's heater sits in the mid-90s and approaches triple-digits on occasion. His curveball's like a gift from Bert Blyleven, one helluva 12-6, knee-buckling offering that's one of the finest in the minor leagues. He'll also throw a slider and a cutter, both solid 60-grade pitches. And his changeup shows tremendous dive-and-fade. The control, repertoire, and build – he's 6-foot-7 and 195-pounds – all suggest elite pitcher, but it's concerning that he's been as limited as he has in terms of workload.

Ceiling: 5.0-win player
Risk: Moderate
MLB ETA: 2020

2. Jose Urquidy, RHP

	FB	CB	SL	CH	Command	Overall
	60	55	50	60	60	50

Born: 05/01/95	Age: 24	Bats: R
Height: 6-0	Weight: 180	Throws: R

YEAR	LVL	IP	W	L	SV	ERA	FIP	WHIP	K/9	K%	BB/9	BB%	K/BB	HR9	BABIP
2019	AA	33.0	2	2	0	4.09	2.26	1.00	10.9	30.08%	1.4	3.76%	8.00	0.55	0.302
2019	AAA	70.0	5	3	0	4.63	4.62	1.19	12.1	32.08%	2.1	5.46%	5.88	1.93	0.311

Background: Part of the conversation with Abraham Toro for biggest riser in the Astros' incredibly deep farm system in 2019. Urquidy, who was known as Jose Luis Hernandez prior to last season, first began showing intriguing promise as a 21-year-old pitching between Low Class A and High Class A in 2016. But a wonky elbow – which eventually resulted in Tommy John surgery – knocked him out for the entire 2017 season. Finally healthy in 2018, Houston sent the hard-throwing right-hander to short-season ball and then onto the Carolina League during his return to action. And while his numbers were good – he averaged 7.5 strikeouts and just 1.6 walks per nine innings – no one could have forecasted his tantalizing showing in 2019. The 6-foot, 180-pound righty ripped through the Texas League and dominated the offensive friendly confines of the Pacific Coast League and spent the last several months of the year yo-yoing between Round Rock and Houston. In total, Urquidy tossed 103.0 innings in the minor leagues, recording 134 strikeouts and just 21 walks with a 4.46 ERA. He made another nine appearances with Houston, posting a 40-to-7 strikeout-to-walk ratio in 41.0 innings of work.

Scouting Report: An extreme strike-thrower before *and* after his Tommy John surgery. Urquidy combines his uncanny ability to find the strike zone with an impressively deep arsenal. His 93- to 94-mph fastball, a plus offering, touched as high as 97 mph on a couple occasions during his work in the minor leagues last season. His devastating changeup, a second genuine swing-and-miss offering, is his go-to offspeed option. He'll complement the duo with a pair of breaking balls: an above-average curveball and a decent slider. #3-type upside.

Ceiling: 3.0-win player
Risk: Moderate
MLB ETA: Debuted in 2019

3. Abraham Toro, IF

	Hit	Power	SB	Patience	Glove	Overall
	50	55	30	60	55	50

Born: 12/20/96	**Age:** 23	**Bats:** B
Height: 6-1	**Weight:** 190	**Throws:** R

YEAR	LVL	PA	1B	2B	3B	HR	SB	CS	AVG	OBP	SLG	BB%	K%	GB%	LD%	FB%
2017	A-	128	17	8	0	6	1	3	0.292	0.414	0.538	14.84%	16.41%	37.6	27.1	23.5
2017	A	158	14	3	2	9	2	0	0.209	0.323	0.463	13.29%	18.99%	29.5	10.5	45.7
2018	A+	349	41	20	1	14	5	1	0.257	0.361	0.473	12.89%	17.77%	38.0	15.2	34.6
2018	AA	202	22	15	2	2	3	3	0.230	0.317	0.371	8.42%	22.77%	34.6	20.3	36.1
2019	AA	435	73	22	4	16	4	1	0.306	0.393	0.513	11.03%	17.70%	37.1	24.8	31.5
2019	AAA	79	18	9	0	1	0	1	0.424	0.506	0.606	12.66%	6.33%	39.0	35.6	20.3

Background: A fifth round pick out of JuCo powerhouse Seminole State College four years ago. Toro flashed some impressive numbers at times, but it wasn't until his massive breakout in the Arizona Fall League where things began to click. A natural catcher who's bounced around the diamond quite a bit in recent years, Toro turned in a mediocre showing in the Appalachian League during his debut as he batted .254/.301/.322. The front office bounced him up to the New York-Penn League to begin the 2017 season and that's when the 6-foot-1, 190-pound switch-hitter began to offer up glimpses of his offensive thump. He slugged .292/.414/.538 with 14 extra-base hits in only 32 games – though, he struggled upon his second half promotion up to the Midwest League. But despite appearing in just 37 games with Quad Cities, Toro was aggressively promoted up to High Class A to start the 2018 season. And after slugging .257/.361/.473 with 35 extra-base hits in 83 games, the front office brass deemed him ready for the minors' toughest challenge: Class AA. He promptly batted .230/.317/.371 in 50 games with Corpus Christi. Then…the breakout happened. Squaring off against the elite competition of the Arizona Fall League, the Canadian-born infielder slugged .348/.463/.561 with six doubles, one triple, and a pair of homeruns in 19 games with the Scottsdale Scorpions – and that proved to just be a harbinger of things to come. Toro ripped through the Texas League pitching to the tune of .306/.393/.513 with 22 doubles, four triples, and 16 homeruns. Per Baseball Prospectus' *Deserved Runs Created Plus*, his overall production topped the league average threshold by 61%. He continued his offensive assault during his brief action in Class AAA. And he earned a 25-game cameo with the big league club down the stretch.

Scouting Report: With respect to his work in Class AA last season, consider the following:

- Since 2006, here's the list of 22-year-old hitters to eclipse the 150 DRC+ threshold in the Texas League (min. 350 PA): Dexter Fowler, Alex Gordon, Chris Carter, and – of course – Abraham Toro.
- Sans Toro, here are the remaining trio's career DRC+ totals: 101 (Fowler), 104 (Gordon) and 112 (Carter).

And just for the record: all four hitters had similar walk and strikeout rates as well. Always a saber-slanted offensive performer, Toro combines plus patience at the plate with 20-homerun thump, strong contact skills, and positional versatility. What's not to like? Houston began shifting him around the infield last season as he spent time between first, second, and third bases. FanGraphs shows he had an average exit velocity of 89 mph, which is slightly better than his mark with Houston. In terms of offensive ceiling, think .280/.350/.460 with 25 homeruns.

Ceiling: 3.0-win player
Risk: Moderate
MLB ETA: Debuted in 2019

4. Cristian Javier, RHP

	FB	CB	SL	CH	Command	Overall
	55	55	50	55	45	50

Born: 03/26/97	**Age:** 23	**Bats:** R
Height: 6-1	**Weight:** 204	**Throws:** R

YEAR	LVL	IP	W	L	SV	ERA	FIP	WHIP	K/9	K%	BB/9	BB%	K/BB	HR9	BABIP
2017	A-	16.7	0	0	0	2.70	2.35	1.20	13.0	32.88%	4.9	12.33%	2.67	0.00	0.282
2017	A	37.7	2	0	1	2.39	3.39	1.06	11.2	31.33%	3.6	10.00%	3.13	0.72	0.265
2017	A+	5.7	1	0	0	0.00	1.80	0.88	14.3	40.91%	4.8	13.64%	3.00	0.00	0.200
2018	A	49.3	2	2	1	1.82	2.54	1.03	14.6	40.61%	4.2	11.68%	3.48	0.55	0.281
2018	A+	60.7	5	4	0	3.41	4.00	1.17	9.8	26.29%	4.0	10.76%	2.44	0.89	0.257
2019	A+	28.7	2	0	1	0.94	2.82	1.08	12.6	33.33%	5.0	13.33%	2.50	0.31	0.226
2019	AA	74.0	6	3	3	2.07	2.91	0.95	13.9	39.04%	4.7	13.36%	2.92	0.61	0.197
2019	AAA	11.0	0	0	0	1.64	3.43	0.82	13.1	36.36%	3.3	9.09%	4.00	0.82	0.182

Background: An unheralded signing out of Santo Domingo, Dominican Republic, for a couple of reasons: (A) at the time of his contract with Houston he was just days away from turning 18-years-old, which is practically ancient on the international free agent market and (B) his bonus, just $10,000, was a relatively paltry sum in baseball terms. But Javier, a promising 6-foot-1, 204-pound right-hander, is proving to be quite the bargain. After spending the first two seasons of his professional career in the foreign and stateside rookie leagues, Javier began jumping through a couple levels per season in 2017. He split time between Tri-City, Quad Cities, and Buies Creek in 2017; spent time with the latter two squads the following year. And then last season Javier dominated the Carolina League in seven appearances, was even better in 17 games with Corpus Christi, and capped off his best professional season with a two-game cameo in Class AAA. In total, Javier tossed a career best 113.2 innings, recording a whopping 170 strikeouts against 59 walks to go along with a 1.74 ERA.

Snippet from The 2018 Prospect Digest Handbook: Just another one of these high ceiling, potentially dominant future big league arms that the club has somehow cornered the market on. Javier's a volatile prospect, but he's the type you bet on though.

Scouting Report: With respect to his work in Class AA last season, consider the following:

- Since 2006, here's the list of 22-year-old pitchers to fan at least 34% of the hitters they faced in any Class AA league (min. 75 IP): Clay Buchholz and Cristian Javier. Buchholz fanned 35% of the hitters he faced. Javier shattered that mark by four percentage points (39%).

Let's expand that a bit...

- Since 2006, here's the of pitchers – at any age – to fan at least 35% of the hitters they faced in any Class AA league (min. 75 IP): Clay Buchholz (35%), Paul Estrada (37% at 23-years-old), and – of course – Cristian Javier.

So...he's clearly good – very, very good. Javier showcases a deep, four-pitch mix: an above-average fastball, curveball, and changeup with a solid-average slider. The problem, of course, is Javier's inability to find the strike zone. He walked nearly 13% of the hitters he faced in 2019. To put that into context, only four qualified pitchers posted a walk percentage of at least 10% in the big leagues last season: Luis Castillo, Julio Teheran, Robbie Ray, and Dakota Hudson. I do think there's some Luis Castillo-type potential with Javier, but the walks will forever remain a concern.

Ceiling: 2.5- to 3.0-win player
Risk: Moderate
MLB ETA: 2020

5. Bryan Abreu, RHP

	FB	CB	SL	CH	Command	Overall
	70	70	65	45	40/45	50

Born: 04/22/97	Age: 23	Bats: R
Height: 6-1	Weight: 204	Throws: R

YEAR	LVL	IP	W	L	SV	ERA	FIP	WHIP	K/9	K%	BB/9	BB%	K/BB	HR9	BABIP
2017	Rk	29.3	1	3	0	7.98	5.09	1.70	12.3	29.63%	6.4	15.56%	1.90	1.23	0.357
2018	A-	16.0	2	0	0	1.13	3.48	1.06	12.4	35.48%	3.4	9.68%	3.67	1.13	0.281
2018	A	38.3	4	1	3	1.64	2.09	1.02	16.0	44.44%	4.0	11.11%	4.00	0.47	0.313
2019	A+	14.7	1	0	0	3.68	3.37	1.02	15.3	42.37%	3.7	10.17%	4.17	1.23	0.292
2019	AA	76.7	6	2	2	5.05	3.98	1.41	11.9	29.97%	5.6	14.24%	2.10	0.70	0.309

Background: Signed off the international scene following the 2013 season. Abreu, a native of Santo Domingo, Dominican Republic, spent several years toiling away in the rookie leagues: two in the foreign ranks and another two stateside. But less than two years after his last appearance in the Appalachian League, the hard-throwing right-hander was toeing the rubber for the Astros. After splitting time between Tri-City and Quad Cities two years ago, Abreu opened up the 2019 season with three absurdly strong starts in High Class A; he fanned 25 and walked just six in 14.2 innings of work. Houston bounced him up to the Texas League where he continued to miss a bevy of bats (as well as the strike zone). In total, Abreu made 23 minor league appearances, 16 of which were starts, throwing 91.1 innings with 126 strikeouts and 54 walks to go along with a 4.83 ERA. He also made seven dominant appearances in the big leagues as well, punching out 13 and walking three in 8.2 innings.

Snippet from The 2018 Prospect Digest Handbook: The control's likely going to keep him out of the rotation long term, but he could be lethal as a fastball/curveball relief arm. The curveball may be the best in the minor leagues. Period. It's absurdly wicked; It's incredible. It may very well get him to the big leagues alone.

Scouting Report: Elite, elite repertoire spearheaded by dual 70-grade offerings: a mid-90s fastball and – arguably – the best curveball in the entire minor leagues. Abreu will also mix in a lethal, near 70-grade slider with late tilting, two-plane break. He's also hesitant to mix in a below-average, incredibly rare changeup. The lead trio all suggest upper echelon starting pitcher, but the problem – which seems to plague more than a few of the Astros' top pitching prospects – is his inability to consistently throw strikes. He's entering his age-23 season, so he'll get a couple more looks at the rotation to figure out the consistency issues before being forced into a dominant bullpen role. Abreu's volatile in sense, because he could be a #2 or an elite closer, but in either scenario he's an impact arm. And just because it bears repeating: elite, elite repertoire.

Ceiling: 3.0-win player
Risk: Moderate to High
MLB ETA: Debuted in 2019

6. Brandon Bailey, RHP

	FB	CB	SL	CU	CH	Control	Overall
	60	55	50	45/50	70	45	45

Born: 10/19/94	**Age:** 25	**Bats:** R
Height: 5-10	**Weight:** 175	**Throws:** R

YEAR	LVL	IP	W	L	SV	ERA	FIP	WHIP	K/9	K%	BB/9	BB%	K/BB	HR9	BABIP
2017	A	57.0	1	1	0	2.68	3.11	1.07	11.5	32.44%	3.3	9.33%	3.48	0.63	0.290
2017	A+	34.0	2	1	1	4.24	3.66	1.12	12.4	33.33%	2.6	7.09%	4.70	1.06	0.304
2018	A+	97.7	5	8	0	2.49	3.32	1.15	10.4	28.18%	4.0	10.72%	2.63	0.55	0.269
2018	AA	24.7	1	0	1	4.01	5.31	1.22	8.4	22.12%	3.3	8.65%	2.56	1.82	0.239
2019	AA	92.7	4	5	0	3.30	4.33	1.22	10.0	27.84%	4.0	11.08%	2.51	1.17	0.271

Background: Easily one of my favorite minor league arms since I began writing about prospects. The book on Bailey is pretty simple: undersized, premium work ethic, high-octane, hard-throwing right-hander. And despite the perceived limitations of a 5-foot-10, 175-pound right-hander, Bailey's been in high demand throughout his professional career. Oakland drafted the Gonzaga product in the sixth round in 2016. A year-and-a-half later the A's flipped him to the Astros for toolsy outfielder Ramon Laureano, who's coming off of a year in which he slugged .288/.340/.521 with 24 homeruns and 13 stolen bases. Bailey's stay in the Astros' organization lasted almost exactly two years. Then the rebuilding Orioles came calling. This time, though, it was in the Rule 5 draft when they used the second overall pick on him. Bailey spent last season – mostly dominating the competition – with the Corpus Christi Hooks in the Texas League. He posted a 103-to-41 strikeout-to-walk ratio in 92.2 innings of work. He tallied a 3.30 ERA and a 4.18 DRA (*Deserved Run Average*). Final Note: Baltimore sent the hard-throwing righty back to Houston midway through Spring Training.

Snippet from The 2018 Prospect Digest Handbook: A nice little hurler to have in the organization, though Laureano may outperform him at the big league level. Bailey's main plan of attack is generating plenty of swings-and-misses by changing a hitter's eye level; typically showcasing his big bending curveball and following it up with a high heater. The control's taken a noticeable step back the past couple of years. And his small stature may eventually push him into a late-inning relief role. But until then Bailey looks like a nice backend option in the rotation.

Scouting Report: Plus fastball, above-average curveball, average slider, and a newly added late-horizontally moving cutter. But make no mistake about it: it's all about that changeup baby. Love it. It's one of the best in the minor leagues. In a perfect world Bailey's control/command upticks half of a grade he graduates in a solid 2.0-win player. In all reality, he's going to be a useful, albeit quite valuable, #4/#5 type arm.

Ceiling: 1.5- to 2.0-win player
Risk: Low to Moderate
MLB ETA: 2020

7. Tyler Ivey, RHP

	FB	CB	SL	CH	Command	Overall
	50+	55	50	55	50	45

Born: 05/12/96	**Age:** 24	**Bats:** R
Height: 6-4	**Weight:** 195	**Throws:** R

YEAR	LVL	IP	W	L	SV	ERA	FIP	WHIP	K/9	K%	BB/9	BB%	K/BB	HR9	BABIP
2017	Rk	2.0	0	0	0	0.00	3.42	1.50	13.5	37.50%	9.0	25.00%	1.50	0.00	0.333
2017	A-	36.3	0	3	0	5.94	3.04	1.46	10.2	25.15%	3.0	7.36%	3.42	0.50	0.368
2018	A	41.7	1	3	2	3.46	2.13	1.06	11.4	30.99%	1.7	4.68%	6.63	0.43	0.315
2018	A+	70.3	3	3	1	2.69	2.56	1.01	10.5	28.87%	2.7	7.39%	3.90	0.38	0.267
2019	A+	3.0	0	0	0	0.00	3.04	0.33	6.0	22.22%	3.0	11.11%	2.00	0.00	0.000
2019	AA	46.0	4	0	0	1.57	3.32	0.96	11.9	33.15%	3.1	8.70%	3.81	0.98	0.228

Background: It was an interesting season for the former third round pick. He opened the year up in the minors' toughest challenge, Class AA, in dominant fashion: he struck out 37 and walked just nine through his first 25.0 innings while surrendering just two earned runs (0.72 ERA). But Ivey, a product of Grayson County College by way of Texas A&M, was suspended for a foreign substance in mid-May, but he wouldn't make it back to Class AA until roughly nine weeks later courtesy of a sprained UCL ligament in his right elbow. He finished the year the same way he started: strong. In total, he made 11 appearances in the Texas League, eight of which were starts, throwing 46.0 innings with 61 strikeouts and 16 walks with a 1.57 ERA and a 2.84 DRA (*Deserved Run Average*).

Snippet from The 2018 Prospect Digest Handbook: At this point it almost borders on absurdity. Houston's somehow cornered the market on pitchers with underrated arsenals and groomed them into legitimate pitching prospects, most of which would rank in the Top 10, even Top 5, for a lot of clubs. Like Ivey. He's very capable of becoming a league average starting pitcher, though he's the type of arm the club typically ships off in a deal.

Scouting Report: Ivey kicks off his windup with a massive step back and then unfurls a solid four-pitch mix out of a wildly herky-jerky, Mike Clevinger-esque motion. His average fastball plays up do to his deception long limbs and deceptive motion. Above-average curveball. Decent, almost bland but workable slider, and a 55-grade changeup with hard diving movement. Ivey's the safest of backend minor league starting options due to a lengthier track record, arsenal, and feel for the strike zone. I still think he gets dealt away as the club tries to lengthen their championship window. Good #4.

Ceiling: 1.5- to 2.0-win player
Risk: Low to Moderate
MLB ETA: 2020

8. Jose Alberto Rivera, RHP

FB	CB	CH	Command	Overall
70	45/55	50/55	45+	55

Born: 02/14/97	Age: 23	Bats: R
Height: 6-3	Weight: 160	Throws: R

YEAR	LVL	IP	W	L	SV	ERA	FIP	WHIP	K/9	K%	BB/9	BB%	K/BB	HR9	BABIP
2017	Rk	36.7	2	3	0	3.44	4.32	1.20	9.1	23.72%	5.9	15.38%	1.54	0.74	0.189
2018	Rk	39.0	1	2	0	3.23	3.75	0.92	9.0	25.00%	1.4	3.85%	6.50	0.92	0.252
2018	A-	10.0	1	2	0	4.50	5.68	1.70	12.6	29.17%	7.2	16.67%	1.75	1.80	0.292
2019	A	75.7	5	5	1	3.81	2.81	1.28	11.3	29.78%	4.3	11.29%	2.64	0.24	0.322

Background: A Valentine's Day Baby. Rivera is – unequivocally – one of my favorite pitchers in all of the minor leagues. The rail-thin right-hander, who stands 6-foot-3 and just 160 pounds, was another one of the club's older international free agent additions; he didn't make his professional debut until his age-20 season. And his numbers in the Dominican Summer League that season, 2017, were mixed – at best. He averaged a punch out per inning but walked nearly six hitters per nine frames. Two years ago, though, Rivera found the strike zone with regular frequency while maintaining a strong ability to miss bats: he fanned 53 and walked just 14 in 49.0 innings between the Gulf Coast and New York-Penn Leagues. The wiry hurler, now 22-years-old, spent last season with the Quad Cities River Bandits in the Midwest League. Making a career high 18 appearances, Rivera averaged 11.3 punch outs and 4.3 walks per nine innings to go along with a 3.81 ERA and a 4.14 DRA (*Deserved Run Average*).

Scouting Report: Rivera has the look of a still-developing 10-year-old little leaguer with his uniform and pants draping off of his wispy frame. But he generates premium velocity as easy – if not *easier* – than any minor league pitching prospect I watched last season – which was over 325 different arms. It's incredibly easy, like walking across the room. Now the less-than-great news: the offspeed offerings – a 12-6 curveball and a firm changeup – are raw. And that's an understatement. The curveball's inconsistent. And it appeared at times he was choking it off. But everyone once in a while he snapped off a beauty that was an easy swing-and-miss, 55-grade. The changeup has some impressive downward action that may reach a 55 as well. He's a high variance arm with the ceiling of a #3/#4 with the floor of a middle relief arm. However, I'm always willing to bet big on the Astros' player development engine.

Ceiling: 2.5-win player
Risk: Moderate to High
MLB ETA: 2021

9. Jairo Solis, RHP

FB	SL	CH	Command	Overall
N/A	N/A	N/A	N/A	50

Born: 12/22/99	Age: 20	Bats: R
Height: 6-2	Weight: 160	Throws: R

YEAR	LVL	IP	W	L	SV	ERA	FIP	WHIP	K/9	K%	BB/9	BB%	K/BB	HR9	BABIP
2017	Rk	26.3	1	1	0	2.73	3.35	1.06	9.6	26.42%	2.7	7.55%	3.50	0.68	0.277
2017	Rk	21.0	1	0	0	3.00	2.89	1.24	10.3	26.09%	3.0	7.61%	3.43	0.43	0.305
2017	Rk	14.0	1	1	0	1.93	2.76	1.29	10.9	28.81%	3.9	10.17%	2.83	0.00	0.333
2018	A	50.7	2	5	0	3.55	3.73	1.60	9.1	22.67%	5.7	14.22%	1.59	0.18	0.345

Background: The timing was a bit poor – though, to be fair, there's never really an ideal time – but Solid underwent the knife in late January last season. The operation repaired a torn UCL in his right elbow – also known as Tommy John surgery. It knocked him out for the entire season. And, while I haven't seen any recent updates, based on the typical recovery schedule the hard-throwing right-hander should return to action around the start of 2020. It's an unfortunate loss of development time for Solis, a 6-foot-2, 160-pound right-hander, as he was coming off of a solid – sometimes impressive – showing as an 18-year-old in the Midwest League: he averaged 9.1 strikeouts and a whopping 5.7 walks per nine innings with a 3.55 ERA and a 5.65 DRA (*Deserved Run Average*).

Snippet from The 2018 Prospect Digest Handbook: An intriguing low-level arm with the potential to operate with three average or better offerings. Solis already shows a plus-fastball that could see a tick-up in grade as his wispy 160-pound matures. His slider is an above-average offering with plus potential. The breaking ball needs a bit of further refinement, though, sometimes it lacks a whole lot of tilt. His changeup figures to be average at his peak. Solis is entering his age-19 season with a solid foundation under his belt. He could be a #4-type arm.

Scouting Report: Obviously, there's nothing to report on. Here's hoping for a full return to health for the promising right-hander. He did battle some control/command issues in 2018, and typically a pitcher's feel for the strike zone takes a hit coming back from Tommy John surgery. Just something to watch for in 2020.

Ceiling: 2.0-win player
Risk: Moderate to High
MLB ETA: 2020

10. Freudis Nova, IF

Hit	Power	SB	Patience	Glove	Overall
40/50	45/50	40	30	50	45

Born: 01/12/00	Age: 20	Bats: R
Height: 6-1	Weight: 180	Throws: R

YEAR	LVL	PA	1B	2B	3B	HR	SB	CS	AVG	OBP	SLG	BB%	K%	GB%	LD%	FB%
2017	RK	190	31	6	0	4	8	3	0.247	0.342	0.355	7.89%	17.37%	36.8	21.1	22.6
2018	RK	157	35	3	1	6	9	5	0.308	0.331	0.466	3.82%	13.38%	45.0	17.8	24.8
2019	A	299	49	20	1	3	10	7	0.259	0.301	0.369	5.02%	22.74%	38.7	24.5	27.4

Background: Part of the club's international free agent class that added Jairo Solis to the fold, Nova, a twitchy infielder from Azua, Dominican Republic, signed with the organization for $1.2 million. Nova made his debut in the foreign rookie league the following season, hitting a disappointing .247/.342/.355 with just 10 extra-base hits in 47 games. The front office bumped the teenager stateside to the Gulf Coast League for the 2018 season. And Nova fared significantly better. In 41 rookie league games, he batted .308/.334/.466 with three triples, one double, six homeruns, and nine stolen bases. Last season Nova was – aggressively – pushed up to Low Class A. And the numbers were...as expected. In a career high 75 games with the Quad Cities Bandits, Nova batted .259/.301/.369 with 20 doubles, one triple, three homeruns, and 10 stolen bases. His overall production, per *Deserved Runs Created Plus*, topped the league average threshold by 5%.

Snippet from The 2018 Prospect Digest Handbook: He shows solid skills across the board: hit tool, power; speed; and glove. He's still more projection rather than production, but he looks capable of holding down a starting job.

Scouting Report: Consider the following:

- Since 2006, only three 19-year-old hitters met the following criteria in the Midwest League (min. 250 PA): 100 to 110 DRC+, a strikeout rate between 18% and 23% with a sub-6.0% walk rate. Those three hitters: Austin Beck, Justin Williams, and Freudis Nova. All – more or less – flawed, albeit toolsy, prospects.

Still more projection over production at this point in his – young – career; Nova does some things well: flashes intriguing power potential for a teenage middle-infielder; runs and his fields his position(s) well. But his inability to work the count and earn more than a rare free pass is already chewing into his overall value. For instance, there were 20 qualified hitters at the big league level to walk fewer than 6% of the time in 2019; nine of them were better than league average hitters. Of those nine, seven of them topped a .170 Isolated Power. So, either Nova's power or his patience will likely have to creep up in the coming years.

Ceiling: 1.5- to 2.0-win player
Risk: Moderate
MLB ETA: 2022

11. Korey Lee, C

Hit	Power	SB	Patience	Glove	Overall
45	45	30	55	50	45

Born: 07/25/98	Age: 21	Bats: R
Height: 6-2	Weight: 205	Throws: R

YEAR	LVL	PA	1B	2B	3B	HR	SB	CS	AVG	OBP	SLG	BB%	K%	GB%	LD%	FB%
2019	A-	259	47	6	4	3	8	5	0.268	0.359	0.371	10.81%	18.92%	52.9	18.0	17.4

Background: There weren't a whole lot of people that would have guessed that Lee, a bit of an offensive disappointment during his first extended look at the University of California, would blossom into a first round pick. But that's exactly what happened. Lee, a 6-foot-2, 205-pound backstop, was sparsely used during his true freshman season, hitting a respectable .277/.338/.338 in 75 trips to the plate. He earned a couple dozen more plate appearances the following season, 2018, as he slugged .238/.328/.426 with just four doubles and five homeruns. Things seemed to click for the California native during the summer in the Northwoods Leagues as he hit .283/.398/.438 with 21 extra-base hits in 60 games with the La Crosse Loggers. Last season, though, Lee became one of the bigger "helium" guys in the draft class. In a career best 51 games for the Pac12 school, Lee slugged .337/.416/.619 with 12 doubles and 15 homeruns. Houston drafted him in the first round, 32nd overall, and signed him to a below-slot deal worth $1.75 million, saving the club a little more than $500,000. Lee spent the entirety of his debut with Tri-City, batting a mediocre .268/.359/.371 with six doubles, four triples, and three homeruns in 64 games.

Scouting Report: With respect to his work in college last season, consider the following:

- Between 2011 and 2018, only two Pac12 hitters met the following criteria (min 200 PA): bat at least .325/.400/.600 with a walk rate between 9% and 12% and a sub-20% strikeout rate. Those two hitters: Michael Conforto and – of course Corey Lee.

The limited track record is concerning, especially considering that he never truly dominated the Northwoods League in either of his stints. And Lee doesn't own a true standout skill. He's similar to former University of California backstop – and 2016 second rounder – Brett Cumberland, though with less patience at the plate. Lee looks like a solid backup, perhaps peaking as a low-end starting option for a non-contending team.

Ceiling: 1.5-win player
Risk: Moderate
MLB ETA: 2022

12. Cionel Perez, LHP

FB	SL	CH	Command	Overall
60	65	50	45	45

Born: 04/21/96	Age: 24	Bats: L
Height: 5-11	Weight: 170	Throws: L

YEAR	LVL	IP	W	L	SV	ERA	FIP	WHIP	K/9	K%	BB/9	BB%	K/BB	HR9	BABIP
2017	A	55.3	4	3	2	4.39	3.01	1.25	8.9	24.23%	2.8	7.49%	3.24	0.33	0.331
2017	A+	25.3	2	1	0	2.84	3.08	1.26	6.4	17.31%	1.8	4.81%	3.60	0.36	0.325
2017	AA	13.0	0	0	0	5.54	4.39	1.54	6.9	16.95%	3.5	8.47%	2.00	0.69	0.341
2018	AA	68.3	6	1	1	1.98	2.60	1.11	10.9	29.96%	2.9	7.94%	3.77	0.40	0.304
2018	AAA	5.3	1	0	0	3.38	4.86	2.06	10.1	23.08%	10.1	23.08%	1.00	0.00	0.357
2019	AAA	47.0	2	1	0	5.36	5.35	1.64	8.2	20.19%	4.6	11.27%	1.79	1.15	0.343

Background: After the back-and-forth between the hurler and organization a deal was finalized – for a second time – adding the hard-throwing left-hander on a $2 million pact seemed like a major coup for the organization. Perez, who had his original $5.15 million deal voided with Houston due to red flags during his physical, was tabbed as an "elite" prospect on the international free agent market. After all, he was coming off of two impressive showings in the Cuban National Series as a 17- and 18-year-old arm. Fast forward three seasons later and the La Habana, Cuba, native was making his stateside debut as he skipped through three separate levels, going from Low Class A to High Class A to Class AA in 2017. Perez continued his rapid ascension to the game's penultimate level the following season as he tossed 16 games for Corpus Christi, another four contests with Fresno, and even settled in for a quick eight-game cameo with Houston. Last season the 5-foot-11, 170-pound southpaw was limited to just 47.0 Class AAA innings due to a troublesome forearm. He posted a 43-to-24 strikeout-to-walk ratio with a 5.36 ERA. He also tossed nine innings with the Astros, recording seven whiffs and two free passes.

Snippet from The 2018 Prospect Digest Handbook: Houston started transitioning Perez into a full-time relief role in the second half as the club geared up for a playoff run, but he has the arsenal to ascend to a #2/#3-type status – as long as his sub-6-foot frame allows him to do so.

Scouting Report: So this is where we're at right now:

- Perez is entering his age-24 season.
- He hasn't eclipsed the 100-inning in a season at any point in his career – which extends all the way back to his two seasons in the Cuban National Series.
- He's a sub-6-foot pitcher.
- Houston's initial physical four years ago flagged some undisclosed concerns. He's coming off of a year in which his forearm flared up.
- Houston was already flirting with the idea of converting him into a full-time reliever.
- He's primarily a two-pitch pitcher: a mid-90s electric fastball and a wipeout slider. His third offering is barely thrown.
- The control/command is below average.

See where I'm heading? If it looks like a duck, walks like a duck, and quacks like a duck, then it's…a duck. In this case, he's a reliever.

Ceiling: 1.5-win player
Risk: Moderate
MLB ETA: Debuted in 2018

13. Enoli Paredes, RHP

FB	CB	SL	CH	Command	Overall
60	50	55+	50	45+	45

Born: 09/28/95	Age: 24	Bats: R
Height: 5-11	Weight: 168	Throws: R

YEAR	LVL	IP	W	L	SV	ERA	FIP	WHIP	K/9	K%	BB/9	BB%	K/BB	HR9	BABIP
2017	A	38.3	1	3	0	2.11	3.81	0.89	7.7	23.08%	3.1	9.09%	2.54	0.70	0.191
2018	A	55.7	2	3	2	1.46	2.38	0.97	11.5	31.56%	4.2	11.56%	2.73	0.00	0.220
2018	A+	13.3	4	1	0	1.35	2.61	0.68	12.8	36.54%	2.0	5.77%	6.33	0.68	0.185
2019	A+	44.0	3	1	0	1.64	3.15	0.95	12.1	34.10%	4.3	12.14%	2.81	0.61	0.205
2019	AA	50.0	2	3	1	3.78	2.51	1.00	12.4	34.33%	3.8	10.45%	3.29	0.18	0.267

Background: Fun Fact: Paredes' old man, Johnny, earned a couple brief cups of big league coffee with the Montreal Expos and Detroit Tigers in the late 1980s and early 1990s. The younger Paredes, a wiry 5-foot-11, loose-armed right-hander, was a bit of an under-the-radar free agent off of the international market in 2015, signing for just $10,000 as a 19-year-old. Since then, though, Paredes has handled himself well in each of his four professional seasons. He whiffed 46 in 33.2 innings in the Gulf Coast League during his debut. And he handed a brief jump up to the Midwest League the following season, posting a 2.11 ERA in eight appearances, six of which were starts. But it was his dynamic showing in 2018 that started opening doors for Paredes. In 69.0 innings as a swing-man between his time with Quad Cities and Buies Creek, Paredes struck out 90 and walked just 29 to go along with a barely-there 1.43 ERA. Last season Paredes – once again – split time between two levels and continued to post impressive strikeout numbers. In 94.0 innings, the Dominican-born hurler averaged a eye-catching 12.3 strikeouts and 4.0 walks per nine innings with a 2.78 ERA.

Scouting Report: With respect to his work in Class AA last season, consider the following:

- Since 2006, here's the list of 23-year-old pitchers to post at least 33% strikeout percentage with a walk percentage between 9% and 12% in the Texas League (min. 50 IP): David McKay, Paul Estrada, and – of course – Enoli Paredes.

An interesting arm that's a bit miscast as a starting pitcher due to his size (he's 5-foot-11 and only 168 pounds) and lack of a strong third weapon and/or strong feel for the strike zone. Paredes attacks hitters with a mid-90s fastball that (A) sneaks up on hitters and (B) is thrown with a fast, whip-like arm. He features a pair of breaking balls, a curveball and slider, though both were inconsistent during the starts I saw in 2019. The slider is the better of the two, showing some sharp, two-plane break when he's staying on top of the ball. His curveball, a 50-grade offering, is loopy and fits best into the "get-me-over" type of breaking ball. Decent, though, forgettable changeup. Again, Paredes fits into the multi-inning relief mode who could handle the rare spot start in crunch time.

Ceiling: 1.5-win player
Risk: Moderate
MLB ETA: 2020

14. Jordan Brewer, CF

Hit	Power	SB	Patience	Glove	Overall
45/50	50	70	45	55	45

Born: 08/01/97	Age: 22	Bats: R
Height: 6-1	Weight: 195	Throws: R

YEAR	LVL	PA	1B	2B	3B	HR	SB	CS	AVG	OBP	SLG	BB%	K%	GB%	LD%	FB%
2019	A-	56	6	0	0	1	2	0	0.130	0.161	0.185	3.57%	10.71%	39.5	18.6	25.6

Background: The reigning Big 10 Conference Player of the Year took the JuCo route to the University of Michigan. The toolsy outfielder spent a couple years dominating the opposition at Lincoln Trail Community College prior to 2019. Last season, the 6-foot-1, 195-pound outfielder was the best hitter on one of the top teams in the country. In 63 games with the Wolverines, Brewer slugged .329/.389/.557 with 20 doubles, 12 homeruns, and 25 stolen bases while racking up a bevy of awards and recognitions including: Second Team All-America (ABCA), Third Team All-America (Baseball America, D1, Perfect Game), ACBA All-Mideast Region First Team, and All-Big 10 First Team. Houston selected the Michigan native in the third round and – of course – signed him to a below-slot deal worth $500,000 – roughly $50,000 below the recommended slot bonus. Brewer appeared in 16 games in the New York-Penn League, hitting a lowly .130/.161/.185 with one homerun during his debut.

Scouting Report: With respect to his work in college last season, consider the following:

- Between 2011 and 2018, only one Big 10 hitters met the following criteria in a season (min. 250 PA): hit at least .300/.375/.550 with a walk rate between 8% and 11% and a strikeout rate between 18% and 21%. That hitter: fellow Astros farmhand Jake Adam, who also took the JuCo route before landing at a Big 10 school.

There's some intriguing power-speed combination here that suggests a poor man's George Springer. Brewer, though, likely won't walk too frequently during his professional career because his patience at the plate with Michigan was below-average for an elite-type hitter. Plus speed that plays well on the base paths and in the outfield. Above-average bat speed. He does look smaller than the 6-foot-1, 195-pounds he's listed at, so he's probably physically maxed out. Fringy starter.

Ceiling: 1.5-win player
Risk: Moderate
MLB ETA: 2022

15. Luis Garcia, RHP

FB	CB	SL	CH	Command	Overall
65	60	50	55	45	45

Born: 12/13/96	Age: 23	Bats: R
Height: 6-1	Weight: 216	Throws: R

YEAR	LVL	IP	W	L	SV	ERA	FIP	WHIP	K/9	K%	BB/9	BB%	K/BB	HR9	BABIP
2018	A-	16.3	0	0	0	0.00	1.52	0.92	15.4	42.42%	4.4	12.12%	3.50	0.00	0.233
2018	A	69.0	7	2	0	2.48	3.72	1.32	9.1	24.14%	4.3	11.38%	2.12	0.52	0.298
2019	A	43.0	4	0	1	2.93	3.03	0.91	12.6	35.93%	3.3	9.58%	3.75	0.84	0.221
2019	A+	65.7	6	4	0	3.02	2.81	1.17	14.8	39.42%	4.7	12.41%	3.18	0.69	0.311

Background: Cut from a power pitcher of yesteryear; Garcia, a husky 6-foot-1, 216-pound righty, garners memories of the old "drop-and-drive" pitchers in the 1970s and 1980s. An older international free agent out of Bolivar, Venezuela, Garcia didn't make his professional debut until 2017, at the age of 20 – in the Dominican Summer League Houston bounced the hard-throwing hurler up to the New York-Penn League to begin the following season. But after five dominant games, in which he averaged 15.4 K/9, he was promoted up to Low Class A for the remainder of the season. He finished the year with a 98-to-41 strikeout-to-walk ratio in 85.1 innings of work. Last season Garcia split time between a return to the Midwest League and a second-half promotion up to High Class A. He tallied a career high 108.2 innings, recording a whopping 168 strikeouts and 50 free passes to go along with a 2.98 ERA. He finished the year with the highest strikeout rate, 13.91 K/9, among all minor league arms with at least 100 IP.

Scouting Report: Heading into the year the knock on Garcia has been a lack of a strong third offering because his slider, in my opinion is fringy; and his changeup was worse. But I have to admit I was genuinely surprised by the quality of Garcia's changeup. There's solid velocity separation with some strong arm-side fade. In one of the game's I scouted last season, Garcia's change generated an impressive amount of swings-and-misses. His fastball, an easy 65-grade, is straight, but explosive. His curveball adds a second plus pitch to his repertoire. He likely winds up in the bullpen, but it won't be because of his arsenal; it'll be because of his fringy command. Because Garcia was an older prospect when he signed, he's already entering his age-23 season, so 2020 will be a massive determining factor in his future role. He could help the bullpen down the stretch.

Ceiling: 1.5-win player
Risk: Moderate
MLB ETA: 2020/2021

16. Brandon Bielak, RHP

FB	CB	SL	CH	Command	Overall
55	55	50	50	45	45

Born: 04/02/96	Age: 24	Bats: L
Height: 6-1	Weight: 210	Throws: R

YEAR	LVL	IP	W	L	SV	ERA	FIP	WHIP	K/9	K%	BB/9	BB%	K/BB	HR9	BABIP
2017	Rk	4.3	1	0	0	0.00	1.80	0.92	10.4	29.41%	2.1	5.88%	5.00	0.00	0.273
2017	A-	29.3	1	1	1	0.92	1.31	0.75	11.4	33.64%	1.2	3.64%	9.25	0.00	0.261
2018	A+	55.7	5	3	2	2.10	2.24	1.10	12.0	33.18%	2.7	7.62%	4.35	0.32	0.331
2018	AA	61.3	2	5	0	2.35	3.56	1.21	8.4	23.08%	3.2	8.91%	2.59	0.59	0.294
2019	AA	36.0	3	0	0	3.75	3.95	1.19	8.3	22.30%	3.5	9.46%	2.36	0.75	0.268
2019	AAA	85.7	8	4	0	4.41	4.60	1.23	9.0	24.43%	3.8	10.23%	2.39	1.05	0.269

Background: One thing the Astros have figured out – perhaps better than any organization not named Cleveland – is their ability to maximize a pitcher's talent. We've seen it with under-the-radar, overlooked international free agents like Cristian Javier and Enoli Paredes, and Brandon Bielak's a shining example of a late-round arm that's developed into a workable big league pitching prospect. Taken in the 11th round, 331st overall, in the 2017 draft after a mostly disappointing collegiate career at the University of Notre Dame, the 6-foot-1, 210-pound right-hander consistently battled subpar control/command issues during extended outings. Two year ago, Bielak's first full season in the Houston organization, he averaged just 3.0 walks per nine innings during 25 appearances with Buies Creek and Corpus Christi. Last season Bielak split time between the upper two levels of the minor leagues, averaging a solid 8.8 strikeouts and 3.7 walks per nine innings. He compiled an aggregate 4.22 ERA across those 23 appearances.

Scouting Report: A workable – though far from dominant – four-pitch mix that's largely built around two similarly shaped breaking balls. The Notre Dame product's curveball is a solid above-average weapon with hard 12-6 bite. And his slider, which shows similar downward movement, isn't as lethal but he commands it well enough to maximize its value. Bielak will also feature an above-average fastball and a decent changeup. He's still not a sound command guy – and subsequently gets lost on a veteran-laden roster like the Astros – but could be a viable innings eater on a non-contending team. Strictly a #5-type arm.

Ceiling: 1.5-win player
Risk: Moderate
MLB ETA: 2020

17. Jeremy Pena, SS

	Hit	Power	SB	Patience	Glove	Overall
	50	45	55	55	50	45

Born: 09/22/97	**Age:** 22	**Bats:** R
Height: 6-0	**Weight:** 179	**Throws:** R

YEAR	LVL	PA	1B	2B	3B	HR	SB	CS	AVG	OBP	SLG	BB%	K%	GB%	LD%	FB%
2018	A-	156	28	5	0	1	3	0	0.250	0.340	0.309	11.54%	12.18%	37.3	23.7	28.8
2019	A	289	54	8	4	5	17	6	0.293	0.389	0.421	12.11%	19.72%	48.9	15.8	28.9
2019	A+	185	35	13	3	2	3	4	0.317	0.378	0.467	6.49%	17.84%	43.7	15.6	33.3

Background: The University of Maine hasn't had a draft pick make it to the big leagues since... Larry Thomas, a second rounder in 1991. Since then the school's had a total of 29 picks selected in the June draft. Jeremy Pena, a 6-foot, 179-pound middle infielder, not only is the highest chosen player in the school since Thomas, but also has a favorable shot at carving out a role at the big league level. A third round pick two years ago, Pena turned in a solid first full season in the Astros' organization. Splitting time between Quad Cities and Fayetteville, the former Black Bear slugged an aggregate .3030/.385/.440 with 21 doubles, seven triples, seven homeruns, and 20 stolen bases in 30 attempts. The club sent the him to the Arizona Fall League where he batted a disappointing .183/.248/.290 in 24 games with the Peoria Javelinas.

Scouting Report: The batted ball data doesn't exactly set off a ton of balls-and-whistles. According to FanGraphs, Pena's average exit velocity was an average-ish 87 mph with a peak of 105 mph. But he's shows a lot of peripheral skills to help bolster his big league hopes. Pena shows an above-average eye at the plate, which is backed by strong contact skills. The power's a 45 and will result in 10 or so homeruns. Above-average speed. Defensive versatility. And a solid glove. He's going to be a solid bench option in the next 18 months or so.

Ceiling: 1.5-win player
Risk: Moderate
MLB ETA: 2021

18. Grae Kessinger, IF

	Hit	Power	SB	Patience	Glove	Overall
	45/50	40/45	50	55	50	45

Born: 08/25/97	**Age:** 22	**Bats:** R
Height: 6-2	**Weight:** 200	**Throws:** R

YEAR	LVL	PA	1B	2B	3B	HR	SB	CS	AVG	OBP	SLG	BB%	K%	GB%	LD%	FB%
2019	A-	45	7	4	0	0	1	1	0.268	0.333	0.366	6.67%	8.89%	37.8	24.3	21.6
2019	A	201	30	6	0	2	8	2	0.224	0.333	0.294	12.94%	15.92%	35.0	20.4	29.9

Background: Originally taken by the Padres in the 26th round coming out of Oxford High School, Kessinger, instead, headed to the University of Mississippi and immediately claimed a starting gig. Except...well...he was abysmal at the plate during his true freshman season as he "hit" a lowly .175/.287/.247 with just seven extra-base hits in 55 games. But the 6-foot-2, 200-pound infielder figured out the SEC during his sophomore season as he slugged .300/.389/.473 with 18 doubles and eight homeruns. And Kessinger, a native of Mississippi, maintained status quo during his final collegiate season in 2019 as well: in 68 games he batted .330/.430/.474 with 18 doubles, seven homeruns, and 16 stolen bases. Houston drafted him in the second round, 68th overall, last June to a below-slot deal worth $750,000 – a smidge over $200,000 below the recommended slot value. After a 12-game cameo in the New York-Penn League, Kessinger batted a lowly .224/.333/.294 with just six doubles and a pair of homeruns in 50 games.

Scouting Report: A patient hitter with strong contact rates, above-average speed, and the defensive chops to bounce around the infield. Kessinger fits the mold of the typical Astros hitting prospect. The power is a touch below –average, but should peak in the 12- or so homerun territory. Lower end starting material with the floor – and likelihood – of a utility guy.

Ceiling: 1.5-win player
Risk: Moderate
MLB ETA: 2022

19. J.J. Matijevic, 1B/LF

Hit	Power	SB	Patience	Glove	Overall
45	50	40	50+	50	40

Born: 11/14/95	Age: 24	Bats: L
Height: 6-0	Weight: 206	Throws: R

YEAR	LVL	PA	1B	2B	3B	HR	SB	CS	AVG	OBP	SLG	BB%	K%	GB%	LD%	FB%
2017	A-	222	28	14	0	6	11	3	0.240	0.302	0.400	8.11%	27.03%	32.2	24.5	36.4
2017	A	26	2	0	0	1	0	1	0.125	0.192	0.250	3.85%	34.62%	33.3	20.0	33.3
2018	A	56	7	6	1	3	3	0	0.354	0.446	0.708	14.29%	17.86%	36.8	26.3	28.9
2018	A+	376	47	20	3	19	10	13	0.266	0.335	0.513	9.57%	27.39%	41.9	17.4	36.4
2019	A+	20	3	1	0	2	0	0	0.333	0.400	0.722	10.00%	20.00%	35.7	21.4	35.7
2019	AA	312	38	21	1	9	8	0	0.246	0.314	0.423	8.65%	31.09%	35.3	31.5	25.5

Background: A product of the University of Arizona byway of a second round selection in 2017. Matijevic always had the look and feel of a potential Houston hitting project. He showed a consistent developmental climb in each of three seasons for the Pac12 school; offered up some defensive versatility, strong peripherals at the plate with average or better power, and – just for fun – he mixed in a little bit of speed as well. Matijevic, a 6-foot, 206-pound first baseman/corner outfielder, put a disappointing debut showing in the rearview mirror as he rebounded with a strong 2018 campaign; he slugged .266/.335/.513 with 42 extra-base hits in only 88 games with Buies Creek. Last season, once again, Matijevic had his season interrupted and appeared in just 78 games, all but five coming in Class AA. He slugged an aggregate .251/.319/.441 with 22 doubles, one triple, and 11 homeruns to go along with eight stolen bases.

Snippet from The 2018 Prospect Digest Handbook: He shows solid skills across the board: hit tool, power; speed; and glove. He's still more projection rather than production, but he looks capable of holding down a starting job.

Scouting Report: His strikeout rate had been bordering on red flag territory from the moment he stepped onto a Houston affiliate field. But last season it toppled over into full blown concern with all the requisite bells and whistles; he whiffed in nearly 32% of his plate appearances. Matijevic has some super-sub offensive qualities but his lack of fluidity and defensive contributions all but doom him into Quad A purgatory.

Ceiling: 1.0- to 1.5-win player
Risk: Moderate
MLB ETA: 2020

20. Nathan Perry, C/1B

Hit	Power	SB	Patience	Glove	Overall
45	50/55	30	55	50	40

Born: 07/07/99	Age: 20	Bats: L	Top CALs:
Height: 6-2	Weight: 195	Throws: R	

YEAR	LVL	PA	1B	2B	3B	HR	SB	CS	AVG	OBP	SLG	BB%	K%	GB%	LD%	FB%
2017	RK	83	11	3	0	2	0	0	0.229	0.325	0.357	12.05%	16.87%	50.0	15.5	29.3
2018	RK	104	14	6	2	0	1	1	0.244	0.337	0.356	11.54%	19.23%	40.8	21.1	15.5
2018	A-	69	6	2	1	2	0	0	0.172	0.217	0.328	5.80%	18.84%	44.2	19.2	21.2
2019	A-	274	32	11	2	12	1	0	0.244	0.354	0.462	13.14%	22.63%	37.2	25.6	25.6

Background: Fun Fact: Prior the ballclub selecting Perry in the fifth round of the 2017 draft, the last time Houston picked a high school catcher that early in the draft was 2006 when they chose Maxwell Sapp with the 23rd overall pick. A product of Bassett High School, the left-swinging catcher / first baseman looked abysmal during his debut in the Gulf Coast League as he batted a lowly .229/.325/.357. And his numbers declined the following year between a return to the rookie league and short-season ball. Last season, though, Perry turned in an impressive breakout campaign during his second stint through the New York-Penn League. In 67 games with the Tri-City ValleyCats, he slugged .244/.354/.462 with 11 doubles, two triples, and 12 homeruns. Per *Deserved Runs Created Plus*, his overall production topped the league average threshold by a whopping 44%.

Scouting Report: Consider the following:

- Since 2006, here's the list of 19-year-old hitters to post a 140 to 150 DRC+ with a double-digit walk rate and a strikeout rate between 21% and 23% in the New York-Penn League (min. 250 PA): B.J. Boyd and Nathan Perry.

As promising as the Perry's breakout appears to be, it needs to be viewed with a level of skepticism – and / or realism. He's not only in an age-appropriate level of competition, but it's his second stint through that level as well. Plus, this is the first time he's shown any signs of life with the bat. Still, though, intriguing power at a premium position. The hit tool is below average, but he compensates by taking a ton of walks. Perry has a ceiling of a bat-first backup.

Ceiling: 1.0- to 1.5-win player
Risk: Moderate
MLB ETA: 2022

Kansas City Royals
Farm System Ranking Trend

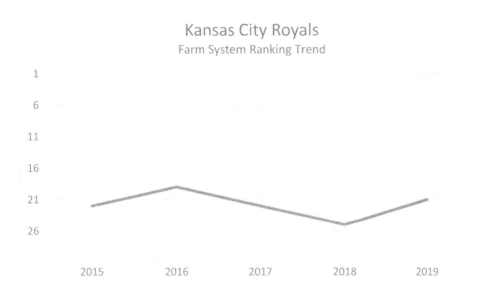

Rank	Name	Age	Pos
1	Bobby Witt Jr.	20	SS
2	Brady Singer	23	RHP
3	Jackson Kowar	23	RHP
4	Daniel Lynch	23	LHP
5	Khalil Lee	22	CF
6	Kyle Isbel	23	CF
7	Yohanse Morel	19	RHP
8	Erick Pena	17	CF
9	Kris Bubic	22	LHP
10	Darryl Collins	18	LF
11	Austin Cox	23	LHP
12	Jonathan Bowlan	23	RHP
13	Yefri Del Rosario	19	RHP
14	Brady McConnell	22	SS
15	MJ Melendez	21	C
16	Nick Pratto	21	1B
17	Brewer Hicklen	24	OF
18	Alec Marsh	22	RHP
19	Carlos Hernandez	23	RHP
20	Michael Gigliotti	24	CF

1. Bobby Witt Jr., SS

Hit	Power	SB	Patience	Glove	Overall
45/55	40/55	55	50	50+	60

Born: 06/14/00	Age: 20	Bats: R
Height: 6-1	Weight: 190	Throws: R

YEAR	LVL	PA	1B	2B	3B	HR	SB	CS	AVG	OBP	SLG	BB%	K%	GB%	LD%	FB%
2019	Rk	180	35	2	5	1	9	1	0.262	0.317	0.354	7.22%	19.44%	53.4	19.1	21.4

Background: It's not easy living up to expectations of having a famous father. Bobby Witt Sr. was the third overall pick out of the University of Oklahoma all the way back in 1986, sandwiched between the likes of B.J. Surhoff (1st overall), Will Clark (2nd), Barry Larkin (4th), and Barry Bonds (6th). The former Sooner star was up in the big leagues by the beginning of the following season and spent parts of the next 16 years as a pitching vagabond. He finished his career with an even 104-104 win-loss record and a 4.83 ERA in 2465.0 innings. Enter: Junior. Primed as a top pick in this last year's draft class for quite some time, Witt Jr., a supremely gifted shortstop from Colleyville-Heritage High School, rose to the occasion. Through the school's first 32 games this season, the burgeoning star slugged an impressive .519/.598/1.160 with 12 doubles, seven triples, and 14 homeruns. And a bevy of awards and recognitions rolled in, including: National Senior Athlete of the Year by the National High School Coaches Association and he became the first high school player to crack the semifinalist list for the USA Baseball Golden Spikes Award. The Royals snagged the prep shortstop in the opening round, 2nd overall, and signed him to a deal worth $7,789,900 – the full recommended slot bonus. Witt spent the entirety of his debut in the Arizona Summer League, hitting a mediocre .262/.317/.354 with just two doubles, five triples, and one homeruns in 37 games. His overall production, as measured by Baseball Prospectus' *Deserved Runs Created Plus*, was 6% below the league average.

Scouting Report: Here's what I wrote about Witt prior to the draft last year:

"A star for 18U Team USA, Witt Jr.'s production line last summer is just as dominant as his high school numbers. In nine games against some of the [most] elite talent available, he slugged a whopping .576/.615/1.121 with just four strikeouts – against a pair of walks – in more than 30 at bats. A patient hitter with explosive bat speed, Witt Jr. possesses the rare gift of true five-tool talent. The hit tool and power look like above-average offerings. And he does a phenomenal job keeping his hands inside of the baseball. He's modified his approach at the plate over the past several months, eliminating a large leg kick in favor of a toe tap and then back to large kick. Defensively, he's smooth with the instincts to remain at the position. He looks like Brendan Rodgers with upside."

One more final note: after starting a bit slowly in the Arizona Summer League, Witt rebounded to slug .304/.347/.435 over his remaining 16 games.

Ceiling: 4.5-win player
Risk: Moderate
MLB ETA: 2020

2. Brady Singer, RHP

FB	SL	CH	Command	Overall
60	55	55	60	60

Born: 08/04/96	Age: 23	Bats: R
Height: 6-5	Weight: 210	Throws: R

YEAR	LVL	IP	W	L	SV	ERA	FIP	WHIP	K/9	K%	BB/9	BB%	K/BB	HR9	BABIP
2019	A+	57.7	5	2	0	1.87	2.80	1.11	8.3	23.25%	2.0	5.70%	4.08	0.16	0.325
2019	AA	90.7	7	3	0	3.47	3.78	1.24	8.4	22.08%	2.6	6.75%	3.27	0.79	0.301

Background: The first of five straight collegiate pitchers taken by the Royals to begin the 2018 draft – as well jumpstarting a depleted farm system – Singer was a key cog of that dominant Florida Gator pitching staff in 2016. Along with current teammate – and fellow 2018 first rounder – Jackson Kowar, the Gators' staff included the likes of Alex Faedo , A.J. Puk, Shaun Anderson, Logan Shore, Scott Moss, and Dane Dunning. Singer, who was originally taken by the Toronto Blue Jays in the second round coming out of high school, didn't make his highly anticipated debut until last season. The front office – aggressively – pushed the 6-foot-5, 210-pound right-hander into High Class A. And he proved to be up to the task. In 10 starts with the Wilmington Blue Rocks, Singer posted a 53-to-13 strikeout-to-walk ratio in 57.2 innings. He was bumped up to Northwest Arkansas on the first of June for his remaining 16 starts. In total, Singer tossed 148.1 innings with 138 strikeouts and just 39 walks to go along with a 2.85 ERA.

Snippet from The 2018 Prospect Digest Handbook: The former Gator has no problem throwing any pitch, at any time in the count. He could front a big league staff and he should certainly move through the minors quickly. Singer will likely debut in High Class A, He's likely to spend a good portion of 2019 in Class AA as well.

Scouting Report: Reminiscent of Corey Kluber in terms of build, physicality, and approach to pitching. Singer owns three above-average or better offerings: a 93- to 94-mph fastball that sneakily leaps from his hand; a late-tilting, tight 83-mph slider; and a solid 55-grade changeup.

The arsenal's not on par with current teammate – and former collegiate rotation-mate – Jackson Kowar, but Singer maximizes his arsenal with pinpoint accuracy. He made a total of 26 starts last season, 22 of those he completed at least five innings. He only walked more than two hitters just three times. He's a burgeoning #2-type arm, maybe a touch better. With respect to his work in Class AA, consider the following:

- Since 2006, here's the list of 22-year-old pitchers to post a strikeout percentage between 21% and 23%; a sub-7.0% walk percentage, and a sub-4.00 DRA (Deserved Run Average) in the Texas League (min. 75 IP): Zack Greinke, Chase De Jong, and – of course – Brady Singer.

Ceiling: 4.0-win player
Risk: Moderate
MLB ETA: 2020

3. Jackson Kowar, RHP

FB	CB	CH	Command	Overall
65	60	80	55	60

Born: 10/04/96	**Age:** 23	**Bats:** R	
Height: 6-5	**Weight:** 180	**Throws:** R	

YEAR	LVL	IP	W	L	SV	ERA	FIP	WHIP	K/9	K%	BB/9	BB%	K/BB	HR9	BABIP
2018	A	26.3	0	1	0	3.42	4.14	1.18	7.5	20.56%	4.1	11.21%	1.83	0.68	0.239
2019	A+	74.0	5	3	0	3.53	3.59	1.22	8.0	21.15%	2.7	7.05%	3.00	0.49	0.305
2019	AA	74.3	2	7	0	3.51	3.67	1.26	9.4	25.16%	2.5	6.77%	3.71	0.97	0.323

Background: Kansas City Royals veteran GM Dayton Moore is a *firm* believer that pitching is the true currency in the professional baseball universe. So, with that mind set and the club's championship window fully closed after one helluva run, the franchise went into the 2018 draft like notorious bank robbers, snatching up as many polished collegiate arms available. And – full disclosure – I didn't like the plan. I thought it (A) presented too much risk due to injury and (B) wasn't overly thrilled with the caliber of arms the club was drafting. While Point (A) is still yet to be determined; I was clearly wrong on Point (B). Enter: enigmatic, overly talented right-hander Jackson Kowar. Taken with the 33rd overall pick two years ago, the former Florida Gator has a history of up-and-down performances – despite owning an upper echelon caliber arsenal. And nothing better exemplifies that than his debut showing in the South Atlantic League when he averaged just 7.5 strikeouts and a disappointing 4.1 walks per nine innings. Last season, though, arguably for the first time in his life, Kowar put it all together for an extended period. And it was remarkable. The 6-foot-5, 180-pound pound fireballer posted a 66-to-22 strikeout-to-walk ratio in 74.0 innings with the Wilmington Blue Rocks. The front office promoted the former first rounder up to Class AA, the toughest challenge in a prospect's path to the big leagues, and Kowar upped the ante. Making 13 starts with the Northwest Arkansas Naturals, Kowar fanned 78 and walked just 21 in 74.1 innings of work.

Snippet from The 2018 Prospect Digest Handbook: The problem with Kowar is that he's too hittable – for some reason. He doesn't generate the swings-and-misses that his arsenal would suggest. There's a little bit of Mark Appel here. And that's not a good thing.

Scouting Report: The electric arsenal is still intact. His fastball was sitting in the mid- to upper-90s. And it touched as high as 98 mph during a mid-season start against the Frisco RoughRiders – which happened to be his first start in Class AA, by the way. His curveball is a knee-buckling, fall-off-the-table secondary weapon that's progressed *tremendously* since his days at the University of Florida. As for his changeup? It's breathtakingly lethal; the best in the minor leagues. Kowar throws it with so much pronation that the movement and fade looks like it's a screwball. The control / command improved as well. Not only is throwing strikes more consistently, but he's throwing quality strikes more consistently. Prior to last year I was concerned about Kowar's being "too hittable." The uptick in command has squashed those ill feelings. Kowar has the chance to be an upper rotation caliber arm.

Ceiling: 4.0-win player
Risk: Moderate
MLB ETA: 2020

4. Daniel Lynch, LHP

FB	CB	SL	CH	Command	Overall
60	50	55	55	55	55

Born: 11/17/96	**Age:** 23	**Bats:** L	
Height: 6-6	**Weight:** 190	**Throws:** L	

YEAR	LVL	IP	W	L	SV	ERA	FIP	WHIP	K/9	K%	BB/9	BB%	K/BB	HR9	BABIP
2018	Rk	11.3	0	0	0	1.59	2.31	0.97	11.1	29.79%	1.6	4.26%	7.00	0.00	0.310
2018	A	40.0	5	1	0	1.58	1.88	1.03	10.6	30.72%	1.4	3.92%	7.83	0.23	0.343
2019	Rk	9.0	1	0	0	4.00	4.63	1.78	7.0	17.95%	3.0	7.69%	2.33	1.00	0.429
2019	Rk	9.0	0	0	0	1.00	2.58	1.00	12.0	37.50%	3.0	9.38%	4.00	0.00	0.294
2019	A+	78.3	5	2	0	3.10	2.99	1.26	8.8	23.62%	2.6	7.06%	3.35	0.46	0.324

Background: Full Disclosure: I was not fond of the Royals drafting Daniel Lynch in the opening round, 34th overall, two years. I had scouted a handful of his games during his senior season and (A) the velocity was fringy for a potential a top flight draft pick and (B) Virginia pitchers haven't exactly lit up the minor league scene over the past several seasons. And then…voila! Instant Velocity. Just add the Kansas City organization. Immediately upon entering the Royals' franchise Lynch's fastball went from the upper-80s to touching the upper-90s with some exceptional late life. After dominating the Class A ball for nine starts, Lynch was ticketed for big things as he shot up prospect lists. And then injury struck – a wonky shoulder, to be exact. The 6-foot-6, 190-pound left-hander was limited to just 15 Class A Advanced starts and a handful of rehab appearances. During his time with the Blue Rocks, the former Cavalier posted a 77-to-23 strikeout-to-walk ratio in 78.1 innings. He compiled a 3.10 ERA and a 4.47 DRA (Deserved Run Average). He also made four brief starts in the Arizona Fall League as well, fanning 19 and walking a quarter in only 14.0 innings.

Snippet from The 2018 Prospect Digest Handbook: Something happened the moment Lynch donned a uniform in Kansas City's organization – his fastball morphed from a fringy offering to one of the better ones I saw last season. His fastball was barely scrapping 92-mph as a junior, but he was regularly sitting the mid- to upper-90s during his time with the Legends. He also showed an above-average slider, which I had not seen during his junior season as well. The curveball and changeup are both average.

Scouting Report: From fringy to explosive to quite solid. The repertoire didn't look quite as good as it did during his debut, though it was markedly better than his time with the Virginia Cavaliers. The fastball lost a tick or two – as well as half of a grade. The slider didn't have the same bite. The curveball looked the same. And the changeup, on the other hand, bumped up for me – going from a 50-grade to a 55. I have (A) little doubt that the after effects of the shoulder injury sapped some of the arsenal's lightning and (B) that he'll be back to form by the start of 2020. A year later, Lynch still looks like a strong bet to ascend to a #3-type gig in the big leagues.

Ceiling: 3.0- to 3.5-win player
Risk: Moderate
MLB ETA: 2020/2021

5. Khalil Lee, OF

	Hit	Power	SB	Patience	Glove	Overall
	45+	50	70	55	45+	50

Born: 06/26/98	Age: 22	Bats: L
Height: 5-10	Weight: 170	Throws: L

YEAR	LVL	PA	1B	2B	3B	HR	SB	CS	AVG	OBP	SLG	BB%	K%	GB%	LD%	FB%
2017	A	532	60	24	6	17	20	18	0.237	0.344	0.430	12.22%	32.14%	49.3	21.0	24.1
2018	A+	301	45	13	4	4	14	3	0.270	0.402	0.406	15.95%	24.92%	47.4	26.3	21.1
2018	AA	118	18	5	0	2	2	2	0.245	0.330	0.353	9.32%	23.73%	59.7	15.6	22.1
2019	AA	546	92	21	3	8	53	12	0.264	0.363	0.372	11.90%	28.21%	59.4	20.3	15.6

Background: While many of the organization's top young hitters took a collective leap backwards last season – not just a step, but a *leap* – Lee, a third round pick in 2016, regained his prospect footing after a disappointing second half in the Texas League two years ago. A product of Flint Hill High School in Oakton, Virginia, (Tommy Doyle, a second round pick out of the University of Virginia is an alumnus), Lee began the 2018 season by slashing a healthy .270/.402/.406 with 13 doubles, four triples, and four homeruns in 71 games with the Wilmington Blue Rocks. His production, however, cratered – massively – following his promotion up to Class AA. He cobbled together a lowly .245/.330/.353 triple-slash line in 29 games. To no one's surprise, Lee found himself back in the Texas League for a do over. And the production, unsurprisingly, improved. In a career high 129 games with the Northwest Arkansas Naturals, the 5-foot-10, 170-pound outfielder batted .264/.363/.372 with 21 doubles, three triples, eight homeruns, and a whopping 53 stolen bases. His production, per *Deserved Runs Created Plus*, topped the league average threshold by 17%.

Snippet from The 2018 Prospect Digest Handbook: At maturity, Lee has the potential to turn into a Lorenzo Cain-type performer (.290/.351/.420) minus the elite level glove. With a strong performance in Class AA, Lee could be positioned to be a late-season call-up.

Scouting Report: Consider the following:

- Since 2006, here's the list of 21-year-old hitters to post a 112 to 122 DRC+ with a double-digit walk rate and a strikeout rate north of 25% in the Texas League (min. 300 PA): Brandon Wood and Khalil Lee.

Well, that's certainly a damning. Wood was once viewed a top prospect in baseball but later flamed out due – largely – to his inability to make consistent contact. Lee, like Wood, has battled swing-and-miss issues throughout the duration of his minor league career. And after showing some positive steps last season, his K-rate regressed above red flag territory. However – *however* – on the other hand, Lee's production against left-handers last season (.268/.336/.412) was – easily – the best of his career. Lee's capable of stuffing the state sheet like few others, offering up average power, plus speed, and a willingness to walk. The tools are incredibly loud. And he still has plenty of youth on his side. In terms of offensive upside think Shin-Soo Choo circa 2019 when he batted .265/.371/.455.

Ceiling: 2.5- to 3.0-win player
Risk: Moderate
MLB ETA: 2020

6. Kyle Isbel, CF

	Hit	Power	SB	Patience	Glove	Overall
	55/60	45/50	60	45+	55	50

Born: 03/03/97	Age: 23	Bats: L
Height: 5-11	Weight: 183	Throws: R

YEAR	LVL	PA	1B	2B	3B	HR	SB	CS	AVG	OBP	SLG	BB%	K%	GB%	LD%	FB%
2018	RK	119	25	10	1	4	12	3	0.381	0.454	0.610	11.76%	14.29%	40.9	29.5	21.6
2018	A	174	30	12	1	3	12	3	0.289	0.345	0.434	6.90%	24.71%	41.9	21.4	26.5
2019	Rk	27	5	2	0	2	3	1	0.360	0.407	0.680	7.41%	18.52%	35.0	30.0	30.0
2019	A+	214	27	7	3	5	8	3	0.216	0.282	0.361	7.01%	20.56%	53.0	16.6	23.2

Background: Buried shoulder deep among the bevy of collegiate arms the franchise hoarded during the 2018 draft. Isbel, a wiry 5-foot-11, 183-pound center fielder, was the first bat taken by the Royals that year. A third round pick out of the University of Nevada-Las Vegas, the 94th overall selection, the former Rebel left the Mountain West Conference school with a career .322/.390/.512 triple-slash line, belting out 40 doubles, 15 triples, and 21 homeruns in 170 games. Isbel continued along a similar offensive profile during his debut as well, batting an aggregate .326/.389/.504 with 22 doubles, two triples, seven homeruns, and 24 stolen bases in 30 total attempts between his stints in Idaho Falls and Lexington. Unfortunately for the potentially fast-moving prospect, several injuries – mainly a hamate issue – limited him to just 52 games in the Carolina League (as well as a few rehab appearances in rookie ball). Isbel batted a disappointing .216/.282/.361 with 15 extra-base knocks. His overall production in High Class A, per *Deserved Runs Created Plus*, was 14% below the league average. He regained his stroke during his 21-game stint in the Arizona Fall League as he slugged an impressive .315/.429/.438.

Snippet from The 2018 Prospect Digest Handbook: Isbel came out firing on all cylinders and didn't show a considerable weakness during his debut. Average plate discipline and bat-to-ball skills; he ran with an equally surprising frequency and success when compared to his collegiate days; and his power transitioned well enough to wood bats. And, perhaps, the best news: after bouncing between in the infield and outfield during his time with the Running Rebels, it looks like he's found a permanent home in center field, where his glove graded out as slightly better-than-average.

Scouting Report: Again, the 2018 draft class is approaching a historic path. Prior to succumbing to the hand / wrist injury, the 5-foot-11, 183-pound center fielder produced – well – like he always has. Through his first 13 games he slugged .348/.423/.630 with extra-base knocks. But he struggled after returning from the disabled list, hitting a pathetic .103/.132/.172 in 22 games. He finally regained his timing and slugged .279/.371/.426 over his remaining 17 games. There's a nonzero chance that Isbel develops a plus hit tool to go along with his plus speed. Average pop with the potential to develop into 15-homer territory in the coming year. Throw in some solid peripherals and strong defense and Isbel looks like a surefire bet to develop into an above-average regular.

Ceiling: 2.5-win player
Risk: Moderate
MLB ETA: 2021

7. Yohanse Morel, RHP

	FB	CB	CH	Command	Overall
	60	55/60	55/60	40/50	50

Born: 08/23/00	Age: 19	Bats: R
Height: 6-0	Weight: 170	Throws: R

YEAR	LVL	IP	W	L	SV	ERA	FIP	WHIP	K/9	K%	BB/9	BB%	K/BB	HR9	BABIP
2018	Rk	43.7	1	2	0	3.71	3.59	1.28	9.7	25.13%	3.3	8.56%	2.94	0.21	0.328
2018	Rk	3.3	0	0	0	8.10	2.29	2.10	13.5	27.78%	2.7	5.56%	5.00	0.00	0.545
2019	A	52.3	2	6	1	6.02	4.75	1.62	9.8	22.98%	3.6	8.47%	2.71	1.20	0.370

Background: The trade that sent hard-throwing, sometimes erratic right-hander Kelvin Escobar was – if I recall correctly – largely panned at the time. And if I'm being truthful: I hated it from the Royals' perspective. Flame-throwing relievers are – typically – worth their weight in gold to a contending team down the stretch. And the Royals sent the free-agent-to-be to the Nationals for a package of three middling and/or unknown prospects: Kelvin Gutierrez, a second tier third baseman without a season OPS north of .800; center fielder Blake Perkins, a toolsy, twitchy former second rounder with a low .200s batting average; and some non-descript, low-level wild card of a pitching prospect. That hurler: Yohanse Morel, who jumped from the Arizona Summer League straight into Low Class A at the ripe ol' age of 18 last year. And Morel shined brightly – despite his 6.02 ERA. In 14 games with the Lexington Legends, 11 of which were starts, the 6-foot, 170-pound righty posted a promising 57-to-21 strikeout-to-walk ratio in only 52.1 innings of work.

Scouting Report: Consider the following:

- Since 2006, only three 18-year-old pitchers met the following criteria in the South Atlantic League (min. 50 IP): a strikeout percentage between 21% and 23% and a walk percentage between 7.5% and 9.5%. Those three pitchers: Anderson Espinoza, who was widely considered a Top 100 Prospect prior to arm issues; Brayan Mata, a Top 100 Prospect heading into 2020; and –

of course – Yohanse Morel, that aforementioned, previously non-descript pitching prospect Kansas City received in the Kelvin Herrera deal with the Nationals.

Really impressive, intriguing arsenal. Fronted by a mid-90s, explosive plus fastball, Morel complements the offering with two offspeed pitches that occasionally flashed plus in 2019. A hard-tilting slider and a changeup that shows tremendous arm side run and fade. And despite a solid walk rate, the command has ways – and *ways* – to go. I think it eventually gets up to a 50-grade over the coming. He's raw. And several years away. But there's an intriguing case to be made that if Morel navigates his way through the injury nexus, he has as high of a ceiling as any arm in the farm system. I really like this kid. A lot. There's a curiously high upside to Morel.

Ceiling: 2.5- to 3.0-win player
Risk: Moderate to High
MLB ETA: 2022

8. Erick Pena, CF

Hit	Power	SB	Patience	Glove	Overall
30/55	40/50	50	50	50	50

Born: 02/20/03	**Age:** 17	**Bats:** L
Height: 6-3	**Weight:** 180	**Throws:** R

Background: With – unfair – Carlos Beltran comparisons swirling about at the time of his signing, KC inked the outfielder to a $3.8 million deal. MLB.com ranked him as the fifth best prospect on the international market.

Scouting Report: Pena didn't make his regular season stateside debut – though he spent the fall putting in work in the Instructs. Loose, easy swing with strong wrists and blazing bat speed. Pena shows above-average power potential and a willingness to shoot the ball from gap-to-gap. He has the chance for loud tools across the board. He currently employees a toe-tap timing mechanism, though the team likely moves him away from that. He could vault himself up as the best hitting prospect in the Royals system within a year or two.

Ceiling: 2.5- to 3.0-win player
Risk: Moderate to High
MLB ETA: 2023

9. Kris Bubic, LHP

FB	CB	CH	Command	Overall
50	50+	55	55	50

Born: 08/19/97	**Age:** 22	**Bats:** L
Height: 6-3	**Weight:** 220	**Throws:** L

YEAR	LVL	IP	W	L	SV	ERA	FIP	WHIP	K/9	K%	BB/9	BB%	K/BB	HR9	BABIP
2018	Rk	38.0	2	3	0	4.03	3.95	1.50	12.6	30.81%	4.5	11.05%	2.79	0.47	0.379
2019	A	47.7	4	1	0	2.08	2.15	0.88	14.2	40.98%	2.8	8.20%	5.00	0.57	0.270
2019	A+	101.7	7	4	0	2.30	2.57	1.01	9.7	29.73%	2.4	7.30%	4.07	0.27	0.286

Background: The final of the club's four first round selections two years, Bubic, who followed Brady Singer, Jackson Kowar, and Daniel Lynch, was taken with the 40th overall pick out of Stanford University. A crafty, 6-foot-3, 220-pound left-hander, Bubic was a mainstay atop the school's rotation for the better part of his three-year career; he finished his amateur career with a stellar 235-to-89 strikeout-to-walk ratio in 223.1 innings of work. Bubic spent his debut twirling games for the Idaho Falls Chukars, averaging 12.6 strikeouts and just 4.5 walks per nine innings. Last season, the herky-jerky southpaw made 26 starts between Lexington and Wilmington, tallying a dominating 185-to-42 strikeout-to-walk ratio in 149.1 innings of work. He finished his sophomore professional season with an aggregate 2.23 ERA.

Snippet from The 2018 Prospect Digest Handbook: The former Gator has no problem throwing any pitch, at any time in the count. He could front a big league staff and he should certainly move through the minors quickly. Singer will likely debut in High Class A, He's likely to spend a good portion of 2019 in Class AA as well.

Scouting Report: Consider the following:

- Since 2006, here's the list of 21-year-old pitchers to post a strikeout percentage between 27% and 30% with a walk percentage between 6% and 8% in the Carolina League (min. 75 IP): Kyle Zimmer, the long term Royals top prospect who finally shook the injury bug last season, and Kris Bubic.

The savvy southpaw has performed better than I would have guessed. His arsenal is largely average – sans a 55-grade changeup. His fastball – once again – hovered in the 91- to 92-mpg range. At times last season his curveball looked a bit sharper than the previous year.

And his above-average changeup adds a nice swing-and-miss dimension to his pitching style. Bubic succeeds on the basic principals of pitching: throw quality strikes and deception. The 6-foot-3, 220-pound hurler is all arms-and-legs and hides the ball well. It's a bit surprising that the Royals didn't bounce Bubic up to Class AA for a brief test. But he's primed to be a late-season callup in 2020. In terms of upside, think Wade Miley, circa 2019: 7.5 K/9, 3.3 BB/9, and a 3.98 ERA.

Ceiling: 2.0-win player
Risk: Low to Moderate
MLB ETA: 2020/2021

10. Darryl Collins, LF

Hit	Power	SB	Patience	Glove	Overall
40/55	30/50	30	50	45/50	50

Born: 09/16/01	Age: 18	Bats: L
Height: 6-2	Weight: 185	Throws: R

YEAR	LVL	PA	1B	2B	3B	HR	SB	CS	AVG	OBP	SLG	BB%	K%	GB%	LD%	FB%
2019	Rk	208	44	7	7	0	1	2	0.320	0.401	0.436	10.58%	14.42%	46.4	19.6	19.6

Background: Unearthed by Nick Leto, the Manager of Arizona Operations for the Royals, in the fall of 2018. Collins, according to an article by *The Athletic's* Alec Lewis, recalls how the precocious then-16-year-old outfielder was competing – and succeeding – in the premier professional league, Honkbal Hoofdklasse, in the Netherlands. Standing a wiry, yet man-child-like 6-foot-2 and 185 pounds, the teenage corner outfielder – who, according to Lewis, was named after Mets great Darryl Strawberry – made one helluva debut in the Arizona Summer League last season. In 48 games, Collins sported a hearty .320/.401/.436 triple-slash line, belting out seven doubles and seven triples. He finished the year with an impressive 30-to-22 strikeout-to-walk ratio. Per Baseball Prospectus' *Deserved Runs Created Plus*, his overall production topped the league average mark by a whopping 51%.

Scouting Report: Consider the following:

- Since 2006, here's the list of 17-year-old hitters to post a DRC+ total between 145 and 160 with a double-digit walk rate and a strikeout below 20% in the Arizona Summer League (min. 175 PA): Jeisson Rosario, a toolsy center fielder in the Padres' system, Jordan Diaz, a raw albeit talented third baseman in the Athletics' organization, Nino Leyja, and Darryl Collins.

Impressive bat speed complemented by some natural loft in his left-handed swing that should generate 15+ homeruns down the line. Collins showed some impressive tools last season during his debut: a solid eye at the plate, strong bat-to-ball ability, and decent, average-ish defense in left. If the power does come to fruition – which, again, I believe it will – he's staring down the path of a league-average starter, maybe more. He has the potential to move quickly in the coming years.

Ceiling: 2.0-win player
Risk: Moderate
MLB ETA: 2023

11. Austin Cox, RHP

FB	CB	SL	CH	Command	Overall
55	55	50	50	50	45

Born: 03/28/97	Age: 23	Bats: L
Height: 6-4	Weight: 185	Throws: L

YEAR	LVL	IP	W	L	SV	ERA	FIP	WHIP	K/9	K%	BB/9	BB%	K/BB	HR9	BABIP
2018	Rk	33.3	1	1	0	3.78	2.76	1.32	13.8	35.66%	4.1	10.49%	3.40	0.27	0.373
2019	A	75.3	5	3	0	2.75	3.21	1.08	9.2	24.76%	2.6	7.07%	3.50	0.60	0.262
2019	A+	55.3	3	3	0	2.77	3.83	1.25	8.5	23.32%	2.6	7.17%	3.25	0.98	0.318

Background: Overlooked and lost in the hullabaloo, Cox – unfortunately for him – was added to the organization in the same draft class as Brady Singer, Jackson Kowar, Daniel Lynch, Kris Bubic, and Jonathan Bowlan. Overshadowed, perhaps, but quite talented. Taken in the fifth round two years ago, 152nd overall, the 6-foot-4, turned in an impressive – sometimes dominant – first full season in professional ball. Splitting time between Lexington and Wilmington, the Mercer University product tossed 130.2 innings across 24 starts whiling racking up plenty of punch outs, 129, and handing out a surprisingly low amount of free passes (38). He finished the year with a stellar 2.76 ERA.

Scouting Report: The 2018 Draft Class is heading down a historical path for the Royals as the club's first five selections all have a shot at contributing considerably to the big league club. But buried down a bit lower is Cox, a sturdy, well-built lefty with a quality four-pitch mix. His fastball bumps 94 mph at times with some sneaky quickness on the tail end. His curveball adds a second above-average weapon to a well-rounded repertoire. He'll also mix in an average changeup and a slider, which he likes to throw against fellow left-handers. Cox was far from consistent strike-thrower at Mercer University, but he honed in on the strike zone with a greater frequency in 2019. If the control / command is repeatable moving forward, Cox looks like a very nice backend starting pitcher.

Ceiling: 1.5- to 2.0-win player
Risk: Moderate
MLB ETA: 2021

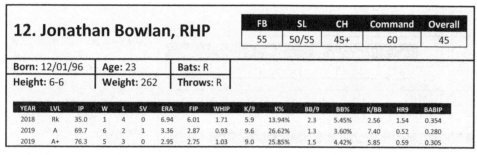

YEAR	LVL	IP	W	L	SV	ERA	FIP	WHIP	K/9	K%	BB/9	BB%	K/BB	HR9	BABIP
2018	Rk	35.0	1	4	0	6.94	6.01	1.71	5.9	13.94%	2.3	5.45%	2.56	1.54	0.354
2019	A	69.7	6	2	1	3.36	2.87	0.93	9.6	26.62%	1.3	3.60%	7.40	0.52	0.280
2019	A+	76.3	5	3	0	2.95	2.75	1.03	9.0	25.85%	1.5	4.42%	5.85	0.59	0.305

	FB	SL	CH	Command	Overall
12. Jonathan Bowlan, RHP	55	50/55	45+	60	45

Born: 12/01/96	Age: 23	Bats: R
Height: 6-6	Weight: 262	Throws: R

Background: If you pause and actually think about it for a second it's actually quite amazing. Certainly, it's odds defying. But the Royals (A) drafted four straight collegiate pitchers to open their 2018 draft and (B) every single one of them has surpassed – by a wide margin – their respective expectations, largely on the backs of their collectively phenomenal 2019 seasons. It was almost like the arms – Brady Singer, Jackson Kowar, Kris Bubic, and Jonathan Bowlan – moved as a cohesive unit. Bowlan, the lone member who wasn't taken in the first round, was beyond abysmal during his debut in the Pioneer League two years ago; he posted a horrible 6.94 ERA while averaging just 5.9 strikeouts per nine innings. Last season, though, the hefty 6-foot-6, 262-pound right-hander hardly resembled the same pitcher. Splitting time between Lexington and Wilmington, Bowlan, whose father owns the only perfect game in the University of Memphis' history, posted an impressive 150-to-23 strikeout-to-walk ratio with a 3.14 ERA in 146.0 innings of work.

Scouting Report: Consider the following:

- Since 2006, here's the list of 22-year-old pitchers to post a strikeout percentage between 25% and 27% and a sub-6.0% walk percentage in the Carolina League (min. 75 IP): Brad Peacock, Max Povse, Tyler Wilson, and Jonathan Bowlan.

Bowlan's the typical polished, crafty collegiate veteran succeeding with a decent arsenal that's backed up with pinpoint accuracy. His heater, an above-average offering, touches 94 mph on occasion. And he commands it to both sides of the plate exceptionally well. His low- to mid-80s slider is his go-to offering. It's not an overly dominating pitch, often settling in as a 50-grade with flashes of a 55. He consistently throws it for quality strikes, even when he's behind in the count. His changeup's not good, but he gets by with it. Bowlan's the typical fast moving, low ceiling arm that eventually settles in as a decent #5. One more final thought: the rotund righty has an interesting windup as he wraps his arms up and around his head.

Ceiling: 1.5-win player
Risk: Low to Moderate
MLB ETA: 2020/2021

	FB	SL	CH	Command	Overall
13. Yefri Del Rosario, RHP	N/A	N/A	N/A	N/A	50

Born: 09/23/99	Age: 20	Bats: R
Height: 6-2	Weight: 180	Throws: R

YEAR	LVL	IP	W	L	SV	ERA	FIP	WHIP	K/9	K%	BB/9	BB%	K/BB	HR9	BABIP
2017	Rk	32.3	1	1	0	3.90	3.14	1.45	8.1	19.73%	2.8	6.80%	2.90	0.28	0.343
2017	Rk	5.0	0	0	0	1.80	2.83	1.00	12.6	77.78%	7.2	44.44%	1.75	0.00	0.333
2018	A	79.0	6	5	0	3.19	4.46	1.24	8.2	21.36%	3.3	8.61%	2.48	1.14	0.263

Background: Caught up in the Braves' international free agent scandal that allowed him to hit the open market a couple years ago. Del Rosario signed with the Royals for $650,000. And he looked poised for big things coming off of an impressive showing in the South Atlantic League in 2018. He averaged 8.2 strikeouts and 3.3 walks per nine innings in 79.0 innings across 15 starts. But a nerve issue in his throwing arm shelved his 2019 campaign before it even got started.

Snippet from The 2018 Prospect Digest Handbook: Hicklen fits the mold of a lot of the other notable bats in the organization: athletic, toolsy, raw, and struggles with contact issues. An above-average defender in left field, Hicklen shows impresses opposite field power to go along with his plus-speed. He's not overly patient at the dish by any stretch of the imagination – despite showing tremendous patience in college.

Scouting Report: Prior to the injury, Del Rosario was sporting two above-average or better pitches – a low-90s fastball that had the potential to jump into plus territory and a strong slider – with a chance for an average changeup. Nerve issues can be tricky – as evidence by Brady McConnell – so Del Rosario's future is a bit cloudy. Here's hoping for a full return to heath in 2020.

Ceiling: 2.0-win player
Risk: High
MLB ETA: 2022

14. Brady McConnell, SS

Hit	Power	SB	Patience	Glove	Overall
35/45	55	30	50	45/50	45

Born: 05/24/98	Age: 22	Bats: R
Height: 6-3	Weight: 195	Throws: R

YEAR	LVL	PA	1B	2B	3B	HR	SB	CS	AVG	OBP	SLG	BB%	K%	GB%	LD%	FB%
2019	Rk	9	0	1	0	1	0	0	0.250	0.333	0.750	11.11%	22.22%	33.3	33.3	33.3
2019	Rk+	169	15	12	1	4	5	3	0.211	0.286	0.382	8.28%	39.05%	46.0	19.5	31.0

Background: Fun Fact: Since 1965 the Kansas City Royals have selected nine players from the University of Florida; three of those players – Brady Singer, Jackson Kowar, and Brady McConnell – were taken in the last two drafts. McConnell, though, lacks the considerable track record of his former teammates. The cause: A nerve blockage. According to Alec Lewis of *The Athletic*, "An artery that pumped blood to the hand had wrapped around a nerve in [his] hand." The doctor, as stated by Lewis, had never seen something like that before. McConnell – against the odds – not only returned for the 2019 season, but he dominated the competition for the SEC powerhouse. In 59 games, the 6-foot-3, 195-pound shortstop slugged an impressive .332/.385/.576 with 11 doubles and 15 homers. He also swiped six bags. KC snagged the healthy middle infielder in the second round, 44th overall. McConnell made a brief two-game cameo in the Arizona Summer League before settling in Rookie Advanced Ball for the remainder of the season. He hit a disappointing .211/.286/.382 with 12 doubles, one triple, and four homeruns in 38 games with the Idaho Chukars. His production, according to *DRC+*, was a whopping 42% below the league average.

Scouting Report: Let's take a look at his production in college last season. Consider the following:

- Between 2011 and 2018, there were 12 hitters in the SEC to meet the following criteria in a second (min. 250 PA): bat at least .325/.375/.550 with 15 homeruns. Those 12 hitters: Mike Zunino, Hunter Renfroe, A.J. Reed, Andrew Benintendi, Dansby Swanson, Jonathan India, Brent Rooker, Kole Cottam, Aaron Westlake, Mason Katz, J.J. Schwarz, and Riley Mahan.
- For those counting at home that's: seven (7) first round picks, including four that went among the top seven selections in the opening round; one (1) second rounder, one (1) third rounder; and two (2) fourth round picks; and one (1) eighth round

Let's continue…

- Among the aforementioned 12 hitters, none of them fanned in more than 18.8% of their plate appearances in those specific seasons. And all but two – Mahan and Schwarz – walked in more than 10% of their plate appearances.

McConnell, by the way, walked in 6.7% of his plate appearances and whiffed 22.4% of the time. So…there's a lot going on here: the injury, the lack of development time, the elite level of production with Florida following basically two seasons off; and – of course – the terrible peripherals. Then…*then*…his swing-and-miss rate during his debut in the Pioneer League adds another whole dimension to this complicated prospect; he K'd in nearly 40% of his plate appearances. The loud tools are clearly in place, but McConnell's far more raw – for obvious reasons – than the typical second round, high pedigreed collegiate player.

Ceiling: 1.5-win player
Risk: Moderate
MLB ETA: 2022

15. MJ Melendez, C

Hit	Power	SB	Patience	Glove	Overall
35/40	50/55	35	50+	55	40

Born: 11/29/98	Age: 21	Bats: L
Height: 6-1	Weight: 185	Throws: R

YEAR	LVL	PA	1B	2B	3B	HR	SB	CS	AVG	OBP	SLG	BB%	K%	GB%	LD%	FB%
2017	RK	198	29	8	3	4	4	2	0.262	0.374	0.417	13.13%	30.30%	48.1	21.3	25.0
2018	A	472	51	26	9	19	4	6	0.251	0.322	0.492	9.11%	30.30%	42.2	19.9	31.9
2019	A+	419	25	23	2	9	7	5	0.163	0.260	0.311	10.50%	39.38%	34.8	16.7	38.7

Background: Took a page out of Nick Pratto's book – which wouldn't have been a bad thing for a young prospect with power already intact prior to 2019. It's remarkable how damn similar the slash lines of Melendez and Pratto stacked up last season – especially considering how they were on opposite of ends of the spectrum heading into the year. Pratto, a first round pick in 2017, cobbled together a toxic .191/.278/.310 triple-slash line with a 64 DRC+ in 124 games with the Wilmington Blue Rocks in 2019. Melendez, a third round pick the same year, batted a rancid .163/.260/.311 with a 51 DRC+ in 110 games with the Blue Rocks.

Snippet from The 2018 Prospect Digest Handbook: At his peak Melendez looks like a .250/.310/.450 type stick with borderline Gold Glove defense – something along the lines of Yadier Molina's production in 2018.

Scouting Report: If one promising hitting prospect looks lost at the plate as his production craters to sub-Mario Mendoza lines it could point to variety of things: undisclosed injury, poor conditioning, mechanical flaws, or – perhaps – a failure of talent. But if two highly drafted hitters fail at the identical subterranean levels, than it can't be a coincidence, right? Because Pratto's hit tool was superior to Melendez prior to their disastrous 2019 season, but the latter's defense adds a dimension. But they're both fighting an uphill battle now. One final note: Melendez threw out 60% of would-be base stealers last season.

Ceiling: 1.0- to 1.5-win player
Risk: Moderate
MLB ETA: 2022

16. Nick Pratto, 1B

Hit	Power	SB	Patience	Glove	Overall
40/50	40	50	50	50	40

Born: 10/06/98	Age: 21	Bats: L
Height: 6-1	Weight: 195	Throws: L

YEAR	LVL	PA	1B	2B	3B	HR	SB	CS	AVG	OBP	SLG	BB%	K%	GB%	LD%	FB%
2017	RK	230	27	15	3	4	10	4	0.247	0.330	0.414	10.43%	25.22%	33.8	24.1	32.4
2018	A	537	87	33	2	14	22	5	0.280	0.343	0.443	8.38%	27.93%	44.5	22.7	26.5
2019	A+	472	49	21	1	9	17	7	0.191	0.278	0.310	10.38%	34.75%	38.2	20.5	36.2

Background: With a lot of the club's top arms surging last season, it was the majority of the better bats that collapsed. Like Nick Pratto, the sweet-swinging first baseman with a high draft pedigree. Taken between Trevor Rogers and J.B. Bukauskas with the 13th overall pick three years ago; Pratto turned in remarkably similar production lines in 2017 and 2018. His overall numbers during those seasons, according to *Deserved Runs Created Plus*, topped the league average mark by 8% and 11%. Last season, though, it was like the 6-foot-1, 195-pound hitter was a victim of a random body snatching and eventually replaced by an inferior being. In 124 games with the Wilmington Blue Rocks, Pratto "hit" a lowly .191/.278/.310 with 21 doubles, one triple, and nine homeruns. He also swiped 17 bags in 24 total attempts. His production, per DRC+, was a whopping 36% *below* the league average threshold.

Snippet from The 2018 Prospect Digest Handbook: The margin for a batting average-driven, first base-only prospect is fairly thin.

Scouting Report: Well, what happens if the batting average-driven prospect, at a power-oriented position, doesn't hit? But here's the most concerning part of his disappointing, lost campaign? He punched out in nearly 35% of his plate appearances last season. Mechanically speaking, he's made some changes. In 2018 the former first round pick kept his hands closer to his torso with his left thumb near ear level height. Last season, though, the hands were pushed back with a lot more jostling prior to the pitch. He also looked noticeably bulking in 2019 as well, and not in a good one. I ultimately think it's just going to be a mechanical flaw, so it's difficult to completely hop off Pratto's bandwagon after an abysmal season (though, you can't really blame someone for doing so). But he has a *long* road ahead of him.

Ceiling: 1.0- to 1.5-win player
Risk: Moderate
MLB ETA: 2022

17. Brewer Hicklen, OF

Hit	Power	SB	Patience	Glove	Overall
40/45	55	55	50+	55	40

Born: 02/09/96	Age: 24	Bats: R
Height: 6-2	Weight: 208	Throws: R

YEAR	LVL	PA	1B	2B	3B	HR	SB	CS	AVG	OBP	SLG	BB%	K%	GB%	LD%	FB%
2017	RK	99	15	8	2	1	3	1	0.299	0.384	0.471	9.09%	22.22%	41.5	32.3	18.5
2017	RK	82	15	3	3	3	13	3	0.348	0.439	0.609	10.98%	29.27%	41.3	15.2	37.0
2018	A	347	56	18	3	17	29	6	0.307	0.378	0.552	6.92%	28.24%	38.2	21.7	32.5
2018	A+	78	10	4	0	1	6	0	0.211	0.263	0.310	5.13%	33.33%	46.8	14.9	21.3
2019	A+	494	76	13	7	14	39	14	0.263	0.363	0.427	11.13%	28.34%	44.7	15.8	33.1

Background: Despite being selected in the seventh round of the 2017 draft, 210th overall, Hicklen was the third highest draft pick to come out of the University of Alabama at Birmingham. He was bested by a pair of sixth round picks: Graham Ashcraft, who was taken by the Reds last June, and former Braves farmhand

Ryan Woolley. Hicklen, who was originally going to be a two-sport player prior to UAB closing their football stadium's doors, ripped through the South Atlantic League by slugging .304/.378/.552 two years ago. But his production stumbled upon a late-season promotion up to High Class A. The 6-foot-2, 208-pound outfielder opened the 2019 season back with Wilmington and the results were quite different. In 125 games with the High Class A affiliate, Hicklen slugged .263/.363/.427 with 13 doubles, seven triples, 14 homeruns, and a whopping 39 stolen bases. Per *Deserved Runs Created Plus*, Hicklen's production topped the league average threshold by 32%.

Snippet from The 2018 Prospect Digest Handbook: Hicklen fits the mold of a lot of the other notable bats in the organization: athletic, toolsy, raw, and struggles with contact issues. An above-average defender in left field, Hicklen shows impresses opposite field power to go along with his plus-speed. He's not overly patient at the dish by any stretch of the imagination – despite showing tremendous patience in college.

Scouting Report: Consider the following:

- Since 2006, here's the list of 23-year-old hitters to post a DRC+ between 127 and 137 with a strikeout rate north of 25% in the Carolina League (min. 300 PA): Brewer Hicklen.

A stat-stuffing, toolsy, albeit flawed baseball player. Hicklen does a lot of things well: above-average power, plus speed, better-than-average defense in the outfield, and the patience that he showed in college came roaring back last season. However, he does the one thing that's likely going to damn his big league prospects: he swings-and-misses too frequently; he K'd in slightly more than 28% of his plate appearances last season. Given his age – he's entering his age-24 season – and the fact that he hasn't squared off against the rigors of Class AA, it's not likely going to improve a lot. He does have the traits of a Charlie Blackmon-type late bloomer, though.

Ceiling: 1.0- to 1.5-win player
Risk: Moderate
MLB ETA: 2021

18. Alec Marsh, RHP

FB	CB	SL	CH	Command	Overall
50	55	50/55	50	45	40

Born: 05/14/98	Age: 22	Bats: R
Height: 6-2	Weight: 220	Throws: R

YEAR	LVL	IP	W	L	SV	ERA	FIP	WHIP	K/9	K%	BB/9	BB%	K/BB	HR9	BABIP
2019	Rk	33.3	0	1	0	4.05	4.05	1.02	10.3	28.79%	1.1	3.03%	9.50	1.35	0.294

Background: Kansas City continued its quest in hording as many collegiate arms as possible in last year's draft as they selected nine older arms among their first 15 selections. The earliest one chosen: Alec Marsh. A product of Arizona State University, the 6-foot-2, 220-pound right-hander was – admittedly – an interesting selection. Taken with the 70th overall pick, Marsh left the Sun Devils with middling peripherals and a less-than-stellar track record: he averaged just 8.2 strikeouts and 3.6 walks per nine innings with a 4.13 ERA in 194.0 career innings. And the crafty right-hander's spent nearly his first season-and-a-half working out of the school's bullpen. Marsh's entire debut was spent with the Idaho Falls Chukars, throwing 33.1 innings across 13 brief starts with 38 strikeouts and just four walks. He compiled a 4.05 ERA.

Scouting Report: The former Sun Devil doesn't seem to fit the mold of the pitcher the front office honed in on early in the 2018 draft class. He doesn't own the pinpoint control / command of a Kris Bubic or Jonathan Bowlan. And his repertoire isn't nearly as loud as a Brady Singer or a Jackson Kowar. Instead, he's mediocre across the board. During his junior season Marsh's fastball sat in the 91- to 93-mph range early in games, but settled in the 88- 89-mph neighborhood in later innings. His curveball shows some solid bite. His slider flashes above-average tilt at times. And his changeup is vanilla with a little bit of fade and run. Throw in some subpar control / command, and it's not an overly exciting recipe. Kansas City was wildly successful in having their quartet of 2018 early round picks take a collective leap forward last season, so there's hope that Marsh fan follow in their footsteps. Right now, though, he looks like a #5 / up-and-down arm.

Ceiling: 1.0- to 1.5-win player
Risk: Moderate
MLB ETA: 2022

19. Carlos Hernandez, RHP

FB	CB	CH	Command	Overall
60	50	50	50	40

Born: 03/11/97	Age: 23	Bats: R
Height: 6-4	Weight: 175	Throws: R

YEAR	LVL	IP	W	L	SV	ERA	FIP	WHIP	K/9	K%	BB/9	BB%	K/BB	HR9	BABIP
2018	A	79.3	6	5	0	3.29	3.56	1.18	9.3	24.77%	2.6	6.95%	3.57	0.79	0.298
2019	Rk	11.0	0	2	0	7.36	4.07	1.55	9.8	25.53%	2.5	6.38%	4.00	0.82	0.387
2019	Rk	10.7	0	0	0	9.28	6.18	2.16	11.0	23.21%	10.1	21.43%	1.08	0.84	0.345
2019	A	36.0	3	3	0	3.50	3.64	1.19	10.8	29.45%	2.3	6.16%	4.78	1.25	0.326

Background: After coming off of two solid, peripherally driven back-to-back seasons in the Appalachian and South Atlantic Leagues, the big right-hander began last on the wrong foot. He had a stress fracture in his rib and was held out of regular season action until the end of June. The 6-foot-4, 175-pound righty made five brief appearances in rookie ball, another three in the Rookie Advanced League, and a final seven starts with the Lexington Legends. In total, Hernandez threw 57.2 innings in 2019, posting a strong 68-to-24 strikeout-to-walk ratio with a 5.31 ERA.

Snippet from The 2018 Prospect Digest Handbook: A plus fastball and two average secondary offerings – it's not a promising mix for future success in a big league rotation but it's not unheard of either. Also aiding Hernandez is his strike-throwing ability, particularly with his mid-90s heater. He's just over 140 innings into his career, so the offspeed stuff could see a tick up in the future. But he's physically maxed out – he's 6-foot-4 and a generously listed 175 pounds – so the fastball's not going to continue to climb.

Scouting Report: One of the few pitchers I wasn't able to scout personally in 2019, so his grades were held firm from the previous season. Here's what we know about Hernandez: (A) he's entering his age-23 season, (B) has only throw a total of 115.1 innings in full-season ball over the past *two seasons*, (C) has continually posted strong peripherals, and (D) has been hit significantly harder than his peripherals and arsenal would suggest. In the end, he's likely staring down a role as a reliever unless he takes a large step forward in 2020.

Ceiling: 1.0- to 1.5-win player
Risk: Moderate
MLB ETA: 2022

20. Michael Gigliotti, CF

Hit	Power	SB	Patience	Glove	Overall
50	30	70	50	55	40

Born: 02/14/96	Age: 24	Bats: L
Height: 6-1	Weight: 180	Throws: L

YEAR	LVL	PA	1B	2B	3B	HR	SB	CS	AVG	OBP	SLG	BB%	K%	GB%	LD%	FB%
2017	RK	191	37	8	3	3	15	5	0.329	0.442	0.477	16.75%	10.99%	56.2	16.8	21.2
2017	A	100	19	5	1	1	7	5	0.302	0.378	0.419	8.00%	20.00%	53.6	20.3	18.8
2018	A	24	2	1	0	1	1	0	0.235	0.435	0.471	25.00%	20.83%	38.5	23.1	15.4
2019	A	279	52	19	1	1	29	7	0.309	0.394	0.411	9.68%	17.56%	51.3	21.0	21.5
2019	A+	99	13	2	1	0	5	3	0.184	0.268	0.230	8.08%	23.23%	53.0	15.2	27.3

Background: A consistent, tools-laden bat during his tenure at Lipscomb University, Gigliotti left the Atlantic Sun Conference school with a .310/.423/.441 career triple-slash line. Kansas City snagged the 6-foot-1, 180-pound outfielder in the fourth round three years ago. And after a strong debut in the Appalachian and South Atlantic Leagues during his debut, Gigliotti slashed .320/.420/.456 with 13 doubles, four triples, and four homeruns and 22 stolen bases in only 64 games. Unfortunately, the speedy center fielder missed all but six games the following season courtesy of an ACL injury. Once again, bumps-and-bruises limited Gigliotti to just 87 games last season. He hit an aggregate .282/.369/.368 with 22 doubles, two triples, one homeruns, and 36 stolen bases – most of the damage coming during his extended stint in Lexington.

Scouting Report: Built from a similar mold as fellow center fielder Kyle Isbel. Gigliotti just can't seem to stay on the field. And his month-long stint in High Class A, where he hit just .184/.268/.230, is just as damning. He's now entering his age-24 season with (A) a total of 93 games played over his past two seasons and (B) only 24 games above Low Class A. He just looks like a low-end fourth / fifth outfielder at this point. One more final thought – prorating his stolen base total with Lexington last year over a full season: 80 stolen bases.

Ceiling: 1.0- to 1.5-win player
Risk: Moderate
MLB ETA: 2022

Los Angeles Angels
Farm System Ranking Trend

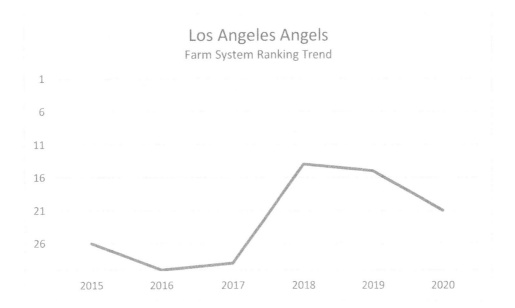

Rank	Name	Age	Pos
1	Jo Adell	21	OF
2	Brandon Marsh	22	OF
3	Patrick Sandoval	23	LHP
4	Jordyn Adams	20	CF
5	Arol Vera	17	SS
6	Jeremiah Jackson	20	2B/SS
7	Chris Rodriguez	22	RHP
8	Jahmai Jones	22	2B
9	Jack Kochanowicz	24	RHP
10	Jose Soriano	21	RHP
11	Hector Yan	21	LHP
12	Orlando Martinez	22	OF
13	Luis Madero	23	RHP
14	Kyren Paris	18	SS
15	Robinson Pina	21	RHP
16	Aaron Hernandez	23	RHP
17	Andrew Wantz	24	RHP
18	D'Shawn Knowles	19	CF
19	Luis Pena	24	RHP
20	Oliver Ortega	23	RHP

1. Jo Adell, OF

	Hit	Power	SB	Patience	Glove	Overall
	60	60	50	50	50	70

Born: 04/08/99	Age: 21	Bats: R
Height: 6-3	Weight: 215	Throws: R

YEAR	LVL	PA	1B	2B	3B	HR	SB	CS	AVG	OBP	SLG	BB%	K%	GB%	LD%	FB%
2018	A	108	17	7	1	6	4	1	0.326	0.398	0.611	10.19%	24.07%	38.6	20.0	31.4
2018	A+	262	35	19	3	12	9	2	0.290	0.345	0.546	5.73%	24.05%	44.1	22.0	30.5
2018	AA	71	7	6	0	2	2	0	0.238	0.324	0.429	8.45%	30.99%	34.1	12.2	31.7
2019	A+	27	4	1	0	2	0	0	0.280	0.333	0.560	3.70%	37.04%	33.3	20.0	40.0
2019	AA	182	26	15	0	8	6	0	0.308	0.390	0.553	10.44%	22.53%	43.7	20.2	29.4
2019	AAA	132	21	11	0	0	1	0	0.264	0.321	0.355	7.58%	32.58%	46.7	28.0	17.3

Background: Looking back at the opening round of the 2017 draft: there's a tremendous amount of talent weaved within the first 10 selections. Brendan McKay, Kyle Wright, Adam Haseley, and Keston Hiura have already reached the big leagues. Royce Lewis, Hunter Greene, and MacKenzie are all widely recognized as Top 100 prospects. Pavin Smith is showing some signs of 50-grade power. And, of course, there's Jo Adell, the tenth overall pick that year. A product of Ballard High School, which is home to former fellow first rounder Jeremy Sowers, Adell is positioned to be the best among the group. A toolsy, 6-foot-3, 215-pound outfielder, Adell ripped through two rookie leagues during his debut as he slugged .325/.376/.532 with 11 doubles, eight triples, and five homeruns. He followed that up by sprinting through three separate levels – he made stops with Burlington, Inland Empire, and Mobile – en route to battering the opposition to the tune of .290/.355/.543 with 32 doubles, four triples, and 20 homeruns. Last season, in an injury shortened campaign, Adell hit .289/.359/.475 with 27 doubles and 10 homeruns and seven stolen bases in as many attempts. The gifted outfielder missed the opening six weeks recovering a from Grade II ankle sprain and a Grade I hamstring strain.

Snippet from The 2018 Prospect Digest Handbook: Easily the best prospect to come through the system since some guy named Mike Trout. Adell's tools are loud and obvious: plus power and a plus hit tool to match with above-average speed. He's destined to contribute in every facet of the game. Adell's lightning quick bat should allow him to turn on inside fastballs with ease, though he's showing a tendency to get too pull happy. Twelve of his homeruns were hit to left field as opposed to just four going the opposite way.

Scouting Report: Consider the following:

- Only two 20-year-old hitters have topped a DRC+ (Deserved Runs Created Plus) total of 160 in the Southern League since 2006 (min. 175 PA): Giancarlo Stanton and – of course – Joe Adell

Now, to be completely fair, (A) Stanton's production line crushed Adell's statistical showing (206 and 168, respectively) and (B) it still falls into a relatively small sample size. However, they're the top two most productive 20-year-old hitters of the past decade-and-a-half in the Southern League, which happens to reside at the minor league's most challenging level. Adell's a budding a star, a bonafide rarity that oozes five tool production: he hits for average, possesses 35-homer power potential, runs well *and* efficiently, can handle all three outfield positions, and shows a powerful throwing arm. Throw in a slightly better-than-average eye at the dish with solid contact skills and the former first round pick looks like – and will be – a super star. Adell's peak exit velocity, 116 mph, was tops according to FanGraphs.

Ceiling: 6.5-win player
Risk: Low to Moderate
MLB ETA: 2020

2. Brandon Marsh, OF

	Hit	Power	SB	Patience	Glove	Overall
	55	40/50	40	60	50	60

Born: 12/18/97	Age: 22	Bats: L
Height: 6-4	Weight: 215	Throws: R

YEAR	LVL	PA	1B	2B	3B	HR	SB	CS	AVG	OBP	SLG	BB%	K%	GB%	LD%	FB%
2017	RK	192	40	13	5	4	10	2	0.350	0.396	0.548	4.69%	18.23%	47.6	23.8	28.0
2018	A	154	23	12	1	3	4	0	0.295	0.390	0.470	13.64%	25.97%	47.3	22.6	29.0
2018	A+	426	67	15	6	7	10	4	0.256	0.348	0.385	12.21%	27.70%	47.2	22.8	26.8
2019	AA	412	78	21	2	7	18	5	0.300	0.383	0.428	11.41%	22.33%	53.0	15.5	29.9

Background: Similarly with Jo Adell and the first round of the 2017 draft, there are several notable players taken in the second round of the 2016 draft: Nolan Jones; a top prospect in the Indians' organization, Bryan Reynolds, who is fresh off a debut rookie showing in which he slugged .314/.377/.503 with the Pirates; Nick Solak, who posted an .884 OPS during his 33-game cameo with the Rangers; Pete Alonso and his prodigious power; Bo Bichette; and – of course – Brandon Marsh. The 60th overall player chosen that year, Marsh has consistently surpassed expectations – despite an aggressive promotion schedule. And he continued to do so as he moved in the Southern League last season. In 96 games with the Mobile BayBears, the 6-foot-4, 215-pound outfielder slugged .300/.383/.428 with 21 doubles, a pair of triples, and seven homeruns. He also swiped 18 bags in 23 total attempts. His overall production, as measured by Baseball Prospectus' *Deserved Runs Created Plus*, topped the league average mark by a whopping 41%.

Snippet from The 2018 Prospect Digest Handbook: The power's still largely untapped, though the doubles and triples will eventually turn into homeruns. Given his speed and propensity to find first base via the free pass, Marsh profiles as a top-of-the-lineup caliber talent.

Scouting Report: Consider the following:

- Since 2006, only two 21-year-old hitters met the following criteria in the Southern League (min. 300 PA): 135 to 145 DRC+, double-digit walk rate, and a strikeout between 21% and 26.5%. Those two hitters are: Tyler O'Neill, who owns a .258/.307/.454 triple-slash line in 121 big league games, and – of course – Brandon Marsh.

Perhaps the most encouraging sign for Marsh and his power potential: over his final 29 games with the BayBears, the former second rounder batted .348/.405/.545 with seven doubles and five of his seven homeruns. And he continued to flash above-average power as he moved into the Arizona Fall League as well, hitting .328/.387/.522 with five doubles, one triple, and two homeruns in only 19 games. I'm still betting big on the continued development of the power. Beyond that, he owns an above-average hit tool and speed, the defensive chops to play all three outfield positions, and a plus eye at the plate. In terms of offensive ceiling, think .300/.380/.490. The lefty-swinger shows no platoon splits.

Ceiling: 4.5-win player
Risk: Moderate
MLB ETA: 2020

3. Patrick Sandoval, LHP

	FB	CB	SL	CH	Command	Overall
	55	60	50	65	45	55

Born: 10/18/96	Age: 23	Bats: L
Height: 6-3	Weight: 190	Throws: L

YEAR	LVL	IP	W	L	SV	ERA	FIP	WHIP	K/9	K%	BB/9	BB%	K/BB	HR9	BABIP
2017	A-	19.0	1	1	0	3.79	1.43	1.32	13.3	34.57%	2.8	7.41%	4.67	0.00	0.404
2017	A	40.0	2	2	1	3.83	2.70	1.35	10.8	27.12%	3.6	9.04%	3.00	0.23	0.333
2017	A+	2.7	0	1	0	10.13	3.02	1.88	6.8	15.38%	3.4	7.69%	2.00	0.00	0.400
2018	A	65.0	7	1	1	2.49	2.60	1.06	9.8	27.00%	1.5	4.18%	6.45	0.55	0.305
2018	A+	14.7	1	0	0	0.00	2.32	0.82	12.9	36.21%	3.7	10.34%	3.50	0.00	0.200
2018	A+	23.0	2	0	1	2.74	2.31	0.70	10.2	30.95%	1.6	4.76%	6.50	0.39	0.216
2018	AA	19.7	1	0	0	1.37	1.84	1.02	12.4	35.06%	3.7	10.39%	3.38	0.00	0.286
2019	AA	20.0	0	3	0	3.60	1.79	1.05	14.4	38.55%	3.2	8.43%	4.57	0.45	0.302
2019	AAA	60.3	4	4	0	6.41	4.95	1.97	9.8	21.85%	5.2	11.59%	1.89	1.04	0.401

Background: It was a deal that barely made a ripple in the headlines – especially outside of the Angels' and Astros' reach. But Halos received a lot more than a just a middle tier prospect – with international bonus slot money – when they dealt veteran backstop Martin Maldonado near the trade deadline two years ago. Sandoval, a 6-foot-3, 190-pound southpaw, continued his rapid ascension through the minor leagues which culminated with his late-season call up to The Show. Taken by the Astros in the 11th round out of Mission Viejo High School five years ago, Sandoval pressed – heavily – on the accelerator beginning in 2017 as he made stops at three different levels (the New York-Penn League, the Midwest League, and the Carolina League). The underrated southpaw – once again – split time across three levels the following year as well, making 14 appearances in Low Class A, eight in both organizations' High Class A affiliates, and capped it off with an impressive four-game stint with Mobile. When the dust finally settled on his second whirlwind campaign Sandoval tossed a career best 122.1 innings with a whopping 145 strikeouts and just 29 walks to go along with a 2.06 ERA. And for the third straight season, Sandoval's 2019 campaign involved stops at three different levels – including a 10-game stint with the Angels. The left-hander tossed 80.1 innings with Mobile and Salt Lake, fanning 98 and walking 42 to go along with a 5.71 ERA. He threw an additional 39.1 innings with the Angels, recording a 42-to-19 K-to-BB ratio.

Snippet from The 2018 Prospect Digest Handbook: Full disclosure: I'm the biggest Patrick Sandoval fan – maybe on earth, sans his parents. Sandoval, despite the lack of a blistering fastball, has the potential to develop into a solid, mid-rotation caliber arm.

Scouting Report: It was – admittedly – a rough year for Sandoval, despite making it to the big leagues for an extended stint. But...but everything is still in place to become a solid, middle-of-the-rotation caliber starting pitcher for the Angels. Only entering his age-23 season, Sandoval's fastball sits in the low-90s, averaging 93 mph during his late season call up. He complements it with a pair of plus secondary pitches: a mid-80s changeup that (A) he'll throw in any count, in any situation and (B) has become one of the better ones in the minor leagues; his curveball, an upper-70s offering, adds a third swing-and-miss offering with sharp, late bite. He'll also mix in a standard, rather vanilla 50-grade slider. The bumps in the road last season were largely from a regression from his normally sharp command / control. The pinpoint accuracy he showed in 2018 may prove to be an anomaly, but last season's showing will be on the opposite side of the spectrum.

Ceiling: 3.0- to 3.5-win player
Risk: Moderate
MLB ETA: 2022

4. Jordyn Adams, CF

Hit	Power	SB	Patience	Glove	Overall
45/55	40/45	50	55	55	50

Born: 10/18/99	Age: 20	Bats: R
Height: 6-2	Weight: 180	Throws: R

YEAR	LVL	PA	1B	2B	3B	HR	SB	CS	AVG	OBP	SLG	BB%	K%	GB%	LD%	FB%
2018	RK	40	6	4	1	0	0	1	0.314	0.375	0.486	10.00%	17.50%	65.5	13.8	20.7
2018	RK	82	13	2	2	0	5	2	0.243	0.354	0.329	12.20%	28.05%	57.4	19.1	14.9
2019	Rk	14	6	1	0	0	4	0	0.538	0.571	0.615	7.14%	21.43%	60.0	20.0	20.0
2019	A	428	69	15	2	7	12	5	0.250	0.346	0.358	11.68%	21.96%	51.6	18.6	22.9
2019	A+	40	5	1	1	1	0	1	0.229	0.325	0.400	12.50%	35.00%	42.9	28.6	23.8

Background: Sandwiched in between a couple of highly touted pitchers in Matthew Liberatore and Brady Singer; Adams, the 17th overall pick two years ago, already reached High Class A before he turned 20-years-old. After batting a respectable .267/.361/.381 in 29 games between both rookie league affiliates, Adams opened up last season with the Burlington Bees in the Midwest League. The front office brass bumped the promising young center fielder up to High Class A in mid-August for the remainder of the year. The 6-foot-2, 180-pounder hit an aggregate .257/.351/.369 with 17 doubles, three triples, eight homeruns, and 16 stolen bases (in 22 attempts) – which includes a three-game cameo in the Arizona Summer League following a brief stint on the disabled list.

Snippet from The 2018 Prospect Digest Handbook: Another gifted athlete patrolling the outfield pastures of the Angels' farm system. Adams' main calling card is his plus speed, which should lead to a bevy of stolen bases and defensive value. Adams may not hit for a ton of extra-base firepower, but he profiles as another top-of-the-lineup table setter.

Scouting Report: Consider the following:

- Since 2006, only two 19-year-old hitters met the following criteria in the Midwest League (min. 300 PA): a DRC+ total between 118 and 128, a double-digit walk rate, and a strikeout rate between 21 and 23%. Those two hitters: Taylor Trammell, who (A) is one of the best prospects in baseball and (B) was highly coveted by the Padres in the Trevor Bauer three-team deal, and – of course – Jordyn Adams.

Very raw, but making plenty of important strides to his offensive game; Adams does a lot of things well with a few – correctable – flaws. He shows above-average patience and a strong nose for first base; blazing speed and the production *and* efficiency to match it on the base paths and in center field; and strong contact skills. The lone lagging skill: the thump in his bat. But it's improving. Adams is beginning to loft the ball more frequently and he has the potential to belt out 15 or so homeruns down the line. He may never develop into a true impact player at the big league level, but he's going to settle in quite nicely as an above-average regular.

Ceiling: 2.5- to 3.0-win player
Risk: Moderate
MLB ETA: 2021/2022

5. Arol Vera, SS

Hit	Power	SB	Patience	Glove	Overall
30/50	35/50+	30	N/A	50	50

Born: 09/12/02	Age: 17	Bats: B
Height: 6-2	Weight: 170	Throws: R

Background: One of the more highly touted players on the international market last summer, Vera, who was picked by MLB.com as the ninth best prospect, agreed to a deal worth $2.2 million – not bad money for a 16-year-old kid.

Scouting Report: Pretty solid swing from either side of the plate. One of the things I look for in teenage hitter is how well they utilize their lower half of their body at the plate. And Vera's significantly better at it than, say, the Angels' 2019 second round pick Kyren Paris. Vera creates a tremendous amount of torque that – barring any contact issues – will lead to 20-homer pop down the line. And the best part: he should be able to remain at third base. Vera could be a Top 100 Prospect within a year or two.

Ceiling: 2.5-win player
Risk: Moderate
MLB ETA: 2024

6. Jeremiah Jackson, 2B/SS

Hit	Power	SB	Patience	Glove	Overall
40/45	60	35	50	45/50	50

Born: 03/26/00	Age: 20	Bats: R
Height: 6-0	Weight: 165	Throws: R

YEAR	LVL	PA	1B	2B	3B	HR	SB	CS	AVG	OBP	SLG	BB%	K%	GB%	LD%	FB%
2018	RK	100	7	6	3	2	4	1	0.198	0.260	0.396	8.00%	34.00%	44.8	12.1	36.2
2018	RK	91	15	4	2	5	6	1	0.317	0.374	0.598	7.69%	27.47%	41.4	22.4	34.5
2019	Rk+	291	29	14	2	23	5	1	0.266	0.333	0.605	8.25%	32.99%	28.9	24.1	39.8

Background: A second round pick out of St. Luke's Episcopal School two years ago; Jackson, a wiry, strong-wristed middle infielder, turned in a solid debut as he split time between the Arizona Summer and Pioneer Leagues. In 43 combined games, he slugged .254/.314/.491 with 10 doubles, five triples, and seven homeruns to go along with 10 stolen bases in 12 attempts. Last season Jackson returned to the Orem Owlz and – simply put – was historic. The 6-foot, 165-pound middle infielder tied the Pioneer League homerun record by belting out 23 dingers in only 65 games. He shares the record with the immortal Gregory Morrison, a 71st round draft pick who slugged .448/.473/.826 in 69 games with the Medicine Hat Blue Jays in 1997. Morrison, by the way, was the 1,632nd player chosen that year. Along with all the dingers, Jackson batted .266/.333/.605 with 14 doubles, two triples, and five stolen bases (in six attempts). His overall production, as determined by *Deserved Runs Created Plus*, topped the league average threshold by just 11%.

Snippet from The 2018 Prospect Digest Handbook: A smooth-fielding defender who has the chops to stay at shortstop. Jackson already stuffs a stat sheet a year into his career. He shows a lightning quick bat, which meets the ball with a noticeable collision. Jackson turns well on inside fastballs thanks to his quick hands. There's some potential to be an everyday guy here.

Scouting Report: Consider the following:

- Since 2006, here's the list of 19-year-old hitters to post a DRC+ total between 105 and 115 in the offensive-friendly environment known as the Pioneer League (min. 250 PA): Jacob Scavuzzo, Stryker Trahan, Chris Dennis, Brandon Allen, Hainley Statie, Julio Carreras, and Jeremiah Jackson. But here's the kicker, unfortunately: only one player's strikeout rate topped 26.5% and that's Jackson's.

Plus power from an up-the-middle position is always sought after. And Jackson offers up plenty of thump – clearly. But then, again, so did Brandon Wood. Jackson's swing-and-miss tendencies were apparent during his debut season as he fanned in 30.8% of his plate appearances. And he upped the ante even further by whiffing in one-third of his plate appearances last season. And that's likely the reason why he found himself back in the advanced rookie league instead of moving up to Low Class A in 2019. He's still young enough to tweak the swing / approach at the plate, but he could very easily get chewed up when he reaches High Class A or Class AA. Boom or bust type prospect – just like Wood.

Ceiling: 2.0-win player
Risk: Moderate to High
MLB ETA: 2022

7. Chris Rodriguez, RHP

FB	CB	SL	CH	Command	Overall
60	50	55	50	45	50

Born: 07/20/98	Age: 21	Bats: R
Height: 6-2	Weight: 185	Throws: R

YEAR	LVL	IP	W	L	SV	ERA	FIP	WHIP	K/9	K%	BB/9	BB%	K/BB	HR9	BABIP
2017	Rk	32.3	4	1	0	6.40	4.14	1.30	8.9	21.92%	1.9	4.79%	4.57	0.28	0.343
2017	A	24.7	1	2	0	5.84	3.17	1.58	8.8	21.62%	2.6	6.31%	3.43	0.36	0.403
2019	A+	9.3	0	0	0	0.00	2.16	1.07	12.5	36.11%	3.9	11.11%	3.25	0.00	0.316

Background: It's been a rough couple of years for the 2016 over-slot fourth rounder. A stress reaction in his back forced him to miss the entirety of the 2018 season. And – for a fleeting moment – it looked like Rodriguez had moved past the injury. Except after three brief starts in the California League, which spanned just 9.1 innings, before a stress fracture forced the promising right-hander under the knife for surgery. He finished the year with 13 punch outs and four walks without surrendering an earned run.

Scouting Report: The good news: Rodriguez's repertoire came roaring back before the stress fracture shut him down for good. During his first start against the Lake Elsinore Storm, the San Diego Padres' High Class A affiliate, the 6-foot-2, 185-pound right-hander's fastball was pumping 94- to 95-mph with added life; his slider flashed some wicked potential as a true swing-and-miss offering; his curveball was a solid 50-grade; and the changeup still looked like he was feeling his way around with it. At this point, Rodriguez remains a true wild card. He could easily vault himself up the organization's prospect list within a year if he can remain healthy. If there is a silver lining to missing two years – or basically two years – it's the fact that it was a non-arm issue. He still looks like a capable #4.

Ceiling: 2.0-win player
Risk: Moderate to High
MLB ETA: 2022/2023

8. Jahmai Jones, 2B/CF

	Hit	Power	SB	Patience	Glove	Overall
	45	40/45	40	50+	55	45

Born: 08/04/97	Age: 22	Bats: R
Height: 5-11	Weight: 205	Throws: R

YEAR	LVL	PA	1B	2B	3B	HR	SB	CS	AVG	OBP	SLG	BB%	K%	GB%	LD%	FB%
2017	A	387	63	18	4	9	18	7	0.272	0.338	0.425	8.27%	16.28%	54.0	11.8	29.4
2017	A+	191	33	11	3	5	9	6	0.302	0.368	0.488	6.81%	22.51%	46.2	13.8	33.8
2018	A+	347	47	10	5	8	13	3	0.235	0.338	0.383	12.39%	18.16%	47.9	18.6	29.7
2018	AA	212	29	10	4	2	11	1	0.245	0.335	0.375	11.32%	24.06%	48.1	17.8	29.6
2019	AA	544	83	22	3	5	9	11	0.234	0.308	0.324	9.19%	20.04%	43.2	17.3	33.3

Background: Added to the organization during the same 2015 draft class that included the likes of Taylor Ward (the 26th overall pick) and David Fletcher (195th). Jones, the 70th overall pick, has had a rough go of it over the past two seasons. Once considered a Top 100 Prospect by some publications, Jones faltered – greatly – in his return to High Class A in 2018 as he batted a lowly .235/.338/.383. But despite the 20-year-old's offensive struggles, the front office – aggressively – pushed him up to Class AA during the second half of the year. He predictably struggled. Last season Jones, unsurprisingly, found himself back with the Mobile BayBears. And the results were…well…the same. In 130 games he batted .234/.308/.324 with 22 doubles, three triples, and five homeruns to go along with nine stolen bases in 20 attempts. His overall production, according to *Deserved Runs Created Plus*, was a whopping 21% *below* the league average mark. Jones' bat did – however – seem to come around during his second stint in the Arizona Fall League as he slugged .302/.377/.509 in 16 games with the Mesa Solar Sox.

Snippet from The 2018 Prospect Digest Handbook: Jones is employing a new, more saber-friendly approach at the dish; he's walking more frequently than he has in the past, going from a fringy-average walk rate to borderline elite. Expect a bounce back offensive campaign in 2018 as Jones gets more comfortable in the field. Plus speed with the ability to fill up a stat sheet. One more thing to remember: thanks to a late birthday he's only entering his age-21 season.

Scouting Report: Well, it wasn't exactly a bounce back season for Jones – and that's putting it mildly. However, he was showing some signs of putting it all together as the season progressed. After batting a lowly .195/.260/.278 over his first 78 games, Jones cobbled together a .292/.370/.391 triple-slash line over his final 55 regular season games. And that's not including his terrific stint in the Arizona Fall League. The power hasn't developed as expected, though he's only entering his age-22 season, but his batted ball data is showing signs of an improvement: he posted his lowest groundball rate of his career (42.1%). One more final note: the former center fielder was otherworldly on the defensive side of the ball during his second season at the keystone. I think it's still too early to give up on him.

Ceiling: 1.5- to 2.0-win player
Risk: Moderate
MLB ETA: 2020/2021

9. Jack Kochanowicz, RHP

	FB	CB	CH	Command	Overall
	55/60	55	50	40/45	45

Born: 12/22/00	Age: 19	Bats: L
Height: 6-6	Weight: 220	Throws: R

Background: After taking North Carolina State University shortstop Will Wilson – who was subsequently dealt to the Giants along with the remaining $12 million on Zack Cozart's contract – and fellow shortstop Kyren Paris with their first two draft picks, the Angels dipped their toes into the pitching pool and fished out tall, lanky right-hander Jack Kochanowicz in the third round. The 92nd overall pick, the 6-foot-6, 220-pound prep star signed for $1.25 million, nearly twice the recommender slot bonus. Kochanowicz was committed to attend collegiate power house University of Virginia.

Scouting Report: A very intriguing prep arm from Harriton High School. Kochanowicz's above-average fastball sits in the low 90s and has considerable room for growth as he adds strength to his slender 6-foot-6 frame. His curveball adds a second above-average, potential swing-and-miss weapon to his arsenal. And the teenage hurler will mix in a solid average changeup. One more final thought: his $1.25 million bonus is equivalent to a mid second round selection, roughly the value assigned to the 57th overall selection.

Ceiling: 1.5- to 2.0-win player
Risk: Moderate
MLB ETA: 2022/2023

10. Jose Soriano, RHP

FB	CB	CH	Command	Overall
70	65	45	40/45	45

Born: 10/20/98	Age: 21	Bats: R
Height: 6-3	Weight: 168	Throws: R

YEAR	LVL	IP	W	L	SV	ERA	FIP	WHIP	K/9	K%	BB/9	BB%	K/BB	HR9	BABIP
2017	Rk	49.0	2	2	0	2.94	4.22	1.16	6.8	18.41%	2.6	6.97%	2.64	0.37	0.281
2017	Rk	3.3	0	0	0	2.70	6.82	2.40	5.4	11.76%	10.8	23.53%	0.50	0.00	0.364
2018	A	46.3	1	6	0	4.47	4.47	1.49	8.2	21.21%	6.8	17.68%	1.20	0.19	0.284
2019	Rk	4.7	0	1	0	1.93	2.75	1.71	15.4	34.78%	5.8	13.04%	2.67	0.00	0.417
2019	A	77.7	5	6	0	2.55	4.03	1.30	9.7	26.01%	5.6	14.86%	1.75	0.58	0.261

Background: Equipped with – arguably – the best heater in the entire Angels farm system. Soriano spent the 2016 and 2017 seasons moving through the foreign and stateside rookie leagues and made the leap up to Low Class A two years ago. The 6-foot-3, 168-pound, firebolt slinging right-hander posted a 42-to-35 strikeout-to-walk ratio in 46.1 innings spread across 14 starts with Burlington. Unsurprisingly, the Dominican hurler found himself back in the Midwest League for a do-over – or at least in hopes of showing signs of improved control / command. And despite missing roughly two months on the disabled list, Soriano tossed a career-best 82.1 innings with 92 strikeouts and 51 walks with the Bees. He compiled a 2.55 ERA and a 4.40 DRA.

Snippet from The 2018 Prospect Digest Handbook: The wispy thin right-hander uncorks a plus-fastball that generally sits in the 96- to 97 mph range. And despite being just 19-years-old last season, Soriano's heater simply overpowered much of the Midwest League, often generating some awkward swings from a lot of table-setters. Soriano's curveball is spotty – when it's on it flashes plus with hard, downward bite. And when it's off it looks like a 19-year-old just getting used to the familiarities of a breaking ball. He reportedly will mix in a changeup, though he was fastball/curveball the times I saw him throw. It's easy to see the plus to plus-plus fastball and impressive hammer and think future starting pitcher. But I'm not entirely certain the control/command comes around enough for that. If that's the case, he could potential be a dominant reliever.

Scouting Report: Along with the – slight – uptick in his ability to throw more consistent strikes, Soriano made a few important developmental strides in 2019. After simply overpowering the Low Class A with his 70-grade fastball two years ago, there were plenty of times where Soriano shook off the catcher's sign for a fastball and wanted to throw an offspeed pitch. And, to me, that's an important building block in the development of a young pitcher. Beyond that, his curveball was simply unhittable at times – easily a plus pitch with fall-off-the-table-type late movement. And he wasn't afraid to mix in his changeup late last season as well. It's not good, but the willingness to mix it in is encouraging. His fastball / curveball combo is reminiscent of Pittsburgh's Mitch Keller. The problem, of course, is that he walks too many hitters. In his 17 appearances with Burlington last season, we walked (A) one or fewer hitters just twice and (B) two or fewer hitters just eight times. He's still likely headed down the relief path, but there's incredible potential as a starting pitcher though it seems like an unreachable dream at this point.

Ceiling: 1.5- to 2.0-win player
Risk: Moderate
MLB ETA: 2022

11. Hector Yan, LHP

FB	CB	CH	Command	Overall
60	60	50	40/45	45

Born: 04/26/99	Age: 21	Bats: L
Height: 5-11	Weight: 180	Throws: L

YEAR	LVL	IP	W	L	SV	ERA	FIP	WHIP	K/9	K%	BB/9	BB%	K/BB	HR9	BABIP
2017	Rk	16.3	0	1	1	4.96	4.59	1.29	11.6	29.17%	6.1	15.28%	1.91	0.00	0.286
2018	Rk	29.7	0	4	0	4.55	6.21	1.65	8.8	21.80%	6.1	15.04%	1.45	0.91	0.342
2019	A	109.0	4	5	1	3.39	3.15	1.16	12.2	33.79%	4.3	11.87%	2.85	0.41	0.298

Background: Fact: Yan, a slight framed left-hander out of La Romana, Dominican Republic, was overlooked, and over-shadowed on the international market when he signed with the club in August 20th, 2015. Fact: the diminutive southpaw looked overmatched and unpolished during his 2018 season with the Orem Owlz in the Pioneer League, averaging 8.8 strikeouts and a whopping 6.1 walks per nine innings. Fact: Yan walked 6.1 hitters every nine innings not only in 2018, but also in limited action in the Arizona Summer League the previous season as well. Fact: Hector Yan, the 5-foot-11, generously listed 180-pound hurler, paced the Midwest League – and finished second among either Low Class A level – in strikeout percentage, 32.3%, last season among all pitchers with at least 100 innings. Fact: Hector Yan is no longer an underrated, unknown prospect in the low levels of the Angels' farm system.

Scouting Report: Consider the following:

- Since 2006, only three 20-year-old pitchers have recorded a strikeout percentage of at least 32% in the either Low Class A league (min. 100 IP): former All-Star Matt Moore, current Giants top prospect Seth Corry, and Hector Yan. All three, by the way, owned walk percentages between 11.4% and 13.4%.

Along with subpar – albeit improving – control / command, Yan has something else working against him: his diminutive size – which, again, is likely inflated. Repertoire wise, it's equipped to slide into a backend of a big league rotation: his fastball was sitting in the 93- to 95-mph range with late, riding life; his curveball is one helluva pitch and he's willing to vary his arm angle to give it some added deception; and he'll mix in an average changeup. It should be noted: over his final 10 games Yan posted a phenomenal 59-to-15 strikeout-to-walk ratio in 45.1 innings of work. The Angels are likely to give Yan every opportunity to succeed as a starter, but unless the control / command continues to improve he's going to settle in as a Tony Sipp / Oliver Perez-type lefty reliever.

Ceiling: 1.5-win player
Risk: Moderate
MLB ETA: 2022

12. Orlando Martinez, OF

	Hit	Power	SB	Patience	Glove	Overall
	50	45/50	40	50	55	45

Born: 02/17/98	Age: 22	Bats: L
Height: 6-0	Weight: 185	Throws: L

YEAR	LVL	PA	1B	2B	3B	HR	SB	CS	AVG	OBP	SLG	BB%	K%	GB%	LD%	FB%
2018	RK	53	11	5	0	2	3	2	0.375	0.415	0.604	7.55%	16.98%	40.0	20.0	27.5
2018	A	238	47	12	1	3	6	5	0.289	0.340	0.394	7.14%	23.53%	41.5	16.5	36.0
2019	A+	422	63	21	4	12	5	4	0.263	0.325	0.434	8.53%	18.72%	42.4	16.6	30.1

Background: A 6-foot, 185-pound outfielder from La Habana, Cuba; Martinez opened some eye on the international scene when he slugged .408/.483/.567 with an 11-to-18 strikeout-to-walk ratio in 143 plate appearances on Cuba's 18U squad four years ago. The Angels signed him for $250,000 at the end of August three years ago. Martinez made his stateside debut in 2018 as he split time between Orem and Burlington, batting an aggregate .305/.354/.432 with 17 doubles, one triple, five homeruns, and nine stolen bases in 16 attempts. Last season the Cuban import spent the entirety of the year squaring off against the California League pitching. In 88 games with the 66'ers Martinez slugged .263/.325/.434 with 21 doubles, four triples, and 12 homeruns. His overall production, as determined by Baseball Prospectus' *Deserved Runs Created Plus*, topped the league average threshold by 11%.

Scouting Report: Martinez started the year off ice cold, going 10-for-44 through his first 10 games, before hitting the disabled list for roughly seven weeks. He came back like a bat out of hell before cooling in July and then regaining some traction in August. Martinez's overall skill set screams future fourth outfielder: he shows a 50-grade hit tool, enough power to keep pitchers honest, an average walk rate, solid contact skills, and the ability to play all three outfield positions above-average. Martinez was rather susceptible to fellow left-handers last season, so that bears watching.

Ceiling: 1.5-win player
Risk: Moderate
MLB ETA: 2021/2022

13. Luis Madero, RHP

	FB	SL	CH	Command	Overall
	50	55	55	55	40

Born: 04/15/97	Age: 23	Bats: R
Height: 6-3	Weight: 185	Throws: R

YEAR	LVL	IP	W	L	SV	ERA	FIP	WHIP	K/9	K%	BB/9	BB%	K/BB	HR9	BABIP
2017	Rk	29.3	3	1	0	3.99	4.76	1.19	8.6	22.58%	1.8	4.84%	4.67	0.92	0.310
2017	A-	19.7	1	1	0	8.24	4.60	1.68	7.8	17.71%	2.3	5.21%	3.40	0.92	0.377
2017	A	26.7	1	2	0	7.76	4.62	1.91	6.1	14.06%	3.0	7.03%	2.00	1.01	0.398
2018	A	61.3	2	7	0	4.26	3.82	1.37	7.2	18.49%	2.2	5.66%	3.27	0.73	0.332
2018	A+	44.3	2	1	0	2.44	3.43	1.20	9.3	25.14%	2.4	6.56%	3.83	0.61	0.314
2019	A+	16.0	1	0	0	1.13	2.10	1.38	12.9	33.82%	3.9	10.29%	3.29	0.00	0.395
2019	AA	89.7	5	11	0	5.72	4.22	1.57	7.5	18.34%	2.4	5.87%	3.13	1.10	0.362

Background: Acquired from the Diamondbacks for veteran vagabond reliever David Hernandez at the trade deadline three years ago. Madero, a 6-foot-3, 185-pound right-hander, capped off a solid showing two years ago with a nine-game cameo in the California League. And – of course – he opened up last season back with the Inland Empire 66'ers. The second tour through the High Class A level lasted all of four starts before he was promoted up to Class AA for the remainder of the season. In 20 games with the Mobile BayBears, 19 of which were starts, the Venezuela hurler tossed 89.2 innings with 75 strikeouts and just 24 walks.

Snippet from The 2018 Prospect Digest Handbook: His slider is what separates him from an up-and-down arm to a potential #4-caliber starter. The slider shows hard, sharp, late bite that has generated a lot of awkward swings in High Class A last season. At the very least, he's capable of developing into a Sergio Romo-slider-based relief arm.

Scouting Report: I'm still quite fond of Madero, but he's looking more like a Sergio Romo, slider-based reliever as opposed to a backend starting pitcher. Madero controls / commands the strike zone exceptionally well, particularly down and away. He'll also vary the break of his slider, showing a sweeping movement as well as a more traditional curveball break. The changeup still needs a bit of refinement due to consistency issues, but it flashes above-average often enough to list it as so. With respect to his work in the Southern League, consider the following:

- Since 2006, here's the list of 22-year-old pitchers that posted a strikeout percentage between 17% and 19% with a sub-7.0% walk percentage in the Southern League (min. 75 IP): Paul Blackburn, Thomas Jankins, Sean Gilmartin, Jon Moscot, Chih-Wei Hu, Nicholas Struck, Jose Urena, and Luis Madero.

The good news: excluding Jankins, who is currently working his way through the minor leagues along with Madero, Struck is the only hurler to not accrue big league time. The bad news: the group is comprised of largely replaceable big league arms.

Ceiling: 1.0- to 1.5-win player
Risk: Moderate
MLB ETA: 2020

14. Kyren Paris, SS

Hit	Power	SB	Patience	Glove	Overall
30/45	30/40	50	N/A	55	40

Born: 11/11/01	Age: 18	Bats: R
Height: 6-0	Weight: 165	Throws: R

YEAR	LVL	PA	1B	2B	3B	HR	SB	CS	AVG	OBP	SLG	BB%	K%	GB%	LD%	FB%
2019	Rk	13	2	1	0	0	0	0	0.300	0.462	0.400	23.08%	30.77%	66.7	33.3	0.0

Background: A bit of a surprise pick by the club in the second round last June; Paris not only failed to make the Under Armour All-America Team two summers ago, but an injury-shortened senior season at Freedom High School further clouded his immediate future – according to the *Los Angeles Times*. Committed to the University of California, Paris, the 55th overall pick, signed for a slightly above-slot bonus. The 6-foot, 165-pound shortstop appeared in just three games in the Arizona Summer League during his debut, going 3-for-10 with a double and three walks.

Scouting Report: I don't love the swing. The bat speed and hand-eye coordination is there, but there's no loft to it. It's raw. And he doesn't utilize a whole lot of his legs. It's like his lower half is completely out of sync with his torso. Defensively, he's smooth with soft hands, plenty of range, and should be able to stay on the left side of the keystone. Right now, he profiles as a bit of glove-first utility guy.

Ceiling: 1.0 to 1.5-win player
Risk: Moderate
MLB ETA: 2023

15. Robinson Pina, RHP

FB	CB	SF	Command	Overall
55+	55	45/50+	40	40

Born: 11/26/98	Age: 21	Bats: R	Top CALs:
Height: 6-4	Weight: 180	Throws: R	

YEAR	LVL	IP	W	L	SV	ERA	FIP	WHIP	K/9	K%	BB/9	BB%	K/BB	HR9	BABIP
2017	Rk	51.3	1	2	0	3.68	2.98	1.15	8.2	21.96%	4.2	11.21%	1.96	0.00	0.250
2018	Rk	14.3	1	1	0	3.14	2.74	1.19	10.7	27.87%	3.1	8.20%	3.40	0.00	0.308
2018	Rk	14.0	1	1	0	3.21	5.03	1.50	11.6	27.69%	5.1	12.31%	2.25	0.64	0.343
2018	Rk	15.7	2	0	1	4.02	1.70	1.15	14.9	40.00%	3.4	9.23%	4.33	0.00	0.387
2019	A	108.0	5	8	1	3.83	3.27	1.35	12.2	30.74%	5.1	12.84%	2.39	0.42	0.315

Background: Signed out of San Cristobal, Dominican Republic a day after Valentine's Day three years ago. Pina, a tall, lanky right-hander, made his debut in the foreign rookie league that summer, posting a mediocre 47-to-24 strikeout-to-walk ratio in 51.1 innings of work. The Angels' front office kept him in the Dominican Summer League to open up the following year, 2018, for eight games before moving him stateside. Pina split the remainder of the year between the club's Arizona Summer League and Pioneer League affiliates. Across all three stops he fanned 61 and walked 19 in 44.0 innings. Last season Pina made his full season debut with the Burlington Bees of the Midwest League. He appeared in 26 games, only five of them coming out of the bullpen, throwing 108.0 innings with an incredible 146 punch outs and 61 free passes. He finished the year with a 3.83 ERA and a solid 4.12 DRA (Deserved Runs Average).

Scouting Report: Consider the following:

- Since 2006, only three 20-year-old pitchers met the following criteria in either Low Class A league (min. 100 IP): a strikeout percentage between 30 and 32% with a walk percentage between 11% and 13%. Those three pitchers; A.J. Alexy, Alexander Smit, and Robinson Pina.

Long, *long* arms that allows his low-90s fastball to play up, Pina also features a snapdragon curveball and an interesting third option, a split-finger fastball which he deploys as a changeup. The splitter is still quite raw and undeveloped; I've seen it move as a traditional circle changeup and other times dive, hard and late like you'd expect a splitter to do. There may be some more gas in the tank as he matures. The control's a definite 40 and it may not ever get up to a true 45 – which likely pushes him into a relief role. One more final note: over his final 48.1 innings with the Bees last season, Pina averaged an incredible 13.8 strikeouts per nine innings.

Ceiling: 1.0- to 1.5-win player
Risk: Moderate
MLB ETA: 2022

16. Aaron Hernandez, LHP

	FB	CB	SL	CH	Command	Overall
	50	50	55	55	40/45	40

Born: 12/02/96	Age: 23	Bats: R
Height: 6-1	Weight: 170	Throws: R

YEAR	LVL	IP	W	L	SV	ERA	FIP	WHIP	K/9	K%	BB/9	BB%	K/BB	HR9	BABIP
2019	A+	72.7	1	4	0	4.46	4.69	1.67	10.0	24.11%	5.7	13.69%	1.76	0.74	0.352

Background: Texas A&M University – Corpus Christi isn't exactly known as a baseball hotbed; prior to the 2018 season, the small Division I school churned out just 12 draft picks since 2005 and only one of them – Dan Minor, a ninth round selection in 2012 – was taken before the 16th round. Enter: Aaron Hernandez, the Angels' third round selection two years ago. Hernandez, a 6-foot-1, 170-pound right-hander, has a bit of an interesting past: he was ruled academically ineligible following his freshman season with the Islanders and was forced to sit out the entire 2017 season. Hernandez made it back to the Southland Conference squad's rotation and turned in a solid, albeit a bit flawed, campaign: he fanned 102 and walked 41 in only 83.0 innings of work. The Angels' front office brass held Hernandez out of pro action until the 2019 and aggressively shoved him straight into High Class A. Hernandez eventually tossed 72.2 innings with the 66'ers, posting an 81-to-46 strikeout-to-walk ratio to go along with a 4.46 ERA and a horrible 6.07 DRA. The organization sent him to the Arizona Fall League where he fanned 25 and walked six in 18.2 innings with the Mesa Solar Sox.

Scouting Report: The control – let alone the command – was worse than advertised and it didn't show any signs of improvement over the course of the regular season. He walked 19 in 27.1 innings over his first eight games; 13 over his next 20.2 innings; and finished with 14 over his final 24.2 innings of work. Repertoire wise, Hernandez shows a standard four-pitch mix: a 92-93 mph fastball; an above-average slider; a curveball, which is essentially a slower version of his slider; and a fading, diving changeup. His build, repertoire, and – assuming it sees an uptick – his control / command are all reminiscent of Boston's right-hander Travis Lakins, who debuted in The Show as a swing-man.

Ceiling: 1.0- to 1.5-win player
Risk: Moderate
MLB ETA: 2022

17. Andrew Wantz, RHP

	FB	SL	CH	Command	Overall
	55	55	55	45	40

Born: 10/13/95	Age: 24	Bats: R
Height: 6-4	Weight: 235	Throws: R

YEAR	LVL	IP	W	L	SV	ERA	FIP	WHIP	K/9	K%	BB/9	BB%	K/BB	HR9	BABIP
2018	Rk	6.0	0	0	0	0.00	1.82	1.00	18.0	46.15%	4.5	11.54%	4.00	0.00	0.273
2018	A	17.0	1	2	0	3.71	3.01	1.35	18.5	47.95%	6.4	16.44%	2.92	1.06	0.375
2019	A+	48.0	5	3	0	3.56	3.52	1.19	10.9	28.57%	3.2	8.37%	3.41	0.75	0.295
2019	AA	48.0	0	6	0	7.13	6.17	1.77	10.1	23.28%	4.9	11.21%	2.08	2.25	0.346

Background: A low leverage, low risk middle-round draft pick as a senior coming out of the University of North Carolina at Greensboro two years ago, Wantz, a well-built 6-foot-4, 235-pound right-hander, already accrued half of a season at Class AA. Acting primarily as a full time reliever during his stint in college, Wantz, who saved 10 games for the Spartans during his final campaign, hadn't made a start since 2016. And it was just one lone start submersed by 33 other relief appearances. The Angels' brass, however, quickly put the big righty on the fast track while concurrently transitioning into a full time starting gig last season. And Wantz made quick work of the California League before getting promoted up to the Southern League in the middle of June. In total, he made 18 starts and six relief appearances, throwing 96.0 innings with an impressive 112 strikeouts against 43 free passes. He compiled an unsightly 5.34 ERA.

Scouting Report: He's eventually going to wind up back in the bullpen in the next year or two. But Wantz has already surpassed any expectations by (A) succeeding as a starting pitcher and (B) quickly reaching Class AA. By stretching him out it allows Wantz to further hone his three above-average offerings as well as improve – hopefully – on some subpar control / command. His fastball sits in the low 90s with some heft, showing some surprising weight behind it. He commands his above-average, 12-6 breaking slider OK. And his changeup shows a ton of pronation with fade. There's a little bit of Brendan Donnelly in him.

Ceiling: 1.0- to 1.5-win player
Risk: Moderate
MLB ETA: 2020/2021

18. D'Shawn Knowles, CF

Hit	Power	SB	Patience	Glove	Overall
40/45	40/45	35	50	50	40

Born: 01/16/01	Age: 19	Bats: B
Height: 6-0	Weight: 165	Throws: R

YEAR	LVL	PA	1B	2B	3B	HR	SB	CS	AVG	OBP	SLG	BB%	K%	GB%	LD%	FB%
2018	RK	130	28	4	1	1	7	4	0.301	0.385	0.381	11.54%	20.77%	44.8	26.4	20.7
2018	RK	123	20	9	2	4	2	3	0.321	0.398	0.550	10.57%	30.89%	46.5	16.9	33.8
2019	Rk+	290	40	11	4	6	5	4	0.241	0.310	0.387	8.97%	26.21%	45.9	18.4	31.4

Background: Signed out of New Providence, Bahamas, in early July 2017 for $850,000. Knowles made his highly anticipated debut the following season as he was thrust into the stateside rookie league. After torching the competition for 30 games, Knowles earned a mid-season promotion up to the rookie advanced league. And he continued to impress. When the season ended the 6-foot, 165-pound Bahamian center fielder was sporting a solid .311/.391/.464 triple-slash line, belting out 13 doubles, a trio of triples, and five homeruns. Last season, in a bit of a surprising move, the front office brass sent the young switch-hitter back down to the Pioneer League, though the results were wildly different. In 64 games with the Owlz, Knowles batted a disappointing .241/.310/.387 with 11 doubles, four triples, and six homeruns. His overall production, per *Deserved Runs Created Plus*, was 30% *below* the league average threshold.

Snippet from The 2018 Prospect Digest Handbook: Already looking like quite the bargain a year into his career, Knowles, who received the second highest bonus handed out by the club on the international market, offers more power as a left-handed hitter, slugging 16 of his 21 extra-base hits (including all five dingers) against right-handed pitching. The then-17-year-old showed a well-rounded approach at the plate featuring an above-average eye, hit tool, and speed to go along with the surprising pop. Defensively, he shifted between all three positions during his debut, but shows the chops to stay in center field long term. After his strong showing in 2018, Knowles is very likely going to spend a significant amount of time in Low Class A as an 18-year-old in 2019. He's poised to shoot up a lot of prospect lists by the end of the year.

Scouting Report: Well, that *clearly* didn't go as expected – or at least as I expected it go. Knowles' production, which benefited greatly from absurdly high BABIPs during his debut, cratered as his BABIP dropped roughly a 100+ points during his sophomore campaign. And he was particularly susceptible to left-handers last season as well. Throw in some borderline red flag strikeout numbers – in both stints in the Pioneer League – and Knowles' future looks pretty cloudy at this point. Right now, he's profiling as a fourth / fifth outfielder.

Ceiling: 1.0 to 1.5-win player
Risk: Moderate
MLB ETA: 2022/2023

19. Luis Pena, RHP

FB	SL	CH	Command	Overall
55	55	50	45	40

Born: 08/24/95	Age: 24	Bats: R
Height: 5-11	Weight: 190	Throws: R

YEAR	LVL	IP	W	L	SV	ERA	FIP	WHIP	K/9	K%	BB/9	BB%	K/BB	HR9	BABIP
2017	Rk	9.3	0	0	0	4.82	5.16	1.82	5.8	13.33%	9.6	22.22%	0.60	0.00	0.241
2017	Rk	4.7	1	0	0	5.79	0.23	1.07	13.5	35.00%	0.0	0.00%	#DIV/0!	0.00	0.385
2017	A+	131.3	6	10	0	5.28	4.55	1.49	10.1	25.52%	4.0	10.00%	2.55	1.03	0.346
2017	AA	20.0	1	3	0	3.15	4.51	1.25	8.6	22.35%	4.1	10.59%	2.11	1.35	0.241
2018	AA	59.0	2	4	0	4.27	4.20	1.20	9.6	25.30%	3.8	10.04%	2.52	1.07	0.258
2018	AAA	46.7	4	3	0	5.59	6.40	1.69	7.3	17.67%	6.2	14.88%	1.19	1.54	0.285
2019	AA	30.3	2	1	2	2.67	3.89	0.96	10.4	28.69%	3.6	9.84%	2.92	1.19	0.183
2019	AAA	14.7	1	1	0	9.20	6.72	2.05	11.0	25.71%	5.5	12.86%	2.00	2.45	0.436

Background: It was eventually going to happen, though it took longer than I would have suspected. But Pena, a thick 5-foot-11, generously listed 190-pound righty, made the move into a relief role last season after several years of giving it a go in the rotation. Pena, a native of Bonao, Dominican Republic, opened his sixth minor league season back with the Salt Lake Bees. But a six-game rough patch where he coughed up 15 earned runs and nine walks in only 14.2 innings forced the front office to demote him back down to Class AA. And, well, Pena looked like the Pena of old after that. He made 18 appearances with the Mobile BayBears, throwing 31.0 innings with 35 strikeouts and 12 walks to go along with a 2.61 ERA and a 3.40 DRA (Deserved Runs Average).

Snippet from The 2018 Prospect Digest Handbook: Strictly a reliever just masquerading as a starting pitcher for the time being. Pena features a typical relief arsenal: two plus-pitches. Equipped with a lively mid-90s fastball and a hellacious slider, Pena's ready to step and handle some sixth or seventh inning duties for the club in 2019. The control's likely to tick up as well in shorter stints.

Scouting Report: Pena's fastball looked a bit slower during his time in the PCL last season, downgrading it from plus to above-average. And his slider lost half of a grade as well, losing a bit of late bite. Pena, for the first time that I can recall, started mixing in third pitch, a changeup, last season as well. Despite the early season speed bump, Pena still looks like a competent sixth / seventh inning reliever at the big league level.

Ceiling: 1.0-win player
Risk: Moderate
MLB ETA: 2020

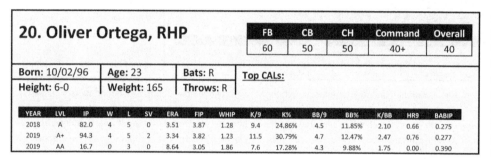

20. Oliver Ortega, RHP

FB	CB	CH	Command	Overall
60	50	50	40+	40

| Born: 10/02/96 | Age: 23 | Bats: R | Top CALs: |
| Height: 6-0 | Weight: 165 | Throws: R | |

YEAR	LVL	IP	W	L	SV	ERA	FIP	WHIP	K/9	K%	BB/9	BB%	K/BB	HR9	BABIP
2018	A	82.0	4	5	0	3.51	3.87	1.28	9.4	24.86%	4.5	11.85%	2.10	0.66	0.275
2019	A+	94.3	4	5	2	3.34	3.82	1.23	11.5	30.79%	4.7	12.47%	2.47	0.76	0.277
2019	AA	16.7	0	3	0	8.64	3.05	1.86	7.6	17.28%	4.3	9.88%	1.75	0.00	0.390

Background: The slender right-hander opened some eyes after returning to regular season action in 2018 after missing the entire previous season. Ortega, who's listed at 6-foot and 165 pounds, fanned 86 and handed out 41 walks through 82.0 innings of work. The front office personnel bumped the Dominican hurler up to the California League to start 2019. But after establishing himself as one of the better strikeout artists in the league, he moved on up to Mobile for his final five starts. Ortega finished the year with a 135-to-57 strikeout-to-walk ratio in a career best 111.0 innings of work. He compiled an aggregate 4.14 ERA.

Scouting Report: Looking at his work with Inland Empire last season, consider the following:

- Since 2006, only three 22-year-old pitchers have posted at least 30% strikeout percentage and a walk percentage north of 10% in an of the three High Class A leagues (min. 75 IP): Drew Pomeranz, an oft-injured former All-Star starter turned dynamic reliever; Wilmer Font, who's fanned a batter-per-inning in his five-year big league career; and Oliver Ortega.

Ortega, like his counterparts, showcases a plus fastball that sits in the mid-90s with riding life. He'll mix in an average power curveball, though he telegraphs the offering by slowing down his body; and a decent changeup. He's battled some control / command demons at various part of his career – especially the last two seasons. There's a remarkable chance that he takes the Wilmer Font career path as a hard-throwing, erratic reliever who may figure things out in the latter part of his 20s.

Ceiling: 1.0-win player
Risk: Moderate
MLB ETA: 2020

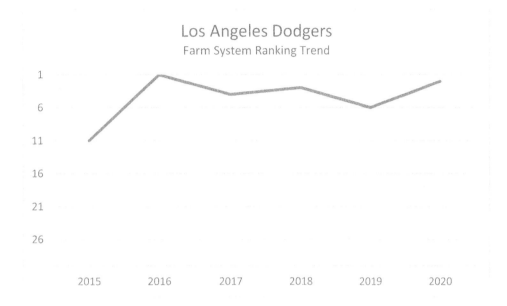

Rank	Name	Age	Pos
1	Gavin Lux	22	2B/SS
2	Dustin May	22	RHP
3	Keibert Ruiz	21	C
4	Diego Cartaya	18	C
5	Tony Gonsolin	26	RHP
6	Brusdar Graterol	22	RHP
7	Josiah Gray	22	RHP
8	Miguel Vargas	20	3B
9	Kody Hoese	22	3B
10	Michael Busch	22	1B/2B
11	Jimmy Lewis	23	RHP
12	Andy Pages	19	OF
13	DJ Peters	24	OF
14	Omar Estevez	22	2B/SS
15	Dennis Santana	24	RHP
16	Michael Grove	23	RHP
17	Devin Mann	23	2B/3B
18	Mitchell White	25	RHP
19	Cristian Santana	23	1B/3B
20	Jacob Amaya	21	2B/SS

1. Gavin Lux, 2B/SS

	Hit	Power	SB	Patience	Glove	Overall
	65	65/70	40	55+	55	80

Born: 11/23/97	Age: 22	Bats: L
Height: 6-2	Weight: 190	Throws: R

YEAR	LVL	PA	1B	2B	3B	HR	SB	CS	AVG	OBP	SLG	BB%	K%	GB%	LD%	FB%
2017	A	501	77	14	8	7	27	10	0.244	0.331	0.362	11.18%	17.56%	53.4	11.9	29.1
2018	A+	404	75	23	7	11	11	7	0.324	0.396	0.520	10.64%	16.83%	41.4	22.3	30.5
2018	AA	120	25	4	1	4	2	2	0.324	0.408	0.495	11.67%	16.67%	41.2	30.6	22.4
2019	AA	291	57	7	4	13	7	3	0.313	0.375	0.521	9.62%	20.62%	50.2	24.1	23.6
2019	AAA	232	43	18	4	13	3	3	0.392	0.478	0.719	14.22%	18.10%	46.4	21.6	26.8

Background: Deep bloodlines: Lux's uncle, Augie Schmidt, was considered one of the top prospects available in the 1982 draft. A dynamic infielder out of the University of New Orleans, Schmidt was taken by the Blue Jays with the second overall pick that year, directly behind Shawon Dunston and ahead of several notable players including: Dwight Gooden, Spike Owen, Duane Ward, Todd Worrell, Ron Karkovice, and Sam Horn. As for Lux, the 20th overall player chosen in 2016, he's already made a strong case that he was one of the top players available that year. The 6-foot-2, 190-pound middle infielder began to show some offensive promise during his professional debut as he slugged an aggregate .296/.375/.399 between the Arizona Summer and Pioneer Leagues. His production stumbled noticeably during his sophomore campaign as he cobbled together a disappointing .244/.331/.362 with 14 doubles, eight triples, seven homeruns, and 27 stolen bases. Undeterred by the speed bump, the front office bounced the lefty-swinging infielder up to the California League. Lo and behold, Lux's production came roaring back: in 88 games with the Rancho Cucamonga Quakes, he slugged a scorching .324/.396/.520. And that stat line was nearly identical during a late season promotion up to Class AA as well (.324/.408/.495). Last season Lux returned to the Texas League with remarkable consistency (.313/.375/.521). His numbers *exploded* during a 49-game stretch in the offensive-friendly Pacific Coast League as he walloped the competition to the tune of .392/.478/.719. He capped off his wildly successful year with a solid 23-game stint with the Dodgers in which he batted .240/.305/.400.

Snippet from The 2018 Prospect Digest Handbook: While Lux's production improved – significantly – in 2018, the fact remains is that fellow lefties still give him all kinds of problems; he hit a lowly .226/.278/.298 against LHP. The good news: it's trending in the right direction. The bad news: it's still *horrible*.

Scouting Report: First and foremost: how'd he fare against left-handers in 2019? He hit a healthy – and career best – .299/.355/.485, though his peripherals remain a bit concerning in a limited sample size (4.7% walk rate and a 31.8% strikeout rate). But…it's progress. Important progress. With respect to his work in Class AAA last season, consider the following:

- Since 2006, only two 21-year-old hitters posted a DRC+ total of at least 160 with a double-digit walk rate and a strikeout rate below 20% in the Pacific Coast League (min. 200 PA): Kyle Tucker and – of course – Gavin Lux. And for the record: Lux's production was a whopping 16-percentage points greater than Tucker's mark.

Above-average to plus tools across the board. As Lux's performance improves against lefties, his ceiling continues to rise. He's burgeoning star. Above-average patience, plus hit tool, plus-plus in-game power, above-average speed, and a strong glove. In terms of offensive ceiling think: Ketel Marte's 2019 season in which he slugged .329/.389/.592.

Ceiling: 7.0-win player
Risk: Low to Moderate
MLB ETA: Debuted in 2019

2. Dustin May, RHP

	FB	CB	CU	CH	Command	Overall
	65	60	70	50	65	60

Born: 09/06/97	Age: 22	Bats: R
Height: 6-6	Weight: 180	Throws: R

YEAR	LVL	IP	W	L	SV	ERA	FIP	WHIP	K/9	K%	BB/9	BB%	K/BB	HR9	BABIP
2017	A	123.0	9	6	0	3.88	3.36	1.20	8.3	21.52%	1.9	4.95%	4.35	0.59	0.306
2017	A+	11.0	0	0	0	0.82	1.47	0.64	12.3	36.59%	0.8	2.44%	15.00	0.00	0.240
2018	A+	98.3	7	3	0	3.29	3.79	1.10	8.6	23.10%	1.6	4.18%	5.53	0.82	0.294
2018	AA	34.3	2	2	0	3.67	3.21	1.14	7.3	19.31%	3.1	8.28%	2.33	0.00	0.267
2019	AA	79.3	3	5	0	3.74	3.12	1.15	9.8	25.83%	2.3	6.01%	4.30	0.57	0.307
2019	AAA	27.3	3	0	0	2.30	3.57	1.10	7.9	21.05%	3.0	7.89%	2.67	0.00	0.276

Background: The great state of Texas is known for its ability to breed big, burly, hard-throwing hurlers. The likes of Nolan Ryan, Roger Clemens, Kerry Wood, Josh Beckett, and Noah Syndergaard immediately jump to the forefront of many minds. And May, a lanky 6-foot-6, 180-pound right-hander from Justin, Texas, is ready to claim his place among the most notable Texans. A third round pick out of Justin High School four years ago, May, who the 101st overall selection, has continued to showcase an elite arsenal with pinpoint control/command. May began his domination as an 18-year-old in the Arizona Summer League as he posted a 34-to-4 strikeout-to-walk ratio in 30.1 innings during his debut. He spent the majority of his sophomore campaign flummoxing the Midwest League competition by averaging 8.3 strikeouts and just 1.9 walks per nine innings. The flame-throwing hurler split time between High Class A and Class AA two years ago, posting a strong 122-to-29 strikeout-to-walk ratio in a 132.2 innings of work. And last season, just his fourth in the Dodgers' organization, May twirled 15 – mostly dominant – starts in the minors' most challenging level, Class AA, before moving up to Oklahoma City and eventually onto Los Angeles. He finished his minor league season with 106.2 innings, fanning 110 and walking just 29 to go along with a 3.38 ERA. He made another 14 appearances in the big leagues, striking out 32 and walking just five with a 3.63 ERA in 34.2 innings.

Snippet from The 2018 Prospect Digest Handbook: May shows poise well beyond his years. He not only fills up the zone with a bevy of strikes, but – more importantly – they're quality strikes. He commands all four pitches well, especially his fastball/cutter.

Scouting Report: Consider the following:

- Since 2006, here's the list of 21-year-old arms to post a strikeout percentage between 25% and 27% with a walk percentage between 5% and 7% in any of the three Class AA leagues (min. 75 IP): Jose Berrios, Nick Neidert, Michael Bowden, and – of course – Dustin May.

The cutter. It's filthy. It's hard with late movement. And he throws it better than any minor leaguer I've seen since I started writing about prospects in 2013. He completely, wholeheartedly trusts the plus-plus offering and will throw it any count. I know this is going to be a bit sacrilege, but its dominance is almost Mariano Rivera-esque. But May isn't just sporting one dominant offering. His explosive, late-lifed fastball sits in the mid-90s with ease *and* it plays up given his long limbs and stride. His curveball's a true 12-6 hammer. And he'll mix in a solid mid-80s changeup that flashes above-average at times. And then there's the pinpoint accuracy. He's not just a strike-thrower; he's a quality strike-thrower. May has a chance to ascend towards true pitching stardom. And he's only scratching the surface of his potential.

Ceiling: 5.5-win player
Risk: Low to Moderate
MLB ETA: Debuted in 2019

3. Keibert Ruiz, C

	Hit	Power	SB	Patience	Glove	Overall
	50/60	40/50	30	50	50+	60

Born: 07/20/98	Age: 21	Bats: B
Height: 6-0	Weight: 200	Throws: R

YEAR	LVL	PA	1B	2B	3B	HR	SB	CS	AVG	OBP	SLG	BB%	K%	GB%	LD%	FB%
2016	RK	206	45	18	2	2	0	0	0.355	0.393	0.503	5.83%	11.17%	36.1	21.9	33.1
2016	RK	39	11	4	1	0	0	0	0.485	0.513	0.667	7.69%	10.26%	45.2	16.1	25.8
2017	A	251	53	16	1	2	0	0	0.317	0.372	0.423	7.17%	11.95%	46.0	19.0	30.0
2017	A+	160	33	7	1	6	0	0	0.315	0.344	0.497	4.38%	14.38%	43.4	24.8	26.4
2018	AA	415	75	14	0	12	0	1	0.268	0.328	0.401	6.27%	7.95%	44.7	23.9	25.1
2019	AA	310	57	9	0	4	0	0	0.254	0.329	0.330	9.03%	6.77%	44.0	22.2	28.4
2019	AAA	40	10	0	0	2	0	0	0.316	0.350	0.474	5.00%	2.50%	48.5	18.2	27.3

Background: The Dodgers have a lengthy, impressive history of talented catchers: Roy Campanella, Mike Piazza, John Roseboro, Mike Scioscia, Steve Yeager, Russell Martin, Paul LoDuca, and Yasmani Grandal immediately jump to the forefront of my mind. And Ruiz, a young, baby-faced switch-hitter, is poised to become the next great Dodger backstop. Signed out of Valencia, Venezuela during the summer of 2014. Since then he's quickly – and efficiently – moved through the Dodgers' farm system like a shark's fin cutting through the ocean. Ruiz torched the Dominican Summer League pitching, hitting a hearty .300/.340/.387 as a 16-year-old. The 6-foot, 200-pound catcher slugged .354/.393/.503 in 48 games in the Pioneer League in 2016. And he didn't miss a beat as he split time between the Midwest and California Leagues the following season. Two years ago Ruiz acquitted himself as a potent, middle-of-the-lineup thumper in the Texas League, batting .268/.328/.401 – as a 19-year-old. Ruiz opened up last season back in Class AA – though the numbers declined down to .254/.329/.330. He spent an additional nine games with Tulsa before an injury – a fractured right pinkie finger – prematurely ended his season.

Snippet from The 2018 Prospect Digest Handbook: In terms of peak seasons, think J.T. Realmuto, circa 2018, when he slugged .277/.340/.484.

Scouting Report: There's an artificially concerning trend in Ruiz's production line: his performances declined in each of the past three seasons. But, of course, he (A) is playing the most rigorous position on a field, (B) against vastly older competition, and (C) his batted ball data and peripherals remain remarkably strong. FanGraphs' data shows he averaged 88 mph on his exit velocity. And he whiffed in less than 7% of his plate appearances last season. Ruiz's power is still largely untapped, grading out a present 40, though he has a future 50. He's still a budding star, though his position, age, and level of competition have dulled his production line.

Ceiling: 4.0-win player
Risk: Moderate
MLB ETA: 2020

4. Diego Cartaya, C

	Hit	Power	SB	Patience	Glove	Overall
	50/55	45/55	20	50	55	55

Born: 09/07/01	Age: 18	Bats: R
Height: 6-2	Weight: 199	Throws: R

YEAR	LVL	PA	1B	2B	3B	HR	SB	CS	AVG	OBP	SLG	BB%	K%	GB%	LD%	FB%
2019	Rk	150	27	10	0	3	1	0	0.296	0.353	0.437	7.33%	20.67%	36.8	16.0	35.8

Background: One of the club's biggest international free agent expenditures two years ago; the Dodgers signed the 6-foot-2, 199-pound backstop to a hefty $2.5 million deal. Cartaya, a native of Maracay, Venezuela, made his pro debut last season. After a brief trip through the foreign rookie league, Cartaya settled in for 36 games in the Arizona Summer League, slugging an impressive .296/.353/.437 with 10 doubles and three triples. Per Baseball Prospectus' *Deserved Runs Created Plus*, his production in the stateside rookie league by 26% – a solid showing for a 17-year-old.

Snippet from The 2018 Prospect Digest Handbook: Cartaya has yet to make his official professional debut. But the teenage backstop shows a clean, smooth right-handed stroke with the potential to generate average power at a premier position. Cartaya starts from an open stance with pull-power from center to left field. Defensively, he shows a quick release and an above-average arm with clean footwork. He has the potential to be a stout defender with fluid actions as well. I think he's going to generally grade out well in pitch framing too.

Scouting Report: Consider the following:

- Since 2006, only three 17-year-old hitters met the following criteria in the Arizona Summer League (min. 150 PA): a 120 to 130 DRC+ with a walk percentage between 6% and 9%. Those three hitters: Kristian Robinson, Jhonkensy Noel, and Diego Cartaya.

Big time pull power. Cartaya shows an incredibly low maintenance swing and keeps his hands inside the well. Smooth. Based on foot speed alone, Cartaya's – maybe – a 35 runner. The young backstop looks like the he's going to move quickly. Plus-throwing arm, both in terms of accuracy and arm strength. He's going to break out in a big way in 2020.

Ceiling: 3.5-win player
Risk: Moderate
MLB ETA: 2022

5. Tony Gonsolin, RHP

	FB	CB	SL	SF	Command	Overall
	60	60	50	65	45	55

Born: 05/14/94	Age: 26	Bats: R
Height: 6-3	Weight: 205	Throws: R

YEAR	LVL	IP	W	L	SV	ERA	FIP	WHIP	K/9	K%	BB/9	BB%	K/BB	HR9	BABIP
2017	A	8.0	0	1	1	3.38	3.75	1.00	13.5	36.36%	0.0	0.00%	N/A	2.25	0.316
2017	A+	62.0	7	5	5	3.92	3.49	1.27	10.6	28.19%	2.6	6.95%	4.06	0.73	0.344
2018	A+	83.7	4	2	0	2.69	2.92	1.17	11.4	30.55%	2.8	7.49%	4.08	0.54	0.319
2018	AA	44.3	6	0	0	2.44	3.26	1.08	9.9	27.22%	3.2	8.89%	3.06	0.61	0.261
2019	AAA	41.3	2	4	0	4.35	4.37	1.50	10.9	26.18%	4.6	10.99%	2.38	0.87	0.327

Background: Fun Pact Part I: During his four seasons at St. Mary's College of California Gonsolin tallied a career ERA of 4.06 while averaging just 7.3 strikeouts and 4.0 walks per nine innings. Fun Fact Part II: During the same time the former two-way star slugged an impressive .305/.383/.453 in 774 plate appearances, belting out 32 doubles, 17 triples, and 11 homeruns while also stealing 21 bags. Los Angeles selected the 6-foot-3, 205-pound athlete in the ninth round, 281st overall, four years ago and they slowly converted him into a full time starting pitcher. Fast forward a couple years, and the hard-throwing right-hander handled himself well in the offensive war zone known as the Pacific Coast League and earned an 11-game cameo in the big leagues. He tossed 41.1 innings with Oklahoma City, posting a 50-to-21 strikeout-to-walk ratio. And another 40.0 innings with the Dodgers, fanning 37 and walking 15.

Snippet from The 2018 Prospect Digest Handbook: Mustachioed like a gnarly '70s movie star. Gonsolin's repertoire and control scream quality big league starting pitcher. His age, though, is a reason for pause. Gonsolin's fastball sits in the low- to mid-90s and touched as high as 97 mph during a game earlier in the season. A converted reliever, Gonsolin's heater lost a little bit of zip as the season progressed, likely a result of the heavier workload. His bread-and-butter secondary offering is fantastic splitter that tunnels exceptionally well with his fastball due to his extreme over-the-top release point. He'll also mix in a mid-80s slider, which is above-average, and a hard-biting 12-6 hammer of a curveball. Gonsolin loves to change a hitter's eye level by bouncing between low splitters and high fastballs. The former St. Mary's stalwart adds some additional deception by hiding the ball well; and he fields his position as well as any pitcher in the minors. There's some solid mid-rotation caliber potential here regardless of his age.

Scouting Report: Still sporting that gnarly facial hair and approaching hitters with his impressive, potentially mid-rotation caliber arsenal. Gonsolin's curveball showed a bit more bite and bend than the previous year and his slider was slightly more flat. But – unfortunately – he's caught in a numbers game as the Dodgers are running out the major's deepest rotation – Walker Buehler, Clayton Kershaw, David Price, Julio Urias, and Alex Wood – and one of the top bullpens (Kenley Jansen, Joe Kelly, Blake Treinen, Pedro Baez, Adam Kolarek, Ross Stripling). And that doesn't include top prospect Dustin May, who's forcing the club to make a spot. I'd love to see a team like the Indians or Rays pull a trade for Gonsolin and let him rack up the innings.

Ceiling: 3.0- to 3.5-win player
Risk: Moderate
MLB ETA: Debuted in 2019

6. Brusdar Graterol, RHP

	FB	SL	CH	Command	Overall
	80	60	45	55/60	50

Born: 08/26/98	Age: 21	Bats: R
Height: 6-1	Weight: 265	Throws: R

YEAR	LVL	IP	W	L	SV	ERA	FIP	WHIP	K/9	K%	BB/9	BB%	K/BB	HR9	BABIP
2017	Rk	20.7	2	1	0	3.92	3.66	1.21	10.5	28.24%	3.9	10.59%	2.67	0.44	0.300
2017	Rk	19.3	2	0	0	1.40	2.85	0.72	9.8	29.17%	1.9	5.56%	5.25	0.47	0.205
2018	A	41.3	3	2	0	2.18	2.90	0.94	11.1	30.54%	2.0	5.39%	5.67	0.65	0.270
2018	A+	60.7	5	2	0	3.12	2.81	1.29	8.3	22.22%	2.8	7.54%	2.95	0.00	0.343
2019	Rk	3.0	0	0	0	0.00	0.83	0.33	12.0	44.44%	0.0	0.00%	N/A	0.00	0.200
2019	AA	52.7	6	0	1	1.71	3.26	1.01	8.5	24.39%	3.6	10.24%	2.38	0.34	0.233
2019	AAA	5.3	1	0	0	5.06	5.12	1.13	11.8	31.82%	3.4	9.09%	3.50	1.69	0.273

Background: For decades – and *decades* – the Twins' pitching philosophy was centered around crafty, make-'em-put-it-play, soft-tossing hurlers. Guys like Brad Radke, Carlos Silva, Eric Milton, and Joe Mays were norm. But over the past several seasons the paradigm shifted in the way the club approached young arms. They began to horde hard throwing, blow-it-by-'em youngsters. And no one better personifies that than Brusdar Grateral, the Zeus-ian right-hander who flicks lightning bolts from the sky with the ferocity of few men. The behemoth 6-foot-1, 265-pound right-hander began to come into his own following his return from Tommy John surgery in 2017. He dominated the stateside rookie leagues by averaging 10.1 strikeouts and just 2.9 walks per nine innings that season. He split the following year with Cedar Rapids and Fort Myers, tallying an absurd 107-to-28 strikeout-to-walk ratio in 102.0 innings of work. The then 20-year-old began the 2019 season in Pensacola's rotation, but after returning from a two-plus month absence he was shifted into a relief role in order to help the big league club down the stretch – and, boy, did he. Graterol posted a 10-to-2 strikeout-to-walk ratio in 9.2 big league innings. Dodgers shipped right-hander Kenta Maeda to the Twins in exchange for Graterol and minor league outfielder Luke Raley.

Snippet from The 2018 Prospect Digest Handbook: Graterol uncorks one of the easiest triple-digit, plus-plus fastballs in baseball – at any level. In term so of pure stuff/arsenal, Graterol's is tops in the minors. He has the rare potential to ascend up towards true ace-dom.

Scouting Report: The fastball is *easily* among the best in baseball. Graterol's heater, which was already a plus-plus weapon as a starter, averaged 99.0 mph during his debut. But it's just not the velocity alone; it's the movement. It darts and cuts and dives and fades. If there were a grade on the scouting scale above an 80, it would certainly be applied here. His slider, an upper 80s offering, is tightly wound with cutter-like movement. And the flame-throwing youngster commands it especially well. He pretty much scrapped the changeup as a reliever, which isn't a surprise. In terms of relief value, only two relievers – Liam Hendricks and Kirby Yates – topped the 3.0-fWAR threshold in 2019. Graterol has a similar ceiling. One final thought: personally, I'd really love to see the organization push him back to the rotation; the below ceiling, though, is based on the assumption that the move won't happen.

Ceiling: 2.5- to 3.0-win player (as a reliever)
Risk: Low to Moderate
MLB ETA: Debuted in 2019

7. Josiah Gray, RHP

	FB	SL	CH	Command	Overall
	60	50/55	50	55	50

Born: 12/21/97	Age: 22	Bats: R
Height: 6-1	Weight: 190	Throws: R

YEAR	LVL	IP	W	L	SV	ERA	FIP	WHIP	K/9	K%	BB/9	BB%	K/BB	HR9	BABIP
2018	Rk	52.3	2	2	0	2.58	3.07	0.88	10.1	28.50%	2.9	8.21%	3.47	0.17	0.219
2019	A	23.3	1	0	0	1.93	2.23	0.86	10.0	29.55%	2.7	7.95%	3.71	0.00	0.241
2019	A+	67.3	7	0	0	2.14	2.58	0.97	10.7	29.96%	1.7	4.87%	6.15	0.40	0.292
2019	AA	39.3	3	2	0	2.75	2.43	1.12	9.4	25.47%	2.5	6.83%	3.73	0.00	0.314

Background: Gray, a 6-foot-1, 190-pound athlete out of LeMoyne College, became one of the trendy picks of the 2018 draft. A former two-way guy that...well...couldn't really hit and didn't have a ton of experience on the mound prior to his junior season. But the hard-throwing right-hander's draft stock shot through the roof with each passing start. After posting a 1.25 ERA across 13 starts and a sparkling 105-to-20 strikeout-to-walk ratio, the Reds drafted Gray in the second round two years ago. Roughly seven months later Cincinnati flipped the young hurler to the Dodgers as part of the massive six-player deal involving Alex Wood, Matt Kemp, Homer Bailey, Kyle Farmer, and fellow top prospect Jeter Downs. Last season, Gray rocketed through three separate levels as he averaged 10.2 strikeouts and just 2.1 walks per nine innings across 26 appearances. He tallied a 2.28 ERA in 130.0 innings of work.

Snippet from The 2018 Prospect Digest Handbook: Gray should be given every opportunity to develop as a starting pitcher early in his professional career; he reminds me a bit of former first rounder Dillon Tate. But I think the fastball/slider repertoire ultimately finds a home in the backend of a bullpen.

Scouting Report: Anchored by a mid-90s fastball, Gray moved efficiently through five Low Class A starts, 12 High Class A appearances, and settled in at the Texas League for another nine games. Plus 94- to 95-mph fastball. Gray's slider was a bit inconsistent during the couple games I saw last season, regularly flashing above-average though he struggled with finishing it. His changeup's firm, but shows some fade. As it stands, the arsenal's not very well-rounded. It's fastball/slider heavy – though everything plays up thanks to his strong feel for the strike zone. The Dodgers develop pitchers as well as any organization, so an uptick in his secondary offerings (A) wouldn't be shocking and (B) something I'm banking on. With respect to his work in High Class A, his longest stretch at a level last season, consider the following:

- Since 2006, here's the list of 21-year-old hurlers to post a strikeout percentage between 29% and 31% with a sub-6.0% walk percentage in any High Class A league (min. 50 IP): Brent Honeywell, Rafael Montero, Edwin Escobar, and Josiah Gray.

Ceiling: 3.0-win player
Risk: Moderate
MLB ETA: 2020

8. Miguel Vargas, 3B

Hit	Power	SB	Patience	Glove	Overall
50/55	40/55	35/30	50	50	50

Born: 11/17/99	Age: 20	Bats: R
Height: 6-3	Weight: 205	Throws: R

YEAR	LVL	PA	1B	2B	3B	HR	SB	CS	AVG	OBP	SLG	BB%	K%	GB%	LD%	FB%
2018	RK	37	9	3	1	0	1	0	0.419	0.514	0.581	13.51%	8.11%	42.9	25.0	28.6
2018	RK	103	23	11	1	2	6	1	0.394	0.447	0.596	7.77%	12.62%	39.5	24.7	33.3
2018	A	89	14	1	1	0	0	0	0.213	0.307	0.253	11.24%	22.47%	53.4	19.0	22.4
2019	A	323	64	20	2	5	9	1	0.325	0.399	0.464	10.84%	13.31%	42.1	19.8	34.7
2019	A+	236	39	18	1	2	4	3	0.284	0.353	0.408	8.47%	16.95%	36.1	22.5	36.7

Background: Signed for a paltry sum of $300,000 after defecting from his native homeland of Cuba, Vargas, who hails from La Habana, put on an offensive display during three abbreviated stops in his debut season. He slugged a hearty .330/.404/.465 with 15 doubles, three triples, a pair of homeruns, and seven stolen bases in 53 games between the Arizona Summer, Pioneer, and Midwest Leagues. Last season Vargas ripped the Low Class A pitching as he returned to the Midwest League, slugging .325/.399/.464 with 20 doubles, two triples, and five homeruns. The front office bumped him up to High Class A in early July. Vargas hit a respectable .284/.353/.408 during his 54-game stint with Rancho Cucamonga.

Snippet from The 2018 Prospect Digest Handbook: Despite the stops being relatively short, Vargas showed an advanced approach at the plate with strong bat-to-ball skills, as evidenced by his contact rates and line-drive numbers. Most of the damage was done in the hitter-friendly confines of the Pioneer League, which inflates offensive numbers like few other environments, but his production topped the league average mark by 41%. Vargas profiles as a potential middle-of-the-lineup thumper with above-average power and the glove to potentially stick at third base. He could be one of the bigger breakouts in 2019.

Scouting Report: With respect to his work in High Class A last season, consider the following:

- Since 2006, only three 19-year-old hitters met the following criteria in the California League (min. 200 PA): a 122 to 132 DRC+ with a walk percentage between 8% and 11%. Those three hitters: Cody Bellinger, Domingo Santana, and – of course – Miguel Vargas.

A few additional notes:

- Cody Bellinger owns a 134 DRC+ in 450 big league games. And Santana is sporting a 102 DRC+ in 492 games.
- Vargas, by the way, owns the best contact rate among the group; he whiffed in just 17% of his plate appearances.

One of the more underrated prospects in the minor leagues. Vargas continues to showcase the type of skills – offensive *and* defensive – to be a perennial All-Star caliber third baseman. Solid patience, phenomenal bat-to-ball skills. And Vargas, who stands 6-foot-3 and 205 pounds, hasn't even tapped into his in-game power. There's 20-homer potential here. In terms of ceiling think .290/.350/.460.

Ceiling: 3.0-win player
Risk: Moderate
MLB ETA: 2021

9. Kody Hoese, 3B

Hit	Power	SB	Patience	Glove	Overall
50	55	30	55	50	50

Born: 07/13/97	**Age:** 22	**Bats:** R	
Height: 6-4	**Weight:** 200	**Throws:** R	

Background: One of the rare draft-eligible sophomores that pop up each season; the Kansas City Royals took a flier on the then-20-year-old third baseman in the 35th round two years ago. And it looks like the Royals' scouting staff knew something the rest of the baseball world didn't: Tulane University slugger Kody Hoese was on the precipice of stardom. A two-time All-Indiana selection as a junior and senior at Griffith High School, Hoese, who was ranked the top shortstop in the state by Prep-Baseball Report and Perfect Game, struggled mightily during his first season with the Green Wave: in 44 games for first-year Head Coach Travis Jewett, the 6-foot-4, 200-pound infielder batted a paltry .213/.287/.279 with just seven extra-base knocks (six doubles and a dinger) in 44 games. Hoese, a native of Griffith, Indiana, had a bit of a coming out party during his follow up sophomore campaign: in 58 games he slugged a healthy .291/.368/.435 with 13 doubles, a pair of triples, and five homeruns while showing solid peripherals at the dish; he posted a 33-to-21 strikeout-to-walk ratio in 262 plate appearances. He spent the ensuing summer playing for the Newport Gulls in the New England Collegiate League, batting .283/.370/.493 with 11 doubles and seven homeruns. But that surge in power only proved to be a harbinger of things to come. In a career-high tying 58 games, the wiry third baseman slugged an impressive .391/.486/.779 triple-slash line while setting career highs in doubles (20), homeruns (23), and walk rate (13.6%). Los Angeles drafted him in the first round, 25th overall, and signed him to a deal worth $2,740,300 – the full slot value. Hoese split his debut between rookie ball and Low Class A, batting .299/.380/.483 with eight doubles, two triples, and five homers.

Scouting Report: Per the usual, here's what I wrote about Hoese heading into the draft last season:

"Consider the following:

- *Between 2011 and 2018 seven Division I hitters have slugged .375/.475/.700 with more walks than strikeouts (min. 250 PA): Deon Stafford, Donnie Dewees, Jason Krizan, D.J. Peterson (twice), Trenton Moses, Andrew Vaughn, Andrew Benintendi, and Kyle Lewis.*

Breaking the group down: there are three first round picks (Peterson, Benintendi, and Lewis and a fourth that is a lock to join them in 2019 (Vaughn). Dewees and Stafford were taken in the second and third rounds, respectively. Krizan was an eighth round pick by the Tigers in 2011. And Moses was a late round flier by the Braves in 2012. Let's approach it in a different way. Consider the following:

- *Between 2011 and 2018, there are 44 instances in which a Division I hitter slugged at least 20 homeruns in a year. Of those 44 instances, only two hitters have fanned in less than 12% of their respective plate appearances: Andrew Benintendi and Andrew Vaughn.*

That'll do... Hoese shows an incredibly rare – obviously – combination of power, patience, and bat-to-ball skills. He owns a simple, smooth right-handed swing and keeps his hands inside the ball well. The Phillies snagged Alec Bohm with the third overall pick last June and Hoese owns a significantly higher ceiling. If the defense grades out as average, he could be a perennial All-Star."

I may have been a little overly optimistic about Hoese's ceiling (as compared to Bohm), but he's a player.

Ceiling: 3.0-win player
Risk: Moderate
MLB ETA: 2021

10. Michael Busch, 1B/2B

Hit	Power	SB	Patience	Glove	Overall
45/50	45/50	35	60	50	50

Born: 11/09/97	Age: 22	Bats: L
Height: 6-0	Weight: 207	Throws: R

YEAR	LVL	PA	1B	2B	3B	HR	SB	CS	AVG	OBP	SLG	BB%	K%	GB%	LD%	FB%
2019	Rk	16	1	0	0	0	0	0	0.077	0.250	0.077	6.25%	12.50%	18.2	27.3	54.5
2019	A	19	2	0	0	0	0	0	0.182	0.474	0.182	31.58%	15.79%	33.3	22.2	33.3

Background: Highly ranked among all Minnesota prep prospects coming out of high school; Perfect Game listed the lefty-swinging infielder / outfielder as the No. 1 shortstop and No. 3 overall player in the state a couple years ago. A 2016 Perfect Game High Honorable Mention All-American following his senior season at Simley High School, Busch looked underwhelming during his first go-round against collegiate pitching: appearing in 55 games for the Tar Heels, the Inner Grove Heights native batted a lowly .215/.349/.341 with eight doubles and a trio of homeruns as a true freshman. Things began to click offensively for him during his tour through the Northwoods League the following summer, though. In 49 games with the St. Cloud Rox, Busch batted a respectable .291/.426/.500 with 17 doubles, one triple, and four homeruns. Listed at 6 feet and 207 pounds, the lefty-swinging Busch carried that offensive momentum into his sophomore campaign for the ACC powerhouse: in 64 games for long-time Head Coach Mike Fox, he slugged an impressive .317/.465/.521 with 10 doubles and 13 homeruns to go along with eight stolen bases in nine attempts. Busch spent the ensuing summer playing for the Chatham Anglers in the premier Cape Cod League, looking quite comfortable against some of the elite college-age pitching. In 27 games, he batted .322/.450/.567 with 10 extra-base hits and a 17-to-19 strikeout-to-walk ratio. Last season Busch's production maintained status quo: he batted .284/.436/.547 with a career high in doubles (14) and homeruns (16). The Dodgers drafted him in the opening round, 31st overall, and signed him to a full slot bonus worth $2,312,000.

Scouting Report: Per the usual, here's what I wrote about Hoese heading into the draft last season:

"Lacking the prototypical size and/or power projection for a first base or corner outfield prospect. Busch, nonetheless, owns an above-average hit tool, 15-homer power potential, and strong on-base peripherals. Consider the following:

- *Between 2011 and 2018, here's the list of ACC hitters to post a .280/.440/.550 with at least a walk rate of at least 17% and a strikeout rate below 15% (min. 200 PA): James Ramsey, Mike Papi, Will Craig (twice), Seth Beer (three times), and Josh Stowers.*

The good news: Ramsey, Papi, Craig, and Beer were all selected in the first round. And Stowers, the lone "outlier", was taken in the second round, 54th overall, last season. The bad news: Ramsey, Papi, and Craig have failed to live up to their lofty draft expectations. Beer and Stowers are only entering their second professional seasons, by the way, so the jury's still out. Busch looks like a solid fourth outfielder-type at full maturity."

Ceiling: 2.0- to 2.5-win player
Risk: Low to Moderate
MLB ETA: 2022

11. Jimmy Lewis, RHP

FB	CB	CH	Command	Overall
60	55/60	45/50	45/50	45

Born: 11/02/00	Age: 19	Bats: R
Height: 6-6	Weight: 200	Throws: R

Background: Fun Fact Part I: Lewis' old man, Jim, starred for Florida State University and was eventually selected by the Houston Astros in the second round of the 1991 draft. Fun Fact Part II: the younger Lewis' alma mater, Lake Travis High School, hadn't produced a draft pick since 2009. Fun Fact Part III: Lake Travis High School had two players, Mets third baseman Brett Baty and Jimmy Lewis, chosen in the opening two rounds last June. The 78th overall selection, Lewis signed for an above-slot deal worth $1.1 million. He was committed to Louisiana State University.

Scouting Report: He didn't appear in a regular season game after signing with the ball club. Lewis flashed a plus offering – a mid-90s fastball – and the potential for a second – a hard, downward biting curveball. He'll also mix in a slightly below-average changeup, which should be a solid 50-grade at maturity. Fast, loose arm with the athleticism and size for a little more in the tank. Lewis remains a wild card, but – again – the Dodgers have a knack for churning out/developing young arms. There's some #4-type potential.

Ceiling: 1.5- to 2.0-win player
Risk: Moderate
MLB ETA: 2022

12. Andy Pages, OF

	Hit	Power	SB	Patience	Glove	Overall
	40/45	60/70	30	50	50	45

Born: 12/08/00	Age: 19	Bats: R
Height: 6-1	Weight: 180	Throws: R

YEAR	LVL	PA	1B	2B	3B	HR	SB	CS	AVG	OBP	SLG	BB%	K%	GB%	LD%	FB%
2018	RK	178	16	8	0	9	9	6	0.236	0.393	0.486	12.92%	17.42%	30.9	15.5	36.4
2018	RK	34	3	1	0	1	1	1	0.192	0.382	0.346	17.65%	11.76%	22.7	18.2	45.5
2019	Rk+	279	27	22	2	19	7	6	0.298	0.398	0.651	9.32%	28.32%	24.5	23.3	42.8

Background: An international free agent summer signing three years ago. Pages, who agreed to terms with the club on a deal worth $300,000, looked quite underwhelming during his professional debut in 2018 as he batted a lowly .229/.392/.464 with nine doubles and 10 homeruns in 52 games between the foreign and stateside rookie leagues. The Dodgers' front office brass aggressively pushed the young power hitter up to the Rookie Advanced League for the 2019 season. And Pages flourished. Big time. A 6-foot-1, 180-pound outfielder from the Dominican Republic, Pages slugged a hearty .298/.398/.651 with 22 doubles, two triples, 19 homeruns, and seven stolen bases. His overall production, according to Baseball Prospectus' *Deserved Runs Created Plus*, topped the league average threshold by a staggering 73%. According to FanGraphs' Kiley McDaniel, Pages would have been included in the non-canceled deal that sent Joc Pederson to the Angels this offseason.

Scouting Report: Consider the following:

- Since 2006, there have been 253 different 18-year-old hitters to appear in the Pioneer League. Eighty-eight of those players earned at least 200 trips to the plate in a season.
- Only one of those aforementioned 88 hitters bested Pages' 173 DRC+ total: Rockies minor league first baseman Grant Lavigne.

Off the charts power thanks to his lightning fast hands. The problem for Pages, however, is his massive swing-and-miss totals; he whiffed in slightly more than 28% of his plate appearances last season. A large, untimely leg kick is clearly causing timing issues as he's struggling to get his foot back down. It's a pretty safe bet that the Dodgers' player development guys are going to eliminate it – or at least quiet it a bit. Mike Stanton type power but the hit tool needs to take several leaps forward.

Ceiling: 1.5- to 2.0-win player
Risk: Moderate to High
MLB ETA: 2021/2022

13. DJ Peters, CF

	Hit	Power	SB	Patience	Glove	Overall
	45	60	30	50+	50	45

Born: 12/12/95	Age: 24	Bats: R
Height: 6-6	Weight: 225	Throws: R

YEAR	LVL	PA	1B	2B	3B	HR	SB	CS	AVG	OBP	SLG	BB%	K%	GB%	LD%	FB%
2016	RK	302	52	24	3	13	5	3	0.351	0.437	0.615	11.59%	21.85%	46.9	20.9	26.5
2017	A+	587	78	29	5	27	3	3	0.276	0.372	0.514	10.90%	32.20%	36.8	22.6	34.6
2018	AA	559	61	23	3	29	1	2	0.236	0.320	0.473	8.05%	34.35%	35.5	20.4	32.9
2019	AA	288	38	10	1	11	1	0	0.241	0.331	0.422	9.72%	32.29%	39.0	17.0	34.0
2019	AAA	255	31	10	1	12	1	1	0.260	0.388	0.490	12.94%	29.41%	34.6	24.8	34.6

Background: Tall and gangly with the athleticism of a prowling jaguar. The Dodgers drafted the 6-foot-6, 225-pound outfielder out of Western Nevada College in the fourth round of the 2016 draft. Peters immediately made an impact on the organization as he slugged a scorching .351/.437/.615 with 40 extra-base knocks in just 66 games in the offensive-friendly Pioneer League. But he didn't miss a beat as the front office bounced him straight up to High Class A for his sophomore campaign as he batted a healthy .276/.372/.514 with 29 doubles, five triples, and 27 homeruns – though he whiffed 189 times. The Glendora, California, native squared off against the minors' toughest challenge, Class AA, in 2018. And his swing-and-miss pockmarks proved too large to overcome as it reared its ugly head against the advanced minor league pitchers. He cobbled together a disappointing .236/.320/.473 triple-slash line in 132 games with Tulsa. Not shockingly, Peters found himself back in the Texas league for some additional seasoning – though, unfortunately, the numbers remained largely the same. He hit .241/.331/.422 with 22 extra-base hits in 68 games. Los Angeles bumped him up to the minors' final stop, Class AAA, in late June. Peters hit an aggregate .249/.358/.453 with 20 doubles, two triple, 23 homeruns, and a pair of stolen bases.

Snippet from The 2018 Prospect Digest Handbook: The problems are two-fold: will he make contact consistently enough to allow his ability to shine *and* how will he adapt when he – inevitably – faces extreme shifts at the big league level?

Scouting Report: At this point I've written – ad nauseam – about (A) Peters' dynamic athleticism which aligns well with Indians snake-bitten outfielder Bradley Zimmer and (B) his propensity to whiff. Peters' strikeout rate in the Pacific Coast League, 29.4%, was the lowest mark of his career since his debut in the Pioneer League in 2016. And now he's staring down an entirely new challenge: The Dodgers' outfield is the best in baseball as its set to run out Mookie Betts, the 2018 A.L. MVP; Cody Bellinger, the 2019 N.L. MVP; and a combination of A.J. Pollock, Joc Pederson, and Chris Taylor in left field. Simply put, there's no room at the inn for Peters. And it's unlikely any potential rebuilding trade partner would view him as anything more than a side dish to the main course. Loud tools that have been undone by his strikeout totals. Perhaps, though, he becomes a bit of a late bloomer.

Ceiling: 1.5-win player
Risk: Moderate
MLB ETA: 2020

14. Omar Estevez, 2B/SS

Hit	Power	SB	Patience	Glove	Overall
50	45	30	50	50	45

Born: 02/25/98	Age: 22	Bats: R
Height: 5-10	Weight: 185	Throws: R

YEAR	LVL	PA	1B	2B	3B	HR	SB	CS	AVG	OBP	SLG	BB%	K%	GB%	LD%	FB%
2016	A	508	77	32	2	9	3	6	0.255	0.298	0.389	5.12%	23.82%	37.6	21.6	27.8
2017	A+	502	86	24	3	4	2	2	0.256	0.309	0.348	6.57%	19.32%	35.4	24.5	27.5
2018	A+	577	83	43	2	15	3	1	0.278	0.336	0.456	7.80%	23.92%	32.4	23.1	33.9
2019	Rk	22	4	2	0	0	0	0	0.300	0.364	0.400	9.09%	36.36%	50.0	16.7	25.0
2019	AA	336	57	24	0	6	0	2	0.291	0.352	0.431	9.23%	20.83%	38.4	25.4	29.3

Background: Added to the organization during the same wave that brought in former top prospect – and current Orioles blue-chipper – Yusniel Diaz, Estevez joined the franchise after signing his name on the dotted line for a cool $6 million deal. And, to be fair, it took the young middle infielder a couple years before he could consistently handle the rigors of the minor leagues. But Estevez, who measures just 5-foot-10 and 185- pound, seemed to put things together during his second stint in the California League two years ago as he batted .278/.336/.456 with a whopping 43 doubles, two triples, and 15 homeruns. The Cuban infielder squared off against the minors' toughest challenge, Class AA, and finished with his finest showing to date. In an injury-shortened year, he batted .291/.352/.431 with 24 doubles and six homeruns in only 83 games of action. According to *Deserved Runs Created Plus*, his overall production topped the league average threshold by 18% - his finest total to date.

Snippet from The 2018 Prospect Digest Handbook: Estevez has always flirted with some impressive power production across his first two seasons, but he finally began to tap into it in 2018; he tied Toronto's Bo Bichette for the second most doubles among all minor league bats. Estevez has all the necessary tools to develop into a league-average starting middle infielder, though he hasn't quite lived up to the hype yet.

Scouting Report: Consider the following:

- Since 2006, here's the list of 21-year-old hitters to post a 113 to 123 DRC+ with a walk rate between 8% and 10% in the Texas League (min. 350 PA): Franmil Reyes, Willie Calhoun, Cheslor Cuthbert, Taylor Lindsey, and – of course – Omar Estevez.

The minor league version of Craig Biggio, a virtual doubles machine. Eventually some of those two-baggers will start turning into long balls more consistently. I've been one of Estevez's biggest fans, but he's now entering his fifth minor league season and it seems like he's never going to take that final step forward. I get the distinct feeling he's going to turn into this generation's version of Carlos Febles.

Ceiling: 1.5-win player
Risk: Moderate
MLB ETA: 2020

15. Dennis Santana, RHP

FB	SL	CH	Command	Overall
55	55	50	45	45

Born: 04/12/96	Age: 24	Bats: R
Height: 6-2	Weight: 190	Throws: R

YEAR	LVL	IP	W	L	SV	ERA	FIP	WHIP	K/9	K%	BB/9	BB%	K/BB	HR9	BABIP
2017	A+	85.7	5	6	0	3.57	3.69	1.27	9.7	24.73%	2.3	5.91%	4.18	0.53	0.340
2017	AA	32.7	3	1	0	5.51	4.24	1.68	10.2	24.03%	6.3	14.94%	1.61	0.55	0.337
2018	AA	38.7	0	2	0	2.56	3.21	1.03	11.9	31.88%	3.3	8.75%	3.64	0.70	0.258
2018	AAA	11.0	1	1	0	2.45	1.74	1.09	11.5	31.11%	1.6	4.44%	7.00	0.00	0.345
2019	AAA	93.3	5	9	0	6.94	5.76	1.76	10.1	23.65%	5.1	11.94%	1.98	1.54	0.364

Background: They say it's always best to have a backup plan, a fallback option. And that's definitely the case with Santana. Originally signed as a shortstop in 2012, the Dodgers quickly changed course after he batted a putrid .198/.312/.256 with just six extra-base hits in 56 games in the Dominican Summer League. Santana spent the next summer dealing in the foreign rookie league as he posted a 38-to-15 strikeout-to-walk ratio with a 1.05 ERA in 34.1 innings of work. And after a control/command hiccup in 2015, he quickly moved through the minor leagues – especially considering his lack of mound experience. Two years ago the San Pedro de Macoris, Dominican Republic, native battled a right shoulder strain – which was originally diagnosed as a lat issue – which limited him to just 11 appearances, including one game with the Dodgers. Santana popped back up with Oklahoma City where he bounced between the club's rotation and pen as he averaged 10.1 strikeouts and a whopping 5.1 walks per nine innings. He also made an additional five relief appearances, fanning six and walking four.

Snippet from The 2018 Prospect Digest Handbook: Santana owns a unique throwing motion, almost short-arming it at times. And it looks like he's a short-strider as well. But he's consistently thrown strikes with all three pitches the past couple of years and should slide into the middle of a big league rotation at maturity (which is very close). Hopefully the shoulder/rotator cuff won't be an issue moving forward.

Scouting Report: I'm not entirely certain the shoulder strain didn't impact Santana's 2019 season. While his fastball remained in the 92- to 93-mph range, his secondary pitches lacked the consistency and typical bite shown in the past. His slider, while it flashed plus on occasion, hovered in the 50- to 55-grade most of the time. And his changeup, which was a strong plus option with tremendous fade in 2018, looked like he completely lost the feel/touch for it. Santana's now entering his age-24 season, coming off of a problematic/disappointing showing the previous year, and looks like a future middle reliever.

Ceiling: 1.5-win player
Risk: Moderate
MLB ETA: Debuted in 2018

16. Michael Grove, RHP

FB	CB	CH	Command	Overall
55	55	45	50	45

Born: 12/18/96	Age: 23	Bats: R
Height: 6-3	Weight: 200	Throws: R

YEAR	LVL	IP	W	L	SV	ERA	FIP	WHIP	K/9	K%	BB/9	BB%	K/BB	HR9	BABIP
2019	A+	51.7	0	5	0	6.10	3.76	1.55	12.7	31.60%	3.3	8.23%	3.84	1.22	0.412

Background: Viewed as a potential first round selection during his first year-and-a-half of collegiate action. Grove's ascension towards the opening round was derailed thanks to a wonky right elbow – an injury that forced him under the knife for Tommy John surgery. The 6-foot-3, 200-pound right-hander would eventually miss his junior season as he was recovering, but that didn't stop the Dodgers from calling his name in the second round that year. Finally healthy, the Wheeling, West Virginia, native began his professional career with an aggressive push up to High Class A. In 21 starts with the Rancho Cucamonga Quakes, Grove struck out 73 and walked 19 in 51.2 innings of work. He compiled an unsightly 6.10 ERA and a slightly better 5.38 DRA (*Deserved Run Average*).

Snippet from The 2018 Prospect Digest Handbook: Assuming he's healthy, Grove could see some time in the California League before year's end.

Scouting Report: A few things to note:

- Grove showed a surprisingly strong feel for the strike zone considering the long layoff and Tommy John recipients typically struggle throwing strikes during their immediate return to action.
- Grove's fastball was a solid 55-grade, sitting in the 92- to 93-mph range. It's straight, but he commands it to all quadrants well.
- Previously, his breaking ball was called a slider; it's not. It's definitely a curveball. And, again, he showed a strong feel for the above-average pitch.
- In a couple brief appearances, I believe I saw his below-average changeup just a handful of time.

So here's where we're at: (A) he's entering his age-23 season; (B) he's thrown below 100 innings since the start of 2017; (C) he battled some homerun issues last season, and (D) he lacks a strong third offering.

Ceiling: 1.5-win player
Risk: Moderate
MLB ETA: 2021

17. Devin Mann, 2B/3B

Hit	Power	SB	Patience	Glove	Overall
50	50	35	50+	50	45

Born: 02/11/97	Age: 23	Bats: R	Top CALs:
Height: 6-3	Weight: 180	Throws: R	

YEAR	LVL	PA	1B	2B	3B	HR	SB	CS	AVG	OBP	SLG	BB%	K%	GB%	LD%	FB%
2018	RK	6	1	0	0	0	0	1	0.200	0.333	0.200	16.67%	50.00%	0.0	100.0	0.0
2018	A	264	38	13	1	2	7	4	0.241	0.348	0.335	12.88%	18.94%	34.1	29.5	28.4
2019	Rk	2	0	0	0	0	0	0	0.000	0.500	0.000	50.00%	0.00%	0.0	0.0	100.0
2019	Rk	14	5	2	0	0	0	1	0.538	0.571	0.692	7.14%	7.14%	41.7	25.0	25.0
2019	A+	424	62	19	2	19	5	4	0.278	0.358	0.496	10.61%	21.93%	31.7	23.8	35.9

Background: A key cog for the University of Louisville's offense for the better part of his three-year career. Mann left the ACC squad with a solid .288/.408/.458 triple-slash line, including slugging .303/.446/.504 with 17 doubles, four triples, and seven homeruns as a junior. Los Angeles selected the 6-foot-3, 180-pound infielder in the fifth round, 164th overall, two years ago. The former Cardinal appeared in 63 games with the Great Lakes Loons during his debut, hitting a mediocre .241/.348/.335. Last season the front office pushed the then-22-year-old infielder up to the Rancho Cucamonga, and his bat awakened. In 98 games with the Quakes, Mann batted .278/.358/.496 with 19 doubles, two triples, and 19 homeruns. He also swiped five bags in nine attempts. Per *Deserved Runs Created Plus*, his overall production topped the league average mark by a whopping 42%. Mann also appeared in 15 games with the Glendale Desert Dogs in the Arizona Fall League; he cobbled together a lowly .191/.339/.340 triple-slash line.

Scouting Report: Consider the following:

- Since 2006, four 22-year-old hitters tallied a 137 to 147 DRC+ with a walk rate between 9% and 11% in the California League (min. 300 PA): Evan White, a top prospect in the Mariners' system; Brad Miller, who's been a league average hitter across his seven-year big league career; Vinnie Catricala, who flamed without reaching the big leagues; and – of course – Devin Mann.

A quietly well-rounded prospect. Mann shows an average hit tool with solid patience and developing power. But perhaps the best news for his future: after a slow start to his 2019 season, the former Louisville Cardinal slugged a solid .295/.366/.523 before hitting the DL for a month beginning in the middle of July. There's so low end starting caliber potential here if everything breaks just right, but he's likely to fall into a bench role. In terms of offensive ceiling think Dansby Swanson's 2019 season in which he batted .251/.325/.422.

Ceiling: 1.5-win player
Risk: Moderate
MLB ETA: 2021/2022

18. Mitchell White, RHP

FB	CB	SL	CH	Command	Overall
55	55	55	45+	50	40+

Born: 12/28/94	Age: 25	Bats: R	Top CALs:
Height: 6-3	Weight: 210	Throws: R	

Background: At one point early in his professional career White looked like a potential #2/#3-type arm. And depending upon whom you asked, his ceiling could have actually been higher. MLB.com reports that Alex Anthopoulos, the former Dodgers vice president of baseball operations and current Braves General Manager, once remarked that the former Santa Clara University ace had the repertoire to go as the first overall pick. Two years into his professional career that assessment looked spot on: White posted a 30-to-6 strikeout-to-walk ratio with a 0.00 ERA in 22.0 innings during his debut and then made it up to Class AA by the end of his sophomore season. But White, a 6-foot-3, 210-pound right-hander, has battled some consistency issues since then. He averaged just 7.5 strikeouts per nine innings in a return to the Texas League in 2018. He looked like he regained his previous form during his third tour of the league to start 2019, but got smacked around quite a bit in 16 appearances in Class AAA. He finished his fourth professional season with 105 punch outs, 31 walks, and a 5.09 ERA in 93.2 innings of work.

Snippet from The 2018 Prospect Digest Handbook: The stuff's seemingly backed up since his phenomenal debut a couple years ago. White's fastball, once viewed as a plus-offering, sat in the low-90s, firmly in the above-average category. His slider was inconsistent, sometimes looking like a strong complementary pitch and other times resembling a fourth option. His curveball, an upper -70s offering, shows solid 12-6 break and is a weapon in his arsenal. He'll also mix in a changeup, which is definitely his fourth pitch. Along with the regression in his stuff, White's ceiling has backed up considerably as well – going from a #3-type arm to a solid backend starting pitcher. He's now entering his age-24 season with two-full seasons on his resume, though he's thrown fewer than 200 total innings in those aforementioned seasons.

Scouting Report: The repertoire never rebounded from the potential ace level he showed a couple seasons ago. And the command, while solid, doesn't compensate. White's fastball, curveball, and slider all grade out as above-average offerings. But his changeup remains subpar – even though he showed a higher willingness to throw it last year. He's a lost man without a future in the Dodgers' organization. And he's seemingly too far down the path of a Chase De Jong type arm, though White's ceiling is a bit higher.

Ceiling: 1.0- to 1.5-win player
Risk: Moderate
MLB ETA: 2020

19. Cristian Santana, 1B/3B

Hit	Power	SB	Patience	Glove	Overall
55	50	30	30	50	40

Born: 02/24/97	Age: 23	Bats: R
Height: 6-2	Weight: 175	Throws: R

YEAR	LVL	PA	1B	2B	3B	HR	SB	CS	AVG	OBP	SLG	BB%	K%	GB%	LD%	FB%
2016	RK	180	28	6	2	8	0	1	0.256	0.278	0.453	2.78%	25.56%	47.7	21.9	23.4
2017	RK	48	14	2	1	5	0	0	0.537	0.583	1.000	12.50%	12.50%	47.2	19.4	30.6
2017	A	180	42	9	0	5	0	1	0.322	0.339	0.460	2.78%	23.33%	52.6	13.5	26.3
2018	A+	580	103	23	0	24	2	2	0.274	0.302	0.447	3.45%	24.66%	46.1	20.9	24.8
2019	AA	413	87	22	1	10	0	0	0.301	0.320	0.436	2.42%	21.31%	54.2	22.9	17.4

Background: It took the Dominican-born slugger three years to make it out of the rookie leagues – he spent the 2014-15 seasons in the foreign level and 2016 in the Arizona Summer League – but he's quickly made up for lost time since. The 6-foot-2, 175-pound corner infielder slugged .363/.390/.563 in 54 games between Ogden and Great Lakes in 2017. And despite appearing in just 44 games in Low Class A that year, Santana handled an aggressive promotion up to High Class A with aplomb the following season as he batted .274/.302/.447. Last season his production maintained status quo as he moved into – and proved himself against – the minors' most important challenge: Class AA. Appearing in 102 games with the Tulsa Drillers, the San Cristobal native slugged .301/.320/.436 with 22 doubles, one triple, and 10 homers. His overall production, according to *Deserved Runs Created Plus*, was 4% *below* the league average.

Scouting Report: The good news: above-average hit tool, solid-average pop, strong bat-to-balls skills, and a little defensive flexibility. The bad news: a career damning inability to work the count. There were 686 minor league hitters that earned at least 400 plate appearances last season; Santana's pitiful 2.4% BB-rate was the second lowest. And to put that into some context: only three big league hitters posted a sub-3.0% walk rate last season (Kevin Pillar, Tim Anderson, and Hanser Alberto). He's probably staring down a role as a Quad-A type hitter unless (A) his hit tool upticks to a 60-grade, (B) there's a power surge, or (C) he doubles his walk rate. Still, though, 22-year-olds that hit a solid .300 with double-digit homeruns in Class AA always have a puncher's chance.

Ceiling: 1.0- to 1.5-win player
Risk: Moderate
MLB ETA: 2020

20. Jacob Amaya, 2B/SS

Hit	Power	SB	Patience	Glove	Overall
45/50	40/45	35	65	50	40

Born: 09/03/98	Age: 21	Bats: R
Height: 6-0	Weight: 180	Throws: R

YEAR	LVL	PA	1B	2B	3B	HR	SB	CS	AVG	OBP	SLG	BB%	K%	GB%	LD%	FB%
2017	RK	140	23	4	1	2	4	2	0.254	0.364	0.356	13.57%	17.86%	64.9	20.2	13.8
2018	RK	155	29	9	3	3	11	4	0.346	0.465	0.535	17.42%	18.71%	38.8	26.5	28.6
2018	A	119	24	1	0	1	3	3	0.265	0.390	0.306	16.81%	15.13%	45.7	27.2	25.9
2019	A	470	66	25	4	6	4	4	0.262	0.381	0.394	15.74%	17.66%	47.2	15.3	31.9
2019	A+	89	14	3	2	1	1	3	0.250	0.307	0.375	7.87%	16.85%	55.2	16.4	26.9

Background: Fun Fact Part I: Frank Amaya, Jacob's grandfather, spent a couple years in the low minor leagues during the mid- to late-1950s. Fun Fact Part II: The elder Amaya was a member of the Dodgers' organization – both in Brooklyn and in Los Angeles – for parts of four seasons. Jacob, an 11th round pick out of South Hills High School, bypassed his commitment to Cal State Fullerton and signed with the organization for roughly $250,000 – not bad money for the 340th overall player chosen. The young middle infielder show a little bit of promise during his debut in the Arizona Summer League, hitting a decent .254/.364/.356 with seven extra-base knocks in 34 games. Two years ago Amaya torched the Pioneer League to the tune of .346/.465/.535 and looked OK during his 27-game cameo in the Midwest League. Amaya returned for a longer look with the Great Lakes loons, hitting .262/.381/.394 with 25 doubles, four triples, six homeruns, and four stolen bases. Per *Deserved Runs Created Plus*, his overall production topped the league average mark by a whopping 46%. Amaya also appeared in 21 games with the Quakes of Rancho Cucamonga, batting .250/.307/.375.

Scouting Report: Consider the following:

- Since 2006, only two 20-year-old hitters met the following criteria in the Midwest League (min. 300 PA): 140 to 150 DRC+; a sub-20% strikeout rate; and a double-digit walk rate. Those two hitters: Vidal Brujan, a top prospect in the Rays system, and – of course – Jacob Amaya.

One of the most patient approaches at the plate in the entire minor leagues; Amaya walked in nearly 16% of his plate appearances in Low Class A last season. And, unfortunately, there's where the overwhelming majority of his value is derived. Slightly below-average power, a little bit of speed, solid glove, and a decent hit tool. Amaya looks like a future utility guy, but he's going to have to prove that he can find first base frequently as he moves up the ladder. Plus, last year was his second stint in Low Class A as well.

Ceiling: 1.0- to 1.5-win player
Risk: Moderate
MLB ETA: 2021/2022

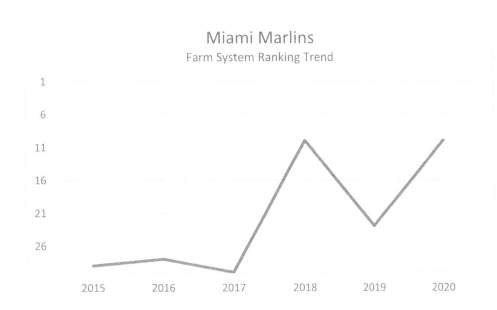

Miami Marlins
Farm System Ranking Trend

Rank	Name	Age	Pos
1	Sixto Sanchez	21	RHP
2	Edward Cabrera	22	RHP
3	JJ Bleday	22	RF
4	Jazz Chisholm	22	SS
5	Jesus Sanchez	22	RF
6	Lewin Diaz	23	1B
7	Braxton Garrett	22	LHP
8	Trevor Rogers	22	LHP
9	Kameron Misner	22	CF
10	Jorge Guzman	24	RHP
11	Peyton Burdick	23	LF
12	Nick Neidert	23	RHP
13	Osiris Johnson	19	SS
14	Monte Harrison	24	CF
15	Connor Scott	20	CF
16	Victor Mesa Jr.	18	CF
17	Tristan Pompey	23	LF
18	Jose Devers	20	2B/SS
19	Jerar Encarnacion	22	RF
20	Victor Victor Mesa	23	CF

1. Sixto Sanchez, RHP

FB	CB	CH	Command	Overall
70	55	70	60	60

Born: 07/29/98	Age: 21	Bats: R
Height: 6-0	Weight: 185	Throws: R

YEAR	LVL	IP	W	L	SV	ERA	FIP	WHIP	K/9	K%	BB/9	BB%	K/BB	HR9	BABIP
2017	A	67.3	5	3	0	2.41	2.35	0.82	8.6	25.00%	1.2	3.52%	7.11	0.13	0.251
2017	A+	27.7	0	4	0	4.55	3.42	1.30	6.5	16.81%	2.9	7.56%	2.22	0.33	0.295
2018	A+	46.7	4	3	0	2.51	2.66	1.07	8.7	23.94%	2.1	5.85%	4.09	0.19	0.295
2019	A+	11.0	0	2	0	4.91	3.94	1.45	4.9	13.04%	1.6	4.35%	3.00	0.82	0.351
2019	AA	103.0	8	4	0	2.53	2.68	1.03	8.5	23.60%	1.7	4.62%	5.11	0.44	0.286

Background: Let's be honest: from the Marlins' point of view the Christian Yelich trade was an utter disaster. Yelich, who is fresh off of his team friendly contract extension, turned in back-to-back otherworldly campaigns. And, well, the Marlins' return has been quite blah. Monte Harrison has been a league average bat in Class AA and Class AAA since 2018. Lewis Brinson owns a laughably poor .189/.238/.294 in 184 big league games with the Marlins. Isan Diaz looked miserable in his debut in Class AA two years, but rebounded in the offense-inducing environment known as the PCL last season. And Jordan Yamamoto looks like a solid #4 starting pitcher. And, to be honest, it looked like the club's mega-deal with the Phillies had the potential to move down the same path when they traded All-Star backstop J.T. Realmuto for an injured – though, admittedly, potentially franchise-altering – pitcher with a worrisome elbow, a finesse left-hander (Will Stewart), and solid big league catcher (Jorge Alfaro). But Sixto Sanchez came roaring back from the wonky elbow like a bat out of hell. After two brief starts in the Florida State League, the 6-foot, 185-pound firebolt-slinging right-hander chewed through the Southern League like a wolf devouring its prey. The Dominican Dandy finished his stint in Class AA, the minors' most important challenge, with 97 strikeouts and just 19 walks with a 2.53 ERA in 103.0 innings of work.

Snippet from The 2018 Prospect Digest Handbook: The lone knock on Sanchez, of course, is his slight 6-foot, 185-pound frame and the potential durability issues that may come along with it. The Phillies have done an incredible job of governing his innings in an effort to carefully navigate him through the injury nexus. Hopefully the elbow/collarbone issues that plagued him last season won't limit him in the coming years. He's a special, special prospect.

Scouting Report: I have to be honest: I'm not sure I would've had the fortitude to make the trade the Marlins did when they acquired Sixto Sanchez. He was limited to just 46.2 early season innings in 2018. And a setback with the elbow curtailed his Arizona Fall League debut before it even began. A few months later Miami's front office pegged him as the centerpiece of a deal involving one of the best backstops in professional baseball. But here we are. And it's proving to be a brilliant deal. Sanchez's repertoire just screams top-of-the-rotation caliber pitcher. His fastball was sitting mid- to upper-90s with the effort of throwing a slow pitch softball. His changeup jumped from a potential plus pitch to a plus-plus weapon. And he showed a level of confidence in the offering that's reminiscent of an in-his-prime Pedro Martinez. And his curveball falls in line with a 55-grade. But what makes Sanchez's high ceiling actually obtainable is his ability to throw – consistent – pitcher's pitches. He's a bonafide, budding ace. As long as the body holds up.

Ceiling: 5.0-win player
Risk: Moderate
MLB ETA: 2020

2. Edward Cabrera, RHP

FB	CB	CH	Command	Overall
70	65	55	55	60

Born: 04/13/98	Age: 22	Bats: R
Height: 6-4	Weight: 175	Throws: R

YEAR	LVL	IP	W	L	SV	ERA	FIP	WHIP	K/9	K%	BB/9	BB%	K/BB	HR9	BABIP
2017	A-	35.7	1	3	0	5.30	3.26	1.40	8.1	19.39%	2.0	4.85%	4.00	0.25	0.350
2018	A	100.3	4	8	0	4.22	4.50	1.47	8.3	21.14%	3.8	9.55%	2.21	0.99	0.329
2019	A+	58.0	5	3	0	2.02	2.20	0.95	11.3	32.16%	2.8	7.93%	4.06	0.16	0.277
2019	AA	38.7	4	1	0	2.56	4.33	1.06	10.0	27.56%	3.0	8.33%	3.31	1.40	0.242

Background: One of the bigger surprises in a now bountiful farm system. The wiry right-hander looked every part of a budding ace during his breakout campaign between the Florida State and Southern Leagues in 2019. A native of Santiago, Dominican Republic, Cabrera showcased some promising peripherals during his stint with Batavia in 2017 (8.1 K/9 and 2.0 BB/9) and his season with Greensboro a year later (8.3 K/9 and 3.8 BB/9). Last season, though, the 6-foot-4, 175-pound loose-armed fireballer began his fourth minor league campaign on a bit of a sour note: he allowed four earned runs and walked more than he fanned in a 4.1-inning start against the Palm Beach Cardinals. From then on he didn't allow a run – earned or unearned – over his next four starts. Miami promoted the baby faced hurler up to Class AA, the minors' toughest challenge, near the end of June. In total, Cabrera tossed 96.1 innings, recording 116 punch outs and just 31 walks to go along with a barely-there 2.23 ERA.

Snippet from The 2018 Prospect Digest Handbook: I think he's going to be special. One more thought: I've personally scouted over 300 pitchers for the book this year; Cabrera's slider the best I've seen. At the very least, he's going to be a dominant backend, shut the doors, turn off the lights type reliever.

Scouting Report: I scouted a handful of Cabrera's games in Class AA season. The main takeaway: he's evolving from a thrower into a full-fledged pitcher. He's always possessed a plus-plus fastball and that wipeout, hard-tilting slider, and a lot his early success was simply from overpowering low level hitters. Last season, though, his changeup progressed into an above-average weapon – one that (A) he showed a significant amount of trust in and (B) adds a third swing-and-miss option to his repertoire. It's power changeup, sitting in the 91- to 92-mph range, with some dive to it. Cabrera has the look, build, and repertoire of a #2/#3-type arm. I really, *really* like him.

Ceiling: 4.0-win player
Risk: Moderate
MLB ETA: 2020

3. J.J. Bleday, RF

Hit	Power	SB	Patience	Glove	Overall
50	60	30	50	50	60

Born: 11/10/97	Age: 22	Bats: L
Height: 6-3	Weight: 205	Throws: R

YEAR	LVL	PA	1B	2B	3B	HR	SB	CS	AVG	OBP	SLG	BB%	K%	GB%	LD%	FB%
2019	A+	151	25	8	0	3	0	0	0.257	0.311	0.379	7.28%	19.21%	36.0	23.4	29.7

Background: The lynchpin in a potent Commodores lineup last season; Bleday, a hulking right field out of Panama City, Florida, teamed with Ethan Paul, Philip Clarke, Austin Martin, Stephen Scott, Cooper Davis, and Pat DeMarco to thrust the school's offense towards the best in college baseball. Out of Mosley High School where he earned Third-Team All-American recognition by Rawlings/Perfect Game, Bleday turned in a solid freshman campaign for the SEC powerhouse three years ago: in 51 games for long-time skipper Tim Corbin, he posted a respectable .256/.384/.341 triple-slash line, belting out eight doubles and a pair of homeruns. Bleday spent the ensuing summer playing for the Newport Gulls in the New England Collegiate League, batting .232/.376/.449.The 6-foot-3, 205-pound corner outfielder showed tremendous strides at the dish during his follow-up campaign en route to slugging .368/.494/.511 with five doubles, one triple, and four homeruns in an injury-abbreviated season. Bleday continued to swing an impressive stick as he moved into the Cape Cod League during the summer as well, hitting .311/.374/.500 with nine doubles, two triples, and five homeruns in 36 games with the Orleans Firebirds. Described by Corbin as a "very low maintenance young man", Bleday's power blossomed into a legitimate plus tool in 2019: he slugged 13 doubles and a career-best 26 homeruns while batting .350/.464/.717. Miami made the former Commodore the fourth overall pick last season, signing him to a deal worth $6.7 million, and pushed him – aggressively into High Class A for his professional debut. He hit .257/.311/.379 in 38 games with the Jupiter Hammerheads.

Scouting Report: Here's what I wrote prior to the draft last season:

"Currently tied with Tulane's Kody Hoese for the lead in homeruns among all DI hitters; Bleday's thump has pushed his prospect status up towards the early part of the opening round. Consider the following:

- *Since 2011 here's the list of SEC hitters to slug at least 20 homeruns in a season: Andrew Benintendi, Jonathan India, A.J. Reed, Brent Rooker, Chad Spanberger, and – of course – J.J. Bleday.*

Let's continue...

- *Of those six players, five of them walked at least 15% of the time and fanned in few than 20% of their plate appearances: Benintendi, India, Reed, Rooker, and Bleday.*
- *Ignoring Bleday momentarily, here's where the remaining members of the group were drafted: seventh overall (Benintendi), fifth overall (India), 35th overall (Rooker), and 42nd overall (Reed).*

Moving along...

Player	Year	Age	PA	AVG	OBP	SLG	K%	BB%
J.J. Bleday	2019	21	216	0.337	0.447	0.750	18.52%	15.74%
Brent Rooker	2017	23	309	0.387	0.495	0.810	18.77%	15.53%
Andrew Benintendi	2015	20	288	0.376	0.488	0.717	11.11%	17.36%
Jonathan India	2018	21	300	0.350	0.497	0.717	18.67%	20.00%

A.J. Reed	2014	21	290	0.336	0.476	0.735	16.55%	16.90%

That's pretty favorable company. Let's take a look at his production in the Cape in 2018. Consider the following:

- *Between 1999 and 2017, here's the list of hitters to post a strikeout rate below 14%, a walk rate under 10%, and hit at least .300/.350/.450 (min. 150 PA): Alec Bohm, Nico Hoerner, A.J. Pollock, Chase Utley, Richie Martin, Lance Niekro, Ross Kivett, and Brandon Trinkwon.*

Bleday shows easy nature loft in his swing which allows his plus-raw power to transition into plus-in-game power. Bleday tends to be too pull happy, so he's likely going to face a plethora of defensive shifts. He looks like a capable starting outfielder, though one not destined for stardom."

Ceiling: 4.0-win player
Risk: Moderate
MLB ETA: 2021

4. Jazz Chisholm, SS

Hit	Power	SB	Patience	Glove	Overall
40/45	55	50	50	45+	60

Born: 02/01/98	Age: 22	Bats: L
Height: 5-11	Weight: 165	Throws: R

YEAR	LVL	PA	1B	2B	3B	HR	SB	CS	AVG	OBP	SLG	BB%	K%	GB%	LD%	FB%
2017	A	125	19	5	2	1	3	0	0.248	0.325	0.358	8.00%	31.20%	39.7	21.9	28.8
2018	A	341	39	17	4	15	8	2	0.244	0.311	0.472	8.80%	28.45%	36.2	17.8	38.0
2018	A+	160	31	6	2	10	9	2	0.329	0.369	0.597	5.63%	32.50%	34.7	31.6	29.6
2019	AA	94	14	4	2	3	3	0	0.284	0.383	0.494	11.70%	25.53%	27.8	29.6	37.0
2019	AA	364	35	6	5	18	13	4	0.204	0.305	0.427	11.26%	33.79%	33.5	18.6	40.7

Background: The Marlins and Diamondbacks got together on an old fashioned challenge trade at the deadline last July. Miami dealt underrated right-hander Zac Gallen – and his sub-3.00 ERA and impressive strikeout rate – for lefty-swinging shortstop Jazz Chisholm. Originally signed out of Nassau, Bahamas, for the relatively modest sum of $200,000 in 2015, Chisholm began shooting up prospect charts after a strong second showing in the Midwest League and an explosion in the hitter-friendly confines of Visalia's home park two years ago when he slugged an aggregate .272/.329/.513 with 54 extra-base hits. Last season, the 5-foot-11, 165-pound shortstop played in 112 games between both organizations' Southern League affiliates, hitting a combined .220/.321/.441 with 10 doubles, seven triples, 21 homeruns, and 16 stolen bases. His overall production, according to Baseball Prospectus' *Deserved Runs Created Plus*, topped the league average threshold by roughly 6%.

Snippet from The 2018 Prospect Digest Handbook: Despite tapping into his potential as an offensive-minded shortstop, not everything's rosy for the Bahamas-native. Fellow southpaws chewed him up and spit out last season, holding him to a lowly .218/.258/.412 mark (vs. the .291/.354/.549 showing against RHP). And this is the third straight season in which he's severely struggled against southpaws. Chisholm contact rates – or lack thereof – are beyond concerning; he posted a 31.2% K-rate during his first go-round in Low Class A and only improved that number barely in his return (28.4%); and he fanned in nearly one-third of his California League PAs too. As easy as it is to buy into the hype, the breaks needed be pumped here – at least until he solves those two issues.

Scouting Report: Consider the following:

- Since 2006, there have been nineteen different 21-year-old hitters to post a DRC+ total between 100 and 110 in the Southern League (min. 300 PA) in a season. Yorman Rodriguez, Taylor Trammell, a current Padres top prospect, and Trent Grisham, whom the Padres just acquired, own the second, third, and fourth highest strikeout rates among the group (23.3%, 22.6%, and 21.5%, respectively). Chisholm sports the worst – by a mile – with his 32.1% whiff rate.

Continuing:

- Using the same parameters for all three Class AA leagues, only two 21-year-old hitters with a DRC+ between 100 and 110 have fanned in more than 30% of their plate appearances: Chisholm and Willy Garcia.

Now, to be completely fair, Chisholm looked completely rejuvenated in his 98-game stint in the Marlins system. But the facts are clear as day, still: he can't hit left-handed pitching and he's fanning way too frequently. And on top of that this is the exact type of trade that the Marlins whiffed on – punned intended – by trading Yelich for a package of volatile prospects. Chisholm owns an intriguing power / speed blend not often seen at shortstop. And the Marlins' development engine has been tremendous strides in the past year in terms of player development, so that adds a layer of hope. A potential saving grace: Chisholm's average exit velocity was a stout 91 mph with a peak of 108 mph. Boom or Bust. Go Big, or Go Home.

Ceiling: 4.0-win player
Risk: Moderate to High
MLB ETA: 2020

5. Jesus Sanchez, RF

	Hit	Power	SB	Patience	Glove	Overall
	50	45/55	35	50	50+	50

Born: 10/07/97	Age: 22	Bats: L
Height: 6-3	Weight: 230	Throws: R

YEAR	LVL	PA	1B	2B	3B	HR	SB	CS	AVG	OBP	SLG	BB%	K%	GB%	LD%	FB%
2018	A+	378	72	24	2	10	6	3	0.301	0.331	0.462	3.97%	18.78%	51.4	17.9	24.5
2019	AA	316	59	11	1	8	5	4	0.275	0.332	0.404	7.59%	20.57%	48.4	22.7	22.2
2019	AAA	71	9	2	1	1	0	0	0.206	0.282	0.317	8.45%	28.17%	63.6	18.2	18.2
2019	AAA	78	11	1	0	4	0	0	0.246	0.338	0.446	11.54%	19.23%	48.0	14.0	30.0

Background: With the new regime in place, the Marlins have been incredibly active on the trade market by adding a bevy of fresh blood to the organization in the likes of Sixto Sanchez, Jazz Chisholm, Lewin Diaz, Monte Harrison, Jordan Yamamoto, Isan Diaz, Lewis Brinson, and – of course – right fielder Jesus Sanchez.

Born in Higuey, Dominican Republic, Sanchez spent the first four-and-a-half years of his professional career grinding through the Rays' system. Miami acquired the well-built 6-foot-3, 230-pound slugger, along with hard-throwing right-hander Ryne Stanek, for right-handers Trevor Richards and Nick Anderson. Sanchez split last season between Class AA and Class AAA, batting an aggregate .260/.325/.398 with 14 doubles, two triples, and 13 homeruns.

Snippet from The 2018 Prospect Digest Handbook: The tools are in place to become an above-average big league outfielder, but, again, similarly performing players haven't fared well in the big leagues.

Scouting Report: So let's take a look at Sanchez's performance in Class AA last season. Consider the following:

- Since 2006, only three 21-year-old hitters have met the following criteria in the Southern League (min. 300 PA): 117 to 127 DRC+; a walk rate between 6% and 8%; and a strikeout rate between 17% and 21%. Those three hitters: Alex Kirilloff, one of the best prospects in baseball; Dustin Peterson, and – of course – Jesus Sanchez.

The power's taking a bit longer to develop, but there's thunder in the bat – something along the lines of 20 to 25 homeruns in a season. The contact rates are solid. The defense is above-average. And the lefty-swinging outfielder isn't showing any problematic platoon splits. Sanchez may not develop into a full-blown star, but he's set to become a reliable, above-average right fielder for many, many years to come. In terms of offensive ceiling, think Corey Seager's 2019 campaign in which he batted .272/.335/.483. One more final thought: per FanGraphs' data, Sanchez's batted ball data was near the top last season as his average exit velocity was 92 mph with a peak of 111 mph.

Ceiling: 3.0-win player
Risk: Moderate
MLB ETA: 2020

6. Lewin Diaz, 1B

	Hit	Power	SB	Patience	Glove	Overall
	50	55+	30	50	50	50

Born: 11/19/96	Age: 23	Bats: L
Height: 6-4	Weight: 225	Throws: L

YEAR	LVL	PA	1B	2B	3B	HR	SB	CS	AVG	OBP	SLG	BB%	K%	GB%	LD%	FB%
2017	A	508	90	33	1	12	2	1	0.292	0.329	0.444	4.92%	15.75%	35.5	14.6	40.3
2018	A+	310	46	11	3	6	1	0	0.224	0.255	0.344	3.23%	18.06%	34.0	20.7	32.0
2019	A+	234	37	11	1	13	0	0	0.290	0.333	0.533	5.98%	17.09%	36.5	15.2	38.8
2019	AA	129	9	6	0	8	0	1	0.200	0.279	0.461	8.53%	21.71%	34.9	16.3	40.7
2019	AA	138	15	16	1	6	0	0	0.302	0.341	0.587	5.80%	16.67%	30.2	20.8	44.3

Background: Oh, just another one of the many new, fresh faces added to the organization's resurgent – and emerging – farm system. Miami acquired the middle-of-the-lineup thumper for hard-throwing right-hander Chris Vallimont, veteran reliever Sergio Romo, and a player to be named later. Diaz, a well-built 6-foot-4, 225-pound first

baseman, rebounded after a terrible 2018 campaign in which he batted a lowly .224/.255/.344 in High Class A. He opened up last season back in the Florida State League. And the results were significantly improved. He slugged .290/.333/.533 with 57 games. Minnesota bounced him up to the Southern League and he hit .302/.341/.587 in 33 games before the trade. Diaz's numbers took a noticeable dive after he slid into the Marlins' system. And he finished the year with an aggregate .270/.321/.530 with 33 doubles, two triples, and a career best 27 homeruns.

Scouting Report: The young first baseman shows an intriguing blend of plus-power potential and strong contact rates. He struggled a bit against left-handers for the first time in his career last season, so a strong bounce back is incredibly likely. And he's surprisingly adapt at spraying the ball around the field. There's a reasonable chance that he repeats his minor league line last season – .270/.321/.530 – at the big league level during his peak. If he's promoted up to The Show in the early part of the 2020 season, Diaz could be a dark horse candidate for the Rookie of the Year.

Ceiling: 3.0-win player
Risk: Moderate
MLB ETA: 2020

7. Braxton Garrett, LHP

	FB	CB	CH	Command	Overall
	50	55	55	50/55	50

Born: 08/05/97	Age: 22	Bats: L	Top CALs:
Height: 6-3	Weight: 190	Throws: L	

YEAR	LVL	IP	W	L	SV	ERA	FIP	WHIP	K/9	K%	BB/9	BB%	K/BB	HR9	BABIP
2017	A	15.3	1	0	0	2.93	5.16	1.24	9.4	24.62%	3.5	9.23%	2.67	1.76	0.250
2019	A+	105.0	6	6	0	3.34	3.72	1.23	10.1	26.94%	3.2	8.45%	3.19	1.11	0.294
2019	AA	1.7	0	1	0	16.20	7.49	4.20	5.4	7.69%	16.2	23.08%	0.33	0.00	0.444

Background: The second prep arm taken in the opening round of the 2016 draft – and second southpaw – Garrett was viewed one of the safer arms available in the class, offering up a strong feel for his offspeed pitches and oozing pitchability. But after a brief four-game stint in the South Atlantic League in 2017 – he tossed just 15.1 innings – the 6-foot-3, 190-pound left-hander succumbed to elbow woes and eventually hit the operating table for Tommy John surgery. He missed the remainder of 2017 season and the entire 2018 season. Finally healthy, Garrett spent the majority of last season working out of the Jupiter Hammerheads' rotation. In 20 starts, the lefty fanned 118 and walked just 37 in 105.0 innings of work. He compiled a 3.34 ERA and a 4.85 DRA (Deserved Runs Average). Garrett also made one disastrous start in the Southern League at the end of the year.

Snippet from The 2018 Prospect Digest Handbook: During his first three starts with the Greensboro Grasshoppers two years ago Garrett was practically unhittable, posted an 11-to-6 strikeout-to-walk ratio while surrendering one earned run in 13.2 innings of work. Garrett did make it back to the mound for the Fall Instructional League. His fastball, an above-average 90- to 92-mph offering, showed some life; his 12-6 curveball was a hammer to be reckoned with, buckling quite a few knees, and his changeup looked average. Despite making just a few appearances two years ago a move up to High Class A by mid-2019 isn't out of the question. Garrett looks like a better version of Trevor Rogers.

Scouting Report: Garrett looked like the prototypical crafty lefty in his return from injury. His fastball continued to sit in the low-90s. His curveball didn't look quite as sharp as years past, though it's still an above-average offering. And his changeup looked better than advertised. Ignoring Braxton's first three starts of the year – due to his long layoff and injury – and his final three starts of the year, where he was clearly tiring, the big southpaw tallied an impressive 91-to-31 strikeout-to-walk ratio in 82.0 innings. He looks like a nice, solid #4-type arm – a league average starting pitcher to help fill out a club's rotation.

Ceiling: 2.5-win player
Risk: Moderate
MLB ETA: 2021

8. Trevor Rogers, LHP

	FB	CB	SL	CH	Command	Overall
	50	50	55	50	55/60	50

Born: 11/13/97	Age: 22	Bats: L
Height: 6-6	Weight: 185	Throws: L

YEAR	LVL	IP	W	L	SV	ERA	FIP	WHIP	K/9	K%	BB/9	BB%	K/BB	HR9	BABIP
2018	A	72.7	2	7	0	5.82	3.03	1.56	10.5	25.99%	3.3	8.26%	3.15	0.50	0.394
2019	A+	110.3	5	8	0	2.53	2.73	1.10	10.0	26.75%	2.0	5.26%	5.08	0.57	0.303
2019	AA	26.0	1	2	0	4.50	3.79	1.31	9.7	25.23%	3.1	8.11%	3.11	1.04	0.314

Background: Taken in between a couple other prep stars – flame-throwing right-hander Shane Baz and sweet-and-sour swinging first baseman Nick Pratto – with the 13th overall pick; Rogers signed for a hefty $3.4 million. The 6-foot-6, 185-pound southpaw wouldn't make his debut until the following season. In 17 starts with the Greensboro Grasshoppers, the Carlsbad High School product posted a promising an 85-to-27 strikeout-to-walk ratio in 72.2 innings of work. Rogers opened up last season with 18 strong starts with the Hammerheads, fanning 122 and walking just 24 in 110.1 innings of work. He capped off his sophomore season with five starts in the minors' toughest level, Class AA. In total, Rogers tossed a 136.1 innings of work, tallying a 150 punch outs and just 33 walks to go along with a 2.90 ERA.

Snippet from The 2018 Prospect Digest Handbook: Rogers handled the club's aggressive promotion up to the South Atlantic League reasonably well, showcasing the ability to miss a lot of bats while keeping the ball around the plate. He's never going to ascend up to true ace status, but he has the potential to be a rock solid mid-rotation caliber arm.

Scouting Report: The fastball velocity's backed up – so much so, in fact, I caught more of Rogers' starts than any other pitcher in the minor leagues last season because, well, I couldn't believe it. Last season it lacked the same type of life he showed the previous year; it was sitting in the upper 80s and would kiss 90 mph on occasion. He complements the average offering with a variety of breaking pitches: an above-average slider that he will vary the break on, sometimes showing it as a true slider and other times it acts as more of a traditional cutter; and he'll throw a fringy curveball. Rogers will also mix in a respectable, average-ish changeup. His large wingspan, long limbs, and pinpoint accuracy allow his repertoire to play up. Equipped with a better fastball two years ago Rogers looked like a #3-type arm. Now, though, he's been downgraded into #4 / #5 territory. With respect to his work in High Class A last season, consider the following:

- Since 2006, here's the list of 21-year-old pitchers to fan between 26% and 28% the hitters they faced in the Florida State League (min. 100 IP): Touki Toussaint, Adonis Medina, Braxton Garrett, and Trevor Rogers.

A few final thoughts: Rogers owned – by far – the best walk percentage among the group, as well as showcasing the lowest graded fastball.

Ceiling: 2.5-win player
Risk: Moderate
MLB ETA: 2020/2021

9. Kameron Misner, CF

	Hit	Power	SB	Patience	Glove	Overall
	50/55	50	60	55	55	50

Born: 01/08/98	Age: 22	Bats: L
Height: 6-4	Weight: 219	Throws: L

YEAR	LVL	PA	1B	2B	3B	HR	SB	CS	AVG	OBP	SLG	BB%	K%	GB%	LD%	FB%
2019	Rk	38	5	2	0	0	3	0	0.241	0.421	0.310	23.68%	18.42%	31.8	22.7	40.9
2019	A	158	28	7	0	2	8	0	0.276	0.380	0.373	13.29%	22.15%	39.4	22.3	30.9

Background: A decorated two-way prospect coming out of Poplar Bluff High School. Misner, a 6-foot-4, 219-pound first baseman / centerfielder, was ranked by Perfect Game as the third best prospect – and top outfielder – in the state of Missouri. Misner slugged a robust .422 with eight doubles, nine triples, and eight homeruns with a whopping 29 stolen bases during his senior season. And he also posted a tidy 2.13 ERA across 32.0 innings on the mound, striking out a team-leading 48 hitters. The Kansas City Royals took a late round flier on the Missouri-native as well. A three-year starter for long time Head Coach Tim Jamieson, Misner earned Freshman All-American honors after batting a hearty .282/.360/.446 with 12 doubles, one triple, and seven homeruns to go along with 17 stolen bases (in 23 attempts). He spent the ensuing summer dominating the New England Collegiate League, hitting a scorching .378/.479/.652 with 13 doubles and eight homeruns for the Newport Gulls. Misner's production jumped up into another stratosphere during his sophomore campaign, but a foot injury knocked him out of the club's final 22 contests. He finished the year with a Ruthian .360/.497/.576 with nine doubles, three triples, and a four homeruns in only 34 games. Last season Misner's production has backed up a touch: the tools-laden first baseman/outfielder hit a solid .286/.440/.481 with 20 extra-base hits (10 doubles and 10 homeruns) while swiping 20 bags against just one caught stealing. Miami drafted Misner in the back up the first round, 35th overall, and sent him to the Midwest League after a quick detour in rookie ball. In 34 games with Clinton, Misner batted .276/.380/.373 with seven doubles and pair of homeruns while going a perfect 8-for-8 in the stolen base department.

Scouting Report: Per the usual, here's what I wrote about him prior to the draft last season:

"With respect to his breakout, injury-shortened 2018 campaign, consider the following:

- *Between 2011 and 2018, only five SEC hitters slugged at least .350/.475/.550 in a season (min. 150 PA): Andrew Benintendi, Jonathan India, Mikie Mahtook, Brent Rooker, and – of course – Kameron Misner. Benintendi, India, Mahtook, and Rooker were all taken in the opening round.*

So know let's take a look at his work thus far in 2019. Consider the following:

- *Between 2011 and 2018, only one other SEC hitter posted a 20% walk rate with a strikeout rate north of 18% (min. 250 PA): University of Florida slugger, and fifth overall pick in 2018, Jonathan India.*

Consider the following:

Player	Age	Year	PA	AVG	OBP	SLG	K%	BB%
Kameron Misner	21	2019	262	0.287	0.443	0.485	21.40%	20.60%
Jonathan India	21	2018	300	0.350	0.497	0.717	18.70%	20.00%

Obviously, India's overall production dwarfs Misner's numbers this season. The University of Missouri star has loud, loud tools: above-average power potential, above-average speed, and a phenomenal eye at the plate. The hit tool, though, is questionable. Misner took some important strides during his sophomore season – he cut his punch out rate down to 16.3% – but the progress has been undone this season. If he can stick in center field, he's an above-average – albeit risky – starting outfielder. He has a lot of Bradley Zimmer in him."

Ceiling: 2.0-win player
Risk: Moderate
MLB ETA: 2021

10. Jorge Guzman, RHP

	FB	SL	CH	Command	Overall
	80	60	40	40	50

Born: 01/28/96	**Age:** 24	**Bats:** R
Height: 6-2	**Weight:** 182	**Throws:** R

YEAR	LVL	IP	W	L	SV	ERA	FIP	WHIP	K/9	K%	BB/9	BB%	K/BB	HR9	BABIP
2017	A-	66.7	5	3	0	2.30	2.47	1.04	11.9	33.46%	2.4	6.84%	4.89	0.54	0.311
2018	A+	96.0	0	9	0	4.03	4.44	1.54	9.5	23.54%	6.0	14.92%	1.58	0.66	0.303
2019	AA	138.7	7	11	0	3.50	4.37	1.20	8.2	22.60%	4.6	12.63%	1.79	0.84	0.241

Background: Equipped with a blistering fastball that ranks among the best in all of professional baseball. Miami acquired the talented, though sometimes erratic, righty in the Giancarlo Stanton money dump with the New York Yankees on December 11th, 2017. Guzman, a native of Las Matas de Santa Cruz, Dominican Republic, made the leap from the New York-Penn League to High Class A two years ago. And the results were…interesting. Throwing 96.0 innings across 21 starts for the Jupiter Hammerheads, the broad-shoulder hurler tallied a 4.03 ERA despite walking 64 hitters – or an average of 6.0 walks every nine innings. Guzman spent last season in the minors' toughest challenge, Class AA, and showed some progress in terms of locating the strike zone. In a career best 138.2 innings of work, he fanned 127 and walked 71 to go along with a 3.50 ERA and a 4.16 DRA (Deserved Runs Average).

Snippet from The 2018 Prospect Digest Handbook: He's very likely to end up as a late-inning power arm. But there's the potential to be an upper-rotation-caliber arm if the control bumps up to even slightly below-average – but I wouldn't count on that happening.

Scouting Report: An easy 80-grade fastball that looks effortless. The Marlins' player development engine saw several players take major strides in 2019, but Guzman honing in on the strike zone more frequently ranks near the top of the list. His slider is a devastating secondary weapon that haunts hitters' nightmares. But at this point he is what he is. And that's a potential late-inning, high leverage, mow-'em-down reliever masquerading as a starting pitcher. His lack of control / command and a third pitch have all but made it official. The Marlins just haven't made the move – yet. He could be the rare reliever that tallies more two wins above replacement – a sort of Dellin Betances type arm.

Ceiling: 2.0-win player
Risk: Moderate
MLB ETA: 2020

11. Peyton Burdick, LF

	Hit	Power	SB	Patience	Glove	Overall
	50	55/60	35	55	50+	50

Born: 02/26/97	**Age:** 23	**Bats:** R	**Top CALs:**
Height: 6-0	**Weight:** 210	**Throws:** R	

YEAR	LVL	PA	1B	2B	3B	HR	SB	CS	AVG	OBP	SLG	BB%	K%	GB%	LD%	FB%
2019	A-	25	5	0	1	1	1	1	0.318	0.400	0.545	8.00%	20.00%	58.8	17.6	23.5
2019	A	288	40	20	3	10	6	6	0.307	0.408	0.542	11.11%	23.26%	39.2	14.0	38.0

Background: A middle-of-the-lineup masher for the duration of his three-year career at Wright State. Burdick, a thick 6-foot, 210-pound corner outfielder, turned in a solid campaign as a true freshman for the Raiders when he slugged .289/.409/.443 with 14 doubles, two triples, and four homeruns. The Batavia, Ohio, native missed the entire following season, 2017, but came roaring back as a redshirt sophomore: he batted a hearty .347/.437/.569 with 19 doubles, two triples, and nine homeruns while earning an invitation to the prestigious Cape Cod League. In 38 games with the Cotuit Kettleers, Burdick hit a respectable .252/.351/.435 with 10 extra-base hits. Last season, Burdick capped off a wildly successful career by hearing his name called in the third round after slashing .407/.538/.729 with 18 doubles, three triples, and 15 homeruns. The hulking left fielder ripped through the New York-Penn League for six games before settling in for 63 games with the Clinton LumberKings. In total, he batted .308/.407/.542 with 20 doubles, four triples, and 11 homeruns. His overall production with the LumberKings, according to Baseball Prospectus' *Deserved Runs Created Plus*, topped the league average mark by a whopping 64%.

Scouting Report: Consider the following:

- Since 2006, only three 22-year-old hitters met the following criteria in the Midwest League (min. 250 PA): at least a 160 DRC+, a double-digit walk rate, and a strikeout rate between 23% and 25%. Those two hitters: Ian Gac and – of course – Peyton Burdick, the former Wright State masher.

Burdick could prove to be one of the bigger steals of last year's draft class. The power's incredible, potentially peaking as a plus in-game tool. Solid peripherals and glove in left field. There's a chance that the Marlins may have unearthed a league average starter in the third round.

Ceiling: 2.0-win player
Risk: Moderate
MLB ETA: 2021/2022

12. Nick Neidert, RHP

FB	CB	CH	Command	Overall
45	50	65	55	45

Born: 11/20/96	Age: 23	Bats: R
Height: 6-1	Weight: 202	Throws: R

YEAR	LVL	IP	W	L	SV	ERA	FIP	WHIP	K/9	K%	BB/9	BB%	K/BB	HR9	BABIP
2017	A+	104.3	10	3	0	2.76	3.39	1.07	9.4	26.14%	1.5	4.08%	6.41	0.60	0.318
2017	AA	23.3	1	3	0	6.56	5.20	1.63	5.0	12.04%	1.9	4.63%	2.60	1.54	0.341
2018	AA	152.7	12	7	0	3.24	3.48	1.13	9.1	25.20%	1.8	5.07%	4.97	1.00	0.309
2019	Rk	3.7	0	0	0	0.00	2.68	0.82	7.4	21.43%	2.5	7.14%	3.00	0.00	0.200
2019	A+	9.3	0	1	0	4.82	5.02	1.50	5.8	14.29%	3.9	9.52%	1.50	0.96	0.300
2019	AAA	41.0	3	4	0	5.05	5.01	1.63	8.1	19.79%	4.8	11.76%	1.68	0.88	0.336

Background: It was a rather trying season for the former second round selection. Neidert, whom I listed among the club's better prospects heading into last season, looked like he was on the precipice of joining the Marlins at some point early in 2020. Disappointment and then disaster struck. The 6-foot-1, 202-pound righty struggled early in the offensive-minded environment in the Pacific Coast League and then hit the disabled list for three months to repair a torn meniscus in his knee. Neidert, who was acquired from the Mariners in the Dee Gordon swap, made a couple low level stops on his rehab tour before making it back the PCL in early August for six final starts. His final Class AAA line for the year: nine starts, 41.0 innings, 37 strikeouts, 22 walks, a 5.05 ERA, and a 5.70 DRA.

Snippet from The 2018 Prospect Digest Handbook: Arguably my favorite pitcher to watch/scout in all the minor leagues. Neidert – despite the gaudy strikeout numbers – is far from a "rear-back and throw by 'em" type of arm. He's a thinking man's pitcher. His fastball's fringe average – and that's being kind – and his curveball looks like it's destined to be a quality breaking ball for a high school arm. But his changeup... Well, it's one helluva swing-and-miss, Bugs Bunny twirl 'em in the ground pitch.

Scouting Report: The fastball backed up even more last season, going from the upper-80s, maybe a tick or two higher, to disappointing 86 mph. The curveball's still questionably fringy. But, damn, that changeup is the type to make you stop, pause, and take note. It's so good, in fact, that it gave his fastball the appearance of a mid-90s offering to several Class AAA hitters. The control / command backed up considerably last season, but given his *lengthy* track record of pinpoint accuracy its likely going to prove to be nothing more than an injury-related blimp. I was too optimistic about his ceiling as a mid-rotation caliber arm. But he could pitch in a Josh Tomlin-type role for a decade.

Ceiling: 1.5-win player
Risk: Low to Moderate
MLB ETA: 2020

13. Osiris Johnson, SS

Hit	Power	SB	Patience	Glove	Overall
40/50	40/45	40	35	50	45

Born: 10/18/00	Age: 19	Bats: R
Height: 6-0	Weight: 181	Throws: R

YEAR	LVL	PA	1B	2B	3B	HR	SB	CS	AVG	OBP	SLG	BB%	K%	GB%	LD%	FB%
2018	RK	111	20	8	2	1	7	2	0.301	0.333	0.447	3.60%	17.12%	40.7	17.4	31.4
2018	A	88	11	3	0	2	0	2	0.188	0.205	0.294	1.14%	38.64%	46.2	13.5	34.6

Background: Fun Fact: the young shortstop's alma mater, Encinal High School in Alameda, California, has churned out a couple of All-Star performers – one of which will be a Hall of Famer – in Jimmy Rollins and Dontrelle Willis. Johnson, who was taken in the second round of the 2018 draft, turned in an impressive debut showing in the Gulf Coast League when he slugged .301/.333/.447 before stumbling – mightily – in Low Class A. Johnson, whose father Marcel was a late round pick by the Mets in 1989, missed the entire 2019 season due to injury: he needed a surgical procedure to repair a right tibial stress fracture.

Snippet from The 2018 Prospect Digest Handbook: Viewed as an offensive-minded shortstop, Johnson shows surprising power potential with impressive bat speed. His swing looks long and robotic; something that will undoubtedly need to be corrected. And I think he's going to continue to battle contact issues as he moves up the ladder, a la his work in the Sally. And it's also not a great sign that he walked just five times in 199 plate appearances.

Scouting Report: There's virtually nothing new to report on because of the injury. But it does bode well for Johnson's future prospects that the Marlins' player development team has had several players take tremendous strides in the last 12 months.

Ceiling: 1.5- to 2.0-win player
Risk: Moderate to High
MLB ETA: 2023

14. Monte Harrison, CF

	Hit	Power	SB	Patience	Glove	Overall
	45	50	60	50	50	45

Born: 08/10/95	Age: 24	Bats: R
Height: 6-3	Weight: 220	Throws: R

YEAR	LVL	PA	1B	2B	3B	HR	SB	CS	AVG	OBP	SLG	BB%	K%	GB%	LD%	FB%
2017	A	261	35	12	1	11	11	3	0.265	0.359	0.475	11.11%	26.82%	47.1	18.5	26.8
2017	A+	252	37	16	1	10	16	1	0.278	0.341	0.487	5.56%	27.38%	46.0	26.7	23.6
2018	AA	583	83	20	3	19	28	9	0.240	0.316	0.399	7.55%	36.88%	51.0	16.5	25.5
2019	AAA	244	41	7	2	9	20	2	0.274	0.357	0.451	10.25%	29.92%	53.8	24.5	18.2

Background: Taken near the top of the second round of the 2014 draft by the Milwaukee Brewers. Harrison, a 6-foot-3, 220-pound center fielder, hails from Lee's Summit West High School – which has produced two other former minor leagues: Matt Fultz and Ryan Hafner. Viewed as a key cog in the return in the Christian Yelich swap, Harrison promptly fell flat on his face as he moved into the Southern League during his first season in the Marlins' organization; he hit a lowly .240/.316/.399 with 20 doubles, three triples, and 19 homeruns in 136 games with the Jacksonville Jumbo Shrimp. Last season, in a bit of a surprising move, the front office promoted the toolsy outfielder up to the hitter-friendly confines of the Pacific Coast League. And, of course, Harrison's production came roaring back. In an injury-shortened campaign, he batted a respectable .270/.357/.451 with seven doubles, two triples, and nine homeruns to go along with 20 stolen bases in only 22 attempts. His overall production, according to *Deserved Runs Created Plus*, was 6% *below* the league average mark.

Snippet from The 2018 Prospect Digest Handbook: He's always battled contact issues, though they were exasperated by the minors' most challenging pitching. Harrison does offer up the always-sought-after combination of power-speed and he plays a solid center field. But at this point, he looks like a fourth outfielder.

Scouting Report: An enigma of sorts. Harrison's always flashed some drool-inducing skills throughout his career. At various stints he's shown a tremendously patient approach at the plate. He's shown incredible efficiency as a base stealer. He can handle center field well. And, of course, there's the power. But here's the thing with him: he's only topped the league average production line in just one season since 2016. Harrison posted a 78 DRC+ total in the Midwest League four years ago; he shined in his return to the level, as well as a second half promotion to High Class A the following season; and he's tallied a 96 and 94 DRC+ in Class AA and Class AAA the past two seasons. Throw in a strikeout rate that seems to hover around 30% and it doesn't paint a rosey picture for his future big league value. Miami's still a year or two away from taking a leap forward, so Harrison will likely get an extended look to prove himself. But his ceiling looks like a .240/.290/.430 type hitter.

Ceiling: 1.5-win player
Risk: Moderate
MLB ETA: 2020

15. Connor Scott, CF

Hit	Power	SB	Patience	Glove	Overall
40/45	35/45	50	50	50	45

Born: 10/08/99	Age: 20	Bats: L
Height: 6-4	Weight: 180	Throws: L

YEAR	LVL	PA	1B	2B	3B	HR	SB	CS	AVG	OBP	SLG	BB%	K%	GB%	LD%	FB%
2018	RK	119	18	1	4	0	8	5	0.223	0.319	0.311	11.76%	24.37%	48.0	20.0	21.3
2018	A	89	13	2	0	1	1	3	0.211	0.295	0.276	11.24%	30.34%	55.8	17.3	23.1
2019	A	413	63	24	4	4	21	9	0.251	0.311	0.368	7.51%	22.03%	49.7	16.0	29.2
2019	A+	111	17	4	1	1	2	1	0.235	0.306	0.327	9.91%	23.42%	43.2	18.9	27.0

Background: Looking back at the opening round of the 2018 draft and it is crystal clear – at least now – the level of impact talent available throughout, especially beyond the top 10 picks. Grayson Rodriguez looks like a future ace. Logan Gilbert is quickly approach big league-readiness. Jordan Groshans, Matthew Liberatore, Jordyn Adams, Nolan Gorman, Bryce Turang, Triston Casas, Bo Naylor, Xavier Edward, and Ethan Hankins all looked strong in their first taste of the full season action. That's not including the likes of Nico Hoerner, Ryan Rolison, Seth Beer, Shane McClanahan, and Kris Bubic. And then there's Connor Scott, who was drafted between Groshans and Gilbert with the 13th overall pick. A product of H.B. Plant High School, which has produced the likes of Pete Alonso, Wade Boggs, John Hudek, and Kyle and Preston Tucker. Scott looked terrible during his debut as he batted a combined .218/.309/.296 between the Gulf Coast and South Atlantic Leagues. Last season the 6-foot-4, 180-pound center fielder split time between a return to Clinton and a promotion to Jupiter. In 122 games he batted .248/.310/.359 with 28 doubles, five triples, and five homers with 23 stolen bases.

Snippet from The 2018 Prospect Digest Handbook: Despite the offensive issues, Scott shows the potential to develop an above-average, spray-it-all-fields hit tool. He has some natural loft to his swing, but the power likely won't come for another year or two. Plus-speed. Solid defender.

Scouting Report: Despite a couple seasons of underwhelming production, it's not quite all doom-and-gloom for the former first rounder. After a slow start with the Clinton LumberKings at the beginning of 2019, the young center fielder's bat warmed up over his last 77 games in Low Class A he batted .279/.337/.397. And after another slow start in the Florida State League (he hit .203/.293/.297 in his first 18 games), but rebounded to bat .294/.333/.382 over his final nine contests. The power's still coming. But he's profiling more like a fourth outfielder at this point. And the Marlins will likely continue to aggressively push him through the system, which might not be the right move either.

Ceiling: 1.5-win player
Risk: Moderate
MLB ETA: 2020

16. Victor Mesa Jr., CF

Hit	Power	SB	Patience	Glove	Overall
45/50	40	40	50	50	45

Born: 09/08/01	Age: 18	Bats: L
Height: 5-11	Weight: 175	Throws: L

YEAR	LVL	PA	1B	2B	3B	HR	SB	CS	AVG	OBP	SLG	BB%	K%	GB%	LD%	FB%
2019	Rk	207	36	9	4	1	7	4	0.284	0.366	0.398	11.59%	14.01%	44.7	20.4	27.0

Background: The young, fresh faced teenager played second fiddle to the other Cuban import the organization signed last offseason – his brother, Victor Victor Mesa, who signed with the Marlins for a $5.25 million. The younger Mesa, on the other hand, settled for a $1 million deal. Standing a wiry 5-foot-11 and 175 pounds, Mesa The Younger made his anticipated debut in the Gulf Coast League last season. In 47 games, he batted a respectable .284/.366/.398 with nine doubles, four triples, and one homerun. Following the conclusion of the season Mesa Jr. was recognized as the squad's Gulf Coast League Most Valuable Player. His overall production, according to *DRC+*, topped the league average threshold by 16%.

Scouting Report: Consider the following:

- Since 2006, here's the list of 17-year-old hitters to post a DRC+ between 110 and 120 with a double-digit walk rate and a whiff rate below 20% in the Gulf Coast League (min. 150 PA): Ramon Flores and Victor Mesa Jr.

Strong wrists but a slapper's mentality at the plate. Mesa Jr.'s not projected to offer up a whole lot of pop – though he should settle in with eight- to 10-homeruns. He's quick, but not fast. The teenage outfielder shows good bat control with the chance to develop an above-average hit tool. The batting average will likely need to carry him to The Show. He looks like a fourth outfielder type.

Ceiling: 1.5-win player
Risk: Moderate
MLB ETA: 2023

Miami Marlins

17. Tristan Pompey, LF

Hit	Power	SB	Patience	Glove	Overall
50	45	40	60	50	45

Born: 03/23/97	Age: 23	Bats: B
Height: 6-4	Weight: 240	Throws: R

YEAR	LVL	PA	1B	2B	3B	HR	SB	CS	AVG	OBP	SLG	BB%	K%	GB%	LD%	FB%
2018	RK	15	3	0	0	0	1	1	0.250	0.400	0.250	20.00%	26.67%	62.5	37.5	0.0
2018	A	103	21	4	0	2	5	3	0.314	0.422	0.430	15.53%	21.36%	56.9	21.5	20.0
2018	A+	101	19	5	0	1	4	1	0.291	0.396	0.384	12.87%	20.79%	46.2	24.6	21.5
2019	Rk	4	1	0	0	0	0	1	0.333	0.500	0.333	25.00%	25.00%	100.0	0.0	0.0
2019	A+	166	19	7	2	0	4	0	0.194	0.295	0.271	12.05%	34.94%	51.7	24.1	18.4

Background: Viewed a safe, low risk, high floor bat with the potential to move quickly through the minor leagues coming out of the University of Kentucky. Pompey, a third round pick two years ago, finished his collegiate career with a .321/.426/.521 triple-slash line. The 6-foot-4, 240-pound corner outfielder blitzed through the Gulf Coast League, Low Class A, and High Class A during his debut, hitting an aggregate .299/.408/.397 with nine doubles, three triples, and 10 stolen bases. Last season, though, was more or less a lost year for Pompey. After just eight games in the Florida State League, he hit the disabled list with a foot injury and wouldn't return until the end of June. And once he was healthy, Pompey looked...terrible. He batted .203/.296/.297 over his final 34 games.

Snippet from The 2018 Prospect Digest Handbook: Pompey looks like a second/third round talent with the ceiling of a fringe big league regular. He could improve his stock if he proves to be an above-average defender in left field or by playing a passable center field.

Scouting Report: Everything went to hell for Pompey last season. A fractured foot limited him to just 42 games in High Class A; his swing-and-miss rate spiked to epic proportions (34.9%); and, frankly, he couldn't hit his way out of brown paper bag. And, now, once-viewed a fast-moving hitter, Pompey's entering his age-23 season with just 66 games above High Class A. It wouldn't be surprising to see the front office push him up to Class AA to start the 2020 season in an effort to make up for lost time. Pompey looks like a poor man's Michael Brantley.

Ceiling: 1.5-win player
Risk: Moderate
MLB ETA: 2021/2022

18. Jose Devers, 2B/SS

Hit	Power	SB	Patience	Glove	Overall
55	20/30	50	50	50	40

Born: 12/07/99	Age: 20	Bats: L
Height: 6-0	Weight: 155	Throws: R

YEAR	LVL	PA	1B	2B	3B	HR	SB	CS	AVG	OBP	SLG	BB%	K%	GB%	LD%	FB%
2017	RK	47	8	2	1	0	1	0	0.239	0.255	0.326	0.00%	34.04%	53.3	6.7	26.7
2017	RK	169	24	7	2	1	15	3	0.246	0.359	0.348	10.65%	12.43%	43.4	14.8	30.3
2018	A	362	76	12	4	0	13	6	0.273	0.313	0.332	4.14%	13.54%	61.8	14.8	14.7
2018	A+	9	2	0	0	0	0	0	0.250	0.333	0.250	11.11%	0.00%	75.0	12.5	0.0
2019	Rk	46	7	3	1	0	3	1	0.275	0.370	0.400	8.70%	8.70%	36.1	22.2	19.4
2019	A	13	3	2	0	0	0	0	0.455	0.538	0.636	15.38%	15.38%	33.3	44.4	0.0
2019	A+	138	37	3	1	0	5	0	0.325	0.384	0.365	5.80%	14.49%	60.4	23.6	10.4

Background: Part of the return – which was unfairly criticized – for Giancarlo Stanton and his massive contract. Devers, who was acquired along with flame-throwing right-hander Jorge Guzman and veteran infielder Starlin Castro, opened some eyes with a solid performance in the South Atlantic League as an 18-year-old two years ago. In 85 games with the Greensboro Grasshoppers, the wiry infielder batted .273/.313/.332 with 12 doubles and four triples. Per *Deserved Runs Created Plus*, his overall production was 9% below the league average. Last season, in an injury-shortened campaign, the young teenager hit an aggregate .322/.391/.390 with eight doubles and a pair of triples in just 47 games split between rookie ball, Low Class A, and High Class A.

Snippet from The 2018 Prospect Digest Handbook: Devers put the ball on the ground 60% of the time last season, the third worst total in the Sally. With that being said, the teenage prospect shows a better-than-average hit tool and matching speed to go along with a nice glove.

Scouting Report: There's a chance for a plus-hit tool, especially considering his age, production, and level of competition. A lot of Devers' future value comes from his (A) his youth, (B) versatility, and (C) speed. Devers is purely a utility only option moving forward. The power's likely never going to turn into much. He's slugged just one homerun in 187 career games. One more note: his line drive rate spiked, massively, albeit in a short sample size.

Ceiling: 1.0- to 1.5-win player
Risk: Low to Moderate
MLB ETA: 2021/2022

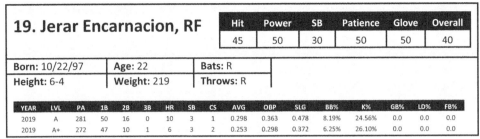

19. Jerar Encarnacion, RF	Hit	Power	SB	Patience	Glove	Overall
	45	50	30	50	50	40

Born: 10/22/97	Age: 22	Bats: R
Height: 6-4	Weight: 219	Throws: R

YEAR	LVL	PA	1B	2B	3B	HR	SB	CS	AVG	OBP	SLG	BB%	K%	GB%	LD%	FB%
2019	A	281	50	16	0	10	3	1	0.298	0.363	0.478	8.19%	24.56%	0.0	0.0	0.0
2019	A+	272	47	10	1	6	3	2	0.253	0.298	0.372	6.25%	26.10%	0.0	0.0	0.0

Background: Signed off the international free agency market at the conclusion of the 2015 season. Encarnacion, a 6-foot-4, 219-pound right fielder, is coming off three – largely – mediocre showings in the lowest levels of the minor leagues. The Dominican outfielder looked abysmal as an 18-year-old in the foreign rookie league four years ago when he batted a lowly .218/.323/.345. His production saw a modest uptick as he moved into the Gulf Coast League in 2017: in 42 games he hit .266/.323/.448 with seven doubles, three triples, and five homeruns. Encarnacion spent the first couple of months of 2018 in the New York-Penn League, slugging a solid .284/.305/.448 with 20 extra-base hits in 43 games. But his production cratered – to epic proportions – the last couple of weeks after he was promoted to the Sally; he went 4-for-54 in 16 games with Greensboro. Back in Low Class A to start last season, Encarnacion put together his finest extended stretch in his pro career as he slugged .298/.363/.478 with 16 doubles and 10 homeruns. He spent the second half of the year in High Class A where he batted .253/.298/.372 in 67 games.

Scouting Report: Encarnacion's always flirted with solid power potential. And last season that in-game thump started showing up on a more consistent basis. The biggest evolution for the young corner outfielder, however, was his ability to make contact more frequently. He fanned in 30.5% of his plate appearances three years ago, and followed that up a 32% whiff rate the next season. Last year, though, Encarnacion posted a K-rate of 24.6% in Low Class A and that number barely moved up during his time in High Class A. He doesn't have a true standout tool, but could serve as a nice bench bat in the coming years.

Ceiling: 1.0- to 1.5-win player
Risk: Moderate
MLB ETA: 2022

20. Victor Victor Mesa, RF	Hit	Power	SB	Patience	Glove	Overall
	35/40	20	40	30	45	40

Born: 07/20/96	Age: 23	Bats: R	Top CALs:
Height: 5-10	Weight: 185	Throws: R	

YEAR	LVL	PA	1B	2B	3B	HR	SB	CS	AVG	OBP	SLG	BB%	K%	GB%	LD%	FB%
2019	A+	390	82	5	3	0	15	2	0.252	0.295	0.283	4.87%	12.31%	60.7	16.0	19.8
2019	AA	113	17	2	0	0	3	0	0.178	0.200	0.196	2.65%	14.16%	64.4	10.0	16.7

Background: The front office bet big on the Mesa brothers last offseason, agreeing to sign Victor Victor Mesa to a deal worth $5.25 million and his younger brother, Victor Mesa Jr., to a pact worth $1 million. The older Mesa turned some heads after parts of six seasons with the Cocodrilos de Matanzas in the Cuban National Series, hitting a combined .275/.334/.38 with 43 doubles, 17 triples, and 10 homeruns in 312 games. The front office sent Mesa to the Florida State League for his debut last season. And in 89 games with the Jupiter Hammerheads, the 5-foot-10, 185-pound center fielder hit a disappointing .252/.295/.283 with just five doubles and three triples and 15 stolen bases in 17 total attempts. His overall production, per *Deserved Runs Created Plus*, was 10% below the league average. Mesa spent the remaining 27 games of the year – looking completely helpless – in the Southern League as he batted .178/.200/.196.

Snippet from The 2018 Prospect Digest Handbook: Physically, Mesa shows a quick, short path to the ball with natural loft that should generate average power at the big league level, though he'll be known more for his gap-to-gap work. He's never going to walk a whole lot; something in the neighborhood of 4.0% to 5.0% should be expected. Scouting reports show that Mesa has the potential to be an above-average defender.

Scouting Report: Consider the following:

- Since 2006, here's the list of 22-year-old hitters to post an 85- to 95- DRC+ total with a sub-5.5% walk rate and a strikeout rate below 16% in the Florida State League (min. 350 PA): Kevin Russo, Michael Bell, Nick Dunn, and – of course – the $5 million, Victor Victor Mesa.

Let's continue:

- Russo, a 20th round pick by the Yankees, eventually made it up to the big leagues for a 54-game cameo in 2010. Bell washed out of affiliated ball a year after his campaign in High Class A. And Dunn, a fifth round pick in 2018, spent last season in High Class A.

Let's be honest: I – and everyone else, for that matter – bought into the Mesa Hype Machine last season. I wasn't as pragmatic as I should have been. He had one strong showing the Cuban National Series when he slugged .354/.399/.539 – but it barely registered a blip on the leader board due to the offense inducing environment. As I suspected, he didn't walk – at all – last season. The power is just as nonexistent. And the defense was close to terrible. And, frankly, he doesn't belong on the club's rejuvenated Top 20 list. But I added him in because (A) I was wrong and wanted to discuss and (B) he's noteworthy enough. He's now entering his age-23 season, and it's clear he's heading down the same path as Rusney Castillo, who signed with the Red Sox for seven years and $72.5 million.

Ceiling: 1.0-win player
Risk: Moderate
MLB ETA: 2021

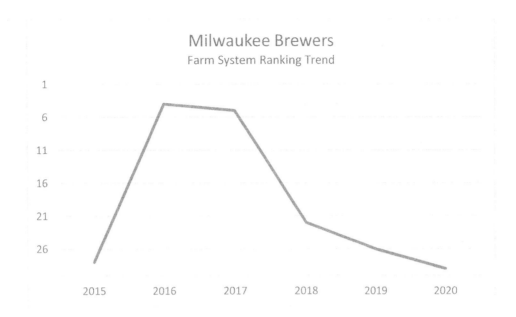

Rank	Name	Age	Pos
1	Brice Turang	20	2B/SS
2	Drew Rasmussen	24	RHP
3	Bowden Francis	24	RHP
4	Ethan Small	23	LHP
5	Aaron Ashby	22	LHP
6	Carlos Rodriguez	19	OF
7	Tristen Lutz	21	OF
8	Mario Feliciano	21	C
9	Antoine Kelly	20	LHP
10	Reese Olson	20	RHP
11	Devin Williams	25	RHP
12	Clayton Andrews	23	LHP
13	Dylan File	24	RHP
14	Alec Bettinger	24	RHP
15	Zack Brown	25	RHP
16	Eduardo Garcia	17	SS
17	Trey Supak	24	RHP
18	Braden Webb	25	RHP
19	Cooper Hummel	25	LF/RF
20	Max Lazar	21	RHP

1. Brice Turang, 2B/SS

	Hit	Power	SB	Patience	Glove	Overall
	55/60	35/45	60	65/60	55	50

Born: 11/21/99	Age: 20	Bats: L
Height: 6-0	Weight: 173	Throws: R

YEAR	LVL	PA	1B	2B	3B	HR	SB	CS	AVG	OBP	SLG	BB%	K%	GB%	LD%	FB%
2018	RK	57	13	2	0	0	8	1	0.319	0.421	0.362	15.79%	10.53%	57.1	19.0	19.0
2018	RK	135	24	4	1	1	6	1	0.268	0.385	0.348	16.30%	20.74%	52.9	20.0	25.9
2019	A	357	68	13	4	2	21	4	0.287	0.384	0.376	13.73%	15.13%	42.7	19.0	31.2
2019	A+	207	25	6	2	1	9	1	0.200	0.338	0.276	16.43%	22.71%	41.9	19.4	31.5

Background: Scouts were quite familiar with the talented prep prospect long before he became an upper classman at Santiago High School. For instance: USA Baseball gave him the Dick Case Award, the first time a player rostered on the 15U team was recognized in such a manner. Turang, the 21st overall pick in the draft two years ago, looked comfortable as he transitioned into the low levels of the minor leagues during his debut. Splitting time between the Arizona Summer and Pioneer Leagues, he batted a respectable .283/.396/.352 with six doubles, one triple, and one homerun to go along with 14 stolen bases in 16 attempts. The 6-foot, 173-pound lefty-swinging infielder opened the year up as a teenager squaring off against the Midwest League. In 82 games with the Wisconsin Rattlers, he batted .287/.384/.376. The front office brass bounced the top prospect up to High Class A in early July for the remainder of the season. Turang batted an aggregate .256/.367/.340 with 19 doubles, six triples, three homeruns, and 30 stolen bases (in 35 attempts).

Snippet from The 2018 Prospect Digest Handbook: Once offering glimpses as a potential face-of-the-franchise type player, Turang's ceiling has cooled a bit in recent years. The bat could eventually join his speed as an above-average skill. But the lefty-swinging shortstop doesn't project to his for a whole lot of extra-base fire power throughout his career. He has a chance to be a Cole Tucker-type of player with better patience.

Scouting Report: Let's take a look at Turang's production in Low Class A last season; consider the following:

- Since 2006, there have been just three 19-year-old hitters to meet the following criteria in the Midwest League (min. 300 PA): a DRC+ total between 137 and 147 and a sub-20% strikeout rate. Those three hitters and their credentials: Corey Seager, a two-time All-Star; Xavier Edwards, a former first round pick and current top prospect who accomplished the feat last season; and – of course – Brice Turang.

An absolute on-base machine thanks to his impeccable patience at the plate; Turang has walked in more than 15% of his plate appearances as a professional. He's not only fast, but he's incredibly efficient on the base paths. He's an above-average defender at either up-the-middle position. The sweet-swinging prospect shows no concerning platoon splits. The lone knock on him: his lack of over-the-fence thump, though it's improving. Turang began elevating the ball more frequently last year, so it wouldn't be surprising to see him belt out 12 or 15-homeruns during his peak. He's a gamer and a potential All-Star.

Ceiling: 3.0-win player
Risk: Moderate
MLB ETA: 2022

2. Drew Rasmussen, RHP

	FB	CB	CH	Command	Overall
	65	55	N/A	45	50

Born: 07/27/95	Age: 24	Bats: R
Height: 6-1	Weight: 225	Throws: R

YEAR	LVL	IP	W	L	SV	ERA	FIP	WHIP	K/9	K%	BB/9	BB%	K/BB	HR9	BABIP
2019	A	2.0	0	0	0	0.00	0.43	0.50	13.5	50.00%	0.0	0.00%	#DIV/0!	0.00	0.333
2019	A+	11.3	0	0	0	1.59	1.08	0.79	12.7	37.21%	1.6	4.65%	8.00	0.00	0.280
2019	AA	61.0	1	3	0	3.54	3.15	1.28	11.4	30.31%	4.3	11.42%	2.66	0.59	0.317

Background: It's been one helluva whirlwind couple of years for the hard-throwing, firebolt-slinging right-hander. The former Oregon State University stud – who, by the way, authored the only perfect game in school history as a freshman – underwent his first Tommy John surgery in March of 2016. Fast forward a little more than a year later and the Tampa Bay Rays called his name near the end of the first round. A routine post-draft physical, however, revealed the 6-foot-1, 225-pound right-hander was going to require a second Tommy John surgery. The two sides failed to come to an agreement, so Rasmussen essentially sat out another year as he recovered from the surgical procedure. The Brewers wisely gambled on the former Beaver in sixth round, 185th overall, in 2018. Finally healthy, Rasmussen made his highly anticipated debut last season. And he quickly made up for lost time. He made one dominant two-inning appearance with Wisconsin before moving up to High Class A. His stint with the Mudcats lasted all of just four starts. And he finally settled in – and dominated – the Class AA level for the remainder of the season. In total, Rasmussen tossed 74.1 innings with 96 strikeouts and just 31 walks to go along with an aggregate 3.15 ERA.

Scouting Report: Various mid-season reports had Rasmussen's fastball back to approaching triple-digits. Personally, I saw him sitting comfortably 92- to 95-mph with a relative amount of ease. His tightly-spun slider was an above-average offering, showing plenty of late bite almost resembling a power-cutter. He reportedly throws a changeup, though I saw him primarily throwing the fastball/slider. And, surprisingly, despite the long layoff and multiple elbow procedures, Rasmussen's control / command looked solid. With respect to his work in Class AA, consider the following:

- Since 2006, only three 23-year-old pitchers posted a strikeout percentage between 29% and 31% with a walk percentage between 10% and 13% in the Southern League (min. 50 IP): Alejandro Chacin, Peter Tago, and – of course – Drew Rasmussen.

It's easy to peg Rasmussen as a hard-throwing pitcher destined for late-inning, high leverage relief work. But it looks like the Brewers are content on stretching him out as a starting option. His arsenal / repertoire is reminiscent of the Marlins' All-Star representative Sandy Alcantara – assuming the former can avoid any more injury issues.

Ceiling: 3.0-win player
Risk: Moderate to High
MLB ETA: 2020

3. Bowden Francis, RHP

	FB	SL	CH	Command	Overall
	60	60/65	50	45	50

Born: 04/22/96	Age: 24	Bats: R
Height: 6-5	Weight: 225	Throws: R

Top CALs:

YEAR	LVL	IP	W	L	SV	ERA	FIP	WHIP	K/9	K%	BB/9	BB%	K/BB	HR9	BABIP
2017	Rk	10.0	0	1	0	8.10	2.82	2.00	11.7	25.00%	2.7	5.77%	4.33	0.00	0.486
2018	A	104.0	5	8	0	4.41	3.67	1.43	8.2	21.02%	2.5	6.42%	3.28	0.78	0.350
2018	A+	24.0	2	2	0	4.88	5.44	1.17	4.1	11.00%	3.4	9.00%	1.22	1.13	0.213
2019	A+	14.0	1	1	0	3.86	2.73	1.36	12.9	33.33%	3.9	10.00%	3.33	0.64	0.364
2019	AA	128.7	7	8	0	3.99	3.76	1.24	10.1	26.70%	3.4	9.02%	2.96	0.98	0.296

Background: The Brewers don't get enough credit for developing collegiate pitchers taken in the middle round rounds of the draft. Brandon Woodruff, an All-Star last season, is the poster boy after being selected in the 11th round of the 2014 draft. Other examples include: Zack Brown, a former fifth round pick, Alec Bettinger, who was added in the tenth round, Dylan File was a 21st round pick, Drew Rasmussen was a sixth round pick (who, admittedly, was taken in the first round the year before), and – of course – Bowden Francis. A product of Florida JuCo powerhouse Chipola College, Francis was one of the bigger surprises in the Brewers' system in 2019. After three dominant starts in High Class A, Francis moved up to – and continued to produce in – Class AA, the most important challenge for a minor leaguer. In 25 appearances with the Biloxi Shuckers, the 6-foot-5, 225-pound right-hander posted a strong 145-to-49 strikeout-to-walk ratio to go along with a 3.99 ERA in 128.2 innings of work. His DRA with the Shuckers was 4.76.

Scouting Report: Quietly impressive – so much so, in fact, that I'm surprised he's not getting more national publicity / notoriety. His fastball is sneaky quick with impressive late life, sitting in the low- to mid-90s without much effort. His slider is a wipeout, swing-and-miss offering that flashes – on occasion – a 65-grade. It's late, sharp with tremendous downward slant. His changeup is a workable, average third option. There's some Brandon Woodruff-type upside here. With respect to his work in Class AA, consider the following:

- Since 2006, here's the list of 23-year-old pitchers to fan between 26% and 28% of the hitters they faced with a walk percentage between 7% and 10% in the Southern League (min. 100 IP): Tucker Davidson, a top prospect in the Braves' system, and Bowden Francis.

Ceiling: 2.5-win player
Risk: Moderate
MLB ETA: 2020

4. Ethan Small, LHP

	FB	CB	CH	Command	Overall
	50+	55	60	55	50

Born: 02/14/97	Age: 23	Bats: L
Height: 6-3	Weight: 214	Throws: L

YEAR	LVL	IP	W	L	SV	ERA	FIP	WHIP	K/9	K%	BB/9	BB%	K/BB	HR9	BABIP
2019	Rk	3.0	0	0	0	0.00	0.92	0.00	15.0	55.56%	0.0	0.00%	#DIV/0!	0.00	0.000
2019	A	18.0	0	2	0	1.00	0.65	0.83	15.5	54.39%	2.0	7.02%	7.75	0.00	0.286

Background: One of the preeminent strikeout artists in college baseball last season, the story on Small is hardly so. A two-time All-American coming out of Lexington High School, Small appeared – briefly – in 15 games for Mississippi State during his freshman season, striking out 20 against 10 walks in only 10 innings of work. The 6-foot-3, 214-pound southpaw spent the ensuing summer hurling games for the Wareham Gatemen in the Cape Cod League, posting a poor 11-to-8 strikeout-to-walk ratio in another 20.0 innings of action. Unfortunately, he succumbed to elbow woes that pushed him under the knife for Tommy John surgery, which knocked him out for the entire 2017 season. Finally healthy, the Tennessee native turned in one of the more surprising seasons two years ago: in a career high 18 starts, Small fanned a remarkable 122 against just 33 free passes to go along with a 3.20 ERA. The Arizona Diamondbacks took a late round gamble on him, though Small opted to head back to school for his redshirt junior season. The lanky left-hander turned in one of the more dominant showings last season: in 17 starts for the Bulldogs, Small fanned 168 and walked just 29 in 102.0 innings of work. Milwaukee used a late first round pick on him. Small would make seven brief appearances during his debut, posting an incredible 36-to-4 strikeout-to-walk ratio in only 21.0 innings. He finished his first taste of pro ball with a 0.86 ERA.

Scouting Report: Per the usual, here's what I wrote prior to the draft last season:

> *"A herky-jerky southpaw with three solid offerings: a low 90s fastball sitting comfortably in the 91- to 92-mph range, a late-breaking sharp 12-6 curveball, and an average changeup. Small commands the inner part of the plate exceedingly well and generates a lot of success working up in the zone – which may not go as well as he transitions into the professional ranks. In terms of production, consider the following:*

> - *Between 2011 and 2018, here's the list of Division I arms that average at least 13 strikeouts and fewer than 3.0 walks per nine innings in a season (min. 70 IP): Trevor Bauer, Logan Gilbert, Robert Broom, and J.P. Sears.*
> - *Bauer and Gilbert were both first round picks. Broom and Sears were late round selections.*

> *Here's the intriguing part though:*

> - *Between 2011 and 2018, here's the list of pitchers to average at least 14 strikeout per nine innings (min. 70 IP): Shane McClanahan. (Small, by the way, is averaging more than 15 strikeouts every nine innings.)*

> *Mississippi's ace doesn't have an eye popping arsenal. But the production is beyond elite. Repertoire-wise Small's similar to former Missouri ace – and current Chicago Cub – Rob Zastryzny, though the former's production is far superior. Small looks like a solid #3/#4-type arm at maturity. One final thought: Love to the bulldog mentality on the mound."*

A few additional notes: his changeup looked far better after he joined Milwaukee's system and, frankly, I'm shocked he missed as many bats as he did. The fastball continues to sneak up on hitters, especially up in the zone.

Ceiling: 2.5-win player
Risk: Moderate
MLB ETA: 2021/2022

5. Aaron Ashby, LHP

FB	CB	SL	CH	Command	Overall
55+	65	50/55	55	45/50	50

Born: 05/24/98	Age: 22	Bats: R
Height: 6-2	Weight: 181	Throws: L

YEAR	LVL	IP	W	L	SV	ERA	FIP	WHIP	K/9	K%	BB/9	BB%	K/BB	HR9	BABIP
2018	Rk	20.3	1	2	1	6.20	5.84	1.28	8.4	21.84%	3.5	9.20%	2.38	1.33	0.273
2018	A	37.3	1	1	0	2.17	2.03	1.31	11.3	30.32%	2.2	5.81%	5.22	0.24	0.398
2019	A	61.0	3	4	0	3.54	3.28	1.23	11.8	31.75%	4.1	11.11%	2.86	0.59	0.319
2019	A+	65.0	2	6	0	3.46	3.50	1.32	7.6	19.78%	4.4	11.51%	1.72	0.14	0.283

Background: One of my favorite pitching prospects in the entire minor leagues. Ashby, who's uncle is former big league veteran Andy Ashby, was a fourth round product out of Crowder College two years ago. A wiry, 6-foot-2, 181-pound southpaw – who, by the way, looks thicker in the lower half – was incredibly dominant during a first half stint in the Midwest League but faltered a bit after his promotion up to High Class A. In total, Ashby made a career best 24 appearances, 23 of them coming via the start, throwing 126.0 innings with 135 punch outs against 60 free passes. He compiled an aggregate 3.50 ERA.

Snippet from The 2018 Prospect Digest Handbook: His fastball is sneaky quick, sitting in the 91-92 mph range and can touch 93 mph on occasion. His two-seamer shows some solid arm-side run as well. His curveball is a bit inconsistent, but flashes plus at times with hard 12-6 bite, giving the illusion of following off the table. His changeup, a quality third pitch, is thrown with tremendous arm speed and dives down-and-away to right-handers. Ashby fires from a high arm slot, somewhere between three-quarter and over-the-top. He's poised to move quickly with the ceiling as a backend starting pitcher. Tremendous, tremendous find in the fourth round.

Scouting Report: Pretty much the same thing a year later – except *better*. Along with looking physically stronger / bulkier in the lower half, Ashby's fastball gained a few ticks on the radar gun, touching – on several occasions – as high as 95 mph. It's a borderline plus pitch that may eventually move into 60-grade territory in the next year or two as he continues to get stronger. His curveball looked sharper with that same late tilt and bite. And his changeup remained in the above-average / 55-grade territory. The lanky lefty also added a fourth pitch: a low-80s slider with a lot of horizontal movement. There's some #4-type potential, maybe more if the command ticks up. With respect to his work in Low Class A, consider the following:

- Since 2006, only two 21-year-old pitchers met the following criteria in the Midwest League (min. 50 IP): a strikeout percentage of at least 30% and a walk percentage between 10% and 13%. Those two pitchers: Dylan Cease, budding Chicago White Sox ace, and – of course – Aaron Ashby.

Ceiling: 2.5-win player
Risk: Moderate
MLB ETA: 2021/2022

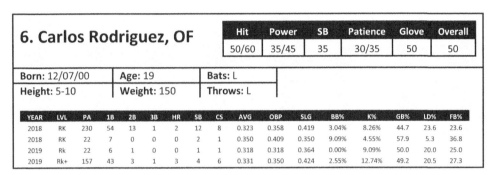

6. Carlos Rodriguez, OF

Hit	Power	SB	Patience	Glove	Overall
50/60	35/45	35	30/35	50	50

Born: 12/07/00	Age: 19	Bats: L
Height: 5-10	Weight: 150	Throws: L

YEAR	LVL	PA	1B	2B	3B	HR	SB	CS	AVG	OBP	SLG	BB%	K%	GB%	LD%	FB%
2018	RK	230	54	13	1	2	12	8	0.323	0.358	0.419	3.04%	8.26%	44.7	23.6	23.6
2018	RK	22	7	0	0	0	2	1	0.350	0.409	0.350	9.09%	4.55%	57.9	5.3	36.8
2019	Rk	22	6	1	0	0	1	1	0.318	0.318	0.364	0.00%	9.09%	50.0	20.0	25.0
2019	Rk+	157	43	3	1	3	4	6	0.331	0.350	0.424	2.55%	12.74%	49.2	20.5	27.3

Background: One of the more recognizable prospects on the international scene three years ago, the Brewers handed the then-16-year-old outfielder a hefty $1.355 million deal. Rodriguez, who measures in at 5-foot-10 and 150 pounds, turned in a dynamic professional debut a year later as he slugged .325/.363/.414 with 13 doubles, one triple, two homeruns, and 14 stolen bases (in 23 attempts) between stints in the foreign and domestic rookie leagues. Rodriguez, who capped off his debut with a brief five-game stint in the Arizona Summer League, opened last season back up in the low level rookie league – though that stint lasted just seven games. Milwaukee bumped the young Venezuelan up to the Pioneer League at the end of July. He popped up for 36 games with Rocky Mountain, hitting a solid .331/.350/.424 with three doubles, one triple, and three homeruns. He swiped four bags in 10 attempts. His overall production in the advanced rookie league, according to Baseball Prospectus' *Deserved Runs Created Plus*, topped the league average mark by 20%.

Snippet from The 2018 Prospect Digest Handbook: Foreign rookie ball stats are worthless. Well, they're really beyond worthless. Take, for example, Rodriguez's overall production in the DSL last summer: he topped the league average threshold by 23%, but that doesn't even crack the Top 60 among all qualified bats in the league last season. Here's what we know: he doesn't strike out a lot; hardly walks; showed above-average speed; and very little power. Right now, Rodriguez has the look and feel as a fourth outfielder – though he's years and years away.

Scouting Report: Consider the following:

- Since 2006, only two 18-year-old hitters met the following criteria in the Pioneer League (min. 150 PA): DRC+ between 115 and 125, a sub-16.0% strikeout rate, and a walk rate below 6.0%. Those two hitters: All-Star outfielder Ender Inciarte and – of course – Carlos Rodriguez.

Let's take it a step further:

NAME	YEAR	AGE	PA	AVG	OBP	SLG	ISO	BB%	K%	DRC+
Ender Inciarte	2009	18	258	0.325	0.358	0.405	0.080	5.81%	15.50%	121
Carlos Rodriguez	2019	18	157	0.331	0.350	0.424	0.093	2.55%	12.74%	120

Rodriguez is a player cut from a similar cloth: a strong hit tool that may peak on the lower end of the plus grade, near nonexistent walk rates, not a ton of power, strong bat-to-ball skills, and above-average speed. Defensively speaking, Rodriguez is no Inciarte; he's average, maybe a tick better in center field. Rodriguez's bat doesn't play as well in a corner spot. If the hit tool continues to perform and approach plus territory, he's a lock to become an above-average regular. If not, he could be a capable fourth outfielder on a contending team.

Ceiling: 2.0-win player
Risk: Moderate
MLB ETA: 2022

7. Tristen Lutz, OF

Hit	Power	SB	Patience	Glove	Overall
40/45	50/55	30	50+	45	50

Born: 08/22/98	Age: 21	Bats: R
Height: 6-2	Weight: 210	Throws: R

YEAR	LVL	PA	1B	2B	3B	HR	SB	CS	AVG	OBP	SLG	BB%	K%	GB%	LD%	FB%
2017	RK	111	23	1	1	6	2	4	0.333	0.432	0.559	10.81%	18.92%	45.2	21.9	31.5
2017	RK	76	9	4	3	3	1	0	0.279	0.347	0.559	5.26%	27.63%	43.8	22.9	25.0
2018	A	503	60	33	3	13	9	3	0.246	0.321	0.421	9.15%	27.63%	45.8	15.1	30.8
2019	A+	477	67	24	3	13	3	2	0.255	0.335	0.419	9.64%	28.72%	46.3	18.7	30.4

Background: Sandwiched between a couple polished collegiate hitters – Kevin Merrell and Brent Rooker – at the end of the first round of the 2017 draft, Lutz has taken the slow-and-steady approach at conquering the minor leagues. He split time between both of the organization's rookie league affiliates during his debut. He followed that up with a decent, semi-strong showing in the Midwest League a year later. And last season the 6-foot-2, 210-pound outfielder squared off against the Carolina League. In 112 games with the Mudcats, the former James W. Martin High School product batted .255/.335/.419 with 24 doubles, three triples, and a career-high tying 13 homeruns. He also swiped a trio of bags and was caught stealing twice. Per *Deserved Runs Created Plus*, his overall production was 9% better than the league average mark.

Snippet from The 2018 Prospect Digest Handbook: Milwaukee's youngster got off to a predictably slow start last season, batting a lowly .167/.244/.282 over his first 20 games. But beginning on May 3rd, he slugged a healthy .262/.337/.451 over his final 99 contests. Lutz has big, big time power potential – as evidenced by his 33 doubles, which will begin to grow some legs in the coming years. His hit tool is a bit underdeveloped, as is his defense as well. But he has a chance to develop into a perennial 30-homer threat.

Scouting Report: Just like his stint in the Midwest League two years ago, Lutz got off to a – say it with me – predictably slow start as he moved into the Carolina League. Across his first 19 games the former first round pick batted a putrid .159/.227/.217 with just a pair of extra-base hits. In comparison, he slugged a healthy .274/.356/.459 over his final 93 contests. While just inching up ever so slightly, Lutz's swing-and-miss issues are becoming problematic; he posted a strikeout rate of 27.6% in 2018 and followed that up with a 28.7% last season. Lutz saw a lot of time as a center fielder last season, but he's eventually going to slide over into a corner spot soon. He has some Khris Davis feel to him with the offensive ceiling as a .245/.320/.480 type hitter.

Ceiling: 2.0-win player
Risk: Moderate
MLB ETA: 2021/2022

8. Mario Feliciano, C

Hit	Power	SB	Patience	Glove	Overall
45	50	35	45	45	45

Born: 11/20/98	Age: 21	Bats: R
Height: 6-1	Weight: 195	Throws: R

YEAR	LVL	PA	1B	2B	3B	HR	SB	CS	AVG	OBP	SLG	BB%	K%	GB%	LD%	FB%
2017	A	446	79	16	2	4	10	2	0.251	0.320	0.331	7.62%	16.14%	48.6	20.4	22.5
2018	A+	165	19	7	1	3	2	0	0.205	0.282	0.329	7.88%	35.76%	46.1	20.2	30.3
2019	A+	482	72	25	4	19	2	1	0.273	0.324	0.477	6.02%	28.84%	40.3	25.7	30.4
2019	AA	14	1	0	1	0	0	0	0.167	0.286	0.333	0.00%	28.57%	50.0	12.5	37.5

Background: Arguably the best prospect to come out of the Carlos Beltran Baseball Academy. Milwaukee snagged the 6-foot-1, 195-pound backstop in the second round of the 2016 draft. Feliciano, a native of Bayamon, Puerto Rico, looked like a burgeoning middle-tier prospect after a solid showing as an 18-year-old in the Midwest League three seasons ago when he batted .251/.320/.331. But his production tanked in an injury-shortened follow up campaign in the Carolina League in 2018; he hit a lowly .205/.282/.329. Milwaukee pushed Feliciano back down to High Class A last season. And his production rebounded – considerably. In 116 games with the Carolina Mudcats, he slugged .273/.324/.477 with career bests in doubles (25), triples (four), and homeruns (19). His overall production with the High Class A squad, per *Deserved Runs Created Plus*, topped the league average mark by 19%. He spent the final three games of the year with Biloxi in the Southern League.

Scouting Report: Consider the following:

- Since 2006, there have been four 20-year-old hitters that posted a DRC+ between 115 and 125 with a strikeout rate north of 25.0% in the Carolina League (min. 350 PA): Anderson Tejeda, Bobby Bradley, Nick Williams, and Mario Feliciano.

Early in his career Feliciano employed a high contact, no power approach at the plate – which resulted in production marks south of the league average threshold. Since entering High Class A two years ago, he's morphed his approach heavily towards more power with high strikeout rates. Defensively, well, he's not good and – frankly – barely passable. The state of catching at the big league level is beyond terrible, so that opens the door – widely – for Feliciano's prospects. If the power holds firm without regressing, he has a chance to be a bat-first option but he's unlikely to ever approach above average status at the big league level.

Ceiling: 1.5- to 2.0-win player
Risk: Moderate
MLB ETA: 2021/2022

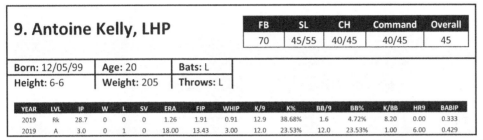

9. Antoine Kelly, LHP

	FB	SL	CH	Command	Overall
	70	45/55	40/45	40/45	45

Born: 12/05/99	Age: 20	Bats: L
Height: 6-6	Weight: 205	Throws: L

YEAR	LVL	IP	W	L	SV	ERA	FIP	WHIP	K/9	K%	BB/9	BB%	K/BB	HR9	BABIP
2019	Rk	28.7	0	0	0	1.26	1.91	0.91	12.9	38.68%	1.6	4.72%	8.20	0.00	0.333
2019	A	3.0	0	1	0	18.00	13.43	3.00	12.0	23.53%	12.0	23.53%	1.00	6.00	0.429

Background: Originally taken by the Padres in the 13th round of the 2018 draft. Instead of joining San Diego's loaded system, Kelly opted to attend JuCo Wabash Valley College last season. Predictably so, the tall, lanky left-hander was practically unhittable: across 52.2 innings, Kelly fanned an incredible 112 – which, for those counting at home, is 19.1 K/9 – to go along with a 1.88 ERA. That production, as well as Kelly's high octane fastball, caught the attention of the Brewers, who would eventually draft him in the second round, 65th overall. Kelly made nine appearances in the Arizona Summer League and one final – disastrous – start in Low Class A during his debut, throwing 31.2 innings with 45 strikeouts and nine walks to go along with a 2.84 ERA.

Scouting Report: Nitrous infused fastball that (A) not only regularly touches 97 mph and sits 94- to 95-mph comfortably, but (B) also has a chance to add a little bit of velocity as his wiry 6-foot-6, 205-pound frame continues to fill out. It's a plus offering that has a chance to blossom into a plus-plus weapon. As far as the secondary pitches are concerned, well, they're raw – very, very raw. I was only able to catch one of Kelly's professional games, the Low Class A contest against the Kane County Cougars. He was primarily – and by that I mean, solely – throwing his 70-grade fastball. I went back to older video of the left-hander to find the secondary offerings: the slider shows nice shape and break, but it's slow and needs to be tightened up. I did not see a changeup at any point. Despite the high draft status, Milwaukee's front office is betting that they can cultivate his slider and changeup to make him a viable starting pitcher. Mechanically, he's an extreme cross-body thrower. His lead foot is hindering his hips and arm to work in sync. It's also causing his control / command issues on the third base side of the plate. Kelly already has a big league fastball, but he could – and likely will – fall into the Taylor Hearn category of one plus pitch, little secondary, perennial noteworthy prospect without making too many waves at the big league level. One final note: David Stearns, the Brewers GM is a former Astros assistant general manager; and Houston really honed in and specialized in their ability to drastically improve pitchers' breaking balls.

Ceiling: 1.5- to 2.0-win player
Risk: Moderate
MLB ETA: 2022/2023

10. Reese Olson, RHP

	FB	CB	CH	Command	Overall
	60	65	50	40/45	45

Born: 07/31/99	Age: 20	Bats: R
Height: 6-1	Weight: 160	Throws: R

YEAR	LVL	IP	W	L	SV	ERA	FIP	WHIP	K/9	K%	BB/9	BB%	K/BB	HR9	BABIP
2018	Rk	10.3	0	2	0	5.23	4.65	1.45	5.2	13.33%	3.5	8.89%	1.50	0.00	0.333
2019	A	94.7	4	7	0	4.66	4.43	1.60	8.0	19.76%	4.5	11.06%	1.79	0.76	0.343

Background: The former 13th round bonus baby has quietly become one of the more intriguing prospects in the Brewers' system, but in the entire minor leagues. The lanky 6-foot-1, 160-pound right-hander signed with the organization for $400,000 two years ago, roughly late fourth / early fifth round money. The North Hall High School product was limited to just four brief appearances in the Arizona Summer League during his debut. And despite the limited action – with, at best, mediocre results, the front office brass aggressively pushed the then-19-year-old up to full season ball to start 2019. And Olson proved up to the task. Making 14 starts and 13 relief appearances with the Wisconsin Timber Rattlers, the hard-throwing righty fanned 84 and walked 47 in 94.2 innings of work. He finished his first full season in pro ball with a 4.66 ERA and a 6.81 DRA (Deserved Runs Average).

Scouting Report: Incredibly intriguing low-level arm. Olson's fastball was sitting – easily – in the 92- to 94-mph range, and touching a 95 at will during a late season start with the Timber Rattlers. His curveball adds a second plus-pitch, showing tremendous hard, late bit. Olson will vary the break from a traditional 12-6 to 1-7 at times. His changeup is solid-average. Olson's control / command still have ways to go. And it's likely to settle in as a 45-grade. He's erratic now, but not wild. With respect to his work in Low Class A last season, consider the following:

- Since 2006, here's the list of 19-year-old pitchers to post a strikeout percentage between 19% and 21% and a walk percentage between 10% and 12% in the Midwest League (min. 75 IP): Max Fried, Fabio Castillo, Robinson Ortiz, Zachary Bird, Zach Phillips, and Reese Olson.

The former prep arm is still quite raw, but he has the potential to help fill out the backend of a big league rotation if the control / command continues to trend in the right direction – perhaps peaking as a #4.

Ceiling: 1.5- to 2.0-win player
Risk: Moderate
MLB ETA: 2022/2023

11. Devin Williams, RHP

FB	SL	CH	Command	Overall
70	45+	55+	45	45

Born: 09/21/94	Age: 25	Bats: R
Height: 6-3	Weight: 165	Throws: R

YEAR	LVL	IP	W	L	SV	ERA	FIP	WHIP	K/9	K%	BB/9	BB%	K/BB	HR9	BABIP
2018	A+	34.0	0	3	0	5.82	4.45	1.82	9.3	21.34%	5.8	13.41%	1.59	0.53	0.380
2019	AA	53.3	7	2	4	2.36	2.86	1.18	12.8	34.55%	4.9	13.18%	2.62	0.51	0.279
2019	AAA	3.7	0	0	0	0.00	1.34	0.82	14.7	46.15%	2.5	7.69%	6.00	0.00	0.333

Background: It was a move that not only was bound to happen, but one that *needed* to happen. And the Brewers – finally – gave up on the dream of Williams' plus, upper-90s fastball and incredibly underrated changeup working out of the club's big league rotation one day and pushed him into a full time relief role at the start of last season. And voila: an instant impact reliever was born. The 6-foot-3, 165-pound right-hander made 34 appearances between Biloxi and San Antonio, throwing 57.0 innings with an incredible 82-to-30 strikeout-to-walk ratio with a 2.21 ERA. Milwaukee called up the firebolt slinging hurler in early August for another 13 brief relief appearances; he would fan 14 and walk six in 13.2 innings of work.

Scouting Report: Since making the transition into a relief role, Williams has – essentially – become a two-pitch pitcher: his plus fastball sits in the mid- to upper-90s, featuring late, riding life; and his changeup, which is better than I recall, is a borderline plus pitch. Both are genuine swing-and-miss options at the big league level. He'll also throw a rare, get-me-over, below-average slider. The lone thing keeping Williams from an eventual closer role – as well as making a ton of future money – is his control / command. He's primed for a late-inning relief role.

Ceiling: 1.5-win player
Risk: Low to Moderate
MLB ETA: Debuted in 2019

12. Clayton Andrews, LHP/CF

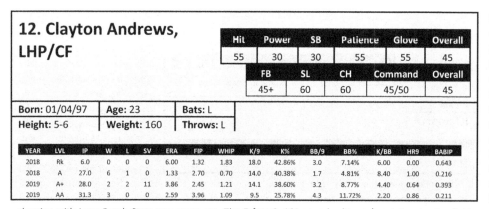

Hit	Power	SB	Patience	Glove	Overall
55	30	30	55	55	45

FB	SL	CH	Command	Overall
45+	60	60	45/50	45

Born: 01/04/97	Age: 23	Bats: L
Height: 5-6	Weight: 160	Throws: L

YEAR	LVL	IP	W	L	SV	ERA	FIP	WHIP	K/9	K%	BB/9	BB%	K/BB	HR9	BABIP
2018	Rk	6.0	0	0	0	6.00	1.32	1.83	18.0	42.86%	3.0	7.14%	6.00	0.00	0.643
2018	A	27.0	6	1	0	1.33	2.70	0.70	14.0	40.38%	1.7	4.81%	8.40	1.00	0.216
2019	A+	28.0	2	2	11	3.86	2.45	1.21	14.1	38.60%	3.2	8.77%	4.40	0.64	0.393
2019	AA	31.3	3	0	0	2.59	3.96	1.09	9.5	25.78%	4.3	11.72%	2.20	0.86	0.211

Background: Unequivocally, without a smidgeon of doubt, I'm the President of the Clayton Andrews fan club. And I'm not ashamed to admit it. He's on the short, short list among my favorite players – not just prospects – of all time; right up there with the Iron Man Cal Ripken Jr. Andrews, a diminutive, do-everything-type of grinder, fell to the Brewers in the 17th round after a stellar showing with Long Beach State two years ago. The 5-foot-6, 160-pound reliever / part-time center fielder posted an impeccable 118-to-17 strikeout-to-walk ratio in 99.2 innings of work and he batted .302/.382/.377 with six doubles and five triples. Andrews continued impress during his debut between Helena and Wisconsin as he struck out an incredible 54 and walked just seven in only 33.0 innings of work. Last season, he split time between the Carolina and Southern Leagues, averaging 11.7 strikeouts and 3.8 walks per nine innings with a 3.19 ERA in 59.1 innings of work. He also hit a combined .333/.391/.381 with a double and a triple with both clubs.

Snippet from The 2018 Prospect Digest Handbook: During his debut Andrews' fastball sat in the 87 to 89 mph. His curveball, a big overhand 12-6 pitch with late break, hovers around 75 mph and it's a plus offering. His changeup provides a third solid offering, which he throws with impressive arm action. He's going to be a solid lefty reliever in the mold of J.P Howell.

Scouting Report: During Andrews' pre-draft analysis, I wrote the following:

"I understand the gravity of what I'm about to type – but I'll do it anyway. Barring any career-altering injury, Clayton Andrews will pitch in the big leagues."

A year later and he's knocking – loudly – on the door to The Show. Not only as a capable lefty reliever, but as a potential two-way player. As a pitching, the small southpaw shows an upper-80s fastball that will occasional break 90 mph. His changeup is phenomenal. And he's scrapped his loopy curveball for a more deceptive, late-tilting slider. As a hitter, he's always had a knack for two things: #1 getting on base and #2 strong, batting average-driven production. And that held firm despite squaring off against the mid- to upper-levels of the minor leagues. He's scrappy. He's going to be productive at the big league level. And he's a hardcore ballplayer. I love everything about him.

Ceiling: 1.5-win player
Risk: Low to Moderate
MLB ETA: 2020

13. Dylan File, RHP

	FB	CB	SL	CH	Command	Overall
	50+	50	55	55	60	45

Born: 06/04/96	**Age:** 24	**Bats:** R
Height: 6-1	**Weight:** 205	**Throws:** R

YEAR	LVL	IP	W	L	SV	ERA	FIP	WHIP	K/9	K%	BB/9	BB%	K/BB	HR9	BABIP
2017	Rk	47.0	1	2	0	4.02	5.80	1.36	7.1	18.05%	2.5	6.34%	2.85	1.34	0.303
2018	A	136.3	8	10	0	3.96	3.94	1.32	7.5	19.96%	1.8	4.90%	4.07	0.99	0.334
2019	A+	66.3	6	4	0	3.80	2.80	1.18	8.5	23.08%	0.9	2.56%	9.00	0.54	0.345
2019	AA	80.7	9	2	0	2.79	3.03	1.10	8.1	22.32%	1.7	4.59%	4.87	0.56	0.301

Background: Fun Fact: Dixie State College of Utah has churned out a surprising – at least to me – trio of big leaguers over the past two decade – former 12-year veteran Brandon Lyon, who earned more than $26 million in his career; Cardinals and Royals swingman Brad Thompson, and 2017 All-Star Brandon Kintzler, who was drafted in the 40th round not once, but twice. Enter: Dylan File, a 21st round pick in the 2017 draft who is poised to be next in line. A 6-foot-1, 205-pound right-hander, File turned some heads with a solid showing in the Midwest League two years ago as he posted a 114-to-28 strikeout-to-walk ratio in 136.1 innings of work. Last season, the crafty right-hander raised the bar even further. In 26 starts between Carolina and Biloxi, the Arizona native averaged 8.3 strikeouts and 1.3 walks per nine innings to go along with a 3.24 ERA.

Scouting Report: With respect to his work in Class AA in the second half of last season, consider the following:

- Since 2006, only three 23-year-old right-handers posted a strikeout percentage between 21% and 23% with a sub-6% walk rate in the Southern League (min. 75 IP): Ross Stripling, a 2018 NL All-Star for the Dodgers, Bernardo Flores, who accomplished the feat last season, and – of course – Dylan File.

File's another one of these mid- to late-round intriguing arms moving their way through the middle of the minor leagues with a legitimate shot at earning significant time in the club's big league rotation. The right-hander features a solid, better-than-average four-pitch mix: a 92-93 mph fastball that he commands exceptionally well; a slider that flashes plus on occasion; a standard 50-grade curveball; and an above-average changeup. File succeeds by doing the little things incredibly well: consistently throwing pitcher's pitches, keeping the ball in the park, and seemingly is always working ahead in the count. The changeup is particularly interesting as it might see another uptick because he didn't start throwing one until he joined the Brewers' system. There's some #4/#5-type starting potential here.

Ceiling: 1.5-win player
Risk: Moderate
MLB ETA: 2020

14. Alec Bettinger, RHP

	FB	CB	CU	Command	Overall
	50	55	50/55	50	45

Born: 07/13/95	**Age:** 24	**Bats:** R
Height: 6-2	**Weight:** 210	**Throws:** R

YEAR	LVL	IP	W	L	SV	ERA	FIP	WHIP	K/9	K%	BB/9	BB%	K/BB	HR9	BABIP
2017	Rk	50.7	3	3	0	4.97	4.62	1.48	6.9	17.73%	4.1	10.45%	1.70	0.18	0.329
2018	A	62.7	5	4	0	3.73	4.04	1.21	7.2	19.46%	2.4	6.61%	2.94	0.86	0.291
2018	A+	54.7	1	6	0	6.91	4.67	1.59	9.2	23.05%	2.8	7.00%	3.29	1.65	0.377
2019	AA	146.3	5	7	0	3.44	3.12	1.07	9.7	26.70%	2.2	5.95%	4.49	0.80	0.286

Background: Another one of the club's mid- to late-round draft homeruns. Milwaukee grabbed the 6-foot-2, 210-pound right-hander out of the University of Virginia in 10th round three years ago. After a rough start to his professional career – he posted a lowly 39-to-23 strikeout-to-walk ratio during his debut – Bettinger's stock has been ascending with every stop along the minor league ladder. He split time between Wisconsin and Carolina two years ago, averaging a combined 8.1 strikeouts and just 2.6 walks per nine innings. He spent the entirety of last season dueling against the Southern League competition. Making a career high 26 starts, the former Cavalier posted a phenomenal 157-to-35 strikeout-to-walk ratio in 146.1 innings of work. He finished the year with a 3.44 ERA and a 4.13 DRA.

Scouting Report: An atypical pitcher of sorts. Bettinger is the only starting pitcher that I've seen to not throw either a changeup or a splitter, which would essentially act as a changeup. Instead, the former Virginia reliever features an average 91- to 92-mph fastball, an above-average, 12-6 curveball, and a cutter (A) that flashes above-average at times and (B) that he'll vary the break and velocity on. Bettinger is a fast, efficient worker that commands the strike zone well. He has the look and feel as a #5-type arm or an ideal partner to work with an opener. Former Brewers right-hander Chase Anderson seems like a very reasonable comp in terms of performance.

Ceiling: 1.5-win player
Risk: Moderate
MLB ETA: 2020

15. Zack Brown, RHP

FB	CB	CH	Command	Overall
55	55	50+	50+	45

Born: 12/15/94	Age: 25	Bats: R
Height: 6-1	Weight: 180	Throws: R

YEAR	LVL	IP	W	L	SV	ERA	FIP	WHIP	K/9	K%	BB/9	BB%	K/BB	HR9	BABIP
2017	A	85.0	4	5	0	3.39	3.90	1.32	8.9	23.80%	3.6	9.63%	2.47	0.74	0.316
2017	A+	25.0	3	0	0	2.16	2.31	1.04	8.3	23.47%	0.7	2.04%	11.50	0.36	0.319
2018	Rk	2.0	0	0	0	0.00	2.57	2.00	13.5	30.00%	4.5	10.00%	3.00	0.00	0.500
2018	AA	125.7	9	1	0	2.44	3.33	1.04	8.3	23.06%	2.6	7.16%	3.22	0.57	0.257
2019	AAA	116.7	3	7	0	5.79	5.67	1.73	7.6	18.15%	4.9	11.85%	1.53	1.23	0.342

Background: An enigmatic pitcher of sorts during his tenure at the University of Kentucky. Milwaukee gambled on the projectable – and somewhat disappointing – right-hander in the fifth round of the 2016 draft. Fast forward two seasons and Brown, who stands 6-foot-1 and 180 pounds, was named the organization's Minor League Pitcher of the Year after posting a 116-to-36 strikeout-to-walk ratio in 125.2 innings in the Southern League. As he entered last season Brown looked like he was on the precipice of making a long term impact in the Brewers' rotation. And then the Pacific Coast League happened. Brown, like numerous other pitchers, struggled in the offense-inflating environment as his control / command backed up considerably. The former Wildcat would average just 7.6 strikeouts and 4.9 walks per nine innings across 23 starts and a pair of relief appearances with San Antonio. He finished the year with a horrible 5.79 ERA and an even worse 6.53 DRA (Deserved Runs Average).

Snippet from The 2018 Prospect Digest Handbook: His homer-prone-ness disappeared; he surrendered just 16 dingers over his last 237.2 innings of work – or roughly .61 HR/9. In terms of arsenal, Brown's fastball gets on hitters quickly. And his devastating breaking ball, called a curveball but moves more like a slider, is incredibly difficult on hitters, showing hard, late lateral movement – often outside the strike zone; it's a true plus offering. He'll mix in the occasional changeup as well. At worst, Brown looks like a late-inning, high-leverage relief arm. But there's some potential as a #3-type arm in the next year or two.

Scouting Report: Consider the following:

- Since 2006, only four 24-year-old pitcher posted a strikeout percentage between 17% and 19% with a walk percentage between 10% and 12% in the Pacific Coast League (min. 100 IP): Luis Cruz, Mike Kickham, Chris Seddon, and Zack Brown.

Ignoring Brown for a moment, it's essentially a group of quasi-big league arms. Along with Brown's once-stellar control / command, the consistent bite on his curveball also disappeared. And one has to wonder if those "new" Class AAA baseballs had anything to do with it. His fastball maintained status quo. And the changeup squeaked up half of a grade, showing more dive and fade than in previous years. Coming off of his breakout 2018 campaign the former Kentucky hurler looked like a potential mid-rotation caliber arm. Now, though, he looks like a fringy #5 – unless the curveball and control / command come storming back.

Ceiling: 1.5-win player
Risk: Moderate
MLB ETA: 2020

16. Eduardo Garcia, SS

	Hit	Power	SB	Patience	Glove	Overall
	20/45	30/40	40	N/A	45/55	45

Born: 07/10/02	Age: 17	Bats: R
Height: 6-2	Weight: 160	Throws: R

Background: The Brewers had to wait a handful days after the July 2nd signing date to officially come to terms with Garcia due to his late birthday. But once he turned 16-year-old on July 8th, the two sides agreed to a pact worth $1M.

Scouting Report: The young Venezuelan shortstop possesses quick hands, though he doesn't drive the ball with authority. He doesn't utilize his lower half well either. Defensively he shows remarkable range with impressive fluidity and has a chance to be an above-average defender. Garcia looks like a potential utility infielder at full maturity, though that may change if he can add some kind of power down the line.

Ceiling: 1.5-win player
Risk: Moderate
MLB ETA: 2023

17. Trey Supak, RHP

	FB	CB	CH	Command	Overall
	50	50	50	50	40

Born: 05/31/96	Age: 24	Bats: R
Height: 6-5	Weight: 240	Throws: R

YEAR	LVL	IP	W	L	SV	ERA	FIP	WHIP	K/9	K%	BB/9	BB%	K/BB	HR9	BABIP
2017	A	41.0	2	2	0	1.76	2.03	0.76	11.6	35.33%	2.2	6.67%	5.30	0.22	0.235
2017	A+	72.3	3	4	1	4.60	5.26	1.29	7.1	18.81%	3.5	9.24%	2.04	1.49	0.261
2018	A+	51.0	2	1	0	1.76	3.10	1.04	8.5	24.12%	2.8	8.04%	3.00	0.35	0.269
2018	AA	86.7	6	6	0	2.91	3.27	1.18	7.8	21.19%	2.9	7.91%	2.68	0.42	0.286
2019	AA	122.7	11	4	0	2.20	3.13	0.87	6.7	19.32%	1.7	4.88%	3.96	0.44	0.226
2019	AAA	30.0	1	2	0	9.30	5.99	1.67	8.1	22.88%	2.7	7.63%	3.00	1.80	0.388

Background: Taken by the Pirates in the second round in what seems like a lifetime ago, Supak continued his slow-and-steady approach through the minor leagues last season. After splitting time between High Class A and Class AA in 2018, the doughy right-hander rattled off 20 strong starts with Biloxi in the Southern League before getting smacked around in the offense-inflating environment known as the Pacific Coast League. The 6-foot-5, 240-pound hurler made a career best 27 starts between both stops, throwing 152.2 innings with just 118 strikeouts and 32 free passes. He compiled an aggregate 3.60 ERA. For his career, Supak is averaging 7.8 strikeouts and a tidy 2.6 walks per nine innings.

Snippet from The 2018 Prospect Digest Handbook: Unlike the typical Texas-born right-hander, Supak's never going to miss a lot of bats on "pure" stuff. But he generally does an impressive job commanding the ball to all four quadrants. He looks like a capable backend end starting pitcher. And one who's less than half-of-a-season away from contributing at the big league level. Think poor man's John Lackey.

Scouting Report: A couple decades ago Supak would have been considered one of the better pitching prospects in the game. He consistently posts low ERAs on the back of his above-average or better control / command. But things have changed. And he's not adapting. His weight's out of control and it's been trending in the wrong direction for years. I went back to The 2015 Prospect Digest Handbook to see his measurements were listed at 6-foot-5 and 210 pounds. He's now being listed as 240 (which is five pounds heavier than last season) – and he's *definitely* carrying more girth. Average offerings across the board with an above-average ability to throw strikes. He's strictly an up-and-down guy.

Ceiling: 1.0- to 1.5-win player
Risk: Low to Moderate
MLB ETA: 2020

18. Braden Webb, RHP

	FB	CB	CH	Command	Overall
	55+	60	60	40	45

Born: 04/25/95	Age: 25	Bats: R
Height: 6-3	Weight: 200	Throws: R

YEAR	LVL	IP	W	L	SV	ERA	FIP	WHIP	K/9	K%	BB/9	BB%	K/BB	HR9	BABIP
2017	A	86.7	6	7	3	4.36	4.11	1.28	9.3	24.39%	4.1	10.57%	2.31	0.83	0.281
2018	A+	100.7	5	8	0	4.20	4.24	1.44	9.3	23.74%	5.0	12.79%	1.86	0.80	0.302
2018	AA	20.0	1	0	0	1.80	2.46	1.15	10.8	30.00%	4.5	12.50%	2.40	0.00	0.283
2019	A+	36.7	1	2	0	3.44	4.52	1.31	7.6	20.39%	6.1	16.45%	1.24	0.49	0.226
2019	AA	15.0	1	4	0	9.00	6.89	2.00	7.8	16.67%	9.0	19.23%	0.87	1.20	0.289

Background: You'd be hard pressed to find a more disappointing showing for a pitching prospect – not only in the Brewers' system, but in *any* system – last season. Webb, a 6-foot-3, 200-pound right-hander, offered up more than the occasional glimpse of dominance over his first two seasons in pro ball: he averaged 9.3 strikeouts per nine innings with Wisconsin in 2017 and he followed that up by whiffing 9.5 hitters every nine innings during his stints in the Carolina and Southern Leagues a year later. Webb, who's always battled control and inconsistency issues through his baseball life, completely fell off the rails last season. The former South Carolina Gamecock opened the year up with six – mostly disastrous – starts in Class AA. He got demoted in early May to High Class A, which lasted eight starts. And then he hit the disabled list for roughly two months before he popped back up in the rookie leagues. In total, Webb posted a hideous 61-to-48 strikeout-to-walk ratio in only 64.1 innings of work.

Snippet from The 2018 Prospect Digest Handbook: On the short list of most underrated pitching prospects in the minor leagues. Webb's control/command still has ways to go, but it's important to remember the time missed due to injury. His repertoire and potential as a late-blooming starting pitcher is reminiscent of Cleveland's unheralded arm Mike Clevinger.

Scouting Report: Well, that didn't go as planned – but what actually does? For the most part Webb's arsenal still looked intact. His fastball was sitting in the low- to mid-90s. His curveball, which he really struggled to command, was a plus offering – when it did happen to find the strike zone. And his changeup shows hard, downward tumble. The arsenal is still quite reminiscent of a Cleveland's ace Mike Clevenger, who – again – was a late-bloomer. But Webb's now entering his age-25 season, so it's likely now or never. What's likely to happen: a shift to the bullpen where he turns into Devin Williams 2.0.

Ceiling: 1.5-win player
Risk: Moderate to High
MLB ETA: 2020

19. Cooper Hummel, LF/RF

Hit	Power	SB	Patience	Glove	Overall
45	50	35	60	55	40

Born: 11/28/94	Age: 25	Bats: B
Height: 5-10	Weight: 198	Throws: R

YEAR	LVL	PA	1B	2B	3B	HR	SB	CS	AVG	OBP	SLG	BB%	K%	GB%	LD%	FB%
2017	A+	239	31	11	2	4	2	2	0.244	0.368	0.381	15.90%	17.57%	42.7	21.7	29.3
2018	A+	404	52	25	0	8	3	1	0.260	0.397	0.410	15.59%	23.02%	38.1	26.3	29.2
2019	AA	419	55	8	5	17	4	7	0.249	0.384	0.450	14.80%	23.87%	42.3	19.5	28.6

Background: Another example of the club's tremendous late-round scouting efforts. Hummel, a former backstop turned corner outfielder, was little-used during his first two seasons at the University of Portland. But he turned in a solid breakout campaign as a junior, slugging .320/.422/.490 with 14 doubles, two triples, and five homeruns. Milwaukee took a flier in the 16th round four years ago. And Hummel has continued to produce at every stop along the way. The 5-foot-10, 198-pound outfielder topped the league average production line by 17% in High Class A in 2017. And his return to the Carolina League produced even better results the following year: he batted .260/.397/.410 with a 140 DRC+. Last season, though, Hummel entered the make-it-or-break-it level of minor league ball, Class AA, and came out with his finest season to date. Appearing in a career best 121 games with the Biloxi Shucker, the former Portland bopper slashed .249/.384/.450 with eight doubles and career highs in triples (five) and homeruns (17). His overall production, as measured by *Deserved Runs Created Plus*, topped the league average mark by 38%.

Scouting Report: Consider the following:

- Since 2006, only five 24-year-old hitters owned a 133 to 143 DRC+ with at least a 12% walk rate in the Southern League (min. 350 PA): Josh Fellhauer, Christian Marrero, Jim Gallagher, Bryan Byrne, and Cooper Hummel.

Incredibly saber-friendly thanks to his bloated walk rates and blossoming average power. Hummel's a gamer that has morphed his former catching skills into an above-average defender in either corner outfield position. Hummel might be able to carve out a semi-useful role as a fourth outfielder / bench bat.

Ceiling: 1.0- to 1.5-win player
Risk: Moderate
MLB ETA: 2020

20. Max Lazar, RHP

FB	CB	CH	Command	Overall
40/45	50	N/A	60	40

Born: 06/03/99	Age: 21	Bats: R
Height: 6-3	Weight: 185	Throws: R

Top CALs:

YEAR	LVL	IP	W	L	SV	ERA	FIP	WHIP	K/9	K%	BB/9	BB%	K/BB	HR9	BABIP
2017	Rk	13.7	0	2	0	5.93	4.29	1.24	9.2	25.00%	0.7	1.79%	14.00	1.32	0.359
2018	Rk	68.0	3	3	0	4.37	4.83	1.31	7.3	18.64%	2.0	5.08%	3.67	0.93	0.312
2019	Rk	6.0	0	1	0	1.50	0.92	0.67	15.0	47.62%	0.0	0.00%	#DIV/0!	0.00	0.364
2019	A	79.0	7	3	1	2.39	2.21	1.04	12.4	36.58%	1.7	5.03%	7.27	0.57	0.353

Background: Just to be completely upfront: I do not believe that Max Lazar is a Top 20 prospect in the Milwaukee Brewers' system. However, I find him so fascinating that I opted to include him on the list as opposed to a guy that likely won't make the big leagues. Standing 6-foot-3 and a generously listed 185 pounds, Lazar's production in the Pioneer League turned some heads two years ago. The then-19-year-old hurler posted a 55-to-15 strikeout-to-walk ratio in 68.0 innings of work. Milwaukee bounced their 2017 11th round draft pick up to the Midwest League to start last season. And Lazar's production leapt into a completely different – and elite – stratosphere: making 19 appearances with the Wisconsin Timber Rattlers, 10 of which were starts, the Florida native struck out a whopping 109 and walking just 15 in only 79.0 innings of work.

Scouting Report: First, let's put some context around just how good Lazar was during his stint in the Midwest League last season; consider the following:

- Since 2006, here's the list of 20-year-old pitchers to surpass a 34% strikeout percentage in the Midwest League (min. 75 IP): Max Lazar.

Max Lazar – or how he should be known: the right-handed version of Jamie Moyer – was otherworldly during his stint in the Midwest League last season, clearly. But he did it with a junior varsity fastball, which was sitting in the 83- to 84-mph range and topping 87 mph; an average grade curveball, and the immaculate control / command of a sniper. The hope, of course, is that Lazar's fastball gains several ticks in velocity as his slender frame fills out. But he's now entering his age-21 season and he may have missed that window. He's a long shot to make it to the big leagues, but if you're looking for an old fashion pitcher in the mold of Jamie Moyer or Charlie Leibrandt, than I would recommend catching a start by Max Lazar

Ceiling: 1.0-win player
Risk: Moderate to High
MLB ETA: 2022/2023

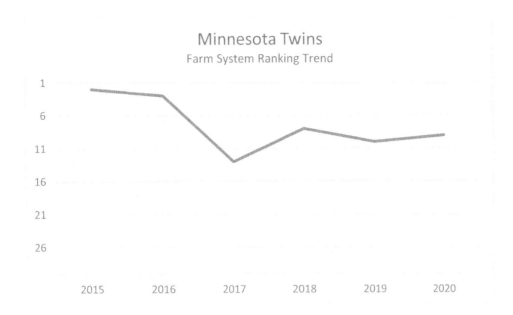

Rank	Name	Age	Pos
1	Alex Kirilloff	22	1B/RF
2	Jhoan Duran	22	RHP
3	Royce Lewis	21	SS
4	Trevor Larnach	23	RF
5	Jordan Balazovic	21	RHP
6	Chris Vallimont	23	RHP
7	Gilberto Celestino	21	CF
8	Keoni Cavaco	26	SS
9	Ryan Jeffers	23	C
10	Brent Rooker	25	1B/LF
11	Ben Rortvedt	22	C
12	Lewis Thorpe	24	LHP
13	Matt Wallner	22	RF
14	Blayne Enlow	21	RHP
15	Matt Canterino	22	RHP
16	Nick Gordon	21	2B/SS
17	Akil Baddoo	21	CF
18	Cole Sands	22	RHP
19	Wander Javier	21	SS
20	Travis Blankenhorn	23	IF/OF

1. Alex Kirilloff, 1B/RF

Hit	Power	SB	Patience	Glove	Overall
60	50/60	35	50	50	60

Born: 11/09/97	Age: 22	Bats: L
Height: 6-2	Weight: 215	Throws: L

YEAR	LVL	PA	1B	2B	3B	HR	SB	CS	AVG	OBP	SLG	BB%	K%	GB%	LD%	FB%
2018	A	281	46	20	5	13	1	1	0.333	0.391	0.607	8.54%	16.73%	45.2	10.1	42.8
2018	A+	280	61	24	2	7	3	2	0.362	0.393	0.550	5.00%	13.93%	40.9	29.3	26.7
2019	AA	411	77	18	2	9	7	6	0.283	0.343	0.413	7.06%	18.49%	47.5	21.0	28.1

Background: If you take a step back and think about it for a moment, it's quite remarkable really. Kirilloff, the 15th overall pick in the 2016, put together a strong debut showing in the Appalachian League when he batted .306/.341/.454 with nine doubles, one triple, and seven homeruns. But a wonky elbow injury – which eventually necessitated Tommy John surgery – forced him out of action the entire following season. The amazing part – and a true testament to his talent – though, is the fact that in his return to action he posted a *Deserved Runs Created Plus* total of 169 between stints in Low Class A and High Class A – despite the major surgery and lengthy time off. Sandwiched between Will Benson and Matt Thaiss as the 15th overall pick, Kirilloff battled a couple injuries in 2019: an early season wrist issue kept him out of action until May 2nd and an undisclosed injury knocked him out of action for several weeks in June as well. When he was in the lineup he did what he always does: bash. In 94 games with the Pensacola Blue Wahoos, the 6-foot-2, 215-pound right fielder/first baseman slugged .283/.343/.413 with 18 doubles, two triples, nine homeruns, and a career best seven stolen bases. Per Baseball Prospectus' *Deserved Runs Created Plus*, his overall production topped the league average threshold by 21%.

Snippet from The 2018 Prospect Digest Handbook: A higher offensive ceiling than teammate and fellow top prospect Royce Lewis. Kirilloff combines his plus-power potential with an amazing ability to put the bat on the ball, leading to phenomenal contact rates. Couple that fact with a hit tool that should be above-average at its peak.

Scouting Report: Consider the following:

- Since 2006, only three 21-year-old hitters met the following criteria in he Southern League (min. 300 PA): 115 to 125 DRC+ total, a sub-20.0% strikeout rate, a walk rate between 6% and 8%, and an Isolated Power total between .130 and .150. Those three hitters: Keston Hiura, Dustin Peterson, and – of course – Alex Kirilloff.
- While Peterson never panned out, Hiura was one of the top performing rookies last season as he posted a 115 DRC+.

Kirilloff got off to a slow start, which isn't surprising given (A) the fact that it's the minors' most challenging level and (B) he missed the opening several weeks of the season. The Pennsylvania native batted a lowly .240/.336/.346 over his first 27 games. But once the calendar flipped to June he slugged .299/.346/.439 the remainder of the season. Southpaws gave Kirilloff a little bit of trouble as well (.244/.301/.333), but it isn't concerning in the least given the track record. Short compact swing with plus bat speed and natural loft to drive out 35 homers in a season at full maturity. In terms of upside, think Rafael Devers' showing in 2019: .311/.361/.555 with 32 homeruns.

Ceiling: 4.5-win player
Risk: Low to Moderate
MLB ETA: 2020

2. Jhoan Duran, RHP

FB	CB	CH	Command	Overall
80	65	60	50+	60

Born: 01/08/98	Age: 22	Bats: R
Height: 6-5	Weight: 230	Throws: R

YEAR	LVL	IP	W	L	SV	ERA	FIP	WHIP	K/9	K%	BB/9	BB%	K/BB	HR9	BABIP
2017	Rk	11.3	0	2	0	7.15	2.98	2.03	10.3	22.03%	3.2	6.78%	3.25	0.00	0.452
2017	A-	51.0	6	3	0	4.24	4.94	1.20	6.4	16.59%	3.0	7.83%	2.12	0.88	0.253
2018	A	64.7	5	4	0	4.73	3.93	1.50	9.9	24.48%	3.9	9.66%	2.54	0.84	0.346
2018	A	36.0	2	1	0	2.00	2.67	0.81	11.0	32.59%	2.5	7.41%	4.40	0.50	0.218
2019	A+	78.0	2	9	0	3.23	3.05	1.21	11.0	29.87%	3.6	9.75%	3.06	0.58	0.317
2019	AA	37.0	3	3	0	4.86	2.75	1.16	10.0	31.54%	2.2	6.92%	4.56	0.49	0.349

Background: From having very few hard-throwing hurlers at any level of the organization to sporting a bevy of talented flame-throwers. And Duran easily fits into the latter group. The Arizona Diamondbacks sent Duran, along with outfielder Ernie De La Trinidad and Gabriel Macias, for veteran infielder Eduardo Escobar. A barrel-chested behemoth out of Esperanza, Dominican Republic, Duran made 15 strong starts with the Fort Myers Miracle to open last season. And he continued to flash elite peripherals – especially for his age – as he moved up for seven final starts with Pensacola. In total, the 6-foot-5, 230-pound right-hander tossed a career-best 115.0 innings, recording 136 strikeouts and just 40 walks. He compiled an aggregate 3.76 ERA.

Snippet from The 2018 Prospect Digest Handbook: Despite a lean pencil-like frame, Duran, who measured 6-foot-5 and only 175 pounds, owns a lightning quick arm that allows his fastball sit hover in the mid- to upper-90s. He'll complement the offering with a slurvy-type breaking pitch that's called a curveball. It's an average offering when he's staying on top and locating it down in the zone. He'll also shows a subpar changeup. More of a strike-thrower than a command guy at this point, Duran has the potential to develop into a sturdy backend starting pitcher with the floor as a high-leverage reliever. He does need one of his secondary offerings to jump up into the above-average range at this point though.

Scouting Report: Everything's changed at this point – including his weight. Duran was listed at 6-foot-5 and 175 pounds last offseason. A year later he's looking noticeably thicker and weighing in at 230 pounds. The fastball velocity increased from sitting in the mid-90s and touching the upper-90s to sitting in the upper-90s with *ease*. His breaking ball, which is called either a slider or curveball depending upon reports, definitely looks like a curveball, sitting in the upper-70s and low-80s with plus movement. But the most intriguing aspect about Duran is his changeup. It's hard with late tumble and downward fade. The movement's incredible. It's another plus pitch. There are very few, if any, pitchers that can match up with Duran's ability to throw strikes and own a deep, potentially elite arsenal. There's some upper rotation caliber potential as long as he doesn't take the Brusdar Graterol route.

Ceiling: 4.0-win player
Risk: Moderate
MLB ETA: 2020

3. Royce Lewis, SS

Hit	Power	SB	Patience	Glove	Overall
40/55	45/55	55	50	50+	60

Born: 06/05/99	Age: 21	Bats: R
Height: 6-2	Weight: 200	Throws: R

YEAR	LVL	PA	1B	2B	3B	HR	SB	CS	AVG	OBP	SLG	BB%	K%	GB%	LD%	FB%
2017	RK	159	25	6	2	3	15	2	0.271	0.390	0.414	11.95%	10.69%	49.1	12.9	29.3
2017	A	80	17	2	1	1	3	1	0.296	0.363	0.394	7.50%	20.00%	44.6	14.3	32.1
2018	A	327	61	23	0	9	22	4	0.315	0.368	0.485	7.34%	14.98%	41.8	11.6	40.2
2018	A+	208	34	6	3	5	6	4	0.255	0.327	0.399	9.13%	16.83%	53.6	19.0	20.3
2019	A+	418	61	17	3	10	16	8	0.238	0.289	0.376	6.46%	21.53%	44.6	15.1	29.5
2019	AA	148	19	9	1	2	6	2	0.231	0.291	0.358	7.43%	22.30%	43.0	17.0	33.0

Background: To the best of my recollection, though perhaps I'm overlooking someone, but I don't recall a prospect that was so widely praised – almost universally – as a top prospect that turned in such a horrible season in which (A) there's no known cause or injury and (B) the reasons for the failures are so different across the board. In last year's Prospect Digest Handbook, I ranked Lewis as the tenth best prospect in the game. *Baseball America* had him as the ninth best. *Baseball Prospectus* listed him one spot better. And MLB.com ranked him as the fifth best minor leaguer. The number overall pick in the 2017 draft, Lewis, a product of JSerra Catholic High School, reached the Midwest League – and acquired himself nicely – during his professional debut. A season later, at the ripe old age of 19, topped the league average mark in the Florida State League. But something went off the rails for him in 2019. Lewis began last season back in the Florida State League, though the results were markedly different; he batted a disappointing .238/.289/.376 with 17 doubles, three triples, and 10 homeruns in 94 games. And his production maintained status quo during his late season promotion up to Class AA: he hit a puny .231/.291/.358 with the Pensacola Blue Wahoos. If there is a silver lining to be had, it's his work in the Arizona Fall League: in 22 games with the Salt River Rafters, Lewis slugged a scorching .353/.411/.565 with nine doubles and three homeruns.

Snippet from The 2018 Prospect Digest Handbook: Not quite as a potent at the plate as Houston's Carlos Correa, but there are quite a few similarities. Lewis has – quietly – become of the best defenders in the minor leagues, saving nine runs above average over the course of his first 175 games. Offensively speaking, he's a budding dynamo – the type of hitter that perches atop a team's big league lineup for the duration of his career: plus speed, plus hit tool, above-average power, strong contact skills, and a decent eye at the plate.

Scouting Report: So...what the hell happened? Statistically speaking, there's really nothing out of whack. His walk rate remained unchanged His strikeout rate jumped a few percentage points and his power dropped a touch, but nothing that isn't within a reasonable norm. And his batted ball data generally seems in line with his career numbers too. Now let's go to the tape... The lightning quick bat speed, strong wrists and forearms are still intact. The problem isn't necessarily his swing, per se. It's this massive leg kick that's creating issues. Sometimes he's late getting his foot down. Sometimes it seems as if his weight is leaning too forward. It's just...bad. I went back and watched old tape from 2018. The leg kick was still prevalent. But the competition of his talent was such that he was able to succeed in spite of it. Lewis possesses the intangibles that made him the top pick in the draft. I think he needs to alter his lower half, rather than the whole swing.

Ceiling: 4.5-win player
Risk: Moderate to High
MLB ETA: 2020/2021

4. Trevor Larnach, RF

Hit	Power	SB	Patience	Glove	Overall
55	50/55	30	55	50	55

Born: 02/26/97	Age: 23	Bats: L
Height: 6-4	Weight: 223	Throws: R

YEAR	LVL	PA	1B	2B	3B	HR	SB	CS	AVG	OBP	SLG	BB%	K%	GB%	LD%	FB%
2018	RK	75	12	5	0	2	2	0	0.311	0.413	0.492	13.33%	14.67%	36.5	30.8	32.7
2018	A	102	15	8	1	3	1	0	0.297	0.373	0.505	10.78%	16.67%	44.6	17.6	36.5
2019	A+	361	68	26	1	6	4	1	0.316	0.382	0.459	9.70%	20.50%	48.0	22.8	27.2
2019	AA	181	35	4	0	7	0	0	0.295	0.387	0.455	12.15%	27.62%	47.1	23.1	26.9

Background: Sandwiched in between a pair of highly touted prep prospects in the opening round 2018 draft, Larnarch, who was taken between Nolan Gorman and Bryce Turnag as the 20th overall pick, was one of the major risers in the entire class. A good, sometime great bat at Oregon State during his sophomore season, the 6-foot-4, 223-pound corner outfielder developed into one of the most feared hitters in the middle of the Beavers' potent lineup during his final campaign. In a career-best 68 games with the Pac12 powerhouse, Larnach belted out personal bests in doubles (19) and homeruns (19), which was 16 more than his entire career total, en route to slugging .348/.463/.652. And that production hasn't slowed since joining the Twins' organization. The California native hit .303/.390/.500 between the Appalachian and Midwest Leagues during his debut. And last season he sprinted through the Florida State and Southern League while batting an aggregate .309/.384/.458 with 30 doubles, one triple, and 13 homeruns.

Snippet from The 2018 Prospect Digest Handbook: As for Larnach, well, he showcases above-average power, perhaps peaking in the 20-homer territory, with a strong eye and the ability to consistently hit .300 – though I do worry a bit about his ability to make consistent contact. He looks like a better version of Pittsburgh's Jordan Luplow, who I ranked as the club's fifth best prospect [heading into 2018].

Scouting Report: On a bit of a side note: Jordan Luplow, forever underrated, slugged .276/.372/.551 with a 126 DRC+ in 85 games with the Indians last season. That level of production seems like a reasonable settling point for the former Oregon State star – perhaps trading some points in batting average for a leaner slugging percentage. With respect to Larnarch's work in High Class A last season, consider the following:

- Since 2006, here's the list of 22-year-old hitters that posted at least a 160 DRC+ total in the Florida State League (min. 300 PA): Brandon Lowe, Nick Solak, Christin Stewart, Brent Keys, and Trevor Larnach.
- Ignoring Larnach for a moment, here are the respective big league career DRC+ totals of the remaining four: 103 (Lowe, in 125 games), 109 (Solak, 33 games), 89 (Stewart, 121 games), and Keys never cracked a big league lineup.

Larnach's made far more consistent contact then I would have guessed, though his K-rate did blow up to nearly 28% in 43 Class AA games. He's still tapping into his above-average power potential as well.

Ceiling: 3.5-win player
Risk: Moderate
MLB ETA: 2020

5. Jordan Balazovic, RHP

FB	SL	CH	Command	Overall
65	55	50	60	55

Born: 09/17/98	Age: 21	Bats: R
Height: 6-5	Weight: 215	Throws: R

YEAR	LVL	IP	W	L	SV	ERA	FIP	WHIP	K/9	K%	BB/9	BB%	K/BB	HR9	BABIP
2017	Rk	40.3	1	3	0	4.91	5.23	1.66	6.5	15.85%	4.5	10.93%	1.45	1.12	0.331
2018	A	61.7	7	3	0	3.94	3.02	1.17	11.4	30.71%	2.6	7.09%	4.33	0.73	0.327
2019	A	20.7	2	1	0	2.18	1.59	0.92	14.4	39.76%	1.7	4.82%	8.25	0.44	0.318
2019	A+	73.0	6	4	0	2.84	2.28	1.00	11.8	32.21%	2.6	7.05%	4.57	0.37	0.283

Background: The fifth round of the 2016 draft produced a surprising amount of talent. Eight of the 30 players have already made it to the big leagues: Cavan Biggio, Twins hurler Devin Smeltzer, Mike Shawaryn, Donnie Walton, Nicky Lopez, Cole Irvin, Jeremy Walker, and Astros top prospect Abraham Toro. Balazovic's likely to add his name to the list in the next year-plus as well. Tall and wiry, the Canadian-born right-hander first caught my attention after a quietly dominant showing in the Midwest League two years ago when he posted a 78-to-18 strikeout-to-walk ratio with a 3.53 DRA (*Deserved Run Average*) as a 19-year-old. But he raised the bar even further when he briefly returned to the Low Class A league to begin 2019. he fanned 33 and walked just a quartet in 20.2 innings. The front office promoted the 6-foot-5, 215-pound right-hander up to High Class A for the remainder of the year. In 15 appearances with the Fort Myers Miracle, Balazovic struck out 96 against 21 free passes in only 73.0 innings.

Snippet from The 2018 Prospect Digest Handbook: Another one of these low level arms in the Twins organization that's incredibly intriguing. The Canadian right-hander locates a plus-fastball well. And he complements it with a slider with vertical break that occasionally flashes above-average and it looks like a curveball as well. He'll also mix in a rare changeup. There's still considerable projection left given his lanky frame and the fact that his innings have been closely governed. Balazovic looks like a solid backend arm, though the development of his changeup remains imperative.

Scouting Report: With respect to his work in High Class A last season, consider the following:

- Since 2006, only four 20-year-old arms posted a strikeout percentage north of 30% with a walk percentage between 6% and 8% in the Florida State League (min. 50 IP): Yovani Gallardo, Will Inman, Sean Reid-Foley, and – of course – Jordan Balazovic.

The former fifth round was light's out from the first inning all the way down to the last in 2019. His 94- to 96-mph fastball is an easy 65-grade with late, riding life. He locates it well and shows a willingness/aptitude to challenge hitters at the top part of the strike zone. His hard, tightly spun, mid-80s slider adds a second swing-and-miss option and it's particularly lethal down and away to right-handed hitters. However, I scouted a few games of Balazovic's last season. And he remains quite hesitant to throw the changeup, which – again – requires further develop. At its best, it's sits in average territory showing some cutting, diving action. After his phenomenal showing in 2019, Balazovic's ceiling now resides – comfortably – in the #3-type starting pitcher. One more thought: the command/control is on the low end of plus with the potential move up as he matures.

Ceiling: 3.0- to 3.5-win player
Risk: Moderate
MLB ETA: 2021

6. Chris Vallimont, RHP

FB	CB	CH	Command	Overall
60	65	50+	55	50

Born: 03/18/97	Age: 23	Bats: R
Height: 6-5	Weight: 220	Throws: R

YEAR	LVL	IP	W	L	SV	ERA	FIP	WHIP	K/9	K%	BB/9	BB%	K/BB	HR9	BABIP
2018	A-	29.0	0	2	0	6.21	5.82	1.59	6.2	15.15%	7.1	17.42%	0.87	0.93	0.235
2019	A	69.3	4	4	0	2.99	3.00	1.07	10.4	29.52%	3.4	9.59%	3.08	0.52	0.273
2019	A+	36.0	2	3	0	3.50	2.97	1.17	10.5	28.57%	2.8	7.48%	3.82	0.75	0.308
2019	A+	22.3	2	2	0	3.63	1.34	0.85	11.3	32.94%	1.6	4.71%	7.00	0.00	0.283

Background: Every year there's a pitcher that completely blows me away when I finally start scouting games. Two years ago it was Miami's Edward Cabrera, whom I touted before his breakout 2019 campaign. Last season, it was Chris Vallimont, a product of Division II Mercyhurst College in Erie, Pennsylvania. A fifth round pick by – coincidentally – the Marlins two years ago, Minnesota acquired Vallimont – with veteran righty reliever Sergio Romo – for slugging first baseman Lewin Diaz. The 6-foot-5, 220-pound hard-throwing right-hander split time the Midwest and Florida State Leagues in 2019, posting a dominating 150-to-41 strikeout-to-walk ratio in only 127.2 innings of work. He compiled an aggregate 3.24 ERA.

Scouting Report: With respect to his work in High Class A last season, consider the following:

- Since 2006, only four 22-year-old arms posted a strikeout percentage north of 30% with a walk percentage between 5.5% and 7.5% in the Florida State League (min. 50 IP): Tarik Skubal, one of baseball's biggest breakouts in 2019, Dellin Betances, Zachary Quate, and – of course – Chris Vallimont. Quate, the odd man out, accomplished it as full time reliever.

Love, love, LOVE him. Plus fastball that he weaponizes at the top of the strike zone like very few hurlers. An even better, fall-off-the-table curveball. And a 50+ grade changeup. Throw in some 55-grade command. And that's a recipe for a solid, better-than-average big league starting pitcher. There's some tremendously sneaky upside here, something along the lines of #3/#4-type arm. I wouldn't be shocked to see him move into several Top 100 lists within a year.

Ceiling: 2.5- to 3.0-win player
Risk: Moderate
MLB ETA: 2021

7. Gilberto Celestino, CF

	Hit	Power	SB	Patience	Glove	Overall
	50	45	45	50	50	50

Born: 02/13/99	Age: 21	Bats: R
Height: 6-0	Weight: 170	Throws: L

YEAR	LVL	PA	1B	2B	3B	HR	SB	CS	AVG	OBP	SLG	BB%	K%	GB%	LD%	FB%
2018	RK	117	23	4	1	1	8	2	0.266	0.308	0.349	5.13%	13.68%	55.3	19.1	18.1
2018	A-	142	29	8	0	4	14	0	0.323	0.387	0.480	7.04%	17.61%	47.6	20.4	27.2
2019	A	503	87	24	3	10	14	8	0.276	0.350	0.409	9.54%	16.10%	51.5	11.7	29.2
2019	A+	33	5	4	0	0	0	0	0.300	0.333	0.433	6.06%	12.12%	48.1	14.8	33.3

Background: A high profile, highly sought after talent on the international market five years ago. Houston signed the toolsy center fielder for a hefty $2.25 million during the July 2nd signing period. Minnesota acquired the Santo Domingo, Dominican Republic, native – along with hard-throwing right-hander Jorge Alcala – near the trade deadline two years ago. The 6-foot, 170-pound prospect spent last season in the Midwest League. In 117 games with the Cedar Rapids Kernels, Celestino slugged .276/.350/.409 with 24 doubles, three triples, 10 homeruns, and 14 stolen bases in 22 total attempts. Per *Deserved Runs Created Plus*, his overall production topped the league average threshold by 37%.

Snippet from The 2018 Prospect Digest Handbook: A raw, toolsy center field lottery ticket. Celestino hasn't quite tapped into his in-game power just yet. But he's not showing a whole lot of red flags either. Decent eye, solid hit tool, and plays a passable center field. He's likely headed for the Midwest League for the entirety of 2018. Hopefully he can carry his impressive showing in short-season ball over with him.

Scouting Report: Consider the following:

- Since 2006, only three 20-year-old hitters met the following criteria in the Midwest League (min. 300 PA): 132 to 142 DRC+, a sub-20% strikeout rate, and a walk percentage between 8.5% and 10.5%. Those three hitters: Alexi Amarista, Jose Fermin, an intriguing prospect in the Indians' system, and Gilberto Celestino.

Celestino was pretty terrible during his first 62 games of the season, hitting a lowly .216/.293/.314 in 263 plate appearance. His stick reached a boiling point shortly thereafter and he slugged .336/.403/.504 with 19 doubles, two triples, and six homeruns. While he doesn't possess a loud tool shed; Celestino's solid-average across the board. He possesses the ceiling as a solid-average regular, maybe a little more. In terms of ceiling, think Oscar Mercado's showing in 2019: .269/.318/.443 with 15 doubles and 15 stolen bases.

Ceiling: 2.5-win player
Risk: Moderate
MLB ETA: 2020

8. Keoni Cavaco, SS

	Hit	Power	SB	Patience	Glove	Overall
	35/50	30/55	35	45	50	50

Born: 06/02/01	Age: 19	Bats: R
Height: 6-2	Weight: 195	Throws: R

YEAR	LVL	PA	1B	2B	3B	HR	SB	CS	AVG	OBP	SLG	BB%	K%	GB%	LD%	FB%
2019	Rk	92	10	4	0	1	1	1	0.172	0.217	0.253	4.35%	38.04%	46.2	15.4	34.6

Background: Eastlake High School in Chula Vista, California, has churned out a surprising amount of talent since 2000: 12 alumni have been drafted. The two most famous: five-time All-Star Adrian Gonzalez, who earned nearly $150,000,000 in his career, and – of course – Keoni Cavaco. In a draft class chock full of premium, high-end talent at the shortstop position, the Twins made Cavaco the third player at the position chosen last June when they selected him with the 13th overall pick. The franchise signed him to a slightly below-slot bonus of $4.05 million, saving the club a little less than $200,000 in their bonus pool. The 6-foot-2, 195-pound middle infielder batted a lowly .172/.217/.253 with just four doubles and a homerun in 25 games in the Gulf Coast League. Per *Deserved Runs Created Plus*, his overall production was a staggering 72% *below* the league average mark.

Scouting Report: There's bad debuts. Then there's awful debut. And there there's Cavaco's showing in the Gulf Coast League last season. Not only was his bat as limp as a wet noodle, but he barely walked – 4.3% – and whiffed way too frequently (38.0%). The former prep star shows an unbelievably short, quick stroke at the plate, allowing his hands to stay inside the ball. Coupled with the plus bat speed, Cavaco shows natural loft and strong wrists, both suggesting he's capable of 15- to 20-homer power. Very quiet approach at the plate with little movement. The abbreviated – and horrible – debut should prove to be an anomaly. I really like the swing.

Ceiling: 2.5-win player
Risk: Moderate
MLB ETA: 2023

9. Ryan Jeffers, C

Hit	Power	SB	Patience	Glove	Overall
45	50	30	50	50	50

Born: 06/03/97	Age: 23	Bats: R
Height: 6-4	Weight: 230	Throws: R

YEAR	LVL	PA	1B	2B	3B	HR	SB	CS	AVG	OBP	SLG	BB%	K%	GB%	LD%	FB%
2018	RK	129	33	7	0	3	0	1	0.422	0.543	0.578	15.50%	12.40%	36.0	39.5	19.8
2018	A	155	26	10	0	4	0	0	0.288	0.361	0.446	9.03%	19.35%	39.4	14.7	36.7
2019	A+	315	51	11	0	10	0	0	0.256	0.330	0.402	8.89%	20.32%	39.3	20.5	34.7
2019	AA	99	16	5	0	4	0	0	0.287	0.374	0.483	9.09%	19.19%	36.9	18.5	33.8

Background: A comically consistent performer during his three-year collegiate career at the University of North Carolina at Wilmington. Jeffers, a broad-shouldered 6-foot-4, 230-pound backstop, posted OPSs between 1.026 and 1.095 in each of his seasons at the Colonial Athletic Association school.

Minnesota snagged Jeffers in the second round, 59th overall, two years ago. The Raleigh, North Carolina, native turned in one of the better debuts that season, slashing .344/.444/.502 with 17 doubles and seven homeruns as he split time between Elizabethton and Cedar Rapids. Jeffers opened up last season with the Fort Myers Miracle in the Florida State League and capped it off with a solid 24-game run in the Southern League. In total, he batted a solid .264/.341/.421 with 16 doubles and 14 homeruns.

Snippet from The 2018 Prospect Digest Handbook: The hulking backstop showed a tremendous eye at the plate, along with matching contact skills, during his collegiate career – and that's carried over into the low levels of the minor leagues as well. Throw in some solid defense and Jeffers has a shot to be a league average starter.

Scouting Report: With respect to his work in High Class A last season, consider the following:

- Since 2006, only five 22-year-old hitters met the following criteria in the Florida State League (min. 300 PA): 117 to 127 DRC+, a walk rate between 8% and 10%, and a strikeout rate between 18% and 22%. Those five hitters: Lorenzo Cain, Todd Frazier, Jared Oliva, Clete Thomas, and – of course – Ryan Jeffers.

For those counting at home:

- Cain owns a career DRC+ total of 105 in 1,045 big league games. Frazier's sporting a 110 DRC+ in 1,186 games. Thomas comes in at 74 in limited action across five levels. And Oliva just posted a 128 DRC+ in Class AA last season.

Not bad. Not bad at all. Solid skills across the board wrapped up at a premium position – likely, the most premium position nowadays. Mitch Garver, my long time personal favorite, has a stranglehold on the catching gig at the big level. But Jeffers could help with spot duty by the end of 2020. In terms of ceiling think Travis d'Arnaud's 2019 season in which he batted .251/.312/.433.

Ceiling: 2.0- to 2.5-win player
Risk: Moderate
MLB ETA: 2020/2021

10. Brent Rooker, 1B/LF

Hit	Power	SB	Patience	Glove	Overall
40+	65	20	55	45	50

Born: 11/01/94	Age: 25	Bats: R
Height: 6-3	Weight: 215	Throws: R

YEAR	LVL	PA	1B	2B	3B	HR	SB	CS	AVG	OBP	SLG	BB%	K%	GB%	LD%	FB%
2017	RK	99	12	5	0	7	2	2	0.282	0.364	0.588	11.11%	21.21%	25.8	30.3	36.4
2017	A+	162	23	6	0	11	0	0	0.280	0.364	0.552	9.88%	29.01%	38.5	20.8	36.5
2018	AA	568	70	32	4	22	6	1	0.254	0.333	0.465	9.86%	26.41%	35.3	25.2	31.4
2019	Rk	7	2	0	0	0	0	0	0.333	0.429	0.333	14.29%	0.00%	66.7	33.3	0.0
2019	AAA	274	34	16	0	14	2	0	0.281	0.398	0.535	12.77%	34.67%	35.8	24.6	32.8

Background: Like a cauldron slowly reaching a boiling point. Rooker's collegiate production reached a scorching temperature during his junior campaign at Mississippi State when he smashed 30 doubles, three triples, and 23 homeruns en route to batting .387/.495/.810 in 67 games. Minnesota snagged the hulking first baseman/left fielder in the opening round, 35th overall, in 2017. Since then Rooker, who stands an imposing 6-foot-3 and 215 pounds, made quick work of the minor leagues: he appeared in 40 games in High Class A during his debut; looked like a middle-of-the-lineup thumper the following season in Class AA; and continued to bash in an injury-shortened season in the International League in 2019. In 65 games with the Rochester Red Wings, Rooker slugged .281/.398/.535 with 16 doubles and 14 homeruns. His overall production, per *Deserved Runs Created Plus*, topped the league average mark by 23%. A right groin contusion ended his season in mid-July.

Snippet from The 2018 Prospect Digest Handbook: Below average hit tool; plus-power; terrible glove – that's not a tremendous recipe for success, especially with average walk rates.

Scouting Report: The franchise broke the homerun record by belting out 307 dingers last season. Brent Rooker is the 2019 Twins incarnate. Offering up 30 double/30 homerun-potential. The problem for Rooker, of course, is simple: where the hell is he going to play at the big league level? Eddie Rosario and Max Kepler are patrolling the corner outfielder positions. Miguel Sano, and his new contract extension, is locked in at first base. And the forever young Nelson Cruz has a strangle hold on the designated hitter spot. In terms of offensive ceiling, think Franmil Reyes showing in 2019: .249/.310/.512.

Ceiling: 2.0-win player
Risk: Low to Moderate
MLB ETA: 2020

11. Ben Rortvedt, C

	Hit	Power	SB	Patience	Glove	Overall
	40	45	20	55	70	45

Born: 09/25/97	Age: 22	Bats: L
Height: 5-10	Weight: 205	Throws: R

YEAR	LVL	PA	1B	2B	3B	HR	SB	CS	AVG	OBP	SLG	BB%	K%	GB%	LD%	FB%
2017	A	336	49	16	0	4	1	0	0.224	0.284	0.315	6.55%	17.86%	56.8	12.4	26.0
2018	A	157	28	9	2	1	1	0	0.276	0.325	0.386	6.37%	22.29%	48.6	11.7	36.0
2018	A+	196	31	7	1	4	0	0	0.250	0.337	0.372	10.71%	14.80%	52.8	18.1	25.0
2019	A+	94	8	8	1	2	0	0	0.238	0.340	0.438	12.77%	17.02%	43.1	12.3	38.5
2019	AA	226	34	8	0	5	0	0	0.239	0.332	0.355	10.18%	22.57%	50.3	16.3	23.1

Background: One of the more lower profile, albeit incredibly fascinating catching prospects in the minor leagues. Rortvedt, a product of Verona High School, has struggled to consistently hit his weight throughout his four minor league seasons, but the one thing that's been as consistent as death and taxes: his trademark stellar defense. A former second round selection in 2016, the lefty-swinging backstop split last season between the Fort Myers Miracle and the Pensacola Blue Wahoos, hitting an aggregate .238/.334/.379 with 16 doubles, one triple, and seven homeruns. For his career, Rortvedt is sporting a .240/.315/.347 triple-slash line.

Snippet from The 2018 Prospect Digest Handbook: Again, Rortvedt's calling has been – is – and will be his work behind the dish. He's phenomenal. The fact that he's showing solid improvement with the bat bodes very well for his career. He's never going to be confused for Mike Piazza but he should have a similar upside as Austin Hedges. Meaning: he's going to be a solid, sturdy capable backup at the big league level, maybe a little more. He's definitely going to see some big league time on his resume though.

Scouting Report: Let's ignore the superficially terrible triple-slash lines for a moment. Let's look at his overall offensive production compared to the league average lines. In three of his last four stops Rortvedt, the "terrible hitter", has bested the league average mark by 15%, 27%, and 14%. The only other time he failed to eclipse the 100-point threshold: he posted a 97 DRC+ in the Florida State League two years ago as a 20-year-old. Now consider the following:

- Since 2006, only four 21-year-old hitters met the following criteria in the Southern League (min. 200 PA): 110 to 120 DRC+; a walk rate between 9% and 11%, and a strikeout rate between 21% and 24%. Those four hitters: Nick Gordon, Arismendy Alcantara, Michael Saunders, and Ben Rortvedt.

How many would have grouped those three hitters along with Ben Rortvedt? I wouldn't have. Now let's talk about Rortvedt's defense: it's crazy good. Clay Davenport's metric had him as a +17 in only 79 games last season. Plus, he threw out 52% of would-be base stealers. The defense alone puts him as a low-tier starter. Throw in a little bit of offensive punch and Rortvedt could be a consistent middle-tier starting option. He's easily one of my favorites.

Ceiling: 1.5- to 2.0-win player
Risk: Low to Moderate
MLB ETA: 2020/2021

Minnesota Twins

12. Lewis Thorpe, LHP

FB	CB	SL	CH	Command	Overall
45	50	45	55	60	45

Born: 11/23/95	Age: 24	Bats: R
Height: 6-1	Weight: 218	Throws: L

YEAR	LVL	IP	W	L	SV	ERA	FIP	WHIP	K/9	K%	BB/9	BB%	K/BB	HR9	BABIP
2017	A+	77.0	3	4	0	2.69	2.92	1.21	9.8	26.75%	3.6	9.87%	2.71	0.35	0.304
2017	AA	6.0	1	0	0	6.00	6.11	1.17	10.5	28.00%	3.0	8.00%	3.50	3.00	0.214
2018	AA	108.0	8	4	0	3.58	3.36	1.25	10.9	28.73%	2.5	6.58%	4.37	1.08	0.327
2018	AAA	21.7	0	3	0	3.32	3.56	1.20	10.8	29.55%	2.5	6.82%	4.33	1.25	0.321
2019	AAA	96.3	5	4	0	4.58	3.72	1.20	11.1	29.53%	2.3	6.20%	4.76	1.21	0.318

Background: After missing more than two full years due to injury, the Australian-born left-hander quickly made up for lost time. He jumped straight back in High Class A and even appeared in a game Class AA in 2017. He spent the majority of the following year back in the Southern League with a three game cameo in Class AAA. And last season the 6-foot-1, 218-pound southpaw yo-yoed between the Rochester Red Wings and the Minnesota Twins as he bounced between starting pitcher and multi-inning reliever. In 20 appearances in Class AAA, Thorpe posted an impressive 119-to-25 strikeout-to-walk ratio. And he fanned 31 and walked 10 in 27.2 innings in the big leagues.

Snippet from The 2018 Prospect Digest Handbook: The lack of a second "out pitch" severely limits his ceiling as a backend starting pitcher. He could very easily end up as a fastball/changeup reliever down the line.

Scouting Report: Thorpe's one of the more intriguing arms in the minor leagues. The quality of the arsenal suggests a middling collegiate pitcher in a power conference: 90- to 91-mph fastball; loopy, average curveball; a subpar cutter-like slider; and an above-average changeup. In spite of the repertoire, Thorpe's continued to miss bats at every single level – including his stint with the Twins. How? The command. It's easily a plus. He can throw whatever pitch, wherever he wants. Based on arsenal alone he'd be a #6-type starting pitcher. But his success and command should push him into regular work – if it's available – as a #5.

Ceiling: 1.5-win player
Risk: Low
MLB ETA: Debuted in 2019

13. Matt Wallner, RF

Hit	Power	SB	Patience	Glove	Overall
45	55	30	50	50	45

Born: 12/12/97	Age: 22	Bats: L
Height: 6-5	Weight: 220	Throws: R

YEAR	LVL	PA	1B	2B	3B	HR	SB	CS	AVG	OBP	SLG	BB%	K%	GB%	LD%	FB%
2019	Rk+	238	31	18	1	6	1	1	0.269	0.361	0.452	7.98%	27.73%	40.8	22.5	28.9
2019	A	53	3	3	1	2	0	0	0.205	0.340	0.455	9.43%	26.42%	43.3	13.3	36.7

Background: If at first you don't succeed, try, try again. And that's exactly what the Twins did with Wallner. Minnesota originally drafted the 6-foot-5, 220-pound corner outfielder in the 32nd round coming out of Forest Lake High School. Wallner – obviously – spurned their interest and attended Southern Mississippi University. After three dynamic seasons at the plate, Minnesota – once again – called Wallner's name last June, except it was in the first round, 39th overall. A career .337/.461/.652 collegiate hitter, he acquitted himself nicely in the Appalachian League as he batted .269/.361/.452 with 18 doubles, one triple, and six homeruns. Wallner also appeared in 12 games with Cedar Rapids in the Midwest League, hitting .205/.340/.455.

Scouting Report: With respect to his work in college last season, consider the following:

- Between 2011 and 2018, only two Conference USA players slugged at least .300/.425/.650 in a season (min. 250 PA): Luke Reynolds, a tenth round pick by the Cubs two years ago, and Matt Wallner, who accomplished the feat twice; once as a freshman and once as a junior.

Remarkably consistent during his three-year collegiate career. Wallner posted OPS totals between 1.093 and 1.127 and nearly three identical strikeout-to-walk ratios. Wallner fanned more frequently during his professional debut, which (A) wasn't expected given his track record and (B) needs to be monitored moving forward. Twenty-five homer power potential, average walk, solid glove, and a strong arm – as evidenced by his work on the mound during his freshman and sophomore seasons. Wallner has the makings of a .245/.315/.450-type hitter.

Ceiling: 1.5- to 2.0-win player
Risk: Moderate
MLB ETA: 2022

14. Blayne Enlow, RHP

	FB	CB	SL	CH	Command	Overall
	60	50/55	55	50/55	50/55	45

Born: 03/21/99	Age: 21	Bats: R
Height: 6-3	Weight: 170	Throws: R

YEAR	LVL	IP	W	L	SV	ERA	FIP	WHIP	K/9	K%	BB/9	BB%	K/BB	HR9	BABIP
2017	Rk	20.3	3	0	0	1.33	3.07	0.69	8.4	24.68%	1.8	5.19%	4.75	0.44	0.176
2018	A	94.0	3	5	1	3.26	3.99	1.37	6.8	17.40%	3.4	8.58%	2.03	0.38	0.315
2019	A	41.3	4	3	0	4.57	3.79	1.38	9.6	23.78%	3.3	8.11%	2.93	0.87	0.317
2019	A+	69.3	4	4	0	3.38	3.84	1.21	6.6	17.53%	3.0	7.90%	2.22	0.52	0.275

Background: Cut from a similar cloth as fellow right-hander Jordan Balazovic. Minnesota unearthed the hard-throwing right-hander in the third round of the 2017 draft. A product of St. Amant High School, the franchise pushed the talented youngster into the Midwest League in 2018. And Enlow, a well built 6-foot-3, 170-pound hurler, compiled a 3.26 ERA and a 5.10 DRA (*Deserved Run Average*) while averaging 6.8 strikeouts and 3.4 walks per nine innings in 20 appearances. The front office took a page out of the Balazovic development plan and kept Enlow in Low Class A at the start of 2019 before promoting him up to the Florida State League. In a career best 21 appearances, 20 of which were starts, Enlow fanned 95 and walked just 38 with a 3.82 ERA in 110.2 innings of work.

Snippet from The 2018 Prospect Digest Handbook: More projection than production as he moved into full-season action last year. Enlow's fastball, which sits in the 93-mph range, shows some life and has some projection left as his thin frame begins to fill out. His curveball flashes above-average, but it's inconsistent – at times getting a bit loopy on him. His changeup is no worse than average. Enlow has the foundation to develop into a league average arm, but his lack of swing-and-miss results – even as a teenager in the Midwest League – brings back memories of another highly touted arm (Kohl Stewart).

Scouting Report: The stuff's ticked up, which was suggested in last year's Handbook. His fastball was sitting in the 94- to 95-mph range and touching as high as 97 mph on occasions. His curveball continued to flash above-average. His slider, which either (A) I didn't see in 2018 or (B) is a new offering, is a solid 55-grade as it sits in the 88-mph to 90-mph territory. His changeup also showed the makings of peaking as above-average too. Command-wise, he's more of a strike-thrower, rather than a quality pitcher-thrower. Enlow has the potential to earn a #4/#5-type role at full maturity. I really like the big bodied right-hander.

Ceiling: 1.5- to 2.0-win player
Risk: Moderate
MLB ETA: 2021/2022

15. Matt Canterino, RHP

	FB	CB	SL	CH	Command	Overall
	55	60	60	45/50	45	45

Born: 12/14/97	Age: 22	Bats: R
Height: 6-2	Weight: 222	Throws: R

YEAR	LVL	IP	W	L	SV	ERA	FIP	WHIP	K/9	K%	BB/9	BB%	K/BB	HR9	BABIP
2019	Rk	5.0	0	0	0	1.80	1.70	0.60	10.8	33.33%	1.8	5.56%	6.00	0.00	0.182
2019	A	20.0	1	1	0	1.35	2.28	0.65	11.3	33.33%	3.2	9.33%	3.57	0.00	0.146

Background: One of the more decorated arms available in the draft class last June. Few pitchers have been able to match the consistently dominant numbers posted by the herky-jerky right-hander. The 6-foot-2, 222-pound Texan struck out a whopping 111 and walked 49 in 96.0 innings as a true freshman. He followed that up with a dynamic showing during his sophomore campaign: making 16 appearances for the Rice Owls, Canterino posted a 116-to-22 strikeout-to-walk ratio in only 94.0 innings. And he continued to dominate the Cape Cod League the ensuing summer as well: 29 K, 10 BB, and a 2.59 ERA 24.1 IP. Last season Canterino maintained status quo for the Conference USA school, averaging 11 strikeouts and just 2.1 walk per nine innings. Minnesota selected him in the second round. After a two-game cameo in the Gulf Coast League, he tossed another 20.0 innings in Low Class A, finishing with a 31-to-8 strikeout-to-walk ratio.

Scouting Report: Three above-average or better offerings with a fourth that could peak as a solid 50-grade. Canterino increases his effectiveness through a lot of mechanical deception. It's difficult to describe, but there's a slight pause in his windup, very herky-jerky. Because Canterino throws strikes and sports two plus breaking balls, he's likely going to quickly chew through the low levels of the minor leagues, so his first test likely won't happen until he reaches Class AA – which may happen by the end of 2020. #4/#5-type potential.

Ceiling: 1.5- to 2.0-win player
Risk: Moderate
MLB ETA: 2021/2022

16. Nick Gordon, 2B/SS

Hit	Power	SB	Patience	Glove	Overall
50	40	50	40	50	40

Born: 10/24/95	Age: 24	Bats: L
Height: 6-0	Weight: 160	Throws: R

YEAR	LVL	PA	1B	2B	3B	HR	SB	CS	AVG	OBP	SLG	BB%	K%	GB%	LD%	FB%
2017	AA	578	94	29	8	9	13	7	0.270	0.341	0.408	9.17%	23.18%	44.2	27.1	25.1
2018	AA	181	36	10	3	5	7	2	0.333	0.381	0.525	6.08%	14.92%	42.4	25.9	30.9
2018	AAA	410	62	13	4	2	13	3	0.212	0.262	0.283	5.61%	20.00%	45.7	19.2	31.8
2019	AAA	319	51	29	3	4	14	4	0.298	0.342	0.459	5.64%	20.38%	53.2	23.4	20.8

Background: It's almost difficult to believe because, well, it just seems like yesterday. But the Twins selected Gordon with the fifth overall pick all the way back in 2014. And to put that into proper context, think about it this way: Of the top 10 players chosen, seven of them have accrued big league time. Those seven: Carlos Rodon (#3), Kyle Schwarber (#4), Alex Jackson (#6), Aaron Nola (#7), Kyle Freeland (#8), Jeff Hoffman (#9), and Michael Conforto (#10). As for Gordon, well, he was able to put a disastrous showing in Class AAA two years ago firmly in the rearview mirror. After hitting a lowly .212/.262/.283 with Rochester in 2018, Gordon slugged a healthier .298/.342/.459 with 29 doubles, three triples, four homeruns, and 14 stolen bases in his return to the International League. Per *Deserved Runs Created Plus*, his overall production was 7% better than the league average.

Snippet from The 2018 Prospect Digest Handbook: From dominant star to burnt out supernova in a heartbeat. Gordon continued his torrid ways for a couple weeks in the International League, but something happened in early June and he – seemingly – forgot how to hit; he batted a laughably bad .186/.243/.243 over his final 82 games – which set off more than a few bells and whistles. Never one to walk all that often, Gordon's always profiled as a slashing, speedy infielder with a better-than-average glove. His lengthy track record is enough of a reason to give him a hall pass on the second half collapse, but he needs to come out firing on all cylinders in 2019.

Scouting Report: At some point the projection of future skills stops and the current tools will be what moves forward. Outside of his torrid 32-game stint in the Southern League in 2018, Gordon's never been a terrific hitter. Hell, he's basically hovered around the league average threshold for the majority of his career. Instead of an above-average hit tool with plus speed, like his brother Dee, Nick's tools are average-ish across the board, sans some disappointing power. He has some defensive versatility, so he could contribute as a solid, cheap bench option.

Ceiling: 1.0- to 1.5-win player
Risk: Low to Moderate
MLB ETA: 2020

17. Akil Baddoo, CF

Hit	Power	SB	Patience	Glove	Overall
40/45	50	60	60	45	45

Born: 08/16/98	Age: 21	Bats: L
Height: 6-1	Weight: 210	Throws: L

YEAR	LVL	PA	1B	2B	3B	HR	SB	CS	AVG	OBP	SLG	BB%	K%	GB%	LD%	FB%
2017	RK	86	12	4	3	1	4	0	0.267	0.360	0.440	10.47%	15.12%	43.5	22.6	32.3
2017	RK	157	25	15	2	3	5	4	0.357	0.478	0.579	17.20%	12.10%	49.1	20.4	26.9
2018	A	517	62	22	11	11	24	5	0.243	0.351	0.419	14.31%	23.98%	43.1	9.1	38.1
2019	A+	131	15	3	3	4	6	2	0.214	0.290	0.393	9.16%	29.77%	41.8	12.7	34.2

Background: One of the trendy picks for a 2019 breakout heading into last season. The former second rounder did the complete opposite. A product of Salem High School in Conyers, Georgia, Baddoo has had one of the bigger roller coaster careers in recent memory. He looked completely abysmal during his debut in the Gulf Coast League as he hit a paltry .178/.299/.271 in 38 games. He looked like a completely different prospect during his return to the league – as well as his promotion up to the Appalachian League – the following season, slugging a scorching .323/.436/.527 in 53 total games. And Baddoo, a 6-foot-1, 210-pound center fielder, held his own as he moved into the Midwest League in 2018 as he batted a saber-friendly .243/.351/.419 with a walk rate north of 14%. Last season a wonky elbow – which eventually forced him under the knife for Tommy John surgery – limited him to just 29 mostly disappointing games in High Class A. He cobbled together a lowly .214/.290/.393 triple-slash line.

Snippet from The 2018 Prospect Digest Handbook: : Still only entering his age-20 season thanks to a late birthday. Baddoo's a fascinating prospect with loud, loud tools and a favorable saber-slant. He owns one of the better eyes in the minor leagues with 20-homer potential and plus-speed. His defense is a liability in center field and the bat doesn't profile as well in a corner spot, so he'll need to show some progress in the coming the years.

Scouting Report: Instead of being a touch young for his levels – despite repeating the rookie leagues in 2017 season – Baddoo's loss of developmental time ensures he'll be playing against age-appropriate competition moving forward. The tools and saber-slant are still prevalent. And it's tough to know how long he battled the elbow injury before shutting it down; meaning: it could have been the cause for the disappointing showing. 20/20 potential, but his defense in center remains a problem. He's looking like a solid fourth outfielder, maybe 80% of a Dexter Fowler type performance.

Ceiling: 1.5-win player
Risk: Moderate to High
MLB ETA: 2022

18. Cole Sands, RHP

FB	CB	CH	Command	Overall
55	60	55	55	40

Born: 07/17/97	Age: 22	Bats: R
Height: 6-3	Weight: 215	Throws: R

YEAR	LVL	IP	W	L	SV	ERA	FIP	WHIP	K/9	K%	BB/9	BB%	K/BB	HR9	BABIP
2019	A	41.3	2	1	0	3.05	2.15	1.26	10.7	28.16%	2.4	6.32%	4.45	0.00	0.373
2019	A+	52.0	5	2	0	2.25	2.79	0.83	9.2	27.60%	1.2	3.65%	7.57	0.69	0.254
2019	AA	4.0	0	0	0	4.50	1.04	1.25	13.5	35.29%	2.3	5.88%	6.00	0.00	0.400

Background: A steady riser during his three-year career at the University of Florida. Sands opened his collegiate career in a spot in the Gators' vaunted rotation as a true freshman, though his peripherals were largely middling (6.5 K/9 and 4.3 BB/9). After a summer in the Cape Cod League, Sands' strikeout rate jumped and his walk rate sagged as he posted a solid 72-to-29 strikeout-to-walk in 83.1 innings of work. And, once again, he spent the summer in the Cape Cod League, posting a 21-to-4 strikeout-to-walk ratio in 17.0 innings with the Falmouth Commodores. Sands continued his development and production during his junior campaign with the Gators as he averaged career bests in strikeout and walk rates (10.5 K/9 and 3.0 BB/9). Minnesota drafted him in the fifth round that year and held him out of professional action until last season. Despite hitting the disabled list three times in 2019 (blister, left calf, and an undisclosed injury), Sands vaulted through three separate levels, totaling 97.1 innings with 108 strikeouts and just 19 walks. He compiled a 2.68 ERA. His older brother, Carson, was a fourth round pick by the Cubs.

Scouting Report: An above-average fastball/changeup combination complemented by a plus slider-like curveball. Sands' repertoire and command suggests a capable backend starting pitcher. But I have doubts as to whether he'll reach that ceiling. He's a low three-quarter slinger that, I believe, will eventually leave him susceptible to left-handed hitters. His likely landing spot is a multi-inning relief-type workhorse with the occasional spot-start thrown his way.

Ceiling: 1.0- to 1.5-win player
Risk: Moderate
MLB ETA: 2020

19. Wander Javier, SS

Hit	Power	SB	Patience	Glove	Overall
40	55	40	45	50	40

Born: 12/29/98	Age: 21	Bats: R	Top CALs:
Height: 6-1	Weight: 165	Throws: R	

YEAR	LVL	PA	1B	2B	3B	HR	SB	CS	AVG	OBP	SLG	BB%	K%	GB%	LD%	FB%
2016	RK	30	3	3	0	2	0	0	0.308	0.400	0.654	13.33%	16.67%	33.3	33.3	19.0
2017	RK	180	29	13	1	4	4	3	0.299	0.383	0.471	10.56%	27.22%	39.4	22.0	29.4
2019	A	342	32	9	1	11	2	0	0.177	0.278	0.323	10.23%	33.92%	45.6	8.8	35.2

Background: Handed a hefty $4 million on the international market during the 2015 summer signing period. In a perfect world Javier would be on the cusp of big league stardom that many had projected – which necessitated the hefty signing bonus. Instead, the Dominican-born shortstop has battled a little of injuries – including a severe labrum issue in his throwing shoulder, which knocked him for the entire 2018 season. The 6-foot-1, 165-pound middle infielder – finally – returned to action in the Midwest League last summer and the results were…beyond terrible. Appearing in 80 games with the Cedar Rapids Kernels, Javier cobbled together a puny, almost comically poor, .177/.278/.323 triple-slash line, though he did manage to belt out 9 doubles, one triple, and 11 homeruns. His overall production, per *Deserved Runs Created Plus*, was a whopping 30% *below* the league average mark.

Scouting Report: In spite of the terrifically poor slash line last season, if you squint hard enough you can make out the tools Javier possesses. Above-average power potential, a solid glove at shortstop, above-average patience. The problem is his inability to make consistent contact. And this isn't a new issue either. He fanned in more than 27% of his plate appearances in the Appalachian League, though he was on an aggressive promotion schedule. But that number ballooned to nearly 34% last season. I'm willing to give him a do over due to his age and length of time he missed. But he needs to show something immediately – like Opening Day immediately.

Ceiling: 1.0- to 1.5-win player
Risk: Moderate
MLB ETA: 2022

Minnesota Twins

20. Travis Blankenhorn, IF/OF

	Hit	Power	SB	Patience	Glove	Overall
	40	55	40	45	50	40

Born: 08/03/96	**Age:** 23	**Bats:** L
Height: 6-2	**Weight:** 228	**Throws:** R

YEAR	LVL	PA	1B	2B	3B	HR	SB	CS	AVG	OBP	SLG	BB%	K%	GB%	LD%	FB%
2017	A	508	64	22	11	13	13	2	0.251	0.343	0.441	9.25%	23.43%	45.8	9.8	37.8
2018	A+	493	61	24	6	11	6	4	0.231	0.299	0.387	6.90%	25.76%	43.8	17.1	30.1
2019	A+	61	9	4	0	1	0	0	0.269	0.377	0.404	14.75%	19.67%	40.0	15.0	37.5
2019	AA	410	70	18	2	18	11	0	0.278	0.312	0.474	4.39%	22.68%	47.1	18.9	29.0

Background: Another one of these guys that seems like they been around forever. The front office drafted Blankenhorn in the third round of the 2015 draft. Since then he's slowly progressed through the club's minor league system. He split time between both rookie leagues during his debut. Began his sophomore campaign back in the Appalachian League before moving up to Low Class A. He was in the Midwest League for the entire 2017 season and spent the ensuing year in High Class A. Last season, after a 15-game refresher course with the Fort Myers Miracle, Blankenhorn finally reached the minors' most challenging level, Class AA, and he more than held his own. In 93 games with Pensacola, the 6-foot-2, 228-pound infielder/outfielder slugged .278/.312/.478 with 18 doubles, two triples, and 18 homeruns. Per *Deserved Runs Created Plus*, his overall production topped the Class AA average mark by 19%.

Scouting Report: With respect to his work in Class AA last season, consider the following:

- Since 2006, only two 22-year-old hitters posted a DRC+ total between 115 and 125 with a sub-6% walk rate in the Southern League (min. 300 PA): Ryan Brett and – of course – Travis Blankenhorn.

The subpar walk rates, which wasn't quite as bad in past years, ultimately chews through his overall value. But he is...well...what he is. A 55-grade power bat with a 40-hit tool, a little bit of speed and some defensive versatility. Likely going to end up as a Quad-A type guy.

Ceiling: 1.0- to 1.5-win player
Risk: Moderate
MLB ETA: 2020/2021

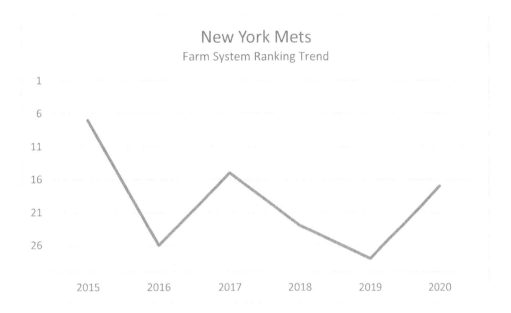

New York Mets
Farm System Ranking Trend

Rank	Name	Age	Pos
1	Andres Gimenez	21	SS
2	Ronny Mauricio	19	SS
3	Brett Baty	20	3B
4	Francisco Alvarez	18	C
5	Matthew Allan	23	RHP
6	Thomas Szapucki	24	LHP
7	David Peterson	24	LHP
8	Josh Wolf	23	RHP
9	Kevin Smith	23	LHP
10	Mark Vientos	20	3B
11	Daison Acosta	21	RHP
12	Dedniel Nunez	24	RHP
13	Alexander Ramirez	17	CF
14	Franklyn Kilome	21	RHP
15	Junior Santos	23	RHP
16	Luis Carpio	22	IF
17	Stephen Gonsalves	26	LHP
18	Shervyen Newton	21	IF
19	Tony Dibrell	24	RHP
20	Ali Sanchez	23	C

1. Andres Gimenez, SS

Hit	Power	SB	Patience	Glove	Overall
60	50	55	40	60	60

Born: 09/04/98 | **Age:** 21 | **Bats:** L | **Top CALs:**
Height: 6-0 | **Weight:** 161 | **Throws:** R |

YEAR	LVL	PA	1B	2B	3B	HR	SB	CS	AVG	OBP	SLG	BB%	K%	GB%	LD%	FB%
2017	A	399	75	9	4	4	14	8	0.265	0.346	0.349	7.02%	15.29%	55.4	18.7	21.4
2018	A+	351	57	20	4	6	28	11	0.282	0.348	0.432	6.27%	19.94%	52.8	16.9	25.4
2018	AA	153	28	9	1	0	10	3	0.277	0.344	0.358	5.88%	14.38%	61.5	12.0	21.4
2019	AA	479	72	22	5	9	28	16	0.250	0.309	0.387	5.01%	21.29%	51.6	15.7	29.7

Background: After struggling to find a capable long term starter at shortstop for the better part of a decade – remember Ruben Tejada, Wilmer Flores, or stopgaps like Omar Quintanilla? – the Mets are now in an enviable position that seemed like nothing more than a pipedream a few years ago: the organization has not one, not two, but three potential above-average starting options at the big league level or currently developing in the pipeline. Amed Rosario, a long time top prospect, quietly turned in a breakout campaign in the Big Apple, hitting .287/.323/.432 while totaling nearly three wins above replacement; the lefty-swinging Gimenez turned in rock solid showing as a 20-year-old squaring off against the minors' most important challenge; and low level top prospect Ronny Mauricio is flashing impressive raw tools. As for Gimenez, in 117 games in Class AA, the Venezuelan native batted .250/.309/.387 with 22 doubles, five triples, and a career best nine homeruns to go along with 28 stolen bases. His overall production, as measured by *Deserved Runs Created Plus* (DRC+), was just 8% below the league average. He also handled himself well in the Arizona Fall League as well, slugging a scorching .371/.413/.586 with nine extra-base hits in 75 plate appearances.

Snippet from The 2018 Prospect Digest Handbook: The power's still a bit underdeveloped, but he slashes the ball from gap-to-gap and has the potential to blossom into a 15- to 20-homerun threat in a couple years. He's also handles lefties and righties equally well. Gimenez looks like a budding star – the type that New Yorkers will gravitate towards as a young, exciting, do-everything player.

Scouting Report: Gimenez's power crept towards that 15- to 20-homerun threat last season, despite being the second youngest everyday regular in the Eastern League. And while the overall numbers appear to be a bit mundane, consider the following:

- Since 2006, here's the list of 20-year-old hitters to post a DRC+ between 85 and 95 in the Eastern League (min. 300 PA): Jose Ramirez, Nick Castellanos, Andrew McCutchen, and – of course – Andres Gimenez.

One other note to consider: the lefty-swinging middle infielder floundered against right-hander pitching to the tune of .223/.274/.365 (as opposed to the .320/.394/.443 triple-slash line he sports against southpaws). Defensively he has a shot to earn multiple Gold Gloves in the not too distant future. In terms of offensive ceiling: think along the lines of .300/.340/.440.

Ceiling: 4.0-win player
Risk: Moderate
MLB ETA: 2020

2. Ronny Mauricio, SS

Hit	Power	SB	Patience	Glove	Overall
50	40/55	30	40	45/50	60

Born: 04/04/01 | **Age:** 19 | **Bats:** B | **Top CALs:**
Height: 6-3 | **Weight:** 166 | **Throws:** R |

YEAR	LVL	PA	1B	2B	3B	HR	SB	CS	AVG	OBP	SLG	BB%	K%	GB%	LD%	FB%
2018	RK	35	4	3	0	0	1	0	0.233	0.286	0.333	8.57%	25.71%	56.5	13.0	26.1
2018	RK	212	36	13	3	3	1	6	0.279	0.307	0.421	4.72%	14.62%	49.7	18.7	25.7
2019	A	504	97	20	5	4	6	10	0.268	0.307	0.357	4.56%	19.64%	53.6	21.6	17.0

Background: The former regime bet big on the Dominican switch-hitting shortstop three years ago, agreeing to a pact worth $2.1 million – a then-record for the organization. Mauricio, a wiry 6-foot-3, 166-pound San Pedro de Macoris, native, was immediately thrust into the stateside rookie leagues the following season. And he passed the club's aggressive challenge with flying colors: spending time between the Gulf Coast and Appalachian Leagues, he batted a combined .273/.304/.410 with 16 doubles, three triples, and three homeruns. To go along with a pair of stolen bases. The front office assigned the precocious prospect up to the South Atlantic last season, where he was just one of two qualified 18-year-old bats. And he consistently impressed before fading down the stretch. Mauricio hit a league-average .268/.307/.357 with 20 doubles, five triples, and four homeruns. He also swiped six bags, though it took 16 total attempts.

Snippet from The 2018 Prospect Digest Handbook: Mauricio's wide range of skills were on full display early in the season, showcasing a potential above-average hit tool, intriguing power potential from an up-the-middle position, and strong contact rates.

Scouting Report: Consider the following:

- Since 2000, there have been just five 18-year-old hitters that met the following criteria in the South Atlantic League (min. 350 PA): 95- to 105-DRC+ and a strikeout rate between 17% and 23%. Those five hitters are Cristian Pache, Anthony Gose, Jay Austin, Francisco Pena, and Ronny Mauricio.

It's a pretty lackadaisical group, sans Pache. But it's important to point out that Mauricio's overall production was significantly better over his first 99 games (.288/.325/.387; as opposed to his final 16 contests when he batted .133/.197/.167). The defense was a bit too spotty at times last season – and it remains to be seen as to whether he can stick as shortstop – but the bat should be no worse than league average. Smooth, easy swing. Plenty of bat speed, so there's a chance the power ticks up into the 20-homer territory. There's a noticeable ease at which he does everything on the field.

Ceiling: 4.0-win player
Risk: Moderate
MLB ETA: 2022/2023

3. Brett Baty, 3B

Hit	Power	SB	Patience	Glove	Overall
30/45	70	30	60	50	60

Born: 11/13/99   **Age:** 20   **Bats:** L   **Top CALs:**
Height: 6-3   **Weight:** 210   **Throws:** R

YEAR	LVL	PA	1B	2B	3B	HR	SB	CS	AVG	OBP	SLG	BB%	K%	GB%	LD%	FB%
2019	Rk	25	3	3	0	1	0	0	0.350	0.480	0.650	20.00%	24.00%	42.9	35.7	21.4
2019	Rk+	186	15	12	2	6	0	0	0.222	0.339	0.437	12.90%	30.11%	49.0	18.6	30.4
2019	A-	17	1	1	0	0	0	0	0.200	0.529	0.300	35.29%	17.65%	57.1	28.6	14.3

Background: One of the older members of the prep class from last season. Baty, a lefty-swinging third baseman out of Lake Travis High School, spent the entirety of the year as a 19-year-old. New York snagged him with the 12th overall pick and signed him to a below-slot deal worth $3.9 million. The Texas native made a quick jaunt through the Gulf Coast League before settling in with Kingsport for the majority of his debut. In 42 games with the club's short-season affiliate, the 6-foot-3, 210-pound Baty batted a power-driven .222/.339/.437 with 12 doubles, two triples, and a six homeruns. Combined with his time in the Gulf Coast and New York-Penn Leagues, the first rounder hit .234/.368/.452 with 16 doubles, two triples, and seven homeruns.

Scouting Report: Baty's opening 15 games in the Rookie Advanced League significantly depressed his value: he hit .132/.258/.283 between July 3rd and July 25th, but rebounded to slug an impressive .254/.371/.505 over his remaining 27 games at the level. The former University of Texas commit owns a thick lower half and is already physically maxed out. The bat speed is off-the-charts with impressive opposite-field power. And he showed a tremendously patient approach as well, walking in more than 15% of the plate appearances. He could very well wind up as a Three True Outcomes hitter if the bat doesn't progress.

Ceiling: 4.0-win player
Risk: Moderate to High
MLB ETA: 2023

4. Francisco Alvarez, C

Hit	Power	SB	Patience	Glove	Overall
55	50/60	30	55	55/50	55

Born: 11/19/01   **Age:** 17   **Bats:** R   **Top CALs:**
Height: 5-11   **Weight:** 220   **Throws:** R

YEAR	LVL	PA	1B	2B	3B	HR	SB	CS	AVG	OBP	SLG	BB%	K%	GB%	LD%	FB%
2019	Rk	31	6	4	0	2	0	1	0.462	0.548	0.846	12.90%	12.90%	36.4	36.4	27.3
2019	Rk+	151	26	6	0	5	1	1	0.282	0.377	0.443	11.26%	21.85%	38.8	21.4	31.6

Background: Built like a brick outhouse already, Alvarez, who tips the scales at 220 pounds spread across his broad-shouldered 5-foot-11 frame, garnered the third highest bonus on the international market two years ago. And that hefty bonus is already paying off in a large way. The then-17-year-old backstop made quick work of the Gulf Coast League, going 12-for-26 with four doubles and a pair of homeruns, before settling in nicely in the Rookie Advanced League. In 35 games with Kingsport, the Venezuelan native slugged hearty .282/.377/.443 with six doubles and five homeruns. His overall production, as measured by *Deserved Runs Created Plus*, topped the league average mark by a whopping 26%. Oh, yeah, he was the only player under the age of 18 to receive at least 100 plate appearances in the Appalachian League.

Scouting Report: Consider the following:

- Since 2011 only 32 different 17-year-old hitters have appeared in the Appalachian League. Of those aforementioned 32, only 14 of them have made at least 150 trips to the plate.

So far, so good. Let's continue, shall we?

- Going back to those 14 players with 150 or more plate appearances, only five have posted at least a 100 *Deserved Runs Created Plus Total* (DRC+): Vladimir Guerrero Jr., Wander Franco, Ozzie Albies, Luis Carpio, and – of course – Francisco Alvarez.

It should be noted that two of the group – Alvarez and Luis Carpio – are currently in the Mets' farm system. It remains to be seen if Alvarez's stocky frame will eventually push him out of his catching duties, but the bat looks like it'll play at any position on the diamond. He looks surprisingly spry behind the dish at this juncture of his career.

Ceiling: 3.5-win player
Risk: Moderate to High
MLB ETA: 2022/2023

5. Matthew Allen, RHP

	FB	CB	CH	Command	Overall
	60	65	50	50/55	50

Born: 04/17/01	Age: 19	Bats: R	Top CALs: N/A
Height: 6-3	Weight: 225	Throws: R	

YEAR	LVL	IP	W	L	SV	ERA	FIP	WHIP	K/9	K%	BB/9	BB%	K/BB	HR9	BABIP
2019	Rk	8.3	1	0	0	1.08	2.30	1.08	11.9	32.35%	4.3	11.76%	2.75	0.00	0.263
2019	A-	2.0	0	0	0	9.00	1.90	3.00	13.5	27.27%	4.5	9.09%	3.00	0.00	0.714

Background: On the short list for top available pitcher in last year's draft class. Allen, a well-built prep arm out of Seminole High School, is already showing a flair for the dramatic: the hard-throwing right-hander fanned 17 en route to cruising to a perfect game against DeLand High School in the semifinal game of the Class 9A District 2 as he propelled the school to the regionals for the first time since 2001. As quoted by the Orlando Sentinel, Allen told Seminole head coach Kenne Brown "just give me one run, that's all I need." Allen, who had a strong commitment to the University of Florida, earned a bevy of awards throughout his amateur career, including:

- 2019 Perfect Game Preseason All-American and All-Region Teams
- 2018 Perfect Game Preseason Underclassmen All-American
- 2017 Perfect Game Preseason Underclassmen All-American
- 2016 Perfect Game Preseason Underclassmen All-American

The Mets snagged the budding ace in the third round as his absorbent asking price scared a lot of teams off. The club signed him for a hefty $2.5 million, roughly end of the first round money. Allen tossed just 10.1 innings during his debut, strikeout out 14 and walking five.

Scouting Report: Per the usual, here's my pre-draft scouting report on Allen:

"The owner of two plus- to plus-plus pitches. Allen attacks hitters with a lethal fastball/curveball combination that was – simply – too overpowering for his current peers. The fastball sits in the mid-90s, touching 96 mph on several occasions, and his knee-buckling curveball hovers in the 79- to 81-mph range. Allen generates the premium velocity without much effort and – generally – commands the zone well. His third offering, an upper-80s changeup, profiles no worse than average. Allen has the build and arsenal to suggest a #2-type ceiling."

Ceiling: 3.0-win player
Risk: Moderate
MLB ETA: 2020/2021

6. Thomas Szapucki, LHP

FB	CB	CH	Command	Overall
55	60	55	45/50	50

Born: 06/12/96	Age: 24	Bats: R
Height: 6-2	Weight: 181	Throws: L

YEAR	LVL	IP	W	L	SV	ERA	FIP	WHIP	K/9	K%	BB/9	BB%	K/BB	HR9	BABIP
2017	A	29.0	1	2	0	2.79	2.91	1.17	8.4	22.88%	3.1	8.47%	2.70	0.00	0.304
2019	A	21.7	0	0	0	2.08	3.20	1.11	10.8	29.55%	4.2	11.36%	2.60	0.42	0.260
2019	A+	36.0	1	3	0	3.25	2.92	1.33	10.5	30.66%	3.8	10.95%	2.80	0.25	0.314
2019	AA	4.0	0	0	0	0.00	3.41	0.75	9.0	22.22%	2.3	5.56%	4.00	0.00	0.182

Background: The fifth round pick in 2015 draft was littered with recognizable, albeit star-powerless names: former Arizona State closer Ryan Burr, Texas workhorse Parker French, Trent Thornton and his high-RPM'd curveball, Jordan Stephens, Joe McCarthy, Chance Adams, Ka'ai Tom, Drew Jackson, Ryan Helsley, Brendon Davis, hard-throwing lefty Taylor Hearn, and – of course – Szapucki, the 149th overall player taken that year. And despite spending parts of five years in the Mets' organization, the lanky southpaw – once again – failed to make it through an entire season of action without some type of malady. Szapucki returned from Tommy John surgery last season, but lasted two starts before being demoted to Extended Spring Training in hopes of building his lagging velocity. And he finished it on another ominous note: he was scratched from the Arizona Fall League for general arm soreness. He finished the year with a career high 61.2 innings, recording 72 whiffs and 26 walks across three separate levels.

Snippet from The 2018 Prospect Digest Handbook: Steven Matz, the poster boy of determination and perseverance, has come back – numerous times – from injury. Here's hoping his fellow lefty can as well.

Scouting Report: The good news is that Szapucki's velocity – as well as his secondary offerings – looked as impressive as ever after the early season hiccup. His fastball showed some exceptional life, sitting in the low 90s with a peak a tick or two higher when needed. The pitch also showed some cut at times throughout a couple separate starts as well, although I'm not sure if it's natural or intended movement. His fall-off-the-table curveball is among the best in the minors. And his changeup is a deceptively strong third weapon, showing some sink and cutting action. The question, of course, is whether Szapucki will be able to handle the rigors of a full season – which hasn't happened yet.

Ceiling: 3.0-win player
Risk: Moderate to High
MLB ETA: 2020/2021

7. David Peterson, LHP

FB	CB	SL	CH	Command	Overall
55	45	60	55	45	50

Born: 09/03/95	Age: 24	Bats: L
Height: 6-6	Weight: 240	Throws: L

YEAR	LVL	IP	W	L	SV	ERA	FIP	WHIP	K/9	K%	BB/9	BB%	K/BB	HR9	BABIP
2018	A	59.3	1	4	0	1.82	2.52	0.96	8.6	24.57%	1.7	4.74%	5.18	0.15	0.283
2018	A+	68.7	6	6	0	4.33	2.98	1.35	7.6	19.27%	2.5	6.31%	3.05	0.13	0.335
2018	AAA	23.7	0	0	0	6.08	4.55	1.82	3.8	8.93%	3.4	8.04%	1.11	0.38	0.375
2019	AA	116.0	3	6	0	4.19	3.18	1.34	9.5	24.55%	2.9	7.44%	3.30	0.70	0.340

Background: The huge lefty turned in one of the more dominant showings in recent memory during his junior campaign with the University of Oregon, fanning an unbelievable 140 hitters – against just 15 free passes – in 100.1 innings of work. New York snagged the huge left-hander in the opening round, 20th overall, three years ago. Peterson spent the entirety of last season twirling games for the Binghamton Rumble Ponies. In a career best 24 starts. The 6-foot-6, 240-pound left-hander posted a 122-to-37 strikeout-to-walk ratio in 116.0 innings of work. Peterson made another four appearances with the Scottsdale Scorpions in the Arizona Fall League, punching out 13 against eight free passes.

Snippet from The 2018 Prospect Digest Handbook: [He] generally avoids the things that can doom a pitcher: he rarely walks anyone, though he's more control rather than command at this point, and he rarely surrenders a homerun thanks to some unearthly groundball rates.

Scouting Report: There's been a disturbing trend as Peterson's progressed up the minor league ladder: his Deserved Run Average, as formulated by *Baseball Prospectus*, has climbed in each of his last three stops going from 3.41 to 3.45 to 4.89 to a horrible 5.65 last season. The former Oregon ace battled bouts of wildness as he remains more of a strike-thrower as opposed to a quality strike-thrower. The repertoire suggests, at minimum, a quality #3 big league starting pitcher. Peterson's fastball is an above-average offering, comfortably resting in the low 90s; his slider hovers in the 83- to 86-mph range with late break; and his changeup is a 55. He also throws a lackluster, below-average bender of a curveball. It might behoove him to scrap the pitch and focus solely on his hellacious slider – pushing his ceiling a bit higher than expected.

Ceiling: 2.5-win player
Risk: Moderate
MLB ETA: 2020

8. Josh Wolf, RHP

FB	CB	CH	Command	Overall
55/60	60	50/55	50/55	50

Born: 09/01/00	Age: 19	Bats: R
Height: 6-3	Weight: 170	Throws: R

YEAR	LVL	IP	W	L	SV	ERA	FIP	WHIP	K/9	K%	BB/9	BB%	K/BB	HR9	BABIP
2019	Rk	8.0	0	1	0	3.38	0.87	1.25	13.5	36.36%	1.1	3.03%	12.00	0.00	0.450

Background: For the second year in a row the Mets dipped into the collegiate ranks and fished out a promising prep arm in the second round. Wolf, a lanky 6-foot-3, 170-pound right-hander from St. Thomas High School, turned in a dominant amateur career, fanning 179 hitters over 108.0 combined innings during junior and senior campaigns. The 53rd overall picked came to terms with the club on a deal worth $2.2 million, becoming just one of five players to eclipse the $2 million mark in the second round last June. Wolf made five brief starts with the organization's Gulf Coast League affiliate, posting a 12-to-1 strikeout-to-walk ratio across eight innings.

Scouting Report: As it stands now the repertoire suggests a solid #4-type starting pitcher, but there's plenty of projection still left in the tank. In a mid-May showcase Wolf's fastball hovered in the 91- to 92-mph range, peaking at 93. The curveball's impressive, showing late downward bite that was difficult to differentiate between his fastball until it was too late. His changeup is surprisingly strong, throwing it in the upper-70s/low-80s that can generate a solid amount of fade when he extends and pronates. The mechanics need cleaned up a bit, but that hasn't stopped him from consistently throwing strikes. Wolf could be one of the better steals in the second round.

Ceiling: 3.0-win player
Risk: Moderate
MLB ETA: 2023

9. Kevin Smith, LHP

FB	SL	CH	Command	Overall
55	55	50	50	50

Born: 05/13/97	Age: 23	Bats: R
Height: 6-5	Weight: 200	Throws: R

YEAR	LVL	IP	W	L	SV	ERA	FIP	WHIP	K/9	K%	BB/9	BB%	K/BB	HR9	BABIP
2018	A-	23.7	4	1	0	0.76	2.42	0.76	10.6	32.94%	2.3	7.06%	4.67	0.38	0.220
2019	A+	85.7	5	5	0	3.05	2.63	1.25	10.7	29.06%	2.5	6.84%	4.25	0.53	0.359
2019	AA	31.3	3	2	0	3.45	3.23	1.28	8.0	22.05%	4.3	11.81%	1.87	0.29	0.289

Background: The big lefty spent his junior and senior seasons at the University of Georgia bouncing between the school's rotation and bullpen, throwing a combined 124.1 innings with 146 strikeouts against 56 walks. The Mets took amid-round flier on the 6-foot-6, 200-pound hurler two years ago. And Smith's proving to be quite the find. The Georgia native breezed through his debut showing in the New York-Penn League, posting an impeccable 28-to-6 strikeout-to-walk ratio in 23.2 innings of work. Smith handled an aggressive promotion up to the Florida State League to start last season, making 17 starts before earning another promotion up to the minors' most challenging level – Class AA. In total he finished the year with 23 starts, throwing 117 innings with 130 punch outs and just 39 free passes to go along with a 3.15 ERA.

Scouting Report: Quietly impressive. Definitely underrated. Smith definitely ticks a lot of important checkboxes for a pitching prospect: underutilized in college, throws strikes, limits walks and homeruns, and missed bats. The big left-hander attacks hitters with a low-90s fastball that plays up because of his gangly limbs. His slider is an above-average offering with a 10-5 sweeping break. And his straight changeup is a solid third weapon. He's the type of cost effective, backend starting pitcher that's becoming increasingly more valuable for teams.

Ceiling: 2.0-win player
Risk: Moderate
MLB ETA: 2020

10. Mark Vientos, 3B

Hit	Power	SB	Patience	Glove	Overall
45	50	30	40	50	45

Born: 12/11/99	Age: 20	Bats: R
Height: 6-4	Weight: 185	Throws: R

YEAR	LVL	PA	1B	2B	3B	HR	SB	CS	AVG	OBP	SLG	BB%	K%	GB%	LD%	FB%
2017	RK	193	29	12	0	4	0	2	0.259	0.316	0.397	7.25%	21.76%	48.9	20.0	24.4
2017	RK	18	3	2	0	0	0	0	0.294	0.333	0.412	5.56%	22.22%	46.2	38.5	7.7
2018	RK	262	41	12	0	11	1	0	0.287	0.389	0.489	14.12%	16.41%	45.9	19.3	28.7
2019	A	454	66	27	1	12	1	4	0.255	0.300	0.411	4.85%	24.23%	40.0	22.6	31.3

Background: The Columbia Fireflies were the worst team in the South Atlantic League last season, finishing with a lowly 52-84 win-loss record. Vientos and fellow infielder Ronny Mauricio were – arguably – the sole reasons worth tuning into the Low Class A affiliates' games after the front office dealt away top prospect Simeon Woods-Richardson in the Marcus Stroman swap. Vientos, a second round pick out of Kempner High School in 2017, quietly turned in one of the better showings in the Sally last season. After slugging a robust .287/.389/.489 with stellar peripherals in the Appalachian League two years ago, the 6-foot-4, 185-pounder looked comfortable as he transitioned to the rigors of full-season action. In a career best 111 games, Vientos batted a healthy .255/.300/.411 with 27 doubles, one triple, and 12 homeruns. His overall production, as measured by *Baseball Prospectus' Deserved Runs Created Plus*, topped the league average mark by a whopping 22%.

Snippet from The 2018 Prospect Digest Handbook: The projectable third baseman also flashed above-average power potential with strong contact skills and uses the whole field well. He also shows impressive opposite field power. Defensively, he was rock solid at the hot corner.

Scouting Report: After taking tremendous strides in working the count during his sophomore season, Vientos looked like an eager child on Christmas morning last season. He walked in a career low 4.8% of his plate appearances, a number that's more in line with his debut showing. And that lack of patience is concerning at this point as well. Consider the following:

- Since 2000, only one other 19-year-old hitter met the following criteria in the South Atlantic League (min. 300 PA): a sub-6.0% walk rate with a strikeout rate between 22% and 24%. That hitter: former top prospect Nick Williams, a toolsy outfielder that's been a slightly below average big league hitter when he's healthy.

Dulling Vientos' shine even further is the fact that Williams' overall production was 8-percentage points better during his time in the South Atlantic League. At his peak, Vientos looks like a starting caliber third baseman on a non-contending team.

Ceiling: 1.5 to 2.0-win player
Risk: Moderate
MLB ETA: 2022

11. Daison Acosta, RHP

	FB	SL	CH	Command	Overall
	55/60	50	50	45	45

Born: 08/24/98	Age: 21	Bats: R
Height: 6-2	Weight: 160	Throws: R

YEAR	LVL	IP	W	L	SV	ERA	FIP	WHIP	K/9	K%	BB/9	BB%	K/BB	HR9	BABIP
2017	Rk	22.0	0	2	0	3.27	2.92	1.14	7.8	21.84%	2.9	8.05%	2.71	0.00	0.305
2018	Rk	42.3	2	5	0	4.46	5.97	1.32	9.8	24.73%	3.8	9.68%	2.56	1.70	0.278
2019	A-	18.3	1	0	0	0.98	1.98	0.82	12.3	36.23%	2.9	8.70%	4.17	0.00	0.250
2019	A	52.3	1	4	0	3.78	4.31	1.45	8.4	20.85%	4.5	11.06%	1.88	0.69	0.303

Background: Signed out of Paraiso, Dominican Republic, in 2016; Acosta made a brief three-game cameo with the club's foreign rookie league affiliate that year, posting an 8-to-6 strikeout-to-walk ratio in 11.2 innings. The front office bounced the wiry teenager up to the Gulf Coast League the following summer. His control improved as he posted a 19-to-7 strikeout-to-walk ratio in 22.0 innings of work. Acosta spent the 2018 season twirling games – and sometimes dominating – for the Kingsport Mets, averaging nearly 10 strikeouts and 3.8 walks per nine innings. Last season the 6-foot-2, 160-pound righty breezed through the New York-Penn League for four appearances, before settling in with Columbia in Low Class A. He totaled a career best 70.2 innings, fanning 74 and walking 32 to go along with an aggregate 3.06 ERA.

Scouting Report: A slightly better, younger version of fellow Mets farmhand Dedniel Nunez; Acosta is still rather raw with some projectable upside in the tank as his body/frame continue to fill out. His fastball sits in the low 90s, showing a bit of unexpected zip at times. His breaking pitch, which he signals as a traditional curveball during warm-ups, has late, downward tilt which often times locks up the inexperienced hitters in the South Atlantic League. In terms of velocity, Acosta's third pitch would be described as a "power changeup", made famous by future Hall of Famer Zack Greinke. It's hard. It's firm. But it shows some sink and has just enough velocity separation to be deceptive. Barring any health issues, Acosta could find himself ranked among the systems Top 5 prospects next year.

Ceiling: 1.5- to 2.0-win player
Risk: Moderate
MLB ETA: 2022/2023

12. Dedniel Nunez, RHP

FB	SL	CH	Command	Overall
55	55	45	50	45

Born: 06/05/96	Age: 24	Bats: R
Height: 6-2	Weight: 180	Throws: R

YEAR	LVL	IP	W	L	SV	ERA	FIP	WHIP	K/9	K%	BB/9	BB%	K/BB	HR9	BABIP
2017	Rk	44.7	1	3	0	5.24	3.51	1.50	9.3	22.66%	3.2	7.88%	2.88	0.60	0.356
2018	Rk	40.3	4	1	1	3.79	4.41	1.34	8.0	20.81%	3.6	9.25%	2.25	0.45	0.316
2019	A	22.3	3	1	0	4.03	2.35	0.76	13.3	38.82%	1.2	3.53%	11.00	0.81	0.267
2019	A+	57.7	2	3	0	4.53	3.11	1.37	9.5	24.11%	3.1	7.91%	3.05	0.47	0.339

Background: In terms of free agents on the amateur market, Nunez didn't hold a whole lot of leverage when the Mets signed him in 2016 thanks to his age; he was 20-years-old. Since then, though, he's consistently – and quietly – climbed the ranks through the low levels of the club's farm system. He posted a 3-to-1 strikeout-to-walk ratio during his debut in the Gulf Coast League in 2017. The hard-throwing right-hander breezed through following season with Kingsport in the Appalachian League. And Nunez was absurdly unhittable in four appearances in the Sally before settling in for 12 final starts in High Class A with St. Lucie. Last season he finished his third professional campaign with a career high 80.0 innings, striking out 94 and walking just 23 to go along with an aggregate 4.39 ERA.

Scouting Report: Nunez shows a three-pitch mix, though he's mainly fastball/slider at this stage of his career due to an underdeveloped changeup. Nunez's fastball sits between 91- to 94-mph with some surprising late, heavy life. He commands it well, especially low and away to right-handed hitters. His slider, which is often mistaken for a curveball, shows a fair amount of depth and hovers in the 80-mph range. Because of Nunez's late signing, he'll be 24-years-old this season with only a couple dozen innings in High Class A. The Dominican righty has some backend starting potential, but the changeup needs to uptick to at least a 50. If the third pitch doesn't come along – and quickly – he could be an eighth inning arm for the big league club.

Ceiling: 1.5 to 2.0-win player
Risk: Moderate
MLB ETA: 2020/2021

13. Alexander Ramirez, OF

Hit	Power	SB	Patience	Glove	Overall
40/50	40/50	60	N/A	N/A	50

Born: 01/13/03	Age: 17	Bats: R	Top CALs:
Height: 6-3	Weight: 170	Throws: R	

Background: Handed a hefty $2.1 million bonus out of the Dominican Republic last summer, Ramirez, who received the third highest in Mets franchise history, is a baby faced center fielder who hails from Santo Domingo.

Scouting Report: Above-average speed with impressively easy bat speed and enough natural loft to grow into above-average power. He's also shown a willingness to shoot the ball the other way, as well. The arm in center field currently grades out as average but might see an uptick as he continues to fill out. Strong wrists.

Ceiling: 2.0-win player
Risk: Moderate to High
MLB ETA: 2020

14. Franklyn Kilome, RHP

FB	CB	CH	Command	Overall
N/A	N/A	N/A	N/A	45

Born: 06/25/95	Age: 25	Bats: R
Height: 6-6	Weight: 175	Throws: R

YEAR	LVL	IP	W	L	SV	ERA	FIP	WHIP	K/9	K%	BB/9	BB%	K/BB	HR9	BABIP
2017	A+	97.3	6	4	0	2.59	3.53	1.37	7.7	20.29%	3.4	9.05%	2.24	0.46	0.325
2017	AA	29.7	1	3	0	3.64	4.27	1.35	6.1	16.26%	4.6	12.20%	1.33	0.61	0.267
2018	AA	102.0	4	6	0	4.24	4.31	1.44	7.3	18.82%	4.5	11.56%	1.63	0.62	0.305
2018	AA	38.0	0	3	0	4.03	3.15	1.08	9.9	27.10%	2.4	6.45%	4.20	0.71	0.289

Background: Acquired from the Phillies near the trade deadline two years ago. The hard-throwing righty lasted just seven starts in his new organization before hitting the DL due to a wonky elbow – which quickly turned into reconstruction surgery. Kilome missed all of the 2019 recovering from Tommy John surgery. He's averaging 8.0 strikeouts and 3.7 walks per nine innings across 471.1 career minor league innings.

Snippet from The 2018 Prospect Digest Handbook: His loss of development time, thanks to the TJ surgery, only tilts the scale towards a shift to the bullpen.

Scouting Report: As noted in last year's Handbook, prior to the injury a potential move into a late-inning, high-leverage relief role was already staring the behemoth right-hander in the eyes. His lack of a third pitch combined with an inability to consistently throw strikes was already putting a death grip on his big league ceiling. Now he's lost a year due to health.

Ceiling: 1.5-win player
Risk: Moderate to High
MLB ETA: 2020/2021

15. Junior Santos, RHP

FB	SL	CH	Command	Overall
70	N/A	N/A	N/A	45

Born: 08/16/01	Age: 18	Bats: R
Height: 6-8	Weight: 218	Throws: R

YEAR	LVL	IP	W	L	SV	ERA	FIP	WHIP	K/9	K%	BB/9	BB%	K/BB	HR9	BABIP
2018	Rk	45.0	1	1	0	2.80	2.84	0.91	7.2	20.69%	1.2	3.45%	6.00	0.20	0.270
2018	Rk	5.0	0	0	0	0.00	2.44	0.80	5.4	16.67%	0.0	0.00%	#DIV/0!	0.00	0.267
2019	Rk	40.7	0	5	0	5.09	5.54	1.75	8.0	18.27%	5.5	12.69%	1.44	0.89	0.333

Background: Signed out of Santiago, Dominican Republic, three years ago, Santos, who was part of the same class that added Ronny Mauricio and his franchise-record-breaking $2.1 million to the organization, came to terms on a deal worth significantly less; the gargantuan righty received $275,000. Standing an impressive 6-foot-6 on the day he became a Mets prospect, Santos has shot up another two inches. He made his debut two years ago, throwing 50.0 innings between the Dominican Summer and Gulf Coast Leagues, posting an impressive 39-to-6 strikeout-to-walk ratio. The front office brass bounced him up to the Rookie Advanced League last June. And the then-17-year-old continued to show promise – despite being the youngest arm in the league. In 40.2 innings of work, he fanned 36 and handed out 25 walks to go along with a 5.09 ERA.

Snippet from The 2018 Prospect Digest Handbook: Already the owner of an above-average fastball, which plays up a tick thanks to his massive wingspan and stride.

Scouting Report: His fastball has grown a bit, both in terms of life and velocity, and it rates as a plus- to plus-plus offering. According to a variety of reports, he'll mix in a slider and a changeup as well – though I didn't see them personally. Mechanically, Santos is fluid with a loose arm that generates easy velocity. Consider the following:

- Since 2010, only two 17-year-old pitchers have thrown at least 40 innings in the Appalachian League: Toronto's Eric Pardinho and Junior Santos.

Santos is still quite raw, and his lack of command was exposed against older competition. But it's difficult to see how he doesn't spend the majority of 2020 in the South Atlantic League. On a final note: I'm conservatively grading Santos, but he could very well become a Top 100 prospect within a year.

Ceiling: 1.5-win player
Risk: Moderate
MLB ETA: 2023

16. Luis Carpio, IF

Hit	Power	SB	Patience	Glove	Overall
55	40	40	55	50	45

Born: 07/11/97	Age: 22	Bats: R
Height: 5-11	Weight: 190	Throws: R

YEAR	LVL	PA	1B	2B	3B	HR	SB	CS	AVG	OBP	SLG	BB%	K%	GB%	LD%	FB%
2017	A	535	86	18	3	3	17	5	0.232	0.308	0.302	9.91%	17.76%	47.5	19.0	27.8
2018	A+	436	52	21	0	12	8	9	0.219	0.289	0.365	9.17%	18.35%	34.3	15.9	36.2
2018	AA	5	1	0	0	0	1	0	0.250	0.400	0.250	20.00%	20.00%	0.0	0.0	66.7
2019	A+	106	25	4	1	1	2	3	0.330	0.396	0.426	9.43%	14.15%	30.0	30.0	25.0
2019	AA	276	46	15	0	3	2	6	0.263	0.347	0.362	10.14%	17.75%	42.2	17.2	31.3

Background: The underrated defensive vagabond quietly put a couple abysmal showings in the rearview mirror. Carpio, who spent time at second and third bases, as well as shortstop and left field in 2019, looked completely overmatched as a 19-year-old in the South Atlantic League three years ago, batting a pathetic .232/.308/.302. The club – for whatever reason – decided to push the once-promising prospect up to High Class A the following year. And, well, he continued to look underwhelming: in 112 games with St. Lucie, Carpio hit .219/.289/.365 though he did manage to belt out 21 doubles and 12 homeruns.

Last season Brodie Van Wagenen and Co. opted to keep the Venezuelan infielder/outfielder in the Florida State League for a refresher course. And Carpio shined. Brightly. In 31 games he slugged .330/.396/.426. And he continued to hold his own as a 21-year-old in Class AA too, hitting .263/.347/.362 with 15 doubles and three homeruns in 82 Eastern League games.

Scouting Report: That spectacular 2015 season in which he slugged .304/.372/.359 as a 17-year-old in the Appalachian League seems like a lifetime ago. But that once-promising hit tool began to show some life in 2019. Consider the following:

- The list of 21-year-old hitters to post a Deserved Runs Created Plus (DRC+) in the Eastern League is rather short since 2000 (min. 250 PA): Clint Frazier, Dominic Smith, Gregory Polanco, Lonnie Chisenhall, Neil Walker, Brandon Moss, Ryan Mountcastle, Bobby Bradley, Thairo Estrada, Alex Romero, Josh Stephen, and Luis Carpio.
- But only three of those hitters posted a double-digit walk rate and a strikeout rate south of 20%: Polanco, Walker, and Carpio.

Carpio's tools took a gargantuan leap forward two years ago, but managed to creep back down towards some expected levels in 2019. The patience is phenomenal. And his infield defense has generally been solid across the board. If the hit tool moves up to a 60 he could become a low-end starting option. But it looks as if the club plans on maximizing his skills in a utility role.

Ceiling: 1.5 win player
Risk: Moderate
MLB ETA: 2020

17. Stephen Gonsalves, LHP

	FB	CB	SL	CH	Command	Overall
	55	N/A	45	50	45	40

Born: 07/08/94	Age: 25	Bats: L	
Height: 6-5	Weight: 220	Throws: L	

YEAR	LVL	IP	W	L	SV	ERA	FIP	WHIP	K/9	K%	BB/9	BB%	K/BB	HR9	BABIP
2017	AA	87.3	8	3	0	2.68	2.88	1.03	9.9	27.27%	2.4	6.53%	4.17	0.72	0.270
2017	AAA	22.7	1	2	0	5.56	4.75	1.54	8.7	21.78%	3.2	7.92%	2.75	1.59	0.343
2018	AA	20.3	3	0	0	1.77	3.66	1.03	11.1	32.89%	4.4	13.16%	2.50	0.89	0.231
2018	AAA	100.3	9	3	0	2.96	4.03	1.20	8.5	23.11%	4.9	13.38%	1.73	0.54	0.237
2019	Rk	9.0	0	1	0	2.00	2.83	0.67	16.0	48.48%	0.0	0.00%	#DIV/0!	2.00	0.267
2019	AA	2.0	0	0	0	13.50	11.29	2.00	13.5	27.27%	9.0	18.18%	1.50	4.50	0.250
2019	AAA	2.0	0	1	0	4.50	9.12	3.00	9.0	18.18%	22.5	45.45%	0.40	0.00	0.250

Background: Unequivocally, this is *exactly* the type of move the Mets, as well as a number of fringy contender teams, should make at every opportunity. It wasn't long ago that Gonsalves, a fourth round pick in 2013, was widely considered a fast-moving Top 100 Prospect. But his control backed up in 2018 and a wonky elbow forced him to miss the majority of last season. The Twins, in a roster crunch, placed him on a waivers and the Mets – wisely – took a no-risk gamble. Gonsalves made eight total appearances last season: one start in Class AAA, two relief appearances in Class AA, and five brief starts in the Gulf Coast League. He fanned 21 and walked seven in 13.0 innings of work. For his career, the big left-hander is averaging an impressive 9.6 strikeouts against 3.6 walks per nine innings with a 2.50 ERA.

Snippet from The 2018 Prospect Digest Handbook: When he's at his best he'll show one above-average pitches (curveball), two solid offerings (fastball and changeup), and a below-average slider that lacks depth. If the control comes back he's a backend arm; if not, well, he'll be riding the minor league bus for quite a while.

Scouting Report: Truth be told: I've seen Gonsalves pitch a lot of the years and his fastball during his one-inning relief appearance at the end of August was the best I've seen from him, showing more late life and explosion. His secondary stuff was rough, which is expected due to the layoff, but there's enough here to be – at worst – a serviceable left arm out of the bullpen. And there's still a reasonable, non-zero probability that Gonsalves carves out a role as a decent #5-type starting pitcher. Very, very savvy move by the Mets' front office brass.

Ceiling: 1.0 to 1.5-win player
Risk: Moderate
MLB ETA: Debuted in 2018

18. Shervyen Newton, IF

Hit	Power	SB	Patience	Glove	Overall
40	50	35	55	45	40

Born: 04/24/99 | **Age:** 21 | **Bats:** B
Height: 6-4 | **Weight:** 180 | **Throws:** R

YEAR	LVL	PA	1B	2B	3B	HR	SB	CS	AVG	OBP	SLG	BB%	K%	GB%	LD%	FB%
2017	RK	303	54	11	9	1	10	4	0.311	0.433	0.444	16.50%	18.81%	48.4	26.6	20.3
2018	RK	266	35	16	2	5	4	0	0.280	0.408	0.449	17.29%	31.58%	41.7	25.8	30.3
2019	A	423	54	15	2	9	1	4	0.209	0.283	0.330	8.75%	32.86%	46.9	23.0	25.9

Background: It's difficult to believe, but the Tilburg, Netherlands, native has already been a part of the Mets' organization for parts of five seasons. Signed on the international market for only $50,000 on July 2nd, 2015, Newton quickly moved past a rocky debut showing in the foreign rookie league with strong back-to-back showings in 2017 and 2018; he batted .311/.433/.444 in a return to the Dominican Summer League and handled an aggressive promotion up to Kingsport with aplomb (.280/.408/.449). Last season, though, Newton got off to a horrid start and never really recovered in his first taste of the South Atlantic League. He went 4-for-51 start and managed to cobble together a lowly a .209/.283/.330 triple-slash line. His production, according to *Deserved Runs Created Plus*, was 14% below the league average.

Snippet from The 2018 Prospect Digest Handbook: He's going to have to start trimming down his swing-and-miss tendencies if he hopes to reach his ceiling as a potential every day starter.

Scouting Report: In short: No, Newton didn't trim down on his red flag-laden strikeout rate. In fact, it worsened slightly during his first year in full season ball as he posted a horrible 32.9% K%. Consider the following:

- Since 2000, there have been 339 20-year-old hitters to eclipse the 350-plate appearance threshold in the South Atlantic League. Of those 339, only 19 of them have struck out at least 30% of the time. At the conclusion of 2019, only one hitter – Kyle Skipworth – made it to the big leagues. Skipworth, who was taken with the sixth overall pick in 2008, received four plate appearances with the Marlins in 2013.

So it's not looking very favorable for the highly touted infielder. He was particularly dreadful against right-handers, hitting .195/.269/.321 against them, and the glove grades out as slightly below-average. If he can run into enough fastballs, he can jack 20 homeruns in a season.

Ceiling: 1.0- to 1.5-win player
Risk: Moderate
MLB ETA: 2023

19. Tony Dibrell, RHP

FB	CB	SL	CH	Command	Overall
50	60	50	50	45	40

Born: 11/08/95 | **Age:** 24 | **Bats:** R
Height: 6-3 | **Weight:** 190 | **Throws:** R

YEAR	LVL	IP	W	L	SV	ERA	FIP	WHIP	K/9	K%	BB/9	BB%	K/BB	HR9	BABIP
2017	A-	19.7	1	1	0	5.03	4.75	1.37	12.8	32.18%	3.7	9.20%	3.50	1.83	0.333
2018	A	131.0	7	6	0	3.50	3.65	1.27	10.1	26.25%	3.7	9.64%	2.72	0.69	0.300
2019	A+	90.3	8	4	0	2.39	3.21	1.21	7.6	20.77%	3.6	9.84%	2.11	0.20	0.285
2019	AA	38.7	0	8	0	9.31	6.40	1.86	8.6	19.79%	4.9	11.23%	1.76	2.33	0.350

Background: An underrated fourth round pick in 2017 out of Kennesaw State University, home to former utility man extraordinaire Willie Harris. At times Dibrell, a 6-foot-3, 190-pound righty, was dominant during his first full season in pro ball two years ago, fanning more than 10 strikeouts and 3.7 walks per nine innings. He spent last season splitting time between the Mets' High Class A and Class AA affiliates, throwing 129.0 innings with 113 whiffs and 57 walks per nine innings. He compiled an aggregate 4.47 ERA.

Snippet from The 2018 Prospect Digest Handbook: Dibrell looks like a low-end #5-type arm at peak and could – and possibly will – slide into a middle relief role in the coming years.

Scouting Report: For the better part of the last two seasons; Dibrell's heater sat comfortably in the 91- to 92-mph range. But it was down to 88- to 89-mph and it took some effort to get up to his usual velocity in a mid-August appearance against the Hartford Yard Goats. Regardless, though, Dibrell's pitchability hinges mainly on his dynamic knee-buckling curveball. It's a plus offering with hard, late, sharp 1-to-7 break. His other two offspeed pitches – an upper 70s slider and a changeup – are average. He's one year closer to moving into that projected relief role.

Ceiling: 1.0 to 1.5-win player
Risk: Moderate
MLB ETA: 2020

20. Ali Sanchez, C

Hit	Power	SB	Patience	Glove	Overall
40	30	30	45	55	40

Born: 01/20/97	Age: 23	Bats: R
Height: 6-0	Weight: 196	Throws: R

YEAR	LVL	PA	1B	2B	3B	HR	SB	CS	AVG	OBP	SLG	BB%	K%	GB%	LD%	FB%
2017	A	200	38	3	0	1	2	3	0.231	0.288	0.264	6.50%	13.00%	59.1	13.2	22.0
2018	A	205	34	11	1	4	1	1	0.259	0.293	0.389	4.88%	11.22%	46.5	19.2	23.8
2018	A+	142	26	9	0	2	1	1	0.274	0.296	0.385	3.52%	10.56%	46.7	13.9	31.1
2019	AA	294	61	13	0	1	1	0	0.278	0.337	0.337	7.82%	17.69%	54.6	20.2	20.6
2019	AAA	65	6	4	0	0	0	1	0.179	0.277	0.250	7.69%	16.92%	48.8	9.3	32.6

Background: There have been moments through Sanchez's six-year career when he's flashed enough production to warrant some consideration as one of the club's Top 10 prospects. Take for example his 71-game sample in the Eastern League last season when he batted .278/.337/.337 with stellar defense behind the plate. His overall production, according to Baseball Prospectus' *Deserved Runs Created* Plus, topped the league average mark by 16%. On the other, though, there are times where he's so underwhelming that he looks like he's on the last leg of his professional career. Like, you know, his 21-game cameo with the Syracuse Mets in the International League as he hit a lowly .179/.277/.250. The Venezuelan-born backstop finished the year with an aggregate .261/.326/.322 triple-slash line, belting out just 17 doubles and one homerun.

Snippet from The 2018 Prospect Digest Handbook: His calling card is above-average to plus-work behind the dish. So much so, in fact, that he could carve out a role as a sturdy backup on a big league squad.

Scouting Report: Again: it's all about his role behind the dish as opposed to his work with a bat. The bat's below average but every now and then he'll squeak out a year with a semi-useful batting average. His patience at the plate jumped from horrific to slightly-below average, so that's progress. But he's still flashing as much power as a Mario Mendoza swinging a piece of Swiss cheese. The defense alone makes him a viable backup option, potentially as early as mid-season 2020.

Ceiling: 1.0-win player
Risk: Low to Moderate
MLB ETA: 2020

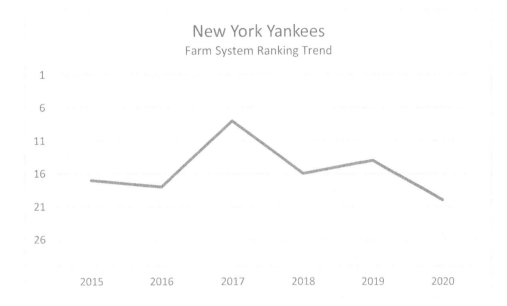

Rank	Name	Age	Pos
1	Deivi Garcia	21	RHP
2	Jasson Dominguez	22	OF
3	Clarke Schmidt	24	RHP
4	Alexander Vizcaino	23	RHP
5	Estevan Florial	22	CF
6	Kevin Alcantara	17	CF
7	Luis Medina	21	RHP
8	Anthony Volpe	19	SS
9	Josh Smith	22	SS
10	Everson Pereira	19	CF
11	Canaan Smith	21	LF
12	Roansy Contreras	20	RHP
13	Antonio Cabello	19	OF
14	Albert Abreu	24	RHP
15	Nick Nelson	24	RHP
16	Josh Breaux	22	C
17	Josh Stowers	23	OF
18	Ezequiel Duran	21	2B
19	T.J. Sikkema	21	LHP
20	Luis Gil	22	RHP

1. Deivi Garcia, RHP

FB	CB	CH	Command	Overall
60	70	45/50	50	60

Born: 05/19/99	Age: 21	Bats: R
Height: 5-9	Weight: 163	Throws: R

YEAR	LVL	IP	W	L	SV	ERA	FIP	WHIP	K/9	K%	BB/9	BB%	K/BB	HR9	BABIP
2017	Rk	28.0	2	1	0	4.50	3.72	1.29	13.8	37.72%	4.2	11.40%	3.31	0.96	0.370
2017	Rk	16.7	3	0	0	3.24	3.96	0.78	13.0	37.50%	2.2	6.25%	6.00	1.62	0.194
2017	Rk	15.3	1	1	0	1.17	2.32	0.78	10.6	33.33%	1.2	3.70%	9.00	0.59	0.281
2018	A	40.7	2	4	0	3.76	3.14	1.01	13.9	37.06%	2.2	5.88%	6.30	1.11	0.302
2018	A+	28.3	2	0	0	1.27	1.95	0.95	11.1	32.11%	2.5	7.34%	4.38	0.00	0.292
2018	AA	5.0	1	0	0	0.00	1.71	0.40	12.6	41.18%	3.6	11.76%	3.50	0.00	0.000
2019	A+	17.7	0	2	0	3.06	0.93	1.25	16.8	45.21%	4.1	10.96%	4.13	0.00	0.438
2019	AA	53.7	4	4	0	3.86	2.20	1.29	14.6	37.02%	4.4	11.06%	3.35	0.34	0.360
2019	AAA	40.0	1	3	0	5.40	5.77	1.48	10.1	25.28%	4.5	11.24%	2.25	1.80	0.307

Background: Not only have I taken a seat on the Garcia hype-train, but I've become the de facto conductor. Originally signed by the Yankees on July 2nd, 2015, the diminutive right-hander, who received a rather paltry bonus of $200,000, has – finally – began rocketing up prospect rankings/lists. The 5-foot-9, 163-pound hurler first popped up on my radar as a fire-bolt slinging, hellacious curveball unfurling 18-year-old dominating the stateside rookie leagues in 2017. Splitting time between the Gulf Coast and Appalachian Leagues, Garcia fanned 67 and walked only 17 in 44.2 innings of work. Heading into the 2018 season I aggressively ranked the Dominican-born pitcher as the Yankees' #3 minor leaguer and among the Top 25 Breakout Prospects. And he did not disappoint. Making stops at three separate levels, Garcia tallied a whopping 105-to-20 strikeout-to-walk ratio to go along with a 2.55 ERA in only 74 innings of work. That's an average of 12.8 strikeouts and just 2.4 walks per nine innings. And that was just a harbinger of things to come. The front office bounced Garcia back down to High Class A for a refresher at the start of the season. But after racking up 33 strikeouts in a little over 17 innings. Garcia's production hardly slowed after his promotion up to Class AA, the most challenging level for a prospect. He fanned a whopping 87 and walked 26 in only 53.2 innings with Trenton. And he capped it off with 11 more strong appearances with Scranton/Wilkes-Barre. One more note: he started the July All-Star Futures Game in Cleveland, Ohio.

Snippet from The 2018 Prospect Digest Handbook: He has front of the rotation talent. The changeup needs refinement. But he's special.

Scouting Report: Garcia's still heavy on the fastball/curveball combo, which is a little disappointing given the rawness of his changeup. But the young right-hander owns two plus pitches – a mid-90s, late-lifed fastball and a monster of a knee-buckling curveball, the latter offering being elite and among the best in the minor leagues. As I noted in last year's Handbook, there's the potential to be special. And Pat Osborn, the Trenton Thunder manager, was quoted by SportsNet New York, that "the way the balls come out, the only name that comes to mind is Pedro Martinez." Now, that's a bit...inflated. But there's a tremendous amount of talent. One more final thought: Garcia's command backed up a bit last season, but it still profiles as at least average. With respect to his work in Class AA last season, consider the following:

- Since 2006, only three 20-year-old pitchers have fanned at least 30% of the hitters they faced in any Class AA league (min. 50 IP): Noah Snydergaard, Phil Hughes, and – of course – Deivi Garcia.

Ceiling: 4.0-win player
Risk: Moderate
MLB ETA: 2020

2. Jasson Dominguez, OF

Hit	Power	SB	Patience	Glove	Overall
45/55	60/70	50	N/A	N/A	60

Born: 02/07/03	Age: 17	Bats: B
Height: 5-10	Weight: 190	Throws: R

Background: The Yankees are used to throwing around big money. After all, the ink on Gerrit Cole's massive $324 million mega-contract is barely dry. But the Yankees took an interesting approach on the international free agent market last summer. The club allotted nearly 95% of their bonus pool towards signing the toolsy, twitchy outfielder. The two sides agreed on a pact worth a whopping $5.1 million. According to reports, the 5-foot-10, 190-pound outfielder is nicknamed "The Martian".

Scouting Report: Massive, massive raw power from both sides of the plate. The young switch-hitter's lightning quick bat's unlike anything I've seen from a 16-year-old, with a natural loft that all but guarantees a floor of 60-grade power with the ceiling of 40 homeruns in full season. There's an awful lot of hand movement during his swing, so it wouldn't be surprising to see the organization quite his hands in the coming years. And, truthfully, I keep circling back to his bat speed. It's almost breathtakingly fast.

Ceiling: 4.5-win player
Risk: Moderate to High
MLB ETA: 2023

3. Clarke Schmidt, RHP

	FB	CB	SL	CH	Command	Overall
	55	55	55	55	55	50

Born: 02/20/96	Age: 24	Bats: R
Height: 6-1	Weight: 200	Throws: R

YEAR	LVL	IP	W	L	SV	ERA	FIP	WHIP	K/9	K%	BB/9	BB%	K/BB	HR9	BABIP
2018	Rk	7.7	0	2	0	7.04	3.38	1.30	14.1	36.36%	2.3	6.06%	6.00	1.17	0.412
2018	Rk	7.3	0	0	0	1.23	2.28	0.82	9.8	30.77%	2.5	7.69%	4.00	0.00	0.250
2018	A-	8.3	0	1	0	1.08	2.16	0.72	10.8	31.25%	2.2	6.25%	5.00	0.00	0.211
2019	Rk	8.3	0	0	0	3.24	2.78	1.08	15.1	43.75%	3.2	9.38%	4.67	1.08	0.357
2019	A+	63.3	4	5	0	3.84	2.86	1.31	9.8	25.46%	3.4	8.86%	2.88	0.28	0.331
2019	AA	19.0	2	0	0	2.37	2.01	0.79	9.0	26.76%	0.5	1.41%	19.00	0.47	0.260

Background: New York took a page out of the Nationals' draft handbook in 2017 by selecting a premium – albeit injured – talent in the early rounds. Enter: Clarke Schmidt, a polished right-hander in the midst of a breakout campaign in the SEC but had his junior season curtailed due to Tommy John surgery. A handful of weeks later New York came calling in the middle of the first round when they selected the 6-foot-1, 200-pound hurler with the 16th overall pick. The former Gamecock didn't make his debut until the following season when he tossed just 23.1 innings of low level action. Last season Schmidt – once again – hit the disabled list for a couple months but managed to make 16 appearances between the Florida State and Eastern Leagues, as well as a trio of rehab games in rookie ball. In total, he tossed 90.2 innings with 102 strikeouts and just 28 walks to go along with a 3.47 ERA.

Snippet from The 2018 Prospect Digest Handbook: By all indications, the promising right-hander returned to full health. A brief cameo in the Eastern League is quite reasonable in 2019.

Scouting Report: 55's across the board: fastball, curveball, slider, changeup, and command. Schmidt has the build, repertoire, and pedigree to slide into a #3/#4 spot at the big league level. And despite missing as much time as he has over the past couple of seasons, Schmidt showed a surprisingly strong feel for his offspeed pitches. In terms of ceiling, think: Mets' right-hander Marcus Stroman, who averaged 7.8 strikeouts and 2.8 walks per nine innings with a 3.22 ERA. Schmidt just needs to prove that he stay healthy.

Ceiling: 2.5- to 3.0-win player
Risk: Moderate
MLB ETA: 2020/2021

4. Alexander Vizcaino, RHP

	FB	CB	CH	Command	Overall
	80	60	60	50/55	50

Born: 05/22/97	Age: 23	Bats: R
Height: 6-2	Weight: 160	Throws: R

YEAR	LVL	IP	W	L	SV	ERA	FIP	WHIP	K/9	K%	BB/9	BB%	K/BB	HR9	BABIP
2017	Rk	51.3	3	5	0	5.79	5.85	1.79	8.6	20.08%	4.0	9.43%	2.13	1.58	0.377
2018	Rk	54.0	3	3	0	4.50	4.97	1.30	9.2	23.81%	3.5	9.09%	2.62	1.17	0.290
2018	A	4.0	0	1	0	13.50	11.21	2.50	4.5	9.09%	4.5	9.09%	1.00	4.50	0.400
2019	A	87.7	5	5	0	4.41	3.29	1.22	10.4	27.15%	2.8	7.26%	3.74	0.62	0.323
2019	A+	27.3	1	1	0	4.28	3.49	1.61	8.9	22.88%	3.6	9.32%	2.45	0.66	0.403

Background: Equipped with one the system's best – if not *the* system's best – fastball. Vizcaino's paltry signing bonus only adds intrigue to his promising ceiling. Handed only $14,000 after signing with New York as a 19-year-old in May of 2016, the 6-foot-2, 160-pound right-hander has taken the slow-and-deliberate approach towards development. The San Cristobal, Dominican Republic, native looked underwhelming during his debut in the foreign rookie league as he averaged just 6.9 strikeouts and 3.3 walks per nine innings in 11 games. He spent the following season, 2017, in the Appalachian League where he averaged 8.6 strikeouts and 4.0 walks every nine innings. And then the front office opted to keep the then-21-year-old back in the Advanced Rookie league for the majority of 2018. At that point, Vizcaino was hardly considered a legitimate prospect. Then 2019 happened. The young Dominican ripped through the South Atlantic League for 16 starts and more than held his own in five additional games in High Class A. When the dust had settled Vizcaino tossed a career best 115.0 innings, recording a whopping 128 strikeouts against just 38 free passes to go along with an aggregate 4.38 ERA.

Scouting Report: Easy heat, like drinking pure capsaicin. Vizcaino's fastball, a true plus-plus offering, was *sitting* 97- to 100-mph as a starting pitcher last season. His upper-80s curveball adds a second (A) bonafide plus offering and (B) another swing-and-miss weapon for hitters to consider. His changeup, a third plus pitch, shows impressive run-and-fade, often times diving out of the strike zone when he was ahead in the count – something that happened quite a bit in 2019. With respect to his work in Low Class A last season, consider the following:

- Since 2006, here's the list of 22-year-old pitchers to post a strikeout percentage between 26% and 28% with a walk percentage between 6% and 8% in the South Atlantic League (min. 75 IP): Andre Wheeler, Chase Huchingson, Ryan Wilson, and – of course – Alexander Vizcaino.

Vizcaino has the repertoire – and now the strike-throwing ability – to slot into a mid-rotation spot at the big league level. But he needs to prove that he can match this type production against the Class AA competition. There's the floor of a Raisel Iglesias-type reliever. If all goes according to plan in 2020, a few spot starts or relief appearances in New York wouldn't be out of the realm of possibility.

Ceiling: 2.5- to 3.0-win player
Risk: Moderate
MLB ETA: 2020/2021

5. Estevan Florial, CF

Hit	Power	SB	Patience	Glove	Overall
45/50	50	60	55	50	50

Born: 11/25/97	Age: 22	Bats: L	Top CALs:
Height: 6-1	Weight: 185	Throws: R	

YEAR	LVL	PA	1B	2B	3B	HR	SB	CS	AVG	OBP	SLG	BB%	K%	GB%	LD%	FB%
2017	A	389	65	21	5	11	17	7	0.297	0.373	0.483	10.54%	31.88%	53.6	21.2	23.9
2017	A+	87	17	2	2	2	6	1	0.303	0.368	0.461	10.34%	27.59%	59.3	18.5	20.4
2018	A+	339	53	16	3	3	11	10	0.255	0.354	0.361	12.98%	25.66%	49.8	26.1	19.3
2019	A+	301	44	10	3	8	9	5	0.237	0.297	0.383	7.97%	32.56%	43.1	15.5	36.8

Background: It's amazing how quickly the status of a prospect can change. Florial, a sweet-swinging, blessed with loud tools center fielder, was reportedly untouchable – or at least nearly untouchable – following his wildly successful breakout season in 2017. The then-19-year-old outfielder slugged a scorching .298/.372/.479 with 23 doubles, seven triples, 13 homeruns, and 23 stolen bases. A broken hamate bone in his hand the following season limited him to just 75 games in High Class A (as well as a handful of rookie league rehab appearances), though the Dominican-born prospect still manage to his .255/.354/.361 with 16 doubles, three triples, three homeruns, and 11 stolen bases. And last season, well, it was more-or-less the same thing: Florial suffered a non-displaced fracture in his right wrist in mid-March – an injury that knocked him out of commission until early June. Once he returned, Florial looked rusty and cobbled together a disappointing .237/.297/.383 triple-slash line with 10 doubles, three triples, eight homeruns, and nine stolen bases. Per Baseball Prospectus' *Deserved Runs Created Plus*, his overall production was 8% *below* the league average mark.

Snippet from The 2018 Prospect Digest Handbook: Despite the noticeable downturn in production [2018] – even before the injury struck – the tools that make Florial so intriguing were still on display: elite eye at the plate, above-average or better speed, strong hit tool, and – of course – the promising power potential, though it came it spurts. The most impressive part of Florial's approach at the plate: his willingness to shoot balls from foul line-to-foul line. Florial has the tools to be a star. And he's taking the proper strides needed as well, including trimming down his problematic strike out rate from full-blown red flag territory to merely concerning.

Scouting Report: Unsurprisingly, Florial's production increased with each passing month. He barely hit his weight during the month of June, posting a lowly .198/.270/.321 mark. He fair significantly better in July, batting .250/.283/.360. And he looked like the Florial of old during the final month of the year: .258/.333/.462. And now the bad news: his strikeout rate *exploded* last season as he fanned in nearly one-third of his plate appearances, though he trimmed that down to 28.5% over his final 20 games. He's only entering his age-22 season and should see some significant time in Class AA, the "make it or break it" level for a prospect. Florial's the definition of high risk, high reward. But you always bet on the talent, and this kid's got a lot it.

Ceiling: 3.0-win player
Risk: Moderate to High
MLB ETA: 2021

6. Kevin Alcantara, CF

Hit	Power	SB	Patience	Glove	Overall
35/50	30/60	40	30/45	50	50

Born: 07/12/02	Age: 17	Bats: R	
Height: 6-6	Weight: 188	Throws: R	

YEAR	LVL	PA	1B	2B	3B	HR	SB	CS	AVG	OBP	SLG	BB%	K%	GB%	LD%	FB%
2019	Rk	128	24	5	2	1	3	3	0.260	0.289	0.358	2.34%	21.09%	51.0	17.7	29.2

Background: I don't even know where to begin with Alcantara. The fact that he's only entering his age-17 season and stands a towering 6-foot-6. Or the fact that he's already spent the majority of a season in the Gulf Coast League – again, *at the age of 16*. Or, according to reports, Alcantara's exit velocity was already kissing triple-digits prior to joining the Yankees. Or what about the seven-figure bonus the Yankees handed him as a free agent? Alcantara, a native of Santo Domingo, Dominican Republic, made a brief detour through the foreign rookie league at the start of 2019 before earning a promotion up to the Gulf Coast. In 32 games, he batted .260/.289/.358 with five doubles, two triples, one homerun, and a trio of stolen bases. His overall production, per *Deserved Runs Created Plus*, was 8% better than the Gulf Coast League average.

Scouting Report: Fun Fact: since 2008, there have been just eleven 16-year-olds to earn at least 100 plate appearances in the Gulf Coast League. Of those aforementioned 11, only four of them posted at least a 100 DRC+. Those four: Domingo Santana, who annihilated the competition with a 160 DRC+, Jonathan Arauz, Carlos Tocci, and Kevin Alcantara. Santana's been a competent big league bat; Tocci reached the big leagues, briefly, in 2018; Arauz reached Class AA last season as a 20-year-old. Very, very raw – both in terms of tools and mechanics. Alcantara takes a Darryl Strawberry-esque high leg kick with a lot of hand movement. It's inconsistent, but not surprising given his age. There's easy plus in-game power brewing with natural loft and strong wrists. And he's likely going to add another 40 pounds onto his rail thin frame. He's the very definition of a low level wild card. He could be a star or flame out early like Tocci. The foundation is set for some powerful tools.

Ceiling: 2.0- to 3.0-win player
Risk: Moderate to High
MLB ETA: 2023

7. Luis Medina, RHP

FB	CB	CH	Command	Overall
70	60	50	35/40	50

Born: 05/03/99 **Age:** 21 **Bats:** R
Height: 6-1 **Weight:** 175 **Throws:** R

YEAR	LVL	IP	W	L	SV	ERA	FIP	WHIP	K/9	K%	BB/9	BB%	K/BB	HR9	BABIP
2017	Rk	23.0	1	1	0	5.09	4.64	1.22	8.6	22.22%	5.5	14.14%	1.57	0.39	0.217
2017	Rk	15.7	1	1	0	5.74	2.98	1.72	9.8	23.29%	5.7	13.70%	1.70	0.00	0.370
2018	Rk	36.0	1	3	0	6.25	6.46	2.17	11.8	25.54%	11.5	25.00%	1.02	0.75	0.337
2019	A	93.0	1	8	0	6.00	4.71	1.65	11.1	26.93%	6.5	15.69%	1.72	0.87	0.339
2019	A+	10.7	0	0	0	0.84	1.90	0.94	10.1	27.91%	2.5	6.98%	4.00	0.00	0.250

Background: Signed out of Nagua, Dominican Republic, during early July four years ago. Medina made his professional debut a few weeks later when he popped up in the foreign rookie league for a trio of games. He split the following season, 2017, between the Dominican Summer and Appalachian Leagues, posting a 39-to-24 strikeout-to-walk ratio in a combined 38.2 innings of work. The front office took the cautious approach and kept the hard-throwing, erratic youngster back in the Advanced Rookie League for a do-over in 2018. And the results were…well…terrible. The good news: he fanned 47 in only 36 innings of work. The bad news: he walked a mindboggling 46 during that same time frame. Last season Medina made 20 starts in the South Atlantic League – as well as a two-game cameo in High Class A at the end of the year – throwing a career best 103.2 innings, racking up an impressive 127 strikeouts and issuing 70 free passes. He finished his fourth minor league season with a 5.47 ERA.

Scouting Report: Medina fits the mold of the type of lottery ticket the front office has been collecting over the past several seasons: hard-throwing hurlers with plus fastballs, wicked breaking balls, and little control, let alone command. Medina's heater was sitting – comfortably, easily – in the upper 90s, touching as high as 98 mph on occasions. He complements the plus-plus pitch with a hard-biting, power curveball with sharp 12-6 break. And he'll mix in a decent changeup for a 20-year-old. The problem, of course, is simple: he's never walked fewer than 5.6 hitters per nine innings in any of his seasons. When he's throwing strikes, he's nearly unhittable; he finished the year with a 29-to-6 strikeout-to-walk ratio and a 0.40 ERA over his final 22.2 innings. But he also walked four or more hitters in half of his appearances as well. He looks like he's going to be Albert Abreu 2.0. His ceiling is predicated on the repertoire, but there's very little chance he actually achieves it.

Ceiling: 3.0-win player
Risk: High
MLB ETA: 2020

8. Anthony Volpe, SS

Hit	Power	SB	Patience	Glove	Overall
45/50	45	40	55	50/55	50

Born: 04/28/01 **Age:** 19 **Bats:** R
Height: 5-11 **Weight:** 180 **Throws:** R

YEAR	LVL	PA	1B	2B	3B	HR	SB	CS	AVG	OBP	SLG	BB%	K%	GB%	LD%	FB%
2019	Rk+	150	15	7	2	2	6	1	0.215	0.349	0.355	15.33%	25.33%	38.4	16.3	40.7

Background: Delbarton High School went 18 years in between draft picks. The White Sox took outfielder Wes Swackhamer in the 19th round all the way back in 2001. And then the New Jersey-based prep school had two players chosen last June: shortstop Anthony Volpe, whom the Yankees selected with the 30th overall pick, and Jack Leiter, who (A) was widely regarded as a top high school pitcher that (B) the Yankees took a late round flier on despite (C) his father, Al, informing teams he would be honoring his commitment to Vanderbilt University. Volpe, a 5-foot-11, 180-pound middle infielder, was pushed up to the Appalachian League; he hit a lowly .215/.349/.355 with seven doubles, two triples, two homeruns, and half-of-a-dozen stolen bases. Per *Deserved Runs Created Plus*, his overall production was exactly the league average mark.

Scouting Report: Fast hands and a short, quick, deliberate path to the ball – which is reminiscent of another Yankees shortstop. Volpe showed more pop than expected during his debut in the Appalachian League, posting a .140 Isolated Power. The New Jersey native also showed a patient approach at the plate, walking in more than 15% of his plate appearances. Defensively, he shows an average arm but soft hands and fluid hips. Volpe looks like a .280/.340/.420 type hitter with slightly better than average defense.

Ceiling: 2.0-win player
Risk: Moderate
MLB ETA: 2023

9. Josh Smith, SS

Hit	Power	SB	Patience	Glove	Overall
55	45	60	50	50+	50

Born: 08/07/97	Age: 22	Bats: L
Height: 5-10	Weight: 172	Throws: R

YEAR	LVL	PA	1B	2B	3B	HR	SB	CS	AVG	OBP	SLG	BB%	K%	GB%	LD%	FB%
2019	A-	141	26	6	1	3	6	3	0.324	0.450	0.477	17.73%	12.06%	42.1	21.1	33.7

Background: Louisiana State University has churned out an impressive collection of middle infielders throughout the school's illustrious history, including: Alex Bregman, Aaron Hill, Ryan Theriot, Jeff Reboulet, Todd Walker, Mike Fontenot, Warren Morris, and Ryan Schimpf are the more recognizeable ballplayers. Now it's time to add Josh Smith's name to the list. A elite performer during his junior campaign with the Tigers, Smith, who slugged a scorching .346/.433/.533 with 17 doubles, two triples, nine homeruns, and 20 stolen bases, was selected by the Yankees in the second round last June. After signing with the franchise for $976,700 – the recommended slot bonus. Smith spent his debut with Staten Island in the New York-Penn League, batting a solid .324/.450/.477 with six doubles, one triple, and three homers. Per *Deserved Runs Created Plus*, his overall production was 107% *better* than the league average mark.

Scouting Report: With respect to his collegiate work last season, consider the following:

- Between 2011 and 2018, here's the list of hitters in the SEC that batted at least .330/.425/.525 with a walk rate between 9% and 11% with a strikeout rate between 13% and 18% (min. 275 PA). Those hitters: Mike Zunino, the third overall pick in 2012, and Josh Smith.

It was a bit of an odd debut for Smith, mainly because he walked far more frequently than his junior season in college – 17.7% vs. 9.3%. There's a chance for an above-average hit tool with 45-grade power and solid defense. Throw in 35-stolen base speed and Smith has the makings of an average starter, maybe more, at the big league level. He ticketed for a start in the Sally and will likely cap it off in High Class A. Jean Segura's 2019 season in which he batted .280/.323/.420 and earned 2.3 fWAR seems like a reasonable ceiling.

Ceiling: 2.0-win player
Risk: Moderate
MLB ETA: 2022

10. Everson Pereira, CF

Hit	Power	SB	Patience	Glove	Overall
40/55	40/50	45	50	50/55	50

Born: 04/10/01	Age: 19	Bats: R	Top CALs:
Height: 6-0	Weight: 191	Throws: R	

YEAR	LVL	PA	1B	2B	3B	HR	SB	CS	AVG	OBP	SLG	BB%	K%	GB%	LD%	FB%
2018	RK	183	31	8	2	3	3	2	0.263	0.322	0.389	8.20%	32.79%	38.9	15.7	39.8
2019	A-	74	8	3	0	1	3	0	0.171	0.216	0.257	5.41%	35.14%	54.5	15.9	22.7

Background: Pereira was a big get off the international market in 2017. The toolsy center fielder signed with baseball's most storied franchise for a hefty $1.5 million. A native of Cabudare, Venezuela, Pereira made his professional debut in the Appalachian League two years ago, acquitting himself nicely as he batted .263/.322/.389 with eight doubles, two triples, and three homeruns in 41 games as a 17-year-old. And heading into last season, plenty of hype began to swirl around Pereira's ceiling. The 6-foot, 191-pound center fielder stumbled out of the gate and his season prematurely ended after a serious collision with the outfield wall in early July. He finished the year with a .171/.216/.257 triple-slash line in 18 games.

Snippet from The 2018 Prospect Digest Handbook: As expected with a 17-year-old making his professional debut in the Appalachian League, there was a lot of good and a lot of bad parts of his game, the latter being quickly exposed by the older competition. The good: the teenage outfielder's tools were on display from the get-go, including impressive power potential, a solid eye, promising hit tool, and a strong glove in center field. The bad: he punched out in nearly one-third of his plate appearances. The Appalachian League – typically – hasn't been overly kind to 17-year-old hitters; since 2006 there have been a total of 17 of them to receive at least 150 plate appearances in a season. Ten of those 17 posted a wRC+ of 88 or below.

Scouting Report: There's really nothing new to report on, thanks to his injury. Pereira's strikeout rate ballooned during his limited action, which isn't concerning given (A) the sample size, (B) his age, and (C) his level of competition. It was more or less a lost season for the talented center fielder. So we'll just take a wait-and-see approach.

Ceiling: 2.0- to 2.5-win player
Risk: Moderate to High
MLB ETA: 2023

11. Canaan Smith, LF

Hit	Power	SB	Patience	Glove	Overall
55	45/50	30	60	50/45	45

Born: 04/30/99	Age: 21	Bats: L
Height: 6-0	Weight: 215	Throws: R

YEAR	LVL	PA	1B	2B	3B	HR	SB	CS	AVG	OBP	SLG	BB%	K%	GB%	LD%	FB%
2017	RK	237	39	10	0	5	5	3	0.289	0.430	0.422	19.41%	18.57%	44.8	17.9	26.9
2018	A-	171	17	8	1	3	0	0	0.191	0.281	0.316	11.11%	30.41%	53.0	14.0	25.0
2019	A	528	92	32	3	11	16	4	0.307	0.405	0.465	14.02%	20.45%	44.2	25.4	24.6

Background: There likely hasn't been a turnaround from one year to the next in last several years – maybe even decades – like the rollercoaster Smith was riding. A fourth round pick out of Rockwall-Heath High School three years ago, Smith looked like junior varsity hitter squaring off against state contenders during his stint in the New York-Penn League two years ago; he "hit" a puny .191/.281/.316 with just eight doubles, one triple, and a trio of homeruns in 45 games with Staten Island. His overall production, per *Deserved Runs Created Plus*, was 22% *below* the league average threshold. At that point he looked like he was heading down the path of non-descript, quickly evaporating prospect bust. And then he totally redeemed himself. Despite the struggles, the front office bumped him up to the South Atlantic League. And Smith not only proved to be up to the challenge, but he established himself as one of the league's premier bats. In a career best 12 games with Charleston, Smith slugged a scorching .307/.405/.465 with 32 doubles, three triples, and 11 homeruns. His overall production was whopping 82% *better* than the league average threshold.

Scouting Report: Consider the following:

- Since 2006, here's the list of 20-year-old hitters to post at least a 175 DRC+ in the South Atlantic League (min. 300 PA): Mookie Betts, Greg Bird, Tyler Austin, and – of course – Canaan Smith.
- Sans Smith, here's their respective big league DRC+ totals: 136 (Betts), 98 (Bird), and 89 (Austin).

So what changed for Smith? Well, to begin, Smith quieted his lower half as he removed some jittery feet and toe tapping and goes straight into his enormous leg kick. His base looks more compact as well. And during the brief time I saw him in 2018 vs. his time in 2019, he looked far more confident at the dish last season. Elite patience with tremendous contact skills. Smith shows above-average or better bat speed with the potential to knock out 15 or homeruns as he continues to matures. Physically, he's maxed out. In terms of ceiling and floor, think Sean Casey and Lenny Harris. The former was a slightly better-than-average bat and the latter is considered one of the best pinch hitters of all time.

Ceiling: 1.5- to 2.0-win player
Risk: Moderate
MLB ETA: 2022

12. Roansy Contreras, RHP

FB	CB	CH	Command	Overall
60	55	50/55	55	45

Born: 11/07/99	Age: 20	Bats: R
Height: 6-0	Weight: 170	Throws: R

YEAR	LVL	IP	W	L	SV	ERA	FIP	WHIP	K/9	K%	BB/9	BB%	K/BB	HR9	BABIP
2017	Rk	31.7	4	1	0	4.26	4.59	1.48	4.8	11.72%	3.4	8.28%	1.42	0.57	0.297
2017	Rk	22.0	0	3	0	3.68	3.55	1.36	7.0	17.35%	2.0	5.10%	3.40	0.82	0.311
2018	A-	28.7	0	0	0	1.26	2.74	0.84	10.0	29.91%	2.8	8.41%	3.56	0.31	0.219
2018	A	34.7	0	2	0	3.38	4.47	1.18	7.3	19.58%	3.1	8.39%	2.33	1.04	0.255
2019	A	132.3	12	5	0	3.33	3.65	1.07	7.7	21.08%	2.4	6.72%	3.14	0.68	0.255

Background: Joined the storied organization for a quarter million dollars during the summer of 2016. Contreras, a wiry right-hander out of Peralvillo, Dominican Republic, rocketed up prospect lists after an impressive 2018 campaign in which he posted a 60-to-21 strikeout-to-walk ratio in 63.1 innings split between Staten Island and Charleston. After a successful seven-game stint in the Sally in 2018, New York opted to keep the hard-throwing youngster in Low Class A last season. And the numbers were…more or less…the same. Making 24 starts with the RiverDogs, Contreras averaged 7.7 strikeouts and just 2.4 walks per nine innings. He finished his third professional season with a 3.33 ERA and a 3.94 DRA (*Deserved Run Average*).

Snippet from The 2018 Prospect Digest Handbook: Contreras looks like a solid, middle-of-the-rotation caliber arm. The Yankees have done a solid job limiting the youngster's workload, so he's probably pegged for 90- to 100-innings next season. And a second-half promotion up to the Florida State League isn't out of the question either.

Scouting Report: Consider the following:

- Since 2006, here's the list of 19-year-olds to post a strikeout percentage between 20% and 22% with a walk percentage between 6% and 8% in the South Atlantic League (min. 100 IP): Aaron Thompson, Brody Colvin, Peter Lambert, and Roansy Contreras.

An interesting low level arm developing for the Yankees – though I'd bet he's more likely ticketed as a trade chip rather than a member of the club's big league roster. Contreras attacks hitters with a loose-armed 93- to 94-mph fastball, an above-average curveball, which he'll vary the velocity and shape; and a changeup that flashes 55. The line between a solid backend starting pitcher and Jeanmar Gomez isn't extraordinarily large, but Contreras looks like a contender to take the multiple-inning relief route. The stuff's solid and he throws strikes. But there's not one true swing-and-miss offering.

Ceiling: 1.5- to 2.0-win player
Risk: Moderate
MLB ETA: 2020/2021

13. Antonio Cabello, OF

	Hit	Power	SB	Patience	Glove	Overall
	40/55	40/45	40	50	50	50

Born: 11/01/00	Age: 19	Bats: R
Height: 5-10	Weight: 160	Throws: R

YEAR	LVL	PA	1B	2B	3B	HR	SB	CS	AVG	OBP	SLG	BB%	K%	GB%	LD%	FB%
2018	RK	30	4	0	1	0	5	1	0.227	0.433	0.318	20.00%	20.00%	50.0	18.8	12.5
2018	RK	162	26	9	4	5	5	5	0.321	0.426	0.555	12.96%	20.99%	40.8	23.3	31.1
2019	Rk+	251	31	10	4	3	5	4	0.211	0.280	0.330	7.57%	30.68%	43.4	12.5	36.2

Background: Named as the 15th best prospect on the international scene during the 2017 signing period. Cabello, a converted catcher, turned in a promising debut two years ago as he slugged a healthy .321/.426/.555 with nine doubles, four triples, and five homeruns in only 40 games of Gulf Coast League action. And the short, stocky outfielder looked poised for a big showing in 2019. But he morphed into the 2018 showing of Canaan Smith. In 56 games with the Pulaski Yankees in the Appalachian League, the 5-foot-10, generously listed 160-pounder batted a lowly .211/.280/.330 with 10 doubles, four triples, and three homeruns. According to *Deserved Runs Created Plus*, his overall production was a staggering 37% *below* the league average threshold.

Snippet from The 2018 Prospect Digest Handbook: The teenager shows impressive bat speed, though not along the lines of fellow Yankees farmhand Clint Frazier, with plenty of loft to tap into his above-average power potential. And Cabello, equipped with above-average speed, handled the move to center field with aplomb. Given some further development/time, he has the potential to be an above-average regular.

Scouting Report: Well, that didn't go as planned. It was a completely lost season for Cabello. His walked rate halved and his strikeout rate went from better-than-average to full-blown red flag territory. And his power, even though it was gap-to-gap, evaporated into a slap-hitting center fielder territory. Mechanically speaking, I don't see any major tweaks from his 2018 showing vs. his disastrous 2019 season. It'll be interesting as to whether Cabello can right the ship like Canaan Smith or fall to the wayside like Gosuke Katoh.

Ceiling: 2.0-win player
Risk: Moderate to High
MLB ETA: 2022

14. Albert Abreu, RHP

FB	CB	SL	CH	Command	Overall
70	60	50	60	40	45

Born: 09/26/95	Age: 24	Bats: R
Height: 6-2	Weight: 175	Throws: R

YEAR	LVL	IP	W	L	SV	ERA	FIP	WHIP	K/9	K%	BB/9	BB%	K/BB	HR9	BABIP
2017	Rk	4.3	0	0	0	2.08	0.42	0.69	16.6	44.44%	0.0	0.00%	#DIV/0!	0.00	0.333
2017	A	14.7	1	0	0	1.84	2.44	0.82	13.5	40.00%	1.8	5.45%	7.33	0.61	0.296
2017	A+	34.3	1	3	0	4.19	3.74	1.40	8.1	20.95%	3.9	10.14%	2.07	0.52	0.316
2018	Rk	2.0	0	1	0	18.00	3.14	2.00	9.0	18.18%	0.0	0.00%	#DIV/0!	0.00	0.500
2018	Rk	3.0	0	2	0	27.00	4.64	4.00	9.0	12.50%	6.0	8.33%	1.50	0.00	0.556
2018	A+	62.7	4	3	0	4.16	4.99	1.32	9.3	23.72%	4.2	10.58%	2.24	1.29	0.274
2018	AA	5.0	0	0	0	0.00	2.31	0.20	7.2	23.53%	1.8	5.88%	4.00	0.00	0.000
2019	AA	96.7	5	8	0	4.28	4.35	1.61	8.5	20.68%	4.9	12.05%	1.72	0.84	0.336

Background: It seems like a lifetime ago at this point. But the tantalizingly enigmatic right-hander has been a member of the Yankees' organization for just the past three seasons. Acquired along with fellow flame-thrower Jorge Guzman, who was dealt to Miami in the Giancarlo Stanton swap, from Houston for All-Star backstop Brian McCann following the 2016 season. Last season – surprisingly – marked the first time in four years that Abreu didn't see action at a High Class A level. Instead, he spent the entirety of 2019 battling the most challenging minor league level, Class AA, with...mixed results. Making a career best 20 starts, along with a trio of relief appearances, the Guayubin, Dominican Republic, native struck out 91 and walked a whopping 53 in only 96.2 innings of work. He compiled a 4.28 ERA and a horrible 6.77 DRA (*Deserved Run Average*).

Snippet from The 2018 Prospect Digest Handbook: Abreu's still only entering his age-23 season, but if another injury-shortened campaign is added to his resume it might be time to start thinking about shifting him into a relief role.

Scouting Report: In terms of pure stuff, there are very few minor league arms that can match up with Abreu's elite repertoire: mid- to upper-90s fastball with exceptional late life; fall-off-the-table power curveball; an underrated plus changeup with plenty of arm-side dive and fade; and – for the first time last season – he unveiled a solid 50-grade slider. But the problem is – and has always been – his ability, or inability, to consistently throw strikes. He walked more than 12% of the batters he faced last season. Abreu has been known to put it all together for brief stints which only whets the appetite, but it quickly comes to an end. New York let Dellin Betances walk via free agency and Abreu could be a dark horse candidate to help fill that role. Mechanically speaking, there's a hitch in lead leg that seems to affect his timing, particularly from the windup. It would behoove the organization to have him throw from the stretch all the time.

Ceiling: 1.5-win player
Risk: Moderate
MLB ETA: 2020

15. Nick Nelson, RHP

FB	CB	SL	CH	Command	Overall
65	55	50	50	40+	45

Born: 12/05/95	Age: 24	Bats: R
Height: 6-1	Weight: 195	Throws: R

YEAR	LVL	IP	W	L	SV	ERA	FIP	WHIP	K/9	K%	BB/9	BB%	K/BB	HR9	BABIP
2017	A	100.7	3	12	0	4.56	3.84	1.52	9.8	24.34%	4.5	11.06%	2.20	0.45	0.356
2018	A	24.7	1	1	0	3.65	2.24	1.01	12.8	34.65%	2.6	6.93%	5.00	0.36	0.304
2018	A+	88.3	7	5	0	3.36	3.11	1.31	10.1	26.26%	4.8	12.47%	2.11	0.10	0.301
2018	AA	8.7	0	0	0	5.19	5.62	2.19	10.4	22.22%	9.3	20.00%	1.11	1.04	0.360
2019	A+	3.7	0	0	0	0.00	0.31	1.36	17.2	46.67%	2.5	6.67%	7.00	0.00	0.571
2019	AA	65.0	7	2	0	2.35	3.26	1.28	11.5	33.20%	4.8	14.00%	2.37	0.55	0.308
2019	AAA	21.0	1	1	0	4.71	3.58	1.29	10.3	26.97%	3.0	7.87%	3.43	0.86	0.321

Background: Taken by the San Francisco Giants in the late, late rounds of the 2014 draft following his senior season at Rutherford High School. Nelson opted to head down the path of the early collegiate draft eligibility and attended JuCo Gulf Coast Community College. Two years later the Yankees called the hard-throwing right-hander's name in the fourth round. Always one for big time strikeouts and wavering, less-than-stellar control/command, Nelson made 18 appearances, 17 of which were starts, between the upper three levels of the minor leagues. The barrel-chested righty tossed 89.2 innings during an injury interrupted campaign, fanning an impressive 114 strikeouts and issuing 43 walks. He finished the year with a 2.81 ERA.

Snippet from The 2018 Prospect Digest Handbook: Nelson falls into a dangerous category: he's a polished prospect equipped with two above-average or better pitches that won't get exposed until he reaches Class AA, the make-it-or-break-it level. Nelson's two above-average or better offerings: a lively fastball that sits in the mid-90s and an 80 mph curveball that he can throw for strikes. His changeup also shows some promise with downward tumble. The problem, though, is Nelson simply doesn't throw enough strikes. He's another one the club's more recognizable arms that will likely get shifted into bullpen as they approach the majors.

Scouting Report: So, Nelson more than proved himself during his 13 appearances in the Eastern League last season. Consider the following:

- Since 2006, only five 23-year-old pitchers posted a strikeout percentage between 29% and 31% in the Eastern League (min. 50 IP: Cory Burns, Alexander Guillen, Humberto Sanchez, Alex Faedo, and Nick Nelson.
- Nelson, by the way, posted the highest walk percentage, 12,8%, by a wide margin; Sanchez, the runner-up posted a 9.6% BB%.

A few notes on the former fourth rounder:

- A lot of reports indicate Nelson throws a splitter. It looks more like a firm, straight changeup. It lacks dive and tumble. And there's no discernible spacing in between his fingers either.
- His fastball, which sits in the 95- to 98-mph range, is tough to get on top off in the upper part of the strike zone. And his curveball shows some impressive bite at times. Both offerings scream late-inning, potential impact relief arm.
- The control/command all but guarantees his move into the pen.

Ceiling: 1.5-win player
Risk: Moderate
MLB ETA: 2020

16. Josh Breaux, C

	Hit	Power	SB	Patience	Glove	Overall
	45	60	30	50	50	45

Born: 10/07/97	Age: 22	Bats: R
Height: 6-1	Weight: 220	Throws: R

YEAR	LVL	PA	1B	2B	3B	HR	SB	CS	AVG	OBP	SLG	BB%	K%	GB%	LD%	FB%
2018	RK	9	1	0	0	0	0	0	0.125	0.222	0.125	11.11%	11.11%	28.6	14.3	42.9
2018	A-	105	19	9	0	0	0	0	0.280	0.295	0.370	2.86%	19.05%	52.4	20.7	15.9
2019	A	216	31	10	0	13	0	0	0.271	0.324	0.518	6.94%	27.31%	45.4	19.1	28.4

Background: Between 2006 and 2017, the Yankees selected a total of two catchers within the opening round rounds of the June draft: Austin Romine, a second round pick out of El Toro High School in 2007 and former Miami Hurricane Peter O'Brien, who was also a second round pick, was taken five years later. It took just one draft class, 2018, for the club to equal that total. New York snagged prep backstop Anthony Siegler with the 23rd pick and then doubled up by selected Josh Breaux 38 picks later. A product of JuCo McLennan Community College, Breaux opened up the 2019 season with the Charleston RiverDogs in the South Atlantic League, but after a couple months of solid production as an elbow injury forced the 6-foot-1, 220-pound backstop to the disabled list for roughly 12 weeks. Breaux hit a respectable .271/.324/.518 with 10 doubles and 13 homeruns in only 51 games of action. Per *Deserved Runs Created Plus*, his overall production topped the league average threshold by 37%.

Snippet from The 2018 Prospect Digest Handbook: Legitimate catching prospects beyond the high school level are scant in [the 2018] draft class, which ultimately helps Breaux's stock. But he's going to struggle in the lower levels of the minor leagues – especially with contact rates

Scouting Report: I was half correct. Breaux – clearly – didn't struggle during his first taste of full season action in 2019. In fact, the numbers are downright impressive, particularly his plus in-game power. However, on the other hand, Breaux's strikeout rate, 27.1%, crept into red flag territory – and it was even worse before the extended layoff (29.1%). With respect to work in the Sally last season, consider the following:

- Since 2006, only two 21-year-old hitters posted a DRC+ total between 132 and 142 with a strikeout rate north of 25% in the South Atlantic League (min. 200 PA): Zoilo Almonte, who had a couple cups of big league coffee with the Yankees in 2013 and 2014, and – of course – Josh Breaux.

Breaux looks like the bat first, power-oriented backstop, though he won't kill a team behind the dish. I still think he's going to continue to battle swing-and-miss issues as he progresses up the ladder. He's going to win a lot of homerun derbies throughout his professional career.

Ceiling: 1.5-win player
Risk: Moderate
MLB ETA: 2023

17. Josh Stowers, OF

	Hit	Power	SB	Patience	Glove	Overall
	45/50	40	60	60	50	45

Born: 02/25/97	Age: 23	Bats: R
Height: 6-0	Weight: 200	Throws: R

YEAR	LVL	PA	1B	2B	3B	HR	SB	CS	AVG	OBP	SLG	BB%	K%	GB%	LD%	FB%
2018	A-	244	32	15	0	5	20	4	0.260	0.380	0.410	15.16%	23.36%	46.3	16.3	25.9
2019	A	460	72	24	2	7	35	16	0.273	0.386	0.400	13.91%	26.74%	36.6	23.3	32.1

Background: A toolsy center fielder out of the University of Louisville, the Mariners originally drafted the dynamic athlete in the second round, 54th overall, two years ago. But Stowers' stay in Seattle's organization was like a screaming meteor: short-lived.

The Mariners sent the 6-foot, 200-pound Chicago native to the Northwest League where he acquitted himself rather nicely as he batted .260/.380/.410 with 15 doubles, five homeruns, and 20 stolen bases. But right before Spring Training the club dealt Stowers to the Yankees for infielder Shed Long (whose tenure as a Yankee was measured in mere hours). Stowers spent last season with the Charleston RiverDogs, batting .273/.386/.400 with 24 doubles, two triples, seven homeruns, and 35 stolen bases in 105 games. His overall production, as measured by Baseball Prospectus' *Deserved Runs Created Plus*, topped the league average threshold by 46%. New York sent him to the Arizona Fall League; he batted a lowly .131/.312/.180 in 20 games with the Surprise Saguaros.

Snippet from The 2018 Prospect Digest Handbook: Oozing premium, top-end speed, Stowers complements it with solid power, a decent hit tool, and a potential plus-eye at the plate; he walked in nearly 18% of his plate appearances with Louisville last season and followed that up with a 15.2% showing in short-season ball.

Scouting Report: Consider the following:

- Since 2006, here's the list of 22-year-olds to post a DRC+ between 140 and 150 with a double-digit walk rate and a strikeout rate north of 25% in the South Atlantic League (min. 300 PA): Tom Murphy, Chris Gittens, Brenden Webb, and Josh Stowers.

The hit tool remains a touch below average, though it profiles as a 50-grade tool as full maturity. And he's still showing solid gap-to-gap power and can run into a handful of fastballs to belt out 10 or so homeruns. And he's a terror on the base paths, though he's not a stout defender. Stowers looks like the prototypical fourth outfielder, maybe a little more given his nose for first base.

Ceiling: 1.5-win player
Risk: Moderate
MLB ETA: 2022

18. Ezequiel Duran, 2B

	Hit	Power	SB	Patience	Glove	Overall
	40/45	50/55	40	50	55	45

Born: 05/22/99	Age: 21	Bats: R
Height: 5-11	Weight: 185	Throws: R

YEAR	LVL	PA	1B	2B	3B	HR	SB	CS	AVG	OBP	SLG	BB%	K%	GB%	LD%	FB%
2017	RK	65	12	5	4	3	4	1	0.393	0.415	0.754	4.62%	23.08%	51.1	36.2	6.4
2018	RK	235	30	8	2	4	7	0	0.201	0.251	0.311	3.83%	27.66%	44.5	10.3	34.2
2019	A-	277	34	12	4	13	11	4	0.256	0.329	0.496	9.03%	27.80%	43.5	20.6	27.1

Background: After a brief – albeit dominating – debut in the foreign rookie league in 2017, Duran, who slugged .393/.415/.754 in 15 games, found himself in the Appalachian League to begin the 2018 season. And like a lot of the other more notable bats in the system, he struggled during his tenure with the Pulaski Yankees, batting a paltry .201/.251/.311 with eight doubles, two triples, and four homeruns in 53 games. Undeterred by his struggles, the front office bumped the 5-foot-11, 185-pound second baseman up to the New York-Penn League. And, well, he finished as the league leader in dingers. In 66 games with Staten Island, Duran slugged .256/.329/.496 with 12 doubles, four triples, and 13 homeruns. He also swiped 11 bags in 15 total attempts. Per *Deserved Runs Created Plus*, his overall production topped the league average threshold by a whopping 60%.

Scouting Report: Consider the following:

- Since 2006, only two 20-year-old hitters met the following criteria in the New York-Penn League (min. 250 PA): 155 to 165 DRC+ and a walk rate between 9% and 11%. Those two hitters: Nathaniel Lowe, who batted .263/.325/.454 during his rookie season with Tampa Bay in 2019, and – of course – Ezequiel Duran.
- It should be noted, of course, that Lowe posted a 13.7% K-rate; Duran, on the other hand, fanned roughly twice as frequently.

Impressive power with a 55-grade glove from an up-the-middle position. It's the foundation for a promising prospect. However, Duran's strikeout rate, 27.8%, is problematic. And he didn't really make any in-season adjustments to help his contact issues either. In terms of ceiling, he looks like a late career Ian Kinsler.

Ceiling: 1.5-win player
Risk: Moderate
MLB ETA: 2022

19. T.J. Sikkema, LHP

FB	CB	CH	Command	Overall
50	55	50	55	45

Born: 07/25/98	Age: 21	Bats: L
Height: 6-0	Weight: 221	Throws: L

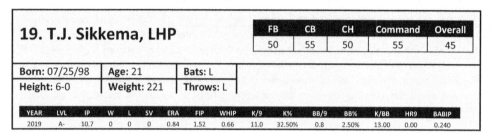

YEAR	LVL	IP	W	L	SV	ERA	FIP	WHIP	K/9	K%	BB/9	BB%	K/BB	HR9	BABIP
2019	A-	10.7	0	0	0	0.84	1.52	0.66	11.0	32.50%	0.8	2.50%	13.00	0.00	0.240

Background: Between 1965 and 2018, the University of Missouri graduated a total of 19 left-handers to the minor leagues. Only a pair of them eventually made it to the big leagues: Dave Otto, a second round pick by the Athletics all the way back in 1985, and Rob Zastryzny, who was also taken in the second round, though it was nearly 30 years later. Sikkema, a doughy southpaw, became (A) the 20th left-hander in school history to be drafted and (B) the only one taken in the first round. A consistent performer throughout his three-year career with the Tigers, Sikkema left the school with a career 258-to-69 strikeout-to-walk ratio in 238.0 innings of work. After joining the Yankees' organization, the 6-foot-1, 221-pound hurler posted a 13-to-1 strikeout-to-walk ratio in 10.2 innings with Staten Island.

Scouting Report: A bit of a curious first round selection by the Yankees. While Sikkema is young for the draft class – he's only now entering his age-21 season – his repertoire and arm slot all scream future reliever – perhaps even a left-handed specialist. Slinging the ball from a crossfire, across his body, low three-quarter slot, Sikkema's fastball sat in the low-90s with some sink. He complements it with an above-average curveball (note: reports indicate it's a slider, but the during warms ups Sikkema, himself, was signaling curveball), and a 50-grade changeup. He's a strike-thrower that's poised to move quickly through the lower ranks of the minor leagues. But he looks almost certain to slide into a relief role. It's just a perplexing pick by the Yankees.

Ceiling: 1.5-win player
Risk: Moderate
MLB ETA: 2020/2021

20. Luis Gil, RHP

FB	CB	CH	Command	Overall
70	45/50	45	40	40

Born: 06/03/98	Age: 22	Bats: R
Height: 6-3	Weight: 176	Throws: R

YEAR	LVL	IP	W	L	SV	ERA	FIP	WHIP	K/9	K%	BB/9	BB%	K/BB	HR9	BABIP
2017	Rk	41.7	0	2	0	2.59	3.30	1.22	10.6	27.68%	4.3	11.30%	2.45	0.43	0.287
2018	Rk	39.3	2	1	0	1.37	3.27	1.17	13.3	35.80%	5.7	15.43%	2.32	0.23	0.256
2018	A-	6.7	0	2	0	5.40	5.13	2.55	13.5	25.64%	8.1	15.38%	1.67	1.35	0.455
2019	A	83.0	4	5	0	2.39	2.48	1.19	12.1	32.00%	4.2	11.14%	2.87	0.11	0.304
2019	A+	13.0	1	0	0	4.85	3.69	1.46	7.6	19.30%	5.5	14.04%	1.38	0.00	0.297

Background: Originally signed by the Twins prior to Spring Training five years ago. Minnesota shipped the flame-throwing right-hander to the Yankees in exchange for Jake Cave, who was designated for assignment following the signing of Neil Walker in early 2018. Gil, a wiry 6-foot-3, 176-pound hurler, showed some enormous potential – and strike zone blindness – during his first season in the Yankees' organization. He posted a 68-to-31 strikeout-to-walk ratio in 46.0 innings between the Appalachian and New York-Penn Leagues. The front office bumped the Dominican-born prospect up to the South Atlantic League where he (A) threw strikes at far more frequently, though not frequent enough and (B) finished with the fourth best strikeout percentage in the league (32.0%). He was promoted up to High Class A for three final starts, fanned 11 and walking eight in 13.0 innings of work.

Scouting Report: The reports didn't match the arsenal, which is a bit disappointing – especially since numerous reports all indicated the same thing. Sure, Gil had a lights out, elite upper-90s fastball. But his secondary weapons were quite raw – raw enough that (A) there's not a ton of hope for future develops and (B) he eventually falls into a single-pitch relief role. The curveball's slow, loopy, and deliberate. And his 45-grade changeup is equally as poor. Zach McAllister carved out a semi-useful role as a seventh-inning reliever, but he showed superior command/control. With respect to his work in Low Class A last season, consider the following:

- Since 2006, only two 21-year-old pitchers posted at least a 30% whiff percentage and a double-digit walk percentage in the South Atlantic League (min. 50 IP): Alberto Tirado and Luis Gil.

Ceiling: 1.0- to 1.5-win player
Risk: Moderate
MLB ETA: 2020

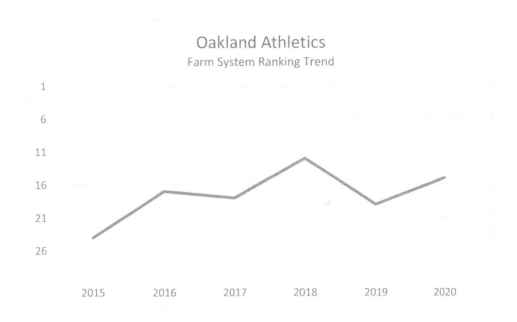

Oakland Athletics
Farm System Ranking Trend

Rank	Name	Age	Pos
1	Jesus Luzardo	22	LHP
2	A.J. Puk	25	LHP
3	Nick Allen	21	SS
4	Sean Murphy	25	C
5	Daulton Jefferies	24	RHP
6	Robert Puason	25	SS
7	Austin Allen	26	C
8	Logan Davidson	22	SS
9	Grant Holmes	24	RHP
10	Jordan Diaz	19	3B
11	Brayan Buelvas	18	CF
12	James Kaprielian	26	RHP
13	Tyler Baum	23	RHP
14	Sheldon Neuse	25	2B/3B
15	Austin Beck	21	CF
16	Hogan Harris	23	LHP
17	Brian Howard	25	LHP
18	Greg Deichmann	25	LF/RF
19	Lazaro Armenteros	21	LF
20	Jeremy Eierman	23	2B/SS

1. Jesus Luzardo, LHP

	FB	CB	CH	Command	Overall
	70	60	55/60	55/60	70

Born: 09/30/97	Age: 22	Bats: L
Height: 6-0	Weight: 209	Throws: L

YEAR	LVL	IP	W	L	SV	ERA	FIP	WHIP	K/9	K%	BB/9	BB%	K/BB	HR9	BABIP
2017	Rk	13.7	1	0	0	1.32	2.17	1.02	9.9	27.78%	0.0	0.00%	N/A	0.66	0.342
2017	Rk	11.7	0	1	0	1.54	2.50	0.86	10.0	28.26%	0.8	2.17%	13.00	0.00	0.290
2017	A-	18.0	1	0	0	2.00	2.93	0.89	10.0	28.17%	2.0	5.63%	5.00	0.50	0.250
2018	A+	14.7	2	1	0	1.23	1.36	0.75	15.3	45.45%	3.1	9.09%	5.00	0.00	0.240
2018	AA	78.7	7	3	0	2.29	2.88	0.97	9.8	27.74%	2.1	5.81%	4.78	0.57	0.268
2018	AAA	16.0	1	1	0	7.31	4.61	2.00	10.1	23.38%	3.9	9.09%	2.57	1.13	0.469
2019	Rk	2.0	0	0	0	0.00	0.75	0.50	22.5	71.43%	0.0	0.00%	N/A	0.00	0.500
2019	A+	10.0	1	0	0	0.90	1.36	0.60	16.2	50.00%	0.0	0.00%	N/A	0.90	0.294
2019	AAA	31.0	1	1	0	3.19	3.63	1.19	9.9	25.95%	2.3	6.11%	4.25	0.87	0.302

Background: It's now a moot point because – well – the Nationals are the World Champions but, man, the 2017 swap involving the clubs had the potential to be quite lopsided. Oakland agreed to trade All-Star reliever Sean Doolittle and veteran Ryan Madson in exchange for Jesus Luzardo, one of the top young arms in baseball, Blake Treinen, who was otherworldly and finished sixth in the Cy Young voting two years ago, and third baseman Sheldon Neuse. Luzardo, a third round pick in 2016 and former Tommy John survivor, inched closer to reaching his status as a perennial Cy Young contender last season. Despite suffering through a shoulder strain, which forced him out of action during the first several months of the year, and then a mid-season lat strain; Luzardo quickly made up for lost time by making his big league debut after just seven starts in Class AAA. Luzardo, who posted a ridiculous 57-to-8 strikeout-to-walk ratio in 43.0 minor league innings, remained equally unhittable in six relief appearances with the A's (12.0 IP, 16 K, and 3 BB).

Snippet from The 2018 Prospect Digest Handbook: Luzardo not only possesses an elite arsenal, but he shows poise beyond his years.

Scouting Report: Elite, *elite* repertoire. Luzardo's left arm, seemingly, has been touched by Sandy Koufax himself. Mid- to upper-90s fastball that sits – *comfortably* – in the 95- to 97-mph range. His sharp, power curveball adds a second plus offering. And his changeup, which didn't look as sharp as previous years, is no worse than above-average. For the record: I had the pitch equal to, if not better, than his curveball heading into the year. The regression in the changeup is likely / probably the result of the time spent on the disabled list. Combined the front-of-the-rotation caliber arsenal with an above-average level of control / command – which flashes plus at times. The only thing standing in Luzardo's way, however, is his ability to remain atop the rubber.

Ceiling: 6.0-win player
Risk: Low to Moderate
MLB ETA: Debuted in 2019

2. A.J. Puk, LHP

	FB	CB	SL	CH	Command	Overall
	70	N/A	70	50/55	45/50	60

Born: 04/25/95	Age: 25	Bats: L
Height: 6-7	Weight: 238	Throws: L

YEAR	LVL	IP	W	L	SV	ERA	FIP	WHIP	K/9	K%	BB/9	BB%	K/BB	HR9	BABIP
2017	A+	61.0	4	5	0	3.69	2.25	1.10	14.5	38.58%	3.4	9.06%	4.26	0.15	0.336
2017	AA	64.0	2	5	0	4.36	2.35	1.39	12.1	30.82%	3.5	8.96%	3.44	0.28	0.380
2019	A+	6.0	0	0	0	6.00	6.99	1.50	13.5	36.00%	6.0	16.00%	2.25	3.00	0.300
2019	AA	8.3	0	0	0	4.32	4.53	1.44	14.0	37.14%	3.2	8.57%	4.33	2.16	0.412
2019	AAA	11.0	4	1	0	4.91	5.52	0.91	13.1	43.24%	2.5	8.11%	5.33	2.45	0.222

Background: Part of the 2016 University of Florida squad that comes around – seemingly – once in a lifetime. The Gators rostered the likes of Puk, Brady Singer, Jackson Kowar, Dane Dunning, Shaun Anderson, Scott Moss, Logan Shore, Pete Alonso, Jonathan India, Buddy Reed, Mike Rivera, J.J. Schwarz, and Dalton Guthrie. Puk, the sixth overall pick in 2016, was on the fast track to big league stardom before Tommy John surgery forced him to take a detour. Coming off of a dominating 2017 season in which he posted a whopping 184-to-48 strikeout-to-walk ratio in only 125.0 innings between the Stockton and Midland, Puk missed the entirety of the following year. Finally healthy, the 6-foot-7, 238-pound southpaw picked right back up where he left. In 18 appearances between the upper three levels of the minors, the former Gator ace struck out 38 and walked 10 in 25.1 innings. Oakland called up the ballyhooed left-hander in late August for the stretch run; he tossed another 11.1 innings with the A's, posting a 13-to-5 strikeout-to-walk ratio with a 3.18 ERA.

Snippet from The 2018 Prospect Digest Handbook: Puk's control took some promising strides forward prior to the elbow injury – so hopefully the surgical procedure, layoff, and rehab work won't stunt that growth for too long. Again, he's a potential front of the rotation caliber arm. Here's hoping for a full recovery.

Scouting Report: Prior to hitting the disabled list with the arm / elbow issues, Puk was featuring a four-pitch repertoire: fastball, curveball, slider, and changeup. As last season progressed – and he was eventually pushed into an innings-governing bullpen role – Puk eliminated the curveball, and to a lesser degree the changeup. He primarily relied upon his plus-plus combination of an upper 90s heater and a hellacious, knee-buckling slider. The changeup, which was rarely thrown, flashed above-averaged, though hard. Puk's in the running – along with teammate Jesus Luzardo – for most dominating left-hander in the minor leagues. He's a potential bonafide ace – if, *if*, he can maintain a sub-4.0 walk rate.

Ceiling: 5.0-win player
Risk: Moderate
MLB ETA: Debuted in 2019

3. Nick Allen, SS

Hit	Power	SB	Patience	Glove	Overall
40/50	35/40	50	50	80	50

Born: 10/08/98	Age: 21	Bats: R
Height: 5-9	Weight: 166	Throws: R

YEAR	LVL	PA	1B	2B	3B	HR	SB	CS	AVG	OBP	SLG	BB%	K%	GB%	LD%	FB%
2017	RK	154	29	3	2	1	7	3	0.254	0.322	0.326	8.44%	18.18%	49.1	17.9	25.9
2018	A	512	87	17	6	0	24	8	0.239	0.301	0.302	6.64%	16.60%	50.5	15.1	24.7
2019	A+	328	54	22	5	3	13	5	0.292	0.363	0.434	8.54%	15.85%	46.3	17.6	29.1

Background: One of my favorite – if not my favorite – prospect in the entire minor leagues. Allen remains (A) incredibly underrated, despite a breakout season in High Class A as a 20-year-old and (B) one of the most talented defensive players – at any position, at any level of baseball. A third round pick out of Parker High School three years ago, Allen looked abysmal at the plate during his professional debut in the Arizona Summer League as he batted a lowly .254/.322/.326. In a bit of a surprising move Oakland's front office brass bumped the defensive wizard up to the Midwest League. And he struggled with the bat, mightily. In 121 games with Beloit, the 5-foot-9, 166-pound shortstop hit .239/.301/.302 with just 23 extra-base hits and 24 stolen bases. Last season the front office continued to aggressively shove the California native through the system. And Allen finally rewarded their faith. In 72 games with the Stockton Ports, the then-20-year-old slugged .292/.363/.434 with career bests in doubles (22) and homeruns (3) as well as legging out five triples and 13 stolen bases. His overall production, as measured by Baseball Prospectus' *Deserved Runs Created Plus*, topped the league average by 35%.

Snippet from The 2018 Prospect Digest Handbook: Defense. Defense. Defense. Allen can pick it as well as any shortstop in the minor leagues – which is a good thing because he hits like your kid sister. The former prep star is all projection at this point. He's not likely to develop any type of meaningful power; the patience is average – at best; and the hit tool is nearly on par with the power.

Scouting Report: Consider the following:

- Since 2006, here's the list of 20-year-old hitters to post a DRC+ between 130 and 140 with a walk rate between 8% and 10% in the California League (min. 300 PA): Colton Welker, Josh Naylor, Edinson Rincon, and – of course – Nick Allen. For those counting at home that's three corner infielders, two of which were/are solid middle-tier prospects (Welker and Naylor), and a defensive-minded shortstop.

Elite levels of value on the defensive side of the ball, Allen's transformed not only into a competent hitter, but a potential table-setter. Strong bat-to-ball skills with an average eye at the plate and plus speed, Allen's added enough gap-to-gap power to be a viable future big league hitter. The defense will carry him to The Show, anything else is just a cherry on top. Allen looks like a .270/.330/.390-type hitter during his peak. He's going to win multiple Gold Gloves too.

Ceiling: 3.0-win player
Risk: Low to Moderate
MLB ETA: 2021

4. Sean Murphy, C

Hit	Power	SB	Patience	Glove	Overall
45	55	30	50	55	50

Born: 10/04/94	Age: 25	Bats: R	Top CALs:
Height: 6-3	Weight: 232	Throws: R	

YEAR	LVL	PA	1B	2B	3B	HR	SB	CS	AVG	OBP	SLG	BB%	K%	GB%	LD%	FB%
2017	A+	178	29	11	0	9	0	0	0.297	0.343	0.527	6.18%	18.54%	48.1	10.5	36.1
2017	AA	217	29	7	0	4	0	0	0.209	0.288	0.309	9.68%	15.67%	52.8	18.0	23.0
2018	AA	289	38	26	2	8	3	0	0.288	0.358	0.498	7.96%	16.26%	49.3	23.0	18.8
2019	AAA	140	20	6	1	10	0	1	0.308	0.386	0.625	10.71%	22.14%	44.6	19.6	31.5

Background: Drafted by the A's in the third round out of Wright State University in 2016, Murphy had flashed some offensive potential in various spurts throughout the early parts of his minor league career. But things finally came together – if ever so briefly – during his breakout 2018 campaign with Midland

RockHounds in the Texas League. Limited to just 68 games at the Class AA level, the 6-foot-3, 232-pound brick wall of backstop slugged a hearty .288/.358/.498 with 26 doubles, two triples, and eight homeruns. Last season, despite a couple stints on the disabled list, Murphy continued to flash above-average offensive production at a premium position. In 31 games in the PCL he slugged .308/.386/.625 with six doubles, one triple, and 10 homeruns. And he held his own in 20 games with Oakland as well, batting .245/.333/.566 with nine extra-base hits.

Snippet from The 2018 Prospect Digest Handbook: Murphy shows a solid offensive foundation built around a high contact approach. Never one to flash a lot of power – even during his collegiate days with the Raiders – Murphy's pop has been trending upward over the past couple of seasons – so much so, in fact, that a 15- to 18-homerun season isn't out of the question

Scouting Report: Despite never stringing together more than 98 games in a professional season, Murphy's power morphed from below-average to a consistent long ball threat last season. And he's done so while maintaining that aforementioned high contact approach at the dish. The hit tool remains below average, but it won't cripple a team's lineup (even if he wasn't flashing the type of power he owns). After opining that his peak season would be.249/.339/.390 last year, I'd bump it something closer to Boston's Christian Vazquez's showing in 2019 (.276/.320/.477). Like a few of the Athletics' other top prospects, he just needs to stay on the field long enough.

Ceiling: 3.0-win player
Risk: Low to Moderate
MLB ETA: Debuted in 2019

5. Daulton Jefferies, RHP

FB	SL	CU	CH	Command	Overall
55+	50	60	55	60	50

Born: 08/02/95	Age: 24	Bats: L
Height: 6-0	Weight: 182	Throws: R

YEAR	LVL	IP	W	L	SV	ERA	FIP	WHIP	K/9	K%	BB/9	BB%	K/BB	HR9	BABIP
2017	A+	7.0	0	0	0	2.57	2.64	1.14	7.7	19.35%	1.3	3.23%	6.00	0.00	0.292
2018	Rk	2.0	0	0	0	0.00	0.93	0.50	22.5	71.43%	0.0	0.00%	N/A	0.00	0.500
2019	A+	15.0	1	0	0	2.40	2.13	0.80	12.6	36.84%	1.2	3.51%	10.50	0.60	0.273
2019	AA	64.0	1	2	0	3.66	3.18	1.09	10.1	27.48%	1.0	2.67%	10.29	0.98	0.327

Background: Persistence is one hell of an attribute, isn't it? Take, for example, Daulton Jefferies. Absurdly dominant over his final two seasons at the University of California, Berkley, Oakland snagged the wiry right-hander in the opening round, 37th overall, in the 2016 draft – despite a shoulder issue that limited him to just 50.0 innings during his junior campaign. Two brief starts into the following season Jefferies hit the disabled list for a different type of serious arm issue: elbow woes that required Tommy John surgery. Injuries and setbacks limited him to just one single, two-inning appearance in the Arizona Rookie League in 2018. And, well, most of the baseball world had completely passed the former first rounder by. Until 2019 happened. Quickly making up for lost time, Jefferies was Bob Gibson-esque during five appearances in High Class A to open the year and he continued to dominate upon a promotion up to the Texas League. The former Golden Bear sported a 93-to-9 K/BB ratio in only 79.0 innings.

Snippet from The 2018 Prospect Digest Handbook: Reports had Jefferies velocity back into the mid-90s over the summer during his rehab work, but he hit the DL right after. Like Kaprielian, you just have to hope that these guys can shake this injury bug and move forward.

Scouting Report: Consider the following:

- Since 2006, here's the list of 23-year-old pitchers to post a strikeout percentage of at least 26.5% with a sub-4.0% in the Texas League (min. 50 IP): Daulton Jefferies. That's it. No one else.

Let's take it one step further:

- Since 2006, only two 23-year-old pitchers met the aforementioned criteria: Daulton Jefferies and Matt Stites, who accomplished the feat as a full time reliever.

Jefferies commands the strike zone with sniper-like precision, something that's hardly believable given his lengthy stints on the disabled list. He attacks hitters with a lively low-90s fastball that will kiss – on occasion – the mid-90s. He'll throw two distinct breaking pitches: a traditional slider that's (A) average and (B) tends to get a little slurvy at times, and the a far superior upper-80s cutter that he spots incredibly well on the first base-side of the bag. Jefferies will also mix in an above-average change up. He's very reminiscent of a Tim Hudson-like competitor. There's #3-type upside, but – again – can he stay on the mound?

Ceiling: 2.5- to 3.0-win player
Risk: Moderate
MLB ETA: 2020

6. Robert Puason, SS

Hit	Power	SB	Patience	Glove	Overall
30/55	30/55	40	50	50	50

Born: 09/11/02	Age: 17	Bats: S
Height: 6-3	Weight: 165	Throws: R

Background: The A's made their infatuation with the young Dominican shortstop abundantly clear – for *everyone* to see. The front office spent slightly more than 86% of their entire international bonus pool on the dynamic, young, switch-hitting shortstop. The final specs on the deal: the then-16-year-old was inked to a deal worth $5.1 million.

Scouting Report: Regarded as one of the top two prospects on the international scene last season; Puason, a 6-foot-3, 165-pound shortstop, physically looks like a ballplayer entering his early 20s. He's lean, yet muscular. Explosive and twitch with fluidity and flair, especially on the defensive side of the ball. Fast hands, but the swing's long and needs to be shortened – especially from the left side. From what I saw, Puason looked a bit overmatched in the Instructional League, but there's gobs of potential as a true five-tool threat in the coming years. One more final thought: he may outgrow shortstop and slide into a comfortable spot as a third baseman.

Ceiling: 3.0-win player
Risk: Moderate to High
MLB ETA: 2023

7. Austin Allen, C

Hit	Power	SB	Patience	Glove	Overall
45	55	20	50	55	50

Born: 01/16/94	Age: 26	Bats: L
Height: 6-2	Weight: 220	Throws: R

YEAR	LVL	PA	1B	2B	3B	HR	SB	CS	AVG	OBP	SLG	BB%	K%	GB%	LD%	FB%
2017	A+	516	77	31	1	22	0	1	0.283	0.353	0.497	8.53%	21.12%	37.9	23.6	31.7
2018	AA	498	78	31	0	22	0	3	0.290	0.351	0.506	7.43%	19.48%	39.5	25.8	29.4
2019	AAA	298	41	27	0	21	0	0	0.330	0.379	0.663	7.38%	18.79%	31.0	26.4	33.8

Background: Locked behind a ridiculous amount of catching depth – Francisco Mejia, Austin Hedges, Luis Torrens, and top prospect Luis Campusano – San Diego flipped the lefty-swinging backstop to the A's in early December as part of the return to the Jurickson Profar. Allen, who was acquired along with outfielder Buddy Reed, split time between San Diego's Class AAA affiliate – the El Paso Chihuahuas – and the big leagues. In 67 games in the Pacific Coast League, Allen slugged a hearty .330/.379/.663 with 27 doubles and 21 homeruns. Per the *Deserved Runs Created Plus*, his overall production topped the league average threshold line by 28%. He also bated .215/.282/.277 with a quarter of doubles in 34 games with the Padres.

Snippet from The 2018 Prospect Digest Handbook: At first Allen was locked behind Austin Hedges. Now it's Austin Hedges *and* Francisco Mejia. The lefty-swinging backstop shows some minor platoon splits, though not enough to hinder playing time. Allen could be used as a trade chip at some time in the next six or so months. There's' some lower-tier, starting caliber potential here.

Scouting Report: The quintessential Oakland A's hitter. Within a year's time, Allen's going to be recognized as one of the better acquisitions in the offseason. The hit tool is below-average, but he compensates with 25-homer thump and solid contact skills wrapped up in a premium position. In terms of upside think Travis d'Arnaud's showing in 2019 when he slugged .251/.312/.433 with 16 homeruns in roughly 400 plate appearances. Really, really like this pick up by Oakland.

Ceiling: 2.0- to 2.5-win player
Risk: Moderate
MLB ETA: Debuted in 2019

8. Logan Davidson, SS

Hit	Power	SB	Patience	Glove	Overall
45	50	40	55	50/55	50

Born: 12/26/97	Age: 22	Bats: B
Height: 6-3	Weight: 185	Throws: R

YEAR	LVL	PA	1B	2B	3B	HR	SB	CS	AVG	OBP	SLG	BB%	K%	GB%	LD%	FB%
2019	A-	238	38	7	0	4	5	0	0.239	0.345	0.332	13.03%	23.11%	40.4	28.1	26.7

Background: Davidson's old man, Mark, starred for Clemson's baseball team during the 1982 season, batting .336 with 16 doubles, a pair of triples, and eight homeruns with 18 stolen bases. The elder Davidson was selected in the 11th round of the draft by the Twins that season and (A) spent parts of six seasons in the big leagues playing for the Twins and Astros and (B) won a World

Series ring with Minnesota in 1987. Logan, who's sister starred as a tennis player at Stanford, has been a consistent – sometimes dominant – performer at the plate for the Tigers during his collegiate career. As a freshman, the 6-foot-3, 185-pound switch-hitting middle infielder batted a hearty .286/.388/.473 with nine doubles and 12 homeruns. But his production faltered mightily during his first trip through the Cape Cod League that summer. In 37 games with the Falmouth Commodores, the Charlotte, North Carolina, native batted a puny .210/.317/.266 while fanning in more than a quarter of his plate appearances. Davidson the Junior raised the bar during his sophomore campaign for Head Coach Monte Lee, batting .292/.408/.544 with 18 doubles and 15 homeruns to go along with 10 stolen bases in 63 games. Once again, however, his numbers cratered once he squared up against the elite Cape Cod League pitching; he hit .194/.292/.266 with another problematic strikeout rate (26.4%). Last season Davidson picked back up where he left off the previous year in the ACC: he slugged .291/.412/.574 with a career best-tying 18 doubles, two doubles, and 15 homeruns. Oakland snagged him in the opening round, 29th, and sent him to the New York-Penn League for his debut; he hit a lowly .239/.345/.332 with seven doubles and four homeruns.

Scouting Report: Here's what I wrote prior to the draft last season:

"Consider the following:

- *Between 2011 and 2018, only nine ACC hitters posted a walk rate between 13% and 16% with a punch out rate between 18% and 21% in a season (min. 250 PA): Richie Shaffer, Richie Martin, Joey Bart, Mike McGee, Shane Kennedy, Joe Cronin, Jackson Leuck, Logan Harvey, Johnny Ruiz, Evan Stephens, and – of course – Logan Davison, who's accomplished the feat twice.*

Taking it one step further:

- *Only three players in the aforementioned group owned at least a .260 Isolated Power: Shaffer, Bart, and Davidson. Shaffer, a former Clemson stud, was the 25th overall pick by the Rays in 2012. And the Giants selected Bart with the second overall pick in 2018.*

A red flag of sorts for Davidson, however, is that his production has largely plateaued during his collegiate career – sans some moderate upgrades in the power department. But it's his performances in the Cape Cod League – both times – that scream caution. His smooth footwork and arm should allow him to stay at short, but there's some concern as to whether he'll make enough contact in the minor leagues.

Ceiling: 2.0-win player
Risk: Moderate
MLB ETA: 2022

9. Grant Holmes, RHP

	FB	CB	CU	CH	Command	Overall
	55	60	50/55	50	45	45

Born: 03/22/96	Age: 24	Bats: L
Height: 6-0	Weight: 224	Throws: R

YEAR	LVL	IP	W	L	SV	ERA	FIP	WHIP	K/9	K%	BB/9	BB%	K/BB	HR9	BABIP
2017	AA	148.3	11	12	0	4.49	4.02	1.42	9.1	23.29%	3.7	9.47%	2.46	0.91	0.328
2018	A+	6.0	0	0	0	4.50	5.25	1.00	12.0	29.63%	3.0	7.41%	4.00	1.50	0.214
2019	AA	81.7	6	5	0	3.31	4.19	1.20	8.4	22.49%	3.0	7.99%	2.81	0.99	0.281
2019	AAA	4.7	0	0	0	1.93	5.08	1.50	9.6	27.78%	1.9	5.56%	5.00	1.93	0.455

Background: With the type of long, luxurious, flowing curly locks that would make Judy Garland jealous, Holmes – finally – returned to the mound after missing the majority of 2018. A shoulder injury forced him out of action until two late season starts with Stockton. Healthy and showing no ill side effects, Holmes made 22 appearances, 16 of which were starts, with the Midland RockHounds of the Texas League. He tossed 81.2 innings while posting a solid 76-to-27 strikeout-to-walk ratio. A first round pick in 2014, Holmes made his Class AAA debut in his final start as well, throwing 4.2 innings against the Tacoma Rainers, fanning five and walking one while surrendering one earned run. The hefty right-hander averaged 8.4 strikeouts and just 2.9 walks per nine innings last season.

Snippet from The 2018 Prospect Digest Handbook: Again, shoulder issues are exponentially more serious that elbow woes. Hopefully Holmes won't have to reinvent himself as a pitcher. Here's hoping for a recovery to full health.

Scouting Report: Holmes didn't need to reinvent himself as a pitcher...but...I have some concerns about his long term future as a starting pitcher. The 6-foot, 224-pound righty looked incredible robotic and stiff last season, lacking a lot of fluidity throughout his hips. And he seems to be relying solely on arm strength alone. The former 22nd overall selection owns a solid starter's repertoire: an above-average fastball that sits consistently in the 93- to 94-mph range; a hard, upper 80s cutter that's become a reliable go-to pitch; a plus, hard curveball in the low 80s; and a power 88-mph changeup that (A) doesn't offer a whole lot of velocity separation and (B) lacks the type of movement that makes Zack Greinke's power changeup a viable big league pitch. With respect to his work in Class AA last season, consider the following:

- Since 2006, only four 23-year-old pitchers met the aforementioned criteria in the Texas League (min. 75 IP): a strikeout percentage between 21.5% and 23.5% and a walk percentage between 7.0% and 9.0%. Those four pitchers: Jerad Eickhoff, Yunior Marte, Ariel Pena, and Grant Holmes

Holmes has been a long, long time personal favorite. But I ultimately think he slides into a high leverage, multiple-inning type of relief arm.

Ceiling: 1.5- to 2.0-win player
Risk: Moderate
MLB ETA: 2020

10. Jordan Diaz, 3B

Hit	Power	SB	Patience	Glove	Overall
40/50	45/55	30	45	50	45

Born: 08/13/00	**Age:** 19	**Bats:** R
Height: 5-10	**Weight:** 175	**Throws:** R

YEAR	LVL	PA	1B	2B	3B	HR	SB	CS	AVG	OBP	SLG	BB%	K%	GB%	LD%	FB%
2017	RK	149	28	7	0	0	2	0	0.255	0.295	0.307	4.03%	14.77%	50.0	22.0	20.3
2017	RK	28	5	0	0	0	1	0	0.185	0.179	0.185	0.00%	14.29%	58.3	8.3	25.0
2018	RK	186	30	11	2	1	0	2	0.277	0.371	0.390	10.22%	11.83%	49.6	16.5	25.9
2019	A-	300	46	17	1	9	2	2	0.264	0.307	0.430	6.00%	15.33%	47.2	21.2	25.5

Background: Signed out of Monteria, Colombia on August 13, 2016, Diaz spent the following year splitting time between the foreign and stateside rookie leagues, hitting a combined .244/.277/.287 with only seven doubles. The front office kept the 5-foot-10, 175-pound third baseman back in the Arizona Summer League for a longer look in 2017. And the results were greatly improved: in 48 games with the AZL Athletics, Diaz slugged .275/.366/.388 with 11 doubles, two triples, and one homerun. Last season the front office bumped the then-18-year-old up to the New York-Penn League. And he continued to take important offensive strides. Playing in a career best 70 games with the Vermont Lake Monsters, the young Colombian batted .264/.307/.430 with 17 doubles, one triple, and nine dingers. His overall production, as measured by Baseball Prospectus' *Deserved Runs Created Plus*, topped the league average threshold by a whopping 44%.

Scouting Report: Consider the following:

- Since 2006, only one other 18-year-old player – former Phillies top prospect and current Royals free agent signing Maikel Franco – posted a DRC+ between 140 and 150 in the New York-Penn League (min. 200 PA). Franco, while never a personal favorite, was typically recognized as a Top 100 prospect multiple times during his minor league career. And while he's never lived up to those lofty expectations, he's quietly been a league average bat and low end starter throughout his career.

As for Diaz: his power is quickly become a legitimate 55-grade threat in the coming years. He consistently makes contact, though his walk rates are slightly below-average. Like Franco, the young third baseman looks like a potential low end starting caliber third baseman, maybe a little more if the hit tool progresses better than expected. One word of warning: his production worsened as the year advanced.

Ceiling: 1.5- to 2.0-win player
Risk: Moderate
MLB ETA: 2023

11. Brayan Buelvas, CF

Hit	Power	SB	Patience	Glove	Overall
45/55	35/45	50	50	45/55	50

Born: 06/08/02	**Age:** 18	**Bats:** R
Height: 5-11	**Weight:** 155	**Throws:** R

YEAR	LVL	PA	1B	2B	3B	HR	SB	CS	AVG	OBP	SLG	BB%	K%	GB%	LD%	FB%
2019	Rk	186	28	10	7	3	12	5	0.300	0.392	0.506	11.83%	24.73%	44.3	18.3	30.4

Background: Signed out of Monteria, Colombia, in early July two years ago. Buelvas made his professional debut last season. The 5-foot-11, 155-pound center fielder opened the 2019 campaign in the Dominican Summer League. But after a 23-game tour through the foreign rookie league, Oakland bounced Buelvas stateside and his offense took off. In 44 games with the organization's Green Team in the Arizona Summer League, he slugged an impressive .300/.392/.506 with 10 doubles, seven triples, and three homeruns. He also swiped 12 bags in 17 total attempts. His overall production, according to Baseball Prospectus' *Deserved Runs Created Plus*, his overall production in the AZL topped the league average mark by 30%.

Scouting Report: Consider the following:

- Since 2006, there were three 17-year-old hitters to meet the following criteria in the Arizona Summer League (min. 150 PA): a DRC+ between 125 and 135 and a strikeout rate between 20% and 25%. Those three hitters: Kristian Robinson, a top prospect in the Diamondbacks' farm system, Diego Cartaya, a personal favorite and to prospect in the Dodgers' organization, and – of course – Brayan Buelvas.

Buelvas' thump really started pounding loudly after his jump to the stateside rookie league. The swing-and-miss numbers – he fanned in nearly a quarter of his plate appearances – are a concern; though he whiffed only 18 times over his final 73 plate appearances. Above-average speed, a chance at 50-grade power, and a solid hit tool.

Ceiling: 2.0-win player
Risk: Moderate to High
MLB ETA: 2023

12. James Kaprielian, RHP

FB	CB	SL	CH	Command	Overall
50+	55	50/55	50	55	45

Born: 03/02/94	Age: 26	Bats: R
Height: 6-3	Weight: 210	Throws: R

YEAR	LVL	IP	W	L	SV	ERA	FIP	WHIP	K/9	K%	BB/9	BB%	K/BB	HR9	BABIP
2019	A+	36.3	2	2	0	4.46	4.43	1.18	10.7	28.29%	2.0	5.26%	5.38	1.49	0.319
2019	AA	27.7	2	1	0	1.63	3.59	0.94	8.5	24.30%	2.6	7.48%	3.25	0.65	0.232
2019	AAA	4.0	0	0	0	2.25	0.79	1.50	13.5	33.33%	0.0	0.00%	N/A	0.00	0.500

Background: It seems like eons ago that Kaprielian, a wiry 6-foot-3, 210-pound right-hander, was lighting up the radar guns at UCLA and generating the type of winds that comes along with leading the PAC-12 in whiffs. The California native ripped through the opposition as a shutdown reliever during his freshman season, blossomed into a bonafide top-of-the-rotation caliber arm the following year, and convinced the Yankees to draft him with the 16th overall pick following his junior campaign in 2015. And then all hell broke loose. Kaprielian's elbow flared up and eventually required Tommy John surgery, and forced him out for the better parts of three full seasons. In the mean time, New York shipped the former Bruin – along with Jorge Mateo and Dustin Fowler – to Oakland for former Vanderbilt ace Sonny Gray. Kaprielian, in no small miracle, made it back to the mound and made dominant stints at three separate levels. Bouncing from High Class A to the Texas League and then on to the PCL, he posted a 75-to-16 strikeout-to-walk ratio with a 3.18 ERA in 68.0 innings.

Snippet from The 2018 Prospect Digest Handbook: Here's hoping 2019 proves to be healthy and fruitful.

Scouting Report: The 2019 season was not only kind to the former collegiate ace, but it was also (A) healthy and (B) fruitful. The repertoire, especially the fastball, isn't quite was it once was. Instead of sitting in the mid-90s and touching close to triple digits, Kaprielian's heated was sitting in the 92- to 93-mph range and kissing 94-mph on occasion. His curveball and slider flash above-average, though the latter is a bit inconsistent (but who wouldn't be after missing three years?). And the changeup is a solid 50-grade. The entire arsenal plays up – considerably – thanks to his pinpoint accuracy. Kaprielian looks like a solid #4/#5-type arm, though he might end up carving out a role as a solid relief specialist a la Ryan Madson.

Ceiling: 1.5- to 2.0-win player
Risk: Moderate to High
MLB ETA: 2020

13. Tyler Baum, RHP

FB	CB	SL	CH	Command	Overall
55	60	50	55	50	45

Born: 01/14/98	Age: 22	Bats: R
Height: 6-2	Weight: 195	Throws: R

YEAR	LVL	IP	W	L	SV	ERA	FIP	WHIP	K/9	K%	BB/9	BB%	K/BB	HR9	BABIP
2019	A-	30.7	0	3	0	4.70	3.75	1.17	10.0	29.57%	2.1	6.09%	4.86	1.17	0.306

Background: A member of the University of North Carolina's rotation for the entirety of his collegiate career. Baum, a 6-foot-2, 195-pound right-hander, progressed from a thrower with middling peripherals as a freshman to an erratic starting pitcher with a big strikeout rate as a sophomore to – finally – putting it all together during his final campaign. Last season the Florida native made a career high 16 starts, as well as one relief appearance, for the Tar Heels, posting a 99-to-25 strikeout-to-walk ratio in 93.0 innings of work. Oakland snagged Baum in the second round, 66th overall, last June. Baum made 11 brief starts with the Vermont Lake Monsters in the New York-Penn League during his debut, fanning 34 and walking seven to go along with a 4.70 ERA and a slightly better 4.42 DRA.

Scouting Report: Prior to the draft Baum's stock was quickly rising on the back of a fastball that reportedly touched the upper 90s on occasion. It's an above-average offering that likely won't come close to reaching that peak on the shortened rest schedules of professional baseball. His curveball's the real deal, a sharp, late, hard-breaking offering that should be a genuine swing-and-miss weapon as he motors his way through the minor leagues. The slider is average. His changeup is underrated and flashes some solid run-and-fade. The former Tar Heel continued his assault on the strike zone after turning pro, a positive sign for his future as a starter. #4/#5-type upside with the floor of a middle reliever.

Ceiling: 1.5-win player
Risk: Moderate
MLB ETA: 2022

14. Sheldon Neuse, 2B/SS

Hit	Power	SB	Patience	Glove	Overall
45	50	40	55	50/55	40

Born: 12/10/94	Age: 25	Bats: R
Height: 6-0	Weight: 218	Throws: R

YEAR	LVL	PA	1B	2B	3B	HR	SB	CS	AVG	OBP	SLG	BB%	K%	GB%	LD%	FB%
2017	A	321	54	19	3	9	12	5	0.291	0.349	0.469	7.79%	20.56%	53.1	15.4	28.9
2017	A+	94	22	3	0	7	2	0	0.386	0.457	0.675	9.57%	26.60%	46.6	20.7	31.0
2017	AA	75	21	4	0	0	0	0	0.373	0.427	0.433	8.00%	28.00%	46.8	40.4	10.6
2018	AAA	537	97	26	3	5	4	1	0.263	0.304	0.357	5.96%	32.03%	39.3	27.0	27.6
2019	AAA	560	98	31	2	27	3	3	0.317	0.389	0.550	10.00%	23.57%	44.5	23.9	28.0

Background: Prior to the season, I co-authored a piece on *The Athletic* with Michael Salfino titled, *"2019 Fantasy Baseball Preview: Top Under-the-Radar Dynasty League Prospects"*. Here's what was written: "His swing-and-miss rate is unconscionably high (172 Ks last year), but the A's are trying to unlock his power by turning him into a fly-ball hitter. That's working. He's entering his age-24 season but slashed .295/.331/.404 over his final 92 games." How'd the former Oklahoma Sooner respond? By feasting on the Pacific Coast League pitching to the tune of .317/.389/.550 with career bests in doubles (31), and homeruns (27). He also added a pair of triples and three stolen bases. His overall production, according to *Deserved Runs Created Plus*, topped the league average mark by 17%.

Snippet from The 2018 Prospect Digest Handbook: During Neuse's rocket through three levels two years ago his swing-and-miss tendencies became increasingly troublesome, going from 20.6% to 26.6% to 28.0%. And that trend continued as it spiked to 32.0% last season. Some of that surge – as well as his dip in production – might be explained by his approach at the plate: Oakland seems to be tweaking his swing-path to allow for fewer ground balls and more fly balls in an effort to tap into the power potential he showed during his junior season with Oklahoma. Neuse, by the way, finished with the lowest groundball rate – by a wide margin – last season (38.2%). Despite entering his age-24 season Neuse isn't a finished product but he's a lot closer than one would believe: he batted .187/.244/.247 over his first 43 games, but slugged a healthy .295/.331/.404 over his remaining 92 games. Neuse is poised for a big 2019 campaign.

Scouting Report: Consider the following:

- Since 2006, here's the list of 24-year-old hitters to post a DRC+ between 112 and 122 with a double-digit walk rate and a punch out rate north of 20% in the Pacific Coast League (min. 300 PA): Chris Carter, Rymer Liriano, Drew Robinson, Jerry Sands, Chad Huffman, and Sheldon Neuse. And here are their respective career DRC+ marks in the big leagues: 112 (Carter), 60 (Liriano), 62 (Robinson), 80 (Sands), and 73 (Huffman).

Obviously, it's not a strong argument for Neuse's future big league success. However, he's consistently added value on the defensive side of the ball and has positional flexibility as well. Neuse's ceiling is likely to hover around .260/.315/.390 with 55-grade defense. He's not a star, far from it actually, but he'll be a useful bench option for the A's.

Ceiling: 1.0- to 1.5-win player
Risk: Low to Moderate
MLB ETA: Debuted in 2019

Oakland Athletics

15. Austin Beck, CF

Hit	Power	SB	Patience	Glove	Overall
40/45	40/45	40	45	55	40

Born: 11/21/98	Age: 21	Bats: R
Height: 6-1	Weight: 200	Throws: R

YEAR	LVL	PA	1B	2B	3B	HR	SB	CS	AVG	OBP	SLG	BB%	K%	GB%	LD%	FB%
2017	RK	174	19	7	4	2	7	1	0.211	0.293	0.349	9.77%	29.31%	46.2	19.2	26.0
2018	A	534	111	29	4	2	8	6	0.296	0.335	0.383	5.62%	21.91%	44.0	21.9	24.2
2019	A+	367	51	22	4	8	2	2	0.251	0.302	0.411	6.54%	34.33%	43.6	15.2	34.1

Background: It's not so much that Beck's failed to live up to his lofty status as the fifth overall pick in the 2017 draft. It's the fact that two of the next three players taken have already established themselves as viable big leaguers (Adam Haseley and Keston Hiura), another one will likely be a solid low end starter (Pavin Smith), and Jo Adell, who was taken four picks later, is a burgeoning star. As for Beck, the North Davidson High School product, has continued to slowly – emphasis on the *slowly* – move up the development ladder. The 6-foot-1, 200-pound center fielder hit a disappointing .211/.293/.349 during his debut in the Arizona Summer League. He followed that up with a batting average-driven production line of .296/.335/.383 as a 19-year-old in the Midwest League. And last season he squared off against the California League, hitting a mediocre .251/.302/.411 with 22 doubles, four triples, and a career best eight homeruns. His overall production, according to *Deserved Runs Created Plus*, was 8% *below* the league average mark.

Snippet from The 2018 Prospect Digest Handbook: In short: the production improved, as did the strikeout rate (dropped from 29.3% to 21.9%), but his power evaporated like a thimble of water in the Sahara Desert. Beck's balls in play remained the same and his power output improved in the second half of the year so – again – there's more hope for the future. Beck uses the field well, spraying balls from foul line to foul line. He's still a bit raw in center field but should be no worse than an average defender at maturity. Beck doesn't look like a future star, but there's enough to a capable starter.

Scouting Report: The former highly touted prep star got off to a solid enough start to the year, batting .262/.308/.448 over his first 53 games. However, a lengthy stint on the disabled list, cooled his bat considerably. He hit a lowly .234/.293/.352 over his final 32 contests. Now the bad news: the bat's below average and has a hole the size of a basketball in it; he punched out in more than a third of his plate appearances last season. Oakland's had some success converting high swing-and-miss hitters to more productive bats as they've progressed (see: Sheldon Neuse), so there's some added hope. He just looks like a poor man's Clint Frazier.

Ceiling: 1.0- to 1.5-win player
Risk: Moderate
MLB ETA: 2022

16. Hogan Harris, LHP

FB	CB	SL	CH	Command	Overall
55	55	50	55	45	40

Born: 12/26/96	Age: 23	Bats: R
Height: 6-3	Weight: 230	Throws: L

YEAR	LVL	IP	W	L	SV	ERA	FIP	WHIP	K/9	K%	BB/9	BB%	K/BB	HR9	BABIP
2019	A-	26.0	1	3	0	3.12	3.01	0.88	12.5	34.62%	3.1	8.65%	4.00	0.69	0.222
2019	A+	28.7	0	2	0	2.51	3.70	0.98	9.1	26.61%	3.1	9.17%	2.90	0.63	0.239

Background: A walking stereotype for a mid-1970s starting pitcher. You know the ones that gave credence to pitchers not being athletes? Harris sports a Fu Manchu facial hair, a doughy, soft midriff, and the windup that looks effortless. Appearance notwithstanding, the 6-foot-3, 230-pound southpaw turned in a solid career at the University of Louisiana at Lafayette which included a summer stint with the Yarmouth-Dennis Red Sox in the Cape Cod League. Oakland drafted the hefty lefty in the third round two years ago, but a non-arm issue delayed his debut until 2019. Splitting time between Vermont and Stockton, Harris struck out 65 and walked 19 in a combined 54.2 innings of work. He complied an aggregate 2.80 ERA in those 15 appearances.

Scouting Report: There were several reports stating that Harris touched the upper-90s at a point during his junior college season, his fastball generally settled in many ticks below that. Harris is difficult to get a good read on. He adds and subtracts velocity from his fastball, taking with it a grade of fringy average to above-average. The curveball flashes plus at times, though it lacks consistency. He'll also mix in a bland slider and an underrated changeup. He could become a JA Happ-type starting pitcher, but that's an absolute best case scenario. In all likelihood he settles In as an up-and-down, #5-type arm.

Ceiling: 1.0- to 1.5-win player
Risk: Moderate
MLB ETA: 2021/2022

17. Brian Howard, RHP

	FB	CB	CU	CH	Command	Overall
	50	50	55	50	50	40

Born: 04/25/95	Age: 25	Bats: R
Height: 6-9	Weight: 185	Throws: R

YEAR	LVL	IP	W	L	SV	ERA	FIP	WHIP	K/9	K%	BB/9	BB%	K/BB	HR9	BABIP
2017	A-	31.3	2	1	1	1.15	1.67	0.73	8.3	25.89%	0.3	0.89%	29.00	0.00	0.268
2018	A+	72.0	7	3	0	2.38	3.90	0.93	9.6	27.30%	1.8	4.96%	5.50	1.13	0.244
2018	AA	67.3	4	4	0	3.48	3.99	1.31	8.4	21.80%	3.1	7.96%	2.74	0.94	0.297
2019	AA	130.0	8	8	0	3.25	3.32	1.35	8.2	21.73%	2.7	7.18%	3.03	0.48	0.348
2019	AAA	14.3	0	1	0	13.81	7.28	2.51	10.0	19.75%	5.0	9.88%	2.00	2.51	0.471

Background: A nice little find – although, to be fair, it's difficult to *not* see him – in the eighth round out of Texas Christian University three years ago. Howard stands a gargantuan 6-foot-9 but only weighs a wispy 185 pounds. The former Horned Frog made a career best 27 starts last season – 23 with Midland and the remaining four with Las Vegas.

He tossed 144.1 innings with a solid 134-to 47 strikeout-to-walk ratio. He compiled an aggregate 4.30 ERA. For his minor league career, the big righty is averaging 8.7 strikeouts and just 2.4 walks per nine innings.

Scouting Report: An enigma of sorts, for several reasons, really. Howard's tall and long limbed. But his fastball barely breaks a window. And unlike the typical massive hurler, he consistently throws strikes – often quality strikes – with all four pitches. Based on velocity alone his fastball is below-average, but it plays up given his 6-foot-9 frame. His cutter is his best overall offering. And he'll mix in a slider and changeup with the latter flashing a 55 at times. Oakland's the type of franchise that will overlook a mediocre repertoire and give Howard several looks at a spot in the rotation. With respect to his production in Class AA last season, consider the following:

- Since 2006, here's the list of 24-year-old pitchers that posted a strikeout percentage between 21% and 23% and a walk percentage between 6% and 8% in any Class AA league (min. 100 IP): Mike Clevinger, Brian Keller, Kevin Hart, Jay Voss, Chris Heston, Michael Rucker, Tom Koehler, and – of course – Brian Howard.

Ceiling: 1.0- to 1.5-win player
Risk: Moderate
MLB ETA: 2020

18. Greg Deichmann, LF/RF

	Hit	Power	SB	Patience	Glove	Overall
	40	55	30	55	45	40

Born: 05/31/95	Age: 25	Bats: L
Height: 6-2	Weight: 190	Throws: R

YEAR	LVL	PA	1B	2B	3B	HR	SB	CS	AVG	OBP	SLG	BB%	K%	GB%	LD%	FB%
2017	A-	195	23	10	4	8	4	1	0.274	0.385	0.530	14.36%	20.51%	35.2	24.8	26.4
2018	A+	185	13	14	0	6	0	1	0.199	0.276	0.392	9.19%	34.05%	38.5	15.4	33.7
2019	AA	340	43	10	2	11	19	5	0.219	0.300	0.375	10.00%	30.29%	34.8	28.4	29.9

Background: A second round pick out of Louisiana State University three years ago; Deichmann left the SEC school after strong back-to-back campaigns. The 6-foot-2, 190-pound corner outfielder continued to batter the competition in the New York-Penn League to the tune of .274/.385/.530 through 46 games. Injuries limited his playing time and effectiveness in High Class A in 2018 as he cobbled together a paltry .199/.276/.392 triple-slash line. And the former Tiger slugger got off to an equally poor start to last year as well, hitting a putrid .199/.286/.333. But things seemed to click for Deichmann at the start of June and he slugged a more Deichmann-like .246/.319/.431 over his remaining 35 games, which also included a lengthy stint on the disabled list due to a shoulder issue. The former early round pick continued to impress during his stint in the Arizona Fall League as well, slugging .256/.347/.634 in 23 games with Mesa.

Snippet from The 2018 Prospect Digest Handbook: Deichmann looks like a low-end Three True Outcomes Hitters, offering up a slightly better-than-average eye at the plate, 25-homerun power potential, and some swing-and-miss issues.

Scouting Report: Again, it comes down to a simple question and a difficult answer. How much impact do the nagging injuries have on Deichmann's production at the plate? Personally, I'm betting on it quite largely. As I stated in last year's book: he looks like a low end Three True Outcomes hitter – the exact type of hitter that flourishes in the A's lineup. Strictly a future designated hitter. But I wouldn't be shocked to see him post a .240/.330/.460 triple-slash line in Oakland if he can shake the injuries. Jack Cust with slightly worse walk rates?

Ceiling: 1.0- to 1.5-win player
Risk: Moderate to High
MLB ETA: 2020

19. Lazaro Armenteros, LF

	Hit	Power	SB	Patience	Glove	Overall
	35/40	50/55	50	55	50	40

Born: 05/22/99	Age: 21	Bats: R
Height: 6-0	Weight: 182	Throws: R

YEAR	LVL	PA	1B	2B	3B	HR	SB	CS	AVG	OBP	SLG	BB%	K%	GB%	LD%	FB%
2017	RK	26	3	0	0	0	2	2	0.167	0.385	0.167	11.54%	34.62%	50.0	20.0	30.0
2017	RK	181	28	9	4	4	10	1	0.288	0.376	0.474	8.84%	26.52%	52.7	10.9	30.9
2018	A	340	63	8	2	8	8	6	0.277	0.374	0.401	10.59%	33.82%	47.5	26.8	22.9
2019	A+	538	58	22	5	17	22	6	0.222	0.336	0.403	13.57%	42.19%	49.1	12.5	36.6

Background: Oakland's never been a stranger to making big, flashy signings on the international market. They added Robert Puason last summer. And years before that they inked former phenom Michael Ynoa to a $5 million deal. Lazarito, a Cuban import, falls into the same category. Added to the organization after agreeing to a deal worth $3 million, the 6-foot, 182-pound corner outfielder known as Lazarito has – well – failed to live up to the hype. After a year in the foreign and stateside rookie leagues, the front office pushed the then-19-year-old into the Midwest League two years ago and the results were mixed – at best. The good: he hit .277/.374/.401 with eight doubles, a pair of triples, eight homeruns, and eight stolen bases. The bad: he whiffed on nearly a third of his plate appearances. Oakland pushed the young outfielder up to the California League and the numbers plummeted. In 126 games with Stockton, Armenteros batted .222/.336/.403 with 22 doubles, five triples, 17 homeruns, and 22 stolen bases. His overall production, according to *Deserved Runs Created Plus*, topped the league average threshold by just 2%.

Snippet from The 2018 Prospect Digest Handbook: Plenty of potential to drool over. Armenteros' free-swinging ways, though, may prove to be too much and eventually slice into his ability to fully tap into his talent. After whiffing 105 times in only 388 plate appearances during his debut, his K-rate spiked to full-blown red flag territory in 2018 (33.8%).

Scouting Report: Consider the following:

- Since 2006, there have been six instances in which a player fanned in at least 40% of their plate appearances in any of the three High Class A leagues (min. 300 PA): Braxton Davidson, Gareth Morgan, Jose Pujols, James Baldwin, Telvin Nash, and – of course – Lazarito. None of them turned out to be anything noteworthy, despite some lofty draft statuses.

On the "positive" side, Armenteros was the youngest player on the list. On the other hand, though, he struck out in 42.2% of the 538 plate appearances he received last season. It doesn't matter if he flashes above-average power and speed with a double-digit walk rate if he can't make consistent contact.

Ceiling: 1.0-win player
Risk: Moderate
MLB ETA: 2022/2023

20. Jeremy Eierman, 2B/SS

	Hit	Power	SB	Patience	Glove	Overall
	35/40	50/55	40	45	45/50	40

Born: 09/10/96	Age: 23	Bats: R
Height: 6-0	Weight: 205	Throws: R

YEAR	LVL	PA	1B	2B	3B	HR	SB	CS	AVG	OBP	SLG	BB%	K%	GB%	LD%	FB%
2018	A-	267	40	8	2	8	10	4	0.235	0.283	0.381	4.87%	26.22%	44.4	20.6	25.0
2019	A+	552	62	22	7	13	11	3	0.208	0.270	0.357	7.07%	32.07%	39.1	9.2	38.8

Background: A product of Missouri State University, Eierman burst onto the scene with a stellar freshman campaign four years ago when he slugged .296/.336/.504 with 13 doubles, four triples, and nine homeruns. He followed that up by blossoming into one of the better power hitters in college baseball in 2017 as he belted out 15 doubles, a pair of triples, and a career best 23 homeruns en route to batting .313/.431/.675. The numbers regressed a bit as a junior – he hit .287/.379/.516 with 17 doubles, two triples, and 10 homeruns – but Oakland saw enough in the middle infielder to use the 70th overall pick on him. Eierman, however, hasn't lived up to his lofty second round draft status. He cobbled together a lowly .235/.283/.381 triple-slash line during his debut in the New York-Penn League. And performed even worst last season as the front office – inexplicably – pushed him straight into the High Class A (.208/.270/.357)

Snippet from The 2018 Prospect Digest Handbook: Eierman is going to battle plate discipline issues, but if [Oakland] can unlock his previous power surge he might be able to carve out a role as a .240/.300/.450-type middle infielder.

Scouting Report: From the onset it was always going to be a risky pick – for any club. There were more than a few red flags. The one glaring one: his horrific, almost humiliating performance in two trips to the Cape Cod League. But taking the former Missouri State University shortstop in the second round, 70th overall, has turned out to be a complete and utter disaster a year later. And Oakland has only compounded the issue by pushing an ill-prepared hitter aggressively through the low levels. Eierman's – essentially – become a one-dimensional player. And even that one dimension – power – isn't all that noteworthy. He's swinging and missing too frequently. The hit tool might not make into 40-grade territory. And his defense backed up as he was jostled around the infield.

Ceiling: 1.0-win player
Risk: Moderate
MLB ETA: 2022

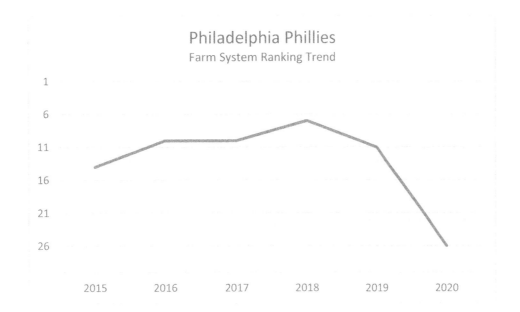

Philadelphia Phillies
Farm System Ranking Trend

Rank	Name	Age	Pos
1	Spencer Howard	23	RHP
2	Alec Bohm	23	1B/3B
3	Josh Stephen	22	LF
4	Francisco Morales	20	RHP
5	Bryson Stott	22	SS
6	Luis Garcia	19	2B/SS
7	Mickey Moniak	22	CF
8	Mauricio Llovera	24	RHP
9	Rodolfo Duran	22	C
10	Kendall Simmons	20	IF
11	Connor Seabold	24	RHP
12	Adonis Medina	23	RHP
13	JoJo Romero	23	LHP
14	Enyel De Los Santos	24	RHP
15	Juan Aparicio	20	C
16	Deivy Grullon	24	C
17	Erik Miller	22	LHP
18	Nick Maton	23	IF
19	Victor Santos	19	RHP
20	Kyle Young	20	LHP

1. Spencer Howard, RHP

FB	CB	CH	Command	Overall
65	55	60	55+	60

Born: 07/28/96	Age: 23	Bats: R
Height: 6-2	Weight: 205	Throws: R

YEAR	LVL	IP	W	L	SV	ERA	FIP	WHIP	K/9	K%	BB/9	BB%	K/BB	HR9	BABIP
2017	A-	28.3	1	1	0	4.45	2.72	1.41	12.7	32.52%	5.7	14.63%	2.22	0.00	0.349
2018	A	112.0	9	8	0	3.78	2.60	1.26	11.8	31.61%	3.2	8.60%	3.68	0.48	0.349
2019	Rk	2.3	0	0	0	11.57	9.07	1.71	11.6	25.00%	3.9	8.33%	3.00	3.86	0.333
2019	Rk	3.0	0	0	0	0.00	1.16	0.67	15.0	50.00%	3.0	10.00%	5.00	0.00	0.200
2019	A+	35.0	2	1	0	1.29	1.53	0.69	12.3	38.40%	1.3	4.00%	9.60	0.26	0.261
2019	AA	30.7	1	0	0	2.35	2.61	0.95	11.2	35.19%	2.6	8.33%	4.22	0.59	0.242

Background: Cal Poly has churned out a handful of notable big leaguers, including: Hall of Famer Ozzie Smith, former All-Star right-hander Mike Krukow, Mariners All-Star Mitch Haniger, and veteran vagabond reliever Bud Norris. After the club dipped into the Mustangs' pool to snag former top prospect Matt Imhof in the second round of the 2014 draft, Philadelphia went back to the same well three years later and plucked hard-throwing right-hander Spencer Howard with the 45th overall pick. The former Big West Conference ace turned in a dynamic first full season in pro ball two years ago when he averaged 11.8 strikeouts and just 3.2 walks across 23 starts with the Lakewood BlueClaws. Last season Howard picked up right when he left off, posting a 30-to-4 strikeout-to-walk ratio through his first 20.0 innings in High Class A. But a wonky shoulder pushed him to the disabled list in late April and it kept him out of action until the end of June. After a couple rehab appearances in the Gulf Coast League, Howard was unhittable in three starts with Clearwater before the front office unleashed him on Class AA. In total, Howard tossed a total of 71.0 innings, posting a ridiculous 94-to-16 strikeout-to-walk with a 2.03 ERA.

Snippet from The 2018 Prospect Digest Handbook: It's a bit surprising that the front office didn't push Howard up to the Florida State League at some point last season, but he's likely to spend at least a portion of 2019 in the Eastern League. At the bare minimum he's a dominant, lights out, shut-em-down reliever. But there's some upside in the rotation along the lines of a good #2/#3. I really, really like him.

Scouting Report: Bonafide ace material in the making. Howard's fastball was sitting in the 94- to 96-mph range, touching as high as 97 mph with a surprising amount of ease – even after his return from the shoulder issue. His curveball remains a firm above-average, swing-and-miss offering. And the changeup (A) ticked up to a plus offering and (B) he trusted it far more than his breakout 2018 campaign. I didn't see his hard cutter, which he featured two years ago, across a couple starts last season. What separates Howard from a lot of high octane hurlers is his above-average control/command. He's just not throwing strikes, but he's throwing quality strikes – *consistently*. And despite missing several months last year, he's quickly nearing big league readiness. I wouldn't be surprised to see the front office call him up down the stretch run as another power arm in the bullpen before sliding him into the rotation in 2021.

Ceiling: 4.5-win player
Risk: Moderate
MLB ETA: 2020

2. Alec Bohm, 1B/3B

Hit	Power	SB	Patience	Glove	Overall
55	60	35	55	50	60

Born: 08/03/96	Age: 23	Bats: R
Height: 6-5	Weight: 225	Throws: R

YEAR	LVL	PA	1B	2B	3B	HR	SB	CS	AVG	OBP	SLG	BB%	K%	GB%	LD%	FB%
2018	RK	10	2	0	0	0	0	0	0.222	0.200	0.222	0.00%	40.00%	66.7	0.0	33.3
2018	RK	27	7	1	1	0	2	0	0.391	0.481	0.522	7.41%	0.00%	60.9	13.0	26.1
2018	A-	121	18	5	1	0	1	0	0.224	0.314	0.290	8.26%	15.70%	56.8	12.5	25.0
2019	A	93	17	9	0	3	3	0	0.367	0.441	0.595	12.90%	15.05%	34.3	26.9	34.3
2019	A+	177	35	10	3	4	1	2	0.329	0.395	0.506	9.60%	11.86%	48.6	13.0	31.9
2019	AA	270	38	11	1	14	2	2	0.269	0.344	0.500	10.37%	14.07%	41.7	18.1	32.7

Background: In just a matter of months the former Wichita State star experienced the all-time highs and then the frustratingly low depths of struggling. The organization crowned the 6-foot-5, 225-pound corner infielder among the best amateur players in world when they selected him in the opening round of the June draft two years ago. Propelled by a stout showing in the Cape Cod League (.351/.399/.513) and a stellar follow up campaign with the Shockers during his junior season, Bohm, who slugged an impressive .339/.436/.625 with 31 extra-base hits, went to the Phillies with the third overall pick. Then minor league pitchers decided to push back. The Omaha, Nebraska, native struggled through two different stops during his debut, batting a lowly .252/.335/.325 in 40 games. Then...he promptly followed that up with a massive showing in 2019. Bohm vaulted through three different levels, going from Low Class A to the Florida State League then settled in nicely in Class AA, en route to slugging a collective .305/.378/.518 with 30 doubles, four triples, and 21 homeruns. He also swiped half-a-dozen stolen bases in 10 attempts.

Snippet from The 2018 Prospect Digest Handbook: Bohm is going to be an above-average big league hitter, peaking around .290/.350/.490 with 20+ homerun potential. Depending upon his defensive chops, he has the potential to turn into an All-Star caliber performer.

Scouting Report: With respect to his showing in Class AA last season, the level where he spent the lion's share of sophomore campaign, consider the following:

- Since 2006, only three 22-year-old hitters met the following criteria in the Eastern League (min. 250 PA): at least a 150 DRC+, a double-digit walk rate, and a sub-20% strikeout rate. Those three hitters: Matt Wieters, Domonic Brown, and Alec Bohm.

Now let's continue...

- Bohm's production line was the worst of the three: 177 (Wieters), 160 (Brown), and 154 (Bohm).
- Despite widely being considered top prospects during their careers, Wieters and Brown own – basically – league average bats during their respective big league careers.

One of the top power bats in the entire minor leagues, an aspect of his game that didn't show up during his debut, Bohm complements the plus-skill with (A) a surprisingly strong ability to make contact and (B) a willingness to spray the ball around the entire field. Throw in a solid-average glove at either corner spot on the infield, and he looks like a safe, low risk contender to develop into a perennial All-Star. Bohm has the floor of a Wieters/Brown-type performer (a.k.a. a league average bat). In terms of ceiling, think Pittsburgh's Josh Bell, who slugged .277/.367/.569 last season.

Ceiling: 4.0-win player
Risk: Moderate
MLB ETA: 2020

3. Josh Stephen, LF

Hit	Power	SB	Patience	Glove	Overall
50	45/50	35	50	45	50

Born: 09/22/97	Age: 22	Bats: L
Height: 6-0	Weight: 185	Throws: L

YEAR	LVL	PA	1B	2B	3B	HR	SB	CS	AVG	OBP	SLG	BB%	K%	GB%	LD%	FB%
2016	RK	184	29	7	3	2	6	6	0.253	0.339	0.370	9.78%	21.20%	50.0	21.0	23.4
2017	A-	253	40	12	5	2	4	3	0.247	0.282	0.364	4.74%	19.76%	40.8	19.9	33.0
2018	A	337	53	17	2	4	4	1	0.242	0.288	0.347	5.64%	21.07%	49.0	19.2	22.4
2019	AA	403	51	29	6	12	7	6	0.271	0.342	0.483	9.68%	27.30%	40.2	18.5	32.9

Background: One of the most intriguing – and arguably underrated – prospects not only in the Phillies system but also the entire minor leagues. Stephen, an 11th round pick four years ago, rocketed from complete obscurity into a dynamic hitting prospect – *all the while skipping High Class A as a 21-year-old*. I've been writing about prospects for the better part of a decade. I don't recall another instance that quite parallels Stephen's (A) jump and (B) level of production. After hitting a disappointing .242/.288/.347 with just 23 extra-base hits in 99 games with Lakewood, Stephen ripped through the Eastern League pitching by slugging .271/.342/.483 with career highs in doubles (29), triples (six), homeruns (12), and stolen bases (seven). Per *Deserved Runs Created Plus*, his overall production topped the league average mark by 24%. That's a whopping 47 percentage point improvement from 2018...in the most difficult level of the minor leagues...despite skipping an entire level.

Scouting Report: Consider the following:

- Since 2006, here's the list of 21-year-old hitters that posted a DRC+ total between 120 and 130 with a walk rate between 8% and 12% in the Eastern League (min. 300 PA): Ke'Bryan Hayes, Clint Frazier, Lonnie Chisenhall, Asdrubal Cabrera, Neil Walker, and – of course – Mr. Breakout, Josh Stephen.

On one hand that's one helluva group to belong too – a lot of big league talent and production. On the other hand, Stephen's strikeout rate, 27.3%, is by far the worst mark among the hitters. There's a lot of potential brewing here. The power really started to shine through during the second half of the season: he slugged 21 doubles, six triples, and eight homeruns over his final 68 games (plus, his strikeout rate was only 24% during that time as well). Now the bad news: he didn't hit lefties. He batted .189/.274/.378 against LHP last season. He didn't show a split in 2018, so there's some hope he rebounds in 2020. I like him a lot. Again, he's one of the most underrated hitters in the minors. Period. One more thought: his defense is beyond bad, like designated hitter bad.

Ceiling: 2.5- to 3.0-win player
Risk: Moderate
MLB ETA: 2020/2021

4. Francisco Morales, RHP

	FB	SL	CH	Command	Overall
	55/60	55/60	45/50	45/50	50

Born: 10/27/99	Age: 20	Bats: R
Height: 6-4	Weight: 185	Throws: R

YEAR	LVL	IP	W	L	SV	ERA	FIP	WHIP	K/9	K%	BB/9	BB%	K/BB	HR9	BABIP
2017	Rk	41.3	3	2	0	3.05	3.64	1.31	9.6	24.44%	4.4	11.11%	2.20	0.22	0.308
2018	A-	56.3	4	5	0	5.27	4.36	1.54	10.9	26.36%	5.3	12.79%	2.06	0.96	0.324
2019	A	96.7	1	8	1	3.82	3.49	1.32	12.0	30.94%	4.3	11.03%	2.80	0.74	0.325

Background: Viewed as the top Latin American pitching prospect during the summer of 2016, the Phillies signed the hard-throwing, baby-faced right-hander to a deal worth $720,000. Morales, a native of San Juan de los Morros, Venezuela, made his debut the following summer. And he did it fashionably. In 10 games with the organization's Gulf Coast League affiliate, the 6-foot-4, 185-pound hurler posted a 44-to-20 strikeout-to-walk ratio in 41.1 innings of work as a 17-year-old. The front office bounced him up to the New York-Penn League the next season. And Morales continued to rack up a bevy of punch outs: he averaged 10.9 strikeouts per nine innings in 13 starts for Williamsport. Morales spent last season dominating the South Atlantic League – *as a 19-year-old*. He posted an absurd 129-to-46 strikeout-to-walk ratio in only 96.2 innings. He finished his first full season of action with a 3.82 ERA and a 4.39 DRA (*Deserved Run Average*).

Snippet from The 2018 Prospect Digest Handbook: Morales' entering his age-19 season with one plus pitch and another that may get there as well, but his control has way – and *ways* – to go. If the changeup progresses up to an average third pitch – as well as several leaps forward in control – Morales has the look of a solid #3/#4-type arm. But, again, there's a lot of risk though.

Scouting Report: Consider the following:

- Since 2006, here's the list of 19-year-old arms that posted a 29% to 32% strikeout percentage in the South Atlantic League (min. 75 IP): Trevor May, Hunter Harvey, Drew Rom, Cody Buckel, Ronny Henriquez, Will Inman, and – of course – Francisco Morales.

Morales' fastball crept up a tick or two in 2019, moving from the low-90s to touching 94 with high regularity in 2019. His mid-80s slider continued to flash plus, though it needs more consistency. And his changeup – which sat 82- to 86-mph – showed some promising arm-side run. The control/command improved last season, particularly through his first 60.0 innings when he walked 26 batters. There's some intriguing #3-type potential, maybe more if his changeup becomes a consistent weapon. One final thought: the front office is likely going to start aggressively challenging Morales next season. It would be shocking to see him spend part of the year in Class AA.

Ceiling: 2.5- to 3.0-win player
Risk: Moderate
MLB ETA: 2021/2022

5. Bryson Stott, SS

	Hit	Power	SB	Patience	Glove	Overall
	50/55	45	50	55	50	50

Born: 10/06/97	Age: 22	Bats: L
Height: 6-3	Weight: 200	Throws: R

YEAR	LVL	PA	1B	2B	3B	HR	SB	CS	AVG	OBP	SLG	BB%	K%	GB%	LD%	FB%
2019	Rk	11	3	1	1	1	0	0	0.667	0.727	1.333	18.18%	0.00%	33.3	33.3	33.3
2019	A-	182	28	8	2	5	5	3	0.274	0.370	0.446	12.09%	21.43%	37.1	19.8	34.5

Background: Garnering some interest from a handful of big time colleges coming out of Desert Oasis High School – including Oregon and Arizona, according to Baseball America – Stott, a 6-foot-3, 200-pound middle infielder was bypassed by a lot of professional scouts throughout his teen years. Fast forward three seasons at UNLV, his parents' alma mater by the way, and the lefty-swinging shortstop positioned himself as one of the top hitters in the entire 2019 draft class. A starter since stepping on campus in 2017, Stott, a native of Las Vegas, slugged an impressive .294/.359/.379 with 11 doubles, a pair of triples, and a one homerun to go along with four stolen bases as a true freshman. The then-19-year-old infielder continued to swing a scorching bat as he squared off against Northwoods League pitching the ensuing summer. In 71 games with the Wisconsin Rapids Rafters, he batted .352/.442/.452 with 17 doubles, one triple, and three homeruns. Stott raised his offensive production into an entire new stratosphere during his sophomore campaign with the Running Rebels: In 59 games for Head Coach Stan Stolte, the burgeoning star hit .365/.442/.556 with a NCAA DI-leading 30 doubles, three triples, and four homeruns. He also swiped 14 bags in only 16 attempts. Perhaps the best part about Stott's breakout campaign: he stuck out just 18 times against 32 walks. Stott spent the following summer with the Team USA National squad and the Wareham Gatemen in the Cape Cod League; he would bat .262/.340/.333 in 13 games with the national team and .275/.383/.325 in a dozen games with the Gatemen. And, once again, Stott's production lurched forward last season: in 58 games, the 6-foot-3, 200-pound middle infielder slugged .356/.486/.599 with 20 doubles, two triples, 10 homeruns, and 16 stolen bases. Philadelphia selected the UNLV star in the opening round, 14th overall. After a brief tour through the Gulf Coast League, Stott spent the remainder of his debut Williamsport in the New York-Penn League, hitting a solid .274/.370/.446 with eight doubles, two triples, five homeruns, and five stolen bases. His overall production, according to Baseball Prospectus' *Deserved Runs Created Plus*, topped the league average mark by 49%.

Scouting Report: Here's what I wrote about the former Rebel heading into the draft last summer:

"First things first let's talk about the elephant in the room: UNLV's home to one of the most hitter-friendly environments in all of college baseball. In fact, consider the following:

- *Between 2011 and 2018 there were eight instances in which a UNLV hitter batted at least .350 in a season (min. 200 PA). Those eight hitters: Trent Cook, Brandon Bayardi, Patrick Armstrong, Payton Squier, Ernie De La Trinidad, Justin Jones, Kyle Isbel, and – of course – Bryson Stott, who accomplished the feat twice.*
- *Let's break the group down: only one player, Kyle Isbel, was selected before the 16th round. Isbel, by the way, the Royals' third round pick two years ago and owns a MiLB line of .329/.394/.523.*

Let's continue. Consider the following junior seasons by Isbel and Stott:

Player	Age	Year	PA	AVG	OBP	SLG	K%	BB%
Bryson Stott	21	2019	228	0.365	0.498	0.652	14.04%	20.18%
Kyle Isbel	21	2018	282	0.357	0.441	0.643	15.25%	12.06%

Defensively speaking, Stott doesn't possess the softest of hands and his bat doesn't profile nearly as well at third base, so he's going to have to remain at shortstop to reach his full potential. His swing shows a bit too much loft for a player that's not likely going to hit for much power in the professional ranks either; he's at his best shooting balls to the gaps. He's very likely to fall into the super-sub type of role as he reaches full maturity."

I was a little pessimistic about Stott's future heading into the draft – mainly the power, which showed up significantly better than I expected. There's some Hunter Dozier type production here.

Ceiling: 2.5-win player
Risk: Moderate
MLB ETA: 2022

6. Luis Garcia, 2B/SS

	Hit	Power	SB	Patience	Glove	Overall
	30/55	35/45	40	50	50	50

Born: 10/01/00	Age: 19	Bats: B
Height: 5-11	Weight: 170	Throws: R

YEAR	LVL	PA	1B	2B	3B	HR	SB	CS	AVG	OBP	SLG	BB%	K%	GB%	LD%	FB%
2018	RK	187	47	11	3	1	12	8	0.369	0.433	0.488	8.02%	11.23%	44.2	25.9	19.7
2019	A	524	66	14	3	4	9	8	0.186	0.261	0.255	8.40%	25.19%	44.4	15.2	25.1

Background: I didn't just tout the young middle infielder in last year's book when (A) I listed him as the club's second best prospect or (B) #1 on The Top 25 Breakout Prospects for 2019 or (C) showed how his production closely paralleled one of the game's best young superstars (Juan Soto). And, of course, Garcia went out and...well...disappointed is not strong enough. So, frankly, he crapped the bed. The Dominican middle infielder, after slugging a scorching .369/.433/.488 during his debut in the Gulf Coast League, barely managed to hit his own weight, cobbling together a puny .186/.261/.255 triple-slash line. According to *Deserved Runs Created Plus*, his overall production was a whopping 42% *below* the league average mark.

Snippet from The 2018 Prospect Digest Handbook: Power notwithstanding, Garcia went toe-to-toe with one of the game's best young stars [Juan Soto] at the same point their respective careers. Yes, the power's a big differentiator, but the rest of the work speaks for itself. Garcia has a plus hit tool, above-average or better speed, and the glove to stick at the most important spot on the infield. The power's still largely untapped, but there's the potential to develop 50-grade pop; he posted a 25.9% line drive rate last season. He could be the top shortstop prospect in a year's time.

Scouting Report: Ugh... there's really no other way to put it. My performance on his analysis went toe-to-toe with Garcia's production in the South Atlantic League last season. But here's the kicker – and, yes, batting average is a rather meaningless stat, but... – Garcia failed to hit .200 in April, June, and July. And – *barely* – eclipsed the threshold in May. The batted ball data is still within reason to his breakout 2018 season. But his power evaporated and his strikeout rate exploded. So let's look at his work through a historical lens. Consider the following:

- Since 2006, been 50 instances in which an 18-year-old hitter received at least 250 plate appearances in the South Atlantic League. Garcia's 58 DRC+ is the third worst showing.
- On the other hand, the second worst show was Juan Lagares, who has had a couple seasons as a production big leaguer.

It's still way too early to jump off of Garcia's bandwagon, but I certainly have one foot hanging off the ride. The front office is certainly responsible for some of the poor showing. It was readily apparent that he wasn't ready for the rigors of Low Class A, but – inexplicably – kept him in the Sally without demoting him. Hopefully he rebounds in 2020 because the basic skill set is still intact.

Ceiling: 2.5-win player
Risk: Moderate to High
MLB ETA: 2022

7. Mickey Moniak, CF

	Hit	Power	SB	Patience	Glove	Overall
	45/50	40/45	45	45	45/50	45

Born: 05/13/98	Age: 22	Bats: L
Height: 6-2	Weight: 185	Throws: R

YEAR	LVL	PA	1B	2B	3B	HR	SB	CS	AVG	OBP	SLG	BB%	K%	GB%	LD%	FB%
2017	A	509	77	22	6	5	11	7	0.236	0.284	0.341	5.50%	21.41%	48.4	18.3	29.5
2018	A+	465	81	28	3	5	6	5	0.270	0.304	0.383	4.73%	21.51%	45.2	19.6	31.1
2019	AA	504	65	28	13	11	15	3	0.252	0.303	0.439	6.55%	22.02%	40.1	22.6	31.1

Background: Just to recap: the Phillies selected Moniak as the #1 overall pick in the 2016 draft, bypassing several top prospects including: Nick Senzel, Ian Anderson, A.J. Puk, Alex Kirilloff, Forrest Whitley, Gavin Lux, and Carter Kieboom – just to name a few. Now that we've discussed the elephant in the room, let's focus on Moniak. After a disappointing showing in the South Atlantic League as a 19-year-old in the 2017, which decimated his prospect status, Moniak has quietly put together solid back-to-back showings over the past two seasons. The 6-foot-2, 185-pound center fielder batted a respectable .270/.304/.383 with 28 doubles, three triples, five homeruns, and six stolen bases in 114 games with Clearwater. And he handled the minors' toughest level, Class AA, last season. In 119 games with the Reading Fightin' Phils, the La Costa Canyon High School product hit .252/.303/.439 with a career high-tying 28 doubles, 13 triples, and 11 homeruns. He also swiped 15 bags in 18 attempts. His overall production, per *Deserved Runs Created Plus*, was 3% below the league average mark. He also popped up in the Arizona Fall League as well, hitting a disappointing .186/.230/.300 in 17 games with the Scottsdale Scorpions.

Snippet from The 2018 Prospect Digest Handbook: After batting a lowly .185/.209/.215 for the first couple of weeks, Moniak slugged a healthy .285/.320/.413 over his remaining 98 games. The former top pick isn't destined to be a future star or a franchise cornerstone. But there's enough of an offensive foundation to suggest a ceiling as a low-end starting center field on a non-contending team. The hit tool still profiles as an above-average skill. But the power and defense have been disappointing.

Scouting Report: That #1 pick label is strung around Moniak's neck like a millstone. So...let's ignore it. And just focus on the player itself. Last season was – by far – his most impressive showing as a professional. Moniak was essentially a league average bat in (A) the most important level for a prospect and (B) at only 21-years-old. And like the previous year, Moniak got off to a putrid slow start before rebounding. He hit .195/.235/.377 over his first 19 games, but managed to slug .265/.316/.451 over his remaining 100 games. Moniak's power took a big leap forward last season. And he's showing some improved efficiency on the base paths, as well as better routes in the outfield. With respect to his work last season, consider the following:

- Since 2006, only four 21-year-old hitters met the following criteria in the Eastern League (min. 300 PA): 95 to 105 DRC+, a walk rate between 5.5% and 7.5% with a strikeout rate between 18% and 23%. Those four hitters: Eddie Rosario, Willie Castro, Austin Romine, and – of course – Mickey Moniak.

Continuing...

- Eddie Rosario owns a 103 DRC+ in his big league career; Castro, who was traded by the Indians to the Tigers, made his big league debut as a 22-year-old last season; and Romine owns a career 78 DRC+.

Again, Moniak's a fine prospect. He's never going to be a star. But he's a grinder, though. And there's something to be said for that. He's flawed, but he's the type of player to get everything out of his talent. He's easy to root for. And he's constantly improving.

Ceiling: 1.5- to 2.0-win player
Risk: Moderate
MLB ETA: 2020/2021

8. Mauricio Llovera, RHP

FB	CB	SL	SF	Command	Overall
60	50+	5	60	45+	45

Born: 04/17/96	Age: 24	Bats: R
Height: 5-11	Weight: 200	Throws: R

YEAR	LVL	IP	W	L	SV	ERA	FIP	WHIP	K/9	K%	BB/9	BB%	K/BB	HR9	BABIP
2017	A	86.0	2	4	0	3.35	2.93	1.33	9.8	25.34%	3.5	8.89%	2.85	0.21	0.332
2018	A+	121.0	8	7	0	3.72	3.90	1.11	10.2	27.02%	2.5	6.71%	4.03	1.04	0.279
2019	AA	65.3	3	4	0	4.55	3.87	1.35	9.9	25.26%	3.9	9.82%	2.57	0.96	0.306

Background: The front office added the hard-throwing, sub-6-foot right-hander to the 40-man roster this offseason. Llovera, a native of El Tigre, Venezuela, has been a consistently, peripherally-driven hurler throughout his tenure in the Phillies' organization. Between 2016 and 2018, the 5-foot-11, 200-pound hurler averaged an impressive 9.93 strikeouts and 2.73 walk per nine innings. And last season, his march towards the big leagues continued in similar fashion. In a shortened campaign, Llovera made 14 appearances with Reading, 12 of which were starts, throwing 65.1 innings with 72 strikeouts and issuing 28 free passes. He finished the season with a 4.55 ERA and 4.70 DRA.

Snippet from The 2018 Prospect Digest Handbook: The fact remains, though, that Llovera's entering his age-23 season, owns three above-average or better pitches, and throws strikes. That's at – bare minimum – the recipe for a backend starting pitcher. Consider the following:

Scouting Report: There's a ton of speculation swirling about that Llovera, and his generously listed midriff, is a prime candidate to break camp as a reliever in the Phillies' pen. And to a certain degree it makes sense: the rotation's basically set with Aaron Nola, Zack Wheeler, Jake Arrieta written in stone as the top three and Zach Efflin, Vince Velasquez, Nick Pivetta, and Cole Irvin fighting for the final two spots. Plus, Llovera's high octane, max-effort approach seems better suited for shorter stints. His fastball is late-lifed with plenty of explosion. He'll mix in two breaking balls – a slider, which has generally graded out better, and a curveball. Last season, though, the latter looked more impressive. He'll also throw one of the better, more underrated splitters in the minor leagues – a bonafide plus pitch. If given the shot, he'd likely be a suitable #4 for a time being as well.

Ceiling: 1.5- to 2.0-win player
Risk: Moderate
MLB ETA: 2020

9. Rodolfo Duran, C

Hit	Power	SB	Patience	Glove	Overall
45	50/55	30	40	50+	45

Born: 02/19/98	Age: 22	Bats: R
Height: 5-9	Weight: 185	Throws: R

YEAR	LVL	PA	1B	2B	3B	HR	SB	CS	AVG	OBP	SLG	BB%	K%	GB%	LD%	FB%
2017	A-	171	28	9	3	0	0	1	0.252	0.298	0.346	4.68%	21.05%	41.9	19.4	30.6
2018	A	336	45	17	1	18	1	1	0.260	0.304	0.495	5.95%	22.32%	40.8	22.1	24.6
2019	A+	245	39	10	1	6	0	0	0.240	0.273	0.369	4.08%	21.63%	33.7	19.3	36.5

Background: Deivy Grullon wasn't the only Phillies catching prospect to take several leaps forward at the plate two years ago. Duran, a 5-foot-9, 185-pound backstop, flashed some plus-power potential during his 88-game stint in the South Atlantic League in 2018. He finished the year with a .260/.304/.495 triple-slash line, belting out 17 doubles, one triple, and 18 homeruns. And, just for fun, here are those numbers prorated for a full 162-game season: 31 doubles, two triples, and 33 homeruns. Last season Duran's offensive firepower backed up a bit as he settled into the Florida State League. In an injury-shortened campaign, the young catcher hit .240/.273/.369 with 10 doubles, one triple, and six homeruns. Per *Deserved Runs Created Plus*, his overall production was 14% *below* the league average threshold.

Snippet from The 2018 Prospect Digest Handbook: The hit tool's nothing to write home about. And he's never shown a patient approach at the plate. But his defense has consistently graded out between above-average and plus. Duran has the potential to develop into a .250/.300/.450-type hitter with strong defense, something along the lines of a Salvador Perez performance.

Scouting Report: Productive big league catching – across the board – is hard to find. Just 11 backstops totaled more than two wins above replacement (FanGraphs' version) – including the Phillies' J.T. Realmuto, who topped MLB with 5.7 fWAR. So the question isn't whether Duran's going to be a star – because he's not – it's whether he has the tools to develop into something close to a league average backstop. The answer: a resounding yes. Defensively, he's above average glove – which already puts him on a short list. Offensively, the hit tool is still subpar, but he runs into enough straight pitches to belt out 15 homeruns or so. The lack of patience chews into his value. But a .250/.300/.450 triple-slash line with 55-grade defense certainly seems reasonable enough. That puts him close to Travis d'Arnaud's showing last season, by the way.

Ceiling: 1.5- to 2.0-win player
Risk: Moderate
MLB ETA: 2022

10. Kendall Simmons, IF

Hit	Power	SB	Patience	Glove	Overall
35/45	50/55	40	50+	45/50	50

Born: 04/11/00	Age: 20	Bats: R
Height: 6-2	Weight: 180	Throws: R

YEAR	LVL	PA	1B	2B	3B	HR	SB	CS	AVG	OBP	SLG	BB%	K%	GB%	LD%	FB%
2018	RK	113	12	7	0	3	2	4	0.232	0.345	0.400	7.96%	26.55%	39.4	19.7	30.3
2019	A-	205	18	7	3	12	5	6	0.234	0.333	0.520	9.76%	26.34%	35.0	19.5	31.7

Background: A raw, toolsy prospect – just like how the Phillies love 'em. The ballclub selected the well-built 6-foot-2, 180-pound infielder with the third pick in the sixth round, 167th overall, two years ago. A product of Tattnall Square Academy in Macon, Georgia,

Simmons showed his flawed approach – and stat-stuffing – ability during his debut in the Gulf Coast League when he slugged .232/.345/.400 with seven doubles, three homeruns, and a pair of stolen bases. Last season the infield vagabond squared off against the New York-Penn League. And the results were…well…better. In 51 games with the Williamsport Crosscutters, the former prep star batted .234/.333/.520 with seven doubles, three triples, 12 homeruns, and five stolen bases. Per *Deserved Runs Created Plus*, his overall production topped the league average threshold by 26%.

Scouting Report: Consider the following:

- Since 2006, only two 19-year-old hitters met the following criteria in the New York-Penn League (min. 200 PA): 120 to 130 DRC+, a walk rate between 9% and 11%, and a strikeout rate between 25% and 27%. Those two hitters: former first rounder Garrett Whitley, who was a top prospect in the Rays system before missing all of 2018 with injury, and Kendall Simmons.

Above-average or better power from an infield position. He's willing to walk. And while the K-rate is slightly concerning, it's nothing that can't be improved upon as the bat continues to mature. He runs a bit and flashes a 50-grade glove around the infield. What's not to like? He's definitely, *definitely* raw. But there's a lot of upside here. A lot of risk too. One more final note: after hitting .169/.235/.324 in his first 21 games; Simmons slugged a healthy .280/.398/.660 over his remaining 30 games. I like him. A lot. He's another potential breakout candidate, though the Sally will be a tough assignment in 2020.

Ceiling: 2.0- to 2.5-win player
Risk: Moderate to High
MLB ETA: 2022

11. Connor Seabold, RHP

FB	SL	CH	Command	Overall
50	55	50	55	45

Born: 01/24/96	Age: 24	Bats: R
Height: 6-2	Weight: 190	Throws: R

YEAR	LVL	IP	W	L	SV	ERA	FIP	WHIP	K/9	K%	BB/9	BB%	K/BB	HR9	BABIP
2017	A-	10.0	2	0	0	0.90	1.43	0.70	11.7	35.14%	1.8	5.41%	6.50	0.00	0.227
2018	A+	71.7	4	4	0	3.77	3.33	0.99	8.5	23.78%	1.8	4.90%	4.86	0.75	0.260
2018	AA	58.7	1	4	0	4.91	4.47	1.26	9.8	25.50%	2.9	7.57%	3.37	1.53	0.290
2019	A+	9.0	1	0	0	1.00	3.19	0.56	10.0	31.25%	1.0	3.13%	10.00	1.00	0.158
2019	AA	40.0	3	1	0	2.25	2.76	1.13	8.1	22.78%	2.3	6.33%	3.60	0.45	0.300

Background: Originally taken by the Baltimore Orioles in the 19th round coming out of Newport Harbor High School in 2017. Seabold spurned the club's interest, instead opting to attend Cal State Fullerton. And he immediately became a dominant force for the Big West Conference squad. He averaged 9.9 strikeouts and just 1.6 walks per nine innings in 22 appearances as a true freshman. He raised the bar even high during his sophomore season, posting a 96-to-9 strikeout-to-walk ratio in only 83.1 innings of work. And after his production regressed a bit (8.6 K/9 and 1.6 BB/9) during his junior campaign, the Phillies snagged the 6-foot-2, 190-pound right-hander in the third round three years ago. Seabold, a native of Newport Beach, California, quickly moved into the upper levels of the minor leagues as he reached Class AA by the end of 2018. An oblique strained knocked him out of first couple months of the year. And after a couple rehab appearances in rookie ball and High Class A, Seabold made seven starts with Reading, throwing 40.0 innings with 36 strikeouts and just 10 walks. Seabold tossed another 17.0 innings in the Arizona Fall League, fanning 22 and issuing just a trio of walks.

Snippet from The 2018 Prospect Digest Handbook: He fits the mold of the typical Cal State Fullerton pitching prospect: he excels by doing things that won't hurt him in the long run, namely throwing strikes. Seabold's arsenal is a bit limited, only his changeup rates better than average, but he has an idea and typically sticks to it by keeping hitters off balance. If everything breaks the right way he could carve out a role as a true #5 or slide into a multiple-inning reliever.

Scouting Report: Seabold's grown on me the more I've watched him throw. His fastball sits in the 90- to 93-mph range with a little bit of life up in the zone. He'll complement that with a mid-80s slider, an above-average weapon, and a low-80s straight changeup. He's like a poor man's

Aaron Nola. There's a solid chance that he could carve out a role as a solid #4-type arm. I wouldn't be surprised to see him put up a couple years of production similar to Jeff Samardzija or Wade Miley circa 2019.

Ceiling: 1.5-win player
Risk: Moderate
MLB ETA: 2020

12. Adonis Medina, RHP

	FB	SL	CH	Command	Overall
	55	55	55	50	45

Born: 12/18/96	Age: 23	Bats: R
Height: 6-1	Weight: 185	Throws: R

YEAR	LVL	IP	W	L	SV	ERA	FIP	WHIP	K/9	K%	BB/9	BB%	K/BB	HR9	BABIP
2017	A	119.7	4	9	0	3.01	3.34	1.19	10.0	26.34%	2.9	7.72%	3.41	0.53	0.306
2018	A+	111.3	10	4	0	4.12	3.81	1.25	9.9	26.06%	2.9	7.63%	3.42	0.89	0.316
2019	AA	105.7	7	7	0	4.94	4.53	1.36	7.0	17.52%	3.5	8.76%	2.00	0.94	0.288

Background: Signed in 2014 out of Santo Domingo Centro, Dominican Republic, the normally aggressive front office has taken the slow-and-steady approach with the talented right-hander. Medina spent a year each at every level beginning with his debut in the Dominican Summer League.

Last season the wiry, 6-foot-1, 185-pound hurler squared off against the minors' toughest challenge, Class AA, and the results were...well...mediocre. Making a career high-tying 22 appearances with Reading, Medina tossed 105.2 innings with just 82 strikeouts and 41 walks. He compiled a 4.94 ERA and a horrible 5.99 DRA (*Deserved Run Average*).

Snippet from The 2018 Prospect Digest Handbook: More of a strike thrower than a command-oriented pitcher, Medina has had no problem filling up the zone throughout the duration of his professional career. He has the potential to grow into a mid-rotation role in the coming years.

Scouting Report: Consider the following:

- Since 2006, only five 22-year-old pitchers posted a strikeout percentage between 16.5% and 18.5% with a walk percentage between 8% and 10% in the Eastern League (min. 100 IP): T.J. House, Stolmy Pimentel, Michael Stutes, T.J. McFarland, and – of course – Adonis Medina.

Sans Medina, the other arms all fall into Quad-A type and/or fringy big leaguers. Now Medina: the lack of command, despite filling up the strike zone, came back to bite him in the butt. His fastball was sitting 92- to 95-mph. His slider showed some solid 2-8 break, hovering in the mid-80s. And his changeup was in the mid-80s. Unfortunately, Medina looks like one of the more overrated pitchers in the minor leagues. And there's a lot more Juan Cruz in him, rather than a consistent big league starter.

Ceiling: 1.5-win player
Risk: Moderate
MLB ETA: 2020

13. JoJo Romero, LHP

	FB	CB	SL	CU	CH	Control	Overall
	55	50	50	50	50	50	40

Born: 09/09/96	Age: 23	Bats: L
Height: 5-11	Weight: 190	Throws: L

YEAR	LVL	IP	W	L	SV	ERA	FIP	WHIP	K/9	K%	BB/9	BB%	K/BB	HR9	BABIP
2017	A	76.7	5	1	0	2.11	2.67	1.07	9.3	26.33%	2.5	7.00%	3.76	0.23	0.299
2017	A+	52.3	5	2	0	2.24	2.91	1.11	8.4	23.33%	2.6	7.14%	3.27	0.34	0.289
2018	AA	106.7	7	6	0	3.80	4.32	1.29	8.4	22.08%	3.5	9.05%	2.44	1.10	0.286
2019	AA	57.7	4	4	0	4.84	2.94	1.21	8.1	21.94%	1.9	5.06%	4.33	0.62	0.321
2019	AAA	53.7	3	5	0	6.88	6.25	1.92	6.7	15.33%	5.9	13.41%	1.14	1.34	0.345

Background: Yavapai College in Prescott, Arizona, has produced a trio of notable ballplayers since 1971. Two of three players – Ken Giles and JoJo Romero – were selected by the Phillies. (Note: the third notable player is current Rangers outfielder Willie Calhoun). Romero, a fourth round pick in 2016, was put on the fast track and reached Class AA in just his second full season; he made 18 starts for Reading that year, throwing 106.2 innings with 100 strikeouts and 41 walks to go along with a 3.80 ERA. Last season the 5-foot-11, 190-pound southpaw split time between Reading and Lehigh Valley, fanning 92 hitters and handing out 47 walks in 111.1 innings of work. He compiled an aggregate 5.82 ERA between both stops. He tossed another 10.2 innings in the Arizona Fall League, posting a disappointing 5-to-4 strikeout-to-walk ratio.

Snippet from The 2018 Prospect Digest Handbook: He succeeds by changing speeds well and never committing himself to a noticeable pattern. Romero should peak as a capable rotational arm, somewhere along the lines of a #4-type starting pitcher.

Scouting Report: A throw-it-up-against-wall-and-see-what-sticks-type of arm. Romero offers a bevy of pitches – five to be exact – and only one of them grades out better than average. His fastball sits in the 91- to 93-mph with a little bit of late life up in the zone. His secondary offerings – a curveball, slider, cutter, and changeup – all fall into the average category. The command has failed to progress and depending upon the day it alternates between below-average and fringy average.

Ceiling: 1.0- to 1.5-win player
Risk: Low to Moderate
MLB ETA: Debuted in 2018

14. Enyel De Los Santos, RHP

	FB	CB	SL	CH	Command	Overall
	55	45	45	55	45+	40

Born: 12/25/95	Age: 24	Bats: R
Height: 6-3	Weight: 170	Throws: R

YEAR	LVL	IP	W	L	SV	ERA	FIP	WHIP	K/9	K%	BB/9	BB%	K/BB	HR9	BABIP
2017	AA	150.0	10	6	0	3.78	3.64	1.19	8.3	22.37%	2.9	7.78%	2.88	0.72	0.290
2018	AAA	126.7	10	5	0	2.63	4.03	1.16	7.8	21.11%	3.1	8.25%	2.56	0.85	0.264
2019	AAA	94.0	5	7	0	4.40	5.31	1.23	7.9	21.34%	3.4	9.00%	2.37	1.53	0.256

Background: Already part of a couple trades in his young career. De Los Santos, who was a late international signing, was traded by the Mariners to the Padres for veteran right-handed reliever Joaquin Benoit after the 2015 season. Two-plus years later San Diego sent the rail-thin hurler to the Phillies in exchange for Freddy Galvis. And that's not the only type of movement that De Los Santos has been making: he's continued his quick ascension through the minor leagues, regardless of which organization he's in. Last season – just like the previous year – De Los Santos split time between Philly's Class AAA affiliate and The Show. He made 19 starts with Lehigh Valley, throwing 94.0 innings with 83 strikeouts and 35 walks to go along with 4.40 ERA. And he made five brief appearances in Philadelphia, posting a 9-to-5 strikeout-to-walk ratio in 11.0 innings.

Snippet from The 2018 Prospect Digest Handbook: De Los Santos will likely work as a spot starter/multiple-inning reliever over the next couple of years, relying solely on the one-two combo of his fastball/changeup. One final note: De Los Santos' curveball averaged 2,145 RPM during his big league stint – well below league average of 2,469 RPMs.

Scouting Report: The good news: De Los Santos pretty much scrapped his crappy curveball – especially during his cup of coffee in the big leagues. The bad news: he still has to throw his equally crappy slider. His fastball declined noticeably last season, going from an average of 94.6 mph to 93.3. His future role is all but determined as a multi-inning reliever where he can focus solely on his fastball/changeup combo.

Ceiling: 1.5- to 1.5-win player
Risk: Low to Moderate
MLB ETA: Debuted in 2018

15. Juan Aparicio, C

	Hit	Power	SB	Patience	Glove	Overall
	40/50	40/50	30	45	50	45

Born: 05/26/00	Age: 20	Bats: R
Height: 5-11	Weight: 175	Throws: R

YEAR	LVL	PA	1B	2B	3B	HR	SB	CS	AVG	OBP	SLG	BB%	K%	GB%	LD%	FB%
2018	RK	119	25	9	1	3	0	1	0.339	0.378	0.518	3.36%	21.85%	37.2	20.9	37.2
2019	A-	121	25	10	4	1	3	2	0.374	0.446	0.570	7.44%	18.18%	38.8	32.9	24.7
2019	A	74	9	3	0	1	0	0	0.191	0.230	0.279	4.05%	25.68%	44.7	8.5	34.0

Background: Signed off the international scene during the summer of 2016, Aparicio, a Maracaibo, Venezuela native, was ranked as the 47th best international prospect by *Baseball America*. The 5-foot-11, 175-pound backstop put an abysmal showing in the Dominican Summer League in the rearview mirror by slugging a robust .339/.378/.518 in the Gulf Coast League the following year. Last season, Aparicio ripped through short-season ball to the tune of .374/.446/.570 with 10 doubles, four triples, and one homerun in only 32 games with Williamsport. His production cratered – massively – in a late season promotion up to the Sally; he batted a lowly .191/.230/.279.

Scouting Report: There's some intriguing upside here. Aparicio was originally signed as a third baseman, but immediately shifted to catching. And – surprisingly – his defense has graded out as average in each of his professional seasons. Plus, he threw out 45% of would-be base stealers last season. There's a chance the hit tool reaches an average peak with 15-homerun thump. There's a low end starting caliber ceiling with the floor of a solid backup option in the coming years.

Ceiling: 1.5-win player
Risk: Moderate
MLB ETA: 2022

16. Deivy Grullon, C

Hit	Power	SB	Patience	Glove	Overall
45	55	30	45+	40	40

Born: 02/17/96	Age: 24	Bats: R
Height: 6-1	Weight: 180	Throws: R

YEAR	LVL	PA	1B	2B	3B	HR	SB	CS	AVG	OBP	SLG	BB%	K%	GB%	LD%	FB%
2016	A	356	56	20	0	6	0	3	0.256	0.320	0.375	8.43%	23.31%	53.9	17.4	24.9
2017	A+	286	47	14	0	8	0	1	0.255	0.287	0.395	4.20%	21.33%	52.8	16.0	28.8
2017	AA	89	12	3	0	4	0	0	0.229	0.270	0.410	5.62%	21.35%	53.8	15.4	26.2
2018	AA	353	53	14	1	21	0	0	0.273	0.310	0.515	5.10%	22.95%	49.2	18.3	28.2
2019	AAA	457	70	24	0	21	1	0	0.283	0.354	0.496	9.85%	29.10%	51.5	20.8	25.9

Background: A mediocre – or worse – offensive performer through the early stages of his minor league career, Grullon, a 6-foot-1, generously listed 180-pound backstop, quietly put together one of the system's bigger breakout campaigns in 2018 – at the most important minor league level, Class AA. In 90 games with Reading, the Dominican catcher batted .273/.310/.515 with gobs of extra-base fire power (14 doubles and 21 homeruns). Some of that production smacked of playing half of his games in one of the Eastern League's more friendly confines. Until he repeated that level of production in 2019. In a career best 108 games with the Lehigh Valley Iron Pigs, Grullon batted .283/.354/.496 with 24 doubles and a career high-tying 21 dingers. His overall production, according to *Deserved Runs Created Plus*, was good enough for 15% better than the league average. He also popped up in the Phillies' lineup for a quarter of games as well.

Scouting Report: Consider the following:

- Since 2006, only three 23-year-old hitters met the following criteria in the International League (min. 350 PA): 110 to 120 DRC+, a walk rate between 9% and 11% and a strikeout rate north of 25%. Those three hitters: Rio Ruiz, Brandon Moss, and Deivy Grullon. Moss owns a career 104 DRC+ in 1,016 big league games. And Ruiz, once considered a solid middle-tier prospect, is sporting a 80 DRC+ in 199 career games.

An offensive-minded backstop that's generally graded out as one of the worst defensive catchers in the minor leagues. Grullon, according to Baseball Prospectus' *Fielding Runs Above Average*, earned a stout -18.9 in 2019. And that porous total was preceded by a -20.0 in 2018. So, clearly, the bat's going to be the driving factor. Grullon's always flashed some intriguing power potential and that began to translate into in-game thump two years ago. He's not all that patient and he battled some swing-and-miss issues for the first time in 2019. And with J.T. Realmuto locked in as a starter, Grullon will likely be competing with former second round pick Andrew Knapp for the backup gig. He looks like a .250/.330/.480-type hitter at his peak. But his defense is such a limited factor at this point.

Ceiling: 1.0- to 1.5-win player
Risk: Moderate
MLB ETA: 2020/2021

17. Erik Miller, LHP

FB	SL	CH	Command	Overall
50+	55	50/55	45	40

Born: 02/13/98	Age: 22	Bats: L
Height: 6-5	Weight: 240	Throws: L

YEAR	LVL	IP	W	L	SV	ERA	FIP	WHIP	K/9	K%	BB/9	BB%	K/BB	HR9	BABIP
2019	Rk	3.0	0	0	0	3.00	1.50	1.33	18.0	46.15%	6.0	15.38%	3.00	0.00	0.400
2019	A-	20.0	0	0	0	0.90	2.15	1.00	13.1	33.72%	3.2	8.14%	4.14	0.00	0.283
2019	A	13.0	1	0	0	2.08	2.47	1.23	11.8	30.91%	4.2	10.91%	2.83	0.00	0.323

Background: The big southpaw made an immediate impact for Stanford. He posted a 3.65 ERA across 13 starts and four relief appearances as a true freshman, despite averaging 5.0 strikeouts and 3.1 walks per nine innings. Miller, a native of Creve Coer, Missouri, nearly doubled his strikeout rate during his sophomore season as he averaged 9.6 punch outs per nine innings, though his control/command wavered at times. He spent the ensuing summer playing for the Orleans Firebirds in the Cape Cod League, posting a 32-to-15 strikeout-to-walk ratio in 23.1 innings of work. Last season, the 6-foot-5, 240-pound left-hander set career highs in strikeout rate (11.1 K/9) as well as walk rate (5.0 BB/9). Philadelphia snagged him in the fourth round last June. Miller made brief stops at three separate levels, fanning 52 against just 15 walks in only 36.0 innings of work. He compiled a barely-there 1.50 ERA as well.

Scouting Report: The big burly southpaw doesn't blow hitters away with a scorching heater. Rather he relies on a little bit of deception and lanky limbs to add some life to his 89- to 92-mph fastball. He'll complement the slightly better-than-average offering with two secondary pitches: an above-average slider and an improving changeup. It looked like Miller was emphasizing his changeup more once he entered the Phillies' organization, likely in an attempt to improve it. The control/command looked vastly improved during his pro debut as well, but I'm not ready to buy it just yet given his lengthy track record of strike zone blindness. He looks like a Brian Tallet-type pitcher.

Ceiling: 1.0- to 1.5-win player
Risk: Moderate
MLB ETA: 2022

18. Nick Maton, IF

	Hit	Power	SB	Patience	Glove	Overall
	50	40	40	55	50	40

Born: 02/18/97	**Age:** 23	**Bats:** L
Height: 6-1	**Weight:** 165	**Throws:** R

YEAR	LVL	PA	1B	2B	3B	HR	SB	CS	AVG	OBP	SLG	BB%	K%	GB%	LD%	FB%
2017	A-	246	41	9	1	2	10	5	0.252	0.350	0.333	12.20%	19.11%	34.9	25.3	34.9
2018	A	466	65	26	5	8	5	3	0.256	0.330	0.404	9.23%	22.10%	34.9	21.6	33.0
2019	A+	384	71	14	3	5	11	8	0.276	0.358	0.380	10.68%	18.49%	35.8	19.2	36.6
2019	AA	72	8	3	0	2	1	1	0.210	0.306	0.355	12.50%	19.44%	26.5	18.4	42.9

Background: A late round pick by the Athletics coming out of Glenwood High School in 2015. Maton, who was taken in the 40th round, headed to in-state school Eastern Illinois. And after slugging .299/.351/.457 with 12 doubles, four triples, and three homeruns, Maton transferred to Lincoln Land Community College. One brief season with the JuCo school, Philadelphia snagged him in the seventh round in 2017. The 6-foot-1, 165-pound infielder looked mediocre during his debut in the New York-Penn League as he hit .252/.350/.333. But he began showing more thump during his season with Lakewood in Low Class A: he slugged .256/.330/.404 with 26 doubles, five triples, and eight homeruns in 114 games. Maton opened last season up with the Clearwater Threshers, hitting a career best .276/.358/.380 with 22 extra-base hits in 93 games. The front office bounced him up to Class AA. And, well, let's just say he struggled over a 21-game cameo; he hit a lowly .210/.306/.355.

Scouting Report: With respect to his work in High Class A, consider the following:

- Since 2006, here's the list of 22-year-old hitters to post a 122 to 132 DRC+ with a double digit walk rate and a sub-20.0% strikeout rate in the Florida State League (min. 300 PA): Hoy Jun Park, Miles Mastrobuoni, Phil Ervin, Reese Havens, Zelous Wheeler, Jeremy Vasquez, and Nick Maton.

Maton falls into that "do everything well without a true standout or noticeable flaw" category. He can run a bit, shoot the gaps well, belt out the occasional dinger, and flash a little leather. Throw in some versatility on defense and an above-average walk rate and Maton looks like a potential Brock Holt type role player. Holt, by the way, owns a career .271/.340/.374 triple-slash line in the big leagues.

Ceiling: 1.0- to 1.5-win player
Risk: Moderate
MLB ETA: 20201

19. Victor Santos, RHP

	FB	SL	CH	Command	Overall
	45	50	50/55	65	40

Born: 07/12/00	**Age:** 19	**Bats:** R
Height: 6-1	**Weight:** 191	**Throws:** R

YEAR	LVL	IP	W	L	SV	ERA	FIP	WHIP	K/9	K%	BB/9	BB%	K/BB	HR9	BABIP
2017	Rk	49.0	4	2	0	2.57	2.25	1.16	7.0	18.81%	0.9	2.48%	7.60	0.18	0.325
2018	Rk	59.3	6	1	0	3.03	2.58	1.13	9.9	27.08%	0.6	1.67%	16.25	0.61	0.355
2019	A	105.3	5	10	0	4.02	3.91	1.18	7.6	20.55%	1.5	4.16%	4.94	0.94	0.310

Background: Signed out of Villa Tapia, Dominican Republic, during the international signing period in 2016, Santos, a savvy right-hander, received a solid $150,000 bonus. The 6-foot-1, generously listed 191-pound right-hander made his debut in the foreign rookie league the following year, posting a phenomenal 38-to-5 strikeout-to-walk ratio in 49.0 innings as a 16-year-old. Philadelphia bounced the strike-throwing machine to the Gulf Coast League the next year. And Santos continued to dominate: he tossed 59.1 innings with an incredible 65-to-4 strikeout-to-walk ratio with a 3.03 ERA. Last season the ballclub aggressively pushed him up to the South Atlantic League. And, well, Santos pitched like a 15-year veteran. Making 27 appearances with the Lakewood BlueClaws, the Dominican righty fanned 89 and walked just 18 in 105.1 innings of work. He compiled a 4.02 ERA and a 5.28 DRA (*Deserved Run Average*).

Scouting Report: The antithesis of the modern day pitching prospect. Santos lacks the high octane fastball that six-figure bonuses are typically reserved for. Rather, he's like the da Vinci of the strike zone, painting the black of the plate like few others in the minor leagues – which allows for his mid- to upper-80s fastball play up several ticks. He'll complement the 45-grade heater with an average slider, and a Bugs Bunny-esque 79-mph changeup. Physically, Santos looks maxed out so there's not a ton of hope that he'll gain some precious ticks on the fastball. Consider the following:

- Since 2006, only two 18-year-old pitchers have posted a strikeout percentage between 19% and 22% with a sub-6.0% walk percentage in the Sally (min. 75 IP): Braves budding ace Mike Soroka and Victor Santos. The former, by the way, owns a significantly better DRA (3.55 vs. 5.28) and a vastly superior arsenal.

Ceiling: 1.0- to 1.5-win player
Risk: Moderate
MLB ETA: 2021/2022

20. Kyle Young, LHP

	FB	SL	CH	Command	Overall
	N/A	N/A	N/A	N/A	40

Born: 12/02/97	Age: 22	Bats: L
Height: 6-10	Weight: 205	Throws: L

YEAR	LVL	IP	W	L	SV	ERA	FIP	WHIP	K/9	K%	BB/9	BB%	K/BB	HR9	BABIP
2017	A-	65.0	7	2	0	2.77	2.20	1.12	10.0	27.38%	2.1	5.70%	4.80	0.14	0.329
2018	Rk	4.0	0	0	0	0.00	3.14	1.00	9.0	25.00%	4.5	12.50%	2.00	0.00	0.200
2018	A-	3.0	0	0	0	0.00	3.14	0.00	6.0	18.18%	0.0	0.00%	#DIV/0!	0.00	0.000
2018	A	52.3	3	3	0	3.10	2.73	1.01	7.6	21.67%	1.2	3.45%	6.29	0.34	0.295
2019	A+	21.0	1	3	0	4.29	2.31	1.05	10.7	29.76%	0.4	1.19%	25.00	0.86	0.339

Background: Built like a young Randy Johnson and blessed with a fastball like an old Tom Glavine. Young combines a gargantuan-sized frame with some pinpoint accuracy. A product of St. Dominic High School in Oyster Bay, New York, the 6-foot-10, 205-pound southpaw consistently posted phenomenal peripherals throughout his career. He finished his debut showing in the Gulf Coast League with a 19-to-2 strikeout-to-walk ratio in 27.0 innings of work. The former 22nd round selection struck out 72 and walked just 15 in 65.0 innings with the Williamsport Crosscutters in the New York-Penn League the following season. And despite missing a good portion of the 2018 season due to injury, Young still managed to average 7.6 strikeouts and just 1.2 walks per nine innings in nine starts with Lakewood. And last season began like any other for Young: he ripped through Dunedin, Fort Myers, and Tampa (twice) by fanning 25 against just one walk. But a wonky elbow forced him out of action at the end of April and eventually under the knife for Tommy John surgery by the end of May.

Snippet from The 2018 Prospect Digest Handbook: Young will continue to get plenty of looks in the rotation – as he should since the production's been great – but he's likely going to settle in as a reliever at some point. He just lacks the arsenal to effectively turn over a lineup multiple times in a game at the upper levels.

Scouting Report: An easy guy to root for because he's an atypical pitching prospect nowadays. Prior to the injury, the redwood-esque southpaw would attack hitters with a bevy of average-ish pitches: a 90 mph fastball that's deceptively quick due to his long limbs, a slider, and a changeup. He's similar to Oakland's 6-foot-9 right-handed pitching prospect Brian Howard: they get outs by doing the little things well, not by throwing it past hitters. He's still likely to wind up as a 40-grade reliever, especially against left-handed hitters. Here's hoping for a healthy and full return from the injury.

Ceiling: 1.0- to 1.5-win player
Risk: Moderate to High
MLB ETA: 2020

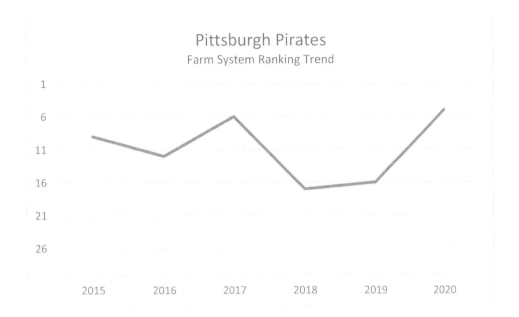

Rank	Name	Age	Pos
1	Mitch Keller	24	RHP
2	Oneil Cruz	21	SS
3	Ke'Bryan Hayes	23	3B
4	Liover Peguero	19	SS
5	Tahnaj Thomas	21	RHP
6	Travis Swaggerty	22	CF
7	Cody Bolton	22	RHP
8	Brennan Malone	23	RHP
9	Quinn Priester	19	RHP
10	Ji-Hwan Bae	20	2B/SS
11	Jack Herman	20	OF
12	Jared Oliva	24	CF
13	Lolo Sanchez	21	CF
14	Cal Mitchell	21	RF
15	Sammy Siani	19	CF
16	Mason Martin	21	1B
17	Travis MacGregor	22	RHP
18	Rodolfo Castro	21	IF
19	Luis Escobar	24	RHP
20	Matt Gorski	21	OF

1. Mitch Keller, RHP

	FB	CB	SL	CH	Command	Overall
	65	80	55	45	55	60

Born: 04/04/96	Age: 24	Bats: R
Height: 6-2	Weight: 210	Throws: R

YEAR	LVL	IP	W	L	SV	ERA	FIP	WHIP	K/9	K%	BB/9	BB%	K/BB	HR9	BABIP
2017	A-	4.0	0	0	0	0.00	1.43	0.75	15.8	43.75%	2.3	6.25%	7.00	0.00	0.286
2017	A+	77.3	6	3	0	3.14	3.54	1.00	7.4	20.92%	2.3	6.54%	3.20	0.58	0.248
2017	AA	34.7	2	2	0	3.12	2.51	1.04	11.7	31.69%	2.9	7.75%	4.09	0.52	0.280
2018	A+	4.0	0	0	0	2.25	3.22	2.00	4.5	10.53%	2.3	5.26%	2.00	0.00	0.438
2018	AA	86.0	9	2	0	2.72	3.72	1.12	8.0	22.22%	3.3	9.36%	2.38	0.73	0.251
2018	AAA	52.3	3	2	0	4.82	3.21	1.55	9.8	24.15%	3.8	9.32%	2.59	0.52	0.366
2019	AAA	103.7	7	5	0	3.56	3.59	1.24	10.7	29.85%	3.0	8.50%	3.51	0.78	0.315

Background: The long, *long* time crown jewel of the Pirates' farm system. Keller was originally selected in the second round of the 2014 draft, sandwiched between a couple of collegiate arms (Spencer Turnbull and Daniel Gossett). Keller, who's older brother Jon once pitched in the Orioles' system, hopped, skipped, and jumped through multiple levels at a time between 2016 and 2018. And that trend continued on through his 2019 campaign as well – except the hard-throwing right-hander reached the game's pinnacle level, multiple times. The younger Keller began the year on a bit of a sour note – he allowed five runs and walked six in 8.2 innings across two brief starts – but quickly got on track and earned his first call up to Pittsburgh for the start of a second game in a doubleheader against Cincinnati. From then on through the remainder of the year the club's top prospect would yo-yo between Indianapolis and the National League Central Division. In total, Keller would make 19 starts in the International League, throwing 103.2 innings with 123 strikeouts and 35 walks. He made an additional 11 starts with the Pirates, tossing 48.0 innings with a 65-to-16 strikeout-to-walk ratio.

Snippet from The 2018 Prospect Digest Handbook: Bred and developed to front the top of a rotation, the only thing the former second rounder is missing is an average third offering. Keller's fastball sits comfortably in the mid-90s, ranging between 93- and -95-mph with a peak of 97. He'll throw it to all four quadrants and isn't afraid to challenge hitters inside or up in the zone. His curveball is a career-defining offering – much in the same way Sandy Koufax's overhand deuce elevated him to mythical proportions. It shows hard, fall-off-the-table tumble and will lead to plenty of swings-and-misses at the big league level. Keller's changeup, though, leaves a lot to be desired. Underdeveloped at this point in his career, it's a straight 88-89-mph offering that lacks enough difference in velocity – or movement/deception – to be an oft-thrown pitch. Keller's likely to see some big league time in 2019, perhaps 15 or so starts, but it's imperative that he develops a workable third offering because that'll be the difference between a #3/#4-type arm and a #1/#2-type ceiling.

Scouting Report: The lack of a solid third offering was incredibly concerning to me, so much so in fact, that I listed Keller behind Oneil Cruz as the club's top prospect heading into last season. But something happened over the winter. Something...career defining. Keller scrapped the crappy changeup – almost altogether – and developed an above-average slider that added a *third* swing-and-miss option to his repertoire. The slider's tight with almost cutter-like movement at time, but his trust in the pitch matches that in his 80-grade curveball. In fact, he threw his slider with nearly double the frequency as his curveball – again, the best deuce in the minor leagues – during his stints in the big leagues. Love him. He's going to win the Rookie of the Year and be on the short list of perennial Cy Young contender barring any career altering injuries.

Ceiling: 5.0-win player
Risk: Low to Moderate
MLB ETA: Debuted in 2019

2. Oneil Cruz, SS

	Hit	Power	SB	Patience	Glove	Overall
	50/55	50/60	50/45	50	55	60

Born: 10/04/98	Age: 21	Bats: R
Height: 6-7	Weight: 175	Throws: R

YEAR	LVL	PA	1B	2B	3B	HR	SB	CS	AVG	OBP	SLG	BB%	K%	GB%	LD%	FB%
2017	A	375	64	9	1	8	8	7	0.240	0.293	0.342	7.47%	29.33%	58.6	15.2	22.4
2017	A	63	7	2	1	2	0	0	0.218	0.317	0.400	12.70%	34.92%	57.6	30.3	12.1
2018	A	443	69	25	7	14	11	5	0.286	0.343	0.488	7.67%	22.57%	53.6	18.6	22.5
2019	Rk	11	5	1	0	0	1	0	0.600	0.636	0.700	9.09%	9.09%	55.6	22.2	22.2
2019	A+	145	27	6	1	7	7	3	0.301	0.345	0.515	5.52%	26.21%	55.1	16.3	25.5
2019	AA	136	20	8	3	1	3	1	0.269	0.346	0.412	11.03%	25.74%	48.2	14.5	32.5

Background: Acquired along with right-hander Angel German from the Dodgers at the trade deadline three years ago, Cruz has blossomed into a bonafide blue chip prospect since entering the Pirates' farm system. The 6-foot-7, 175-pound man-child slugged a healthy .286/.343/.488 with 25 doubles, seven triples, and 14 homeruns – as well as 11 stolen bases – in a return to Low Class A in 2018. Last season the Dominican infielder split time between the Florida State and Eastern Leagues, as well as spending roughly two months on the disabled list. In total, the budding star slugged an impressive .298/.356/.475 with 15 doubles, four triples, and eight homeruns in 73 games. And just for good measure: he swiped 11 bags in 15 attempts.

Snippet from The 2018 Prospect Digest Handbook: Cruz is going to be the biggest breakout prospect in 2019. Bar none. He's likely going to shift over to third base. After all, how many 6-foot-6 shortstops are running around? The bat, though, will play anywhere. He's a game changer.

Scouting Report: Just for fun, here are his counting stats prorated over a full 162-game season: 33 doubles, nine triples, 18 homeruns, and 24 stolen bases. The big – pun intended – elephant in the room, obviously, is Cruz's massive frame size. Standing 6-foot-7, not only would he become the tallest shortstop in big league history (according to *Baseball Reference's* Play Index), but there's only one player who's played at least 25 games at the position who was 6-foot-5: Mike Morse, who lasted just one season as a shortstop for the Mariners. Cruz is just beginning to tap into his massive, plus power potential. There's 30- to 35-homer thunder brewing in his bat. Above-average speed, OK-ish contact rates, above-average defense, and proven production against significantly older competition. Ke'Bryan Hayes is the long term answer at the hot corner. So Cruz will have to beat out former top prospect Cole Tucker for the starting shortstop gig. He could – and should – become a full fledged star, a potential face of the franchise. At his peak, Cruz looks like a .280/.350/.480 type hitter.

Ceiling: 4.5-win player
Risk: Moderate
MLB ETA: 2020/2021

3. Ke'Bryan Hayes, 3B

	Hit	Power	SB	Patience	Glove	Overall
	45/50	40/45	40	50+	60	55

Born: 01/28/97	Age: 23	Bats: R
Height: 6-1	Weight: 210	Throws: R

YEAR	LVL	PA	1B	2B	3B	HR	SB	CS	AVG	OBP	SLG	BB%	K%	GB%	LD%	FB%
2017	A+	482	92	16	7	2	27	5	0.278	0.345	0.363	8.51%	15.77%	49.3	19.1	23.5
2018	AA	508	83	31	7	7	12	5	0.293	0.375	0.444	11.22%	16.54%	41.6	16.0	34.4
2019	AAA	480	71	30	2	10	12	1	0.265	0.336	0.415	8.96%	18.75%	46.9	19.2	26.8

Background: Fun Fact: Hayes' old man, Charlie, tied with Andy Benes for fifth in the 1989 National League Rookie of the Year Award, trailing Jerome Walton (the winner), Dwight Smith, Gregg Jefferies, and Derek Lilliquist. The younger Hayes, who patrols the same position as his father, was originally taken by the Pirates in the first round, 32nd overall, of the 2015 draft. Sandwiched between Chris Shaw and Nolan Watson, Hayes has handled a relatively aggressive promotion schedule. Last season the 6-foot-1, 210-pound third baseman – who often masquerades as the great Brooks Robinson – spent the entirety of the year in the International League, sans a three-game rehab stint in the New York-Penn League. In 110 games with the Indianapolis Indians, the slick fielding Hayes batted .265/.336/.415 with 30 doubles, two triples, and 10 homeruns while swiping 12 stolen bases in only 13 attempts. His overall production, per Baseball Prospectus' *Deserved Runs Created Plus*, was 4% below the league average threshold.

Snippet from The 2018 Prospect Digest Handbook: With each passing season Hayes makes a strong argument as one of the game's better third base prospects – even if he lacks the traditional in-game power typically required at the position, at least for now anyways.

Scouting Report: Hayes got off to a bit of a rocky start to the year in 2019, batting a lowly .241/.333/.388 with 20 doubles, two triples, and three homeruns through his first 58 contests. However, once he returned from a fractured left index finger he slugged a hearty .291/.339/.443 with 10 doubles and seven homeruns in 52 games. A slightly better than average eye with phenomenal contact skills, Hayes – for some reason – has been a bit susceptible to left-handers through his career. Beginning in 2017 through last season, here are his yearly OPS totals against southpaws (with his production vs. RHP in parenthesis: .639 (.731), .693 (.855), and .680 (.768). The power is still developing, though it may never get to a 50-grade tool. Defensively, he's going to win multiple – three, four, five, or more – Gold Gloves and a handful of Platinum Gloves in his career. In terms of offensive ceiling, think Jonathan Villar's 2019 campaign with the Orioles: .274/.339/.453.

Ceiling: 3.5-win player
Risk: Low to Moderate
MLB ETA: 2020

4. Liover Peguero, SS

	Hit	Power	SB	Patience	Glove	Overall
	45/55	35/50	45	50	50	55

Born: 12/31/00	Age: 19	Bats: R
Height: 6-1	Weight: 160	Throws: R

YEAR	LVL	PA	1B	2B	3B	HR	SB	CS	AVG	OBP	SLG	BB%	K%	GB%	LD%	FB%
2018	RK	90	18	3	3	1	4	1	0.309	0.356	0.457	6.67%	13.33%	42.3	22.5	28.2
2018	RK	71	13	0	0	0	3	2	0.197	0.254	0.197	7.04%	23.94%	69.4	14.3	14.3
2019	Rk+	156	37	7	3	5	8	1	0.364	0.410	0.559	7.69%	21.79%	56.4	21.8	19.1
2019	A-	93	16	4	2	0	3	1	0.262	0.333	0.357	8.60%	18.28%	53.7	17.9	20.9

Background: Overshadowed by two highly touted amateurs – Kristian Robinson and Jorge Barrosa – as part of the Diamondbacks' haul on the international scene, Peguero, nonetheless, is developing into quite the prospect himself. After quickly handling the foreign league competition, but floundering in a late season promotion to the stateside rookie league, Peguero ripped through the Pioneer League in the opening half of 2019. In 38 games with Missoula, the 6-foot-1, 160-pound shortstop slugged .264/.410/.559 with seven doubles, three triples, and five homeruns with eight stolen bases. His numbers declined – predictably – upon his promotion up to Hillsboro; he batted .262/.333/.357 with four doubles and a pair of triples with the Hops. Pittsburgh acquired the young shortstop, along with 2019 first rounder Brennan Malone and international bonus money, from the Diamondbacks in exchange for outfielder Starling Marte this offseason.

Scouting Report: With respect to his work in the Pioneer League last season, consider the following:

- Since 2006, here's the list of 18-year-olf hitters to post a 150 to 165 DRC+ in the Pioneer League (min. 150 PA): Jesse Winker, Caleb Gindl, and Liover Peguero.

The offensive numbers in the opening portion of the year are a bit misleading. The Pioneer League tends to inflate numbers quite a bit. But…Peguero's batted ball data was nothing short of phenomenal. According to FanGraphs, the then-18-year-old posted an average exit velocity of 90 mph with a peak of 105 mph. Solid speed, glove, and a hit tool that could climb to a 55-grade. Arizona's front office seems determined to push Peguero aggressively through the system as long as he proves himself at a level over a reasonable amount of time. It wouldn't be shocking to see the Pirates take a similar approach. Very intriguing upside.

Ceiling: 3.0- to 3.5-win player
Risk: Moderate
MLB ETA: 2022

5. Tahnaj Thomas, RHP

FB	CB	CH	Command	Overall
65	55	N/A	50	55

Born: 06/16/99	Age: 21	Bats: R
Height: 6-4	Weight: 190	Throws: R

YEAR	LVL	IP	W	L	SV	ERA	FIP	WHIP	K/9	K%	BB/9	BB%	K/BB	HR9	BABIP
2017	Rk	33.0	0	3	0	6.00	6.49	1.82	7.9	18.83%	6.8	16.23%	1.16	1.09	0.330
2017	Rk	5.3	0	2	0	3.38	5.86	2.06	8.4	18.52%	13.5	29.63%	0.63	0.00	0.214
2018	Rk	19.7	0	0	0	4.58	4.32	1.17	12.4	33.75%	4.6	12.50%	2.70	0.92	0.275
2019	Rk	48.3	2	3	0	3.17	3.64	1.12	11.0	29.50%	2.6	7.00%	4.21	0.93	0.292

Background: Originally signed out of Freeport, Bahamas, as a shortstop by the Indians and immediately converted into a pitcher. The Pirates acquired the promising, albeit raw project with utility infielder Erik Gonzalez for Jordan Luplow, Max Moroff, and big right-hander Dante Mendoza. Thomas, a 6-foot-4, 190-pound right-hander, is coming off of two strong back-to-back seasons in the low levels of the minor leagues. After struggling through his first tour in the Arizona League, Thomas returned to the stateside rookie league with a vengeance in 2018; he averaged 12.4 strikeouts and 4.6 walks per nine innings during his final season in the Cleveland farm system. Last season Pittsburgh pushed him up to the Appalachian League and the Bahamian fireballer took some promising developmental steps forward. In 12 starts with Bristol, he posted a 59-to-14 strikeout-to-walk ratio in 48.1 innings of work. He compiled a 3.17 ERA and a 3.77 DRA (Deserved Runs Average).

Scouting Report: Originally a low level lottery ticket that's increasing his odds of paying off – in a large way. Consider the following:

- Since 2006, here's the list of 20-year-old pitchers to post at least a 29.0% strikeout percentage and a sub-7.0% walk percentage in the Appalachian League (min. 45 IP): Josiah Gray, a top prospect in the Dodgers' system; Boone Whiting; Ross Francis; Martire Garcia; and Tahnaj Thomas.

Explosive plus- to plus-fastball with riding, late life. A curveball that may eventually climb into 60-grade territory. And he'll mix in a changeup, though I didn't see one. Throw in some improving control / command and Thomas is quietly becoming a legitimate top pitching prospect. The wiry right-hander may see another slight uptick in velocity as he gains experience and strength. This is a bit of an aggressive ranking, but he could eventually settle in as a mid-rotation caliber arm with the floor of a high-leverage relief arm.

Ceiling: 3.0- to 3.5-win player
Risk: Moderate
MLB ETA: 2022

6. Travis Swaggerty, CF

Hit	Power	SB	Patience	Glove	Overall
55	40/45	50	50	60	50

Born: 08/19/97	Age: 22	Bats: L
Height: 5-11	Weight: 180	Throws: L

YEAR	LVL	PA	1B	2B	3B	HR	SB	CS	AVG	OBP	SLG	BB%	K%	GB%	LD%	FB%
2018	A-	158	26	9	1	4	9	3	0.288	0.365	0.453	9.49%	25.32%	41.6	24.8	27.7
2018	A	71	5	1	1	1	0	0	0.129	0.225	0.226	9.86%	25.35%	40.0	8.9	40.0
2019	A+	524	89	20	3	9	23	8	0.265	0.347	0.381	10.88%	22.14%	50.7	14.4	26.8

Background: Despite a bit of downturn in production during his junior campaign the Pirates drafted for the South Alabama center fielder with the tenth overall selection, bypassing top prospects like Logan Gilbert, Grayson Rodriguez, Nolan Gorman, or Brice Turang – just to name a few.

Swaggerty, a wiry 5-foot-11, 180-pound center fielder, split time between the New York-Penn and South Atlantic Leagues during his debut, batting a disappointing .239/.322/.383 with 10 doubles, two triples, and five homeruns. The front office opted to push the young outfielder straight into the California League – in spite of his late season struggles with the West Virginia Power during his debut. And the results were…as expected, more or less. Swaggerty batted a mediocre .265/.347/.381 with 20 doubles, three triples, and nine homeruns. He also swiped 23 bags in 31 attempts. His overall production, per *Deserved Runs Created Plus*, topped the league average mark by 24%.

Snippet from The 2018 Prospect Digest Handbook: Swaggerty's offensive foundation is enough to push him into starting material at the big league level. And while he hasn't consistently played against top notch talent as other prospects in the SEC or PAC12, his work for Team USA helps allay some fears. In terms of big league ceiling, think .280/.330/.400 with a dozen or so homeruns and stolen bases.

Scouting Report: Consider the following:

- Since 2006, here's the list of 21-year-old hitters to post a DRC+ between 120 and 130 with a strikeout rate between 21% and 23% in the Florida State League (min. 300 PA): Marcell Ozuna, Chris Parmelee, Kirk Nieuwenhuis, and – of course – Travis Swaggerty. Sans Swaggerty, here are their respective big league career DRC+ totals: 108 (Ozuna), 96 (Parmelee), and 74 (Nieuwenhuis).

A few random-ish thoughts:

- The former South Alabama star fits the mold as many of the club's other top center fielders: a toolsy, defensive-minded athlete.
- After a slow start to the year in which he batted .213/.311/.311 over his first 64 games, Swaggerty's production leapt in another stratosphere over his final 57 contests as he slugged .324/.389/.460.
- I'm betting on the second half production; the first half was – likely – due to a learning curve and aggressive promotion schedule.
- The power may never push the needle above a 45.

He's borderline elite in center field with a floor as a low end starter and I think the ceiling still resides in the .280/.330/.400 neighborhood as I wrote in last year's book.

Ceiling: 3.0-win player
Risk: Moderate
MLB ETA: 2020/2021

7. Cody Bolton, RHP

FB	SL	CU	CH	Command	Overall
60	60	60	45	50+	50

Born: 06/19/98	Age: 22	Bats: R
Height: 6-3	Weight: 185	Throws: R

YEAR	LVL	IP	W	L	SV	ERA	FIP	WHIP	K/9	K%	BB/9	BB%	K/BB	HR9	BABIP
2017	Rk	25.7	0	2	0	3.16	3.14	1.21	7.7	20.56%	2.8	7.48%	2.75	0.35	0.286
2018	A	44.3	3	3	0	3.65	3.73	1.13	9.1	25.14%	1.4	3.91%	6.43	1.22	0.308
2019	A+	61.7	6	3	0	1.61	1.96	0.86	10.1	28.87%	2.0	5.86%	4.93	0.15	0.245
2019	AA	40.0	2	3	0	5.85	4.66	1.33	7.4	19.76%	3.6	9.58%	2.06	1.35	0.277

Background: Just another one of the examples of how well the Pirates find – and sign – talent outside the first few rounds of the draft. Pittsburgh selected the 6-foot-3, 185-pound right-hander in the sixth round, 178th overall, in the 2017 June draft and – of course – signed him to an above-slot bonus. Bolton immediately started paying dividends. He posted a 22-to-8 strikeout-to-walk ratio in 25.2 innings of work in the Gulf Coast League during his debut. The front office bumped the hard-throwing youngster up to the South Atlantic League the following year, 2018, and he dominated in an injury-shortened campaign. He averaged 9.1 strikeouts and just 1.7 walks per nine innings to go along with a 3.65 ERA. Despite the shortened tenure in Low Class A – he tossed fewer than 50 innings – the Pirates' brass, once again, challenged Bolton by sending him directly up to High Class A to start last season. After 12 absurdly strong starts he earned a promotion up to the minors' toughest challenge, Class AA, for the remainder of the year. In all, the Tracy High School product posted an impeccable 102-to-30 strikeout-to-walk ratio in 101.2 innings of work.

Snippet from The 2018 Prospect Digest Handbook: As far as the production is concerned, consider the following:

- Between 2006 and 2016, only three 20-year-old pitchers posted a strikeout percentage between 24% and 26% with a sub-6.0% walk percentage in the Sally (min. 40 IP): Felix Doubront, Brooks Pounders, and Luis Severino. It's incredibly promising that all three went on to eventually make the big leagues – though Bolton slides next to Doubront and Pounders.

Scouting Report: Easily, easily the best pitcher you've never heard of. Bolton looks like a bonafide upper-part-of-the-rotation caliber arm in the making. I scouted a handful of his games last season. His fastball was sitting – *effortlessly* – in the 94- to 96-mph range and touching 98 mph several times. He features two types of breaking pitches, though they're quasi-similar. His slider is a wipeout swing-and-miss offering, sitting in the 87- to 88-mph neighborhood. He'll also feature a hard, low-90s cutter that he throws the same way as his slider. Bolton, like Mitch Keller, throws a subpar, too firm changeup; though the former's does show some promising fade and arm-side run. Bolton has the feel of a #3 / #4 type pitcher. With respect to his work in High Class A last season, consider the following:

- Since 2006, here's the list of 21-year-old pitchers to post a strikeout percentage between 27% and 30% with a sub-% walk percentage in the Florida State League (min. 50 IP): Brent Honeywell, Wade Davis, Daniel Norris, Cole Sands, Rafael Montero, Victor Arano, and Cody Bolton.

Ceiling: 3.0-win player
Risk: Moderate
MLB ETA: 2020

8. Brennan Malone, RHP

	FB	CB	SL	CH	Command	Overall
	65	50	55/60	45/50	45/50	55

Born: 09/08/00	Age: 19	Bats: R
Height: 6-4	Weight: 205	Throws: R

YEAR	LVL	IP	W	L	SV	ERA	FIP	WHIP	K/9	K%	BB/9	BB%	K/BB	HR9	BABIP
2019	Rk	7.0	1	2	0	5.14	4.39	1.29	9.0	24.14%	6.4	17.24%	1.40	0.00	0.176
2019	A-	1.0	0	0	0	0.00	1.62	0.00	9.0	33.33%	0.0	0.00%	#DIV/0!	0.00	0.000

Background: Along with Jack Leiter and Matthew Allen, Malone's name belonged in the conversation for top prep arm in the months heading into last year's draft. Malone, who committed verbally to the University of North Carolina in the fall of 2016, was lights out for Indian Trail Porter Ridge High School two years ago; in 51.1 innings the hard-throwing right-hander fanned a whopping 76 and compiled a barely there 1.36 ERA. The broad-shouldered right-hander spent the following summer playing for the 18U Team USA National squad, throwing 8.1 innings of working with nine punch outs and nine walks. He was particularly dominant against the Dominican Republic (4.1 innings and 4 strikeouts) and helped propel Team USA to the gold medal game by working three innings against a solid Nicaragua team. Malone transferred to IMG academy prior to his senior season. Perfect Game tabbed him as a 2019 Preseason All-American and All-Region Teams. The Diamondbacks snagged him near the back of the first round, 33rd, and limited his debut to just 8.0 innings between the Arizona Summer and Northwest Leagues; he fanned eight and walked five.

Scouting Report: Huge, burly frame that looks like he should be playing professionally as a tight end or a linebacker. Malone attacks hitters with an impressive four pitch mix: his explosive fastball sits comfortably in the mid-90s with significant run on his two-seamer; his curveball shows solid 12-6 break; his slider, often times resembling a cutter, flashes plus; and his changeup should become an average weapon in his arsenal. Malone's an interesting prospect because his max effort and massive frame suggest a future reliever. Bu the has the potential to develop into a strong – pun intended – starting pitcher.

Ceiling: 2.5- to 3.0-win player
Risk: Moderate
MLB ETA: 2022/2023

9. Quinn Priester, RHP

FB	CB	CH	Command	Overall
60	60	N/A	45/50	50

Born: 09/15/00	Age: 19	Bats: R
Height: 6-3	Weight: 195	Throws: R

YEAR	LVL	IP	W	L	SV	ERA	FIP	WHIP	K/9	K%	BB/9	BB%	K/BB	HR9	BABIP
2019	Rk	32.7	1	1	0	3.03	2.91	1.19	10.2	26.43%	2.8	7.14%	3.70	0.28	0.318
2019	A-	4.0	0	0	0	4.50	5.15	1.75	9.0	21.05%	9.0	21.05%	1.00	0.00	0.300

Background: A two-sport star for Cary-Grove High School. Priester, who stands 6-foot-3 and 195 pounds, switched from quarterback to wide receiver and defensive back prior to his final go-round on the grid iron. The squad finished with a perfect 14-0 record, including 8-0 in conference play, as they captured the school's first state championship since 2009. A commit to Big12 Conference powerhouse Texas Christian University, who locked him in verbally during his sophomore season, Priester went to the Pirates in the opening round, 18th overall, last June. The two sides agreed to a pact worth $3.4 million, just a smidgeon below the assigned slot value of $3,481,300. Priester made eight appearances in the Gulf Coast League and one final, four-inning start in the New York-Penn League during his debut, posting an impressive 41-to-14 strikeout-to-walk ratio in 36.2 innings of work. He compiled a 3.19 ERA.

Scouting Report: Here's what I wrote about the hard-throwing right-hander prior to the draft last season:

"Showing easily repeatable, almost effortless mechanics; Priester attacks hitters with a deadly combination of a lively low- to mid-90s fastball and a sharp, late-breaking curveball – both grading out as plus pitches. His heater will show some solid arm side run at times as well. Reports indicate that he'll mix in a changeup at times, though he's mainly a two-pitch hurler at this point. As with a lot of young arms, his third pitch – the changeup – hasn't been used frequently. Priester looks like a potential mid-rotation caliber arm."

Ceiling: 2.5-win player
Risk: Moderate
MLB ETA: 2022

10. Ji-Hwan Bae, 2B/SS

Hit	Power	SB	Patience	Glove	Overall
55/60	20/40	60	55	50	50

Born: 07/26/99	Age: 20	Bats: L
Height: 6-1	Weight: 170	Throws: R

YEAR	LVL	PA	1B	2B	3B	HR	SB	CS	AVG	OBP	SLG	BB%	K%	GB%	LD%	FB%
2018	RK	152	27	6	2	0	10	4	0.271	0.362	0.349	9.87%	10.53%	55.2	14.7	28.4
2019	A	380	76	25	5	0	31	11	0.323	0.403	0.430	11.32%	20.26%	52.2	20.9	24.5

Background: A representative of South Korea in the 2017 U18 Baseball World Cup, Bae, who batted a respectable .286 with a handful of RBIs and a pair of stolen bases, signed with Pittsburgh for a hefty $1.25 million. He made his stateside debut in the Gulf Coast League two years ago, hitting .271/.362/.349 with six doubles, a pair of triples, and 10 stolen bases (in 14 total attempts). His overall production, according to *Deserved Runs Created Plus*, topped the league average threshold by 24%. The front office maintained status quo and aggressively challenged the youngster by assigning him to the South Atlantic League last season. And the 6-foot-1, 170-pound lefty-swinging middle infielder answered the challenge – resoundingly. Despite missing six weeks at the start of the year, Bae went on to slug .323/.403/.430 with 25 doubles, five triples, and 31 stolen bases. His production topped 58% above the league average mark.

Scouting Report: Consider the following:

- Since 2006, only two 19-year-old hitters posted a 150 DRC+ or better in the South Atlantic League (min. 300 PA): former Orioles top prospect Chance Sisco, who's been disappointing in three stints in the big leagues, and Ji-Hwan Bae.

The potential to have a 60-grade hit tool and some defensive versatility. The Eiffel Tower-sized red flag, of course, has been Bae's lack of thunder in his bat. He's slugged exactly *zero* homeruns in 121 career minor league games. On the other hand, Bae belted out 30 extra-base hits in only 86 games last season. Prorating those numbers over a 162 game season: 47 doubles and nine triples. Meaning: the power's on its way in terms of over the fence production. He's very intriguing as a potential starting caliber infielder. But the pop has to start showing up in the next couple of years.

Ceiling: 2.5-win player
Risk: Moderate
MLB ETA: 2022

11. Jack Herman, OF

Hit	Power	SB	Patience	Glove	Overall
45	50	35	50	60	50

Born: 09/30/99	Age: 20	Bats: R	
Height: 6-0	Weight: 190	Throws: R	

YEAR	LVL	PA	1B	2B	3B	HR	SB	CS	AVG	OBP	SLG	BB%	K%	GB%	LD%	FB%
2018	RK	169	34	9	3	2	2	2	0.340	0.435	0.489	13.61%	14.20%	45.0	22.5	27.5
2019	A	300	41	12	2	13	6	6	0.257	0.340	0.464	9.33%	29.33%	46.6	21.8	28.7

Background: If unearthing Mason Martin's thunder in the 17th round wasn't impressive enough, the Pirates dipped way down in the 2018 draft and grabbed Jack Herman in the 30th round, making him the 894th overall player taken. A product of Eastern High School, who's churned out just four other players that eventually got drafted, Herman went all Ty Cobb on the Gulf Coast League during his debut two years ago when he slashed a scorching .340/.435/.489 with nine doubles, three triples, two homeruns, and a pair of stolen bases. And similarly with Martin, the front office – aggressively – pushed him straight up to the South Atlantic League for his sophomore campaign. Herman, though, fared spectacularly better. In 75 games with the Greensboro Grasshoppers, the 6-foot, 190-pound outfielder batted a more than respectable .257/.340/.464 with 12 doubles, two triples, 13 homeruns, and half of a dozen stolen bases. Per Baseball Prospectus' *Deserved Runs Created Plus*, his overall production topped the league average mark by 25%.

Scouting Report: Consider the following:

- Since 2006, only three 19-year-old hitters met the following criteria in the South Atlantic League (min. 250 PA): a DRC+ between 120 and 130 and a strikeout rate between 27% and 30%. Those three hitters: Austin Riley, who made his big league debut after years of being listed among the Braves' top prospects; Nick Williams, roughly a league-average bat in two of his three big league seasons and long time top prospect; and Jack Herman, the former 30th round pick.

Like Mason Martin, Herman's showed some serious swing-and-miss issues last season, whiffing on 29.3% of his plate appearances. However, there's two major differentiating factors: #1 Herman whiffed far less during their debuts in the rookie league (14.2% vs. 24.7%) and #2 Herman fanned less during each of their respective first stints in the Sally (29.3% vs. 35.8%). Herman also adds a tremendous amount of value in the outfield; he was an elite defender in either corner outfield spot last season. Nick Williams, a toolsy outfielder in his own right, is a solid comparison moving forward.

Ceiling: 2.5-win player
Risk: Moderate
MLB ETA: 2022

12. Jared Oliva, CF

Hit	Power	SB	Patience	Glove	Overall
50	45	65	50	50	50

Born: 11/27/95	Age: 24	Bats: R	Top CALs:
Height: 6-3	Weight: 203	Throws: R	

YEAR	LVL	PA	1B	2B	3B	HR	SB	CS	AVG	OBP	SLG	BB%	K%	GB%	LD%	FB%
2017	A-	254	42	10	7	0	15	4	0.266	0.327	0.374	6.69%	22.44%	51.1	21.0	22.2
2018	A+	454	72	24	4	9	33	8	0.275	0.354	0.424	8.81%	20.04%	46.5	15.7	30.4
2019	AA	507	88	24	6	6	36	10	0.277	0.352	0.398	8.28%	20.51%	48.9	14.0	29.4

Background: An up-and-down production line during his first two seasons at the University of Arizona, Oliva's collegiate career culminated in a seventh round selection after slugging .321/.385/.498 with 2 doubles, three triples, and four homeruns during his junior campaign. And not including a mediocre showing in the New York-Penn League during his professional debut in 2017, Oliva's offense hasn't missed a beat. He handled the aggressive assignment up to Bradenton at the start of 2018 by hitting .275/.354/.424. And the 6-foot-3, 203-pound center fielder acquitted himself nicely in the minors' toughest challenge, Class AA, last season. In a career best 123 games with the Altoona Curve, Oliva hit .277/.352/.398 with 24 doubles, six triples, and six homeruns with a career best 36 stolen bases. He continued to surpass expectations in the Arizona Fall League as well, slugging .312/.413/.473 in 26 games.

Snippet from The 2018 Prospect Digest Handbook: If Oliva's defense improves a bit, he's starting caliber material. Otherwise, he's very strong fourth outfield option for any club.

Scouting Report: Consider the following:

- Since 2006, only four 23-year-old hitters met the following criteria in the Eastern League (min. 350 PA): 123 to 133 DRC+; a walk rate between 7% and 10%; and a strikeout rate between 19% and 22%. Those four hitters and their big league career DRC+ totals are: Christian Walker (107), Eric Thames (104), Luis Antonio Jimenez (69 in only 18 PA).

So...the defense improved a bit last season, going from below average to average – which is exactly what needed to happen for the former Wildcat. He'll run into enough pitches at the big league level to belt out 8- to 12-homeruns in a year. But his speed is a game changer. In terms of offensive peak, Oliva's likely to be a .260/.340/.420 – something close to Andrew Benintendi's 2019 season.

Ceiling: 2.0-win player
Risk: Low to Moderate
MLB ETA: 2019

13. Lolo Sanchez, CF

Hit	Power	SB	Patience	Glove	Overall
45/55	35/45	60	50	55	50

Born: 04/23/99	Age: 21	Bats: R
Height: 5-11	Weight: 168	Throws: R

YEAR	LVL	PA	1B	2B	3B	HR	SB	CS	AVG	OBP	SLG	BB%	K%	GB%	LD%	FB%
2017	RK	234	11	2	4	4	14	7	0.284	0.359	0.417	8.97%	8.12%	51.1	13.7	24.2
2018	A	441	69	18	1	4	30	13	0.243	0.322	0.328	9.30%	16.33%	44.0	18.9	24.8
2019	A	263	48	10	6	4	20	10	0.301	0.377	0.451	6.46%	10.65%	51.5	13.6	21.8
2019	A+	195	25	3	3	1	13	5	0.196	0.300	0.270	9.23%	15.90%	50.4	11.1	28.9

Background: Pittsburgh inked the toolsy center fielder during the summer signing period in 2015 for $450,000. Sanchez, who stands a wiry 5-foot-11 and 168 pounds, looked dreadfully underwhelming during his debut in the foreign rookie league the following year, hitting a lowly .235/.359/.275 in 45 games.

The front office, nonetheless, pushed the then-18-year-old outfielder stateside in 2017. And his bat finally started showing some signs of life. He hit a respectable .284/.359/.417 with 17 extra-base hits in 51 games. Sanchez spent the 2018 campaign squaring off against the South Atlantic League competition – though he came up mostly on the losing end (.243/.322/.328). Of course, Sanchez found himself back with Greensboro to start last season. And the results were significantly improved: he slugged .301/.37/.451 with 10 doubles, six triples, four homeruns and 20 stolen bases in only 61 games. He was promoted up to the Florida State League near the end of June, but looked as bad as ever for the remainder of the year; he hit .196/.300/.270 in 52 games.

Snippet from The 2018 Prospect Digest Handbook: Sanchez's bat wasn't just cold during the opening couple months of the year, it was downright arctic. He batted a putrid .165/.242/.243 over his first 31 games. But beginning on May 17th, he batted an impressive .278/.355/.365 with a 111 wRC+. A speed demon who is just learning how to tap into his potential on the base paths and in center field. Sanchez has the potential to be an elite defender with double-digit homer potential. He's still incredibly raw, but there's starting caliber potential here; it's just years away.

Scouting Report: As streaky as ever – clearly. Let's take a look at how his production in a do-over of Low Class A stacks up against his peers. Consider the following:

- Since 2006, only three 20-year-old hitters met the following criteria in the South Atlantic League (min. 250 PA): 138 to 148 DRC+; a sub-15% strikeout rate; and a walk rate below 7%. Those three hitters: Jose Altuve, Malquin Canelo, and Lolo Sanchez.

Now let's take a look at his work in the Florida State League:

- Since 2006, Sanchez is the only 20-year-old hitter to post a sub-70 DRC+ with a sub-15% strikeout rate and a walk rate between 8% and 10% in the Florida State League (min. 175 PA).

Tremendously talented, but – again – quite streaky. When's he's clicking on all cylinders he flashes an above-average hit tool, plus speed, 15-homerun power potential, tremendous contact skills, a solid eye at the plate, and above-average defense in center field. That's the recipe for an All-Star performer at the big league level. The problem, of course, is that he hasn't put it all together for an entire year. He's heading back to High Class A to start 2019 but will likely spend a good portion of the year in Class AA as well.

Ceiling: 2.0-win player
Risk: Moderate
MLB ETA: 2021/2022

14. Cal Mitchell, RF

	Hit	Power	SB	Patience	Glove	Overall
	45	50/55	30	45+	50	50

Born: 03/08/99	Age: 21	Bats: L
Height: 6-0	Weight: 209	Throws: L

YEAR	LVL	PA	1B	2B	3B	HR	SB	CS	AVG	OBP	SLG	BB%	K%	GB%	LD%	FB%
2017	RK	185	26	11	0	2	2	3	0.245	0.351	0.352	12.97%	18.92%	33.9	18.5	34.7
2018	A	495	82	29	3	10	4	5	0.280	0.344	0.427	8.28%	22.02%	39.7	27.9	25.6
2019	A+	493	75	21	2	15	1	1	0.251	0.304	0.406	6.49%	28.80%	35.4	19.9	37.0

Background: With handsome, chiseled good looks of a young, up-and-coming actor, the 6-foot, 209-pound outfielder's notoriety shot through the roof after a tremendous showing in the South Atlantic League as a teenager in 2018. Mitchell, a second round pick out of Rancho Bernardo High School in 2017, slugged an impressive .280/.344/.427 with 29 doubles, three triples, and 10 homeruns in 119 games. His overall production, per *Deserved Runs Created Plus*, topped the league average mark by 27%. Gaining some traction in national publications heading into last season, the organization pushed the young right fielder up to the Florida State – where his numbers, unsurprisingly, stumbled a bit. In 118 with the Bradenton Marauders, Mitchell batted .251/.304/.406 with 21 doubles, two triples, and a career best 15 homeruns. This time his production line topped the league average threshold by just 4%.

Snippet from The 2018 Prospect Digest Handbook: His monthly OPS totals beginning with April are: 1.043, .791, .709, .611, and .672. Certainly a disturbing trend for a bat-first prospect. Mitchell isn't very patient and won't add any value on the defensive side of the ball, so it's all going to come down to his power. Right now, he looks like a fringy starter on a non-contender.

Scouting Report: Just the like the year before Mitchell's production cratered as the season wore on. The former second rounder batted a healthy .279/.315/.453 with 25 extra-base hits through his first 63 games. He promptly followed that up with a .212/.290/.342 triple-slash line over his remaining 55 contests. What's the cause? After back-to-back seasons like this it could very well be that he's not making any adjustments or not making them quickly enough. Above-average power potential, but his swing-and-miss issues bumped up to full blown red flag territory last season. With respect to his production, consider the following:

- Since 2006, only two 20-year-old hitters posted a DRC+ total between 100 and 110 with a strikeout rate north of 25% in the Florida State League (min. 300 PA): Yankees top prospect Estevan Florial and – of course – Cal Mitchell, who walks nearly has as often as his counterpart.

Mitchell's still a borderline starting outfielder contender. He still has plenty of youth on his side and is set to enter Class AA.

Ceiling: 2.0-win player
Risk: Moderate
MLB ETA: 2022

15. Sammy Siani, CF

	Hit	Power	SB	Patience	Glove	Overall
	35/45	30/45	50	50	50	45

Born: 12/14/00	Age: 19	Bats: L
Height: 6-0	Weight: 195	Throws: L

YEAR	LVL	PA	1B	2B	3B	HR	SB	CS	AVG	OBP	SLG	BB%	K%	GB%	LD%	FB%
2019	Rk	164	26	3	3	0	5	0	0.241	0.372	0.308	15.85%	25.00%	52.1	19.1	23.4

Background: The younger brother of Cincinnati Reds top prospect Michael Siani, who was taken in the fourth round two years ago, Sammy holds the family distinction of hearing his name called three rounds earlier last June. The 37th overall pick, Siani, who signed for an above-slot bonus of $2.15 million, went out with a bang at William Penn Charter School as he slugged .457 with 25 RBIs and 16 stolen bases during his senior season. After signing with the Pirates, Siani moved into the Gulf Coast League and batted a mediocre .241/.372/.308 with just six extra-base hits (three doubles and three triples) in 39 games. His overall production was 5% below the league average mark according to *Deserved Runs Created Plus*. He was previously committed to Duke University.

Scouting Report: Just oozing athleticism with plus speed to spare, Siani has the physical tools in place to effective patrol center fielder for a long time. The question with the younger Siani is if he'll hit enough to justify the everyday spot in the lineup in the coming years. The bat speed is, without question, legit. But the ability to make consistent contact might be an issue moving forward – and that's before factoring in his whiff rate during his debut (25%). One final note: it looks like he has a tendency to chase pitches and regularly miss "his pitch".

Ceiling: 1.5- to 2.0-win player
Risk: Moderate
MLB ETA: 2022/2023

16. Mason Martin, 1B

Hit	Power	SB	Patience	Glove	Overall
40/45	65	35	55	55	45

Born: 06/02/99	Age: 21	Bats: L
Height: 6-0	Weight: 201	Throws: R

YEAR	LVL	PA	1B	2B	3B	HR	SB	CS	AVG	OBP	SLG	BB%	K%	GB%	LD%	FB%
2017	RK	166	20	8	0	11	2	2	0.307	0.457	0.630	19.28%	24.70%	29.2	15.7	46.1
2018	RK	269	31	10	1	10	2	2	0.233	0.357	0.422	15.61%	32.34%	39.1	18.1	34.1
2018	A	173	18	8	0	4	1	1	0.200	0.302	0.333	10.40%	35.84%	47.2	20.2	25.8
2019	A	355	34	19	3	23	8	2	0.262	0.361	0.575	12.96%	29.01%	37.9	20.2	37.4

Background: Plucked out of Southridge High School all the way in the 17th round, 508th overall, and handed a hefty $350,000 bonus. Martin, a former two-sport star during his high school days, was just recognized by *Baseball America* as the Pirates' Minor League Player of the Year. A well-built, quick-twitch athlete, Martin first opened some eyes after an explosive landing in the Gulf Coast League during his debut, slugging a hefty .307/.457/.630 with eight doubles and 11 homeruns. The Washington native promptly fell on his face as the front office aggressively shoved him into the South Atlantic League the following year, hitting a lowly .200/.302/.333 before getting demoted down to Bristol. Unsurprisingly, the 6-foot, 201-pound first baseman found himself back in the Sally for a do over. This time, though, the results were wildly different. Appearing in 82 games with the Greensboro Grasshoppers, Martin battered the competition to the tune of .262/.361/.575 with 19 doubles, three triples, and 23 homeruns. Pittsburgh bounced him up to High Class A in early July; he hit .239/.333/.528 with the Marauders the rest of the way.

Scouting Report: With respect to his work in the Sally last season, consider the following:

- Since 2006, only here's the list of 20-year-old hitters that posted a DRC+ of at least 150 and a double-digit walk rate in either Low Class A league (min. 300 PA): Nolan Jones, Mookie Betts, Derek Norris, Greg Bird, Rosell Herrera, Tyler Austin, Clint Coulter, Canaan Smith, Will Swanner, and Mason Martin.

There's a lot of intriguing names mixed in the aforementioned group, so let's continue:

- Among the aforementioned group, here's the list of players to fan in at least 25% of their plate appearances: Will Swanner and Mason Martin.

That's pretty damning, no? Of course, it's going to come down to Martin's ability – or inability – to make consistent contact. He's fanned in 30.8% of his career plate appearances and that includes whiffing in 30.2% of the time last season. Game changing, plus-plus in-game power, above-average patience at the plate, and a solid glove at first base. He's a TTO (Three True Outcomes) hitter, and that likely won't change.

Ceiling: 1.5- to 2.0-win player
Risk: Moderate to High
MLB ETA: 2022

17. Travis MacGregor, RHP

FB	CB	CH	Command	Overall
N/A	N/A	N/A	N/A	45

Born: 10/15/97	Age: 22	Bats: R
Height: 6-3	Weight: 180	Throws: R

YEAR	LVL	IP	W	L	SV	ERA	FIP	WHIP	K/9	K%	BB/9	BB%	K/BB	HR9	BABIP
2017	Rk	41.3	1	4	0	7.84	5.11	1.96	7.0	15.31%	4.4	9.57%	1.60	0.65	0.389
2018	Rk	7.0	0	0	0	2.57	4.64	1.00	7.7	20.69%	1.3	3.45%	6.00	1.29	0.250
2018	A	63.7	1	4	0	3.25	3.79	1.24	10.5	27.11%	3.0	7.69%	3.52	0.99	0.307

Background: MacGregor, who was taken between A.J. Puckett and Matthias Dietz in the second round of the 2016 draft, was a disappointment through his first two seasons in pro ball. His debut in the Gulf Coast League ended with a nice enough 3.13 ERA, but was clouded by a troubling low strikeout rate; he averaged just under 5.5 K/9 in 31.2 innings. The front office bounced the 6-foot-3, 180-pound right-hander up to Appalachian League the following year, and – well – his whiff rate improved (7.0 K/9) but he battled some control demons (4.4 BB/9). Regardless, MacGregor found himself in the Sally to start the 2018 season. And he turned in a stellar, albeit injury-shortened, breakout campaign with the West Virginia Power. In 15 starts, the hard-throwing righty fanned 74 and walked just 21 in just 63.2 innings of work. Unfortunately for all parties involved, he underwent the knife for Tommy John surgery after the year and he didn't make it back to regular season action in 2019.

Snippet from The 2018 Prospect Digest Handbook: Mitch Keller without the curveball – which, unfortunately, doesn't paint a rosy picture for MacGregor and his professional trajectory. MacGregor's secondary offerings haven't developed as expected since entering the Pirates' organization a couple years ago. Like Keller, his changeup is a below-average offering, though it does flash average rarely. His curveball is slow and lacks depth. And during the time I saw him pitch, it looked like he was attempting a slider, which mostly spun on the same plane.

Scouting Report: Here's the simple truth: the Pirates have a lot of young arms that have some level of hype revolving around their draft status. Guys like Steven Jennings, Michael Burrows, and Braxton Ashcraft. But they're all flawed and likely will peter out in the mid levels of the minor leagues. Jennings' fastball was 86- to 89-mph when I saw him in early June. Burrows' fastball was average, his changeup was not great, and he got hit around a bit in the New York-Penn League. And Ashcraft showed a solid fastball and projection, but hasn't missed any bats in two years. So we're back around on MacGregor, who owns – or owned before the surgery – a plus, big league fastball. I think there's still hope that he adds a second reliable pitch to help push him into a relief role eventually.

Ceiling: 1.5- to 2.0-win player
Risk: Moderate to High
MLB ETA: 2022/2023

18. Rodolfo Castro, IF

	Hit	Power	SB	Patience	Glove	Overall
	40/45	50/55	35	45	50+	45

Born: 05/21/99	Age: 21	Bats: B
Height: 6-0	Weight: 200	Throws: R

YEAR	LVL	PA	1B	2B	3B	HR	SB	CS	AVG	OBP	SLG	BB%	K%	GB%	LD%	FB%
2017	RK	211	30	12	4	6	4	3	0.277	0.344	0.479	7.58%	22.27%	50.0	16.0	29.2
2018	A	426	54	19	4	12	6	3	0.231	0.278	0.395	6.10%	23.47%	43.8	20.7	28.4
2019	A	246	23	13	2	14	6	5	0.242	0.306	0.516	7.32%	27.64%	43.9	17.4	34.8
2019	A+	215	30	13	1	5	1	0	0.243	0.288	0.391	6.05%	25.12%	47.9	21.9	26.0

Background: A switch-hitting infielder out of Los Llanos, Dominican Republic, Castro has always flirted by showing some intriguing skills. He batted .271/.360/.411 with 20 extra-base hits in the foreign rookie league during his debut in 2016. He put together an even better showing as an 18-year-old in the Gulf Coast League the following year, slugging .277/.344/.479 with 22 extra-base hits in 53 games. But his production hit the skids as he entered the South Atlantic League two years ago. The then-19-year-old hit a pitiful .231/.278/.395, though he flashed some intriguing power potential with 19 doubles, four triples, and 12 homeruns in 105 games. Pittsburgh kept the infield vagabond down in Low Class A to begin last season. And Castro responded with a thunder-punched triple-slash line: .242/.306/.516 with 13 doubles, two triples, and 14 homeruns. He spent the second half of the year looking helpless against the Florida State League pitching. In total, Castro batted .242/.298/.456 with 26 doubles, three triples, and 19 homeruns.

Scouting Report: The perfect analogy to describe Castro: in 2018 he looked incredibly poor against left-handers to the tune .179/.188/.321 and looked competent against RHP with a .243/.299/.411 mark. Last season, those splits flipped. Let's take a look at his production in the Sally last season. Consider the following:

- Since 2006, only three 20-year-old hitters have totaled a DRC+ between 122 and 132 with a strikeout rate between 24% and 28% in the South Atlantic League (min. 200 PA): Josh Ockimey, Drew Robinson, and Rodolfo Castro. And it needs to be noted that the former two had walk rates that were at least 16% and Castro tallied only at 7.3%.

The power is certainly nice, especially for a potential up-the-middle position. But his swing-and-miss issues crossed over into the low end of red flag territory last season. The hit tool is underdeveloped. He also handles second base, shortstop, and third base equally well. He looks like a potential super-sub type of bench player. One who's value is tied to his power and versatility.

Ceiling: 1.5-win player
Risk: Moderate
MLB ETA: 2022

19. Luis Escobar, RHP

	FB	CB	CH	Command	Overall
	60	60	55	40	40

Born: 05/30/96	Age: 24	Bats: R
Height: 6-1	Weight: 205	Throws: R

YEAR	LVL	IP	W	L	SV	ERA	FIP	WHIP	K/9	K%	BB/9	BB%	K/BB	HR9	BABIP
2017	A	131.7	10	7	0	3.83	3.53	1.19	11.5	29.89%	4.1	10.68%	2.80	0.62	0.282
2018	A+	92.7	7	6	0	3.98	4.39	1.23	8.3	22.02%	3.7	9.84%	2.24	0.87	0.272
2018	AA	35.7	4	0	0	4.54	5.22	1.43	6.3	15.92%	5.3	13.38%	1.19	1.01	0.248
2019	A+	13.3	0	0	3	0.00	2.86	0.90	10.1	27.78%	4.1	11.11%	2.50	0.00	0.194
2019	AAA	55.0	2	1	1	4.09	5.06	1.56	9.3	24.15%	5.2	13.56%	1.78	1.15	0.329

Background: Always up for titillating the powers that be with some sensational starts and some eye-catching peripherals. The problem with Escobar, a rotund right-hander, is quite simple: he could throw (A) enough strikes and (B) enough consistent quality strikes. So after five minor league seasons as a member of a variety of rotations within the Pittsburgh organization, the front office – finally – made the move and shifted the Colombian hurler into the bullpen full time last season.

Escobar tossed 68.1 innings in the minor leagues, positing an Escobar-esque 72-to-38 strikeout-to-walk ratio with a 3.29 ERA. He also made four relief appearances with the big league club, fanning a pair and walking four.

Snippet from The 2018 Prospect Digest Handbook: Quietly owns one of the better curveballs in the minor leagues. Escobar unfurls a hard, 12-6 snap-dragon with incredibly downward bite that generated a lot of awkward looking swings. That plus-offering sits in the 80-mph range. His fastball, another plus-offering, is explosive and touches as high as 95 mph. His changeup is an underrated pitch: it's hard, straight, and but shows a lot of downward sink. Based on stuff alone, Escobar looks like a #3-type arm in the making. But his control – which, admittedly, has come a long way over the past couple of seasons – will likely push him into a relief role in the next two or three years, which is a shame.

Scouting Report: He has the repertoire to provide value as a starting pitcher on a number of big league clubs. It's just…well…he sucks at throwing strikes. There's really no way around it. He's now entering his age-24 and has walked more than five hitters per nine innings in the upper two levels of the minor leagues. The stuff's good, but not *that* good to compensate for those control demons. Mid-90s fastball. Mid-80s diving changeup. Upper 70s curveball. No command. One more final thought: he posted a 20-to-11 strikeout-to-walk ratio in 22.1 innings as a starting pitcher last season; on the other hand he averaged 5.4 walks per nine innings as a reliever.

Ceiling: 1.0- to 1.5-win player
Risk: Moderate
MLB ETA: Debuted in 2019

20. Matt Gorski, OF

Hit	Power	SB	Patience	Glove	Overall
45	55	50/45	50	50	40

Born: 12/22/97	Age: 22	Bats: R	
Height: 6-4	Weight: 198	Throws: R	

YEAR	LVL	PA	1B	2B	3B	HR	SB	CS	AVG	OBP	SLG	BB%	K%	GB%	LD%	FB%
2019	A-	202	26	9	2	3	11	3	0.223	0.297	0.346	9.41%	23.76%	47.7	12.9	30.3

Background: Equipped with a pair of selections in the second round of the draft last June, Pittsburgh opted for two polished collegiate bats: they snagged outfielder Matt Gorski with #57 and chose infielder Jared Triolo with #72. A product of Indiana University – which has churned out several notable hitters in recent years, like Kyle Schwarber, Alex Dickerson, and Sam Travis – Gorski left the school on a bit of a sour note: he finished his sophomore campaign on a scorching note as he batted .356/.404/.554 but saw his production decline to .271/.374/.498 last season. After signing the former Hoosier to a below-slot deal, which saved the club roughly $250,000, Gorski headed to the West Virginia Black Bears for his debut. In 49 games with the club's New York-Penn League affiliate, Gorski cobbled together a lowly .223/.297/.346 triple-slash line with just nine doubles, two triples, and three homeruns. His overall production, per *Deserved Runs Created Plus*, was 15% *below* the league average.

Scouting Report: Taking Gorski in the early part of the second round was a reach. The former Hoosier was already showing signs of having problematic swing-and-miss totals in college; he fanned in roughly 24% of his plate appearances as a junior – which was a dramatic increase from his stellar sophomore campaign (14.7%). His performance during his stint in the Cape Cod League was mediocre, though his strikeout total was problematic there too (33.3%). And he's going to have to consistently prove that contact issues won't be a hinderance moving forward. He looks like a fourth outfield-type at this point.

Ceiling: 1.0- to 1.5-win player
Risk: Moderate
MLB ETA: 2022

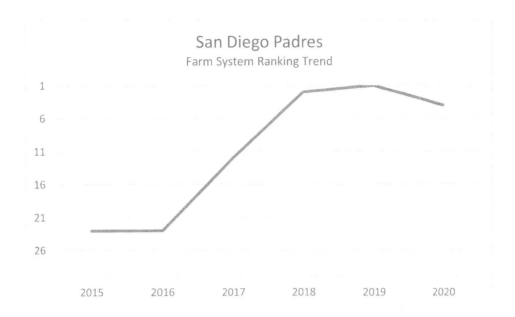

Rank	Name	Age	Pos
1	MacKenzie Gore	21	LHP
2	Luis Patino	20	RHP
3	CJ Abrams	19	SS
4	Luis Campusano	21	C
5	Taylor Trammell	22	OF
6	Adrian Morejon	21	LHP
7	Ryan Weathers	20	LHP
8	Owen Miller	23	IF
9	Michel Baez	24	RHP
10	Joey Cantillo	20	LHP
11	Gabriel Arias	20	SS
12	Luis Torrens	24	C
13	Joshua Mears	19	RF
14	Reggie Lawson	22	RHP
15	Hudson Potts	21	3B
16	Edward Olivares	24	OF
17	Efrain Contreras	20	RHP
18	Ronald Bolanos	23	RHP
19	Jeisson Rosario	20	CF
20	Yeison Santana	19	SS

1. MacKenzie Gore, LHP

	FB	CB	SL	CH	Command	Overall
	60	55	50	60	60	80

Born: 02/24/99	Age: 21	Bats: L
Height: 6-3	Weight: 195	Throws: L

YEAR	LVL	IP	W	L	SV	ERA	FIP	WHIP	K/9	K%	BB/9	BB%	K/BB	HR9	BABIP
2017	Rk	21.3	0	1	0	1.27	2.16	0.98	14.3	40.48%	3.0	8.33%	4.86	0.00	0.333
2018	A	60.7	2	5	0	4.45	3.25	1.30	11.0	28.35%	2.7	6.90%	4.11	0.74	0.354
2019	A+	79.3	7	1	0	1.02	2.38	0.71	12.5	38.19%	2.3	6.94%	5.50	0.45	0.211
2019	AA	21.7	2	1	0	4.15	4.18	1.29	10.4	37.88%	3.3	12.12%	3.13	1.25	0.308

Background: For several decades Whiteville High School's claim to fame was centered around a couple of former big leaguers: former All-Star right-hander Tommy Greene, who authored a no-hitter against the Expos as a member of the Phillies on May 23rd, 1991; and shortstop Pat Lennon – both players, by the way, were taken in that early parts of the opening rounds of the 1986 and 1985 drafts. But over the last couple of seasons the high school's been known for something else: the home of left-hander MacKenzie Gore, one of the best young arms in the minor leagues. After a dynamic prep career, the Padres drafted the high-stepping, smooth-throwing southpaw in the opening round, third overall, and handed him a hefty, then-Padres record of $6.7 million. And the talented left-hander proved to be better than advertised during his debut: he posted an absurd 34-to-7 strikeout-to-walk ratio in 21.1 innings in the Arizona Summer League. San Diego sent the then-19-year-old hurler up to the Midwest league. And, well, he continued to dominate as he averaged 11.0 strikeouts and 2.7 walks per nine innings with a 4.45 ERA in 60.1 innings of work. Last season the front office began to ease the reins a bit as Gore's workload increased up to 101.0 innings as he split time between Lake Elsinore and Amarillo. He finished the year with a sparkling 1.69 ERA while averaging 12.0 strikeouts and just 2.5 walks per nine innings.

Snippet from The 2018 Prospect Digest Handbook: San Diego has – generally – done a fine job in keeping their young arms healthy. And if Gore can navigate his way carefully through the injury nexus, he has a chance to ascend to a true #1.

Scouting Report: Gore was particularly dominating during his 15-start cameo in the California League. Let's see how his numbers stack up to his peers through a historical lens. Consider the following:

- Since 2006, there have been eight 20-year-old pitchers to post a strikeout percentage north of 30% in any of the three High Class A leagues (min. 75 IP): Yovani Gallardo, Tyler Glasnow, Jake McGee, DL Hall, Jeremy Jeffress, Cody Buckel, Will Inman, and – of course – MacKenzie Gore.

Continuing...

- And here's the list of arms to eclipse the 34% strikeout percentage threshold: MacKenzie Gore.

Gore, by the way, fanned a *staggering* 38.2% of the hitters he faced in High Class A last season. He didn't just surpass top all other 20-year-olds. He – unequivocally – made sure no other 20-year-old will ever reach that threshold again (well, he tried to do that, anyway). Three plus pitches – fastball, slider, changeup – backed up by and swing-and-miss, strong 55-grade curveball. Gore's fastball sits in the 92-93 mph range and touched 94 on occasion last season, but it plays up due to his elite feel for the strike zone. He's a bonafide, legitimate budding ace who likely ascends to true ace-dom. In terms of ceiling, think of an in-his-prime Zack Greinke when he averaged 9.5 K/9 and 2.0 BB/9 for the Royals in 2009.

Ceiling: 7.0-win player
Risk: Moderate
MLB ETA: 2020

2. Luis Patino, RHP

	FB	CB	SL	CH	Command	Overall
	70	55/60	55	45/50	50/55	60

Born: 02/24/99	Age: 21	Bats: L
Height: 6-3	Weight: 195	Throws: L

YEAR	LVL	IP	W	L	SV	ERA	FIP	WHIP	K/9	K%	BB/9	BB%	K/BB	HR9	BABIP
2017	Rk	40.0	2	1	0	2.48	4.07	1.20	9.7	25.60%	3.6	9.52%	2.69	0.45	0.286
2017	Rk	16.0	2	1	0	1.69	1.73	0.81	8.4	25.00%	1.1	3.33%	7.50	0.00	0.256
2018	A	83.3	6	3	0	2.16	2.32	1.07	10.6	29.70%	2.6	7.27%	4.08	0.11	0.320
2019	A+	87.0	6	8	0	2.69	2.87	1.09	11.7	31.65%	3.5	9.52%	3.32	0.41	0.278
2019	AA	7.7	0	0	0	1.17	2.40	1.57	11.7	28.57%	4.7	11.43%	2.50	0.00	0.381

Background: Blessed with one of the best arms in the minor leagues, Patino, who employees a high reaching leg kick modeled after friend and teammate MacKenzie Gore, is just the latest example of the front office's astute work on the international free agent market. Handed just $130,000 as a 16-year-old in 2016, the Barranquilla, Colombia, native has rocketed through San Diego's farm system, reaching the vaunted Class AA challenge last season as a 19-year-old. The hard-throwing right-hander began the year a bit slowly in the California League as he walked 12 hitters through his first eight starts. But after that, though, Patino handed out just 22 free passes – to go along with a whopping 100 punch outs – over his remaining 15 games with the Lake Elsinore Storm. He also made a couple brief sub-5.0-inning appearances with the Sod Poodles of Amarillo. In total, Patino tossed a career best 94.2 innings, recording a dominating 123-to-28 strikeout-to-walk ratio with a 2.57 ERA.

Snippet from The 2018 Prospect Digest Handbook: Even in an organization as tightly condensed with blue chip arms, Patino doesn't have a problem standing out. One could make the argument – and potentially win – that Patino's the highest ceiling pitcher in the minor leagues.

Scouting Report: Consider the following:

- Since 2006, only three 19-year-old arms have fanned at least 30% of the hitters they faced in any High Class A league (min. 75 IP): Tyler Skaggs, Triston McKenzie, and – of course Luis Patino.

An elite combination of control, eventual command, and high octane arsenal. Patino continues to consistently showcase his rare ability to blow hitters away and, simply, take games over. Late season his fastball sat in the mid-90s with his trademark ease, though he could reach back for several additional ticks when needed. The curveball remains an above-average offering, though he did snap off a couple plus knee-bucklers. The slider didn't look at sharp when I saw him, but the shape/bend and velocity was consistent from years past. One of the large improvements for Patino was his willingness to throw his changeup. It's still too firm, still too straight. But the willingness, itself, is important because (A) he shows an improving maturity and (B) gives hope that consistent use will help its development. Upper echelon ceiling.

Ceiling: 5.0-win player
Risk: Moderate
MLB ETA: 2020

3. CJ Abrams, SS

	Hit	Power	SB	Patience	Glove	Overall
	55/65	45/50	70	45+	55	60

Born: 10/03/00	Age: 19	Bats: L
Height: 6-2	Weight: 185	Throws: R

Background: Lurking quietly in the shadows of another talented prep shortstop – Colleyville-Heritage High School's Bobby Witt Jr. – Abrams has a long history of playing against elite levels of competition. He spent some time on four different 14U

YEAR	LVL	PA	1B	2B	3B	HR	SB	CS	AVG	OBP	SLG	BB%	K%	GB%	LD%	FB%
2019	Rk	156	34	12	8	3	14	6	0.401	0.442	0.662	6.41%	8.97%	50.0	15.6	28.9
2019	A	9	1	1	0	0	1	0	0.250	0.333	0.375	11.11%	0.00%	37.5	0.0	37.5

Perfect Game Tournament Teams in 2015 – the East Cobb Invitational All-Tournament Team, the Invitational All-Tournament Team, the National Championship All-Tournament Team, and the World Series All-Tournament Team. He followed that up with a bevy of performances for the 15U and 16U squads as well, including: WWBA 16U National Championship All-Tourney Team, WWBA 15U National Championship All-Tourney Team, and The 15U Perfect Game BCS Finals All-Tournament Team. The speedy middle infielder spent the 2017 season as a member of the 17U USA Baseball Team Development Program too. And that progress reached a crescendo two summers ago summer as he started nine games for the 18U National Team. Abrams batted .297/.395/.324 with just one double in 37 at bats. San Diego drafted the Blessed Trinity High School product in the opening round last June, sixth overall, and sent him to the Arizona Summer League. And, damn, was it a debut showing. In 32 games the 6-foot-2, 185-pound slugged .401/.442/.662 with 12 doubles, eight triples, and a trio of homeruns with 14 stolen bases. He also popped up to Low Class A for a couple of games.

Scouting Report: Per the usual, here's what I wrote about Abrams prior to the draft:

"Yes, the sample size is incredibly small/limited. But...it's very telling how Abrams numbers stacked up against his Team USA peers last summer: He has the third lowest batting average, the third lowest on-base percentage, and the lowest slugging percentage among the 11 hitters. Abrams shows a slashing approach at the plate that, combined with his slight frame, won't likely allow for much power development – even at his peak. The hit tool is raw as well, especially for a potential early first round pick. The elite speed is apparent. But his work at shortstop suggests a possible move to second base, where he showed some fluidity turning two. He could go the sturdy starter route just as easily as a utility guy."

Yikes...I couldn't have been more wrong. The batted ball data was impressive: according to FanGraphs, his average exit velocity was 89 mph. The hit tool has the makings of a plus weapon to match his elite speed with average power. It's embarrassing how wrong I was with this.

Ceiling: 4.5-win player
Risk: Moderate
MLB ETA: 2021

4. Luis Campusano, C

Hit	Power	SB	Patience	Glove	Overall
55	50	20	55	50	60

Born: 09/29/98	Age: 21	Bats: R
Height: 5-10	Weight: 215	Throws: R

YEAR	LVL	PA	1B	2B	3B	HR	SB	CS	AVG	OBP	SLG	BB%	K%	GB%	LD%	FB%
2017	RK	98	20	4	0	1	0	1	0.278	0.327	0.356	6.12%	14.29%	49.4	19.5	24.7
2017	RK	53	8	0	0	3	0	1	0.250	0.377	0.455	16.98%	20.75%	48.5	24.2	21.2
2018	A	284	61	11	0	3	0	1	0.288	0.345	0.365	6.69%	15.14%	51.8	22.0	18.8
2019	A+	487	90	31	1	15	0	0	0.325	0.396	0.509	10.68%	11.70%	45.4	20.7	28.0

Background: Fun Fact: There have been exactly two ballplayers in the history of the game named Luis Campusano; both were catchers. San Diego's young backstop, though, has given the impression there's some star quality level of talent developing in his powerful stick. A second round pick in 2017, 39th overall, Campusano turned in a solid debut showing in the Arizona Summer League as he batted .269/.344/.388 with a quarter of doubles and homeruns. His production maintained status quo in a concussion-shortened sophomore campaign in the Midwest League two years; he hit .288/.345/.365 with 11 doubles and a trio of homeruns. Last season, though, Campusano – quietly – put together one of the bigger breakouts in the minor leagues. Appearing in 110 games with the Lake Elsinore Storm, the 5-foot-10, 215-pound catcher slugged a scorching .325/.396/.509 with a whopping 31 doubles and 15 homeruns. Per Baseball Prospectus' *Deserved Runs Created Plus*, his overall production topped the league average line by an eye-catching 68%.

Snippet from The 2018 Prospect Digest Handbook: A bat-first backstop who looked a little sieve-like behind the dish on defense last season, Campusano's power backed up noticeably as he moved in the Midwest League against older pitching last season. He still projects to have average-ish pop at maturity, though, but he's going to have to put the ball in the air more frequently.

Scouting Report: Consider the following:

- Since 2006, only three 20-year-old hitters have tallied at least a 160 DRC+ in the California League (min. 300 PA): Corey Seager, Ryan McMahon, and – of course – Luis Campusano.
- And, for those counting at home: Seager owns a career 115 DRC+ in 489 big league games and McMahon is coming off of his full season for the Rockies, slugging .250/.329/.450.

Another fun fact: Campusano failed to hit at least .320 in only one month last season (May); he still slugged .275/.372/.543. But his offensive firepower wasn't the only development; he defense took tremendous leaps forward as well. In terms of offensive ceiling, think something along the lines of J.T. Realmuto's 2018 season with the Marlins in which he batted .277/.340/.484.

Ceiling: 4.0-win player
Risk: Moderate
MLB ETA: 2021

5. Taylor Trammell, OF

Hit	Power	SB	Patience	Glove	Overall
55	50	50	60	50	60

Born: 09/13/97	Age: 22	Bats: L
Height: 6-2	Weight: 215	Throws: L

YEAR	LVL	PA	1B	2B	3B	HR	SB	CS	AVG	OBP	SLG	BB%	K%	GB%	LD%	FB%
2016	RK	254	52	9	6	2	24	7	0.303	0.374	0.421	9.06%	22.44%	55.0	21.1	18.1
2017	A	571	91	24	10	13	41	12	0.281	0.368	0.450	12.43%	21.54%	42.9	15.5	30.4
2018	A+	461	79	19	4	8	25	10	0.277	0.375	0.406	12.58%	22.78%	43.7	18.8	32.4
2019	AA	133	18	4	1	4	3	4	0.229	0.316	0.381	9.77%	27.07%	40.7	22.2	32.1
2019	AA	381	58	8	3	6	17	4	0.236	0.349	0.336	14.17%	22.57%	40.5	16.9	32.5

Background: One of the most athletic prospects in the entire minor leagues. Cincinnati selected the toolsy outfielder at the backend of the first round of the 2016 draft – 35th overall, to be exact. Soon after, the legend of Taylor Trammell was born. He ripped through the Pioneer League to the tune of .303/.374/.421 during his debut. And he posted some incredibly impressive numbers the following year as a 19-year-old in the Midwest League: .281/.368/.450 with 24 doubles, 10 triples, 13 homeruns, and 41 stolen bases. Cincinnati bumped him up to the Florida State League in 2018. And, once again, he proved up to the test as he batted a saber-friendly .277/.375/.406 with 19 doubles, four triples, eight homeruns, and 25 stolen bases. Last season Trammell squared off against the minors' toughest challenge, Class AA, and the results were...well...not what we're used to seeing. Trammell, who was acquired as part of the three-team mega-trade involving the Reds and Indians, batted an aggregate .234/.340/.349 with 12 doubles, four triples, 10 homeruns, and 20 stolen bases between both organizations' Class AA affiliate.

Snippet from The 2018 Prospect Digest Handbook: Loud tools with a sabermetric tinge. Trammell profiles as a potential perennial All-Star at the big league level. The bat itself will be an above-average or better skill during his peak years; his power has a chance to blossom into 20-homer territory; and he's consistently displayed plus to plus-plus speed on the base paths and in the outfield. His route running – particularly in center field – needs to improve though.

Scouting Report: A few thoughts:

- The front office is betting *big* on the underlying skills, as opposed to last season's performance, because they gave up a lot of talent (Franmil Reyes, Logan Allen, and Victor Nova).
- Despite the lackluster production line, all of Trammell's batted ball data remains strong: according to FanGraphs, his average exit velocity was 88 mph with a peak exit velocity of 108 mph. His flyball, line drive, and groundball percentages are where you'd want them to be.
- Finally, he's using the entire field effectively.

So why did the numbers decline as much as they did in 2019? I think a lot of it has to do with bad luck. It seems like a quick answer. But it's the truth. He's still (A) consistently hitting the ball hard and (B) spraying it around. And his near 60-point decline in BABIP seems to only back that up. There's some Carl Crawford type potential, though with more walks.

Ceiling: 4.5-win player
Risk: Moderate to High
MLB ETA: 2020

6. Adrian Morejon, LHP

	FB	CB	CH	Command	Overall
	60	60	55/60	45	50

Born: 02/27/99	Age: 21	Bats: L
Height: 6-0	Weight: 175	Throws: L

YEAR	LVL	IP	W	L	SV	ERA	FIP	WHIP	K/9	K%	BB/9	BB%	K/BB	HR9	BABIP
2017	A-	35.3	2	2	0	3.57	2.96	1.13	8.9	23.97%	0.8	2.05%	11.67	0.51	0.337
2017	A	27.7	1	2	0	4.23	4.29	1.48	7.5	19.17%	4.2	10.83%	1.77	0.65	0.321
2018	Rk	2.7	0	1	0	6.75	1.07	1.88	13.5	30.77%	0.0	0.00%	#DIV/0!	0.00	0.556
2018	A+	62.7	4	4	0	3.30	4.10	1.24	10.1	26.62%	3.4	9.13%	2.92	0.86	0.302
2019	AA	36.0	0	4	0	4.25	3.58	1.22	11.0	28.57%	3.8	9.74%	2.93	0.75	0.292

Background: A few years back the Padres established a mini pipeline to Cuba as they added the likes of Adrian Morejon, Ronald Bolanos, and Michel Baez at various points in 2016. Morejon, a slight-framed southpaw from La Habana, Cuba, agreed to join the organization for a hefty $11 million deal. Since making his highly anticipated stateside debut in 2017, Morejon has continued to jump through the minor league ranks – despite a rather limited track record, some of which was by design, others due to injury. San Diego governed his workload at just 63.0 innings between Tri-City and Fort Wayne during his debut. He made just 13 starts with the Lake Elsinore Storm in the California League the following season. And last year the Padres deployed an usual approach to his workload: beginning in late April/early May, Morejon tossed no more than 2.1 innings in each of his 18 starts. A late season left shoulder impingement ended his year in early August. One final note: he made his big league debut beginning in late July, throwing 8.0 innings with nine punch outs and three walks.

Snippet from The 2018 Prospect Digest Handbook: There are some concerns as to whether Morejon's small stature will allow him to compete after fifth day, but until proven otherwise, he looks quite promising.

Scouting Report: It's difficult to get a good feel for Morejon's ceiling. When he's on, he's flashing three plus pitches: an explosive mid-90s fastball, a late biting low-80s curveball, and a changeup that shows some nice downward cutting action. The problem, of course, is that (A) he's entering his fourth year in the organization and hasn't topped more than 65.1 innings in a season and (B) the left shoulder impingement is quite concerning. His command backed up as well. He's one of the more talented, yet high variance prospects in the minor leagues. He could settle in as a #2/#3 type arm or bottom out as a high leverage reliever. Given his youth, I'm still betting on his ability as a starting pitcher.

Ceiling: 3.0-win player
Risk: Moderate
MLB ETA: Debuted in 2019

7. Ryan Weathers, LHP

	FB	CB	SL	CH	Command	Overall
	60	55	50	55	55/60	50

Born: 12/17/99	Age: 20	Bats: L
Height: 6-1	Weight: 230	Throws: L

YEAR	LVL	IP	W	L	SV	ERA	FIP	WHIP	K/9	K%	BB/9	BB%	K/BB	HR9	BABIP
2018	Rk	9.3	0	2	0	3.86	6.21	1.18	8.7	21.43%	2.9	7.14%	3.00	1.93	0.222
2018	A	9.0	0	1	0	3.00	1.81	1.33	9.0	21.95%	1.0	2.44%	9.00	0.00	0.355
2019	A	96.0	3	7	0	3.84	3.15	1.24	8.4	22.78%	1.7	4.56%	5.00	0.56	0.347

Background: Fun Fact Part I: Ryan's old man, veteran reliever David Weathers, earned a smidge over $25 million over the course of his 19-year big league career. Fun Fact Part II: The younger Weather tallied slightly more than 20% of his father's career earnings before even throwing a professional pitch thanks to his hefty $5.23 million draft bonus. The seventh overall pick out of Loretto High School two years ago, the young southpaw earned a trip back up to the Midwest League in 2019 – after spending half of his abbreviated debut in Low Class A. In 22 starts with the Fort Wayne TinCaps, the hefty lefty fanned 90 and walked just 18 in 96.0 innings of work. He tallied a 3.84 ERA and a 5.46 DRA (*Deserved Run Average*).

Snippet from The 2018 Prospect Digest Handbook: Surprisingly enough, Weathers, the seventh pick last June, falls well short of being able to light up a radar gun; his fastball sat in the 89-91 mph range, topping 92 during his time in Low Class A. But that only tells half the story. While it's not a traditional above-average fastball, Weathers' heater is more sneaky quick and it's heavy, like hitting a bowling ball. He'll mix in a pair of solid offspeed pitches, as well: a mid- to upper-70s curveball with some bite and a nice little changeup. Weathers doesn't look as wiry, athletic, or projectable as many prep arms taken in the opening rounds, but he should develop into a nice league average arm.

Scouting Report: Consider the following:

- Since 2006, only two 19-year-old arms met the following criteria in the Midwest League (min. 75 IP): a 22% to 24% strikeout percentage with a sub-6.0% walk percentage. Those two arms: Phillies reliever Victor Arano, who's average 9.6 strikeouts and just 2.8 walks in 74.2 career big league innings, and – of course – Ryan Weathers.

Everything – and I mean *everything* – is different for Weathers as he's entering his third professional season. His fastball, which sat in the upper 80s/low 90s during his debut, was significantly livelier as he sat in the 93- to 94-mph range and topped 95 mph during a few starts I scouted. His curveball and changeup both remain strong 55-grade options. He also added a fourth pitch: a low- to mid-80s slider with cutter/sweeping movement. He's a future #3/#4-type innings eater arm.

Ceiling: 3.0-win player
Risk: Moderate
MLB ETA: 2022

8. Owen Miller, IF

	Hit	Power	SB	Patience	Glove	Overall
	55	45	35	50	55	50

Born: 11/15/96	Age: 23	Bats: R
Height: 6-0	Weight: 190	Throws: R

YEAR	LVL	PA	1B	2B	3B	HR	SB	CS	AVG	OBP	SLG	BB%	K%	GB%	LD%	FB%
2018	A-	216	51	8	3	2	4	4	0.335	0.395	0.440	6.94%	11.11%	43.9	24.6	25.7
2018	A	114	23	11	0	2	0	0	0.336	0.368	0.495	3.51%	14.91%	51.6	17.6	26.4
2019	AA	560	104	28	2	13	5	5	0.290	0.355	0.430	8.21%	15.36%	44.4	25.1	22.2

Background: A consistent, oft-times dominant presence in Illinois State University's lineup for the duration of his three-year collegiate career. San Diego picked the overachieving infielder in the third round, 84th overall, two years ago. Miller, who left the school as a career .345/.383/.511 hitter, didn't miss a beat as he slugged a healthy .336/.386/.460 with 19 doubles, three triples, and four homeruns between his time with Tri-City and Fort Wayne. The front office – aggressively – shoved the 6-foot, 190-pound infielder straight into the minors' toughest challenge, Class AA, and he more than held his own. In 130 games with the Amarillo Sod Poodles, Miller batted a solid .290/.355/.430 with 28 doubles, two triples, and 13 homeruns. His overall production, per *Deserved Runs Created Plus*, topped the league average threshold by 12%.

Scouting Report: Consider the following:

- Since 2006, only four 22-year-old hitters tallied a DRC+ between 107 and 117 with a sub-20.0% strikeout rate in the Texas League (min. 350 PA): Jean Segura, Peter Bourjos, Erick Mejia, and Owen Miller.

Miller maintained his trademark consistency last season, despite leaping up to Class AA: he posted monthly OPS totals between .732 and .833 in every month of the year. Above-average hit tool and defense to match. Miller will run into enough pitches to approach 15 homeruns in a full season with a handful of stolen bases and average patience. He's a low ceiling/high floor bet to develop into a super-sub and/or quietly underrated starter. Spray hitter that shoots line drives from gap-to-gap. He's going to push recently acquired Jurickson Profar for playing time by the middle of 2020. In terms of offensive ceiling, think: 2019 Adam Frazier, who slugged .278/.336/.417.

Ceiling: 2.0-win player
Risk: Low to Moderate
MLB ETA: 2020

9. Michel Baez, RHP

	FB	CB	SL	CH	Command	Overall
	70	55	50	60	50	50

Born: 01/21/96	Age: 24	Bats: R
Height: 6-8	Weight: 220	Throws: R

YEAR	LVL	IP	W	L	SV	ERA	FIP	WHIP	K/9	K%	BB/9	BB%	K/BB	HR9	BABIP
2017	Rk	5.0	1	0	0	3.60	5.22	0.80	12.6	38.89%	3.6	11.11%	3.50	1.80	0.125
2017	A	58.7	6	2	0	2.45	2.99	0.84	12.6	36.44%	1.2	3.56%	10.25	1.23	0.264
2018	A+	86.7	4	7	0	2.91	3.66	1.22	9.6	25.34%	3.4	9.09%	2.79	0.52	0.297
2018	AA	18.3	0	3	0	7.36	6.28	1.85	10.3	24.14%	5.9	13.79%	1.75	1.96	0.375
2019	AA	27.0	3	2	1	2.00	2.56	1.22	12.7	33.04%	3.7	9.57%	3.45	0.33	0.333

Background: Part of the club's massive influx of Cuban talent during the 2016 season. The redwood-esque right-hander, who stands 6-foot-8 and weighs just 220 pounds, showed some impressive peripherals during his first two stateside professional seasons: he averaged 12.6 K/9 and just 1.4 BB/9 during his debut in 2017, and posted a 113-to-45 strikeouts-to-walk ratio in 105.0 innings the following season. Last season, though, was a first for the hard-throwing hurler: he spent the year working primarily as a late-inning, high leverage reliever. Baez spent the first half of 2019 dealing out of the Sod Poodles' pen as he averaged a whopping 12.7 strikeouts and 3.7 walks per nine innings to go along with a sparkling 2.00 ERA and a 3.42 DRA (*Deserved Run Average*). He also made 24 appearances for the Padres as well, posting a 28-to-14 strikeout-to-walk ratio in 29.2 innings of work.

Snippet from The 2018 Prospect Digest Handbook: Despite his age – he's now entering his age-23 season – Baez remains quite raw, though he has the potential to be a #3/#4-type arm with the floor of a power-armed backend reliever.

Scouting Report: Still sporting a strong middle-of-the-rotation caliber arsenal, Baez didn't shy away from his offspeed offerings – despite manhandling the minor league competition. Upper-90s heater. Low-80s curveball. Mid-80s tightly wound slider. And a changeup that sits 88- to 89-mph, which upticked noticeable last season as it showed more deceptive sink and arm-side fade. The Padres bullpen, which is going to feature Kirby Yates, Andres Munoz, Drew Pomeranz, and Baez, among others, is going to be downright scary. I still think it's too early to move him away from the rotation permanently.

Ceiling: 2.0-win player
Risk: Low to Moderate
MLB ETA: Debuted in 2019

10. Joey Cantillo, LHP

	FB	CB	CH	Command	Overall
	50	55	60	55	50

Born: 12/18/99	Age: 20	Bats: L
Height: 6-4	Weight: 220	Throws: L

YEAR	LVL	IP	W	L	SV	ERA	FIP	WHIP	K/9	K%	BB/9	BB%	K/BB	HR9	BABIP
2017	Rk	8.0	1	0	0	4.50	3.72	1.38	15.8	37.84%	6.8	16.22%	2.33	0.00	0.333
2018	Rk	45.3	2	2	0	2.18	2.50	0.99	11.5	31.69%	2.4	6.56%	4.83	0.00	0.300
2018	A	3.7	0	1	0	9.82	3.20	1.91	12.3	27.78%	7.4	16.67%	1.67	0.00	0.400
2019	A	98.0	9	3	0	1.93	2.13	0.87	11.8	34.69%	2.5	7.32%	4.74	0.28	0.264
2019	A+	13.7	1	1	0	4.61	4.98	1.39	10.5	25.40%	4.6	11.11%	2.29	1.32	0.270

Background: The earliest draft pick taken in Kailua High School history – and, to be frank, it's not even that impressive. San Diego selected the big left-hander in the 16th round, 468th overall, and convinced the young Hawaiian to sign. Fast forward a couple of seasons and Cantillo turned in one of the most dominant showings in 2019. Making 19 starts with the Fort Wayne TinCaps, the 6-foot-4, 220-pound lefty struck out a whopping 128 and handed out a curmudgeon-like 27 free passes in only 98 innings of work. He compiled a barely-there 1.93 ERA and an equally impressive 2.18 DRA (*Deserved Run Average*). He also made a trio of starts with Lake Elsinore in the California League at the end of the year, posting a 16-to-7 strikeout-to-walk ratio in 13.2 innings of work.

Scouting Report: Consider the following:

- Since 2006, here's the list of hurlers to fan at least 32% of the hitters they faced with a sub-3.00 DRA in the Midwest League (min. 75 IP): Neftali Feliz, Pedro Avila, and – of course – Joey Cantillo. Feliz and Avila were both 20-years-old during their aforementioned season. Cantillo, on the other hand, was just 19.

Unlike Feliz and Avila, Cantillo doesn't possess a plus mid-90s or better fastball. Instead, Cantillo is a pitcher's pitcher who gets by on poise, guile, and pitchability. A decent average fastball that he manipulates the strike zone with, the big left-hander features a pair of quality secondary pitches: an above-average curveball and a plus-Vulcan changeup. The latter is particularly devastating. He's an efficient, quick worker whose arsenal plays up due to his control/command. It's not surprising to see an advanced arm – regardless of age – dominate Low Class A. Meaning: Cantillo's going to have to prove himself in High Class A and – definitely – Class AA. There's some #4/#5-type potential here, something along the lines of poor man's Jose Quintana.

Ceiling: 2.0-win player
Risk: Moderate
MLB ETA: 2020

11. Gabriel Arias, SS

Hit	Power	SB	Patience	Glove	Overall
50	50	40	40/45	45	50

Born: 02/27/00	Age: 20	Bats: R
Height: 6-1	Weight: 201	Throws: R

YEAR	LVL	PA	1B	2B	3B	HR	SB	CS	AVG	OBP	SLG	BB%	K%	GB%	LD%	FB%
2018	A	504	73	27	3	6	3	3	0.240	0.302	0.352	8.13%	29.56%	53.7	18.2	24.9
2019	A+	511	102	21	4	17	8	4	0.302	0.339	0.470	4.89%	25.05%	43.9	21.4	28.8

Background: A highly touted prospect on the international scene in 2016, San Diego signed the toolsy infielder to a hefty $1.6 million. And Arias, a 6-foot-1, 201-pound athlete from La Victoria, Venezuela, looked comfortable during his debut in rookie ball the falling season as he batted .275/.329/.353 as a 17-year-old. The front office aggressively pushed him up to Low Class A for the final two-plus weeks of the year. Arias' production took a noticeable – albeit expected – nosedive in his return to the Midwest League in 2018 as he batted a lowly .240/.302/.352 with 27 doubles, three triples, and six homeruns. And he didn't fare that well in the Venezuelan Winter League either: .254/.323/.288 in 24 games. So last season's massive showing in the California League was *clearly* a surprise. In 120 games with the Storm of Lake Elsinore, he slugged a hearty .302/.339/.470 with 21 doubles, four triples, and 17 homeruns. He also swiped eight bags in 12 attempts. His overall production, according to *Deserved Runs Created Plus*, topped the league average threshold by 22%.

Scouting Report: Consider the following:

- Since 2006, only two 19-year-old hitters posted a DRC+ between 117 and 127 with a sub-6.0% walk rate in the California League (min. 300 PA): Franklin Barreto and Gabriel Arias.

A few additional notes:

- Barreto, a widely recognized Top 100 prospect during his minor league career, has been abysmal in three brief cups of coffee with the Athletics.
- Arias fanned far more frequently during their respective stints in the California League: 25.1% to 18.4%.

The peripherals aren't spectacular: he's always combined low walk rates and troublesome – albeit improving – strikeout numbers. Meaning: he's going to go as far as his batting average and power carry him. The defense, which has been decent in past years, was abysmal last season. He's quite raw and incredibly athletic, so I wouldn't rule out a move to the outfield or third base if the power continues to grow. League average, maybe more depending upon how the BABIPs bounce.

Ceiling: 2.0-win player
Risk: Moderate
MLB ETA: 2021

12. Luis Torrens, C

Hit	Power	SB	Patience	Glove	Overall
50	45+	30	50+	55	45

Born: 05/02/96	Age: 24	Bats: R
Height: 6-0	Weight: 175	Throws: R

YEAR	LVL	PA	1B	2B	3B	HR	SB	CS	AVG	OBP	SLG	BB%	K%	GB%	LD%	FB%
2016	A-	50	10	4	0	0	1	1	0.311	0.360	0.400	8.00%	14.00%	41.0	23.1	35.9
2016	A	164	24	6	0	2	1	1	0.230	0.348	0.317	13.41%	15.85%	54.9	17.7	21.2
2018	A+	515	88	36	3	6	1	1	0.280	0.320	0.406	5.05%	14.95%	46.8	20.4	28.8
2019	AA	397	66	23	1	15	1	2	0.300	0.373	0.500	10.58%	16.88%	53.0	20.4	21.8

Background: Originally signed by the Yankees all the way back during the summer of 2012. A native of Valencia, Venezuela, Torrens was passed around by a few teams following the 2016 season. The 6-foot, 175-pound backstop was taken by the Reds with the second overall pick of the Rule 5 draft and then quickly flipped him to the Padres. After moonlighting with San Diego that following season, the Padres bounced Torrens down to the California League for the 2018 season. And his bat came alive. In 122 games with the Lake Elsinore Storm, Torrens slugged a healthy .280/.320/.406 with a whopping 36 doubles, three triples, and six homeruns. Last season the front office bumped the young backstop up to the Texas League. And Torrens – quietly – had his finest showing to date as he slugged .300/.373/.500 with 23 doubles, one triple, and 15 homeruns in only 97 games of action. Per *Deserved Runs Plus*, his overall production topped the league average threshold by 35%.

Scouting Report: Consider the following:

- Since 2006, only five 23-year-old hitters have tallied a 135- to 145- DRC+ in the Texas League (min. 350 PA):Andrew Knizner, Mitch Moreland, Kyle Parker, Ryan Casteel, and Luis Torrens.

In many other organizations, not only would Torrens be one of the systems better prospects, but he'd also have a clear cut path to a starting gig at the big league level. Unfortunately, though, he's locked in behind an offensive-minded backstop – Francisco Mejia – and a defensive wizard (Austin Hedges). Torrens is a do-everything-well-without-a-true-standout type of prospect. He'll handle himself well at the plate and behind the dish. There's definite starting material here. And Wilson Ramos' 2019 season with the Mets – he batted .288/.351/.416 – seems reasonable.

Ceiling: 1.5- to 2.0-win player
Risk: Low to Moderate
MLB ETA: Debuted in 2017

13. Joshua Mears, RF

Hit	Power	SB	Patience	Glove	Overall
40/45	55/65	50	50+	50	50

Born: 02/21/01	Age: 19	Bats: R
Height: 6-3	Weight: 230	Throws: R

YEAR	LVL	PA	1B	2B	3B	HR	SB	CS	AVG	OBP	SLG	BB%	K%	GB%	LD%	FB%
2019	Rk	195	28	4	3	7	9	1	0.253	0.354	0.440	11.79%	30.26%	45.9	15.6	30.3

Background: A product of Federal Way High School, Mears became the school's earliest draft pick since right-hander Dan Spillner was chosen in the second round all the way back in 1970. And what team drafted Spiller? Coincidentally, the San Diego Padres. A chiseled 6-foot-3, 230-pound corner outfielder, Mears appeared in 43 games with the ballclub's Arizona Summer League affiliate, slugging a respectable .253/.354/.440 with four doubles, three triples, seven homeruns, and nine stolen bases in 10 total attempts. Per Baseball Prospectus' *Deserved Runs Created Plus*, Mears' production was exactly 100. Meaning: he was the quintessential average offensive performer. Mears signed for a slightly below-slot deal worth $1 million.

Scouting Report: Consider the following:

- Since 2006, only two 18-year-old hitters tallied a DRC+ between 95 and 105 with a strikeout rate north of 28% in the Arizona Summer League (min. 175 PA): Cabrera Weaver and Joshua Mears.

Growing up I distinctly remember the way the bat would slam against Mike Piazza's at the completion of his swing. It was powerful. And that's the same type of swing Mears showed during his debut last season. Strong, like natural God-given strength, with tree trunks for legs and a surprising amount of speed. There's a chance for 65-grade power. The problem for Mears, though, are the punch outs. He whiffed in more than 30% of his plate appearances last season. If he can keep that mark on the right side of 25% moving forward, he could be special.

Ceiling: 2.0-win player
Risk: Moderate to High
MLB ETA: 2022

14. Reggie Lawson, RHP

FB	CB	CH	Command	Overall
N/A	N/A	N/A	N/A	45

Born: 08/02/97	Age: 22	Bats: R
Height: 6-4	Weight: 205	Throws: R

YEAR	LVL	IP	W	L	SV	ERA	FIP	WHIP	K/9	K%	BB/9	BB%	K/BB	HR9	BABIP
2017	A	73.0	4	6	0	5.30	4.00	1.37	11.0	28.34%	4.3	11.15%	2.54	0.99	0.317
2018	A+	117.0	8	5	0	4.69	4.33	1.55	9.0	22.37%	3.9	9.75%	2.29	0.85	0.348
2019	AA	27.7	3	1	0	5.20	4.13	1.48	11.7	29.75%	4.2	10.74%	2.77	1.30	0.353

Background: The type of hurler that owns a track record of impressive peripherals that tends to get clouded by some unsightly ERAs. Lawson, a second round pick out of Victor Valley High School four years ago, averaged an impressive 11.0 strikeouts and 4.3 walks per nine innings with a 5.30 ERA in 17 starts in the Midwest League as a 19-year-old. He followed that up with a 117-to-51 strikeout-to-walk ratio with a 4.69 ERA in 117.0 innings of work in the California League I 2018. And last season, Lawson continued down a similar path: he fanned 36 and walked 13 through his first six appearances. But a wonky elbow prematurely ended his season in the middle of May. Fortunately, the 6-foot-4, 205-pound right-hander was able to avoid any surgical procedures after receiving a platelet-rich plasma injection and requisite rehab work. He popped up in the Arizona Fall League for a trio of brief appearances.

Snippet from The 2018 Prospect Digest Handbook: Lawson has the repertoire to slide comfortably into a slot in the middle of a big league rotation: his fastball shows exceptional life up in the zone; his curveball is a late-breaking, heavily tilted weapon; and his changeup flashes above-average. His control/command, though, has ways to go. If the control remains as is, Lawson still becomes a #4/#5-type pitcher.

Scouting Report: According to reports, Lawson's heater was back in the 93- to 96-mph range, which is a definite plus in terms of his long term future. The command hasn't quite developed as expected and the long layoff/loss of development time won't aid him. The front office has been eager to push some of the more recognizable young arms into the bullpen – see: Adrian Morejon and Michel Baez – and Lawson seems like a prime candidate. For now, though, he looks like a solid backend starter with a touch higher upside if the command/control sees an uptick.

Ceiling: 1.5- to 2.0-win player
Risk: Moderate
MLB ETA: 2020

15. Hudson Potts, 3B

Hit	Power	SB	Patience	Glove	Overall
40+	50/55	30	45+	45+	45

Born: 10/28/98	Age: 21	Bats: R
Height: 6-3	Weight: 205	Throws: R

YEAR	LVL	PA	1B	2B	3B	HR	SB	CS	AVG	OBP	SLG	BB%	K%	GB%	LD%	FB%
2017	A	522	77	23	4	20	0	1	0.253	0.293	0.438	4.41%	26.82%	43.3	16.7	34.3
2018	A+	453	61	35	1	17	3	1	0.281	0.350	0.498	8.17%	24.72%	44.4	20.2	29.0
2018	AA	89	10	0	0	2	1	0	0.154	0.258	0.231	11.24%	37.08%	35.6	17.8	26.7
2019	AA	448	53	23	1	16	3	1	0.227	0.290	0.406	7.14%	28.57%	40.8	24.5	23.4

Background: Fun Fact: Carroll High School in Southlake, Texas, has produced two famous baseball alums: former Texas Christian University right-hander Tyler Alexander and John Curtiss, a former Texas Longhorn. Potts, though, is the highest drafted Carroll High School product. The 24th overall selection in the 2016 draft, the hulking young third baseman has been a consistent power threat during his four-year career. Last season, his first in Class AA, Potts' sagged as he slugged .227/.290/.406 with 23 doubles, one triple, and 16 homeruns in 107 games. Per Baseball Prospectus' *Deserved Runs Created Plus*, his overall production was a staggering 42% *below* the league average threshold. San Diego sent the former first rounder to the Arizona Fall League where he – largely – looked overwhelmed as he batted .182/.191/.250 in 13 games with Peoria.

Snippet from The 2018 Prospect Digest Handbook: The hit tool's never going to be an above-average weapon, but his potent thump helps to compensate – especially if he's walking near the league average.

Scouting Report: If Baseball Prospectus wasn't responsible for tabulating *Deserved Runs Created* I absolutely wouldn't believe that Potts' production line – as compared to the league average – was a staggering poor as it was. It bears repeating: he was 42% *below the league average threshold*. He maintained some impressive thump and average-ish walk rates. The bad news: he whiffed in nearly 29% of his plate appearances. But there is a silver lining of sorts: over his final 56 games with the Sod Poodles, he batted .248/.298/.467 with 11 doubles, one triple, and 11 homeruns. The power spikes up to plus territory, he's a low end starter. If not, he's a Quad-A bat.

Ceiling: 1.5-win player
Risk: Moderate
MLB ETA: 2020/2021

16. Edward Olivares, RF

Hit	Power	SB	Patience	Glove	Overall
50	50	60	50	50+	45

Born: 03/06/96	Age: 24	Bats: R
Height: 6-2	Weight: 186	Throws: R

YEAR	LVL	PA	1B	2B	3B	HR	SB	CS	AVG	OBP	SLG	BB%	K%	GB%	LD%	FB%
2017	A	464	66	26	9	17	18	7	0.277	0.330	0.500	4.74%	17.67%	45.8	15.9	26.2
2017	A+	77	13	1	1	0	2	2	0.221	0.312	0.265	10.39%	22.08%	51.0	17.6	27.5
2018	A+	575	100	25	10	12	21	8	0.277	0.321	0.429	5.04%	17.74%	47.2	18.3	26.1
2019	AA	551	93	25	2	18	35	10	0.283	0.349	0.453	7.80%	17.79%	43.2	24.6	23.6

Background: Originally signed by the Blue Jays all the way back during the 2014 summer signing period. Toronto flipped the toolsy – albeit flawed – outfielder to San Diego two years ago as part of the return for veteran infielder Yangervis Solarte. Olivares, who was acquired along with right-hander Jared Carkuff, spent the entirety of 2019 battling – and succeeding – against the minors' toughest challenge: Class AA. In 127 games with the Amarillo Sod Poodles, the 6-foot-2, 186-pound outfielder slugged a healthy .283/.349/.453 with 25 doubles, two triples, and a career best 18 dingers. He also set a new personal best with 35 stolen bases (in 45 total attempts). Per *DRC+*, his overall production topped the league average threshold by 14%.

Scouting Report: Consider the following:

- Since 2006, only four 23-year-old hitters met the following criteria in the Texas League (min. 350 PA): 110 to 120 DRC+, a sub-20% strikeout rate, and a walk rate between 7% and 9%. Those four hitters: Richie Martin, Tommy Edman, Peter Ciofrone, and – of course – Edward Olivares.

Quintessential fourth outfielder type. Olivares does it everything well enough: average hit tool, 15-homer pop, plus speed, and some defensive versatility in the outfield. He's going to struggle finding time – let alone consistent time – in San Diego, so he could be a nice cheap pick up for a rebuilding club. Similar to former Tribe outfielder Jody Gerut.

Ceiling: 1.5-win player
Risk: Moderate
MLB ETA: 2020

17. Efrain Contreras, RHP

FB	CB	SL	CH	Command	Overall
60	55	50	50	55	45

Born: 01/02/00	Age: 20	Bats: R
Height: 5-10	Weight: 210	Throws: R

YEAR	LVL	IP	W	L	SV	ERA	FIP	WHIP	K/9	K%	BB/9	BB%	K/BB	HR9	BABIP
2018	Rk	43.0	1	3	0	2.72	3.77	1.05	9.2	25.73%	1.9	5.26%	4.89	0.63	0.295
2018	Rk	19.3	0	0	1	1.40	2.19	0.78	11.6	33.78%	1.4	4.05%	8.33	0.47	0.250
2018	A-	6.0	1	0	0	0.00	2.22	0.50	10.5	35.00%	3.0	10.00%	3.50	0.00	0.091
2019	A	109.7	6	6	0	3.61	3.68	1.18	9.9	27.94%	2.6	7.39%	3.78	0.98	0.306

Background: Even if his production was incredibly dominating over the past two seasons – because it definitely was – Contreras' inclusion on the Padres' Top 20 list for this season was a near lock as soon as I heard his badass nickname: The Embalmer – which is nod to his family mortuary business. A slight-framed right-hander out of Ciudad Juarez, Mexico, Contreras flashed some incredible potential as he skipped through three low levels two years ago: he posted a 76-to-14 strikeout-to-walk ratio with a 2.11 ERA in only 68.1 innings of work. Last season Contreras moved up to the Midwest League, but that didn't slow his lightning quick arm. Making 25 appearances with the TinCaps, 23 of which were starts, the hard-throwing righty whiffed 121 and walked just 32 in 109.2 innings. He finished his second season with a 3.61 ERA and a 4.25 DRA (*Deserved Run Average*).

Scouting Report: Consider the following:

- Since 2006, here's the list of 19-year-old arms to post a K% between 25.5% and 27.5% with a BB% between 7% and 10% in either Low Class A league (min. 100 IP): Trevor Cahill, Randall Delgado, Michael Bowden, and – of course – Efrain Contreras.

I caught a couple of Contreras' April starts, as well as his final start of the year. The difference: his fastball. Contreras' heater was sitting 91- to 92-mph early in the year and was sitting – comfortably – in the 93- to 94-mph range at season's end. He'll mix in an above-average 12-6 bending curveball; an upper 80s slider; and a 50-grade changeup. Contreras throws a lot of strikes, though he's not a genuine command guy. At 5-foot-10 and 200 pounds, he's physically maxed out. He looks like a backend starting pitcher unless the slider/changeup upticks.

Ceiling: 1.5-win player
Risk: Moderate
MLB ETA: 2022

18. Ronald Bolanos, RHP

FB	CB	SL	CH	Command	Overall
60	50	50	45+	45	40

Born: 08/23/96	Age: 23	Bats: R
Height: 6-3	Weight: 220	Throws: R

YEAR	LVL	IP	W	L	SV	ERA	FIP	WHIP	K/9	K%	BB/9	BB%	K/BB	HR9	BABIP
2017	A	69.3	5	2	0	4.41	4.15	1.43	6.6	17.23%	4.4	11.49%	1.50	0.39	0.301
2018	A+	125.0	6	9	0	5.11	4.65	1.50	8.5	21.15%	3.6	8.96%	2.36	0.94	0.341
2019	A+	53.7	5	2	0	2.85	4.07	1.12	9.1	24.66%	3.9	10.50%	2.35	0.67	0.244
2019	AA	76.7	8	5	0	4.23	3.90	1.32	10.3	26.99%	3.5	9.20%	2.93	0.82	0.335

Background: Part of the club's big free agent expenditures in 2016. Bolanos, who hails from Santa Cruz del Norte, Cuba, has quickly climbed the minor league ladder during his stateside career – despite some mediocre performances. After an underwhelming showing in the Midwest League where he averaged a disappointingly mediocre 6.6 strikeouts and 4.4 walks per nine innings, the 6-foot-3, 220-pound right-hander blossomed into a viable big league pitching prospect in the California League in 2018. The then-21-year-old struck out 118 and walked 50 in 125.0 innings of work – though he was hit around a bit as he posted a 5.11 ERA. Bolanos opened last season back up in High Class A – with far better results: 9.1 K/9, 3.9 BB/9, and a 2.85 ERA in 10 starts. The front office bumped the enigmatic hurler up to the Texas League in early June for another 15 appearances; he tossed 76.2 innings with 88 strikeouts and 30 free passes with the Sod Poodles. Bolanos made five final appearances with the Padres late in the season, posting a 19-to-12 strikeout-to-walk ratio.

Scouting Report: The arsenal is a bit underwhelming. His fastball, which averaged a smidgeon over 94 mph during his MLB debut, was far too hittable last season; it's straight and "lite". His two-seamer shows some arm-side run. His 12-6 bending curveball will – rarely – flash above-average when he's locating low, but it's inconsistent. He'll mix in a low- to mid-80s cutter-like slider and a straight changeup. The production, arsenal, and control/command don't gel well, so he's likely headed to the pen – potentially peaking as a Rafael Betancourt type arm.

Ceiling: 1.0- to 1.5-win player
Risk: Moderate
MLB ETA: Debuted in 2019

19. Jeisson Rosario, CF

Hit	Power	SB	Patience	Glove	Overall
45/50	35/40	55	55	55	40

Born: 10/22/99	Age: 20	Bats: L
Height: 6-1	Weight: 191	Throws: L

YEAR	LVL	PA	1B	2B	3B	HR	SB	CS	AVG	OBP	SLG	BB%	K%	GB%	LD%	FB%
2017	RK	224	45	10	0	4	8	6	0.299	0.404	0.369	14.73%	16.07%	52.6	18.8	23.4
2018	A	521	93	17	5	3	18	12	0.271	0.368	0.353	12.67%	20.73%	50.6	19.0	24.0
2019	A+	525	83	14	4	3	11	4	0.242	0.372	0.314	16.57%	21.71%	51.6	19.2	23.9

Background: The front office went hog wild on the amateur free agent market during the 2016 season, committing – according to *Baseball America* – more than $80 million in their quest for top end talent. And Rosario, a wiry center fielder out of Santo Domingo, Dominican Republic, was one of the bigger names acquired that year. Standing 6-foot-1 and 191 pounds, Rosario showed some offensive promise during his professional debut in 2017 as he batted a respectable .299/.404/.369 as a 17-year-old in the stateside rookie league. The front office promoted the teenager up to the Midwest League the following season. And he looked...solid. In 117 games with Fort Wayne, Rosario batted .271/.368/.353 with 17 doubles, five triples, and a trio of homeruns to go along with 18 stolen bases. Per *Deserved Runs Created Plus*, his overall production was 3% below the league average mark. Rosario spent last season squaring off against the California League pitching. He responded with a .242/.372/.314 triple-slash line, belting out 14 doubles, four triples, three homeruns, and 11 stolen bases. And despite the lackluster slash line, his overall production topped the league average mark by 18%.

Snippet from The 2018 Prospect Digest Handbook: The question for Rosario – and it could determine whether he develops into a starting vs. backup outfielder – is whether he develops any type of power.

Scouting Report: Same story, different year. Rosario's still showing little thump in his bat. And the fact that he's putting the ball on the ground 50% of the time, suggests that won't change without a swing remake. Rosario actually performed solidly for three months of the season as he batted .253/.341/.354, .307/.381/.347, and .304/.453/.446 in May, June, and August. The problem, though is he tallied sub-.600 OPS the other two months. Extreme patience at the plate – which is where he generates the majority of his value. Although he's only entering his age-20 season, he's quickly heading down the path of a fourth/fifth outfielder.

Ceiling: 1.0- to 1.5-win player
Risk: Moderate
MLB ETA: 2021/2022

20. Yeison Santana, SS

Hit	Power	SB	Patience	Glove	Overall
40/45	40/45	40	55	50	40

Born: 12/07/00	Age: 19	Bats: R
Height: 5-11	Weight: 170	Throws: R

YEAR	LVL	PA	1B	2B	3B	HR	SB	CS	AVG	OBP	SLG	BB%	K%	GB%	LD%	FB%
2018	RK	173	28	1	5	0	5	5	0.258	0.405	0.341	19.08%	17.34%	43.9	22.4	26.2
2019	Rk	192	43	5	5	3	4	5	0.346	0.429	0.494	11.98%	19.79%	53.9	20.3	21.9

Background: An unheralded signing out of Azua, Dominican Republic, three years ago – although, Padres outfielder Franchy Cordero did share the announcement on Twitter at the time – Santana has shown a solid offensive foundation during his brief professional career. The 5-foot-11, 170-pound shortstop batted an IBO-driven .258/.405/.341 during his debut in the foreign rookie league in 2018, belting out one double and five triples. Last season Santana moved stateside to battle the Arizona Summer League. In 41 games, he hit a scorching .346/.429/.494 with five doubles, five triples, and a trio of homeruns to go along with a quarter of stolen bases. Per *Deserved Runs Created Plus*, his overall production line topped the league average threshold by a whopping 48%.

Scouting Report: Consider the following:

- Since 2006, here's the list of 18-year-old hitters to post a DRC+ between 143 and 153 with a double-digit walk rate and a strikeout rate between 18% and 22% in the Arizona Summer League (min. 150 PA): B.J. Boyd, Raynel Delgado, Brandon Diaz, and – of course – Yeison Santana.

Does. Not. Get. Cheated. The wiry shortstop swings like a bonafide 40-homerun threat. And, subsequently, the swing's a bit too long. But there's some bat speed and natural loft in place. He could wind up belting out 15 homeruns or so. Strong patience and decent contact skills with a solid glove. Santana's one of the more interesting low level wild cards in the Padres' system. He's profiling more as a utility guy, but there's a bit more headroom in the ceiling.

Ceiling: 1.0- to 1.5-win player
Risk: Moderate
MLB ETA: 2022/2023

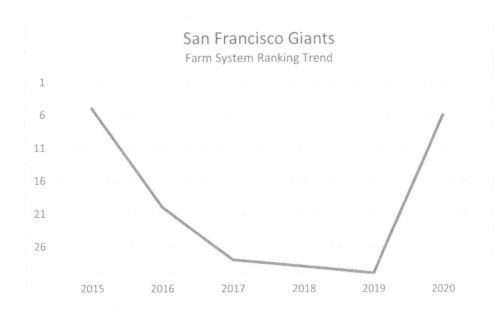

San Francisco Giants
Farm System Ranking Trend

Rank	Name	Age	Pos
1	Marco Luciano	18	SS
2	Joey Bart	23	C
3	Heliot Ramos	20	CF
4	Seth Corry	21	LHP
5	Logan Webb	23	RHP
6	Hunter Bishop	22	CF
7	Luis Matos	18	CF
8	Alexander Canario	20	OF
9	Luis Toribio	19	3B
10	Jairo Pomares	19	RF
11	Mauricio Dubon	25	2B/SS
12	Will Wilson	21	SS
13	Logan Wyatt	22	1B
14	Sean Hjelle	23	RHP
15	Gregory Santos	20	RHP
16	Tristan Beck	24	RHP
17	Diego Rincones	21	LF/RF
18	Kai-Wei Teng	21	RHP
19	Blake Rivera	22	RHP
20	Jake Wong	23	RHP

1. Marco Luciano, SS

Hit	Power	SB	Patience	Glove	Overall
50/60	55/70	45	65	45/50	70

Born: 09/10/01	Age: 18	Bats: R
Height: 6-2	Weight: 178	Throws: R

YEAR	LVL	PA	1B	2B	3B	HR	SB	CS	AVG	OBP	SLG	BB%	K%	GB%	LD%	FB%
2019	Rk	178	26	9	2	10	8	6	0.322	0.438	0.616	15.17%	21.91%	43.0	14.0	37.4
2019	A-	38	3	4	0	0	1	0	0.212	0.316	0.333	13.16%	15.79%	37.0	14.8	40.7

Background: The Giants landed the top middle infield prospect on the international scene two years ago, agreeing to sign the 6-foot-2, 178-pound teenager to a hefty $2.6 million pact. The young shortstop bypassed the Dominican Summer League last season and headed stateside to begin his professional career. Luciano played in 38 games in the Arizona Summer League in 2019, slugging an impressive .322/.438/.616 with nine doubles, a pair of triples, and a whopping 10 homeruns to go along with eight stolen bases in 14 total attempts. His overall production, according to Baseball Prospectus' *Deserved Runs Created Plus*, topped the league average threshold by a whopping 95%. The San Francisco de Macoris, Dominican Republic native also spent the final nine games of the year in the Northwest League, approaching the league average production line despite a depressed .212/.316/.333 triple-slash line.

Scouting Report: Consider the following:

- Since 2006, only three 17-year-old hitters posted at least a 190 DRC+ in the Arizona Summer League (min. 150 PA): Mike Trout, Dorssys Paulino, and – of course – Marco Luciano.

Ignoring Luciano momentarily, that's two players on the complete ends of the spectrum: a player who's on pace to be the greatest in history and Paulino, who washed out of professional baseball two years ago. As for Luciano, he flashed tremendous potential as a dynamic top-of-the-lineup bat with an extreme saber-slant. He walked in nearly 15% of his plate appearances during his debut. Mix in solid contact rates, above-average speed, strong defense at an up-the-middle position, and plus- to plus-plus power potential and there's *A LOT* to love about this kid. One more brief note: Luciano's 195 DRC+ is the fifth best mark for a 17-year-old in any stateside rookie league since 2006, trailing (in order): Mike Trout, Dorssys Paulino, Juan Soto, and Luis Garcia. For those counting at home that's: one Hall of Famer (Trout), a player who could very well wind up in the Hall of Fame (Soto), one of the best prospects in the game (Garcia, who spent the entire 2019 in Class AA as a teenager), and a bust (Paulino). Per FanGraphs, Luciano's average exit velocity, 92 mph, last season was tied as the seventh best among all measured minor league hitters (304 total). Again, he was 17-years-old.

Ceiling: 6.5-win player
Risk: Moderate
MLB ETA: 2022

2. Joey Bart, C

Hit	Power	SB	Patience	Glove	Overall
55	65	30	45	55	60

Born: 12/15/96	Age: 23	Bats: R
Height: 6-3	Weight: 235	Throws: R

YEAR	LVL	PA	1B	2B	3B	HR	SB	CS	AVG	OBP	SLG	BB%	K%	GB%	LD%	FB%
2018	RK	25	4	1	1	0	0	0	0.261	0.320	0.391	4.00%	28.00%	43.8	25.0	18.8
2018	A-	203	25	14	2	13	2	1	0.298	0.369	0.613	5.91%	19.70%	51.4	10.6	31.7
2019	A+	251	38	10	2	12	5	2	0.265	0.315	0.479	5.58%	19.92%	42.9	16.8	31.5
2019	AA	87	16	4	1	4	0	2	0.316	0.368	0.544	8.05%	24.14%	44.1	16.9	32.2

Background: In the history of the modern June draft only nine catchers have been chosen with the first or second overall selection: Steve Chilcott, who was famously chosen one pick in front of Reggie Jackson, Mike Ivie, Danny Goodwin, who was selected with the top overall pick twice, Joe Mauer, Adley Rutschman, John Stearns, Tyler Houston, Ben Davis, and – of course – Joey Bart. An absolute monster at the plate during his three-year career at Georgia Tech, Bart left the ACC school as a lifetime .321/.407/.544 hitter, offering up a bevy of game-changing skills. At the time of his signing, Bart was handed the largest signing bonus for a position player – a hefty $7.025 million. The Georgia native – and a product of Buford High School – Bart's professional career got off to a fantastic start: he slugged .294/.364/.588 with 15 doubles, three triples, and 13 homeruns in 51 games between rookie ball and the Northwest League. Last season, though, was a bit of a roller coaster for the former Yellow Jacket. He missed significant time at the start of the year due to a broken bone courtesy of a wild pitch. And his successful stint in the Arizona Fall League ended in a similar manner: an errant pitch. A 96 mph heater, from Pirates hurler Blake Cederlind, fractured his thumb. Outside of the injuries, the 6-foot-3, 235-pound backstop batted a combined .278/.328/.495 between stints with San Jose and Richmond.

Snippet from The 2018 Prospect Digest Handbook: A lot of my trepidation surrounding Bart was, simply, his future ability to make contact. He fanned in slightly more than 20% of his plate appearances last season against vastly inferior competition. And I suspected – and still do – that it's incredibly likely that number will eventually go up as he climbs the minor league ladder. Though, it should be noted it was a pedestrian

19.7% in short-season ball, which offers hope down the line as well. Bart should also provide plenty of value behind the dish as well: he threw out 42% of would-be base stealers with Salem-Keizer and was a plus-3 defender in an admittedly brief stint.

Scouting Report: The overall numbers are solid, not great, until his injuries are factored into the analysis. After returning to San Jose in early June after missing nearly two months Bart struggled – unsurprisingly – at the plate; he hit a lowly .205/.271/.455 in 12 games. However, over the remainder of the regular season his slash line was an impressive .293/.337/.496. And he raised his offensive production through his limited 10-game cameo in the Arizona Fall League, slugging .333/.524/.767. Bart's strikeout rates continue to be a nonfactor. Combine those strong contact rates with plus-power and above-average defense and Bart's ceiling resides in the neighborhood of a perennial All-Star. The lone knock on him: his below-average walk rates, which chews into his overall ceiling. He's like the Adam Jones the catching. Low walk rates, 30-homer power potential, 55-grade hit tool.

Ceiling: 4.5-win player
Risk: Low to Moderate
MLB ETA: 2020

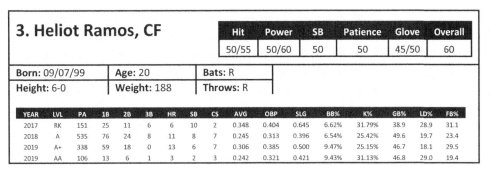

	Hit	Power	SB	Patience	Glove	Overall
3. Heliot Ramos, CF	50/55	50/60	50	50	45/50	60

Born: 09/07/99	Age: 20	Bats: R
Height: 6-0	Weight: 188	Throws: R

YEAR	LVL	PA	1B	2B	3B	HR	SB	CS	AVG	OBP	SLG	BB%	K%	GB%	LD%	FB%
2017	RK	151	25	11	6	6	10	2	0.348	0.404	0.645	6.62%	31.79%	38.9	28.9	31.1
2018	A	535	76	24	8	11	8	7	0.245	0.313	0.396	6.54%	25.42%	49.6	19.7	23.4
2019	A+	338	59	18	0	13	6	7	0.306	0.385	0.500	9.47%	25.15%	46.7	18.1	29.5
2019	AA	106	13	6	1	3	2	3	0.242	0.321	0.421	9.43%	31.13%	46.8	29.0	19.4

Background: One of the youngest players in the 2017 draft class, Ramos' youth belied his production during his debut: in 35 games in the Arizona Summer League the then-17-year-old slugged a scorching .348/.404/.645 with 11 doubles, six triples, and six homeruns to go along with 10 stolen bases. The production generated gobs of hype and hoopla. And then he crashed – *hard* – upon his promotion to the South Atlantic League the following season. The toolsy, albeit raw, center fielder cobbled together a disappointing .245/.313/.396 triple-slash line, though he belted out 43 extra-base hits (24 doubles, eight triples, 11 homeruns, and eight stolen bases). Then the hype faded. Despite the struggles, though, the front office correctly decided to push the former first round pick up to the California League. And, viola, recaptured magic. The 6-foot, 188-pound center fielder slugged an impressive .306/.385/.500 with 18 doubles and 13 homeruns. San Francisco bumped the then 19-year-old up to Class AA – the most challenging minor league level – and he handled himself well by batting .242/.321/.421.

Snippet from The 2018 Prospect Digest Handbook: So there are a few things to note with the young center fielder:

1. Despite swinging one of the hottest bats in organized baseball during his debut, he still whiffed in nearly 32% of his plate appearances. But he was able to trim that down significantly – 25.4% – as he skipped several levels in 2018.
2. Not unusual – especially for young prospects making a big leap – Ramos struggled out of the gate as he transitioned into the Sally, hitting a depressingly poor .220/.297/.358 over his first 45 games. He was able to right the ship near the beginning of May and batted .260/.322/.417 over his remaining 79 contests.
3. The list of 18-year-old hitters with a modicum of success in the Sally isn't incredibly long, which also plays into his favor as well.

Scouting Report: Consider the following:

- Since 2006, here's the list of 19-year-old hitters that posted a DRC+ between 138 and 148 in the California League (min. 300 PA): Addison Russell, Luis Urias, Hudson Potts, and Heliot Ramos.

Incredibly toolsy with a matching ceiling. Ramos has a do-everything-well type of game. The hit tool will be an above-average weapon; the power's already average and could – conceivably – grow into a plus skill; 20-stolen base potential; and solid patience at the plate. He's still quite raw in center field – and the metrics match that assessment – but he should be no worse than average at full maturity. The lone pockmark (still): his borderline problematic strikeout rates. He whiffed in more than a quarter of his plate appearances in High Class A.

Ceiling: 4.0-win player
Risk: Moderate
MLB ETA: 2020/2021

4. Seth Corry, LHP

	FB	CB	CH	Command	Overall
	55+	60	50	40/45	60

Born: 11/03/98	Age: 21	Bats: L
Height: 6-2	Weight: 195	Throws: L

YEAR	LVL	IP	W	L	SV	ERA	FIP	WHIP	K/9	K%	BB/9	BB%	K/BB	HR9	BABIP
2017	Rk	24.3	0	2	0	5.55	5.99	1.48	7.8	19.09%	8.1	20.00%	0.95	0.37	0.203
2018	Rk	38.0	3	1	0	2.61	3.70	1.45	9.9	24.85%	4.0	10.06%	2.47	0.24	0.349
2018	A-	19.7	1	2	0	5.49	4.92	1.47	7.8	19.54%	6.9	17.24%	1.13	0.46	0.245
2019	A	122.7	9	3	0	1.76	2.85	1.07	12.6	33.86%	4.3	11.42%	2.97	0.29	0.265

Background: A third round pick out of Lone Peak High School in 2017, Corry battled some control demons over his first two stints in the minor leagues. As a baby-faced 18-year-old, the 6-foot-2, 195-pound southpaw walked 22 in only 24.1 innings in the Arizona Summer League. Corry followed that up by averaging 5.0 walks per nine innings between a return to the rookie league and Salem-Keizer. Last season the promising left-hander's control continued its trend in the right direction. Appearing in full-season action for the first time in his career, Corry made 27 appearances with the Augusta GreenJackets, throwing 122.2 innings while averaging 12.6 strikeouts and a career best 4.3 walks per nine innings of work. He compiled a barely-there 1.76 ERA and a 3.32 DRA (Deserved Run Average).

Snippet from The 2018 Prospect Digest Handbook: Young left-handed pitchers with three above-average pitches don't grow on trees. The fact that he's battling some control issues will only dull his prospect shine a bit. There's some #3/#4-type potential brewing in Corry's left arm. But, again, it's going to come down to his ability – or inability – to consistently throw strikes with all three pitches. He's very promising, but very raw.

Scouting Report: Consider the following:

- Since 2006, only three 20-year-old pitchers have fanned at least 30% of the hitters they faced in the South Atlantic League (min. 100 IP): former All-Star Matt Moore, A.J. Alexy, and – of course – Seth Corry.

Let's take it one step further:

NAME	YEAR	AGE	IP	DRA	K%	BB%
Matt Moore	2009	20	123.0	3.59	33.72%	13.41%
Seth Corry	2019	20	122.7	3.32	33.86%	11.42%

Not a bad comparison – at all. Corry attacks hitters with a heavy low-90s fastball; that patented hammer of a curveball, and a solid changeup. Corry's control – not command, though – took some important strides in the second half of last season. He walked just 18 hitters over his final 68.2 innings of work. It's a very encouraging sign that could point to better things in the future. He's a volatile prospect because he'll either wind up as a solid league-average starting or a solid reliever depending upon the control.

Ceiling: 3.5-win player
Risk: Moderate to High
MLB ETA: 2022

5. Logan Webb, RHP

	FB	SL	CH	Command	Overall
	60	65	45	50	50

Born: 11/18/96	Age: 23	Bats: R
Height: 6-2	Weight: 220	Throws: R

YEAR	LVL	IP	W	L	SV	ERA	FIP	WHIP	K/9	K%	BB/9	BB%	K/BB	HR9	BABIP
2017	A-	28.0	2	0	0	2.89	2.89	1.18	10.0	26.50%	2.3	5.98%	4.43	0.32	0.325
2018	A+	74.0	1	3	0	1.82	3.56	1.22	9.0	24.50%	4.4	11.92%	2.06	0.24	0.274
2018	AA	30.7	1	2	0	3.82	4.49	1.34	7.6	19.70%	3.2	8.33%	2.36	1.17	0.289
2019	A	10.0	1	0	0	0.90	2.87	0.70	8.1	24.32%	2.7	8.11%	3.00	0.00	0.167
2019	AA	41.3	1	4	0	2.18	2.39	1.28	10.2	30.13%	2.6	7.69%	3.92	0.44	0.333
2019	AAA	7.0	0	0	0	1.29	2.22	1.00	9.0	25.93%	0.0	0.00%	#DIV/0!	0.00	0.368

Background: "Webb's poised to be one of the bigger breakout prospects in 2019." That's what I wrote in last year's Handbook when I – clearly – became quite smitten with the former fourth round pick. A star two-way player at Rocklin High School, Webb, who threw 38 touchdowns during his three-years on the gridiron, did make it up to the big league for eight starts. The bad news: he got popped early in the season for a performance enhancing drug – Dehydrochlormethyltestosterone. It was the same drug that Daniel Stumpf and Chris Colabello tested positive for a couple years ago. Suspended for 80 games last season; the 6-foot-2, 220-pound right-hander made stops at four different minor league levels as he pitched himself back into shape before getting the call up to The Show in mid-August. Webb finished his sixth minor league season with a 69-to-15 strikeout-to-walk ratio in 63.1 innings. He made an additional eight starts with the Giants, throwing 39.2 innings with 37 strikeouts and 14 walks to go along with a 5.22 ERA and a 4.17 DRA.

Snippet from The 2018 Prospect Digest Handbook: A bit of a forgotten arm in the Giants' system because he was limited to just 70.0 innings the previous two seasons. Webb's fastball looked explosive during his time in Class AA reaching upwards of 95 mph on occasion. His slider, an above-average pitch that could see an uptick in grade as he polishes it more, is a filthy late-breaking offering. And his changeup will show some nice run to it, though it's clearly a below-average offering at this time. Given his limited experience – he tossed just 134.2 innings before this season – Webb still has some projection left in his right arm.

Scouting Report: If not for the PED suspension, Webb could have very easily been one of the more talked about rookies in 2019. The former over-slot signing shows two-plus pitches (fastball and slider), an improved changeup, and the ability to consistently throw strikes. Webb's one of the rare pitchers that shows a distinct visible difference between his four-seam and two-seam fastballs. He uses the four-seam fastball belt high and above to challenge hitters. And his two-seamer shows incredible sink and arm-side run. The difference between the offerings is similar to a fastball and cut-fastball. His slider is lethal, one of the best in the minor leagues. His changeup, which I had graded as a 45 with a chance to develop into a 50 last year, is a clear 50 now. Assuming he's beyond the arm issues in the past – he underwent Tommy John previously – Webb has the build and repertoire to become a #2/#3-type pitcher.

Ceiling: 3.0-win player
Risk: Moderate
MLB ETA: 2022

6. Hunter Bishop, CF

Hit	Power	SB	Patience	Glove	Overall
45	55	40	60	50	50

Born: 06/25/98	Age: 22	Bats: L
Height: 6-5	Weight: 210	Throws: R

YEAR	LVL	PA	1B	2B	3B	HR	SB	CS	AVG	OBP	SLG	BB%	K%	GB%	LD%	FB%
2019	Rk	29	1	3	0	1	2	0	0.250	0.483	0.550	31.03%	37.93%	33.3	11.1	55.6
2019	A-	117	13	1	1	4	6	2	0.224	0.427	0.400	24.79%	23.93%	43.6	9.1	27.3

Background: A two-sport star and middle-of-the-lineup thumper during his tenure at Junipero Serra High School, Bishop, a well-built 6-foot-5, 210-pound outfielder, slugged an impressive .426/.512/.663 during his senior season and had a football scholarship – which he ultimately declined – to attend the University of Washington. Bishop, who's older brother Braden was a third round pick by the Mariners in 2016, earned the distinction of playing for two state champions during his prep career: the Junipero Serra football team captured the crown in 2015 and the school's baseball squad accomplished the feat a year later. A mainstay in the middle of Arizona State's lineup throughout the duration of his colligate career, Bishop sported a healthy .301/.363/.484 triple-slash line with 14 extra-base hits and a handful of stolen bases during his freshman campaign, earning an All-Conference Honorable Mention along the way. He spent the ensuing summer playing for the Brewster Whitecaps in the Cape Cod League, hitting a paltry .212/.344/.308. Bishop's numbers declined noticeably during his sophomore campaign as his production line sagged to a mediocre .250/.352/.407 to go along with a ballooning strikeout rate (30.3%). And, once again, he spent the summer playing with the Whitecaps – though his production only improved modestly; he hit .233/.369/.350 with another concerning punch out rate (30.2%). Last season Bishop transformed his approach at the plate, improving his plate discipline vastly (21.8% K-rate and 17.9% BB-rate) while bashing the competition to the tune of .342/.479/.748 with career highs in doubles (16), triples (four), homeruns (22), and stolen bases (12). San Francisco snagged the raw, talented outfielder in the opening round, 10th overall. Bishop batted .229/.438/.429 during his debut.

Scouting Report: Here's what I wrote prior to the draft last season:

"Consider the following:

- *Between 2011 and 2018, only one other junior Division I hitter met the following criteria (min. 200 PA): 16% walk rate, a strikeout rate between 17% and 20%, and slugged at least .350/.450/.700. That hitter: former Florida Gator star – and the fifth overall pick in the 2018 draft – Jonathan India.*

Here's how their respective junior campaigns have measured up thus far:

Player	Year	Age	PA	AVG	OBP	SLG	BB%	K%
Hunter Bishop	2019	21	211	0.369	0.498	0.815	17.54%	19.43%
Jonathan India	2018	21	300	0.350	0.497	0.717	20.00%	18.67%

Obviously the numbers are nearly identical with the overall production value tilting in Bishop's direction. So let's take a look at their work throughout their respective collegiate careers:

Player	PA	AVG	OBP	SLG	BB%	K%
Hunter Bishop	547	0.310	0.412	0.581	12.80%	24.68%
Jonathan India	815	0.310	0.411	0.530	12.88%	17.30%

Again, the numbers closely parallel each other sans the strikeout rate, which was concerning during Bishop's early on. And that's not the only red flag for the Sun Devil either: he's faltered – significantly – during both of his stints in the Cape Cod, hitting a collective .223/.358/.330 in 278 total plate appearances. Bishop shows solid bat speed and enough loft in his swing to belt out 20 homeruns in a professional season. His swing-and-miss tendencies, despite the dramatic improvement, are still a bit concerning. But he should have no problems developing into a league average starting outfielder, particularly if he can stay in center field.

For the record: he fanned in nearly 27% of his plate appearances during his debut.

Ceiling: 3.0-win player
Risk: Moderate
MLB ETA: 2022

7. Luis Matos, CF

	Hit	Power	SB	Patience	Glove	Overall
	40/55	40/50	50/45	45	50	50

Born: 01/28/02	Age: 18	Bats: R
Height: 5-11	Weight: 160	Throws: R

Background: The Giants added the toolsy center fielder to the fold during the 2018 international signing date. Matos, a native of Valera, Venezuela, earned a payday just shy of three-quarters of a million dollars. Standing 5-foot-11 and 160 pounds, Matos made his professional debut with the organization's foreign rookie league affiliate last season: in 55 games with the DSL Giants, he scorched the competition to the tune of .362/.430/.570 with 24 doubles, a pair of triples, and seven homeruns. San Francisco bumped Matos up to the stateside rookie league for five brief games; he would go 7-for-16 with a double.

Scouting Report: Like a blade quickly and quietly moving through the air, Matos' swing looks almost effortless. Impressive bat speed and the type of lean, projectable frame that should only add layers of athleticism as he matures. Matos – basically – ran at will during his stint in the Dominican Summer League, but the thick lower half and large plodding steps has me doubting if he'll continue to do so as he matures. There's a chance for average or better tools across the board.

Ceiling: 2.5-win player
Risk: Moderate
MLB ETA: 2023

8. Alexander Canario, OF

	Hit	Power	SB	Patience	Glove	Overall
	45/50	50/55	45	50	45/50	50

Born: 05/07/00	Age: 20	Bats: R
Height: 6-1	Weight: 165	Throws: R

YEAR	LVL	PA	1B	2B	3B	HR	SB	CS	AVG	OBP	SLG	BB%	K%	GB%	LD%	FB%
2017	RK	274	43	17	4	5	18	10	0.294	0.391	0.464	12.04%	14.60%	48.5	16.8	21.9
2018	RK	208	31	5	2	6	8	5	0.250	0.357	0.403	12.98%	24.52%	47.2	13.4	26.8
2019	Rk	46	6	3	1	7	1	0	0.395	0.435	1.000	4.35%	19.57%	23.5	11.8	52.9
2019	A-	219	31	17	1	9	3	1	0.301	0.365	0.539	8.22%	32.42%	30.2	27.0	33.3

Background: In terms of baseball signing bonuses, Canario's $60,000 sum is a mere small pittance. But the young Dominican outfielder is quickly becoming one of the more exciting players in a developing San Francisco farm system. Measuring in at a wiry 6-foot-1 and 165 pounds, Canario turned in a solid debut in the foreign rookie league three years ago, bating .294/.391/.464 with 27 doubles, four triples, and five homeruns to go along with 18 stolen bases. His production declined a bit as the front office pushed him stateside the following year; he hit .250/.357/.403 with 13 extra-base knocks. In a bit of a surprising move the front office bounced the then-19-year-old back down to the Arizona Summer League before bumping up to the Northwest League, a more age-appropriate level. In 49 games with the Salem-Keizer Volcanoes, Canario posted a .301/.365/.539 triple-slash line with 17 doubles, one triple, and nine homeruns. His overall production with the short-season squad topped the league average threshold by a whopping 58%.

Snippet from The 2018 Prospect Digest Handbook: Canario has an intriguing power/speed foundation wrapped up in a potentially saber-friendly package. He remains incredibly raw – and several years away – but there's starting outfielder potential here.

Scouting Report: Canario's once saber-friendly ways pulled a 180-degree turn last season. He was far more aggressive at the plate as he posted – by far – the worst strikeout and walk rate of his career with Salem-Keizer (32.4% and 8.2%, respectively). On the other hand, he began to tap into his full power potential as he lofted the ball far more frequently (his GB% was a low 27.8%) and he stopped running on the base paths.

- Since 2006, only two 19-year-old hitters bested the 150 DRC+ mark in the Northwest League (min. 200 PA): Tyson Gillies, who accomplished the feat in 2008 and eventually petered out in Class AAA, and – of course – Alexander Canario.

Canario's morphed from a one side of the spectrum to the complete opposite. He's no longer that speedy, walk rate-driven outfielder. Instead he's playing like a slow, plodding power-hitter with contact issues. One more quick study:

- During the same time frame (2006-2019), there were forty 19-year-old hitters to whiff in at least 30% of their plate appearances in either short-season league (min. 200 PA). Of those 40, only two – Marcell Ozuna and Will Middlebrooks – turned into viable big leaguers.

Not great odds. But Canario owns loud tools that can be an impact – if he can make enough contact.

Ceiling: 2.5- to 3.0-win player
Risk: Moderate to High
MLB ETA: 2022

9. Luis Toribio, 3B

Hit	Power	SB	Patience	Glove	Overall
40/50	40/50	35/30	60/55	50	50

Born: 09/28/00	Age: 19	Bats: L
Height: 6-1	Weight: 165	Throws: R

YEAR	LVL	PA	1B	2B	3B	HR	SB	CS	AVG	OBP	SLG	BB%	K%	GB%	LD%	FB%
2018	RK	274	34	13	1	10	4	1	0.270	0.423	0.479	18.61%	22.63%	37.7	24.7	30.5
2019	Rk	234	34	15	3	3	4	5	0.297	0.436	0.459	19.23%	23.08%	43.6	19.5	29.3
2019	A-	13	2	1	0	0	0	0	0.273	0.385	0.364	15.38%	38.46%	16.7	50.0	0.0

Background: San Francisco signed the lefty-swinging third baseman for $300,000 as part of their haul on the international scene three years ago. The San Francisco de Macoris, Dominican Republic native made his debut in the foreign rookie league a season later, batting a power-drive .270/.423/.479 with 13 doubles, one triple, and 10 homeruns to go along with a quartet of stolen bases. The front office brass bounced the teenage third baseman to the stateside rookie league. And Toribio responded by slugging .297/.436/.459 with 15 homeruns, three triples, and three homeruns with four stolen bases (in nine attempts). His overall production, according to Baseball Prospectus' *Deserved Runs Created Plus*, topped the league average mark by a whopping 66%. Toribio also popped up in the Northwest League for his final three games.

Scouting Report: Consider the following:

- Since 2006, only three 18-year-old hitters posted a DRC+ between 160 and 175 with a walk rate of at least 15% in the Arizona Summer League (min. 200 PA): Clint Coulter, Cedric Hunter, and Luis Toribio.

Incredibly saber-friendly. Toribio, in 51 games in the rookie league last season, sported a near one-to-one strikeout-to-walk ratio, which is nearly unheard of. Solid contact rates with power that could develop into 20-homer territory in the coming years. The lone red flag for the lefty-swinging third baseman: he looked completely helpless against fellow southpaws in 2019, hitting a lowly .133/.341/.167 in limited action. Toribio is incredibly raw, but one of the more promising bats in the Giants' system. There's some starting caliber potential here.

Ceiling: 2.0- to 2.5-win player
Risk: Moderate
MLB ETA: 2022/2023

10. Jairo Pomares, RF

Hit	Power	SB	Patience	Glove	Overall
40/55	35/55	30	50	50	50

Born: 08/04/00	Age: 19	Bats: L
Height: 6-1	Weight: 185	Throws: R

YEAR	LVL	PA	1B	2B	3B	HR	SB	CS	AVG	OBP	SLG	BB%	K%	GB%	LD%	FB%
2019	Rk	167	40	10	4	3	5	3	0.368	0.401	0.542	5.99%	15.57%	45.0	19.1	31.3
2019	A-	62	9	3	0	0	0	0	0.207	0.258	0.259	1.61%	27.42%	41.5	29.3	17.1

Background: Signed out of Sancti Spiritus, Cuba, for just shy of a million dollars as part of the organization's haul on the international market two years ago. Pomares, a lefty-swinging corner outfielder, made his highly anticipated debut last season as the club pushed the teenage prospect straight into the Arizona Summer League. Appearing in 37 games in rookie ball, the 6-foot-1, 185-pound Cuban slugged a Ruthian .368/.401/.542 with 10 doubles, four triples, and a trio of homeruns. He also swiped five bags in eight attempts. His overall production, as measured by *Deserved Runs Created Plus*, topped the league average threshold by an impressive 69%. Pomares also spent 14 – mostly disastrous – games with Salem-Keizer in the Northwest League.

Scouting Report: Consider the following:

- Since 2006, only four 18-year-old hitters met the following criteria in the Arizona Summer League (min. 150 PA): a DRC+ between 165 and 175 and a sub-16% strikeout rate. Those four hitters are: Cedric Hunter, Teodoro Martinez, Yu-Cheng Chang, and – of course – Jairo Pomares. Interesting note: sans Pomares, two of the remaining three – Hunter and Chang – have popped up in the big leagues.

Big leg kick with a lightning quick bat that was touted for his power potential prior to signing with the club. Pomares has yet to fully tap into his over-the-fence pop, but showed a knack for consistently barreling up the baseball. And while his walk rates are slightly below-average, Pomares showed a solid eye at spitting on offspeed pitches under the strike zone / in the dirt. The Cuban teenage is still wiry, so his body's likely to continue to fill out as he matures. He looked incredibly overmatched during his stint in the Northwest League, so that bears watching as well. If you're a believer in the power potential – which, personally, I am – than there's a starting caliber ceiling, likely more.

Ceiling: 2.0- to 2.5-win player
Risk: Moderate
MLB ETA: 2023

11. Mauricio Dubon, 2B/SS

	Hit	Power	SB	Patience	Glove	Overall
	55	45	40	40	55	50

Born: 07/19/94	Age: 25	Bats: R
Height: 6-0	Weight: 160	Throws: R

YEAR	LVL	PA	1B	2B	3B	HR	SB	CS	AVG	OBP	SLG	BB%	K%	GB%	LD%	FB%
2017	AA	304	58	14	0	2	31	9	0.276	0.338	0.351	8.22%	13.82%	49.4	19.7	24.5
2017	AAA	244	40	15	0	6	7	6	0.272	0.320	0.420	5.74%	13.93%	40.7	18.0	27.3
2018	AAA	114	22	9	2	4	6	3	0.343	0.348	0.574	1.75%	16.67%	46.2	15.1	31.2
2019	AAA	112	24	4	0	4	1	2	0.323	0.391	0.485	8.93%	8.04%	39.3	21.3	29.2
2019	AAA	427	81	22	1	16	9	6	0.297	0.333	0.475	4.22%	13.82%	38.7	21.7	29.2

Background: Now onto his third organization, Dubon, who was originally drafted in the 26th round of the 2013 draft, was flipped to Milwaukee four years ago as part of that ridiculously lopsided deal that sent Tyler Thornburg to the Red Sox. San Francisco acquired the middle infielder at the trade deadline last season for 100 mph bullet-throwing right-hander Ray Black and All-Star southpaw Drew Pomeranz. Dubon, a native of San Pedro Sula, Honduras, had a successful comeback from a season-ending ACL injury in 2018. In 123 games between both organizations' Pacific Coast League affiliates, the 6-foot, 160-pound infielder slugged .302/.345/.477 with 26 doubles, one triple, and a career best 20 homeruns. His overall production, according to *Deserved Runs Created Plus*, topped the league average mark by 3%. He also spent a combined 30 games in the big leagues as well, batting .274/.306/.464 with five doubles and four homers.

Snippet from The 2018 Prospect Digest Handbook: A brief 62-game stint in High Class A three years ago notwithstanding, Dubon's never been a patient hitter. But he owns an above-average bat with the potential to be a solid .280 hitter in the big leagues. His power has developed from nonexistent to below-average over the past couple of years. There's enough of a foundation to carve out a spot as a low end everyday regular.

Scouting Report: So...about that power. It literally came out of nowhere last season. Most of that thump, of course, can be attributed to (A) the PCL's typical hitter-friendly environment and (B) those damn, new minor league balls. Dubon did belt out another four homeruns in 30 big league games, but the batted ball data was pretty atrocious (average exit velocity is 84.8 mph, Hard Hit % was just 19.8%). Dubon didn't run as frequently as in past years and he's still not walking often either. But the hit tool is above-average and he – generally – can play above-average defense on either side of the keystone. At his peak he looks like a .280/.315/.400-ish hitter – which is solid value for an up-the-middle position. With respect to his work in Class AAA last season, consider the following:

- Since 2006, here's the list of 24-year-old hitters to post a DRC+ between 98 and 108 with a sub 6.0% walk rate in the Pacific Coast League (min. 350 PA): Chris Shaw, Tyrone Taylor, Chad Pinder, Francisco Pena, Charlie Culberson, Chris Johnson, Wes Bankston, and Mauricio Dubon.

Ceiling: 2.0-win player
Risk: Low to Moderate
MLB ETA: Debuted in 2019

11. Will Wilson, 2B/SS

Hit	Power	SB	Patience	Glove	Overall
45/50	50	30	50	50	50

Born: 07/21/98	Age: 21	Bats: R
Height: 6-0	Weight: 184	Throws: R

YEAR	LVL	PA	1B	2B	3B	HR	SB	CS	AVG	OBP	SLG	BB%	K%	GB%	LD%	FB%
2019	Rk+	204	34	10	3	5	0	0	0.275	0.328	0.439	6.86%	23.04%	55.6	23.2	16.2

Background: Before becoming a mainstay atop the North Carolina State University's lineup Wilson put together one of the more absurd production lines during his senior season at Kings Mountain High School: in only 26 games the 6-foot, 184-pound middle infielder belted out a 21 extra-base hits (five doubles, two triples, and a whopping 14 homeruns) en route to slugging a mindboggling .535/.673/1.253. Wilson was inserted into the heart of N.C. State's lineup as a true freshman – he batted sixth – and immediately paid dividends; he went 3-for-4 with two doubles during his college debut against Hawaii. Becoming one of only a handful of freshman to start every game in the ACC, he compiled an impressive .300/.377/.504 triple-slash line, finishing the year with 21 doubles, two triples, and eight homeruns. And he cracked Team USA's star-studded lineup during the summer as well, hitting .208/.208/.208 in limited action. Collegiate Baseball and D1Baseball recognized him as a Freshman All-American after his stellar campaign. Wilson pushed his production line up to an even higher level during his follow up season, hitting .307/.376/.588 with 16 doubles, three triples, and 15 homeruns while shaving off three-percentage points from his strikeout rate. He would be named as a Dick Howser Trophy Semifinalist and Collegiate Baseball tabbed him as a Second Team All-American. Last season the talented shortstop put together his finest showing for Head Coach Elliot Avent: in 55 games, the North Carolina native slugged .339/.429/.665 with career highs in doubles (20) and homeruns (16). The Los Angeles Angels drafted the former Wolfpack star in the opening round, 15th. And after hitting a respectable .275/.328/.439 during his debut in the Pioneer League, the Halos flipped Wilson to the Giants – as well as Zack Cozart's bloated contract – for Garrett Williams.

Scouting Report: Here's what I wrote about him heading into the draft last season:

"Let's take a look at how his production as a freshman stacks up through a historic lens. Consider the following:

- *Between 2011 and 2018, here's the list of ACC players that hit at least .290/.370/.500 with a walk ratio between 8.0% and 10.5% and a strikeout rate of 8.0% to 10.5% (min. 200 PA): Chris Okey, Cameron Simmons, Sam Fragale, and – of course – Will Wilson. Okey was a second round pick; Simmons was a late round pick by the Rangers two years ago; and Fragale went undrafted.*

And it should be noted that Okey and Simmons accomplished the feat during their sophomore seasons and Fragale did it during his junior year. Now let's take a look at Wilson's sophomore campaign. Consider the following:

- *Between 2011 and 2018, only two hitters batted at least .300/.370/.580 with a walk rate between 9% and 11% in the ACC in a year (min. 200 PA): Will Wilson and Stuart Fairchild, a second round pick by the Reds in 2017. Fairchild, by the way, accomplished the feat during his junior year at Wake Forest.*

Finally, let's take a look at Wilson's numbers thus far in 2019. Consider the following:

- *Again, between 2011 and 2018, here's the list of ACC hitters to bat at least .320/.400/.600 with a walk rate between 10% and 14% in a year (min. 200 PA): Daniel Palka, a third round pick in 2013, David Thompson, a fourth round pick in 2015, and Stuart Fairchild.*

And here are Wilson's numbers against Fairchild's production during his junior season:

Player	Age	Year	PA	AVG	OBP	SLG	K%	BB%
Will Wilson	21	2019	205	0.331	0.410	0.657	18.10%	11.20%
Stuart Fairchild	21	2017	304	0.360	0.439	0.636	17.80%	10.20%

Fairchild, by the way, owns a decent .269/.350/.395 over his first 205 minor league games. Wilson shows incredible bat speed with enough power to belt out 15 or so homeruns in the professional ranks. The lone question hovering around Wilson's ceiling is whether his borderline red flag strikeout rates will balloon up in the minor leagues. Some of that concern will be negated a bit by his up-the-middle position. If the hit tool proves to be average, he's a league average or better starter. One more final thought: Oakland snagged former Missouri State University shortstop Jeremy Eierman in the second round last June; Wilson is a far superior prospect."

Ceiling: 2.0-win player
Risk: Moderate
MLB ETA: 2022

13. Logan Wyatt, 1B

Hit	Power	SB	Patience	Glove	Overall
50/60	40/50	30	60	50	50

Born: 11/15/97	Age: 22	Bats: L
Height: 6-4	Weight: 230	Throws: R

YEAR	LVL	PA	1B	2B	3B	HR	SB	CS	AVG	OBP	SLG	BB%	K%	GB%	LD%	FB%
2019	Rk	29	8	1	0	0	0	1	0.375	0.448	0.417	13.79%	20.69%	63.2	5.3	31.6
2019	A-	78	15	2	0	2	0	1	0.284	0.385	0.403	12.82%	11.54%	55.6	14.8	25.9
2019	A	76	10	3	0	1	0	0	0.233	0.368	0.333	15.79%	18.42%	64.6	14.6	16.7

Background: A potent middle of the lineup force over his final two seasons at the University of Louisville. Wyatt's career, however, began on a sour note with the Cardinals: he batted a lowly .167/.273/.222 in limited time as a true freshman. The 6-foot-4, 230-pound, lefty-swinging first baseman had a massive breakout campaign the following year. In 64 games with the ACC squad, Wyatt slugged .339/.490/.522 with 22 doubles, one triple, and six homeruns while displaying an absurd level of patience and bat control; he posted a 37-to-63 strikeout-to-walk ratio. The Kentucky native continued to swing a hot stick as he moved into the Cape Cod League that summer as well, hitting .305/.458/.438 with five double, four homeruns, and an impressive strikeout-to-walk ratio (24-to-29) against some of the elite amateur pitching in the nation. Last season Wyatt's overall production backed up a touch as he slashed to the tune of .291/.458/.470 with 12 doubles, one triple, and a career high nine dingers. He did, however, maintain his spectacular peripherals: 47 strikeouts and a whopping 68 walks. San Francisco snagged him in the second round last June. He made three brief stops during his debut, batting an aggregate .278/.388/.377.

Scouting Report: It's a simple question with a fairly difficult answer: Will Wyatt develop any type of meaningful power that will allow him to play at the preeminent power position (first base)? The answer: maybe. Wyatt shows an unparalleled short stroke at the plate, but he doesn't generate a ton of natural loft. The hit tool has a chance to climb into 60-grade territory. And the patience is already there. Throw in some average defense and that's a recipe for a Brendan Belt-type first baseman. And I think he eventually develops 20-homer in-game pop.

Ceiling: 2.0-win player
Risk: Moderate
MLB ETA: 2023

14. Sean Hjelle, RHP

FB	CB	SL	CH	Command	Overall
60+	50	50	55	55	45

Born: 05/05/97	Age: 23	Bats: R
Height: 6-6	Weight: 225	Throws: R

YEAR	LVL	IP	W	L	SV	ERA	FIP	WHIP	K/9	K%	BB/9	BB%	K/BB	HR9	BABIP
2018	A-	21.3	0	0	0	5.06	4.63	1.31	9.3	23.40%	1.7	4.26%	5.50	1.69	0.317
2019	A	40.7	1	2	0	2.66	3.00	1.23	9.7	25.58%	2.0	5.23%	4.89	0.66	0.333
2019	A+	77.7	5	5	0	2.78	3.29	1.18	8.6	22.77%	2.2	5.85%	3.89	0.23	0.326
2019	AA	25.3	1	2	0	6.04	3.32	1.86	7.5	17.65%	3.2	7.56%	2.33	0.36	0.430

Background: A tall redwood-esque hurler from the University of Kentucky. Hjelle, which is pronounced like jelly, strapped a missile to his 6-foot-11 frame and rocketed through three levels of competition during his first full year in the minors. Opening the year up with nine dominant starts in the South Atlantic League, the front office bumped the former Wildcat up to the California League at the end of May for 14 – mostly dominant – starts. He capped up his wild ride with five games with the Richmond Flying Squirrels. He made 28 starts in totality, throwing 143.2 innings while recording 139 punch outs and just 37 walks. He compiled a 3.32 ERA.

Snippet from The 2018 Prospect Digest Handbook: Hjelle offers up a standard four-pitch mix: a 91-92 mph fastball that grades up thanks to his long limbs and stride length, an above-average changeup that should confound hitters in the lower- to middle-levels of the minor leagues, a curveball and slider, the latter both grading out as average. Again, he looks like a serviceable #4/#5-type arm.

Scouting Report: Hjelle took some big strides last season – no pun intended. His fastball velocity, which was fringy average prior to the draft as well as his professional debut, was regularly touching the mid-90s last season. Throw in his long limbs and giant strides, and it's an easy 60+ grade. The curveball and slider were average. And the changeup remains his best secondary weapon. Hjelle throws a surprising amount of strikes for a massively-framed pitcher. And he generally commands the strike zone with all four pitches well. He still looks like a #4/#5-type arm unless one of the breaking balls takes a step forward.

Ceiling: 1.5- to 2.0-win player
Risk: Moderate
MLB ETA: 2020

15. Gregory Santos, RHP

FB	SL	CH	Command	Overall
60	50/55	50	50	45

Born: 08/28/99	Age: 20	Bats: R
Height: 6-2	Weight: 190	Throws: R

YEAR	LVL	IP	W	L	SV	ERA	FIP	WHIP	K/9	K%	BB/9	BB%	K/BB	HR9	BABIP
2017	Rk	18.7	1	0	0	1.93	3.61	1.39	8.2	20.48%	2.4	6.02%	3.40	0.96	0.322
2017	Rk	30.3	2	0	0	0.89	3.23	1.22	7.1	23.08%	4.5	14.42%	1.60	0.00	0.243
2018	A-	49.7	2	5	0	4.53	3.45	1.59	8.3	20.26%	2.7	6.61%	3.07	0.54	0.379
2019	A	34.7	1	5	0	2.86	4.25	1.24	6.8	18.18%	2.3	6.29%	2.89	1.04	0.288

Background: Originally signed by the Red Sox for $275,000, San Francisco acquired the burly right-hander – along with fellow hurler Shaun Anderson – for veteran Eduardo Nunez three years ago. Santos, a 6-foot-2, 190-pound prospect, spent the first two years of his career in the foreign rookie league – first battling control and command issues and then dominating the league without stellar peripherals. The San Cristobal, Dominican Republic native moved stateside to the Northwest League two years ago and it all finally started coming together. In 12 starts with Salem-Keizer, Santos averaged 8.3 strikeouts and just 2.7 walks per nine innings as an 18-year-old. San Francisco bumped him up to full-season action for the 2019 season. And despite battling shoulder issues prior to the year, as well as midway through the campaign, Santos made eight starts in the Sally. He posted a 26-to-9 strikeout-to-walk ratio in 34.2 innings of work.

Scouting Report: Santos throws a surprising amount of strikes for a couple reasons: #1 his age and level of competition the past two seasons and #2 young power arms are typically erratic more often than not. Santos' fastball sits in the mid-90s. And he complements it with a solid slider that flashes above-average and workable changeup. Shoulder issues at any age are concerning at age, but Santos' comes very early in his career, lingered throughout the season, and eventually curtailed his 2019 after eight starts. Santos has the upside as a #4-type starting pitcher, but he could easily wind up in the bullpen in a few years.

Ceiling: 1.5- to 2.0-win player
Risk: Moderate to High
MLB ETA: 2022

16. Tristan Beck, RHP

FB	CB	CH	Command	Overall
55+	60	55	50	45

Born: 06/24/96	Age: 24	Bats: R
Height: 6-4	Weight: 165	Throws: R

YEAR	LVL	IP	W	L	SV	ERA	FIP	WHIP	K/9	K%	BB/9	BB%	K/BB	HR9	BABIP
2018	Rk	4.7	0	0	0	0.00	1.93	1.29	13.5	36.84%	3.9	10.53%	3.50	0.00	0.400
2019	Rk	9.0	0	0	0	4.00	1.72	1.44	14.0	35.90%	4.0	10.26%	3.50	0.00	0.429
2019	A+	35.7	3	2	0	2.27	3.13	1.29	9.3	25.17%	3.3	8.84%	2.85	0.25	0.337
2019	A+	36.7	2	2	0	5.65	3.03	1.61	9.6	24.53%	3.4	8.81%	2.79	0.49	0.413

Background: Beck turned in one of the more memorable freshman campaigns at Stanford University in recent memory. Not only was he just the third freshman to start Opening Day for the Cardinal (Mike Mussina and Cal Quantrill also accomplished the feat), but the then-20-year-old right-hander posted a 2.48 ERA for the PAC12 squad across 83.1 innings with a stellar 76-to-26 strikeout-to-walk ratio. A stress fracture in his back knocked him out for the entirety of the following season (2017). Beck's production took a downturn during his return to Stanford in 2018 and the Atlanta Braves eventually capitalized on his low draft stock by selecting him in the fourth round. San Francisco acquired him as part of the return for Mark Melancon last season. Beck made 16 starts between both organizations' High Class A affiliate in 2019, posting a 90-to-31 strikeout-to-walk ratio in 81.1 innings of work.

Snippet from The 2018 Prospect Digest Handbook: Right now, though, he looks like a #3/#4 starting pitcher. There's risk though.

Scouting Report: Beck's fastball showed a bit more life last season than in previous years, pushing his 93- to 94-mph heater on the fringe of a plus offering. He complements the fastball with two above-average or better secondary offerings: a 12-6 snapdragon curveball, though he needs to clean up his command, and a running changeup that adds a third swing-and-miss pitch. Injuries – once again – flared up and cost Beck some precious development time; he missed two months due to a severe groin issue early in the year. There's some #4-type potential, but - just as I wrote last year – there's risk. It should be noted, though, that while he's spent a lot of time on the DL over the past several years, none of it has been due to arm/shoulder/elbow issues.

Ceiling: 1.5- to 2.0-win player
Risk: Moderate to High
MLB ETA: 2021

17. Diego Rincones, LF/RF

Hit	Power	SB	Patience	Glove	Overall
55/60	40/45	30	45	50	45

Born: 06/14/99	Age: 21	Bats: L
Height: 6-0	Weight: 175	Throws: R

YEAR	LVL	PA	1B	2B	3B	HR	SB	CS	AVG	OBP	SLG	BB%	K%	GB%	LD%	FB%
2017	RK	180	37	8	1	3	0	1	0.308	0.372	0.428	7.78%	11.11%	37.3	16.2	38.7
2018	A-	277	59	15	0	7	0	0	0.315	0.357	0.455	3.61%	11.55%	37.9	15.9	36.6
2019	A	442	84	25	4	5	0	0	0.295	0.346	0.415	6.11%	12.67%	41.0	19.4	26.3
2019	A+	88	12	4	0	2	0	0	0.247	0.375	0.384	12.50%	9.09%	35.4	15.4	30.8

Background: Quietly one of the more productive bats in the South Atlantic League last season. Rincones, a 6-foot, 175-pound corner outfielder, has been incredibly consistent since making the leap to the stateside rookie league in 2017. As an 18-year-old that year, Rincones hit a solid .308/.372/.428 with eight doubles, one triple, and three homeruns. He spent the following year with the Salem-Keizer Volcanoes in the Northwest League, batting .315/.357/.455 with 15 doubles and seven homeruns. Last season, the Ciudad Bolivar, Venezuela, native moved into full-season action for the first time. Appearing in 105 games with the Augusta GreenJackets, Rincones slugged .295/.346/.415 with 25 doubles, four triples, and five homeruns. His overall production, according to *Deserved Runs Created Plus*, topped the league average mark by 28%. The baby-faced outfielder was promoted up to High Class A in mid-August for the remainder of the year; he hit .247/.375/.384 with four doubles and a pair of homeruns.

Scouting Report: Consider the following:

- Since 2006, only three 20-year-old hitters posted a DRC+ between 123 and 133 with a sub-7.0% walk rate and a strikeout rate below 15% in the South Atlantic League (min. 350 PA): Josh Reddick, Grenny Cumana, and Diego Rincones.

Rincones is an interesting prospect. His main skill is an extreme bat-to-ball ability, but lacks the requisite power or bloated walk rates typically needed for a corner outfield spot. And his lack of foot speed keeps him out of center field. Rincones looks like a competent fourth outfield. But if the power takes a step forward, something close to an average skill, is instantly a starting contender.

Ceiling: 1.5-win player
Risk: Moderate
MLB ETA: 2021/2022

18. Kai-Wei Teng, RHP

FB	CB	SL	CH	Command	Overall
50+	55	50	50	55	40

Born: 12/01/98	Age: 21	Bats: R
Height: 6-4	Weight: 260	Throws: R

YEAR	LVL	IP	W	L	SV	ERA	FIP	WHIP	K/9	K%	BB/9	BB%	K/BB	HR9	BABIP
2018	Rk	42.7	3	3	0	3.59	2.78	1.20	9.9	26.26%	3.2	8.38%	3.13	0.00	0.319
2019	A	50.7	4	0	0	1.60	2.88	1.07	8.7	23.33%	2.5	6.67%	3.50	0.18	0.277
2019	A	29.0	3	0	0	1.55	1.82	0.79	12.1	35.45%	2.2	6.36%	5.57	0.00	0.262

Background: Originally signed by the Twins near the end of 2017 for $500,000 plus an additional $80,000 for future tuition expenses. Teng made his stateside debut in the Gulf Coast League the following season, posting a strong 47-to-15 strikeout-to-walk ratio in 42.2 innings as a 19-year-old. San Francisco acquired the crafty right-hander, along with Jaylin Davis and Prelander Berroa, for hard-throwing right-hander Sam Dyson at the trade deadline last season. Teng, a well-built 6-foot-4 and 260 pounds, spent the year working between both organizations' Low Class A affiliates: in a combined 14 appearances, 13 of which were starts, he fanned 88 and walked just 21 in 79.2 innings of work.

Scouting Report: A savvy right-hander that gets by on moxie, pitchability, and a strong feel for the strike zone. Teng sports a standard four-pitch mix: an average low 90s fastball, an above-average curve with late bite, a solid slider with similar, though tighter, breaker; and a changeup. Teng commands the zone incredibly well with all four pitches. He's successful moving his fastball to all four quadrants and keeping his offspeed low. Teng's changeup – which may bump up to a 55-grade – already plays up because of his feel for the pitch. There's some backend starting caliber potential here, though he's likely to fall into the Quad A / up-and-down arm. With respect to his work last season, consider the following:

- Since 2006, only six 20-year-old pitchers met the following criteria in either Low Class A league (min. 75 IP): a strikeout percentage between 26.5% and 28.5% with a walk percentage between 6.5% and 8.5%. Those six pitchers are: Jake Odorizzi, David Bromberg, Luis Lugo, Resly Linares, and Hansel Rodriguez.

Ceiling: 1.0- to 1.5-win player
Risk: Low to Moderate
MLB ETA: 2022

19. Blake Rivera, RHP

FB	CB	CH	Command	Overall
55	60	50	40	40

Born: 01/09/98	Age: 22	Bats: R
Height: 6-4	Weight: 225	Throws: R

YEAR	LVL	IP	W	L	SV	ERA	FIP	WHIP	K/9	K%	BB/9	BB%	K/BB	HR9	BABIP
2018	A-	19.0	0	0	0	6.16	5.65	1.63	6.6	15.38%	5.2	12.09%	1.27	0.95	0.295
2019	Rk	2.0	0	1	0	18.00	7.25	3.00	0.0	0.00%	9.0	18.18%	0.00	0.00	0.444
2019	A	73.0	4	6	0	3.95	3.31	1.34	10.7	27.44%	4.8	12.30%	2.23	0.37	0.301

Background: A fourth round pick out of Wallace State Community College two years ago. Rivera, a 6-foot-4, 225-pound right-hander, looked abysmal during his debut in the Northwest League. Making nine brief appearances, the Alabama native posted a 14-to-11 strikeout-to-walk ratio in only 19.0 innings of work. Last season Rivera turned in a campaign more suggestive of his lofty draft status. Despite missing nearly seven weeks due to an injury, the young right-hander made 16 appearances – 15 of which were starts – with the Augusta GreenJackets, throwing 73.0 innings with 87 punch outs and 39 walks. He compiled a 3.95 ERA and a 5.06 DRA (Deserved Runs Average).

Scouting Report: Rivera's heater sits in the 94 mph range, but it's a soft 94 mph. There's a lot of natural cut where you can almost see his fingers sliding off the ball on the side instead of pulling backwards on the strings. It's just one of those offerings that *should* be a plus a pitch, but it just doesn't play as well as the velocity would suggest. His curveball is a 12-6 hammer, easily a plus pitch. And he'll mix in an average changeup. Already entering his age-22 season, it's unlikely that the former JuCo star's control – let alone his command – develops enough to keep him in the rotation long term. Consider the following:

- Since 2006, only three 21-year-old pitchers have fanned between 26.5% and 28.5% of the hitters they faced in the South Atlantic League to go along with a walk percentage between 11% and 13% (min. 100 IP): Ryne Slack, Yorvin Pantoja, and Blake Rivera.

Ceiling: 1.5-win player
Risk: Moderate
MLB ETA: 2022

20. Jake Wong, RHP

FB	CB	CH	Command	Overall
55	50/55	50	50	40

Born: 09/03/96	Age: 23	Bats: R
Height: 6-2	Weight: 215	Throws: R

YEAR	LVL	IP	W	L	SV	ERA	FIP	WHIP	K/9	K%	BB/9	BB%	K/BB	HR9	BABIP
2018	A-	27.3	0	2	0	2.30	2.93	1.24	8.9	22.88%	2.0	5.08%	4.50	0.33	0.329
2019	A	40.7	2	1	0	1.99	3.32	0.91	7.5	22.08%	2.4	7.14%	3.09	0.44	0.226
2019	A+	72.3	3	2	0	4.98	4.09	1.38	8.3	22.87%	3.0	8.19%	2.79	0.75	0.345

Background: A member of Grand Canyon's rotation for three seasons, Wong, a 6-foot-2, 215-pound right-hander, was one of the bigger breakout players in college baseball in 2018. The Chandler, Arizona, native averaged nearly a punch out per inning with a sub-3.0 walk rate in 15 starts. San Francisco snagged Wong in the third round, 80th overall, two years ago. Last season the former Lopes hurler split time between Low Class A and High Class A, throwing a combined 113.0 innings while fanning 101 and walking 35. He compiled an aggregate 3.90 ERA.

Scouting Report: Looking at Wong's repertoire today hardly screams early round draft selection: his fastball is slightly better than average, hovering in the 92- to 93-mph range; his curveball has nice shape and might eventual climb into an above-average offering; and his changeup is run-of-the-mill average. Wong profiles as a middle relief arm, primarily succeeding on his fastball/curveball/command trio.

Ceiling: 1.0- to 1.5-win player
Risk: Moderate
MLB ETA: 2021/2022

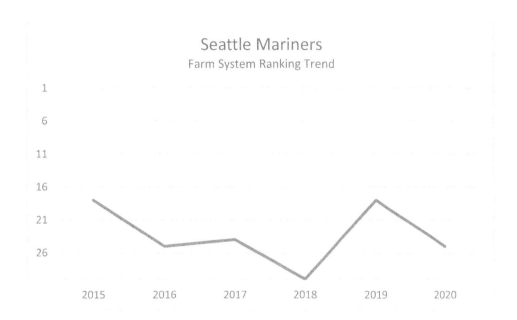

Seattle Mariners
Farm System Ranking Trend

Rank	Name	Age	Pos
1	Jarred Kelenic	20	CF
2	Julio Rodriguez	19	RF
3	Evan White	24	1B
4	Logan Gilbert	23	RHP
5	George Kirby	22	RHP
6	Justus Sheffield	24	LHP
7	Justin Dunn	24	RHP
8	Jake Fraley	25	OF
9	Cal Raleigh	23	C
10	Isaiah Campbell	21	RHP
11	Kyle Lewis	24	OF
12	Ljay Newsome	23	RHP
13	Ricardo Sanchez	23	LHP
14	Brayan Perez	19	LHP
15	Brandon Williamson	22	LHP
16	Devin Sweet	23	RHP
17	Juan Then	20	RHP
18	Damon Casetta-Stubbs	20	RHP
19	Sam Delaplane	22	RHP
20	Joey Gerber	23	RHP

1. Jarred Kelenic, CF

Hit	Power	SB	Patience	Glove	Overall
55/60	50/60	30	50	50	70

Born: 07/16/99	Age: 20	Bats: L
Height: 6-0	Weight: 196	Throws: L

YEAR	LVL	PA	1B	2B	3B	HR	SB	CS	AVG	OBP	SLG	BB%	K%	GB%	LD%	FB%
2018	RK	51	14	2	2	1	4	0	0.413	0.451	0.609	7.84%	21.57%	50.0	19.4	27.8
2018	RK	200	27	8	4	5	11	1	0.253	0.350	0.431	11.00%	19.50%	48.1	23.0	25.9
2019	A	218	31	14	3	11	7	4	0.309	0.394	0.586	11.47%	20.64%	43.8	18.5	28.1
2019	A+	190	29	13	1	6	10	3	0.290	0.353	0.485	8.95%	25.79%	42.0	19.3	32.8
2019	AA	92	10	4	1	6	3	0	0.253	0.315	0.542	8.70%	18.48%	38.8	17.9	29.9

Background: There are very – very – few organizations that (A) can boast the talent Seattle has in their Top 2 prospects and (B) would rank Julio Rodriguez as the second best minor leaguer in their system. Times are changin' for Seattle. No. Doubt. About. It. Tradin' Jerry Dipoto acquired the former seventh overall pick last offseason in a megadeal with the Mets. The Mariners received Kelenic, Justin Dunn (another of the club's best prospects), Gerson Bautista, Anthony Swarzak, and Jay Bruce for future Hall of Famer (maybe?) Robinson Cano, All-Star closer Edwin Diaz, and cash. Kelenic, a 6-foot, 196-pound center fielder out of Waukesha West H.S., looked comfortable in his new surroundings as he vaulted through three separate levels during his first full professional season. The young center fielder finished the year with an aggregate .291/.364/.540 triple-slash line with 31 doubles, five triples, 23 homeruns, and 20 stolen bases.

Snippet from The 2018 Prospect Digest Handbook: A twitchy hitter that already shows surprising power to the opposite field. Kelenic showed a well-rounded approach at the plate during his debut: above-average patience, hit tool, and power while flashing plus speed and matching instincts on the base paths and running down balls in center field. He shows a short compact swing with impressive bat speed. Kelenic has the loud, impactful tools to make a splash at the big league level in the coming years. There's some Christian Yelich-type potential brewing here.

Scouting Report: With respect to his work in Low Class A last season, consider the following:

- Since 2006, here's the list of 19-year-old hitters to post a *Deserved Runs Created Plus* total of at least 170 in any Low Class A league (min. 200 PA): Bo Bichette, Byron Buxton, Oscar Taveras, Jaff Decker, and Jarred Kelenic. It should be noted that Kelenic is the lone player to accomplish the feat in the South Atlantic League.

Now let's take a look at his work in High Class A:

- Since 2006, here's the list of 19-year-old hitters to post a *Deserved Runs Created Plus* total between 133 and 143 in any High Class A league (min. 175 PA): Jo Adell, Carlos Correa, Heliot Ramos, Jake Bauers, Billy McKinney, and Jarred Kelenic. Again, it should be noted that only four did so in the California League (Adell, Correa, Ramos, and Kelenic).

If you're only as good as the company you keep, then Kelenic is pretty damn good. As I noted in last year's Handbook there's a lot of Christian Yelich brewing here. Above-average, maybe plus hit tool, 30 homerun potential, 30-stolen-base threat; solid glove.

Ceiling: 6.5-win player
Risk: Moderate
MLB ETA: 2020/2021

2. Julio Rodriguez, OF

Hit	Power	SB	Patience	Glove	Overall
55/60	50/60	30	50	50	70

Born: 12/29/00	Age: 19	Bats: R
Height: 6-4	Weight: 225	Throws: R

YEAR	LVL	PA	1B	2B	3B	HR	SB	CS	AVG	OBP	SLG	BB%	K%	GB%	LD%	FB%
2018	RK	255	42	13	9	5	10	0	0.315	0.404	0.525	11.76%	15.69%	51.4	17.1	22.7
2019	A	295	46	20	1	10	1	3	0.293	0.359	0.490	6.78%	22.37%	47.7	19.3	28.9
2019	A+	72	19	6	3	2	0	0	0.462	0.514	0.738	6.94%	13.89%	49.1	27.3	18.2

Background: From dominating the Dominican Summer League – as well as being named the league's Most Valuable Player – to reaching the California League within a year. It's been an incredible season for the talented prospect out of Loma de Cabrera, Dominican Republic. And that's before his age even enters the conversation. Rodriguez, by the way, is still only entering his age-19 season. With far less of a baby face, the 6-foot-4, 225-pound outfielder ripped through the South Atlantic League by slugging .293/.359/.490 with 20 doubles, one triple, and 10 homeruns. And he continued his torrid pace upon his promotion to High Class A: he slugged a Ruthian .462/.514/.738 with another 11 extra-base hits (six doubles, three triples, and a pair of homeruns) in only 17 games. When the dust finally cleared on just his second professional season, Rodriguez, who was a finalist for MiLB's Breakout Prospect of the Year, batted an aggregate .326/.390/.540 with 26 doubles, four triples, and a dozen homeruns in 84 games. The budding star missed roughly two months at the start of the year with a hand injury, which makes the production all the more impressive. Seattle sent the young outfielder to the Arizona Fall League after the season; Rodriguez batted a more-than-respectable .288/.397/.365 with four doubles in 15 games with Peoria.

Snippet from The 2018 Prospect Digest Handbook: Rodriguez's toolkit provides a strong foundation: above-average hit tool with room to grow, solid average plate discipline, and 20/20 potential.

Scouting Report: Rodriguez is not only a man amongst boys already at this stage of his minor league career, but he grew an inch and put on 45 pounds since the last Prospect Digest Handbook. And at 6-foot-4 and 225 pounds, he's now pushing the limits of his physical maturity. With respect to his production in Low Class A, consider the following:

- Since 2006, here's the list of 18-year-old hitters to post a *Deserved Runs Created Plus* total of at least 160 in any Low Class A league (min. 250 PA): Mike Trout, Bryce Harper, and – of course – Julio Rodriguez.

Enough said, right? Rodriguez is a budding star, though he doesn't have nearly the same patient approach as his two aforementioned counterparts. The Mariners' future face-of-the-franchise does everything else at an above-average or plus level. He's going to be a perennial .300/.370/.550 type hitter, though he likely slides over into right field permanently. One more thought: per Fangraphs, Rodriguez's average exit velocity was a stellar 92 mph with a peak of 109 mph.

Ceiling: 6.5-win player
Risk: Moderate
MLB ETA: 2021

3. Evan White, 1B

Hit	Power	SB	Patience	Glove	Overall
55	55	30	50	55	55

Born: 04/26/96	Age: 24	Bats: R
Height: 6-3	Weight: 205	Throws: L

YEAR	LVL	PA	1B	2B	3B	HR	SB	CS	AVG	OBP	SLG	BB%	K%	GB%	LD%	FB%
2017	A-	55	8	1	1	3	1	1	0.277	0.345	0.532	10.91%	10.91%	48.8	20.9	23.3
2018	A+	538	99	27	7	11	4	3	0.303	0.375	0.458	9.67%	19.14%	50.1	19.6	23.1
2018	AAA	18	2	2	0	0	0	0	0.222	0.222	0.333	0.00%	27.78%	53.8	30.8	7.7
2019	AA	400	74	13	2	18	2	0	0.293	0.350	0.488	7.25%	23.00%	43.3	22.5	27.3

Background: In a move, frankly, they I didn't think a Jerry Dipoto-led club would make – for a variety of reasons, like, say, most guys pass through Seattle as quickly as the changing weather. But Seattle inked the former first round pick to a hefty six-year, $24 million pact that includes three club options. It's incredible financial security for a prospect that (A) hasn't played above Class AA, (B) is essentially a one-dimension player, and (C) didn't start showing any type of meaningful power until this season. Here we are, though. White, the 17th overall player taken in 2017 draft, spent the entirety of last season squaring off against the Texas League competition; in a shortened 92-game campaign, the 6-foot-3, 205-pound first baseman slugged .293/.350/.488 with 13 doubles, two triples, and a career best 18 homeruns. His overall production, according Baseball Prospectus' *Deserved Runs Created Plus*, topped the league average threshold by a staggering 53%, the best mark of his young career.

Snippet from The 2018 Prospect Digest Handbook: A very typical Jerry Dipoto acquisition as the veteran General Manager places an unreasonably high value on on-field production at the cost of future projection. In doing so, Dipoto broke one of the Draft's Golden Rules: never burn a first round selection on a first baseman.

Scouting Report: Dipoto doubled down – clearly. So let's take a look at how White's stats measure up to his peers. Consider the following:

- Since 2006, there have been just two 23-year-old hitters to post a DRC+ between 150 and 160 in the Texas League (min. 300 PA): former top prospect – who never quite figured it out at the big league level – Mike Olt and Evan White. The duo have nearly the same swing-and-miss rate (24% and 23%), though Olt walked twice as often (14.5% vs. 7.25%).

The good news: White's power surge appears to be organic. His home ballpark was (A) the lowest run-scoring environment and (B) the most difficult place to drop a bomb in the Texas League. The bad news: the Texas League was the most friendly of three Class AA leagues in terms of offense. In the grand scheme of things if White turns out to be a bust, it's a small financial commitment.

Ceiling: 3.0- to 3.5-win player
Risk: Low to Moderate
MLB ETA: 2020

4. Logan Gilbert, RHP

FB	CB	SL	CH	Command	Overall
65	50	55	55	50/55	55

Born: 05/05/97	Age: 23	Bats: R
Height: 6-6	Weight: 225	Throws: R

YEAR	LVL	IP	W	L	SV	ERA	FIP	WHIP	K/9	K%	BB/9	BB%	K/BB	HR9	BABIP
2019	A	22.7	1	0	0	1.59	2.37	0.66	14.3	43.37%	2.4	7.23%	6.00	0.79	0.184
2019	A+	62.3	5	3	0	1.73	2.62	1.03	10.5	30.04%	1.7	4.94%	6.08	0.43	0.320
2019	AA	50.0	4	2	0	2.88	2.87	0.98	10.1	28.72%	2.7	7.69%	3.73	0.36	0.271

Background: The powers that be at Stetson University should really think about capitalizing on the school's – quiet – ability to churn out quality pitching. Perhaps a name change to Cy Young University after Corey Kluber captured two of the awards in a four-year span and Mets ace Jacob deGrom won the prodigious hardware in back-to-back campaigns. Gilbert, an alumnus of Stetson University, continued to make some massive waves in his second professional season. The 14th overall pick two years ago, Gilbert rocketed through three separate levels last season, going from the Sally to the California before settling in for a – *dominant* – nine-game cameo in the Texas League. The 6-foot-6, 225-pound right-hander finished the year with 135.0 innings of work, recording an impressive 165-to-33 strikeout-to-walk ratio with a 2.13 ERA.

Snippet from The 2018 Prospect Digest Handbook: [Jerry] Dipoto & Co. hit a homerun with the selection of Gilbert in the middle of the first round last June.

Scouting Report: Every time I watch Gilbert throw – and it's been quite a few times over the past two seasons – the immediate comparison that jumps to mind, at least physically, are the Weaver brothers (Jeff and Jered). Long and gangly, but athletic. Gilbert attacks hitters with a standard four-pitch mix: a 60-grade fastball that sits in the mid-90s with some heft to it; an above-average slider and changeup, and a slower, loopy-ish curveball. Gilbert's more of a strike-thrower than a command guy, but if it continues on the same trajectory he should wind up with 55-command. I thought the slider would wind up as a plus-offering, but it seems to have settled in comfortably a tick below. He's a mid-rotation, true #3 arm for a decade plus.

Ceiling: 3.5-win player
Risk: Moderate
MLB ETA: 2022

5. George Kirby, RHP

FB	CB	SL	CH	Command	Overall
55/60	55	50	55	55	50

Born: 02/04/98	Age: 22	Bats: R
Height: 6-4	Weight: 201	Throws: R

YEAR	LVL	IP	W	L	SV	ERA	FIP	WHIP	K/9	K%	BB/9	BB%	K/BB	HR9	BABIP
2019	A-	23.0	0	0	0	2.35	2.01	1.04	9.8	29.41%	0.0	0.00%	#DIV/0!	0.39	0.355

Background: The New York Metropolitans had a wildly successful 2016 draft, landing hard-throwing right-hander Justin Dunn and savvy southpaw Anthony Kay in the opening round and plucking hulking cornerstone Peter Alonso in the second. But taken all the way down the draft, as the 970th overall pick, the club called out a prep right-hander's name: George Kirby from Rye High School – though the two-sides never came to an agreement. Kirby, a lanky 6-foot-4, 201-pound righty from Rye, New York, has been a sensation throughout his tenure for the Elon Phoenix. In 16 games for long time Head Coach Mike Kennedy, five of which were starts, Kirby posted an impressive 55-to-17 strikeout-to-walk ratio in 61.0 innings of work. He also saved a pair of games for the Colonial Athletic Association school during his freshman season as well. Kirby, who's father George played baseball for Florida International University, followed that up with an even better showing during sophomore campaign: in 90.2 innings the promising youngster fanned 96, walked just 27, and posted a 10-3 win-loss record to go along with a sparkling 2.89 ERA. But that was just a smattering of dominance that Kirby had buried in his right arm. Pitching in relief for the Harwich Mariners in the Cape Cod League, he posted an absurd 24-to-1 strikeout-to-walk ratio with a barely-there 1.38 ERA against an elite level of competition. And then he continued to get better...In 14 starts for the Phoenix last season, Kirby posted a 107-to-6 strikeout-to-walk ratio in 88.1 innings of work. Seattle snagged the young righty in the opening round, 20th overall, last June and signed him for the exact slot amount ($3,242,900). Kirby made nine brief appearances in the Northwest League during his pro debut, fanning 25 without a walk to go along with a 2.35 ERA.

Scouting Report: My pre-draft analysis:

Fun Fact: Kirby's ridiculous 17.5-to-1 strikeout-to-walk ratio leads all Division I pitchers by a wide margin. Runner up Matt Waldron of Nebraska owns an 11.7-to-1 strikeout-to-walk ratio. Just how special has Kirby been in 2019? Consider the following:

- *Between 2011 and 2018, only Division I pitchers averaged at least 11 strikeouts and fewer than 1.5 walks per nine innings in a season (min. 75 IP): Casey Mize (twice), David Peterson, Kyle Freeland, Taylor Clarke, and Miller Hogan.*

Mize, of course, was the top pick in the draft in 2018. Peterson and Freeland were taken with the 20th and 8th overall selections. Clarke was a third rounder in 2015. And Hogan was a sixth round pick by the Rays last season.

Let's continue...

- *Only one of those pitches, Mize, fanned at least 11 and walked fewer than a batter per inning – a la Kirby this season.*

Kirby attacks hitters with four average or better offerings: his fastball sits comfortably in the low 90s without much effort and may have some additional growth as his lanky frame begins to fill out; his curveball is a tightly spun 12-6 bender; his slider shows cutter-like characteristics; and his changeup flashes plus with tremendous dive and fade. Kirby has the potential to grow into a solid #3-type arm at his peak. One final thought: his changeup, when it's on, could be among the best in the draft.

Ceiling: 2.5-win player
Risk: Low to Moderate
MLB ETA: 2022

6. Justus Sheffield, LHP

	FB	SL	CH	Command	Overall
	60	65	50	45	50

Born: 05/13/96	Age: 24	Bats: L
Height: 6-0	Weight: 200	Throws: L

YEAR	LVL	IP	W	L	SV	ERA	FIP	WHIP	K/9	K%	BB/9	BB%	K/BB	HR9	BABIP
2017	AA	93.3	7	6	0	3.18	4.58	1.36	7.9	20.25%	3.2	8.15%	2.48	1.35	0.293
2018	AA	28.0	1	2	0	2.25	2.49	1.07	12.5	34.82%	4.5	12.50%	2.79	0.32	0.259
2018	AAA	88.0	6	4	0	2.56	3.12	1.16	8.6	23.14%	3.7	9.92%	2.33	0.31	0.264
2019	AA	78.0	5	3	0	2.19	2.63	1.03	9.8	27.87%	2.1	5.90%	4.72	0.46	0.293
2019	AAA	55.0	2	6	0	6.87	7.17	1.82	7.9	18.25%	6.7	15.59%	1.17	1.96	0.292

Background: There are dream seasons in which everything goes better than expected – perfect. Think Julio Rodriguez, Jarred Kelenic, or Logan White. And there's the opposite of that: nightmares. Think Justus Sheffield. Passed around more times than expected for a perennial top prospect, Sheffield, who started in Cleveland, moved to New York and then settled in with Seattle last season, simply couldn't find it. And when he did have one of those moments they were all too fleeting. He begin the year in Class AAA, got promoted up to Seattle for a brief three-inning stint, and then was demoted back Tacoma. And that's where things took a turn for the worse. Sheffield struggled to get out of the third inning against Salt Lake and then rattled off a stretch in which he allowed 32 earned runs in 34.0 innings. Seattle bumped him back down to the Texas League where things got predictably better. Sheffield finished off the year fairly decent stretch of seven starts back in the big leagues.

Snippet from The 2018 Prospect Digest Handbook: The lone knock on Sheffield: his control can waiver at times. He has the arsenal – two plus pitches and an average third offering – to develop into a #2/#3 type arm. But his control/command needs to take a step forward.

Scouting Report: I caught a few of his minor league games in the early and middle parts of the season and his stuff lacked the crisp, late life that it showed in 2018. Two years ago his fastball was up to 98 mph at times and his slider had that hard, fall-off-the-table downward bite consistently. Last season, though, his fastball was 92- to 94-mph and he clearly didn't have the same feel for his trademark offspeed pitch, one that ranks near the top – or at the top - in the minor leagues. The major league data would back that up as well: his fastball was down 1.5 mph (though he was pitching in relief in his debut in New York). And then there's his command, which hasn't developed as expected. The list of MiLB left-handers that own two plus-pitches and a solid third option are far-and-few between. Even if Sheffield doesn't progress any further he's going to be a solid #4.

Ceiling: 2.5- to 3.0-win player
Risk: Moderate
MLB ETA: Debuted in 2018

7. Justin Dunn, RHP

FB	CB	SL	CH	Command	Overall
55	50	55	50	50	50

Born: 09/22/95	Age: 24	Bats: R
Height: 6-2	Weight: 185	Throws: R

YEAR	LVL	IP	W	L	SV	ERA	FIP	WHIP	K/9	K%	BB/9	BB%	K/BB	HR9	BABIP
2017	A+	95.3	5	6	0	5.00	4.15	1.56	7.1	17.32%	4.5	11.09%	1.56	0.47	0.322
2018	A+	45.7	2	3	0	2.36	2.99	1.27	10.1	25.89%	3.0	7.61%	3.40	0.39	0.325
2018	AA	89.7	6	5	0	4.22	3.36	1.36	10.5	27.70%	3.7	9.76%	2.84	0.70	0.345
2019	AA	131.7	9	5	0	3.55	3.42	1.19	10.8	28.57%	2.7	7.05%	4.05	0.89	0.314

Background: The second big piece acquired in the mega-swap with the Mets last season. Dunn – quietly – put together his finest season to date in 2019, doing so at the most important minor league level. Originally taken by New York in the opening round, 19th overall, out of Boston College four years ago, the 6-foot-2, 185-pound right-hander made a career best 25 starts, throwing 131.2 innings while recording a whopping 159 strikeouts and handing out just 39 free passes to go along with a 3.55 ERA. The former BC Eagle finished his second stint in Class AA with a 4.61 *Deserved Runs Average*. Dunn also made four brief appearances with Seattle as well, tossing another 6.2 innings with five strikeouts and an incredible nine walks.

Snippet from The 2018 Prospect Digest Handbook: Dunn has the makings of a nice mid-rotation caliber starting pitcher with a little bit more in the tank if his control/command ticks up a notch or two in the coming years.

Scouting Report: The good news for Dunn – as well as for the Mariners' long term future – is that the wiry right-hander's control / command improved significantly last season. He was not only throwing more strikes, but he was throwing better strikes more consistently. The bad news: in all of the games I personal saw Dunn throw, his fastball lacked the added oomph that it picked up the previous season. His fastball, which was consistently touching 95 mph in 2018, settled in around 91 mph last season. And the data from his brief MLB stay backs that up as well; he averaged a smidgeon over 92 mph. The curveball's average and the changeup improved to a 50-grade as well. The slider is a strong 55. Dunn still looks like a #3/#4-type arm, though he needs to repeat his new found control / command, especially if the fastball is sitting 91-92. With respect to his work in the Texas League last season, consider the following:

- Since 2006, here's the list of 23-year-old pitchers to post a strikeout percentage between 27% and 30% with a sub-8.5% walk percentage in any Class AA league (min. 100 IP): Brandon Woodruff, Alex Faedo, Eric Surkamp, and Justin Dunn.

Ceiling: 2.5-win player
Risk: Moderate
MLB ETA: 2022

8. Jake Fraley, OF

Hit	Power	SB	Patience	Glove	Overall
50	55	50	50	50	50

Born: 05/25/95	Age: 25	Bats: L
Height: 6-0	Weight: 195	Throws: L

YEAR	LVL	PA	1B	2B	3B	HR	SB	CS	AVG	OBP	SLG	BB%	K%	GB%	LD%	FB%
2017	RK	17	3	3	0	1	3	1	0.467	0.529	0.867	11.76%	17.65%	0.0	16.7	66.7
2017	A+	105	11	3	1	1	1	3	0.170	0.238	0.255	6.67%	22.86%	43.1	19.4	29.2
2018	A+	260	48	19	7	4	11	8	0.347	0.415	0.547	10.00%	16.92%	41.4	20.4	33.3
2019	AA	259	44	15	2	11	16	5	0.313	0.386	0.539	8.88%	21.24%	32.4	26.7	30.1
2019	AAA	168	19	12	3	8	6	2	0.276	0.333	0.553	6.55%	20.24%	31.4	20.3	36.4

Background: It was a deal that was highlighted more about Jerry Dipoto reacquiring Mallex Smith a year after trading him to the Tampa Bay Rays. But Fraley, who was generally panned as a throw-in, secondary-tier minor leaguer quietly turned in one of the most dominant minor league showings in 2019. Taken by the Rays with the last pick in the second round in 2016, Fraley battled a litany of injuries that limited him to just 96 games between 2017 and 2018. And while he topped the 100-game threshold for the first time in his professional career last season, Fraley's offense more than made up for the absence. He stroked .298/.365/.545 with 27 doubles, five triples, and 19 homeruns while swiping 22 bags in 99 games with Arkansas and Tacoma. And he earned a 12-game cameo with Seattle as well.

Snippet from The 2018 Prospect Digest Handbook: His power and speed continue to be standout tools, but now he's handling southpaws significantly better; he batted .297/.379/.432 against them last season. Plus, his defense in left or center fields remains steady. The Rays have typically had a lot of success develops outfielders of the same ilk, so Fraley will provide a solid testing ground for Seattle's player development engine. He looks like a capable fourth outfielder, though he's trending up. Class AA will be a make-it-or-break-it challenge.

Seattle Mariners

Scouting Report: Consider the following:

- Since 2006, here's the list of 24-year-olds to post a DRC+ of at least 180 with a walk rate between 8.0% and 10% in any Class AA league (min. 250 PA): Kevin Kouzmanoff, Joey Meneses, Ty France, and Jake Fraley. Kouzmanoff was a league average bat during his eight-year big league career. Meneses spent last season playing in Japan. And France appeared in 69 games as a rookie for the Padres last season.

Average or better tools across the board. The question isn't whether Fraley can be a productive big league player in all facets of the game. He can. The question is whether he can stay in the lineup consistently. Even in Seattle's cavernous park he's capable of putting up Mark Canha circa 2018 numbers (.249/.328/.449 with 17 homeruns).

Ceiling: 2.0-win player
Risk: Moderate
MLB ETA: Debuted in 2019

9. Cal Raleigh, C

Hit	Power	SB	Patience	Glove	Overall
45	50	30	50	45+	45

Born: 11/26/96	Age: 23	Bats: B
Height: 6-3	Weight: 215	Throws: R

YEAR	LVL	PA	1B	2B	3B	HR	SB	CS	AVG	OBP	SLG	BB%	K%	GB%	LD%	FB%
2018	A-	167	23	10	1	8	1	1	0.288	0.367	0.534	10.78%	17.37%	33.9	16.1	33.9
2019	A+	348	40	19	0	22	4	0	0.261	0.336	0.535	9.48%	19.83%	33.3	15.2	38.7
2019	AA	159	20	6	0	7	0	0	0.228	0.296	0.414	8.81%	29.56%	27.8	20.6	36.1

Background: Raleigh turned in a spectacular freshman season at Florida State University four years ago: he slugged a robust .301/.412/.511 with 16 doubles, one triple, and 10 homeruns to go along with a nearly 1-for-1 strikeout-to-walk ratio. But the switch-hitting backstop's bat failed – miserably – in the Cape Cod League that summer and that lack of production bled over into his sophomore campaign for the Seminoles; he batted a lowly .227/.330/.397 in 69 games. The North Carolina native – and his once potent stick – reemerged from the ashes during his junior campaign, hitting a healthy .326/.447/.583 with career highs in doubles (18) and homeruns (13). Seattle snagged the underrated prospect in the third round two years ago. After a strong pro debut in the Northwest League (.288/.367/.534), Raleigh handled the aggressive promotion up to High Class A with aplomb: he hit .261/.336/.535 with 19 doubles and 22 homeruns. His bat did cool a bit during a late season promotion up to Arkansas. He finished the year with an aggregate .251/.323/.497 line.

Snippet from The 2018 Prospect Digest Handbook: For his part, Raleigh was able to maintain his saber-friendly ways during his transition to pro ball as well, showcasing a better than average eye at the plate and surprising power from a premium defensive position. Raleigh will never be confused with Yadier Molina behind the dish, but there's enough offensive potential to suggest a starting caliber backstop.

Scouting Report: Consider the following:

- Since 2006, here's the list of 22-year-old to post a DRC+ of at least 145 with a walk rate between 8.5% and 10.5% and a strikeout rate between 19 and 23% in the California League (min. 300 PA): Chris Shaw, Mac Williamson, and Cal Raleigh.

See a trend? Polished collegiate hitters feasting off of an age-appropriate level of competition. Another pattern: Shaw's been abysmal in limited action with the Giants and Williamson, a former Giants farmhand, owns a career 74 DRC+ in 160 games. Raleigh's a 45-bat, 55-power, and slightly below-average work behind the dish. Catching is in dire need of production across the MLB. So Raleigh's likely going to get more than enough opportunities. There's some starting caliber potential, but he won't be a star.

Ceiling: 1.5- to 2.0-win player
Risk: Moderate
MLB ETA: 2021

10. Isaiah Campbell, RHP

FB	CB	SL	SF	Command	Overall
55	55	55	50	50	45

Born: 08/15/97	Age: 22	Bats: R
Height: 6-4	Weight: 225	Throws: R

Background: The epitome of perseverance. Campbell, a broad-shouldered right-hander from Olathe, Kansas, turned in a mediocre campaign at the University of Arkansas during his true freshman season: he posted a 23-to-11 strikeout-to-walk ratio in 31.2 innings spread between the rotation and bullpen. Elbow woes limited Campbell to just one appearance during his sophomore season before he hit the DL. Healthy for the 2018 season, the big Razorback tossed 69.2 innings while fanning 75 and walking 29 walks to go along with a 4.26 ERA. The Angels took a late round flier on Campbell, who bet big on himself and returned to school for his redshirt junior season. And he was all aces. In 17 starts for the SEC squad, Campbell averaged 9.3 strikeouts against just 1.6 walks per nine innings with a 2.26 ERA. Seattle snagged Campbell at the end of the second round last June and signed him for $850,000.

Scouting Report: A little bit of Jon Duplantier in him. Campbell attacks hitters with a solid four-pitch repertoire: a low- to mid-90s fastball; an above-average curveball that rests in the low 80s; a 55-grade slider; and a decent splitter that he uses as a changeup. With respect to his work in college last season, consider the following:

- Between 2011 and 2018, here's the list of SEC pitchers to post a strikeout rate between 8.5 K/9 and 10.5 K/9 with a walk rate below 2.0 BB/9 (min. 75 IP): Aaron Nola (twice), Brady Singer, Alex Wood, Dane Dunning, Hunter Martin, Blaine Knight, Michael Plassmeyer.

Ceiling: 1.5- to 2.0-win player
Risk: Moderate
MLB ETA: 2022/2023

11. Kyle Lewis, OF

Hit	Power	SB	Patience	Glove	Overall
45	55	30	50	45	45

Born: 07/13/95	Age: 24	Bats: R
Height: 6-4	Weight: 210	Throws: R

YEAR	LVL	PA	1B	2B	3B	HR	SB	CS	AVG	OBP	SLG	BB%	K%	GB%	LD%	FB%
2017	RK	46	6	2	1	1	1	0	0.263	0.348	0.447	8.70%	30.43%	50.0	3.8	34.6
2017	A+	167	28	4	0	6	2	1	0.255	0.323	0.403	8.98%	22.75%	54.0	16.8	26.5
2018	A+	211	18	18	0	5	0	0	0.260	0.303	0.429	5.21%	26.07%	43.4	25.2	30.8
2018	AA	152	17	8	0	4	1	0	0.220	0.309	0.371	11.18%	21.05%	42.2	22.5	32.4
2019	AA	517	82	25	2	11	3	2	0.263	0.342	0.398	10.83%	29.40%	41.4	26.3	29.3

Background: The second collegiate player taken in the 2016 draft, Lewis, the 11th overall pick, has had one helluva difficult road to navigate since entering the professional ranks. He shredded his right ACL just 30 games into his professional career and was limited to just 49 games the following year due to recovery and rehab. And another knee injury forced him out of action until mid-May in 2018. Finally healthy, the 6-foot-4, 210-pound outfielder appeared in 122 games with the Arkansas Travelers, batting a solid .263/.342/.398 with 25 doubles, two triples, and 11 homeruns. He also swiped three bags in five attempts. Per Baseball Prospectus' *Deserved Runs Created Plus*, his overall production topped the league average by 11%. Seattle bumped up the once-dynamic prospect in early September; Lewis would hit .268/.293/.592 in 75 plate appearances.

Snippet from The 2018 Prospect Digest Handbook: At this point, it's an all but foregone conclusion that he slides over into a corner outfield position permanently thanks to multiple knee issues, which only further limits his value. If the power takes another step forward, Lewis looks like a starting caliber corner outfielder. But that's far from a certainty.

Scouting Report: Each time I start to write the former Mercer University star off there's something that causes me to do a quick double take. Take, for example, his production in Class AA last system. It was OK. Maybe if you squint hard enough you could convince yourself that, yes, he has the potential to produce at the big league level. But, again, it's far from a certainty. Here's where it get incredibly interesting. Class AA is the hardest transition for a prospect. And there's often a learning curve. Lewis is no different. The former first rounder hit a paltry .211/.316/.325 over his first 44 games in Class AA. After that he slugged a healthy .292/.358/.440 with 26 extra-base hits over his final 78 contests. The hit tool is below-average and he swings-and-misses too often. The power is average, maybe a touch better. One more thing: yes, it's incredibly small and equally unreliable, but Lewis posted a Hard Hit% of 46.5% with an average exit velocity of 90.3 mph during his brief tenure in the bigs. Low end starting caliber potential.

Ceiling: 1.5-win player
Risk: Moderate
MLB ETA: Debuted in 2019

12. Ljay Newsome, RHP

	FB	CB	SL	CH	Command	Overall
	50	50	50	50	70	40

Born: 11/08/96	Age: 23	Bats: R
Height: 5-11	Weight: 210	Throws: R

YEAR	LVL	IP	W	L	SV	ERA	FIP	WHIP	K/9	K%	BB/9	BB%	K/BB	HR9	BABIP
2017	A	129.7	8	9	0	4.10	3.60	1.13	7.7	20.94%	1.1	3.02%	6.94	0.97	0.302
2018	A+	138.7	6	10	0	4.87	4.59	1.31	8.0	20.71%	0.8	2.19%	9.46	1.56	0.337
2018	AAA	5.0	0	0	0	5.40	3.54	0.80	3.6	10.53%	1.8	5.26%	2.00	0.00	0.188
2019	A+	100.7	6	6	0	3.75	2.89	1.13	11.1	30.39%	0.8	2.21%	13.78	0.98	0.357
2019	AA	48.7	3	4	0	2.77	3.57	0.99	6.5	20.71%	1.3	4.14%	5.00	0.74	0.270
2019	AAA	5.7	0	0	0	6.35	3.09	1.06	15.9	43.48%	1.6	4.35%	10.00	1.59	0.364

Background: At what point does Ljay Newsome become a legitimate big league prospect? It wasn't when he was coming out of Chopticon High School; the Mariners took a flier on him in the 26th round in 2015. It wasn't went he cruised through the Northwest League at 19-years-old or when he posted a 111-to-16 strikeout-to-walk ratio in 129.2 innings in the Midwest League a year later. And it definitely wasn't after he averaged 8.0 strikeouts and just 0.8 walks per nine innings in High Class A two years ago. But now, though, it's time to consider if the short, stocky right-hander has some big league value developing in his right arm. Standing just 5-foot-11 and 210-pounds, Newsome headed back to the California League to open up the 2019 season. He rattled off an impressive 18-game span in which he posted a 124-to-9 strikeout-to-walk ratio in only 100.2 innings of work. Seattle bumped him up to Arkansas for a quick – and successful – nine-game span; he posted a 2.77 ERA and he also popped up for a quick cameo in Class AAA as well.

Scouting Report: Tree trunk legs that look like he could squat a Buick; Newsome's fastball has ticked up. His fastball, once sitting in the upper 80s, touched as high as 93 mph. And he uses it effectively by consistently challenging hitters in the upper half of the strike zone. If I'm guessing, Newsome probably got some Rapsodo data on his fastball showing an above-average amount of spin, which allows these types of fastballs to succeed at the upper part of the zone. His slider is his go-to secondary weapon. It's tight with a little wrinkle but he locates it well. He'll also mix in a mid-80s changeup and a mid-70s curveball. He looks like a competent #5-type starting pitcher. Pinpoint accuracy; likely the best in the entire minor leagues.

Ceiling: 1.0 to 1.5-win player
Risk: Low to Moderate
MLB ETA: 2020

13. Ricardo Sanchez, LHP

	FB	SL	CH	Command	Overall
	50	50	50	55	40

Born: 04/11/97	Age: 23	Bats: L
Height: 5-11	Weight: 215	Throws: L

YEAR	LVL	IP	W	L	SV	ERA	FIP	WHIP	K/9	K%	BB/9	BB%	K/BB	HR9	BABIP
2017	A+	100.0	4	12	0	4.95	4.06	1.63	9.1	22.00%	4.1	10.02%	2.20	0.90	0.358
2018	AA	57.7	2	5	0	4.06	3.87	1.54	6.9	16.99%	3.7	9.27%	1.83	0.47	0.333
2019	AA	146.0	8	12	0	4.44	3.39	1.34	8.3	22.02%	2.3	6.20%	3.55	0.62	0.348

Background: Similar to fellow southpaw – and teammate – Justus Sheffield, Sanchez has already popped up in a trio of organizations. The doughy-bodied hurler was signed by the Angels for a more than $500,000 out of Venezuela in July of 2013. The club flipped him to the Braves for Kyle Kubitza and Hate Hyatt less than two years later. And, finally, the Mariners acquired the lefty for cash after he was designated for assignment. The 5-foot-11, 215-pound hurler spent the entirety of the season pitching out of the Arkansas Travelers rotation in the Texas League. Making a career best 27 starts, Sanchez posted an impressive 135-to-38 strikeout-to-ratio in 146.0 innings of work. He finished the year with a 4.44 ERA and a 5.66 DRA (*Deserved Runs Average*).

Scouting Report: Consider the following:

- Since 2006, here's the list of 22-year-old pitchers to post a strikeout percentage between 21% and 23% with a sub-7% walk percentage in the Texas League (min. 100 IP): Zack Greinke, Brett Kennedy, Chase De Jong, and Ricardo Sanchez.

Which name does not belong? Sanchez is no Greinke. Clearly. And it should be noted that Sanchez's DRA (5.66) is roughly 1.5 runs worse than the next pitcher (Kennedy). Average stuff across the board: vanilla fastball, bland lollypop of a curveball, and his changeup couldn't be less exciting. But Sanchez throws a lot of strikes, most of which are pitcher's strikes. He can take the ball every fifth day and generally keep his team in the game. Remember Indians left-hander Jeremy Sowers? He's like that. But better.

Ceiling: 1.0- to 1.5-win player
Risk: Low to Moderate
MLB ETA: 2020

14. Brayan Perez, LHP

	FB	SL	CH	Command	Overall
	50/55	50/55	50/55	50/55	45

Born: 09/05/00	Age: 19	Bats: L
Height: 6-0	Weight: 170	Throws: L

YEAR	LVL	IP	W	L	SV	ERA	FIP	WHIP	K/9	K%	BB/9	BB%	K/BB	HR9	BABIP
2018	Rk	53.0	1	3	0	3.57	2.34	1.15	9.8	26.48%	1.9	5.02%	5.27	0.17	0.336
2019	Rk	36.7	4	1	0	3.44	3.98	1.09	8.1	22.60%	2.0	5.48%	4.13	0.49	0.297
2019	A-	30.7	4	1	0	3.23	3.65	1.57	8.5	21.64%	2.6	6.72%	3.22	0.59	0.402

Background: Signed out of Venezuela in early July 2017, Perez, who came to terms with the organization on deal worth $300,000, turned in a dominant debut season in the foreign rookie league two years ago. Making 15 appearances with the organization's Dominican Summer League affiliate, the 6-foot, 170-pound southpaw tossed 53.0 innings with 58 strikeouts and just 11 free passes. Seattle bounced the youngster stateside for 2019. He would make eight appearances in the Arizona Summer League and tossed seven additional games in the Northwest League, throwing 67.1 innings while fanning 62 and walking just 17 to go along with a 3.34 ERA.

Scouting Report: The potential to sport three above-average or better offerings with pitchability oozing from his fingertips. Using a three-quarter slinging arm action, Perez shows a sneaky quick fastball that likely settles in the 55-grade territory at full maturity. His slider shows solid spin, though he struggles with a consistent release point. The changeup was better than advertised. Perez has a game plan and an idea on how to implement it. He's going to start moving quickly. He'll likely spend a portion of 2020 in High Class A with significant time in Class AA by 2021. One thing to watch: the low arm slot may result in some wonky splits that could push him into a relief role.

Ceiling: 1.5-win player
Risk: Moderate to High
MLB ETA: 2022/2023

15. Brandon Williamson, LHP

	FB	CB	SL	CH	Command	Overall
	55	50	50	55	45	40

Born: 04/02/98	Age: 22	Bats: L
Height: 6-6	Weight: 210	Throws: L

YEAR	LVL	IP	W	L	SV	ERA	FIP	WHIP	K/9	K%	BB/9	BB%	K/BB	HR9	BABIP
2019	A-	15.3	0	0	0	2.35	1.53	0.91	14.7	40.98%	2.9	8.20%	5.00	0.00	0.310

Background: Originally taken by the Milwaukee Brewers in the 36th round coming out of Martin County West High School in 2016, Williamson, a 6-foot-6, 210-pound southpaw, spent the following two seasons pitching for North Iowa Area Community College. After an especially dominating season in 2018 – he posted a 104-to-34 strikeout-to-walk ratio in only 66.0 innings – Williamson transferred to Texas Christian University for his junior season. And he didn't miss a beat. In 16 starts for the Horned Frogs, the big lefty posted an 89-to-36 strikeout-to-walk ratio across 77.0 innings of work. Seattle drafted him in the second round, 59th overall, and sent him to the Northwest League. Williamson made 10 brief appearances with the Aqua Sox, striking out 25 and walking just five in 15.0 innings.

Scouting Report: The redwood-esque owns a solid four pitch mix: a low-90s fastball with some arm-side run; a loopy-ish mid-70s curveball; an infrequent, average curveball; and an above-average changeup that made grade out a tick better in the professional ranks. He's had a lengthy track record of subpar control / command, so that's likely going to continue into the professional ranks. Consider the following:

- Between 2011 and 2018, here's the list of BIG12 pitchers to average at least 10 strikeouts and 3.8 walks per nine innings (min. 75 IP): Alec Hansen, Sam Stafford, and Ryan Zeferjahn.

Williamson still has a little bit of project left as he begins to fill out his lanky frame. Brian Tallet-type lefty.

Ceiling: 1.0- to 1.5-win player
Risk: Moderate
MLB ETA: 2022/2023

16. Devin Sweet, RHP

	FB	SL	CH	Command	Overall
	50	50	65	55	40

Born: 09/06/96	Age: 23	Bats: B
Height: 5-11	Weight: 183	Throws: R

YEAR	LVL	IP	W	L	SV	ERA	FIP	WHIP	K/9	K%	BB/9	BB%	K/BB	HR9	BABIP
2018	Rk	8.3	1	1	2	4.32	3.35	1.20	13.0	34.29%	4.3	11.43%	3.00	0.00	0.353
2018	A-	8.0	1	0	0	3.38	1.55	1.50	12.4	30.56%	2.3	5.56%	5.50	0.00	0.435
2018	A	3.0	0	0	0	9.00	7.14	1.67	3.0	7.14%	0.0	0.00%	#DIV/0!	3.00	0.333
2019	A	108.7	7	5	0	3.06	2.74	1.13	10.8	29.84%	1.9	5.24%	5.70	0.66	0.336
2019	A+	18.7	1	0	0	0.96	2.75	0.86	10.1	30.00%	1.9	5.71%	5.25	0.48	0.250

Background: Seattle signed the short, stocky right-hander as an undrafted free agent coming out of North Carolina Central University in mid-June 2018. Sweet, a 5-foot-11, 183-pound hurler, quietly turned in a solid senior season for the Mid-Eastern Athletic Conference school: in 16 appearances, 14 of which were starts, he posted an 87-to-20 strikeout-to-walk ratio in 85.1 innings of work. Sweet, a native of Greensboro, North Carolina, quickly assimilated to life as a professional pitcher. He made stops at three separate levels during his debut. And spent time with West Virginia and Modesto during his sophomore season in 2019. In 127.1 combined innings, Sweet fanned a whopping 152 and walked just 27 to go along with a 2.76 ERA.

Scouting Report: A fastball / slider combination that's flavored like vanilla ice cream. Sweet's sweetness comes from his fantastical changeup. Thrown his tremendous arm deception, the offering shows a large amount of velocity separation and strong arm-side run and fade. It's a plus pitch – one that's likely among the Top 10 or so in the entire minor leagues. The fastball's straight but he commands it well enough where it might play up a half of a grade. And he's not afraid to challenge hitters up-and-in. The slider shows some two-plane depth. Best case scenario: Josh Tomlin with a plus-pitch (changeup).

Ceiling: 1.0- to 1.5-win player
Risk: Moderate
MLB ETA: 2022

17. Juan Then, RHP

	FB	CB	SL	CH	Command	Overall
	55	55	45	50	50	45

Born: 07/22/99	Age: 20	Bats: R
Height: 6-4	Weight: 225	Throws: R

YEAR	LVL	IP	W	L	SV	ERA	FIP	WHIP	K/9	K%	BB/9	BB%	K/BB	HR9	BABIP
2017	Rk	61.3	2	2	0	2.64	2.87	1.06	8.2	22.86%	2.2	6.12%	3.73	0.44	0.278
2018	Rk	50.0	0	3	0	2.70	3.20	0.98	7.6	21.54%	2.0	5.64%	3.82	0.36	0.259
2019	Rk	2.0	0	0	0	0.00	2.25	1.00	9.0	28.57%	0.0	0.00%	#DIV/0!	0.00	0.400
2019	A-	30.3	0	3	0	3.56	2.83	1.09	9.5	26.89%	2.7	7.56%	3.56	0.30	0.299
2019	A	16.0	1	2	0	2.25	3.66	0.69	7.9	22.95%	2.3	6.56%	3.50	0.56	0.150

Background: Apparently Jerry Dipoto just can't quit Juan Then. The franchise shipped off the teenage pitching prospect – as well left-hander, and long time personal favorite of mine, JP Sears to the Yankees for right-hander Nick Rumbelow in the middle of November in 2017. Roughly a year-and-a-half later Dipoto & Co. reacquired the hard-throwing right-hander from New York in exchange for Edwin Encarnacion and cash considerations. Then spent last season between three different levels – the Arizona Summer League, the Northwest League, and the Sally – as he tossed 48.1 innings while fanning 48 and walking just 13 to go along with an aggregate 2.98 ERA.

Scouting Report: Like a lot of the lower level arms in the system Then is an intriguing wild card. He can pump his heater into the mid-90s with relative ease. His curveball has progressed over the past year to when it's flashing above-average more consistently. His slider, which looks to be recently added, is still a work in progress. And he'll mix in a changeup as well. He's a bit reminiscent in stature and stuff to former Cubs top prospect Juan Cruz.

Ceiling: 1.5-win player
Risk: High
MLB ETA: 2022/2023

18. Damon Casetta Stubbs, RHP

	FB	CB	SL	CH	Command	Overall
	55/60	55/60	45	45	50	45

Born: 07/22/99	Age: 20	Bats: R
Height: 6-4	Weight: 225	Throws: R

YEAR	LVL	IP	W	L	SV	ERA	FIP	WHIP	K/9	K%	BB/9	BB%	K/BB	HR9	BABIP
2018	Rk	6.7	0	2	0	13.50	4.67	2.85	9.5	17.07%	5.4	9.76%	1.75	0.00	0.536
2019	A-	70.0	3	3	0	4.11	4.72	1.13	8.6	22.56%	3.5	9.09%	2.48	0.90	0.247
2019	A	44.3	3	5	0	7.11	4.26	1.67	7.5	18.05%	2.6	6.34%	2.85	0.81	0.393
2019	A+	2.3	0	0	0	0.00	4.95	1.71	11.6	21.43%	7.7	14.29%	1.50	0.00	0.250

Background: One of the more raw, albeit intriguing arms in the entire Seattle system. The Mariners bet big on the big right-hander out of King's Way Christian Schools two years ago. After taking a late round flier on Casseta-Stubbs, the club signed him to a hefty $325,000 deal – roughly middle of the fifth round money.

Casetta-Stubs, the 328th player chosen, popped up in six brief games in the Arizona Summer League during his debut, posting a 7-to-4 strikeout-to-walk ratio in 6.2 innings of work. Last season the 6-foot-4, 225-pound righty bound around between three levels (short-season ball, Low Class A and High Class A), throwing 116.2 innings with 107 strikeouts and 42 walks.

Scouting Report: Really, really raw. Liked uncooked chicken. But there's a lot of intriguing bits-and-pieces working in Casetta-Stubbs' favor: (A) he looks the part of a potential John Lackey-type starting pitcher; (B) he handled himself well in the Northwest League; and (C) he shows a solid aptitude for pitching, despite his youth. Casetta-Stubbs owns an above-average fastball that will eventually grade-up to a plus-offering. His curveball shows hard, late tilt. His slider, which was reportedly the best of his offspeed weapons, looked flat, lacked depth, and was hit pretty hard during the outings I watched. He'll also work in a changeup. Again, he's very raw. But there's something about him that intrigues me.

Ceiling: 1.5-win player
Risk: High
MLB ETA: 2022/2023

19. Sam Delaplane, RHP

	FB	SL	Command	Overall
	60	55	50	40

Born: 09/06/96	Age: 23	Bats: B
Height: 5-11	Weight: 183	Throws: R

YEAR	LVL	IP	W	L	SV	ERA	FIP	WHIP	K/9	K%	BB/9	BB%	K/BB	HR9	BABIP
2017	Rk	31.0	2	1	0	2.90	2.80	1.13	13.6	36.15%	2.3	6.15%	5.88	0.58	0.342
2018	A	59.7	4	2	10	1.96	2.42	1.27	15.1	38.76%	3.3	8.53%	4.55	0.75	0.380
2019	A+	31.7	3	2	2	4.26	1.99	1.14	17.6	48.44%	4.0	10.94%	4.43	0.57	0.417
2019	AA	37.0	3	1	5	0.49	1.99	0.59	14.1	43.28%	2.2	6.72%	6.44	0.49	0.177

Background: I typically make it a point to not include relief pitchers among a club's Top 20 List – unless they're a top pick, reach triple digits, or put up absurd numbers. Enter: Delaplane, a 23rd round pick out of Eastern Michigan University in 2017. Seattle took a late round flier on the senior and it's immediately paying dividends. The hard-throwing right-hander was nearly unhittable in Low Class A two years ago, averaging 15.1 strikeouts and 3.3 walks per nine innings. He split time between Modesto and Arkansas last season as he continued to miss a ridiculous amount of bats: he posted an eye-popping 120-to-23 strikeout-to-walk ratio in only 68.2 innings. He finished his third professional season with an aggregate 2.23 ERA.

Scouting Report: A deadly fastball / slider combination coupled with a decent feel for the strike zone. Delaplane's fastball sits in the 94- to 96-mph range with late, explosive life. His slider is tight, almost cutter-like, and sits in the upper 80s. On a lower end big league team Delaplane could snipe some saves, but he's probably better suited for a seventh-inning role.

Ceiling: 1.0-win player
Risk: Moderate
MLB ETA: 2020

20. Joey Gerber, RHP

	FB	SL	Command	Overall
	65	50	45	40

Born: 07/22/99	Age: 20	Bats: R
Height: 6-4	Weight: 225	Throws: R

YEAR	LVL	IP	W	L	SV	ERA	FIP	WHIP	K/9	K%	BB/9	BB%	K/BB	HR9	BABIP
2018	A-	14.0	1	0	6	1.93	1.83	1.07	13.5	38.89%	3.9	11.11%	3.50	0.00	0.333
2018	A	11.7	0	0	2	2.31	0.99	1.20	17.0	46.81%	3.9	10.64%	4.40	0.00	0.450
2019	A+	26.0	0	2	8	3.46	2.16	1.12	13.5	36.11%	4.2	11.11%	3.25	0.00	0.304
2019	AA	22.7	1	2	0	1.59	3.00	1.24	11.9	32.26%	2.8	7.53%	4.29	0.79	0.352

Background: A dominant closer during his tenure at the University of Illinois; Seattle drafted the 6-foot-4, 215-pound right-hander in the eighth round two years ago. Gerber, who averaged a whopping 12.1 strikeouts and an equally large 4.9 walks per nine innings during his collegiate career, was absurdly good during his debut with Everett and Clinton: he fanned 43 and walked just 11 in only 25.2 innings of work. Last season Gerber split time with Modesto and Arkansas, throwing a career best 48.2 innings while recording 69 punch outs against 19 walks to go along with an aggregate 2.59 ERA.

Scouting Report: Aggressive, short-arming reliever with a lively mid-90s fastball that kisses the upper-90s on occasion and an average-ish upper-80s slider. He lacks the wipeout secondary option to thrust him into a legitimate high-leverage big league option. And his control/command is subpar and wavers at times. But Gerber should be a serviceable seventh-inning option as soon as 2020.

Ceiling: 1.0-win player
Risk: Moderate
MLB ETA: 2020

Rank	Name	Age	Pos
1	Dylan Carlson	21	OF
2	Nolan Gorman	20	3B
3	Ivan Herrera	20	C
4	Matthew Liberatore	21	LHP
5	Andrew Knizner	25	C
6	Genesis Cabrera	23	LHP
7	Zack Thompson	22	LHP
8	Elehuris Montero	21	3B
9	Malcom Nunez	19	3B
10	Lane Thomas	24	OF
11	Mateo Gil	25	SS
12	Justin Williams	24	LF/RF
13	Johan Oviedo	22	RHP
14	Trejyn Fletcher	23	CF
15	Jhon Torres	20	OF
16	Angel Rondon	22	RHP
17	Junior Fernandez	23	RHP
18	Edmundo Sosa	24	IF
19	Luken Baker	23	1B
20	Tony Locey	21	RHP

1. Dylan Carlson, OF

	Hit	Power	SB	Patience	Glove	Overall
	55	50/55	50/45	60	50	60

Born: 10/23/98	Age: 21	Bats: B
Height: 6-3	Weight: 205	Throws: L

YEAR	LVL	PA	1B	2B	3B	HR	SB	CS	AVG	OBP	SLG	BB%	K%	GB%	LD%	FB%
2016	RK	201	27	13	3	3	4	2	0.251	0.313	0.404	7.96%	25.87%	48.5	22.7	27.3
2017	A	451	66	18	1	7	6	6	0.240	0.342	0.347	11.53%	25.72%	43.8	17.5	32.1
2018	A	57	6	3	0	2	2	0	0.234	0.368	0.426	17.54%	17.54%	51.4	13.5	35.1
2018	A+	441	62	19	3	9	6	3	0.247	0.345	0.386	11.79%	17.69%	44.1	21.1	29.3
2019	AA	483	66	24	6	21	18	7	0.281	0.364	0.518	10.77%	20.29%	39.3	26.0	30.3
2019	AAA	79	15	4	2	5	2	1	0.361	0.418	0.681	7.59%	22.78%	29.6	16.7	44.4

Background: The California-based Elk Grove High School has helped mold a surprising amount of baseball talent since the beginning of the 21st century. Four big leaguers have walked through the hallowed halls of The Thundering Herd: veteran reliever David Hernandez, who's earned more than $14 million in his 10-year career; J.D. Davis, who's coming off of a breakout season with the Mets in which he slugged 22 dingers en route to batting .307/.369/.527; hulking Blue Jays first baseman Rowdy Tellez, and – of course – the immortal Dom Nunez, a sixth round pick by the Rockies in 2013. And that list doesn't include a trio highly touted draft picks: current Tigers center fielder Derek Hill was the 23rd overall pick six years ago; Nick Madrigal, who was originally drafted by the Indians in the 17th round in 2015 and the tabbed as the fourth overall pick by the White Sox after a stellar career at collegiate powerhouse Oregon State; and then there's Dylan Carlson, whose dynamic showing in 2019 has him shooting up prospect lists. The 33rd overall pick in 2016, Carlson was a solid minor league outfielder over his previous three minor league seasons, showing a severe saber-slant with burgeoning power potential. And Carlson, finally, put it all together last season. Squaring off against the minors' toughest challenge, Class AA, the 6-foot-3, 205-pound switch-hitter slugged a hearty .281/.364/.518 with 24 doubles, six triples, 21 homeruns, and – just for good measure – he swiped 18 bags in 25 attempts. Per Baseball Prospectus' *Deserved Runs Created Plus*, his overall production topped the league average threshold by a whopping 51%. Carlson spent the final couple of weeks in the Pacific Coast League as well, batting a scorching .361/.418/.681.

Snippet from The 2018 Prospect Digest Handbook: A really intriguing projection-over-production type prospect. Carlson's approach at the plate is similar to a young Jesse Winker, Cincinnati's young star outfielder. The Elk Grove High School product shows an above-average eye at the plate with strong bat-to-ball skills with a line-drive slashing swing. His numbers have been slowly trending upward the past couple of seasons, though an immediate breakout isn't likely as he's probably headed to the minors' toughest challenge, Class AA. He could, though, be one of 2020's biggest risers. Carlson could wind up being a lite version of Jesse Winker, peaking around .270/.340/.415.

Scouting Report: So...he *was* one of the biggest riser's in 2019. I was, simply, a year off. With respect to his work in Class AA last season, consider the following:

- Since 2006, there have been 58 instances in which a 20-year-old posted a 145 DRC+ or better in a minor league season (min. 350 PA).
- Of those aforementioned 58, only seven of them accomplished the feat in Class AA or Class AAA.
- Of those seven, five of them accomplished the feat in the Texas League: Cody Bellinger, the 2017 N.L. Rookie of the Year and reigning N.L. MVP; Colby Rasmus, Oscar Taveras, Jon Singleton, and – of course – Dylan Carlson.

For those counting at home that's: one of this generation's greatest ballplayers (Bellinger), a perennial top prospect whose life was tragically cut short (Taveras), a long-time league average hitter who topped the average production line by at least 15% on separate occasions (Rasmus), and a failed top prospect who battled personal demons and contact issues (Singleton). As for Carlson, he's a doing everything well – like, really well – type of ballplayer, a legitimate five-tool burgeoning star. He'll hit for average with a silky smooth swing from both sides of the plate, belt out 20- to 25-homeruns as he continues to turn on the inside pitch, and avoid outs thanks to his innate ability to sniff out first base. Throw in above-average speed and glove to match, and the kid has the makings of a star at the big league level. And, personally, I think he's just beginning to tap into his power potential. In terms of ceiling, think Justin Turner's showing with the Dodgers last season in which he slugged .290/.372/.509 with 27 homeruns.

Ceiling: 4.5-win player
Risk: Low to Moderate
MLB ETA: 2020

2. Nolan Gorman, 3B

Hit	Power	SB	Patience	Glove	Overall
45+	55/65	30	55	65	60

Born: 05/10/00		**Age:** 20		**Bats:** L	
Height: 6-1		**Weight:** 210		**Throws:** R	

YEAR	LVL	PA	1B	2B	3B	HR	SB	CS	AVG	OBP	SLG	BB%	K%	GB%	LD%	FB%
2018	RK	167	28	10	1	11	1	3	0.350	0.443	0.664	14.37%	22.16%	38.7	15.1	39.6
2018	A	107	10	3	0	6	0	2	0.202	0.280	0.426	9.35%	36.45%	26.3	12.3	49.1
2019	A	282	31	14	3	10	2	0	0.241	0.344	0.448	11.35%	28.01%	32.3	15.2	47.0
2019	A+	230	31	16	3	5	0	1	0.256	0.304	0.428	5.65%	31.74%	28.6	26.4	37.9

Background: A highly touted power hitting infielder out of Sandra Day O'Connor High School. Gorman was well known on the scouting and tournament circuits early in his amateur career. For example: he committed to the University of Arizona a few months after his freshman season concluded. He promptly went out and bashed 11 homeruns and batted .490 as a sophomore for the Arizona-based school. But it wasn't until his conclusion of his junior season when Gorman really began to take off. In a matter of months, he won a couple homerun derbies and starred for the 18U National Squad. Following another impressive showing during his senior season, St. Louis drafted the lefty-swinging third baseman in the opening round, 19th overall, and signed him to a barely below-slot deal worth $3,231,000 – which saved the club a whopping $700. After signing, Gorman ripped through the Appalachian League like a pit bull mauling a sofa as he slugged .350/.443/.664 with 21 extra-base hits in 38 contests. He also spent nearly a month in the Midwest League, though the results were far less impressive. Last season, unsurprisingly, Gorman found himself back in Low Class A – though, this time the results fell more in line with expectations. He slugged .241/.344/.448 in 67 games. He spent the second half of the year in the Florida State League, batting .256/.304/.428. He finished the year with 30 doubles, six triples, and 15 homeruns.

Snippet from The 2018 Prospect Digest Handbook: The concern with Gorman heading into the draft was whether he'd make consistent enough contact to fully take advantage of his plus-plus power potential. And he helped alleviate some of those concerns with his performance in the Appalachian League, though he did punch out in more than a third of his plate appearances in Low Class A. Gorman also struggled against left-handers as well, batting .250/.291/.462 against them in a small sample size. Strong, quick-snapping wrists help generate easy bat speed. . A year into his pro career and I'd peg his ceiling at .250/.340/.540.

Scouting Report: A few notes:

- The swing-and-miss issues were borderline concerning, but they weren't full-blown alarming. He fanned in 28% of his plate appearances in Low Class A and posted a 31.7% K-rate in High Class A.
- He was able to solve left-handers last season, which alleviates a lot of my concern. He posted a triple-slash line of .248/.331/.437 s. RHP and a .244/.308/.439 mark vs. LHP.
- Unreal power.

Gorman's one of the more underrated defenders – as well as being one of the best defensive infielders – in the minor leagues. There's the potential to earn a few Gold Gloves at the major league level. Last year I remarked how Gorman's ceiling resides in the .250/.340/.540 neighborhood. Throw in some plus-defensive value and all of a sudden you're staring down the ceiling of a Matt Chapman. He's headed back to High Class A to start 2020, but should finish the year in Class AA. Wait till he fully taps into his in-game power.

Ceiling: 4.5-win player
Risk: Moderate to High
MLB ETA: 2021/2022

3. Ivan Herrera, C

Hit	Power	SB	Patience	Glove	Overall
50	50/55	30	50+	50	55

Born: 06/01/00		**Age:** 20		**Bats:** R	
Height: 6-0		**Weight:** 180		**Throws:** R	

YEAR	LVL	PA	1B	2B	3B	HR	SB	CS	AVG	OBP	SLG	BB%	K%	GB%	LD%	FB%
2017	RK	201	41	15	0	1	2	2	0.335	0.425	0.441	8.96%	17.91%	62.0	16.8	15.3
2018	RK	130	28	6	4	1	1	1	0.348	0.423	0.500	8.46%	15.38%	44.7	29.8	19.1
2018	AA	5	0	0	0	0	0	0	0.000	0.200	0.000	0.00%	40.00%	100.0	0.0	0.0
2019	A	291	53	10	0	8	1	1	0.286	0.381	0.423	12.03%	19.24%	45.6	16.9	27.7
2019	A+	65	15	0	0	1	0	0	0.276	0.338	0.328	7.69%	24.62%	36.6	19.5	31.7

Background: Signed out of Panama, Panama, on July 7th, 2016. Herrera's been one of the minors' most consistent, oft-times well above-average bats through his three-year professional career. He torched the foreign rookie league with a .335/.425/.441 triple-slash line; didn't slow one iota as he moved into the Gulf Coast League two years ago (.348/.423/.500), and he acquitted himself quite nicely in 69 games Low Class A games in 2019. He hit .286/.381/.423 with 10 doubles and eight homeruns with Peoria. Per *Deserved Runs Created Plus*, his overall production topped the league average threshold by a whopping 38%.

He also spent a handful of weeks in the Florida State League, batting .276/.338/.328. He finished the year by slugging .324/.439/.382 in 10 games with Glendale in the Arizona Fall League.

Snippet from The 2018 Prospect Digest Handbook: Herrera's pretty advanced in terms of his offensive skill set and it wouldn't be out of the question for and him to spend a significant amount of time in Low Class A in 2019. Solid tools across the board.

Scouting Report: First things first: I was pretty bearish on Herrera's showing in the Gulf Coast League in last year's Handbook. I was clearly wrong and he – easily – surpassed my expectations. With respect to his work in Low Class A last season, consider the following:

- Since 2006, here's the list of 19-year-old hitters to post a 133 to 143 DRC+ total with a sub-20% strikeout rate and a double-digit walk rate in the Midwest League (min. 250 PA): Jesse Winker, Bryce Turang, and – of course – Ivan Herrera. For those counting at home: Winker has topped the MLB average line by at least 12% in each of his three big league seasons; and Turang is one of the best middle infielder prospects in the minor leagues.

St. Louis governed Herrera's playing time last season – particularly in the early parts of the year. There's a solid possibility that Herrera develops into a 50-grade hit tool with 20-homerun thump with a solid enough glove to stay behind the dish. I don't expect the type of patience he displayed to remain at the peak level it was in Low Class A, but it should settle in around 9% to 10% in the coming years.

Ceiling: 3.0- to 3.5-win player
Risk: Moderate
MLB ETA: 2021/2022

4. Matthew Liberatore, LHP

	FB	CB	SL	CH	Command	Overall
	55	60	55+	50	50	50

Born: 11/06/99	Age: 20	Bats: L
Height: 6-5	Weight: 200	Throws: L

YEAR	LVL	IP	W	L	SV	ERA	FIP	WHIP	K/9	K%	BB/9	BB%	K/BB	HR9	BABIP
2018	Rk	27.7	1	2	0	0.98	2.85	0.98	10.4	29.63%	3.6	10.19%	2.91	0.00	0.258
2018	Rk	5.0	1	0	0	3.60	3.19	1.40	9.0	26.32%	3.6	10.53%	2.50	0.00	0.417
2019	A	78.3	6	2	0	3.10	3.16	1.29	8.7	22.89%	3.6	9.34%	2.45	0.23	0.311

Background: St. Louis got together with a familiar trade partner this offseason when they agreed to send slugging first baseman/corner outfielder Jose Martinez, bashing minor league outfielder Randy Arozarena, and a 2020 supplemental first round pick to the Tampa Bay Rays for Matthew Liberatore, backstop Edgardo Rodriguez, and a 2020 second round supplemental selection. The Mountain Ridge High School product, the 16th overall pick two years ago, showed a ton of promise during his debut between the Gulf Coast and Appalachian League as he fanned 37 and walked just 13 in 32.2 innings of work. Tampa Bay bounced the lanky lefty up to the Midwest League and he looked comfortable against the vastly older competition. Making 16 appearances, the 6-foot-5, 200-pound hurler posted a 76-to-31 strikeout-to-walk ratio in 78.1 innings.

Snippet from The 2018 Prospect Digest Handbook: Poised beyond his years, the lanky left-hander shows an incredibly well-rounded, polished arsenal that still has a bit of projection left. There's some #2/#3-type potential here. He could move quickly, especially for a prep arm.

Scouting Report: Consider the following:

- Since 2006, here's the list of 19-year-old pitchers to post a strikeout percentage between 21% and 23% with a walk percentage between 8% and 10% in the Midwest League (min. 75 IP): Jose Berrios, one of the top young pitchers in baseball; Travis Wood, who had a couple solid MLB seasons; Shaun Garceau, a former Cardinals farmhand, and Matthew Liberatore.

Again, very polished for his age. Liberatore, who's a long time best friend of new teammate Nolan Gorman, begins games in the 93- to 94-mph range, but will settle in a tick or two below later on. When I saw him his curveball was a bit rough, though it's easy to see a potential plus offering given the shape and depth. His slider was better than it was two years ago, showing hard late action when it was thrown in the mid-80s with more bend and break when it was sitting 81-82. The changeup's a solid average pitch. St. Louis has generally done well in cultivating young arms and Liberatore could begin to move quickly once the training wheels are removed. A year after prognosticating a potential #2 ceiling, I'm more inclined to bump him down to a true #3, unless some extra velocity develops and/or above-average control/command.

Ceiling: 3.0-win player
Risk: Moderate
MLB ETA: 2021/2022

5. Andrew Knizner, C

Hit	Power	SB	Patience	Glove	Overall
50	45	30	45+	45	50

Born: 02/03/95	Age: 25	Bats: R	
Height: 6-1	Weight: 200	Throws: R	

YEAR	LVL	PA	1B	2B	3B	HR	SB	CS	AVG	OBP	SLG	BB%	K%	GB%	LD%	FB%
2017	A	191	31	10	1	8	1	1	0.279	0.325	0.480	4.71%	11.52%	40.8	23.6	28.7
2017	AA	202	42	13	0	4	0	1	0.324	0.371	0.462	6.93%	13.37%	47.8	18.9	30.2
2018	AA	313	68	13	0	7	0	1	0.313	0.365	0.434	7.35%	12.78%	48.6	19.4	22.7
2018	AAA	61	12	5	0	0	0	0	0.315	0.383	0.407	6.56%	13.11%	42.6	21.3	29.8
2019	AAA	280	46	10	0	12	2	0	0.276	0.357	0.463	8.57%	13.21%	39.8	18.5	33.2

Background: The club's been in search of the Molina's heir apparent for the last several seasons. And it one point it looked like the duo of Andrew Knizner and Carson Kelly would duke it out for the position. But (A) Molina still remains a viable big league backstop well into his 30s and (B) Kelly was dealt away to the Diamondbacks as part of the package to fetch slugging first baseman Paul Goldschmidt. Knizner, a product of North Carolina State University, spent the majority of last season with the Redbirds in the Pacific Coast League, batting a respectable .276/.357/.463 with 10 doubles and 12 homeruns. His overall production, per *Deserved Runs Created Plus*, topped the league average mark by 12%. The 6-foot-1, 200-pound backstop also earned a couple trips up to The Show as well, hitting a lowly .226/.293/.377 with a pair of doubles and two homeruns in 58 plate appearances.

Snippet from The 2018 Prospect Digest Handbook: He shows a short, slashing swing at the plate with solid bat-to-ball skills. His swing doesn't create much loft, so homeruns will be a rarity for him though.

Scouting Report: A hitter that would likely get slapped with that old "professional" label that was seemingly thrown around a decade or two ago. Knizner is a bat-first catcher whose defense hasn't graded out exceptionally well the past couple of seasons. And some fringy walk rate will ultimately chew into his overall offensive value. The N.C. State product could be paired with a defensive-minded backup to provide some quality value for the club in the coming years. In terms of ceiling, think something along the lines of Brian McCann's production in 2019: .249/.323/.412.

Ceiling: 2.5-win player
Risk: Low to Moderate
MLB ETA: Debuted in 2019

6. Genesis Cabrera, LHP

FB	CB	CH	Command	Overall
60	55/60	50	45	50

Born: 10/10/96	Age: 23	Bats: L	
Height: 6-2	Weight: 190	Throws: L	

YEAR	LVL	IP	W	L	SV	ERA	FIP	WHIP	K/9	K%	BB/9	BB%	K/BB	HR9	BABIP
2017	A+	69.7	4	5	0	2.84	3.35	1.00	7.8	21.90%	3.2	9.12%	2.40	0.39	0.230
2017	AA	64.7	5	4	0	3.62	4.13	1.58	7.1	17.29%	3.8	9.15%	1.89	0.84	0.332
2018	AA	113.7	7	6	0	4.12	4.00	1.29	9.8	26.16%	4.5	12.03%	2.18	0.87	0.282
2018	AA	24.7	1	3	0	4.74	4.90	1.50	7.7	19.63%	4.7	12.15%	1.62	1.09	0.300
2018	AAA	2.0	0	0	0	0.00	2.24	0.50	13.5	42.86%	4.5	14.29%	3.00	0.00	0.000
2019	AAA	99.0	5	6	0	5.91	5.61	1.47	9.6	24.42%	3.5	8.99%	2.72	1.82	0.330

Background: St. Louis and Tampa Bay have pulled off three trades during their respective histories: #1 The Tino Martinez swap that sent the aging slugger to the Devil Rays for a pair of non-descript prospects; #2 The July 31st, 2018 deal where St. Louis acquired Genesis Cabrera, Justin Williams and Roel Ramirez for Tommy Pham and international bonus money; #3 The most recent trade that sent Matthew Liberatore and change to the Rays for Jose Martinez and change. Cabrera, a wiry 6-foot-2, 190-pound southpaw, made 20 appearances in the Pacific Coast League, 18 of which were starts, throwing 99.0 innings with 106 punch outs and 39 walks. He finished his sixth professional season with a 5.91 ERA and a 5.11 DRA (*Deserved Run Average*). Cabrera also tossed an additional 20.1 innings with the Cardinals as well, fanning 19 and walking 11 with a 4.87 ERA in.

Snippet from The 2018 Prospect Digest Handbook: Cabrera's more Jeremy Hellickson than Jose Berrios. Meaning: he should settle in as #4/#5.

Scouting Report: With respect to his work in Class AAA last season, consider the following:

- Since 2006, only two 22-year-old pitchers met the following criteria in the Pacific Coast League (min. 75 IP): 23.5% and 25.5% strikeout percentage with a walk percentage between 8% and 10%. Those two hurlers: Yordano Ventura, who tallied 6.9 fWAR in 547.2 career innings, and – of course – Genesis Cabrera.

In a late season start with the Memphis Redbirds Cabrera's fastball showed a lot more life than I remembered in previous years. It's a genuine plus-offering that is a borderline 65-grade. His curveball is still inconsistent. But when he stays on top it shows hard, downward bite while flashing plus. And his changeup is a firm, upper-80s 50-grade. The control/command – even at its best – is slightly below-average. After an uptick in on his two primary offerings, Cabrera has the ceiling as a low-end #3 with the floor as a dominant, dominant late-inning relief arm.

Ceiling: 2.5- to 3.0-win player
Risk: Moderate
MLB ETA: Debuted in 2019

7. Zack Thompson, LHP

	FB	CB	SL	CH	Command	Overall
	55	60	55	50	50	50

Born: 10/28/97	Age: 22	Bats: L
Height: 6-2	Weight: 225	Throws: L

YEAR	LVL	IP	W	L	SV	ERA	FIP	WHIP	K/9	K%	BB/9	BB%	K/BB	HR9	BABIP
2019	Rk	2.0	0	0	0	0.00	0.50	1.50	18.0	40.00%	0.0	0.00%	#DIV/0!	0.00	0.500
2019	A+	13.3	0	0	0	4.05	2.03	1.50	12.8	33.93%	2.7	7.14%	4.75	0.00	0.455

Background: Prior to last season, the list of first round picks taken out of the University of Kentucky is quite small: since 1965 only five Wildcats have been taken in the opening round of the June draft. Three of those players – James Paxton, Joe Blanton, and Alex Meyer – were pitchers, all of whom made it to the big leagues with the Paxton and Blanton establishing themselves as viable big league starters and the latter, Meyer, was widely recognized as a Top 100 prospect for several seasons. Enter: Zack Thompson. A well-built left-hander measuring in at 6-foot-3 and 225 pounds, Thompson was originally taken in the 11th round by the Tampa Bay Rays coming out of high school. Recognized by Perfect Game as the No. 23 best left-handed pitcher, the two sides couldn't come to an agreement so Thompson packed his bags and slid into the SEC. A native of Anderson, Indiana, Thompson made 20 appearances for first-year Head Coach Nick Mingione during his debut collegiate season, throwing 75.2 innings while recording a whopping 96 strikeouts and just 38 walks to go along with a 3.45 ERA. He was named to the Freshman All-American squad by Baseball America. And Perfect/Rawlings named him as a First-Team Freshman All-American award as well. An elbow injury limited Thompson to just 31.0 innings for the Wildcats during his sophomore campaign, though he did manage to strikeout 42 and walk 20. He split the ensuing summer playing for Team USA (8.2 IP, 7 K, and 5 BB) and the Brewster Whitecaps in the Cape Cod League (5.2 IP, 4 K, and 3 BB). Finally healthy, Thompson was been lights out in 2019: in a career high 14 starts, he tallied a dominating 130-to-34 strikeout-to-walk ratio with an impeccably diminutive 2.40 ERA in only 90.0 innings of work. St. Louis snagged Thompson with the 19th overall pick last June. Thompson tossed 15.1 innings during his debut, most of which came in the Florida State League, fanning 23 and walking four with a 3.52 ERA.

Scouting Report: Per the usual, here's what I wrote prior to the draft last June:

"In a draft class as perilously thin as this year's group, Thompson – easily – stands out with TCU's Nick Lodolo and Mississippi State's Ethan Small as the top left-handers available. Kentucky's ace showcases three above-average or better offerings – fastball, curveball, and slider – and a solid fourth option (changeup). Thompson commands his low- to mid-90s fastball well, showing the ability to pitch to all four quadrants. His curveball provides a second strikeout offering. His mid-80s slider will resemble a cutter at times. And his changeup is a workable pitch that might tick up as he gains more experience. With respect to his production this season, consider the following:

- *Between 2011 and 2018, here's the list of Division I pitchers that averaged at least 12.25 strikeouts and between 2.75 and 3.25 walks every nine innings (min. 70 IP): Carlos Rodon, Matt Hall, Eli Morgan, Robert Broom, and Kyle Brnovich. Rodon was the third overall pick in the 2014 draft. Morgan, Hall, and Broom were all mid-round selections. And Brnovich is currently a junior at Elon.*

Morgan and Hall are both soft-tossing finesse pitchers. And Broom was a dominant, multi-inning reliever. So let's take a look at how Thompson's production stacks up against Rodon's numbers during their aforementioned seasons. Consider the following:

Player	Year	Age	IP	K/9	BB/9	ERA
Zack Thompson	2019	21	71.2	12.81	3.01	1.88
Carlos Rodon	2013	20	132.0	12.51	3.06	2.99

Thompson's not quite on the same level as Rodon was. However, in a thin pitching crop the Kentucky ace could go within the top 15 or so selections. The elbow injury from last season does cause some concern, but he's not showing any side effects thus far. Thompson looks like a good #3 at his peak."

Ceiling: 2.5- to 3.0-win player
Risk: Moderate
MLB ETA: 2022

St. Louis Cardinals

8. Elehuris Montero, 3B

Hit	Power	SB	Patience	Glove	Overall
55	55	30	45	50	50

Born: 08/17/98	Age: 21	Bats: R
Height: 6-3	Weight: 215	Throws: R

YEAR	LVL	PA	1B	2B	3B	HR	SB	CS	AVG	OBP	SLG	BB%	K%	GB%	LD%	FB%
2017	RK	208	26	16	1	5	0	2	0.277	0.370	0.468	10.58%	15.87%	32.9	19.9	37.0
2018	A	425	77	28	3	15	2	0	0.322	0.381	0.529	7.76%	19.06%	37.4	24.3	30.5
2018	A+	106	18	9	0	1	1	0	0.286	0.330	0.408	4.72%	20.75%	39.0	24.7	24.7
2019	Rk	15	4	0	0	0	0	0	0.308	0.400	0.308	6.67%	13.33%	45.5	18.2	18.2
2019	AA	238	27	8	0	7	0	1	0.188	0.235	0.317	5.88%	31.09%	46.3	23.1	25.2

Background: I wasn't only a member of the Montero Hype Train heading into last season; I was the damn conductor, engineer, dining-car service attendant, and that one guy that walks up-and-down the aisles punching holes in everyone's tickets. And, well, Montero put together a disastrous – albeit injury-riddled – showing in 2019.

Coming off of a season in which he bashed 37 doubles, three triples, and 16 homeruns with a .315/.371/.504 triple-slash line between Low Class A and High Class A, Montero looked poised to become the next big Cardinals homegrown hitter. St. Louis moved him up to the Texas League – as a 20-year-old – and got off to a slow start, hit the disabled list with a wrist issue for month, looked pretty good for a handful of games, and then returned to the DL for nearly two months with a broken hamate. When the dust had finally settled, Montero was sporting a lowly .194/.245/.316 triple-slash line.

Snippet from The 2018 Prospect Digest Handbook: Montero shows a nice-and-easy approach at the plate that generates impressive bat speed, though his swing is more geared towards scorching line drives than hitting towering fly balls. Only entering his age-20 season, Montero's just scratching the surface of what could eventually turn into plus-power, perhaps peaking in the 25-homer territory. He shows decent patience at the plate that may peak slightly better than average with phenomenal bat-to-ball skills as well. Defensively speaking, it looks like he may be able to stay at the hot corner, only further increasing his value. At maturity Montero looks like a bonafide middle-of-the-lineup thumper capable of putting together a .280/.340/.500 triple-slash line, essentially putting him in the Eduardo Escobar/Eugenio Suarez camp.

Scouting Report: See...I told you I was president of the Montero fan club. It was, unequivocally, a lost developmental season for Montero. Not only did he leap up to Class AA as a 20-year-old with just 24 games in High Class A, but he battled two severe hand/wrist issues. And the second injury, a broken hamate, is known to sap a hitter's power for months upon months. Prior to his disastrous season, the Dominican-born third baseman was coming off of back-to-back stellar seasons at the plate, showing 20-homer power potential with solid contact. The lone concern I have about Montero moving forward: his K-rate spiked tremendously last season (31.1%). His status has taken a (significant) hit, but I'm still betting on a rebound in 2020 – particularly the second half.

Ceiling: 2.5- to 3.0-win player
Risk: Moderate to High
MLB ETA: 2020/2021

9. Malcom Nunez, 3B

Hit	Power	SB	Patience	Glove	Overall
40/50	40/55	30	45	50	50

Born: 03/09/01	Age: 19	Bats: R
Height: 5-11	Weight: 205	Throws: R

YEAR	LVL	PA	1B	2B	3B	HR	SB	CS	AVG	OBP	SLG	BB%	K%	GB%	LD%	FB%
2018	RK	199	37	16	2	13	3	0	0.415	0.497	0.774	13.07%	14.57%	36.0	31.7	25.2
2019	Rk+	146	20	11	0	2	3	2	0.254	0.336	0.385	8.90%	21.92%	56.1	20.4	21.4
2019	A	77	12	1	0	0	0	0	0.183	0.247	0.197	6.49%	19.48%	51.8	14.3	19.6

Background: Fellow third baseman Elehuris Montero wasn't the only promising bat in the system to struggle with an aggressive promotion in 2019. Nunez, a stocky 5-foot-11, 205-pound corner infielder, looked otherworldly during his debut in the Dominican Summer League two years ago when he slugged .415/.497/.774 with 16 doubles, two triples, and 13 homeruns in only 44 games – numbers that stood out even in a crazy offense-inducing environment. The front office pushed the young teenager directly up to the Midwest League to start 2019. But after going 13-for-71, he was demoted down to the Rookie Advanced League. In 37 games with Johnson City he batted .254/.336/.385 with 11 doubles and a pair of homeruns.

Snippet from The 2018 Prospect Digest Handbook: Incredible bat speed generated through his massive forearms and tree trunk-like legs. Nunez looks like a grown man despite only entering his age-18 season. Plus skills sprinkled across the board – specially the bat and prodigious power potential – with a solid approach at the plate. Physically, he looks like a young Bo Jackson. I'd be surprised if he sticks at the hot corner, but the bat/power potential plays anywhere. On any planet. He's stiff and robotic and defense, lacking fluidity and agility. His hands look like concrete too.

Scouting Report: Nunez went on an absolute tear during his first couple weeks in the Appalachian League following his demotion as he slugged a scorching .345/.402/.536 in 22 contests. But he finished out the year by going a frigid 4-for-46 which absolutely cratered his final slash-line at the level. There's a ton of talent here, strictly as a potential power-hitter, but looked far rawer than what I thought he was a year ago. I'd put Nunez's ceiling in the Jesus Aguilar territory.

Ceiling: 2.5-win player
Risk: Moderate to High
MLB ETA: 2020/2021

10. Lane Thomas, OF

Hit	Power	SB	Patience	Glove	Overall
50	50	40	50	55	45

Born: 08/23/95	Age: 24	Bats: R
Height: 6-1	Weight: 210	Throws: R

YEAR	LVL	PA	1B	2B	3B	HR	SB	CS	AVG	OBP	SLG	BB%	K%	GB%	LD%	FB%
2017	A+	308	47	12	6	4	8	7	0.252	0.319	0.383	8.77%	27.27%	49.2	17.9	25.1
2017	A+	39	8	0	1	0	2	2	0.257	0.308	0.314	7.69%	25.64%	46.2	19.2	26.9
2018	AA	435	59	16	4	21	13	9	0.260	0.337	0.487	9.89%	23.22%	43.8	21.9	26.7
2018	AAA	140	21	7	2	6	4	1	0.275	0.321	0.496	5.00%	23.57%	41.8	20.4	32.7
2019	AAA	304	42	17	2	10	11	6	0.268	0.352	0.460	10.53%	26.32%	42.0	21.8	27.7

Background: It's a pretty stark difference. The pre-St. Louis Cardinals version of Thomas was a light-hitting, often lost hitter at the plate – a shell of the player the Blue Jays thought they were drafting in the fifth round six years ago. But the post-trade outfielder – the prospect on full display right now – is something entirely different. The Cardinals acquired Thomas for international bonus money in early July 2017. Since then he's slugged .264/.333/.489 with 23 doubles, six triples, and a massive surge in homerun power (27 dingers, 19 more than his previous high) in 2018. Thomas spent the majority of last season with the Memphis Redbirds in the hitter-friendly confines of the Pacific Coast League, batting .265/.352/.460 with 17 doubles, two triples, and 10 homeruns in 75 games. Per *Deserved Runs Created Plus*, his overall production was slightly below the league average. Thomas also appeared in 34 games with the Cardinals, hitting an impressive .316/.409/.684 in 44 plate appearances.

Snippet from The 2018 Prospect Digest Handbook: It's clear to see some of the mechanical changes the organization has made in Thomas' stance at the plate: he's more upright now with less bend in his lower half; his hands are quieter; and his bat path shows a bit more loft. There's some potential starting caliber value to be had here.

Scouting Report: A poor man's starter kit for five-tool potential. Thomas does everything well without owning a true standout skill. He'll hit .250 or .260, take the occasional walk, belt out 20 homeruns, swipe 15 bags, and play 55-grade defense. That's starting caliber potential wrapped up in a bargain basement price. In terms of offensive ceiling, think Nick Ahmed's showing in 2019 when he batted .254/.316/.437 with 19 homeruns.

Ceiling: 1.5- to 2.0-win player
Risk: Low to Moderate
MLB ETA: Debuted in 2019

11. Mateo Gil, SS

Hit	Power	SB	Patience	Glove	Overall
50	45/50	30	50	50	45

Born: 07/24/00	Age: 19	Bats: R
Height: 6-1	Weight: 180	Throws: R

YEAR	LVL	PA	1B	2B	3B	HR	SB	CS	AVG	OBP	SLG	BB%	K%	GB%	LD%	FB%
2018	RK	194	35	6	1	1	2	2	0.251	0.340	0.316	10.31%	26.29%	43.3	17.5	30.8
2019	Rk+	225	38	8	2	7	1	3	0.270	0.324	0.431	7.56%	24.89%	46.4	16.6	24.5
2019	A+	6	0	0	0	0	0	0	0.000	0.000	0.000	0.00%	33.33%	100.0	0.0	0.0

Background: A product of Timer Creek High School in Fort Worth, Texas, Gil owns some impressive bloodlines: the young shortstop's father, Benji, not only spent parts of eight years in the big leagues with the Rangers and Angels but was chosen as the 19th overall pick in 1991 – just a few selections after Manny Ramirez, Cliff Floyd, and Shawn Green. The younger Mateo, the Cardinals' third round selection two years ago, turned in a mediocre debut showing in the Gulf Coast League as he batted .251/.340/.316 with six doubles, one triple, and one homerun. The front office bumped the 6-foot-1, 180-pound middle infielder up to Johnson City last season. And Gil's bat began to show some signs of life. In 51 games with the club's Appalachian League affiliate, he slugged .270/.324/.431 with eight doubles, two triples, and seven homeruns. Per *Deserved Runs Created Plus*, his overall production topped the league average threshold by 12%. He also earned a two-game cameo in High Class A as well.

Scouting Report: Consider the following:

- Since 2006, here's the list of 18-year-old hitters to post a 107 to 117 DRC+ with a single-digit walk rate and a punch out rate between 22% and 25% in the Appalachian League (min. 200 PA): Chris Carter, Jorge Bonifacio, Moises Gomez, and Mateo Gil.

It's a surprisingly strong set of hitters that Gil's production lines up with. Carter and Bonifacio made it to the big leagues. And all three showed some average or better power. Gil, himself, shows intriguing power potential as a middle infielder and has the potential to develop into 15-homer territory down the line. Throw in a decent glove and hit tool, and Gil looks like a fringy starting shortstop. Plus, there's plenty of youth on his side as he was one of the younger players in the 2018 draft class.

Ceiling: 1.5- to 2.0-win player
Risk: Moderate
MLB ETA: 2022

12. Justin Williams, LF/RF

Hit	Power	SB	Patience	Glove	Overall
50	50/60	30	45+	55	45

Born: 08/20/95	Age: 24	Bats: L
Height: 6-2	Weight: 215	Throws: L

YEAR	LVL	PA	1B	2B	3B	HR	SB	CS	AVG	OBP	SLG	BB%	K%	GB%	LD%	FB%
2017	AA	409	72	21	3	14	6	2	0.301	0.364	0.489	9.05%	16.87%	54.5	22.3	20.3
2018	AAA	386	66	18	0	8	4	3	0.258	0.313	0.376	6.48%	20.98%	53.1	19.5	24.9
2018	AAA	76	9	3	0	3	0	1	0.217	0.276	0.391	6.58%	22.37%	43.4	24.5	30.2
2019	AA	61	9	1	0	1	1	0	0.193	0.246	0.263	6.56%	27.87%	57.5	25.0	17.5
2019	AAA	119	24	5	0	7	0	0	0.353	0.437	0.608	13.45%	25.21%	40.6	24.6	29.0

Background: There are guys that take out frustrations on watercoolers or bat racks or even dugout walls. And then there's Justin Williams, *who punched a damn television set during the offseason.* The result: fractured fingers and a painful hand that knocked him out of action until early May. The former 2013 returned to action for a couple weeks, but hit the disabled list for another five weeks. He then returned to action in late June, which lasted for a little more than a week, and soon hit the DL again – this time sitting out another three weeks. Finally healthy, with much of the season lost, Williams returned on July 30th and spent the remainder of the season back with Memphis. In total, Williams batted the Class AAA pitching to the tune of .353/.437/.608 with five doubles and seven homeruns in only 36 games.

Snippet from The 2018 Prospect Digest Handbook: Given the work the organization did by resurrecting Lane Thomas' career trajectory, I wouldn't be surprised to see St. Louis sprinkle the same magic dust over Williams. He's a boom or bust type of guy: either he figures it out and develops into an above-average outfielder or he doesn't and languishes in the upper minors for the rest of his career.

Scouting Report: Williams is exactly the type of prospect that can't afford to lose a season, especially considering (A) he was already entering his age-23 campaign, (B) coming off of a disappointing showing the previous year, and (C) was caused by a foolish, easily preventable injury. The tools remain intact to be a star, but he can't shake inconsistency issues. The power potential is definitely a plus, but he just can't get it to translate into in-game power. At points, he'll flirt with a solid 50-grade hit tool and then moments later look like he should be back in the low minors. Still boom or bust. But I'm hoping the Cardinals can unlock his full potential. Above-average glove certainly makes him an interesting bet to develop into a low-end league average starter.

Ceiling: 1.5- to 2.0-win player
Risk: Moderate
MLB ETA: 202

13. Johan Oviedo, RHP

FB	CB	SL	CH	Command	Overall
60	45	55/60	45+	40/45	45

Born: 03/02/98	Age: 22	Bats: R
Height: 6-6	Weight: 210	Throws: R

YEAR	LVL	IP	W	L	SV	ERA	FIP	WHIP	K/9	K%	BB/9	BB%	K/BB	HR9	BABIP
2017	Rk	27.7	2	1	0	4.88	4.05	1.45	10.1	24.80%	5.9	14.40%	1.72	0.00	0.306
2017	A-	47.3	2	2	0	4.56	3.81	1.50	7.4	18.75%	3.4	8.65%	2.17	0.57	0.340
2018	A	121.7	10	10	1	4.22	4.20	1.54	8.7	21.77%	5.8	14.58%	1.49	0.44	0.304
2019	A+	33.7	5	0	0	1.60	2.86	1.22	9.4	24.82%	3.2	8.51%	2.92	0.27	0.308
2019	AA	113.0	7	8	0	5.65	4.13	1.63	10.2	26.12%	5.1	13.06%	2.00	0.72	0.366

Background: The front office handed the Cuban import a hefty $1.9 million deal in early July 2016, after defecting. The mammoth righty continues to offer up glimpses of pure dominance mixed with utter frustration. The source: some wavering control. The then-18-year-old posted a 29-to-6 strikeout-to-walk ratio during his debut in the foreign rookie league in 2016. Oviedo split time between Johnson City and State College the following year, averaging 8.4 strikeouts and 4.3 walks per nine innings. The La Habana, Cuba, native spent the 2018 season squaring off against the Midwest League competition. In 25 appearances with Peoria he fanned 118 but handed out a whopping 79 walks in only 121.2 innings of work. The front office bumped Oviedo up to the Florida State League to begin last season, but after six ridiculously strong appearances he was promoted up to the Texas League. He rattled off 23 starts with Springfield, posting a 128-to-64 strikeout-to-walk with a 5.65 ERA and a 6.32 DRA (*Deserved Run Average*) in 113.0 innings of work.

Snippet from The 2018 Prospect Digest Handbook: Physically maxed out with no projection left. Only entering his age-21 season, Oviedo's quickly heading down the path of org. arm.

Scouting Report: The fastball bumped up a couple ticks, improving from 91-92 mph up to 93-94 mph range. And it plays up even more given long stride, lanky arms. The changeup is fringy average. And his curveball is below-average – so much so, in fact, he should probably just scrap it all together. But the big difference in Oviedo's arsenal is his lethal slider. A hard-tilting, late breaking, downward biting offering that adds a swing-and-miss offspeed dimension that he previously lacked. The control/command is still terrible and could ultimately push him toward an eighth or ninth inning relief role. With respect to his work in Class AA last season, consider the following:

- Since 2006, here's the list of 21-year-old pitchers to post a strikeout percentage between 24% and 26% with a double-digit walk percentage in the Texas League (min. 100 IP): Kyle Muller, Mauricio Robles, and Johan Oviedo.

Ceiling: 1.5- to 2.0-win player
Risk: Moderate
MLB ETA: 2020/2021

14. Trejyn Fletcher, CF

Hit	Power	SB	Patience	Glove	Overall
30/45	50/60	60	45	50	45

Born: 04/30/01	Age: 19	Bats: R
Height: 6-2	Weight: 200	Throws: R

YEAR	LVL	PA	1B	2B	3B	HR	SB	CS	AVG	OBP	SLG	BB%	K%	GB%	LD%	FB%
2019	Rk	42	6	3	0	2	0	0	0.297	0.357	0.541	9.52%	40.48%	47.6	14.3	38.1
2019	Rk+	133	21	4	1	2	7	1	0.228	0.271	0.325	5.26%	44.36%	43.9	19.7	31.8

Background: Earliest drafted high school outfielder by the organization since they selected current top prospect Dylan Carlson with the 33rd overall pick in 2016. Fletcher, who was committed to Vanderbilt, was named by USA Today as an All-USA High School Baseball selection last season. St. Louis drafted the 6-foot-2, 200-pound athlete in the second round, 58th overall, and signed him to an above-slot deal worth $1.5 million. Fletcher opened up his professional career with a quick – and successful – showing in the Gulf Coast League; he hit .297/.357/.541 with a trio of doubles and a pair of homeruns. The front office pushed him up to the Appalachian League in early July for the remainder of the year – though the production tumbled quite a bit (.228/.271/.325).

Scouting Report: Very short, compact, powerful swing with natural loft that should allow him to belt out 20 or so homeruns at his peak. Fletcher looked far less robotic during the months leading up to the draft than his showing on the showcase circuits. He's physically mature with a muscular build. And now the bad news: he whiffed – A LOT. Like, a lot, a lot. He struck out in 76 of his 175 plate appearances last season. That's 43.4% of the time. Frankly, that's going to be tough to come back from. There's some George Springer-type potential, but (A) he needs to solve the swing-and-miss issues first.

Ceiling: 1.5- to 2.0-win player
Risk: Moderate to High
MLB ETA: 2023

15. Jhon Torres, OF

Hit	Power	SB	Patience	Glove	Overall
40/50	50/60	30	55	55/50	45

Born: 03/29/00	Age: 20	Bats: R
Height: 6-4	Weight: 199	Throws: R

YEAR	LVL	PA	1B	2B	3B	HR	SB	CS	AVG	OBP	SLG	BB%	K%	GB%	LD%	FB%
2017	RK	226	32	7	3	5	4	4	0.255	0.363	0.408	12.39%	18.14%	52.7	11.3	26.0
2018	RK	111	20	3	0	4	3	0	0.273	0.351	0.424	9.91%	21.62%	42.7	24.0	25.3
2018	RK	75	15	6	0	4	1	1	0.397	0.493	0.683	10.67%	17.33%	38.0	26.0	26.0
2019	Rk+	133	17	9	0	6	0	2	0.286	0.391	0.527	14.29%	27.07%	31.2	22.1	37.7
2019	A	75	8	3	0	0	0	1	0.167	0.240	0.212	9.33%	38.67%	46.2	7.7	30.8

Background: Originally signed by the Indians during the summer of 2016 for $150,000. Torres, a well-built, broad-shouldered outfielder out of Sincelejo, Columbia, turned in a solid debut in the foreign rookie league the following season as he batted .255/.363/.408. Midway through his sophomore campaign the Tribe dealt the

6-foot-4, 199-pound prospect – along with fellow outfielder Conner Capel – to the Cardinals for Oscar Mercado. Torres finished the year with an aggregate .321/.409/.525 triple-slash line between both organizations' stateside rookie leagues. St. Louis aggressively pushed the teenager up to the Midwest League to begin 2019. But after struggling – mightily – over 21 games, Torres was demoted down to the Advanced Rookie League. He finished the year with an aggregate .242/.337/.410 with 12 doubles and six homeruns in 54 games.

Scouting Report: It's easy to dream upon Torres' plus-power potential. He's tall and physically strong, shows above-average bat speed, and the natural loft requisite to drive out 20 homeruns or so in a full season. The problem for Torres, however, is he displayed some problematic swing-and-miss issues last season; he whiffed in nearly 38% of his Midwest League plate appearances and sported a concerning 27.1% K-rate during his stint in the Appalachian League. He's cut from the Justin Williams mold.

Ceiling: 1.5-win player
Risk: Moderate
MLB ETA: 2022

16. Angel Rondon, RHP

FB	SL	CH	Command	Overall
55	55	50	50	45

Born: 12/01/97	Age: 22	Bats: R
Height: 6-2	Weight: 185	Throws: R

YEAR	LVL	IP	W	L	SV	ERA	FIP	WHIP	K/9	K%	BB/9	BB%	K/BB	HR9	BABIP
2017	Rk	47.7	3	3	0	2.64	3.44	1.32	7.7	20.40%	3.2	8.46%	2.41	0.38	0.317
2017	Rk	5.7	0	1	0	4.76	3.76	1.24	9.5	25.00%	4.8	12.50%	2.00	0.00	0.308
2017	Rk	4.0	0	0	0	6.75	10.90	2.25	11.3	23.81%	6.8	14.29%	1.67	4.50	0.400
2018	A-	29.0	0	4	0	3.72	4.17	1.24	7.1	19.01%	2.2	5.79%	3.29	0.93	0.302
2018	A	59.0	3	2	0	2.90	4.15	1.12	8.7	23.08%	2.6	6.88%	3.35	1.07	0.259
2019	A+	45.0	5	1	0	2.20	3.35	0.96	9.4	26.26%	3.4	9.50%	2.76	0.60	0.209
2019	AA	115.0	6	6	0	3.21	3.97	1.23	8.8	23.28%	3.3	8.73%	2.67	0.86	0.283

Background: It took a couple seasons of floundering before the Dominican-born right-hander started to make some traction, but Rondon has quickly made up for lost time since the middle of 2018. Standing a wiry 6-foot-2 and 185-pounds, Rondon spent parts of two seasons in the foreign rookie league, some more time in the Gulf Coast, Appalachian, and New York-Penn Leagues between 2016 and the first half of 2018. Since then, though, Rondon blitzed through the Midwest League – he posted a 57-to-17 strikeout-to-walk ratio in 59.0 innings of work – in the second half of 2018. He spent only eight games in High Class A at the start of last year before settling in for 20 appearances in Class AA. In total, Rondon tossed a career-high 160.0 innings in 2019, posting a 159-to-59 K-to-BB ratio.

Scouting Report: With respect to his work in Class AA last season, consider the following:

- Since 2006, only two 21-year-old pitchers met the following criteria in the Texas League (min. 100 IP): 22.5% and 24.5% strikeout percentage with a walk percentage between 8% and 10%. Those two hurlers: Grant Holmes, a top prospect in the Athletics' system, and – of course – Angel Rondon.

Two above-average pitches backed up by a firm, though, decent changeup. Rondon's more of a strike-thrower rather a command guy. Simply put: there's really nothing that stands out with Rondon. Good build, but not great. Above-average fastball, which he attacks the upper part of the strike zone, but it's straight and doesn't miss a ton of bats. His slider shows nice two-plane break, almost like a power curveball, but – again – it's not a genuine swing-and-miss pitch. And the changeup is...OK.

Ceiling: 1.5-win player
Risk: Moderate
MLB ETA: 2020

17. Junior Fernandez, RHP

FB	SL	CH	Command	Overall
70	50	55+	45	40

Born: 03/02/97	Age: 23	Bats: R
Height: 6-1	Weight: 180	Throws: R

YEAR	LVL	IP	W	L	SV	ERA	FIP	WHIP	K/9	K%	BB/9	BB%	K/BB	HR9	BABIP
2017	A+	90.3	5	3	0	3.69	4.27	1.34	5.8	15.14%	3.9	10.18%	1.49	0.50	0.281
2018	A+	9.7	1	0	3	0.00	3.26	1.14	6.5	17.95%	1.9	5.13%	3.50	0.00	0.321
2018	AA	21.0	0	0	0	5.14	4.73	1.67	7.3	17.89%	6.9	16.84%	1.06	0.43	0.295
2019	A+	11.7	0	0	4	1.54	3.73	1.37	8.5	21.57%	6.2	15.69%	1.38	0.00	0.258
2019	AA	29.0	1	1	5	1.55	1.79	1.00	13.0	36.52%	3.4	9.57%	3.82	0.00	0.295
2019	AAA	24.3	2	1	2	1.48	3.18	1.15	10.0	26.47%	4.1	10.78%	2.45	0.00	0.274

Background: I spent a lot of time over the past several years writing about the promising right-hander. Here's a piece of my analysis from 2016: "He's a big time power arm with the uncanny ability to hit the zone on a regular basis. Here's one of the bolder predictions I will make in this year's book: Junior Fernandez, a soon-to-be 19-year-old right-hander with 85.2 professional innings under his belt, is the best pitching prospect you've never heard of. Yet." Bold – very bold. And it didn't exactly pan out as expected. But I doubled down the following year as well. In 2018 Handbook, I backed down a bit as I wrote, "I do wonder if a move to the bullpen, at least temporarily, would be the best course of action." Well, the club converted him into a full time reliever and...he struggled. Big time. But finally – *finally* – things seemed to click last season. Sprinting through the final three minor league levels, as well as earning a 13-game cameo with the big league club, Fernandez was quite good. He posted an 80-to-30 strikeout-to-walk ratio with a 1.52 ERA in 65.0 minor league innings. And he fanned 16 against six free passes in 11.2 innings with the Cardinals.

Scouting Report: And wouldn't you know it? The moment I stop writing about Fernandez – I didn't list him among the club's Top 20 Prospects – he puts it all together. Fernandez attacks hitters with a hard, lively 96- to 97-mph fastball, an above-average changeup that flashes plus at times, and a fringy cutter-ish slider. The control has regressed from his early strike-throwing days, but he could slide into a solid seventh-inning gig tomorrow.

Ceiling: 1.0- to 1.5-win player
Risk: Low to Moderate
MLB ETA: Debuted in 2019

18. Edmundo Sosa, IF

	Hit	Power	SB	Patience	Glove	Overall
	50	45	40	40	50	40

Born: 03/06/96 | **Age**: 24 | **Bats**: R
Height: 5-11 | **Weight**: 170 | **Throws**: R

YEAR	LVL	PA	1B	2B	3B	HR	SB	CS	AVG	OBP	SLG	BB%	K%	GB%	LD%	FB%
2017	RK	23	6	1	0	1	0	0	0.364	0.391	0.545	4.35%	8.70%	50.0	30.0	20.0
2017	A+	211	44	10	1	0	3	0	0.285	0.329	0.347	5.69%	16.11%	53.7	14.6	21.3
2017	AA	5	0	0	0	0	0	0	0.000	0.200	0.000	20.00%	0.00%	50.0	0.0	50.0
2018	AA	279	47	17	1	7	1	2	0.276	0.308	0.429	3.23%	18.64%	39.9	21.6	26.8
2018	AAA	209	32	13	0	5	5	2	0.262	0.321	0.408	6.22%	20.10%	39.3	28.7	26.7
2019	AAA	496	92	18	5	17	2	3	0.291	0.335	0.466	3.43%	19.35%	43.7	23.4	26.6

Background: There are very few legitimate prospects – if any – that have maintained their rookie status longer than the Cardinals long time minor league infielder. Signed out of Panama, Panama, in early July of 2012 (2012!), Sosa spent the next five years toiling away in the low to middle levels of the minor leagues, only popping up at the Class AA for one brief showing in 2017. The 5-foot-11, 170-pound utility man extraordinaire split time between Springfield and Memphis during the 2018 season, hitting an aggregate .270/.313/.420 with 30 doubles, one triple, and 12 homeruns. Last season, Sosa appeared in 118 games with the Memphis Redbirds, hitting a league-inflated .291/.335/.466 with 18 doubles, five triples, and a career best 18 dingers. His overall production, according to *Deserved Runs Created Plus*, was 5% *below* the league average threshold. And for the second straight year he appeared in a handful of games with the Cardinals.

Snippet from The 2018 Prospect Digest Handbook: The writing's clearly on the wall and it's pointing towards utility-dom. A fair comparison might be a better version of ex-MLB'er Enrique Wilson.

Scouting Report: Sosa earned a couple of brief mentions in my first two books – all the way back in 2014 and 2015 – before cracking the club's Top 10 list in 2016. And it seems like every year the same analysis still holds firm for Sosa: bad walk rates that sap his OBPs, decent pop for a utility guy, 50-grade hit tool, a little bit of speed, and a workable glove around the horn. Enrique Wilson, as mentioned above and in last year's Handbook, hit .257/.299/.354 over his three best seasons in 1999-2001, and – frankly – I can't imagine Sosa besting that mark by much.

Ceiling: 1.0- to 1.5-win player
Risk: Low to Moderate
MLB ETA: Debuted in 2018

19. Luken Baker, 1B

	Hit	Power	SB	Patience	Glove	Overall
	45	50/55	30	55	50	40

Born: 03/10/97 | **Age**: 23 | **Bats**: R
Height: 6-4 | **Weight**: 265 | **Throws**: R

YEAR	LVL	PA	1B	2B	3B	HR	SB	CS	AVG	OBP	SLG	BB%	K%	GB%	LD%	FB%
2018	RK	28	9	2	0	1	0	0	0.500	0.536	0.708	10.71%	14.29%	42.9	33.3	4.8
2018	A	156	28	9	0	3	0	0	0.288	0.359	0.417	10.26%	19.87%	47.7	20.2	22.9
2019	A+	496	64	32	1	10	1	1	0.244	0.327	0.390	10.48%	22.58%	35.9	20.2	31.3

Background: Snake-bitten for the majority of his collegiate career – particularly over his final two seasons with the Texas Christian Horned Frogs. He suffered a horrific arm injury during his sophomore season and lower body injuries derailed his junior season. St. Louis took a gamble on the hulking first baseman in the second round two years ago. And after a strong – albeit limited – debut in the Midwest League, Baker was pushed straight up to High Class A for the 2019 season. In 122 games with the Palm Beach Cardinals, the 6-foot-4, 265-pound slugger batted

.244/.327/.390 with 32 doubles, one triple, and 10 homeruns. Per *Deserved Runs Created Plus*, his overall production topped the league average mark by 18%.

Snippet from The 2018 Prospect Digest Handbook: Baker has the makings of a solid, saber-friendly hitter in the minor leagues.

Scouting Report: In short, outside of his hot month of August – where he batted .346/.413/.654 with four bombs – Baker was pretty terrible for the majority of the season. He's walking an above-average amount of time with 20- to 25-homer power potential. But the limited collegiate experience – combined with the body woes – seems like it's finally caught up to him. Poor Man's Paul Goldschmidt, maybe 70% of Goldschmidt.

Ceiling: 1.0- to 1.5-win player
Risk: Moderate
MLB ETA: 2021

20. Tony Locey, RHP

FB	CB	SL	CH	Command	Overall
60	50	55	45+	40+	40

Born: 07/29/98	Age: 21	Bats: R
Height: 6-3	Weight: 239	Throws: R

YEAR	LVL	IP	W	L	SV	ERA	FIP	WHIP	K/9	K%	BB/9	BB%	K/BB	HR9	BABIP
2019	Rk	2.0	0	0	0	0.00	3.50	1.50	13.5	33.33%	9.0	22.22%	1.50	0.00	0.250
2019	A	15.0	1	2	0	6.00	2.56	1.67	16.8	41.18%	6.0	14.71%	2.80	0.60	0.483

Background: An up-and-down career with the Georgia Bulldogs. Locey spent his freshman season bouncing between the school's rotation and bullpen, tallying a terrible 37-to-31 strikeout-to-walk ratio in 42.1 innings of work. Despite then terrible peripherals, however, Locey spent the ensuing summer playing for the Brewster Whitecaps in the Cape Cod League. And this time he was throwing far more strikes: he posted a 38-to-14 strikeout-to-walk ratio in 36.0 innings. The 6-foot-3, 239-pound right-hander spent his sophomore season with the SEC squad as a reliever, making 22 relief appearances and only five starts. He averaged 9.9 strikeouts and 4.9 walks per nine innings. Last season, Locey maintained status quo: he averaged 9.8 strikeouts and 4.6 walks per nine innings – though he transitioned into a full time starting gig. St. Louis grabbed Locey in the third round last June. He made 12 relief appearances in the lower levels, fanning 31 and walking 12.

Scouting Report: A bit of a risky pick because (A) Locey's never thrown a ton of strikes, (B) he's a max-effort guy, and (C) two of his four offerings are fringy – at best. Locey was sitting 94-95 during his pro debut. His slider, an above-average offering, was 80- to 83-mph with a bit of bite. The curveball's loopy and won't miss many bats. And it's a 45+ changeup.

Ceiling: 1.0-win player
Risk: Moderate
MLB ETA: 2022

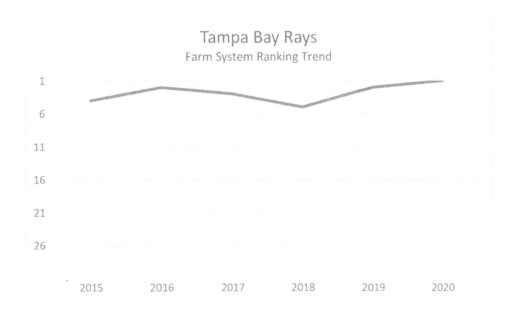

Tampa Bay Rays
Farm System Ranking Trend

Rank	Name	Age	Pos
1	Wander Franco	18	SS
2	Brendan McKay	25	1B/LHP
3	Shane McClanahan	22	LHP
4	Josh Lowe	21	OF
5	Brent Honeywell	22	RHP
6	Shane Baz	20	RHP
7	Vidal Brujan	21	2B/SS
8	Xavier Edwards	19	2B/SS
9	Randy Arozarena	24	OF
10	Anthony Banda	25	LHP
11	Greg Jones	21	SS
12	Joe Ryan	23	RHP
13	Ronaldo Hernandez	21	C
14	Seth Johnson	20	RHP
15	Taylor Walls	22	SS
16	JJ Goss	23	RHP
17	Kevin Padlo	22	3B
18	John Doxakis	20	LHP
19	Tyler Frank	22	IF
20	Nick Schnell	19	CF

1. Wander Franco, SS

	Hit	Power	SB	Patience	Glove	Overall
	70	50/60	50	60	55	80

Born: 03/01/01	Age: 19	Bats: B
Height: 5-10	Weight: 189	Throws: R

YEAR	LVL	PA	1B	2B	3B	HR	SB	CS	AVG	OBP	SLG	BB%	K%	GB%	LD%	FB%
2018	RK	273	57	10	7	11	4	3	0.351	0.418	0.587	9.89%	6.96%	44.9	15.1	32.4
2019	A	272	47	16	5	6	14	9	0.318	0.390	0.506	11.03%	7.35%	48.2	15.0	30.0
2019	A+	223	49	11	2	3	4	5	0.339	0.408	0.464	11.66%	6.73%	49.7	18.4	27.4

Background: Franco comes from a long, rather impressive lineage of baseball bloodlines: His father, also named Wander, played some minor league ball during the 1990s; both of the young shortstop's brothers, also named Wander and Wander, played some affiliated ball in the Giants' organization in 2019; and – of course – two of his uncles, Erick and Willy Aybar spent several years in The Show with the former earning nearly $50 million over his 12-year career and the latter appearing in 405 career games with the Dodgers, Braves, and Rays. As for the youngest Franco, well, the sky is limit. A much ballyhooed international prospect, the typically thrifty Rays signed then-16-year-old switch-hitter to a hefty $3.85 million deal on July 2nd, 2017. Franco, a native of Bani, Dominican Republic, set the world ablaze the following year as he was aggressively sent to the Appalachian League. He responded by slugging a scorching .351/.418/.587 with 10 doubles, seven triples, 11 homeruns, and four stolen bases. Per Baseball Prospectus' *Deserved Runs Created plus*, his overall production topped the league average threshold by a whopping 66%. Tampa Bay moved the dynamic, five-tool prospect up to the Midwest League for the start of 2019. And he made quick work of the significantly older pitching by batting .318/.390/.506. He earned a second half promotion up to the Florida State League, and his bat didn't cool one iota as he hit .339/.408/.464. In total, the teenage superstar slugged an aggregate .327/.398/.487 with 27 doubles, seven triples, nine homeruns, and 18 stolen bases.

Snippet from The 2018 Prospect Digest Handbook: Franco does *everything*: plus hit tool, plus power potential, above-average speed, and a glove that should peak as slightly-above average. He's a perennial All-Star in the making and should be the next franchise cornerstone. A brief stop in Class AA in 2019 isn't out of the realm of possibility either.

Scouting Report: With respect to his work in Low Class A last season, consider the following:

- Since 2006, here's the list of 18-year-old hitters to post a DRC+ between 150 and 165 with a sub-20.0% strikeout rate in the Midwest League (min. 250 PA): Carlos Correa, who's sporting a career DRC+ of 123 in the big leagues, and – of course – Wander Franco.

Now let's look at his work in High Class A, consider the following:

- Since 2006, here's the list of 18-year-old hitters to post a DRC+ of at least 170 in any High Class A league (min. 200 PA): Vladimir Guerrero Jr. and Wander Franco.

Elite tools across the board. Lightning quick bat that can turn on 80-grade fastballs. Natural loft that suggests a peak of 30 to 35 homeruns at full maturity. A willingness to shoot outside pitches the other way. Plus speed. Above-average glove. And some of the best bat-to-ball skills I've ever seen. He's going to be a superstar, one of this generation's greats. His ceiling's going to reside around .330/.410/.600.

Ceiling: 8.0-win player
Risk: Low to Moderate
MLB ETA: 2021/2022

2. Brendan McKay, 1B/LHP

	Hit	Power	SB	Field	Overall
	35/50	60	20	50	55

	FB	CB	CU	CH	Control	Overall
	55	55	55+	50	60	60

Born: 12/18/95	Age: 24	Bats: L
Height: 6-2	Weight: 212	Throws: L

YEAR	LVL	IP	W	L	SV	ERA	FIP	WHIP	K/9	K%	BB/9	BB%	K/BB	HR9	BABIP
2017	A-	20.0	1	0	0	1.80	4.03	0.75	9.5	28.77%	2.3	6.85%	4.20	1.35	0.159
2018	Rk	6.0	0	0	0	1.50	1.14	0.50	13.5	40.91%	1.5	4.55%	9.00	0.00	0.167
2018	A	24.7	2	0	0	1.09	1.00	0.41	14.6	47.06%	0.7	2.35%	20.00	0.36	0.167
2018	A+	47.7	3	2	0	3.21	2.51	1.17	10.2	28.13%	2.1	5.73%	4.91	0.38	0.350
2019	AA	41.7	3	0	0	1.30	1.66	0.82	13.4	39.74%	1.9	5.77%	6.89	0.43	0.280
2019	AAA	32.0	3	0	0	0.84	2.56	0.81	11.3	32.79%	2.5	7.38%	4.44	0.28	0.229

Background: One of the most prolific two-way players in the college baseball history. McKay did everything but tend the watercooler during his three-year career at the University of Louisville. The 6-foot-2, 212-pound first baseman/left-handed starting pitcher compiled some impressive career statistics: he slugged an a hefty .328/.430/.536 with 48 doubles, three triples, and 28 homeruns while finishing with a phenomenal 114-to-107 strikeout-to-walk ratio in 796 plate appearances; and as a moundsmen he fanned 391, walked just 111, and tallied a 32-10 win-loss record to go along with a 2.23 ERA in 315.1 innings of work. Tampa Bay drafted the former Cardinal in the opening round, 3rd overall, and signed him to a deal in excess of $7 million. The Rays have continued to allow McKay to develop as a potential dual threat, though his work on the mound *easily* surpasses anything he's done in the batter's box. Last season the Pennsylvania native split time between Montgomery and Durham, hitting .200/.298/.331 with four doubles and five homeruns in 58 combined games; as a pitcher he tossed 73.2 innings while recording an absurd 102-to-18 strikeout-to-walk ratio with a sparkling 1.10 ERA. McKay also spent a couple weeks with Tampa Bay as well, hitting .200/.273/.500 while fanning 56 and walking just 16 in 49.0 innings on the bump.

Snippet from The 2018 Prospect Digest Handbook (Pitcher): McKay's far more advanced as a pitching prospect. His fastball showed more life than I expected, regularly touching the mid-90s with a surprising amount of ease. His curveball adds a second plus weapon to his arsenal. And his cutter and changeup both grade out as above-average offerings. Throw in a strong feel for the strike zone and McKay looks like a potential mid-rotation caliber starting pitcher.

Snippet from The 2018 Prospect Digest Handbook (Hitter): This is where things get a bit murkier. McKay combined a tremendous eye at the plate with plus-power potential. But the hit tool has been subpar. McKay's still more projection than production at this point. And I'm not convinced he ever achieves his full potential if he's not concentrating on hitting exclusively. McKay will get another year or so to develop on both aspects of the game before the organization makes a decision as to whether he becomes a pitcher (highly likely) compared to a hitter. One more thing to remember: it's highly unlikely the club let's McKay's sagging development as a hitter hinder his ability to quickly move through the minors as a pitcher.

Scouting Report (Pitcher): McKay commands the strike zone as well as any prospect in the minor leagues, showing the consistent ability to throw his entire repertoire for quality strikes. The problem for the big left-hander, though, is the arsenal seemed to regress a bit from the previous year. McKay was throwing – *easily* – in the mid-90s with a sharp, late-tilting curveball. Last season, though, he was 91- to 93-mph during the minor leagues (though he averaged 93 mph in the big leagues) with a slightly inconsistent curveball. The cutter remains a borderline plus-offering and has become a real equalizer. Despite the small dip in velocity, McKay still has the makings of a very good #3-type arm.

Scouting Report (Hitter): The in-game power has – and will always be – a plus weapon. And he continues to show an incredibly patient approach at the plate. But the swing-and-miss issues that first popped up in High Class A two years ago continued their upward trend in 2019. He fanned in slightly more than 30% of his minor league plate appearances. Hitting a baseball at the professional level is the single most difficult skill to master in all of professional sports. And that's not taking into account the fact that McKay's developmental time is split between pitching and hitting. I don't think the K-rates will be an issue long term, but I do wonder how long the Rays – with a loaded lineup – will allow McKay to work on both sides of the ball.

Ceiling: 4.0-win player
Risk: Low to Moderate
MLB ETA: Debuted in 2019

3. Shane McClanahan, LHP

FB	SL	CH	Control	Overall
70	60	50	45+	60

Born: 04/28/97	Age: 23	Bats: L
Height: 6-1	Weight: 200	Throws: L

YEAR	LVL	IP	W	L	SV	ERA	FIP	WHIP	K/9	K%	BB/9	BB%	K/BB	HR9	BABIP
2018	Rk	4.0	0	0	0	0.00	1.24	0.75	15.8	50.00%	2.3	7.14%	7.00	0.00	0.333
2018	Rk	3.0	0	0	0	0.00	0.36	0.33	18.0	60.00%	0.0	0.00%	N/A	0.00	0.250
2019	A	53.0	4	4	0	3.40	3.13	1.30	12.6	33.18%	5.3	13.90%	2.39	0.51	0.304
2019	A+	49.3	6	1	0	1.46	1.72	0.83	10.8	34.30%	1.5	4.65%	7.38	0.18	0.250
2019	AA	18.3	1	1	0	8.35	4.11	1.96	10.3	23.33%	2.9	6.67%	3.50	1.47	0.450

Background: Originally taken by the Mets in the 26th round coming out of Cape Coral High School in 2015. McClanahan, of course, opted to take the collegiate route and headed to the University of South Florida. But the hard-throwing southpaw missed the entire 2016 season, his freshman campaign, as he recovered from Tommy John surgery.

Finally healthy, the Florida native made it back to regular season action the following year and he looked better than ever; he averaged 12.3 strikeouts and 4.3 walks per nine innings in 15 starts. McClanahan continued his – erratic – dominance during his junior campaign two years ago, posting a 120-to-48 strikeout-to-walk ratio in only 76.1 innings of work. Tampa Bay selected him in the opening round, 31st overall, and signed him to a deal worth $2.2 million. Last season the 6-foot-1, 200-pound left-hander blitzed through three separate levels, going from Bowling Green up to Charlotte before settling in for a quarter of starts with Montgomery. He tallied 120.2 innings across 24 appearances, fanning a whopping 154 and walking 45 to go along with a 3.36 ERA.

Snippet from The 2018 Prospect Digest Handbook: McClanahan has genuine front-of-the-rotation caliber talent. It'll be up to his new organization to unlock and/or improve upon his ability to throw more consistent strikes. Needless to say, there is a bit more risk given his control issues.

Scouting Report: Consider the following:

- Since 2006, there were three 22-year-old pitchers that met the following criteria in the Florida State League (min. 40 IP): at least a 30% strikeout percentage, a sub-6.0% walk percentage, and a DRA (*Deserved Run Average*) below 3.00. Those three pitchers: Trevor Stephan, Jordan Yamamoto, and – of course – Shane McClanahan.

Incredibly easy plus-plus, premium velocity – especially from the left side. McClanahan sits in the upper 90s, generally 96 to 98 mph, early in the games and will settle in around 94- to 95 mph later on. He'll complement the 70-grade offering with a plus, tightly-wound low- to mid-80s slider and a upper 80s changeup. The command/control last season upticked several notches. If that holds firm moving forward, there's some early career Scott Kazmir type potential, something along the lines of 10 K/9 and 3.5 BB/9 with a low 3.00s ERA.

Ceiling: 4.0-win player
Risk: Moderate
MLB ETA: 2020

4. Josh Lowe, CF

Hit	Power	SB	Patience	Glove	Overall
45+	50/60	60	55	55	60

Born: 02/02/98	Age: 22	Bats: L
Height: 6-4	Weight: 205	Throws: R

YEAR	LVL	PA	1B	2B	3B	HR	SB	CS	AVG	OBP	SLG	BB%	K%	GB%	LD%	FB%
2016	RK	114	15	6	1	2	1	1	0.258	0.386	0.409	17.54%	23.68%	43.3	17.9	34.3
2016	RK	100	14	0	2	3	1	1	0.238	0.360	0.400	17.00%	32.00%	49.0	19.6	25.5
2017	A	507	86	26	2	8	22	8	0.268	0.326	0.386	8.28%	28.40%	49.2	19.0	25.5
2018	A+	455	61	25	3	6	18	6	0.238	0.322	0.361	10.33%	25.71%	38.0	19.5	33.1
2019	AA	519	68	23	4	18	30	9	0.252	0.341	0.442	11.37%	25.43%	36.8	22.6	34.4

Background: Fun Fact Part I: Lowe's old man, David, was a fifth round pick out of Satellite Beach High School by the Seattle Mariners in 1986. Fun Fact Part II: Lowe's older brother, Brandon, was a third round pick by the Rays out of the University of Maryland in 2015 and finished third in the American League Rookie of the Year voting after slugging .270/.336/.514 in 82 games last season. Josh, who bested his father and brother by earning the distinction of a first round pick, turned in a dynamic showing at the minors' toughest challenge in 2019. Appearing in a career best 121 games with the Montgomery Biscuits, the 6-foot-4, 205-pound lefty-swinging center fielder slugged an impressive .252/.341/.442 with 23 doubles, four triples, 18 homeruns, and 30 stolen bases (in 39 total attempts). His overall production, according to *Deserved Runs Created Plus*, topped the league average mark by 28%. He also appeared in 15 games with the Salt River Rafters in the Arizona Fall League, batting a hearty .327/.379/.558 in 58 plate appearances.

Snippet from The 2018 Prospect Digest Handbook: A league average bat for the majority of his three-year professional career. Lowe falls into the same category as fellow saber-slanted outfielders in the system like Garrett Whitley: strong walk rates, tools oozing, and questionable strikeout rates – though Lowe did trim nearly three-percentage points from his K-rate from the previous season. He still hasn't quiet tapped into his raw power just yet, despite having the batted ball profile to belt out 15- to 20-homeruns.

Scouting Report: Consider the following:

- Since 2006, here's the list of 21-year-old hitters that tallied a DRC+ total between 123 and 133 with a double-digit walk rate in the Southern League (min. 350 PA): Joc Pederson, Chris Young, Matt Davidson, and – of course – Josh Lowe.
- Sans Lowe, here are their respective career DRC+ totals in the big leagues: 111 (Pederson), 94 (Davidson), and 97 (Young).

Lowe's 2019 season helped alleviate my biggest concern: his strikeout rate held firm, despite moving up into the make-it-or-break-it level. There's plenty of more power in the bat as he's just scratching the surface, something along the lines of 25- to 30-homer thump. Solid patience. Above-average glove work. Plus-speed that he utilizes efficiently on the base paths. He's going to force his way into the Rays' 2020 plan, despite a glut of outfield talent. In terms of offensive ceiling: .250/.345/.500. One more final thought: very strong batted ball date as he averaged 90 mph on his exit velocity with a peak of 110 mph.

Ceiling: 4.0-win player
Risk: Moderate
MLB ETA: 2020

5. Brent Honeywell, RHP

	FB	SC	CB	SL	CH	Control	Overall
	N/A	N/A	N/A	N/A	N/A	N/A	60

Born: 03/31/95	Age: 25	Bats: R
Height: 6-2	Weight: 195	Throws: R

Background: It's been a terrible couple of years for the former budding ace. Honeywell, a second round pick out of Walters State Community College in 2014, looked like he was on the precipice of stardom. He blitzed through the minor leagues, spending nearly the entire 2017 season in Class AAA. But a wonky elbow, which eventually forced him under the knife for Tommy John surgery, knocked him out for the entire 2018 campaign. Fine. It happens to a lot of arms, particularly young, vulnerable ones. Honeywell hit the comeback trail, but he was struck by several setbacks. There was some uneasiness in his surgically repaired elbow and some concern about nerve irritation. Then it went from bad to worse. Honeywell was closing in on a return to game action, but another massive elbow injury struck: he fractured a bone in his elbow while throwing a bullpen session.

Scouting Report: At this point, we can only hope Honeywell (A) gets past this snake-bitten couple of years and (B) returns to something close to his pre-injury ceiling. Fingers crossed for the now-25-year-old right-hander.

Ceiling: 5.0-win player
Risk: High
MLB ETA: 2021 – Maybe?

6. Shane Baz, RHP

	FB	CB	SL	CH	Control	Overall
	70	55	60	50	40/45	55

Born: 06/17/99	Age: 21	Bats: R
Height: 6-2	Weight: 190	Throws: R

YEAR	LVL	IP	W	L	SV	ERA	FIP	WHIP	K/9	K%	BB/9	BB%	K/BB	HR9	BABIP
2017	Rk	23.7	0	3	0	3.80	4.81	1.69	7.2	18.10%	5.3	13.33%	1.36	0.76	0.348
2018	Rk	45.3	4	3	0	3.97	3.90	1.50	10.7	26.09%	4.6	11.11%	2.35	0.40	0.344
2018	Rk	7.0	0	2	0	7.71	7.42	2.43	6.4	13.51%	7.7	16.22%	0.83	1.29	0.417
2019	A	81.3	3	2	0	2.99	3.64	1.23	9.6	25.44%	4.1	10.82%	2.35	0.55	0.279

Background: It's a deal that looked like it had the potential to be remarkably bad for Pittsburgh. And, vice versa, incredibly strong for Tampa Bay. The Rays dealt away long time ace, and two-time All-Star, Chris Archer to Pittsburgh for outfielder Austin Meadows, flame-throwing right-hander Tyler Glasnow, and Shane Baz. That potential turned into a full-blown theft as Meadows slugged a scorching .291/.364/.558 with 29 doubles, seven triples, and 33 homeruns and Glasnow posted a 1.78 ERA while averaging 11.3 strikeouts and just 2.1 walks through 12 starts. And that's not even including Baz's future contributions. Sandwiched between Jake Burger and Trevor Rogers as the 12th overall pick three years ago, Baz moved into the Midwest League for the first time in 2020, offering up a glimpse as a future impact big league arm. In a career high 17 appearances with the Hot Rods, he fanned 87 and walked 37 in 81.1 innings of work. He compiled a 2.99 ERA and a 3.88 DRA (*Deserved Run Average*). Baz appeared in eight games with the Salt River Rafters, posting a 14-to-8 strikeout-to-walk ratio in 11.0 innings in the Arizona Fall League.

Snippet from The 2018 Prospect Digest Handbook: Baz has the type of arsenal that resembles the man he was trade for, Chris Archer, whom the organization was able to corral into a strike-throwing machine. They might be able to work the same magic again.

Scouting Report: Consider the following:

- Since 2006, here's the list of 20-year-old pitcher to post a 24.5% and 26.5% strikeout percentage with a walk percentage between 10% and 12% in the Midwest League (min. 75 IP): Daniel Norris, Dennis Santana, Wily Peralta, Matt Megill, Victor Gonzalez, Jordan Norberto, and – of course – Shane Baz.

Unharnessed lightning. Or straight filth. Whichever you prefer, though both perfectly describe Baz's high octane repertoire. His fastball shows sudden late life, sitting in the mid- to upper-90s. His upper 80s slider is difficult to differentiate from his fastball out of his hand, adding a second dominant plus offering. His curveball's a solid 55-grade complementary offering. And he'll mix in a decent changeup. Loose arm, but there's some effort in the mechanics. There's some Mike Clevenger-type potential here, but the control/command may force him towards the #3/#4-type potential. He's not far from being – widely – regarded as a Top 100 prospect. He's poised to spend half of 2020 in Class AA.

Ceiling: 3.5-win player
Risk: Moderate
MLB ETA: 2021/2022

7. Vidal Brujan, 2B/SS

	Hit	Power	SB	Patience	Glove	Overall
	50/60	40/45	80	50	55	55

Born: 02/09/98	Age: 22	Bats: B
Height: 5-9	Weight: 155	Throws: R

YEAR	LVL	PA	1B	2B	3B	HR	SB	CS	AVG	OBP	SLG	BB%	K%	GB%	LD%	FB%
2016	RK	223	39	12	5	1	8	5	0.282	0.344	0.406	6.28%	6.73%	52.1	13.8	27.1
2016	A-	9	0	0	0	0	2	0	0.000	0.111	0.000	11.11%	11.11%	57.1	14.3	14.3
2017	A-	302	51	15	5	3	16	8	0.285	0.378	0.415	11.26%	11.92%	45.4	16.7	26.9
2018	A	434	90	18	5	5	43	15	0.313	0.395	0.427	11.06%	12.21%	51.5	22.0	22.3
2018	A+	114	21	7	2	4	12	4	0.347	0.434	0.582	13.16%	13.16%	57.1	14.3	21.4
2019	A+	196	39	8	3	1	24	5	0.290	0.357	0.386	8.67%	13.27%	59.6	13.2	22.5
2019	AA	233	39	9	4	3	24	8	0.266	0.336	0.391	8.58%	15.02%	47.7	22.7	20.9

Background: Signed off the international free agency market all the way back in 2014. Brujan, a native of San Pedro de Macoris, Dominican Republic, flashed some offensive firepower during his debut in the foreign rookie league the following season as he batted .301/.411/.401 with nine doubles, a quartet of triples, two homeruns, and 11 stolen bases. The young switch-hitter's production maintained status quo as he moved stateside in 2016 as he batted .271/.335/.390 in 49 contests in the Gulf Coast League and a pair of late-season contests in short-season ball. Brujan spent the 2017 season with the Hudson Valley Renegades, posting similar numbers (.285.378/.415). At that point Brujan was a nice, complementary low level bat who was – simply – tracking as a utility guy. And then he had turned in one of the bigger breakouts in the organization. Splitting time between Bowling Green and Charlotte, the 5-foot-9, 155-pound infielder slashed an impressive .320/.403/.459 with 25 doubles, seven triples, nine homeruns, and a whopping 55 stolen bases. Brujan opened up last season back in the Florida State League, hitting a solid – albeit not spectacular - .290/.357/.386. Tampa Bay promoted the Dominican middle infielder up to the minors' toughest challenge, Class AA, and he held his own by posting a .266/.336/.391 line. He also appeared in 22 games with the Salt River Rafters in the Arizona Fall League, slugging .256/.380/.463.

Scouting Report: One the big "helium" guys in the minor leagues this offseason, Brujan's shooting up a ton of prospect lists – which is surprising because (A) his production line regressed noticeably from his breakout campaign in 2018 and (B) a lot of the underlying skills weren't as sharp; his walk rate decline, his power shrank a bit. Some of that, though, is the result of moving up to Class AA as a 21-year-old, but what explains the decline in the Florida State League? The batted ball data, according to FanGraphs, is OK, perhaps a bit on the lite side: his average exit velocity was 87 mph with a peak of 104 mph. That's good, but far from great. Brujan shows a short, slashing swing with strong gap-to-gap power and plus-plus speed. If everything breaks the right way, Brujan could be reminiscent of young Johnny Damon.

Ceiling: 3.0- to 3.5-win player
Risk: Moderate
MLB ETA: 2020

8. Xavier Edwards, 2B/SS

	Hit	Power	SB	Patience	Glove	Overall
	55/65	30/40	80	50	55	55

Born: 08/09/99	Age: 20	Bats: B
Height: 5-10	Weight: 175	Throws: R

YEAR	LVL	PA	1B	2B	3B	HR	SB	CS	AVG	OBP	SLG	BB%	K%	GB%	LD%	FB%
2018	RK	88	23	4	1	0	12	1	0.384	0.471	0.466	14.77%	11.36%	72.3	12.3	12.3
2018	A-	107	23	4	0	0	10	0	0.314	0.438	0.360	16.82%	14.02%	56.2	21.9	19.2
2019	A	344	85	13	4	1	20	9	0.336	0.392	0.414	8.72%	10.17%	46.8	19.1	27.7
2019	A+	217	50	5	4	0	14	2	0.301	0.349	0.367	6.45%	8.76%	57.9	18.5	20.8

Background: The phenom certainly left an indelible mark on his alma mater as he became the highest drafted player in North Broward Preparatory High School's history when the Padres drafted him in the opening round, 38th overall, two years ago. Edwards, who slashed a scorching .406 during his senior season with the Florida high school, was previously committed to collegiate powerhouse Vanderbilt University. Standing a wiry 5-foot-10 and 175 pounds, Edwards ripped through the Arizona Summer and Northwest Leagues during his debut as he slugged a sizzling .346/.453/.409 with eight doubles, one triple, and 22 stolen bases in 23 attempts. The Padres' brass bounced the then-19-year-old up to the Midwest League to begin 2019. Edwards continued his onslaught. In 77 games with the Fort Wayne TinCaps, he batted .336/.392/.414. And his bat continued to turn some heads in a second half promotion up to High Class A: he hit .301/.349/.367. San Diego shipped the young infielder, along with outfielder Hunter Renfroe and a PTBNL, to the Rays in exchange for infielder Jake Cronenworth and Tommy Pham this offseason.

Scouting Report: Consider the following:

- Since 2006, here's the list of 19-year-old hitters to post a 135 to 145 DRC+ total with a sub-20% strikeout rate in the Midwest League (min. 300 PA): Bryce Turang, a top prospect in the Brewers' farm system, and – of course – Xavier Edwards.

Short, quick, slashing swing in the same mold as current Rays prospect Vidal Brujan. Edwards, like his fellow infielder, doesn't profile for much extra-base thump – though he compensates for elite speed on the base paths. Edwards, however, does have a chance to develop a 70-grade hit tool. Tremendous bat-to-ball skills, solid patience. But the power is almost non-existent at this point; he's slugged just one homerun in his young career. Mallex Smith's 2018 season with the Rays seems like a reasonable ceiling; he batted .296/.367/.406. Two more final thoughts: #1. the bat path just doesn't offer up too much hope in terms of future power and #2. the batted ball data, according to FanGraphs, was pretty terrible (84 average exit velocity and 100 peak exit velocity). Meaning: there's some risk.

Ceiling: 3.5-win player
Risk: Moderate to High
MLB ETA: 2020

9. Randy Arozarena, OF

	Hit	Power	SB	Patience	Glove	Overall
	55	45	50	50	50	50

Born: 02/28/95	Age: 25	Bats: R
Height: 5-11	Weight: 170	Throws: R

YEAR	LVL	PA	1B	2B	3B	HR	SB	CS	AVG	OBP	SLG	BB%	K%	GB%	LD%	FB%
2017	A+	295	40	22	3	8	10	4	0.275	0.333	0.472	4.41%	17.97%	47.0	20.3	24.4
2017	AA	195	27	10	1	3	8	3	0.252	0.366	0.380	13.85%	17.44%	50.4	11.5	26.7
2018	AA	102	24	5	0	7	9	3	0.396	0.455	0.681	5.88%	24.51%	52.2	25.4	20.9
2018	AAA	311	41	16	0	5	17	5	0.232	0.328	0.348	9.00%	18.97%	55.9	12.7	25.4
2019	AA	116	18	7	2	3	8	5	0.309	0.422	0.515	11.21%	19.83%	56.8	25.7	14.9
2019	AAA	283	56	18	2	12	9	7	0.358	0.435	0.593	8.48%	16.96%	47.0	18.0	28.5

Background: For the second time in a year-and-a-half the Rays and Cardinals got together on a pretty notable trade. After agreeing to the Tommy Pham deal at the trade deadline two years ago, the clubs agreed on a four-player, two-draft-pick swap this offseason. The pieces: St. Louis Cardinals acquired former first rounder Matthew Liberatore, catcher Edgardo Rodriguez, and a 2020 supplemental second round pick for outfielder Randy Arozarena, first baseman/corner outfielder Jose Martinez, and a 2020 supplemental first round selection. Arozarena, who originally signed with the Cardinals in 2016 after defecting from Cuba, began last season back in Class AA for his third tour. But after batting a solid .309/.422/.515 in 28 contests, St. Louis bumped him up to the PCL for the reminder of the year. He hit .358/.435/.593 in 64 games with Memphis. He also appeared in 19 games with the Cardinals.

Snippet from The 2018 Prospect Digest Handbook: The good news: Arozarena completely obliterated the Texas League, slugging a Ruthian .396/.455/.681 in 24 games. The bad news: he was absolutely, completely and utterly subpar in 89 games with Memphis, hitting .232/.328/.348. Arozarena's similar to fellow outfielder Justin Williams in a sense: he puts the ball on the ground too frequently to full take advantage of his power potential. Decent eye and the hit tool looked like it could be an above-average weapon at one point, but it's backed up into an average territory. Arozarena looks like a fringy starting caliber outfielder, one that would start on a non-contender and a fourth outfielder on a championship team like St. Louis.

Scouting Report: His batted ball data in the minor leagues is pretty impressive: his average exit velocity was 90 mph with a peak exit velocity of 109 mph. But the same problem persists: he puts the ball on the ground far too frequently to take advantage of his above-average raw power. And now that he's entering his age-25 season, there's not too much hope for a massive shift in his approach – though the Rays were able to coax 14 homeruns in 79 games out of Yandy Diaz last season. Complicating matters: The Rays are chock full of outfielders with Hunter Renfroe, Kevin Kiermaier, Austin Meadows, Manuel Margot rostered. Final thought: after a solid rebound in Class AAA in 2019, Arozarena looks like a safe, competent league average starter.

Ceiling: 2.5- to 3.0-win player
Risk: Low to Moderate
MLB ETA: Debuted in 2019

10. Anthony Banda, LHP

	FB	CB	SL	CH	Control	Overall
	60	50	55	55	45	50

Born: 08/10/93	Age: 26	Bats: L
Height: 6-2	Weight: 225	Throws: L

YEAR	LVL	IP	W	L	SV	ERA	FIP	WHIP	K/9	K%	BB/9	BB%	K/BB	HR9	BABIP
2017	AAA	122.0	8	7	0	5.39	4.72	1.44	8.6	21.85%	3.8	9.60%	2.27	1.11	0.317
2018	AAA	42.0	4	3	0	3.64	3.28	1.45	10.5	26.92%	3.9	9.89%	2.72	0.64	0.360
2019	Rk	2.3	0	1	0	7.71	3.92	3.86	15.4	25.00%	11.6	18.75%	1.33	0.00	0.667
2019	A+	2.7	0	0	0	0.00	1.81	0.38	6.8	22.22%	0.0	0.00%	#DIV/0!	0.00	0.143
2019	AAA	28.3	2	3	0	6.04	6.20	1.38	8.6	22.50%	3.5	9.17%	2.45	2.22	0.284

Background: If there's one thing you remember about Anthony Banda it's this: Don't' ever bet against him. Why? Because he's had one helluva career and he's only entering his age-26 season. Drafted by the Brewers in the 10th round out of San Jacinto College, North Campus all the way back in 2012. Milwaukee flipped Banda and Mitch Haniger to the Diamondbacks for veteran outfielder Gerardo Parra two years later. Banda's stint with Arizona lasted 3.5 years before he was dealt to Tampa Bay as part of a three-team deal involving the Yankees. A handful of months later the 6-foot-2, 225-pound southpaw succumbed to

Tommy John surgery, which knocked him out for the remainder of 2018 and the opening couple of months of 2019. Finally healthy, with a full return to pre-injury form, Banda made a handful of rehab appearances before settling in for nine games in the International League. He also popped back up with the Rays in early September for three final games.

Snippet from The 2018 Prospect Digest Handbook: He's likely not going to pop back up at the big league level until early 2020. He could be a solid-average starter, maybe a tick below. He also seems to be a poster boy for having one of the "Openers" start games for him and enter in the second inning.

Scouting Report: The fastball came roaring back as it sat in the 93- to 95-mph range during his abbreviated stint in the International League. Banda favored his slider, which was as good as I've seen it, hovering in the 87- to 89-mph neighborhood. And his changeup adds a third swing-and-miss option. Baseball Savant shows the former 10th rounder featuring a low 80s curveball, but I didn't see one. There's some definite backend starting potential, maybe a little more depending upon his control/command. Again, it wouldn't be surprising to see him paired with one of the Rays' Openers. He's going to surprise a lot of people in 2020.

Ceiling: 2.5-win player
Risk: Low to Moderate
MLB ETA: Debuted in 2017

11. Greg Jones, SS

	Hit	Power	SB	Patience	Glove	Overall
	50/55	40/45	70	50	55	50

Born: 03/07/98	Age: 22	Bats: B
Height: 6-2	Weight: 175	Throws: R

YEAR	LVL	PA	1B	2B	3B	HR	SB	CS	AVG	OBP	SLG	BB%	K%	GB%	LD%	FB%
2019	A-	218	46	13	4	1	19	8	0.335	0.413	0.461	10.09%	25.69%	52.9	29.4	15.4

Background: A rare draft-eligible sophomore, though he turned 21-years-old last season, Jones was originally taken by the Baltimore Orioles in the 17th round coming out of Cary High School three years ago. A switch-hitting, twitchy shortstop, Jones was highly touted as a prep prospect heading into his senior season: Baseball America and Perfect Game ranked him as the 75th and 133rd best prospect, respectively. Jones turned in a solid, though pockmarked freshman campaign at UNC Wilmington. In 60 games for long time Head Coach Mark Scalf, the 6-foot-2, 175-pound infielder batted .278/.412/.370 with just 11 extra-base hits (five doubles, two triples, and four homeruns) to go along with 16 stolen bases. The problem, of course, was Jones' inability to consistently make contact; he fanned in nearly a quarter of his plate appearances. The North Carolina native spent the ensuing summer playing for the Chatham Anglers, posting a decent .259/.374/.353 with a triple and three homeruns in 37 contests. Last season Jones' peripherals at the plate improved greatly: he tallied an impressive 44-to-55 strikeout-to-walk ratio en route to slugging a hearty .341/.491/.543 with 12 doubles, nine triples, five homeruns, and a whopping 42 stolen bases (in 52 attempts). Tampa Bay drafted the speedy switch-hitting in the opening round, 22nd, and signed him to a full-slot deal worth $3,027,000. Jones spent the entirety of his debut in the New York-Penn League, slashing a scorching .335/.413/.461 with 13 doubles, four triples, one homer, and 19 stolen bases. Per *Deserved Runs Created Plus*, his production topped the league average mark by 74%.

Scouting Report: Here's what I wrote about the UNC Wilmington star heading into the draft last June:

"Consider the following:

- *Between 2011 and 2018 there were three Colonial Athletic Association hitters that met the following criteria (min. 250 PA): 15% walk rate, a sub-17% strikeout rate, and slug at least .330/.450/.500. Those three hitters are Johnny Bladel, Jared Hammer, and Brady Policelli.*

Policelli, by the way, was the only one to play affiliated ball; he was taken by the Tigers in the 13th round three years ago. Let's continue...

- *Between 2011 and 2018 only seven Division I hitters met the following criteria in a season (min. 250 PA): at least a 16% walk rate, a strikeout rate between 14% and 17%, and an Isolated Power between .180 and .220. Those seven hitters are Mike Papi, Devin Mann, Wade Hinkle, Connor Owings, Rob Lind, Travis Swaggerty, and Matt Whatley.*

- *Papi and Swaggerty were first rounders. Whatley was a third round pick by the Rangers two years ago. Mann was taken in the fifth round by the Dodgers last season. Hinkle and Owings were late round selections. And Lind went undrafted.*

Jones possesses a silky smooth swing and a surprising amount of bat speed. But the hit tool and power are questionable. His plus-speed and raw athleticism make him an intriguing prospect nonetheless."

A few additional notes:

- The hit tool was better than I suspected, though the power remains firmly in the below-average category – especially for a hitter that puts the ball on the ground more than 50% of the time.
- I'm still concerned a bit by the strikeout rate – which was an issue during his freshman campaign. He whiffed in more than a quarter of his plate appearances during his debut. And that's as a pedigreed, early draft pick squaring off against an age-appropriate level of competition.
- In terms of ceiling, I would put it at .280/.330/.400 with 30 doubles, 35 stolen bases, and above-average defense.

Ceiling: 2.5-win player
Risk: Moderate
MLB ETA: 2021/2022

12. Joe Ryan, RHP

FB	CB	SL	CH	Control	Overall
60	50/55	50	50	45+	50

Born: 06/05/96	Age: 24	Bats: R
Height: 6-1	Weight: 185	Throws: R

YEAR	LVL	IP	W	L	SV	ERA	FIP	WHIP	K/9	K%	BB/9	BB%	K/BB	HR9	BABIP
2018	A-	36.3	2	1	0	3.72	3.15	1.10	12.6	34.69%	3.5	9.52%	3.64	0.74	0.303
2019	A	27.7	2	2	0	2.93	2.27	1.08	15.3	40.87%	3.6	9.57%	4.27	0.65	0.315
2019	A+	82.7	7	2	0	1.42	1.68	0.71	12.2	35.90%	1.3	3.85%	9.33	0.33	0.244
2019	AA	13.3	0	0	0	3.38	2.54	1.13	16.2	44.44%	2.7	7.41%	6.00	1.35	0.375

Background: One of the better value picks in the entire 2018 draft. Tampa Bay unearthed the wiry right-hander in the seventh round out California State University Stanislaus – which, by the way, produced long time big league coach Rusty Kuntz. Ryan, who missed all but five games during his junior collegiate season, came back strong during his final campaign with the Big West Conference squad two years ago as he posted a dominating 127-to-13 strikeout-to-walk ratio with a 1.65 ERA in 98.1 innings of work. The California native was able to keep that momentum moving forward during his debut with the Hudson Valley Renegades as well, averaging an impressive 12.6 strikeouts and 3.5 walks per nine innings in 12 appearances. But that brief display of dominance was just a harbinger of things to come. Ryan shot through three levels during his breakout 2019 campaign, appearing in six starts with Bowling Green, another 15 dominating appearances with Charlotte, and he settled in for three final contests in Class AA. When the dust finally settled Ryan was sporting a tidy, barely-there 1.96 ERA while averaging 13.3 strikeouts and just 2.0 walks per innings.

Scouting Report: Fastball. Fastball. Fastball. Even when his backstop flashed an offspeed sign, Ryan was likely to shake him off in search of old number one. Explosive, plus mid-90s heater that he (A) commands reasonably well and (B) elevates frequently when he's ahead in the count. Ryan's phenomenal showing last season is a bit superficial in terms of development. He was wary of throwing his secondary offerings, most of which need some fine tuning. His curveball, a tightly would 12-6 breaking pitch, flashed above-average a few times. His slider, which showed some decent horizontal movement, lacked consistency. And his changeup, another 50-grade offering, has solid arm-side run. But here's the truth: he's entering his age-24 season with unproven, inconsistent secondary pitches and 45+ command/control. Ryan is a prime candidate to partner with an opener. One final thought: if a secondary pitch – or two – ticks up or if he shows an increased level of confidence in them, Ryan has the ceiling as a #4-type arm.

Ceiling: 2.0-win player
Risk: Low to Moderate
MLB ETA: 2020

13. Ronaldo Hernandez, C

Hit	Power	SB	Patience	Glove	Overall
50	50	30	45	50	50

Born: 11/11/97	Age: 22	Bats: R
Height: 6-1	Weight: 185	Throws: R

YEAR	LVL	PA	1B	2B	3B	HR	SB	CS	AVG	OBP	SLG	BB%	K%	GB%	LD%	FB%
2016	RK	229	52	12	0	6	3	5	0.340	0.406	0.485	8.73%	5.24%	49.0	27.3	18.0
2017	RK	246	46	22	1	5	2	2	0.332	0.382	0.507	6.50%	15.85%	46.0	23.0	23.5
2018	A	449	73	20	1	21	10	4	0.284	0.339	0.494	6.90%	15.37%	39.4	19.8	27.4
2019	A+	427	73	19	3	9	7	0	0.265	0.299	0.397	3.98%	15.22%	39.8	17.1	32.9

Background: From a consistent well above-average offensive performer and in the conversation for top catching prospect in the entire minor leagues to...well...anything but. Hernandez, a 6-foot-1, 185-pound backstop from Arjona, Colombia, ripped through the foreign rookie leagues as an

18-year-old in 2016 when he slugged .340/.406/.485 with 18 extra-base knocks. Tampa Bay bounced the spry catcher straight up to the Appalachian League the following season and his bat remained scorching hot; he batted .332/.382/.507 in 54 games with Princeton. Hernandez moved up to full season ball two years ago, as a 20-year-old, and continued to impressed as he slashed .284/.339/.494 with 20 doubles, one triple, and 21 long balls. And the baseball world began to take notice. Then...he lost his footing in High Class A. Appearing in 103 games with the Charlotte Stone Crabs, Hernandez cobbled together a mediocre .265/.299/.397 triple-slash line, belting out 19 doubles, three triples, and nine homeruns. Per *Deserved Runs Created Plus*, his overall production topped the league average mark by 5%. Hernandez appeared in 11 games with the Salt River Rafters in the Arizona Fall League following the season, going 14-for-39 with three doubles and a dinger.

Snippet from The 2018 Prospect Digest Handbook: Hernandez combines above-average power with strong contact rates and a decent eye. Defensively speaking, he grades out as above-average with the ability to control the running game. Yadier Molina's performance in 2018 seems like a good fit for Hernandez at the big league level: .260/.317/.436.

Scouting Report: Consider the following:

- Since 2006, here's the list of 21-year-old hitters to post a 100 to 110 DRC+ with a sub-6.0% walk rate and a strikeout rate below 20% in the Florida State League (min. 350 PA): Jose Miranda, Tony Cruz, Calten Daal, and – of course – Ronaldo Hernandez.

Not exactly a stellar collection of comps, is it? Everything seemingly backed up on Hernandez last season: his power regressed, his walk rate declined all the way down to a laughably poor 4.0%, and his power dried up as well. The young backstop showed some flashes of his former offensive thump as he tallied OPS totals north of .800 during the months of May and July. But the season's other three months caused his stat line to crumble. The track record is long enough to suggest that a rebound is more than likely, but he's also – likely – headed to the minors' toughest challenge, Class AA, at some point in 2020.

Ceiling: 2.0-win player
Risk: Moderate
MLB ETA: 2021

14. Seth Johnson, RHP

	FB	CB	SL	CH	Control	Overall
	55/60	50	55	50	50	45

Born: 09/19/98	Age: 21	Bats: R
Height: 6-1	Weight: 200	Throws: R

YEAR	LVL	IP	W	L	SV	ERA	FIP	WHIP	K/9	K%	BB/9	BB%	K/BB	HR9	BABIP
2019	Rk	10.0	0	0	0	0.00	2.70	0.90	6.3	17.95%	1.8	5.13%	3.50	0.00	0.233
2019	Rk	7.0	0	1	0	5.14	1.60	1.57	11.6	30.00%	1.3	3.33%	9.00	0.00	0.500

Background: Fun Fact Part I: Campbell University, which resides in Buies Creek, North Carolina, has had 35 players drafted since 1967 – including two players Marvin Townsend and Wayne Dale, who were drafted twice. Fun Fact Part II: Johnson, the second last pick in the opening round last June, is the highest draft player in school history (in the June draft). Standing 6-foot-1 and 200-pounds, Johnson has a pretty unique background story. The North Carolina native spent the first two seasons as a light-hitting shortstop at Louisburg College – where he, famously, tossed just six innings. Johnson transferred to Campbell for his junior campaign, focused solely on pitching, and heard his name called as the 40th overall player chosen. Johnson tossed 66.1 innings, recording 81 strikeouts and 30 walks with a 4.61 ERA. After signing with the club, he tossed 17.0 rookie league innings, fanning 16 and walking three.

Scouting Report: Impressive athleticism that's readily apparent through his controlled mechanics. Because of his limited experience on the mound, as well as his youth, Johnson has significantly more projection as compared to the typical three-year collegiate arm. Johnson's fastball sat in the low-90s, peaking in the mid-90s. As he continues to hone his craft, there's a solid chance his fastball grades out as a firm 60-grade. His 12-6 curveball is slow and loopy. The slider flashes above-average. And his firm changeup adds a second average weapon. There's some #4/#5-type potential here with the floor of a middle reliever. I like this pick quite a bit.

Ceiling: 1.5 to 2.0-win player
Risk: Moderate
MLB ETA: 2020

15. Taylor Walls, SS

Hit	Power	SB	Patience	Glove	Overall
55	45	60	55	55	45

Born: 07/10/96	Age: 23	Bats: B
Height: 5-10	Weight: 180	Throws: R

YEAR	LVL	PA	1B	2B	3B	HR	SB	CS	AVG	OBP	SLG	BB%	K%	GB%	LD%	FB%
2017	A-	197	25	9	0	1	5	4	0.213	0.330	0.287	14.72%	26.90%	49.1	21.9	21.1
2018	A	540	102	28	6	6	31	12	0.304	0.393	0.428	12.22%	14.81%	45.6	22.3	28.7
2019	A+	180	29	7	2	4	13	6	0.269	0.339	0.417	10.56%	15.56%	38.3	15.0	38.3
2019	AA	243	30	16	5	6	15	9	0.270	0.346	0.479	10.70%	20.99%	34.8	26.1	32.9

Background: Fun Fact Part I: When the Rays drafted Walls in the third round, 79th overall, in 2017 he became the earliest drafted player from Florida State since 2015. Fun Fact Part II: Walls is the third earliest draft pick from FSU since 2012. A career .284/.426/.400 hitter during his three-year career with the Seminoles, Walls continued to show a heavy slant towards his saber-friendly approach as he moved in the Midwest League two years ago when he batted .304/.393/.428 with 28 doubles, six triples, six homeruns, and 31 stolen bases. Last season, the 5-foot-10, 180-pound switch-hitter slugged a respectable .270/.343/.452 with 23 doubles, seven triples, 10 homeruns, and 28 stolen bases during his time with Charlotte and Montgomery.

Scouting Report: A bit of an underrated prospect for a couple of reasons:

1. He's lost in the sheer depth of the Rays' farm system.
2. He shows a well-rounded offensive approach, though his lack of power makes him a candidate to get easily overlooked.
3. A solid amount of his value is going to come from the defensive side of the ball.

Walls takes a slashing approach as a hitter, shooting the indiscriminately from gap-to-gap. Plus-speed. 10 or so homerun pop. Above-average patience. And he owns a strong glove at short. Add it all up and that's a recipe for a league-average starter, even if it is on the low end of the league average.

Ceiling: 1.5- to 2.0-win player
Risk: Moderate
MLB ETA: 2020

16. JJ Goss, RHP

FB	SL	CH	Control	Overall
55/60	60	50/55	45+	45

Born: 12/25/00	Age: 19	Bats: R
Height: 6-3	Weight: 185	Throws: R

YEAR	LVL	IP	W	L	SV	ERA	FIP	WHIP	K/9	K%	BB/9	BB%	K/BB	HR9	BABIP
2019	Rk	17.0	1	3	0	5.82	2.91	1.24	8.5	22.54%	1.1	2.82%	8.00	0.53	0.353

Background: Equipped with a trio of first round selections last June, the Rays grabbed prep right-hander JJ Goss between a couple of collegiate prospects. Goss, the 36th overall pick, sparkled like a well polished diamond during his senior season at Cypress Ranch High School as he tallied an 11-2 win-loss record with a tidy, barely-there 0.64 ERA. Previously committed to attend Texas A&M University, Goss signed with the savvy franchise for a hefty $2.05 million, roughly $40,000 below the recommended slot bonus. Goss made nine brief appearances in the Gulf Coast League during his debut, posting a 16-to-2 strikeout-to-walk ratio in 17.0 innings.

Scouting Report: Tall and thin, which suggests there may be a little more in the tank once he begins to fill out. Goss attacks hitters with a low-90s fastball, peaking in the 94-mph range which projects as a plus-offering at full maturity. He'll also show a mid-80s change that shows the makings of a potential above-average offering. But it's his late-tilting slider that separates Goss from the rest of his talented peers. Also of note: Goss showed a decent 12-6 curveball prior to his senior season, though he seems to have shelved it in favor of throwing the slider exclusively.

Ceiling: 1.5 to 2.0-win player
Risk: Moderate
MLB ETA: 2020

17. Kevin Padlo, 3B

Hit	Power	SB	Patience	Glove	Overall
45	55	40	60	50+	45

Born: 07/15/96	Age: 23	Bats: R
Height: 6-2	Weight: 205	Throws: R

YEAR	LVL	PA	1B	2B	3B	HR	SB	CS	AVG	OBP	SLG	BB%	K%	GB%	LD%	FB%
2016	A	509	54	22	3	16	14	9	0.229	0.358	0.413	15.52%	26.33%	34.7	22.6	30.2
2017	RK	21	1	0	1	0	1	0	0.118	0.286	0.235	14.29%	4.76%	50.0	6.3	25.0
2017	A+	259	27	13	3	6	4	5	0.223	0.324	0.391	13.51%	23.17%	37.2	11.6	34.1
2018	A+	449	52	26	0	8	5	0	0.223	0.318	0.353	10.47%	26.50%	36.0	17.6	32.4
2019	AA	277	23	20	0	12	11	4	0.250	0.383	0.505	16.97%	25.27%	32.7	25.6	29.5
2019	AAA	155	17	11	1	9	1	0	0.290	0.400	0.595	13.55%	29.68%	34.9	20.5	28.9

Background: The Rays – and their savvy, underrated front office – don't make a lot of poor deals. But you have to wonder if the front office would do it all over again when it comes to how they acquired the power-hitting third baseman. The Rays acquired Padlo as the complementary sidekick to slugging outfielder Corey Dickerson, who (A) was phenomenal during his abbreviated stint in Tampa Bay, (B) but was traded two years later to the Pirates for Daniel Hudson and Tristan Gray. Heading back to Colorado was hard-throwing lefty Jake McGee with one-year of team control left and German Marquez, who (A) hadn't made his big league debut yet and (B) has been worth nearly 10 wins above replacement since 2017. Padlo, a fifth round pick out of Murrieta Valley High School in 2014, split last season between Montgomery and Durham, slugging .265/.389/.538 with 331 doubles, one triple, and 21 homeruns in only 110 games.

Scouting Report: With respect to his production in Class AA last, where he spent the majority of the time, consider the following:

- Since 2006, here's the list of 22-year-old hitters to post a DRC+ between 160 and 175 with a double-digit walk rate and a strikeout rate of at least 22% in any Class AA league (min. 250 PA): Pedro Alvarez, who was a league average hitter during his nine-year big league career, and Kevin Padlo.

Padlo's always shown some borderline concerning strikeout totals without actually teetering over into a full blown meltdown. But he compensates with impressive 20+ homer pop and phenomenal walk rates. He's likely going to wind up as a Three True Outcomes Hitter, something along the lines of a lesser Joey Gallo, pre-2019.

Ceiling: 1.5-win player
Risk: Moderate
MLB ETA: 2020

18. John Doxakis, LHP

FB	SL	CH	Control	Overall
50	55	55	55	45

Born: 08/20/98	Age: 21	Bats: L
Height: 6-4	Weight: 215	Throws: L

YEAR	LVL	IP	W	L	SV	ERA	FIP	WHIP	K/9	K%	BB/9	BB%	K/BB	HR9	BABIP
2019	A-	32.7	0	0	0	1.93	2.78	0.95	8.5	23.85%	3.0	8.46%	2.82	0.00	0.235

Background: After struggling through a disappointing, pock-marked freshman campaign for Texas A&M – where he was mostly used as a relief option – Doxakis found his footing as a full-time starting pitcher the following year. In 17 appearances for the SEC squad, the 6-foot-4, 215-pound southpaw posted a solid 92-to-29 strikeout-to-walk ratio in 93.1 innings of work. The Houston, Texas, native raised the bar a bit during his junior campaign in 2019 as he averaged 9.9 strikeout and 2.2 walks per nine innings with a 2.06 ERA in 16 starts. The Rays selected Doxakis in the second round, 61st overall, and signed to him a deal worth $1.13 million, the recommended slot bonus. Doxakis made 12 brief appearances in the New York-Penn League, posting a 31-to-11 strikeout-to-walk ratio with a 1.93 ERA in 32.2 innings of work.

Scouting Report: With respect to his work in college last season, consider the following:

- Between 2011 and 2018, only seven SEC pitchers met the following criteria in a season (min. 100 IP): 9 K/9 to 11 K/9, a sub-3.0 BB/9 and a homerun below 0.5 HR/9. Those seven pitchers: Walker Buehler, Kevin Gausman, Aaron Nola, Brady Singer, Kyle Wright, Dakota Hudson, and Brigham Hill. All but Hill, who was a fifth round pick by the Nationals in 2017, were first round selections.

If you looked up the definition of a crafty left-hander, you'd likely find a picture of Doxakis there. Average low-90s fastball, above-average slider, 50-grade changeup with a strong feel for the strike zone. Purely a backend option that could flourish in the Rays' system if he's teamed with an Opener. Very similar to Rays' Ryan Yarbrough. Low ceiling, high floor. Very safe. One more final thought: he was young for a three-year collegiate player.

Ceiling: 1.5-win player
Risk: Moderate
MLB ETA: 2021/2022

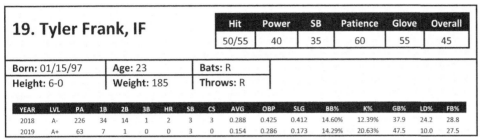

19. Tyler Frank, IF

	Hit	Power	SB	Patience	Glove	Overall
	50/55	40	35	60	55	45

Born: 01/15/97	Age: 23	Bats: R
Height: 6-0	Weight: 185	Throws: R

YEAR	LVL	PA	1B	2B	3B	HR	SB	CS	AVG	OBP	SLG	BB%	K%	GB%	LD%	FB%
2018	A-	226	34	14	1	2	3	3	0.288	0.425	0.412	14.60%	12.39%	37.9	24.2	28.8
2019	A+	63	7	1	0	0	3	0	0.154	0.286	0.173	14.29%	20.63%	47.5	10.0	27.5

Background: Florida Atlantic University has churned out a surprising number of draft picks in recent years. In fact, the Conference USA school had 23 players taken since 2015, including a pair of shortstops picked in the second round: the Red Sox selected C.J. Chatham with the 51st overall pick four years ago and the Rays nabbed Tyler Frank, the 56th player chosen, in 2018. A wiry 6-foot, 185-pound infielder from Tamarac, Florida, Frank left the school as a three-year starter with a solid .310/.433/.504 with 43 doubles, one triple, and 25 homeruns in 165 total games. He continued to produce as he moved into the New York-Penn League during his debut, batting .288/.425/.412 with 14 doubles, one triple, and a pair of homeruns. Per *Deserved Runs Created Plus*, his overall production topped the league average mark by 78%. An undisclosed left arm injury curtailed his sophomore professional campaign in early April after just 16 games with the Charlotte Stone Crabs.

Scouting Report: A saber-slanted offensive performer with a nose for first base who's likely slotted for a super-sub type role. Frank fits the mold – typically not taken by the Rays – of a low ceiling, high floor, quick moving collegiate prospect. I'm not sold on the power due to the average bat speed and slight frame. He does compensate by a short bat path. Purely backup. And one that's going to have to hit the ground running in 2020 to make up for lost time.

Ceiling: 1.5-win player
Risk: Moderate
MLB ETA: 2021

20. Nick Schnell, CF

	Hit	Power	SB	Patience	Glove	Overall
	40/45	45/55	40	50+	50	40

Born: 03/27/00	Age: 20	Bats: L
Height: 6-3	Weight: 180	Throws: R

YEAR	LVL	PA	1B	2B	3B	HR	SB	CS	AVG	OBP	SLG	BB%	K%	GB%	LD%	FB%
2018	RK	82	10	4	1	1	2	6	0.239	0.378	0.373	17.07%	28.05%	54.5	20.5	22.7
2019	Rk	21	2	0	2	0	0	0	0.190	0.190	0.381	0.00%	42.86%	25.0	33.3	41.7
2019	Rk+	166	23	11	3	5	5	2	0.286	0.361	0.503	10.84%	30.72%	39.2	26.8	29.9
2019	A	60	9	3	1	0	0	1	0.236	0.271	0.327	3.33%	40.00%	36.4	21.2	33.3

Background: The 32nd overall player chosen in the 2018 draft. Schnell, a product of Roncalli High School, looked a bit overwhelmed during his 19-game cameo in the Gulf Coast League as he batted a lowly .239/.378/.373 in 82 trips to the plate. Schnell returned to the rookie league – briefly – to begin the 2019 season, but was promoted up to the Appalachian League in early July. Appearing in 37 games with the Princeton Rays, the 6-foot-3, 180-pound center fielder slugged an impressive .286/.361/.503 with 11 doubles, three triples, five homeruns, and five stolen bases (in seven attempts). His overall production, according to *Deserved Runs Created Plus*, topped the league average mark by 18%. He spent the final few weeks with the Bowling Green Hot Rods of the Midwest League, hitting .236/.271/.327 in 60 plate appearances.

Snippet from The 2018 Prospect Digest Handbook: During his limited time in pro ball Schnell looked uncomfortable against breaking pitches, especially ones thrown for strikes; he was able to lay off the ones in the dirt well enough. Hitting from a closed stance, Schnell should develop average power which combines well with his above-average speed. He looks to be in the same mold as current Rays prospect Garrett Whitley. Meaning: toolsy but raw.

Scouting Report: Unfortunately, the early signs of trouble with breaking balls was just a harbinger of things to come. The lefty-swinging center fielder whiffed 84 times in just 247 plate appearance – or an average of 34% of the time. Solid patience, 55-grade pop at full maturity, and decent speed. It's going to come down to how well the hit tool develops moving forward. One more final thought: he's already showing some concerning platoon splits. Beware.

Ceiling: 1.0- to 1.5-win player
Risk: Moderate
MLB ETA: 2022

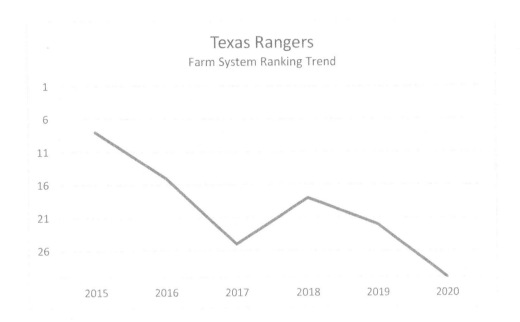

Texas Rangers
Farm System Ranking Trend

Rank	Name	Age	Pos
1	Josh Jung	22	3B
2	Nick Solak	25	2B/3B
3	Hans Crouse	21	RHP
4	Ronny Henriquez	20	RHP
5	Cole Winn	20	RHP
6	Brock Burke	23	LHP
7	Bubba Thompson	22	OF
8	Leody Taveras	21	CF
9	Davis Wendzel	19	3B
10	Yerry Rodriguez	22	RHP
11	Keithron Moss	18	IF
12	A.J. Alexy	22	RHP
13	Joe Palumbo	25	LHP
14	Sam Huff	22	C
15	Steele Walker	24	CF
16	Demarcus Evans	23	RHP
17	Ryan Garcia	21	RHP
18	Jonathan Hernandez	23	RHP
19	Tyler Phillips	22	RHP
20	Sherten Apostel	21	1B/3B

1. Josh Jung, 3B

Hit	Power	SB	Patience	Glove	Overall
55	50	35	50	50	55

Born: 02/12/98	Age: 22	Bats: R
Height: 6-2	Weight: 215	Throws: R

YEAR	LVL	PA	1B	2B	3B	HR	SB	CS	AVG	OBP	SLG	BB%	K%	GB%	LD%	FB%
2019	Rk	19	7	1	1	1	0	0	0.588	0.632	0.941	10.53%	15.79%	64.3	14.3	21.4
2019	A	179	31	13	0	1	4	1	0.287	0.363	0.389	8.94%	16.20%	48.8	24.4	24.4

Background: Jung turned in a prolific career for MacArthur High School: he was a four-time All-District honoree and was recognized as an All-District and All-State selection three times. The 6-foot-2, 215-pound third baseman was also named by Rawlings/Perfect Game as an Honorable All-American and Louisville Slugger handed him three All-American Awards as well. But despite the hardware Jung, a native of San Antonio, Texas, went undrafted. Three short seasons later he positioned himself as an early first round selection. Cracking the Red Raiders' lineup as a true freshman, Jung batted an impressive .306/.395/.453 with 14 doubles, a pair of triples, and six homeruns to go along with some promising plate discipline; he sported a 45-to-36 strikeout-to-walk ratio in 289 plate appearances. He spent the following summer dominating the California Collegiate League to the tune of .368/.454/.521 with 11 extra-base hits in 34 games with the Santa Barbara Foresters. The young third baseman raised the bar even further during his sophomore campaign for Head Coach Tim Tadlock at Texas Tech: in 65 games for the Raiders – a squad, by the way, which finished fifth in the nation – Jung slugged a Ruthian .392/.491/.639 with 17 doubles, one triple, and 12 homeruns with four stolen bases. And, once again, he showed remarkable plate discipline by posting more walks than strikeouts (39 vs. 32). Jung spent the 2018 summer playing with Adley Rutschman, Shea Langeliers, and Andrew Vaughn on Team USA; the budding star held his own by batting .283/.377/.377 in 15 games. Last season Jung's production maintained status quo: he batted a .342/..476/.636, belting out a career high 22 doubles, one triple, and 14 homeruns – also a homerun – to go along with a 39-to-52 strikeout-to-walk ratio. The Rangers drafted the 6-foot-2, 215-pound third baseman in opening round, 8th overall. Jung spent the majority of his debut with the Hickory Crawdads, hitting a respectable .287/.363/.389 with 13 doubles and a homerun with the South Atlantic League affiliate. His overall production, per Baseball Prospectus' *Deserved Runs Created Plus*, was 37% better than the league average mark.

Scouting Report: Here's what I wrote prior to the draft last June:

"Let's just jump right into the production. With respect to his sophomore season in 2018, consider the following:

- Between 2011 and 2018, there were 1,322 instances in which a Division I player earned at least 275 plate appearances in a season. His .392 batting average tied for the 29th best mark.

Obviously, batting average alone is misleading. Let's continue:

- Between 2011 and 2018, here's the list of Division I hitters that batted at least .375/.475/.600 with a walk rate between 11% and 13% and a whiff rate between 9% and 12% (min. 275 PA): D.J. Peterson, the 12th overall pick in 2013, and – of course – Josh Jung.

What separates the two, though, are their home fields. New Mexico's ballpark, Santa Ana Star Field, is a notorious bandbox that inflates offense like few others. Texas Tech, on the other hand, plays in a far less-offensive-inducing palace. Now let's take a look at his work thus far in 2019. Consider the following:

- Between 2011 and 2018, here's the list of Division I hitters that batted at least .340/.450/.600 with a walk rate between 19% and 21% and a strikeout rate between 13% and 15% (min. 200 PA): Keston Hiura, James Ramsey, and Will Craig – all three being first round picks.

Jung shows above-average bat speed and a big leg kick at the plate The natural loft in his swing, coupled with the bat speed, should allow him to be a perennial 20-homerun threat as he transitions into the professional ranks. He has a long history – extending all the way back through his prep career – of above-average to elite production against top tier talent. Defensively, he's a little stiff with a slightly better-than-average arm at the hot corner. He'll never be mistaken for a Brooks Robinson, but he shouldn't have to worry about shifting away from the position. At his peak, he looks like a .280/.340/.480 type hitter."

Ceiling: 3.5-win player
Risk: Moderate
MLB ETA: 2021/2022

2. Nick Solak, 2B/3B

Hit	Power	SB	Patience	Glove	Overall
55	50	35	55	50	50

Born: 01/11/95	Age: 25	Bats: R
Height: 5-11	Weight: 190	Throws: R

YEAR	LVL	PA	1B	2B	3B	HR	SB	CS	AVG	OBP	SLG	BB%	K%	GB%	LD%	FB%
2016	A-	279	60	13	1	3	8	0	0.321	0.412	0.421	10.75%	13.98%	56.4	23.8	16.8
2017	A+	406	73	17	4	10	13	4	0.301	0.397	0.460	13.05%	18.72%	54.2	15.4	27.1
2017	AA	132	22	9	1	2	1	1	0.286	0.344	0.429	7.58%	18.18%	59.8	12.4	21.6
2018	AA	565	96	17	3	19	21	6	0.282	0.384	0.450	12.04%	19.82%	53.4	17.0	23.7
2019	AAA	349	49	13	1	17	3	2	0.266	0.353	0.485	11.17%	22.92%	52.4	17.8	25.8
2019	AAA	128	25	6	0	10	2	0	0.347	0.386	0.653	4.69%	19.53%	46.7	23.9	26.1

Background: An oddity of sorts because he's been destined for a starting gig at the big league level since he was taken in the second round, 62nd overall, in 2016 by the Yankees. But the former University of Louisville standout has moved around more than expected in four professional seasons. New York flipped the offensive-minded infielder to Tampa as part of a three-team deal that also involved the Diamondbacks. A little more than a year later the Rays dealt Solak to the Rangers for hard-throwing right-handed reliever Peter Fairbanks. All along the way, though, Solak did what Solak always does: hit. Splitting time between both organizations' Class AAA affiliates, the 5-foot-11, 190-pound second / third baseman slugged .289/.362/.532 with 19 doubles, one triple, and 27 homeruns in only 115 games. Texas promoted Solak up to The Show at the end of the year. And, of course, he continued to hit. He batted a Solak-esque .293/.393/.491 with six doubles, one triple, and five homeruns in 33 games.

Snippet from The 2018 Prospect Digest Handbook: Solak's the type of player that you look up one season and he's quietly become one of the better second basemen in baseball. The former Louisville star does everything well – but now he's showing some impressive power potential too. In terms of big league ceiling think something along the lines of .280/.340/.430.

Scouting Report: Solak continues to fly under the radar – despite sporting a .294/.383/.468 minor league triple-slash line. The former Louisville Cardinal's power leapt up from a *potential* average skill into full blown 50-grade territory. He has a long history of impressive peripherals, a little bit of speed, and solid up-the-middle glove. Again, he's the type of player that comes to ballpark, quietly produces, and you look up 12 years later and begin to appreciate a borderline perennial All-Star caliber infielder. He's going to be this generation's Jason Kipnis.

Ceiling: 3.0-win player
Risk: Low to Moderate
MLB ETA: Debuted in 2018

3. Hans Crouse, RHP

FB	SL	CH	Command	Overall
70	65	50/55	50/55	50

Born: 09/15/98	Age: 21	Bats: L
Height: 6-4	Weight: 180	Throws: R

YEAR	LVL	IP	W	L	SV	ERA	FIP	WHIP	K/9	K%	BB/9	BB%	K/BB	HR9	BABIP
2017	Rk	20.0	0	0	0	0.45	3.22	0.70	13.5	40.54%	3.2	9.46%	4.29	0.45	0.176
2018	A-	38.0	5	1	0	2.37	2.63	0.95	11.1	31.13%	2.6	7.28%	4.27	0.47	0.253
2018	A	16.7	0	2	0	2.70	4.06	1.56	8.1	19.74%	4.3	10.53%	1.88	0.54	0.333
2019	A	87.7	6	1	0	4.41	4.44	1.20	7.8	21.90%	2.0	5.48%	4.00	1.23	0.297

Background: The third highest drafted player out of Dana Hills High School in Dana Point, California, Crouse, who was bested by fellow pitchers Peter Tago and Blake Taylor, should – easily – surpass some of the school's more famous alums, which also includes Tanner Scheppers and Seth Etherton, as the most noteworthy player. Taken in the second round, 66th overall, in 2017, the lanky, long-limbed right-hander was nearly unhittable during his debut that summer in rookie ball: he posted a 30-to-7 strikeout-to-walk ratio in only 20.0 innings of work. He split his follow up campaign between Spokane and Hickory, throwing a combined 54.2 innings with 62 strikeouts and just 19 free passes. Last season Texas pushed Crouse back into the Sally for the entire year. The 6-foot-4, 180-pound youngster started a career best 19 games, averaging 7.8 strikeouts and just 2.0 walks per nine innings. He finished the year with a 4.41 ERA and a 5.12 DRA.

Snippet from The 2018 Prospect Digest Handbook: There's front-of-the-rotation caliber potential here, but he'll need to further refine his changeup. Tremendous, tremendous find in the second round two years ago.

Scouting Report: Consider the following:

- Since 2006, only seven 20-year-old pitchers met the following criteria in the South Atlantic League (min. 75 IP): a strikeout percentage between 20% and 22% and a sub-6% walk percentage. Those seven pitchers: Will Stewart, Alejandro Requena, Alex Wells, Marcos Frias, Zack Von Rosenberg, Vicente Campos, and – of course – Hans Crouse.

The arsenal's a potential elite, power-based repertoire. And after a strong five-game cameo in the Sally two years ago, I was a bit surprised that the Rangers didn't explore the possibility of pushing their top young arm up to High Class A early in 2019. But then I took note of Crouse's pitch sequencing – and a certain emphasis – last season. After showing a raw, though potentially promising changeup in 2018, Crouse seemed to feature the offering a bit more frequently last year – likely in an effort to improve it. And it certainly did. There were times he choked it, throwing it a solid 55 feet. But when it was on, it was impressive. The fastball's one of the better ones showcased by a starting pitching in the minor leagues, as is his slider. Given the emphasis on his changeup, as well as his 55-grade control/command, I'd expect Crouse's strikeout percentage to leap several degrees in 2020. Again, there's some potential #3 caliber status here.

Ceiling: 3.0-win player
Risk: Moderate
MLB ETA: 2022

4. Ronny Henriquez, RHP

FB	SL	SF	Command	Overall
60	55/60	55	50	50

Born: 06/20/00	Age: 20	Bats: R
Height: 5-10	Weight: 155	Throws: R

YEAR	LVL	IP	W	L	SV	ERA	FIP	WHIP	K/9	K%	BB/9	BB%	K/BB	HR9	BABIP
2018	Rk	58.0	5	0	0	1.55	1.62	0.78	12.3	36.07%	1.2	3.65%	9.88	0.31	0.269
2019	A	82.0	6	6	0	4.50	3.11	1.44	10.9	29.55%	3.0	8.06%	3.67	0.66	0.384

Background: In retrospect, it's amazing how money is doled out on the international market. Sure, there are a lot of flashy, big dollar free agents, but I'm always fascinated how guys with five-figure bonuses sneak in under-the-radar and immediately become a bonafide top prospects. You know, like, Ronny Henriquez – a diminutive, slight-framed right-hander with a big time arsenal who was handed just $10,000 a couple years ago. Henriquez, a native of Bonao, Dominican Republic, made the gigantic leap from the foreign rookie league straight into the Sally. And the promising youngster didn't miss a beat. Making 21 appearances for the Hickory Crawdads, the 5-foot-10, 155-pound righty posted a dominating 99-to-27 strikeout-to-walk ratio in only 82.0 innings of work. Not too shabby for the then-19-year-old. He compiled a 4.50 ERA and a 5.91 DRA (*Deserved Run Average*).

Scouting Report: Consider the following:

- Since 2006, here's the list of 19-year-old pitchers to post a strikeout percentage between 27.0% and 29.0% with a walk percentage between 6.5% and 8.5% in the South Atlantic League (min. 75 IP): Lucas Giolito, the long time perennial top prospect and 2019 AL All-Star, and – of course – Ronny Henriquez.

Now, to be fair, Giolito's *Deserved Run Average*, a metric for true performance, was significantly better (2.37 vs. 5.91). But the peripherals are nearly identical. Henriquez, a wiry right-hander with plenty of room to grow, showcases a lively, high octane three-pitch arsenal: a mid-90s, plus fastball; an above-average slider that may tick up another half grade as he matures; and one of the better splitters in the minor leagues. And the youngster shows a surprisingly solid feel for the strike zone. Something else to consider: Among Henriquez's 21 appearances, two of them were particularly poor – a July 6th start against the Fireflies and an August 9th starts against the RiverDogs. Ignoring those from his season, his ERA drops to just 3.41. Similarly with any small hurler, Henriquez is will have to continually prove he can withstand the rigors of grabbing the ball every fifth day. But there's some #3/#4-type potential brewing in his right arm.

Ceiling: 2.5- to 3.0-win player
Risk: Moderate
MLB ETA: 2021/2022

5. Cole Winn, RHP

FB	CB	SL	CH	Command	Overall
60	55/60	50/55	50	50	50

Born: 11/25/99	Age: 20	Bats: R
Height: 6-2	Weight: 190	Throws: R

YEAR	LVL	IP	W	L	SV	ERA	FIP	WHIP	K/9	K%	BB/9	BB%	K/BB	HR9	BABIP
2019	A	68.7	4	4	0	4.46	4.36	1.43	8.5	21.81%	5.1	13.09%	1.67	0.66	0.290

Background: Orange Lutheran High School in Orange, California, has churned out a few big leaguers: New York Yankees ace – and three-time All-Star, Gerrit Cole; right-handed reliever Brandon Maurer; and outfielder Jason Martin. Fun Fact: All three of the aforementioned players have accrued time in the Pittsburgh Pirates organization. Cole Winn, the 15th overall pick in 2018, has a strong chance to add his name to the list. Taken between fellow top prospects Logan Gilbert of the Seattle Mariners and Matthew Liberatore, who was selected by the Rays and traded to the Cardinals this offseason; Winn didn't make his professional debut until last season. Making 14 starts with the Hickory Crawdads, the 6-foot-2, 190-pound right-hander fanned 65 and walked 39 in 68.2 innings of work. He compiled a 4.46 ERA and a 5.47 DRA (*Deserved Runs Average*).

Snippet from The 2018 Prospect Digest Handbook: His fastball sits comfortably in the 93- to 95-mph range with late life. His changeup, a plus-pitch, is thrown with tremendous arm action and shows solid sink and fade. The change sits in the 85- to 87-mph range and had many hitters out front on it. He'll also mix in a 12-6 curveball, another plus-offering, and an average slider. Winn also commanded the ball reasonably well, though he has a tendency to choke his changeup a bit. There's definite #2/#3-type potential here.

Scouting Report: Consider the following:

- Since 2006, here's the list of 19-year-old hurlers to post a strikeout percentage between 21% and 23% and a double-digit walk percentage in the South Atlantic League (min. 50 IP): Josh Hader, Brad Hand, Luke Jackson, Wilmer Font, Jesse Biddle, Ryan Tucker, Ofelky Peralta, and – of course – Cole Winn.

Ignoring Winn momentarily, notice the trend among the group? Each of the aforementioned arms eventually relinquished their holds onto their spot in the rotation. And all but one of them – Ofelky Peralta – has spent time on a big league roster with a couple becoming above-average or better MLB relievers (Hader, Hand, Jackson). As for Winn: the control/command was a battle all season long and in nearly half of his starts he walked three of more batters. The repertoire – like many of his counterparts – would slide into a #3/#4 type role in the future. Mid-90s, plus fastball; a tight 12-6 curveball that flashes plus; a slider that offered glimpses of being an above-average offering; and a decent little changeup. The Rangers are known for aggressive minor league assignments for the better prospects, so a quick cameo in Class AA at some point in 2020 isn't out of the question.

Ceiling: 2.5- to 3.0-win player
Risk: Moderate
MLB ETA: 2022

6. Brock Burke, LHP

	FB	CB	SL	CH	Command	Overall
	55	50	50/55	50	50+	50

Born: 08/04/96	Age: 23	Bats: L
Height: 6-4	Weight: 180	Throws: L

YEAR	LVL	IP	W	L	SV	ERA	FIP	WHIP	K/9	K%	BB/9	BB%	K/BB	HR9	BABIP
2017	A	57.3	6	0	0	1.10	2.49	0.99	9.3	26.22%	3.1	8.89%	2.95	0.00	0.253
2017	A+	66.0	5	6	0	4.64	3.96	1.38	6.7	17.13%	2.2	5.59%	3.06	0.82	0.329
2018	A+	82.0	3	5	0	3.84	3.19	1.40	9.5	24.10%	3.3	8.31%	2.90	0.44	0.343
2018	AA	55.3	6	1	0	1.95	2.19	0.96	11.5	32.13%	2.3	6.33%	5.07	0.33	0.282
2019	A	5.0	0	0	0	7.20	3.07	1.80	1.8	4.55%	0.0	0.00%	N/A	0.00	0.429
2019	AA	45.3	3	5	0	3.18	2.78	1.01	9.7	30.63%	2.4	7.50%	4.08	0.40	0.262
2019	AAA	8.0	0	0	0	7.88	5.29	2.25	12.4	26.19%	6.8	14.29%	1.83	1.13	0.478

Background: Originally taken in the third round by the Rays in the 2014 draft. Texas acquired the savvy southpaw as part of the three-team deal that involved Tampa and the Oakland A's two years ago. Burke, who stands a lanky 6-foot-4 and 180 pounds, was one of the bigger surprises in the Rays' system in 2018 when he tallied a 158-to-44 strikeout-to-walk ratio in 137.1 innings between the Florida State and Southern Leagues. Last season, the Evergreen High School product was limited to just 13 minor leagues starts, which were spread amongst four separate levels, and half-a-dozen big league starts. An early season blister problem nagged him for a couple months. And then a "shoulder impingement" forced the Rangers to prematurely end his 2019 season in September. In total, Burke tossed 62.1 minor league innings, recording 64 strikeouts against just 18 walks. He tossed another 26.2 innings in The Show, posting a 14-to-11 strikeout-to-walk ratio to go along with a horrible 7.43 ERA.

Snippet from The 2018 Prospect Digest Handbook: Burke – quietly – became one of the minors' most competent left-handers last season, showing a knack for missing bats while doing things not to hurt himself. He looks like a potential #3/#4-type arm moving forward.

Scouting Report: The offspeed stuff didn't look as crisp last season as in years past. Some of that dullness, undoubtedly, can be attributed to the long layoffs and – perhaps – tweaking grips in an effort to avoid those pesky blister issues. As long as the shoulder impingement doesn't prove to be a lingering issue, Burke still looks like a potential backend arm – though he looks more like a #4/#5 instead of someone that settles in near the middle of a rotation. One more final thought: At times, he looked hesitant to throw his curveball last season, which I prefer to his slider/cutter. Update: Burke underwent the knife in late February to repair of a torn labrum, an injury that will knock him out of action until 2021.

Ceiling: 2.0-win player
Risk: Moderate to High
MLB ETA: Debuted in 2019

7. Bubba Thompson, OF

Hit	Power	SB	Patience	Glove	Overall
35/45	40/55	50	50	50	45

Born: 06/09/98	Age: 22	Bats: R	
Height: 6-1	Weight: 180	Throws: R	

YEAR	LVL	PA	1B	2B	3B	HR	SB	CS	AVG	OBP	SLG	BB%	K%	GB%	LD%	FB%
2017	RK	123	17	7	2	3	5	5	0.257	0.317	0.434	4.88%	22.76%	52.9	16.5	24.7
2018	A	363	65	18	5	8	32	7	0.289	0.344	0.446	6.34%	28.65%	44.3	21.3	27.8
2019	A+	228	21	8	2	5	12	3	0.178	0.261	0.312	9.21%	31.58%	42.3	12.3	33.1

Background: I gushed about Thompson's raw athleticism in last year's Handbook. And I pegged the former first rounder, in an article I co-authored with Michael Salfino on *The Athletic*, for Top Under the Radar Dynasty League Prospects. So...clearly...things didn't go as I would have expected. A product of McGill-Toolen Catholic High School, Thompson, the 26th overall selection, turned in an impressive – albeit a bit flawed – showing as a 20-year-old in the South Atlantic League two years ago when he slugged a healthy .289/.344/.446 with 18 doubles, five triples, eight homeruns, and 32 stolen bases in only 84 games. Per *Deserved Runs Created Plus*, his overall production topped the league average mark by 18%. He looked – or so I thought – like the perfect candidate to become a legitimate top prospect. And then 2019 clapped back. Thompson started out a bit slow, going 6-for-40 in his first 12 games with the Down East Wood Ducks. But things quickly went from bad to worse. He fractured his hamate bone, an injury that typically saps a hitter's power for quite awhile, and underwent the knife to have it surgically repaired. He came back in mid-June and promptly fanned in seven of his first 13 plate appearances. He hit the DL again after just four games and missed another month. In total he batted a lowly .178/.261/.312 in 57 games. His production sort of returned during his stint with the Surprise Saguaros in the Arizona Fall League as he hit .254/.337/.394.

Snippet from The 2018 Prospect Digest Handbook: Not only did Thompson make the leap from the lowest level of stateside ball up to the Sally, but he missed the first month-plus of the season and came out raking. He finished third in the league in stolen bases – despite appearing in roughly 30 fewer games than two players that bested him (Kirvin Moesquit and Yonny Hernandez).

Scouting Report: It was – in every regard – a complete and utter lost season for Thompson. Not only did he miss the majority of the year due to injury, but his offensive approach at the plate was wrecked. He fanned in a career worst 31.6% of his plate appearances. And the hit tool looked like it was a junior varsity level grade. The raw ability is still apparent, but his status took a significant hit last season. Assuming he can shake the injuries and the poor 2019 season – which is far from a certainty – he looks like a Nick Williams-esque type performer. Williams, a former Rangers farmhand, owns a .254/.313/.420 career big league line.

Ceiling: 1.5- to 2.0-win player
Risk: Moderate
MLB ETA: 2022

8. Leody Taveras, CF

Hit	Power	SB	Patience	Glove	Overall
45/50	40	70	50	55+	45

Born: 09/08/98	Age: 21	Bats: B	
Height: 6-1	Weight: 171	Throws: R	

YEAR	LVL	PA	1B	2B	3B	HR	SB	CS	AVG	OBP	SLG	BB%	K%	GB%	LD%	FB%
2017	A	577	95	20	7	8	20	6	0.249	0.312	0.360	8.15%	15.94%	50.0	17.9	23.4
2018	A+	580	100	16	7	5	19	11	0.246	0.312	0.332	8.79%	16.55%	48.0	21.0	23.8
2019	A+	290	62	7	4	2	21	5	0.294	0.368	0.376	10.69%	21.38%	45.2	19.8	29.4
2019	AA	293	51	12	4	3	11	8	0.265	0.320	0.375	7.85%	20.48%	42.5	18.4	31.9

Background: One of the club's big midseason expenditures on the international market four years ago. The Rangers handed the then-16-year-old a hefty $2.1 million. Since then, well, Taveras has continued to offer up fleeting glimpses of that promise enveloped by a mix of frustration and disappoint. The Rangers have aggressively challenged the young center fielder – he spent the 2017 in the South Atlantic League as an 18-year-old and reached Class AA last season as a 20-year-old – but the results have largely been mixed. Last season, though, was Taveras' finest showing to date. He opened the year back up in High Class A and ripped through the league by batting .294/.368/.376. He was promoted up the Texas League in the second half and hit a mediocre .265/.320/.375. The Dominican outfielder hit an aggregate .279/.344/.376 with 19 doubles, eight triples, five homeruns and 32 stolen bases (in 45 attempts).

Snippet from The 2018 Prospect Digest Handbook: [His] top asset is his speed, which is a legitimate game-changer, and defense. Otherwise, the rest of the physical tools range from average (hit tool, eye at the plate) to below-average (power). The fact that he contributes on the defensive side of the ball pads his sagging status a bit, but there's not a whole lot that differentiates Taveras and former Phillies top prospect – and current Ranger – Carlos Tocci.

Scouting Report: With respect to his work in Class AA last season, consider the following:

- Since 2006, only three 20-year-old hitters posted a DRC+ total between 92 and 107 in the Texas League (min. 250 PA): Wil Myers, Bryan Anderson, and Leody Taveras.

Perhaps there's no better analogy for Taveras than the above comparison. On one hand you have an above-average big league bat who has a long term deal in his back pocket. On the other hand you have a failed fourth round pick who cracked a big league lineup 40 times in five brief stints. Boom or bust. And that's what Leody Taveras is. The hit tool could peak as an average weapon. The power below that. And, again, it's all about his speed. Defensively, he's come a *long* way in the last two years, going from a poor center fielder to borderline plus at times. I've never been particularly fond of his big league outlook. And he's certainly young enough to take a couple more gigantic leaps forward. But the only time's he's cracked the league offensive production since 2017 was in last year's do-over of High Class A.

Ceiling: 1.5- to 2.0-win player
Risk: Moderate
MLB ETA: 2020

9. Davis Wendzel, 3B

Hit	Power	SB	Patience	Glove	Overall
50	50	35	60	50	45

Born: 05/23/97	Age: 23	Bats: R
Height: 6-0	Weight: 205	Throws: R

YEAR	LVL	PA	1B	2B	3B	HR	SB	CS	AVG	OBP	SLG	BB%	K%	GB%	LD%	FB%
2019	Rk	11	2	1	0	1	0	0	0.444	0.545	0.889	18.18%	27.27%	16.7	33.3	33.3
2019	A-	13	2	0	0	0	2	1	0.200	0.385	0.200	23.08%	23.08%	57.1	42.9	0.0

Background: Talk about improving one's draft status. The Red Sox drafted the 6-foot, 205-pound infielder in the 37th round following his sophomore campaign in which he slugged .310/.435/.532 at Baylor University. And with little to lose, Wendzel headed back to the school. And he put together an even better showing during his age-22 season. In 46 games for the Big12 Conference squad, the California native hit a career best .367/.484/.610 with 19 doubles, eight homeruns, and 11 stolen bases. Texas drafted him in the opening round, 41st overall, and signed him to a deal worth $1.6 million – just slightly below the recommended bonus. Wendzel appeared in just seven games between the Arizona Summer and Northwest Leagues, going 6-for-19 with a double and a dinger.

Scouting Report: A stocky, well-built third baseman. Wendzel has always shown a saber-slanted approach at the plate, offering up a bevy of walks with some power potential and solid contact rates. The problem, of course, is his age: he's already entering his age-23 season and has just seven professional games on his resume. With respect to his work in college last season, consider the following:

- Between 2011 and 2018, here's the list of Big12 hitters to slash at least .350/.450/.600 in a season (min. 200 PA): fellow 2019 first rounder – and current Rangers top prospect – Josh Jung, Sheldon Neuse, Grant Little, Kyle Gray, Matt Oberste, and Davis Wendzel.

The differentiator, of course, is his aforementioned age. Jung, for example, accomplished the feat as a 20-year-old. There's 50-grade power potential with a matching bat and plenty of walks. He's going to have to start to move quickly, but there's a non-zero chance he develops into a .270/.340/.430-type hitter.

Ceiling: 1.5- to 2.0-win player
Risk: Moderate
MLB ETA: 2022

10. Yerry Rodriguez, RHP

FB	SL	CH	Command	Overall
60	50/55	50/55	55	45

Born: 10/15/97	Age: 22	Bats: R
Height: 6-2	Weight: 198	Throws: R

YEAR	LVL	IP	W	L	SV	ERA	FIP	WHIP	K/9	K%	BB/9	BB%	K/BB	HR9	BABIP
2017	Rk	6.0	1	0	0	0.00	2.73	1.17	4.5	13.64%	1.5	4.55%	3.00	0.00	0.333
2018	Rk	38.3	2	2	0	3.52	1.93	1.07	12.9	34.81%	0.7	1.90%	18.33	0.23	0.381
2018	A-	24.7	3	0	0	1.82	3.14	1.09	9.9	26.47%	1.8	4.90%	5.40	0.73	0.299
2019	A	73.7	7	3	0	2.08	3.11	0.90	10.4	30.04%	2.6	7.42%	4.05	0.61	0.240

Background: Another one of the bargains the club's unearthed on the international scene. Rodriguez, a 6-foot-2, 198-pound right-hander out of Santiago, Dominican Republic, agreed to join the organization for just $60,000 in early September of 2015. Rodriguez languished in the foreign rookie league for two seasons, though he was limited to just a pair of appearances during his second stint, before moving stateside in 2018. He spent that year splitting time between the Arizona Summer and Northwest Leagues, throwing 63.0 innings with a whopping 82 punch outs against just eight free passes. The front office moved the slinging right-hander into the South Atlantic League last season. And the then-21-year-old more than held hisown. Unfortunately, a sprained UCL in his right elbow cut his season short. Rodriguez averaged 10.4 strikeouts and just 2.6 walks per nine innings in 13 starts. He finished the season with a 2.08 ERA and a dominating 2.57 DRA.

Scouting Report: Consider the following:

- Since 2006, only four pitchers have met the following criteria in the South Atlantic League (min. 50 IP): a strikeout percentage of at least 29% with a walk percentage between 6.5% and 8.5%. Those four pitchers: Miguel Del Pozo, Carlos Diaz, Eric Surkamp, and Yerry Rodriguez.

Prior to sustaining the elbow injury, Rodriguez showed a solid three-pitch mix: a plus, mid-90s fastball, a slider, and a changeup. Both secondary offerings are inconsistent, but show a lot of promise. (Note: many scouting reports I've seen refer to Rodriguez's breaking ball as a curveball; it appears to be a slider. The catcher signals with three fingers.) His slider will range from a solid-average grade to flashing plus depending on the day. And his changeup looked significantly better during one of his final starts than earlier in the year. Rodriguez is a strike-slinging machine with a loose arm. Assuming the sprained UCL won't hinder him in the future; Rodriguez looks like a potential backend starting pitcher with the floor of a high leverage setup reliever.

Ceiling: 1.5- to 2.0-win player
Risk: Moderate
MLB ETA: 2021/2022

11. Keithron Moss, IF

Hit	Power	SB	Patience	Glove	Overall
45/55	40/50	50	50/55	50	50

Born: 08/20/01	Age: 18	Bats: B
Height: 5-11	Weight: 165	Throws: R

YEAR	LVL	PA	1B	2B	3B	HR	SB	CS	AVG	OBP	SLG	BB%	K%	GB%	LD%	FB%
2018	RK	204	20	11	1	0	8	7	0.196	0.350	0.276	17.16%	30.39%	41.7	21.4	28.2
2019	Rk	147	28	4	3	2	8	2	0.308	0.425	0.442	14.29%	27.21%	48.8	25.6	25.6

Background: Over the past several summers there's been a variety of intriguing, athletically gifted ballplayers hailing from the Bahamas that have signed with big league organizations like: Lucius Fox, Jazz Chisholm, Kristian Robsinson, Tahnaj Thomas, D'Shawn Knowles, and Trent Deveaux immediately jump to the forefront of my mind. And it's time to add Keithron Moss's name to the list. From New Providence, Bahamas, the Rangers signed the switch-hitting infielder for $800,000 a couple years ago. After an absolutely, disgustingly atrocious debut in the Dominican Summer League in 2018 (he hit .196/.350/.276), the front office aggressively challenged the then-17-year-old and sent him into the Arizona Summer League. Moss promptly responded with one of top offensive showings in 2019. He slugged .308/.425/.442 with four doubles, three triples, two homeruns, and eight stolen bases (in 10 attempts) in only 34 games. Per *Deserved Runs Created Plus*, his overall production topped the league average threshold by a staggering 71%.

Scouting Report: How's this for impressive? Consider the following:

- Since 2006, here's the list of 17-year-old hitters to eclipse the 170 DRC+ threshold in the Arizona Summer League (min. 125 PA): Mike Trout, Marco Luciano, Heliot Ramos, Dorssys Paulino, and – of course – Keithron Moss, the youngster who barely hit his weight the previous season.

It's not all roses and bumblebees for Moss, however. His strikeout rate was ridiculously poor during his stint in the foreign rookie league (30.4%) and barely improved in the stateside rookie league last season (27.2%). And he gets a pass on some of that given the fact he's a young switch-hitter, but the K-rate needs to continue to trend downward as he progresses through the system. There's an intriguingly solid-across-the-board mix of tools for the young infielder. The potential for an above-average hit tool, something that approaches average power, some speed, and defensive chops.

Ceiling: 2.0-win player
Risk: Moderate to High
MLB ETA: 2022

12. A.J. Alexy, RHP

	FB	CB	CH	Command	Overall
	65	60	55	35/40	45

Born: 04/21/98	Age: 22	Bats: R
Height: 6-4	Weight: 195	Throws: R

YEAR	LVL	IP	W	L	SV	ERA	FIP	WHIP	K/9	K%	BB/9	BB%	K/BB	HR9	BABIP
2017	A	73.7	2	6	0	3.67	3.52	1.13	10.5	28.38%	4.5	12.21%	2.32	0.37	0.254
2017	A	20.7	1	1	0	3.05	5.12	1.35	11.8	30.34%	6.5	16.85%	1.80	1.31	0.233
2018	A	108.0	6	8	0	3.58	3.17	1.31	11.5	30.53%	4.3	11.50%	2.65	0.42	0.337
2019	A+	19.3	0	3	0	5.12	3.99	1.40	10.7	27.06%	6.1	15.29%	1.77	0.47	0.283

Background: Part of the mega-deal that sent Yu Darvish to the Dodgers for the stretch run in 2017. Alexy, who was acquired along with Willie Calhoun and Brendan Davis, was originally selected in the 11th round of the 2016 draft out of Twin Valley High School. The 6-foot-4, 195-pound right-hander showed some incredible promise as a 20-year-old in the South Atlantic League two years ago when he averaged 11.5 strikeouts and 4.3 walks per nine innings across 20 starts and a pair of relief appearances for the Hickory Crawdads. Texas bounced the hard-throwing youngster up to the Carolina League last season. And things went off the rails almost immediately. He didn't make it out of the fifth inning until his fourth start of the year and was shut down one appearance later with a severe lat strain – which would eventually cut his season short.

Snippet from The 2018 Prospect Digest Handbook: The control/command needs to continue to progress as he moves up the ladder, but it's been trending in the right direction. And despite some higher walk rates, Alexy isn't just a thrower only relying on a dominating fastball; he's not afraid to throw the curveball. As CAL pointed out, there's some Zack Wheeler/Aaron Sanchez type ceiling here.

Scouting Report: In terms of across the board arsenal, there are very few pitching prospects in the minor leagues that can go pitch-for-pitch, grade-for-grade with Alexy. His fastball is full of late life action and is thrown with a surprising amount of ease. His curveball is an absolute hammer, a gift from the baseball greats. And his changeup shows some impressive fade and downward run. But it doesn't really matter how awesome the repertoire is if he can't throw strikes. Alexy is still only entering his age-22 season, so there's some time left on his developmental clock. But he has to start showing some serious progress. He has the floor of a dominant, dominant high leverage, late-inning reliever – something along the lines of Luke Jackson's showing for the Braves in 2019.

Ceiling: 1.5- to 2.0-win player
Risk: Moderate to High
MLB ETA: 2021

13. Joe Palumbo, LHP

	FB	CB	CH	Command	Overall
	60	60	50	45	45

Born: 10/26/94	Age: 25	Bats: L
Height: 6-1	Weight: 168	Throws: L

YEAR	LVL	IP	W	L	SV	ERA	FIP	WHIP	K/9	K%	BB/9	BB%	K/BB	HR9	BABIP
2017	A+	13.7	1	0	0	0.66	1.05	0.59	14.5	44.00%	2.6	8.00%	5.50	0.00	0.167
2018	Rk	9.0	0	0	0	4.00	2.85	0.67	15.0	44.12%	1.0	2.94%	15.00	1.00	0.267
2018	A+	27.0	1	4	0	2.67	3.28	1.11	11.3	29.57%	2.0	5.22%	5.67	1.00	0.304
2018	AA	9.3	1	0	0	1.93	2.59	0.96	9.6	27.03%	2.9	8.11%	3.33	0.00	0.261
2019	AA	53.7	0	0	0	3.19	3.59	1.27	11.6	30.80%	4.2	11.16%	2.76	0.84	0.309
2019	AAA	27.0	3	0	0	2.67	4.05	0.85	13.0	38.24%	3.3	9.80%	3.90	1.33	0.188

Background: Joe Palumbo was selected in the 30th round, 910th overall, all the way back in 2013. Just to put that into proper perspective: that was the same draft class where Mark Appel and Kris Bryant went #1 and #2. So, yeah, it feels like an eternity ago. The oft-injured, seemingly always banged up southpaw spent time at the three highest levels of professional baseball last season, beginning with 10 starts in Class AA and then yo-yoing between Nashville and the Rangers. In total, he made 17 minor league appearances – all but one coming via the start – tossing 80.2 innings with a whopping 108 strikeouts and 35 walks. He made an additional seven appearances in The Show, fanning 21 and walking only eight to go along with a horrific-looking 9.18 ERA.

Snippet from The 2018 Prospect Digest Handbook: A little bit of Tim Collins in him. Palumbo isn't overly big – especially in the waist area – but he generates an above-average fastball and a wicked hammer-of-a-curveball. He'll also show an average changeup with some cutter-like movement down in the zone where it can be particularly deceptive. The Rangers have tried to handle Palumbo with the softest of kid gloves, but he's now entering his age-24 season without (A) a 100-inning campaign or (B) a year in which he's made more than 11 starts on his resume. Meaning: he's likely going to be ticketed as a three-pitch, long-man relief option. It's a shame, really, because there's some intriguing #4-type production if his body could hold up.

Scouting Report: Same story, different year. The New Jersey-native shows two plus-pitches – a 94 mph fastball and one helluva power curveball – and complements it with a workable changeup. And while his control/command isn't good, it's decent enough to work as a solid backend starting pitcher. But, again, he's worked almost exclusively as a starting pitcher as a professional, but he's failed to eclipse the 100-inning-threshold in seven seasons. Texas has Corey Kluber, Mike Minor, Lance Lynn, Kyle Gibson slotted as the top four starts with Jordan Lyles and Ariel Jurado duking it out for the fifth spot. Palumbo could fall – or be pushed – into that multiple inning, power-lefty role out of the pen.

Ceiling: 1.5-win player
Risk: Moderate
MLB ETA: Debuted in 2019

14. Sam Huff, C

	Hit	Power	SB	Patience	Glove	Overall
	40	60	35	45	55	45

Born: 01/14/98	**Age:** 22	**Bats:** R	
Height: 6-4	**Weight:** 230	**Throws:** R	

YEAR	LVL	PA	1B	2B	3B	HR	SB	CS	AVG	OBP	SLG	BB%	K%	GB%	LD%	FB%
2016	RK	117	20	10	1	1	0	0	0.330	0.436	0.485	13.68%	24.79%	59.4	26.1	14.5
2017	RK	225	29	9	2	9	3	2	0.249	0.329	0.452	10.67%	29.33%	34.3	18.7	38.1
2018	A	448	57	22	3	18	9	1	0.241	0.292	0.439	5.13%	31.25%	37.2	22.4	32.9
2019	A	114	16	5	0	15	4	1	0.333	0.368	0.796	5.26%	32.46%	29.6	26.8	36.6
2019	A+	405	64	17	2	13	2	5	0.262	0.326	0.425	6.67%	28.89%	46.0	18.4	31.2

Background: In a system chock full of high variance hitters that seemed to collectively ebb instead of flow last season, Huff stood out as a man among men. Taken by the franchise in the seventh round of the 2016 draft, the 6-foot-4, 230-pound backstop has always flirted with above-average or better power potential. He slugged .485 as an 18-year-old during his debut in the Arizona Summer League. Two years later he belted out 43 extra-base hits in 118 games with the Hickory Crawdads in the South Atlantic League. And last season his tool kit developed enough to where he was able to put together his finest campaign to date. Back in the Sally to start the year, Huff's Low Class A do over lasted 30 games before he was promoted up to the Carolina League. In total, the Arcadia High School product slugged .278/.335/.509 with 22 doubles, a pair of triples, and 28 homeruns. He also swiped six bags in 12 attempts as well.

Snippet from The 2018 Prospect Digest Handbook: Solid, above-average power from a position typically deficient of any type of wallop. But here's the problem: Huff's plate discipline continued its downward march from saber-friendly to Hell's Kitchen. And last year's peripherals – 5.1% walk rate; 31.3% strikeout rate – are downright scary.

Scouting Report: With respect to his work in High Class A, where he spent 97 of his 120 games in 2019, consider the following:

- Since 2006, here's the list of 21-year-old hitters to post a DRC+ total between 105 and 115 with at least a strikeout rate of 26% in the Carolina League (min. 350 PA): Jake Gatewood, Trayce Thompson, Isan Diaz, and – of course – Sam Huff.

Ignoring Huff momentarily, what do the other three hitters have in common? Toolsy, talented, athletic hitters that are – frankly – flawed. So what about Huff? Well, as I stated in last year's Handbook: "You're only as good as the company you keep." Plus in-game power that's become a consistent 25- to 30-homer threat each season. A cannon for an arm that threw out 48% of would-be base stealers last season. Strong glove behind the dish. But, of course, his contact issues are damning. He fanned in nearly a third of his plate appearances in his *do-over* in the Sally and he whiffed in just under 29% of the time in High Class A. Since 2017 his punch out rates have hovered between 29.9% and 32.5%. Throw in some subpar patience and the narrative for his future big league prospects are as dim as a fog-enveloped Bay Area shoreline. One final note: he fanned in 24 of his final 56 plate appearances.

Ceiling: 1.5-win player
Risk: Moderate
MLB ETA: 2021/2022

15. Steele Walker, CF

	Hit	Power	SB	Patience	Glove	Overall
	50	45	40	50	50	45

Born: 07/30/96	**Age:** 23	**Bats:** L	
Height: 5-11	**Weight:** 190	**Throws:** L	

YEAR	LVL	PA	1B	2B	3B	HR	SB	CS	AVG	OBP	SLG	BB%	K%	GB%	LD%	FB%
2018	RK	38	4	1	0	2	1	1	0.206	0.263	0.412	2.63%	18.42%	35.7	21.4	39.3
2018	RK	13	5	0	0	0	0	0	0.455	0.538	0.455	7.69%	7.69%	60.0	0.0	40.0
2018	A	126	13	5	0	3	5	1	0.186	0.246	0.310	6.35%	23.02%	39.1	17.2	34.5
2019	A	87	14	10	3	0	4	1	0.365	0.437	0.581	9.20%	17.24%	29.5	31.1	32.8
2019	A+	441	65	26	2	10	9	5	0.269	0.346	0.426	9.52%	14.29%	41.5	13.3	35.3

Background: In a bit of an odd trade that seems like the Rangers...didn't quite get enough of a return. Texas dealt young slugging outfielder – and former top prospect – Nomar Mazara to the White Sox for center fielder Steele Walker. Taken round pick out of the University of Oklahoma two years ago, Walker, who stands 5-foot-11 and 190 pounds, looked completely abysmal during his debut two years ago: he hit a lowly .209/.271/.342 with just 11 extra-base hits in 44 games between the Pioneer and South Atlantic Leagues. Last season, though, his production rebounded to match his lofty draft status – or at least, it came close to matching it. Walker ripped through the Sally to the tune of .365/.437/.581 in 20 games. And he settled in nicely for the remainder of the year in the Carolina League as he batted a respectable .269/.346/.426 with 26 doubles, two triples, 10 homeruns, and nine stolen bases. His overall production with the Winston-Salem Dash, per *Deserved Runs Created Plus*, was 26% better than the league average.

Snippet from The 2018 Prospect Digest Handbook: Walker has the potential to develop into a fringy starting outfielder – especially if he can stay in center field. He'll likely be a late first or early second round pick.

Scouting Report: Consider the following:

- Since 2006, here's the list of 22-year-old hitters to post a 120 to 130 DRC+ with a sub-16.0% strikeout rate in the Carolina League (min. 350 PA): Raudy Reed, Jordan Smith, and Steele Walker.

The former sooner looked like a 45-grade center fielder coming out of college. And nothing's changed since then. It's a bit surprising that the Rangers were enamored enough to deal away perennial 20-homer threat in Nomar Mazara, but maybe they know something we don't. Walker looks like a .270/.320/.390-type center fielder, playing solid defense and sprinkling in a handful of stolen bases. One more thought: the lefty-swinging outfielder – much like the man he was traded for – struggled *mightily* against fellow southpaws.

Ceiling: 1.5-win player
Risk: Moderate
MLB ETA: 2022

16. Demarcus Evans, RHP

FB	CB	Command	Overall
60	65	40	45

Born: 10/22/96	Age: 23	Bats: R
Height: 6-4	Weight: 270	Throws: R

YEAR	LVL	IP	W	L	SV	ERA	FIP	WHIP	K/9	K%	BB/9	BB%	K/BB	HR9	BABIP
2017	Rk	5.7	0	1	0	11.12	4.92	2.12	15.9	33.33%	9.5	20.00%	1.67	0.00	0.500
2017	A-	24.3	0	2	0	2.59	2.96	0.99	9.2	25.00%	3.3	9.00%	2.78	0.00	0.231
2017	A	29.7	2	5	0	4.85	3.80	1.58	14.0	32.86%	7.6	17.86%	1.84	0.30	0.328
2018	A	56.0	4	1	9	1.77	1.51	0.98	16.6	46.82%	4.3	12.27%	3.81	0.16	0.307
2019	A+	22.3	4	0	6	0.81	2.08	1.16	16.1	44.44%	6.9	18.89%	2.35	0.00	0.273
2019	AA	37.7	2	0	6	0.96	2.70	0.96	14.3	42.86%	5.3	15.71%	2.73	0.48	0.203

Background: Fun Fact Part I: Evans, a 25th round pick by the ballclub in 2015, finished third in strikeout percentage (42.5%) and fourth in strikeout rate (15.0 K/9) among all minor league arms with at least 50.0 innings pitched last season. Fun Fact Part II: Since converting into a full-time reliever at the start of 2018, the rotund right-hander has whiffed 44.5% of all the hitters he's faced. That's an incredible, mind-numbingly absurd number. To put that into a bit of context: Josh Hader led all MLB arms with a 47.8% K-percentage in 2019 (min. 50 IP). And now the bad news: Evans has walked – on average – 5.12 hitters every nine innings over the past two years. Or in other words: just a smidgeon over 14.5% of the hitters he's faced. Last season, he split time between Down East and Frisco, posting a 100-to-39 strikeout-to-walk ratio in only 60.0 innings of work. He tallied an aggregate 0.90 ERA.

Scouting Report: I've watched hundreds of minor league pitchers last season, something upwards of 350. Evans' heater is the single most fascinating pitch I've scouted. He's a full-time, all-the-time, max-effort reliever. And judging by the continual late swings-and-misses by the hitters, you'd guess his fastball would be sitting – easily – in the upper-90s, maybe even reaching triple digits at times. But it's not even close to that. I saw him blow a fastball by a quality minor league bat at 90 mph. It'll generally hover in the 93-mph range. But it's the heaviest, liveliest fastball I scouted. The RPMs, I'm assuming, are off the chart. High fastballs, wipeout plus curveballs low. Everyone in the park knows his pattern and hitters still can't touch him. 40-control is generous. And his weight is bordering on a concern. But there's some high leverage innings brewing in his 270-pound, 6-foot-4 frame. I love this kid.

Ceiling: 1.5-win player
Risk: Moderate
MLB ETA: 2020

17. Ryan Garcia, RHP

FB	CB	SL	CH	Command	Overall
50	50	55	50	55/60	45

Born: 01/24/98	Age: 22	Bats: R
Height: 6-0	Weight: 180	Throws: R

YEAR	LVL	IP	W	L	SV	ERA	FIP	WHIP	K/9	K%	BB/9	BB%	K/BB	HR9	BABIP
2019	Rk	1.0	0	0	0	9.00	3.25	2.00	18.0	40.00%	9.0	20.00%	2.00	0.00	0.500
2019	A-	4.0	0	0	0	2.25	1.37	0.75	13.5	42.86%	2.3	7.14%	6.00	0.00	0.286

Background: A stalwart and consistent mainstay atop the UCLA Bruins' rotation for his final two seasons in college. The slight-framed right-hander was particularly dominant during his junior campaign for the Pac12 ballclub. Making a career high 13 starts, along with three additional relief appearances, the California native posted an absurd 117-to-26 strikeout-to-walk ratio with a barely-there 1.44 ERA with a dominating 10-1 win-loss record. And that performance comes on the heels of his ridiculous showing in the Cape Cod League the previous summer when he averaged 10.6 strikeouts and just 2.9 walks per nine innings for the Wareham Gatemen. Texas grabbed the right-hander in the second round last June. He pitched just five brief low level innings during his debut.

Scouting Report: Sort of a dying breed. Garcia's the type of pitcher that, say, five to ten years ago, would have been a lock as a mid-first round selection. He's a pitcher's pitcher. He commands the strike zone incredibly well, shows four average or better offerings, and has a solid idea on how he wants to approach each hitter. Plus, he has a lengthy track record against some of the best collegiate talent around. The reality of the situation, however, is pitchers with average 88- to 90-mph fastballs that bump 92 at times just aren't viewed in the same light as they once were. He complements the heater with a plus slider, a curveball, and changeup – the latter two firmly in the 50-grade territory. Best case scenario: He's Mike Leake. Worst case: Adam Plutko, which still provides plenty of value to a big league team. Garcia should move quickly.

Ceiling: 1.5-win player
Risk: Moderate
MLB ETA: 2021

18. Jonathan Hernandez, RHP

FB	SL	CH	Command	Overall
60	55	45	45	40

Born: 07/06/96	Age: 23	Bats: R
Height: 6-2	Weight: 175	Throws: R

YEAR	LVL	IP	W	L	SV	ERA	FIP	WHIP	K/9	K%	BB/9	BB%	K/BB	HR9	BABIP
2017	A	46.3	2	5	0	4.86	3.79	1.47	8.9	23.12%	2.5	6.53%	3.54	0.97	0.370
2017	A+	65.3	3	6	0	3.44	3.35	1.48	8.8	22.70%	4.3	10.99%	2.06	0.28	0.350
2018	A+	57.3	4	2	0	2.20	2.97	0.94	12.1	35.16%	2.7	7.76%	4.53	0.94	0.263
2018	AA	64.0	4	4	0	4.92	4.76	1.47	8.0	20.58%	5.1	13.00%	1.58	0.84	0.299
2019	AA	96.0	5	9	0	5.16	4.30	1.44	8.9	22.73%	3.6	9.09%	2.50	1.03	0.331

Background: An international free agent that was added to the organization for $300,000 in 2013. And since then, the wiry right-hander has slowly moved through the Rangers' farm system – something that's become an oddity for young, promising prospects in the organization. Hernandez spent his first two seasons in the Dominican Summer League, parts of two seasons in Low Class A, another two stints in High Class A, and – finally – parts of two seasons in Class AA. Last season, the Memphis, Tennessee, native split time between the Texas League and a nine-game cameo with the Rangers. He made 22 appearances with the Frisco RoughRiders, 16 of which were starts, throwing 96.0 innings with 95 strikeouts, 38 walks, and a 5.16 ERA. He compiled an unsightly 5.16 DRA (*Deserved Runs Average*). In his brief stint with the Rangers, Hernandez posted a 19-to-13 strikeout-to-walk ratio in 16.2 innings of work.

Snippet from The 2018 Prospect Digest Handbook: He's more of a control pitcher, rather than one that commands the zone. He's still incredibly young – he's entering his age-22 season with sometime in Class AA – but he looks like future middle relief option, at best.

Scouting Report: Consider the following:

- Since 2006, here's the list of 22-year-old pitchers to post a strikeout percentage between 22% and 24% with a walk percentage between 8% and 10% in the Texas League (min. 75 IP): Jon Gray, the former top prospect and current Rockies stud, and – surprisingly – Jonathan Hernandez.

Well...I didn't see that one coming. And, frankly, I'm not sure anyone else would have suspected that comparison either. The differentiating factor, though, is the arsenal. Hernandez's three-pitch mix simply doesn't match up. The Rangers' young hurler shows a mid- to upper-90s fastball, an above-average upper-80s slider, and a below-average, too firm changeup. The Rangers' rotation is currently filled with the likes of Corey Kluber, Mike Minor, Lance Lynn, Kyle Gibson, and the fifth spot will come down to Jordan Lyles or Ariel Jurado – which, of course, leaves Hernandez back in the minor leagues or fighting for a spot in the pen. Hernandez has a chance to be a backend starting pitcher, though he's going to end up as a nice eighth inning arm.

Ceiling: 1.0- to 1.5-win player
Risk: Low to Moderate
MLB ETA: Debuted in 2019

19. Tyler Phillips, RHP

	FB	CB	CH	Command	Overall
	50	50	60	60	40

Born: 10/27/97	Age: 22	Bats: R
Height: 6-5	Weight: 191	Throws: R

YEAR	LVL	IP	W	L	SV	ERA	FIP	WHIP	K/9	K%	BB/9	BB%	K/BB	HR9	BABIP
2017	A-	73.0	4	2	0	3.45	3.21	1.22	9.6	25.24%	1.4	3.56%	7.09	0.74	0.338
2017	A	25.3	1	2	0	6.39	5.03	1.46	5.3	12.82%	3.2	7.69%	1.67	0.71	0.302
2018	A	128.0	11	5	0	2.67	2.33	1.02	8.7	24.22%	1.0	2.73%	8.86	0.28	0.308
2018	A+	5.0	1	0	0	1.80	3.96	0.80	5.4	15.79%	3.6	10.53%	1.50	0.00	0.154
2019	A+	37.7	2	2	0	1.19	2.79	0.90	6.7	20.00%	1.4	4.29%	4.67	0.24	0.260
2019	AA	93.3	7	9	0	4.73	4.72	1.23	7.1	19.12%	1.9	5.17%	3.70	1.45	0.292

Background: A sixteenth round selection out of Bishop Eustace Preparatory School in Pennsauken, New Jersey, five years ago. Phillips, a 6-foot-5, 191-pound crafty right-hander, leapt up a lot of prospect lists after a dynamite 2018 campaign when he posted a 127-to-16 strikeout-to-walk ratio in 133.0 innings – all but five of them coming in the South Atlantic League. Last season Phillips picked up right where he left off in High Class A: he struck out 28 and walked just six in 37.2 innings. The front office bumped the changeup artist up to Class AA, the minors' toughest challenge, in the middle of May for the remainder of the year. He would make a total of 18 appearances for the Frisco RoughRiders, throwing 93.1 innings with 74 strikeouts and just 20 walks to go along with a 4.73 ERA and a 5.29 DRA (*Deserved Run Average*).

Snippet from The 2018 Prospect Digest Handbook: Control/command pitchers like this tend to feast off of the lesser experienced hitters in the lower levels of the minor leagues, but there's a #4-type ceiling here.

Scouting Report: Consider the following:

- Since 2006, here's the list of 21-year-old pitchers to post a strikeout percentage between 18% and 20% with a sub-6.0% walk percentage in any of the Class AA leagues (min. 75 IP): Henderson Alvarez, Collin Balester, Alex Sanabia, and Tyler Phillips.

Elite-type control/command with a plus, sometimes devastatingly tricky changeup. The fastball and curveball are average, bland, nothing to write home about. Phillips is now staring down a #5-type starting gig. The heater and breaking ball need to be perfect because there's not a lot of room for error.

Ceiling: 1.0- to 1.5-win player
Risk: Moderate
MLB ETA: 2020

20. Sherten Apostel, 1B/3B

	Hit	Power	SB	Patience	Glove	Overall
	45	55	30	55	45+	40

Born: 03/11/99	Age: 21	Bats: R
Height: 6-4	Weight: 200	Throws: R

YEAR	LVL	PA	1B	2B	3B	HR	SB	CS	AVG	OBP	SLG	BB%	K%	GB%	LD%	FB%
2017	RK	259	26	12	4	9	4	5	0.258	0.422	0.495	21.62%	18.92%	47.4	18.4	27.6
2018	RK	175	22	7	0	7	3	1	0.259	0.406	0.460	18.29%	24.00%	54.1	17.3	25.5
2018	A-	49	11	1	0	1	0	1	0.351	0.469	0.459	18.37%	16.33%	51.6	25.8	19.4
2019	A	319	44	13	1	15	2	1	0.258	0.332	0.470	8.78%	22.26%	40.5	21.9	31.2
2019	A+	159	22	5	1	4	0	0	0.237	0.352	0.378	14.47%	30.82%	47.1	23.5	27.1

Background: A trade deadline pickup with Taylor Hearn from the Pittsburgh Pirates for veteran right-hander reliever Keone Kela two years ago. Apostel, who was the Player To Be Named Later in the deal, showed some offensive promise during his stints with Bristol and Spokane in 2018 when he batted .287/.420/.460 with eight doubles and eight homeruns. Last season the 6-foot-4, 200-pound corner infielder split time between Hickory and Down East, slugging an aggregate .251/.339/.440 with 18 doubles, a pair of triples, and 19 homeruns. He also swiped a pair of bags in three attempts as well.

Scouting Report: With respect to his work in the Sally last season, consider the following:

- Since 2006, here's the list of 20-year-old hitters to post a 115 to 125 DRC+ with a walk percentage between 8% and 10% strikeout percentage between 21% and 24% in the South Atlantic League (min. 300 PA): Deivi Grullon, Brandon Snyder, Darren Ford, and Sherten Apostel.

Exactly the type of player a team should gamble as a PTBNL. The 6-foot-4, 200-pound first/third baseman offers up an intriguing power bat with some average-ish contact numbers and some damn fine walk rates. Most guys don't like this don't pan out, but if Apostel can maintain his positional versatility – or stay at the hot corner – it significantly improves Apostel's odds. One final thought: he shows a willingness to spray the ball all around the field.

Ceiling: 1.0- to 1.5-win player
Risk: Moderate
MLB ETA: 2022

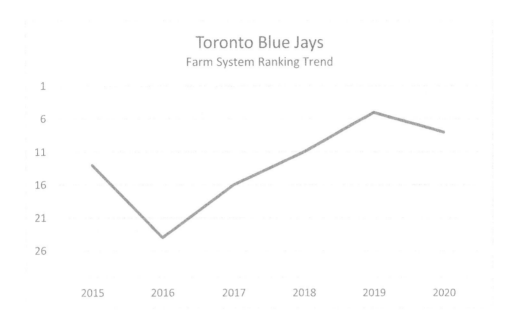

Toronto Blue Jays
Farm System Ranking Trend

Rank	Name	Age	Pos
1	Nate Pearson	23	RHP
2	Jordan Groshans	20	SS
3	Simeon Woods Richardson	19	RHP
4	Orelvis Martinez	18	3B/SS
5	Gabriel Moreno	20	C
6	Eric Pardinho	19	RHP
7	Alejandro Kirk	21	C
8	Anthony Kay	25	LHP
9	Alek Manoah	22	RHP
10	Adam Kloffenstein	19	RHP
11	Kendall Williams	25	RHP
12	Miguel Hiraldo	19	2B/SS
13	Maximo Castillo	21	RHP
14	Otto Lopez	21	2B/SS
15	Leonardo Jimenez	19	2B/SS
16	Yennsy Diaz	23	RHP
17	Reese McGuire	25	C
18	Riley Adams	24	C
19	Hector Perez	24	RHP
20	Griffin Conine	22	RF

1. Nate Pearson, RHP

FB	CB	SL	CH	Command	Overall
80	50	65	50	50/55	70

Born: 08/20/96	Age: 23	Bats: R
Height: 6-6	Weight: 245	Throws: R

YEAR	LVL	IP	W	L	SV	ERA	FIP	WHIP	K/9	K%	BB/9	BB%	K/BB	HR9	BABIP
2017	Rk	1.0	0	0	0	0.00	-0.58	1.00	18.0	50.00%	0.0	0.00%	N/A	0.00	0.500
2017	A-	19.0	0	0	0	0.95	2.05	0.58	11.4	35.82%	2.4	7.46%	4.80	0.00	0.158
2018	A+	1.7	0	1	0	10.80	10.07	3.00	5.4	10.00%	0.0	0.00%	N/A	5.40	0.500
2019	A+	21.0	3	0	0	0.86	1.64	0.62	15.0	46.67%	1.3	4.00%	11.67	0.86	0.229
2019	AA	62.7	1	4	0	2.59	2.89	0.99	9.9	28.28%	3.0	8.61%	3.29	0.57	0.250
2019	AAA	18.0	1	0	0	3.00	4.07	0.83	7.5	21.74%	1.5	4.35%	5.00	1.00	0.208

Background: Not all paths to stardom are the same. Coming out of Bishop McLaughlin Catholic High School, the flame-throwing right-hander (A) didn't possess a plus-plus fastball and (B) wasn't highly recruited. Instead, Pearson settled in for a season at Florida International University, showing decent production as a full-time reliever; he posted a 33-to-12 strikeout-to-walk ratio in 33.1 innings of work. Following his freshman season the 6-foot-6, 245-pound hurler transferred to Central Florida Community College where – of course – he posted absurdly ridiculous numbers: he was named JuCo Pitcher of the Year by *Perfect Game* while fanning 118 to go along with a 1.56 ERA. And, yet, the world wasn't clamoring. The triple-digit-touching Pearson lasted until the back of the first round, 28th overall, three years ago. The Odessa, Florida, native dominated the low levels during his debut, and looked poised for big things in 2018. But a line drive broke his right ulna, ending his campaign in early May. And that comes on the heels of an earlier oblique injury. Last season, though, Pearson quickly made up for any lost time – finding the deserving hype along the way. Making stops at the three highest minor league levels, he started 25 games, throwing 101.2 innings with 119 strikeouts against just 27 walks. He compiled an aggregate 2.30 ERA.

Snippet from The 2018 Prospect Digest Handbook: Unlike a lot of other throwers who show the potential to touch triple-digits, Pearson – generally – keeps the ball around the strike zone. He has the arsenal to ascend towards the top of a rotation, but he'll need to continue to prove he can consistently throw his breaking pitches for quality strikes – which he's done thus far.

Scouting Report: An abnormally strong feel for the strike for a pitcher with a premium arsenal. Pearson, who works entirely from the stretch, pounded the zone with the regularity of a crafty, 15-year veteran. The fastball's an easy 80-grade. His slider showed improved tilt and late bite, pushing it closely to a second plus-plus offering. His curveball and firm, upper-80s changeup are solid average weapons. Pearson has a legitimate chance to ascend to a bonafide, true #1 starting pitcher. With respect to his work in Class AA, where he spent the lion's share of 2019, consider the following:

- Since 2006, only two 22-year-old pitchers posted a strikeout percentage between 27% and 29% with a walk percentage between 7.5% and 9.5% in the Eastern League (min. 50 IP): Mike Pelfrey, the ninth overall pick in the 2005 draft who pitched 12 seasons in the big leagues, and – of course – Nate Pearson.

Ceiling: 6.0-win player
Risk: Moderate
MLB ETA: 2020

2. Jordan Groshans, SS

Hit	Power	SB	Patience	Glove	Overall
50/55	50/55	30	50+	50	60

Born: 11/10/99	Age: 20	Bats: R
Height: 6-3	Weight: 205	Throws: R

YEAR	LVL	PA	1B	2B	3B	HR	SB	CS	AVG	OBP	SLG	BB%	K%	GB%	LD%	FB%
2018	RK	48	6	1	0	1	0	0	0.182	0.229	0.273	4.17%	16.67%	45.9	13.5	32.4
2018	RK	159	31	12	0	4	0	0	0.331	0.390	0.500	8.18%	18.24%	44.3	13.9	35.7
2019	A	96	20	6	0	2	1	1	0.337	0.427	0.482	13.54%	21.88%	48.4	30.6	19.4

Background: The first high school shortstop off the board two years ago. Groshans, the 12th overall pick, made the transition into the professional ranks look as smooth and easy as water drops dripping off a freshly waxed Camaro. The 6-foot-3, 205-pound middle infielder slugged an impressive .296/.353/.446 during stints in the Gulf Coast and Appalachian Leagues – though the overwhelming majority of damage was done in former. Last season Groshans picked up right where he left off: he posted an eye-catching .337/.427/.482 with six doubles and a pair of homeruns in only 23 games. A stress injury to the navicular bone in his left foot curtailed his hot start and prematurely ended his season in early May.

Snippet from The 2018 Prospect Digest Handbook: A lean prospect who's likely going to fill out in the coming years, which could ultimately push him to the hot corner permanently, Groshans looks fluid in the field, showing smooth reflexes. The 6-foot-3, 178-pound infield has a short, compact swing at the plate with natural loft that should allow him to his 20 to 25 homeruns during his peak. And he didn't show any major red flags during his debut, including during his stumble in the Appalachian League.

Scouting Report: A year later and there's really nothing else to add to the scouting report because the sample sizes are still unreliable at this point. But Groshans is flashing an impressive skill set that may end up with two above-average tools (hit and power) and a couple strong 50-grades in his glove and speed. And despite the limited – albeit dominating – 2019 season, it wouldn't be surprising to see the Blue Jays push the young shortstop up to High Class A at the start of 2020.

Ceiling: 4.0-win player
Risk: Moderate to High
MLB ETA: 2022

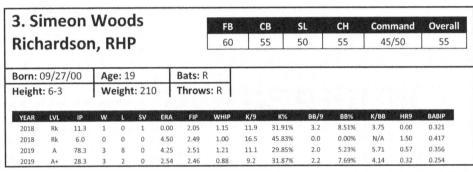

3. Simeon Woods Richardson, RHP

FB	CB	SL	CH	Command	Overall
60	55	50	55	45/50	55

Born: 09/27/00	Age: 19	Bats: R
Height: 6-3	Weight: 210	Throws: R

YEAR	LVL	IP	W	L	SV	ERA	FIP	WHIP	K/9	K%	BB/9	BB%	K/BB	HR9	BABIP
2018	Rk	11.3	1	0	1	0.00	2.05	1.15	11.9	31.91%	3.2	8.51%	3.75	0.00	0.321
2018	Rk	6.0	0	0	0	4.50	2.49	1.00	16.5	45.83%	0.0	0.00%	N/A	1.50	0.417
2019	A	78.3	3	8	0	4.25	2.51	1.21	11.1	29.85%	2.0	5.23%	5.71	0.57	0.356
2019	A+	28.3	3	2	0	2.54	2.46	0.88	9.2	31.87%	2.2	7.69%	4.14	0.32	0.254

Background: Part of the return the Jays received from the Mets in the Marcus Stroman megadeal near the trade deadline last July. Woods Richardson, who was acquired along with promising left-hander Anthony Kay, capped off a wildly successful first full season in professional ball by reaching High Class A during his age-19 season. Taken with the fifth pick of the second round two years ago, the broad-shouldered, "built-like a NFL tight end" right-hander began the year on a sour note: he failed to make it out of the second inning against the Charleston RiverDogs. And a few starts later Woods Richardson hit a rough patch by allowing 25 earned runs in 20.2 innings of work. After that, though, it was smooth, dominat sailing. He finished the year by posting an 82-to-17 strikeout-to-walk ratio with a 2.27 ERA over his final 71.1 innings of work – which included six strong starts with Dunedin.

Snippet from The 2018 Prospect Digest Handbook: The Kempner High School product shows a plus-fastball and a pair of secondary offerings that flash above-average on occasion – a sharp curveball and a fading changeup, the latter showing more promise as another swing-and-miss pitch. Wood Richardson's shown the rare ability of throwing both offspeed pitches for strikes, which may necessitate a quick rise through the lower levels. The promising youngster looks like a solid bet to develop into amid-rotation-caliber starting pitcher.

Scouting Report: An absolute bulldog on the mound that would make peak-career Orel Hershiser pause for a double take. Woods Richardson was on the short, short list of pitchers that I most looked forward to scouting in 2019. The former second rounder aggressively challenges hitters with an explosive mid-90s fastball, an above-average curveball, and a changeup that may peak as a plus-offering. He'll also mix in the rare 50-grade slider as well. With respect to his work in Low Class A last season, consider the following:

- Since 2006, only two 18-year-old pitchers posted a strikeout percentage between 29% and 31% with a walk percentage between 5% and 8% in either Low Class A league (min. 75 IP): Luis Patino, who's widely recognized as one of the top right-handed pitching prospects in baseball, and – of course Mr. Simeon Woods Richardson.

Barring any injuries or catastrophes, Toronto's going to come out far better in the Marcus Stroman trade.

Ceiling: 3.5-win player
Risk: Moderate
MLB ETA: 2020

4. Orelvis Martinez, 3B/SS

Hit	Power	SB	Patience	Glove	Overall
45/50	50/55	40/35	50	50	50

Born: 11/19/01	Age: 18	Bats: R
Height: 6-1	Weight: 188	Throws: R

YEAR	LVL	PA	1B	2B	3B	HR	SB	CS	AVG	OBP	SLG	BB%	K%	GB%	LD%	FB%
2019	Rk	163	19	8	5	7	2	0	0.275	0.352	0.549	8.59%	17.79%	44.3	16.5	33.0

Background: The normally reserved front office pushed all their chips to the center of the table and went all in – both literally and figuratively – when they signed the toolsy infielder during the 2018 summer. The cost: a hefty $3.5 million. Martinez, a native of Santo Domingo, Dominican Republic, made his highly anticipated professional debut in the Gulf Coast League last season; in 40 games the 6-foot-1, 188-pound shortstop/third baseman slugged an impressive .275/.352/.549 with eight doubles, five triples, seven homeruns, and a pair of stolen bases. Per *Deserved Runs Created Plus*, topped the league average mark by a whopping 40%.

Scouting Report: Consider the following:

- Since 2006, only three 17-year-old hitters met the following criteria in the Gulf Coast League (min. 150 PA): 135 to 145 DRC+; sub-20% K-rate; and a BB-rate between 6% to 9%. Those three hitters: Delvin Perez, Thairo Estrada, and Orelvis Martinez.

Really impressive power for a teenage bat, regardless of the level. Martinez may develop 25- to 30-homer thump in the coming years. And he combines that with surprisingly strong contact skills. Martinez also showed a willingness to walk as well. Defensively speaking, he's solid. Martinez has some above-average starting caliber potential. Perhaps even peaking as a borderline All-Star. Short quick swing with impressive bat speed due to his strong, twitchy wrists. He doesn't get cheated either.

Ceiling: 3.0-win player
Risk: Moderate
MLB ETA: 2022

5. Gabriel Moreno, C

	Hit	Power	SB	Patience	Glove	Overall
	50	50/55	40	45	50	50

Born: 02/14/00	Age: 20	Bats: R
Height: 5-11	Weight: 160	Throws: R

YEAR	LVL	PA	1B	2B	3B	HR	SB	CS	AVG	OBP	SLG	BB%	K%	GB%	LD%	FB%
2017	RK	135	26	4	1	0	5	4	0.248	0.274	0.296	4.44%	3.70%	54.0	14.5	24.2
2018	RK	66	10	5	0	2	1	0	0.279	0.303	0.459	4.55%	19.70%	36.0	28.0	30.0
2018	RK	101	22	12	2	2	1	1	0.413	0.455	0.652	3.96%	6.93%	39.5	23.3	32.6
2019	A	341	52	17	5	12	7	1	0.280	0.337	0.485	6.45%	11.14%	37.6	19.3	34.7

Background: A fascinating tale, as told by John Lott of *The Athletic*, Moreno is a recent convert to catching. Originally a middle infielder, a Jays scout saw Moreno during a workout and immediately envisioned a smooth operating backstop. And that scout, Francisco Plasencia, was spot on. Handed just $25,000 when the club signed him, Moreno put a mediocre debut showing in the foreign Dominican Summer League behind him by dominating – convincingly – a couple stateside rookie leagues: he slugged a scorching .359/.395/.575 with 17 doubles, a pair of triples, and a quartet of homeruns in 40 games. Last season Moreno continued to show some offensive firepower as he squared off against the Midwest League – as a 19-year-old. In 82 games with Lansing, the 5-foot-11, 160-pound catcher batted .280/.337/.485 with 17 doubles, five triples, 12 homeruns, and – just for good measure – seven stolen bases in eight attempts. Per Baseball Prospectus' *DRC+*, his overall production topped the league average mark by 30%.

Scouting Report: Consider the following:

- Since 2006, here's the list of 18-year-old hitters to post a DRC+ between 125 and 135 with a sub-8% walk rate and a strikeout rate of 15% of less in the Midwest League (min. 300 PA): Jorge Polanco, Hank Conger, Jake Hager, and – of course – Mr. Former Infielder Gabriel Moreno. Sans Moreno, here are their respective career DRC+ totals at the big league level: 103 (Polanco), Conger (89), and Hager never made it to The Show.

Here's the best part about Moreno's prospect status: he's graded out as a solid-average defender at each of his stops thus far and he's throwing out roughly one-third of all would-be base stealers as well. Offensively speaking, there's a whole lot to like – especially at a premier position. There's surprising thump in his wiry, 5-foot-11 frame; it's an easy 50 with maybe a little more in the tank. He can hit for average, run a little bit, and – most importantly – he wasn't overmatched against significantly older competition. There's definite starting caliber potential here with the ceiling of a .270/.330/.450 type hitter.

Ceiling: 3.0-win player
Risk: Moderate
MLB ETA: 2022

6. Eric Pardinho, RHP

	FB	CB	SL	CH	Command	Overall
	55	55	50/55	50	60	50

Born: 01/05/01	Age: 19	Bats: R
Height: 5-10	Weight: 155	Throws: R

YEAR	LVL	IP	W	L	SV	ERA	FIP	WHIP	K/9	K%	BB/9	BB%	K/BB	HR9	BABIP
2018	Rk	50.0	4	3	0	2.88	3.75	1.06	11.5	31.53%	2.9	7.88%	4.00	0.90	0.274
2019	Rk	4.0	1	0	0	0.00	3.25	1.00	11.3	35.71%	6.8	21.43%	1.67	0.00	0.167
2019	A	33.7	1	1	0	2.41	3.19	1.25	8.0	22.06%	3.5	9.56%	2.31	0.27	0.304

Background: The most poised teenage arm I've ever seen. Toronto signed the savvy youngster off the international free agent market for a hefty $1.4 million in early July 2017. The front office pushed the advanced prospect up to the Appalachian League for his debut two years ago. And

Pardinho, a 5-foot-10, 155-pound hurler, showcased the calm of a 15-year veteran. He made 11 starts for Bluefield, posting a 2.88 ERA and an impeccable 64-to-16 strikeout-to-walk ratio in 50.0 innings of work. It looked like he was poised for a multi-level, fast-paced 2019 season. But then a ligament in his elbow flared up. Elbow tightness, which would eventually be diagnosed as a strain, kept him out of action – though he did manage to avoid the surgeon's table – until late June. After a brief tune-up in the Gulf Coast League, Pardinho made seven solid starts with the Lansing Lugnuts, fanning 30 and walking 13 in 33.2 innings of work. Update: Pardinho underwent Tommy John surgery in mid-February.

Snippet from The 2018 Prospect Digest Handbook: Not only does Pardinho control *and* command the strike zone impressively well for any age, but he has the type of arsenal that screams future upper-rotation-type arm. His fastball sits comfortably in the low 90s and should see an uptick as he begins to fill out. His curveball, a solid 12-6 breaking ball, flashes plus. And his changeup is a strong third offering. The lone knock on Pardinho is his slight frame.

Scouting Report: Despite some impressive numbers in Low Class A as an 18-year-old last season, Pardinho, who averaged eight strikeouts and 3.5 walks per nine innings, didn't seem to fully trust his healed elbow. In a late-July start Pardinho's fastball was touching 94 with a surprising amount of ease and fluidity. A couple weeks later his heater was sitting in the 87- to 88-mph range. Pardinho is the type of pitcher to add and subtract velocity from his fastball, but it certainly needs to be monitored. Above-average fastball and curveball. A 50-grade changeup. And a slider that flashes above-average at times. One more thought: he's physically maxed out so the velocity's not likely going to climb much higher.

Ceiling: 3.0-win player
Risk: Moderate
MLB ETA: 2021/2022

7. Alejandro Kirk, C

	Hit	Power	SB	Patience	Glove	Overall
	50/55	45	30	45+	50	50

Born: 11/06/98	Age: 21	Bats: R	
Height: 5-9	Weight: 220	Throws: R	

YEAR	LVL	PA	1B	2B	3B	HR	SB	CS	AVG	OBP	SLG	BB%	K%	GB%	LD%	FB%
2017	RK	3	0	0	0	0	0	0	0.000	0.333	0.000	0.00%	0.00%	50.0	0.0	0.0
2018	RK	244	52	10	1	10	2	0	0.354	0.443	0.558	13.52%	8.61%	52.7	21.3	20.2
2019	A	96	13	6	1	3	1	0	0.299	0.427	0.519	18.75%	8.33%	44.3	12.9	32.9
2019	A+	276	38	25	0	4	2	0	0.288	0.395	0.446	13.77%	11.23%	41.5	25.0	30.5

Background: A short, stocky, almost loveable bowling ball of a backstop. The Mexican-born catcher burst onto the scene – largely out of the thin blue air – two years ago in the Appalachian League. The then-19-year-old slugged a hefty .354/.443/.558 with 10 doubles, a triple, and 10 homeruns in only 58 games of action. Kirk began last season in the Midwest League, but after slashing a healthy .299/.427/.519 in 21 games the front office bumped him up a level. In 71 games with the Dunedin Blue Jays, the young backstop slugged .288/.395/.446 with 25 doubles and four homeruns. According to *Deserved Runs Created Plus*, his overall production in High Class A topped the league average threshold by a whopping 54%.

Snippet from The 2018 Prospect Digest Handbook: Simply put, the 5-foot-9, 220-pound backstop was an unstoppable force at the plate, showcasing an impressive hit tool, above-average power, and elite bat control/patience. Plus, he was solid behind the dish as well.

Scouting Report: Consider the following:

- Since 2006, here's the list of 20-year-old hitters to post a 150 to 160 DRC+ with a double-digit walk rate and a strikeout rate below 20% in any High Class A league (min. 250 PA): Carter Kieboom, an easy Top 50 Prospect, Logan Morrison, who owns a 108 DRC+ in nearly 1,000 big league games, Chance Sisco, and Alejandro Kirk.

Quietly good, bordering on fantastic, and definitely underrated – even in his own system. Kirk's a do-everything-well-type of backstop without any glaring red flags: he's handled aggressive promotions; flashes solid pop; makes consistent, hard contact; and the hefty prospect moves efficiently behind the plate. Plus, he's thrown on nearly 40% of would-be base stealers in his young career. If there is a knock on Kirk, it's his weight. He's tipping the scales at a hearty 220 pounds, which wouldn't be terrible for someone over 6 feet. Kirk stands just 5-foot-9. There's a chance for a 55-grade hit tool and 50-grade power – a rare combination for a backstop.

Ceiling: 3.0-win player
Risk: Moderate
MLB ETA: 2021/2022

8. Anthony Kay, LHP

	FB	CB	CH	Command	Overall
	60	70	55	45	50

Born: 03/21/95	Age: 25	Bats: L
Height: 6-0	Weight: 218	Throws: L

YEAR	LVL	IP	W	L	SV	ERA	FIP	WHIP	K/9	K%	BB/9	BB%	K/BB	HR9	BABIP
2018	A	69.3	4	4	0	4.54	3.55	1.37	10.1	26.00%	2.9	7.33%	3.55	0.78	0.356
2018	A+	53.3	3	7	0	3.88	3.66	1.46	7.6	19.48%	4.6	11.69%	1.67	0.17	0.321
2019	AA	66.3	7	3	0	1.49	2.71	0.92	9.5	26.72%	3.1	8.78%	3.04	0.27	0.224
2019	AAA	31.3	1	3	0	6.61	6.21	1.63	7.5	18.57%	3.2	7.86%	2.36	2.01	0.355
2019	AAA	36.0	2	2	0	2.50	4.54	1.53	9.8	24.53%	5.5	13.84%	1.77	0.75	0.323

Background: The deal that sent Marcus Stroman to the Mets last trade deadline is atypical because the return wasn't based upon one blue chip caliber prospect and a lesser minor leaguer or two. Instead, the Blue Jays received Prospect 1A and Prospect 1B. Kay, who was acquired along with fast-rising teenage right-hander Simeon Woods Richardson, quickly made up for missed time from his successful Tommy John surgery. After missing all of 2017 recovering from the procedure, the stocky southpaw split time between the South Atlantic and Florida State Leagues during his return to action. And last season the former University of Connecticut ace spent time in Class AA, Class AAA, and earned a three-game cameo with the Jays down the stretch. In total, he tossed 133.2 innings in the minor leagues, posting a 135-to-56 strikeout-to-walk ratio. And he fanned 13 and walked five in 14.0 big league innings.

Snippet from The 2018 Prospect Digest Handbook: Kay's progressing towards that #3/#4-type ceiling. Last season his fastball looked a bit quicker than advertised, using a combination of tunneling/deception/a healthy elbow to generate a lot of late swings. His command/control wasn't as sharp as it's been in the past, though some of that's due to the elbow procedure and time off. He also fields the position well and shows a strong pickoff move to first.

Scouting Report: Once again Kay's heater surpassed my expectations. Multiple times during his minor league stint Kay's fastball was bumping 95 with some impressive late life. His curveball, a plus-plus pitch, is similar to that of veteran southpaw Rich Hill – except hard, with more bite. And his changeup, a strong 55-grade, shows consistent dive and – at times – cutting action. Kay has nothing left to prove at the minor league level. And he's coming off of back-to-back years in which he's thrown at least 120.0 innings, so any lingering concerns about the elbow should be quelled. In terms of ceiling/production think of something similar to Joey Lucchesi's 2019 showing with the Padres when he averaged 8.69 K/9 and 3.18 BB/9 with a 4.18 ERA.

Ceiling: 2.5-win player
Risk: Low to Moderate
MLB ETA: Debuted in 2019

9. Alek Manoah, RHP

	FB	SL	CH	Command	Overall
	60	60	50/55	45+	50

Born: 01/09/98	Age: 22	Bats: R
Height: 6-6	Weight: 260	Throws: R

YEAR	LVL	IP	W	L	SV	ERA	FIP	WHIP	K/9	K%	BB/9	BB%	K/BB	HR9	BABIP
2019	A-	17.0	0	1	0	2.65	2.44	1.06	14.3	45.00%	2.6	8.33%	5.40	0.53	0.379

Background: The burly righty accomplished something that only one other player has done in West Virginia University school history, Manoah joined Chris Enochs as the only members of Mountaineers to hear their names called in the first round. Enochs, by the way, was the 11th overall player chosen in the 1997 draft. Standing a barroom brawler-esque 6-foot-6 and 260 pounds, Manoah, a native of Miami, Florida, began turning heads as a junior playing for South Dade. That year, 2015, he was named to the First-Team ABCA Rawlings All-American and Under Armour All-American Teams. And he would eventually be ranked by Perfect Game as the 82nd overall best prospect nationally and 27th best right-hander. Manoah spent his first two seasons with the Mountaineers bouncing between the school's rotation and bullpen, making a total of 42 appearances, 18 of which were starts. As a true freshman the big right-hander posted a mediocre 45-to-33 strikeout-to-walk ratio in 55.2 innings of work. He followed that up with an impressive sophomore campaign: in a career-best 23 appearances for skipper Randy Mazey, Manoah struck out 60 and walked 28 in 54.0 innings. He spent the ensuing summer, 2018, playing with Michael Busch and Kyle McCann on the Chatham Anglers. In seven starts the hard-throwing hurler posted a dominating 48-to-11 strikeout-to-walk ratio in just over 33 innings while leading the league in punch outs. Last season Manoah, who's older brother Erik Jr pitches in the Angels' organization, honed in on the strike zone with ace-like precision: he finished his collegiate career with a 144-to-27 strikeout-to-walk ratio with a 2.08 ERA in 108.1 innings of work. Toronto drafted Manoah with the 11th overall pick last June. He made six brief starts in the Northwest League, throwing 17.0 innings with 27 strikeouts and five walks.

Scouting Report: Here's what I wrote prior to the draft last June:

"Not overly worked at this point in his collegiate career, Manoah's very likely going to be limited to just a handful of appearances this season – if any at all – once he officially enters the professional thanks to the increase in his workload. Working primarily from the stretch, Manoah shows an impressive three-pitch repertoire: a lively low- to mid-90s fastball, a hard-breaking slider with two-plane depth, and a decent fading changeup. With respect to his production thus far in 2019, consider the following:

- *Between 2011 and 2018, here's the list of Division I hurlers to average 11.5 to 12 K/9 and 2.75 to 3.25 BB/9 (min. 75 IP): Oliver Jaskie, Luke Leftwich, and Mariano Rivera, the Hall of Famer's son. Jaskie was taken in the sixth round in 2017. Leftwich was drafted in the seventh round in 2015. And Rivera was snagged by the Nationals in the fourth round four years ago.*

Obviously, it's a less-than-stellar collection of arms. Manoah's an interesting prospect: there's still a little bit of projection left thanks to his limited work as a starting pitcher over his first two seasons. The changeup and command to need to another step forward if he's going to reach his full potential as a #3/#4-type starting pitcher. There's some risk, though, as he could very easily slide back into a relief role eventually."

Ceiling: 2.5- to 3.0-win player
Risk: Moderate
MLB ETA: 2022

10. Adam Kloffenstein, RHP

	FB	CB	SL	CH	Command	Overall
	60	50/55	55	55	50	50

Born: 08/25/00	Age: 19	Bats: R
Height: 6-5	Weight: 243	Throws: R

YEAR	LVL	IP	W	L	SV	ERA	FIP	WHIP	K/9	K%	BB/9	BB%	K/BB	HR9	BABIP
2018	Rk	2.0	0	0	0	0.00	2.64	1.50	18.0	44.44%	9.0	22.22%	2.00	0.00	0.333
2019	A-	64.3	4	4	0	2.24	3.70	1.09	9.0	24.71%	3.2	8.88%	2.78	0.56	0.262

Background: The young right-hander hit every check box imaginable coming out of the draft two years ago: big and projectable; a bevy of quality pitches; solid control; and at 17-years-ohd, he was young for the draft. And Kloffenstein, who stands 6-foot-5 and 243 pounds, is continuing to hit the necessary check boxes. Last season the then-18-year-old hurler posted an impressive 64-to-23 strikeout-to-walk ratio in 64.1 innings across 13 starts in the Appalachian League. He finished his tenure with the Vancouver Canadians with a 2.24 ERA and a 3.03 DRA (*Deserved Run Average*). He was particularly dominant over his final four starts of the year as well, fanning 27 and walking just five in 23.0 innings of work.

Snippet from The 2018 Prospect Digest Handbook: Already owning four pitches with above-average or better potential. Kloffenstein shows impressive composure and clean, repeatable mechanics. His fastball overpowered fellow prep prospects and he commanded his tightly-spun slider exceptionally well. Kloffenstein has the make and build as a mid-rotation caliber arm.

Scouting Report: Consider the following:

- Since 2006, only two 18-year-old pitchers post a strikeout percentage between 24% and 26% in the Appalachian League (min. 50 IP): Alex Burnett, who spent parts of four seasons in the big leagues, and – of course – Adam Kloffenstein.

Kloffenstein's fastball was touching the mid-90s last season; his curveball showed flashes of above-average; his slider's a swing-and-miss pitch; and his changeup is quietly strong. Throw in a solid feel for the strike zone and Kloffenstein has the makings of a #4-type starting pitcher. He's poised to be one of the bigger breakouts in 2020.

Ceiling: 2.0- to 2.5-win player
Risk: Moderate
MLB ETA: 2022

11. Kendall Williams, RHP

FB	CB	CH	Command	Overall
55/60	55/60	50	45	50

Born: 08/24/00	Age: 19	Bats: R
Height: 6-6	Weight: 205	Throws: R

YEAR	LVL	IP	W	L	SV	ERA	FIP	WHIP	K/9	K%	BB/9	BB%	K/BB	HR9	BABIP
2019	Rk	16.0	0	0	0	1.13	2.62	0.81	10.7	30.16%	3.9	11.11%	2.71	0.00	0.167

Background: Last year was an exceptional one for Bradenton, Florida, force IMG Academy. The school had not one, not two, not three – but *six* players chosen in the June amateur draft, including one first rounder (Brennan Malone, Arizona Diamondbacks), and a pair of second rounders (Rece Hinds, Cincinnati Reds) and Kendall Williams (Toronto Blue Jays). Williams, the 52nd overall selection, was committed to the Vanderbilt University – a.ka. Pitcher U. – before the club signed him to a hefty $1.55 million deal – just slightly above the recommended bonus. The 6-foot-6, 205-pound right-hander tossed 46.0 innings during his senior season, posting a 69-to-15 strikeout-to-walk ratio with a 0.91 ERA. Williams made six brief appearances in the Gulf Coast League, posting a 19-to-7 strikeout-to-walk ratio in 16.0 innings of work.

Scouting Report: There's plenty of optimism surrounding Williams. He's tall, long-limbed, and quite projectable due to his thin frame. Williams' fastball generally sits in the 93 mph range and touches 94 mph regularly. It wouldn't be surprising to see his velocity creep into 95-mph range as he gets stronger in the coming years. His curveball, which also flashes plus, shows some late tilt and downward bite. It'll get a little slurvy on him at times. He'll also mix in a solid changeup. Mechanically, he's still, a bit robotic. Williams has the potential to develop into a solid #4-type arm.

Ceiling: 2.0-win player
Risk: Moderate
MLB ETA: 2022/2023

12. Miguel Hiraldo, 2B/SS

Hit	Power	SB	Patience	Glove	Overall
50	50	50	45	50	50

Born: 09/05/00	Age: 19	Bats: R
Height: 5-11	Weight: 170	Throws: R

YEAR	LVL	PA	1B	2B	3B	HR	SB	CS	AVG	OBP	SLG	BB%	K%	GB%	LD%	FB%
2018	RK	40	5	4	0	0	3	0	0.231	0.250	0.333	2.50%	30.00%	63.0	11.1	22.2
2018	RK	239	44	18	3	2	15	6	0.313	0.381	0.453	9.62%	12.55%	47.0	23.2	24.3
2019	Rk+	256	43	20	1	7	11	3	0.300	0.348	0.481	5.47%	14.06%	44.6	20.8	27.2
2019	A	4	0	0	1	0	0	0	0.250	0.250	0.750	0.00%	0.00%	25.0	25.0	25.0

Background: Signed from the international market during the same 2017 class that added Eric Pardinho and Leonardo Jimenez; Hiraldo received a $750,000 bonus from the organization. The 5-foot-11, 170-pound middle infielder turned in an impressive debut in the foreign rookie league two years ago when he batted .313/.381/.453. And he capped off his successful season with a 10-game cameo in the Gulf Coast League. Last season Hiraldo made the jump straight up the Appalachian League; he slugged .300/.348/.481 with 20 doubles, one triple, and seven homeruns to go along with 11 stolen bases in 14 attempts. His overall production, according to *Deserved Runs Created Plus*, topped the league threshold by 25%. He also earned a brief one-game call-up to the Midwest League.

Scouting Report: Consider the following:

- Since 2006, only two 18-year-old hitters posted a DRC+ between 120 and 130 with a sub-20% strikeout rate in the Appalachian League (min. 200 PA): teammates Leonardo Jimenez and Miguel Hiraldo, both of whom were added to the organization as part of the same international signing class.

Impressive power that could peak in 20-homer territory in the coming years. Throw in some average defense and Hiraldo already has the makings of a legitimate prospect. The best part about Hiraldo, though, is his ability to consistently square up the baseball. He's poised to be one of the bigger breakouts in 2020.

Ceiling: 2.0-win player
Risk: Moderate
MLB ETA: 2022

13. Maximo Castillo, RHP

FB	CB	CH	Command	Overall
60	50	55	55	45

Born: 05/04/99	Age: 21	Bats: R
Height: 6-2	Weight: 256	Throws: R

YEAR	LVL	IP	W	L	SV	ERA	FIP	WHIP	K/9	K%	BB/9	BB%	K/BB	HR9	BABIP
2017	Rk	47.3	6	0	0	3.80	3.31	1.29	9.9	26.00%	1.3	3.50%	7.43	0.76	0.368
2018	A	131.3	10	5	1	4.52	4.03	1.40	7.9	20.25%	2.9	7.39%	2.74	0.82	0.332
2019	A+	130.3	11	5	0	2.69	3.09	1.10	7.9	21.80%	1.9	5.35%	4.07	0.55	0.290

Background: Signed off the international free agent market at the conclusion of the 2015 season, Castillo, who received a rather paltry sum of $10,000, has quickly and efficiently moved through the lower levels of the minor leagues. The poised youngster, who tips the scales at a hefty 256 pounds, split his professional debut between the foreign and rookie leagues in 2016. He followed that up with a dominating 52-to-7 strikeout-to-walk ratio performance in 47.1 innings in the Appalachian League. But his production – and velocity – regressed a bit during his season in the Midwest League in 2018 as he averaged 7.9 strikeouts and 2.9 walks per nine innings. Last season, though, the rotund righty regained his velocity and showed his trademark impeccable control/command as he fanned 114 and walked just 28 in 130.1 innings of work. He compiled a 2.69 ERA and a 3.81 DRA (*Deserved Run Average*).

Scouting Report: Two years ago Castillo's fastball was sitting in the 91- to 92-mph range, but last season the large – and in charge – hurler was sitting 93 mph and bumping 94 mph frequently. He complements the now-plus-pitch with a solid 50-grade curveball, which shows 2-to-8 break, and an above-average changeup. With respect to his work last season consider the following:

- Since 2006, here's the list of 20-year-old pitchers to post a 21% to 23% strikeout percentage with a sub-6% walk percentage in any of the High Class A leagues (min. 100 IP): Zach Davies, Antonio Senzatela, Peter Lambert, Kyle Smith, and – of course – Maximo Castillo. And it should be noted that Castillo's the only one to accomplish the feat the Florida State League.
- For those keeping track at home: Davies has earned at least 2.5 fWAR in two separate seasons; Senzatela's been a decent #5 arm for the Rockies; Lambert struggled through his rookie season in Colorado; and Smith petered out in Class AAA.

Davies seems like a fair ceiling for Castillo. The latter lacks a dominant swing-and-miss secondary option, though the pinpoint accuracy helps to compensate some. He's going to have to monitor his weight moving forward as well.

Ceiling: 1.5- to 2.0-win player
Risk: Moderate
MLB ETA: 2021

14. Otto Lopez, 2B/SS

Hit	Power	SB	Patience	Glove	Overall
50/55	40/45	50	45	50	45

Born: 10/01/98	Age: 21	Bats: R
Height: 5-10	Weight: 160	Throws: R

YEAR	LVL	PA	1B	2B	3B	HR	SB	CS	AVG	OBP	SLG	BB%	K%	GB%	LD%	FB%
2017	RK	203	39	6	3	1	7	3	0.275	0.361	0.360	9.36%	11.33%	53.2	17.9	19.2
2018	RK	34	5	5	2	0	1	0	0.364	0.382	0.636	0.00%	14.71%	46.4	42.9	10.7
2018	A-	206	38	7	4	3	13	6	0.297	0.390	0.434	12.62%	10.19%	50.3	15.3	26.8
2019	A	492	115	20	5	5	20	15	0.324	0.371	0.425	6.91%	12.80%	55.6	18.7	18.5

Background: Another one of the club's top prospects signed off the international market. Lopez, who inked his pact in 2016, put together a decent debut in the Gulf Coast League the following summer when he batted .275/.361/.360. The 5-foot-10, 160-pound infielder spent the majority of the 2018 season with Vancouver, hitting a solid .297/.390/.434 with seven doubles, four triples, and a trio of homeruns to go along with 13 stolen bases in 51 games. Last season Lopez, a native of Santo Domingo, Dominican Republic, turned in his finest showing to date – despite moving into full-season action. Appearing in a career-high 108 games with the Lugnuts, Lopez slugged a scorching .324/.371/.425 with 20 doubles, five triples, and five homeruns. He also swiped 20 bags in 25 attempts. Per *Deserved Runs Created Plus*, his overall production topped the league average mark by a whopping 37%.

Snippet from The 2018 Prospect Digest Handbook: If Lopez's power sees an uptick in the coming years, he might be able to slide into a solid starting gig at the keystone. Otherwise, he should have no problems becoming a capable super-sub.

Scouting Report: Consider the following:

- Since 2006, here's the list of 20-year-old hitters to post a 132 to 142 DRC+ with a strikeout rate below 15% in the Midwest League (min. 300 PA): Vidal Brujan, Alexi Amarista, Johnny Giavotella, Gerardo Parra, Jose Fermin, Michael Collins, and Otto Lopez.

- For those counting at home: Brujan a top prospect in the Rays' system; Amarista and Giavotella are MLB vagabonds; and Parra was once an above-average outfielder.

So, similarly performing players at this age more often than not made it to the big leagues – which his great. Lopez still looks like a utility-type guy with the same caveat: if the power continues to creep forward as will his prospect ceiling. Strong bat-to-ball skills. Above-average speed, though he doesn't use it efficiently. And a solid glove.

Ceiling: 1.5- to 2.0-win player
Risk: Moderate
MLB ETA: 2022

15. Leonardo Jimenez, 2B/SS

Hit	Power	SB	Patience	Glove	Overall
45/55	20/40	30	50	50	45

Born: 05/17/01	Age: 19	Bats: R
Height: 5-11	Weight: 160	Throws: R

YEAR	LVL	PA	1B	2B	3B	HR	SB	CS	AVG	OBP	SLG	BB%	K%	GB%	LD%	FB%
2018	RK	150	23	8	2	0	0	0	0.250	0.333	0.341	10.67%	11.33%	40.5	16.4	36.2
2019	Rk+	245	49	13	2	0	2	1	0.298	0.377	0.377	8.57%	17.14%	43.4	26.3	24.0
2019	A	6	1	0	0	0	0	0	0.167	0.167	0.167	0.00%	33.33%	50.0	25.0	25.0

Background: The organization added quite a bit of talent to its flourishing system during the 2017 season: they drafted top prospect Nate Pearson, as well as Logan Warmoth, Riley Adams, and Kevin Smith; and then they went out and signed Eric Pardinho, Miguel Hiraldo, and Leonardo Jimenez on the international free agent market. Jimenez, a wiry 5-foot-11, 160-pound middle infielder out of Chitre, Panama, earned an $875,000 bonus. He young infielder made his professional debut in the Gulf Coast League two years ago, batting a respectable .250/.333/.341 with eight doubles and a pair of triples in 37 games. Last season Jimenez appeared in 56 games with the Bluefield Blue Jays in the Appalachian League, hitting .298/.377/.377 with 13 doubles, a pair of triples, and two stolen bases. His overall production, according to *Deserved Runs Created Plus*, topped the league average mark by 20%. Jimenez also appeared in two Midwest League games at the end of the year as well.

Scouting Report: Jimenez keeps the ball off the ground far more frequently than one would expect, especially considering he's yet to slug a dinger in his professional career. The young Panamanian has made some noticeable tweaks to his stance at the plate since signing with the club: he's opened up his lower half and his hands are held more closely to his head. He's also looks noticeably thicker, stronger. Jimenez uses a slashing approach at the plate with a gap-to-gap approach and a solid eye at the plate. Solid glove on either side of second base too. With respect to his production last season, consider the following:

- Since 2006, only four 18-year-old hitters met the following criteria in the Appalachian League (200 PA): 115 to 125 DRC+, a single-digit walk rate, and a sub-20.0% strikeout rate. Those four hitters: Mike Siani, a top prospect in the Reds' organization, Mario Martinez, fellow Jays prospect Miguel Hiraldo, and Leonardo Jimenez.

Unless Jimenez's power develops better than expected, he profiles best as a solid up-the-middle utility bat.

Ceiling: 1.5-win player
Risk: Moderate
MLB ETA: 2023

16. Yennsy Diaz, RHP

FB	CB	CH	Command	Overall
70	55	50	50	40

Born: 11/15/96	Age: 23	Bats: R
Height: 6-1	Weight: 202	Throws: R

YEAR	LVL	IP	W	L	SV	ERA	FIP	WHIP	K/9	K%	BB/9	BB%	K/BB	HR9	BABIP
2017	A	77.0	5	2	0	4.79	4.73	1.45	9.6	24.70%	4.8	12.35%	2.00	1.17	0.310
2018	A	47.7	5	1	0	2.08	4.44	0.99	7.9	21.99%	4.7	13.09%	1.68	0.76	0.151
2018	A+	99.7	5	4	0	3.52	3.36	1.19	7.5	20.34%	2.5	6.86%	2.96	0.45	0.297
2019	AA	144.3	11	9	0	3.74	3.93	1.23	7.2	19.05%	3.3	8.70%	2.19	0.75	0.270

Background: Signed by the club all the way back on July 3rd, 2014 – which seems forever ago, doesn't it? – for a little more than $1.5 million. And after a couple seasons of cautiously handling the hard-throwing right-hander, the front office began easing the reins on the talented youngster. Born in Azua, Dominican Republic; Diaz split the 2018 season between Lansing and Dunedin, showing a new found ability to throw strikes he fanned 125 and walked 53 in 147.1 innings of work. Last season the 6-foot-1, 202-pound well-built righty squared off against the Eastern League and came out...OK. In 26 appearances, 24 of which were starts, Diaz tossed 144.1 innings while recording 116 strikeouts and 53 walks. He compiled a 3.74 ERA and a 4.82 DRA. Toronto also promoted him up to The Show for one disastrous relief appearance against Baltimore in early August.

Scouting Report: Consider the following:

- Since 2006, here's the list of 22-year-old hurlers to post a 18% to 20% strikeout percentage with a walk percentage between 8% and 10% in the Eastern League (min. 100 IP): Frankie De La Cruz, Shawn Morimando, Devin Jones, Ronald Bay, and Yennsy Diaz.

The collection of arms only cements the notes I scribed in watching Diaz pitch: he's better suited as a hard-throwing, dare-ya-to-hit-it reliever, rather than a mediocre/fringy starting pitcher. Diaz sports a nitrous-infused, plus-plus fastball that sits in the upper 90s, even as a starting pitcher. He complements it with an average changeup and an inconsistent 55-grade curveball. The problem with Diaz as a starting pitcher: the secondary options aren't strong enough to consistently rely and his control/command doesn't help compensate for it. He's an 8th inning guy all the way.

Ceiling: 1.0- to 1.5-win player
Risk: Low to Moderate
MLB ETA: Debuted in 2019

17. Reese McGuire, C

Hit	Power	SB	Patience	Glove	Overall
45	45	30	45+	50	40

Born: 03/02/95	Age: 25	Bats: L
Height: 6-0	Weight: 215	Throws: R

YEAR	LVL	PA	1B	2B	3B	HR	SB	CS	AVG	OBP	SLG	BB%	K%	GB%	LD%	FB%
2017	RK	26	7	2	0	0	0	1	0.409	0.462	0.500	11.54%	3.85%	40.9	18.2	40.9
2017	A+	13	2	1	0	0	0	0	0.250	0.308	0.333	7.69%	15.38%	70.0	10.0	20.0
2017	AA	136	20	5	1	6	2	1	0.278	0.366	0.496	11.76%	13.97%	54.0	12.0	29.0
2018	AAA	369	57	9	2	7	3	2	0.233	0.312	0.339	8.94%	20.87%	47.0	22.1	22.5
2019	AAA	277	42	12	1	5	4	0	0.247	0.316	0.366	9.03%	15.88%	42.2	22.3	24.3

Background: Taken in the same draft as Kris Bryant, Jon Gray, former teammate Austin Meadows, and Tim Anderson; McGuire, who was chosen by the Pirates with the 14th overall pick seven years, has been mired in baseball purgatory the past couple seasons as he's proved himself worthy in brief stints in the big leagues, but has been shuffled back to Class AAA. Acquired by Toronto, along with Francisco Liriano and Harold Ramirez in exchange for Drew Hutchison on August 1st, 2016; McGuire appeared in 72 games with the Buffalo Bisons of the International League last season, hitting .247/.316/.366 with 12 doubles, one triple, and five homeruns. Per *Deserved Runs Created Plus*, his overall production was 23% *below* the league average threshold. The lefty-swinging backstop also popped up to Toronto for 30 games as well, batting a solid .299/.346/.526 with seven doubles and five homeruns.

Scouting Report: A solid defensive backstop and a slightly better than average pitch framer, McGuire now has two brief – and incredibly successful – stints with Toronto over the past couple of seasons; he slugged an aggregate .297/.343/.539 in 44 games – numbers vastly better than his minor league showings. And his batted ball data all suggest it's a bit of a mirage as well. His Hard Hit% has been about 12-percentage points below the league average. And his exit velocity has been just 85.4 mph. Still, though, given the dearth of production from behind the plate at the big league level, there's no reason that McGuire couldn't be a low end starting option for a number of teams. Once his numbers normalize, McGuire looks like a Tucker Barnhart-type contributor (.250/.328/.371) with a little better defense.

Ceiling: 1.0- to 1.5-win player
Risk: Low to Moderate
MLB ETA: Debuted in 2018

18. Riley Adams, C

Hit	Power	SB	Patience	Glove	Overall
45	50	30	50	50	40

Born: 06/26/96	Age: 24	Bats: R
Height: 6-4	Weight: 225	Throws: R

YEAR	LVL	PA	1B	2B	3B	HR	SB	CS	AVG	OBP	SLG	BB%	K%	GB%	LD%	FB%
2017	A-	227	42	16	1	3	1	1	0.305	0.374	0.438	7.93%	22.03%	50.6	16.9	29.2
2018	A+	409	55	26	1	4	3	0	0.246	0.352	0.361	12.22%	22.74%	44.2	19.0	29.5
2019	A+	83	12	3	0	3	1	0	0.277	0.434	0.462	16.87%	21.69%	48.9	17.0	29.8
2019	AA	332	46	15	2	11	3	1	0.258	0.349	0.439	9.64%	31.63%	36.1	18.3	35.6

Background: The 2017 draft will forever been known as draft that added one of baseball's top pitching prospects, flame-throwing right-hander Nate Pearson, to Toronto's mix. But Riley Adams, a backstop out of the University of San Diego, is quietly adding his name to the list as well. A .305/.411/.504 hitter coming out of college, Adams, who was taken in the third round, made the transition to wooden bats with aplomb as he hit .305/.374/.438 during his 52-game debut in the Northwest League. The front office aggressively challenged him the following season by sending him straight up to High Class A. And the results were...OK. He batted a respectably mediocre .246/.352/.361 with 26 doubles, one triple, and four homeruns. The 6-foot-4, 225-pound backstop began last season back in High Class A, but after hitting .277/.434/.462 for the better part of a month – as well as the front office shuffling their impressive depth of catchers – Adams was promoted up to Class AA for the remainder of the year. He hit .258/.349/.439 with 15 doubles, two triples, and 11 homeruns in 81 games with New Hampshire. His overall production – per *Deserved Runs Created Plus* – was 31% better than the average.

Scouting Report: Consider the following:

- Since 2006, only three 22-year-old hitters posted a DRC+ between 125 to 135 with a strikeout rate north of 28% in the Eastern League (min. 300 PA): Bradley Zimmer, Jacob Heyward, and – of course – Riley Adams.

There's a reason why I consider Class AA the "make-it-or-break-it" level for a prospect. And Adams' strikeout rate last season with New Hampshire only cements that. Prior to his promotion, his career K-rate was roughly 22%. In 81 games in Class AA, the former University of San Diego star struck out in nearly a third of his plate appearances. The contact issues notwithstanding, Adams flashes the necessary tools to be a serviceable backup: 50-grade hit tool and power, solid walk rates, and a good glove. He's very likely going to get stuck behind the guys currently ahead of him – Reese McGuire and Danny Jansen – and the guys below him – Alejandro Kirk and Gabriel Moreno.

Ceiling: 1.0- to 1.5-win player
Risk: Moderate
MLB ETA: Debuted in 2018

19. Hector Perez, RHP

	FB	CB	SL	SF	Command	Overall
	60	55	55	55	40	40

Born: 06/06/96	Age: 24	Bats: R
Height: 6-3	Weight: 218	Throws: R

YEAR	LVL	IP	W	L	SV	ERA	FIP	WHIP	K/9	K%	BB/9	BB%	K/BB	HR9	BABIP
2017	A	18.0	1	1	0	2.50	4.11	1.11	12.0	33.33%	5.5	15.28%	2.18	1.00	0.200
2017	A+	89.3	6	5	2	3.63	4.39	1.52	10.5	26.46%	6.8	17.05%	1.55	0.60	0.300
2018	A+	72.7	3	3	2	3.84	3.74	1.24	10.3	27.48%	5.0	13.25%	2.08	0.62	0.263
2018	AA	25.7	0	1	0	3.86	3.43	1.29	11.2	29.36%	5.6	14.68%	2.00	0.35	0.276
2018	AA	16.7	0	1	0	3.24	2.72	1.20	9.7	26.09%	4.3	11.59%	2.25	0.00	0.279
2019	AA	121.3	7	6	0	4.60	3.96	1.62	8.7	21.51%	5.0	12.32%	1.75	0.67	0.349

Background: The Jays did well in the Roberto Osuna deal with Houston – considering the baggage the righty is/was carrying. Toronto received hard-throwing closer Ken Giles, who averaged 14.1 K/9 last season, David Paulino, and Hector Perez. A 6-foot-3, 218-pound right-hander out of Santo Domingo, Dominican Republic, Perez was an interesting return for the Jays. The hard-throwing hurler has a lengthy – *lengthy* – history of dominating strikeout rates and problematic, career-limiting control/command issues. And last season, his fifth in professional baseball, was more or less the same. Perez made a career-high 24 starts – as well as a pair of relief appearances – for the New Hampshire Fisher Cats, throwing 121.2 innings with 117 strikeouts and a whopping 67 free passes. He finished the year with a 4.60 ERA and a 6.70 DRA (*Deserved Run Average*).

Snippet from The 2018 Prospect Digest Handbook: The problem, of course, with Perez is his inability to find the strike zone with any type of regularity. And that fact that his walk rates have plateaued is concerning and it explains why Houston dealt him away. Perez is reminiscent of a young Chris Archer, both showing a fantastic, yet uncontrolled arsenal. But Archer was able to hone his weaponry during his age-23 season. It remains to be see if Perez can.

Scouting Report: So it seems like a long, lost dream at this point. Almost unattainable. Perez owns a career 5.2 BB/9 rate. And he's averaged exactly five walks per nine innings since 2018. There's little hope that he develops even fringy 45-grade control – let along command – to allow his impressive arsenal to remain in the rotation. 93- to 95-mph fastball with some giddy up. An above-average mid-80s slider. A 55-grade snapdragon for a curveball. And a better than average splitter. Not many pitchers can boast four above-average or better pitches. Perez is one of them. Then on the other hand, not many pitchers are given as many tries to figure out the strike zone either. One more final though: when he does happen to find the strike zone, rarely are they quality strikes.

Ceiling: 1.0- to 1.5-win player
Risk: Moderate
MLB ETA: 2020

20. Griffin Conine, RF

Hit	Power	SB	Patience	Glove	Overall
40+	60	35	5521	55	40

Born: 07/11/97	Age: 22	Bats: L
Height: 6-1	Weight: 200	Throws: R

YEAR	LVL	PA	1B	2B	3B	HR	SB	CS	AVG	OBP	SLG	BB%	K%	GB%	LD%	FB%
2018	RK	9	2	1	0	0	0	0	0.375	0.444	0.500	11.11%	22.22%	50.0	33.3	16.7
2018	A-	230	26	14	2	7	5	0	0.238	0.309	0.427	8.26%	27.39%	46.9	15.9	29.7
2019	A	348	43	19	2	22	2	0	0.283	0.371	0.576	10.92%	35.92%	41.2	21.5	32.8

Background: Jeff's kid was a trendy pick as a potential early first round selection heading into his junior season at Duke University. But a slow start to the 2017 season forced Conine's stock to tumble – despite a resurgence later in the year – until the second round. He finished his junior campaign with a .286/.410/.608 triple-slash line, belting out 15 doubles, two triples, and 18 homeruns. Unfortunately, he didn't carry that surging momentum into his debut in the Northwest League as he hit a mediocre .238/.309/.427 with 14 doubles, a pair of triple, and seven homeruns in 55 games. The 6-foot-1, 200-pound chiseled corner outfielder spent last season – albeit a shortened one – with the Lugnuts in Low Class A. In 80 games the former Duke star slugged .283/.371/.576 with 19 doubles, two triples, and 22 homeruns to go along with a pair of stolen bases. His overall production, according to *Deserved Runs Created*, was a whopping 55% above the league average threshold. Conine was suspended at the start of the year for taking a banned stimulant (ritalinic acid).

Snippet from The 2018 Prospect Digest Handbook: Conine's going to struggle making contact upon entering the professional ranks. And he doesn't have enough power – though, it's solid – to compensate. I'd expect him to go in round four. He has a ceiling as a backup outfielder.

Scouting Report: Well, I was clearly wrong about (A) his eventual draft slot and (B) the amount of thump in his bat. However, Conine did struggle – *massively* – with contact issues last season. He fanned in 35.9% of his plate appearances with the Lugnuts, the third highest total among all Midwest League bats (min. 300 PA). Consider the following:

- Since 2006, here's the list of 21-year-old hitters to post at least a 150 DRC+ in the Midwest League (min. 300 PA): Boog Powell, Kyler Burke, Eliezer Alvarez, Myles Straw, and Griffin Conine.
- For the record: Conine's strikeout rate is nearly double that of the runner up (Eliezer Alvarez, 19.24%).

In all likelihood Conine's going to travel down the path of a poor man's Three True Outcomes hitter. He's going (continue) to whiff a lot. And he's already showing borderline plus-plus power. The problem, of course, is that he doesn't walk all that frequently.

Ceiling: 1.0- to 1.5-win player
Risk: Moderate
MLB ETA: Debuted in 2018

Rank	Name	Age	Pos
1	Carter Kieboom	22	IF
2	Luis Garcia	20	2B/SS
3	Jackson Rutledge	21	RHP
4	Seth Romero	23	LHP
5	Andry Lara	17	RHP
6	Mason Denaburg	20	RHP
7	Tim Cate	22	LHP
8	Israel Pineda	20	C
9	Jeremy De La Rosa	19	OF
10	Wil Crowe	25	RHP
11	Matt Cronin	22	LHP
12	Steven Fuentes	23	RHP
13	Tres Barrera	25	C
14	Yasel Antuna	20	IF
15	Joan Adon	21	RHP
16	Drew Mendoza	22	1B
17	Reid Schaller	23	RHP
18	Jackson Tetreault	24	RHP
19	KJ Harrison	23	1B
20	Nick Raquet	24	LHP

1. Carter Kieboom, IF

	Hit	Power	SB	Patience	Glove	Overall
	55/60	50/60	30	50	50	60

Born: 09/03/97	Age: 22	Bats: R
Height: 6-2	Weight: 190	Throws: R

YEAR	LVL	PA	1B	2B	3B	HR	SB	CS	AVG	OBP	SLG	BB%	K%	GB%	LD%	FB%
2017	RK	16	2	3	0	0	0	0	0.417	0.563	0.667	18.75%	0.00%	50.0	8.3	33.3
2017	A-	29	5	1	0	1	1	0	0.250	0.276	0.393	3.45%	6.90%	53.8	19.2	11.5
2017	A	210	33	12	0	8	2	2	0.296	0.400	0.497	13.33%	19.05%	53.2	14.4	24.5
2018	A+	285	47	15	0	11	6	1	0.298	0.386	0.494	12.63%	17.54%	47.5	20.7	25.3
2018	AA	273	43	16	1	5	3	1	0.262	0.326	0.395	8.06%	21.61%	42.6	16.8	36.3
2019	AAA	494	82	24	3	16	5	2	0.303	0.409	0.493	13.77%	20.24%	46.0	22.2	27.3

Background: The first round of the 2016 draft will certainly be remembered for several things: #1 more than a few teams got burned with their selections, especially among the early picks of the round (Mickey Moniak, Riley Pint, Corey Ray, Zack Collins, Kyle Lewis, and Will Benson immediately jump to mind) and #2 the prep talent has produced a bevy of top prospects including Matt Manning, Alex Kirilloff, Forrest Whitley, Taylor Trammell, Gavin Lux, and – of course – Carter Kieboom, the 28th overall pick. A product of Walton High School in Marietta, Georgia, which has produced a couple other big leaguers in Billy Burns and Blaine Boyers, Kieboom offered up glimpses of his potential as a baby faced 18-year-old in the Gulf Coast League, hitting .244/.323/.452 in 36 contests. Injuries limited the young infielder to just 61 games the following season, most of which was spent in the South Atlantic League, as he managed to slug .297/.396/.492. His "official" breakout campaign didn't happen until two years ago as he ripped through the Carolina League and looked comfortable in the minors' toughest challenge, Class AA. Last season, the former full time shortstop bounced around a bit in the infield, though that didn't slow his production at the plate. In 109 games with the Fresno Grizzlies he batted .303/.409/.593 with 24 doubles, three triples, and 16 homeruns. His overall production, according to Baseball Prospectus' *Deserved Runs Created Plus*, topped the league average mark by 26%. He spent an additional 11 games with the Nationals as well, going 5-for-39.

Snippet from The 2018 Prospect Digest Handbook: A do-everything-type shortstop knocking – loudly – on the door to stardom. The 6-foot-2, 190-pound shortstop shows an advanced approach at the plate, offering up an elite level of patience, strong contact skills, and 25- to 30-homer potential. Defensively speaking, he shows enough promise to remain at the position, though he'll never be a Gold Glove recipient.

Scouting Report: Consider the following:

- Since 2006, only two 21-year-old hitters have posted a DRC+ between 120 and 130 with a double-digit walk rate and a strikeout rate between 18% and 23% in the Pacific Coast League (min. 300 PA): Prince Fielder and – of course – Carter Kieboom. For the record: Fielder owns a career 131 DRC+ mark in over 1,600 big league games.

Obviously, that's a pretty promising comp in terms of his offensive similarities. Kieboom continued to show the trademark skills that's made him one of the best prospects in the game: above-average to borderline elite walk rates; above-average power especially for an up-the-middle position; phenomenal bat control / bat-to-ball skills; and the defensive chops to play any skilled position on the infield. The Nationals – obviously – have a glaring at the keystone or the hot corner, so depending upon the rest of the offseason Kieboom will be handed one of those.

Ceiling: 5.5-win player
Risk: Low to Moderate
MLB ETA: Debuted in 2019

2. Luis Garcia, 2B/SS

	Hit	Power	SB	Patience	Glove	Overall
	50/60	40/50	40	40	50	60

Born: 05/16/00	Age: 20	Bats: L
Height: 6-2	Weight: 190	Throws: R

YEAR	LVL	PA	1B	2B	3B	HR	SB	CS	AVG	OBP	SLG	BB%	K%	GB%	LD%	FB%
2018	A	323	67	14	4	3	8	5	0.297	0.335	0.402	5.88%	15.17%	54.9	20.0	20.8
2018	A+	221	48	7	2	4	4	1	0.299	0.338	0.412	5.43%	14.93%	51.4	12.6	29.7
2019	AA	553	105	22	4	4	11	5	0.257	0.280	0.337	3.07%	15.55%	51.1	18.0	26.8

Background: The quantity of generational / perennial All-Star caliber talent the Nationals have signed on the international market, drafted, and developed out over the past several seasons is really mindboggling: Bryce Harper, Stephen Strasburg, Anthony Rendon, Juan Soto, Carter Kieboom, Victor Robles, and Luis Garcia. And that's *not* including the guys they've traded for (Trea Turner) or traded away (Jesus Luzardo and to a lesser extent Blake Treinen). A lefty-swinging middle-infielder from New York, New York; Garcia burst onto the scene with a dynamic showing in the Gulf Coast League as a 17-year-old; he slugged .32/.330/.387 in 49 games. The Washington brass aggressively pushed the teenager up to – and eventually through – the South Atlantic League a year later. And last season the 6-foot-2, 190-pound infielder spent the entirety of the year battling against the toughest minor league challenge, Class AA, at the ripe ol' age of 19. In a career best 129 games with the Harrisburg Senators, Garcia slugged .257/.380/.337 with 22 doubles, four triples, and four homeruns. He also swiped 11 bags in 16 attempts. Per *Deserved*

Runs Created Plus, his overall production was a disappointing 31% below the league average. Garcia spent the ensuing autumn playing for the Surprise Saguaros in the Arizona Fall League; he hit a solid .276/.345/.382.

Snippet from The 2018 Prospect Digest Handbook: Not everything is rosy for the talented youngster. The left-handed swinging Garcia was incredibly susceptible to southpaws last season, cobbling together a lowly .234/.250/.287 triple-slash line (as opposed to a .330/.377/.465 showing vs. RHP). And that comes on the heels of his horrific performance against lefties in 2017 as well (.184/.244/.289). The bat is a plus, which helps soothe any concern over his platoon splits, and the power is above-average.

Scouting Report: Despite the overall disappointing showing at the plate last season, there are a few silver linings to suggest far better times are on the immediate horizon: his production against southpaws upticked for the second consecutive season (he hit .248/.283/.315 against them) and after a slow start to the year in which he batted .213/.246/.249 in his first 51 games, his stick rebounded in early June to post a .284/.301/.390 triple-slash line over his final 78 games. The walk rates / patience at the plate are beyond atrocious, but the hit tool will be – at least – a 60-grade with 50-power and average-ish defense. In an ideal world, Garcia and Kieboom would both seize the openings at second and third bases during the spring.

Ceiling: 4.0- to 4.5-win player
Risk: Moderate to High
MLB ETA: 2020

3. Jackson Rutledge, RHP

	FB	CB	SL	CH	Command	Overall
	70	55/60	60	45	45	50

Born: 04/01/99	Age: 21	Bats: R
Height: 6-8	Weight: 250	Throws: R

YEAR	LVL	IP	W	L	SV	ERA	FIP	WHIP	K/9	K%	BB/9	BB%	K/BB	HR9	BABIP
2019	Rk	1.0	0	0	0	27.00	5.50	5.00	18.0	22.22%	9.0	11.11%	2.00	0.00	0.800
2019	A-	9.0	0	0	0	3.00	6.28	0.78	6.0	17.65%	3.0	8.82%	2.00	2.00	0.091
2019	A	27.3	2	0	0	2.30	2.52	0.91	10.2	29.25%	3.6	10.38%	2.82	0.00	0.222

Background: The big 6-foot-8, 250-pound right-hander took a bit of an unusual route to the first round last June. The Missouri native began his collegiate career at the University of Arkansas two years ago. He made 12 appearances for the Razorbacks, two of which were starts, throwing 15.2 innings with a 14-to-11 strikeout-to-walk ratio. Rutledge transferred to San Jacinto Junior College with the plan, according to reports, to head to the University of Kentucky for his junior season. Except he didn't make it to the land of the Wildcats. Washington drafted the gargantuan righty in the opening round, 17th overall, after a predictably dominating showing against the JuCo competition; in 13 starts he punched out 134 hitters in only 82.2 innings of work to go along with a barely-there 0.87 ERA. Rutledge made brief stops at three separate levels during his pro debut, throwing another 37.1 innings, recording 39 punch outs against 15 walks en route to totaling a 3.13 ERA.

Scouting Report: Tall and wiry with a loose arm and some projection left thanks to his age (he's only entering his age-21 season). Rutledge owns two plus pitches (fastball and slider), an above-average offering that likely moves into plus territory (curveball), and a below-average changeup. Rutledge's heater sits – easily, with little to no effort – in the mid- to upper-90s. It was a bit more hittable than expected down in the zone, but was generally untouchable in his Low Class A stint when he was locating above the belt. His slider is wicked with hard, late bit and 1-7 break. The curveball, a 12-6 breaking ball, provides a third swing-and-miss option. And the changeup, which is too firm, shows a touch of arm-side run. If the command ticks up toward a 50-grade he becomes a potential #2-type arm. If not, he has the floor as a hard-throwing, sometimes erratic #4.

Ceiling: 3.0-win player
Risk: Moderate
MLB ETA: 2022

4. Seth Romero, LHP

	FB	SL	CH	Command	Overall
	N/A	N/A	N/A	N/A	55

Born: 04/19/96	Age: 24	Bats: L
Height: 6-3	Weight: 240	Throws: L

YEAR	LVL	IP	W	L	SV	ERA	FIP	WHIP	K/9	K%	BB/9	BB%	K/BB	HR9	BABIP
2017	Rk	2.0	0	0	0	0.00	3.42	1.00	13.5	37.50%	9.0	25.00%	1.50	0.00	0.000
2017	A-	20.0	0	1	0	5.40	1.13	1.25	14.4	37.65%	2.7	7.06%	5.33	0.00	0.404
2018	A	25.3	0	1	0	3.91	3.74	1.11	12.1	30.91%	2.8	7.27%	4.25	1.07	0.279

Background: Enigmatic. Oft-dominant. Perhaps a bonafide upper-rotation caliber big league arm. Problematic – on multiple occasions. Historically a pain in the ass with the maturity level of toddler throwing a temper tantrum. Injured. That's Seth Romero in a nutshell. He was suspended multiple times during his rocky collegiate career at the University of Houston before he was eventually dismissed from the team. The Nationals took a flier on the hard-throwing southpaw near the end of the opening round in 2017 and continued to deal with his behavioral issues. He was sent home during Spring Training in 2017 for violating team policy. And Romero ultimately succumbed to elbow woes, which pushed him under the knife for Tommy John surgery, and missed the entire 2018 season.

Snippet from The 2018 Prospect Digest Handbook: Ignoring the glaring red flag of immaturity issues, Romero's a supremely gifted, talented pitcher. He's a legitimate top-of-the-rotation caliber arm. His entire arsenal can be succinctly described as...electric. His fastball sits comfortably in the 92- to 94-mph range with a peak of 97. The plus offering shows incredible late life and explosion. His slider, a hellacious mid-80s offering, provides another swing-and-miss pitch. And his changeup sits comfortably in above-average territory with a little room to grow. Based merely on talent and ability alone, Romero could easily ascend up to the top of a rotation. But now he's battling health issues on top of a novel of indiscretions.

Scouting Report: To be frank: who the hell knows what to expect from Romero? He's gifted. And everyone knows it, including himself. But he also can't get out of his own way. Prior to the elbow surgery I had his fastball *and* slider grading out as 65 with an above-average changeup that flashed plus. He could very easily be what Jesus Luzardo is going to become.

Ceiling: 3.5- to 4.0-win player
Risk: High to Extremely High
MLB ETA: 2021

5. Andry Lara, RHP

FB	CB	CH	Command	Overall
60/65	55/60	N/A	N/A	50

Born: 01/06/03	Age: 17	Bats: R
Height: 6-4	Weight: 180	Throws: R

Background: Always busy and willing to hand out big money on the international market – which, by the way, has worked out well for the organization – the Nationals inked the 6-foot-4, 180-pound right-hander to a deal worth $1.25 million.

Scouting Report: Big, projectable, and equipped with two offerings that have a chance to be at least 60-grade. Lara features a standard three-pitch mix: a low-90s fastball that projects to sit – comfortably – in the mid-90s at full maturity; a hard, late-snapping breaking ball that should creep into plus territory; and a changeup (which I did not witness personally). Note: because of the angle, I couldn't differentiate if the breaking pitch was a curveball or slider; it had the typical slider velocity but more of a curveball break. It's not difficult to imagine that if Lara was entering the 2021 draft that he wouldn't be an early- to mid-first round selection.

Ceiling: 2.0-win player
Risk: Moderate
MLB ETA: 2023

6. Mason Denaburg, RHP

FB	SL	CH	Command	Overall
N/A	N/A	N/A	N/A	50

Born: 08/08/99	Age: 20	Bats: R
Height: 6-4	Weight: 195	Throws: R

YEAR	LVL	IP	W	L	SV	ERA	FIP	WHIP	K/9	K%	BB/9	BB%	K/BB	HR9	BABIP
2019	Rk	20.3	1	1	0	7.52	5.22	1.82	8.4	18.81%	6.2	13.86%	1.36	0.44	0.361

Background: Selected between two of the more notable power bats taken in the opening round two years ago, Denaburg, the 27th overall selection, was sandwiched between Red Sox up-and-coming first baseman Triston Casas and former Astro-turned-Diamondback saber-superstar Seth Beer. The 6-foot-4, 195-pound right-hander signed for an above-slot deal worth $3 million, roughly half-of-a-million north of the recommended bonus. Denaburg, a product of Merritt Island High School, was held out of regular season action due to a troublesome right bicep muscle. He did make his debut in the Gulf Coast League last season, but another arm issue – a wonky shoulder – shut him down after seven appearances.

Snippet from The 2018 Prospect Digest Handbook: The projectable right-hander already owns two plus pitches: an explosive mid-90s fastball with some run and a fall-off-the-table caliber curveball. It was almost comical watching high school-aged hitters attempt to make contact on the 12-to-6, hard-biting breaking ball. In terms of upside, Denaburg looks far more projectable and polished than Orioles first round Grayson Rodriguez, who was taken 16 picks earlier. There's some mid-rotation caliber talent here, maybe a bit more.

Scouting Report: While Baltimore's Grayson Rodriguez took off like a bat out of hell last season, Denaburg sputtered to another injury shortened campaign. Denaburg's production really fell off the table beginning with his fourth start in the rookie league; he allowed 15 earned runs and posted an 8-to-8 strikeout-to-walk ratio in only 10.1 innings of work. At this point he's a complete wild card – an expensive, supremely talented wild card, but a wild card nonetheless.

Ceiling: 2.0-win player
Risk: Moderate to High
MLB ETA: 2023

7. Tim Cate, LHP

	FB	CB	CH	Command	Overall
	50	70	50+	55	45

Born: 09/30/97	Age: 22	Bats: L
Height: 6-0	Weight: 185	Throws: L

YEAR	LVL	IP	W	L	SV	ERA	FIP	WHIP	K/9	K%	BB/9	BB%	K/BB	HR9	BABIP
2018	A-	31.0	2	3	0	4.65	3.38	1.42	7.5	18.84%	2.9	7.25%	2.60	0.29	0.333
2018	A	21.0	0	3	0	5.57	5.13	1.38	8.1	20.43%	2.6	6.45%	3.17	1.71	0.306
2019	A	70.3	4	5	0	2.82	2.32	1.05	9.3	26.16%	1.7	4.66%	5.62	0.26	0.309
2019	A+	73.3	7	4	0	3.31	3.06	1.23	8.1	23.49%	2.3	6.76%	3.47	0.49	0.324

Background: A bonafide ace throughout his tenure as a Connecticut Husky. The club drafted the safe, low ceiling, fast-moving southpaw in the second round of the 2018 draft. Cate, the 65th overall pick that year, left the school with a career 14-8 win-loss record while averaging an impressive 11.5 strikeouts and 3.3 walks per nine innings to go along with a 2.99 ERA. The crafty southpaw split his debut between Auburn and Hagerstown, throwing an additional 52.0 innings with 45 strikeouts and 16 walks. Last season Cate – once again – split time between two different levels: he opened the year up with 13 dominating starts back in the South Atlantic League and finished it with 13 starts with Potomac. He tossed a total of 143.2 innings, recording 139 strikeouts against 32 walks with a 3.07 ERA.

Snippet from The 2018 Prospect Digest Handbook: There's some #3/#4-type caliber potential. He owns one of the better curveballs in the minors.

Scouting Report: Cate's level of production and success are built upon the very basic building blocks of pitching: throw quality strikes, pitch to your strengths, and own one hellacious curveball. The 6-foot, 185-pound southpaw's fastball is fringy, at best. But he moves it around and commands it low-and-away especially well. Along with his curveball, his changeup has improved half-of-a-grade as well, going from a firm 50 to a 50+. And there's a non-zero chance that it moves into full blown above-average territory. Cate's becoming an anomaly of sorts as a soft-tossing hurler, so he'll have to continue to fight the good fight.

Ceiling: 1.5- to 2.0-win player
Risk: Moderate
MLB ETA: 2021

8. Israel Pineda, C

	Hit	Power	SB	Patience	Glove	Overall
	50/60	40/50	40	40	50	45

Born: 04/03/00	Age: 20	Bats: R
Height: 5-11	Weight: 190	Throws: R

YEAR	LVL	PA	1B	2B	3B	HR	SB	CS	AVG	OBP	SLG	BB%	K%	GB%	LD%	FB%
2017	RK	65	10	5	2	0	0	0	0.288	0.323	0.441	6.15%	20.00%	45.8	27.1	22.9
2018	A-	185	34	7	0	4	0	0	0.273	0.341	0.388	6.49%	18.92%	40.9	24.2	29.5
2019	A	411	62	12	0	7	1	2	0.217	0.278	0.305	7.30%	24.82%	42.9	16.8	30.8

Background: Following the company's modus operandi of aggressively shoving young bats through the minors as quickly as possible, Pineda, a native of Maracay, Venezuela, found himself squaring off against the South Atlantic League competition as a 19-year-old. Predictably so, his offensive production faltered. Coming off of a solid showing with Auburn in the New York-Penn League two years ago, Pineda battled through an early stint on the disabled list and hit a paltry .217/.278/.308 with 12 doubles and seven homeruns. His overall production, according to *Deserved Runs Created Plus*, was a whopping 32% *below* the league average threshold.

Snippet from The 2018 Prospect Digest Handbook: Pineda looks like a fringy starter at this point. But, remember, backstops typically take a lot longer to develop.

Scouting Report: Despite the disappointingly putrid offensive showing last season, Pineda still looks like a low-end starting caliber option. He's a better than average defender, offers up 50-grade power, shuts down the opposition's running game like few others; and has consistently –

albeit with mixed results – battled significantly older competition. It wouldn't be all that shocking if the front office brass opted against the conservative approach and push him up to High Class A at the start of 2020.

Ceiling: 1.5- to 2.0-win player
Risk: Moderate
MLB ETA: 2022

9. Jeremy De La Rosa, OF

Hit	Power	SB	Patience	Glove	Overall
45	45/50	30	55	50	45

Born: 01/16/02	Age: 18	Bats: L
Height: 5-11	Weight: 160	Throws: L

YEAR	LVL	PA	1B	2B	3B	HR	SB	CS	AVG	OBP	SLG	BB%	K%	GB%	LD%	FB%
2019	Rk	99	14	1	2	2	3	2	0.232	0.343	0.366	12.12%	29.29%	50.9	9.1	29.1

Background: Another one of the ballclub's international expenditures; De La Rosa, a wiry sub-6-foot outfielder, signed with the Nationals for $300,000 on July 2nd, 2018. A native of Santo Domingo, Dominican Republic, De La Rosa – unsurprisingly – bypassed the foreign rookie league and made his professional debut with Washington's Gulf Coast League affiliate last season. In 26 games, the teenage outfielder batted a disappointing .232/.343/.366 with one doubles, two triples, and two homeruns. He also swiped three bags in five total attempts. Per *Deserved Runs Created Plus*, his overall production was 15% *below* the league average.

Scouting Report: Warning: small sample size analysis to follow. Understandably so, De La Rosa struggled during the first half of his aggressive assignment; he batted a lowly .132/.283/.132 through the month of July (13 games). However, in the second half of his debut, which happened to be 13 games in August, he slugged .318/.396/.568 with his five extra-base knocks. De La Rosa needs to clean up the lower half of his swing in order to take full advantage of his natural loft and above-average bat speed. Above-average foot speed. He's also made some adjustments to his swing since signing with the organization: he's more closed off with a wider base; he holds his hands higher, closer to his ear and know shows a more pronounced leg kick. Despite the five-tool potential there is one red flag: his swing-and-miss issues; even during his second half hot streak he fanned in more than 26% of his plate appearances.

Ceiling: 1.5- to 2.0-win player
Risk: Moderate to High
MLB ETA: 2023

10. Wil Crowe, RHP

FB	CB	SL	CH	Command	Overall
55	55	50	55	45	45

Born: 09/09/94	Age: 25	Bats: R
Height: 6-2	Weight: 240	Throws: R

YEAR	LVL	IP	W	L	SV	ERA	FIP	WHIP	K/9	K%	BB/9	BB%	K/BB	HR9	BABIP
2017	Rk	3.7	0	0	0	4.91	3.14	1.09	4.9	14.29%	2.5	7.14%	2.00	0.00	0.273
2017	A-	20.7	0	0	0	2.61	4.44	1.02	6.5	18.29%	1.3	3.66%	5.00	1.31	0.250
2018	A-	3.0	0	0	0	0.00	4.81	1.33	3.0	9.09%	6.0	18.18%	0.50	0.00	0.250
2018	A+	87.0	11	0	0	2.69	3.63	1.16	8.1	21.61%	3.1	8.31%	2.60	0.62	0.267
2018	AA	26.3	0	5	0	6.15	6.08	1.78	5.1	12.61%	5.5	13.45%	0.94	1.37	0.325
2019	AA	95.3	7	6	0	3.87	3.14	1.12	8.4	23.24%	2.1	5.74%	4.05	0.76	0.294
2019	AAA	54.0	0	4	0	6.17	5.46	1.70	6.8	16.40%	4.3	10.40%	1.58	1.17	0.337

Background: Taken in the second round of the 2017 draft out of the University of South Carolina, Crowe looked the part of a fast-moving, safe, low-ceiling pitcher. Three years later and, well, basically the same thing can be said. The 6-foot-2, 240-pound right-hander split time between two levels during his debut. He followed that up by reaching Class AA – albeit with terrible results – by the end of the 2018 season. The former Gamecock opened the 2019 campaign back in Class AA for a do-over, which lasted 16 starts, before settling in at Class AAA. Crowe made a career best 26 starts last year, throwing a career high 149.1 innings with a 130-to-48 strikeout-to-walk ratio. He compiled an aggregate 4.70 ERA.

Scouting Report: At first glance it's a bit surprising that Crowe hasn't missed many bats in the professional ranks; he's averaged just 7.5 punch outs per nine innings in 57 career games. He owns three above-average pitches – fastball, curveball, and changeup – and will mix in a solid slider. The problem, of course, is how well he commands them. In short, he doesn't. And the PCL hitters – with their newly minted inflated baseballs – took full advantage of it last season. The hefty 6-foot-2, 240-pound righty is now entering his age-25 season, so there's little reason to expect his control – let alone his command – to tick up a bit. He's strictly a fifth starter and could slide into a long-man relief role.

Ceiling: 1.5-win player
Risk: Moderate
MLB ETA: 2020

11. Matt Cronin, LHP

FB	CB	Command	Overall
60	70	45	45

Born: 09/20/97	Age: 22	Bats: L
Height: 6-2	Weight: 195	Throws: L

YEAR	LVL	IP	W	L	SV	ERA	FIP	WHIP	K/9	K%	BB/9	BB%	K/BB	HR9	BABIP
2019	A	22.0	0	0	1	0.82	1.97	1.00	16.8	53.25%	4.5	14.29%	3.73	0.41	0.345

Background: A stout, shut-'em-down type reliever throughout the duration of his three-year career at the University of Arkansas. Cronin, a well-built 6-foot-2, 195-pound left-hander, was a key cog in the Razorbacks' bullpen as a true freshman: he appeared in 15 games, throwing 18.0 innings while recording a whopping 31 punch outs against 12 free passes. The Florida native, however, was just getting started. The following year he broke former closer – and 2013 second round pick by the Miami Marlins – Colby Suggs' school record for saves, eclipsing the previous mark of 13 by one. Cronin finished the year with a 59-to-14 strikeout-to-walk ratio in 48.1 innings en route to totaling a 3.54 ERA. Last season the big lefty's command regressed a bit as his walk rate nearly doubled from the previous year – it went from 2.6 BB/9 to 4.5 BB/9 – though he still managed to fan 41 in only 28.0 innings of work. Washington selected Cronin in the fourth round, 123rd overall. He made 17 appearances with Hagerstown in the South Atlantic League, averaging 16.8 strikeouts and 4.5 walks per nine innings.

Scouting Report: Mid-90s fastball and one helluva power curveball that buckled more than a few knees in Sally. Cronin's command has backed up a bit since his record-setting season two years ago. And even if it doesn't prove to be an anomaly, the hard-throwing southpaw has the makings of a solid seventh or eighth inning setup arm. He's herky-jerky, which adds several layers of deception, and throws with a max effort on each offering. Very solid pick by the Nationals. The curveball's already on the short, short list for best in the minor leagues.

Ceiling: 1.5-win player
Risk: Moderate
MLB ETA: 2021/2022

12. Steven Fuentes, RHP

FB	SL	CH	Command	Overall
50	50	60	55	40

Born: 05/04/97	Age: 23	Bats: R
Height: 6-2	Weight: 175	Throws: R

YEAR	LVL	IP	W	L	SV	ERA	FIP	WHIP	K/9	K%	BB/9	BB%	K/BB	HR9	BABIP
2017	A	63.3	4	3	2	4.41	4.60	1.47	7.5	18.73%	1.8	4.59%	4.08	1.28	0.351
2017	A+	2.3	0	1	0	7.71	8.53	2.57	0.0	0.00%	15.4	30.77%	0.00	0.00	0.222
2018	A	23.0	2	1	3	2.35	1.37	0.83	10.6	30.34%	0.8	2.25%	13.50	0.00	0.283
2018	A+	45.0	3	3	3	3.00	2.93	1.09	8.6	23.12%	3.2	8.60%	2.69	0.20	0.258
2019	A+	17.0	1	1	1	0.53	1.73	0.88	13.8	38.81%	3.7	10.45%	3.71	0.00	0.242
2019	AA	63.7	5	4	0	2.69	2.24	1.23	8.9	23.16%	2.1	5.51%	4.20	0.14	0.326

Background: An unheralded arm slowly making his way through the club's farm system for the past several years. Fuentes, a 6-foot-2, generously listed 175 pounds right-hander, began his career in a bit of a swingman type role; he made 15 starts and 11 relief appearances over his first two seasons in the foreign and stateside rookie leagues. After that, though, the front office transitioned the Panamanian hurler into a full-time reliever – a position that he held for two-and-a-half seasons. Fuentes opened up the 2019 season in the Carolina League, his third tour through High Class A. But after eight dominant multi-inning relief appearances, Washington bounced him up to Class AA. Just four appearances into his stint with the Harrisburg Senators, Fuentes moved back to the rotation and he blossomed. He made 11 starts with the Eastern League squad, throwing 57.2 innings with an impeccable 54-to-11 strikeout-to-walk ratio to go along with a 2.81 ERA. The most impressive part: he had one clunker of a start in which he allowed seven earned runs. Removing that game, he posted a 1.80 ERA.

Scouting Report: With respect to his work as a starting pitcher in Class AA last season, consider the following:

- Since 2006, here's the list of 22-year-old hurlers that posted a strikeout percentage between 21% and 23% with a sub-5.0% walk percentage in any Class AA league (min. 50 IP): Shane Bieber, Liam Hendriks, and Rudy Owens. For those counting at home: that's two All-Stars (Bieber and Hendriks) and Owens, who briefly spent time with Houston six years ago.

Fuentes isn't the same caliber of pitcher as Bieber and Hendriks; mainly because the All-Star duo sport above-average or better heaters. However, Fuentes owns one plus to plus-plus-pitch – his devastating changeup – and trusts it as much – if not more – than anyone I've seen. The Panamanian righty will throw it at any time, in any count. It's not on par to Chris Paddack's changeup, but it's not far from it. Fuentes owns a 90- to 94-mph fastball and a decent, average-ish slider. I'm not sure he slides into a full time starting gig, but there's definite MLB value here.

Ceiling: 1.0- to 1.5-win player
Risk: Low to Moderate
MLB ETA: 2020

13. Tres Barrera, C

Hit	Power	SB	Patience	Glove	Overall
40	40	30	50	55	40

Born: 09/14/94	Age: 25	Bats: R	
Height: 6-0	Weight: 215	Throws: R	

YEAR	LVL	PA	1B	2B	3B	HR	SB	CS	AVG	OBP	SLG	BB%	K%	GB%	LD%	FB%
2016	A-	190	27	9	1	3	0	0	0.244	0.337	0.366	7.89%	11.58%	47.2	16.0	24.3
2017	A	268	39	18	1	8	1	0	0.278	0.354	0.464	8.58%	21.64%	40.9	19.9	28.2
2018	A+	288	48	14	0	6	3	0	0.263	0.334	0.386	7.64%	18.40%	40.1	15.9	35.7
2019	AA	403	58	23	0	8	1	2	0.249	0.323	0.381	8.93%	17.12%	44.1	19.0	27.9

Background: A sixth round pick out of the University of Texas, at Austin in 2016. Barrera, a stocky catcher, turned in his finest offensive campaign to date in the Nationals' organization – which climaxed with a brief two-game cameo with the big league club. A career .279/.370/.444 bat for the Longhorns, Barrera, known for his defensive aptitude, appeared in 101 games with the Harrisburg Senators, batting a respectable .249/.323/.381 with a career best 23 doubles and a career-high tying eight homeruns. His overall production for the Eastern League squad, per *Deserved Runs Created Plus*, topped the league average mark by 18%.

Scouting Report: Consider the following:

- Since 2006, only five 24-year-old hitters posted a DRC+ between 113 and 123 a walk rate between 8% and 10% with a strikeout rate between 16% and 20% in the Eastern League (min. 300 PA): Jose Marmolejos, Jeff Fiorentino, Daniel Ortmeier, Jose Bautista, and Tres Barrera.

Obviously, ignoring Bautista (for good reason), the reminder of the group is comprised of minor leaguers and role players. Fortunately for Barrera, he plays one helluva backstop. He's going to be a glove-first back up but the offensive contributions won't kill a big league team in extended spurts either.

Ceiling: 1.0- to 1.5-win player
Risk: Low to Moderate
MLB ETA: Debuted in 2019

14. Yasel Antuna, IF

Hit	Power	SB	Patience	Glove	Overall
40/45	40/50	40/35	50	40/45	45

Born: 10/26/99	Age: 20	Bats: B	
Height: 6-0	Weight: 170	Throws: R	

YEAR	LVL	PA	1B	2B	3B	HR	SB	CS	AVG	OBP	SLG	BB%	K%	GB%	LD%	FB%
2017	RK	199	40	8	3	1	5	5	0.301	0.382	0.399	11.56%	14.57%	43.2	22.6	24.0
2018	A	362	49	14	2	6	8	7	0.220	0.293	0.331	8.84%	21.82%	47.2	14.9	30.6
2019	Rk	8	1	0	0	0	0	0	0.167	0.375	0.167	25.00%	12.50%	20.0	20.0	20.0

Background: Just the latest example of the difficulties involved with evaluating prospects, particularly young, unproven teenagers. The Nationals signed a pair of Dominican shortstops on the international scene four years ago: Yasel Antuna, who received a deal worth $3.9 million, and Luis Garcia, who was signed for just $1.3 million. Garcia's rocketed through the minor leagues, spending last season as a teenager in Class AA. And, well, Antuna tore up the Gulf Coast League in 2017, looked completely underwhelming and overmatched in an aggressive promotion to Low Class A the following season, and missed all but three Gulf Coast League games as he underwent Tommy John surgery.

Snippet from The 2018 Prospect Digest Handbook: There's an awful lot to consider with Antuna: (A) his age and level of competition, (B) the fact that he's a switch-hitter, who – by the way – showed a massive platoon split in the Gulf Coast League two years ago, and (C) his production at the plate was trending in the right direction before his season ended prematurely in mid-July. Antuna's clearly not on the same developmental curve as, say, Luis Garcia. But the skill set is intriguing, albeit incredibly raw. Just give him time.

Scouting Report: There's really nothing else to add at this point. The Nationals were already experimenting with him around the infield. With Trea Turner, Carter Kieboom, and Luis Garcia in front of him as up-the-middle options, Antuna's likely going to have to shift to third base. Like last season, just give him time.

Ceiling: 1.5-win player
Risk: Moderate to High
MLB ETA: 2022/2023

15. Joan Adon, RHP

FB	SL	CH	Command	Overall
50/55	50/55	45/50	45/50	40

Born: 08/12/98	Age: 21	Bats: R
Height: 6-2	Weight: 185	Throws: R

YEAR	LVL	IP	W	L	SV	ERA	FIP	WHIP	K/9	K%	BB/9	BB%	K/BB	HR9	BABIP
2017	Rk	28.0	2	1	1	3.54	3.09	1.18	10.0	26.50%	2.9	7.69%	3.44	0.32	0.329
2018	Rk	19.7	2	0	2	2.29	3.59	1.68	13.3	28.71%	5.9	12.87%	2.23	0.00	0.377
2018	A-	11.0	1	1	0	7.36	7.11	2.00	9.0	19.64%	7.4	16.07%	1.22	1.64	0.355
2019	A	105.0	11	3	0	3.86	4.23	1.30	7.7	20.98%	3.8	10.26%	2.05	0.69	0.289

Background: Signed out of Santo Domingo, Dominican Republic on July 2nd, 2016, for the relatively small sum of $50,000; Adon, a wiry, projectable right-hander, is proving to be quite the bargain. The 6-foot-2, 185-pound youngster made his debut in the foreign rookie league the following year, averaging 10.0 strikeouts and just 2.9 walks per nine innings in 13 relief appearances. The front office brass immediately put him on the fast track to Washington a year later. Adon began the 2018 season in the Gulf Coast League with 13 solid relief appearances and capped it off with another seven games in the New York-Penn League. Last year Adon transitioned into a full-time starting gig as he was promoted up to Low Class A. In 22 appearances, all but one of them coming via the start, he posted a 90-to-44 strikeout-to-walk ratio in 105.0 innings. He finished the year with a 3.86 ERA and a 5.27 DRA (Deserved Runs Average).

Scouting Report: A variety of reports had Adon's fastball sitting in the mid-90s and touching the lower end of the upper-90s in previous years – albeit in short stints. Last season his fastball was sitting – comfortably – in the 90- to 93-mph range. His slider, a mid-80s offering, shows some promise and flashes above-average at times. And he seemed to hone in on the development of his below-average changeup at the latter part of the year (as opposed to not throwing it as frequently in earlier games). There's really nothing extraordinary about Adon: it's a decent repertoire; he throws a decent amount of strikes and misses some bats; and he handled his promotion to Low Class A well. There's not a lot that separates Adon from mediocre pitching prospects like long time vagabond Keury Mella.

Ceiling: 1.0 to 1.5-win player
Risk: Moderate
MLB ETA: 2022

16. Drew Mendoza, 1B

Hit	Power	SB	Patience	Glove	Overall
45	45/50	30	55	50	40

Born: 10/10/97	Age: 22	Bats: L
Height: 6-5	Weight: 230	Throws: R

YEAR	LVL	PA	1B	2B	3B	HR	SB	CS	AVG	OBP	SLG	BB%	K%	GB%	LD%	FB%
2019	A	239	37	12	0	4	3	0	0.264	0.377	0.383	14.23%	23.85%	42.6	14.2	40.4

Background: A middle of the lineup thumper for Florida State for the entirety of his collegiate career. Mendoza put together a solid triple-slash line as a freshman, batting .270/.400/.534 with nine doubles and 10 homeruns. He spent the following summer, 2017, playing – and struggling – in the Cape Cod League; he cobbled together a paltry .171/.218/.220 in 28 games with the Yarmouth-Dennis Red Sox. Mendoza, a hulking 6-foot-5, 230-pound corner infielder, maintained status quo during his sophomore campaign with the Seminoles: in 62 games, he slugged .313/.440/.491 with 17 doubles and seven homeruns. And, once again, he struggled – mightily – in the Cape Cod League; he slashed .232/.365/.348 with just four extra-base hits in 29 games with the Chatham Anglers. Last season Mendoza's performance returned with FSU: in a career-best tying 62 games, the Florida native hit .319/.484/.620 with 12 doubles, two triples, and 16 homeruns. Washington selected him in the third round, 94th overall, and sent him to the Sally – which produced mixed results. He batted .264/.377/.383 with 12 doubles and four homers in 55 games. His production, as determined by *Deserved Runs Created Plus*, topped the league mark by 27%.

Scouting Report: A bit of a surprising pick because Mendoza owns several red flags and / or pockmarks:

- His battled some swing-and-miss issues at various parts of his collegiate career, including whiffing in more than 24% of his plate appearances as a junior.
- He was *horrible* in two separate stints in the Cape Cod League, hitting .171/.218/.220 and .232/.365/.348, respectively.
- He owns limited power (50-grade) for a corner infielder.
- He's likely going to be only a first base prospect – if he's not already there.

Mendoza likely slides into a Quad-A role in the coming years – nothing more, nothing less.

Ceiling: 1.0- to 1.5-win player
Risk: Moderate
MLB ETA: 2022

17. Reid Schaller, RHP

	FB	SL	CH	Command	Overall
	50	50	45	45	40

Born: 04/02/97	Age: 23	Bats: R
Height: 6-3	Weight: 210	Throws: R

YEAR	LVL	IP	W	L	SV	ERA	FIP	WHIP	K/9	K%	BB/9	BB%	K/BB	HR9	BABIP
2018	Rk	11.7	0	1	0	1.54	3.04	1.03	12.3	34.04%	2.3	6.38%	5.33	0.77	0.308
2018	A-	29.0	2	2	0	5.90	3.41	1.34	5.0	12.90%	2.8	7.26%	1.78	0.00	0.306
2019	A	52.0	4	3	0	3.29	4.41	1.21	8.1	21.96%	4.3	11.68%	1.88	0.87	0.243

Background: A highly touted prep arm coming out of Lebanon High School, Schaller, who would eventually go undrafted thanks to injury concerns, hit the disabled list for Tommy John surgery and played at Vanderbilt University for just one season. The 6-foot-3, 210-pound right-hander made 21 appearances for the Commodores in 2018, only two of them coming via the start, throwing 28.2 innings with an impressive 39-to-9 strikeout-to-walk ratio and a 3.77 ERA. Washington drafted the Indiana native in the third round, 101st overall, and began to extend him out in stints in the Gulf Coast and New York-Penn Leagues. He would throw a total of 40.2 innings, fanning 32 and walking 12 to go along with a 4.65 ERA. Schaller got off to a late start to 2019 season; he wouldn't make his first appearance in the South Atlantic League until the end of June. He would eventually start 12 games, posting a mediocre 47-to-25 strikeout-to-walk ratio in 52.0 innings. He finished the year with a 3.29 ERA and a 4.41 DRA (Deserved Runs Average).

Snippet from The 2018 Prospect Digest Handbook: Schaller's fastball will touch triple-digits in short stints, but his secondary offerings – a slider and changeup – remain quite raw. The slider will flash plus at times, but he doesn't always finish the pitch, leaving it hanging at times. The changeup shows a little bit of run, though it's a below-average offering. Washington, reportedly, has designs of moving Schaller into a full-time starter. And given his lack of experience – due to the elbow issue – there's still considerable projection left. The most probably outcome is that Schaller slides back into a relief role – potentially becoming a dominant closer.

Scouting Report: After showcasing a plus- to plus-plus-fastball during his relief outings in college, Schaller's fastball was moving as quickly as a governed go-cart. The *average* offering was sitting in the 90- to 92-mph range, consistently. His slider still lacks considerable depth and bite. And his changeup is as raw as ever. He's likely headed back into a relief role, although not a late-inning reliever. He might be able to serve as a seventh-inning arm. One more note: he's an extreme short-armer, along the same lines as Lucas Giolito's newly minted arm action last year.

Ceiling: 1.0-win player
Risk: Moderate
MLB ETA: 2022

18. Jackson Tetreault, RHP

	FB	CB	SL	CH	Command	Overall
	50	50	55	50	45	40

Born: 06/03/96	Age: 24	Bats: R
Height: 6-5	Weight: 189	Throws: R

YEAR	LVL	IP	W	L	SV	ERA	FIP	WHIP	K/9	K%	BB/9	BB%	K/BB	HR9	BABIP
2017	Rk	2.0	0	0	0	4.50	9.42	1.00	9.0	25.00%	4.5	12.50%	2.00	4.50	0.000
2017	A-	38.3	2	2	0	2.58	3.14	1.25	8.5	21.82%	3.8	9.70%	2.25	0.23	0.277
2018	A	110.0	3	8	0	4.01	3.56	1.29	9.7	24.95%	2.8	7.19%	3.47	0.82	0.320
2018	A+	22.7	1	1	0	4.37	3.67	1.24	7.9	21.05%	2.8	7.37%	2.86	0.79	0.288
2019	A+	37.7	4	2	0	1.91	3.03	1.12	6.9	19.08%	3.1	8.55%	2.23	0.00	0.269
2019	AA	85.7	4	5	0	4.73	4.38	1.61	6.6	16.49%	4.2	10.47%	1.58	0.84	0.335

Background: One of the bigger surprises in the system two years ago. Tetreault, a wiry 6-foot-5, 189-pound righty, spent time with organization's South Atlantic and Carolina League affiliates, throwing 132.2 innings with an impeccable 138-to-41 strikeout-to-walk ratio. And, to be frank, I was completely enamored with the former State College of Florida, Manatee-Sarasota product. Then he fell flat on his face. Tetreault opened the year back up with Potomac in dominating fashion by posting a 1.23 ERA across four starts. The front office brass bounced the former seventh rounder up to Class AA, the most difficult challenge for a minor leaguer, and the results were – largely – disappointing. In 18 starts with Harrisburg he fanned just 63 and walked 40 in only 85.2 innings of work. After a string of disappointing starts Tetreault was demoted back to the Carolina League for three final starts.

Snippet from The 2018 Prospect Digest Handbook: A nice little find in the middle part of the draft two years ago – kudos to the Nationals scouting department – Tetreault showcases two plus-offerings: a 93-94 mph fastball, though it tends to be a touch too straight, and a wipeout slider with hard, late bite. The slider has a chance to be one of the better sliders in the minor leagues. The big right-hander will also show an above-average changeup in the 86-87 mph range and big bending 12-6 curveball, which flashes plus as well. There's a chance Tetreault develops into a low-end #3 or good #4-type arm in a big league rotation. Highly, highly underrated.

Scouting Report: Boy, was I wrong – in a big way. Tetreault's entire repertoire backed up across the board. His fastball was down to 92-mph; his slider downgraded to above-average; his curveball was – barely – average, lacking the bite it showed the previous season; and his changeup maintained its 50-grade showing. Tetreault's first 11 starts in the Eastern League weren't terrible – he posted a 42-to-16 strikeout-to-walk ratio with a 3.88 ERA in 51.0 innings – so there's hope that either (A) he was pitching hurt or (B) there's a chance for a bounce back. At this point, based on what I saw last season, he looks like an up-and-down arm or a multi-inning reliever.

Ceiling: 1.0-win player
Risk: Moderate
MLB ETA: 2020/2021

19. KJ Harrison, 1B

Hit	Power	SB	Patience	Glove	Overall
45	50	30	55	45	40

Born: 08/11/96	Age: 23	Bats: R
Height: 6-0	Weight: 208	Throws: R

YEAR	LVL	PA	1B	2B	3B	HR	SB	CS	AVG	OBP	SLG	BB%	K%	GB%	LD%	FB%
2017	RK	214	33	14	0	10	0	0	0.308	0.388	0.546	10.75%	25.70%	40.6	20.3	32.3
2018	A	466	54	29	0	12	2	2	0.228	0.298	0.384	8.37%	31.55%	31.3	21.5	33.8
2019	A	66	13	8	0	2	0	0	0.404	0.485	0.649	12.12%	15.15%	25.5	29.8	40.4
2019	A+	413	54	21	1	11	2	1	0.244	0.344	0.401	12.35%	23.73%	36.7	14.1	35.2

Background: A stout offensive contributor throughout his career for PAC-12 powerhouse Oregon State University. The Brewers originally drafted the part-time catcher / first baseman in the third round three years ago. The Nationals acquired Harrison – as well as former international bonus baby turned prospect bust Gilbert Lara – for veteran left-hander Gio Gonzalez and international bonus money at the August trade deadline in 2018. The 6-foot, 208-pound former Beaver ripped through the Sally to start last season – of course, that's after a complete an utter failure in Low Class A the previous year – and continued to hold his own in High Class A. In 101 games with the Potomac Nationals, Harrison slugged .244/.344/.401 with 21 doubles, one triple, and 11 homeruns. His overall production at High Class A, per *Deserved Runs Created Plus*, topped the league average mark by 26%.

Snippet from The 2018 Prospect Digest Handbook: Harrison's career trajectory has taken a significant hit because he's no longer (1.) a bat-first prospect and, most importantly, (2.) a catcher. Milwaukee moved the former Oregon State star away from the dish and to first base – the place where prospects go to die – in roughly two-third of his games. It also didn't help that 90% of would-be base stealers were successful in their attempts. Harrison can run into a handful of pitches to drive out 15- to -20 homeruns in a full season. And he's willing to take the occasional walk. But his ability to make consistent contact proved to be problematic last season.

Scouting Report: Consider the following:

- Since 2006, only five 22-year-old hitters posted a DRC+ between 120 and 130 with a double-digit walk rate in the Carolina League (min. 300 PA): Nicky Lopez, Mike Papi, Jordan Smith, Jodd Carter, and – of course – KJ Harrison.

As I opined in last year's Handbook, Harrison's value took a tremendous hit as he moved away from behind the dish – a move, for what it's worth, that had to be made thanks to his defensive shortcomings. There's a little bit of Oakland A's-type hitter slant to him: he walks a lot, doesn't strikeout all that much, and will flash average or better power. Unfortunately, it's not going to be enough for a first base only prospect. I wouldn't be shocked to see him start bouncing around a bit – perhaps to a corner outfielder spot – to expand his limited value.

Ceiling: 1.0-win player
Risk: Moderate
MLB ETA: 2021

20. Nick Raquet, LHP

FB	CB	SL	CH	Command	Overall
55	50	45	50	45+	35

Born: 12/12/95	Age: 24	Bats: R
Height: 6-0	Weight: 215	Throws: L

YEAR	LVL	IP	W	L	SV	ERA	FIP	WHIP	K/9	K%	BB/9	BB%	K/BB	HR9	BABIP
2017	Rk	2.0	0	0	0	0.00	1.42	1.00	9.0	25.00%	0.0	0.00%	#DIV/0!	0.00	0.333
2017	A-	51.3	3	2	0	2.45	3.54	1.23	3.9	10.58%	1.2	3.37%	3.14	0.35	0.307
2018	A	67.7	4	6	0	2.79	2.88	1.27	7.4	19.86%	2.4	6.38%	3.11	0.13	0.327
2018	A+	55.0	5	3	0	4.91	4.01	1.69	5.9	14.34%	3.4	8.37%	1.71	0.49	0.365
2019	A+	130.3	11	9	0	4.07	3.87	1.32	8.4	21.86%	3.0	7.71%	2.84	0.83	0.314

Background: The Nationals took collegiate arms in the third round in back-to-back years, first selecting Raquet in the 2017 draft and following it up with former Vanderbilt project Reid Schaller a year later. Raquet, a 6-foot, 215-pound soft-bodied left-hander, split time between two separate colleges prior to joining the Nationals' organization. He spent his freshman season as a little-used, albeit effective, reliever for the University of North Carolina. And after sitting out a year, he joined William & Mary's squad. Last season the crafty southpaw made a career best 25 starts in the Carolina League, averaging 8.4

strikeouts and 3.0 walks per nine innings to go along with a 4.07 ERA and a 5.54 DRA. He spent the fall playing for the Surprise Saguaros, posting a 12-to-9 strikeout-to-walk ratio in 11.2 innings of work.

Scouting Report: Purely a reliever in the end. One that, unfortunately, will have to survive on an above-average fastball and deception. His curveball is bland, quite generic. His slider only shows lateral movement, which will likely be an issue as he continues up the ladder. And his change is decent. The control and command are solid, nothing spectacular.

Ceiling: 0.5- to 1.0-win player
Risk: Moderate
MLB ETA: 2021

Made in the USA
Monee, IL
10 April 2020